T0142046

Lecture Notes in Computer Science 12972

Founding Editors

Gerhard Goos
Karlsruhe Institute of Technology, Karlsruhe, Germany
Juris Hartmanis
Cornell University, Ithaca, NY, USA

Editorial Board Members

Elisa Bertino
Purdue University, West Lafayette, IN, USA
Wen Gao
Peking University, Beijing, China
Bernhard Steffen
TU Dortmund University, Dortmund, Germany
Gerhard Woeginger
RWTH Aachen, Aachen, Germany
Moti Yung
Columbia University, New York, NY, USA

More information about this subseries at http://www.springer.com/series/7410

Elisa Bertino · Haya Shulman ·
Michael Waidner (Eds.)

Computer Security – ESORICS 2021

26th European Symposium
on Research in Computer Security
Darmstadt, Germany, October 4–8, 2021
Proceedings, Part I

 Springer

Editors
Elisa Bertino (iD)
Purdue University
West Lafayette, IN, USA

Michael Waidner (iD)
National Research Center for Applied
Cybersecurity ATHENE
Technische Universität Darmstadt,
Fraunhofer Institute for Secure Information
Technology SIT
Darmstadt, Germany

Haya Shulman (iD)
National Research Center for Applied
Cybersecurity ATHENE
Fraunhofer Institute for Secure Information
Technology SIT
Darmstadt, Germany

ISSN 0302-9743   ISSN 1611-3349 (electronic)
Lecture Notes in Computer Science
ISBN 978-3-030-88417-8   ISBN 978-3-030-88418-5 (eBook)
https://doi.org/10.1007/978-3-030-88418-5

LNCS Sublibrary: SL4 – Security and Cryptology

© Springer Nature Switzerland AG 2021
This work is subject to copyright. All rights are reserved by the Publisher, whether the whole or part of the material is concerned, specifically the rights of translation, reprinting, reuse of illustrations, recitation, broadcasting, reproduction on microfilms or in any other physical way, and transmission or information storage and retrieval, electronic adaptation, computer software, or by similar or dissimilar methodology now known or hereafter developed.
The use of general descriptive names, registered names, trademarks, service marks, etc. in this publication does not imply, even in the absence of a specific statement, that such names are exempt from the relevant protective laws and regulations and therefore free for general use.
The publisher, the authors and the editors are safe to assume that the advice and information in this book are believed to be true and accurate at the date of publication. Neither the publisher nor the authors or the editors give a warranty, expressed or implied, with respect to the material contained herein or for any errors or omissions that may have been made. The publisher remains neutral with regard to jurisdictional claims in published maps and institutional affiliations.

This Springer imprint is published by the registered company Springer Nature Switzerland AG
The registered company address is: Gewerbestrasse 11, 6330 Cham, Switzerland

Preface

The 26th European Symposium on Research in Computer Security (ESORICS 2021) was held together with the affiliated workshops during the week of October 4–8, 2021. Due to the COVID-19 pandemic the conference and the workshops took place digitally, hosted by the Fraunhofer Institute for Secure Information Technology (Fraunhofer SIT), within the National Research Center for Applied Cybersecurity ATHENE, Germany.

This year's ESORICS introduced for the first time in the ESORICS conference series two review cycles: a winter cycle and a spring cycle. This follows the general trends for conferences of providing multiple submission deadlines and is not only more convenient for the authors but also allows revision and resubmission for papers. In the case of ESORICS, papers submitted in the winter cycle could be recommended for revision and resubmission to the spring cycle.

In response to the call for papers 351 papers were submitted to the conference. These papers were peer reviewed and subsequently discussed based on their novelty, quality, and contribution by the members of the Program Committee. The submissions were single blind, and all the members of the Program Committee had access to all the submissions and their reviews at all times to facilitate discussions among the members. The submission of the papers and the review process were carried out using the Easychair platform. Based on the reviews and the discussion 71 papers were selected for presentation at the conference. As a result ESORICS had an interesting program covering timely and interesting security and privacy topics in theory, systems, networks, and applications.

The papers that were selected for presentation at ESORICS 2021 were published in a two volume set of proceedings: LNCS 12972 and LNCS 12973.

ESORICS is a flagship European security conference. The aim of ESORICS is to advance the research in computer security and privacy by establishing a European forum, bringing together researchers in these areas, and promoting the exchange of ideas with the developers, standardization bodies, and policy makers and by encouraging links with researchers in related fields.

We were honoured to have four keynote speakers: Shafi Goldwasser, Christof Paar, Nicolas Papernot, and Yuval Yarom. Their talks provided interesting insights and research directions in important research areas. The program was complemented by six tutorials given by Anna Cinzia Squicciarini, Yossi Oren, Michael Schwarz, Avishai Wool, and Daphne Yao. For tutorials, ESORICS introduced a novel organization, in that tutorials were given in advance with respect to the conference dates, with the first tutorial given on June 30, 2021, and the last one on September 8, 2021. Tutorial presentations were recorded and are available online. This arrangement takes advantage of today's availability of content dissemination platforms and allows researchers to access the tutorial contents at their own pace.

The Program Committee consisted of 185 members across 31 countries. There were submissions from a total of 1150 authors across 41 countries, with 25 countries represented among the accepted papers. We would like to thank the members of the Program Committee and the external referees for their hard work in supporting the review process as well as everyone who supported the organization of ESORICS. We are grateful to the workshops chairs, Adrian Perrig and David Hay, and all of the workshop co-chairs, the poster chair, Simone Fischer-Hübner, and the ESORICS Steering Committee. We are also grateful to Huawei and IBM Research – Haifa, Israel, for supporting the organization of ESORICS 2021. Finally, we would like to thank the authors for submitting their papers to ESORICS 2021. We hope that the proceedings will promote the research and facilitate future work in the field of security.

September 2021

Elisa Bertino
Haya Shulman
Michael Waidner

Organization

General Chair

Michael Waidner   National Research Center for Applied Cybersecurity
ATHENE/Technische Universität
Darmstadt/Fraunhofer SIT, Germany

Program Committee Chairs

Elisa Bertino   Purdue University, USA
Haya Shulman   National Research Center for Applied Cybersecurity
ATHENE/Fraunhofer SIT, Germany

Steering Committee

Joachim Biskup
Véronique Cortier
Frédéric Cuppens
Sabrina De Capitani di Vimercati
Joaquin Garcia-Alfaro
Dieter Gollmann
Sokratis Katsikas
Mirosław Kutyłowski
Javier Lopez
Jean-Jacques Quisquater
Peter RYAN
Pierangela Samarati
Einar Arthur Snckkenes
Michael Waidner

Program Committee

Ruba Abu-Salma   International Computer Science Institute / University
of California, Berkeley, USA
Yehuda Afek   Tel Aviv University, Israel
Mitsuaki Akiyama   NTT, Japan
Cristina Alcaraz   UMA, Spain
Mark Allman   International Computer Science Institute, USA
Vijay Atluri   Rutgers University, USA
Erman Ayday   Case Western Reserve University, USA
Guangdong Bai   University of Queensland, Australia
Lejla Batina   Radboud University, The Netherlands

Steven M. Bellovin	Columbia University, USA
Antonio Bianchi	Purdue University, USA
Marina Blanton	University at Buffalo, USA
Carlo Blundo	Università degli Studi di Salerno, Italy
Tamara Bonaci	Northeastern University, USA
Nora Boulahia Cuppens	Polytechnique Montréal, Canada
Alejandro Cabrera Aldaya	Tampere University of Technology, Finland
Lorenzo Cavallaro	King's College London, UK
Berkay Celik	Purdue University, USA
Aldar C.-F. Chan	BIS Innovation Hub Hong Kong Centre, Hong Kong
Liqun Chen	University of Surrey, UK
Rongmao Chen	National University of Defense Technology, China
Xiaofeng Chen	Xidian University, China
Yu Chen	School of Cyber Science and Technology, Shandong University, China
Sherman Chow	Chinese University of Hong Kong, Hong Kong
Mauro Conti	University of Padua, Italy
Scott Coull	FireEye, Inc., USA
Bruno Crispo	University of Trento, Italy
Michel Cukier	University of Maryland, USA
Frédéric Cuppens	Polytechnique Montréal, Canada
George Danezis	University College London, UK
Sanchari Das	University of Denver, USA
Sabrina De Capitani di Vimercati	Università degli Studi di Milano, Italy
Hervé Debar	Télécom SudParis, France
Roberto Di Pietro	Hamad Bin Khalifa University, Qatar
Wenrui Diao	Shandong University, China
Tassos Dimitriou	Computer Technology Institute, Greece/Kuwait University, Kuwait
Shlomi Dolev	Ben-Gurion University, Israel
Josep Domingo-Ferrer	Universitat Rovira i Virgili, Spain
Changyu Dong	Newcastle University, UK
Haixin Duan	Tsinghua University, China
François Dupressoir	University of Surrey, UK
Pardis Emami Naeini	Carnegie Mellon University, USA
Paulo Esteves-Veríssimo	Université du Luxembourg, Luxembourg
Jose-Luis Ferrer-Gomila	University of the Balearic Islands, Spain
Sara Foresti	Università degli Studi di Milano, Italy
Michael Franz	University of California, Irvine, USA
David Galindo	University of Birmingham, UK
Debin Gao	Singapore Management University, Singapore
Joaquin Garcia-Alfaro	Telecom SudParis, France
Siddharth Garg	New York University, USA
Thanassis Giannetsos	Technical University of Denmark, Denmark
Dieter Gollmann	Hamburg University of Technology, Germany

Neil Gong	Duke University, USA
Stefanos Gritzalis	University of Piraeus, Greece
Daniel Gruss	Graz University of Technology, Austria
Zhongshu Gu	IBM T.J. Watson Research Center, USA
Thomas Haines	Norwegian University of Science and Technology, Norway
Feng Hao	University of Warwick, UK
Juan Hernández-Serrano	Universitat Politècnica de Catalunya, Spain
Xinyi Huang	Fujian Normal University, China
Syed Hussain	Pennsylvania State University, USA
Sotiris Ioannidis	Technical University of Crete, Greece
Tibor Jager	Bergische Universität Wuppertal, Germany
Philipp Jeitner	Fraunhofer SIT, Germany
Yuseok Jeon	Ulsan National Institute of Science and Technology, South Korea
Shouling Ji	Zhejiang University, China
Ghassan Karame	NEC Laboratories Europe, Germany
Sokratis Katsikas	Norwegian University of Science and Technology, Norway
Aggelos Kiayias	University of Edinburgh, UK
Hyoungshick Kim	Sungkyunkwan University, South Korea
Ryan Ko	University of Queensland, Australia
Juliane Krämer	TU Darmstadt, Germany
Steve Kremer	Inria France
Marina Krotofil	Honeywell Industrial Cyber Security Lab, USA
Christopher Kruegel	University of California, Santa Barbara, USA
Yonghwi Kwon	University of Virginia, USA
Costas Lambrinoudakis	University of Piraeus, Greece
Shir Landau-Feibish	The Open University of Israel, Israel
Kyu Hyung Lee	University of Georgia, USA
Corrado Leita	VMware, UK
Shujun Li	University of Kent, UK
Zitao Li	Purdue University, USA
Kaitai Liang	Delft University of Technology, The Netherlands
Xiaojing Liao	Indiana University Bloomington, USA
Hoon Wei Lim	Trustwave, Singapore
Zhiqiang Lin	Ohio State University, USA
Xiangyu Liu	Alibaba Group, China
Joseph Liu	Monash University, Australia
Rongxing Lu	University of New Brunswick, Canada
Xiapu Luo	Hong Kong Polytechnic University, Hong Kong
Shiqing Ma	Rutgers University, USA
Leandros Maglaras	De Montfort University, UK
Fabio Martinelli	IIT-CNR, Italy
Sjouke Mauw	Université du Luxembourg, Luxembourg
Weizhi Meng	Technical University of Denmark, Denmark

Nele Mentens	KU Leuven, Belgium
Mira Mezini	TU Darmstadt, Germany
Chris Mitchell	Royal Holloway, University of London, UK
Tal Moran	Interdisciplinary Center Herzliya, Israel
Tatsuya Mori	Waseda University, Japan
Johannes Mueller	University of Luxembourg, Luxembourg
Max Mühlhäuser	TU Darmstadt, Germany
David Naccache	Ecole normale suprieure, France
Siaw-Lynn Ng	Royal Holloway, University of London, UK
Nick Nikiforakis	Stony Brook University, USA
Jianting Ning	National University of Singapore/Singapore Management University, Singapore
Satoshi Obana	Hosei University, Japan
Martín Ochoa	AppGate Inc., Colombia
Rolf Oppliger	eSECURITY Technologies, Switzerland
Rebekah Overdorf	Ecole Polytechnique Fédérale de Lausanne, Switzerland
Sikhar Patranabis	Visa Research, Palo Alto, USA
Jiaxin Pan	Norwegian University of Science and Technology, Norway
Radia Perlman	Dell EMC, USA
Günther Pernul	Universität Regensburg, Germany
Tran Viet Xuan Phuong	University of Wollongong, Australia
Frank Piessens	KU Leuven, Belgium
Joachim Posegga	University of Passau, Germany
Jean-Jacques Quisquater	Université Catholique de Louvain, Belgium
Siddharth Prakash Rao	Nokia Bell Labs, USA
Awais Rashid	University of Bristol, UK
Michael Reiter	Duke University, USA
Kui Ren	Zhejiang University, China
Junghwan Rhee	University of Central Oklahoma, USA
Giovanni Russello	University of Auckland, New Zealand
Peter Ryan	University of Luxembourg, Luxembourg
Reihaneh Safavi-Naini	University of Calgary, Canada
Merve Sahin	SAP Security Research, France
Amin Sakzad	Monash University, Australia
Pierangela Samarati	Università degli Studi di Milano, Italy
Damien Sauveron	University of Limoges/CNRS, France
Sebastian Schinzel	FH Münster, Germany
Steve Schneider	University of Surrey, UK
Bruce Schneier	BT, USA
Dominique Schröder	Friedrich-Alexander-Universität Erlangen-Nürnberg, Germany
Michael Schwarz	CISPA Helmholtz Center for Information Security, Germany
Joerg Schwenk	Ruhr-Universität Bochum, Germany

Kent Seamons   Brigham Young University, UK
Bardin Sébastien   CEA LIST, France
Jean-Pierre Seifert   TU Berlin, Germany
Siamak F. Shahandashti   University of York, UK
Kris Shrishak   TU Darmstadt, Germany
Radu Sion   Stony Brook University, USA
Nigel Smart   KU Leuven, Belgium
Einar Snekkenes   Norwegian University of Science and Technology,
                               Norway
Juraj Somorovsky   Ruhr-Universität Bochum, Germany
Thorsten Strufe   KIT, Germany
Willy Susilo   University of Wollongong, Australia
Paul Syverson   U.S. Naval Research Laboratory, USA
Qiang Tang   Luxembourg Institute of Science and Technology,
                               Luxembourg
Qiang Tang   University of Sydney, USA
Dave Tian   Purdue University, USA
Laura Tinnel   SRI International, USA
Nils Ole Tippenhauer   CISPA Helmholtz Center for Information Security,
                               Germany
Jacob Torrey   Amazon Web Services, USA
Ari Trachtenberg   Boston University, USA
Helen Treharne   University of Surrey, UK
Aggeliki Tsohou   Ionian University, Greece
Mathy Vanhoef   New York University Abu Dhabi, Abu Dhabi
Luca Viganò   King's College London, UK
Michael Waidner   Fraunhofer SIT/National Research Center for Applied
                               Cybersecurity ATHENE, Germany
Cong Wang   City University of Hong Kong, Hong Kong
Haining Wang   Virginia Tech Research Center - Arlington, USA
Lingyu Wang   Concordia University, Canada
Weihang Wang   SUNY University at Buffalo, USA
Bing Wang   University of Connecticut, USA
Edgar Weippl   University of Vienna/SBA Research, Austria
Avishai Wool   Tel Aviv University, Israel
Christos Xenakis   University of Piraeus, Greece
Yang Xiang   Swinburne University of Technology, Australia
Minhui Xue   University of Adelaide, Australia
Guomin Yang   University of Wollongong, Australia
Jie Yang   Florida State University, USA
Kang Yang   State Key Laboratory of Cryptology, China
Yuval Yarom   University of Adelaide, Australia
Xun Yi   RMIT University, Australia
Yu Yu   Shanghai Jiao Tong University, China
Fengwei Zhang   SUSTech, China
Kehuan Zhang   The Chinese University of Hong Kong, Hong Kong

Yang Zhang	CISPA Helmholtz Center for Information Security, Germany
Yinqian Zhang	Southern University of Science and Technology, China
Yuan Zhang	Fudan University, China
Zhenfeng Zhang	Chinese Academy of Sciences, China
Yunlei Zhao	Fudan University, China
Jianying Zhou	Singapore University of Technology and Design, Singapore
Sencun Zhu	Pennsylvania State University, USA

Workshop Chairs

| David Hay | Hebrew University of Jerusalem, Israel |
| Adrian Perrig | ETH Zurich, Switzerland |

Posters Chair

| Simone Fischer-Hübner | Karlstad University, Sweden |

Publication Chairs

| Philipp Jeitner | Fraunhofer SIT, Germany |
| Hervais Simo | Fraunhofer SIT, Germany |

Publicity Chairs

| Oliver Küch | Fraunhofer SIT, Germany |
| Anna Spiegel | Fraunhofer SIT, Germany |

Sponsorship Chair

| Ute Richter | Fraunhofer SIT, Germany |

Local Arrangements Chair

| Linda Schreiber | National Research Center for Applied Cybersecurity ATHENE, Germany |

Web Chair

| Ingo Siedermann | Fraunhofer SIT, Germany |

Posters Program Committee

Patricia Arias	KIT, Germany
Xinlei He	CISPA Helmholtz Center for Information Security, Germany
Juliane Krämer	TU Darmstadt, Germany
Erwin Quiring	TU Braunschweig, Germany
Neta Shiff Rozen	Hebrew University of Jerusalem, Israel
Tobias Urban	Westphalian University of Applied Sciences, Germany
Di Wang	King Abdullah University of Science and Technology, Saudi Arabia
Zhikun Zhang	CISPA Helmholtz Center for Information Security, Germany

Additional Reviewers

Alexopoulos, Nikolaos
Amiri Eliasi, Parisa
Andreina, Sebastien
Angelogianni, Anna
Avizheh, Sepideh
Bag, Samiran
Bagheri, Sima
Bamiloshin, Michael
Bampatsikos, Michail
Baumer, Thomas
Baumgärtner, Lars
Binun, Alexander
Bolgouras, Vaios
Bonte, Charlotte
Brighente, Alessandro
Böhm, Fabian
Cao, Yanmei
Caprolu, Maurantonio
Catuogno, Luigi
Cecconello, Stefano
Chen, Jinrong
Chen, Long
Chen, Min
Chen, Xihui
Ciampi, Michele
Cicala, Fabrizio
Dang, Hai-Van
Daudén, Cristòfol
Davies, Gareth

Diemert, Denis
Ding, Hailun
Divakaran, Dinil Mon
Dolev, Shlomi
Dong, Naipeng
Du, Jianqi
Du, Minxin
Duman, Onur
Dutta, Sabyasachi
Eckhart, Matthias
Ehsanpour, Maryam
El Kassem, Nada
Empl, Philip
Esgin, Muhammed F.
Feng, Qi
Ferrag, Mohamed Amine
Freisleben, Bernd
Gaballah, Sarah
Gangwal, Ankit
Gellert, Kai
Ghaedi Bardeh, Navid
Gong, Boru
Han, Donggyun
Handirk, Tobias
Hao, Shuai
Hassan, Fadi
Hatzivasilis, George
Hou, Huiying
Huang, Mengdie

Huang, Zonghao
Ismail, Maliha
Jiang, Hetong
Jiang, Shaoquan
Judmayer, Aljosha
Junming, Ke
Kantarcioglu, Murat
Karim, Imtiaz
Kasinathan, Prabhakaran
Kasra Kermanshahi, Shabnam
Kelarev, Andrei
Kern, Andreas
Kern, Sascha
Kim, Hyungsub
Klement, Felix
Komissarov, Rony
Koutroumpouchos, Nikolaos
Kuchta, Veronika
Kumar, Manish
Kwon, Yonghwi
Köstler, Johannes
Lai, Jianchang
Lakka, Eftychia
Lal, Chhagan
Lampropoulos, Konstantinos
Lee, Jehyun
Li, Rui
Li, Yanan
Li, Yannan
Liber, Matan
Lima Pereira, Hilder Vitor
Lin, Chengyu
Lin, Yan
Liu, Guannan
Liu, Lin
Livsey, Lee
Lopez, Christian
Loss, Julian
Lyu, Lin
Ma, Haoyu
Ma, Jack P. K.
Ma, Mimi
Makriyannis, Nikolaos
Mariot, Luca
Marson, Giorgia Azzurra
Martínez, Sergio

Mateu, Victor
Merzouk, Mohamed-Amine
Mestel, David
Mitropoulos, Charalambos
Mohammadi, Farnaz
Niehues, David
Noorman, Job
O'Connell, Sioli
Oppermann, Alexander
Palamidessi, Catuscia
Pan, Jing
Pang, Bo
Panwar, Nisha
Park, Jeongeun
Petroulakis, Nikolaos
Poeplau, Sebastian
Pradel, Gaëtan
Qiu, Tian
Qiu, Zhi
Rabbani, Md Masoom
Ramírez-Cruz, Yunior
Ringerud, Magnus
Rivera, Esteban
Rizomiliotis, Panagiotis
Román-García, Fernando
Saha, Sayandeep
Sanchez-Rola, Iskander
Schindler, Philipp
Schlette, Daniel
Sentanoe, Stewart
Setayeshfar, Omid
Sharifian, Setareh
Shen, Jun
Shen, Xinyue
Silde, Tjerand
Singla, Ankush
Skrobot, Marjan
Song, Zirui
Spolaor, Riccardo
Stifter, Nicholas
Striecks, Christoph
Struck, Patrick
Tabatabaei, Masoud
Tan, Teik Guan
Teague, Vanessa
Tengana, Lizzy

Tian, Guangwei
Trujillo, Rolando
Tschorsch, Florian
Tu, Binbin
Turrin, Federico
Van Strydonck, Thomas
Vielberth, Manfred
Wang, Coby
Wang, Jiafan
Wang, Kailong
Wang, Qian
Wang, Xiaofeng
Wang, Xiaolei
Wang, Yi
Watanabe, Yohei
Wen, Rui
Wisiol, Nils
Wong, Harry W. H.
Wu, Chen
Wu, Huangting

Xu, Fenghao
Xu, Jia
Yang, Rupeng
Yang, S. J.
Yang, Shishuai
Yang, Xu
Yang, Xuechao
Yang, Zheng
Ying, Jason
Yung, Moti
Zhang, Cong
Zhang, Min
Zhang, Wenlu
Zhang, Yanjun
Zhang, Yubao
Zhang, Yuexin
Zhang, Zhiyi
Zhao, Yongjun
Zou, Yang
Zuo, Cong

Additional Reviewers for Posters

Alexopoulos, Nikolaos
Ma, Yihan
Wang, Cheng-Long

Wen, Rui
Xiang, Zihang
Zhang, Minxing

Keynotes

Algorithms and the Law

Shafi Goldwasser

Massachusetts Institute of Technology (MIT),
Weizmann Institute of Science (WIS)

Abstract. Today, algorithms are proposed to replace several key processes governed by laws, regulations and policies. This requires mathematical definitions of regulations and proofs of algorithmic adherence. We will discuss several such developments.

The Politics and Technology of (Hardware) Trojans

Christof Paar

Ruhr University

Abstract. Over the last decade or so, hardware Trojans have drawn increased attention by the scientific community. They have been mainly considered a technical problem that arises in the context of the globalized semiconductor supply chain. However, low-level Trojans and other forms of backdoors have also a fascinating societal and political component. In this keynote we will present some interesting technical issues of hardware Trojans, especially if they are designed to avoid detection. We will also summarize some of the reported cases of cryptographic backdoors and put them in a political context.

Increasing Trust in ML Through Governance

Nicolas Papernot

University of Toronto

Abstract. The attack surface of machine learning is large: training data can be poisoned, predictions manipulated using adversarial examples, models exploited to reveal sensitive information contained in training data, etc. This is in large parts due to the absence of security and privacy considerations in the design of ML algorithms. Designing secure ML requires that we have a solid understanding as to what we expect legitimate model behavior to look like. We illustrate these directions with recent work on adversarial examples, model stealing, privacy-preserving ML, machine unlearning, and proof of learning.

The Science of Computer Science: An Offensive Research Perspective

Yuval Yarom

School of Computer Science at the University of Adelaide

Abstract. Is computer science a real science? Is offensive security research a scientific activity? To answer these questions, in this talk we explore the state of the art in hardware security research. We discuss anecdotes, directions, and methods and draw parallels to established sciences. Finally, we reach somewhat non-surprising conclusions.

Contents – Part I

Malware

User Behaviour and Underground Economy

Blockchain

Machine Learning

Automotive

Anomaly Detection

Contents – Part II

Cryptography

Privacy

Differential Privacy

Zero Knowledge

Key Exchange

Multi-party Computation

Posters

Network Security

More Efficient Post-quantum KEMTLS with Pre-distributed Public Keys

Peter Schwabe[1,2], Douglas Stebila[3], and Thom Wiggers[2(✉)]

[1] Max Planck Institute for Security and Privacy, Bochum, Germany
`peter@cryptojedi.org`
[2] Radboud University, Nijmegen, The Netherlands
`thom@thomwiggers.nl`
[3] University of Waterloo, Waterloo, Canada
`dstebila@uwaterloo.ca`

Abstract. While server-only authentication with certificates is the most widely used mode of operation for the Transport Layer Security (TLS) protocol on the world wide web, there are many applications where TLS is used in a different way or with different constraints. For example, embedded Internet-of-Things clients may have a server certificate pre-programmed and be highly constrained in terms of communication bandwidth or computation power. As post-quantum algorithms have a wider range of performance trade-offs, designs other than traditional "signed-key-exchange" may be worthwhile. The KEMTLS protocol, presented at ACM CCS 2020, uses key encapsulation mechanisms (KEMs) rather than signatures for authentication in the TLS 1.3 handshake, a benefit since most post-quantum KEMs are more efficient than PQ signatures. However, KEMTLS has some drawbacks, especially in the client authentication scenario which requires a full additional roundtrip.

We explore how the situation changes with *pre-distributed public keys*, which may be viable in many scenarios, for example pre-installed public keys in apps, on embedded devices, cached public keys, or keys distributed out of band. Our variant of KEMTLS with pre-distributed keys, called KEMTLS PDK, is more efficient in terms of both bandwidth and computation compared to post-quantum signed-KEM TLS (even cached public keys), and has a smaller trusted code base. When client authentication is used, KEMTLS-PDK is more bandwidth efficient than KEMTLS yet can complete client authentication in one fewer round trips, and has stronger authentication properties. Interestingly, using pre-distributed keys in KEMTLS-PDK changes the landscape on suitability of PQ algorithms: schemes where public keys are larger than ciphertexts/signatures (such as Classic McEliece and Rainbow) can be viable, and the differences between some lattice-based schemes is reduced. We also discuss how using pre-distributed public keys provides privacy benefits compared to pre-shared symmetric keys in TLS.

Keywords: Post-quantum cryptography · Transport Layer Security

© Springer Nature Switzerland AG 2021
E. Bertino et al. (Eds.): ESORICS 2021, LNCS 12972, pp. 3–22, 2021.
https://doi.org/10.1007/978-3-030-88418-5_1

1   Introduction

The Transport Layer Protocol (TLS) is among the most-used secure channel protocols. In August 2018, the most recent version was standardized as TLS 1.3 [38]. TLS 1.3 uses an (elliptic curve) Diffie–Hellman key exchange to establish an ephemeral shared secret with forward secrecy. Server (and optionally client) authentication is provided by digital signatures. Long-term signature public keys are exchanged in certificates during the handshake. The most commonly used signature algorithm is RSA, although elliptic curve signatures are also supported.

Migrating to Post-quantum TLS. To protect against quantum adversaries, effort has been made to move the TLS handshake towards post-quantum cryptography. The focus has largely been on upgrading the key exchange to post-quantum security. In [8], Bos, Costello, Naehrig and Stebila showed how to replace Diffie–Hellman by lattice-based key agreement in TLS 1.3. The lattice-based scheme was improved in the NewHope proposal [2], which was used in the first real-world post-quantum TLS experiment by Google in 2016 [9]. A second, more wide-scale, post-quantum TLS experiment by Google and Cloudflare has been running since 2019 [29,31]. Post-quantum authentication in TLS is widely believed to be less urgent, as attacks against authentication cannot be mounted retroactively. However, several works also investigated the use of post-quantum signature schemes and certificates in TLS [5,6,44] by dropping in replacements of post-quantum primitives into the existing TLS 1.3 handshake and PKI infrastructure.

KEMTLS [43] is a recent proposal that makes more radical changes to the TLS 1.3 handshake. Instead of Diffie–Hellman and signatures, KEMTLS uses key-encapsulation mechanisms (KEMs) not just for confidentiality, but also for authentication. The main motivation for this design is that most post-quantum KEMs are much more efficient, both computationally and in terms of bandwidth requirements, than post-quantum signature schemes. Additional advantages are a smaller trusted code base and offline deniability. We give a high-level overview of KEMTLS in comparison to the TLS 1.3 handshake in Appendix A.

1.1   Pre-distributed Keys

Both TLS 1.3 and KEMTLS assume that the client does not know the server's long-term public-key when sending the ClientHello message; the certificate is transmitted as part of the handshake, even if the client already knows the public key. We refer to the scenario when a client already knows the server's public key as the *pre-distributed-key* or *cached-key* scenario. This occurs, for example, when web browsers cache certificates of frequently accessed servers; when mobile apps store certificates of the limited number of servers they connect to; when TLS is used by IoT devices that only ever connect to one or a handful of servers and have those certificates pre-installed; or when certificates have been distributed out of band, for example, through DNS [24].

In fact, the TLS cached information extension [41] allows the client to inform the server that it already knows certain certificates so they need not be transmitted. However, this RFC is not widely implemented, perhaps because (pre-quantum) certificates are fairly short and thus bandwidth savings are limited.

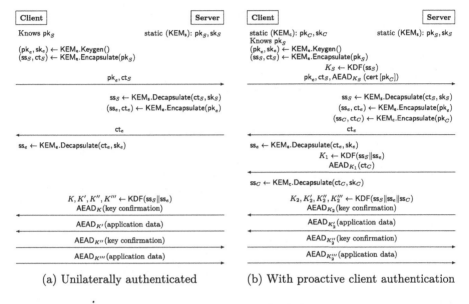

(a) Unilaterally authenticated   (b) With proactive client authentication

Fig. 1. Overview of KEMTLS-PDK variants

Contributions of This Paper. In this paper we investigate how this situation changes with the move to post-quantum cryptography, both when caching signature-based certificates in the TLS 1.3 handshake, but more importantly when using KEM-based authentication as used in KEMTLS. More specifically,

- we introduce KEMTLS-PDK, a variant of KEMTLS that makes use of pre-distributed keys for earlier authentication in the protocol flow;
- we describe KEMTLS-PDK with proactive client authentication and show that the benefits of earlier authentication are even more significant;
- we analyse the security properties of KEMTLS-PDK (a complete proof in the standard model is in the full version of the paper, available online);
- we implement KEMTLS-PDK in the Rustls library using different instantiations of the KEMs with NIST PQC round-3 candidates; and
- we evaluate the performance of KEMTLS-PDK in comparison to TLS 1.3 instantiated with different post-quantum primitives and pre-distributed (cached) server certificates, and in comparison to KEMTLS.

We give a sketch of KEMTLS-PDK in Fig. 1a. The central property to observe is that, like in TLS 1.3, but unlike in KEMTLS, the first message from the server

Table 1. Summary of performance characteristics of KEMTLS, signed-KEM TLS 1.3 with cached server certificate, and KEMTLS-PDK

	KEMTLS	Cached TLS	KEMTLS-PDK
Unilaterally authenticated			
Round trips until client receives response data	3	3	3
Size (bytes) of public key crypto objects transmitted:			
• Minimum PQ	932	499	561
• Module-LWE/Module-SIS (Kyber, Dilithium)	5,556	3,988	2,336
• NTRU-based (NTRU, Falcon)	3,486	2,088	2,144
Mutually authenticated			
Round trips until client receives response data	4	3	3
Size (bytes) of public key crypto objects transmitted:			
• Minimum PQ	1,431	2,152	1,060
• MLWE/MSIS	9,554	10,140	6,324
• NTRU	5,574	4,365	4,185

serves as key confirmation. This means that in this variant on KEMTLS, like in TLS 1.3, the server is explicitly authenticated after a single round trip. Also like TLS 1.3, the server can send data to the client first. The version of KEMTLS-PDK with proactive client authentication is shown in Fig. 1b.

We give a brief summary how this affects performance in Table 1, for a variety of post-quantum algorithm combinations. We see that client authentication in KEMTLS-PDK is just as efficient in terms of round trips as in TLS 1.3. However, in terms of bandwidth requirements, KEMTLS-PDK is *more* efficient than TLS 1.3 with cached certificates (Cached TLS) for most instantiations. We will discuss this in more detail in Sect. 5, but the unilaterally authenticated "Minimum PQ" instantiation actually shows another interesting effect of considering TLS with cached keys: KEMs and signature schemes with small ciphertexts/signatures, such as Classic McEliece [1] or Rainbow [16], not only become viable but are the most efficient instantiation.

Related Work. The KEMTLS and KEMTLS-PDK proposals follow a long line of work on authenticated key exchange (AKE) that started from early works by Bellare and Rogaway [4] and Canetti and Krawczyk [10]. Many earlier works already considered AKE protocols that do not use signatures for authentication; often authentication is then obtained from long-term Diffie–Hellman (DH) keys. See, for example [25,30,33,36]. The approach of constructing AKE with long-term DH keys for authentication has been considered for TLS in the OPTLS proposal by Krawczyk and Wee in [28], and in a subsequent IETF draft [39]. Unfortunately, there is no efficient post-quantum instantiation for non-interactive key exchange required by those DH-based constructions, which means that the closest proposals to KEMTLS and KEMTLS-PDK are generic AKE constructions using KEMs or public-key encryption schemes, such as the protocols described in [14,21,22]. While [14] mentions as an application (post-quantum) TLS, none of these earlier works on KEM-based AKE actually present an integration (or implementation) as part of the TLS handshake. This means that they work in the typical setting for AKE that all long-term keys are distributed beforehand – not just the server's keys as in KEMTLS-PDK. Also those earlier works do not present concrete TLS handshake performance results.

Availability of Software. Our implementation, measurement software, and data are available at https://thomwiggers.nl/publication/kemtlspdk/ under permissive open-source licenses.

2   Preliminaries

Notation. The TLS protocol has named messages, such as `ClientHello`, which we abbreviate like `CH`. Encrypted messages are written as $\{\texttt{Message}\}_{key}$. We write the transcript constructed by concatenating a sequence of TLS messages like `CH`...`SF`. $\emptyset$ denotes an empty value.

Symmetric Cryptography. We rely on standard definitions such as collision-resistant hash functions, authenticated encryption, and pseudorandom functions. In the proof we use message-authentication codes with existential unforgeability under chosen message attacks (EUF-CMA). The key schedule is based on HKDF [26, 27], which consists of two functions, HKDF.Extract and HKDF.Expand. HKDF.Extract takes a random *salt* and *input keying material*; the output is a *pseudorandom key* that is fed to HKDF.Expand along with *context*, to derive keys of specified length for use in the handshake. The key schedule in TLS sets up a chain of these operations. It passes along the internal state via the salt argument to HKDF.Extract. New shared secrets are incorporated via the other argument. The context given to HKDF.Expand is provided as an operation-specific constant value and the current hash of the transcript. For ease of presentation, we will write these as if they are separate arguments and omit the desired output length. Our security analysis of KEMTLS-PDK relies on HKDF.Expand being a *dual PRF* (a PRF in either of its two arguments, salt and input keying material).

Key Encapsulation Mechanisms. A key encapsulation mechanism (KEM) is an asymmetric primitive that abstracts a basic key exchange and is a focus of the NIST post-quantum standardization project. A KEM consists of: a key generation algorithm KEM.Keygen() which generates a public and private keypair $(\mathsf{pk}, \mathsf{sk})$; an encapsulation algorithm KEM.Encapsulate(pk) which generates a shared secret ss in a shared secret space $\mathcal{K}$ and ciphertext (encapsulation) ct against a given public key pk; and a decapsulation algorithm KEM.Decapsulate(ct, sk) which decapsulates to obtain the shared secret ss'. Decapsulation might fail; in a δ-correct scheme, $\mathsf{ss}' = \mathsf{ss}$ with probability at least $1-\delta$. Our security analysis of KEMTLS-PDK relies on standard IND-CCA-security of the KEMs used for client and server authentication, and IND-1CCA-security (i.e., IND-CCA restricted to a single decapsulation query) for the KEM used for ephemeral key exchange.

3   KEMTLS with Pre-distributed Long-Term Keys

Even though one of the strengths of the TLS protocol is its ability to establish a secure channel with a previously unknown party, it is very often not the case that the communicating party is completely unknown. TLS 1.3's pre-shared key mechanism can be used with session tickets to enable fast resumption after an initial full handshake [38, Fig. 3]. These mechanisms rely mostly on symmetric cryptography, although TLS 1.3 allows an optional additional ephemeral key exchange in resumption for forward secrecy. There is nothing precluding the use of these mechanisms, including the "0-RTT" client-to-server data flow in the resumption message in KEMTLS.

However, because TLS 1.3 resumption relies on symmetric cryptography, it is not very flexible. The security properties of a resumed session are tied to the previous session. This includes, e.g., if the session was mutually authenticated. For these reasons session tickets expire quickly, after at most 7 days [38, Sect. 4.6.1]. There are also privacy issues, as the tickets, which are opaque to the client, might contain tracking information. To prevent such tracking, Sy et al. [46] even suggested limiting session lifetime to only 10 min.

Because externally distributed pre-shared keys are symmetric, we quickly run into concerns there as well. If clients have a common installation profile and share keys, when a single client is compromised there will be no security for any client anymore. A client that also acts as a server also needs to use different keys in each role to prevent the Selfie attack [19]. This means we need a key for each client and server pair, quickly turning this into a key-management nightmare.

In our proposed KEMTLS-PDK, we employ a more flexible approach by distributing a server's long-term KEM public key instead of a symmetric key. A detailed protocol flow diagram of KEMTLS-PDK is given in Fig. 2.

Like in KEMTLS, the client encapsulates to the server's long-term KEM public key pk_S, obtaining a ciphertext ct_S and a shared secret ss_S. However, as we assume that the client already has pk_S, it can do this *at the start* of the connection and send ct_S in a ClientHello extension. We plug ss_S into the key derivation schedule at the earliest possible stage when deriving the Early Secret ES. Deriving ES from ss_S avoids changing the key schedule. It also intuitively makes sense, as data encrypted under traffic keys derived from ES has no forward secrecy or replay protection; just as in TLS 1.3 with PSK and 0-RTT data [38, Sect. 2.3]. The only server who can read a message encrypted under a key derived from ES is the server that has access to sk_S; we consider such keys *implicitly authenticated*. For forward secrecy we also send an ephemeral public key pk_e in the ClientHello message.

Except for the additional extension transmitting ct_S, the CH message is the same as in KEMTLS. This allows a handshake to fall back to the regular KEMTLS handshake protocol, e.g., if the client has an out-of-date certificate.

The server replies with the encapsulation ct_e of ephemeral shared secret ss_e in the ServerHello message. It also indicates in an extension that it has accepted ciphertext ct_S and is proceeding with KEMTLS-PDK. Then it proceeds in a similar fashion as the original TLS 1.3 handshake. The server derives HS from

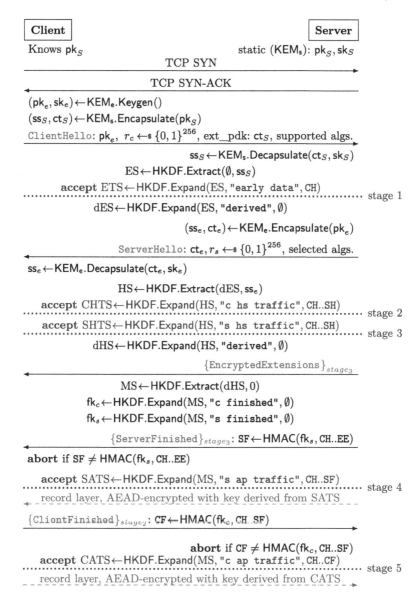

Fig. 2. The KEMTLS-PDK handshake for unilateral (server-only) authentication with pre-distributed server public keys

ES and ss_e and sends the `EncryptedExtensions` message encrypted under a key derived from HS. It then immediately finishes its part the handshake by sending a MAC over the message transcript in the `ServerFinished` message. This confirms the server's view of the handshake to the client and explicitly authenticates the server. The server can now start sending application data. The client follows up by also confirming its view of the handshake in a `ClientFinished` message. This means the client is now ready to communicate as well.

3.1   Proactive Client Authentication

In some applications, such as in a VPN, the client already knows that the server will require mutual authentication. This means that a client can *proactively* authenticate by sending its certificate as early in the handshake as possible, and in particular before the server requests the certificate. For privacy reasons, client authentication in TLS requires that we verify the identity of the server and send the certificate encrypted [38, Sect. E.1.2]. Performing client authentication in KEMTLS thus requires a full additional round-trip: we can only send the client certificate after authenticating the server and the server cannot send the ciphertext before it receives pk_C.

In KEMTLS-PDK the client already posesses the server's long-term public key. We can use the shared secret obtained from encapsulating to the corresponding long-term key to send a client certificate along in the `ClientHello` message. This gives us mutual authentication within a single round-trip. The server supplies the challenge ciphertext ct_C to the client and derives the confirmation and traffic keys from ss_e, ss_S, and ss_C. At this point the server can start sending application data to the client. The client is implicitly authenticated, as they have not yet confirmed that they derived the same keys. As the keys are derived from ss_C, only the client who possesses sk_C can read these messages. To finish the handshake the client sends its own key confirmation message before proceeding to the application traffic. KEMTLS-PDK with mutual authentication is shown in Fig. 3.

4   Security Analysis

As KEMTLS-PDK is an authenticated-key-exchange protocol, the main security property it aims for is that keys established should be indistinguishable from random keys, however there are many subtleties that arise in KEMTLS-PDK. In this section we describe in greater detail the specific security properties that KEMTLS-PDK achieves.

Security Model. Following the approach of Dowling et al. [18] for the analysis of TLS 1.3, we model KEMTLS-PDK as a multi-stage key-agreement protocol [20], where each session has several *stages* in each of which a shared secret key is established. This model is an adaptation of the Bellare–Rogaway security model for authenticated key exchange [4]. The formal model appears in the full version;[1] we describe it briefly here.

Each party (client or server) has a long-term public-key/secret-key pair, and we assume there exists a public-key infrastructure for certifying these public keys. Each party can run multiple instances of the protocol simultaneously or

---

[1] The full version is available from thomwiggers.nl/publication/kemtlspdk/.

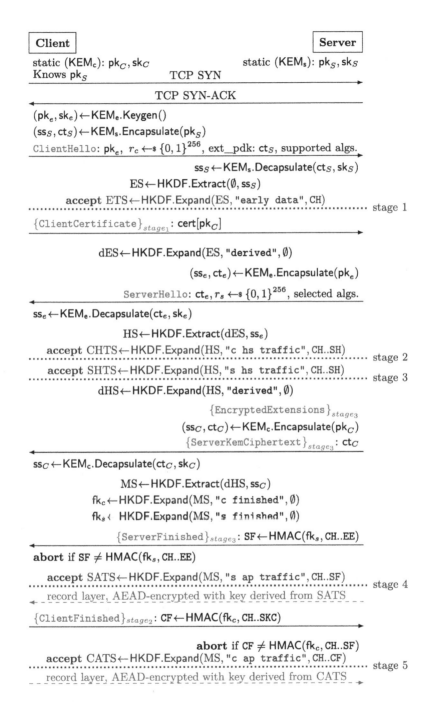

Fig. 3. The KEMTLS-PDK handshake for proactive client authentication with pre-distributed server public keys

in parallel, each of which is called a *session*. During each party's execution of a session, it maintains a variety of state variables, tracking the configuration of the session, status of execution, and intermediate values of the protocol itself. One important session variable is the *session identifier*, which will be used in the model to identify pairs of sessions that are partnered to each other. In general the session identifier consists of all of the protocols transmitted up until that point; as KEMTLS-PDK permits pre-distributed public keys, those pre-distributed values will be included in the session identifier.

The adversary controls all communications between parties, and can arbitrarily relay, change, drop, reorder, or insert messages. The adversary activates all sessions (via a NewSession query) and delivers all messages (via a Send query). It may compromise keys established during a stage (Reveal query) and parties' long-term keys (Corrupt query). The security model tracks the Reveal and Corrupt queries, and marks some sessions *unfresh* if too much information has been revealed and security can no longer be expected. The adversary may issue a Test query to a particular session and stage, and obtain either (a) the real key established for that stage, or (b) a uniformly random key; the choice of (a) or (b) depends on a hidden (uniform) bit chosen at the start of the experiment. There are some additional details in the full model in how queries are processed. Stage keys are marked as for *internal* or *external* use; internal-use keys may be used in subsequent parts of the protocol (e.g., to encrypt handshake messages), so the adversary must decide whether to Test an internal-use key when it is accepted.

Key Indistinguishability. The Test query captures that keys established should be indistinguishable from random: the goal of the adversary is to guess the hidden bit in the Test query, thereby distinguishing real keys form random. The experiment restricts the adversary from issuing the Test query to stages where the key has been exposed via a Reveal query, including partnered sessions.

Implicit Authentication and Forward Secrecy. Following [43], the security model captures three levels of forward secrecy for stage keys, which simultaneously incorporate notions of implicit authentication, meaning that only the intended party *could* know the shared secret.

- *Weak forward secrecy level 1* (wfs1): The stage key is indistinguishable to adversaries who were passive in the test stage, even if the adversary obtains the peer's long-term key at any point in time. These keys offer no implicit authentication. KEMTLS-PDK achieves wfs1 for server stages 2–5.
- *Weak forward secrecy level 2* (wfs2): The stage key is indistinguishable to adversaries who were passive in the test stage (wfs1) or who never corrupted the peer's long-term key; in the latter case this yields implicit authentication. KEMTLS-PDK achieves wfs2 for client stages 2–3.
- *Forward secrecy* (fs): The stage key is indistinguishable to adversaries who were passive in the test stage (wfs1) or who did not corrupt the peer's long-term key before the stage accepted; in the latter case this yields implicit authentication. KEMTLS-PDK achieves fs for client stages 4 and 5, and for server stages 4 and 5 in the mutually authenticated version.

The model captures *retroactive* revision of forward secrecy: a stage-i key may have a weaker form of forward secrecy at the time it is accepted, but may have a stronger form of forward secrecy after some subsequent stage accepts. In KEMTLS-PDK, earlier stage keys are upgraded to the level of forward secrecy achieved by later stages once the later stage accepts.

In the unilaterally authenticated version of KEMTLS-PDK (Fig. 2), the client gets full fs one round trip earlier than in KEMTLS.

Explicit Authentication. The security model also tracks at what point in time each party receives explicit authentication of its peer; explicit authentication goes a step further than implicit authentication in that the party has received explicit evidence (e.g., a MAC tag) that the intended peer actually is live. The model also includes retroactive authentication, in which an earlier stage may be regarded as explicitly authenticated once a later stage accepts. Client sessions in KEMTLS-PDK receive explicit authentication right before the stage-4 key is accepted, one round trip earlier than in KEMTLS. Server sessions, in mutually authenticated KEMTLS-PDK, receive explicit authentication right before the stage-5 key is accepted, again one round tip earlier than KEMTLS. In particular, this means that KEMTLS-PDK gives explicit authentication for all client application data (although only implicit authentication for the client certificate).

Downgrade Resilience. [43] observed that implicit authentication characteristics of early stages of keys in KEMTLS meant that some application data would be transmitted prior to the client having received explicit authentication from the server of the symmetric encryption algorithms negotiated during the handshake. This meant that it would be possible for an adversary to cause a downgrade to a suboptimal (from the server's perspective) algorithm—although still only to an algorithm that the client offered to use. In KEMTLS-PDK, explicit server authentication happens one round trip earlier, and in particular prior to client transmission of application data, so KEMTLS-PDK offers full downgrade resilience.

Replayability. The model tracks that some stages are not protected against replays: in particular, stage-1 keys are not guaranteed to be unique at server instances since an adversary can replay the same ClientHello message multiple times to induce the same stage-1 key; all subsequent stages are replay-protected.

Anonymity. Like TLS 1.3 and KEMTLS, KEMTLS-PDK does not offer full anonymity, in particular due to the presence of the ServerNameIndicator extension in the ClientHello message. Our implementation also identifies the server certificate that was encapsulated to. (This identifier could be omitted by using trial-decryption at the server, though if the server has many public keys, this could be prohibitive.) The TLS working group is considering an "Encrypted ClientHello" mechanism that relies on the client obtaining a server public key out-of-band to enable identity protection for the server. KEMTLS-PDK's use of a pre-distributed key for encryption of part of the initial client message may be compatible with a variant of encrypted `ClientHello`, which we leave as future work since encrypted `ClientHello` has not yet been finalized even for TLS 1.3.

Deniability. As KEMTLS-PDK avoids the use of signatures for authentication, like KEMTLS and unlike TLS 1.3, KEMTLS-PDK offers *offline deniability* [15], meaning that a judge, when given a transcript of a protocol execution and all of the keys involved, cannot tell whether the transcript is genuine or forged. KEMTLS-PDK does not have the harder-to-achieve online deniability property [17] when one party tries to frame the other or collaborates with the judge.

5 Instantiation and Evaluation

In this section we describe how we instantiate and implemented KEMTLS-PDK and compare the performance with KEMTLS and cached TLS.

For a fair comparison with cached TLS we proceed as follows. RFC 7924 [41] proposes a caching mechanism for certificates, which lets the client indicate that it already knows the server's certificate by including the hash of the `ServerCertificate` (SCRT) message in the `ClientHello` message. In TLS 1.2 this amounts to a hash of the certificate chain. In TLS 1.3, however, the SCRT message was extended, and may include certificate transparancy [32] or OCSP [40] status information. This means that the hash value for the message is no longer stable. For our experiments, we adapt the mechanism of RFC 7924 to TLS 1.3 by using hashes for each individual certificate, instead. The server does not omit the SCRT message, but the certificates are replaced by their hashes. This allows the client to use those hashes to look up and replace the certificates by the originals for validation purposes. When instantiating TLS 1.3 with post-quantum primitives, we replace ephemeral DH by a KEM as described in [8] (for TLS 1.2) and implemented in post-quantum TLS experiments [9,29,31].

5.1 Choice of Primitives

Table 2 shows the scenarios and primitives considered in our evaluation. We also show the sizes of the cryptographic objects that need to be transmitted, such as public keys, ciphertexts and signatures. All experiments require a KEM public key and ciphertext for ephemeral key exchange. In KEMTLS, we need a full certificate (signed KEM public key) and a ciphertext for authentication. For the TLS 1.3 with caching experiments, we only transmit a signature for authentication; certificates are withheld. Finally, for the KEMTLS-PDK instantiations, we withold the certificate and only transmit the ciphertext for authentication.

To instantiate KEMs and signatures we choose NIST PQC round-3 candidates at "level 1 security" (equivalent to AES-128). Kyber-512 [42], LightSABER [13], and NTRU-HPS-2048 [12] are all finalists, efficient KEMs and suitable for both ephemeral key exchange and authentication. Classic McEliece 348864 [1] is the remaining finalist KEM, but its large public key makes it only suitable for authentication in KEMTLS-PDK. We include alternate candidate SIKEp434-compressed [23] as it is the KEM with the smallest sum of

Table 2. Sizes (in bytes) of public-key cryptography objects transmitted and cached/ pre-distributed in KEMTLS, TLS 1.3 with cached certificates, and KEMTLS-PDK, for server-only and mutual authentication.

		Server-only authentication			+ Client authentication			
		Ephem. key ex. (pk+ct)	Server auth.	Trans-mitted	Cached @client (server pk)	Client auth. (pk+ct/sig)	CA (sig)	Trans-mitted	Cached @server (CA pk)
KEMTLS	Minimum	SIKE 197 236	SIKE/Rai. crt+ct 499	932	–	SIKE 433	Rainbow 66	1,431	Rainbow 161,600
	Assumption: MLWE/MSIS	Kyber 800 768	Kyber/Dil. crt+ct 3,988	5,556	–	Kyber 1,568	Dilithium 2,420	9,554	Dilithium 1,312
	Assumption: NTRU	NTRU 699 699	NTRU/Fal. crt+ct 2,088	3,486	–	NTRU 1,398	Falcon 690	5,574	Falcon 897
Cached TLS	TLS 1.3	X25519 32 32	RSA-2048 sig 256	320	RSA-2048 272	RSA-2048 528	RSA-2048 256	1,104	RSA-2048 272
	Minimum	SIKE 197 236	Rainbow sig 66	499	Rainbow 161,600	Falcon 1,587	Rainbow 66	2,152	Rainbow 161,600
	Assumption: MLWE/MSIS	Kyber 800 768	Dilithium sig 2,420	3,988	Dilithium 1,312	Dilithium 3,732	Dilithium 2,420	10,140	Dilithium 1,312
	Assumption: NTRU	NTRU 699 699	Falcon sig 690	2,088	Falcon 897	Falcon 1,587	Falcon 690	4,365	Falcon 897
KEMTLS-PDK	Minimum	SIKE 197 236	McEliece ct 128	561	McEliece 261,120	SIKE 433	Rainbow 66	1,060	Rainbow 161,600
	Finalist: Kyber	Kyber 800 768	Kyber ct 768	2,336	Kyber 800	Kyber 1,568	Dilithium 2,420	6,324	Dilithium 1,312
	Finalist: NTRU	NTRU 699 699	NTRU ct 699	2,097	NTRU 699	NTRU 1,398	Falcon 690	4,185	Falcon 897
	Finalist: SABER	SABER 672 736	SABER ct 736	2,144	SABER 672	SABER 1,408	Dilithium 2,420	5,972	Dilithium 1,312

public key and ciphertext. For the signature schemes we consider the finalists Dilithium II [34], Falcon-512 [37], and Rainbow I Classic [16]. We align the chosen instantiations based on similar assumptions.

These scenarios immediately expose trade-offs that may or may not be feasible in real-world implementations. For example, the public keys for Rainbow ($\approx 160\,\mathrm{KB}$) and McEliece ($\approx 260\,\mathrm{KB}$) are very large, so they are probably not suitable for scenarios where the public keys are cached for shorter amounts of time, such as TLS resumption. If the cached public key needs to be updated, for example by having a KEMTLS-PDK handshake fall back to the regular KEMTLS, sending a certificate with a McEliece or Rainbow public key could be prohibitive.

5.2   Implementation

For our experiments, we implemented KEMTLS-PDK by extending the Rustls TLS library [7]. It is based on our prior implementation of KEMTLS. We also extend the TLS 1.3 protocol with the certificate caching for server certificates, as described in the previous paragraph. The measured post-quantum KEMs and signature algorithms are provided by the Open Quantum Safe project's liboqs library [45]. This library includes optimized, AVX2-accelerated implementations for every primitive measured, except for Rainbow. For a fair comparison, we ad-hoc integrated the AVX2 implementation from the Rainbow submitters into the version of `liboqs` used.

5.3 Handshake Sizes

Table 2 shows the sizes of the public-key cryptographic objects transmitted in KEMTLS, TLS 1.3 with certificate caching, and KEMTLS-PDK. For KEMTLS, a full leaf certificate is transmitted (but no intermediate or root certificate); for TLS 1.3 with caching and KEMTLS-PDK we assume server certificates are cached. For client authentication, we have not included caching for the end-point certificate, as servers would presumably talk to many clients.

In scenarios where we aim to minimize communication, TLS 1.3 with caching transmits 433 fewer bytes of public-key cryptography objects than KEMTLS. It needs 66 fewer bytes on the wire than KEMTLS-PDK for unilaterally authenticated handshakes. When client authentication is included, KEMTLS-PDK reduces the number of bytes transmitted in the handshake by 51% (1092 B) compared to TLS 1.3 with caching, however. Compared to KEMTLS it saves 25% (371 B). The minimum scenarios for TLS 1.3 with caching and KEMTLS-PDK both heavily rely on the fact that the (very large) Rainbow and McEliece public keys do not need to be transmitted. This probably makes this scenario only practical for those cases where these keys can be used for very long times, such as when the keys are embedded in IoT devices.

The other instantiations are based on much faster lattice-based cryptography. These also have more managable public keys. This allows applications where the handshake is initially done without caching, after which the client remembers the certificate. In these instantiations, the Kyber instantiation of KEMTLS-PDK reduces transmission by 58% (3220 B) over KEMTLS for unilaterally authenticated handshakes and by 33% (3230 B) in mutually authenticated handshakes. For NTRU and Falcon—the two lattice-based schemes based on NTRU lattices— we see that KEMTLS-PDK performs better than cached TLS in terms of bandwidth requirements only when used with client authentication. This is expected as NTRU ciphertexts have essentially the same size (699 bytes) as Falcon signatures in the worst case (690 bytes). Note the average signature size of Falcon is advertised as 666 bytes [37], but our API does not use variable-size signatures.

5.4 Handshake Times

We measured the times to complete the handshakes for each of our considered scenarios over both a low-latency, high-bandwidth connection and a high-latency, low-bandwidth connection. We follow the same methodology as [43], which is in turn using the methodology from [35]. Table 3 shows the timings of unilaterally authenticated handshakes. We see there is little difference between the three scenarios, although compressed SIKE has noticable performance overhead. The lattice schemes perform very similarly.

For mutually authenticated handshakes, as shown in Table 4, things change. The extra round-trip for client authentication in KEMTLS is clearly visible.

Table 3. Average time in ms for unilaterally authenticated handshakes of TLS 1.3 with cached leaf certificates and of KEMTLS-PDK.

Unilaterally authenticated	31.1 ms RTT, 1000 Mbps			195.6 ms RTT, 10 Mbps		
	Client sent req.	Client recv. resp.	Server expl. auth.	Client sent req.	Client recv. resp.	Server expl. auth.
KEMTLS Minimum	75.2	**115.9**	115.9	408.2	**616.3**	616.2
MLWE/MSIS	63.2	**94.7**	94.6	397.2	**594.3**	594.3
NTRU	63.1	**94.7**	94.6	395.6	**592.6**	592.6
Cached TLS TLS 1.3	66.3	**97.5**	66.2	396.6	**592.8**	396.5
Minimum	70.0	**101.2**	69.9	402.0	**598.2**	401.9
MLWE/MSIS	63.9	**95.1**	63.8	396.8	**593.0**	396.7
NTRU	64.8	**96.1**	64.7	396.7	**592.9**	396.7
PDK Minimum	66.1	**97.3**	66.1	397.8	**594.0**	397.7
Kyber	63.0	**94.3**	63.0	395.1	**591.3**	395.0
NTRU	63.0	**94.3**	62.9	395.0	**591.2**	394.9
SABER	63.1	**94.3**	63.0	395.1	**591.2**	395.0

For a comparison of CPU cycles spent on the asymmetric cryptography, results for KEMTLS-PDK are similar to those of KEMTLS [43, Table 2 (left)]. The comparison made there also holds for KEMTLS-PDK and TLS 1.3 with caching, as the same cryptographic operations still need to be done and there have not been significant changes since round 2 of the NIST competition. In other words, KEMTLS-PDK offers the same massive savings compared to TLS 1.3 with pre-distributed certificates as KEMTLS offers in comparison to plain TLS 1.3.

6 Discussion

In this paper we presented the first investigation of post-quantum TLS with pre-distributed server public keys, both with traditional signature-based authentication and in the KEM-based authentication setting of KEMTLS. We believe that the results show that a combination of KEMTLS and KEMTLS-PDK may be the more efficient option for the post-quantum future of TLS. However, this will need to be confirmed (or refuted) through real-world experiments; one such experiment is currently underway in collaboration with Cloudflare; see [11].

There are some aspects of KEMTLS-PDK that we have not discussed so far but that deserve being mentioned.

We did not compare KEMTLS-PDK to TLS session resumption using a symmetric pre-shared key (for authentication) and DH (or KEMs) for forward secrecy. The reason is that in this scenario clients need to keep a sensitive secret key that is shared with the server; see the related discussion in Sect. 3.

For proactive client authentication, the client needs to pick some symmetric ciphersuite to use for encrypting and authenticating its certificate; this decision

Table 4. Average time in ms for mutually authenticated handshakes of TLS 1.3 with cached leaf certificates and of KEMTLS-PDK.

Mutually authenticated	31.1 ms RTT, 1000 Mbps			195.6 ms RTT, 10 Mbps		
	Client sent req.	Client recv. resp.	Server expl. auth.	Client sent req.	Client recv. resp.	Server expl. auth.
KEMTLS Minimum	129.6	**160.8**	122.9	630.4	**826.8**	621.9
MLWE/MSIS	95.1	**126.5**	95.0	598.0	**794.3**	597.8
NTRU	95.0	**126.4**	94.8	595.7	**792.1**	595.5
Cached TLS TLS 1.3	68.6	**100.1**	66.0	399.4	**597.0**	396.7
Minimum	71.0	**102.6**	69.9	403.4	**601.9**	402.1
MLWE/MSIS	64.4	**96.1**	63.8	399.7	**616.1**	399.2
NTRU	66.1	**98.0**	64.7	398.3	**597.4**	396.9
PDK Minimum	84.9	**116.0**	84.9	420.4	**616.7**	420.4
Kyber	63.5	**94.8**	63.4	399.4	**595.6**	399.3
NTRU	63.6	**94.9**	63.5	397.2	**593.4**	397.1
SABER	63.6	**94.9**	63.5	400.6	**597.1**	400.5

must be made before any ciphersuite negotiation has taken place. In our implementation we use a "default" ciphersuite; for example, TLS_AES_128_GCM_SHA256 must be implemented by any TLS 1.3-compliant application [38, Sec. 9.1]. Another option would be to store information about the ciphersuite to use alongside the certificate – one could even consider integrating ciphersuite information inside certificates. This would clearly constitute a bigger change to the TLS infrastructure, but is not unprecedented (c.f. HPKE [3]).

Interestingly, if KEMTLS uses KEMs with different cryptographic assumptions for the ephemeral and the long-term KEM, we obtain hybrid confidentiality in the following sense: even if the assumption used for the ephemeral KEM is cryptographically broken at some point in the future, handshakes retain confidentiality as long as the long-term KEM keys are not compromised. With KEMTLS-PDK some interesting combinations of ephemeral and long-term KEMs—e.g., McEliece and Saber, Kyber, or NTRU—may become feasible. We leave it to future work to investigate this further and to formalize the notion of hybrid confidentiality sketched here.

Acknowledgements. The authors gratefully acknowledge insightful discussions with Patrick Towa on the security model, proof, and pre-distributed keys scenario. This work has been supported by the European Research Council through Starting Grant No. 805031 (EPOQUE) and the Natural Sciences and Engineering Research Council of Canada through Discovery grant RGPIN-2016-05146 and a Discovery Accelerator Supplement.

A   KEMTLS

Figure 4 presents KEMTLS [43] side-by-side with TLS 1.3. Establishing an ephemeral shared secret happens in a similar way in TLS 1.3 and KEMTLS. The client submits a public key g^x (TLS 1.3) or pk_e (KEMTLS) to the server in the ClientHello message. The server then replies with its key share g^y (TLS 1.3) or ciphertext ct_e (KEMTLS). At this point, the server has the information to derive the handshake shared secret. This shared secret ss_e is used to encrypt the server's certificate before transmitting it to the client.

In TLS 1.3, this certificate contains a long-term public key for a digital signature algorithm pk_S. The server signs the transcript of all the transmitted messages so far and submits this signature in the ServerCertificateVerify message. This allows the client to immediately verify the server's identity: the signature proves the server posesses the private key corresponding to the certificate. The server then finishes the handshake by sending the key confirmation message. The client replies with its own key confirmation message.

When using long-term public keys for KEMs in certificates, signing the transcript is not possible. So, in KEMTLS, the client encapsulates a new shared secret ss_S to the server's long-term public key pk_S. It then sends over the corresponding ciphertext ct_S to the server. Only if the server can decapsulate the shared secret from the ciphertext, can it prove posession of the private key corresponding to the certificate. The server mixes in the new shared secret with the ephemeral secret key and derives new handshake keys. The server's key confirmation message then proves posesion of the long-term key.

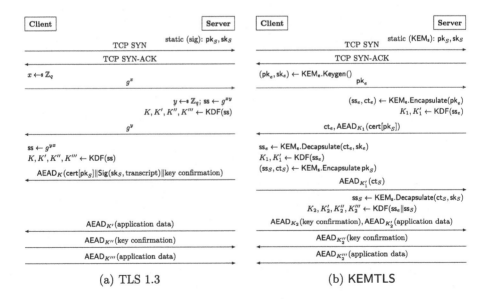

(a) TLS 1.3   (b) KEMTLS

Fig. 4. Overview of TLS 1.3 and KEMTLS

If the client were to wait for the server to prove that it has decapsulated the ciphertext, KEMTLS would need a full extra round-trip over TLS 1.3. However, before the confirmation message, the client already knows that only the intended server would be able to read any data that is encrypted with keys derived from ss_S. KEMTLS uses this to allow the client to send data to the *implicitly authenticated* server before it has received the server's key confirmation message. Once the key confirmation is received, the server is *explicitly authenticated* and the client then knows the server is present.

References

1. Albrecht, M.R., et al.: Classic McEliece. Technical report, National Institute of Standards and Technology (2020). urlhttps://csrc.nist.gov/projects/post-quantum-cryptography/round-3-submissions
2. Alkim, E., Ducas, L., Pöppelmann, T., Schwabe, P.: Post-quantum key exchange - a new hope. In: Holz, T., Savage, S. (eds.) USENIX Security 2016, pp. 327–343. USENIX Association, August 2016
3. Barnes, R.L., Bhargavan, K., Lipp, B., Wood, C.A.: Hybrid public key encryption. Internet-draft, Internet Research Task Force (2021), https://datatracker.ietf.org/doc/html/draft-irtf-cfrg-hpke-08
4. Bellare, M., Rogaway, P.: Entity authentication and key distribution. In: Stinson, D.R. (ed.) CRYPTO 1993. LNCS, vol. 773, pp. 232–249. Springer, Heidelberg (1994). https://doi.org/10.1007/3-540-48329-2_21
5. Bindel, N., Braun, J., Gladiator, L., Stöckert, T., Wirth, J.: X.509-compliant hybrid certificates for the post-quantum transition. J. Open Sour. Softw. 4(40), 1606 (2019). https://doi.org/10.21105/joss.01606
6. Bindel, N., Herath, U., McKague, M., Stebila, D.: Transitioning to a quantum-resistant public key infrastructure. In: Lange, T., Takagi, T. (eds.) PQCrypto 2017, vol. 10346, pp. 384–405. Springer, Heidelberg (2017). https://doi.org/10.1007/978-3-319-59879-6_22
7. Birr-Pixton, J.: A modern TLS library in Rust. https://github.com/ctz/rustls. Accessed 29 Apr 2021
8. Bos, J.W., Costello, C., Naehrig, M., Stebila, D.: Post-quantum key exchange for the TLS protocol from the ring learning with errors problem. In: 2015 IEEE Symposium on Security and Privacy, pp. 553–570. IEEE Computer Society Press, May 2015. https://doi.org/10.1109/SP.2015.40
9. Braithwaite, M.: Experimenting with post-quantum cryptography. Posting on the Google Security Blog (2016). https://security.googleblog.com/2016/07/experimenting-with-post-quantum.html
10. Canetti, R., Krawczyk, H.: Analysis of key-exchange protocols and their use for building secure channels. In: Pfitzmann, B. (ed.) EUROCRYPT 2001. LNCS, vol. 2045, pp. 453–474. Springer, Heidelberg (2001). https://doi.org/10.1007/3-540-44987-6_28
11. Celi, S., Wiggers, T.: KEMTLS: post-quantum TLS without signatures. Posting on the Cloudflare Blog (2021). https://blog.cloudflare.com/kemtls-post-quantum-tls-without-signatures/
12. Chen, C., et al.: NTRU. Technical report, National Institute of Standards and Technology (2020). https://csrc.nist.gov/projects/post-quantum-cryptography/round-3-submissions

13. D'Anvers, J.P., et al.: SABER. Technical report, National Institute of Standards and Technology (2020). https://csrc.nist.gov/projects/post-quantum-cryptography/round-3-submissions
14. de Saint Guilhem, C.D., Smart, N.P., Warinschi, B.: Generic forward-secure key agreement without signatures. In: Nguyen, P.Q., Zhou, J. (eds.) ISC 2017. LNCS, vol. 10599, pp. 114–133. Springer, Heidelberg (2017)
15. Di Raimondo, M., Gennaro, R., Krawczyk, H.: Deniable authentication and key exchange. In: Juels, A., Wright, R.N., De Capitani di Vimercati, S. (eds.) ACM CCS 2006, pp. 400–409. ACM Press, October–November 2006. https://doi.org/10.1145/1180405.1180454
16. Ding, J., et al.: Rainbow. Technical report, National Institute of Standards and Technology (2020). https://csrc.nist.gov/projects/post-quantum-cryptography/round-3-submissions
17. Dodis, Y., Katz, J., Smith, A., Walfish, S.: Composability and on-line deniability of authentication. In: Reingold, O. (ed.) TCC 2009. LNCS, vol. 5444, pp. 146–162. Springer, Heidelberg (2009). https://doi.org/10.1007/978-3-642-00457-5_10
18. Dowling, B., Fischlin, M., Günther, F., Stebila, D.: A cryptographic analysis of the TLS 1.3 handshake protocol candidates. In: Ray, I., Li, N., Kruegel, C. (eds.) ACM CCS 2015, pp. 1197–1210. ACM Press, October 2015. https://doi.org/10.1145/2810103.2813653
19. Drucker, N., Gueron, S.: Selfie: reflections on TLS 1.3 with PSK. Cryptology ePrint Archive, Report 2019/347 (2019). https://eprint.iacr.org/2019/347
20. Fischlin, M., Günther, F.: Multi-stage key exchange and the case of Google's QUIC protocol. In: Ahn, G.J., Yung, M., Li, N. (eds.) ACM CCS 2014, pp. 1193–1204. ACM Press, November 2014. https://doi.org/10.1145/2660267.2660308
21. Fujioka, A., Suzuki, K., Xagawa, K., Yoneyama, K.: Strongly secure authenticated key exchange from factoring, codes, and lattices. In: Fischlin, M., Buchmann, J., Manulis, M. (eds.) PKC 2012. LNCS, vol. 7293, pp. 467–484. Springer, Heidelberg (2012). https://doi.org/10.1007/978-3-642-30057-8_28
22. Fujioka, A., Suzuki, K., Xagawa, K., Yoneyama, K.: Practical and post-quantum authenticated key exchange from one-way secure key encapsulation mechanism. In: Chen, K., Xie, Q., Qiu, W., Li, N., Tzeng, W.G. (eds.) ASIACCS 2013, pp. 83–94. ACM Press, May 2013
23. Jao, D., et al.: SIKE. Technical report, National Institute of Standards and Technology (2020). https://csrc.nist.gov/projects/post-quantum-cryptography/round-3-submissions
24. Josefsson, S.: Storing Certificates in the Domain Name System (DNS). RFC 4398, March 2006. https://doi.org/10.17487/RFC4398
25. Krawczyk, H.: HMQV: a high-performance secure Diffie-Hellman protocol. In: Shoup, V. (ed.) CRYPTO 2005. LNCS, vol. 3621, pp. 546–566. Springer, Heidelberg (2005). https://doi.org/10.1007/11535218_33
26. Krawczyk, H.: Cryptographic extraction and key derivation: the HKDF scheme. In: Rabin, T. (ed.) CRYPTO 2010, LNCS, vol. 6223, pp. 631–648. Springer, Heidelberg (2010). https://doi.org/10.1007/978-3-642-14623-7_34
27. Krawczyk, H., Eronen, P.: HMAC-based Extract-and-Expand Key Derivation Function (HKDF). RFC 5869, May 2010. https://doi.org/10.17487/RFC5869
28. Krawczyk, H., Wee, H.: The OPTLS protocol and TLS 1.3. In: EuroS&P 2016. IEEE (2017). https://eprint.iacr.org/2015/978.pdf
29. Kwiatkowski, K.: Towards post-quantum cryptography in TLS. Posting on the Cloudflare Blog (2019). https://blog.cloudflare.com/towards-post-quantum-cryptography-in-tls/

30. LaMacchia, B.A., Lauter, K., Mityagin, A.: Stronger security of authenticated key exchange. In: Susilo, W., Liu, J.K., Mu, Y. (eds.) ProvSec 2007. LNCS, vol. 4784, pp. 1–16. Springer, Heidelberg (2007)
31. Langley, A.: Cecpq2. Posting on the ImperialViolet Blog (2018). https://www.imperialviolet.org/2018/12/12/cecpq2.html
32. Laurie, B., Langley, A., Kasper, E.: Certificate transparency. RFC 6962, June 2013. https://doi.org/10.17487/RFC6962
33. Law, L., Menezes, A., Qu, M., Solinas, J., Vanstone, S.: An efficient protocol for authenticated key agreement. Des. Codes Crypt. **28**(2), 119–134 (2003)
34. Lyubashevsky, V., et al.: CRYSTALS-DILITHIUM. Technical report, National Institute of Standards and Technology (2020). https://csrc.nist.gov/projects/post-quantum-cryptography/round-3-submissions
35. Paquin, C., Stebila, D., Tamvada, G.: Benchmarking post-quantum cryptography in TLS. In: Ding, J., Tillich, J.P. (eds.) 11th International Conference on Post-Quantum Cryptography, PQCrypto 2020, pp. 72–91. Springer, Heidelberg (2020). https://doi.org/10.1007/978-3-030-44223-1_5
36. Perrin, T.: Noise protocol framework, July 2018. https://noiseprotocol.org/noise.html. Accessed 29 Apr 2021
37. Prest, T., et al.: FALCON. Technical report, National Institute of Standards and Technology (2020). https://csrc.nist.gov/projects/post-quantum-cryptography/round-3-submissions
38. Rescorla, E.: The Transport Layer Security (TLS) Protocol Version 1.3. RFC 8446, August 2018. https://doi.org/10.17487/RFC8446
39. Rescorla, E., Sullivan, N., Wood, C.A.: Semi-static Diffie-Hellman key establishment for TLS 1.3. Internet-draft, Internet Engineering Task Force (2020). https://tools.ietf.org/html/draft-rescorla-tls-semistatic-dh-02
40. Santesson, S., Myers, M., Ankney, R., Malpani, A., Galperin, S., Adams, D.C.: X.509 internet public key infrastructure Online Certificate Status Protocol - OCSP. RFC 6960, June 2013. https://doi.org/10.17487/RFC6960
41. Santesson, S., Tschofenig, H.: Transport Layer Security (TLS) Cached Information Extension. RFC 7924, July 2016. https://doi.org/10.17487/RFC7924
42. Schwabe, P., et al.: CRYSTALS-KYBER. Technical report, National Institute of Standards and Technology (2020). https://csrc.nist.gov/projects/post-quantum-cryptography/round-3-submissions
43. Schwabe, P., Stebila, D., Wiggers, T.: Post-quantum TLS without handshake signatures. In: Ligatti, J., Ou, X., Katz, J., Vigna, G. (eds.) ACM CCS 20, pp. 1461–1480. ACM Press, November 2020. https://doi.org/10.1145/3372297.3423350
44. Sikeridis, D., Kampanakis, P., Devetsikiotis, M.: Post-quantum authentication in TLS 1.3: a performance study. In: NDSS 2020. The Internet Society , February 2020
45. Stebila, D., Mosca, M.: Post-quantum key exchange for the internet and the open quantum safe project. In: Avanzi, R., Heys, H.M. (eds.) SAC 2016. LNCS, vol. 10532, pp. 14–37. Springer, Heidelberg (2016). https://doi.org/10.1007/978-3-319-69453-5_2
46. Sy, E., Burkert, C., Federrath, H., Fischer, M.: Tracking users across the web via TLS session resumption. In: ACM ACSAC 2018, pp. 289–299. ACM Press (2018). https://doi.org/10.1145/3274694.3274708

How to (Legally) Keep Secrets from Mobile Operators

Ghada Arfaoui[1], Olivier Blazy[2], Xavier Bultel[3], Pierre-Alain Fouque[4],

Thibaut Jacques[4], Adina Nedelcu[1,4], and Cristina Onete[2(✉)]

[1] Orange Labs, Cesson-Sévigné, France
[2] XLIM, University of Limoges, Limoges, France
[3] INSA Centre Val-de-Loire, Bourges, France
[4] IRISA, University of Rennes 1, Rennes, France

Abstract. Secure-channel establishment allows two endpoints to communicate confidentially and authentically. Since they hide all data sent across them, good or bad, secure channels are often subject to mass surveillance in the name of (inter)national security. Some protocols are constructed to allow easy data interception . Others are designed to preserve data privacy and are either subverted or prohibited to use without trapdoors.

We introduce LIKE, a primitive that provides secure-channel establishment with an exceptional, session-specific opening mechanism. Designed for mobile communications, where an operator forwards messages between the endpoints, it can also be used in other settings. LIKE allows Alice and Bob to establish a secure channel with respect to n authorities. If the authorities all agree on the need for interception, they can ensure that the session key is retrieved. As long as at least one honest authority prohibits interception, the key remains secure; moreover LIKE is versatile with respect to who learns the key. Furthermore, we guarantee non-frameability: nobody can falsely incriminate a user of taking part in a conversation; and honest-operator: if the operator accepts a transcript as valid, then the key retrieved by the authorities is the key that Alice and Bob should compute. Experimental results show that our protocol can be efficiently implemented.

1 Introduction

For almost a decade mass surveillance has caused controversy, widespread protests, and scandals; and yet, it is on the rise. The NSA, for instance, illegally collected phone-call data from all Verizon customers, and the data of all calls occurring in the Bahamas and Afghanistan [28]. During the present COVID-19 pandemic, Germany used contact-tracing data to pursue criminal investigations [26]. The need for privacy-enhancing solutions that provide transparency and limit mass surveillance has never been greater.

User privacy is a human right acknowledged by Article 12 of the Universal Declaration for Human Rights [42]: "No one shall be subjected to arbitrary interference with his privacy [...] or correspondence [...]. Everyone has the right to the protection of the law against such [...] attacks." The European General Data Protection Regulation (GDPR) and e-Privacy both aim to protect privacy in digital environments, requiring

© Springer Nature Switzerland AG 2021
E. Bertino et al. (Eds.): ESORICS 2021, LNCS 12972, pp. 23–43, 2021.
https://doi.org/10.1007/978-3-030-88418-5_2

minimal, transparent, secure, and user-controlled storage of data. Increasingly aware of mass surveillance, users now choose more frequently to secure their communications by using, *e.g.*, WhatsApp and Viber. In mobile networks, data is encrypted by mobile network operators, which have an incentive to improve the privacy they offer their users.

Unfortunately, mobile data remains at risk, especially when exceptional access to it lies with a single entity. In 2016, only the integrity of Tim Cook (Apple CEO) and his awareness of the danger of such a precedent prevented encrypted phone data to be given to the FBI [30]. His refusal was not a deterrent, and risks to privacy and encryption grow every day [25].

Law-enforcement agencies argue that mobile data can be pivotal to investigations, which are undermined by individuals "going dark" [21]. Even strong privacy advocates, such as Abelson *et al.* [6] agree that *targeted* investigations, *limited in scope and motivation*, can be legitimate and useful (see the corruption-scandal regarding Nicolas Sarkozy's campaign funds). It is this type of limited Lawful Interception (LI) that emerging EU legislation advocates [24].

Recent research [45] has tried to find a middle ground between privacy and lawful interception, enabling the latter at high cost. Unfortunately, that approach sacrifices a crucial real-world requirement: timely (exceptional) decryption [2]. In this paper we define and instantiate Lawful-Interception Key-Exchange (LIKE), a novel primitive allowing mobile users to E2E encrypt their conversation, but providing exceptional lawful interception. This would remove the "[...] need to choose between compliance and strong encryption" (cf. Joel Wallenstrom).

LIKE combats mass surveillance in multiple ways. It *fine-grains* the window of interception to a single session, such that one exceptional opening will not affect past or future conversations. Moreover, the freshness used in the protocol is user- not authority-generated, thus *removing the need* for a centralized, secure party storing all the keys. We also divide the responsibility of exceptional opening between multiple authorities that *must agree* to lawfully intercept communications. Finally, we make the primitive *versatile*, allowing only one, or only several authorities to ultimately retrieve the session key. This makes our solution more privacy-preserving than mobile protocols today, while at the same time remaining compatible to the strictest LI-supporting 3GPP texts [2].

Lawful Interception. Regardless of one's stand on it, Lawful Interception (LI) is part of our world, regulated by laws and standards. Ignoring it can lead to privacy threats (subversion or mass surveillance). Solutions that provide privacy but no LI are discarded as unlawful, regardless of their merits. We take the alternative approach: we analyze LI requirements and technically provide for them, while still maximizing data privacy.

LI requirements in mobile communications are authored by 3GPP and standardized by organizations, *e.g.*, ETSI. LI is the procedure through which a law enforcement agency, holding a legal warrant, can obtain information about phone calls: either metadata (time of calls, identity of callers) or contents (of conversations happening in real time). By law, a mobile operator *must* provide the data requested and specified by a warrant. Three main types of requirements regulate LI: user-privacy requirements, LI-security requirements, and requirements on encryption.

R1 User Privacy: the interception is limited in time (as dictated by the warrant) and to a targeted user. The law enforcement agency should not get data packages or conversations outside the warrant, from the same or other users.

R2 LI Security: LI must be undetectable by either users (whose quality of service should stay the same) or non-authorized third parties (including other law-enforcement agencies). Intercepted data must be provided promptly, with no undue delay.

R3 Special case: if it implements encryption, the operator must provide either decrypted content, or a means to decrypt it (*e.g.*, a decryption key). However, if the users employ other means of encryption, not provided by the operator, the latter is not obliged to provide decrypted (or decryptable) conversations.

1.1 Our Contributions

LIKE. Based on these requirements, we define a novel cryptographic primitive called Lawful-Interception Key Exchange (LIKE, in short). This protocol allows (only) the end users to compute session keys in the presence of a variable number n of authorities (*e.g.*, a court of justice, a law enforcement agency, operators), which all parties must agree on; the operators output a public *session state*. Given the session state, authorities may each extract a trapdoor. The use of all n trapdoors can yield a session key. Importantly, unless they are an authority, operators *cannot* recover the end users' key; instead they forward and verify the compliance of exchanged messages (else the operator aborts).

We also formalize the following strong properties:

C Correctness: Under normal conditions, Alice and Bob obtain the same key. Moreover, this will be the key retrieved by the collaboration of all the authorities by means of lawful interception (requirement R2)

KS Key-security: If at least one authority and both users are honest for a given session, that session's key remains indistinguishable from a random key of the same length with respect to an adversary that can control all the remaining parties (including the other authorities and the operator); (requirements R1 and R2)

NF Non-frameability: The collusion of malicious users, the authorities, and the operator cannot frame an honest user of participating to a session she has not been a party to (requirement R2);

HO Honest Operator: If an honest operator forwards the so-called session state (see below) of a session it deems correct, then the key recovered by the authorities is the one that the session transcript should have yielded (requirement R3). Thus operators can prove that this protocol is compliant with LI specifications.

Our Protocol and Implementation. As our second contribution, we describe an instantiation of LIKE using standard building blocks (signatures, zero knowledge proofs and signatures of knowledge) which we prove secure, provided the Bilinear Decisional Diffie-Hellman problem is intractable, the signature scheme is unforgeable, and our zero-knowledge proofs/signatures are secure.

Mindful of practical requirements, we place most of the burden during AKE on the operator (not on the endpoints). Our proofs and signatures of knowledge can be simply implemented based on Schnorr and respectively Chaum and Pedersen proofs (with Fiat-Shamir). The two endpoints do have to compute a pairing operation –however, we explain that the actual computation can actually be delegated to the mobile phone, leaving a single exponentiation (in the target group) to be performed on the USIM card.

The complexity of the opening procedure is reduced. Some steps are parallelizable and run in constant time (trapdoor generation), but others are linear (combining the trapdoors). Even so the computational burden remains minimal and in line with requirements R2 (constant quality of service, since only authorities run LI, not the operator) and R3 (no undue delay would be incurred by the operator, and only minimal delays occur at the authorities). A proof-of-concept implementation given in Sect. 7 illustrates this point.

1.2 Related Work

Existing encryption in mobile networks is not E2E secure, only providing privacy with respect to non-authorized third parties. This solution is compliant to LI requirements [3–5] because the secure channel it provides is between the user and the operator (rather than user-to-user); thus the operator has unrestricted access to all user communications. Our LIKE protocol provides much stronger privacy in that respect.

LIKE also provides much stronger guarantees than key-escrow [8, 11, 19, 20, 22, 27, 32–35, 37, 38, 40, 41, 44]: we can handle malicious authority input; we fine-grain exceptional opening so that it only holds for one session at a time; we allow authorities to remain offline at all times except for exceptional opening; we minimize storage and computational costs for users and authorities; we have no central key-generation authority which knows all secret keys; and we guarantee the new properties of non-frameability and honest operator, which are tailored to the LI requirements analyzed above. In return, our use-case is narrower than typically considered in key-escrow: by considering the case of mobile communications, we can safely assume that parties always use the operator as a proxy, unlike in generic key-escrow settings.

Our work is motivated by the same problem handled by [12, 45], but we take a different approach: rather than make LI computationally costly, we limit its scope, divide exceptional opening between several authorities, and fine-grain access. Our setup also resembles that of reverse firewalls [36] – which builds on related work pioneered by Young and Yung [23, 31, 46]. Although apparently similar, the setup of these works is complementary to ours. Kleptography describes ways for users to abuse protocols such that the latter appear to be running normally, while subliminal information is allowed to leak. For instance in key-exchange, a government agency could substitute the implementation of the protocol by one with a backdoor, to make the key recoverable even without formal LI. We also consider the case that Alice and Bob might be malicious (the HO property). However, rather than wanting to exfiltrate information –which is the adversarial goal in typical reverse-firewalls– in our case, Alice and Bob aim to cheat by choosing protocol contributions that might make LI malfunction. To be provably-secure, LIKE protocols must prevent this.

2 Preliminaries

Notations. By $x \leftarrow y$ we mean that variable x takes a value y, while $x \overset{\$}{\leftarrow} X$ indicates x is chosen from the uniform distribution on X. The notation $[\![1, n]\!]$ is short for $\{1, 2, \cdots, n\}$. Let $\mathsf{A}(x) \rightarrow a$ express that algorithm A, running on input x, outputs a, and $\mathsf{P}\langle \mathsf{A}(x), \mathsf{B}(y)\rangle(z) \rightarrow (a, b)$ to express that protocol P implements the interactions of $\mathsf{A}(x) \rightarrow a$ and $\mathsf{B}(y) \rightarrow b$, where z is an additional public input of A and B. Let λ be a security parameter.

Building Blocks. We assume the reader's familiarity with the notion of unforgeability for signature schemes (EUF-CMA), also visible in our full version [7]. We denote by $\mathsf{Adv}_{\mathsf{DS}}^{\mathsf{EUF\text{-}CMA}}(\lambda)$ the maximal advantage an adversary has against the signature scheme that we employ.

Definition 1 (BDDH Assumption [15]). *Let* $\mathbb{G}_1 = \langle g_1 \rangle$, $\mathbb{G}_2 = \langle g_2 \rangle$, *and* $\mathbb{G}_T$ *be groups of prime order* p *of length* λ. *Let* $e : \mathbb{G}_1 \times \mathbb{G}_2 \rightarrow \mathbb{G}_T$ *be a type 3 bilinear map. The* Bilinear decisional Diffie-Hellman problem *(BDDH) assumption holds in* $(\mathbb{G}_1, \mathbb{G}_2, \mathbb{G}_T, e)$ *if, given* $(a, b, c, d_1) \overset{\$}{\leftarrow} (\mathbb{Z}_p^*)^4$, $d_0 \leftarrow abc$, *and* $\beta \overset{\$}{\leftarrow} \{0, 1\}$, *no PPT adversary* $\mathcal{A}$ *can guess* β *from* $(g_1^a, g_2^a, g_1^b, g_2^b, g_1^c, g_2^c, e(g_1, g_2)^{d_\beta})$ *with non-negligible advantage. We denote by* $\mathsf{Adv}^{\mathsf{BDDH}}(\lambda)$ *the maximum advantage over all PPT adversaries.*

Signature of Knowledge. Let $\mathcal{R}$ be a binary relation and let $\mathcal{L}$ be a language such that $s \in \mathcal{L} \Leftrightarrow (\exists w, (s, w) \in \mathcal{R})$. A Non-Interactive Proof of Knowledge (NIPoK) [10] allows a prover to convince a verifier that he knows a witness w such that $(s, w) \in \mathcal{R}$. Here, we follow [16] and write $\mathsf{NIPoK}\{w : (w, s) \in \mathcal{R}\}$ for the proof of knowledge of w for the statement s and the relation $\mathcal{R}$. A *signature of knowledge* essentially allows one to sign a message and prove in zero-knowledge that a particular statement holds for the key [17]. In this paradigm, w is a secret key and s is the corresponding public key.

Definition 2 (Signature of Knowledge). *Let* $\mathcal{R}$ *be a binary relation and* $\mathcal{L}$ *be a language such that* $s \in \mathcal{L} \Leftrightarrow (\exists w, (s, w) \in \mathcal{R})$. *A* Signature of Knowledge *for* $\mathcal{L}$ *is a pair of algorithms* $(\mathsf{SoK}, \mathsf{SoKver})$ *with* $\mathsf{SoK}_m\{w : (s, w) \in \mathcal{R}\} \rightarrow \pi$ *and* $\mathsf{SoKver}(m, s, \pi) \rightarrow b$, *such that:*

- *Perfect Zero Knowledge: There exists a polynomial time algorithm* Sim, *the simulator, such that* $\mathsf{Sim}(m, s)$ *and* $\mathsf{SoK}_m\{w : (s, w) \in \mathcal{R}\}$ *follow the same probability distribution.*
- *Knowledge Extractor: There exists a PPT knowledge extractor* Ext *and a negligible function* ϵ_{SoK} *such that for any algorithm* $\mathcal{A}^{\mathsf{Sim}(\cdot, \cdot)}(\lambda)$ *having access to a simulator that forges signatures for chosen instance/message tuples and that outputs a fresh tuple* (s, π, m) *with* $\mathsf{SoKver}(m, s, \pi) = 1$, *the extractor* $\mathsf{Ext}^{\mathcal{A}}(\lambda)$ *outputs* w *such that* $(s, w) \in \mathcal{R}$ *having access to* $\mathcal{A}(\lambda)$ *with probability at least* $1 - \epsilon_{\mathsf{SoK}}(\lambda)$.

We omit the definition of NIPoK which is the same as SoK without the messages.

3 LIKE Protocols

Lawful-interception (authenticated) key-exchange (LIKE) consists of two mechanisms: a multiparty AKE protocol between 2 mobile subscribers (users) and a (number of) mobile network operators (performing the same actions), and an Extract-and-Open mechanism for LI between a number of *authorities*.

Intuition. Our AKE component allows user Alice, subscribing to operator O_A, and Bob, subscribing to O_B, to compute a session key in the presence of O_A and O_B. The operators do not compute the session key, just some auxiliary *session state*, which allows for session authentication and ulterior key-recovery.

In the Extract-and-Open component, each authority uses its secret key to *extract* a trapdoor from the session state. The trapdoors are then used together to *open* the session key.

Formalization. Let USERS be a set of mobile users and OPS be a set of operators, such that each user is affiliated to precisely one operator. We also consider a set of authorities AUTH of cardinality |AUTH|, with elements indexed as $\Lambda_1, \ldots, \Lambda_{|AUTH|}$.

Let PARTIES be the set of all participants: USERS $\cup$ OPS $\cup$ AUTH. Mobile users have no super-role: USERS $\cap$ AUTH $= \emptyset =$ USERS $\cap$ OPS. Syntactically, OPS $\cap$ AUTH $= \emptyset$; however, operators can act as authorities by registering a second set of (authority) credentials and using those for opening. This is described in the full version.

Parties, attributes, and oracles are formally introduced in the next section. We use a dot notation to refer to *attributes* of a party P: A.PKis Alice's public key and Λ_i.SK is the secret key of the i-th authority. We write O_A to indicate Alice's operator even though we have no user registration and can run the protocol with *any* two operators chosen by the users. The operators are assumed to transit all communication (as is the case today). The parties can agree on a variable number n of (distinct) authorities, with $1 \leqslant n \leqslant |AUTH|$.

Definition 3. *A* lawful interception key exchange (LIKE) *protocol is defined by the following algorithms:*

- Setup(1^λ) $\rightarrow$ pp: *Takes as input a security parameter and outputs public system parameters* pp, *known to all parties.*
- UKeyGen(pp) $\rightarrow$ (U.PK, U.SK): *Takes as input the public parameters* pp *and outputs a user key pair.*
- OKeyGen(pp) $\rightarrow$ (O.PK, O.SK): *Takes as input the public parameters* pp *and outputs an operator key pair.*
- AKeyGen(pp) $\rightarrow$ (Λ.PK, Λ.SK): *Takes as input the public parameters* pp *and outputs an authority key pair.*
- AKE$\langle$A(A.SK), $O_A(O_A$.SK), $O_B(O_B$.SK), B(B.SK)$\rangle$(PK$_{A \rightarrow B}$) $\rightarrow$ (k_A, sst$_A$, sst$_B$, k_B): *An authenticated key-exchange protocol between users* (A, B) $\in$ USERS^2 *and their operators* $(O_A, O_B) \in$ OPS^2, *the latter providing active middleware at all times. The parties each take as input a secret key, and they all have access to the same set of public values* PK$_{A \rightarrow B}$ *containing: parameters* pp, *public keys* (A.PK, B.PK), *and a vector of authority public keys* APK $= (\Lambda_i.$PK$)_{i=1}^n$ *with (distinct)* $\Lambda_i \in$ AUTH *for all* i. *At the end of the protocol,* A *(resp.* B*) returns a session*

secret key k_A *(resp. k_B) and the operator O_A (resp. O_B) returns a (public) ses-sion state sst_A (resp. sst_B). In case of failure, the parties output a special symbol $\perp$ instead.*

- $\mathsf{Verify}(pp, sst, A.PK, B.PK, O.PK, APK) \to b$: *Takes as input session state sst, user public keys $A.PK$ and $B.PK$, an operator public key $O.PK$, a set of authority public keys $APK = (\Lambda_i.PK)_{i=1}^n$, outputting a bit $b = 1$ if sst was correctly generated and authenticated by O, and $b = 0$ otherwise.*

- $\mathsf{TDGen}(pp, \Lambda.SK, sst) \to \Lambda.t$: *Takes as input authority secret key $\Lambda.SK$ and session state sst, and outputs trapdoor $\Lambda.t$.*

- $\mathsf{Open}(pp, sst, APK, \mathcal{T}) \to k$: *Takes as input session state sst, two vectors $APK = (\Lambda_i.PK)_{i=1}^n$ with n distinct public keys, and $\mathcal{T} = (\Lambda_i.t)_{i=1}^n$ (authority public keys and corresponding trapdoors), and outputs either a session key k, or a symbol $\perp$.*

We defer the full correctness definition to Appendix A. It essentially states that if parameters are normally generated, for an honestly-run protocol session: both operators approve it, both users accept computing the same key, and that same key is extracted from either of the operators' session states.

To use a LIKE scheme, keys are generated based on the parties' role: UKeyGen for users, OKeyGen for operators, and AKeyGen for authorities. Then, Alice, Bob, and the operators run AKE as described above. At the end, Alice and Bob share a session key (unknown to the operator), and each operator returns a public session state sst. The values included in sst are protocol-dependent, and they must allow the authorities to verify that the session was run correctly and recover the session key. The verification is not exclusively meant for authorities: the algorithm Verify checks the validity of the session and authenticates its participants.

The authorities may later retrieve session keys. Each authority verifies the soundness of a given sst, then extracts a trapdoor to the session key, using its secret key. Given all the trapdoors, the algorithm Open retrieves the session key. Depending on the LI scenario, the Open algorithm may be run by one or multiple parties (thus, whoever has all the trapdoors extracts the key). Our protocol is versatile and can adapt to many cases, some of which are shown in the full version.

4   Security Model

This section formalizes LIKE security: an essential contribution to the paper, which pro-vides much stronger guarantees than regular authenticated key exchange or key-escrow. We begin by giving the adversarial model, then list the oracles which adversaries can use to manipulate honest parties, and formalize security games for each property.

The Adversarial Model. We assume all parties (users, operators, authorities) have unique and unchanging roles. Parties may still play multiple roles if the same physi-cal entity registers as multiple users in our scheme (an authority and an operator, for instance). Each party P is associated with these attributes:

- (SK, PK): long-term private (resp. public) keys SK (resp. PK). Such keys are output by UKeyGen, OKeyGen, or AKeyGen.

- γ: a corruption flag, indicating whether that party has been corrupted (1) or not (0). The flag starts out as 0, and if it changes to 1, it can never flipped back to 0.

Alice, Bob, and their operators run AKE in *sessions*. At each new session, a new *instance* of each party is created (yielding four instances per session). We denote by π_P^i the i-th instance generated during the experiment, where P denotes the corresponding party. In addition to the long-term keys and corruption bits of the party, instances keep track of the following attributes:

- sid: a session identifier consisting of a tuple of session-specific values, like public parameters or randomness. This attribute stores only state pertinent to that session, does not include secret values, and is computable by the instances running the session. The value of sid is initially set to $\bot$ and changes during the protocol run.
- PID: partner identifiers. If $P \in \mathsf{USERS}$, then $\mathsf{PID} \in \mathsf{USERS}$ such that $P \neq \mathsf{PID}$, else $P \in \mathsf{OPS}$ and $\mathsf{PID} \in \mathsf{USERS}^2$ including two distinct parties.
- OID: operator identifiers. If $P \in \mathsf{USERS}$ then $\mathsf{OID} \in \mathsf{OPS}^2$. Else $\mathsf{OID} \in \mathsf{OPS}$.
- AID: distinct authority identifiers such that $\mathsf{AID} \in \mathsf{AUTH}^n$.
- α: an accept flag, undefined ($\alpha = \bot$) until the instance terminates, either in an abort (setting $\alpha = 0$) or without error ($\alpha = 1$).
- k: the session key, initialized to $\bot$, and modified if the protocol terminates without error. Operator instances do not have this attribute.
- sst: a set of values pertaining to the instance's view of the session, initialized to $\bot$ and modified if the protocol terminates without error. User instances do not have this attribute.
- ρ: a reveal bit, initialized to 0 and set to 1 if the adversary reveals a session key $k \neq \bot$. Operator instances do not have this attribute.
- b: a bit chosen uniformly at random upon the creation of the instance.
- τ: the transcript of the session, initialized as $\bot$, turning to the ordered list of messages sent and received by that instance in the same order.

An auxiliary function IdentifySession (sst, π) is defined, taking as input session state sst and a party instance π, outputting 1 if π took part in the session where sst was created, and 0 otherwise. We need this at opening, when authorities must extract and verify the session identifier for themselves.

Notice that, unlike in typical AKE, we have two types of parties running each session (users and operators), and three attributes that describe partners: mobile user partners in PID, operator partners in OID, and authorities partnering it in AID. Moreover, IdentifySession and sst are protocol dependent, *i.e.*, they will have a different instantiation depending on the protocol we analyse.

We define matching conversation defined as follows:

Definition 4 (Matching Instances). *For any $(i, j) \in \mathbb{N}^2$ and $(A, B) \in \mathsf{USERS}^2$ such that $A \neq B$, we say that π_A^i and π_B^j have matching conversation if all the following conditions hold: $\pi_A^i.\mathsf{sid} \neq \bot$, $\pi_A^i.\mathsf{sid} = \pi_B^j.\mathsf{sid}$, and $\pi_A^i.\mathsf{AID} = \pi_B^j.\mathsf{AID}$. If two instances π_A^i and π_B^j have matching conversation, we sometimes say, by abuse of language, that π_A^i matches π_B^j.*

Oracles. We define LIKE security in terms of games played by an adversary plays against a challenger. In each game, the adversary $\mathcal{A}$ may query some or all of the oracles below. Intuitively, $\mathcal{A}$ may register honest or malicious participants (using Register), initiate new sessions (using NewSession), interact in the AKE protocol (using Send), corrupt parties (using Corrupt), reveal session keys (using Reveal), or reveal LI trapdoors (using RevealTD). Finally, the adversary has to query a testing oracle (Test) and tell whether the output was the real session key or a random one. Each oracle *aborts* if queried with ill-formatted input, or if insufficient information exists for the response.

- Register$(\mathsf{P}, \mathtt{role}, \mathsf{PK}) \to \perp \cup \mathsf{P.PK}$: On input party $\mathsf{P} \notin \mathsf{USERS} \cup \mathsf{OPS} \cup \mathsf{AUTH}$, role $\mathtt{role} \in \{\mathtt{user}, \mathtt{operator}, \mathtt{authority}\}$, and public key PK:
  - If $\mathtt{role} = \mathtt{user}$ (resp. $\mathtt{operator}, \mathtt{authority}$), add P to the set USERS (resp. OPS, AUTH).
  - If $\mathtt{role} = \mathtt{user}$ (resp. $\mathtt{operator}$ and $\mathtt{authority}$) and $\mathsf{PK} = \perp$, run UKeyGen$(\mathsf{pp}) \to (\mathsf{P.PK}, \mathsf{P.SK})$ (resp. OKeyGen and AKeyGen).
  - If $\mathsf{PK} \neq \perp$, set the $\mathsf{P}.\gamma = 1$, $\mathsf{P.PK} = \mathsf{PK}$, and $\mathsf{P.SK} = \perp$.
  Finally, return $\mathsf{P.PK}$.
- NewSession$(\mathsf{P}, \mathsf{PID}, \mathsf{OID}, \mathsf{AID}) \to \pi_\mathsf{P}^i$: On input party $\mathsf{P} \in \mathsf{USERS} \cup \mathsf{OPS}$, if $\mathsf{P} \in$ USERS then $\mathsf{PID}, \mathsf{OID}$ and AID must be such that: $\mathsf{PID} \in$ USERS with $\mathsf{P} \neq \mathsf{PID}$; $\mathsf{OID} \in \mathsf{OPS}^2$; and $\mathsf{AID} \in \mathsf{AUTH}^*$ with $|\mathsf{AID}| \neq 0$. If $\mathsf{P} \in$ OPS, then $\mathsf{PID}, \mathsf{OID}$, and AID are such that $\mathsf{PID} \in \mathsf{USERS}^2$; $\mathsf{OID} \in$ OPS; and $\mathsf{AID} \in \mathsf{AUTH}^*$ such that $|\mathsf{AID}| \neq 0$. On the i-th call to this oracle, return new instance π_P^i with already-set values for $\mathsf{PID}, \mathsf{OID}$, and AID.
- Send$(\pi_\mathsf{P}^i, m) \to m'$: Send message m to instance π_P^i and return message m' according to protocol (potentially $\perp$ for inexistent, aborted, or terminated instance, for ill-formed m, or if $\mathsf{P.SK} = \perp$).
- Reveal$(\pi_\mathsf{P}^i) \to \mathsf{k}$: For accepting user instance π_P^i, return the session key $\pi_\mathsf{P}^i.\mathsf{k}$ and set $\pi_\mathsf{P}^i.\rho = 1$. For accepting operator instance π_P^i return the session state $\pi_\mathsf{P}^i.\mathsf{sst}$ and set $\pi_\mathsf{P}^i.\rho = 1$. If π_P^i is not an accepting instance ($\alpha \neq 1$), return $\perp$.
- Corrupt$(\mathsf{P}) \to \mathsf{P.SK}$: Return $\mathsf{P.SK}$ of input party P (all roles) and set $\mathsf{P}.\gamma = 1$ for all instances of this party.
- Test$(\pi_\mathsf{P}^i) \to \widetilde{\mathsf{k}}$: Return $\perp$ if input instance π_P^i is not an accepting user instance or if this oracle has been queried before, outputting a value that is non-$\perp$. Else, if $\pi_\mathsf{P}^i.\mathsf{b} = 0$, return $\pi_\mathsf{P}^i.\mathsf{k}$, and otherwise return randomly-sampled r from the same domain as $\pi_\mathsf{P}^i.\mathsf{k}$. This oracle can only be called once during an experiment, which means that only one instance bit b is actually used.
- RevealTD$(\mathsf{sst}, \mathsf{A}, \mathsf{B}, \mathsf{O}, (\Lambda_i)_{i=1}^n, l) \to \Lambda_l.t$: If Verify$(\mathsf{pp}, \mathsf{sst}, \mathsf{A.PK}, \mathsf{B.PK}, \mathsf{O.PK}, (\Lambda_i.\mathsf{PK})_{i=1}^n) = 1$, run $\Lambda_l.t \leftarrow$ TDGen$(\mathsf{pp}, \Lambda_l.\mathsf{SK}, \mathsf{sst})$, return $\Lambda_l.t$; else return $\perp$.

Notice that the operators do not contribute in a traditional sense to the security of the key; instead they verify the soundness of the exchanges and produce a session state sst, which proves the operator's honesty to the authorities. The two operators need not agree on sst, and only one sst is required for the opening procedure (as is the case in most applications). However, if during AKE one operator validates, but not the other, then ultimately the session is aborted.

We define LIKE security in terms of three properties: key-security (KS), non-frameability (NF), and honest operator (HO). For the reader's convenience, some useful notations from the model may also be found summarized in Appendix A.

Key-Security. Our KS game extends AKE security [13]. The adversary may query all the oracles above (subject to *key-freshness* as defined below) and must distinguish a real session key from one randomly chosen from the same domain.

The KS notion is much stronger than traditional 2-party AKE. The attacker can adaptively corrupt all but the users targeted in the challenge, all but one out of the n selected authorities, and all the operators; $\mathcal{A}$ may also register malicious users, retroactively corrupt users (thus ensuring forward secrecy), and learn all but one trapdoor in the challenge session. Thus, the session key is only known by the endpoints, and by the collusion of *all* the n authorities (LI); all other (collusions of) parties fail to distinguish it from a random key. More formally, the tested target instance must be key-fresh with respect to Definition 5. The full game $\mathsf{Exp}^{\mathsf{KS}}_{\mathsf{LIKE},\mathcal{A}}(\lambda)$ is given in Table 1.

Definition 5 (Key Freshness). *Let π_{P}^{j} be the j-th created instance, associated to party* $\mathsf{P} \in \mathsf{USERS}$. *Let $\mathcal{A}$ be a PPT adversary against* LIKE. *Parse π_{P}^{j}.PID as P' and π_{P}^{j}.AID as $(\Lambda_i)_{i=1}^{n}$. The key π_{P}^{j}.k is fresh if all the following conditions hold:*

Table 1. Games for key-security (KS, left) and non-frameability (NF, right).

$\mathsf{Exp}^{\mathsf{KS}}_{\mathsf{LIKE},\mathcal{A}}(\lambda)$:	$\mathsf{Exp}^{\mathsf{NF}}_{\mathsf{LIKE},\mathcal{A}}(\lambda)$:
pp $\leftarrow$ Setup(1^λ);	pp $\leftarrow$ Setup(1^λ)
$\mathcal{O}_{\mathsf{KS}}$ $\begin{cases} \mathsf{Register}(\cdot,\cdot,\cdot), \mathsf{Send}(\cdot,\cdot), \\ \mathsf{NewSession}(\cdot,\cdot,\cdot), \\ \mathsf{Reveal}(\cdot), \mathsf{RevealTD}(\cdot,\cdot), \\ \mathsf{Corrupt}(\cdot,\cdot), \mathsf{Test}(\cdot) \end{cases}$;	$\mathcal{O}_{\mathsf{NF}}$ $\begin{cases} \mathsf{Register}(\cdot,\cdot,\cdot), \mathsf{Send}(\cdot,\cdot), \mathsf{Reveal}(\cdot), \\ \mathsf{NewSession}(\cdot,\cdot,\cdot), \mathsf{RevealTD}(\cdot,\cdot), \mathsf{Corrupt}(\cdot,\cdot) \end{cases}$;
$(i, \mathsf{P}, d) \leftarrow \mathcal{A}^{\mathcal{O}_{\mathsf{KS}}}(\lambda, \mathsf{pp})$;	$(\mathsf{sst}, \mathsf{P}) \leftarrow \mathcal{A}^{\mathcal{O}_{\mathsf{NF}}}(\lambda, \mathsf{pp})$;
If π_{P}^i.k is fresh and π_{P}^i.b = d, return 1;	If $(\mathsf{A}, \mathsf{B}) \in \mathsf{USERS}^2, n \in \mathbb{N}, \mathsf{O} \in \mathsf{OPS}, (\Lambda_i)_{i=1}^n \in \mathsf{AUTH}^n$ s.t.:
Else $b' \xleftarrow{\$} \{0,1\}$, return b'.	$\quad$ Verify(pp, sst, A.PK, B.PK, O.PK, $(\Lambda_i.\mathsf{PK})_{i=1}^n) = 1$;
	$\quad \mathsf{P} \in \{\mathsf{A}, \mathsf{B}\}$;
	$\quad \mathsf{P}.\gamma = 0$;
	$\quad \forall i$, if $\pi_{\mathsf{P}}^i \neq \perp$: IdentifySession(sst, π_{P}^i) $= 0$ or $\pi_{\mathsf{P}}^i.\alpha = 0$,
	Then return 1,
	Else return 0.

- $\pi_{\mathsf{P}}^{j}.\alpha = 1$, $\mathsf{P}.\gamma = 0$ when $\pi_{\mathsf{P}}^{j}.\alpha$ became 1, and $\pi_{\mathsf{P}}^{j}.\rho = 0$.
- if π_{P}^{j} matches $\pi_{\mathsf{P}'}^{k}$, for $k \in \mathbb{N}$, then: $\pi_{\mathsf{P}'}^{k}.\alpha = 1$, $\mathsf{P}'.\gamma = 0$ when $\pi_{\mathsf{P}'}^{k}.\alpha$ became 1, and $\pi_{\mathsf{P}'}^{k}.\rho = 0$.
- if no $\pi_{\mathsf{P}'}^{k}$ matches π_{P}^{j}, $\mathsf{P}'.\gamma = 0$.
- $\exists\ l \in [\![1, n]\!]$ such that for any $\mathsf{O} \in \pi_{\mathsf{P}}^{j}.\mathsf{OID}$, $\mathcal{A}$ has never queried RevealTD(sst, A, B, O, $(\Lambda_i')_{i=1}^{n'}, l'$) and:
  - $\Lambda_l.\gamma = 0$ and $\Lambda_l = \Lambda_{l'}'$;
  - IdentifySession(sst, π_{P}^{j}) $= 1$.

Definition 6. *For an adversary $\mathcal{A}$ the value:*

$$\mathsf{Adv}^{\mathsf{KS}}_{\mathsf{LIKE},\mathcal{A}}(\lambda) := \left| \mathbb{P}\left[\mathsf{Exp}^{\mathsf{KS}}_{\mathsf{LIKE},\mathcal{A}}(\lambda) = 1\right] - \frac{1}{2} \right|$$

denotes its advantage *against* $\mathsf{Exp}^{\mathsf{KS}}_{\mathsf{LIKE},\mathcal{A}}(\lambda)$. *A lawful-interception authenticated key-exchange scheme* LIKE *is* key-secure *if for all PPT* $\mathcal{A}$, $\mathsf{Adv}^{\mathsf{KS}}_{\mathsf{LIKE},\mathcal{A}}(\lambda)$ *is a negligible function of the security parameter* λ.

Non-frameability. In this game, $\mathcal{A}$ attempts to frame a user P^* for running an AKE session (with session state sst) which P^* rejected or did not take part in. The adversary may corrupt all parties apart from P^*, as formalized in Table 1.

Definition 7. *The advantage of an adversary* $\mathcal{A}$ *in the non-frameability experiment* $\mathsf{Exp}^{\mathsf{NF}}_{\mathsf{LIKE},\mathcal{A}}(\lambda)$ *in Table 1 is defined as:*

$$\mathsf{Adv}^{\mathsf{NF}}_{\mathsf{LIKE},\mathcal{A}}(\lambda) = \mathbb{P}\left[\mathsf{Exp}^{\mathsf{NF}}_{\mathsf{LIKE},\mathcal{A}}(\lambda) = 1\right].$$

A lawful interception authenticated key-exchange scheme LIKE *is* non-frameable *if all PPT adversaries* $\mathcal{A}$, *have negligible* $\mathsf{Adv}^{\mathsf{NF}}_{\mathsf{LIKE},\mathcal{A}}(\lambda)$ *as a function of* λ.

Table 2. The honest-operator HO game, where q_r is the number of queries to Register, and P_i is the party input as the i-th such query.

$$\mathsf{Exp}^{\mathsf{HO}}_{\mathsf{LIKE},\mathcal{A}}(\lambda):$$

pp $\mathsf{Setup}(1^\lambda)$;
$\mathcal{O}_{\mathsf{HO}}$ $\left\{\begin{array}{l}\mathsf{Register}(\cdot,\cdot,\cdot),\mathsf{NewSession}(\cdot,\cdot,\cdot),\mathsf{Send}(\cdot,\cdot),\\ \mathsf{Reveal}(\cdot),\mathsf{RevealTD}(\cdot,\cdot),\mathsf{Corrupt}(\cdot,\cdot)\end{array}\right\}$;
$(j,\mathsf{sst},\mathsf{A},\mathsf{B},\mathsf{O},(\Lambda_i,\Lambda_i.t)_{i=1}^n)$ $\mathcal{A}^{\mathcal{O}_{\mathsf{HO}}}(\lambda,\mathsf{pp})$;
If $\mathsf{O}.\gamma = 1$ then return $\perp$;
If $\mathsf{Verify}(\mathsf{pp},\mathsf{sst},\mathsf{A}.\mathsf{PK},\mathsf{B}.\mathsf{PK},\mathsf{O}.\mathsf{PK},(\Lambda_i.\mathsf{PK})_{i=1}^n) = 0$ then return $\perp$;
If $\mathsf{IdentifySession}(\mathsf{sst},\pi_{\mathsf{O}}^j.\mathsf{sid}) = 0$ then return $\perp$;
k_* $\mathsf{Open}(\mathsf{pp},\mathsf{sst},(\Lambda_i.\mathsf{PK})_{i=1}^n,(\Lambda_i.t)_{i=1}^n)$;
Return $(k_*,\pi_{\mathsf{O}}^j,\{\mathsf{P}_i.\mathsf{PK}\}_{i=1}^{q_r})$.

Honest Operator. The HO game captures the fact that honest operators will abort if they detect ill-formed or non-authentic messages. The adversary must create a valid session state sst, accepted by the operators, for which the authorities Open to an incorrect session key. The attacker can provide some trapdoors and corrupt all the parties except the operator that approves sst.

Ideally, LIKE schemes should guarantee that if the (honest) operator approves a session, then the extracted key (output in $\mathsf{Exp}^{\mathsf{HO}}_{\mathsf{LIKE},\mathcal{A}}(\lambda)$, see Table 2) will be the one used by Alice and Bob. However, malicious endpoints could run a protocol perfectly, then use a different key (*e.g.*, exchanged out of band) to encrypt messages. This flaw is universal to secure-channel establishment featuring malicious endpoints. The best a LIKE protocol can guarantee is that the extracted key is the one that *would have resulted* from an honest protocol run yielding sst. We express this in terms of a *key extractor*, which, given an operator instance and a set of public keys, outputs the key k associated with the session in which the instance took part.

Definition 8 (Key Extractor). *For any* LIKE, *a key extractor* Extract$(\cdot, \cdot)$ *is a deterministic unbounded algorithm such that, for any users* A *and* B, *operators* O_A *and* O_B, *and set of* n *authorities* $(\Lambda_i)_{i=1}^n$, *any set* $\{$pp, A.PK, A.SK, B.PK, B.SK, O_A.PK, O_A.SK, O_B.PK, O_B.SK, k, sst, APK $= (\Lambda_i.PK)_{i=1}^n, (\Lambda_i.SK)_{i=1}^n, \tau_A, \tau_B, $ PPK$\}$ *generated as follows:*

> pp $\leftarrow$ Setup(λ); (A.PK, A.SK) $\leftarrow$ UKeyGen(pp); (B.PK, B.SK) $\leftarrow$ UKeyGen(pp);
> $(O_A.PK, O_A.SK) \leftarrow$ OKeyGen(pp); $(O_B.PK, O_B.SK) \leftarrow$ OKeyGen(pp);
> $\forall i \in [\![1, n]\!], (\Lambda_i.PK, \Lambda_i.SK) \leftarrow$ AKeyGen(pp);
> $(k, sst_A, sst_B, k) \leftarrow$ AKE$\langle$A(A.SK), $O_A(O_A.SK)$,
> $O_B(O_B.SK)$, B(B.SK)$\rangle$(pp, A.PK, B.PK, APK);
> τ_A *is the transcript of the execution yielding* sst_A *from* O_A*'s point of view;*
> τ_B *is the transcript of the execution yielding* sst_B *from* O_B*'s point of view;*
> PPK $\leftarrow \{O_A.PK, O_B.PK, A.PK, B.PK\} \cup \{\Lambda_i.PK\}_{i=1}^n$;

it holds that $\forall(U, P) \in \{A, B\}^2$ *such that* $U \neq P$ *and any instance* π_{O_U} *such that* $\pi_{O_U}.\tau = \tau_U$, $\pi_{O_U}.$PID $= P$, $\pi_{O_U}.$AID $= (\Lambda_i)_{i=1}^n$, *and* $\pi_{O_U}.$sst $=$ sst, *then:*
Pr$[$Extract$(\pi_{O_U}, PPK) = k] = 1$.

Notice that our extractor is unbounded, as it must be in order to preserve key security (otherwise the extractor would allow the operator to find the session key).

Definition 9. *For any lawful interception key-exchange scheme* LIKE *that admits a key extractor* Extract *the advantage of an adversary* $\mathcal{A}$ *in the honest-operator game* $\mathsf{Exp}_{\mathsf{LIKE},\mathcal{A}}^{\mathsf{HO}}(\lambda)$ *in Table 2 is defined as:* $\mathsf{Adv}_{\mathsf{LIKE},\mathcal{A}}^{\mathsf{HO}}(\lambda) =$

$$\mathbb{P}\left[\begin{array}{l}(k_*, \pi_O, \mathsf{PPK}) \leftarrow \mathsf{Exp}_{\mathsf{LIKE},\mathcal{A}}^{\mathsf{HO}}(\lambda); \\ k \leftarrow \mathsf{Extract}(\pi_O, \mathsf{PPK})\end{array} : \begin{array}{l}k \neq \bot \wedge k_* \neq \bot \\ \wedge k \neq k_*\end{array}\right].$$

A LIKE *scheme is* honest-operator secure *if, for all adversaries running in time polynomial in* λ, $\mathsf{Adv}_{\mathsf{LIKE},\mathcal{A}}^{\mathsf{HO}}(\lambda)$ *is negligible as a function of* λ.

5   Our Protocol

Our LIKE schemerequires a signature scheme DS $= (\mathsf{SGen}, \mathsf{SSig}, \mathsf{SVer})$; a signature of knowledge scheme (SoK, SoKver) allowing to prove knowledge of a discrete logarithm in group $\mathbb{G}_2 = \langle g_2 \rangle$; and two NIZK proofs of knowledge – one denoted NIPoK$\{x : y = g_1^x\}$ that allows to prove knowledge of the discrete logarithm of $y = g_1^x$ in a cyclic group $\mathbb{G}_1 = \langle g_1 \rangle$ for private witness x; and another denoted NIPoK$\{x : y_1 = g_1^x \wedge y_T = g_T^x\}$ that allows to prove knowledge of the discrete logarithm of values $y_1 = g_1^x$ and $y_T = g_T^x$ in same-size groups $\mathbb{G}_1 = \langle g_1 \rangle$ and $\mathbb{G}_T = \langle g_T \rangle$ for private witness x.

The proof and the signature of knowledge of a discrete logarithm can be instantiated by using Fiat-Shamir on Schnorr's protocol [39]. For the proof, we use the hash of the statement and the commitment as a challenge; for the signature of knowledge, we add the message into the hash [17]. The proof of the discrete logarithm equality can be instantiated by using Fiat-Shamir on the Chaum and Pedersen protocol [18].

Our scheme follows the syntax in Sect. 3. We divide its presentation into four components: (a) setup and key generation, (b) authenticated key-exchange, (c) public verification, and (d) lawful interception.

Setup and Key Generation. This part instantiates the four following algorithms of the LIKE syntax presented in Sect. 3.

- Setup(1^λ): Based on λ, chooses $\mathbb{G}_1 = \langle g_1 \rangle$, $\mathbb{G}_2 = \langle g_2 \rangle$, and $\mathbb{G}_T$, three groups of prime order p of length λ, $e : \mathbb{G}_1 \times \mathbb{G}_2 \to \mathbb{G}_T$ a type 3 bilinear mapping, and outputs $\mathsf{pp} = (1^\lambda, \mathbb{G}_1, \mathbb{G}_2, \mathbb{G}_T, e, p, g_1, g_2)$.
- UKeyGen(pp): Runs (U.PK, U.SK) $\leftarrow$ SGen(pp) and returns (U.PK, U.SK).
- OKeyGen(pp): Runs (O.PK, O.SK) $\leftarrow$ SGen(pp) and returns (O.PK, O.SK).
- AKeyGen(pp): Picks $\Lambda.\mathsf{SK} \xleftarrow{\$} \mathbb{Z}_p^*$, sets $\Lambda.\mathsf{pk} \leftarrow g_1^{\Lambda.\mathsf{SK}}$ and $\Lambda.\mathsf{ni} \leftarrow \mathsf{NIPoK}\{\Lambda.\mathsf{SK} : \Lambda.\mathsf{pk} = g_1^{\Lambda.\mathsf{SK}}\}$, lets $\Lambda.\mathsf{PK} \leftarrow (\Lambda.\mathsf{pk}, \Lambda.\mathsf{ni})$, and returns $(\Lambda.\mathsf{PK}, \Lambda.\mathsf{SK})$.

The setup algorithm is run only once; key-generation is run once per party. The users and operators generate signature keys required in the authenticated key-exchange step. Authorities generate private/public keys, then prove (in zero-knowledge) that they know the private key. This prevents attacks in which authorities choose keys that cancel out other authority keys, breaking key security.

Alice: A(A.SK)	Operator: O_P(O_P.SK) where P $\in$ {A, B}	Bob: B(B.SK)
	precomputation: all parties parse APK as $(\Lambda_i.\mathsf{pk}, \Lambda_i.\mathsf{ni})_{i=1}^n$; **check all** $\Lambda_i.\mathsf{ni}$; $\omega \leftarrow \mathsf{A}\|\mathsf{B}\|(\Lambda_i)_{i=1}^n$; $\Lambda.\mathsf{pk} \leftarrow \prod\limits_{i=1}^{n} \Lambda_i.\mathsf{pk}$	

$$x \xleftarrow{\$} \mathbb{Z}_p^*; X_1 \leftarrow g_1^x; X_2 \leftarrow g_2^x;$$
$$\mathsf{ni}_X \leftarrow \mathsf{SoK}_\omega \{x : X_2 = g_2^x\};$$
$$m_X \leftarrow (X_1\|X_2\|\mathsf{ni}_X);$$
$\xrightarrow{\quad m_X \quad}$ Verify ni_X;

$$y \xleftarrow{\$} \mathbb{Z}_p^*; Y \leftarrow g_2^y;$$
$$\mathsf{ni}_Y \leftarrow \mathsf{SoK}_\omega \{y : Y = g_2^y\};$$
$$m_Y \leftarrow (Y\|\mathsf{ni}_Y);$$

Check $e(X_1, g_2) = e(g_1, X_2)$; $\xrightarrow{\quad m_X \quad}$ Verify ni_X;

Check $e(X_1, g_2) = e(g_1, X_2)$;

Verify $\sigma_Y^1, \mathsf{ni}_Y$;   Verify $\sigma_Y^1, \mathsf{ni}_Y$; $\xleftarrow{\quad m_Y, \sigma_Y^1 \quad}$ $\sigma_Y^1 \leftarrow \mathsf{SSig}(\mathsf{B.SK}, \omega\|m_X\|m_Y)$;

$M \leftarrow \omega\|m_X\|m_Y\|\sigma_Y^1$ $\xleftarrow{\quad m_Y, \sigma_Y^1 \quad}$ Verify σ_X; $\xrightarrow{\quad \sigma_X \quad}$ Verify σ_X;

$\sigma_X \leftarrow \mathsf{SSig}(\mathsf{A.SK}, M)$; $\xrightarrow{\quad \sigma_X \quad}$ ⌐ If P = O_B send σ_Y^2 to O_A ⌐ $\xleftarrow{\quad \sigma_Y^2 \quad}$ $\hat{M} \leftarrow \omega\|m_X\|m_Y\|\sigma_Y^1\|\sigma_X$

⌐ Verify σ_Y^2; $\sigma_Y^2 \leftarrow \mathsf{SSig}(\mathsf{B.SK}, \hat{M})$;

$m \leftarrow (\omega\|m_X\|m_Y\|$
$\sigma_Y^1\|\sigma_X\|\sigma_Y^2)$;

Return $k \leftarrow e(\Lambda.\mathsf{pk}, Y)^x$; $\sigma_{(O,P)} \leftarrow \mathsf{SSig}(O_P.\mathsf{SK}, m)$;   Return $k' \leftarrow e(\Lambda.\mathsf{pk}, X_2)^y$;
Return $\mathsf{sst}_P \leftarrow (m\|\sigma_{(O,P)})$;

Fig. 1. The AKE component of LIKE, with operators O_A and O_B under a single heading. Operators run protocol steps in turn, forwarding messages to the next participant. If some verification fails, we assume operators instantly abort. The only message *not* forwarded by O_A to Alice is marked in the dashed box. Note that X_1 is not used during this protocol; we will see later that this element is required to generate the trapdoors.

Authenticated Key Exchange. Whenever two users communicate, they run the AKE component of our LIKE syntax, AKE$\langle$A(A.SK), O_A(O_A.SK), O_B(O_B.SK),

$B(B.SK)\rangle$ $(pp, A.PK, B.PK, APK)$. Our protocol is described in Fig. 1. For readability we "merge" O_A and O_B since they act almost identically. Neither O_A, nor O_B computes session keys.

In Fig. 1, Alice, Bob, and the operators first verify the public keys of the n authorities, aborting if their NIZK proofs are incorrect. Notice that in the figure we omit to state that any failed verification leads to an abort. If a user has already performed these verifications, future sessions with those authority keys can proceed directly.

The heart of the protocol is the exchange between Alice and Bob. Alice generates a secret x and sends $X_1 = g_1^x, X_2 = g_2^x$, with an associated signature of knowledge linking this key share to ω. Bob proceeds similarly, sampling y and sending $Y = g_2^y$ and a signature of knowledge. The endpoints also send a signature over the transcript, thus authenticating each other and their conversation.

The two operators verify the messages they receive, aborting in case of failure, and otherwise forwarding the messages. An exception is Bob's last message, verified by both operators, but not forwarded to Alice. The operators check the signatures and signatures of knowledge and the equality of the exponents in Alice's DH elements.

Given Bob's public value Y, all the authority public keys, and her private exponent x, Alice computes her session key as a pairing of the product of all authority public keys and Y, all raised to her secret x: $k = e(\prod_{i=1}^n \Lambda_i.pk, Y)^x$. Due to bilinearity, this is equal to $e(\prod_{i=1}^n \Lambda_i.pk, g_2^y)^x = e(\prod_{i=1}^n \Lambda_i.pk, g_2^x)^y = e(\prod_{i=1}^n \Lambda_i.pk, X_2)^y$, which is Bob's key. Thus our scheme is correct for the endpoints. Note that all endpoint computations including secret values can be done by a SIM card except the pairing. Since the pairing is on public values, it can be delegated to a less secure environment (like the phone); then the exponentiation can be done on the SIM card. The operator's output is the session state sst, the signed session transcript from the their point of view.

Verification. We instantiate Verify as follows:

- Verify$(pp, sst, A.PK, B.PK, O.PK, APK) \rightarrow b$: Parse APK as a set $(\Lambda_i.PK)_{i=1}^n$ and parse each $\Lambda_i.PK$ as $(\Lambda_i.pk, \Lambda_i.ni)$, set $\omega \leftarrow A\|B\|(\Lambda_i)_{i=1}^n$. Parse sst as $\omega'\|m_X\|m_Y\|\sigma_Y^1\|\sigma_X\|\sigma_Y^2\|\sigma_O$, m_X as $X_1\|X_2\|ni_X$ and m_Y as $Y\|ni_Y$. if:
  - $\forall i \in [\![1, n]\!]$, NIPoKver$(\Lambda_i.pk, \Lambda_i.ni) = 1$;
  - $e(X_1, g_2) = e(g_1, X_2)$;
  - SoKver$(\omega, (g_2, X_2), ni_X) = $ SoKver$(\omega, (g_2, Y), ni_Y) = 1$;
  - SVer$(B.PK, \sigma_Y^1, \omega\|m_X\|m_Y) = 1$;
  - SVer$(A.PK, \sigma_X, \omega\|m_X\|m_Y\|\sigma_Y^1) = 1$;
  - SVer$(B.PK, \sigma_Y^2, \omega\|m_X\|m_Y\|\sigma_Y^1\|\sigma_X) = 1$;
  - SVer$(O.PK, \sigma_O, \omega\|m_X\|m_Y\|\sigma_Y^1\|\sigma_X\|\sigma_Y^2) = 1$;

  then the algorithm returns 1, else it returns 0.

Intuitively, the signatures authenticate Alice, Bob, and the operator outputting sst. The Verify algorithm retraces the operator's verifications of the authorities' proofs, of the signatures and SoKs, and of the equality of the discrete logarithms for X_1 and X_2.

Lawful Interception. Lawful interception employs two algorithms, one for trapdoor generation, and another which uses all the trapdoors to extract a key.

- TDGen(pp, Λ.SK, sst): Parse sst as $(\omega\|m_X\|m_Y\|\sigma_Y^1\|\sigma_X \quad \|\sigma_Y^2\|\sigma_O)$. Compute $\Lambda.t_1 \leftarrow e(X_1, Y)^{\Lambda.\text{SK}}, \Lambda.t_2 \leftarrow \text{NIPoK}\{\Lambda.\text{SK} : \Lambda.\text{pk} = g_1^{\Lambda.\text{SK}} \wedge \Lambda.$
  $t_1 = e(X_1, Y)^{\Lambda.\text{SK}}\}$ and $\Lambda.t \leftarrow (\Lambda.t_1, \Lambda.t_2)$, and return $\Lambda.t$.
- Open(pp, sst, APK, $\mathcal{T}$): Parse $\mathcal{T}$ as $(\Lambda_i.t)_{i=1}^n$, parse sst as $\text{A}\|\text{B}\|(\Lambda_i)_{i=1}^n$ $\|m_X\|m_Y\|\sigma_Y^1\|\sigma_X\|\sigma_Y^2\|\sigma_O$, m_X as $X_1\|X_2\|\text{ni}_X$ and m_Y as $Y\|\text{ni}_Y$, APK as $(\Lambda_i.\text{PK})_{i=1}^n$, parse each $\Lambda_i.\text{PK}$ as $(\Lambda_i.\text{pk}, \Lambda_i.\text{ni})$, each $\Lambda_i.t$ as $(\Lambda_i.t_1, \Lambda_i.t_2)$ and verify the non-interactive proof of knowledge: NIPoKver $((g_1, \Lambda_i.\text{pk}, (X_1, Y), \Lambda_i.t_1), \Lambda_i.t_2)$; if any verification fails, the Open algorithm returns $\bot$. Compute and return $\text{k} \leftarrow \prod_{i=1}^n (\Lambda_i.t_1)$.

Informally, each authority Λ_i generates a trapdoor $\Lambda_i.t_1 = e(X_1, Y)^{\Lambda_i.\text{SK}}$ as well as a proof $\Lambda_i.t_2$ that ensures that $\Lambda_i.t_1$ has been generated correctly, using the same $\Lambda_i.\text{SK}$ that is associated at key-generation with that authority (e.g., $\log_{g_1}(\Lambda_i.\text{pk}) = \log_{e(X_1,Y)}(\Lambda_i.t_1)$). The session key is recovered by multiplying all the trapdoors from $\Lambda_1.t_1$ to $\Lambda_n.t_1$, i.e., $\prod_{i=1}^n \Lambda_i.t_i = \prod_{i=1}^n e(X_1, Y)^{\Lambda_i.\text{SK}} = \prod_{i=1}^n e(g_1^x, g_2^y)^{\Lambda_i.\text{SK}} = e(g_1, g_2^{xy})^{\sum_{i=1}^n \Lambda_i.\text{SK}} = e(g_1^{\sum_{i=1}^n \Lambda_i.\text{SK}}, g_2^{x \cdot y}) = e(\prod_{i=1}^n \Lambda_i.\text{pk}, X_2)^y$. This is indeed Bob's key, proving correctness with respect to LI.

Complexity. Due to the NIZK verification and computing the product of the n authority public keys, the AKE protocol runs in linear time with respect to n. If, however, authorities do not change between protocol runs (as is likely in practice), the runtime will be constant with respect to n.

6 Security

We present our main theorem in this section, provide proof sketches in Appendix B, and give full proofs in the full version [7].

In the following, let sid $:= X_2\|Y$, and define IdentifySession(sst, π_P^j) for some party P and integer j as follows. Parsing sst as:

$$\text{A}\|\text{B}\|(\Lambda_i)_{i=1}^n\|X_1\|X_2\|\text{ni}_X\|Y\|\text{ni}_Y\|\sigma_Y^1\|\sigma_X\|\sigma_Y^2\|\sigma_O,$$

the algorithm IdentifySession(sst, π_P^j) returns 1 iff:

- $X_2\|Y = \pi_\text{P}^i.\text{sid}$,
- if π_P^j plays the role of Alice then $\text{P} = \text{A}$ and $\pi_\text{P}^j.\text{PID} = \text{B}$, else $\pi_\text{P}^j.\text{PID} = \text{A}$ and $\text{P} = \text{B}$, and
- $\pi_\text{P}^j.\text{AID} = (\Lambda_i)_{i=1}^n$.

Theorem 1. *Suppose LIKE is instantiated with an EUF-CMA signature scheme DS, extractable and zero-knowledge proofs/signature of knowledge, and let pp be chosen such that the BDDH assumption holds. Then:*

- *Our protocol is key-secure and, for all PPT adversaries $\mathcal{A}$ making at most q_r queries to Register, q_{ns} queries to NewSession, q_s queries to Send and q_t queries to RevealTD:*

$$\mathsf{Adv}^{\mathsf{KS}}_{\mathsf{LIKE},\mathcal{A}}(\lambda) \leq \frac{q_s^2}{p} + q_{\mathsf{ns}} \cdot q_r^2 \cdot \left(\mathsf{Adv}^{\mathsf{EUF\text{-}CMA}}_{\mathsf{DS}}(\lambda) + q_{\mathsf{ns}} \cdot q_r \cdot \right.$$

$$\left. \left((2 \cdot q_t + q_s) \cdot \epsilon_{\mathsf{SoK}}(\lambda) + q_r \cdot \epsilon_{\mathsf{NIPoK}}(\lambda) + \mathsf{Adv}^{\mathsf{BDDH}}(\lambda)\right)\right).$$

- *Our protocol is non-frameable, and for all PPT adversaries $\mathcal{A}$ making at most q_r queries to* Register*, we have:* $\mathsf{Adv}^{\mathsf{NF}}_{\mathsf{LIKE},\mathcal{A}}(\lambda) \leq q_r \cdot \mathsf{Adv}^{\mathsf{EUF\text{-}CMA}}_{\mathsf{DS}}(\lambda).$
- *Our protocol is honest-operator, and for all PPT adversaries $\mathcal{A}$ making at most q_r queries to* Register*, we have* $\mathsf{Adv}^{\mathsf{HO}}_{\mathsf{LIKE},\mathcal{A}}(\lambda) \leqslant q_r \cdot \epsilon_{\mathsf{NIPoK}}(\lambda) + \mathsf{Adv}^{\mathsf{EUF\text{-}CMA}}_{\mathsf{DS}}(\lambda).$

An important ingredient in our protocol are the proofs and signatures of knowledge. We start with the latter. Without Alice's and Bob's signatures of knowledge, given honestly-generated X_1, X_2, Y from the challenge session, $\mathcal{A}$ could choose random values r, s, run the protocol using $X_1' \leftarrow X_1^r$, $X_2' \leftarrow X_2^r$ and $Y' \leftarrow Y^s$ for two corrupted users and the same authorities, obtain sst, and run RevealTD on sst for each authority. Using Open, the adversary obtains: $\mathsf{k}' = \prod_{i=1}^{n}(X_1', Y_2')^{\Lambda_i.\mathsf{SK}} = \left(\prod_{i=1}^{n}(X_1, Y_2)^{\Lambda_i.\mathsf{SK}}\right)^{r \cdot s}$, and can compute the targeted key as $\mathsf{k} = (\mathsf{k}')^{1^{-r \cdot s}}$. This attack does not work if $\mathcal{A}$ must prove knowledge of the discrete logarithm of X_2' and Y'. Moreover, $\mathcal{A}$ cannot reuse X_2 and Y together with the signature of the honest user, since that signature uses the identity of the users as a message.

Each authority must prove knowledge of its secret key. Without this proof, an authority Λ_j could pick random r and compute: $\Lambda_j.\mathsf{pk} = g_1^r / \left(\prod_{i=1;i\neq j}^{n} \Lambda_i.\mathsf{pk}\right).$ In this case, Alice's session key becomes: $\mathsf{k} = e\left(\prod_{i=1}^{n} \Lambda_i.\mathsf{pk}, Y\right)^x = e(g_1^r, g_2^y)^x = e(X_1, Y)^r$, and the authority computes it as $e(X_1, Y)^r$. This attack is not possible if the authority must prove the knowledge of its secret key.

Finally, each authority must prove that the trapdoor is well-formed. This is essential for the HO property: otherwise, the authority can output a fake trapdoor, distorting the output of the algorithm Open.

7 Proof-of-Concept Implementation

We provide a proof-of-concept C-implementation of LIKE, which runs the entire primitive from setup to key-recovery, but omitting network exchanges. The implementation features: two authorities, Alice, Bob, and a single operator (since both operators would have to perform the same computations). The choice of two authorities was arbitrary: one for the justice system, and another for law-enforcement. More authorities would translate into a slightly higher runtime for the endpoints (one exponentiation per added authority), and a higher runtime for LI, depending on which authorities may view the session key (see also the full version [7]). However, even the worst added complexity would only involve an increased number of multiplications and potentially, the establishment of a secure multiparty channel. We measure the time-complexity of various operations during key-exchange and recovery, and provide averaged results in Table 2.

Setup. All tests are done on a Debian GNU/Linux 10 (buster) machine with an AMD Ryzen 5 1600 Six-Core Processor and 8GB RAM. We use the Ate pairing [43] over the

BN462 Barreto-Naehrig curve [29] with 128-bit security, thus following the recommendations of [9] for pairing curve parameters. We use the base points described in [29] as the generators of groups $\mathbb{G}_1$ and $\mathbb{G}_2$.

For the signature scheme, we use ed25519 [14], SHA-256 as our hash function, and we implement the signatures/proofs of knowledge as explained in Sect. 5. We use mcl [1] for our elliptic-curve and pairing computations. For the ed25519 signature scheme and SHA-256 we used openssl.

Results. Table 2 shows our results, averaged over 5000 protocol runs. The protocol steps involving the authorities (trapdoor generation/opening) have linear complexity in the number of authorities n ($n = 2$ in our case) because *all* trapdoors are necessary to open, and opening is linear in n. In the table, A, B, and O denote the total runtimes of Alice, Bob, and the operator respectively, during AKE (omitting the pre-computation). Verification, TDGen, and Open represent the runtime for those algorithms – which could be improved through parallelization for the last two algorithms. The runtime given for TDGen is a cumulation for the two authorities we consider; thus, each authority has a runtime of about half that value. For reference we also include the runtime of a single pairing, since it is our most expensive computation.

Operations	A	B	O	Verification	TDGen	Open	Pairing
CPU time (ms)	9.1	15.2	10.9	12.9	12.7	10.4	3.3

Fig. 2. Average CPU time (in milliseconds) for 5000 trials.

Our results above are promising, but insufficient for protocol deployment. An immediate next step would be to implement it on a mobile phone. Stronger security might even require long-term secrets for Alice and Bob to be stored in a secure element, like the SIM card, possibly delegating some computations to the mobile phone as described in Sect. 5. Moreover our protocol (and LIKE at large) would require further testing and standardization prior to deployment.

8 Conclusion

In this paper we bridge the gap between privacy and fine-grained lawful interception by introducing LIKE, a new primitive ensuring channel-establishment that is secure except with respect to: Alice, Bob, or a collusion of n legitimate authorities. In addition, users cannot be framed of wrong-doing, even by a collusion of all the authorities and operators. Finally, both the operator and the authorities are guaranteed that the LI procedure will reveal the key that Alice and Bob should have computed in any given session.

We instantiate LIKE by using efficient NIZK proofs and signatures of knowledge, and signatures. As our proof-of-concept implementation also demonstrates, the protocol is fast, and even problematic computations could be delegated on a mobile phone.

So far, our protocol only works for domestic communications, with both operators subject to an identical authority set. An extension to multiple authority sets is not obvious and we thus leave this as an open question.

40   G. Arfaoui et al.

Acknowledgement. Ghada Arfaoui, Olivier Blazy, Pierre-Alain Fouque, and Cristina Onete are grateful for the support of the ANR, through project ANR MobiS5 (ANR-18-CE39-0019).

A   Model Complements

Symbol	Meaning
pp	Global public parameters
Λ_i	The i-th authority
γ	Corruption bit, indicates if a party is corrupted
α	Accept bit, indicates if a party instance has terminated in an accepting state or not
ρ	Reveal bit, indicates if a party's session key was revealed
k	Session key, computed by endpoints or by collusion of authorities
sst	Session state, computed by operators
PID	Users partnered to a given instance
AID	Authorities implicitly partnered to a given instance (may open key)
OID	Operators partnered to a given instance

Fig. 3. Useful notations from our model and their significance

Definition 10 (Correctness). *Let* λ *a security parameter and* n *an integer. Run* pp $\leftarrow$ Setup(1^λ), (A.PK, A.SK) $\leftarrow$ UKeyGen(pp), (B.PK, B.SK) $\leftarrow$ UKeyGen(pp), (O_A.PK, O_A.SK) $\leftarrow$ OKeyGen(pp), (O_B.PK, O_B.SK) $\leftarrow$ OKeyGen(pp). *For all* $i \in [\![1, n]\!]$, (Λ_i.PK, Λ_i.SK) $\leftarrow$ AKeyGen(pp). *Let* APK $\leftarrow$ (Λ_i.PK)$_{i=1}^n$. *Then:*

- PK$_{A \to B}$ $\leftarrow$ (pp, A.PK, B.PK, APK);
- (k$_A$, sst$_A$, sst$_B$, k$_B$) $\leftarrow$
  AKE$\langle$A(A.SK), O_A(O_A.SK), O_B(O_B.SK), B(B.SK)$\rangle$(PK$_{A \to B}$);
- b$_A$ $\leftarrow$ Verify(pp, sst$_A$, A.PK, B.PK, O_A.PK, APK);
- *For all* i *in* $[\![1, n]\!]$, Λ_i.t$_A$ $\leftarrow$ TDGen(pp, Λ_i.SK, sst$_A$);
- k$_A^*$ $\leftarrow$ Open(pp, sst$_A$, (Λ_i.PK)$_{i=1}^n$, (Λ_i.t$_A$)$_{i=1}^n$);
- b$_B$ $\leftarrow$ Verify(pp, sst$_B$, A.PK, B.PK, O_B.PK, APK);
- *For all* i *in* $[\![1, n]\!]$, Λ_i.t$_B$ $\leftarrow$ TDGen(pp, Λ_i.SK, sst$_B$);
- k$_B^*$ $\leftarrow$ Open(pp, sst$_B$, APK, (Λ_i.t$_B$)$_{i=1}^n$).

For any (b$_A$, b$_B$, k$_A$, k$_A^*$, k$_B$, k$_B^*$) *generated as above:* Pr[b$_A$ = b$_B$ = 1 $\wedge$ k$_A$ = k$_A^*$ = k$_B$ = k$_B^*$] = 1.

B   Proof Sketches

Our main theorem includes three statements; we prove these in order below.

First Statement: KS. We begin by proving that the adversary has a negligible probability of winning the key-security experiment by querying the oracle Test on an instance that matches no other instance. Notably, if the tested instance does not abort the protocol, the adversary will have to break the EUF-CMA of the signature scheme to generate the expected signatures without using a matching session.

Thus, the targeted instance must have a matching one. By key-freshness, $\mathcal{A}$ must test a key generated by two honest users, such that the trapdoor of at least one honest authority has never been queried to the oracle RevealTD. We prove (by a reduction) that $\mathcal{A}$ can only win by breaking the BDDH assumption. Let $(W_*, X_*, Y_*, W'_*, X'_*, Y'_*, Z_*)$ be a BDDH instance. We set W_* as the part of the public key Λ.pk of the honest authority, and we set X_2 as X'_*, X_1 as X_* and Y as Y'_* for the session that matches the tested instance. Then, we build the key as follows, where Λ is the honest authority: $k \leftarrow Z_* \prod_{i=1; \Lambda_i \neq \Lambda}^{n} e(X_*, Y'_*)^{\Lambda_i.\text{SK}}$. To compute the secret keys of the authorities controlled by the adversary, we run the extractor on the proofs of knowledge of the discrete logarithm of the public keys Λ_i.PK. If Z_* is a random value, k will be random for the adversary, else $Z_* = e(X_*, Y'_*)^{\Lambda.\text{SK}}$. Moreover, we simulate the oracle RevealTD on sessions with values X and Y chosen by the adversary by using the extractor on the signatures of knowledge of their discrete logarithms.

Second Statement: NF. To win the non-frameability experiment, the adversary has to build a valid session state sst for a given user, containing a valid signature of this user. We prove this theorem by reduction: assuming that an adversary is able to break the non-frameability, since this adversary generates a valid signature for a user, we can use it to break the EUF-CMA security.

Third Statement: HO. The first step of the HO proof is to design a key extractor, which takes in input a session state sst, brute-forces the discrete logarithm of Bob's Y, then computes the key as Bob would: $k = e(\prod_{i=1}^{n} \Lambda_i.\text{pk}, X_2)^y$. Our goal is to prove that this is the key the authorities would retrieve.

We first show (by reduction) that the adversary can only build by itself a valid sst (that may match a fake authority set) with negligible probability. Namely, if an adversary can output valid signatures for an honest operator, then we can use it to break the EUF-CMA of the signature scheme.

Moreover, for any authority Λ and any values X_1 and Y, the proof of knowledge of a trapdoor ensures that $g_1^{\Lambda.\text{SK}} = \Lambda$.pk and $\Lambda.t_1 = e(X_1, Y)^{\Lambda.\text{SK}}$, which implies that $\Lambda.t_1 = e(\Lambda.\text{pk}, X_2)^y$ and: $k_* = \prod_{i=1}^{n} \Lambda_i.t_1 = e(\prod_{i=1}^{n} \Lambda_i.\text{pk}, X_2)^y$. Thus, to win the HO experiment (and return a key such that $k \neq k_*$), the adversary must produce a proof on a false statement, which happens with negligible probability.

References

1. MCL (2020). https://github.com/herumi/mcl
2. 3GPP: TS 33.106 3rd Generation Partnership Project; Technical Specification Group Services and System Aspects; 3G security; Lawful interception requirements (R. 15), June 2018
3. 3GPP: TS 33.126 3GPP; Technical Specification Group Services and System Aspects; Security; Lawful Interception requirements (R. 16), September 2019
4. 3GPP: TS 33.127 3GPP; Technical Specification Group Services and System Aspects; Security; Lawful Interception (LI) Architecture and Functions (R. 16), March 2020

5. 3GPP: TS 33.128 3GPP; Technical Specification Group Services and System Aspects; Security; Protocol and procedures for Lawful Interception (LI); Stage 3 (R. 16), March 2020
6. Abelson, H., et al.: Keys under doormats. Commun. ACM **58**(10), 24–26 (2015)
7. Arfaoui, G., et al.: Legally keeping secrets from mobile operators: lawful interception key exchange (LIKE). IACR ePrint (2020). https://eprint.iacr.org/2020/684
8. Azfar, A.: Implementation and performance of threshold cryptography for multiple escrow agents in VoIP. In: Proceedings of SPIT/IPC, pp. 143–150 (2011)
9. Barbulescu, R., Duquesne, S.: Updating key size estimations for pairings. J. Cryptol. **32**, 1298–1336 (2019)
10. Bellare, M., Goldreich, O.: On defining proofs of knowledge. In: Brickell, E.F. (ed.) CRYPTO 1992. LNCS, vol. 740, pp. 390–420. Springer, Heidelberg (1992). https://doi.org/10.1007/3-540-48071-4_28
11. Bellare, M., Goldwasser, S.: Verifiable partial key escrow. In: CCS 1997. ACM (1997)
12. Bellare, M., Rivest, R.L.: Translucent cryptography - an alternative to key escrow, and its implementation via fractional oblivious transfer. J. Cryptol. **12**(2) (1999)
13. Bellare, M., Rogaway, P.: Entity authentication and key distribution. In: Stinson, D.R. (ed.) CRYPTO 1993. LNCS, vol. 773, pp. 232–249. Springer, Heidelberg (1993). https://doi.org/10.1007/3-540-48329-2_21
14. Bernstein, D.J., Duif, N., Lange, T., Schwabe, P., Yang, B.Y.: High-speed high-security signatures. In: Proceedings of CHES 2011, pp. 124–142 (2011)
15. Boyen, X.: The uber-assumption family. In: Galbraith, S.D., Paterson, K.G. (eds.) Pairing 2008. LNCS, vol. 5209, pp. 39–56. Springer, Heidelberg (2008). https://doi.org/10.1007/978-3-540-85538-5_3
16. Camenisch, J., Stadler, M.: Efficient group signature schemes for large groups (extended abstract). In: Kaliski, B.S. (ed.) CRYPTO 1997. LNCS, vol. 1294, pp. 410–424. Springer, Heidelberg (1997). https://doi.org/10.1007/BFb0052252
17. Chase, M., Lysyanskaya, A.: On signatures of knowledge. In: Dwork, C. (ed.) CRYPTO 2006. LNCS, vol. 4117, pp. 78–96. Springer, Berlin, Heidelberg (2006). https://doi.org/10.1007/11818175_5
18. Chaum, D., Pedersen, T.P.: Wallet databases with observers. In: Brickell, E.F. (ed.) CRYPTO 1992. LNCS, vol. 740, pp. 89–105. Springer, Heidelberg (1993). https://doi.org/10.1007/3-540-48071-4_7
19. Chen, L., Gollmann, D., Mitchell, C.J.: Key escrow in mutually mistrusting domains. In: Proceedings of Security Protocols, pp. 139–153 (1996)
20. Chen, M.: Escrowable identity-based authenticated key agreement in the standard model. Chin. Electron. J. **43**, 1954–1962 (10 2015)
21. Comey, J. (FBI) (2014). https://www.fbi.gov/news/speeches/going-dark-are-technology-privacy-and-public-safety-on-a-collision-course
22. Denning, D.E., Branstad, D.K.: A taxonomy for key escrow encryption systems. Commun. ACM **39**(3) (1996)
23. Desmedt, Y.: Abuses in cryptography and how to fight them. In: Goldwasser, S. (ed.) CRYPTO 1988. LNCS, vol. 403, pp. 375–389. Springer, New York (1990). https://doi.org/10.1007/0-387-34799-2_29
24. EU: Draft council resolution on encryption - security through encryption and security despite encryption (2020). https://files.orf.at/vietnam2/files/fm4/202045/783284_fh_st12143-re01en20_783284.pdf
25. Europol. https://www.europol.europa.eu/newsroom/news/europol-and-european-commission-inaugurate-new-decryption-platform-to-tackle-challenge-of-encrypted-material-for-law-enforcement
26. FairTrials (2020). https://www.fairtrials.org/news/short-update-police-germany-defend-use-contact-tracing-criminal-investigations

27. Fan, Q., Zhang, M., Zhang, Y.: Key escrow scheme with the cooperation mechanism of multiple escrow agents (2012)
28. Franceschi-Bicchierai, L.: The 10 biggest revelations from Edward Snowden's leaks (2014). https://mashable.com/2014/06/05/edward-snowden-revelations/?europe=true
29. IETF: Pairing-friendly curves (2020). https://datatracker.ietf.org/doc/draft-irtf-cfrg-pairing-friendly-curves/
30. Kahney, L.: The FBI wanted a back door to the iPhone. Tim cook said no (2019). https://www.wired.com/story/the-time-tim-cook-stood-his-ground-against-fbi/
31. Kilian, J., Leighton, F.T.: Fair Cryptosystems, revisited: a rigorous approach to key-escrow (extended abstract). In: Coppersmith, D. (ed.) CRYPTO 1995. LNCS, vol. 963, pp. 208–221. Springer, Heidelberg (1995). https://doi.org/10.1007/3-540-44750-4_17
32. Long, Y., Cao, Z., Chen, K.: A dynamic threshold commercial key escrow scheme based on conic. Appl. Math. Comput. **171**(2), 972–982 (2005)
33. Long, Y., Chen, K., Liu, S.: Adaptive chosen ciphertext secure threshold key escrow scheme from pairing. Informatica Lith. Acad. Sci. **17**(4), 519–534 (2006)
34. Martin, K.M.: Increasing efficiency of international key escrow in mutually mistrusting domains. In: Darnell, M. (ed.) Cryptography and Coding 1997. LNCS, vol. 1355, pp. 221–232. Springer, Heidelberg (1997). https://doi.org/10.1007/BFb0024467
35. Micali, S.: Fair public-key cryptosystems. In: Brickell, E.F. (ed.) CRYPTO 1992. LNCS, vol. 740, pp. 113–138. Springer, Heidelberg. https://doi.org/10.1007/3-540-48071-4_9
36. Mironov, I., Stephens-Davidowitz, N.: Cryptographic reverse firewalls. In: Oswald, E., Fischlin, M. (eds.) EUROCRYPT 2015. LNCS, vol. 9057, pp. 657–686. Springer, Heidelberg (2015). https://doi.org/10.1007/978-3-662-46803-6_22
37. Museum, C.: Clipper chip. https://www.cryptomuseum.com/crypto/usa/clipper.htm
38. Ni, L., Chen, G., Li, J.: Escrowable identity-based authenticated key agreement protocol with strong security. Comput. Math. Appl. **65**(9), 1339–1349 (2013)
39. Schnorr, C.: Efficient identification and signatures for smart cards. In: Brassard, G. (ed.) CRYPTO 1989. LNCS, vol. 435, pp. 239–252. Springer, New York (1989). https://doi.org/10.1007/0-387-34805-0_22
40. Shamir, A.: Partial key escrow: a new approach to software key escrow. Presented at Key Escrow Conference (1995)
41. Shamir, A.: Identity-based cryptosystems and signature schemes. In: Blakley, G.R., Chaum, D. (eds.) CRYPTO 1984. LNCS, vol. 196, pp. 47–53. Springer, Heidelberg (1984). https://doi.org/10.1007/3-540-39568-7_5
42. UN (1948). https://www.un.org/en/universal-declaration-human-rights/
43. Vercauteren, F.: Optimal pairings. IEEE Trans. Inf. Theory **56**(1), 455–461 (2010)
44. Wang, Z., Ma, Z., Luo, S., Gao, H.: Key escrow protocol based on a tripartite authenticated key agreement and threshold cryptography. IEEE Access **7**, 149080–149096 (2019)
45. Wright, C.V., Varia, M.: Crypto crumple zones: enabling limited access without mass surveillance. In: Proceedings of EuroS&P 2018. IEEE (2018)
46. Young, A.L., Yung, M.: Kleptography from standard assumptions and applications. In: Proceedings of SCN, pp. 271–290 (2010)

A Formal Security Analysis of Session Resumption Across Hostnames

Kai Gellert and Tobias Handirk[(✉)]

Bergische Universität Wuppertal, Wuppertal, Germany
{kai.gellert,tobias.handirk}@uni-wuppertal.de

Abstract. The TLS 1.3 session resumption handshakes enables a client
and a server to resume a previous connection via a shared secret, which
was established during a previous session. In practice, this is often done
via *session tickets*, where the server provides a "self-encrypted" ticket
containing the shared secret to its clients. A client may resume its session by sending the ticket to the server, which allows the server to retrieve
the shared secret stored within the ticket.

Usually, a ticket is only accepted by the server that issued the ticket.
However, in practice, servers that share the same hostname, often share
the same key material for ticket encryption. The concept of a server
accepting a ticket, which was issued by a different server, is known as
session resumption across hostnames (SRAH). In 2020, Sy *et al.* showed
in an empirical analysis that, by using SRAH, the time to load a webpage can be reduced by up to 31% when visiting the page for the very
first time. Despite its performance advantages, the TLS 1.3 specification
currently discourages the use of SRAH.

In this work, we formally investigate which security guarantees can be
achieved when using SRAH. To this end, we provide the first formaliza-
tion of SRAH and analyze its security in the multi-stage key exchange
model (Dowling *et al.*; JoC 2021), which proved useful in previous analyses of TLS handshakes. We find that an adversary can break authentication if clients do not specify the intended receiver of their first protocol
message. However, if the intended receiver is specified by the client, we
prove that SRAH is secure in the multi-stage key exchange model.

1 Introduction

If two parties want to securely establish a common key over an insecure channel,
they typically execute a key exchange protocol. The most used key exchange
protocol is the Transport Layer Security (TLS) protocol, whose most recent
version, TLS 1.3, was standardized in 2018 [18]. The TLS 1.3 protocol provides
two variants of key establishment: (i) the full handshake where two users can
establish a fresh key, and (ii) the resumption handshake (also called pre-shared
key handshake) where two users may derive a new key from preexisting key

Supported by the German Research Foundation (DFG), project JA 2445/2-1.

© Springer Nature Switzerland AG 2021
E. Bertino et al. (Eds.): ESORICS 2021, LNCS 12972, pp. 44–64, 2021.
https://doi.org/10.1007/978-3-030-88418-5_3

material (e.g., key material from an earlier session, or key material that was established out-of-band).

One of the main motivations to use the resumption handshake instead of the full handshake, is a reduction of computational complexity. That is, the resumption handshake does not require the expensive verification of signatures to authenticate the server. Instead authentication is provided implicitly by knowledge of the *pre-shared key* (PSK). In fact, according to Cloudflare in 2017[1], 40% of handshakes are users resuming a previous connection, which further illustrates the resumption handshakes form one of the cornerstones of secure connection establishments over the Internet.

Session Resumption Across Hostnames. In practice, a client rarely only establishes one connection to a server, but rather has to open multiple connections in order to retrieve additional data distributed across multiple servers, requiring several *full* handshakes. These additional handshakes often slow down the TLS connection establishment and are desirable to avoid.

An interesting observation is that not all of the additional handshakes request data from external services but some request data from the same content provider, only under a different hostname. For example, a user could request the web page *www.webpage.com* and could be required to load additional content from subdomains such as *assets.webpage.com*. Even though the subdomain may share the certificate of the original domain, a full handshake would need to be executed. Naturally, it would be interesting to investigate whether connection establishment could be accelerated if such handshakes could rely on a resumption-based handshake rather than a full handshake. This approach is called *session resumption across hostnames* (SRAH).

In 2020, Sy *et al.* [19] conducted a study investigating the potential performance improvement when using SRAH. They found that 59% of the (on average) 20 full TLS handshakes required to retrieve a website can be converted into handshakes based on resumption across hostnames. According to them, this would reduce 44% of the computational complexity and accelerate the connection establishment by 31%

SRAH in TLS 1.3. The typical session resumption can be described as follows: After a client and a server have completed a full TLS 1.3 handshake, both parties derive a PSK which can be used in future resumption handshakes. Typically, the server does not want to keep track of each of those PSKs for each user and encrypts the PSK under a symmetric key only known to the server. This ciphertext is called *ticket* and sent to the client at the end of the original full handshake. Note that this enables the server to delete the PSK as it can always retrieve it from the issued ticket. That is, when the client sends back the ticket to the server, both parties can take the PSK as basis to derive a new session key.

The above approach can be extended to capture the conceptual approach of SRAH as well. To this end, the client would not only send the ticket back

---

[1] See https://blog.cloudflare.com/introducing-0-rtt/.

to the server, but the client would also indicate which hostname it wants to establish a connection with. This indication can be given in form of a Server Name Indication (SNI) value chosen by the client, providing leverage to choose for which server (sharing the same symmetric ticket encryption key) a ticket should be used. The TLS 1.3 standard specifies in Sect. 4.2.11:

> *"In TLS 1.3, the SNI value is always explicitly specified in the resumption handshake, and there is no need for the server to associate an SNI value with the ticket. Clients, however, SHOULD store the SNI with the PSK to fulfill the requirements of Sect. 4.6.1."*

We remark that we find the first part of this quote worrying, as the standard does not indicate that the SNI value *must* be set in the resumption handshake. While we agree that the SNI value is not necessary if connections are only resumed with the server that issued a ticket, this formulation also opens room for interpretation how the SNI value should be used when considering SRAH. We are concerned that this ambiguity might lead to wrong conclusions when implementing TLS 1.3.

Furthermore, the standard states in Sect. 4.6.1:

> *"Clients MUST only resume if the new SNI value is valid for the server certificate presented in the original session and SHOULD only resume if the SNI value matches the one used in the original session. [...] Normally, there is no reason to expect that different servers covered by a single certificate would be able to accept each other's tickets; [...] If such an indication is provided (externally or by any other means)*[2]*, clients MAY resume with a different SNI value."*

We can observe that the latter half of the above excerpt allows to use SRAH without need to change the standard. However, the standard does not yet elaborate what consequence a resumption across hostnames could have and how those consequences should be dealt with. A potential reason for this might be that the security of SRAH has never been formally analyzed and we currently do not understand its advantages and disadvantages well enough.

Our Contributions. In this work, we formally investigate the security of SRAH. We summarized our contributions as follows:

- We give the first formal definition of secure SRAH, as an abstraction of the construction that can be used in TLS 1.3. This approach enables us to carefully investigate what security for SRAH means and how we can achieve it, without being overwhelmed by the complexity of protocols such as TLS 1.3.

---

[2] We remark that this indication can either be provided by the server via the `subjectAltName` field in a server's certificate, or via an extension providing this information within the `ClientHello` message of the original full handshake as recommended by Sy *et al.* [19].

- We show security in the most recent version of multi-stage key exchange model [9], which has been proven useful in many analyses of TLS handshakes [3,6,7,11]. Specifically, we show that a misinterpretation of the TLS 1.3 standard leads to an attack on authentication when two servers share the same certificate and symmetric ticket key. Furthermore, we provide an SRAH protocol which constitutes an abstraction of the TLS 1.3 resumption protocol and prove its security.

Related Work. The security of the TLS 1.3 resumption handshake has been analyzed in many previous works. Most notably are the works by Dowling *et al.* [9], and Drucker and Gueron [10] who analyzed the security of the standardized handshake, and Arfaoui *et al.* [1] who analyzed privacy aspects of the resumption handshake. Furthermore, Aviram *et al.* [2,3] proposed an improvement of the resumption handshake, which achieves forward security for the 0-RTT variant of the handshake. Note, however, that none of the related works consider the case of SRAH.

2   Preliminaries

2.1   Building Blocks

Hash Functions, MACs, and PRFs. In this work, we use standard definitions for hash functions and their collision resistance, MACs and their strong unforgeability. Due to space constraints, we cannot formally define all of those building blocks and hence only define further non-well-known properties in the sequel.

Definition 1. *Let* $f : \{0,1\}^* \times \{0,1\}^{i(\lambda)} \to \{0,1\}^{o(\lambda)}$ *be an efficient function with. We call* f *pseudorandom if for all PPT adversaries* $\mathcal{A}$ *the advantage*

$$\mathsf{Adv}^{\mathsf{PRF\text{-}sec}}_{f,\mathcal{A}}(\lambda) := \left| \Pr[\mathcal{A}^{f(k,\cdot)}(1^\lambda) = 1] - \Pr[\mathcal{A}^{g(\cdot)}(1^\lambda) = 1] \right|$$

is negligible in λ, *where* $k \xleftarrow{\$} \{0,1\}^\lambda$, *and* g *is chosen randomly from the set of all functions mapping* $\{0,1\}^{i(\lambda)} \to \{0,1\}^{o(\lambda)}$. *Additionally we say* f *achieves dual PRF security if the advantage*

$$\mathsf{Adv}^{\mathsf{dual\text{-}PRF\text{-}sec}}_{f,\mathcal{A}}(\lambda) := \mathsf{Adv}^{\mathsf{PRF\text{-}sec}}_{f^{\mathsf{swap}},\mathcal{A}}(\lambda)$$

is a negligible function in the security parameter λ, *where* $f^{\mathsf{swap}}(k,l) := f(l,k)$.

HMAC-based Key Derivation. The *HMAC-based key derivation function* (HKDF) [15,16] is a key derivation scheme and is used, e.g., in TLS 1.3 [18]. The HKDF scheme is based on the HMAC construction [4,17] and follows the *extract-then-expand* paradigm, i.e., from some given source key material first a pseudorandom key of fixed length is extracted, which is then expanded to a pseudorandom key of the desired length. Formally, HKDF.Extract(salt, src) given a (potentially fixed) salt salt and a source key material src outputs a pseudorandom key prk. HKDF.Expand(prk, ctxt) given a pseudorandom key prk and a (potentially empty) context info ctxt outputs a new pseudorandom key.[3] In our security analysis we rely on the assumption that both HKDF.Extract and HKDF.Expand are pseudorandom functions [16].

PRF-ODH Assumption. An important security assumption in the analysis of TLS 1.2 and 1.3 is the PRF-ODH assumption first introduced by Jager *et al.* [14]. Brendel *et al.* [5] analyzed and generalized the PRF-ODH assumption into several variants. In this work we will need the dual-snPRF-ODH assumption.

Definition 2. *Let $\lambda \in \mathbb{N}$, $\mathbb{G}$ be a cyclic group of prime order q with generator g and PRF : $\{0,1\}^* \times \mathbb{G} \rightarrow \{0,1\}^\lambda$ be a pseudorandom function keyed with the second input. Consider the following game $G_{\mathsf{PRF},\mathbb{G},\mathcal{A}}^{\mathsf{dual\text{-}snPRF\text{-}ODH}}(\lambda)$ played between a challenger $\mathcal{C}$ and an adversary $\mathcal{A}$:*

1. *$\mathcal{C}$ samples $b \xleftarrow{\$} \{0,1\}$, $u,v \xleftarrow{\$} \mathbb{Z}_q$ and outputs $\mathbb{G}, g, g^u, g^v$ to $\mathcal{A}$. $\mathcal{A}$ then outputs a challenge label $x^\star$.*
2. *$\mathcal{C}$ computes $y_0^\star = \mathsf{PRF}(x^\star, g^{uv})$ and samples $y_1^\star \xleftarrow{\$} \{0,1\}^\lambda$ uniformly at random and outputs $y_b^\star$ to $\mathcal{A}$.*
3. *$\mathcal{A}$ may query a pair (x, S). If $S \notin \mathbb{G}$ or $(x, S) = (x^\star, g^v)$, $\mathcal{C}$ returns $\perp$. Otherwise $\mathcal{C}$ returns $y \leftarrow \mathsf{PRF}(x, S^u)$.*
4. *At some point $\mathcal{A}$ outputs a guess $b' \in \{0,1\}$.*

We say that $\mathcal{A}$ wins the game $G_{\mathsf{PRF},\mathbb{G},\mathcal{A}}^{\mathsf{dual\text{-}snPRF\text{-}ODH}}(\lambda) = 1$ if $b = b'$. A pseudorandom function PRF is secure under the dual-snPRF-ODH assumption if for PPT adversaries $\mathcal{A}$ the advantage

$$\mathsf{Adv}_{\mathsf{PRF},\mathbb{G},\mathcal{A}}^{\mathsf{dual\text{-}snPRF\text{-}ODH}}(\lambda) := \Pr[G_{\mathsf{PRF},\mathbb{G},\mathcal{A}}^{\mathsf{dual\text{-}snPRF\text{-}ODH}}(\lambda) = 1] - \frac{1}{2}$$

is a negligible function in the security parameter λ.

2.2 Multi-Stage Key Exchange

We briefly recap the multi-stage key exchange (MSKE) model in its pre-shared secret variant from [9], which has been used in previous analyses of resumption handshakes in TLS 1.3 [3,7–9,12].

The following description of the model is taken verbatim from [9], except for the following minor changes. We modified the NewSecret query such that a pre-shared secret can be shared between more than two users with the restriction that only a single user uses the pre-shared secret in the initiator role. As a consequence we modified the maps storing all pre-shared secrets as well as the input to the NewSession and Corrupt query to properly identify the pre-shared secret to be used in the session, resp. the pre-shared secret to corrupt.

---

[3] Formally, HKDF.Expand is given an additional input L. This third parameter determines the length of the output pseudorandom key. For simplicity we omit this parameter and assume that $L = \lambda$ unless stated otherwise.

Preliminaries. In the MSKE model, properties are separated into *protocol-specific* and *session-specific* properties. The protocol-specific properties are defined by a vector $(\mathsf{M}, \mathsf{AUTH}, \mathsf{USE}, \mathsf{FS}, \mathsf{REPLAY})$ denoting the following:

- $\mathsf{M} \in \mathbb{N}$: the number of stages (i.e., the number of keys derived).
- $\mathsf{AUTH} \subseteq \{((u_1, m_1,) \ldots, (u_{\mathsf{M}}, m_{\mathsf{M}})) | u_j, m_j \in \{1, \ldots, \mathsf{M}, \infty\}\}$: a set of vectors of pairs, where each vector encodes a supported scheme for authentication and authentication upgrades. The i-th entry (u_i, m_i) of a vector indicates that the session key of stage i initially is unauthenticated, then becomes unilaterally authenticated at stage u_i, and finally reaches mutual authentication at stage m_i. Entries in each pair must be non-decreasing, and $u_i = \infty$ or $m_i = \infty$ denotes that unilateral, respectively mutual, authentication is never reached for stage i.
- $\mathsf{USE} \in \{\mathsf{internal}, \mathsf{external}\}^{\mathsf{M}}$: the usage indicator for each stage. We denote with USE_i the usage of the key of stage i. An internal key is used within the key exchange protocol (but possibly also outside of it), while an external key must not be used within the protocol.
- $\mathsf{FS} \in \{1, \ldots, \mathsf{M}, \infty\}$: the stage $j = \mathsf{FS}$ from which on keys are forward secure (or ∞ in case of no forward security).
- $\mathsf{REPLAY} \in \{\mathsf{replayable}, \mathsf{nonreplayable}\}^{\mathsf{M}}$: the replayability indicator for each stage. We denote with REPLAY_i whether the stage i is replayable meaning that an adversary is able to force identical session identifiers and keys in this stage.

We denote the set of users by $\mathcal{U}$, where each user is uniquely identified by some $U \in \mathcal{U}$. Protocol sessions are uniquely identified by a *label* label $\in \mathsf{LABELS} = (\mathcal{U} \times \mathcal{U} \times \mathbb{N})$, where label $= (U, V, k)$ indicates the k-th local session of the *session owner* U with V as the intended communication partner. Each session holds an identifier pssid $\in \{0, 1\}^*$ for the pre-shared secret pss $\in \mathcal{P}$ (for some pre-shared secret space $\mathcal{P}$) used in the session. All pre-shared secrets are stored in maps $\mathsf{pss}_{U,\mathcal{V}} : \{0, 1\}^* \to \mathcal{P}$ mapping pre-shared secret identifiers to the corresponding pre-shared secrets pss. A pre-shared secret pss stored in a map $\mathsf{pss}_{U,\mathcal{V}}$ is shared between the participants U and all $V \in \mathcal{V} \subseteq \mathcal{U}$ where U uses pss only in the initiator role and all $V \in \mathcal{V}$ use pss only in the responder role.

All sessions are stored in the *session list* $\mathsf{List}_{\mathsf{S}}$ with each entry holding the following information:

- label $\in \mathsf{LABELS}$: the unique session label.
- id $\in \mathcal{U}$: the session owner.
- pid $\in \mathcal{U}$: the intended communication partner.
- role $\in \{\mathsf{initiator}, \mathsf{responder}\}$: the role of the session owner.
- auth $\in \mathsf{AUTH}$: the intended authentication type vector, where auth_i indicates the authentication level pair for stage i, and $\mathsf{auth}_{i,j}$ its j-th entry.
- pssid $\in (\{0, 1\}^* \cup \{\bot\})$: the identifier of the pre-shared secret to be used in this session.

- $\mathsf{st_{exec}} \in (\mathsf{RUNNING} \cup \mathsf{ACCEPTED} \cup \mathsf{REJECTED})$: the state of execution, where $\mathsf{RUNNING} = \{\mathsf{running}_i \,|\, i \in \mathbb{N}_0\}$, $\mathsf{ACCEPTED} = \{\mathsf{accepted}_i \,|\, i \in \mathbb{N}\}$, $\mathsf{REJECTED} = \{\mathsf{rejected}_i \,|\, i \in \mathbb{N}\}$. $\mathsf{st_{exec}}$ is initialized to $\mathsf{running}_0$. It is set to $\mathsf{accepted}_i$ when the i-th key is accepted, set to $\mathsf{running}_i$ when the protocol continues after accepting the i-th key, and set to $\mathsf{rejected}_i$ if the session rejects the i-th key (we assume a session does not continue after rejecting a key in any stage).
- $\mathsf{stage} \in [\mathsf{M}]_0$: the current stage. stage is initialized to 0 and set to i when $\mathsf{st_{exec}}$ is set to $\mathsf{accepted}_i$ or $\mathsf{rejected}_i$.
- $\mathsf{sid} \in (\{0,1\}^* \cup \{\bot\})^\mathsf{M}$: sid_i indicates the session identifier of stage i, that is set once when $\mathsf{st_{exec}}$ is set to $\mathsf{accepted}_i$. sid is initialized to $(\bot, \ldots, \bot)$.
- $\mathsf{cid} \in (\{0,1\}^* \cup \{\bot\})^\mathsf{M}$: cid_i indicates the contributive identifier of stage i, that may be set multiple times until $\mathsf{st_{exec}}$ is set to $\mathsf{accepted}_i$. cid is initialized to $(\bot, \ldots, \bot)$.
- $\mathsf{key} \in (\{0,1\}^* \cup \{\bot\})^\mathsf{M}$: key_i indicates the established session key of stage i. key is initialized to $(\bot, \ldots, \bot)$.
- $\mathsf{st_{key}} \in \{\mathsf{fresh}, \mathsf{revealed}\}^\mathsf{M}$: $\mathsf{st_{key},i}$ indicates the state of the session key in stage i. $\mathsf{st_{key}}$ is initialized to $(\mathsf{fresh}, \ldots, \mathsf{fresh})$.
- $\mathsf{tested} \in \{\mathsf{true}, \mathsf{false}\}^\mathsf{M}$: tested_i indicates whether the session key of stage i has been tested. tested is initialized to $(\mathsf{false}, \ldots, \mathsf{false})$.
- $\mathsf{corrupted} \in \{0, \ldots, \mathsf{M}, \infty\}$: indicates the stage the session was in when a $\mathsf{Corrupt}$ query for the pre-shared secret used in the session was issued. $\mathsf{corrupted}$ may be set to 0, indicating that the pre-shared secret was corrupted before the session started, and to ∞, indicating that the pre-shared secret is not corrupted. $\mathsf{corrupted}$ is initialized to ∞.

Whenever an incomplete tuple $(\mathsf{label}, \mathsf{id}, \mathsf{pid}, \mathsf{role}, \mathsf{auth}, k, \mathsf{pss}, \mathsf{pssid})$ is added to $\mathsf{List_S}$ the missing entries are initialized as described above. As a shorthand notation we use $\mathsf{label.sid}$ for the entry sid of the tuple with the unique label in $\mathsf{List_S}$. Two distinct sessions label and $\mathsf{label'}$ are defined to be *partnered* in stage i if $\mathsf{label.sid}_i = \mathsf{label'.sid}_i \neq \bot$. For correctness two sessions having a non-tampered joint execution are required to be partnered in all stages upon acceptance.

Upgradeable Authentication. The rectified authentication level $\mathsf{rect\_auth}_i$ of some stage i in a session currently in stage stage with the intended authentication vector auth_i and the corruption indicator $\mathsf{corrupted}$ is defined as follows:

$$\mathsf{rect\_auth}_i := \begin{cases} \mathsf{mutual} & \text{if } \mathsf{stage} \geq \mathsf{auth}_{i,2} \text{ and } \mathsf{corrupted} \geq \mathsf{auth}_{i,2} \\ \mathsf{unilateral} & \text{if } \mathsf{stage} \geq \mathsf{auth}_{i,1} \text{ and } \mathsf{corrupted} \geq \mathsf{auth}_{i,1} \\ \mathsf{unauth} & \text{otherwise} \end{cases}$$

Adversary Model. We consider a probabilistic polynomial-time adversary $\mathcal{A}$ that controls the communication between all participants and can intercept, inject, and drop messages. We use a flag lost to capture actions by $\mathcal{A}$ where it trivially loses, e.g., revealing and testing the session key in partnered sessions. The flag lost is initialized to false. The adversary is given access to the following queries:

- NewSecret($U, \mathcal{V}$, pssid): Generates a pre-shared secret pss with identifier pssid. pss is shared between the user U and all users $V \in \mathcal{V} \subseteq \mathcal{U}$ with $\mathcal{V} \neq \emptyset$. U uses pss in the initiator role and all $V \in \mathcal{V}$ use pss in the responder role. If the value $\text{pss}_{U,\mathcal{V}}(\text{pssid})$ is already defined, return $\bot$. Otherwise, sample pss uniformly at random from the pre-shared secret space $\mathcal{P}$ and define $\text{pss}_{U,\mathcal{V}}(\text{pssid}) := \text{pss}$.

- NewSession($U, V, \mathcal{V}$, role, auth, pssid): Creates a new session with a unique new label label with U as the session owner in the role role, V as the intended communication partner, and aiming at authentication type auth. pssid indicates the pre-shared secret to be used in the session. If role = initiator, it must hold that $V \in \mathcal{V}$ and the session then uses $\text{pss}_{U,\mathcal{V}}(\text{pssid})$. If role = responder, it must hold that $U \in \mathcal{V}$ and the session then uses $\text{pss}_{V,\mathcal{V}}(\text{pssid})$. Add (label, U, V, role, auth, pssid) to Lists. If label is corrupted, set corrupted to 0. Return label.

- Send(label, m): Sends a message m to the session with label label. If no session with label label exists in Lists, return $\bot$. Otherwise, run the protocol on behalf of the session owner U on input of the message m and return the response as well as the updated state of execution label.st$_{\text{exec}}$. If label.role = initiator and m = init the protocol is initiated without any input message.

  If, during the protocol execution, label.st$_{\text{exec}}$ is changed to accepted$_i$ for some stage $i \in [\text{M}]$, the protocol execution is suspended and accepted$_i$ is returned to the adversary. In order to let the protocol execution resume and receive the next protocol message and execution state, the adversary may send a special message m = continue to the session.

  If, during the protocol execution, label.st$_{\text{exec}}$ is changed to accepted$_i$ for some $i \in [\text{M}]$ and there exists a session label$' \neq$ label partnered in stage i, i.e., label.sid$_i$ = label$'$.sid$_i$, in Lists with label$'$.tested$_i$ = true, then label.tested$_i$ is set to true as well. Moreover, if USE$_i$ = internal, label.key$_i$ is set to label$'$.key$_i$. If, during protocol execution, label.st$_{\text{exec}}$ is changed to accepted$_i$ for some $i \in [\text{M}]$ and the session label is corrupted, set label.st$_{\text{key},i}$ to revealed.

- Reveal(label, i): Reveals the session key label.key$_i$ of the session with label label in stage i. If no session with label label exists in Lists or label.stage $< i$, return $\bot$. Otherwise, set label.st$_{\text{key},i}$ to revealed and return label.key$_i$ to the adversary.

- Corrupt($U, \mathcal{V}$, pssid): Provides the pre-shared secret $\text{pss}_{U,\mathcal{V}}(\text{pssid})$ to the adversary. Add the global pre-shared secret identifier $(U, \mathcal{V}, \text{pssid})$ to the set of corrupted entities $\mathcal{C}$. For all sessions label with label.(role, id, pid, pssid) $\in \{(\text{initiator}, U, V, \text{pssid}), (\text{responder}, V, U, \text{pssid})\}$ and label.corrupted $\neq \infty$ for some $V \in \mathcal{V}$, set label.corrupted := label.stage. For stage-j forward secrecy, in any such session label, set st$_{\text{key},i}$ to revealed for all $i < j$ and all $i >$ label.stage. For the non-forward secure case, in any such session label set st$_{\text{key},i}$ to revealed for all $i \in [\text{M}]$.

- Test(label, i): Tests the session key of stage i of the session with label label. The Test oracle stores a bit b_{test}, which is fixed throughout the game. If no session with label label exists in Lists or if label.st$_{\text{exec}} \neq$ accepted$_i$ or if label.tested$_i$ = true, return $\bot$. If USE$_i$ = internal and there exists a session label$' \neq$ label partnered in stage i, i.e., label.sid$_i$ = label$'$.sid$_i$, in Lists with label$'$.st$_{\text{exec}} \neq$ accepted, set lost to true. If label.rect_auth$_i$ = unilateral and label.role = responder or if label.rect_auth$_i$ = unauth, but there exists no session label$' \neq$ label in List$_S$ with label.cid$_i$ = label$'$.cid$_i$, then the flag lost is set to true. Otherwise, set label.tested$_i$ to true.

If $b_{\text{test}} = 0$, a key $K \xleftarrow{\$} S$ is drawn uniformly at random from the session key space S. If $b_{\text{test}} = 1$, set K to the real session key label.key$_i$. If USE$_i$ = internal, label.key$_i$ is set to K.

If there exists a partnered session label$' \neq$ label in stage i, i.e., label.sid$_i$ = label$'$.sid$_i$, in List$_S$ with label.st$_{\text{exec}}$ = label$'$.st$_{\text{exec}}$ = accepted$_i$, then label.tested$_i$ is set to true, and if USE$_i$ = internal, label$'$.key$_i$ is set to label.key$_i$ as well. Return K.

Match Security. The notion of Match security ensures that session identifiers properly identify partnered sessions. The Match security game $G_{\text{MSKE},\mathcal{A}}^{\text{Match}}(\lambda)$ is defined as follows.

Definition 3 (Match security). *Let* MSKE *be a multi-stage key exchange protocol with properties* (M, AUTH, USE, FS, REPLAY) *and* $\mathcal{A}$ *a PPT adversary interacting with* MSKE *in the following game* $G_{\text{MSKE},\mathcal{A}}^{\text{Match}}(\lambda)$:

1. *The adversary* $\mathcal{A}$ *is given access to the queries* NewSecret, NewSession, Send, Reveal, Corrupt, Test.
2. *At some point* $\mathcal{A}$ *stops without any output.*

We say that $\mathcal{A}$ *wins the game, denoted by* $G_{\text{MSKE},\mathcal{A}}^{\text{Match}}(\lambda) = 1$, *if at least one of the following conditions holds:*

1. *There exist two distinct labels* label, label$'$ $\in$ List$_S$ *with* label.sid$_i$ = label$'$.sid$_i$ $\neq$ $\perp$ *for some stage* $i \in$ [M], *but* label.key$_i$ $\neq$ label$'$.key$_i$. *(Different session keys in some stage of partnered sessions.)*
2. *There exist two distinct labels* label, label$'$ $\in$ List$_S$ *with* label.sid$_i$ = label$'$.sid$_i$ $\neq$ $\perp$ *for some stage* $i \in$ [M], *but* label.role = label$'$.role *and* REPLAY$_i$ = nonreplayable *or* label.role = label$'$.role = initiator *and* REPLAY$_i$ = replayable. *(Non-opposite roles of partnered sessions in non-replayable stage.)*
3. *There exist two distinct labels* label, label$'$ $\in$ List$_S$ *with* label.sid$_i$ = label$'$.sid$_i$ $\neq$ $\perp$ *for some stage* $i \in$ [M], *but* label.auth$_i$ $\neq$ label$'$.auth$_i$. *(Different authentication types in some stage of partnered sessions.)*
4. *There exist two distinct labels* label, label$'$ $\in$ List$_S$ *with* label.sid$_i$ = label$'$.sid$_i$ $\neq$ $\perp$ *for some stage* $i \in$ [M], *but* label.cid$_i$ $\neq$ label$'$.cid$_i$ *or* label.cid$_i$ = label$'$.cid$_i$ = $\perp$. *(Different or unset contributive identifiers in some stage of partnered sessions.)*
5. *There exist two distinct labels* label, label$'$ $\in$ List$_S$ *with* label.sid$_i$ = label$'$.sid$_i$ $\neq$ $\perp$ *and* label.sid$_j$ = label$'$.sid$_j$ $\neq$ $\perp$ *for some stages* $i, j \in$ [M] *with* $j \leq i$, *with* label.role = initiator, *and* label$'$.role = responder *such that*
   - label.auth$_{j,1} \leq i$ *(unilateral authentication), but* label.pid $\neq$ label$'$.id, *or*
   - label.auth$_{j,2} \leq i$ *(mutual authentication), but* label.id $\neq$ label$'$.pid.

(Different authenticated partner or different key identifiers in mutual authentication)

6. *There exist two (not necessarily distinct) labels* label, label' $\in$ Lists *with* label.sid$_i$ = label'.sid$_j$ $\neq$ $\perp$ *for some stages* $i, j \in$ [M] *with* $i \neq j$. *(Different stages share the same session identifier.)*

7. *There exist three pairwise distinct labels* label, label', label'' $\in$ Lists *with* label.sid$_i$ = label'.sid$_i$ = label''.sid$_i$ $\neq$ $\perp$ *for some stage* $i \in$ [M] *with* REPLAY$_i$ = nonreplayable. *(More than two sessions share the same session identifier in a non-replayable stage.)*

We say MSKE *is* Match-*secure if for all PPT adversaries* $\mathcal{A}$ *the advantage*

$$\mathsf{Adv}^{\mathsf{Match}}_{\mathsf{MSKE},\mathcal{A}}(\lambda) := \Pr[\mathsf{G}^{\mathsf{Match}}_{\mathsf{MSKE},\mathcal{A}}(\lambda) = 1]$$

is a negligible function in the security parameter λ.

Multi-Stage Security. The notion of Multi-Stage security ensures that established session keys are indistinguishable from randomly sampled keys.

Definition 4 (Multi-Stage security). *Let* MSKE *be a multi-stage key exchange protocol with key space* $\mathcal{S}$ *and properties* (M, AUTH, USE, FS, REPLAY) *and* $\mathcal{A}$ *a PPT adversary interacting with* MSKE *in the following game* $\mathsf{G}^{\mathsf{Multi\text{-}Stage}}_{\mathsf{MSKE},\mathcal{A}}(\lambda)$:

1. *The challenger samples the bit* b_{test} $\xleftarrow{\$}$ $\{0, 1\}$ *and sets the flag* lost *to* false.
2. *The adversary* $\mathcal{A}$ *is given access the the queries* NewSecret, NewSession, Send, Reveal, Corrupt, Test. *Note that such queries may set* lost *to* true.
3. *At some point* $\mathcal{A}$ *stops and ouputs a guess* b. *The challenger sets the flag* lost *to* true *if there exist two (not necessarily distinct) labels* label, label' $\in$ Lists *and some stage* $i \in$ [M] *with* label.sid$_i$ = label'.sid$_i$, label.st$_{\mathsf{key},i}$ = revealed, *and* label'.tested$_i$ = true, *i.e., the adversary has tested and revealed the key of some stage in a single session or in two partnered sessions.*

We say that $\mathcal{A}$ *wins the game, denoted by* $\mathsf{G}^{\mathsf{Multi\text{-}Stage}}_{\mathsf{MSKE},\mathcal{A}}(\lambda) = 1$, *if* $b = b_{\mathsf{test}}$ *and* lost = false. *We say* MSKE *with properties* (M, AUTH, USE, FS, REPLAY) *is* Multi-Stage-*secure if* MSKE *is* Match-*secure and for all PPT adversaries* $\mathcal{A}$ *the advantage*

$$\mathsf{Adv}^{\mathsf{Multi\text{-}Stage}}_{\mathsf{MSKE},\mathcal{A}}(\lambda) := \Pr[\mathsf{G}^{\mathsf{Multi\text{-}Stage}}_{\mathsf{MSKE},\mathcal{A}}(\lambda) = 1] - \frac{1}{2}$$

is a negligible function in the security parameter λ.

3 Breaking the Security of Session Resumption Across Hostnames in TLS 1.3

In this section we show that session resumption across hostnames in TLS 1.3 is not a secure MSKE protocol if clients do not include the SNI value of the intended receiver in the ClientHello. As mentioned before, the TLS 1.3 specification [18] does not precisely state that resumption handshakes require an SNI value to be sent by the client. We therefore assume that in practice this may not always be seen as an absolute requirement for implementations and it may happen that clients do not specify an SNI value in their ClientHello.

We will exploit this lack of an SNI value to break the authentication of TLS 1.3 if two servers share the same certificate and symmetric ticket encryption key. Our attack targets a client C that wants to perform SRAH with some server S_A. The core idea of the attack is for the adversary to reroute any messages from C to a different server S_B that is able to execute the session resumption. This results in S_B implicitly authenticating itself by its ability to accept the session ticket while from the view of C it was S_A that implicitly authenticated itself.

3.1   Modeling TLS 1.3 Session Resumption as an MSKE Protocol

We begin by formally modeling the TLS 1.3 session resumption as an MSKE protocol. We consider both the PSK-only as well as the PSK-(EC)DHE handshake variants of TLS 1.3. We illustrate both variants in Fig. 1.

The TLS 1.3 session resumption protocol proceeds as follows. The client's first message ClientHello contains the protocol version, a random nonce, and a list of supported cryptographic algorithms. Moreover, it contains a pre_shared_key extension that indicates the identity of the PSK used in this handshake. In the PSK-(EC)DHE handshake it additionally contains the client's Diffie–Hellman share in the key_share extension. Additionally, the client may use the server_name extension to specify the SNI value of the intended receiver. In several derivation steps the client computes the early secret ES, the binder key bk, the key fk_0, the early traffic secret ets, and the early traffic key tk_{ets}. Using fk_0 the client computes the Fin_0 message, which constitutes a MAC over the ClientHello. The client may use tk_{ets} to encrypt early application data and send them to the server. However, note that this is not part of the handshake protocol itself.

Stage 2 only consists of deriving the early exporter master secret EEMS. In stage 3 the server responds with the ServerHello containing the protocol version, a random nonce, the selected cryptographic algorithms, and the pre_shared_key extension confirming the identity of the PSK. In the PSK-(EC)DHE handshake it additionally contains the server's Diffie–Hellmann share in a key_share extension. Other optional extensions are sent separately in an EncryptedExtensions message, although we omit that message for simplicity. In several derivation steps the derived early secret dES, the handshake secret HS, the client, respectively server, handshake traffic secret chts and shts, as well as the keys tk_{chts} and tk_{shts} are computed. Note that in the PSK-(EC)DHE handshake HS is derived from dES and the shared Diffie–Hellman key DHE.

In stage 4 the keys fk_S, fk_C, the derived handshake secret dHS, the master secret MS, the client, respectively server, application traffic secret cats and sats, as well as the client, respectively server, application traffic key tk_{cats} and tk_{sats} are derived. Using fk_S the server computes the message Fin_S, which constitutes a MAC over all previously exchanged messages. The server encrypts Fin_S under tk_{shts} and sends it to the client. The keys tk_{cats} and tk_{sats} are used to encrypt

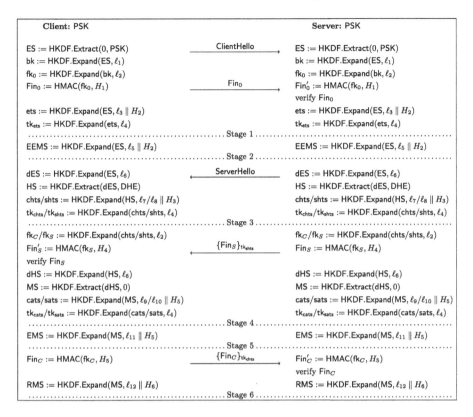

Fig. 1. The TLS 1.3 session resumption protocol. The client and server possess a pre-shared secret PSK. A dotted line indicates the key of the stage noted at that line being accepted. The values $\ell_1, \ldots, \ell_{11}$ are publicly known string labels. The values $H_1, \ldots, H_6$ are hash values computed from the transcript of the communication. We provide the exact listing of messages for each hash value in Table 1. In the PSK-only variant DHE is set to 0 and in the PSK-(EC)DHE variant DHE is the shared (elliptic curve) Diffie–Hellman key. $\{m\}_k$ denotes a message m being encrypted with key k.

any exchanged application data, although again note that this is not part of the handshake protocol itself.

Stage 5 only consists of deriving the exporter master secret EMS. In stage 6 using fk_C the client computes Fin_C, which again constitutes a MAC over all previously exchanged messages, encrypts it under $\mathsf{tk}_{\mathsf{chts}}$ and sends it to the server. As the last step of the protocol the resumption master secret RMS is derived from MS.

For completeness we provide an exact listing of the messages over which the MACs are computed in Table 1. In Fig. 1 for readability we separated the Fin_0 message from the ClientHello, although according to the standard it is contained in the ClientHello as the *PSK binder* (cf. [18, Sect. 4.2.11.2]). Moreover, note that both participants possess a pre-shared key PSK. The value PSK is derived from the RMS computed in the previous handshake and a random nonce, which is provided by the server via the NewSessionTicket message. The NewSessionTicket message is encrypted under tk_{sats} and additionally contains an opaque label ticket, which is used as the PSK identifier in the pre_shared_key extension.

Similar to previous security analyses of TLS 1.3 [8,9,12], we capture neither the NewSessionTicket message nor the derivation of PSK. In order to simplify the analysis the previous works treat tk_{sats} as an external key that can be used in an arbitrary symmetric protocol. To capture the transmission of the NewSessionTicket message, tk_{sats} would have to be treated as an internal key. Instead it is assumed that some out-of-band mechanism is used to establish a mapping between PSK identifiers and the PSK values. We follow the same approach and assume the same out-of-band mapping.

Table 1. List of the hash values and the transcript messages used to compute them in the TLS 1.3 session resumption handshake.

Hash value	Messages
H_1	ClientHello
H_2	ClientHello, Fin_0
H_3	ClientHello, Fin_0, ServerHello
H_4	ClientHello, Fin_0, ServerHello, EncryptedExtensions
H_5	ClientHello, Fin_0, ServerHello, EncryptedExtensions, Fin_S
H_6	ClientHello, Fin_0, ServerHello, EncryptedExtensions, Fin_S, Fin_C

Protocol Properties. The protocol properties of the TLS 1.3 PSK-only and PSK-(EC)DHE handshakes in the MSKE model are as follows:

- $M = 6$. Both handshake variants comprise 6 stages deriving the keys tk_{ets}, EEMS, tk_{chts}/tk_{shts}, tk_{cats}/tk_{sats}, EMS, and RMS.
- The authentication properties AUTH are different for each handshake variant. We explain the reasoning for the difference in detail in Remark 5.
  - for PSK-only AUTH = $\{((1,1),(2,2),(3,3),(4,4),(5,5),(6,6))\}$: all keys are immediately mutually authenticated.
  - for PSK-(EC)DHE AUTH = $\{((1,1),(2,2),(4,4),(4,4),(5,5),(6,6))\}$: the keys tk_{chts} and tk_{shts} are at first unauthenticated and reach mutual authentication in stage 4, while all other keys are immediately mutually authenticated.
- The forward security is different for the two handshake variants:
  - for PSK-only FS = ∞. The PSK-only variant does not provide forward security.
  - for PSK-(EC)DHE FS = 3. The PSK-(EC)DHE variant provides forward security for all stages $i \geq 3$.

- USE = (external, external, internal, external, external, external). The handshake traffic keys $\mathsf{tk_{chts}}$ and $\mathsf{tk_{shts}}$ are used internally to encrypt some handshake messages. All other keys are used externally.
- REPLAY = (replayable, replayable, nonreplayable, nonreplayable, nonreplayable, nonreplayable). The stages 1 and 2 with the keys $\mathsf{tk_{ets}}$ and EEMS are replayable. All other stages are non-replayable.

Remark 5. In the PSK-EC(DHE) handshake the keys $\mathsf{tk_{chts}}$ and $\mathsf{tk_{shts}}$ of stage 3 only reach mutual authentication in stage 4 due to the following attack. An adversary can intercept the ServerHello, replace the server's Diffie–Hellman share with its own share, and then send the modified ServerHello to the client. After corrupting the pre-shared secret the adversary can then compute $\mathsf{tk_{chts}}$ and $\mathsf{tk_{shts}}$ from the pre-shared secret, the client's Diffie–Hellman share and its own Diffie–Hellman share. Note that the adversary cannot execute a similar attack by replacing the client's Diffie–Hellman share instead of the server's share since in contrast to the Fin_S message, which is sent separately from the ServerHello, the Fin_0 message is included in the ClientHello.

To prevent this attack we at first treat $\mathsf{tk_{chts}}$ and $\mathsf{tk_{shts}}$ as unauthenticated and as mutually authenticated once the server authenticated its Diffie–Hellman share in stage 4. An alternative approach is to prohibit the adversary from corrupting the pre-shared secret during stage 3 by treating stage 3 as non-forward secure. However, this would be a counterintuitive solution as both parties contributed ephemeral key material to the key of stage 3. Thus, the straightforward choice is to treat $\mathsf{tk_{chts}}$ and $\mathsf{tk_{shts}}$ as unauthenticated in stage 3.

Session and Contributive Identifiers. We define the session identifiers of each stage to comprise all handshake messages sent up to that stage. In order to have different session identifiers for each stage, we add a label string if in some stage no handshake message is sent. Formally, the session identifiers are defined as follows:

$$\mathsf{sid}_1 = (\mathsf{ClientHello}, \mathsf{Fin}_0) \quad \mathsf{sid}_2 = (\mathsf{sid}_1, \text{"EEMS"}) \quad \mathsf{sid}_3 = (\mathsf{sid}_2, \mathsf{ServerHello})$$
$$\mathsf{sid}_4 = (\mathsf{sid}_3, \mathsf{Fin}_S) \quad \mathsf{sid}_5 = (\mathsf{sid}_4, \text{"EMS"}) \quad \mathsf{sid}_6 = (\mathsf{sid}_5, \mathsf{Fin}_C)$$

For all stages $i \in \{1, 2, 4, 5, 6\}$ we set $\mathsf{cid}_i = \mathsf{sid}_i$ when sid_i is set. For stage 3 on sending (resp. receiving), the ClientHello, the client (resp. server) sets $\mathsf{cid}_3 = (\mathsf{ClientHello}, \mathsf{Fin}_0)$. Similarly, on sending (resp. receiving) the ServerHello, the server (resp. client) extends cid_3 to $(\mathsf{ClientHello}, \mathsf{Fin}_0, \text{"EEMS"}, \mathsf{ServerHello})$.

3.2 The Attack

We now proceed to describe the attack breaking the security of SRAH in TLS 1.3 in the MSKE model. To this end, we give a sequence of query calls that allows us to win the Match security game $\mathsf{G}^{\mathsf{Match}}_{\mathsf{TLS\text{-}1.3\text{-}SRAH}, \mathcal{A}}$ with a probability of 1, proving that SRAH in TLS 1.3 is not a Match-secure protocol. The attack is applicable to both the PSK-only handshake as well as the PSK-(EC)DHE handshake.

Theorem 6. *If the client does not include the SNI value of the intended communication partner in the* ClientHello, *the TLS 1.3 PSK-only and the TLS 1.3 PSK-(EC)DHE handshakes with SRAH are not* Match-*secure and we can construct an adversary* $\mathcal{A}$ *with the advantage*

$$\mathsf{Adv}^{\mathsf{Match}}_{\mathsf{TLS\text{-}1.3\text{-}SRAH},\mathcal{A}}(\lambda) = 1.$$

Proof. We construct $\mathcal{A}$ as follows. Let $\mathsf{pssid} \in \{0,1\}^*$ be a pre-shared key identifier, $C, S, S' \in \mathcal{U}$ be participant identities, and $\mathsf{auth} \in \{((1,1),(2,2),(3,3),(4,4),(5,5),(6,6)),((1,1),(2,2),(4,4),(4,4),(5,5),(6,6))\}$ depending on the handshake variant. We proceed as follows:

1. $\mathsf{NewSecret}(C, \{S, S'\}, \mathsf{pssid})$. We begin by generating a new pre-shared secret with the identifier pssid shared between C, S, and S'.
2. $\mathsf{NewSession}(C, S, \{S, S'\}, \mathsf{initiator}, \mathsf{auth}, \mathsf{pssid})$. We create a new session with the label $\mathsf{label} = (C, S, 1)$ for the client C with the server S as the intended communication partner, where the session is resumed based on the pre-shared secret we created in step 1.
3. $\mathsf{NewSession}(S', C, \{S, S'\}, \mathsf{responder}, \mathsf{auth}, \mathsf{pssid})$. We then create a new session with the label $\mathsf{label}' = (S', C, 1)$ for the server S' with the client C as the intended communication partner, where the session is resumed based on the pre-shared secret we created in step 1.
4. $\mathsf{Send}((C, S, 1), \mathsf{init})$. We send the special message init to the client C, which initiates the protocol. After C accepts the key of stage 1, it sets $\mathsf{sid}_1 = (\mathsf{ClientHello}, \mathsf{Fin}_0)$ and suspends the execution we send the special message continue to C to obtain the messages ClientHello and Fin_0.
5. $\mathsf{Send}((S', C, 1), (\mathsf{ClientHello}, \mathsf{Fin}_0))$. We send the messages ClientHello and Fin_0 to the server S'. Since we did not modify either of the messages, the Fin_0 message will successfully be verified. Therefore, S' accepts the key of stage 1, sets $\mathsf{sid}_1 = (\mathsf{ClientHello}, \mathsf{Fin}_0)$ and suspends the protocol execution.

The above sequence of query calls results in the game $\mathsf{G}^{\mathsf{Match}}_{\mathsf{TLS\text{-}1.3\text{-}SRAH},\mathcal{A}}$ being won with probability 1. The session label is partnered with the session label' and we have $\mathsf{label}.\mathsf{auth}_{1,1} = 1$ but $\mathsf{label}.\mathsf{pid} \neq \mathsf{label}'.\mathsf{id}$. Observe that this fulfills condition 5 in $\mathsf{G}^{\mathsf{Match}}_{\mathsf{TLS\text{-}1.3\text{-}SRAH},\mathcal{A}}$ and we therefore have

$$\mathsf{Adv}^{\mathsf{Match}}_{\mathsf{TLS\text{-}1.3\text{-}SRAH},\mathcal{A}}(\lambda) = 1.$$

4   Secure SRAH Protocols

In this section we formally define secure SRAH protocols, which will resemble an abstraction of the TLS 1.3 session resumption. While in TLS 1.3 multiple keys are derived for many different purposes (e.g., partial encryption of the handshake, or multiple keys for application-based encryption), we start with a reduced approach to SRAH, which generates two keys only: one "temporary" key to send (optional) data within the first protocol message[4] and one potentially stronger "main" key as result of the handshake. Reducing the complexity of the protocol in comparison to TLS 1.3 will later allow us to achieve a simpler security proof compared to the security proofs of the full TLS 1.3 protocol by Dowling et al. [9].

Definition 7. A session resumption across hostnames protocol with key space S is a tuple of five PPT algorithms $\mathsf{SRAH} = (\mathsf{KeyGen}, \mathsf{TicketGen}, \mathsf{SessionRes}_{\mathsf{init}}^{\mathsf{client}}, \mathsf{SessionRes}_{\mathsf{refresh}}^{\mathsf{server}}, \mathsf{SessionRes}_{\mathsf{refresh}}^{\mathsf{client}})$.

$\mathsf{KeyGen}(1^{\lambda}) \to k$. On input of a security parameter λ the algorithm outputs a long–term key k.

$\mathsf{TicketGen}(s) \to t$. On input of a secret s the algorithm outputs a session ticket t.

$\mathsf{SessionRes}_{\mathsf{init}}^{\mathsf{client}}(s, t, j) \to (s_{\mathsf{tmp}}, m_C)$. On input of a secret $s \in S$, a ticket $t \in \{0,1\}^*$ and a server identifier j the algorithm outputs a temporary secret s_{tmp} and a message m_C.

$\mathsf{SessionRes}_{\mathsf{refresh}}^{\mathsf{server}}(k, m_C) \to (s_{\mathsf{tmp}}, s_{\mathsf{main}}, m_S)$. On input of a long-term key k and a message m_C the algorithm outputs a temporary secret s_{tmp}, a secret s_{main}, and a message m_S.

$\mathsf{SessionRes}_{\mathsf{refresh}}^{\mathsf{client}}(m_S) \to s_{\mathsf{main}}$. On input of a message m_S the algorithm outputs a secret s_{main}.

We say a session resumption across hostnames protocol is correct if for all $k \xleftarrow{\$} \mathsf{KeyGen}(1^{\lambda})$, all $s \xleftarrow{\$} S$, and all $t \xleftarrow{\$} \mathsf{TicketGen}(k, s)$ it holds that $s_{\mathsf{tmp}} = s'_{\mathsf{tmp}}$ and $s_{\mathsf{main}} = s'_{\mathsf{main}}$, where $(s_{\mathsf{tmp}}, m_C) \xleftarrow{\$} \mathsf{SessionRes}_{\mathsf{init}}^{\mathsf{client}}(s, t, j)$, $(s'_{\mathsf{tmp}}, s'_{\mathsf{main}}, m_S) \xleftarrow{\$} \mathsf{SessionRes}_{\mathsf{refresh}}^{\mathsf{server}}(k, m_C)$, and $s_{\mathsf{main}} \xleftarrow{\$} \mathsf{SessionRes}_{\mathsf{refresh}}^{\mathsf{client}}(m_S)$.

We use the modified version of the MSKE security model described in Sect. 2.2 to define the security of SRAH protocols.

Definition 8. We say a SRAH protocol is secure if it is Multi-Stage-secure.

Using an SRAH protocol. The flow of an SRAH protocol is shown in Fig. 2.

---

[4] This captures the optional zero round-trip time feature of TLS 1.3 resumption handshakes, where a client may send encrypted early data with its first flight of messages. Note that due to the lack of interaction, this often comes at the cost of forward security for this message.

Fig. 2. Execution of an SRAH protocol between a client C_i and a server S_j where $t = \mathsf{TicketGen}(k, s)$, computed by a server $S_\ell \neq S_j$.

4.1   Constructing Secure SRAH Protocols

In this section we show a construction of a secure SRAH protocol. Our construction essentially resembles an abstraction of the TLS 1.3 session resumption protocol with the addition of a mandatory server identifier in the client's first message, which identifies the intended recipient of the message. By adding the server identifier we prevent an adversary from applying the attack described in Sect. 3.2.

Recall that the main idea of the attack in Sect. 3.2 is to reroute the messages sent by the client to a different server than the intended receiver. This is unnoticed by both the client and the server receiving the message since the client's messages do not include any information on the intended recipient. However, if the message m_C contains the identifier of the intended receiver and an adversary reroutes it to a different server, that server recognizes that it is not the intended recipient of the message and aborts the handshake. Moreover, we use a MAC to prevent the adversary from modifying the server identifier.

With the `server_name` extension TLS 1.3 already provides a mechanism to indicate the intended receiver of a ClientHello. We recommend to make the `server_name` extension mandatory in session resumption handshakes to prevent the attack as described intuitively above. In the following we formally prove that this change prevents the attack by showing that our construction, which abstracts TLS 1.3 session resumption with a mandatory `server_name` extension, is a secure MSKE protocol.

Definition 9. *Let $\Pi = (\Pi.\mathsf{KeyGen}, \Pi.\mathsf{Enc}, \Pi.\mathsf{Dec})$ be a symmetric encryption scheme, HMAC be the HMAC construction, HKDF the HKDF scheme, $\mathbb{G}$ a cyclic group of prime order p, and g a generator of $\mathbb{G}$. We construct a SRAH protocol $\mathsf{SRAH} = (\mathsf{KeyGen}, \mathsf{TicketGen}, \mathsf{SessionRes}_{\mathsf{init}}^{\mathsf{client}}, \mathsf{SessionRes}_{\mathsf{refresh}}^{\mathsf{server}}, \mathsf{SessionRes}_{\mathsf{refresh}}^{\mathsf{client}})$ as follows.*

$\mathsf{KeyGen}(1^\lambda)$. *Returns $k \xleftarrow{\$} \Pi.\mathsf{KeyGen}(1^\lambda)$.*
$\mathsf{TicketGen}(k, s)$. *Returns $t \xleftarrow{\$} \Pi.\mathsf{Enc}(k, s)$.*
$\mathsf{SessionRes}_{\mathsf{init}}^{\mathsf{client}}(s, t, \mathsf{ID})$. *Samples $x \xleftarrow{\$} \mathbb{Z}_p^*, r_C \xleftarrow{\$} \{0,1\}^\lambda$, computes*

$$s_{\mathsf{tmp}} := \mathsf{HKDF.Extract}(\text{``tmp''}, s),$$
$$s_{\mathsf{MAC}} := \mathsf{HKDF.Extract}(\text{``MAC''}, s),$$
$$\tau_C := \mathsf{HMAC}(s_{\mathsf{MAC}}, g^x \parallel r_C \parallel j \parallel t),$$

and returns (s_{tmp}, m_C), *where* $m_C := (g^x, r_C, j, \tau_C, t)$.

$\mathsf{SessionRes}^{\mathsf{server}}_{\mathsf{refresh}}(k, m_C)$. *Parses* m_C *as* $(g^x, r_C, j', \tau_C, t)$. *If* j' *is not the identifier of the executing server, returns* $\bot$. *Otherwise computes*

$$s = \Pi.\mathsf{Dec}(k, t),$$
$$s_{\mathsf{MAC}} = \mathsf{HKDF.Extract}(\text{``}MAC\text{''}, s).$$

If $\mathsf{HMAC}(s_{\mathsf{MAC}}, g^x \parallel r_C \parallel j' \parallel t) \neq \tau_C$, *returns* $\bot$. *Otherwise samples* $y \xleftarrow{\$} \mathbb{Z}_p^*, r_S \xleftarrow{\$} \{0,1\}^\lambda$, *computes*

$$s_{\mathsf{tmp}} := \mathsf{HKDF.Extract}(\text{``}tmp\text{''}, s),$$
$$s_{\mathsf{main}} := \mathsf{HKDF.Extract}(s, g^{xy}),$$
$$\tau_S := \mathsf{HMAC}(s_{\mathsf{MAC}}, m_C \parallel g^y \parallel r_S)$$

and returns $(s_{\mathsf{tmp}}, s_{\mathsf{main}}, m_S)$, *where* $m_S := (g^y, r_S, \tau_S)$.

$\mathsf{SessionRes}^{\mathsf{client}}_{\mathsf{refresh}}(m_S)$. *Parses* m_S *as* (g^y, r_S, τ_S). *If* $\mathsf{HMAC}(s_{\mathsf{MAC}}, m_C \parallel g^y \parallel r_S) \neq \tau_S$, *returns* $\bot$. *Otherwise computes*

$$s_{\mathsf{main}} := \mathsf{HKDF.Extract}(s, g^{xy})$$

and returns s_{main}.

We set the following protocol-specific properties for the MSKE model:

- $\mathsf{M} = 2$: *The number of stages is equal to two, where* s_{tmp} *is the key of stage 1, and* s_{main} *the key of stage 2.*
- $\mathsf{AUTH} = \{((1,1),(2,2))\}$: *All keys are mutually authenticated.*
- $\mathsf{USE} = (\mathsf{external}, \mathsf{external})$: *Both keys are used only externally.*
- $\mathsf{FS} = 2$: *The main key is forward secure, while the temporary key is not forward secure.*
- $\mathsf{REPLAY} = (\mathsf{replayable}, \mathsf{nonreplayable})$: *stage 1 is replayable while stage 2 is non-replayable.*

Moreover, we define the session identifiers of both stages to comprise all messages sent up to that stage. Formally, the session identifiers are defined as $\mathsf{sid}_1 = (m_C)$ *and* $\mathsf{sid}_2 = (m_C, m_S)$. *For stage 1 we set the contributive identifier* $\mathsf{cid}_1 = \mathsf{sid}_1$ *when* sid_i *is set. On sending (resp. receiving) the message* m_C, *the client (resp. server) sets* $\mathsf{cid}_2 = (m_C)$. *Similarly, on sending (resp. receiving) the message* m_S, *the server (resp. client) sets* $\mathsf{cid}_2 = (m_C, m_S)$.

Theorem 10. *The above construction* SRAH *is* Match-secure *with properties* $(\mathsf{M}, \mathsf{AUTH}, \mathsf{USE}, \mathsf{FS}, \mathsf{REPLAY})$ *given above. For each PPT adversary* $\mathcal{A}$, *there exists an algorithm* $\mathcal{B}$ *such that*

$$\mathsf{Adv}^{\mathsf{Match}}_{\mathsf{SRAH}, \mathcal{A}}(\lambda) \leq \mathsf{Adv}^{\mathsf{collision}}_{\mathsf{HMAC}, \mathcal{B}}(\lambda) + \frac{n_p^2}{|\mathcal{P}|} + n_s^2 \cdot \frac{1}{p} + 2^{-\lambda}.$$

Proof. (Sketch) Due to space restrictions we only give a sketch and provide a detailed proof in the full version [13]. Recall the seven conditions for Match-security from Definition 3. The conditions 3, 4, and 6 trivially hold by definition of the authentication vector, the contributive identifiers, and session identifiers. Since the pre-shared secret and the Diffie–Hellman shares are contained in all session identifiers and they uniquely determine all derived keys, two sessions with the same session identifier hold the same key and condition 1 holds. Condition 2 holds since in a replayable stage by condition 7 there are at most two sessions holding the same session identifier and sessions do not accept messages intended for the opposite role. Condition 7 holds since the probability of two sessions drawing the same Diffie–Hellman share and the same random nonce is negligible.

Since servers do not accept messages that are intended for a different server, clients are always partnered with their intended communication partner. To show that servers are always partnered with their intended communication partner, we consider HMAC as an unkeyed hash function, which implies that two sessions agreeing on τ_C also agree on the value of pss. Since moreover pre-shared secrets collide with negligible probability, pss must originate from the same call to NewSecret, which to a server identifies its communication partner as its intended partner, and hence condition 5 holds.

Theorem 11. *The above construction* SRAH *is* Multi-Stage-*secure with the properties* (M, AUTH, USE, FS, REPLAY) *given above. For each efficient adversary* $\mathcal{A}$, *there exist efficient algorithms* $\mathcal{B}_1, \ldots, \mathcal{B}_8$ *such that*

$$\mathsf{Adv}_{\mathcal{A},\mathsf{SRAH}}^{\mathsf{Multi\text{-}Stage}}(\lambda) \leq 2n_s \cdot \left(n_p \cdot \left(\mathsf{Adv}_{\Pi,\mathcal{B}_1}^{\mathsf{CPA}} + \mathsf{Adv}_{\mathsf{HKDF.Extract},\mathcal{B}_2}^{\mathsf{dual\text{-}PRF\text{-}sec}}(\lambda) \right. \right.$$

$$\left. + \mathsf{Adv}_{\mathsf{HMAC},\mathcal{B}_3}^{\mathsf{sEUF\text{-}CMA}}(\lambda) \right) + n_p \cdot n_s \cdot \left(\mathsf{Adv}_{\Pi,\mathcal{B}_4}^{\mathsf{CPA}}(\lambda) + \mathsf{Adv}_{\mathsf{HKDF.Extract},\mathcal{B}_5}^{\mathsf{dual\text{-}PRF\text{-}sec}}(\lambda) \right.$$

$$\left. \left. + \mathsf{Adv}_{\mathsf{HMAC},\mathcal{B}_6}^{\mathsf{sEUF\text{-}CMA}}(\lambda) + \mathsf{Adv}_{\mathsf{HKDF.Extract},\mathcal{B}_7}^{\mathsf{dual\text{-}PRF\text{-}sec}}(\lambda) \right) + n_s \cdot \mathsf{Adv}_{\mathsf{HKDF.Extract},\mathcal{B}_8}^{\mathsf{dual\text{-}snPRF\text{-}ODH}}(\lambda) \right)$$

where n_s *is the maximum number of sessions and* n_p *is the maximum number of pre-shared secrets.*

Proof. (Sketch) Due to space restrictions we give a sketch and provide a full proof in the full version [13]. We use a sequence of hybrid security games to prove Theorem 11. Starting from the original security game $\mathsf{G}_{\mathsf{SRAH},\mathcal{A}}^{\mathsf{Multi\text{-}Stage}}$ we first restrict the adversary to a single Test query. As shown by Dowling *et al.*, this reduces the adversary's advantage by a factor of at most $\mathsf{M} \cdot n_s$ where n_s is the number of sessions [9, Lemma A.1]. Next we split our analysis into the following cases:

1. the session label tested by $\mathcal{A}$ has no contributive partner
2. $\mathcal{A}$ tests a session label in stage 1 and label has a contributive partner
3. $\mathcal{A}$ tests a session label in stage 2 and label has a contributive partner

The main ideas for the proofs in the different cases are as follows. In the first case we reduce the adversary's to 0 by aborting the game when the tested session accepts without a contributive partner hence preventing $\mathcal{A}$ from issuing a Test query. This allows us to bound the adversary's advantage by bounding the probability that the game is aborted. We then show that the probability of aborting the game is negligible by proving that we can break the sEUF-CMA security of HMAC if the tested session accepts without a contributive partner.

In the second case we primarily rely on the dual-PRF-sec security of the HKDF scheme to replace the key s_{tmp} with a truly random value, which results in the advantage of $\mathcal{A}$ being reduced to 0. Additionally, we use the sEUF-CMA security of HMAC to prove that the message m_C can only be accepted by the intended parter of the tested session.

In the third case we rely on the dual-snPRF-ODH security of HKDF to replace the session key s_{main} with a truly random value, which again reduces the adversary's advantage to 0. It is necessary to use the dual-snPRF-ODH since an adversary may be able to corrupt a server after it accepted in stage 2 and then replace the Diffie–Hellman share g^y in the message m_S with some $g^{y'}$. In order to simulate all queries by the adversary in that case we need to use the oracle provided by the dual-snPRF-ODH assumption to compute $g^{xy'}$.

References

1. Arfaoui, G., Bultel, X., Fouque, P.-A., Nedelcu, A., Onete, C.: The privacy of the TLS 1.3 protocol. PoPETs **2019**(4), 190–210 (2019)
2. Aviram, N., Gellert, K., Jager, T.: Session resumption protocols and efficient forward security for TLS 1.3 0-RTT. In: Ishai, Y., Rijmen, V. (eds.) EUROCRYPT 2019, Part II. LNCS, vol. 11477, pp. 117–150. Springer, Cham (2019). https://doi.org/10.1007/978-3-030-17656-3_5
3. Aviram, N., Gellert, K., Jager, T.: Session resumption protocols and efficient forward security for TLS 1.3 0-RTT. J. Cryptol. **34**(3), 1–57 (2021)
4. Bellare, M., Canetti, R., Krawczyk, H.: Keying hash functions for message authentication. In: Koblitz, N. (ed.) CRYPTO 1996. LNCS, vol. 1109, pp. 1–15. Springer, Heidelberg (1996). https://doi.org/10.1007/3-540-68697-5_1
5. Brendel, J., Fischlin, M., Günther, F., Janson, C.: PRF-ODH: relations, instantiations, and impossibility results. In: Katz, J., Shacham, H. (eds.) CRYPTO 2017. LNCS, vol. 10403, pp. 651–681. Springer, Cham (2017). https://doi.org/10.1007/978-3-319-63697-9_22
6. Diemert, D., Jager, T.: On the tight security of TLS 1.3: theoretically sound cryptographic parameters for real-world deployments. J. Cryptol. **34**(3), 1–57 (2021)
7. Dowling, B., Fischlin, M., Günther, F., Stebila, D.: A cryptographic analysis of the TLS 1.3 handshake protocol candidates. In: Ray, I., Li, N., Kruegel, C. (eds.) ACM CCS 2015, pp. 1197–1210. ACM Press (2015)
8. Dowling, B., Fischlin, M., Günther, F., Stebila, D.: A cryptographic analysis of the TLS 1.3 draft-10 full and pre-shared key handshake protocol. Cryptology ePrint Archive, Report 2016/081 (2016). http://eprint.iacr.org/2016/081
9. Dowling, B., Fischlin, M., Günther, F., Stebila, D.: A cryptographic analysis of the tls 1.3 handshake protocol. Cryptology ePrint Archive, Report 2020/1044 (2020). https://eprint.iacr.org/2020/1044
10. Drucker, N., Gueron, S.: Selfie: reflections on TLS 1.3 with PSK. J. Cryptol. **34**(3), 1–18 (2021). https://doi.org/10.1007/s00145-021-09387-y

11. Fischlin, M., Günther, F.: Replay attacks on zero round-trip time: the case of the TLS 1.3 handshake candidates. In: 2017 IEEE European Symposium on Security and Privacy, EuroS&P 2017, Paris, France, April 26–28, 2017, pp. 60–75. IEEE (2017)
12. Fischlin, M., Günther, F.: Replay attacks on zero round-trip time: the case of the TLS 1.3 handshake candidates. In: 2017 IEEE European Symposium on Security and Privacy (EuroS&P), pp. 60–75. IEEE (2017)
13. Gellert, K., Handirk, T.: A Formal Security Analysis of Session Resumption Across Hostnames. Cryptology ePrint Archive, Report 2021/987 (2021). https://eprint.iacr.org/2021/987
14. Jager, T., Kohlar, F., Schäge, S., Schwenk, J.: On the security of TLS-DHE in the standard model. In: Safavi-Naini, R., Canetti, R. (eds.) CRYPTO 2012. LNCS, vol. 7417, pp. 273–293. Springer, Heidelberg (2012). https://doi.org/10.1007/978-3-642-32009-5_17
15. Krawczyk, H., Eronen, P.: HMAC-based Extract-and-Expand Key Derivation Function (HKDF). RFC 5869, IETF (2010)
16. Krawczyk, H.: Cryptographic extraction and key derivation: the HKDF scheme. In: Rabin, T. (ed.) CRYPTO 2010. LNCS, vol. 6223, pp. 631–648. Springer, Heidelberg (2010). https://doi.org/10.1007/978-3-642-14623-7_34
17. Krawczyk, H., Bellare, M., Canetti, R.: HMAC: keyed-hashing for message authentication. IETF Internet Request for Comments 2104 (1997)
18. Rescorla, E.: The Transport Layer Security (TLS) Protocol Version 1.3. RFC 8446, IETF (2018)
19. Sy, E., Moennich, M., Mueller, T., Federrath, H., Fischer, M.: Enhanced performance for the encrypted web through TLS resumption across hostnames. In: Proceedings of the 15th International Conference on Availability, Reliability and Security, ARES 2020, New York, NY, USA. Association for Computing Machinery (2020)

Attacks

Caught in the Web: DoS Vulnerabilities in Parsers for Structured Data

Shawn Rasheed[1]([✉])(iD), Jens Dietrich[2](iD), and Amjed Tahir[1](iD)

[1] Massey University, Palmerston North, New Zealand
{s.rasheed,a.tahir}@massey.ac.nz
[2] Victoria University of Wellington, Wellington, New Zealand
jens.dietrich@vuw.ac.nz

Abstract. We study a class of denial-of-service (DoS) vulnerabilities that occur in parsing structured data. These vulnerabilities enable low bandwidth DoS attacks with input that causes algorithms to execute in disproportionately large time and/or space. We generalise the characteristics of these vulnerabilities, and frame them in terms of three aspects, TTT: (1) the TOPOLOGY of composite data structures formed by the internal representation of parsed data, (2) the presence of recursive functions for the TRAVERSAL of the data structures and (3) the presence of a TRIGGER that enables an attacker to activate the traversal.

An analysis based on this abstraction was implemented for one target platform (Java), and in our study, we found that the impact of the results obtained with this method goes beyond Java. The inputs from our investigation revealed several similar vulnerabilities in programs written in other languages such as Rust and PHP. As a result we have reported 11 issues (of which seven have been accepted as issues), and obtained four CVEs for some of those issues in PDF, SVG and YAML libraries across different languages.

Keywords: DoS · Security · Vulnerabilities · Analysis

1 Introduction

Denial-of-service (DoS) attacks based on algorithmic complexity have received increasing attention recently [26,29].[1] Unlike classical DoS attacks based on flooding an application with network requests, or exploiting bugs that crash applications, algorithmic complexity-based DoS attacks target the exhaustion of computational resources such as CPU or memory, with small inputs that cause worst-case performance behaviour in a program [7]. Some of the more well-known attacks based on this class of vulnerabilities are regular expression DoS (*ReDoS*) [29] that target regular expression engines, and *HashDos* [7] that target hash functions.

---

[1] https://blog.cloudflare.com/cloudflare-outage/ [Accessed 08-October-2020].

The work of the second author was supported by Oracle Labs, Australia.

© Springer Nature Switzerland AG 2021
E. Bertino et al. (Eds.): ESORICS 2021, LNCS 12972, pp. 67–85, 2021.
https://doi.org/10.1007/978-3-030-88418-5_4

A complexity-related DoS vulnerability can be due to programs recursively traversing composite data structures. Tree and graph-like data structures that are composed of parts are common in programs, and when such structures are defined recursively, it is practical to define recursive operations over them. Such an operation can potentially run in exponential time or/and space if redundant traversals are not (or cannot be) controlled. These performance-related vulnerabilities can be exploited to carry out DoS attacks on systems. Serialisation,[2] which externalises a program's internal data structures to disk or for transmission over a network, and external format parsers that utilise these data structures present opportunities for DoS attacks based on these vulnerabilities [9].

Static and dynamic analysis techniques have been used for detecting performance-related bugs in programs. However, most existing approaches for detecting them are domain-specific - for instance, detection techniques for regular expression engines [33]. Fuzzing has been used to detect performance defects in programs. However, fuzzers are inefficient by nature with normal turnaround times in hours or more [16]. Constraint-based techniques such as symbolic execution are limited when it comes to producing complex inputs and there is little work on using them to detect performance bugs, especially for complex inputs [20,23].

This work presents a characterisation of a class of vulnerabilities along with a novel approach to detect them. Our approach is based on modelling the vulnerabilities, implementing the analysis for the Java language and constructing payloads to verify the analysis reports. Finally, the constructed payloads are used to check if other libraries are vulnerable as well. We characterise some of the program structures that facilitate such an attack. This is broken down into three parts (we refer to these parts as the three T's):

1. **Topology:** a data structure that has a topology which allows the redundant execution of recursive code/methods.
2. **Traversal:** the presence of recursive methods that operate on the elements in the data structures identified in step one.
3. **Trigger:** an execution path, in a program, from an entry point method for the program, typically a method that loads and evaluates data, to a recursive method identified in step two.

We implemented this analysis for Java and then evaluated it on a set of 16 Java parser libraries for different data formats. The scope and impact of this study goes beyond the vulnerabilities found in the Java libraries as these libraries are used in numerous applications. We validated the vulnerabilities by constructing malicious inputs, and it turns out that some of these reveal vulnerabilities in libraries and applications written in other languages such as Rust and PostScript.

In our study, we found a total of *11* vulnerabilities: Four new vulnerabilities in Java libraries using the analysis, (i.e. Apache PDFBox, PDFxStream, Apache

---

[2] Java serialisation, https://docs.oracle.com/javase/tutorial/jndi/objects/serial.html [Accessed 08-October-2020].

Batik and SnakeYAML), and seven vulnerabilities in non-Java libraries found during the evaluation. All 11 issues were reported to the vendors (7 were accepted as security bugs) and four CVEs were obtained as a result. We have made the implementation and results publicly available for replication.[3]

2 Motivation

The vulnerabilities that we study are closely related to the well-known *billion laughs* attack on XML parsers [6] where the payload consists of an XML document with nested XML entities where each entity's definition contains references to the preceding definition. Parsing the document results in an output, which has a length exponential in the depth of the nesting, that causes the service to degrade or fail from memory exhaustion.

The basic idea of billion laughs can be ported to an attack on Java programs as shown by Coekaert's SerialDoS vulnerability [5]. In SerialDoS, shown in Listing 1.1, the equivalent of the nested entity references in an XML element is a serialised collection of nested sets.

Listing 1.1. SerialDoS payload construction

```
1   import java.util.*;
2   ...
3   Set root = new HashSet();
4   Set s1 = root;
5   Set s2 = new HashSet();
6   for (int i = 0; i < depthN; i++) {
7       Set child1 = new HashSet();
8       Set child2 = new HashSet();
9       child1.add("foo");
10      s1.add(child1);
11      s1.add(child2);
12      s2.add(child1);
13      s2.add(child2);
14      s1 = child1;
15      s2 = child2;
16  }
17
18  root.hashCode();
```

The problem occurs if `root.hashCode()` is invoked. The `hashCode` of `HashSet` is recursive, i.e., it is computed using the hash values of the elements of the respective sets. This leads to a computation that is exponential in `depthN`.

The first enabling property for this attack is the shape of the data structure, forming a network of cross-referencing parent-child relationships, where each child node is referenced by more than one (in this case: two) parent objects. The resulting object graph for the listing is shown in Fig. 1. The second ingredient is the recursive method that operates on this structure, `hashCode()` in this case.

Finally, there must be a way to parse the format to an internal representation with the same topology and trigger the traversal over it. The fact that the method can be reached from the entry point of a program can be statically determined

---

[3] https://bitbucket.org/unshorn/ciwstudy/.

by examining direct paths from the entry point method to the target method in the call graph.

In the case of SerialDoS, the trigger is the deserialisation API. Serialisation is a common attack surface for Java applications as demonstrated by Frohoff et al. [2,10]. The deserialisation of the `HashSet` instances encountered in the stream will then invoke `hashCode()` via a call graph chain from `readObject()`, and the malicious computation is activated.

Redundant traversals can be solved using dynamic programming in some cases. However, a solution is not available in the case of SerialDoS where it is not a programming defect that gives rise to the vulnerability. In SerialDoS, each method invocation happens within another context (i.e., state of the stack), and for a programmer to cache intermediate results would require knowledge about the state of the heap and stack during each invocation.

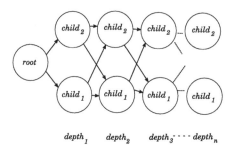

Fig. 1. Many-to-many topology in object graphs – each vertex represents an object and an edge represents a reference. Note that parents have two children, but children also have two parents. The graph is abstracted in the sense that intermediate references to elements in `java.util.HashSet` are not shown.

3   Characteristics of the Vulnerability

In this section, we discuss the three defining characteristics, TTT, needed to craft DoS attacks based on vulnerabilities in code recursively traversing data structures: *topologies, traversals* and *triggers*.

3.1   Topologies

In Java-like languages, an instance of a data structure forms a graph of objects as depicted in Fig. 1. An object, *parent*, references $child_1$ if $child_1$ is the value of a field of *parent*. Often, references are indirect via intermediate objects, in particular arrays or collections. Given an object graph, we are particularly interested in subgraphs formed by objects of some type T, where these objects have more than one predecessor and/or successor of type T. These structures can be described as following a many-to-many pattern.[4] Examples of this are common in the Java collection library, where, for instance, lists can be elements of multiple other lists.

A pattern that is very widely used, and conceptually similar to many-to-many, is *composite* [11]. A composite has containers with elements that are either containers as well, or leaf nodes. Usually, there are dedicated container and child types subtyping a more abstract component type, but variations of this pattern are common.[5]

Whether a composite can form a many-to-many graph depends on how the parent-child relationships are represented and controlled. Often it is an implicit precondition for an operation with a composite as an input, that at most, the composite has a single reference to any of its children. This is often enforced by an explicit parent reference in the children, and an API that maintains the consistency of the parent-child and child-parent references.[6]

3.2   Traversals

A many-to-many pattern in an object graph describes the data structure that can be exploited in SerialDoS-style attacks. To actually launch an attack, a function that operates recursively on this structure must be present. Regarding these functions, or methods as they are called in object-oriented languages, there are two aspects to consider. Firstly, recursion can be simply described by the presence of strongly-connected components in the call graph.

Secondly, the recursive method needs to traverse the many-to-many object graph. Consider such a method m with formal parameters $m.this, m.arg_1, m.arg_n$. Then, there must be a call graph chain linking m to itself. Additionally, at this invocation there is a parameter that points to a child of an object that the respective parameter points to at the previous invocation.

This captures several common *traversal patterns* found in real world programs. The most obvious one is direct recursion, where the many-to-many elements are always referenced by `this`.

There are more complicated traversal patterns though. For instance, it is possible to implement traversals using static methods in some class, where the traversed data structure is only passed as a parameter. This can be used to program traversals implemented outside the data structure being traversed. A more standardised way to achieve this is using the *visitor* pattern [11], which factors out the operation to be performed on a data structure from its implementation.

---

[4] Many-to-many relationships, in the database community, describe one type of cardinality of relationships between two entities.

[5] For instance, in `java.io.File`, state is used to determine whether an element is a container (a directory) or a child (a file). This can be considered a case of a composite that uses structural instead of nominal typing.

[6] A good example for this is how the parent reference is maintained in the `java.awt.Container.add*` methods which add a child component to the visual component hierarchy.

Note that the component of traversals we have discussed so far concerns traversing the graph depth-wise. Another aspect is how a method traverses the children of each parent. In our example, this is accomplished through the for-loop which iterates over the children in `elements`. A generalised technique is to use the iterator pattern [11], which abstracts the traversal of different implementations of collection types.

3.3 Triggers

The presence of the topology and the traversals itself is not sufficient to launch an attack. It is also necessary to create objects that instantiate the many-to-many pattern, and to trigger the traversal. This requires an external data structure to be translated to a vulnerable internal representation of the object graph in a data format, interpreted or otherwise processed, and in this process the traversal is activated. The activation refers to an invocation chain from a method that is called by the library or the framework when the data is processed, to the actual traversal method (e.g., deserialisation in SerialDoS). In general, a trigger is a method in the public API of a library that is invoked when data is processed (either by a client program, or by the library itself), and that leads to the invocation of the traversal (method).

4   Modelling the Analysis

In this section, we describe how we model the topology, traversal and trigger pattern for our analysis. We formalise the analysis in graph-theoretic terms using three graphs that model different aspects of program behaviour. These definitions are language-agnostic, and are applicable to languages with common object-oriented language features. We occasionally refer to Java for illustrative purposes.

4.1   Preliminaries

The Type Graph. A type graph models classes and their relationships in a program written in an object-oriented programming language, formally defined as follows:

Definition 1. *The **type graph** of a program is a directed labelled graph $\langle T, E \rangle$ where*

- *T is a set of vertices representing classes and (nested) arrays of classes that occur in the program, we represent vertices using their class name, with the suffix [ ] for array types as usual. For the sake of brevity, we identify those names with the respective vertices from now on.*
- *$E \subseteq T \times T$ are the graph edges. We consider edges of two kinds, i.e., $E = E_{subtype} \cup E_{assoc}$, representing subtype and association relationships, respectively.*

Subtype edges between vertices represent subtype relationships. The particular rules differ between languages, for Java, they are defined in [13, Sect. 4.10]. We use the simplified notion "B is subtype of A" to say that there is a path consisting of subtype edges linking B to A. That is, the edge $(B \rightarrow A) \in E_{subtype}$. If $C \in T$ is either representing an array, or a class that is a subtype of a container type (such as Java's java.util.Collection), then we call C a container type. If a container type is an array A[] then A is called the component type of the container. If the language supports the declaration of component types for container types, using some mechanism like Java's generics [13, Sect. 8.1.2], C<A>, then A is called the component type of C. Association edges represent the relationships between container types and their respective component types.

The Points-To Graph. A points-to graph models the memory during program executions. There are several versions of points-to analysis, our representation is used in an Andersen-style, field-sensitive analysis [30]. In a points-to graph, object abstractions and variables are represented by vertices, and allocations, assignments, field or array stores and loads are represented by edges which define the flow of values in the program being represented.

Definition 2. *The **points-to graph** of a program is a directed labelled bipartite graph $\langle O, V, E_{alloc}, E_{assign}, E_{load}, E_{store} \rangle$ where*

- *V is the set of vertices representing the variables in the program*
- *O is the set vertices representing object allocation sites in the program*
- *$E_{alloc} \subseteq O \times V$ is a set of allocation edges, modelling memory allocation*
- *$E_{assign} \subseteq V \times V$, a set of assignment edges modelling variable assignment*
- *$E_{load} \subseteq V \times V$, a set of field load edges modelling field loads, labelled with the respective field name*
- *$E_{store} \subseteq V \times V$, a set of field store edges modelling field stores, labelled with the respective field name*

Array access can be modelled similarly to field access. We omit details for the sake of brevity here.

Given a points-to graph, the objective of a points-to analysis is to infer additional *flowsTo* edges $E_{flowsTo} \subseteq O \times V$ describing the relationship between abstract values and variables pointing to them.[7] This is a computational complex problem, usually solved by computing CFL-reachability via a fixpoint algorithm [8,28].

One of the main uses of the points-to graph is alias analysis. Two variable vertices v_1, v_2 *alias* if there is an object vertex $o \in O$ and paths consisting of *flowsTo* edges from o to both variable vertices v_1 and v_2. Aliasing means that both variables can point to the same memory location. Furthermore, this can be used to define a *heap access path* between variables. A heap access path between v_1 and v_2 consists of a sequence of load edges where the destination (sink) of an edge in the sequence aliases with the source of the next edge, v_1 is the source

---

[7] Sometimes, the reverse *points-to* edges are inferred.

of the first and v_2 the destination of the last edge in the sequence. This models (nested) field access in a programming language, i.e. statements like `foo.f.g`. By accounting for aliases, this also covers field access with intermediate variables, in programs like `x = foo.f; x.g;`.

The Call Graph. A call graph statically models the interprocedural calling (invocation) behaviour of a program. Methods are represented by vertices and interprocedural calls by edges.

Definition 3. *The **call graph** of a program is a directed graph $\langle M, I \rangle$ where*

- *M is the set of methods in the program*
- *$I \subseteq M \times M$ is a set of edges, $(m, n) \in I$ means that method m has a call site with an invocation of n.*

A call graph can be constructed by analysing invocation instructions found in program code. To model runtime behaviour in languages with dynamic dispatch, additional edges must be inferred (devirtualisation). There are various algorithms available for this purpose differing in their precision and efficiency (e.g. CHA, VTA) [30]. The more precise methods require points-to information to determine the type of the objects a receiver points to in a method invocation, a process often referred to as call graph construction on-the-fly.

Cross-Referencing Graphs. The three models defined above are widely used in static program analysis. In practice, they are often combined. There are certain relationships between these models we will exploit in our analysis.

Firstly, for a given method m, the variables in the points-to graph include the return value and the parameters of this method. We denote the parameters, including the receiver of an invocation (in Java, the `this` reference), as $param(m) \subseteq V$. Secondly, call graph vertices can be associated with type graph vertices via the types that define those methods. We refer to those types as the owner of a method m, $owner(m) \in T$. Finally, allocation vertices $o \in O$ in the points-to graph can be associated with the types they instantiate, $type(o) \in T$.

4.2   Analysis Specification

Topologies. Given a type graph $\langle T, E \rangle$, we describe an instance of *composite* as a mapping between the two roles in the composite design pattern [11] and actual types that occur in the program.[8]

Definition 4. *Given a type graph $TG = \langle T, E \rangle$, a composite is a mapping $\{cont, comp\} \rightarrow TG$ such that the following two conditions are satisfied:*

- *$(composite(cont), composite(comp)) \in E_{assoc}$*
- *$(composite(cont), composite(comp)) \in E_{subtype}$*

---

[8] The *cont* role corresponds to the *Container* role in the design pattern, whereas the *comp* roles corresponds to the *Component* role. We do not consider a particular leaf type.

Traversals. We define a traversal as the presence of a recursive invocation in the call graph and the flow of an object from a field of a composite to an argument of the recursive call.

Definition 5. *Given the type graph $TG = \langle T, E \rangle$, the call graph $CG = \langle M, I \rangle$ and the points-to graph $PG = \langle V, O, E_{alloc}, E_{assign}, E_{load}, E_{store} \rangle$, a traversal is a method $m \in CG$ such that:*

- *$m \in M$ is recursive in CG, i.e. CG contains a path connecting m to itself*
- *there is a composite c and $c(comp) \in param(m)$*
- *there is a heap access path in PG from some parameter of $v \in param(m)$ to the respective argument in the recursive call site for m*

Triggers. We define a trigger as the presence of a method that instantiates a *composite* through a chain of method invocations. Once the composite is instantiated it would also trigger the recursive traversal with the *composite* as an argument.

Definition 6. *Given a call graph $CG = \langle M, I \rangle$ and the points-to graph $PG = \langle V, O, E_{alloc}, E_{assign}, E_{load}, E_{store} \rangle$, a trigger is a method trigger $\in M$ in the call graph that is reachable from a program entry point $ep \in M$. There must also be a path in the CG from the trigger to a traversal method with the instantiated composite as an argument in PG.*

5   Experimental Setup and Evaluation

5.1   Approach

The approach focuses on first running the static analysis to detect instances of the TTT pattern in Java parser libraries, then using the analysis results to confirm whether we can construct payloads to exploit vulnerabilities, and finally using the payload for non-Java parsers (e.g., C, Python, Rust etc.) to check if these parsers are also vulnerable. The payloads were constructed manually using format specifications, source code indicated by analysis results. The effort required to construct payloads varied across different libraries, and this process is discussed in more detail in Sect. 5.5.

5.2   Implementation

The analysis was implemented as an extension of DOOP [1], a state-of-the-art static analysis framework for Java, which encodes static analyses declaratively in the Datalog [4] language. Datalog programs are a natural way to express the graph-based algorithms [35] used in the specification of our analysis. Datalog-based formulations of static analyses have been used successfully in bug and vulnerability detection [14,18,27]. The underlying analyses in DOOP compute points-to information and call graphs from an input program, and they can also be used to obtain the type graph.

5.3   Libraries for Analysis

We evaluated the analysis on a set of 16 widely used Java parser libraries for different data formats (Table 1). These popular libraries are known to parse external data formats, and are therefore prone to the vulnerabilities we study. These libraries process data used in messaging, object serialisation and document representation, represented in various text and binary formats. We covered libraries for parsing or processing XML, JSON and YAML, PDF and external DSLs. Table 1 also contains usage data showing how many Maven artefacts depend on those libraries. This provides some indication of the impact vulnerabilities in these libraries have based on usage statistics.[9]

Table 1. Java libraries for analysis

Library	Input format	Version	Usage
batik	SVG	1.1	115
gson	JSON	2.8.5	11,900
jackson	JSON	2.9.8	6,829
jettison	JSON	1.4.0	753
jfxrt	FXML	1.8	N/A
mongo	BSON	3.9.1	1,048
mvel2	MVEL2	2.4.3	395
ognl	OGNL	3.2.10	339
pdfbox	PDF	2.0.12	403
pdfxstream	PDF	3.7.0	N/A
protobuf	Protocol	3.6.1	2,407
sanselan	Images	0.97	52
snakeyaml	YAML	1.23	1,962
stringtemplate	StringTemplate	3.2	270
xbean	SOAP/XMLBean	3.0.2	632
xstream	XStream	1.4.11.1	1,711

After analysing these 16 libraries, we proceeded to evaluate whether libraries for other languages, shown in Table 2 were vulnerable using the payloads constructed. These libraries were selected based on availability and popularity. librsvg is used in the GNOME desktop,[10] Ghostscript is widely deployed and used for processing PDFs, a popular vector-based illustration software - Inkscape uses librsvg and cairo.[11] Inkscape[12] is also used by ImageMagick for SVG processing. We looked at solutions for sanitising SVG files, and found that svg-sanitizer is the most widely used (e.g. WordPress, drupal).

---

[9] Maven usage statistics (obtained on 12 Feb. 2020).
[10] https://www.gnome.org.
[11] https://cairosvg.org/.
[12] https://inkscape.org/.

Table 2. Non-Java libraries investigated

Library	Language	Input format	Version
Qt	C++	SVG	5.14.1
librsvg	Rust	SVG	2.46
PDFtk	GCJ	PDF	2.0.2
qpdf	C++	PDF	9.1.1
PDFium	C++	PDF	N/A
ghostscript	PostScript	PDF	9.25
svg-sanitizer	PHP	SVG	0.13.2
resvg	Rust	SVG	0.8.0
cairosvg	Python	SVG	2.4.2

5.4 Triggers or Entry Points

Identifying a trigger is a manual step that requires domain knowledge of the library under analysis. For image formats this could be the rasterisation/conversion process that would require traversals of the structure. Some libraries have command line interfaces which initiate calls to the trigger methods. In the case where we analysed libraries without command line interfaces, a driver was required as an entry point for the input program for the analysis. We have written custom drivers for libraries that are not bundled with a command line interface. The driver provides an entry point as well as a facility to interact with the library's API. In the case of SnakeYAML, the driver consists of statements to instantiate the parser and load a file. Only MVEL2, PDFBox, Batik and PDFxStream come with built-in command line interfaces and did not require custom drivers.

5.5 Evaluation

Static Analysis. The experiments were performed on an Intel(R) Core(TM) i7-8700 CPU @ 3.20 GHz with 64 GB of RAM on Linux Ubuntu 18.04.3. DOOP was run using the Java 8 platform as implemented in Oracle's version 8 of the JDK. We used a context-insensitive analysis. the following options for the analysis:

- analysis: `-a context-insensitive`
- main class: `-main` option was used with the driver class as an argument.

For each project, we extracted facts from the input library, and then executed DOOP with custom rules to compute:

- Composites (i.e., facts instantiating the Composite rule).
- Recursive methods.
- Heap flows to refine the list of recursive methods, i.e. an object that is of composite type must flow to the parameter of a recursive method.

– Methods with heap flows from the previous step, and that are reachable via the entry point.

Manual Evaluation of Analysis Results. At the end of the static analysis we find a set of candidate instances, i.e. bindings of the concepts used in TTT to concrete artefacts within the program under analysis. However, these may contain false positives as the malicious computation is effectively prevented by some program logic. While we cannot accurately eliminate false positives, we conducted a manual step to identify true positives, by constructing payloads that expose the respective vulnerability. This consisted of inspection of the program's source code, debugging and reviewing specifications against the implementation for the particular parser library.

6   Results and Discussion

Table 3 shows a summary of the outcomes of the experiment, including the static analysis run times for the 16 libraries. Methods and composites from the library and their dependencies are shown. The **Topology** column lists all composite types in the library. The **Methods (Composite)** column lists only those methods that have a composite type as a parameter. From these methods, the **Traversal** column lists methods that have a value flow within the composite field to the recursive callsite. The **Triggered Traversals** column lists reachable traversals for the identified topologies. In the following sections, we discuss some of the vulnerabilities detected in more detail.

Table 3. Overview of experiments (composites and direct recursion)

Library	Format	Time (sec)	Topology	Methods (composite)	Traversal	Triggered traversals
batik	SVG	505	430	595	34	34
gson	JSON	300	27	25	1	1
jackson	XML	404	126	167	10	10
jettison	JSON/XML	296	19	8	1	1
jfxrt	XML	784	0	0	0	0
mongo	BSON	433	275	224	0	0
mvel2	MVEL	173	93	135	4	2
ognl	OGNL	317	29	64	4	4
pdfbox	PDF	703	480	247	11	11
pdfxstream	PDF	334	115	118	3	3
protobuf	Protobuf	383	199	202	5	5
sanselan	Image	307	35	6	0	0
snakeyaml	YAML	307	30	13	3	3
stringtemplate	Template	306	32	18	0	0
xbean	XML	492	363	230	0	0
xstream	XML	331	120	100	1	1

6.1   PDF Vulnerabilities

The analysis detected 11 triggered traversals that recurse on a parameter in the PDFBox library. From these results, a vulnerability was confirmed in Apache PDFBox, the most used Java PDF library in the Maven repository.[13]

A PDF document's format, Carousel Object Structure (COS), is described in the PDF Reference [24]. It supports basic types such as booleans, integers, real numbers, strings, names and more crucially, arrays and dictionaries. The particular composite topology in the library consists of `COSDictionary` as the container and `COSBase` as the component where the children are stored in an object that implements the `Map` interface. The recursive method that traverses this structure is `checkPagesDictionary(COSDictionary pagesDict)` defined in `org.apache.pdfbox.pdfparser.COSParser`, which is invoked when the PDF file is parsed. The only constraint in the path condition from the entry into the method to the recursive call is the presence of child objects that are of the same type as the passed parameter.

Manual inspection of the source code and the PDF specification [24] revealed that the root of a PDF document, the catalog, points to a dictionary referred to as a *Page Tree*, which can in turn refer to another *Page Tree*. This structure parses to a `COSDictionary` composite and we can craft a PDF document that parses into an object graph with the many-to-many pattern.

Passing the crafted PDF to the application revealed that it can result in attacks on responsiveness and disk space as the application can also be used to convert the pages in a PDF to disk as images. The issue was reported and it has been accepted with the identifier CVE-2018-11797.

The same PDF document was used to confirm the vulnerability in PDFxStream (CVE-2019-17063), and it also revealed the same vulnerability in PDFtk[14], the PDF toolkit. They both use a `HashMap` to store the COS structure, which in principle makes a DoS attack possible.

We also tested the PDF document on Ghostscript [12], a PostScript and PDF interpreter. Using the crafted PDF as an input to Ghostscript resulted in DoS. This bug was accepted as a security vulnerability (CVE-2018-19478). The PDF parser in Ghostscript is implemented in PostScript and the traversal of the COS was for an entirely different purpose when compared to the previous cases, which was to detect cycles in the *Page Tree* that had caused a security vulnerability in Ghostscript. This suggests that traversals of the form that we have studied occur across multiple languages.

6.2   Scalable Vector Graphics (SVG) Vulnerability

SVG [31] is an XML-based format for two-dimensional graphics supported by web browsers and is used in illustration programs. SVG is processed by the Batik library. The analysis reported 34 triggered traversals for the library. One

---

[13] https://mvnrepository.com/.

[14] https://www.pdflabs.com/tools/pdftk-the-pdf-toolkit/ [Accessed 08-October-2020].

particular composite topology in the library consists of `Node` as the container with children or parents of the same type. The recursive method that traverses this structure is `String getCascadedXMLBase (Node node)` defined in `org.apache.batik.anim.dom.SVGOMElement`, which is invoked when the SVG file is parsed. The only constraint in the path condition from the entry into the method to the recursive call is the presence of child objects that are of the same node type as the passed parameter (i.e. XML element nodes).

Any SVG graphics element is potentially a template object that can be reused (i.e., instanced) in the SVG document via a `<use>` element. The `<use>` element references another element and indicates that the graphical contents of that element is included/drawn at that given point in the document. The `<g>` element can be used to specify a grouped container of elements. The `<g>` element in conjunction with the `<use>` element can be used to construct a nested structure to trigger the detected vulnerability. The `<use>` element can also be used to construct the SVG version for SerialDoS as shown in Listing 1.2. We based our SVG file on this ability to nest references using `<g>` and `<use>` elements. There is an additional way to reference elements, as shown in Listing 1.3, which uses the pattern tag and its fill attribute set to a `url` function containing the reference id for an element in the document.

Listing 1.2. Nested References in SVG

```
1  <g id="t0a">
2  <use xlink:href="#t1a"/>
3  <use xlink:href="#t1b"/>
4  </g>
5
6  <g id="t0b">
7  <use xlink:href="#t1a"/>
8  <use xlink:href="#t1b"/>
9  </g>
```

Listing 1.3. References with use() function in SVG

```
1  <pattern id="h" ... >
2        <rect   fill="url(#g)"  stroke="green" />
```

The same SVG document was used to verify vulnerabilities in web browsers, and a core Linux SVG rendering library (librsvg[15]). The issue was reported for librsvg and fixed by the vendor (CVE-2019-20446). We found the crafted file to impact all tested browsers (e.g. Mozilla Firefox (version 73.0), Google Chrome (Version 77.0.3865.120, Official Build) by excessively consuming resources (memory and CPU) for Firefox and crashing the active browser tab in Chrome. This can be used by malicious parties to craft client-DoS for websites that allow links to SVG code in user input (e.g. Markdown with links to external SVG files in user comments). We confirmed this observation for the StackOverflow[16] Q&A platform, GitLab[17] and GitHub[18] issue trackers. The impact on these services

---

[15] https://wiki.gnome.org/action/show/Projects/LibRsvg   [Accessed   08-October-2020].

[16] https://stackoverflow.com.

[17] https://gitlab.com.

[18] https://github.com.

is that they can render the page inaccessible to users if it has malicious SVG content.

We also considered svg-sanitizer[19], which performs server-side sanitisation of SVG content (used in Drupal and WordPress as a plugin). On passing the crafted SVG file as input, svg-sanitizer, entered a non-terminating computation which make services using the plugin susceptible to DoS attacks. This issue was reported to the developer and it was fixed by adding a check to limit levels of **use** recursion during SVG sanitisation.

6.3 YAML Vulnerability

YAML is a popular and widely used (human readable) serialisation language for data interchange and application configuration. It supports primitives and common data structures such as maps and lists [34]. We looked at the SnakeYAML library in Java and the analysis reported three triggered traversals, one of which involves the composite `MappingNode` with a list of `NodeTuple` as children that can potentially have the same type as the parent.

The code is the implementation of the << merge key feature in YAML, which is used to indicate that all the keys of one or more specified maps should be inserted into the current map. If the value associated with the key is a single map, each of its key/value pairs is inserted into the current map, unless the key already exists in it. If the value associated with the merge key is a sequence, then this sequence is expected to contain multiple maps and each of these are merged in order. Listing 1.4 shows the use of YAML merge as well as the use of YAML aliases in constructing SerialDoS type inputs, which were detected as vulnerabilities by the analysis.

Listing 1.4. Merging map keys in YAML

```
1  ? - &t2a
2      - &t3a [lol]
3      - &t3b [lol]
4    - &t2b
5      - *t3a
6      - *t3b
7  : value
8  --
9  { << { << { key: value} } }
```

We created a YAML file with nested merges and nested lists with aliases forming the topology, and passed the file as input to our SnakeYAML driver to confirm that it crashed from stack exhaustion for the nested merges case, and entered a long-running computation for nested lists. Consequently, this issue has been reported to the maintainer.

6.4 Newly Discovered Security Vulnerabilities

Following the guidelines for responsible disclosure, we have reported all vulnerabilities to the libraries' developers/maintainers. We provide a timeline and the statuses of each of these vulnerabilities below (Table 4).

---

[19] https://github.com/darylldoyle/svg-sanitizer [Accessed 08-October-2020].

Table 4. Status of reported bugs and vulnerabilities status.

Library	Version	Status	Fixed date
PDFBox	2.0.12	CVE-2018-11797	6-Oct-18
PDFxStream	3.6.0	CVE-2019-17063	27-Feb-19
PDFTk	2.02	Pending	
GhostScript	9.25	CVE-2018-19478	20-Nov-2018
Svg-sanitizer	0.13.0	CVE requested (pending)	20-Jan-20
Batik	1.11	Won't fix	–
Firefox	69	Duplicate	–
Drupal	6.x–8.x	–	25-June-20
Snakeyaml	1.23	Won't fix	
Qtsvg	5.14.1	Bug	29-Feb-20
Librvg	2.46.2	CVE-2019-20446	15-Oct-19

6.5   Threats to Validity

Manual confirmation of the vulnerabilities reported by the tool poses a threat to
the validity of the evaluation. However, for the most likely candidates, we were
able to construct payloads and confirm that the reports are actual bugs. Even
though a hand-selected set of projects was used in the evaluation, the generality
of the model and the discovery of related bugs in other libraries are encouraging.

7   Related Work

7.1   Detecting Algorithmic Complexity Vulnerabilities

Wuestholz et al. [33] discuss an approach to statically detect DoS vulnerabilities
in programs that use regular expressions. The analysis has multiple stages and
is conceptually similar to the analysis proposed in this paper: they first build a
model to detect vulnerable structures (by reasoning about the worst-case complexity of NFAs), and then devise a separate (taint) analysis to establish whether
a vulnerable regular expression can be matched against an input string. The tool
they have developed, Rexploiter, finds 41 exploitable security vulnerabilities in
Java web applications. Holland et al. [15] propose a hybrid approach to detect
algorithmic complexity vulnerabilities. In a static pre analysis step, they use a
loop call graph to detect nested loop structures that are susceptible to algorithmic complexity vulnerabilities. The first step is similar to our approach, but
uses a different model. Our approach is based on the presence of higher level
data structures and recursive methods which then implicitly create the nested
traversals.

7.2   Traversals/Performance Bugs

The detection of performance bugs and in particular redundant traversal is a problem related to DoS vulnerabilities. Olivo et al. [21] study redundant traversal performance bugs in Java code, limited to traversals in non-recursive functions, and a static analysis, CLARITY, to detect them. Burnim et al. [3] present WISE, automated test generation for detecting worst-case complexity in programs. WISE uses symbolic test generation. Jiayi et al. [32] describe Singularity, another input generation technique for detecting worst-case performance bugs in Java programs. Singularity uses a greybox fuzzing technique that looks for critical input patterns modelled as recurrent computation graphs (RCGs). Their technique reveals performance and DoS-related bugs in real world programs. Other fuzzing approaches include SlowFuzz and PerfFuzz [17,25]. Nistpor et al. [19] propose Toddler, an example of dynamic analysis to detect performance bugs. Toddler instruments loops and read instructions, and uses the data collected using inserted code to detect similar memory-access patterns. Padhye and Sen [22] describe Travioli, a dynamic analysis technique for detecting data-structure traversals. It is also based on instrumenting code in order to harvest trace data, from which the analysis model is built. The purpose is similar to what we try to achieve in this paper with the topologies and traversal steps of our model, however this being a dynamic model, it has different tradeoffs between precision and recall, and its quality depends on the existence of drivers (such as unit tests) that exercise a large part of the program under analysis.

8   Conclusion

We presented an approach to classify and detect a class of DoS vulnerabilities in parsing data structures. We evaluated this approach on a set of 16 Java parser libraries with a Datalog-based formulation of a static analysis using the DOOP analysis framework for Java. The study revealed four new vulnerabilities in widely used Java PDF, SVG and YAML libraries. A further evaluation also revealed seven more vulnerabilities in parser libraries for Rust, PHP, C++ and PostScript. Out of these reports, we have obtained four CVEs and reported a total of 11 security issues to vendors (7 of which have been accepted). The results confirm that a lightweight static analysis can be useful in uncovering vulnerabilities that belong to this class. Possible directions for future work include using micro-fuzzing to fuzz the recursive functions reported by the static analysis for more precise results, and using constraint-based approaches to more precisely identify the topology and traversal patterns reported by the analysis.

References

1. Bravenboer, M., Smaragdakis, Y.: Strictly declarative specification of sophisticated points-to analyses. In: Proceedings of the 24th ACM SIGPLAN Conference on Object Oriented Programming Systems Languages and Applications, OOPSLA 2009, Association for Computing Machinery, New York, NY, USA, pp. 243–262 (2009). https://doi.org/10.1145/1640089.1640108

2. Breen, S.: What Do WebLogic, WebSphere, JBoss, Jenkins, OpenNMS, and Your Application Have in Common? This Vulnerability (2015). https://goo.gl/cx7X4D. Accessed on 08 Oct 2020
3. Burnim, J., Juvekar, S., Sen, K.: WISE: automated test generation for worst-case complexity. In: Proceedings of the ICSE 2009. IEEE (2009)
4. Ceri, S., Gottlob, G., Tanca, L.: What you always wanted to know about Datalog (and never dared to ask). IEEE TKDE 1(1), 146–166 (1989)
5. Coekaerts, W.: SerialDOS (2015). https://gist.github.com/coekie/a27cc406fc9f 3dc7a70d. Accessed on 08 Oct 2020
6. CVE-2003-1564 (Billion Laughs) (2003). https://cve.mitre.org/cgi-bin/cvename. cgi?name=CVE-2003-1564. Accessed on 14 Jan 2020
7. Crosby, S.A., Wallach, D.S.: Denial of service via algorithmic complexity attacks. In: Proceedings of the USENIX Security 2003. USENIX Association (2003)
8. Dietrich, J., Hollingum, N., Scholz, B.: Giga-scale exhaustive points-to analysis for Java in under a minute. In: Proceedings of the OOPSLA 2015. ACM (2015)
9. Dietrich, J., Jezek, K., Rasheed, S., Tahir, A., Potanin, A.: Evil Pickles: DoS attacks based on object-graph engineering. In: Proceedings of the ECOOP 2017 (2017)
10. Frohoff, C., Lawrence, G.: Marshalling Pickles (2015). http://frohoff.github.io/ appseccali-marshalling-pickles/. Accessed on 08 Oct 2020
11. Gamma, E., Vlissides, J., Johnson, R., Helm, R.: Design Patterns: Elements of Reusable Object-oriented Software. Addison-Wesley (1994)
12. GhostScript: An interpreter for the PostScript language and for PDF (2019). https://www.ghostscript.com/. Accessed on 14 Jan 2020
13. Gosling, J., Joy, B., Steele, G., Brache, G., Buckley, A.: The Java® Language Specification Java SE 8 Edition (2015). https://docs.oracle.com/javase/specs/jls/ se8/jls8.pdf. Accessed on 08 Oct 2020
14. Grech, N., Smaragdakis, Y.: P/Taint: unified points-to and taint analysis. In: Proceedings of the OOPSLA 2017. ACM (2017)
15. Holland, B., Santhanam, G.R., Awadhutkar, P., Kothari, S.: Statically-informed dynamic analysis tools to detect algorithmic complexity vulnerabilities. In: Proceedings of the SCAM 2016. IEEE (2016)
16. Klees, G., Ruef, A., Cooper, B., Wei, S., Hicks, M.: Evaluating fuzz testing. In: Proceedings of the CCS 2018. ACM (2018)
17. Lemieux, C., Padhye, R., Sen, K., Song, D.: PerfFuzz: automatically generating pathological inputs. In: Proceedings of the ISSTA 2018. ACM (2018)
18. Livshits, V.B., Lam, M.S.: Finding security vulnerabilities in Java applications with static analysis. In: Proceedings of the USENIX Security 2014. USENIX Association (2005)
19. Nistor, A., Song, L., Marinov, D., Lu, S.: Toddler: detecting performance problems via similar memory-access patterns. In: Proceedings of the ICSE 2013. IEEE (2013)
20. Noller, Y., Kersten, R., Păsăreanu, C.S.: Badger: complexity analysis with fuzzing and symbolic execution. In: Proceedings of the ISSTA 2018. ACM (2018)
21. Olivo, O., Dillig, I., Lin, C.: Static detection of asymptotic performance bugs in collection traversals. In: Proceedings of the PLDI 2015. ACM (2015)
22. Padhye, R., Sen, K.: Travioli: a dynamic analysis for detecting data-structure traversals. In: Proceedings of the ICSE 2017. IEEE (2017)
23. Păsăreanu, C.S., Kersten, R., Luckow, K., Phan, Q.S.: Symbolic execution and recent applications to worst-case execution, load testing, and security analysis. Adv. Comput. 113, 289–314 (2019). https://doi.org/10.1016/bs.adcom.2018.10. 004

24. PDF Reference 6th edition (2006). https://www.adobe.com/content/dam/acom/en/devnet/-pdf/pdf_reference_archive/pdf_reference_1-7.pdf. Accessed on 14 Jan 2020
25. Petsios, T., Zhao, J., Keromytis, A.D., Jana, S.: SlowFuzz: automated domain-independent detection of algorithmic complexity vulnerabilities. In: Proceedings of the CCS 2017. ACM (2017)
26. Rasheed, S., Dietrich, J., Tahir, A.: Laughter in the wild: a study into DoS vulnerabilities in YAML libraries. In: Proceedings of the TrustCom 2019. IEEE (2019)
27. Scholz, B., Jordan, H., Subotić, P., Westmann, T.: On fast large-scale program analysis in datalog. In: Proceedings of the 25th International Conference on Compiler Construction, CC 2016, Barcelona, Spain, March 12–18, 2016. ACM (2016)
28. Sridharan, M., Gopan, D., Shan, L., Bodík, R.: Demand-driven points-to analysis for Java. In: Proceedings of the OOPSLA 2005. ACM (2005)
29. Staicu, C.A., Pradel, M.: Freezing the web: a study of ReDoS vulnerabilities in Javascript-based web servers. In: Proceedings of the USENIX Security 2018. USENIX Association (2018)
30. Sundaresan, V., et al.: Practical virtual method call resolution for Java. In: Proceedings of the OOPSLA 2000. ACM (2000)
31. Scalable Vector Graphics (SVG) 1.1, 2nd edn. (2011). https://www.w3.org/TR/SVG11/REC-SVG11-20110816.pdf. Accessed on 14 Jan 2020
32. Wei, J., Chen, J., Feng, Y., Ferles, K., Dillig, I.: Singularity: pattern fuzzing for worst case complexity. In: Proceedings of the ESEC/FSE 2018. ACM (2018)
33. Wüstholz, V., Olivo, O., Heule, M.J.H., Dillig, I.: Static detection of DoS vulnerabilities in programs that use regular expressions. In: Legay, A., Margaria, T. (eds.) TACAS 2017. LNCS, vol. 10206, pp. 3–20. Springer, Heidelberg (2017). https://doi.org/10.1007/978-3-662-54580-5_1
34. YAML Ain't Markup Language (YAML) Version 1.2 (2019). https://yaml.org/spec/1.2/spec.html. Accessed on 08 Oct 2020
35. Yannakakis, M.: Graph-theoretic methods in database theory. In: Proceedings of the PODS 1990. ACM (1990)

PoW-How: An Enduring Timing Side-Channel to Evade Online Malware Sandboxes

Antonio Nappa[1,2,3], Panagiotis Papadopoulos[4(✉)], Matteo Varvello[5],
Daniel Aceituno Gomez[2], Juan Tapiador[2], and Andrea Lanzi[6]

[1] UC Berkeley, Berkeley, USA
[2] Universidad Carlos III de Madrid, Getafe, Spain
[3] Zimperium zLabs Team, Dallas, USA
[4] Telefonica Research, Miami, USA
panagiotis.papadop@telefonica.com
[5] Nokia Bell Labs, Murray Hill, USA
[6] University of Milan, Milan, Italy

Abstract. Online malware scanners are one of the best weapons in the arsenal of cybersecurity companies and researchers. A fundamental part of such systems is the sandbox that provides an instrumented and isolated environment (virtualized or emulated) for any user to upload and run unknown artifacts and identify potentially malicious behaviors. The provided API and the wealth of information in the reports produced by these services have also helped attackers test the efficacy of numerous techniques to make malware hard to detect.

The most common technique used by malware for evading the analysis system is to monitor the execution environment, detect the presence of any debugging artifacts, and hide its malicious behavior if needed. This is usually achieved by looking for signals suggesting that the execution environment is not belong to a the native machine, such as specific memory patterns or behavioral traits of certain CPU instructions.

In this paper, we show how an attacker can evade detection on such online services by incorporating a Proof-of-Work (PoW) algorithm into a malware sample. Specifically, we leverage the asymptotic behavior of the computational cost of PoW algorithms when they run on some classes of hardware platforms to effectively detect a non bare-metal environment of the malware sandbox analyzer. To prove the validity of this intuition, we design and implement the PoW-How framework, a tool to automatically implement sandbox detection strategies and embed a test evasion program into an arbitrary malware sample. Our empirical evaluation shows that the proposed evasion technique is durable, hard to fingerprint, and reduces existing malware detection rate by a factor of 10. Moreover, we show how bare-metal environments cannot scale with actual malware submissions rates for consumer services.

© Springer Nature Switzerland AG 2021
E. Bertino et al. (Eds.): ESORICS 2021, LNCS 12972, pp. 86–109, 2021.
https://doi.org/10.1007/978-3-030-88418-5_5

1   Introduction

Malware attacks have a significant financial cost, estimated around $1.5 trillion dollars annually (or $2.9 million dollars per minute) [39], with predictions hinting at this cost to reach $6 trillion dollars by 2021 [27]. Due to the sheer amount of known malware samples [25,73], manual analysis neither scales nor allows to build any comprehensive threat intelligence around the detected cases (e.g., malware clustering by specific behavior, family or infection campaign). To address this problem, security researchers have introduced *sandboxes* [16]: isolated environments that automate the dynamic execution of malware and monitor its behavior under different scenarios. Sandboxes usually comprise a set of virtualized or emulated machines, instrumented to gather fundamental information of the malware execution, such as system calls, registry keys accessed or modified, new files created, and memory patterns.

As a next step, online services came to bring malware analysis from security experts to the common users [63]. Online malware scanners are not only useful for the users but also for the attackers. In fact by allowing an artefact to be checked multiple times against various state-of-the-art of malware analysis sandboxes, attackers can tune the evasiveness of their malware samples by exploiting the feedback reported by these services and try various techniques before making the sample capable of detecting the presence of a sandbox. Specific CPU instructions, registry keys, memory patterns, and *red pills* [55,64,67] are only a few of the signals used by attackers for identifying glitches of the emulated environment that can disclose the presence of a sandbox environment. These techniques have triggered an arms-race, with the more sophisticated web malware scanners rushing to spoof any such exploitable signals [40].

In this work, we show how an attacker can evade malware analysis of these scanning services by leveraging Proof-of-Work (PoW) [32] algorithms. Our intuition lies on the fact that, like NP-class problems [76], the asymptotic behavior of a PoW algorithm is constant in terms of computational power [32], e.g., CPU and memory consumption which remain stable over time. Accordingly, PoW algorithms are perfect candidates for benchmarking the computation capability of the underlying hardware. In such scenario the benchmark can be leveraged as a fingerprint of the underlying computing infrastructure, revealing the presence of a sandbox since it shows a statistical deviation compared with the native hardware platform. Moreover, current defensive techniques that aim at spoofing the virtualization signals present in contemporary sandboxes cannot act as countermeasures against the stable timing side-channels that our technique exploits.

A key advantage of using PoW techniques is that they are a time-proof and self-contained mechanism compared to other more fine-grained timing side-channel approaches that try to detect the underlying hardware machine. In fact, our system does not require access to precise timing resources for detecting the emulated environment (e.g., network or fine-grained timers). In our evaluation we empirically validate that a PoW-based technique can detect an emulated environment with high precision just by looking at the output of the algorithm (i.e., execution time, and number of successful iterations). Furthermore, PoW implementations do not raise any suspicion to automated malware sandboxes compared with the stalling code (e.g., infinite loops and/or sleep) that is easier to detect because of CPU idleness [49]. Fingerprinting PoW algorithms as a malware component is feasible e.g., by checking the usage of particular cryptographic instructions. However, using it as a proxy signal for detecting malware would produce a large number of false positives since PoW algorithms are part of legitimate applications such as Filecoin [65] and Hashcash [6].

Contributions. In this paper, we make the following contributions:

1. We design and implement PoW-How: a framework to automatically create, inject, and evaluate PoW-based evasion strategies in arbitrary programs. PoW-How operates as a three-step pipeline. First (step 1) multiple PoW algorithms are thoroughly tested across different hardware platforms (Raspberry Pi 3, Dual Intel Xeon, Intel i9), operating systems (Linux Ubuntu 18.03 and Windows 10), and machine loads. The outcome of these tests (step 2) is used to build a statistical characterization of each PoW's execution time under each setting. We use the Bienaymé–Chebyshev inequality [8] to obtain statistical evidence about the expected execution time. Next, a miscreant can upload its malware to the PoW-How framework and select the evasion mechanism to be used. Finally (step 3), PoW-How automatically evaluates the accuracy of the evasion mechanism selected and embedded in the uploaded malware via several tests on multiple online sandbox services [63].

2. We empirically evaluate each step of PoW-How's pipeline. For the PoW threshold estimation, we have tested three popular PoW algorithms (Catena [24], Argon2 [17,18] and Yescrypt [7]) using multiple configurations. During 24 h of testing, we find Chebyshev inequality values higher than 97% regardless of PoW and setting. This result verifies high determinism in PoW execution times on real hardware, thus validating the main intuition behind this work. We test our technique on top of two known ransomware families by submitting to three sandboxes several variants that include PoW-based evasion. The results demonstrate how PoW-based evasion reduces the number of detections, even in the presence of anti-analysis techniques such as code virtualization or packing.

3. To further quantify the efficacy of PoW-based evasion with real-world sandboxes, we wrote a fully functional malware sample, integrated with an evasion mechanism based on Argon2, and submitted it to several online sandboxes. All the reports from each sandbox mark our malware as *clean*. We further discuss the behavioral analysis for our malware, as well as potential countermeasures to this novel PoW-based evasion mechanism we have proposed. To ensure the reproducibility of our results and foster further research on this topic, we make the source code of our system publicly available [13][1].

---

[1] https://github.com/anonnymousubmission/Esorics2021_Paper159.

2   Background

2.1   Malware and Malware Analysis

Together with the evolution of malicious software, researchers and professionals have tried to improve their tools and skills to understand malware and counter its consequences. There is a huge amount of literature devoted to analyze and counter malware [21, 36, 43, 44, 57, 59, 74, 77]. Every aspect of this phenomenon has been taken into consideration, from its network infrastructure, to the code that gets reused among samples, unexplored paths in the control-flow, sandbox design and instrumentation. Nonetheless the arms race keeps running, while new analysis evasion techniques are found, new countermeasures get developed.

Anti-Analysis Techniques: There are several anti-analysis techniques which have been developed during the years by miscreants, and promptly countered by our community: e.g., packers [53, 72], emulators [68], anti-debugging and anti-disassembly tricks and stalling code. Among all these techniques the only one that seems to resist is stalling code, which is very difficult to detect [47]. Indeed, over 70% of all malware attacks involved evasive zero-day malware in Q2 of 2020: a 12% rise on the previous quarter [26]. This denotes that evasive malware is a phenomenon that will hardly disappear and there will always be continuous research in evading analysis systems.

2.2   PoW for Malware Analysis Evasion

Proof-of-Work (PoW) [32] is a consensus mechanism that imposes computation workload on a node. A key feature of such algorithms is their asymmetry: the work imposed on the node is moderately hard but it is easy for a server to check the computed result. There are two types of PoW protocols: (a) *challenge-response* protocols, which require an interactive link between the server and the client, and (b) *solution-verification* protocols, which allow the client to solve a self-imposed problem and send the solution to the server to verify the validity of the problem and its solution. Such PoW protocols (also known as CPU cost functions) leverage algorithms like hashcash with doubly iterated SHA256 [48], momentum birthday collision [46], cuckoo cycle [70], and more.

In PoW-HoW we use Argon2, which guarantees that by using the same input parameters, the amount of computation performed is asymptotically constant; hence, the variance of Argons2's execution time T is very small on the same platform. Moreover, Argon2 is based on a memory-hard function which, even in the case of parallel or specialized execution (e.g., ASICs or FPGAs), will not enhance scalability, and hence remains computationally bounded due to its asymptotic behavior.

The Argon2 algorithm takes the following input:

- A message string P, which is a password for password hashing applications. Its length must be within 32-bit size.

- A nonce S, which is used as salt for password hashing applications. Its length must be within 32-bit size.
- A degree of parallelism p that determines how many independent (but synchronized) threads can be run. Its value should be within 24-bit size (minimum is 1).
- A tag, which length should be within 2 and 32-bit.
- A memory size m, which is a number expressed in Kibibytes.
- A number of internal iterations t, which is used to tune the running time independently of the memory size. Its value should be within 32-bit size (minimum is 1).

These input parameters are used in our framework to define the computational boundary of the algorithm execution on a specific class of hardware machines. Once the parameters are set, the output of the PoW algorithm only depends on the hardware platform.

2.3 Side-Channel Measurement

Various techniques have been proposed to detect if applications are running inside a sandbox/virtualizer/emulator. The most reliable of them is based on timing measurements [42]. Indeed, fine grained timers help also to build microarchitectural attacks such as Spectre and Meltdown [41,51]. The intuition behind our work is that PoW algorithms offer strong cryptographic properties with a very stable complexity growth, which make the approach very resilient to any countermeasure, such as using more powerful bare-metal machines to enhance performance and reduce the space for time measurements.

By exploiting the asymptotic behavior of the PoW algorithms, we build a statistical model that can be used to guess the class of environment where the algorithm is running and consequently distinguish between physical and virtualized, emulated or simulated architectures, like different flavors of malware sandboxes. Indeed, even fine grained red-pills techniques [64] such as CPU instruction misbehavior can be easily fixed in the sandbox or spoofed to thwart evasion techniques. On the other hand PoW stands on top of well defined mathematical and well defined computational behavior. Moreover, a simple modification of the PoW library avoids the malware sample to be fingerprinted by static techniques. If we take as an example of PoW complexity the one that is run in the crypto currency environment, we know that by design the computation complexity of the algorithm is increased for each new block of the blockchain transaction [58]. Such an increase of computation shows the asymptotic behavior that can be exploited by our technique. By applying PoW as a malware sandbox evasion technique, we get an off-the-shelf technique which improves the malware resilience and limits its analysis.

3   Our Approach: POW-HOW

This section describes our threat model before describing our approach in detail. We first provide an overview of the technique (Sect. 3.2) and its main workflow.

We then describe how the key parameters are estimated (Sects. 3.3 and 3.4) and how an arbitrary sample can be equipped with the evasion module (Sect. 3.5).

3.1 Threat Model

In this paper, we assume a malware scanning service based on virtualized or emulated sandboxes, which allows users to upload and scan their individual files for free as many times as they need. Such a service joins together results from various state-of-the-art malware analysis sandboxes before responding back to the user with a detailed report about the detection outcome of each and every sandbox scanner used.

On the other hand, we assume an attacker who developed a program that includes (i) some malicious payload along with (ii) a technique to pause or alter the execution of the malicious program itself, when a possible malware analysis environment is detected. Before distributing the malicious program to the victims, the attacker may use a malware scanning service to assess its evasiveness.

3.2 System Design

As described in Sect. 2, PoW puzzles have moderately high solving cost and a very small verification time, like problems in the NP complexity class [76]. This implies that their asymptotic behavior is constant in terms of computational cost [32], e.g., CPU and memory consumption. PoW-How exploits this asymptotic behavior to build a statistical model that can be used to identify the class of hardware machines where the algorithm is running. Such a model can later be used to distinguish between physical and virtualized architectures, like those present in malware sandboxes. PoW-How is a three-step pipeline (see Fig. 1):

1. *Performance Profiling.* It executes multiple PoW algorithms on several hardware and operating systems using different configuration settings and system loads.
2. *Model estimation.* The previous step provides the system with a measurement of the amount of time needed to execute the PoW on real hardware. By using the Bienaymé–Chebyshev [8] inequality, it then estimates the time (threshold) expected for a particular configuration to run on a given architecture.
3. *Integration.* Once the models are built, a malware developer can select a specific PoW and parameters to associate with an arbitrary malware sample. PoW-How then generates a module with the chosen PoW, which is integrated with the sample by building a single statically-linked executable.

As ground truth, our methodology leverages a custom Cuckoo Sandbox [37] and popular crowd-sourced malware scanning services (like VirusTotal or similar [63]), as a testbed to report on the accuracy of the evasiveness of the malware in real-world settings.

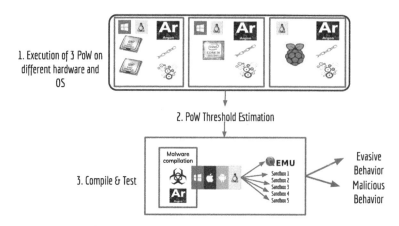

Fig. 1. High level overview of PoW-How. Step 1: execution of the PoW on several hardware/OSes using different configuration settings and system load. Step 2: threshold estimation based on execution time per configuration/architecture. Step 3: malware integration and test.

3.3   Performance Profiling

The first step in PoW-How's pipeline produces a number of PoW executions using different algorithms, parameters, hardware, operating systems, and load settings:

Hardware: PoW-How leverages three machines representative of low, medium, and high-end platforms. The high-end machine is a desktop equipped with an Intel(R) Core(TM) i9-9900X CPU @ 3.50 GHz with 10 physical cores and 20 threads equipped with a PCI-e M2 512 GB disk and 32 GB of RAM. The medium-end machine is a workstation equipped with a Dual Intel(R) Xeon(R) CPU E5-2643 0 @ 3.30 GHz with 16 physical cores and 64 GB of RAM. Finally, the low-end device is a Raspberry Pi 3 which comes with a quad core ARMv7 Processor rev 4 (v7l) and 1 GB of RAM.

Systems and Loads: With the exception of the Raspberry Pi 3, the other hardware platforms are setup in dual boot, supporting both Linux Ubuntu 18.04.3 (64 bits) and Windows 10 (64 bits). Each platform can be further configured in *idle* and *busy* mode. The latter is achieved using `iperf` [31] a CPU bound network traffic generator to keep the operating system and the CPU occupied.

PoW and Parameters: PoW-How currently supports three popular PoW algorithms: Catena [24], Argon2 [17,18], and Yescrypt [7]. Each PoW algorithm is executed multiple times with different input parameters on each hardware platform, operating system, and load setting. The parameters of each algorithm allow to control the amount of memory, parallelism, and complexity of the PoW. Our selection is based on common configuration of COTS hardware devices, with respect to memory and CPU. However, not all the selected algorithms have these parameters available for tuning and in some cases, their tuning is more coarse grained [24].

3.4 Threshold Estimation

The second step in PoW-How's pipeline aims at estimating the PoW thresholds for different settings (PoW algorithm, parameters, hardware, operating system, and load). This is achieved through a statistical characterization of the execution time in each setting using the Bienaymé–Chebyshev inequality [8]. This is a well-known result in probability theory stating that for a large class of distributions, no more than $\frac{1}{k^2}$ values of a distribution X can be more than k standard deviations (σ) away from the mean (μ):

$$Pr(|X - \mu| \geq k\sigma) \leq \frac{1}{k^2} \tag{1}$$

Using the empirical distribution of execution time observed in the previous step, this inequality allows us to select a threshold T (*i.e.*, a maximum execution time) which guarantees a high sample population coverage. The previous deduction enables us to determine with high probability the time T it will take for a PoW to run if the underlying platform is not virtualized. To reduce false positives, the evasion rule can be generalized to "the execution environment is virtualized if the PoW does not complete N executions in less than T seconds".

3.5 Malware Integration and Testing

The final step in PoW-How's pipeline is PoW integration with a malware sample provided as input. At this step, the attacker can upload its sample to PoW-How and select the PoW-based evasion mechanism to be used, along with its parameters. PoW-How further informs the attacker about the predicted accuracy of this selection.

PoW-How integrates the uploaded malware with the PoW selected and the Boost C++ libraries [62], which ease the OS interaction to build a single statically-linked executable. The compilation stage is automated as an Ansible [66] playbook and clang [52]. The integration is achieved at linking stage, so the malware will have a stub call to an external symbol that will be linked with the chosen PoW. PoW-How's pipeline then starts the Ansible scripts, which runs some tests and launch the compilation of the final binary for multiple platforms automatically.

Testing: To evaluate the accuracy of the newly generated evasion mechanism, we rely both on a local sandbox—a custom Cuckoo Sandbox [37] equipped with Windows 10 (64 bits), which is the most targeted OS for malware campaigns [75]—and several on-line free-of-charge sandbox services [63]. Once this step is completed, PoW-How offers to the user access to the set of reports generated by each sandbox.

Table 1. Number of consecutive PoW executions per hardware and OS combination over 24 h. For a given platform, the first line refers to results obtained with the *idle* setting, while the second line refers to *busy* setting.

Platform	Status	Win 10	Ubuntu 18.03
Intel i9	*idle*	4,500	9,325
	busy	3,642	8,867
Dual Intel Xeon	*idle*	6,005	7,897
	busy	4,320	7,012
Raspberry Pi 3	*idle*	–	300
	busy	–	143

Table 2. Statistical measurement results for Catena.

Garlic graph size	Min	Max	Sigma	Mean	K	Chebyshev
15	0.12	5.35	0.503	0.209	9.99	99.00%
18	1.13	35.61	4.22	1.86	7.94	98.41%
20	5.11	165.57	19.01	8.26	8.26	98.54%

4 Evaluation

In this section, we evaluate PoW-How's pipeline. We first analyze the combination of PoWs and their parameters currently supported by PoW-How. The outcome of this evaluation are the parameters N (cycle of execution made in less than T second) and T (maximum execution time) to be associated with the malware sample. We then discuss the accuracy of our evasion mechanism across using various case studies across three public malware scanning services: [9–11], along with our own Cuckoo Sandbox instance.

4.1 Threshold Estimation and PoW Algorithm Choice

For each PoW, we have selected different configurations with respect to memory footprint, parallelism, and algorithm internal iterations (see Tables 2 for Catena and 3 for Argon2i and Yescryot). Argon2i and Yescrypt have similar parameters (memory, number of threads, blocks) whereas Catena's only parameter is a graph size which grows in memory and will make its computation harder as the graph size increases.

PoW-How executes each PoW configuration on the low-end (Raspberry Pi 3), medium-end (Dual Intel Xeon), and high-end (Intel i9) machines. All PoW configurations are executed sequentially during 24 h on each machine for both idle and busy conditions. As pointed out in Sect. 3, with the exception of the Raspberry Pi 3, all tests are performed on two operating system per hardware platform: Linux Ubuntu 18.04.3 (64 bits) and Windows 10 (64 bits).

Table 1 shows the total number of PoW executed over 24 h per hardware, operating systems, and CPU load (*idle* or *busy*). Regardless of the CPU load on each machine, we observe two key insights. First, there is a significant drop in the number of PoW executions when considering Linux vs Windows, which is close to a 50% reduction in the high-end machine. This is due to operating system interaction, ABI and binary format, and ultimately idle cycle management. Second, a 30x reduction in the number of PoW executions when comparing high-end and low-end platforms, e.g., under no additional load the Raspberry Pi 3 completes 300 executions versus an average of 8,611 executions on both the high and medium-end machines. Finally, extra load on the medium and high-end machines causes a reduction in number of proofs computation of about 6–10%, averaging out to 7,300 executions between the two machines. A more dramatic 50% reduction was instead measured for the Raspberry Pi 3.

Next, we statistically investigate PoW execution times by mean of the Bienaymé–Chebyshev inequality (see Sect. 3.4). To balance equally sized datasets, we sampled 150 random executions (*i.e.*, the total number of executions that were possible to complete on the low-end platform) from the 9,325 executions available from both the medium and high-end platforms. Tables 2 and 3 show for each PoW and configuration, several statistics (min, max, σ, and K, Chebyshev inequality) of the PoW execution time computed across hardware platforms, OSes (when available), and load condition (idle, busy). Overall, we measured Chebyshev inequality values higher than 97% regardless of the PoW and its configuration. This confirms high determinism in the PoW execution times on real hardware, validating the main intuition behind this work.

Algorithm Choice: The results above provide the basis to select a PoW algorithm along with its parameters to integrate with the input malware sample. These results indicate that PoW selection has minimal impact on the expected accuracy of the proposed evasion mechanism. We then selected Argon2i (with 8 threads, 100 internal functions and 4KiB of memory) motivated by its robustness and maturity. We leverage the results from Table 3 (top, second line) to set the parameters N (PoW execution) and T (evasion threshold) of an Argon-based evasion mechanism. The table shows that $K = 8.1\,s$ allows a good coverage for the execution time population (98.3%). We opted for a more conservative value of $T = 10$ and further performed multiple tests on our internal Cuckoo Sandbox. Given that our Cuckoo Sandbox could not even execute 1 PoW with $T = 10$, we simply set $N > 1$. We will use this configuration for the experimentation described in the remaining of this paper.

4.2 Case Study: Known Malware

We first analyze the effect of adding our PoW-based evasion strategy to the code of two well-known ransomware samples: Relec and Forbidden Tear. The use of real-world malwares, which are well know and thus easy to detect, allows us to comment on the impact that PoW-based evasion has on *malware reuse*, the practice of recycling old malware for new attacks. We use POW-HOW to generate various combinations of each original ransomware with/without PoW-based evasion strategy, code virtualization[2], and packing offered by Themida, a well-known commercial packer [61]. We verify that all the malicious operations of the original malwares were preserved across the generated versions.

---

[2] This cannot be applied to ForbiddenTear since it is written in .NET.

Table 3. Statistical measurement results for Argon2i (top) and Yescrypt (bottom). Thr. = number of threads. It. = number of algorithm steps. Mem. = amount of memory used in KiB. Cheb. = Chebyshev coverage.

Thr.	It.	Mem.	Min	Max	Sigma	Mean	K	Cheb.
1	10	1 KB	0.01	0.70	0.09	0.02	7.9	98.4%
8	100	4 KB	0.20	9.28	1.07	0.46	8.1	98.3%
16	500	8 KB	2.03	88.8	10.5	3.85	7.9	98.4%
1	1K	8 KB	0.00	0.02	0.00	0.01	6.1	97.3%
8	2K	32 KB	0.03	0.56	0.05	0.05	10.5	99.1%
16	4K	64 KB	0.08	5.00	0.51	0.19	9.4	98.9%

Table 4. Online Sandbox detection results for 2 ransomware samples (Relec and Forbidden Tear) and a benign test program using various anti-analysis configurations.

Test	Relec	Forbidden tear	Hello world
Original	23/72	26/72	3/72
Original+Code virtualizer	32/72	n/a	19/72
Original+Themida	33/72	21/72	17/72
Original+PoW+ Code virtualizer	29/72	n/a	0/72
Original+PoW+ Themida	32/72	18/72	9/72
Original+PoW	**3/71**	**3/72**	**2/72**

We submitted all malware variants to three online sandboxes for analysis and checked how many AV engines (antivirus products) flag each variant as malicious (see Table 4). In the case of Relec, adding code virtualization or packing, results in more AV engines detecting the sample as malicious. This is likely due to the engines flagging such protections, not the malware sample itself. In all cases, the addition of PoW decreases the number of detections by a factor of 10 [14], reaching a level where the difference between the label *malicious* and *false positive* is evanescent.

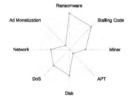

Fig. 2. Behavioral map of the malware PoC *without* PoW and *without* full static protection enabled.

Fig. 3. Behavioral map of the malware PoC *without* PoW and *with* full static protection enabled.

Fig. 4. Behavioral map of the malware PoC *with* PoW and *with* full static protection enabled.

Table 4 also show results when submitting several variants of a standard Hello World program. Note that the original code has been flagged as malicious by 3 AV engines, though as it is possible to see from the report the detections are mislabeled *i.e.,* Relec is not recognized. This false positive could be due to a large number of submissions of the same code hash (due to its simplicity and popularity), our source IP being flagged, and other unknown factors which may influence the scoring. The table also shows that adding code virtualization or packing translates into a substantial increase in false positive detections even of a simple Hello World program, confirming our intuition above. Instead, adding our PoW-based evasion strategy results in less false positives, one less than the original code. This is likely due to the fact that our code on top of Hello World has more entropy, respect to a very simple one line program, looking more legit to engines that measure such kind of parameters.

Overall, these three case studies show that a PoW-based evasion strategy reduces the number of detections by 10x with known malware by preventing the sample from executing in the analysis sandbox. This result demonstrates large potential for malware reuse by coupling it with PoW-based evasion strategy. In the next section, we perform more controlled experiments based on *fresh* (*i.e.*, previously unseen) malware.

4.3   Case Study: Fresh Malware Sample

In order to further explore the results obtained in the previous case studies, we wrote a simple malware PoC (roughly 150 LoC) for Windows 10 (VC++) and Linux (C++). Our malware sample implements a basic ransomware functionality which scans the entire hard drive and encrypts all its files. This behavior should be easy to detect by any malware scanning services.[3] Using PoW-How, we automatically embed a PoW (Argon2i, as we will discuss below) and make sure to exhibit its malicious activity only if the PoW is successfully executed at least N times before a timeout T. Finally, we submitted different variants of our malware sample (with PoW, without PoW, with static sanitization) to several on-line sandboxes and the results were disheartening (see Table 5). For the static sanitation we remove the symbol tables and debugging symbols. Note that very similar results were also achieved with our local Cuckoo Sandbox. It is important to note that to check the execution of the malware payload we insert a *create-file* function at the beginning of the malware payload itself. Such file creation is visible on the behavioral report of the analyzed sandboxes in case the malware payload is executed[4]. We used such a simple test to check whether the PoW algorithm detects the emulated environment and so validate our technique. In case such a file is not present on the behavioral report, it means the PoW algorithm detects the emulated environment and stops the payload execution. None of the analyzed sandboxes is able to execute more than 1 PoW during $T = 10$ (or even $T = 20$ s), which is worse than what a Raspberry Pi 3 can do even in presence of some extra load (e.g., see max value in the top of Table 1).

We made all the reports of our analysis publicly available, including screenshots of evasive malware samples[5]. It has to be noted that not all sandboxes

---

[3] The malware detection report for this malware without our PoW-based evasive measure has been anonymized [1, 12].

[4] This reference has been anonymized not to violate the terms of service of sandbox vendors [1].

[5] The references have been anonymized not to violate the terms of service of sandbox vendors [1, 1, 1–5].

report are the same, but they all signal the hard drive scan (Ransomware behavior) without full static protection (i.e., with the default compiler options). In Table 5 the number of PoW executed is visible only if a screenshot of the sandbox is available. As for the sandbox execution timeout, not all the analysis services had it available for selection.

Detection Rate Decrease: As it is possible to see PoW-How's approach is capable of reducing to zero the detection rate of roughly 70 antiviruses run by the tested sandboxes [9–11] for any sample that we have tested. We have investigated the multiple facets of our technique (static and dynamic). Thus we conclude after looking also at the behavioural results of our samples that the whole technique is capable of reducing the detection rate to zero. The behavioural part plays a fundamental role as it is possible to see from the Hello World example and the behavioural maps generated by AV labels of Figs. 2, 3 and 4.

5 Security Analysis

The results shown in the previous section demonstrate that a PoW-How-ed malware can effectively detect a sandbox and abort the execution of any malicious payload. This strategy is effective in getting a malware sample marked as "clean" by all sandboxes tested by PoW-How (see Table 5). **PoW-How's technique is simple to deploy, it does not require precise timing measurements and, thanks to its algorithmic properties, it will last for many years as a potential threat.**

We next discuss in detail the *behavioral* analysis of our malware. This is an analysis produced by a sandbox related to how a malware interacts with file system, network, and memory. If any of the monitored operations matches a known pattern, the sandbox can raise an alarm.

Figures 2, 3, and 4 show the behavioral analysis of our malware on a radar plot, labelled with most prevalent AV labels. The samples were submitted with different combinations of PoW and static protection. In Fig. 2, the radar plot is mostly "green" (benign) with respect to some operations like phishing, banker and adware for which we would not expect otherwise. However, four "suspicious" (orange) behaviors are reported with respect to evader, spyware, ransomware, Trojan operations. While our malware PoC is not labeled as "malicious" (red), the suspicious flags for our binary would trigger further manual analysis that coukd reveal its maliciousness. It is thus paramount to investigate and mitigate such suspicious flags.

Our intuition is that the suspicious flags are due to the fact that our malware is neither packed nor stripped, and hence some of its functionality *i.e.,* exported functions, linked libraries, and function names are visible through basic static analysis that is usually also implemented in the dynamic sandbox environment. Accordingly, we strip out the whole static information from our binary and resubmit it as a new binary. Figure 3 shows the behavioral analysis of our PoC malware without PoW-based sandbox detection but with full static protection enabled. As expected, various signals have dropped from the behavioral report.

Table 5. Execution results of a custom ransomware sample on various sandboxes

Sandbox	Evasion timeout	PoW timeout	# of PoW executed	Timeout	Notes
Sandbox1	10 s	50	1	120	Clean
Sandbox1	15 s	45	1	180	Clean
Sandbox1	20 s	40	1	240	Clean
Sandbox1	20 s	15	1	500	Clean
Sandbox2	20 s	15	0	N/A	Clean
Sandbox3	20 s	45	N/A	N/A	Clean
Sandbox3	20 s	15	N/A	N/A	Clean

Finally, Fig. 4 shows the result of adding PoW to the last binary. A completely green radar plot which does not raise any suspicion illustrates the evasion effect of PoW-How.

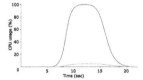 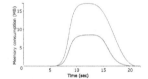 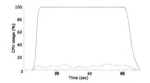

Fig. 5. CPU consumption of our malware PoC (Argon2d) Malware: red line, System Idle (PID 0): green line. (Color figure online)

Fig. 6. Memory consumption of our malware PoC (Argon2d) Malware: red line, System Idle (PID 0): green line. (Color figure online)

Fig. 7. CPU consumption of our malware PoC. T = 60 s and 0.5 s between each PoW execution. Malware: red line, System Idle (PID 0): green line. (Color figure online)

CPU and Memory Usage: The main downside of associating a PoW with a malware sample is an increase in both CPU and memory consumption. We here report on CPU and memory consumption as measured by our sandbox. Figures 5 and 6 compare, respectively, CPU and memory utilization of our malware (red line) with System Idle (PID 0). With respect to CPU usage, the PoW associated with our malware causes an (expected) 100% utilization for the whole duration of the PoW ($T = 10$ s). With respect to memory utilization, our malware only requires about 17 MB versus the 7 MB that utilizes a sample system process like System Idle (PID 0). This is a minor increase, unlikely to raise any suspicion.

Next, we investigate whether we can reduce the CPU usage of our PoC ransomware by setting a longer T (e.g., 60 s) and a sleep of 0.5 s between each PoW execution. Despite such sleeps, Fig. 7 still shows 100% CPU utilization for the whole T (60 s in this test). The lack of CPU reduction associated with the extra sleeps is counter-intuitive. The likely explanation is that the sandbox leverages a coarse CPU monitoring tool and, thus, the CPU reduction associated with our extra sleeps gets averaged out. These results provide a foundation to detect evasion techniques based on PoW. A sandbox could attempt heuristics based on a binary's CPU and memory consumption. We argue, however, that this is quite challenging because of the potential high number of false positives that can be generated.

6   Countermeasures

Evasion techniques are easily comparable with other anti-analysis techniques like *packing*. Packing techniques have evolved to such sophistication that it has become practically impossible to unpack a malware sample without dynamically executing it [38,72]. However, dynamically executing a sample can indeed trigger evasion techniques like stalling code. To counter evasion techniques, and especially the ones that PoW-How implements, one idea would be to fingerprint the algorithms, e.g., CPU and memory footprint. However, it would be very easy for attackers to apply code polimorphism techniques and produce variants that diverge from the original implementation, as it is done with packers. This will constitute a challenge for the sandbox, which could generate a false negative by not being able to spot the algorithm. In Table 4, the Hello World program is detected as malicious and our technique reduces its detection rate and with a code virtualizer it makes the sample completely stealth.

Fingerprinting Evasion: A common solution against red pills [64] is to reduce the amount of instructions failing due to emulation. As Martignoni et al. [54,55] show, the analysis can be automated and the fixes can be easily produced. However, with PoW the computational model is not seeking for emulation/virtualization failures or malfunctions. Instead, PoW is acting as a probe to spot a side channel in the execution time of the algorithm, which in this case is time-based.

Virtualized Instructions Set: Native execution of the cryptographic instructions is another potential countermeasure that could be considered to mitigate our approach. In such a case, the cryptographic instructions of the PoW algorithm are not emulated by the sandbox environment, but directly executed on the native CPU. Avoiding the emulation of the cryptographic instructions could clearly improve the computational performance of the PoW algorithm and reduce the success probability of the evasive behavior showed by PoW-How. The technique described in the Inspector Gadget paper [43], which works at the program analysis level, may also work to avoid the execution of our evasion code. Once the sample is unpacked, it would be possible to extract and execute only the malware branch of the code as a gadget and analyze its behavior in isolation. However, a sufficiently complex packer or emulator would make such process very tedious and require manual effort, which makes this solution excessively complex to be implemented in an automated malware analysis service.

Specialized Hardware: Even if our choice, Argon2, is resilient to specialized circuits for mining (ASICs and FPGAs), other PoW algorithms are not, and hence an analyst could equip his sandbox with a miner [71]. Such a dedicated hardware is expensive for a non-professional user (around $3,000 at the time of writing). Nonetheless, if the phenomenon of sandbox evasion due to PoW proliferate, having such a platform would be of great help to offload the PoW calculations, through a tailored interface, and continue the execution of the malware sample inside the sandbox. The cost/benefit trade-off of adopting such a measure really depends on the intended scale of the analysis platform. For example, according to VirusTotal statistics [25], the service receives weekly more than 3M PE binaries. Hence, a dedicated hardware to defeat PoW evasion based techniques seem a good compromise, since it allows to analyze and discover new malicious behaviors.

Spoofing Timers: The sandbox that gets a POW-HOW-ed malware could try to delay the time, which could mean to make our $T = 10\,s$ last much longer to achieve the payload execution. This approach may work well. Though, if we expect a total of at least 50 PoW iterations (see Sect. 3.4) and the sandbox is not able to execute more than one in about a minute for a unique malware sample, the analysis would take more than one hour. This will eventually extract the payload that will then require extra work to be reverse engineered, understood, and fingerprinted. Hence, this approach may not scale in terms of time/cost for the large number of samples that online sandboxes analyze daily.

Bare-Metal Sandboxes: Using bare metal hardware represents a reasonable solution that might be adopted within corporate companies but it is not possible to use such technology at Internet scale, *i.e.,* cloud-based solutions like Virus Total. Also, isolated sandboxes do not benefit of the information that on-line in cloud services have which leverages large scale cross-correlations.

7   Discussion

7.1   Ethical Considerations

The results obtained by POW-HOW regarding the analyzed publicly available sandboxes, normally used by malware analysts under their term of service (ToS), demonstrate that our technique works consistently either in our custom Cuckoo Sandbox implementation or in proprietary solutions. Our aim, though, is not to disrupt any business nor to difficult the operation of companies that profit from providing malware behavior analysis. We contacted all the platforms and vendors that we have tested with POW-HOW and we notified them about our findings. Part of the vendors were very positive and agreed to further collaborate to work on practical countermeasures. Unfortunately, the response we received from other vendors opposed any dissemination of our results, adopting a short-sighted security-through-obscurity approach which is not novel in our community. Consequently, tested vendors have been anonymized to avoid violation of their ToS. We purposely maintained the number of new variants submitted to the bare minimum, but our approach may transform easily any existing sample into a new one. The authors are available for contact for further information disclosure.

7.2 Bare-Metal Environments

In [40] the authors present BareCloud a bare-metal system which helps to detect evasive malware. This system in order to execute malware trades visibility against transparency. In other words it makes the analysis system transparent (non-detectable by malware) and produces less powerful analysis data (limited instrumentation). Indeed their detection technique leverages hierarchical similarity [33] comparison between different malware execution traces (virtualized and emulated) systems i.e., (Ether [29], Anubis [16], and VirtualBox [37]). One of the biggest problem of hierarchical similarity algorithms is scalability, which means that the algorithm should be polynomial in time and space. An example [60] of application and analysis of hierarchical similarity for binary program comparison shows $O(n^2)$ complexity. Hence using BareCloud as a production system for example for VirusTotal which claims [25] about 1.5M daily submissions means that the hierarchical comparison would approximate 2.250 billion of operations daily to detect evasive malware with bare metal equipment. It is evident that BareCloud can be useful in special cases, as briefly stated above, where also a manual analyst can make the difference. For the sake of scalability though virtualization and emulation methods cannot be fully replaced, even if it would be possible to instrument in hardware an entire system [49], the approach would suffer many other issues, for instance having a lot of physical hardware and maintaining it.

7.3 Economical Denial of Sustainability

Online sandboxes, like any other business, have costs to sustain. Ignoring evasive malware to avoid an additional cost is (for now) understandable. Unfortunately, malware that exploits PoW-How's technique implies additional energy and memory costs, especially if submitted in large scale to such systems, opening avenues to EDoS attacks, which will try to make the on-line service not sustainable economically. These on-line services receive on average 1.5M samples daily. It is not difficult to imagine how much energy just a tenth of the total submissions can consume if it is running PoW. Such algorithm is one of the most energy intensive operation that a computer can perform. For instance, the yearly energy consumption of Bitcoin's blockchain is comparable to the one of a country such as Tunisia or Czech Republic [28]. We strongly recommend that not all evasion techniques are the same, and every technique that exploits hardware consumption side channels should be properly analyzed to avoid service disruption.

8 Related Work

There is a significant body of research [20, 22, 35, 45, 68, 69, 78] focusing on both designing novel evasion techniques for malware and also providing mechanisms to detect them. We next discuss the most relevant works related to ours.

Fingerprinting emulated environments: By recognizing the sandboxes of different vendors, malware can identify the distinguishing characteristics of a given emulated environment and alter its behavior accordingly. The work in [67] introduced the notion of *red pill* and released a short exploit code snippet that could be used to detect whether the code is executed under a VM or in a real platform. In [64], the authors propose an automatic and systematic technique (based on EmuFuzzer [54]) to generate red pills for detecting whether a program is executed inside a CPU emulator. In [55], the authors build KEmuFuzzer, which leverages protocol-specific fuzzing and differential analysis. KEmuFuzzer forces the hosting virtual machine and the underlying physical machine to execute specially crafted snippets of user- and system-mode code before comparing their behaviors. In [19] authors presented AVLeak, a tool that can fingerprint emulators running inside commercial antivirus (AV) software, which are used whenever AVs detect an unknown executable. The authors developed an approach that allows them to deal with these emulators as black boxes and then use side channels for extracting fingerprints from each AV engine. Instead, we show that even with completely transparent analysis programs, the real environment can be used by the malware to determine that it is under analysis. In [56] authors propose a ML-based approach to detect emulated environments. This technique is based on the use of features such as the number of running processes, shared DLLs, size of temporary files, browser cookies, etc. These features are named by the authors "wear-and-tear artifacts" and are present in real system as opposed to sandboxes. The authors use such features to train an SVM classifier. We also rely on modeling a distinguishing feature, in our case is a time channel arising from the asymptotic behavior of a Pow, not the presence or absence of system artefacts.

In [34], authors introduce the virtual machine monitor (VMM) detection and they propose a fuzzy benchmark approach that works by making timing measurements of the execution time of particular code sequences executed on the remote system. The fuzziness comes from heuristics which they employ to learn characteristics of the remote system's hardware and its configuration. In [23], the authors present a technique that leverages TCP timestamps to detect anomalous clock skews in VMs. A downside of the approach is that it requires the transmission of streams of hundreds of SYN packets to the VM, something that can be detected in the case of a honeypot VM and flagged as malicious behavior. Compared to the previous approaches, POW-HOW is more principled and offers a solid basis founded on cryptographic primitives (PoW) with a predictable and reproducible computational behavior on different tested platforms.

Detecting Evasive Malware: In [30], the authors propose Ether, a malware analyzer that eliminates in-guest software components vulnerable to detection. Ether leverages hardware virtualization extensions such as Intel VT, thus residing outside of the target OS environment. In [40], the authors present an automated evasive malware detection system based on bare-metal dynamic malware analysis. Their approach is designed to be transparent and thus robust against sophisticated evasion techniques. The evaluation results showed that it could automatically detect 5,835 evasive malware out of 110,005 tested samples. In [15], authors propose a technique to detect malware that deploys evasion mechanisms. Their approach works by comparing the system call trace recorded when running a malware program on a reference system with the behavior observed in the analysis environment. In [50], authors propose a system for detecting environment-sensitive malware by comparing its behavior in multiple analysis sandboxes in an automated way. Compared to previous techniques, our approach is agnostic to system artifacts and cannot be recognized by only monitoring the system operations.

9 Conclusion

Online malware scanning services are becoming more and more popular, allowing users to upload and scan artefacts against AV engines and malware analysis sandboxes. Common mechanisms used by malware samples to avoid detection include the inspection of signals that imply the existence of a virtualized or emulated environment. These strategies triggered an arms-race where online malware scanners patch such signals to make virtualization transparent. In this paper, we leverage PoW techniques as the basis for a novel malware evasion technique due to their ability to fingerprint real hardware. We provide empirical evidence of how it can be used to evade online malware analysis sandboxes and discuss potential countermeasures. The implementation of our approach goes beyond a simple proof-of-concept, showing that injecting evasion modules can be easily automated on any arbitrary sample. We make our code and results publicly available in an attempt to increase reproducibility and stimulate further research in this area.

References

1. Evasive malware analysis report (2020). anonymized
2. Evasive malware analysis report - 1 (2020). anonymized
3. Evasive malware analysis report - 2 (2020). anonymized
4. Evasive malware analysis report - 3 (2020). anonymized
5. Evasive malware analysis sandbox (2020). anonymized
6. Adam Back: Hashcash: antin-spam tool (2020). http://www.hashcash.org/

7. Alexander Peslyak, T.H.: yescrypt - scalable KDF and password hashing scheme (2015). www.openwall.com/yescrypt
8. Alsmeyer, G.: Chebyshev's inequality. In: Lovric, M. (eds.) International Encyclopedia of Statistical Science. Springer, Heidelberg (2011). https://doi.org/10.1007/978-3-642-04898-2_167
9. anonymized: Sandbox 1 (2020). anonymized
10. anonymized: Sandbox 2 (2020). http://www.anonymized
11. anonymized: Sandbox 3 (2020). http://www.anonymized
12. Nappa, A., et al.: PoC Behaviour (No Evasion) - anonymized (2020). http://www.anonymized
13. Nappa, A., Papadopoulos, P., Varvello, M., Gomez, D.A., Tapiador, J., Lanzi, A.: Artifact repository. https://github.com/anonnymousubmission/Esorics2021_Paper159 (2021)
14. Nappa, A., Papadopoulos, P., Varvello, M., Gomez, D.A., Tapiador, J., Lanzi, A.: Relec + PoW + static sanitization - anonymized (2021). http://www.anonymized
15. Balzarotti, D., Cova, M., Karlberger, C., Vigna, G.: Efficient detection of split personalities in malware. In: Proceedings of the 17th Annual Network and Distributed System Security Symposium (NDSS) (2010)
16. Bayer, U., Comparetti, P.M., Hlauschek, C., Krügel, C., Kirda, E.: Scalable, behavior-based malware clustering. In: NDSS. The Internet Society (2009). http://dblp.uni-trier.de/db/conf/ndss/ndss2009.html#BayerCHKK09
17. Biryukov, A., Dinu, D., Khovratovich, D.: Argon2: new generation of memory-hard functions for password hashing and other applications. In: IEEE European Symposium on Security and Privacy, EuroS&P 2016, Saarbrücken, Germany, 21–24 March 2016 (2016)
18. Biryukov, A., Dinu, D., Khovratovich, D., Josefsson, S.: Argon2 rfc (2019). www.tools.ietf.org/id/draft-irtf-cfrg-argon2-05.html
19. Blackthorne, J., Bulazel, A., Fasano, A., Biernat, P., Yener, B.: AVLeak: fingerprinting antivirus emulators through black-box testing. In: 10th USENIX Workshop on Offensive Technologies (WOOT 16), Austin, TX. USENIX Association, August 2016. https://www.usenix.org/conference/woot16/workshop-program/presentation/blackthorne
20. Brengel, M., Backes, M., Rossow, C.: Detecting hardware-assisted virtualization. In: Caballero, J., Zurutuza, U., Rodríguez, R.J. (eds.) DIMVA 2016. LNCS, vol. 9721, pp. 207–227. Springer, Cham (2016). https://doi.org/10.1007/978-3-319-40667-1_11
21. Caballero, J., Grier, C., Kreibich, C., Paxson, V.: Measuring pay-per-install: the commoditization of malware distribution. In: Proceedings of the 20th USENIX Security Symposium (2011)
22. Canali, D., Lanzi, A., Balzarotti, D., Kruegel, C., Christodorescu, M., Kirda, E.: A quantitative study of accuracy in system call-based malware detection. In: Heimdahl, M.P.E., Su, Z. (eds.) International Symposium on Software Testing and Analysis, ISSTA 2012, Minneapolis, MN, USA, 15–20 July 2012, pp. 122–132. ACM (2012). https://doi.org/10.1145/2338965.2336768
23. Chen, X., Andersen, J., Mao, Z.M., Bailey, M., Nazario, J.: Towards an understanding of anti-virtualization and anti-debugging behavior in modern malware. In: 2008 IEEE International Conference on Dependable Systems and Networks with FTCS and DCC (DSN), pp. 177–186. IEEE (2008)
24. Forler, C., Lucks, S., Wenzel, J.: The catena password-scrambling framework (2015). www.uni-weimar.de/fileadmin/user/fak/medien/professuren/Mediensicherheit/Research/Publications/catena-v3.1.pdf

25. Chronicle Security: File statistics during last 7 days (2020). https://www.virustotal.com/en/statistics/
26. Coker, J.: Evasive malware threats on the rise despite decline in overall attacks (2020). https://www.infosecurity-magazine.com/news/evasive-malware-rise-decline/
27. Cybersecurity Ventures: Global cybercrime damages predicted to reach $6 trillion annually by 2021 (2018). https://cybersecurityventures.com/cybercrime-damages-6-trillion-by-2021/
28. Digiconomist: Yara Signature Detector (2007). https://digiconomist.net/bitcoin-energy-consumption
29. Dinaburg, A., Royal, P., Sharif, M., Lee, W.: Ether: malware analysis via hardware virtualization extensions. In: Proceedings of the 15th ACM Conference on Computer and Communications Security, CCS 2008, New York, NY, USA, pp. 51–62. Association for Computing Machinery (2008). https://doi.org/10.1145/1455770.1455779
30. Dinaburg, A., Royal, P., Sharif, M., Lee, W.: Ether: malware analysis via hardware virtualization extensions. In: Proceedings of the 15th ACM Conference on Computer and Communications Security, pp. 51–62 (2008)
31. Dugan, J., Elliott, S., Mah, B.A., Poskanzer, J., Prabhu, K.: iPerf - the ultimate speed test tool for TCP, UDP and SCTP (2020). https://iperf.fr/
32. Dwork, C., Naor, M.: Pricing via processing or combatting junk mail. In: Brickell, E.F. (ed.) CRYPTO 1992. LNCS, vol. 740, pp. 139–147. Springer, Heidelberg (1993). https://doi.org/10.1007/3-540-48071-4_10
33. Feldman, R., Dagan, I.: Knowledge discovery in textual databases (KDT). In: Proceedings of the First International Conference on Knowledge Discovery and Data Mining, KDD 1995, pp. 112–117. AAAI Press (1995)
34. Franklin, J., Luk, M., McCune, J.M., Seshadri, A., Perrig, A., Van Doorn, L.: Remote detection of virtual machine monitors with fuzzy benchmarking. ACM SIGOPS Oper. Syst. Rev. **42**(3), 83–92 (2008)
35. Graziano, M., Canali, D., Bilge, L., Lanzi, A., Balzarotti, D.: Needles in a haystack: mining information from public dynamic analysis sandboxes for malware intelligence. In: Proceedings of the 24rd USENIX Security Symposium (USENIX Security), August 2015
36. Gu, G., Yegneswaran, V., Porras, P., Stoll, J., Lee, W.: Active botnet probing to identify obscure command and control channels. In: Proceedings of 2009 Annual Computer Security Applications Conference (ACSAC 2009), December 2009
37. Guarnieri, C.: Cuckoo sandbox (2010). https://cuckoosandbox.org/
38. Haq, I.U., Chica, S., Caballero, J., Jha, S.: Malware lineage in the wild. Comput. Secur. **78**(C), 347–363, August 2018. https://doi.org/10.1016/j.cose.2018.07.012
39. Infosecurity Magazine: Cybercrime costs global economy $2.9m per minute (2019). https://www.infosecurity-magazine.com/news/cybercrime-costs-global-economy/
40. Kirat, D., Vigna, G., Kruegel, C.: BareCloud: bare-metal analysis-based evasive malware detection. In: 23rd USENIX Security Symposium (USENIX Security 14), San Diego, CA, pp. 287–301. USENIX Association, August 2014. https://www.usenix.org/conference/usenixsecurity14/technical-sessions/presentation/kirat
41. Kocher, P., et al.: Spectre attacks: exploiting speculative execution. In: 40th IEEE Symposium on Security and Privacy (S&P 2019) (2019)
42. Kocher, P.C.: Timing attacks on implementations of Diffie-Hellman, RSA, DSS, and other systems. In: Koblitz, N. (ed.) CRYPTO 1996. LNCS, vol. 1109, pp. 104–113. Springer, Heidelberg (1996). https://doi.org/10.1007/3-540-68697-5_9

43. Kolbitsch, C., Holz, T., Kruegel, C., Kirda, E.: Inspector gadget: automated extraction of proprietary gadgets from malware binaries. In: 31st IEEE Symposium on Security and Privacy, S&P 2010, Berleley/Oakland, California, USA, 16–19 May 2010, pp. 29–44. IEEE Computer Society (2010). https://doi.org/10.1109/SP.2010.10

44. Kotzias, P., Bilge, L., Caballero, J.: Measuring PUP prevalence and pup distribution through pay-per-install services. In: Proceedings of the 25th USENIX Security Symposium (2016)

45. Lanzi, A., Balzarotti, D., Kruegel, C., Christodorescu, M., Kirda, E.: AccessMiner: using system-centric models for malware protection. In: Al-Shaer, E., Keromytis, A.D., Shmatikov, V. (eds.) Proceedings of the 17th ACM Conference on Computer and Communications Security, CCS 2010, Chicago, Illinois, USA, 4–8 October 2010, pp. 399–412. ACM (2010). https://doi.org/10.1145/1866307.1866353

46. Larimer, D.: Momentum-a memory-hard proof-of-work via finding birthday collisions. Technical report (2014)

47. Lastline Inc.: Not so fast my friend - using inverted timing attacks to bypass dynamic analysis (2014). www.lastline.com/labsblog/not-so-fast-my-friend-using-inverted-timing-attacks-to-bypass-dynamic-analysis/

48. Laurie, B., Clayton, R.: Proof-of-work proves not to work; version 0.2. In: Workshop on Economics and Information, Security (2004)

49. Li, L.W., Duc, G., Pacalet, R.: Hardware-assisted memory tracing on new SoCs embedding FPGA fabrics. In: Proceedings of the 31st Annual Computer Security Applications Conference, ACSAC 2015, New York, NY, USA, pp. 461–470. Association for Computing Machinery (2015). https://doi.org/10.1145/2818000.2818030

50. Lindorfer, M., Kolbitsch, C., Milani Comparetti, P.: Detecting environment-sensitive malware. In: Sommer, R., Balzarotti, D., Maier, G. (eds.) RAID 2011. LNCS, vol. 6961, pp. 338–357. Springer, Heidelberg (2011). https://doi.org/10.1007/978-3-642-23644-0_18

51. Lipp, M., et al.: Meltdown: Reading kernel memory from user space. In: 27th USENIX Security Symposium (USENIX Security 18) (2018)

52. LLVM: Clang: a C language family frontend for LLVM (2020). https://clang.llvm.org/

53. Martignoni, L., Christodorescu, M., Jha, S.: Omniunpack: Fast, generic, and safe unpacking of malware. In: ACSAC 2007 (2007)

54. Martignoni, L., Paleari, R., Fresi Roglia, G., Bruschi, D.: Testing CPU emulators. In: Proceedings of the 2009 International Conference on Software Testing and Analysis (ISSTA), Chicago, Illinois, USA, pp. 261–272. ACM (2009)

55. Martignoni, L., Paleari, R., Fresi Roglia, G., Bruschi, D.: Testing system virtual machines. In: Proceedings of the 2010 International Symposium on Testing and Analysis (ISSTA), Trento, Italy (2010)

56. Miramirkhani, N., Appini, M.P., Nikiforakis, N., Polychronakis, M.: Spotless sandboxes: evading malware analysis systems using wear-and-tear artifacts. In: 2017 IEEE Symposium on Security and Privacy (SP), pp. 1009–1024, May 2017. https://doi.org/10.1109/SP.2017.42

57. Moser, A., Krügel, C., Kirda, E.: Exploring multiple execution paths for malware analysis. In: 2007 IEEE Symposium on Security and Privacy (S&P 2007), Oakland, California, USA, 20–23 May 2007, pp. 231–245. IEEE Computer Society (2007). https://doi.org/10.1109/SP.2007.17

58. Nakamoto, S.: Bitcoin: a peer-to-peer electronic cash system. http://bitcoin.org/bitcoin.pdf

59. Nappa, A., Xu, Z., Rafique, M.Z., Caballero, J., Gu, G.: Cyberprobe: towards internet-scale active detection of malicious servers. In: Proceedings of the 21st Annual Network and Distributed System Security Symposium (NDSS 2014), February 2014
60. Oprişa, C., Ignat, N.: A measure of similarity for binary programs with a hierarchical structure. In: 2015 IEEE International Conference on Intelligent Computer Communication and Processing (ICCP), pp. 117–123 (2015). https://doi.org/10.1109/ICCP.2015.7312615
61. Oreans: Advanced windows software protection system (2020). https://www.oreans.com/themida.php
62. The Boost organization: Boost C++ libraries (2020). https://www.boost.org/
63. Ozarslan, S.: Online malware sandboxes (2016). www.medium.com/@su13ym4n/15-online-sandboxes-for-malware-analysis-f8885ecb8a35
64. Paleari, R., Martignoni, L., Roglia, G.F., Bruschi, D.: A fistful of red-pills: How to automatically generate procedures to detect cpu emulators. In: Proceedings of the 3rd USENIX Conference on Offensive Technologies, WOOT 2009, USA, p. 2. USENIX Association (2009)
65. Protocol Labs: Filecoin: a decentralized storage network (2020). https://filecoin.io/
66. Red Hat Inc.: Ansible it automation (2020). https://github.com/ansible
67. Rutkowska, J.: Red pill ... or how to detect VMM using (almost) one CPU instruction (2004). https://securiteam.com/securityreviews/6z00h20bqs/
68. Sharif, M., Lanzi, A., Giffin, J., Lee, W.: Automatic reverse engineering of malware emulators. In: IEEE Symposium on Security and Privacy, vol. 0, pp. 94–109 (2009). http://doi.ieeecomputersociety.org/10.1109/SP.2009.27
69. Tanabe, R., Ueno, W., Ishii, K., Yoshioka, K., Matsumoto, T., Kasama, T., Inoue, D., Rossow, C.: Evasive malware via identifier implanting. In: Giuffrida, C., Bardin, S., Blanc, G. (eds.) DIMVA 2018. LNCS, vol. 10885, pp. 162–184. Springer, Cham (2018). https://doi.org/10.1007/978-3-319-93411-2_8
70. Tromp, J.: Cuckoo cycle: a memory bound graph-theoretic proof-of-work. In: Brenner, M., Christin, N., Johnson, B., Rohloff, K. (eds.) FC 2015. LNCS, vol. 8976, pp. 49–62. Springer, Heidelberg (2015). https://doi.org/10.1007/978-3-662-48051-9_4
71. Tuwiner, J.: Bitmain antminer s9 review (2017). https://www.buybitcoinworldwide.com/mining/hardware/antminer-s9/
72. Ugarte-Pedrero, X., Balzarotti, D., Santos, I., Bringas, P.G.: SoK: deep packer inspection: a longitudinal study of the complexity of run-time packers. In: 2015 IEEE Symposium on Security and Privacy, pp. 659–673, May 2015. https://doi.org/10.1109/SP.2015.46
73. VirusShare: Virusshare.com - because sharing is caring (2020). https://virusshare.com/1
74. Wang, T., Wei, T., Gu, G., Zou, W.: TaintScope: a checksum-aware directed fuzzing tool for automatic software vulnerability detection. In: Proceedings of the 31st IEEE Symposium on Security and Privacy (Oakland 2010), May 2010
75. Wikipedia: Wannacry ransomware hits prevalently windows (2017). https://en.wikipedia.org/wiki/WannaCry_ransomware_attack/
76. Wong, D.: Np complexity (2013). https://www.cryptologie.net/article/43/np-complexity/

77. Xu, Z., Nappa, A., Baykov, R., Yang, G., Caballero, J., Gu, G.: AutoProbe: towards automatic active malicious server probing using dynamic binary analysis. In: Proceedings of the 21st ACM Conference on Computer and Communication Security (2014)

78. Yokoyama, A., et al.: SandPrint: fingerprinting malware sandboxes to provide intelligence for sandbox evasion. In: Monrose, F., Dacier, M., Blanc, G., Garcia-Alfaro, J. (eds.) RAID 2016. LNCS, vol. 9854, pp. 165–187. Springer, Cham (2016). https://doi.org/10.1007/978-3-319-45719-2_8

Characterizing GPU Overclocking Faults

Eldad Zuberi[(⊠)] and Avishai Wool[(⊠)]

School of Electrical Engineering, Tel Aviv University, 69978 Ramat Aviv, Israel
EldadZuberi@gmail.com, yash@eng.tau.ac.il

Abstract. Graphics Processing Units (GPUs) are powerful parallel processors that are becoming common on computers. They are used in many high-performance tasks such as crypto-mining and neural-network training. It is common to overclock a GPU to gain performance, however this practice may introduce calculation faults. In our work, we lay the foundations to exploiting these faults, by characterizing their formation and structure. We find that temperature is a contributing factor to the fault rate, but is not the sole cause. We also find that faults are a byte-wide phenomenon: individual bit-flips are rare. Surprisingly, we find that the vast majority of byte faults are in fact byte-flips: all 8 bits are simultaneously negated. Finally, we find strong evidence that faults are triggered by memory-remnant reads at an alignment of a 32 byte memory transaction size.

Keywords: CUDA · GPU · Nvidia · Fault injection · DFA · Overclocking

1 Introduction

1.1 Background

GPUs are parallel processors capable of high performance computations. They were originally designed for computer graphics acceleration, but are now commonly used for general purpose computation such as crypto-mining [10,33], deep learning [12], crypto-acceleration [25], cryptanalysis [21] and password cracking [27]. To achieve this, GPUs are built to handle instructions in a SIMD fashion. Such processors perform the same instruction over multiple data, thus accelerating calculations by a factor of the number of cores. Adding a GPU to a system expands the system's attack surface and introduces a new world of security holes: vulnerabilities can be found in drivers and control codes [43], side channel attacks can be performed over multiple number of variables [17], and even the intended design of the GPU can lead to information leakage [22]. In this paper we investigate a less explored part of the GPU's attack surface, dealing with fault injection.

The field of fault injections investigates the threats to a system where faults are introduced during its execution. Fault injection can be applied in many scenarios, such as breaking encryption algorithms [6,7,13] and escalation of privileges in an OS [39,40].

© Springer Nature Switzerland AG 2021
E. Bertino et al. (Eds.): ESORICS 2021, LNCS 12972, pp. 110–130, 2021.
https://doi.org/10.1007/978-3-030-88418-5_6

1.2   Related Work

GPU Security. Researching the security of GPUs was done in many fields. For example, Lee et al. have shown that it is possible to discover the websites last visited by the user [22]. This is possible because the GPU doesn't reset the contents of freed memory. By reallocating all available memory right after the termination of another context, remnants of the first context's data can be extracted and compared with the expected fingerprints of specific websites.

Zhu et al. presented multiple attacks on the GPU [43]. In their work, they managed to run malicious code in two ways: (1) by dynamically patching the GPU driver; and (2) by editing the microcode of a peripheral chip that resides inside the GPU. The chip was accessed using *base address registers*, a set of registers that hold special addresses, and allow the CPU to access other devices' memory layout.

Jiang et al. were able to leak a full AES key in a program that used the GPU to encrypt packets [17], using a timing side channel attack that correlated between the execution time and the data access behaviour.

Work was also done in the field of reverse engineering GPUs: Bialas et al. have researched the way thread divergence is implemented in Nvidia GPUs [5]. Wong et al. have researched Nvidia's GPU architecture through benchmarking [42].

Fault Injection. Much research has been done in the field of injecting faults into encryption algorithms. Boneh et al. showed that by comparing the signature of a correct and a faulty message it is possible to recover the secret key used to generate the signature [7]. Their idea was extended further, leading up to the developing of DFA, a similar technique which can be successfully applied to break DES and AES encrypted messages [6,13]. Since then, many DFA attacks and algorithms were published with the target of decreasing the number of faulty cipher-texts required in order to break the system [9]. While some papers aimed at improving the existing algorithms by reducing the number of required faulty ciphertexts, other investigated the effects of different fault models on the output. For example, algorithms for applying DFA on AES were developed assuming a byte-wide faults model [23,32], a single bit-flip faults model [1,2,13], and even an hybrid-fault model, where faults can happen in a single-byte or in a multi-byte [24].

Many of these algorithms rely on the assumption that the attacker has a way to inject a specific fault (e.g., a byte-level fault) at a precise timing (e.g., between the 8th MixColumn and the 9th MixColumn). However, introducing such faults usually require physical access to the system and sophisticated devices, for example a laser beam [1]. To match other systems, where the faults are intrinsic and less controllable by nature, another model is required. In these systems the faults may occur more randomly, in the sense that they can appear in any round of AES, and that the fault itself is not always predictable. Research has shown both practical setups that are breakable under the random faults assumptions [4,36], and theoretical work to improve the analysis and algorithms used to break such systems [23,32].

Beyond its serious implications on encryption algorithms, the research of fault injection exploitation was also conducted in other areas. Timmers et al. demonstrated achieving code execution by injecting faults during the boot loader stage of an ARM based embedded chip [40]. Their injection led to changing the operands of *load/store* instructions which they leveraged to take control over the *program counter (PC)* register. Later on, it was shown that similar techniques can be applied to Linux kernel running on a chip, leading to privilege escalation [39]. The faults can happen in any stage of the *fetch-decode-execute* instruction processing cycle.

Recently Sabbagh et al. demonstrated a fault injection model which allows breaking AES that is implemented on an AMD GPU, resulting in a complete key recovery [35]. To do so, they developed a tailored DFA for the AES GPU implementation. To inject faults, a combination of overclocking and undervolting (to which they refer as "overdriving") was used. They also found that on the AMD GPU they used, the *load* instruction was the most susceptible to faults. While laying the foundations to breaking AES implemented on a GPU, their work relies on a stringent fault model in which faults can be introduced in "precise" words or rounds. This goes against of the nature of "overdriving" - which introduces random faults that can happen in any stage during the encryption process [36]. To enforce the faults' occurrence location, they added checkpoints to the victim's kernel and discarded any fault that occurred in an undesired location - resulting in an instrumented AES encryption setup that can't be seen in the wild. Additionally, their research was conducted on an AMD GPU, where ours focuses an Nvidia GPU.

Complementing the work of Sabbagh et al. [35], our research further unveils the behaviour of faults generated on an Nvidia GPU in an overclocking situation. Our work supports the infrastructure of many fault injections attacks, including global DFA analysis, and is intended to help the development of exploitation techniques, similar to the work presented by Sabbagh et al. [35]. Our insights on the formation of faults and faults' values may allow future works to become more efficient, and overcome the challenges and assumptions raised by Sabbagh et al. [35]. As our work is general to Nvidia GPUs and not AES-specific, this work should also help to the exploitation of fault injection against other algorithms.

1.3   Contributions

The common ground to exploiting all of these injections is understanding and characterizing the faults behaviour. As far as we know, we are the first to characterize the effects of overclocking on faults formed in an Nvidia GPU. We focus on "global" fault injection, similar to the work done by Selmane et al. [36], where faults occur randomly while the system is executing its algorithm, and the attacker can not control the faults' timing and localization.

We find that temperature is a contributing factor to the fault rate and present the probabilities of a fault when performing a *load* instruction, for multiple temperatures. We also find that faults are a byte-wide phenomenon, and not a bit-wide one. Multi-byte faults occur at a much lower frequency, yet the probability of multi-byte faults increases with temperature as well. We further study the values received when a fault is encountered. Surprisingly, we find that the vast majority of byte faults are in fact byte-flips: all 8 bits are simultaneously negated. The byte-flip class of fault constitutes nearly 92% of the faults. In 7% of the faults, the fault value is composed of a bit-flips, where all the flipped bits are contained in the same byte. Additionally, we see that multi-byte faults appear in around 1% of the samples. Finally, we find strong evidence that faults are triggered by memory-remnant reads. We find the minimal *memory load transaction* size, and show that the memory-remnants that lead to faults are aligned with it.

2   Preliminaries

2.1   CUDA

CUDA is a general purpose parallel computing platform and programming model that leverages the parallel compute engine in Nvidia GPUs. CUDA C++ extends the language by allowing the programmer to define C++ functions, called *kernels*, that, when called, are executed N times by N different CUDA threads [28]. The threads run on up to M hardware cores in the GPU (the number of cores differs between GPU models). Further details can be found in Appendix A.1.

2.2   General GPU Setup

Display. The GPU is capable of two broad tasks: displaying and rendering the screen, and doing general calculations (functioning as a GPGPU). Unless specifically installed otherwise (e.g., [11]) the GPU allows both. In our work, we work with the default setup.

Memory Consistency. GPUs include their own memory. The basic programming model assumes different memory spaces for the *host* (PC) and the *device* (GPU), and therefore an interface is provided by CUDA to manage memory transfers between the device and the host. On early versions of CUDA, if a programmer wanted to transfer a set of data from the device to the host (or vice versa), an explicit action was needed. Functions such as cudaMemcpy combined with flags of the type cudaMemcpyHostToDevice were used to make the desired transfer. This memory type is called "page-locked" or "pinned" memory [28]. Starting with the Kepler architecture and CUDA 6, GPUs support a new type of memory called *unified memory* [15]. This memory is can be shared between the *host* and the *device* by a mechanism of page migration. The existence of such mechanism shifts the responsibility of managing and mirroring the memory from the programmer to the GPU driver [31]. Since the two different types of memory behave differently [8,20] in this paper we focus on characterizing faults in the more basic *pinned memory*.

Temperature Control. Like any modern processor, the GPU has its own set of fans that allow it to cool down during long and intensive executions. The default fan speed changes dynamically according to the temperature.

Nvidia provides APIs to set and query advanced GPU options, e.g., set clock speed and fan speed or query the temperature. Querying these values can be done by a non-root user, but setting them requires root privileges to enable editing them, as they are disabled by default. To enable them the *coolbits* in the *xorg* file have to be turned on [3]. To set and query the relevant properties we used the command line utilities **nvidia-smi** and **nvidia-settings** [29,30].

The *xorg* file can be accessed using the **nvidia-xconfig** utility, or be manually edited. On Ubuntu 18.04 this file can be found at /etc./X11/xorg.conf. To edit this file, *root* permissions are required. However once the respective coolbits are enabled in the *xorg* file, any unprivileged linux user can modify the fan speed values.

2.3   Overclocking

Overclocking means increasing the clock frequency of a chip beyond its factory-default setting. Overclocking is done for various reasons, including enhanced gaming, bitcoin mining and so on. However overclocking has the risk of shortening the cycle time below some critical value such that some instructions execute incorrectly, producing faulty results. In GPUs, overclocking in itself is not considered an adversarial action: in fact, it is a very popular action with many dedicated guides and tools available online [16,18,19], and Nvidia GPUs provide documented APIs and tools to control the overclocking. In modern Nvidia GPUs two different clocks can be overclocked: the *Graphics* Clock and the *Memory Transfer Rate* Clock. In this paper, we only treat the *Memory Transfer Rate* clock.

To find out one's preferred overclocking rates, tutorials are available online (e.g., [37]). These tutorials guide the users through the process of tweaking their GPU's clock value to balance between speed and correctness of calculations. In order to simulate an innocent user in our tests, we followed [37] to find a typical overclocking range a user is likely to receive from such tutorial. It is important to mention that an overclocking rate which still allows the GPU to function properly is unique to each GPU, and differs between different GPU brands, models and even between different GPUs of the exact same model. As with temperature controls, overclocking needs to be enabled by root in the coolbits in the *xorg* file.

2.4   Attack Model

Our attack target is a computer that has a GPU. The attack model assumes that root enabled the "coolbits" to gain enhanced performance. The malicious code is running on the same host with non-root privileges, however it can increase the overclocking frequency and run heavy load programs that can lead to faulty calculations by the GPU. Therefore legitimate GPU-based tasks that the user runs simultaneously are at risk of breach (in case of security tasks e.g., encryption of files/videos) or at risk of malfunctioning. In this way, an attacker can utilize fault injection on background tasks, (e.g., break encryption that runs simultaneously) without the need of high privileges, and without the need to communicate with other processes - which provides a high degree of stealthiness.

3   GPU Faults and Temperature Dependency

3.1   Setup

For this research we used a *GeForce GTX-1660* graphics card with 6 GB RAM and 1408 *CUDA Cores*, using Nvidia Driver version 440.100 and CUDA Version 10.2. The tests were conducted on a PC using an *Intel i7-8700 CPU @ 3.20 GHz* running Ubuntu 18.04. On our system by default the *Memory Transfer Rate* varies between 3 levels, depending on the GPU load. In our tests the GPU immediately shifted to level 3 when kernel code started executing. The level 3 clock rate is 8,002 MHz. The minimal and maximal overclocking rates for our GPU are $[-2000\,\text{MHz}, 6000\,\text{MHz}]$. The selected overclocking rate is added to the default clock, resulting in possible frequencies in the range of $[6{,}002\,\text{MHz}, 14{,}002\,\text{MHz}]$ at level 3. The overclocking values for our GPU were found by following [37], which recommended using values between $[1960\,\text{MHz}–2000\,\text{MHz}]$ for our GPU. The reason for working with a range rather than a specific value is because occasionally with high overclocking the faults were severe enough to cause the GPU to crash/hang. Crashes and hangs usually happened during tests which perform multiple long runs of the program. Most likely, in some stages of these tests high temperature was reached by the GPU which affected its operation in multiple ways. When encountering such situations we rebooted the whole system. To avoid GPU damage, the temperature and faults rate were constantly monitored, and experiments were terminated if thresholds were exceeded.

3.2   Initial Tests

The guide in [37] relies on a complex graphics and data calculation, and it suggests to increase the overclocking as high as possible until visual errors start to appear. We used this method to establish the rough overclocking rate. Then we used a publicly available stress test [41]. This stress test is based on another complex calculation (large floating-point matrix multiplication): we observed that faults indeed occur during the stress test at an overclocking of 2,000 MHz.

We then switched to an encryptor [34] which uses the GPU to parallelize AES in CTR mode. We instrumented the program to repeatedly encrypt the same data, and added a kernel that compares the output to the valid ciphertext. The encryptor was fed with a 1 GB array of random data. With an overclocking of 2,030 MHz, we observed faults that manifested themselves as an incorrect ciphertext bytes after 50 loops (i.e., after encrypting 50 GB of data).

Our first step in characterizing the faults was replacing the stress test code by a much simpler calculation. We switched from floating point to integers,

---

Algorithm 1. The testLoad kernel and its execution configuration syntax

---

```
1   __global__  void  testLoad(int * A, int * A_duplicate, ...)
2   {
3       // ... //
4       if (A[i] != A_duplicate[i])
5           recordFault(A[i], A_duplicate[i], ...);
6   }
7   #define NUM_OF_ELEMENTS (5000000)
8       size_t threads = 256;
9       size_t blocks = (NUM_OF_ELEMENTS + threads - 1) /
        threads;
10      // ... //
11      for (size_t loop_num; loop_num < MAX_LOOPS; loop_num++)
12      {
13          testLoad<<<blocks, threads >>>(...);
14          cudaDeviceSynchronize(); // wait for GPU to finish
15          // ... //
16      }
```

---

and investigated a simple kernel which only performs a single comparison. We randomized a vector with 5 million cells of an integer type, duplicated it to be used for comparison, and tested whether the values loaded from matching cells of the vectors were indeed equal, using the kernel in Algorithm 1. Each execution of the testLoad kernel compared the full content of the vectors. The recordFault function analyzes every fault and records it. The kernels' *execution configuration syntax* were chosen according to Nvidia's suggestion. The choice of the number of threads per block (256), was arbitrary: the kernels have no memory contention. Once allocated on the host device, the vectors were copied to the GPU using cudaMalloc and cudaMemCpy. This means the GPU accessed a copy of the vectors that resided in the GPU's global memory space.

Since faults occur even with this simple kernel, we conclude that when overclocked, it is the *load* instruction that is being executed incorrectly, and not, for instance, the arithmetic floating point instructions.

3.3 Basics of Faults

After establishing that overclocking causes faults in memory loads, we examine the effect of the overclocking on the fault occurrence rate. In Fig. 1 we can see the cumulative number of faults as a function of the time, expressed as the total number of kernel iterations done. In our setup, the connection between time and loop number is roughly $10,000\ [loops] = 2.2\ [s]$. The graph shows results for various overclocking frequencies. From the figure we can see three things:

1. As the overclocking frequency increases, the fault rate increases.
2. Faults begin to appear only after a certain amount of time passes.
3. The fault rate increases in a super-linear fashion over time.

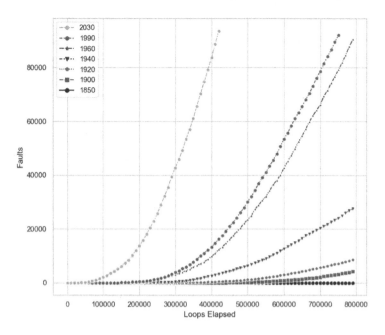

Fig. 1. The total number of faults as a function of the running time, expressed as loop number, for 7 overclocking frequencies. Some curves end early due reaching a cutoff threshold of 90,000 faults.

3.4   The Relationship Between Faults and Temperature

It is well known that GPU computations cause it to heat up. One may hypothesize that faults occur due to the higher temperature rather than because of the overclocking. To test this hypothesis, we ran multiple experiments and changed the GPU's fan speed during the execution. Each experiment had a different threshold temperature that once reached, triggered the fan to run at 99% speed instead of its normal operating point of around 40%. The results of these experiments can be seen in Fig. 2. The bottom graph shows the temperature rising over time, for all 3 temperature thresholds, and stabilizing to a flat line once the fan trigger is reached. The top graph shows the cumulative number of faults for the same experiments. The graph shows that the temperature has a significant effect on the faults' occurrence rate: even though the curves start out with very similar pace, they diverge once the fan is introduced. The introduction of the fan largely prohibits the increase in the temperature, and when the temperature is steady - the fault rate becomes fixed, showing as a linear cumulative curve. This is evident in the curves for 56 and 58°; for 62° the experiment was halted before reaching the threshold temperature.

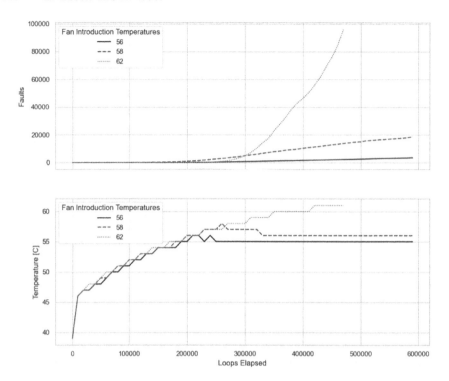

Fig. 2. The cumulative number of faults and temperature as a function of the loop number, for different fan introduction temperatures and for overclocking of 2,000 MHz.

Now that we established that the temperature has a significant impact on the fault rate, we ask whether the results presented in Fig. 1 were affected by the overclocking itself or whether the overclocking just caused the temperature to rise faster, which contributed to the fault rate. To answer this question we provide Fig. 3. In this figure we can see the fault probability as a function of the temperature, for multiple overclocking rates. The figure clearly shows that while higher temperature causes more faults - the overclocking rate is crucial: at the same temperature, higher overclocking produces significantly more faults. Therefore it is evident that the temperature itself is not enough to determine the fault rate. The fault rate is rather determined by a combination of both the overclocking and temperature, and as we shall see, by additional factors.

4   Faults Boundaries and Values

4.1   The Boundaries of Faults

Understanding the faults boundaries is vital for the analysis of and exploitation fault injection, as mentioned in Sect. 1.2. To understand the fault boundaries we conducted the following test. We filled the arrays with random data, used the

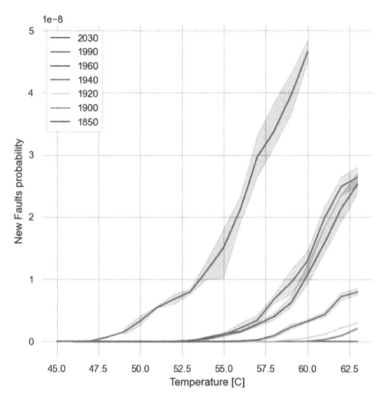

Fig. 3. Faults probabilities versus temperature, for 7 different overclocking rates. The faults threshold was 90,000, and the maximal loop counter was 800,000. The lines represent the average and the shaded area represents 95% confidence intervals.

kernels of Algorithm 1, and tested which bits within each integer cell flipped. The experiments were halted at reaching the fault threshold.

Figure 4 shows the number of times each bit in an integer was flipped. From the figure it is clear that the boundary of a byte has a significant impact on the probability of a bit flip: each consecutive 8 bits exhibit the same flipping behaviour (although not precisely the same number). The figure presents 3 different executions, and we can see that location of the more "faulty-prone" bytes is not constant across different executions.

Next, in Fig. 5 we see the probability of a multi-byte faults out of the total faults encountered, versus the temperature. The figure shows that at low temperature (and low fault frequency), the faults are almost entirely contained in a single byte. Moreover, the probability of multi-byte faults increases with the temperature. This is as expected since we have seen in Sect. 3 that faults become more frequent as the temperature increases, hence the probability that two faults will occur in the same load instruction increases as well.

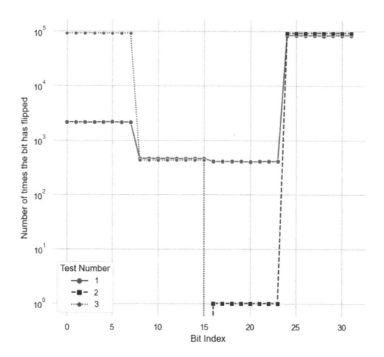

Fig. 4. The number of times each bit has flipped, where bit 0 is the LSB, and bit 31 is the MSB (logarithmic scale). Note that the Y-axis is logarithmic. The experiments were performed with an overclocking of 2,000 MHz, a fault threshold of 90,000 and maximal loop counter of 820,000.

4.2 Byte-Flips and Bit-Flips

When we examined the values read from bytes at which faults occur, we discovered a surprising phenomenon: The vast majority of faultily-read byte values are in fact a **bitwise negation** of the actual byte's value. We call this type of fault a *byte-flip*. In *byte-flip* faults, all the bits of the read byte are flipped simultaneously, e.g., the *load* instruction reads $\neg A[i]_j$ instead of $A[i]_j$, where j indicates the byte within the integer. Thus we classify each faulty read of an integer into 4 classes:

(i) *Byte-flip* - exactly one of the four bytes was negated; (ii) *Multi-byte flip* - two or more of the bytes were negated; (iii) *Bit-flip* - some, but not all of the bits in one of the bytes were flipped; and (iv) *Multi-byte bit-flip* - any fault that doesn't fall in the above categories.

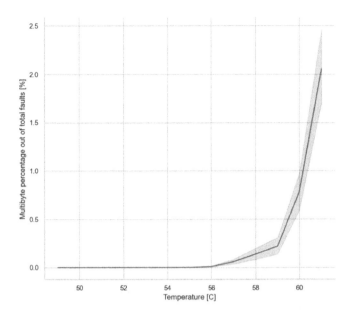

Fig. 5. The percentage of multi-byte faults out of total faults versus temperature. 8 tests were performed at an overclocking of 1,970 MHz, with a fault threshold of 200,000 and a maximal loop counter of 900,000. The line indicates the average, and the shaded area represents the 95% confidence intervals.

Figure 6 shows the total number of times a fault occurred as a function of the number of bits flipped within the boundary of that integer. The figure shows that the most prevalent number of bits flipped is 8. Practically all these occurrences are caused by an entire "byte-flip". The figure also shows that 1–7 bit-flips do occur but at a frequency smaller by two orders of magnitude than byte-flips. Faults with more than 8 bit-flips are usually composed of a byte-flip and an additional fault (either another byte-flip or a smaller bit-flip). The graph shows that the values between 9–16 bit-flips have the same qualitative shape as the values between 1–8 bit-flips, but with smaller absolute values: we observed that 16 bit flips are composed of two byte-flips. Notice that faults that involve more than 2 bytes were not observed.

The percentage of each class of fault can be seen in Table 1: we find that 92% of all faults were *byte-flips*. We observed the same phenomenon across multiple experiments, with various methods of randomizing the array contents, and also when dealing with floats (graphs omitted). We are unable to explain **why** byte-flips occur, but the evidence is quite overwhelming. We believe that incorporating byte-flips into a fault attack can lead to more efficient attacks.

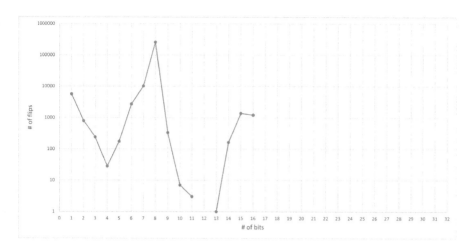

Fig. 6. The number of times N bits flip occurred (logarithmic scale). The test was performed with an overclocking of 2,000 MHz, with a fault threshold of 250,000.

Table 1. The distribution of fault class. The overclocking was 2,000 MHz, and total of 281,087 faults occurred after 820,000 loops.

Fault boundary	Single byte		Multi byte	
Fault type	Byte flips	Bit flips	Byte flips	Bit flips
Fault prevalence [%]	91.9	7.0	0.4	0.7

5   Memory Remnants and Transaction Size

5.1   The Basic Memory Transaction Size

During our experimentation we observed that the data values in the array cells had an impact on the fault rate. In particular, we found that when the array was completely filled with the same value we observed no faults whereas when the values were random we observed many faults. Therefore, we hypothesized that the faults may be influenced by the similarity between the cell's value and a memory remnant: if the array only contains copies of the same value, all the remnants will have this value and faults will not be triggered. A memory-remnant hypothesis, in turn, is impacted by the size and alignment of memory transactions. To understand the possible values of a misread, we would have to find out the size of the transaction in which data is loaded from global memory. For that the following test was designed: we generated a fixed list R of 32 random values, and filled the array, cyclically with values from this list. Specifically, for a given cycle length CL, we filled the array with the values of $R[1], \ldots, R[CL]$, as follows:

```
1    int  R_list[32] = {  /* random data */ };
2    A[i] = R_list[i % CL];
```

5.2 A Model of the Memory Remnants Hypothesis:

Suppose memory access is done in memory transaction of M integers, and that on a memory access at time t to an address in memory block m_a, there is a fault probability p. If a fault occurs then the observed memory contents will not be of m_a but of the contents of some remnant block m_b accessed at a time $t' < t$.

We then used Algorithm 1 to count the faults on this cyclically filled array. As we shall see, this experiment allows us to evaluate the memory-remnant hypothesis, and identify the memory transaction size.

As explained above, we fill the memory with a cyclic pattern $1, 2, \ldots, c, 1, 2, \ldots$, consisting of c different integers, and access the memory. We assume that when a fault occurs on access to some m_a, the read memory content will be of a block m_b which also includes part of the cycle, depending on the offset of m_b into the pattern. If the alignment of m_a, relative to the cycle length c, is the same as that of m_b—the observed content will be equal. But if the alignment of m_a and m_b is different we will observe inequalities in all the positions of m_a where the corresponding values in m_b are different.

If $c|M$ (the cycle length c divides the block length M) then all blocks m_b will have exactly the same contents and we will observe zero inequalities even if faults occur. Otherwise, m_a and m_b can have up to c possible relative alignments: however not all of them will exhibit inequalities. E.g., when $M = 8$ and $c = 6$ (and using the values 1–6 as an illustration) there are only 3 possible contents of the remnant block m_b: 12345612; 34561234; 56123456, of which one will be identical to m_a.

In general, if $g = gcd(c, M)$ is the greatest common divisor, then $r = c/g$ is the total number of contents of possible contents of m_b, of which 1 will be equal to m_a and $r - 1$ will be different. So the expected fraction of block inequalities for cycle length c is $R_c = (r - 1)/r$. Note that this expression covers the case of $c|M$ as well: then $g = gcd(c, M) = c$, then $r = 1$, and so $R_c = 0$.

There is an interesting special case when $c = M$. Clearly $R_c = 0$ because $c|M$. But for $c' = 2c = 2M$ we get $g = gcd(c', M) = M$, $r' = c'/g = 2$, and $R_{c'} = 1/2 > 0$; and $c = M$ is the minimal c for which this holds. I.e., let

$$c_{min} = \min_c \text{ s.t. } R_c = 0 \text{ and } R_{2c} > 0, \tag{1}$$

Then $M = c_{min}$, which gives a simple criterion to determine the block size M.

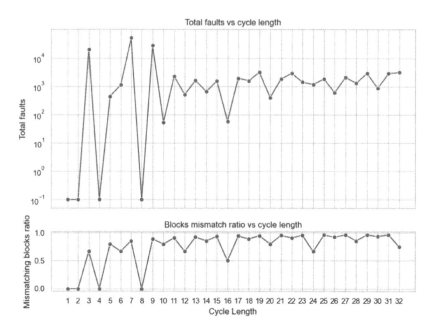

Fig. 7. Top: The total number of faults as a function of the cycle's length (logarithmic scale). The number of loops was restricted to 370,000, and the overclocking was 1960 MHz. The results are an average of 5 executions. Cycle lengths that exhibited no faults were artificially set to have $TotalFaults = 0.1$. **Bottom**: the expected ratio of mismatching blocks (R_c) assuming a basic transaction size of 8 cells (32 bytes).

5.3   Experimental Results

We ran the experiment using cycle lengths of $[1-32]$ integers, and compared the results to the model. The results can be seen in the upper graph in Fig. 7. The figure shows the total number of faults that occurred as a function of the cycle length. The figure also presents the expected values of R_c when $M = 8$. The graph shows that the number of faults is 0 for $CL \in 1, 2, 4, 8$ and non-zero in all other cases (including $CL = 16$). Note also how the fault numbers at even cycle lengths are lower than at odd cycle lengths, and the "dip" at $CL = 16 = 2M$ is indeed deeper than at other lengths where $R_c > 0$ - almost exactly as the model predicts. Therefore we conclude, first, that the memory remnants hypothesis is correct, and secondly, based on Eq. 1 that the process of memory fetching is done with a transaction size of $M = 8$ cells. Since in our case a cell is an integer, we come to the conclusion that the basic transaction size is 32 **bytes**. According to the CUDA documentation, *"device memory is accessed via 32-, 64-, or 128-byte memory transactions"* [28]. This clearly agrees with our conclusion. We may further conclude out that according to our test a 128-byte memory transaction is composed of four smaller components, each of which executes the basic 32-byte memory transaction individually.

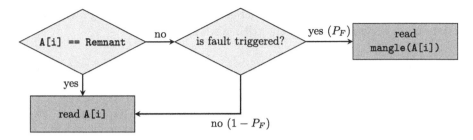

Fig. 8. Schematic model of the value read in a load instruction. P_F is the fault probability, as mentioned in Sect. 3.4.

Table 2. The distribution of fault classes for multiple cycle lengths. The overclocking was 1,970 MHz, and the maximal loop counter was 370,000.

Cycle length	3	5	7	9	18	24
Byte flip [%]	95.7	99.4	95.4	96.0	100.0	97.2
Multi-byte flip [%]	3.2	0.6	2.7	2.8	0	2.8
Single-byte bit-flip [%]	0.7	0	1.0	0.4	0	0
Multi-byte bit-flip [%]	0.4	0	0.9	0.8	0	0

5.4   A Unified Fault Model

At first glance the memory-remnant model seems to conflict the byte-flip phenomenon, since reading memory remnants would not produce a high frequency of byte-flips. However this is not the case. In Table 2 we see the distribution of fault classes for various cycle lengths using the experiment scenario of Sect. 5.1. The table clearly shows that byte-flips for all the cycle lengths in this experiment are as frequent as when the data in the arrays is random (compare Table 1). We conclude that while the memory remnants *trigger* the fault, the read value is not the remnant itself - it is primarily a mangling of the memory cell. So we end with a fault model as in Fig. 8, where `mangle()` is a function that with high probability flips whole bytes.

6   Countermeasures and Conclusions

6.1   Countermeasures

The main countermeasure to these attacks would be to limit the control that processes have over the GPU - as it is risky to allow all processes to change delicate GPU settings even if overclocking is generally allowed. Control mechanisms can include a special authorization to change advanced GPU settings, or by granting special permissions to processes that are expected to legitimately modify the overclocking. A second countermeasure is to control overclocking rates (that were set by an authenticated user) and automatically block rates that cause faults:

The driver should reject dangerous overclocking rates, perhaps by occasionally performing a test to verify that the GPU work is not faulty.

6.2   Conclusions

In our work we showed the first characterization of faults on Nvidia GPUs, and lay the foundations for future exploitation research which is based on GPUs overclocking. Our attack model is very realistic: we only assumed that the GPU is already in an overclocked setup, i.e., the administrator enabled overclocking in general. Under these conditions unprivileged user processes can control the overclocking rate. We demonstrated that such a setup is exposed to fault based attacks, including triggering faults in non-instrumented encryption code.

We showed that the faults rate is affected by the overclocking rate and by the temperature: increasing either one causes more faults. We also showed that the faults are a byte-wide phenomenon, and surprisingly, that the vast majority of the faults are byte-flips, in which the negation of a byte is read instead of its actual value. Lastly, we demonstrated that faults are triggered by memory-remnant reads at an alignment of a 32 byte memory transaction size: to do so we developed a theoretical model for remnant-read faults on cyclic data and validated it experimentally.

Given the explosion of GPGPU usage and the popularity of overclocking, we therefore believe that our findings are a real threat to overclocked setups.

A   Appendix

A.1   CUDA basics

CUDA *Kernels* are declared using the `__global__` declaration specifier and can be invoked using the syntax in Algorithm 2. Kernels are executed in *blocks* where each block consists of multiple *threads*. The parameters `numBlocks` and `threadsPerBlock` specify the *execution configuration syntax*. Each thread that executes the kernel is given unique thread/block IDs that are accessible within the kernel through built-in variables. All threads of a block reside on the same processor core and must share the memory resources of that core. Therefore, the number of threads per block is limited (up 1024 on current GPUs). Instructions are issued and executed in groups of 32 threads, called *warps*.

Thread blocks are required to execute independently: It must be possible to execute them in any order, in parallel or in series. Threads within a block can cooperate by sharing data through some *shared memory* and by synchronizing their execution to coordinate memory accesses. Synchronization points can be declared using intrinsic functions, e.g., `__syncthreads()`.

Algorithm 2. CUDA kernel definition.

```
1   __global__   void  KernelName(arg1 ,  ...)
2   {
3       // Kernel Code //
4   }
5
6   int  HostFunction(arg1 ,  ...)
7   {
8       // ... //
9       KernelName<<<numBlocks , threadsPerBlock>>>(arg1 ,  ...)
10      // ... //
11  }
```

A.2   Future Work

Future work involves leveraging the characterization of faults presented in this paper towards the development of efficient tailored exploitation algorithms and methods. Examples include:

Breaking Cryptographic Calculations Implemented on GPUs. One can speculate that using the byte-flip phenomenon may be incorporated with the work done by Sabbagh et al. [35]. As their work relies on exploiting an instrumented-AES, our characterization might enable the attack to target non-instrumented kernels, as well as reducing the number of messages required to break the encryption. Also it seems that byte-flips may be used to improve attacks on public-key calculations done in a GPU.

Faulty Instructions. During our tests we observed that as the faults rate increased, occasionally the graphics card stopped responding (API calls failed), crashed, or acted extremely slow. We also received kernel crashes with error codes such as: *"An illegal instruction was encountered"* and *"Invalid program counter"*. This suggests that the GPU is not only vulnerable to data corruption, but also to instruction corruption [14,26,38–40], since code-registers (apart from data-registers) are also vulnerable to the faults caused by overclocking.

The knowledge in this paper may allow an attacker to develop code which triggers precise and predictable faults - effectively allowing it to hide malicious instruction in a legitimate code. To design this, the attacker could create a more "prone-to-errors" region of the code (e.g., by performing many loops in a specific alignment). The attacker also knows that it is likely the fault value will be a byte-flip. By studying of GPU opcodes and their inverse, the attacker can then craft his own command in the **misread CUDA code**. Similar technique can be used to leverage the faults to modification of the *Program Counter* register.

Other GPUs. Our tests were conducted on an Nvidia GPU, similar work can be carried out to characterize the faults on other GPUs.

References

1. Agoyan, M., Dutertre, J., Mirbaha, A., Naccache, D., Ribotta, A., Tria, A.: Single-bit DFA using multiple-byte laser fault injection. In: 2010 IEEE International Conference on Technologies for Homeland Security (HST), pp. 113–119 (2010)
2. Agoyan, M., Dutertre, J.-M., Naccache, D., Robisson, B., Tria, A.: When clocks fail: on critical paths and clock faults. In: Gollmann, D., Lanet, J.-L., Iguchi-Cartigny, J. (eds.) CARDIS 2010. LNCS, vol. 6035, pp. 182–193. Springer, Heidelberg (2010). https://doi.org/10.1007/978-3-642-12510-2_13
3. ArchWiki. NVIDIA/Tips and tricks. https://wiki.archlinux.org/index.php/NVIDIA/Tips_and_tricks
4. Barenghi, A., Bertoni, G.M., Breveglieri, L., Pellicioli, M., Pelosi, G.: Low voltage fault attacks to AES. In: 2010 IEEE International Symposium on Hardware-Oriented Security and Trust (HOST), pp. 7–12. IEEE (2010)
5. Bialas, P., Strzelecki, A.: Benchmarking the cost of thread divergence in CUDA. In: Wyrzykowski, R., Deelman, E., Dongarra, J., Karczewski, K., Kitowski, J., Wiatr, K. (eds.) PPAM 2015. LNCS, vol. 9573, pp. 570–579. Springer, Cham (2016). https://doi.org/10.1007/978-3-319-32149-3_53
6. Biham, E., Shamir, A.: Differential fault analysis of secret key cryptosystems. In: Kaliski, B.S. (ed.) CRYPTO 1997. LNCS, vol. 1294, pp. 513–525. Springer, Heidelberg (1997). https://doi.org/10.1007/BFb0052259
7. Boneh, D., DeMillo, R.A., Lipton, R.J.: On the importance of checking cryptographic protocols for faults. In: Fumy, W. (ed.) EUROCRYPT 1997. LNCS, vol. 1233, pp. 37–51. Springer, Heidelberg (1997). https://doi.org/10.1007/3-540-69053-0_4
8. Nvidia developer forum. Unified Memory vs Pinned Memory. https://forums.developer.nvidia.com/t/unified-memory-vs-pinned-host-memory-vs-gpu-global-memory/34640
9. Dusart, P., Letourneux, G., Vivolo, O.: Differential fault analysis on A.E.S. In: Zhou, J., Yung, M., Han, Y. (eds.) ACNS 2003. LNCS, vol. 2846, pp. 293–306. Springer, Heidelberg (2003). https://doi.org/10.1007/978-3-540-45203-4_23
10. Ekbote, B., Hire, V., Mahajan, P., Sisodia, J.: Blockchain based remittances and mining using CUDA. In: 2017 International Conference On Smart Technologies for Smart Nation (SmartTechCon), pp. 908–911. IEEE (2017)
11. Nvidia Forum. Run CUDA on dedicated GPU. https://forums.developer.nvidia.com/t/solved-run-cuda-on-dedicated-nvidia-gpu-while-connecting-monitors-to-intel-hd-graphics-is-this-possible/47690/2/
12. Gawande, N.A., Daily, J.A., Siegel, C., Tallent, N.R., Vishnu, A.: Scaling deep learning workloads: NVIDIA DGX-1/Pascal and intel knights landing. Future Gener. Comput. Syst. **108**, 1162–1172 (2020)
13. Giraud, C.: DFA on AES. In: Dobbertin, H., Rijmen, V., Sowa, A. (eds.) AES 2004. LNCS, vol. 3373, pp. 27–41. Springer, Heidelberg (2005). https://doi.org/10.1007/11506447_4
14. Gratchoff, J.: Proving the wild jungle jump. Technical report, University of Amsterdam (2015). https://homepages.staff.os3.nl/~delaat/rp/2014-2015/p48/report.pdf

15. Harris, M.: Unified Memory in CUDA 6. https://developer.nvidia.com/blog/unified-memory-in-cuda-6/
16. integralfx. DDR4 Overclocking Guide. https://github.com/integralfx/MemTestHelper/blob/master/DDR4
17. Jiang, Z.H., Fei, Y., Kaeli, D.: A complete key recovery timing attack on a GPU. In: 2016 IEEE International Symposium on High Performance Computer Architecture (HPCA), pp. 394–405. IEEE (2016)
18. Kemal. Scripts to overclock & start bitcoin miners on boot. https://gist.github.com/disq/995082
19. Kovacs, B.: Nvidia overclock scripts. https://github.com/brandonkovacs/nvidia-overclock-scripts
20. Landaverde, R., Zhang, T., Coskun, A.K., Herbordt, M.: An investigation of unified memory access performance in CUDA. In: 2014 IEEE High Performance Extreme Computing Conference (HPEC), pp. 1–6. IEEE (2014)
21. Lapid, B., Wool, A.: Cache-attacks on the ARM TrustZone implementations of AES-256 and AES-256-GCM via GPU-based analysis. In: Cid, C., Jacobson Jr. M. (eds.) SAC 2018. LNCS, vol. 11349, pp. 235–256. Springer, Cham (2019). https://doi.org/10.1007/978-3-030-10970-7_11
22. Lee, S., Kim, Y., Kim, J., Kim, J.: Stealing webpages rendered on your browser by exploiting GPU vulnerabilities. In: 2014 IEEE Symposium on Security and Privacy, pp. 19–33. IEEE (2014)
23. Liao, N., Cui, X., Liao, K., Wang, T., Yu, D., Cui, X.: Improving DFA attacks on AES with unknown and random faults. Sci. China Inf. Sci. **60**(4), 1–14 (2016). https://doi.org/10.1007/s11432-016-0071-7
24. Liu, Y., Cui, X., Cao, J., Zhang, X.: A hybrid fault model for differential fault attack on AES. In: 2017 IEEE 12th International Conference on ASIC (ASICON), pp. 784–787. IEEE (2017)
25. Manavski, S.A.: CUDA compatible GPU as an efficient hardware accelerator for AES cryptography. In: 2007 IEEE International Conference on Signal Processing and Communications, pp. 65–68. IEEE (2007)
26. Moro, N., Dehbaoui, A., Heydemann, K., Robisson, B., Encrenaz, E.: Electromagnetic fault injection: towards a fault model on a 32-bit microcontroller. In: 2013 Workshop on Fault Diagnosis and Tolerance in Cryptography, pp. 77–88. IEEE (2013)
27. Murakami, T., Kasahara, R., Saito, T.: An implementation and its evaluation of password cracking tool parallelized on GPGPU. In: 2010 10th International Symposium on Communications and Information Technologies, pp. 534–538. IEEE (2010)
28. Nvidia. Cuda-C-Programming-Guide. https://docs.nvidia.com/cuda/cuda-c-programming-guide/index.html/
29. Nvidia. Nvidia System Management Interface. https://developer.nvidia.com/nvidia-system-management-interface/
30. Nvidia. Using the nvidia-settings Utility. https://download.nvidia.com/XFree86/Linux-x86_64/396.51/README/nvidiasettings.html/
31. Nvidia. Everything you need to know about unified memory. https://on-demand.gputechconf.com/gtc/2018/presentation/s8430-everything-you-need-to-know-about-unified-memory.pdf, 2018
32. Piret, G., Quisquater, J.-J.: A differential fault attack technique against SPN structures, with application to the AES and KHAZAD. In: Walter, C.D., Koç, Ç.K., Paar, C. (eds.) CHES 2003. LNCS, vol. 2779, pp. 77–88. Springer, Heidelberg (2003). https://doi.org/10.1007/978-3-540-45238-6_7

33. Gerardo Ravago. CUDA bitcoin miner. https://github.com/geedo0/cuda_bitcoin_miner
34. Jan S. CUDA-AES. https://github.com/franneck94/CUDA-AES
35. Sabbagh, M., Fei, Y., Kaeli, D.: A novel GPU overdrive fault attack. In: 2020 57th ACM/IEEE Design Automation Conference (DAC), pp. 1–6 (2020)
36. Selmane, N., Guilley, S., Danger, J.: Practical setup time violation attacks on AES. In: 2008 Seventh European Dependable Computing Conference, pp. 91–96 (2008)
37. Online tech tips. How to overclock your GPU safely to boost performance. https://www.online-tech-tips.com/computer-tips/overclock-gpu-safely-boost-performance/
38. George Thessalonikefs. Electromagnetic fault injection characterization. Master's thesis, University of Amsterdam (2014). https://homepages.staff.os3.nl/~delaat/rp/2013-2014/p67/report.pdf
39. Timmers, N., Mune, C.: Escalating privileges in Linux using voltage fault injection. In: 2017 Workshop on Fault Diagnosis and Tolerance in Cryptography (FDTC), pp. 1–8 (2017)
40. Timmers, N., Spruyt, A., Witteman, M.: Controlling PC on ARM using fault injection. In: 2016 Workshop on Fault Diagnosis and Tolerance in Cryptography (FDTC), pp. 25–35. IEEE (2016)
41. Ville Timonen. GPU Burn. https://github.com/wilicc/gpu-burn
42. Wong, H., Papadopoulou, M.-M., Sadooghi-Alvandi, M., Moshovos, A.: Demystifying GPU microarchitecture through microbenchmarking. In: 2010 IEEE International Symposium on Performance Analysis of Systems & Software (ISPASS), pp. 235–246. IEEE (2010)
43. Zhu, Z., Kim, S., Rozhanski, Y., Hu, Y., Witchel, E., Silberstein, M.: Understanding the security of discrete GPUs. In: Proceedings of the General Purpose GPUs, pp. 1–11 (2017)

Fuzzing

ARIstoteles – Dissecting Apple's Baseband Interface

Tobias Kröll[1], Stephan Kleber[2], Frank Kargl[2], Matthias Hollick[1], and Jiska Classen[1][(✉)]

[1] Secure Mobile Networking Lab, TU Darmstadt, Darmstadt, Germany
{tkroell,mhollick,jclassen}@seemoo.de
[2] Institute of Distributed Systems, Ulm University, Ulm, Germany
{stephan.kleber,frank.kargl}@uni-ulm.de

Abstract. Wireless chips and interfaces expose a substantial remote attack surface. As of today, most cellular baseband security research is performed on the *Android* ecosystem, leaving a huge gap on *Apple* devices. With *iOS* jailbreaks, last-generation wireless chips become fairly accessible for performance and security research. Yet, *iPhones* were never intended to be used as a research platform, and chips and interfaces are undocumented. One protocol to interface with such chips is Apple Remote Invocation (ARI), which interacts with the central phone component `CommCenter` and multiple user-space daemons, thereby posing a Remote Code Execution (RCE) attack surface. We are the first to reverse-engineer and fuzz-test the ARI interface on *iOS*. Our *Ghidra* scripts automatically generate a *Wireshark* dissector, called *ARIstoteles*, by parsing closed-source *iOS* libraries for this undocumented protocol. Moreover, we compare the quality of the dissector to fully-automated approaches based on static trace analysis. Finally, we fuzz the ARI interface based on our reverse-engineering results. The fuzzing results indicate that ARI does not only lack public security research but also has not been well-tested by *Apple*. By releasing *ARIstoteles* open-source, we also aim to facilitate similar research in the future.

Keywords: Apple remote invocation · Baseband · iPhone · Fuzzing

1 Introduction

Any component on a mobile system that is reachable over the air poses a security risk. On smartphones, the largest attack surface is functionality related to the cellular baseband—they pose the longest wireless range and most complex codebase. However, many wireless components are closed-source and undocumented, such as wireless firmware and vendor-specific system extensions on all mobile platforms or wireless daemons on *iOS*. Thus, these complex components are often untested by public security research.

We focus on *iOS* since it experienced significantly less public testing than *Android*. Recent *iPhones* come with basebands from either *Qualcomm* or *Intel*.

© Springer Nature Switzerland AG 2021
E. Bertino et al. (Eds.): ESORICS 2021, LNCS 12972, pp. 133–151, 2021.
https://doi.org/10.1007/978-3-030-88418-5_7

Intel basebands are predominant on the European market and are at least shipped in the *iPhone 7, 8, Xs, 11*, and *SE2* models. The same chip as in the *iPhone 11* and *SE2* is used by the *iPad Air 2020*, but telephony functionality is restricted. Moreover, the *Apple Watch 6 GPS+Cellular* has a feature-reduced *Intel* baseband variant. The management protocol for *Qualcomm* chips is called Qualcomm MSM Interface (QMI), which open-source libraries support [12]. On *Android* devices, *Intel* chips use AT commands as control interface [6]. Likely for better interoperability and a feature set closer to QMI, *Apple* introduced Apple Remote Invocation (ARI). Security of the ARI interface is unstudied, even though it resides in the heart of the *iOS* baseband ecosystem.

Understanding ARI enables baseband research on *Apple* devices. Via debug profiles [3], it supports passive baseband analysis on non-jailbroken devices. Moreover, on jailbroken devices, this knowledge can be used to control the baseband chip. Basic protocol structure information is already sufficient to inject mutated ARI payloads for fuzzing purposes. However, more fine-grained control requires understanding all protocol internals in detail. To establish the understanding, we reverse-engineered *iOS* ARI parsing libraries. We instrumented them with our *Ghidra* scripts to automatically extract type information to generate a *Lua*-based *Wireshark* dissector [19,28], which we name *ARIstoteles*. More precisely, the contributions of this paper are as follows:

- We are the first to publicly **reverse-engineer and document the ARI protocol**, resulting in the *Wireshark* dissector *ARIstoteles*.
- Our *Ghidra* scripts generate *ARIstoteles*, which **automatically detect new protocol fields** added in future *iOS* updates.
- We compare the *Ghidra*-based dissector generation approach to fully automated dissector **generation based on static analysis of protocol traces**.
- By fuzzing the ARI interface in user space with Fʀɪᴅᴀ [20], we encounter various **parsing errors and crashes in *iOS* binaries**.

Overall, we identify 42 unique crashes in CommCenter and ARI-related parsing libraries. Due to the central role of CommCenter within *iOS*—the telephony daemon in the *iPhone*—these crashes caused by the fuzzer also affect 12 daemons communicating with CommCenter via Cross-Process Communication (XPC). We emphasize that we disclosed all fuzzing results to *Apple*, who started patching in *iOS 14.2* and added further patches in *iOS 14.6*. *ARIstoteles* and crashing example payloads are available online[1].

This paper is structured as follows. Section 2 explains the baseband security model and security research in this field. Before diving into further details, Sect. 3 describes the basic ARI packet structure, which helps understanding why static traffic-based approaches are not optimal to dissect ARI automatically in Sect. 4. Thus, we create *Ghidra* scripts in Sect. 5, which extract protocol information from shared libraries. These scripts work across 10 different *iOS* versions. We use this protocol knowledge to fuzz CommCenter via ARI in Sect. 6 and show that the *ARIstoteles* dissector can be used to understand these crashes. We conclude our results and outline the security impact in Sect. 7.

---

[1] https://github.com/seemoo-lab/aristoteles.

2   Background and Related Work

The following section provides background information on the *iOS* baseband architecture as well as previous security-related research in this area.

2.1   Baseband Security Architecture

When a wireless packet from a base station reaches a modern smartphone, it usually passes several data processing layers. First, the baseband chip performs initial processing. Then, it passes management information and data to the mobile operating system kernel running on the main processor. Usually, the kernel component is as minimalistic as possible since it runs with high privileges. Hence, most protocol parsing is outsourced to sandboxed daemons running in user space.

A concrete example of this separation on modern *iOS* devices is shown in Fig. 1. The baseband chip processes data, which in turn passes information to CommCenter. Due to intermediate data processing, some contents are not directly passed on to *iOS*. This abstraction layer might prevent some over-the-air attacks but can also introduce further mistakes. For example, the baseband chip scans for nearby cells and measures their signal strength, and then further assembles this information into a list sent to CommCenter. Parsing issues could be on-chip, when directly processing cell information, but also within CommCenter, when parsing the list reported by the chip. If abstraction by the chip prevents exploitation, an on-chip RCE is required to escalate into *iOS*. Typically, wireless chips are optimized towards performance rather than security. Thus, baseband chips miss common mitigation mechanisms and are a common exploitation target [5, 9, 14, 22]. In the following, we assume that the attacker either already has code execution on the baseband chip (e.g., they can create an arbitrary list of cells with invalid entries and report it to CommCenter) or that data injected by an over-the-air attacker is not abstracted by the baseband chip (e.g., the cell identifiers are not further processed by the chip and directly forwarded to CommCenter).

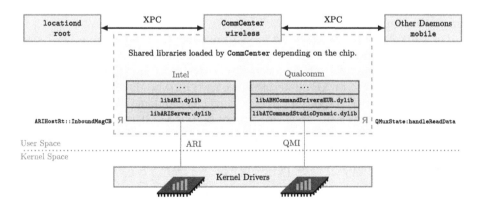

Fig. 1. Simplified baseband packet parsing architecture on *iOS 12–14*.

Depending on the chip type, *Intel* or *Qualcomm*, ARI or QMI is the baseband management interface.

While this paper does not cover *Android* in detail, the overall architecture is very similar. However, *Android* has a more diverse device landscape and enables vendors to add new wireless chips. To this end, *Android* defines a Radio Interface Layer (RIL) [2]. Depending on the chip, a vendor-specific library parses custom chip commands and translates them to RIL calls. Data between these components is passed as *Binder* parcels. *Binder* abstracts communication between kernel and user space. Thus, it has been a popular research target for automated fuzzing in the past [13, 26].

In contrast to *Android*, baseband components on *iOS* were not extensively researched. In 2009, Mulliner and Miller approached *iOS* fuzzing over the air by injecting SMS [18]. Besides Denial of Service (DoS), they were able to gain code execution via an SMS parsing issue in CommCenter [17]. This bug was found on one of the very first *iOS* releases—the first *iPhone* was released in 2007—and *iOS 2* already had a CommCenter daemon but running as root without sandboxing. Inspired by this bug, Silvanovich revisited SMS parsing on the significantly more hardened *iOS 11* but could not find any issues [25]. SMS fuzzing is related to ARI fuzzing, since ARI also carries SMS payloads. Apart from SMS parsing, we are not aware of any public security research revolving around CommCenter, which is surprising given that it poses a zero-click RCE attack surface.

2.2 Baseband Interface Analysis Options on iOS

Apple provides a baseband debug profile on the developer website [3]. After installation on any *iPhone*, it is possible to observe the baseband–CommCenter interface. Not all capabilities of debug profiles are documented. The documentation for the baseband debug profile only states the location of baseband chip crash logs, which are stored in the undocumented Intel System Trace Protocol (ISTP) format. Surprisingly, after installing a baseband debug profile on an *iPhone*—even if not jailbroken—all QMI respectively ARI packets are printed to the system log as hexadecimal bytes. Packets can be interpreted on the fly by parsing the log during runtime.

On jailbroken devices, it is furthermore possible to inject custom QMI and ARI payloads. Silvanovich instrumented an undocumented XPC interface for internal SMS testing [25], which injects SMS without passing the QMI and ARI parsing layer. Instead of XPC interfaces, we use FꓤIDA to directly hook into the CommCenter libraries responsible for parsing baseband messages [20]. Similar to a debugger, FꓤIDA can attach to a running process. It features support for modifying a process, injecting payloads, and tracing program execution. Thus, by hooking into a process with FꓤIDA, we are not restricted to pre-defined XPC interfaces and can even rewrite parts of the program code.

2.3   IOS Shared Libraries

Usually, *iOS* shared libraries are stored within one large `dyld_shared_cache` binary file. After attaching an *iPhone* to *Xcode* on *macOS* and setting it up for development, separated shared library files are extracted to the folder `~/Library/Developer/Xcode/iOS DeviceSupport/`. In contrast to most other *iOS* binaries, shared libraries are meant to be loaded and called by external processes. Thus, they export many function signatures, making them easily accessible with tools like *Ghidra* despite being closed-source. The shared libraries handling ARI are called `libARIServer.dylib` and `libARI.dylib`.

`libARIServer.dylib` is the last instance aware of protocol internals before passing packets to kernel drivers. Thus, it is the perfect library for injecting arbitrary payloads. When sending information to the baseband, the function `AriHostRt::SendRaw` is called, and the opposite direction uses the function `AriHostRt::InboundMsgCB`. We will use these library functions for fuzzing in Sect. 6. However, this library only performs a few final checks, such as checking sequence numbers, likely to prevent out-of-order packets caused by multithreading.

`libARI.dylib` is closer to `CommCenter` and performs most of the parsing and message abstraction. It contains human-readable names of all message groups as well as definitions of most Type Length Value (TLV) types. Hence, it is a great resource to automatically generate a *Wireshark* dissector, as shown in Sect. 5.

3   Apple Remote Invocation Protocol

ARI is an *Apple*-internal protocol without any public documentation. While we are the first to analyze ARI, it would be hard to follow our reverse engineering process and problems encountered using different approaches without a basic understanding of the protocol structure. Technical details about how most of the information was obtained will follow in Sect. 5.

As a management protocol, ARI only carries commands and information of a more general nature without large amounts of data. For example, it signals incoming phone calls—but the audio is sent over a different interface. Moreover,

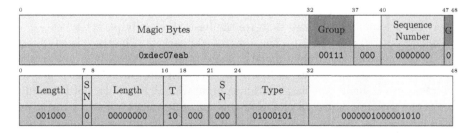

Fig. 2. ARI header format, 12 B split into according bits with example values.

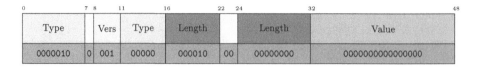

Fig. 3. ARI TLV format with example payloads.

network traffic is not handled by ARI. Nonetheless, ARI carries lightweight information besides connection management, including SMS, location, and time. Each ARI packet has a fixed-length header with a group and type identifier. The group defines the overall purpose, e.g., SMS processing, making calls, SIM access, diagnostics, and more. Group types define further actions, such as acknowledging an SMS, a request to send an SMS, or the delivery status of an SMS. Furthermore, the header defines the remaining packet length, which is filled with multiple Type Length Value (TLV) structures. TLVs can be mandatory or optional. The minimum packet length is 12 B for packets that only have a header and no TLV payload.

Since ARI is for *Apple*-internal use only, the protocol structure has grown historically. This shows in the header format in Fig. 2. For example, the sequence number was probably added to unused bits within three non-consecutive bytes. This makes the header extremely hard to understand.

TLVs following the header are shown in Fig. 3. In addition to a type, length, and value, they also have a version number. This packet structure still does not reflect protocol semantics. However, it outlines that ARI is rather complex and historically grown, making further security research challenging.

4   Fully-Automated Protocol Dissection

Manually analyzing large packet traces and spotting patterns is a tedious task. Despite being experienced with protocol reverse engineering, we failed to identify most fields in the header manually in the beginning when we did not have the information from Sect. 3. Thus, as a first step, we use a heuristics-based segmentation only relying on traffic traces, which has been very successful on various other protocols, including the proprietary Apple Wireless Direct Link (AWDL) protocol [27]. In this process, which is based on NEMESYS and NEMETYL [10,11], we identify segment boundaries that are the basis to classify packet types.

We run both algorithms on a trace with 1000 packets. The trace is collected from an *iPhone* when making a phone call and receiving SMS. The overall trace contains 2497 packets, and we reduce it by subsampling the recorded trace to 1000 messages to make the classification computationally feasible. For retaining most of the variance across the reduced amount of messages, we select the most dissimilar packets. We measure the dissimilarity by the number of uncommon byte sequences per message. Subsampling reduces the groups from 22 to 20. The by far most frequent group is net_cell (labels obtained during later analysis) with 312 occurrences. Almost 95 % of all messages are of 9 different groups.

Figure 4 shows the manually reverse-engineered header format on top and the result of the NEMESYS segmentation on the bottom. With one exception in the magic bytes, all segment boundaries are correct. However, the segmentation algorithm only tries to find boundaries on a byte level and not on a bit level. Moreover, the segmentation algorithm is not aware of non-continuous segments.

It is important to note that these two properties, bit-level and non-continuous segments, are scarce for most protocols, with a few exceptions like flag fields that would not lead to such a high fragmentation. While bit-level segmentation would be easy to integrate into the existing segmentation algorithm, identifying split segments and grouping them into one seems hard to achieve. Adding more freedom to segmentation also increases the likelihood of detecting additional false segment boundaries in general. Especially the bit-fragmented fields spread over multiple offsets are particular to ARI and very uncommon for other protocols. These disjoint short chunks of bits make it almost impossible to apply statistical methods in static traffic analysis.

Next, we use NEMETYL to identify the message type automatically. In contrast to a traditional packet parser, NEMETYL does not rely on detecting the group and type field in the header. Thus, even if the header segmentation with NEMESYS fails, correctly segmenting parts of the remaining packet and classifying them by the overall message similarity can be successful. As shown in Fig. 5, NEMETYL

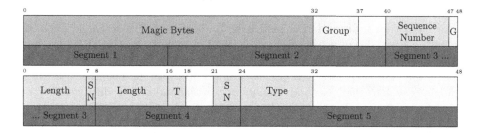

Fig. 4. Heuristic-based analysis results for the ARI header.

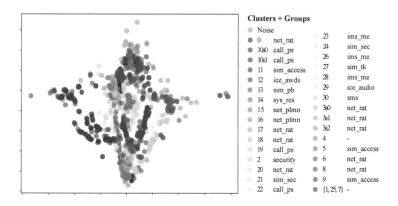

Fig. 5. Message type classification results showing multiple clusters.

indeed locates multiple clusters in the message trace. A unique color indicates a cluster. To plot the dissimilarities of the messages, their relative positions to each other are projected into a two-dimensional plane using Multi-dimensional Scaling (MDS) [24]. The absolute positions in the plot are insignificant, therefore we omit any axis labels. NEMETYL identifies 32 clusters. Only two of these clusters contain messages of multiple groups, and the remaining 30 clusters belong to exactly one group, meaning that the group classification is highly accurate. Some of the correctly identified group clusters contain multiple message types. Six group clusters contain two message types, and one group contains four message types. Such mistakes can be explained with similar packets belonging to different groups or types, for example, an SMS in send versus receive direction.

We conclude that static traffic analysis shows a high potential to identify message types correctly. Since ARI is a protocol with uncommon properties, the analysis would need further optimizations and very specific adaptions to work properly. Some of the required changes are likely to only apply for ARI. Thus, instead of overfitting the heuristics, we continue with manual reverse-engineering and automate these findings with *Ghidra* scripts. As future work, we plan to improve the static traffic analysis method with the insights gained in this use case to ease its application for other specialized unknown protocols.

5   Automated Reverse-Engineering

Packet structure information is sufficient for basic security research, such as generation-based fuzzing. However, to understand what exactly ARI does and utilize the baseband, additional information is required. *iOS* needs some of this information since it parses ARI packets coming from the baseband and creates commands sent to the baseband. Depending on the underlying chip, *Qualcomm* or *Intel*, CommCenter loads shared libraries for parsing QMI or ARI. In the following, we automatically analyze ARI parsing in the libARI.dylib library to create a *Lua*-based dissector. First, we manually locate and reverse-engineer the central data structures and functions, which we then parse automatically. The automated analysis even enables us to track protocol changes in *iOS* updates. While the initial parser generation needs manual work, it could be applied for other proprietary protocols parsed by shared libraries. In addition to shared libraries, some *macOS* binaries contain more symbols than *iOS* binaries. Sometimes, *Apple* accidentally releases a kernel without stripping symbols like in an early *iOS 14 Beta* release.

5.1   Group and TLV Definitions

Message parsing starts at the function AriMsg::AriMsg. After checking that the message starts with the magic bytes 0xdec07eab and is at least 12 B long, it passes the message to Ari::MsgDefById. This function assigns group information via a lookup in the array called ARIMSGDEF_GROUPS. This array contains 63 pointers to group definitions on *iOS 14.5*. Each group definition contains an array of fixed-length message type objects. Likely, they were structures and arrays before compilation and only contained data, no code.

Figure 6 shows one of these message type objects in the net_cell group. Each object contains the group number, which is the same as the array index. This is followed by a unique message type identifier. Moreover, each group definition contains three pointers: a list of mandatory TLVs, a full list including optional TLVs, and a human-readable type name.

The first entry in the list of TLVs is shown in Fig. 7. Each TLV definition starts with an incrementing index number and a type identifier. Then, the actual definition follows, consisting of a pointer to the encoding and the name.

We extract both structures, shown in Fig. 6 and 7, with a *Ghidra* script. This way, we can access all information with a decompiler despite not having any source code. The script starts at the symbol ARIMSGDEF_GROUPS in libARI.dylib, which is exported and, thus, easy to locate. Then, the script follows the pointers to the group and TLV definitions. Since the actual definition structure is removed during the compilation process, we apply the reverse-engineered structural information from Fig. 6 and 7. The script finishes information extraction when a null entry terminates a list. Finally, all information is written into a *Lua* table, which is included by the *Wireshark* dissector.

5.2 Type Definitions

As of *iOS 14.5*, the shared ARI library defines 290 asString methods. The method definitions differ by the parameter type, which corresponds to an encoding. An encoding specifies a human-readable format of a type. For example, a phone call can be disconnected due to 226 reasons, represented by an integer, and the corresponding asString method transforms this number to a more descriptive reason. The asString methods are code and, thus, do not follow the same simple memory structure as the group and TLV definitions. Moreover, likely due to compiler optimizations, each asString method looks slightly different. During a manual comparison, we identify three variants:

1. A lookup table, where the input is used as index in a list of strings.
2. An if-not construct, where strings are set to a default value and changed if the default does not apply in a fall-through manner.
3. A switch-case construct containing early returns, if statements, and jumps.

0	4	8	16	24	32	48
Group	Type	Padding	Mandatory TLVs	Available TLVs	Unknown	Name
0x9	0x101	0x0	0x1C6B4D468	0x1D9507480	0x0003...00	0x1C6B847E0
			msg101_mtlvs	msg101_tlvs		IBINetSet...

Fig. 6. First message object in _ARIMSGDEF_GROUP09_net_cell, defining the message structure of IBINetSetRadioSignalReportingConfiguration.

Index	Type	Padding	Encoding	Name
0	4	8	16	24
0x1	0x101	0x0	0x1DE283508	0x1C6B666E5
			ARI_IBIUInt32_1_CODEC	nInstance_t1

Fig. 7. First TLV object in `msg101_tlvs`, defining the type structure of `nInstance_t1`.

The first two variants account for 240 of 290 `asString` methods and can be automatically extracted with *Ghidra*. Due to the inconsistent structure of the third variant, we have to extract these definitions manually. It would also be possible to emulate the `asString` methods. However, their input range is undefined, and without analyzing their code, emulation might miss some inputs.

```
1  char* asString(IBIImsMEAudioEVSBandWidthType t) {  // at address 0
       x1e0d2ab38
2    if (t - 1 < 8) {
3      return *(char **)((long)&PTR_s_IBI_IMS_ME_AUDIO_BAND_NB_1e0d2ab38 + (long)(int
           )(t - 1) * 8);
4    }
5    return "???";
6  }
```

Listing 1.1. `asString` method with a look-up table (variant 1).

```
1  (unique, 0x7fe0, 4) INT_SUB (register, 0x4000, 4), (const, 0x1, 4)
2  (unique, 0x1d0, 1) INT_LESS (unique, 0x7fe0, 4), (const, 0x8, 4)
3    --- CBRANCH (ram, 0x1c9c4d8d4, 1), (unique, 0x1d0, 1)
4  (unique, 0xbf0, 8) INT_SEXT (unique, 0x10000011, 4)
5  (unique, 0xe40, 8) INT_MULT (unique, 0xbf0, 8), (const, 0x8, 8)
6  (unique, 0x1000001d, 8) INT_ADD (unique, 0x10000015, 8), (unique, 0xe40,
       8)
7  (register, 0x4000, 8) LOAD (const, 0x1b1, 4), (unique, 0xeb0, 8)
8  (unique, 0x10000009, 8) PTRSUB (const, 0x0, 8), (const, 0x1e0d2ab38, 8)
```

Listing 1.2. *Ghidra P-Code* representation of the same function.

We show how to extract the first variant, but all scripts and the *Wireshark* dissector are available online. Each lookup table has a wrapper function like the one shown in Listing 1.1. It optionally adds an offset to the type prior to the lookup in the string list. If the value is undefined, the string ??? is returned. Mapping strings requires locating the lookup table as well as the range of input values. To this end, we need to interpret *Ghidra P-Code* instructions, which are the internal architecture-independent code representation within *Ghidra*. On a more detailed level, the extraction script works by iterating over all *P-Code* operands of the `asString` function.

The extractor collects all INT_ADD and INT_SUB commands that occur before the last INT_LESS operand. The INT_LESS operand represents the "less than" comparison in the if (t - 1 < 8) condition. The condition's right value is a parameter to the comparison operand. For our example from Listing 1.1 this value (8) can be found in the example *P-Code* in line 2 in Listing 1.2. We can see that the function in Listing 1.1 always subtracts 1 from the input parameter. This subtraction will be transformed to a INT_SUB *P-Code* instruction, as can be seen in line 1 of Listing 1.2. And thus, if we happen to find further addition (INT_ADD) and subtraction (INT_SUB) operands, we will have to take these offsets into account for our iteration boundary when calculating the offset and range of possible asString type values. We do this because we assume that all subtractions and additions that happen before a INT_LESS comparison belong to the left value of the condition's expression.

5.3   Integrating Existing Dissectors

ARI embeds further formats that are well-known, such as SMS. After adding these dissectors manually, the *Wireshark* output becomes even more readable. Figure 8 shows how the resulting dissector looks after adding TLV and type definitions as well as SMS parsing.

Fig. 8. *ARIstoteles* dissecting an SMS.

5.4   iOS Version Change Tracking

Using the resulting *Ghidra* scripts enables tracking changes in the ARI protocol over multiple *iOS* versions. The results in Table 1 show that automated *Wireshark* dissector generation does not only save manual reverse-engineering overhead during initial dissector generation but with every *iOS* update. This especially applies to TLV types. The similar numbers indicate that the scripts run flawless, independent of slight differences introduced by the different compilation processes. Tracking changes within ARI allows determining if and when new features were added to the protocol and test these in specific. Interestingly, the last ARI update was applied in *iOS 13.5*, released in parallel to the *iPhone SE 2020*.

Table 1. Extracted data structures for different *iOS* versions.

iOS Version	Types	asString (total)	asString (extracted)
12.5.1 (16H22)	783	290	249
13.3 (17C54)	874	290	249
13.5 (17F75)	879	290	249
6 versions skipped	—	—	—
14.5 (18E199a)	879	290	249

6   Fuzzing

Based on the protocol knowledge, we can now inject messages into `CommCenter`. We leverage this for smart fuzzing, compare ARI results to QMI, and outline how to build high-performance *iOS* fuzzers. Finally, we analyze these crashes.

6.1   Initial Fuzzing Considerations

There are only a few options for fuzzing closed-source *iOS* daemons. *Corellium*, the most advanced commercial *iOS* emulation, does not support cellular daemons and hardware as of May 2021 [4]. Open-source emulators can only boot parts of the kernel but not the entire system [1]. Thus, we need to fuzz `CommCenter` on a physical *iPhone*. Non-emulated fuzzing has various drawbacks [16], such as non-scalability and no possibility to reset the system state. Nonetheless, running on physical hardware can find more realistic bugs. Given these circumstances, we present the considerations that led to our setup for fuzzing ARI messages in the following.

In-process Fuzzing on a Physical Device. Our fuzzer is based on Fʀɪᴅᴀ, which injects a new thread into the target process. This means that a partial or complete fuzzer is running within the CommCenter process. Listing 1.3 shows a minimal code example that injects a single message using the *JavaScript* API. The payload is injected into the target function AriHostRt::InboundMsgCB within the libARIServer.dylib shared library. The example only calls the target function once. For fuzzing, payloads would need to be generated and the function had to be called repeatedly. Moreover, we attach a so-called interceptor to the target function, which can read and modify input parameters before execution. This is necessary to keep track and adjust the sequence numbers since the physical baseband continues sending messages during the fuzzing process, resulting in out-of-order sequence numbers. Additionally, the Fʀɪᴅᴀ stalker can trace executed functions or code blocks, enabling coverage collection [21]. Execution is traced by dynamic binary rewriting during runtime and executing copies of the original code that have additional tracing instructions.

Payload Injection. Payloads can either be generated (1) by an external device and sent to the target or (2) within the Fʀɪᴅᴀ thread. The first option enables fast development and reusing existing fuzzing libraries without adapting them to Fʀɪᴅᴀ. If the target process CommCenter crashes, the external device is still aware of the last packet sent prior to the crash. Furthermore, the external device might have larger storage for packet and crash logs. However, the second option is significantly faster. We explore and compare both strategies in the next section.

Payload Mutation. Creating new payloads requires a mutation strategy, which can be (1) coverage-based, (2) generation-based, or a combination of both. Even without much knowledge about a protocol, the Fʀɪᴅᴀ stalker can collect basic block coverage and use this as a metric to improve the quality of injected packets. Whenever a packet reaches a new basic block, it is added to the corpus. However, collecting coverage with Fʀɪᴅᴀ slows down the fuzzer. Another issue that arises is inconsistent coverage. Most binary parsers that process files would always produce the same coverage for the same input, and processing the current file does not depend on the previous file. Protocols are very different and highly state-dependent. For example, if a multi-part SMS is injected, the last message part would increase the coverage, but injecting this message part again would not increase the coverage. Thus, even injecting the same packet twice in a row can lead to different coverages. Furthermore, processes have an inconsistent state that is not solely controlled by packets injected by the fuzzer but configurations, external daemons, or user interaction like enabling a mobile hotspot and dialing a number, again leading to inconsistent coverage. The second option, which is generating new messages based on protocol knowledge, is significantly faster and does not lead to any issues with inconsistent coverage. We also compare coverage-based to generation-based approaches.

```
1  // define hook for ARI messages chip (BB) -> iOS (AP)
2  var InboundMsgCb_addr = Module.getExportByName('libARIServer.dylib', '
      _ZN9AriHostRt12InboundMsgCBEPhm');
3  var InboundMsgCb = new NativeFunction(InboundMsgCb_addr, "int64", ["pointer",
      "int64"]);
4
5  Interceptor.attach(InboundMsgCb_addr, {    // optional hook customization
6      onEnter: function(args) {
7           // fix ARI sequence number, collect basic block coverage, etc.
8  }});
9
10 InboundMsgCb(payload, length);              // call the target once
```

Listing 1.3: Injecting an ARI packet within the CommCenter process with FRIDA.

6.2 Building and Optimizing Fuzzers

We compare five fuzzers with multiple injection and mutation strategies. These variants lead to significantly different speeds, as we verified by fuzzing a comparable SMS payload with the performance results presented in Table 2. These fuzzers do not only differ in speed but also type of crashes they are able to find.

The prior reverse-engineering of the protocol internals enables us to fix certain aspects of the message, such as the sequence number. Moreover, we leave the magic bytes in the header intact, and have options to only mutate the TLVs.

(1) Replacing Existing Messages. This approach randomly changes a few bytes after a random amount of messages. Ideally, the target *iPhone* has a SIM card installed and is actively used to make phone calls, send messages, browse the Internet, and so on. The total amount of messages highly depends on user interaction, thus, we do not list it in Table 2, but it is significantly slower than all other variants. When setting a good ratio of mutated versus original messages, the *iPhone* works almost normally, and the fuzzer can reach states rather deep within the protocol. Using this method, we found various crashes that cannot

Table 2. Fuzzing speed depending on the setup on an *iPhone 7* with an *iOS 14.3 Beta* and *14.1.2*.

Speed test scenario	Fuzz cases per second
(5a) Local *JavaScript* SMS bit flipper	17000
(5b) Local *JavaScript* SMS bit flipper with additional array copy	11000
(4) Local *JavaScript* SMS bit flipper collecting basic block coverage	250
(2) External *Python* SMS injection	400
(3b) External *Python* SMS injection collecting basic block coverage	100
(3a) External *ToothPicker* variant with radamsa mutator and coverage	20

be reproduced by replaying a message trace. For example, one null pointer issue in the audio controller can only be triggered when the user previously initiated a phone call—which requires user interaction and cannot be reproduced by injecting ARI messages alone.

(2) External Message Generation. In this approach, we collect a large message corpus from typical baseband interaction. Then, we replay this corpus, either ordered or unordered, and mutate a subset of the messages based on the protocol structure. All messages are logged on the external device since some crashes only occur on a packet sequence. This fuzzer reaches around 400 fuzz cases per second (fcps).

(3) External Coverage-based. radamsa Mutation One of our previous projects, *ToothPicker*, fuzzes the Bluetooth daemon on *iOS* [8]. We adapt it to fuzz CommCenter and observe a slightly slower speed than for the Bluetooth daemon, around 20 fcps *(3a)*. Note that when injecting payloads without the smart radamsa mutation strategy, this could be improved up to 100 fcps *(3b)*. Even when initializing the radamsa mutator with different payloads, it tends to find the same crashes over and over again. Usually, mutators are trying to fuzz crashes again to determine the underlying issue further. However, in the case of an in-process fuzzer based on FЯIDA, crashing *CommCenter* also leads to a crash of the fuzzer. A CommCenter restart takes around 20–30 s. After a crash, we remove the payload that lead to the crash from the corpus and reinitialize the fuzzer by collecting coverage. On a large corpus, this can take several minutes, further reducing the fuzzer's speed.

(4) Local Coverage-based. AFL++ Mutation Another option is to mutate the payloads with AFL++ on the target device. This is meanwhile supported by *fpicker* [7], and we were allowed to use an early pre-release version. Running locally leads to a significant speedup of around 250 fcps, now primarily limited by the FЯIDA stalker collecting coverage. This fuzzer is 10 × faster than *Tooth-Picker* while supporting a similar feature set.

(5) Local High-speed Mutation. We test the upper limit of achievable fuzzing speed by randomly flipping bits within a provided message. This is not a powerful mutator but shows that the fuzzing speed could be increased up to 17 000 fcps *(5a)*. Already very small changes, such as copying the payload array slightly more inefficient *(5b)*, lead to a speed reduction, as shown in Table 2.

Overall, we found the rather naive second approach the best to uncover new crashes. Mutating payloads based on a large corpus and keeping structural protocol information intact reaches both a comparably fast fuzzing speed and high bug density. Approaches collecting coverage were rather slow and suffered from inconsistent coverage information, thereby not compensating massive slowdown introduced by coverage collection.

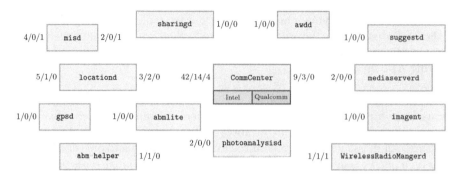

Individual crashes found: Total / Replayable / Fixed in iOS 14.3. Colors indicate ARI vs. QMI fuzzing.

Fig. 9. Fuzzing results, also affecting various daemons due to XPC.

Fig. 10. Crash within reported network cells during a scan.

6.3   Crash Evaluation

Every time a process crashes, *iOS* creates a crash log containing the exception type, the name of the crashed thread within the process, as well as a backtrace of each thread. Thus, we can identify unique crashes even without coverage-based fuzzing. Figure 9 shows all crashes found by fuzzing QMI and ARI, including processes that communicate with CommCenter using XPC. Even though QMI has fewer bugs, components residing on top of the QMI protocol parser and in external daemons crash as well, sometimes similar as during ARI fuzzing.

Due to state issues, not all crashes are replayable by injecting the same messages as during fuzzing. For example, we find a crash in the Mobile Internet Sharing Daemon misd, caused by invalid memory access to an address that looks like a configuration string. This bug frequently occurs on *Qualcomm* and *Intel iPhones*, meaning that it is chip-independent. However, it cannot be reproduced by replaying packets. *Apple* rated the `misd` parsing issue as security-critical but did not assign a Common Vulnerabilities and Exposures (CVE) number since they discovered it in parallel to our research. This bug was present in *iOS 13.7* and fixed in *iOS 14.2*.

Even when a bug is replayable, it is often hard to understand its root cause. In contrast to the shared library we were parsing in Sect. 5, `CommCenter` itself does not contain exported symbols. Thus, we only know the crash location in a binary without function or variable names. Reading code in the binary is further complicated by inaccuracies in the decompilation process, resulting in wrong pseudo-code output. Understanding payloads significantly speeds up manual crash analysis.

We illustrate this with a crash that occurs in the `CellMonitor` thread. It accesses an invalid offset in the function `processGsmCellInfo`. Converting the crashing packet into a *Wireshark* dump and opening it reveals which part of the payload causes the crash, as shown in Fig. 10, detailing the `IBIGsmCellInfoT` contents. This bug is stateless, meaning that its payload can be replayed at any time. Moreover, cell information might not only be injected with on-chip RCE but even with a rogue base station setup. However, *Apple* did not assign a CVE number without a full proof of concept showing if this bug is actually exploitable beyond denial of service.

While not assigning high priority to most bugs identified by our fuzzer, *Apple* did indeed fix all replayable crashes as of *iOS 14.6*. We did not receive any feedback which bug was fixed in which specific version. However, *Apple* assigned *CVE-2021-1770* to one of our `CommCenter`-related bugs and fixed it in *iOS 14.5*, categorized as a Wi-Fi security issue that leads to arbitrary code execution. Moreover, we assume that they were running our fuzzer, which we provided to them, and most likely with further internal analysis tools.

7   Conclusion

Proprietary and undocumented interfaces pose a huge security risk if not tested thoroughly by manufacturers. Our fuzzing results let us assume that *Apple* did not perform any fuzz testing on ARI. Given that this interface is reachable via wireless components, this is surprising. We hope that *Apple* will improve wireless interface security in future releases and run—among other security testing—internal fuzzing campaigns.

The *Wireshark* dissector we provide will be a helpful research tool also after ARI parsing issues got fixed within *iOS*. It enables debugging baseband interactions on the fly and provides insights on network operation, SIM interaction, and more. We hope that the open-source release of *ARIstoteles* will support wireless security research in general. It is the first step towards a low-level cellular experimentation framework comparable to projects that already exist for Bluetooth and Wi-Fi [15,23]. Additionally, the *Ghidra* scripts will enable researchers to build similar dissectors based on shared library information or leaked symbols.

Availability

The *ARIstoteles* source code as well as the *Ghidra* extraction scripts are available on https://github.com/seemoo-lab/aristoteles. This repository also contains the FЯIDA scripts that can record ARI packets during runtime and inject packets, including replayable crashing packets and packet sequences found with the fuzzers.

Acknowledgments. This work has been funded by the German Federal Ministry of Education and Research and the Hessen State Ministry for Higher Education, Research and the Arts within their joint support of the National Research Center for Applied Cybersecurity ATHENE.

References

1. Afek, J.: Simplifying iOS research: booting the iOS kernel to an interactive bash shell on QEMU (2020). https://www.offensivecon.org/speakers/2020/jonathan-afek.html
2. Android Open Source Project: RIL Refactoring (2021). https://source.android.com/devices/tech/connect/ril
3. Apple: Profiles and Logs - Bug Reporting - Apple Developer (2021). https://developer.apple.com/bug-reporting/profiles-and-logs/
4. Corellium: Introduction to iOS Devices (2021). https://support.corellium.com/hc/en-us/articles/360053569554-Introduction-to-iOS-Devices
5. Golde, N.: There's Life in the Old Dog Yet: Tearing New Holes into Intel/iPhone Cellular Modems (2018). https://comsecuris.com/blog/posts/theres_life_in_the_old_dog_yet_tearing_new_holes_into_inteliphone_cellular_modems/
6. Guy: Burned in Ashes: Baseband Fairy Tale Stories (2019). https://cfp.recon.cx/reconmtl2019/talk/7A7TBA/
7. Heinze, D.: fpicker (2021). https://github.com/ttdennis/fpicker
8. Heinze, D., Classen, J., Hollick, M.: ToothPicker: apple picking in the iOS Bluetooth Stack. In: 14th USENIX Workshop on Offensive Technologies (WOOT 20). USENIX Association (2020). https://www.usenix.org/conference/woot20/presentation/heinze
9. Hernandez, G., Muench, M.: Emulating Samsung's Baseband for Security Testing. BlackHat USA 2020 (2020)
10. Kleber, S., van der Heijden, R.W., Kargl, F.: Message type identification of binary network protocols using continuous segment similarity. In: IEEE INFOCOM 2020 - IEEE Conference on Computer Communications, pp. 2243–2252 (2020). https://doi.org/10.1109/INFOCOM41043.2020.9155275
11. Kleber, S., Kopp, H., Kargl, F.: NEMESYS: network message syntax reverse engineering by analysis of the intrinsic structure of individual messages. In: 12th USENIX Workshop on Offensive Technologies (WOOT 18). USENIX Association, Baltimore (2018)
12. libqmi Developers: QMI modem protocol helper library (2021). https://github.com/freedesktop/libqmi
13. Liu, B., Zhang, C., Gong, G., Zeng, Y., Ruan, H., Zhuge, J.: FANS: fuzzing android native system services via automated interface analysis. In: 29th USENIX Security Symposium (USENIX Security 20), pp. 307–323. USENIX Association (2020). https://www.usenix.org/conference/usenixsecurity20/presentation/liu

14. Maier, D., Seidel, L., Park, S.: BaseSAFE: baseband sanitized fuzzing through emulation. In: The 13th ACM Conference on Security and Privacy in Wireless and Mobile Networks (WiSec '20) (2020)
15. Mantz, D., Classen, J., Schulz, M., Hollick, M.: InternalBlue - bluetooth binary patching and experimentation framework. In: The 17th Annual International Conference on Mobile Systems, Applications, and Services (MobiSys '19) (2019). https://doi.org/10.1145/3307334.3326089
16. Muench, M., Stijohann, J., Kargl, F., Francillon, A., Balzarotti, D.: What you corrupt is not what you crash: challenges in fuzzing embedded devices. In: 25th Annual Network and Distributed System Security Symposium (NDSS 2018). The Internet Society (2018)
17. Mulliner, C.: Fuzzing the phone in your phone. https://media.ccc.de/v/26c3-3507-de-fuzzing_the_phone_in_your_phone
18. Mulliner, C., Miller, C.: Fuzzing the phone in your phone. https://www.blackhat.com/presentations/bh-usa-09/MILLER/BHUSA09-Miller-FuzzingPhone-PAPER.pdf
19. National Security Agency: Ghidra (2021). https://ghidra-sre.org/
20. Ravnås, O.A.V.: Frida - a world-class dynamic instrumentation framework (2020). https://frida.re/
21. Ravnås, O.A.V.: Frida - stalker (2020). https://frida.re/docs/stalker/
22. Ruge, J., Classen, J., Gringoli, F., Hollick, M.: Frankenstein: advanced wireless fuzzing to exploit new bluetooth escalation targets. In: 29th USENIX Security Symposium (USENIX Security 19). USENIX Association (2020)
23. Schulz, M., Wegemer, D., Hollick, M.: Nexmon: the C-based firmware patching framework (2017). https://nexmon.org
24. scikit-learn Developers: sklearn.mainfold.MDS - scikit-learn 0.24.2 documentation (2021). https://scikit-learn.org/stable/modules/generated/sklearn.manifold.MDS.html
25. Silvanovich, N.: iOS Messaging Tools (2019). https://github.com/googleprojectzero/iOS-messaging-tools
26. Stone, M.: Bad binder: android in-the-wild exploit (2019). https://googleprojectzero.blogspot.com/2019/11/bad-binder-android-in-wild-exploit.html
27. Stute, M., et al.: A billion open interfaces for eve and mallory: MitM, DoS, and tracking attacks on iOS and macOS through apple wireless direct link. In: 28th USENIX Security Symposium (USENIX Security 19), pp. 37–54. USENIX Association, Santa Clara (2019)
28. Wireshark Foundation: Wireshark (2021). https://www.wireshark.org/

webFuzz: Grey-Box Fuzzing
for Web Applications

Orpheas van Rooij$^{(\boxtimes)}$, Marcos Antonios Charalambous, Demetris Kaizer,
Michalis Papaevripides, and Elias Athanasopoulos

University of Cyprus, Nicosia, Cyprus
{ovan-r01,mchara01,dkaize01,mpapae04,eliasathan}@cs.ucy.ac.cy

Abstract. Fuzzing is significantly evolved in analysing native code, but web applications, invariably, have received limited attention until now. This paper designs, implements and evaluates webFuzz, a *gray-box fuzzing* prototype for discovering vulnerabilities in web applications.

webFuzz is successful in leveraging instrumentation for detecting cross-site scripting (XSS) vulnerabilities, as well as covering more code faster than black-box fuzzers. In particular, webFuzz has discovered *one* zero-day vulnerability in WordPress, a leading CMS platform, and *five* in an online commerce application named CE-Phoenix.

Moreover, in order to systematically evaluate webFuzz, and similar tools, we provide the first attempt for automatically synthesizing reflective cross-site scripting (RXSS) vulnerabilities in vanilla web applications.

1 Introduction

Automated software testing, or fuzzing, is an established technique for analyzing the behaviour of applications, and recently has been focused, among others, in finding unknown vulnerabilities in programs. The drive to discover bugs in software through an automated process has progressed with the introduction of American Fuzzy Lop (AFL) [47], a state-of-the-art fuzzer that leverages the coverage feedback from the *instrumented* target program. In creating this *feedback loop*, fuzzers can significantly improve their performance by determining whether an input is interesting, namely, it triggers a new code path, and use that input to produce other test cases.

Although automated software testing has become a burgeoning field of research, it still has a long way to go, especially for web applications [17]. On the other hand, the proliferation of the web attracts many more malicious attacks on web applications. This predicates a strong need for the development of automated vulnerabilities scanners that target web applications as well as for automated vulnerabilities injection tools to evaluate the former.

Traditionally, fuzzers come under three categories; black-, white- or grey-box depending on the level of awareness they have of the target program's structure. Black-box fuzzers are unaware of the internal program structure, that is, their

© Springer Nature Switzerland AG 2021
E. Bertino et al. (Eds.): ESORICS 2021, LNCS 12972, pp. 152–172, 2021.
https://doi.org/10.1007/978-3-030-88418-5_8

target is a black-box, no feedback other than what is directly observable is provided. One of their main advantages is their low overhead which allows them to exercise the program under test with millions of inputs. In this way their chances of triggering a bug increases. On the other hand, their lack of knowledge on the program's structure comes with a cost. *AFL* Fuzzer has shown that its feedback loop that uses previously generated interesting inputs to built new test cases is a key idea for successful bug discovery [13,47]. Black-box fuzzers though lack the ability to make sound judgements on what is considered interesting input [35,39]. As a result they either do not retain generated inputs for further mutation or the heuristic used to identify favorable inputs is insufficient as it can only rely on what is observable in the application response. This limits the effectiveness of black-box solutions.

On the other end of the scale exist the white-box solutions that require access to source code and rely heavily on static-analysis. Most of these approaches utilize constraint-solving and a combination of symbolic and concolic execution [3,4,6] to identify vulnerable code statements. Although sophisticated in their approach, their inherent limitation lies in the computationally demanding constraint solver. For instance, tools such as Chainsaw [3] and Navex [4] utilise static analysis to perform a mapping between source variables such as URL parameters to sink statements, that is, server-side code statements (such as the `print` command) that output the source back to the client. Creating this source-sink pair link and identifying whether sanitisation happens along the way is the key ingredient in exposing a vulnerability. For each associated pair to be created though lies an expensive constraint solving operation, and the magnitude of this problem only increases with the number of sources and sinks.

Coverage-based grey box fuzzing comes at an ideal compromise between sophistication and scalability. Instead of statically analysing the source code, it relies on input mutations and lightweight coverage feedback to explore the input-space within a limited time frame. Given that the input-space can be enormous, a fuzzer can leverage the instrumentation feedback to identify interesting inputs and built new test cases from them. Ways of defining an interesting input can be if it explores new unobserved code paths or if it exercises the business logic of the application and does not fail early on in the input-format checks. In this way, it maximises code coverage, whether that is on a global or function level [12], thus increasing the chances of triggering a vulnerability.

In this paper, we design, implement and evaluate a coverage-based *grey-box* fuzzing solution for web applications aimed at detecting reflective and stored cross-site scripting vulnerabilities. For native applications, instrumentation is carried out at the intermediate representation of the application's code (e.g., at the LLVM's IR), when the source code is available, or directly to the binary [47]. For web applications, instrumentation is challenging, since (a) several different frameworks are used to realize web applications, (b) applications are executed through a web server and (c) there is no standard intermediate representation of web code. webFuzz applies all instrumentation at the abstract-syntax tree layer of PHP applications. Therefore, our instrumentation can cover a significant amount of available web code, while it is generic enough – labeling basic blocks, collecting feedback, and embedding the feedback to a shared resource can all be translated to other web languages without facing many challenges.

Evaluating fuzzing is another challenging task [28], since migrating known vulnerabilities to existing software, in order to test the capabilities of the fuzzer in finding bugs, can be a tedious process [32]. Thus, for evaluating webFuzz, but also other fuzzers for web applications, we develop a methodology for automatically injecting bugs in web applications written in PHP. Our methodology is inspired by LAVA [15] and targets web applications instead of native code. Injecting vulnerabilities in web code, again, is challenging, since important tools used for analyzing native code and injecting vulnerabilities (e.g., taint-tracking and information-flow frameworks) are not available for web applications. To overcome this lack of available tools, our vulnerability injection methodology leverages the instrumentation infrastructure we use for building webFuzz, in the first place.

1.1   Contributions

In this paper, we make the following contributions.

1. We design, implement and evaluate webFuzz, a prototype grey-box fuzzer created for discovering vulnerabilities in web applications. We thoroughly evaluate webFuzz in terms of efficiency in finding unknown bugs, of code coverage and throughput. Indicatively, webFuzz can cover about 27% of WordPress (almost half a million LoCs of PHP), in 1.4 days (2,000 min) of fuzzing. It has additionally managed to uncover *1* zero-day RXSS bug in the latest version of WordPress, and *5* zero-day XSS bugs in an active commerce application named CE-Phoenix. Compared to Wfuzz, a prominent open-source black-box fuzzer, webFuzz also finds more real-life and artificial XSS bugs.
2. We design and implement a methodology for automated bug injection in web applications written in PHP. Our bug-injection methodology is *not only* essential for evaluating webFuzz but also vital for the progression of further research in vulnerability finding for web software.
3. To foster further research in the field, we release all of our contributions, namely the toolchain for instrumenting PHP applications, the actual fuzzer, and the toolchain for injecting bugs in web applications, as open-source. The source code can be found at: https://bitbucket.org/srecgrp/webfuzz-fuzzer

2   webFuzz

This section describes the architecture of webFuzz. We begin by discussing how webFuzz instruments a target application before analysis, and then elaborate on how a fuzzing analysis works by expanding on how inputs are mutated, responses are analyzed and vulnerabilities are detected. We also discuss how we minimize fuzz targets in order to favor the ones that lead eventually to better code coverage.

2.1 Instrumentation

webFuzz instruments PHP applications in the Abstract Syntax Tree (AST) level of the code to provide coverage information in the form of *basic block* or *branch coverage* [5]. To achieve this, it parses the AST of each PHP source file using the PHP-Parser [36] library, it identifies basic blocks during the AST traversal process, and lastly appends to each block identified extra stub code. In order to output the coverage feedback at the end of the execution, stub code is also inserted at the beginning of every source file. We elaborate more on this mechanism, below.

Instrumentation Level. Basic blocks are maximal sequences of consecutive statements that are always executed together (i.e., contain no branching statements) [2]. In a Control Flow Graph (CFG), the basic blocks correspond to the nodes in the graph. In order to measure code coverage, it is sufficient to identify the executed blocks and their order of execution. Identification of the blocks happens during the AST traversal process, in which the type of each statement encountered is inspected and modified accordingly. webFuzz identifies the beginning of a basic block as:

- the first statement in a function definition;
- the first statement in a control statement;
- the exit statement in a control statement.

Control statements are all conditional, looping and exception handling constructs. Although expressions with logical operators can also be composed out of multiple basic blocks due to short-circuit evaluation, for the sake of performance webFuzz does not instrument them.

Coverage. Basic-block coverage provides the least granularity as it only measures which basic blocks get executed irrespective of their order. Branch coverage enhances the accuracy by measuring the pairs of consecutive blocks executed. The latter method is also known as *edge coverage* method, as one pair corresponds to an edge in the CFG of a program. We further focus on the implementation of the most complex case, namely the edge coverage.

Inspired by the AFL [47] method of providing edge coverage information, we have adapted a similar approach for web applications. Listing 1.1 shows the instrumented version of a function `foo`. At the beginning of every basic block, a unique randomly generated number (the basic block's label) is XORed with the label of the previously visited block. The result of this operation represents the edge label. The edge label is used as index in the global `map` array where the counter for the edge is incremented.

The last statement in the stub code performs a right bitwise shifting on the current basic block label and stores the result as the label of the previously visited block. The shifting is needed to avoid cases where a label is XORed with itself thus giving zero as a result. This can happen for instance with simple loops that do not contain control statements in their body [47]. The super-global variable of PHP (`GLOBALS`) allows us to have access to the instrumentation data structures anywhere in the code, regardless of scope.

```
1  <?php
2  function foo(int $x, int $y) {
3      # BEGIN instrumentation code for basic block A
4      # $_key represents Edge CallSite->A
5      $_key = BASIC_BLOCK_A_LABEL ^ $GLOBALS["_instr"]["prev"];
6      $GLOBALS["_instr"]["map"][$_key] += 1;
7      $GLOBALS["_instr"]["prev"] = BASIC_BLOCK_A_LABEL >> 1;
8      # END instrumentation code
9
10     $z = 0;
11     if ($x == $y) {
12         # BEGIN instrumentation code for basic block B
13         # $_key represents Edge A->B
14         $_key = BASIC_BLOCK_B_LABEL ^ $GLOBALS["_instr"]["prev"];
15         $GLOBALS["_instr"]["map"][$_key] += 1;
16         $GLOBALS["_instr"]["prev"] = BASIC_BLOCK_B_LABEL >> 1;
17         # END instrumentation code
18
19         $z = 1
20     }
21     # BEGIN instrumentation code for basic block C
22     # $_key represents Edge A->C or B->C
23     $_key = BASIC_BLOCK_C_LABEL ^ $GLOBALS["_instr"]["prev"];
24     ...
```

Listing 1.1. Sample of an instrumented function **foo** for measuring edge coverage.

Feedback. Coverage information is reported at the end of program execution. To achieve this, we prepend to every source file additional header stub code that will be the first statements executed in a program. We additionally utilize the inbuilt function **register_shutdown_function**, where a custom function is specified that will automatically get called at the end of the program. In this header stub, a function is registered that will write the resulting **map** array to a file, HTTP headers or shared memory region and the instrumentation data structures are initialised. Listing 1.2 shows the header stub code for outputting coverage information in a file. webFuzz will place this stub after any **Namespace** and **Declare** statements present in the source file, as PHP dictates that these must be the top-most statements. The header stub follows that will only be called once during program execution (guarded by the enclosing **if**) and the remaining statements in the source file come next.

```
1  <?php
2  # Namespace and Declare statements of source file
3  if (! array_key_exists('_instr', $GLOBALS)) {
4      $GLOBALS['_instr']['map'] = array();
5      $GLOBALS['_instr']['prev'] = 0;
6      function instr_out() {
7          $f = fopen("/var/instr/map." . $_SERVER['HTTP_REQ_ID'], "w+");
8          foreach ($GLOBALS["_instr"]["map"] as $edge => $count) {
9              fwrite($f, $edge . "-" . $count . "\n");
10         }
11         fclose($f);
12     }
13     register_shutdown_function('instr_out');
14 }
15 # Remaining source file statements follow
16 ...
```

Listing 1.2. The instrumentation header stub inserted at the beginning of each source file. This particular stub will write the coverage report in a file.

2.2   Fuzzing Analysis

webFuzz is a mutation based fuzzer that employs incremental test case creation guided by the coverage feedback it receives from the instrumented web application. It additionally features a dynamic builtin crawler, a proxy for intercepting browser requests, easy session cookie retrieval and a low false-positive XSS detector. We expand on all of these aspects below.

Workflow. A fuzzing session consists of multiple workers continuously sending requests and analysing their responses. The high-level process that each worker performs is as follows. Initially, webFuzz fetches an unvisited GET or POST request that has been uncovered by the builtin crawler. If no such request exists, webFuzz will create a new request by mutating the most favorable previous one. It then sends the request back to the web application and reads its HTTP response and coverage feedback. Furthermore, webFuzz parses the HTML of the response to uncover new links from anchor and form elements and scans the document for XSS vulnerabilities. Finally, if the request is favorable (deduced from its coverage feedback) webFuzz computes its rank and stores it for future mutation and fuzzing.

The fuzzing session can be run as an authenticated user by spawning a browser window for the user to login and for webFuzz to retrieve the session cookies.

Mutation. Mutating inputs is a necessary step in the fuzzing process in order to maximize the number of paths explored and to trigger bugs lying in vulnerable pieces of code. The choice of mutation functions is both a challenging and empirical task. Aggressive mutating functions can destroy much of the input data structure which will result in the test case failing early on during program execution. On the other hand, too conservative mutations may not be enough to trigger new control flows [46]. Conversely to many fuzzers that employ malicious payload generation via the use of a specific attack grammar [18,39], webFuzz takes a mutation-based approach [37]. It starts with the default input values of an application (e.g., specified by the value attribute in a HTML input element), and performs a series of mutations on them. Currently five mutation functions are employed which modify the GET and/or POST parameters of a request. They are as follows.

- Insertion of real-life XSS payloads found in the wild;
- Mixing GET or POST parameters from other favourable requests (in evolutionary algorithms this is similar to *crossover*);
- Insertion of randomly generated strings;
- Insertion of HTML, PHP or JavaScript syntax tokens;
- Altering the type of a parameter (from an Array to a String and vice versa).

Some parameters may also get randomly opted out from the mutation process. This can be useful in cases where certain parameters need to remain unchanged for certain areas of the program to execute.

Proxy Server. Due to the heavy utilization of client-side code in most web applications, multiple URL links are generated on the fly by the browser's JavaScript engine instead of being present in the HTML response of the server. Since webFuzz only searches for new URL links in the HTML response and does not execute any client-side code, such JavaScript generated URLs will be missed from the fuzzing process. To solve this issue, webFuzz provides an option to initiate a proxied session before the fuzzing process begins, where the web application loads in a web browser environment and the user is given the ability to exercise the functionality of the web application manually by submitting new requests. As soon as the proxied web browser session is closed by the user, web-Fuzz retrieves all the URL links send during this session, adds them as possible fuzz targets and begins the fuzzing process.

Dynamic Crawling Functionality. Every HTML response received from the web applications is parsed and analysed in order to effectively crawl the whole application. HTML parsing is performed using the lenient *html5lib* [24] library which adheres to the HTML specification thus ensures similar results with that of web browsers. Using the parsed result, webFuzz can dynamically extract new fuzz targets from links in `anchor` and `form` elements, while also retrieve inputs from `input`, `textarea` and `option` elements. The crawler module additionally filters out any previously observed links to avoid crawling the same links repeatedly.

Vulnerability Detection. webFuzz is currently designed to detect stored and reflective cross-site scripting bugs produced by faulty server-side code. To ensure a low false positive rate webFuzz utilizes lightweight JavaScript code analysis. To identify whether a link is vulnerable, JavaScript code present in the HTML responses is parsed to its AST representation using the *esprima* [19] library. As every HTML document is parsed, identifying the executable HTML elements and attributes is trivial. webFuzz will look for code in the following locations in the HTML.

- Link attributes (e.g., `href`) that start with the *javascript:* label;
- Executable attributes that start with the *on* prefix (e.g. `onclick`);
- Script elements.

The XSS payloads webFuzz injects to `GET` and `POST` parameters are designed to call the JavaScript `alert` function with a unique keyword (having a fixed prefix) as input. The goal for the detector is to find the corresponding `alert` function call during the AST traversal process. If such a function call exists, it can infer that the XSS payload is executable, thus proving that the responsible link is vulnerable.

Additionally, in order to pinpoint which link triggers a found vulnerability, webFuzz will search in the request history and look for the request that contained the unique keyword present in the executable `alert` function call. Since this request history bookkeeping is a memory intensive process, webFuzz provides an option to limit the history size up to a maximum size.

Culling the Corpus. The majority of the mutations performed on requests are unsuccessful at triggering new code paths. It is thus essential to shrink the corpus of fuzz targets and store only the most favorable. In this way, webFuzz can reduce its memory footprint and ensure test case diversity.

Algorithm 1. Algorithm to decide whether a new request will be kept for future fuzzing

---

function ADDREQUEST(*hashTable, heapTree, newRequest*)
   for (*label, hitCount*) **in** *newRequest.coverage* **do**
      bucket ← *floor*(*log2*(*max*(*hitCount*, 128)))

      existingRequest ← *hashTable*[*blockLabel*][*bucket*]
      if *existingRequest* == ∅ **then**
         hashTable[*blockLabel*][*bucket*] ← *newRequest*

      else if *newRequest* **is lighter than** *existingRequest* **then**
         hashTable[*blockLabel*][*bucket*] ← *newRequest*

         if *existingRequest* ∉ *hashTable* **then**
            remove *existingRequest* **from** *HeapTree*
         end if
      end if
   end for
   if *newRequest* ∈ *hashTable* **then**
      add *newRequest* **to** *HeapTree*
   end if
end function

Algorithm 1 shows the *AFL*-inspired algorithm that determines if a new request is kept for future fuzzing or is discarded. The coverage feedback of a new request is checked against a hash table that holds information about all the instrumentation points (labels) that have been observed. Each entry in the table is split to *8* buckets, with each bucket corresponding to the number of times the label was executed in a single run. At each label-bucket entry, the lightest request that triggered this combination is stored. The use of buckets aims to distinguish requests that have executed a label a few times versus triggering it many more times [47].

When the hit-count of a label falls in a bucket that has already been observed, there is a clash for the same bucket in the same entry in the dictionary. The two requests are compared in terms of execution time and request size and the lightest of the two gets the entry.

As soon as a request has no longer entries in the table it is removed from the fuzzing session. This is done by removing it from an internal heap tree that stores the available fuzz targets in a semi-ordered fashion.

On the other hand, if a request has successfully acquired at least one entry in the hash table, it is inserted to a heap tree that contains all the favorable requests. This tree is consulted every time webFuzz has run out of new unvisited links, and thus requests the most favorable previous request to mutate. To rank requests we calculate a weighted difference score based on their attributes. The metrics it uses are listed below. Note that a (+) symbol indicates higher values are better while the opposite applies to (-).

- **Coverage Score** (+): total number of labels it has triggered;
- **Mutated Score** (+): approximation on the difference of code coverage with its parent request (the request it got mutated from);
- **Sinks Present** (+): whether injected GET or POST parameters managed to find their way in the HTML response;
- **Execution Time** (-): round-trip time of the request;
- **Size** (-): total number of characters in the GET and POST parameters;
- **Picked Score** (-): the number of times it has been picked for further mutation (this ensures that all requests in the heap tree will eventually be fuzzed).

3   Bug Injection

In this section we discuss a technique for injecting synthetic bugs in PHP. Such synthetic bugs can be useful not only for evaluating webFuzz, but also other bug-finding techniques for web applications. Our methodology is inspired by LAVA [15], a tool which is widely used to inject bugs into native code. Web vulnerabilities are different from memory-corruption ones, however the underlying mechanics of LAVA are still useful. In practice, we can inject hundreds of common web vulnerabilities, such as reflective cross-site scripting, and file inclusion, in a reasonable time period.

The artificial bugs should have several characteristics. They must be easy to inject, be plenty, span throughout the code, and be triggerable using only a limited set of inputs [15]. The vulnerability should also be injected in appropriate places by adding new code or modifying existing one. Lastly each injected bug should come with an input that serves as an existence proof.

3.1   Analysis and Injection

Using our custom instrumentation toolkit, we analyze the PHP source code dynamically to identify potential basic blocks and input parameters suitable for bug injection. Static analysis techniques using control flow and data flow graphs is also an option, however it would be more challenging due to the dynamically typed nature of PHP.

```
 1 <?php
 2 if ($_POST['v1'] == 2) {
 3    # Basic Block A
 4    if ($_POST['v2'] == 3) {
 5       # Basic Block B
 6       ...
 7    } else {
 8       # Basic Block C
 9       ...
10    }
11 } else {
12    // Basic Block D
13    ...
14 }
15 ?>
```

Listing 1.3. Example of PHP code where different set of inputs trigger different blocks.

In PHP, users' input is largely given using the *super-global* arrays the language provides, such as _POST, _GET and _REQUEST. By definition these variables contain the users' input unmodified. Discovering input variables that do not alter the execution path taken by a request is useful, as those variables can be used to synthesize an artificial bug.

For instance, in Listing 1.3 we present a possible pattern that can occur inside a PHP program. Specifically, variable _POST['v2'] can be used to synthesize a bug in basic block D as its value is not used inside the branch decisions to reach the block. On the contrary, in basic blocks A, B and C, the variable _POST['v1'] cannot be used to synthesize a bug inside these blocks, as any changes to the variable value would cause the blocks to not get executed. For this reason, finding the right input parameters and basic blocks to inject a bug into requires analyzing the branch decisions that reach it.

Due to the complexity in performing such analysis, our tool instead relies on a random, trial and error technique to determine the right input and basic block pairs to inject a bug. The bug injection process is as follows. The tool firstly crawls the web application and finds all the unique URLs. For each URL, it will extract the input fields from HTML forms and URL parameters, together with all the basic blocks triggered from this request. Using some block selection criteria (e.g. basic block nested level), it selects one of the blocks reported and it inserts a *candidate* bug in its location in the source code. The same request is sent to the web application with the input parameters modified to trigger the candidate bug, and if the bug is triggerable it is then considered a working artificial bug. This can only happen if the input parameters used in the artificial bug still trigger the execution path to the selected basic block.

3.2 Bug Template

Each candidate bug is created from a bug template that represents its general structure. The template can consist of one to three input fields from either GET or POST parameters. An example of a template is shown in Listing 1.4.

```
1  <?php
2
3  if ( ($_POST['v1'] % 10)  == (MAGIC % 10) ) {
4    if ( ($_POST['v1'] % 100) == (MAGIC % 100) ) {
5      if ( ($_POST['v1'] % 1000) == (MAGIC % 1000) ) {
6          # Vulnerable Sink
7          # Examples:
8          # 1) echo $_POST['v2']
9          # 2) print '<div class="' . $_POST['v2'] . '"></div>'
10         # 2) include $_POST['v2']
11       }
12     }
13 }
```

Listing 1.4. Construction of a bug using two variables. The exploiting input must contain the magic value in v1 and the bug payload in v2.

The *MAGIC* value in Listing 1.4 is a random number that needs to be guessed to execute the bug. This magic number must be placed in POST variable v1 and the bug payload in variable v2.

The format of the template is designed to mimic how a real-world bug may be hidden inside a deeply nested block. The stacked if statements also help in the process of guessing the magic number by rewarding with a new basic block (i.e. increase in code coverage) every time a correct digit is found. A bug finding tool that has access to information on the executed basic blocks can identify which inputs are closer to executing an artificial bug.

The aim of the stacked if approach is similar to the *value profile* feature provided by libfuzzer [40], with the difference that libfuzzer inherently supports instrumenting comparison instructions whereas webFuzz requires explicit unrolling of the comparison instruction as a series of stacked if statements.

The vulnerability the sink aims to introduce ranges from cross-site scripting bugs due to unsafe use of **echo** and **print** statements to **include** statements for file inclusion bugs. A plethora of different sink formats are also available which can further test the bug finding tool's ability in generating the correct bug payload format. Some examples for cross-site scripting bugs include unsafe code inside JavaScript block and unsafe code inside HTML attributes.

Using our bug injection tool, we have added numerous triggerable bugs in popular web applications, such as WordPress. In Sect. 4 we evaluate webFuzz's performance in finding these bugs.

4   Evaluation

In this section we evaluate webFuzz and the bug injection methodology. Our evaluation aims to answer the following research questions (RQ).

- **RQ1** Does our approach of coverage-guided input selection and mutation achieve high code coverage? Do we still notice an increase in code coverage after the initial crawling process is finished (i.e., are the input mutations effective in triggering new paths)?
- **RQ2** What is the combined overhead of our solution (instrumentation and webFuzz processing) in terms of throughput, and how does this compare with black-box approaches?

- **RQ3** Can webFuzz detect more artificial and real-life XSS bugs in comparison to other fuzzers within a limited time frame?

For *RQ1* we measure how the accumulated code coverage develops in our test subjects for a fuzzing session lasting 35 h in each. The experiment is thoroughly analysed in Sect. 4.1. For *RQ2-3*, we compare webFuzz with Wfuzz [31], one of the most prominent open-source black-box fuzzers, and we present the results in Sects. 4.2 and 4.3. Finally, we use the following web applications for all experiments: (1) CE-Phoenix 1.0.5 (e-commerce application), (2) Joomla 3.7.0 (CMS), (3) WackoPicko (a web application with known vulnerabilities), (4) WeBid 1.2.1 (online auctions application), and (5) WordPress 4.6.19 (CMS).

All experiments are executed on four identical Ubuntu 18.04 LTS Linux machines that possess a quad-core Intel Xeon W-2104 Processor @3.20 GHz and 64 GB of RAM. In total, we have spend around *1000* computational hours in running our experiments.

The amount of manual effort needed in setting up the experiments varies depending on the application. Applications such as WeBid and CE-Phoenix are more susceptible to damage caused by sending unexpected input and thus all sensitive endpoints need to be firstly identified and blocked from the fuzzing process. Additionally, webFuzz has a number of tunable parameters such as the weight of each attribute when calculating the request's rank and the weight of each mutation strategy. Although webFuzz comes with sane defaults for these values, we have tweaked these parameters in each of our experiments to increase the throughput and code coverage but at the cost of more manual effort.

4.1 Code Coverage

Code coverage is an important metric for a fuzzer, as higher coverage entails higher chances of triggering vulnerabilities. Thus is justifiable as to trigger a given bug the fuzzer must be able to reach the associated code path where the bug lies. In addition, code coverage can provide feedback on the effectiveness of the mutation functions employed and, in particular, whether they trigger new code paths.

Methodology. All *five* web applications are instrumented using the hybrid node-edge method, that provides coverage information for both the basic-blocks and the pairs of consecutive blocks (edges) executed. Since the actual number of all possible edges is not known (as that requires CFG generation), we can use the block count to get an estimate on the code coverage as a percentage. In addition, we run the proxy feature as described in Sect. 2.2 in all *five* projects to include the JavaScript generated URLs in the list of fuzzing targets.

Analysis. Figure 1 shows how the accumulated code coverage progresses with time in the five applications. webFuzz managed to trigger more than 20% of the total basic blocks in all five applications, with CE-Phoenix managing to reach code coverage as high as 34% and with WackoPicko reaching 41%. The lenient and sometimes non-existent input validation rules with CE-Phoenix makes the

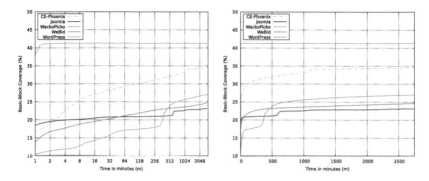

Fig. 1. Accumulated Basic-Block coverage achieved with webFuzz in *five* web applications. The figure on the left shows the coverage in logarithmic time scale, and on the right in linear time scale.

fuzzing process particularly effective as seen from the high code coverage. web-Fuzz can mutate form inputs with much freedom without requiring the input to adhere to stringent validation rules. The minimalistic nature of the WackoPicko app on the other hand, allowed webFuzz to quickly crawl the application within the first few minutes, while the input mutations only slightly increased the code coverage with time.

With WordPress, at around 350 min in the fuzzing session the mutation process kicks in as webFuzz finished the initial crawling process. The code coverage is seen to take a steep increase, indicating that the mutation functions employed are largely effective in triggering new code paths. A similar pattern can be observed with Joomla, albeit on a smaller scale. Long after the initial crawling finished, at 600 min in, the mutation functions manage to trigger multiple new basic blocks increasing the code coverage by 1%.

The code coverages reached by webFuzz is comparable to that of native application fuzzers such as AFL, AFL-Fast, TortoiseFuzz, FairFuzz and MOPT. Wang et al. have measured the code coverage of seven native fuzzers in 12 applications in their evaluation of TortoiseFuzz [44]. Their work showed that the average coverage reached for a application ranged from 4.55% ± 1.26 up to 76% ± 0.3 and with an average coverage throughout all fuzzers and applications being at 27.4%. webFuzz in the five test subjects tested reached 32.8% on average.

4.2 Throughput

One reason for the effectiveness of fuzzers in discovering vulnerabilities is their ability to test millions of inputs in a short time frame. For this reason we conduct an experiment to test the difference in throughput (requests/sec) between the black-box fuzzer Wfuzz and webFuzz.

Methodology. We measure the throughput of the two fuzzers during fuzzing sessions lasting 1 h for each web application. We further measure how the throughput varies with different worker counts, i.e., number of parallel connections used. webFuzz uses the instrumented whereas Wfuzz uses the original versions of the web applications. In addition, because Wfuzz requires explicit definition of the fuzzing payloads to use, we have instructed it to generate XSS payloads in a similar fashion to webFuzz. Lastly, due to Wfuzz's limited crawling functionality, we assist the fuzzer by crawling each web application using our tools. We then instruct Wfuzz to fuzz each link in the crawler's result in a round-robin fashion.

Table 1. Average and Maximum throughout achieved with webFuzz and Wfuzz using different worker counts. Each cell states the throughput (requests/sec) at the particular scenario.

Fuzzer workers	webFuzz						Wfuzz					
	4		8		16		4		8		16	
	Avg	Max	Avg	Max	Avg	Max	Avg	Max	Avg	Max	Avg	Max
CE-Phoenix	83	141	70	183	62	182	133	392	137	446	133	453
Joomla	36	50	46	74	45	74	272	896	61	174	63	250
WackoPicko	52	260	45	170	128	152	480	976	491	1008	496	1004
WeBid	29	75	26	89	18	81	143	418	43	57	27	30
WordPress	8	33	8	34	10	36	17	142	72	194	62	176

Analysis. In Table 1 we see the average and maximum throughput achieved by the two fuzzers. Depending on the size of the web application, the bottleneck factor that limits the throughput is either the web server or the fuzzer. With WeBid, a relatively small project, we notice with both fuzzers a slight decrease in throughput when increasing the number of workers. The bottleneck in both situations is the fuzzer, where due to their single-core nature, the core is utilized at the fullest with just 4 worker counts, thus not benefiting from higher worker counts. On the other hand, WordPress benefits from higher worker counts due to its large project size. The average round-trip time is relatively high, thus both fuzzers can benefit from more workers as more requests are sent in parallel and the fuzzing process does not stall.

In general, the introduction of instrumentation, HTML parsing, and coverage analysis takes a toll on the performance, as Wfuzz is seen to reach throughputs up to ten times higher than webFuzz. Section 4.3 shows that this overhead is outweighed by the improved detection speed of webFuzz.

4.3 Vulnerability Detection

The crucial test for webFuzz is whether it can outperform black-box fuzzers in detecting XSS vulnerabilities. To test this, we fuzz the set of web applications using webFuzz and Wfuzz and we compare the findings. To further evaluate our bug injection tool, we artificially inject XSS vulnerabilities in the *five* web applications and measure the number of artificial bugs found by both fuzzers.

Methodology. We fuzz every web application for at least 50 hours with each fuzzer. We again assist Wfuzz in crawling and payload selection as described in Sect. 4.2.

Table 2. Number of real-life (known from CVE records) and artificial XSS bugs found with webFuzz and Wfuzz. Each cell states the number of bugs found in respect to the total bugs present. The zero-day bugs found by each fuzzer are additionally stated.

Fuzzer	webFuzz			Wfuzz		
Bug type	Zero-day	Real-life	Artificial	Zero-day	Real-life	Artificial
CE-Phoenix	5	14/15	23/541	1	13/15	2/541
Joomla	0	1/32	2/64	0	0/32	0/64
WackoPicko	0	3/3	2/48	0	3/3	0/48
WeBid	1	7/7	3/72	1	7/7	0/72
WordPress	1	2/4	3/241	0	1/4	3/241

Analysis. Table 2 shows the results of our experiments. webFuzz outperforms Wfuzz in all five applications. webFuzz additionally manages to find *zero-day* XSS bugs in the latest versions of WordPress and CE-Phoenix. We have reported all found vulnerabilities to their developers, they have acknowledged our findings, and we have been awarded $500 from WordPress for our responsible disclosure. The official WordPress bug report is Report 1103740 and will be publicly disclosed as soon as a bug fix is available.

Beginning with CE-Phoenix, both fuzzers manage to uncover multiple bugs. In total webFuzz found *14* real XSS bugs and *5* zero-day bugs which were not listed in CVE records. Interestingly, webFuzz has found more XSS bugs in this project than Wfuzz. One reason for this lies in the request ranking mechanism employed by webFuzz that prioritizes requests that have high code coverage and contain sinks. As a result, the vulnerable URLs receive more fuzzing time than in the round-robin approach used by Wfuzz.

The input validations and heavy utilization of client-side JavaScript code in Joomla has proven to be an obstacle in the fuzzing process as webFuzz found just one out of the 32 real XSS bugs present.

In the WackoPicko application, both fuzzers manage to find all three XSS vulnerabilities that it contained. The required XSS payload structure is relatively simple so the main feature needed to find the bugs is a good crawler. For this reason, if Wfuzz was not extended with additional crawler functionality, it would not be able to find the multi-step XSS present in the application.

Continuing with WeBid, this inactive project was known to contain *7* XSS vulnerabilities from the CVE [14] records on it. Since the complexity of the real bugs present in this project is relatively simple – required simple payload format and little crawling – both fuzzers manage to find all known real-life XSS bugs and an additional unlisted XSS bug.

With WordPress, we enable four third-party plugins that each contained one XSS vulnerability. webFuzz uncovers *two* out of the *four* plugin bugs, as the other two bugs require complex JSON formatted XSS payload or a GET parameter not present in the HTML responses.

The *zero-day* RXSS bug in WordPress consisted of finding a vulnerable GET parameter in a link and inserting a specially formatted payload to effectively bypass any sanitization steps. Two features employed by webFuzz have accelerated the finding of this bug, which are the source-sink identification and the executed basic block count. Firstly, by analysing the HTML response and finding out that the GET parameter is outputted in the response, webFuzz prioritized the request using its request ranking mechanism. Additionally, the needed payload format exercised more code paths in the input parsing process in comparison to other types of payload formats which meant that webFuzz would be rewarded with extra basic blocks when the right format was guessed. More specifically, in order for the payload to avoid getting sanitized, it had to contain a leading hashtag character which the input parsing code would mistakenly treat as a URL fragment. When the URL fragment parsing code got executed though, webFuzz received in its coverage feedback more basic blocks. These two features allowed webFuzz to guess the right XSS payload faster as the request with the vulnerable GET parameter containing a leading hashtag character scored higher.

Concerning the artificial RXSS bugs, webFuzz also finds more bugs than Wfuzz due to the different XSS payload creation mechanisms. As it has been described in Sect. 3.2, an artificial bug requires that a fuzzer finds the correct XSS payload format and also guesses the right magic number. Since correctly guessing a digit from the magic number triggers a new instrumentation point, webFuzz detects this change and prioritizes the request that causes it. With this method, the finding of a magic number is done incrementally, one correct digit at a time, which is faster than Wfuzz's blind fuzzing approach. As a real-world analogy for this process, each digit of the magic number can represent one correct mutation that gets us closer to the vulnerable sink.

5   Limitations

Concerning the Bug Injection tool, our prototype is currently limited to injecting surface-level bugs that rely on magic byte guessing to increase their complexity. Because the algorithm works by crawling the web application and semi-randomly picking an executed basic block to inject a vulnerability to, the resulting bugs do not rely on a complex internal application state for a bug to be triggered. More work needs to be done to improve the bug injection algorithm by enhancing it with means to monitor the application's state (located in the document cookies and in the database) and thus be able to expand its bug types to vulnerabilities that rely on a series of dependent requests.

Limitations in our fuzzer also exist, with the main limitation being the inability for webFuzz to fuzz Single Page Applications (SPA). These types of web applications heavily rely on JavaScript and the server responses are usually not in HTML format. Since webFuzz will not execute client-side JavaScript code, which in SPA applications is fully responsible for the HTML document creation and rendering, our fuzzer will not be applicable in such situations.

6   Future Work

As it can be seen from Sect. 4.2, the instrumentation overhead and webFuzz's request processing introduces high overheads. Multiple research papers have explored innovative ways to decrease the instrumentation overhead [1,10,43]. One common solution is to perform probe pruning which consists of finding the minimum set of basic blocks, where instrumenting only these blocks still provides us enough information to distinguish all executions from each other, i.e., no coverage information is lost. To perform this, CFG analysis must be performed which is possible in PHP [7].

There are also plans to extend our detection capabilities to SQL injection (SQLi) attacks which occur when untrusted data are sent to an interpreter or database as part of a query. To achieve this, SQLi related attack payloads found in the wild can be used as the base of the payload. To detect an SQLi vulnerability, webFuzz can scan the HTML response for database related keywords or for database hangs which can occur when a call to the database SLEEP command successfully slips through the query.

Finally, we are also planning on introducing netmap [38], a tool to effectively bypass the operating system's expensive network stack and allow the client and server to communicate faster.

7   Related Work

Native Fuzzing. Fuzzing has been perceived through several techniques and algorithms over the years, initially with fuzzing native applications. There exist the Black-box fuzzers [23,41,45] that are unaware of the fuzz target's internals, and the white- and grey-box fuzzers that leverage *program analysis* and *instrumentation* respectively to obtain feedback concerning the inputs' precision in discovering unseen paths [21,22,37,42,47] Additionally directed-based fuzzers use the coverage feedback to direct the fuzzer towards particular execution paths [21].

Web-app Fuzzing. Even though a huge effort is directed toward building fuzzers with the aim to weed out vulnerabilities in *native code*, little attention has been given to web application bugs. Tools currently available that target web application vulnerabilities behave predominantly in a black-box fashion that are subject to limitations due to limited knowledge of the application's state [9,17]. Some examples are: *Enemy of the State* [16], a black-box fuzzer that attempts to recreate the web application's state machine from the application responses and uses it to drive the fuzzing session. and *KameleonFuzz* [18], an evolutionary algorithm based black-box fuzzer.

There have been attempts to overcome the shortcomings of black-box techniques. White-box approaches for instance, utilize access to the web application's source code to create test cases intelligently [3, 4, 7, 8, 25–27, 29, 30]. Artzi et al. [6] developed a tool for discovering web application vulnerabilities by collecting information about the target extracted through concrete and symbolic execution. Another tool combining static and dynamic analysis is Saner [8] which tries to identify any sanitization processes that do not work as expected to, resulting in allowing attackers to introduce exploits. Similarly other work [3, 4], rely on static analysis and constraint solving to identify vulnerable source-sink pairs that contain insufficient sanitization. Backes et al. in their PHP aimed tool on the other hand, rely on Code Property Graphs and on modeling of vulnerabilities as graph traversals [7].

Contrary to the above research work for identifying web vulnerabilities, our technique adopts the grey-box approach. webFuzz *instruments* the fuzz target in order to create a feedback loop.

Vulnerability Injection. When evaluating automated vulnerability scanners, there is this great need of ground truth corpora, programs that have realistic vulnerabilities in known places. An example of such effort is Juliet [11], a suite that consists of thousands of small programs in C/C++ and Java, that contain various vulnerabilities (e.g., buffer overflows, NULL pointer dereference). Another example of such suite is BugBox [33], a vulnerability corpus for PHP web applications. However, these examples are pre-defined sets of vulnerable programs, that while being helpful for evaluating vulnerability scanners, they cannot simulate real world scenarios because of their small size. In contrast, automated bug injection tools can simulate real world scenarios because they are capable of injecting bugs in real-world programs. Main example of such tool and the inspiration of our automated bug injection tool is LAVA [15] which can automatically synthesize and inject thousands of bugs in native code programs. Some other examples include SolidiFI [20], an automated vulnerability injection tool targeted for evaluating smart contracts and EvilCoder [34], a framework that finds and modifies potentially vulnerable source code.

8   Conclusion

In this paper we presented webFuzz, the first *grey-box* fuzzer for discovering vulnerabilities in web applications. webFuzz applies instrumentation on the target web application for creating a *feedback loop* and utilizing it in order to increase code coverage. Consequently it increases the number of potential vulnerabilities found.

Acknowledgements. We thank the anonymous reviewers for helping us to improve the final version of this paper. This work was supported by the European Union's Horizon 2020 research and innovation programme under grant agreements No. 786669 (ReAct), No. 830929 (CyberSec4Europe) and No. 101007673 (RESPECT).

References

1. Agrawal, H.: Dominators, super blocks, and program coverage. In: Proceedings of the 21st ACM SIGPLAN-SIGACT Symposium on Principles of Programming Languages, pp. 25–34 (1994)
2. Aho, A., Lam, M., Ullman, J., Sethi, R.: Compilers: Principles, Techniques, and Tools. Pearson Education (2011). https://books.google.com.cy/books?id=NTIrAAAAQBAJ
3. Alhuzali, A., Eshete, B., Gjomemo, R., Venkatakrishnan, V.: Chainsaw: chained automated workflow-based exploit generation. In: Proceedings of the 2016 ACM SIGSAC Conference on Computer and Communications Security, pp. 641–652 (2016)
4. Alhuzali, A., Gjomemo, R., Eshete, B., Venkatakrishnan, V.: NAVEX: precise and scalable exploit generation for dynamic web applications. In: 27th USENIX Security Symposium (2018)
5. Ammann, P., Offutt, J.: Introduction to Software Testing. Cambridge University Press, Cambridge (2016)
6. Artzi, S., et al.: Finding bugs in web applications using dynamic test generation and explicit-state model checking. IEEE Trans. Softw. Eng. **36**, 474–494 (2010)
7. Backes, M., Rieck, K., Skoruppa, M., Stock, B., Yamaguchi, F.: Efficient and flexible discovery of PHP application vulnerabilities. In: 2017 IEEE European Symposium on Security And Privacy (EuroS&P), pp. 334–349. IEEE (2017)
8. Balzarotti, D., et al.: Saner: composing static and dynamic analysis to validate sanitization in web applications. In: 2008 IEEE Symposium on Security and Privacy (SP 2008) (2008)
9. Bau, J., Bursztein, E., Gupta, D., Mitchell, J.: State of the art: automated blackbox web application vulnerability testing. In: 2010 IEEE Symposium on Security and Privacy (2010)
10. Ben Khadra, M.A., Stoffel, D., Kunz, W.: Efficient binary-level coverage analysis. In: Proceedings of the 28th ACM Joint Meeting on European Software Engineering Conference and Symposium on the Foundations of Software Engineering, pp. 1153–1164 (2020)
11. Black, P.E., Black, P.E.: Juliet 1.3 test suite: changes from 1.2. US Department of Commerce, National Institute of Standards and Technology (2018)
12. Böhme, M., Pham, V.T., Nguyen, M.D., Roychoudhury, A.: Directed greybox fuzzing. In: Proceedings of the 2017 ACM SIGSAC Conference on Computer and Communications Security, pp. 2329–2344 (2017)
13. Cornelius Aschermann et al.: REDQUEEN: fuzzing with input-to-state correspondence. In: NDSS, vol. 19, pp. 1–15 (2019)
14. Corporation, T.M.: Common vulnerabilities and exposures (CVE) (2020). https://cve.mitre.org/
15. Dolan-Gavitt, B., et al.: LAVA: large-scale automated vulnerability addition. In: 2016 IEEE Symposium on Security and Privacy (SP). IEEE (2016)

16. Doupé, A., Cavedon, L., Kruegel, C., Vigna, G.: Enemy of the state: a state-aware black-box web vulnerability scanner. In: 21st USENIX Security Symposium (USENIX Security 12), Bellevue, WA, pp. 523–538. USENIX Association, August 2012. https://www.usenix.org/conference/usenixsecurity12/technical-sessions/presentation/doupe
17. Doupé, A., Cova, M., Vigna, G.: Why Johnny can't pentest: an analysis of black-box web vulnerability scanners. In: Kreibich, C., Jahnke, M. (eds.) DIMVA 2010. LNCS, vol. 6201, pp. 111–131. Springer, Heidelberg (2010). https://doi.org/10.1007/978-3-642-14215-4_7
18. Duchene, F., Rawat, S., Richier, J.L., Groz, R.: KameleonFuzz: evolutionary fuzzing for black-box XSS detection. In: Proceedings of the 4th ACM Conference on Data and Application Security and Privacy, CODASPY 2014, New York, NY, USA, p. 3748. Association for Computing Machinery (2014). https://doi.org/10.1145/2557547.2557550
19. Germán Méndez Bravoi, A.H.: esprima-python (2017). https://github.com/Kronuz/esprima-python
20. Ghaleb, A., Pattabiraman, K.: How effective are smart contract analysis tools? Evaluating smart contract static analysis tools using bug injection. arXiv preprint arXiv:2005.11613 (2020)
21. Godefroid, P., Klarlund, N., Sen, K.: Dart: directed automated random testing. In: Proceedings of the 2005 ACM SIGPLAN Conference on Programming Language Design and Implementation, PLDI 2005, New York, NY, USA, pp. 213–223. Association for Computing Machinery (2005). https://doi.org/10.1145/1065010.1065036
22. Godefroid, P., Levin, M.Y., Molnar, D.: SAGE: whitebox fuzzing for security testing. Queue (2012)
23. Householder, A.D., Foote, J.M.: Probability-based parameter selection for black-box fuzz testing, Technical report. Carnegie-Mellon Univ Pittsburgh PA Software Engineering Inst. (2012)
24. James Graham, S.S.: html5lib-python (2007). https://github.com/html5lib/html5lib-python
25. Jovanovic, N., Kruegel, C., Kirda, E.: Pixy: a static analysis tool for detecting web application vulnerabilities. In: 2006 IEEE Symposium on Security and Privacy (S&P 2006), pp. 6-pp. IEEE (2006)
26. Jovanovic, N., Kruegel, C., Kirda, E.: Precise alias analysis for static detection of web application vulnerabilities. In: Proceedings of the 2006 Workshop on Programming Languages and Analysis for Security, PLAS 2006, New York, NY, USA, pp. 27–36. Association for Computing Machinery (2006). https://doi.org/10.1145/1134744.1134751
27. Kieyzun, A., Guo, P.J., Jayaraman, K., Ernst, M.D.: Automatic creation of SQL injection and cross-site scripting attacks. In: 2009 IEEE 31st International Conference on Software Engineering, pp. 199–209 (2009)
28. Klees, G., Ruef, A., Cooper, B., Wei, S., Hicks, M.: Evaluating fuzz testing. In: Proceedings of the 2018 ACM SIGSAC Conference on Computer and Communications Security, CCS 2018, New York, NY, USA, pp. 2123–2138. Association for Computing Machinery (2018). https://doi.org/10.1145/3243734.3243804
29. Medeiros, I., Neves, N., Correia, M.: DEKANT: a static analysis tool that learns to detect web application vulnerabilities. In: Proceedings of the 25th International Symposium on Software Testing and Analysis, pp. 1–11 (2016)

30. Medeiros, I., Neves, N.F., Correia, M.: Automatic detection and correction of web application vulnerabilities using data mining to predict false positives. In: Proceedings of the 23rd International Conference on World Wide Web, WWW 2014, pp. 63–74, New York, NY, USA. Association for Computing Machinery (2014). https://doi.org/10.1145/2566486.2568024
31. Mendez, X.: Wfuzz - the web fuzzer (2011). https://github.com/xmendez/wfuzz
32. Mu, D., Cuevas, A., Yang, L., Hu, H., Xing, X., Mao, B., Wang, G.: Understanding the reproducibility of crowd-reported security vulnerabilities. In: 27th USENIX Security Symposium (USENIX Security 18), Baltimore, MD. pp. 919–936. USENIX Association, August 2018. https://www.usenix.org/conference/usenixsecurity18/presentation/mu
33. Nilson, G., Wills, K., Stuckman, J., Purtilo, J.: BugBox: a vulnerability corpus for PHP web applications. In: 6th Workshop on Cyber Security Experimentation and Test (CSET 13). USENIX Association, Washington, D.C., August 2013. https://www.usenix.org/conference/cset13/workshop-program/presentation/nilson
34. Pewny, J., Holz, T.: EvilCoder: automated bug insertion. In: Proceedings of the 32nd Annual Conference on Computer Security Applications, ACSAC 2016, New York, NY, USA, p. 214225. Association for Computing Machinery (2016). https://doi.org/10.1145/2991079.2991103
35. Pham, V.T., Böhme, M., Santosa, A.E., Caciulescu, A.R., Roychoudhury, A.: Smart greybox fuzzing. IEEE Trans. Softw. Eng. (2019)
36. Popov, N.: PHP parser. https://github.com/nikic/PHP-Parser
37. Rawat, S., Jain, V., Kumar, A., Cojocar, L., Giuffrida, C., Bos, H.: VUzzer: application-aware evolutionary fuzzing. In: NDSS, vol. 17, pp. 1–14 (2017)
38. Rizzo, L., Landi, M.: Netmap: Memory mapped access to network devices. SIGCOMM Comput. Commun. Rev. **41**(4), 422–423 (2011). https://doi.org/10.1145/2043164.2018500
39. Seal, S.M.: Optimizing web application fuzzing with genetic algorithms and language Theory. Master's thesis, Wake Forest University (2016)
40. Serebryany, K.: Libfuzzer-a library for coverage-guided fuzz testing (2015). https://llvm.org/docs/LibFuzzer.html
41. Sparks, S., Embleton, S., Cunningham, R., Zou, C.: Automated vulnerability analysis: leveraging control flow for evolutionary input crafting. In: Twenty-Third Annual Computer Security Applications Conference (ACSAC 2007), pp. 477–486 (2007)
42. Stephens, N., et al.: Driller: augmenting fuzzing through selective symbolic execution. In: NDSS, vol. 16, pp. 1–16 (2016)
43. Tikir, M.M., Hollingsworth, J.K.: Efficient instrumentation for code coverage testing. ACM SIGSOFT Softw. Eng. Notes **27**(4), 86–96 (2002)
44. Wang, Y., et al.: Not all coverage measurements are equal: fuzzing by coverage accounting for input prioritization. In: NDSS (2020)
45. Woo, M., Cha, S.K., Gottlieb, S., Brumley, D.: Scheduling black-box mutational fuzzing. In: Proceedings of the 2013 ACM SIGSAC Conference on Computer & Communications Security, pp. 511–522 (2013)
46. Zalewski, M.: Binary fuzzing strategies: what works, what doesn't, August 2014. https://lcamtuf.blogspot.com/2014/08/binary-fuzzing-strategies-what-works.html
47. Zalewski, M.: More about AFL - AFL 2.53b documentation (2019). https://afl-1.readthedocs.io/en/latest/about_afl.html

My Fuzzer Beats Them All! Developing a Framework for Fair Evaluation and Comparison of Fuzzers

David Paaßen[✉], Sebastian Surminski, Michael Rodler, and Lucas Davi

University of Duisburg-Essen, Duisburg, Germany
{david.paassen,sebastian.surminski,michael.rodler,lucas.davi}@uni-due.de

Abstract. Fuzzing has become one of the most popular techniques to identify bugs in software. To improve the fuzzing process, a plethora of techniques have recently appeared in academic literature. However, evaluating and comparing these techniques is challenging as fuzzers depend on randomness when generating test inputs. Commonly, existing evaluations only partially follow best practices for fuzzing evaluations. We argue that the reason for this are twofold. First, it is unclear if the proposed guidelines are necessary due to the lack of comprehensive empirical data in the case of fuzz testing. Second, there does not yet exist a framework that integrates statistical evaluation techniques to enable fair comparison of fuzzers.

To address these limitations, we introduce a novel fuzzing evaluation framework called SENF (Statistical EvaluatioN of Fuzzers). We demonstrate the practical applicability of our framework by utilizing the most wide-spread fuzzer AFL as our baseline fuzzer and exploring the impact of different evaluation parameters (e.g., the number of repetitions or run-time), compilers, seeds, and fuzzing strategies. Using our evaluation framework, we show that supposedly small changes of the parameters can have a major influence on the measured performance of a fuzzer.

1 Introduction

Fuzzing approaches aim at automatically generating program input to assess the robustness of a program to arbitrary input. The goal of a fuzzer is to trigger some form of unwanted behavior, e.g., a crash or exception. Once a program fault occurs during the fuzzing process, a developer or analyst investigates the fault to identify its root cause. Subsequently, this allows the software vendor to improve the quality and security of the software. One of the most prominent fuzzers, called American Fuzzy Lop (AFL) [41], has discovered hundreds of security-critical bugs in a wide variety of libraries and programs.

Following the success of AFL, various other fuzzers have been proposed which aim to outperform AFL by implementing new and improved fuzzing techniques (e.g., [8,19,27,29]). However, it remains largely unclear whether the claim of

© Springer Nature Switzerland AG 2021
E. Bertino et al. (Eds.): ESORICS 2021, LNCS 12972, pp. 173–193, 2021.
https://doi.org/10.1007/978-3-030-88418-5_9

improving the overall fuzzing performance is indeed true. This is because accurately evaluating a fuzzer is challenging as the fuzzing process itself is nondeterministic. Hence, comparing single runs or multiple runs using simple statistical measurements such as average values can lead to false conclusions about the performance of the evaluated fuzzer. Similarly, deriving the number of potentially discovered bugs based solely on coverage measurements and the number of program crashes does not necessarily map to the effectiveness of a fuzzer. For instance, Inozemtseva et al. [25] show that there is no strong correlation between the coverage of a test suite and its ability to detect bugs. Additionally, there are fuzzing approaches that prioritize certain program paths instead of maximizing the overall coverage [7,10,39]. Such approaches cannot be evaluated using overall code coverage as a measurement.

A study by Klees et al. [26] shows that existing evaluation strategies do not consider state-of-the-art best practices for testing randomized algorithms such as significance tests or standardized effect sizes. They also provide a list of recommendations. However, these recommendations are mainly derived from known best practices from the field of software testing or from a small set of experiments on a small test set. Nevertheless, as we will show in Sect. 4, recent fuzzing proposals still do not consistently follow recommendations regarding the employed statistical methods and evaluation parameters (e.g., run-time or number of trials). Since the goal of the recommendations is to ensure that the reported findings are not the results of randomness, it remains unclear whether we can trust existing fuzzing experiments and conclusions drawn from those experiments.

Another important aspect of any fuzzer evaluation concerns the employed test set. Several research works introduced test sets such as LAVA-M [14], Magma [22], or the Google Fuzzer Suite [20]. Ideally, a test set should contain a wide variety of different programs as well as a set of known bugs covering various bug types including a proof-of-vulnerability (PoV). This is crucial to enable accurate assessment on the effectiveness and efficiency of a fuzzer as a missing ground truth may lead to overestimating or underestimating the real performance of a fuzzer. We analyze these test sets in detail in Sect. 5.2 as the test set selection is crucial for evaluating and comparing fuzzers.

Lastly, existing evaluation strategies lack uniformity for evaluation parameters such as the number of trials, run-time, and size of the employed test set and the included bugs. As it is still unknown how these parameters affect the fuzzer evaluation in practice, fuzzing experiments are commonly executed using a wide variety of different parameters and evaluation methods. This may not only affect the soundness (e.g., due to biases caused by the choice of parameter) of the results but also makes it even harder to compare results across multiple studies.

Our Contributions. In this study, we address the existing shortcomings of fuzzing evaluations. To do so, we review current fuzzing evaluation strategies and introduce the design and implementation of a novel fuzzing evaluation framework, called SENF (Statistical EvaluatioN of Fuzzers), which unifies state-of-the-art statistical methods and combines them to calculate a ranking to compare an arbitrary number of fuzzers on a large test set. The goal of our framework is twofold. First, we aim to provide a platform that allows us to easily compare a large number of fuzzers (and configurations) on a test set utilizing statistical significance tests and standardized effect sizes. Contrary to existing frameworks, such as UNIFUZZ [28], SENF provides a single ranking which allows for an easy comparison of the overall performance of fuzzers. Second, due to the lack of comprehensive empirical data we test if following the recommended best practices is necessary or if we can loosen the strict guidelines to reduce the computational effort needed to compare different fuzzing algorithms without impairing the quality of the evaluation which was not possible with the data provided by Klees et al. [26].

To show the applicability of SENF, we build our evaluation based on the most prominent fuzzer, namely AFL [41] and its optimizations, as well as the popular forks AFLFast [8], Fairfuzz [27], and AFL++ [15]. This allows us to argue about the usefulness and impact of the proposed methods and techniques as AFL is commonly used as the baseline fuzzer in existing fuzzing evaluations. We ensure that all tested fuzzers share the same code base which allows us to precisely attribute performance differences to the changes made by the respective fuzzer or optimization technique.

We provide an extensive empirical evaluation of the impact of fuzzing parameters. In total, we ran over 600 experiments which took over 280k CPU hours to complete. To the best of our knowledge, this is currently the largest study of fuzzers published in academic research.

In summary, we provide the following contributions:

- We implement a fuzzing evaluation framework, called SENF, which utilizes state-of-the-art statistical evaluation methods including p-values and standardized effect sizes to compare fuzzers on large test sets.
- We conduct a large-scale fuzzer evaluation based on a test set of 42 different targets with bugs from various bug classes and a known ground truth to quantify the influence of various evaluation parameters to further improve future fuzzer evaluations.
- We open-source SENF [32], containing the statistical evaluation scripts, the result data of our experiments, and seed files to aid researchers to conduct fuzzer evaluations and allowing reproducibility of our study.

2   Background

In this section, we provide background information on the most relevant fuzzing concepts and discuss how these are implemented in case of the popular fuzzer AFL [41].

Fuzzers are programs that need to decide on a strategy to generate inputs for test programs. The inputs should be chosen in such a way that they achieve as much coverage of the program's state space as possible to be able to detect abnormal behavior that indicates an error. Fuzzers are commonly categorized into black-box, white-box, and grey-box fuzzers. Where black-bock fuzzers (e.g., zzuf [23]) try to maximizes the number of executions while white-box fuzzers (e.g., KLEE [9]) make heavy use of instrumentation and code analysis to generate more significant input. Grey-box fuzzers (e.g., AFL [41]) try to find a balance between the executions per second and time spend on analysis.

One of the most well-known fuzzers is called American fuzzy lop (AFL) and is a mutation-based coverage-guided grey-box fuzzer. It retrieves coverage feedback about the executed program path for a corresponding test input. Since its creation, AFL discovered bugs in more than 100 different programs and libraries [41] confirming its high practical relevance to improve software quality and security.

Given the influence of AFL in the fuzzing area, we take a closer look at its architecture. AFL includes a set of tools that act as drop-in replacements for known compilers, e.g., as a replacement for gcc AFL features afl-gcc which is used to add code instrumentation. The instrumentation provides crucial information such as the branch coverage and coarse-grained information about how often a specific branch has been taken.

The fuzzing process can be divided into four different core components which can also be found in many existing mutations-based grey-box fuzzers, including forks of AFL: ① *Search strategy*: The search strategy selects an input (e.g., one of the initial seeds) that is used in the mutation stage to generate more test inputs. ② *Power schedule*: The power schedule assigns an energy value which limits the number of new inputs generated in the mutation stage. The idea is to spend more time mutating input that is more likely to increase the code coverage. ③ *Mutations*: The mutation stage changes (part of) the selected input to produce new inputs which are then executed by the program under test. AFL has two different mutation stages. The *deterministic stage* does simple bit flips or inserts specific values such as INT_MAX. In the *havoc stage*, AFL executes a loop that applies different mutations on the selected input, e.g., inserting random data or trimming the input. ④ *Select interesting input*: After executing a new input, the fuzzer collects the feedback data and decides if the newly generated input is interesting, i.e., whether or not the input should be mutated to generate new inputs.

Successors of AFL commonly implement their improvements as part of one or more of the discussed core components. In Sect. 6.1 we describe the changes implemented by the different fuzzers we test in our evaluation in more detail.

To address the problem of inputs being rejected due to rigorous input checks, fuzzer leverage seed files which provide initial coverage and useful inputs for the mutation stage. Thus, a fuzzer does not need to learn the input format from scratch. To generate a set of seed files, one can either collect sample files from the public sources or manually construct them. AFL prefers seeds with high code coverage, a small file size, and low execution time. To minimize the seed set, AFL provides a tool called afl-cmin which one can use to remove useless seed files. However, if it is not possible to collect a sophisticated seed set one can always employ an empty file as the only initial seed file.

3   Statistical Evaluations

As the main purpose of fuzzers is to find bugs, the naive approach to compare two or more fuzzers, is to fuzz a target program for a fixed amount of time and then either compare the time it took to find bugs or compare the number of bugs a fuzzer discovered. However, the fuzzing process itself is non-deterministic. For instance, in AFL, the non-deterministic component is the havoc stage which is part of the mutation module. Thus, executing multiple trials with the same fuzzer may yield different results. As a consequence, using only a single execution might lead to a false conclusion. Other utilized evaluation metrics such as the average and median can be affected by similar issues. The common problem of these simple techniques is that they ignore randomness, i.e., they do not consider the non-deterministic nature of fuzzing. The most common method to address this problem is to calculate the statistical significance, i.e., the p-value which was popularized by Fisher [17]. If the p-value is below a predefined threshold we assume that the observed difference between to fuzzers is genuine and consider the results statistically significant.

When comparing two fuzzers, it is not only relevant to know whether the performance differences are statistically significant but also to properly quantify the difference, namely, we have to calculate the effect size. However, when comparing fuzzers on multiple targets non-standardized effect sizes are affected by the unit of measurement which may result in unwanted biases. To address this issue a standardized effect size should be used [2].

In general, we can differentiate between statistical tests for dichotomous and interval-scale results which require a different set of statistical evaluation methods. In the following, we describe both result types and the recommended approach to calculate statistical significance and the corresponding effect size as discussed by Arcuri et al. [2]. For more details about the employed statistical methods, we refer the interested reader to the relevant literature [16,30,38].

An interval-scale result in the context of fuzzing is the time a fuzzer needs to detect a specific bug. In such a case it is recommended to use the Mann-Whitney-U test to calculate the p-value to test for statistical significance. Contrary to the popular *t-test* the Mann-Whitney-U test does not assume that the underlying data follows the normal distribution. To quantify the effect size for interval-scale results, one can utilize the Vargha and Delaneys $\hat{A}_{12}$ statistic.

A dichotomous result can only have two outcomes, usually *success* or *failure*. In the context of a fuzzer evaluation, a dichotomous result simply states whether a specific bug has been discovered in the given time limit. To calculate the statistical significance, Arcuri et al. [2] recommend using the Fisher exact test. As the name suggests, this statistical test is exact which means that it is precise and not just an estimation for the actual p-value. To calculate the effect size for dichotomous results, it is recommended to calculate the odds ratio.

4   Problem Description and Related Work

The evaluation of fuzzers was first analyzed by Klees et al. [26] who demonstrate that simply comparing the number of crashes found using a single trial on a small set of targets is misleading as it gives no insight into whether the fuzzer finding more crashes discovers more bugs in practice. Thus, it is preferred to use a test set with a ground truth, i.e., a set of inputs that trigger a known bug or vulnerability inside the test program. To improve fuzzer evaluations, Klees et al. [26] provided a set of recommendations for evaluating fuzzers based on best practices from the field of software engineering. They recommend 30 trials, a run-time of 24 h and use of the Mann-Whitney-U test for statistical significance, and the $\hat{A}_{12}$ statistic as an effect size. However, as we show in Table 1, these recommendations are only partially followed by current fuzzing evaluations. As it is unknown how much influence each evaluation parameter has on the results, it is unclear whether or not these results are reproducible in practice. Contrary to Klees et al. [26], we conduct comprehensive experiments to be able to argue about the influence of different evaluation parameters based on empirical data.

To discuss the state of current fuzzer evaluations we analyze the evaluations from previous work published in reputable security conferences. The experiments gathered from the evaluation sections of different studies based on the following criteria: ① the experiment is used to compare the overall performance of the respective approach to at least one different fuzzers ② we exclude experiments that are used to either motivate the work or certain design choices as well as case studies. The results are summarized in Table 1. Note that we use the term *Crashes* as an evaluation metric for all evaluations that do not utilize a ground truth and rely on a de-duplication method which tries to correlate crashes to a root cause. However, de-duplication methods are prone to errors and cannot sufficiently estimate the correct number of bugs [26]. We use the term *Bugs* when the authors evaluate fuzzers with a set of targets that contain known vulnerabilities, i.e., it is possible to determine which inputs trigger which bug without utilizing a de-duplication technique.

We observe that none of the fuzzing proposals strictly follows all best practices in their evaluations. For instance, none of the listed studies uses 30 trials per experiment and only a single study employs a standardized effect size. Another problem is the lack of uniformity. This is especially prevalent when real-world programs are used to evaluate fuzzers which regularly use different sets of programs or program versions which may introduce unwanted biases and also makes it hard to compare these results. Furthermore, most studies either do not provide any statistical significance results or only for some of the conducted experiments.

A work that partially addresses similar issues has been introduced by Metzman et al. [31] from Google who published FuzzBench, an evaluation framework for fuzzers. FuzzBench generates a report based on coverage as an evaluation metric including a statistical evaluation. However, as the main purpose of a fuzzer is to find bugs, the coverage is only a proxy metric and therefore less meaningful than comparing the number of bugs found on a ground truth test set and thus not recommended [26, 34, 37].

Table 1. Analysis of current fuzzer evaluations. Entries with a question mark mean that we were unable to find the respective information in the related study. Test set: *RW* = real-world programs, *Google* = Google fuzzing suite. The number following the test sets corresponds to the number of targets used. Effect Size: *Avg.* = average, *Max.* = maximum value of all trials. Statistical significance: *CI* = confidence intervals, *MWU* = Mann-Whitney-U test.

Fuzzer	No	Test set	Run-time	Trials	Eval. metric	Effect size	Stat. significance
Hawkeye [10]	1	RW (19)	8 h	20	Bugs	Average	–
	2	RW (1)	4 h	8	Bugs	Average, $\hat{A}_{12}$	–
	3	RW (1)	4 h	8	Bugs	Average, $\hat{A}_{12}$	–
	4	Google (3)	4 h	8	Coverage	Average, $\hat{A}_{12}$	–
Intriguer [13]	1	LAVA-M (3)	5 h	20	Bugs	Median, Max	
	2	LAVA-M (1)	24 h	20	Bugs	Median	CI, MWU
	3	RW (7)	24 h	20	Coverage	Median	CI[b], MWU
DigFuzz [42]	1	CGC (126)	12 h	3	Coverage	Norm. Bitmap[a]	-
	2	CGC (126)	12 h	3	Bugs	–	–
	3	LAVA-M (4)	5 h	3	Bugs	?	–
	4	LAVA-M (4)	5 h	3	Coverage	Norm. Bitmap[a]	–
REDQUEEN [3]	1	LAVA-M (4)	5 h	5	Bugs	Median	CI[c]
	2	CGC (54)	6 h	?	Bugs	–	–
	3	RW (8)	10 h	5	Coverage	Median	CI, MWU
	4	RW (8)	10 h	5	Bugs	–	–
GRIMOIRE [5]	1	RW (8)	48 h	12	Coverage	Median	CI, MWU[d]
	2	RW (4)	48 h	12	Coverage	Median	CI, MWU
	3	RW (3)	48 h	12	Coverage	Median	CI, MWU
	4	RW (5)	?	?	Bugs	–	–
EcoFuzz [40]	1	RW (14)	24 h	5	Coverage	Average	p-value[e]
	2	RW (2)	24 h	5	Coverage	Average	–
	3	RW (2)	24 h	?	Crashes	–	–
	4	LAVA-M (4)	5 h	5	Bugs	–	–
GREYONE [18]	1	RW (19)	60 h	5	Crashes[f]	–	–
	2	RW (19)	60 h	5	Coverage	–	–
	3	LAVA-M (4)	24 h	5	Bugs	Average	-
	4	LAVA-M (4)	24 h	5	Crashes	Average	–
	5	RW (10)	60 h	5	Coverage	Average	-
Pangolin [24]	1	LAVA-M (4)	24 h	10	Bug	Average	MWU
	2	RW (9)	24 h	10	Crashes	–	–
	2	RW (9)	24 h	10	Coverage	Average	MWU

[a] Normalized Bitmap size describes the relative size of the bitmap compared to the bitmap found by all tested fuzzers.
[b] Confidence intervals only given for five of the seven targets.
[c] Confidence intervals are only provided for Redqueen.
[d] The Appendix further provides: mean, standard deviation, skeweness, and kurtosis.
[e] We were unable to determine the exact statistical test which has been used to obtain the p-value.
[f] The evaluation compares de-duplicated crashes as well as unique crashes as reported by AFL-style fuzzers.

UNIFUZZ is a platform to compare different fuzzers based on 20 real-world programs [28]. The evaluation metrics are based on crashes which are de-duplicated using the last three stack frames which is known to be unreliable because stack frames might be identical even though they trigger different bugs or stack frame may be different while triggering the same bug [26]. UNIFUZZ provides an overview of the fuzzer performance on each test program which makes it hard to assess the overall performance. SENF goes one step further and summarizes the results in a single ranking which allows us to easily compare all tested fuzzers. Therefore, it is not required to manually analyze the results on each target separately. However, if needed one can still get the target specific data from the results database of SENF.

5   Our Methodology

In this section, we provide an overview of the most important aspects of a fuzzer evaluation. We describe our choice of fuzzers, seeds, test set, and test machine setup which we use to test our framework to quantify the influence of various evaluation parameters.

5.1   Comparing Fuzzers

Comparing fuzzers with each other is not straightforward due to the various fuzzer designs and the wide variety of available testing methods. A fuzzer design is usually highly complex and given that a fuzzer executes millions of test runs, even small differences can have a huge impact on the performance. Some fuzzers are based on completely novel designs which makes it hard to attribute performance improvements to a specific change. For example, Chen and Chen proposed Angora [11] a mutation-based fuzzer that is written in Rust instead of C/C++ like AFL. Angora implements various methods to improve the fuzzing process: byte-level taint tracking, a numeric approximation based gradient descent, input length exploration, and integration of call stacks to improve coverage mapping. Due to the considerable differences to other fuzzers, it is impossible to accurately quantify the respective contribution of each technique when comparing it with AFL or other fuzzer which do not share the same code base. As a consequence, it is important to evaluate fuzzers based on common ground. Given the high popularity of AFL, we opted to focus on fuzzers that are based on the AFL code base. Note however that our evaluation framework is not specifically tailored to AFL in any way. Thus, it can be used to evaluate an arbitrary selection of fuzzers.

5.2   Test Set Selection

A crucial aspect of any fuzzer evaluation is the underlying test set, i.e., the target programs for which the fuzzer aims to discover bugs. In what follows, we study four different test sets available at the time of testing and argue why we decided to use the CGC test set for our evaluation. Note that we focus on test sets that provide a form of ground truth as there is currently no way to reliably match crashes to the same root cause as proper crash de-duplication is still an open problem (see Sect. 4).

LAVA-M. In 2016, Brendan et al. presented LAVA [14], a method to inject artificial bugs into arbitrary programs. The corresponding *LAVA-M* test set was the first ground truth test set to evaluate fuzzers that has been published in academia. It consists of four different programs with hundreds of injected bugs. Each bug has a specific bug-id that is printed before deliberately crashing the program. Due to its rather small size, the *LAVA-M* test set lacks the diversity found in real-world programs. Further, recent fuzzers such as Redqueen [3] and Angora [11] solve the test set by finding all injected bugs. This is possible because LAVA-M only features a single bug type which requires that the fuzzer solves magic byte comparisons, missing the bug diversity found in real-world software.

Google Fuzzing Suite. The Google Fuzzer Suite [20] consists of 22 different real-world programs with 25 different challenges that fuzzers are expected to solve. All challenges are documented and may include seed files. However, the test suite is not suitable for our use case as the majority of the bugs can be discovered by existing fuzzers in a very short time span (seconds or minutes). Furthermore, some of the challenges do not contain any bugs. Instead, the goal of these challenges is for the fuzzer to reach a certain path or line of code (i.e., a coverage benchmark) which is not compatible with our evaluation metric as we are interested in the number of bugs found. Additionally, the included bugs are partially collected from other fuzzing campaigns which might introduce biases.

Magma. The Magma fuzzing benchmark is a ground truth test set [22] that is based on a set of real-world programs. At the time of testing, the test set contains six different targets each containing a set of known bugs. Similar to LAVA-M, Magma uses additional instrumentation in the form of bug oracles to signal whether a bug condition has been triggered by a specific input. However, we do not use the Magma test set because at the time of testing it did not provide a sufficiently large test set. Further, not all bugs include a proof-of-vulnerability (PoV) which makes it impossible to know if a fault can be triggered by any means.

CGC. The DARPA Cyber Grand Challenge[1] (CGC) was a capture-the-flag style event where different teams competed by writing tools that are able to detect and subsequently fix bugs in a test corpus of close to 300 different programs with a prize pool of nearly 4 million USD. Each challenge has been designed carefully and consists of one or more binary which mirror functionality known from real-world software. CGC challenges contain at least one bug of one of two types: Type 1 bugs allow an attacker to control the instruction pointer and at least one register. Type 2 bugs allow reading sensitive data such as passwords. The challenges are written by different teams of programmers and do not rely on automatically injected bugs. As a result, the CGC test set offers great bug diversity which are similar to bugs found in real-world software and is therefore not susceptible to the same limitations as the LAVA-M test set.

Instead of the original binaries which were written for *DECREE*, we use the multi OS variant published by Trail of Bits [21] which allows us to execute the challenge binaries on Linux. All challenges and bugs are very-well documented and contain a PoV and a patched version of the respective challenge program(s).

---

[1] https://github.com/CyberGrandChallenge/.

Each bug is categorized into their respective CWE classes[2]. Further, challenges include test suits that we can use to ensure that the compiled program works as intended which can be especially helpful when using code instrumentation.

Given the greater bug and program diversity of CGC in combination with its great documentation and comprehensive test suites, we select a subset of the ported version of the CGC test set based on the following criteria: ① All tests (including the PoV) are successfully executed on our test servers. ② The target only contains one vulnerability. ③ The vulnerability is of type 1 as type 2 bugs do not lead to a crash. ④ The challenge consists of only one binary as fuzzers usually do not support to fuzz multiple binaries.

We are using targets with only one vulnerability as this allows us to verify the discovered crashing inputs using differential testing (see Sect. 5.6). This process does not require any additional instrumentation (e.g., bug oracles) which may significantly change the program behavior and lead to non-reproducible bugs [28]. Furthermore, we do not need to correlate crashes to their root cause using de-duplication methods. Our complete test set is composed of 42 targets including bugs of 21 different CWE types. We provide a complete list of all targets including their bug types in our public repository [32]. Note that it is not required to use CGC to be able to use SENF because the framework is not specifically tailored to the test set but can used with any test set. Furthermore, SENF can also be used to evaluate fuzzers based on the code coverage, e.g., when testing how long it takes a fuzzer to reach a certain basic block. We provide further details in the public repository [32].

5.3   Seed Sets

To evaluate fuzzers, we opted to use two sets of seed files. The first set of seed files contains sample input which we extract from the test inputs that are shipped with each CGC challenge. We minimize each seed set using `afl-cmin`. As it might not always be possible for users to create a comprehensive seed set for their target, we use an empty file as a second seed set.

5.4   Statistical Evaluation

To evaluate the results of our experiments, we employ the statistical methods described in Sect. 3. SENF supports both, dichotomous and interval-scale statistics as their usage depends on the use case. Dichotomous results provide an answer to the question which fuzzer finds the most bugs in a certain time frame, but ignores the time it took to find a bug. These types of evaluations are relevant for use cases such as OSS-Fuzz [1] where fuzzing campaigns are continuously run for months without a fixed time frame. Statistical tests on interval-scale results are useful in practical deployments when the amount of time to fuzz a target is

---

[2] Common Weakness Enumeration (CWE) is a list of software and hardware problem types (https://cwe.mitre.org/).

limited, e.g., when running tests before releasing a new software version. We use R [35] to calculate statistical significance tests as well as effect sizes.

When comparing multiple fuzzers or fuzzer configurations on a large set of targets, we encounter two problems. First, due to the large number of comparisons, it is not practical to publish all p-values and effect sizes as part of a study. Secondly, even if one publishes all values, it is not trivial to assess if a fuzzer actually outperforms another. Therefore, we implement a scoring system, which is inspired by Arcuri et al. [2], to summarize the results in a single score. The scoring system follows the intuition that the fuzzer which finds the most bugs the fastest, on the most of the targets is overall the best fuzzer. To determine the best fuzzer, the algorithm compares all fuzzers using the statistical significance tests and standardized effect sizes. For each target, it generates a ranking based on the time it took each fuzzer to find a specific bug. The final score is the average ranking of each fuzzer over the whole test set. For a more detailed description of the scoring algorithm we refer the interested reader to the respective publication [2].

5.5   Fuzzing Evaluation Setup

In Fig. 1 we provide an overview of our fuzzing evaluation setup. At its core, our design features a management server that runs a controller which provides the target program and seed set to one of the available experiment servers. On each experiment server, a dedicated executor starts the fuzzer and monitors the fuzzing process. The monitoring includes logging the CPU utilization and number of executions of the fuzzer. Thus, we can detect hangs and crashes of the fuzzer itself and restart a run if necessary.

After the pre-defined run-time, the executor stops the fuzzer and sends a success message to the controller program. Using the data from all successful fuzzing runs, SENF evaluates the reported results using evaluation methods which compare all executed runs of an arbitrary number of fuzzers and calculates statistical significance, effect size, the ranking based on dichotomous and interval-scale statistical tests.

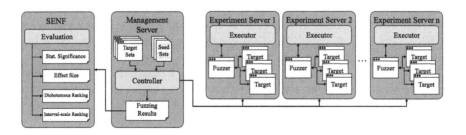

Fig. 1. Conceptual overview of the fuzzing evaluation setup.

5.6 Test Runs

Note that we conduct each experiment (i.e., a combination of fuzzers, targets, and seeds) for a maximum of 24 h. As each target only contains a single bug, we stop fuzzing when an input has been found by a fuzzer that triggers the bug of the respective target. To avoid false positives [3], we verify each crash using differential analysis, i.e., we execute a potential crashing input on the vulnerable and patched version of the respective binary and check whether the input crashes the binary.

SENF itself only requires a database which contains the result data, i.e., the time it took until a specific bus has been triggered, and a list of targets/seeds that should be used in the evaluation. Therefore, our framework can be used to evaluate other fuzzers or test sets. With minimal modifications one can also use other evaluation metrics (e.g., block coverage) to compare fuzzers with SENF.

6   Experiments

We run extensive fuzzing campaigns to systematically quantify the influence of various parameters used in fuzzing evaluations while following state-of-the-art statistical evaluation methodology. We test the influence of the following parameters: the seed set, number of trials, run-time, and number of targets as well as bugs. In total we run 616 fuzzing experiments with an accumulated run-time of over 284k CPU hours.

If not stated otherwise we use the following parameters as a default configuration for the statistical evaluation: a p threshold of 0.05, a non-empty seed set, interval-scale statistical tests, with 30 trials per experiment and a run-time of 24 h. Further, experiments for a specific target are always run on the same hardware configuration to ensure uniform test conditions. Note that when testing with an empty seed we have to exclude seven targets of our test set of 42 programs as these targets do not properly process an empty file thus fail initial tests done in AFLs initialization routine.

We execute all experiments on a cluster of 13 servers. To ensure equal conditions for all fuzzers, we use Docker containers and assign them one CPU core each and a ramdisk to minimize the overhead caused by I/O operations. We utilize Ubuntu 18.04 LTS as an operating system. If not stated otherwise we use fuzzers AFL/Fairfuzz in version 2.52b and AFLFast in version 2.51b as well as AFL++ in version 2.65c. The CGC test set was built using the code from commit e50a030 from the respective repository from Trail of Bits.

Due to the extensive amount of data in our evaluation and the inherent space limitations, we cannot publish all results (e.g., comparing different p-value thresholds) as part of this publications. We provide an extended version of our work in our public repository [32].

6.1 Fuzzers

We test a total of four fuzzers (❶ AFL [41], ❷ AFLFast [8], ❸ Fairfuzz [27], ❹ AFL++ [15]), two AFL-based compiler optimizations (❺ AFL-CF, ❻ AFL-

LAF), and two modes of AFL (❼ -d and ❽ -q) which provide a wide range of different performances. In the following, we explain the different fuzzers and modes of AFL we tested including the different compiler optimizations.

❶ **AFL.** The general purpose fuzzer AFL supports various different optimizations and parameters which change one or more its core components: ❼ **AFL (-d).** If the -d flag is enabled, AFL skips the deterministic part of the mutation stage and directly proceeds with the havoc stage. ❽ **AFL (-q)** The -q flag enables the *qemu mode*. Using this mode, AFL can fuzz a target without access to its source code. The necessary coverage information is collected using QEMU. According to the AFL documentation[3], the performance may decrease substantially due to the overhead introduced by the binary instrumentation.

❺ **AFL-CF.** As described in Sect. 2, AFL ships with various compilers that add the coverage feedback instrumentation when compiling a target program from source code. Using the alternative compiler `afl-clang-fast`, the instrumentation is added on the compiler level, instead of the assembly level, using a LLVM pass which improves the performance.

❻ **AFL-LF.** Based on `afl-clang-fast`, one can try to improve the code coverage by using the LAF LLVM passes[4]. For instance, these passes split multi-byte comparisons into smaller ones which AFL can solve consecutively.

❷ **AFLFast.** AFLFast [8] is a fork of AFL that investigates fuzzing *low-frequency paths*. These are paths that are reached by only a few inputs following the intuition that these inputs solve a path constraint that may lead to a bug. The implementation is part of the power schedule with an optimized search strategy. Note that AFL incorporated improvements from AFLFast starting with version 2.31b.

❸ **Fairfuzz.** Fairfuzz [27] is also based on AFL. Similar to AFLFast, it aims at triggering branches that are rarely reached by other testing inputs. However, it does not utilize a Markov chain model but rather relies on a dynamic cutoff value (i.e., a threshold for the number of hits) to decide which branches are considered *rare*. Further, Fairfuzz uses a heuristic that checks if certain bytes can be modified while still executing the same respective rare branch. Fairfuzz implements these changes as part of the search strategy and the mutation stage of AFL.

❹ **AFL++.** The AFL++ fuzzer [15] is a novel variation of AFL that improves usability and enables easy customization. It implements various improvements from academia as well as the fuzzing community (e.g., the AFLFast power schedules and the LAF LLVM passes). The goal is to introduce a new baseline fuzzer that is used for future fuzzing evaluations.

6.2 Seed Set

First, we evaluate the influence of the seed set by comparing an empty with a non-empty seed set (see Sect. 5.3). The results are depicted in Table 2 which

---

[3] https://github.com/mirrorer/afl/blob/master/qemu_mode/README.qemu.
[4] https://gitlab.com/laf-intel/laf-llvm-pass/tree/master.

lists the number of times that a fuzzer performed statistically better with the empty and non-empty seed set. We find that with the majority of targets the non-empty seed set either outperforms the empty seed or performs equally well on both statistical tests. We find that AFL is able to detect five bugs using the empty seed set that AFL is unable to detect when using the non-empty seed set. We believe that the main reason for this is that AFL spends less time in the deterministic stage when using an empty seed as the file is only a single byte. Note that even though the performance with a proper seed set is significantly better, testing an empty seed is still useful in cases where it is favorable to minimize the number of variables which may influence the fuzzing process [26] as well as scenarios where one cannot compile a comprehensive sets of inputs for the tested programs.

Table 2. Comparison of the non-empty and empty seed sets using interval-scale and dichotomous tests. Listed are the number of times the performance of the non-empty seed set was statistically better than the empty seed set and vice versa.

Fuzzer	Interval-scaled		Dichotomous	
	Non-empty	Empty	Non-empty	Empty
afl	12	6	6	2
afl (-Q)	8	4	7	1
afl (-d)	18	2	8	1
fairfuzz	13	4	7	1
afl-li	13	6	5	3
afl-cf	12	6	5	2
aflfast	12	5	6	0
afl++	12	5	5	2

6.3   Run-Time

To show the impact of differences in run-time, we calculate the ranking for maximum run-times between 1 h and 24 h. For each ranking, we only consider crashes that have been found in the respective time frame. We present the results in Fig. 2a. We observe that the run-time has a significant influence on the results. Interestingly, we find that even though all fuzzers are based on the same code base there is no uniform trend when increasing the run-time. For example, AFL without its deterministic stage consistently improves, in total by 0.45 in the average ranking from 1 h to 24 h. In the same time the performance of Fairfuzz, AFLFast, and AFL may increase or decrease slightly which also changes the relative ranking of these fuzzers depending on the maximum run-time. *We observe that on our test set, the run-time should be at least 8 h as lower run-times may lead to false conclusions of the fuzzer performance.*

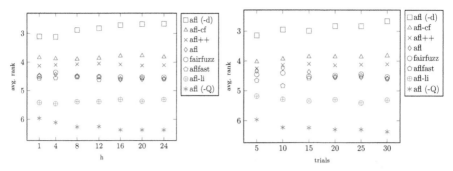

(a) Run-times varying between 1h and 24h.   (b) Trials varying between 5 and 30.

Fig. 2. Average ranking when using different run-times and number of trials.

6.4 Number of Trials

To calculate a p-value, one has to repeat every experiment multiple times. The number of trials also influences the minimum p-value that can be achieved. We compare the average ranking of each fuzzer and configuration considering between the first 5 and all 30 trials. In Fig. 2b, we can see that the performance may vary significantly depending on the number of trials used. For example, using 10 trials AFL++ has a slightly better performance than AFL and Fairfuzz, both of which clearly outperform AFLFast. Analyzing the results after 30 trials we find that AFL++ now outperforms AFL and Fairfuzz which both perform as well as AFLFast. *We conclude that the number of trials has significant impact on the results and if under serious resource constraints one should prioritize a higher number of trials over longer run-times.*

6.5 Number of Bugs/Targets

Another parameter that one can adjust is the number of targets a fuzzer is evaluated on. As we use targets with a single bug, the number of targets is equal to the number of bugs in our test set. We evaluate all fuzzers on test sets between five and 35 different targets. For each test set size, we randomly sample 1000 different target combinations and calculate the ranking including maximum and minimum. Note that given larger test sets, the spread will naturally decrease as we sample from a maximum of 42 different targets. In Fig. 3, we can see that the performance may vary substantially depending on the used test set. We further analyze the results and find randomly sampled test sets with 15 targets where AFL-CF outperforms AFL without the deterministic stage or test sets where the performance of Fairfuzz is second to last. Even when we use 35 targets, we find randomly sampled test sets that result in a substantially different rankings compared to the 42 target test set. For example, we observe test sets where AFL++ outperforms AFL-CF or test sets where Fairfuzz performs better than AFL++. *Our results show that target and bug selection should not be taken lightly as it can introduce significant biases when testing fuzzers.*

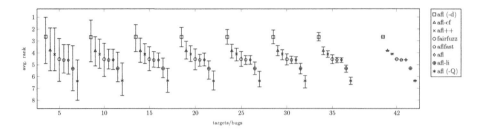

Fig. 3. Average ranking when using varying numbers of targets/bugs. Whiskers correlate to the minimum and maximum rank.

6.6 Further Insights

Next, we compare the SENF-ranking with a ranking that utilizes the *average* as commonly found in fuzzer evaluations (see Sect. 4). The results are shown in Table 3. Notably, when we only consider the average, the overall ranking changes drastically with the exception of the best and worst performing fuzzers. *This shows the influence of statistically insignificant results on the overall performance results which further confirms the choice of using righteous statistical methods as employed in SENF.*

Table 3. Comparison of the SENF-ranking and avg. number of bugs found over all targets.

SENF ranking		Ranking based on Avg.	
Fuzzer	Avg. ranking	Fuzzer	Avg. #bugs found
afl (-d)	2.67	afl (-d)	16.86
afl-cf	3.82	fairfuzz	14.17
afl++	4.11	afl-cf	13.55
fairfuzz	4.54	aflfast	13.26
aflfast	4.60	afl	12.60
afl	4.60	afl-li	12.60
afl-li	5.31	afl++	12.48
afl (-Q)	6.37	afl (-Q)	9.21

To test the *consistency* of each fuzzer, we take a closer look at the time it takes a fuzzer to detect a bug in Fig. 4. To improve the readability of the figure we plot the difference between the shortest and longest time a fuzzer needs to find a bug over all trials for each target. If a fuzzer is not able to find a bug, we set the execution time to 24h. When a fuzzer was not able to find a bug in a target over all trials, we omitted the result to increase readability. For all fuzzers and configurations, randomness plays a significant role when searching for bugs with differences between minimum and maximum time close to our run-time of 24 h. *No fuzzer in our evaluation is able to consistently find bugs over all trials.*

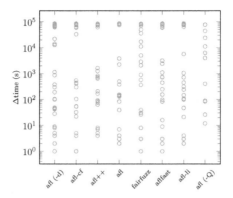

Fig. 4. Difference between min. and max. exec. time for each fuzzer and target over all trials.

7 Discussion

Test Set Selection. Our framework SENF in combination with a ground truth test set significantly increases the probability that the reported results are reproducible. Even though our test set of 42 different programs and 21 different bug types ensures a certain level of diversity in our evaluation, the resulting ranking could potentially differ if a larger, representative test set of real-world programs with a ground truth is used because programs from the CGC test set do not provide the same level complexity. Note that other test sets can easily be evaluated with SENF as we only require a database containing the experiment results as input.

Resource Limitations. Due to unavoidable limitations of resources, we cannot analyze the full range of parameters used in existing fuzzing evaluations, e.g., run-times of 60 h (see Sect. 4). Therefore, we limit our experiments to values recommended in fuzzing literature [26]. For the same reason, we do not conduct experiments with multiple concurrent fuzzer instances testing the same target. The experiments of Chen et al. [12] as well as Böhme and Falk [6] suggest that the performance of fuzzers varies significantly when fuzzing with multiple instances simultaneously.

Fuzzer Selection. Due to the aforementioned resource constraints, we have to limit the selection of fuzzers as the experiments in Sect. 6 already required over 280k CPU hours. We opted to focus on AFL, AFL-based fuzzers, and various optimizations as this allows us to easily attribute performance differences. Furthermore, AFL is the most popular baseline fuzzer, e.g., it is recommended by Klees et al. [26] and used in all evaluations we studied in Sect. 4. Additionally, AFL is commonly used as a code base to implement new fuzzers [8,19,27,29,33,36]. For these reasons, we argue that focusing on AFL-style fuzzers is more significant for common fuzzer evaluations compared to other fuzzers. However, since our implementation is open-source one can easily use SENF to evaluate any set of fuzzers. We provide detailed guidelines in our public repository [32].

Scoring Algorithm. The scoring algorithm we use in our evaluation adopts the commonly used intuition that the fuzzer which outperforms the other fuzzers (i.e., finds more bugs) on the most targets has the best overall performance. However, other evaluation metrics may be useful for other use cases, e.g., when testing a target with a section of different fuzzers one may not only be interested in the fuzzer that finds the most bugs but also fuzzers that find a unique set bugs which all other fuzzers are unable to detect. However, calculating the unique set of bugs for each fuzzer does not require complex statistical evaluations as provided by SENF.

Furthermore, our evaluation does not take into account by how much a fuzzer A improves over a different fuzzer B. SENF addresses this problem by supporting a variable effect size thresholds. Thus, interested parties can set a custom minimum effect size which SENF takes into account when calculating the score of a fuzzer. We provide more detailed information on the effect size and its influence in the extended version of this paper.

Threshold of the p-value. In our evaluation, we opted to use the widely established p threshold of 0.05 which is commonly used in software engineering evaluations [26]. However, this threshold is generally considered a trade-off between the probability of false positive and false negative results. Other scientific communities opted to use lower thresholds or other methods of statistical evaluation [4]. SENF addresses this and lets the user set an arbitrary threshold to calculate the average ranking of each fuzzer.

8   Conclusion

Our analysis of recent fuzzing studies shows that fuzzers are largely evaluated with various different evaluation parameters which are not in line with the recommendations found in academic literature. To address these issues, we presented SENF, which implements dichotomous and interval-scale statistical methods to calculate the p-value and effect sizes to compute a ranking to asses the overall performance of all tested fuzzers.

Based on extensive empirical data, we quantified the influence of different evaluation parameters on fuzzing evaluations for the first time. We demonstrate that even when we utilize the recommended statistical tests, using insufficient evaluation parameters—such as a low number of trials or a small test set—may still lead to misleading results that in turn may lead to false conclusions about the performance of a fuzzer. Thus, the choice of parameters for fuzzing evaluations should not be taken lightly and existing recommendations should be followed to lower the chance of non-reproducible results. We described and open-sourced a practical evaluation setup that can be used to test the performance of fuzzers.

Acknowledgements. Funded by the Deutsche Forschungsgemeinschaft (DFG, German Research Foundation) under Germany's Excellence Strategy – EXC 2092 CASA – 390781972.

This work has been partially funded by the Deutsche Forschungsgemeinschaft (DFG, German Research Foundation) – SFB 1119 – 236615297.

References

1. Aizatsky, M., Serebryany, K., Chang, O., Arya, A., Whittaker, M.: Announcing OSS-Fuzz: continuous fuzzing for open source software (2016)
2. Arcuri, A., Briand, L.: A Hitchhiker's guide to statistical tests for assessing randomized algorithms in software engineering. Softw. Test. Verif. Reliab. **24**, 219–250 (2014)
3. Aschermann, C., Schumilo, S., Blazytko, T., Gawlik, R., Holz, T.: REDQUEEN: fuzzing with input-to-state correspondence. In: Symposium on Network and Distributed System Security (NDSS) (2019)
4. Benjamin, D.J., Berger, J.O., Johannesson, M., Nosek, B.A., Wagenmakers, E.J., et al.: Redefine statistical significance. Hum. Nat. Behav. **2**, 6–10 (2017)
5. Blazytko, T., et al.: GRIMOIRE: synthesizing structure while fuzzing. In: USENIX Security Symposium (2019)
6. Böhme, M., Falk, B.: Fuzzing: on the exponential cost of vulnerability discovery. In: Symposium on the Foundations of Software Engineering (FSE) (2020)
7. Böhme, M., Pham, V.T., Nguyen, M.D., Roychoudhury, A.: Directed greybox fuzzing. In: ACM Conference on Computer and Communications Security (CCS) (2017)
8. Böhme, M., Pham, V.T., Roychoudhury, A.: Coverage-based greybox fuzzing as markov chain. In: ACM Conference on Computer and Communications Security (CCS) (2016)
9. Cadar, C., Dunbar, D., Engler, D.: KLEE: unassisted and automatic generation of high-coverage tests for complex systems programs. In: USENIX Conference on Operating Systems Design and Implementation (2008)
10. Chen, H., et al.: Hawkeye: towards a desired directed grey-box fuzzer. In: ACM Conference on Computer and Communications Security (CCS) (2018)
11. Chen, P., Chen, H.: Angora: efficient fuzzing by principled search. In: IEEE Symposium on Security and Privacy (S&P) (2018)
12. Chen, Y., et al.: EnFuzz: ensemble fuzzing with seed synchronization among diverse fuzzers. In: USENIX Security Symposium (2019)
13. Cho, M., Kim, S., Kwon, T.: Intriguer: field-level constraint solving for hybrid fuzzing. In: ACM Conference on Computer and Communications Security (CCS) (2019)
14. Dolan-Gavitt, B., et al.: LAVA: large-scale automated vulnerability addition. In: IEEE Symposium on Security and Privacy (S&P) (2016)
15. Fioraldi, A., Maier, D., Eißfeldt, H., Heuse, M.: Afl++: combining incremental steps of fuzzing research. In: USENIX Workshop on Offensive Technologies (WOOT) (2020)

16. Fisher, R.: On the Interpretation of χ^2 from contingency tables, and the calculation of P. J. R. Stat. Soc. **85**, 87–94 (1922)
17. Fisher, R.: Statistical Methods for Research Workers. Oliver and Boyd, Edinburgh (1925)
18. Gan, S., et al.: GREYONE: data flow sensitive fuzzing. In: USENIX Security Symposium (2020)
19. Gan, S., et al.: CollAFL: path sensitive fuzzing. In: IEEE Symposium on Security and Privacy (S&P) (2018)
20. Google: fuzzer-test-suite (2016). https://github.com/google/fuzzer-test-suite/
21. Guido, D.: Your tool works better than mine? Prove it (2016). https://blog.trailofbits.com/2016/08/01/your-tool-works-better-than-mine-prove-it/
22. Hazimeh, A., Herrera, A., Payer, M.: Magma: a ground-truth fuzzing benchmark. In: Proceedings of the ACM on Measurement and Analysis of Computing Systems 4 (2020)
23. Hocevar, S.: zzuf (2006). https://github.com/samhocevar/zzuf/
24. Huang, H., Yao, P., Wu, R., Shi, Q., Zhang, C.: Pangolin: incremental hybrid fuzzing with polyhedral path abstraction. In: IEEE Symposium on Security and Privacy (S&P) (2020)
25. Inozemtseva, L., Holmes, R.: Coverage is not strongly correlated with test suite effectiveness. In: International Conference on Software Engineering (ICSE) (2014)
26. Klees, G., Ruef, A., Cooper, B., Wei, S., Hicks, M.: Evaluating fuzz testing. In: ACM Conference on Computer and Communications Security (CCS) (2018)
27. Lemieux, C., Sen, K.: FairFuzz: a targeted mutation strategy for increasing greybox fuzz testing coverage (2018)
28. Li, Y., et al.: UNIFUZZ: a holistic and pragmatic metrics-driven platform for evaluating fuzzers. In: USENIX Security Symposium (2021)
29. Lyu, C., et al.: MOPT: optimized mutation scheduling for fuzzers. In: USENIX Security Symposium (2019)
30. Mann, H., Whitney, D.: On a test of whether one of two random variables is stochastically larger than the other. Ann. Math. Stat. **18** (1947)
31. Metzman, J., Arya, A., Szekeres, L.: FuzzBench: Fuzzer Benchmarking as a Service (2020). https://opensource.googleblog.com/2020/03/fuzzbench-fuzzer-benchmarking-as-service.html
32. Paaßen, D., Surminski, S., Rodler, M., Davi, L.: Public github respository of SENF. https://github.com/uni-due-syssec/SENF
33. Pham, V.T., Böhme, M., Santosa, A.E., Căciulescu, A.R., Roychoudhury, A.: Smart greybox fuzzing. IEEE Trans. Softw. Eng. (2019)
34. Pham, V.-T., Khurana, S., Roy, S., Roychoudhury, A.: Bucketing failing tests via symbolic analysis. In: Huisman, M., Rubin, J. (eds.) FASE 2017. LNCS, vol. 10202, pp. 43–59. Springer, Heidelberg (2017). https://doi.org/10.1007/978-3-662-54494-5_3
35. R Core Team: R: A Language and Environment for Statistical Computing. R Foundation for Statistical Computing, Vienna, Austria (2019).https://www.R-project.org/
36. Schumilo, S., Aschermann, C., Gawlik, R., Schinzel, S., Holz, T.: kAFL: hardware-assisted feedback fuzzing for OS kernels. In: USENIX Security Symposium (2017)
37. van Tonder, R., Kotheimer, J., Le Goues, C.: Semantic crash bucketing. In: ACM/IEEE International Conference on Automated Software Engineering (2018)
38. Vargha, A., Delaney, H.D.: A critique and improvement of the CL common language effect size statistics of McGraw and Wong. J. Educ. Behav. Stat. 25, 10—132 (2000)

39. Wang, Y., et al.: Not all coverage measurements are equal: fuzzing for input prioritization. In: Symposium on Network and Distributed System Security (NDSS) (2020)
40. Yue, T., et al.: EcoFuzz: adaptive energy-saving greybox fuzzing as a variant of the adversarial multi-armed bandit. In: USENIX Security Symposium (2020)
41. Zalewski, M.: Technical "whitepaper" for afl-fuzz. https://lcamtuf.coredump.cx/afl/technical_details.txt
42. Zhao, L., Duan, Y., Yin, H., Xuan, J.: Send hardest problems my way: probabilistic path prioritization for hybrid fuzzing. In: Symposium on Network and Distributed System Security (NDSS) (2019)

Malware

.

Rope: Covert Multi-process Malware Execution with Return-Oriented Programming

Daniele Cono D'Elia[(✉)], Lorenzo Invidia, and Leonardo Querzoni

Department of Computer, Control, and Management Engineering,
Sapienza University of Rome, Rome, Italy
delia@diag.uniroma1.it

Abstract. Distributed execution designs challenge behavioral analyses of anti-malware solutions by spreading seemingly benign chunks of a malicious payload to multiple processes. Researchers have explored methods to chop payloads, spread chunks to victim applications through process injection techniques, and orchestrate the execution. However, these methods can hardly be practical as they exhibit conspicuous features and make use of primitives that anti-malware solutions and operating system mitigations readily detect. In this paper we reason on fundamental requirements and properties for a stealth implementation of distributed malware. We propose a new covert design, Rope, that minimizes its footprint by making use of commodity techniques like transacted files and return-oriented programming for covert communication and payload distribution. We report on how synthetic Rope samples eluded a number of state-of-the-art anti-virus and endpoint security solutions, and bypassed the opt-in mitigations of Windows 10 for hardening applications. We then discuss directions and practical remediations to mitigate such threats.

Keywords: Malware · Distributed execution · Anti-virus · EDR · Injection · Code reuse · Application hardening · ROP · TxF · WDEG

1 Introduction

Malicious software is a plague on users and organizations as it can compromise the availability and integrity of computer systems. To shield machines from the overwhelming amount of new threats appearing every year, anti-malware solutions devise dynamic analyses to flag untrusted software as potentially malicious by monitoring its execution traits. In particular, Anti-Virus (AV) and, more recently, Endpoint Detection and Response (EDR) solutions protect home and business computers by combining traditional signature-based mechanisms for binaries with behavioral detection techniques to forestall new threats.

In principle, threat actors may bypass behavioral analysis by diluting the temporal and spatial features of a malicious computation in multiple execution

ⓒ Springer Nature Switzerland AG 2021
E. Bertino et al. (Eds.): ESORICS 2021, LNCS 12972, pp. 197–217, 2021.
https://doi.org/10.1007/978-3-030-88418-5_10

units. This approach requires partitioning a payload into coordinated components so that no one of them causes an AV/EDR system to raise an alert [40].

Some academic literature [8,21,26,40] explores distributed malware execution designs that, using manual or automated methods, craft components that execute as independent processes and coordinate between themselves, possibly through covert channels. Using dedicated processes as units, however, is a conspicuous trait that exposes every process to immediate analysis and, depending on the ignition method, to correlation attempts from security solutions. Even recent designs where each process imitates benign applications in a mimicry fashion [8] need to create no less than 18–20 processes to avoid detection.

Two recent proposals [20,37] make a leap forward by distributing a payload across pre-existing, benign processes through the use of process injection techniques. Such designs bring a strictly harder problem for defenders [20], as they need to correlate actions (e.g., API calls) that are spread out in the event streams for both the victim processes and the entire system. Unfortunately, as we elaborate in more detail later, both designs exhibit conspicuous features and build on primitives that make them an easy prey of state-of-the-art AV/EDR solutions. Also, they both conflict with modern operating system (OS) mitigations that users can enable to harden applications against subversion attempts.

Our approach. In this work we introduce Rope, a new covert design for multi-process malware execution. Rope meets real-world requirements for deploying distributed malware on victims where both behavioral analyses and application hardening mitigations are in place. To this end, Rope builds on commodity OS features (Transactional NTFS) and attack techniques (Return-oriented Programming) for covert communication and for payload encoding and distribution, minimizing the footprint and in turn the conspicuous features of the execution runtime. Rope further raises the bar for defenders as threat actors can replace individual components of the implementation with alternative primitives.

In our tests, Rope eludes the latest version of state-of-the-art AV/EDR products and complies with common opt-in hardening mitigations available on Windows 10. As part of a responsible disclosure process, we reported to Microsoft three flaws (and bypasses) for Windows Defender Exploit Guard and cooperated with one vendor to extend their EDR product so as to detect the implementation solutions that we use. Finally, the paper points out several directions and practical remediations to anticipate and mitigate threats like Rope.

Contributions. In summary, this paper proposes the following contributions:

- an analysis of the challenges that lie along the way to practical multi-process execution of malware;
- a new design, Rope, to meet such challenges using commodity means;
- an evaluation of Rope in the presence of state-of-the-art security solutions and application hardening mitigations, where Rope successfully eludes both.

2   Background

This section details fundamental traits of anti-malware defenses for systems and applications, and depicts the state of the art in distributed malware execution.

2.1   Defenses for Systems and Applications

To detect an incoming untrusted program as malicious, anti-malware solutions use two primary techniques [39]: signature scanning and behavioral analysis.

Signature scanning looks for distinctive patterns in the binary representation of a program, and is challenged both by new threats and by obfuscation and polymorphism applied to known malware strains [35]. Behavioral analysis attempts a controlled execution in emulators [3] and even in the real system by shepherding the use of specific APIs. Unlike signature scanning, it can periodically kick in for long-running programs, e.g., as soon as those exercise operations red-flagged and monitored by the anti-malware solution. In a broader connotation of behavioral analysis, we include also in-memory scanning techniques that dynamically look for patterns in the code and data of processes.

While the inner workings of AV/EDR solutions are undisclosed, prior research [15] reports on behavioral analysis concepts involving feature extraction for sequences of performed API calls, graph representations that capture relations also between their parameters or return values, and variants of these ideas. Correlation is usually limited to single execution units or to their descendants.

Typically, on Windows systems the monitoring of AV/EDR solutions operates through hooks for user-space APIs and minifilters for I/O events, while kernel-level hooks that vendors used to apply on, e.g., the System Service Descriptor Table are no longer allowed since the introduction of PatchGuard [27].

We also note that EDR solutions are nowadays popular among enterprise users as they embody a multifaceted approach, extending the protection of AV engines with improved monitoring capabilities (e.g., remote telemetry) and complementary solutions (e.g., whitelisting, threat detection and response).

Recently available OS mitigations for hardening applications can then serve as a further line of defense. Introduced with Windows 10 version 1709, Windows Defender Exploit Guard (WDEG) blocks several behaviors commonly used in malware attacks [29], offering orthogonal protection alongside AV/EDR solutions. WDEG supersedes and widens the exploit-oriented protection of Microsoft EMET with a number of opt-in hardening mitigations [28], including:

- **ACG** (*Arbitrary Code Guard*), to block the allocation of executable memory as well as permission changes to host dynamically generated code;
- **CIG** (*Code Integrity Guard*), to block the loading of non-signed code;
- **EAF** (*Export Address Filtering*) and **IAF** (*Import Address Filtering*), to block code not from a disk-backed module when accessing the export and import address table of any loaded module (e.g., to locate API addresses);

- **ROP** mitigations (*CallerCheck*, *SimExec*, *StackPivot*), to validate upon an invocation of a sensitive API its call and return sites and the stack pointer value against typical traits of return-oriented programming attacks.

2.2 Distributed Malware

The idea of using multiple processes to deliver a malicious computation dates back at least to 2007 with the formal model of k-ary malicious codes by Filiol [13], and has seen multiple uses in the wild over the years [15]. As we mentioned in Sect. 1, a rather rich academic literature explores variants of this idea: initially to thwart signature scanning [39], but soon enough behavioral detection became the main target (e.g., [15,21,26]). Multi-process execution can be effective against behavioral analyses as their "dynamic" signatures often involve sequences of events that are not short (or the risk of false positives could be very high [26]): henceforth attackers may spread smaller parts to separate execution units.

Most distributed designs require the creation of new processes, which brings a few practical problems. As several AV/EDR products can look for correlations among processes and their descendants as a form of spatial locality [40], a distributed runtime should try to spawn each execution unit as a sibling process of the others, which is non-trivial to achieve. Also, untrusted executables may run with low integrity levels or be subject to restrictions for, e.g., network access. Recent studies in ransomware design [8] suggest that a high number of processes is required to avoid special-purpose detectors—we picture those as part of an EDR ecosystem—even when attempting mimicry strategies.

Researchers have also explored how to leverage existing processes instead, an approach that brings several benefits at once if successful. For instance, the malicious actions get further spread among the own activities of each victim application, and an execution unit can inherit the access rights of the victim to get around, e.g., application whitelisting or Egress filtering policies [31].

Process injection techniques may offer an avenue to this end. malWASH [20] chops an existing binary into chunks of variable length (e.g., one per basic block) and, from a loader component, injects them into pre-existing processes along with an emulator that orchestrates their execution from a dedicated thread. D-TIME [37] ameliorates malWASH in two respects: it replaces the (conspicuous) remote thread created for emulator dispatching with a mechanism that injects Windows APC calls, and simplifies the communication channel creation.

Unfortunately, both systems would struggle with deployment requirements as we consider the sophistication of ever-improving defenses. malWASH and D-TIME place their emulators and chunks in executable memory regions: a design trait that is fundamentally incompatible, depending on the injection method, with either ACG or CIG-like policies. Their very same complex emulator (5,500 hand-written assembly lines in malWASH, which need orthogonal diversification techniques to avoid fingerprinting) is conspicuous, as it uses multiple shared regions to host data segments, heap, and stack for the payload, and others for metadata required to coordinate chunk execution. As we will see later in the paper, these and other practical traits make even such recent designs an easy prey of sophisticated AV/EDR solutions.

3 Challenges for Covert Distributed Malware

This section identifies as challenges a number of requirements and properties, missed in prior works, behind covert designs and implementations of distributed malware abstractions. We believe that, in the lack of a principled approach to cope with real-world deployment requirements, such abstractions would end up being thwarted by narrow-scope remediations from anti-malware solutions, as already happened even for promising concepts like malWASH and D-TIME.

While the list presented in the following may not be exhaustive, we hope it can advance the knowledge in malware design and favor the development of comprehensive mitigations for upcoming threats. We assume a generic design skeleton where an initial component, the *loader*, initiates the distribution of the payload among the leveraged execution units. Each unit executes pieces (*chunks*) of the whole computation with the assistance of a local *bootstrap* component. Due to the inherent limitations of process creation-based designs (Sect. 2), our main focus for the discussion will be injection-based designs, but the considerations we are about to present are mostly general and apply to both.

[C1] Use a flexible delivery technique. This point is important especially for injection-based designs, as threat actors and researchers regularly come up with new injection techniques [23] to slip through the cracks of evolving AV/EDR solutions and OS mitigations. The covertness of the method used to deliver the chunks to execution units can be almost as important as its ease of replacement, which in turn can also favor the diversification of malware instances.

[C2] Minimize the footprint of the runtime. There are at least two factors that contribute to making a distributed runtime conspicuous: the size of the bootstrap component and the dispatching of the chunks for execution.

The first aspect is a proxy of the complexity of the coordination tasks that the component implements. A small size for it brings a less conspicuous footprint against in-memory detections and fingerprints. Depending on the delivery technique, it may even be accommodated in caves of benign modules. The engineering effort in malWASH to support the execution of already existing payloads is commendable, yet we would argue for a less complex runtime eased by payload writing choices. Compatibility is an important requirement, for instance, for obfuscations meant to protect legitimate software, but in the context of malware we find it fair to assume that a threat actor would be willing to comply with the runtime to ease the payload chopping and coordination processes.

The second aspect involves spreading the actions from the chunks among those of a whole process[1]. Having the loader—or the bootstrap—component attempt the creation of remote threads (malWASH) or entries in the APC queue

---

[1] This is relevant also for mimicry attacks from process creation-based approaches.

of a process (D-TIME) are actions that trigger the real-time behavioral monitoring components of AV/EDR solutions. A covert design may instead attempt to make the process itself dispatch the execution of the chunks, ideally choosing among multiple primitives or even diversifying them among the execution units.

[C3] Ensure compliance with hardening mitigations. This point affects the loader and the bootstrap components, the placement of chunks, but also specific actions from distributed payloads. Avoiding the use of RWX regions (or 'W⊕X' permission changes) is essential in the presence of hardening mitigations. It also has benefits against behavioral detection, as dynamic code changes are a prerogative of specific classes of applications, such as browsers, that a security solution can whitelist. Similarly, covert strategies used in either component or in the payload to locate APIs covertly need retrofitting work so as not to conflict with mitigations like EAF and IAF meant to block such attempts.

[C4] Keep code and data hidden as much as possible. Along with [C1,2], this point is instrumental to minimize both the indicators of compromise on a machine and to which extent the distributed execution is exposed to in-memory inspection. Ideally, the runtime may expose the code and data for a payload portion only for the fraction of time needed for its execution. As noted in [20], leaving the bootstrap component visible in memory may possibly make defenders move towards detecting the distributed mechanism instead of the target payload, but has the advantage of hiding the true functionality of the latter. Special care is advised also for covert communication channels, so as to hinder the inspection of their contents through, e.g., dynamic signatures from behavioral analysis.

[C5] Limit the footprint of any unavoidable suspicious action. While suspicious behaviors from a payload may be effectively spread out to multiple execution units, there are actions carried in the loader or the bootstrap component that may alert a behavioral detection. Their design may thus seek to reduce the extent of information that an AV/EDR solution receives for their actions by, for instance, circumventing API hooks in place. While such anti-analysis tricks may not suffice to deceive a behavioral analysis of a standalone full payload, as AV/EDR solutions also access other sources (Sect. 2.1), they can bring instead marginal gains to the overall stealthiness of a distributed concept.

Discussion. The five challenges depicted above are meant to capture the operation of present defenses, and also possible straightforward combinations or extensions of current detection capabilities and fingerprints. Hence, they may be seen as forward-looking targets. Nonetheless, as we detail in Sect. 6, present AV/EDR solutions already block recently proposed distributed concepts.

Alongside covertness aspects, other issues exist for supporting a distributed execution paradigm. Thankfully, prior literature tackles such aspects well. These include, for instance, feature distribution based on process characteristics and restrictions [31], split communication channels so as to expose only pairwise links between units [26], object marshaling and descriptor duplication [20,26], resilience to termination of single units [20], and drop-in replacements for APIs that provide or work on process-specific information [20,37]. Our Rope concept is orthogonal to such research and can fully benefit from it in an implementation.

4   Rope

In this paper we propose a novel design, Rope, to advance the state of the art in distributed malware execution and overcome the challenges of Sect. 3. To this end, we pursue a radically different approach compared to prior works.

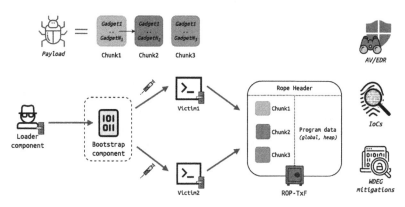

Fig. 1: Architecture of Rope: chunks, runtime components, defenses in place.

Rope uses a standard attack technique, return-oriented programming [41] (ROP), and a commodity Windows feature, Transactional NTFS [1, 42] (TxF), to encode the required computations and distribute them through a covert channel that also hosts program data. Rope sidesteps the issue of having to allocate or modify executable memory, and uses ROP as an effective and versatile tool to bypass other hardening mitigations of Windows and to raise the bar against in-memory inspections. Rope comes with a small runtime footprint and is amenable to different implementation choices and delivery techniques, as well as to known obfuscation and diversification techniques for both its ROP and non-ROP parts.

Before presenting the general traits of the design, we define which are the defenses that we assume to be in place on a machine where Rope is deployed.

Attack Target. We target a machine equipped with an AV/EDR solution with behavioral detection. No previous threat compromised the machine, as the detection capabilities of the AV/EDR could otherwise be affected. The targets for injection by Rope are already running processes that may have opted in for hardening mitigations conceptually akin to[2] the WDEG ones listed in Sect. 2.1.

The exploitation of a human or system vulnerability necessary to ignite the loader component, and the evasion of possible fine-grained analyses (e.g., malware sandboxes) along the way to a victim, are orthogonal problems. Rope is compatible with existing means for achieving both ends; the goal of Rope and prior works in the area [20] is that the execution stays undetected on the victim.

---

[2] Necessary to overcome present implementation gaps in WDEG, e.g., with concomitant use of ACG and ROP mitigations [28], or with ACG and remote allocations [19].

4.1 Architecture

Fig. 1 presents the architecture of Rope. As in the generic skeleton for distributed malware depicted in Sect. 3, we use a loader component to infect a set of (pre-existing) victim execution units. We then deliver the bootstrap component to each victim using an injection primitive. Rope encodes this component as a ROP chain. However, if the injection primitive is capable of eluding CIG (we discuss one in Sect. 5), also a short shellcode is a possibility. The malicious payload comes as a sequence of chunks expressed as ROP chains. Along with runtime metadata, we lay them out in a transacted NTFS file: the ROP-TxF.

Transactional NTFS is a Windows feature to atomically manipulate files and directories, where a series of operations (including content changes) can form a transaction to commit or abort as a whole in the surrounding system. Kulkarni and Jagdale observe in [24] how this provides a form of read-committed isolation. Until a transaction is committed, transient changes are visible only to the processes that created or obtained a handle to the transaction (and to the Windows Kernel Transaction Manager that backs the TxF functionality [1]). AV/EDR products can make a minifilter driver enlist for TxF commit events (e.g., to detect a TxF-based strategy to infect files on disk [24]); however, any content transiently stored in a TxF file will stay hidden to them, and Rope does not need commit operations to support its distributed execution.

The loader component of Rope creates the ROP-TxF on a random file, alters its contents, and duplicates a handle for it for every victim process. Each instance of the bootstrap component uses its own duplicate handle to access and modify the ROP-TxF contents, dispatching the execution of the chunks in it in a coordinated manner. The Rope paradigm is general enough to allow for (at least) the following execution modes, which may also be mixed in the same payload:

- one follows a *feature-agnostic* scenario where the Rope runtime, similarly as in malWASH and D-TIME, aids in explicit coordination of the chunks without making distinctions about the characteristics of their actions;
- the other follows a *feature-aware* scenario: the Rope runtime offloads sequences of chunks to victims based on their capabilities and/or with a separation in functionally distinct units, similarly to malware seen in the wild.

In the following we detail the different components and how Rope meets the [C1–5] challenges on the way to covert multi-process malware execution.

4.2 Loader Component

The loader component initiates the distributed execution by first looking for pre-existing processes to target as victims. Compared to standard injection practices from malware, Rope does not add any special requirement for process selection. In the feature-aware scenario, the malware writer can specify preferred targets (for instance, browsers are suitable for chunks that need to establish network connections). The loader component has then to accomplish three main tasks:

1. creates the ROP-TxF and duplicates the TxF handles for the victims;
2. injects the bootstrap component in each victim;
3. tampers with each victim to dispatch the bootstrap component.

The first task is straightforward. For the second task, we must avoid the use of any executable memory. As we will detail when presenting a possible implementation in Sect. 5, we inject a short ROP chain to have the victim process itself load the bootstrap component. This chain also accomplishes the third task, choosing among different dispatching strategies. In more detail, we may make the victim create an own thread or schedule an APC (neither of which is suspicious, unlike the remote variants used in malWASH and D-TIME), or we may tamper with its IAT to realize an API call target hijacking.

The implementation can use off-the-shelf techniques to place the chain in the address space of a victim. A reader may wonder if such an action should be blocked by a behavioral detection, or if it may undermine the stealthiness of the approach. Denying the use of WriteProcessMemory, NtWriteVirtualMemory, or other commodity OS features (e.g., Atom tables) that malware abuses as write-what-where primitives may break the functioning of legitimate applications. Such an action should definitely be part of behavioral signatures but, most likely, together with other conspicuous criteria to be met. Also, techniques like Ghost Writing can write to a process without even having to open it [23]. Nonetheless, Rope may also resort to evasion techniques for API hooks to reduce the footprint of specific actions: we defer their discussion to Sect. 5.

Similarly, no Rope-specific provisions are necessary to make the victim execute the initial short ROP chain: for instance, we may hijack a thread, overwrite a return address in a stack frame, or use other standard techniques.

4.3   Chunk Crafting and ROP-TxF Layout

Rope is the first design to use a covert communication channel for hosting both instructions and program state: as even chunks take the form of data, the execution runtime can host both using a single RW region. We use NTFS transactions to keep the contents of ROP-TxF hidden as much as possible, but as we will discuss in Sect. 4.5 also other standard means can provide hosting in its place.

As the top part of Fig. 1 shows, a payload that Rope spreads out takes the form of a series of ROP chains of user-defined length, with each chain embodying a chunk. In the implementation, we use chunks that encompass a single API call, as in the eyes of behavioral detection API calls are the unit of interaction with the OS. Trade-offs with larger chunks should also be possible [20,37].

Careful choices in payload designing help in keeping the execution runtime small and with fewer conspicuous features. For starters, we want to avoid the creation of multiple memory regions (e.g., stack, heap, data, rodata), each with different permissions and relocations as for the typical segments of an executable. The design point that we follow is radically simple: we model global, heap, and stack memory as part of a flat space in the ROP-TxF. We promote each stack variable[3] to global storage, and we encapsulate all global variables and objects (e.g., strings) as fields of a single data structure. Every access to a program variable undergoes a level of indirection in a base+offset computation, and upon loading the ROP-TxF we control the value that the runtime exposes for base.

To encode ROP chains, we can pick gadgets from a code module that the victim processes share already before or as a consequence of the actions of the loader or the bootstrap component. Another important issue in chunk crafting is the sharing of OS resources among execution units. Well-studied in [20], this issue involves Windows HANDLE, registry, and socket objects as they are unique per process (i.e., other units cannot access them). Since we already wrap program variables, we can identify the involved handles and then duplicate them via standard OS features, exposing to each unit its own copies.

We can now detail the layout of the ROP-TxF, which hosts three adjacent areas: *header*, *chunks*, and *program memory*. The header aids the runtime in bookkeeping tasks. It holds the index of the last executing unit and of the current chunk, the addresses of the Windows APIs that the payload may use, and a per-unit structure hosting duplicated handles (for TxF and program resources), scratch locations for ROP gadgets, and other runtime metadata (e.g., for the feature-aware scenario). Chunks are indexed and laid out consecutively, then program memory follows as it can expand by appending to the ROP-TxF file.

4.4 Bootstrap Component

The bootstrap component serves two main purposes: scheduling the chunks in coordination with the other units and loading the ROP-TxF to memory.

For execution coordination, Rope can benefit from well-studied techniques to implement locks in increasingly covert ways [6,20,37]. Once a victim execution unit acquires the lock, it updates the ROP-TxF header and advances chunk execution. Upon execution termination, the bootstrap component may actively wait for new chunks to process or go dormant for some time. In the latter scenario, the bootstrap component arranges for its rescheduling if the loader used a method with a limited lifetime (e.g., an APC call—Section 4.2) to dispatch it.

As for the ROP-TxF loading, we identify two alternative strategies:

a) Use the ROP-TxF as a memory-mapped file and access its contents directly. Any change will be readily visible to the other units. The mapping may be active persistently or recreated whenever about to execute a chunk.
b) Read the strictly needed portions from the ROP-TxF file and copy them to process-local memory (e.g., heap), then write them back to propagate any updates (e.g., program state values) to the other units.

The two strategies come with a different trade-off between stealthiness (i.e., visibility of the full ROP-TxF contents to in-memory scanning techniques) and bookkeeping work (i.e., explicit synchronization of contents). Present AV/EDR

---

[3] Only recursive functions would require semantic changes to their code: e.g., the attacker may use a stack data structure to host and reference each stack frame.

solutions do not appear to be equipped with ROP-aware analyses that may benefit from any available memory contents. Hence, we believe that for now, a malware writer would choose one of the two based on factors beyond the goals of Rope, such as trying to hinder forensic analysis during incident response.

Irrespective of such choice, the functionality that the component will enact is the same: it changes the stack pointer to point to the beginning of the first chunk to execute, dispatches one or more chunks, and eventually reacquires control.

Finally, we give the bootstrap component a further and more practical task: solving in a covert way the APIs used in the payload, filling currently unassigned address fields in the ROP-TxF header. While handling API resolution in the loader would be simpler (e.g., by importing such APIs statically or by solving them dynamically), it would give away hints on the actions (e.g., crypto, network) that the payload may perform. Also, it may get in the way with more complex payloads where, e.g., a sample receives from the network a functional update that exercises APIs not initially considered. Instead, the processes that Rope abuses typically use the enclosing DLLs already for their activities. Therefore, the bootstrap component can scan their memory covertly to look up APIs.

4.5   Discussion

Rope brings new advances to the malware design literature by meeting the five open challenges we identified along the way to covertness (Sect. 3) with original solutions. These include, among others, the flattening of code and program data as relocatable elements of a single region, the covert dispatching of the bootstrap component as part of the own activities of the process, and forfeiting the introduction of executable regions and other forms of dynamic code generation.

Along with careful design choices for the components of the architecture, code reuse techniques turn out to be decisive to achieve all these ends and properties. The means to deliver chunks to execution units sees no Rope-specific constraints [C1], and we do not even inject code but data (Sect. 4.2). The bootstrap component, thanks to payload crafting choices such as indirection for data accesses and clear fields for handles (Sect. 4.3), is conceptually simple and in turn compact [C2]. As Sect. 5 will detail for [C3], ROP offers a means to bypass hardening mitigations like EAF and IAF and to make Rope comply with others by design. The loading strategies for the ROP-TxF contents and the use of TxF can go a long way for [C4]. Finally, as we observed in our experiments, only the actions of the loader may need special countermeasures to limit their footprint [C5]. Indeed, unlike for the bootstrap component and the chunks, we cannot disguise its actions as if they were from pre-existing processes.

Another design advantage of Rope is that the technical means that we use are virtually interchangeable. For instance, we may replace or combine ROP with other code reuse techniques, and use different methods in each victim to dispatch the bootstrap component. We may possibly replace even the ROP-TxF using a standard file or a shared memory, albeit with a loss of covertness for its contents against minifilters from AV/EDR solutions or in-memory scans. As we will argue in Sect. 7, defenders should equip with comprehensive detections for distributed malicious executions, as mitigating only individual components may turn out insufficient.

On a different note, a few research works have explored uses of ROP in malware design, e.g., for split-personality [44] and polymorphism [34] schemes. Those works make a surgical use of ROP to target weaknesses in static code analysis schemes: both the adversary (e.g., AV signatures in [34]) and the extent of the ROP encoding (i.e., limited to few parts) are different than in our work.

To the best of our knowledge, Rope is the first work successfully targeting Windows systems hardened with AV/EDR solutions and the opt-in mitigations of WDEG. The design behind Rope is general: we believe that with implementation adaptations one may explore it also on other platforms, such as Linux [16] and Android [22], for which injection techniques recently started to emerge.

As anticipated at the end of Sect. 3, when presenting the design of Rope we did not touch on aspects such as split communication channels or resilience to termination, as for those problems Rope can adopt existing solutions.

5 Implementation

This section illustrates the choices that we followed in a prototype implementation of Rope, and reports on the bypass techniques for the WDEG mitigations that we created and responsibly disclosed to Microsoft in February 2021. A companion technical report [10] covers details of the implementations of both Rope and the bypass techniques that we omitted in the following for brevity.

Injection and Gadget Source. As described in Sect. 4.2, the loader component needs to inject in each victim process a short ROP chain to make it load the bootstrap component of Rope. To this end, we resort to a standard technique in malware for hijacking one of the threads of the victim. We retrieve the CPU context, alter the stack pointer to make room for the chain, write the chain to the victim's stack along with the saved CPU context, and update the instruction pointer so as to execute the first gadget. Upon thread resumption, the chain loads the bootstrap component, dispatches it for execution, and eventually restores the saved CPU context to resume the victim's activities.

In Sect. 4.3 we also discussed the possibility of using as a gadget source a DLL module that all victims load as a consequence of the actions of either the loader or of the bootstrap component. In the implementation, we foresaw an opportunity for a shortcut to ease the loading of both the bootstrap component and such DLL module: when TxF-ed files are involved, the CIG mitigation of Windows struggles with operations that are not self-contained. In particular, while WDEG causes a checksum error for NtCreateSection if a CIG-enabled process tries to map a section object from a TxF-ed file, it currently does not stop it from mapping a view of a section object created in another process.

Hence, we make the Rope loader create another transacted file on a signed Microsoft DLL, add to it any required gadgets using code caves, and embed also the bootstrap component (as a ROP chain or even as a shellcode placed in RX caves) in it[4]. Then we create a section object and duplicate the handle to it.

The initial ROP chain that we inject uses 6 one-instruction gadgets from ntdll.dll. To make the victim load the transacted DLL it uses the system call NtMapViewOfSection, as the ROP mitigations of WDEG do not shepherd it. Then it executes a helper sequence of the bootstrap component that creates a thread for it to run, and readily returns to the chain.

The bootstrap component uses the ROP-TxF as a memory-mapped file and a simple mutex to coordinate the execution. As the transacted DLL can see different base addresses due to the non-standard loading that we use, before executing a chunk the component applies relocations to gadget addresses and saves the current base address for the DLL in the ROP-TxF header. In this way, the next execution unit can perform its own relocations with the same technique.

API Calls. The interaction with APIs from the OS brings three problems: locating them covertly in the presence of EAF/IAF mitigations, eluding the ROP mitigations of WDEG for sensitive APIs, and evading AV/EDR hooks.

The EAF and IAF mitigations (Sect. 2.1) monitor accesses to the export and import address tables of loaded code modules: those are recurring traits in covert API resolution methods. To avoid suspicious imports in the loader or uses of noisy OS means (i.e., GetProcAddress) for API resolution, we designed and responsibly disclosed to Microsoft two bypass techniques for EAF and IAF, respectively, that the bootstrap component can alternatively use. In both techniques, we disguise accesses to the export/import address table of the victim program by using a ROP gadget that can read from an arbitrary address, searching it within any loaded DLL (e.g., kernel32.dll). The current implementations of EAF and IAF whitelist such an access, erroneously assuming it originated in a legitimate module. Further details can be found in [10].

Our implementation complies with the WDEG ROP mitigations for sensitive APIs (Sect. 2.1) that a chunk or the bootstrap component may invoke. In particular, WDEG shepherds invocations of several APIs that are typically used for manipulating memory, processes, and code modules [28]. To get around those mitigations, for *StackPivot* we switch the stack pointer so as to have any API calls (i.e., also non-sensitive ones) take place on the native program stack, while for *CallerCheck* and *SimExec* we use suitable gadgets described in prior works [5,33].

Finally, eluding API hooks may be useful for setup activities that may arouse suspicion in a behavioral engine [C5]. In our tests, only the loader seemed to benefit from hook evasion: indeed, due to its standalone and intrusive nature, the loader can be the weak link in distributed malware concepts. Our implementation may call standard high-level APIs, use their low-level Nt counterparts from ntdll.dll, or attempt hook evasion. On 64-bit victims, "direct" system

---

[4] A more conservative and covert implementation may target an already-loaded module (e.g., kernel32.dll) and encode the bootstrap component and the chunks with, e.g., microgadgets [17] that are abundant [32]. However, this was not necessary for validating the stealthiness of our approach on the currently available tested defenses.

calls [11] can elude user-space hooks for Nt functions by solving the ordinal for each system call and invoking it with an own ASM stub. However, for 32-bit victims evasion is harder in Windows 10, as system calls (like the whole kernel) are 64-bit code and take place in the WOW64 compatibility layer. As evasion strategy we opted to use the wow64ext helper library[5] to make a transition (colloquially known as "Heaven's gate") into 64-bit code and call the 64-bit Nt functions directly, as AV/EDR products may neglect them. As future work, we would like to stress such security solutions further by issuing direct system calls after Heaven's gate.

Payload Encoding. Manually encoding a ROP payload can be a lengthy task [2]. The current implementation assumes that the attacker encodes the payload as one or more C functions, delimits the chunks manually (e.g., with an inlined ASM nop), and compiles it to object code using a standard compiler (we used Visual Studio 2019). With careful compilation settings [12], such as omitting the generation of stack canaries, the output resembles a position-independent code for which we can partially automate the ROP translation.

In more detail, we look up or introduce suitable gadgets in the target DLL for one instruction at a time, and wrap constructs like conditional transfers and API calls with templates. Promoting stack variables to global storage in the design sidesteps difficulties that would emerge here and that are known in the ROP practice, as in general translating stack manipulations may require non-trivial program analyses or the use of a parallel stack [4]. While implementing a fully automated translation goes beyond the scope of proving the effectiveness of Rope in avoiding detection, we believe it is a realistic goal also in light of the recent advances in ROP-based program obfuscation [4,32]. Also, capable attackers have already written and released fully-ROP malware in the past [9,14].

6 Evaluation

This section details the findings of our experimental validation. First, we present the methodology for testing AV/EDR products and the WDEG mitigations, and illustrate the PoC Rope samples that we exercised. We then report on our findings and on interactions that we had with a vendor of a popular EDR solution.

Design of Experiments. As the inner workings of commercial AV/EDR solutions are undisclosed and fingerprinting them through manual reverse engineering is difficult [3], we follow a black-box approach to test the success of the covert distribution. We craft several standalone payloads involving different tasks typical of malware (e.g., download and execute) and verify that each security solution would detect them as malicious via behavioral analysis. We then encode equivalent sequences in Rope and test if they avoid detection as expected. For presenting the results, we chose one minimal representative sample for either Rope execution mode (i.e., feature-agnostic and feature-aware, Sect. 4.1).

---

[5] https://github.com/rwfpl/rewolf-wow64ext.

As for WDEG mitigations, we test different combinations to rule out possible interferences among them: we found one between ACG and IAF and reported it. Also, for each employed bypass technique we verified that a violation was indeed detected for an alternate payload that did not make use of it. To rule out false positives from implementation gaps, we test the mitigations in audit mode and review the Windows Event Logs for any report originating from the own activities of the application. These may happen, e.g., when an application loads a legitimate module that was not signed by Microsoft or the Windows Store, or when a browser uses dynamic code generation without liaising with ACG/CIG.

Subjects. For testing, we use three versions of Windows 10 (2004, 20H2, and an Insider build from January 2021) running in a VMware Fusion appliance. All versions come with the following system-wide mitigations enabled: DEP, ASLR, Mandatory ASLR, Bottom-up ASLR, High-entropy ASLR, SEHOP, Validate Heap Integrity, and CFG [28]. We pick our victims from 9 popular applications of varying complexity (Table 1) in their 32-bit releases to allow for a direct comparison with prior solutions, and we make them opt-in for (combinations of) the mitigations that Rope targets (ACG, CIG, EAF, IAF, and ROP—Section 2.1).

As state-of-the-art security solutions, we evaluate Rope on 6 AV and 4 EDR products (Table 1) for which we could obtain a trial version. We run each application and the Rope loader with medium integrity level. We use distinct VM instances for each product, and restore their state after each test.

For the feature-agnostic mode, we use a payload that tampers with the Windows registry by introducing a key entry to achieve persistence for the loader or, alternatively, to invoke a privileged system utility like `bcdedit`. The victim processes (two already sufficed) can race in any order to execute every chunk. For the feature-aware mode, we create a download-and-execute scenario where one network-active process executes chunks that download a PowerShell script from a remote C2 server and drop it to the `%TEMP%` folder, while a normal process executes chunks that read the file path from the ROP-TxF and run the script.

Results. None of the security solutions detected Rope, and no alerts were raised for WDEG as expected. In more detail, we found that the injection primitive that we use in the loader went unnoticed by 7 of the 10 products even when using high-level APIs. One product instead aggressively flags any attempt to open a process and write to its memory: calling the 64-bit `Nt` functions with Heaven's gate suffices to elude it. Finally, two products cause errors (5: `Access Denied`) when trying to open a process. By further investigation, we observed that both `OpenProcess` and `DuplicateHandle` see flawed outputs and errors. This behavior is coherent with prior research on inconsistencies in AV emulators [3]; also, it seems to suggest that these security solutions initially run an untrusted binary as with low integrity and/or in a sandbox-like fashion, shepherding its interactions with the OS in the early execution stages. Unfortunately, direct system calls and other evasions may be effective in defeating even this approach.

On a different note, during our experiments we had several fruitful interactions with one of the EDR vendors, who graciously granted us a trial for testing their product with new concepts and eventually extended it to cope with

Table 1: Tested AV/EDR solutions and victim applications.

	Security solution	Version	Application	Version
AV	Avast	2.1.27.0	Adobe Reader DC	19.010.20098
	Bitdefender Total Security	25.0.10.52	Chrome	86.0.4240.198
	Kaspersky Total Security	21.2.16.590	Discord	0.0.309
	Intezer Endpoint Scanner	1.0.1.8	Dropbox	112.4.321
	Malwarebytes	4.1.1.167	Firefox	83.0
	Windows Defender	January 2021	Opera	73.0.3856.257
EDR	Comodo Client Security	12.5.0.8351	Steam	2.10.91.91
	Microsoft Defender ATP	January 2021	Skype	8.66.0.77
	Sophos Intercept X	2.0.18	Telegram	2.4.7
	Webroot SecureAnywhere	9.0.29.62		

our implementation tactics. The information that they shared with us on their remote telemetry and detections confirmed the truthfulness of our black-box findings.

Finally, to compare with prior research in the field, we distributed the standalone version of the two test payloads using D-TIME: only 3 of the 10 AV/EDR products did not block it. The result is not surprising, as the novelty of remote APC injection wore off shortly after the paper was published. Also, we note that Windows 10 already in its 1809 version added sensors for more complex forms of APC injection (e.g., Defender ATP uses them to detect DoublePulsar-like APC attacks [30]). We do not test malWASH for covertness: while it provides a robust distributed execution runtime, it uses a very conspicuous delivery primitive that D-TIME already improves. In general, revamping either system with more cutting-edge injections would only bring short-lived benefits: vendors will add detections for new injections, while their emulators and chunks will remain an issue in the eyes of AV/EDR analyses and hardening mitigations.

7   Countermeasures and Wrap-Up

Our experiments suggest that Rope hits a blind spot in the characteristics of AV/EDR solutions, even in the presence of application hardening mitigations meant to reduce the attack surface for malware. A fundamental question is how to counter this and similar threats in anti-malware defenses running on machines.

Caveat: As the details of AV/EDR solutions are undisclosed, nuances of the ideas that we outline next may be already present in them in ineffective or incomplete forms, whereas none aided the systems that we tested with Rope*. Also, we do not claim to cover in the following all possible methods to detect* Rope.

From a methodological perspective, we foresee three complementary avenues. The first involves enriching process correlation heuristics in behavioral detection by monitoring primitives that are instrumental to distributed computations. As making a real-time detection scale to multiple units for correlation is computationally expensive [26], heuristics may "draw its fire" to candidate groups of seemingly unrelated processes for close monitoring as a whole. These heuristics should conjecture links by tracking not only process injection primitives (which are continuously evolving and thus hard to cover exhaustively) but also—and possibly with a major emphasis—those OS features that distributed execution designs would need for sharing objects (e.g., handle duplication) and hosting data contents (e.g., TxF, shared memories, memory-mapped files).

The second involves extending the dynamic signatures and in-memory analyses of security solutions with techniques for detecting [38] and analyzing [9,14] payloads encoded with ROP or other weird machines. For instance, a solution may look for repeated gadget sequences used to invoke API calls or for the arrangement of typical constants as API call arguments. On the other hand, attackers may experiment with gadgets more complex than the ones we use in Rope, for instance by playing with gadget diversification and dynamically dead code [4]. We observe that in this setting ROP-aware analyses may serve a more general purpose, as the recent availability of systems for encoding whole programs in ROP for obfuscation [4,32] may also encourage threat actors to experiment more with ROP in standalone malware too (e.g., for polymorphism [34]).

The third involves stronger means to intercept the execution footprint of any kind of malware. The evasion of user-mode API hooks can be a customary practice for the stealthiest malware strains. In addition to minifilters, the Windows kernel provides notifications for events like process creation and termination[6], which AV/EDRs and other systems (e.g., anti-cheat engines) use also to intercept subversion attempts. However, Ciholas et al. show in [7] that a user-mode process can outrun them. A more resilient approach to monitoring application-level events may be using hardware-assisted virtualization features, such as multiple EPT views [18,25] to insert hooks in the physical pages for OS and processes [11].

Albeit the design of Rope leaves much leeway to implementation diversification, stopgap measures may in the meantime help for immediate remediation. As mentioned early on, we reported several flaws in WDEG to Microsoft, suggesting practical countermeasures for each. Adding detection logic to AV/EDR engines based on the implementation solutions detailed in this paper may help as well.

Security solutions may also explore fine-grained detections of ROP execution via hardware assistance. For instance, the HitmanPro. Alert proactive detection system can use the Last Branch Record feature of Intel processors to heuristically detect ROP (as much academic literature explored in the past [36]), albeit false positives may be frequent on, e.g., browsers. Windows 10 with its 2004 version landed instead the first complete implementation of hardware-enforced stack protection by using the Intel Control-Flow Enforcement Technology (CET). We note, however, that the first processor supporting CET became available at the end of 2020, and that CET still leaves room for attacks [43].

On a different note, Rope poses interesting challenges also for reverse engineering and fine-grained analyses. For instance, the combination of ROP with

---

[6] Also the ETW (Event Tracing for Windows) system offers useful tracing capabilities.

NTFS transactions may be interesting for fileless malware concepts, and forensic analyses may need tools to carve out TxF contents that are not directly mapped in memory. Offline systems like Panorama [45] that perform expensive system-wide information flow analyses may instead be useful to track computations spread among execution units, so as to shed light in a black-box fashion on the internal working of Rope samples or other distributed malware instances.

We hope that the ideas presented in this paper may contribute to raise awareness on the effectiveness and practicality of covert distributed malware attacks, to foster research on defensive countermeasures, and to improve the implementation of current AV/EDR solutions. The technical details omitted from the paper for brevity can be found in our companion technical report [10]. The Rope samples from our tests will be made available to AV/EDR vendors upon request.

References

1. Allred, C.: Understanding Windows file system transactions. In: Storage Developer Conference 2009. SNIA (2009). https://www.snia.org/sites/default/orig/sdc_archives/2009_presentations/tuesday/ChristianAllred_UnderstandingWindowsFileSystemTransactions.pdf
2. Angelini, M., et al.: ROPMate: visually assisting the creation of ROP-based exploits. In: Proceedings of the 15th IEEE Symposium on Visualization for Cyber Security. VizSec 2018 (2018). https://doi.org/10.1109/VIZSEC.2018.8709204
3. Blackthorne, J., Bulazel, A., Fasano, A., Biernat, P., Yener, B.: AVLeak: fingerprinting antivirus emulators through black-box testing. In: 10th USENIX Workshop on Offensive Technologies. WOOT 2016, USENIX Association (2016)
4. Borrello, P., Coppa, E., D'Elia, D.C.: Hiding in the particles: when return-oriented programming meets program obfuscation. In: Proceedings of the 51st Annual IEEE/IFIP International Conference on Dependable Systems and Networks, pp. 555–568. DSN 2021. IEEE (2021). https://doi.org/10.1109/DSN48987.2021.00064
5. Borrello, P., Coppa, E., D'Elia, D.C., Demetrescu, C.: The ROP needle: hiding trigger-based injection vectors via code reuse. In: Proceedings of the 34th ACM/SIGAPP Symposium on Applied Computing, pp. 1962–1970. SAC 2019. ACM (2019). https://doi.org/10.1145/3297280.3297472
6. Botacin, M., de Geus, P.L., Grégio, A.: "VANILLA" malware: vanishing antiviruses by interleaving layers and layers of attacks. J. Comput. Virol. Hack. Techn. 15(4), 233–247 (2019). https://doi.org/10.1007/s11416-019-00333-y
7. Ciholas, P., Such, J.M., Marnerides, A.K., Green, B., Zhang, J., Roedig, U.: Fast and furious: outrunning Windows kernel notification routines from user-mode. In: Maurice, C., Bilge, L., Stringhini, G., Neves, N. (eds.) DIMVA 2020. LNCS, vol. 12223, pp. 67–88. Springer, Cham (2020). https://doi.org/10.1007/978-3-030-52683-2_4
8. De Gaspari, F., Hitaj, D., Pagnotta, G., De Carli, L., Mancini, L.V.: THE NAKED SUN: malicious cooperation between benign-looking processes. In: Conti, M., Zhou, J., Casalicchio, E., Spognardi, A. (eds.) ACNS 2020. LNCS, vol. 12147, pp. 254–274. Springer, Cham (2020). https://doi.org/10.1007/978-3-030-57878-7_13
9. D'Elia, D.C., Coppa, E., Salvati, A., Demetrescu, C.: Static analysis of ROP code. In: Proceedings of the 12th European Workshop on Systems Security. EuroSec 2019, ACM (2019). https://doi.org/10.1145/3301417.3312494

10. D'Elia, D.C., Invidia, L.: Rope: Bypassing behavioral detection of malware with distributed ROP-driven execution. Black Hat USA (2021). https://i.blackhat. com/USA21/Wednesday-Handouts/us-21-Rope-Bypassing-Behavioral-Detection-Of-Malware-With-Distributed-ROP-Driven-Execution-wp.pdf

11. D'Elia, D.C., Nicchi, S., Mariani, M., Marini, M., Palmaro, F.: Designing robust API monitoring solutions. arXiv abs/2005.00323 (2020)

12. Doniec, A.: From a C project, through assembly, to shellcode (by hasherezade). VX Underground (2020). https://github.com/vxunderground/VXUG-Papers

13. Filiol, E.: Formalisation and implementation aspects of K-ary (malicious) codes. J. Comput. Virol. **3**, 75–86 (2007). https://doi.org/10.1007/s11416-007-0044-2

14. Graziano, M., Balzarotti, D., Zidouemba, A.: ROPMEMU: a framework for the analysis of complex code-reuse attacks. In: Proceedings of 11th Asia Conference on Computer and Communications Security, pp. 47–58. ASIACCS 2016. ACM (2016). https://doi.org/10.1145/2897845.2897894

15. Hăjmăşan, G., Mondoc, A., Portase, R., Creţ, O.: Evasive malware detection using groups of processes. In: De Capitani di Vimercati, S., Martinelli, F. (eds.) SEC 2017. IAICT, vol. 502, pp. 32–45. Springer, Cham (2017). https://doi.org/10.1007/978-3-319-58469-0_3

16. Hendrick, A.: Fileless malware and process injection in Linux. Hack.lu (2019). http://archive.hack.lu/2019/Fileless-Malware-Infection-and-Linux-Process-Injection-in-Linux-OS.pdf

17. Homescu, A., Stewart, M., Larsen, P., Brunthaler, S., Franz, M.: Microgadgets: Size does matter in Turing-complete return-oriented programming. In: 6th USENIX Workshop on Offensive Technologies. WOOT 2012, USENIX Association (2012)

18. Hong, J., Ding, X.: A novel dynamic analysis infrastructure to instrument untrusted execution flow across user-kernel spaces. In: Proceedings of the 2021 IEEE Symposium on Security and Privacy, pp. 402–418. SP 2021. IEEE Computer Society (2021). https://doi.org/10.1109/SP40001.2021.00024

19. ired.team: ProcessDynamicCodePolicy: Arbitrary Code Guard (ACG). Red Teaming Experiments GitBook (2020). https://www.ired.team/offensive-security/defense-evasion/acg-arbitrary-code-guard-processdynamiccodepolicy

20. Ispoglou, K.K., Payer, M.: malWASH: washing malware to evade dynamic analysis. In: 10th USENIX Workshop on Offensive Technologies. WOOT 2016, USENIX Association (2016)

21. Ji, Y., He, Y., Zhu, D., Li, Q., Guo, D.: A mulitiprocess mechanism of evading behavior-based bot detection approaches. In: Huang, X., Zhou, J. (eds.) ISPEC 2014. LNCS, vol. 8434, pp. 75–89. Springer, Cham (2014). https://doi.org/10.1007/978-3-319-06320-1_7

22. Kaspersky: Dvmap: the first Android malware with code injection. SecureList (2017). https://securelist.com/dvmap-the-first-android-malware-with-code-injection/78648/)

23. Klein, A., Kotler, I.: Process injection techniques - gotta catch them all (Windows process injection in 2019). Black Hat USA (2019). https://i.blackhat.com/USA-19/Thursday/us-19-Kotler-Process-Injection-Techniques-Gotta-Catch-Them-All-wp.pdf

24. Kulkarni, A.P., Jagdale, P.D.: Adapting to TxF. VirusBulletin, January 2010. https://www.virusbulletin.com/virusbulletin/2010/05/adapting-txf

25. Lengyel, T.K., Maresca, S., Payne, B.D., Webster, G.D., Vogl, S., Kiayias, A.: Scalability, fidelity and stealth in the DRAKVUF dynamic malware analysis system. In: Proceedings of the 30th Annual Computer Security Applications Conf. (ACSAC 2014), pp. 386–395. ACM (2014). https://doi.org/10.1145/2664243.2664252

26. Ma, W., Duan, P., Liu, S., Gu, G., Liu, J.C.: Shadow attacks: automatically evading system-call-behavior based malware detection. J. Comput. Virol. **8**(1), 1–13 (2012). https://doi.org/10.1007/s11416-011-0157-5
27. MDSec: Bypassing user-mode hooks and direct invocation of system calls for red teams (2020). https://www.mdsec.co.uk/2020/12/bypassing-user-mode-hooks-and-direct-invocation-of-system-calls-for-red-teams/
28. Microsoft: Exploit protection reference. https://docs.microsoft.com/en-us/microsoft-365/security/defender-endpoint/exploit-protection-reference?view=o365-worldwide
29. Microsoft: Windows Defender Exploit Guard: Reduce the attack surface against next-generation malware (2017). https://www.microsoft.com/security/blog/2017/10/23/windows-defender-exploit-guard-reduce-the-attack-surface-against-next-generation-malware/
30. Microsoft Defender Security Research Team: From alert to driver vulnerability: Microsoft Defender ATP investigation unearths privilege escalation flaw. https://www.microsoft.com/security/blog/2019/03/25/from-alert-to-driver-vulnerability-microsoft-defender-atp-investigation-unearths-privilege-escalation-flaw/
31. Min, B., Varadharajan, V.: Design and analysis of a new feature-distributed malware. In: 2014 IEEE 13th International Conference on Trust, Security and Privacy in Computing and Communications, pp. 457–464 (2014). https://doi.org/10.1109/TrustCom.2014.58
32. Nakanishi, F., De Pasquale, G., Ferla, D., Cavallaro, L.: Intertwining ROP gadgets and opaque predicates for robust obfuscation. arXiv abs/2012.09163 (2020)
33. Nemeth, Z.L.: Modern binary attacks and defences in the Windows environment - fighting against Microsoft EMET in seven rounds. In: 2015 IEEE 13th International Symposium on Intelligent Systems and Informatics, pp. 275–280. SYSY 2015 (2015). https://doi.org/10.1109/SISY.2015.7325394
34. Ntantogian, C., Poulios, G., Karopoulos, G., Xenakis, C.: Transforming malicious code to ROP gadgets for antivirus evasion. IET Inf. Security **13**(6), 570–578 (2019). https://doi.org/10.1049/iet-ifs.2018.5386
35. Or-Meir, O., Nissim, N., Elovici, Y., Rokach, L.: Dynamic malware analysis in the modern era - a state of the art survey. ACM Comput. Surv. **52**(5) (2019). https://doi.org/10.1145/3329786
36. Pappas, V., Polychronakis, M., Keromytis, A.D.: Transparent ROP exploit mitigation using indirect branch tracing. In: 22nd USENIX Security Symposium, pp. 447–462. USENIX Security 2013, USENIX Association (2013)
37. Pavithran, J., Patnaik, M., Rebeiro, C.: D-TIME: Distributed threadless independent malware execution for runtime obfuscation. In: 13th USENIX Workshop on Offensive Technologies. WOOT 2019, USENIX Association (2019)
38. Polychronakis, M., Keromytis, A.D.: ROP payload detection using speculative code execution. In: 2011 6th International Conference on Malicious and Unwanted Software, pp. 58–65. IEEE Computer Society (2011). https://doi.org/10.1109/MALWARE.2011.6112327
39. Ramilli, M., Bishop, M.: Multi-stage delivery of malware. In: 2010 5th Int. Conference on Malicious and Unwanted Software, pp. 91–97 (2010). https://doi.org/10.1109/MALWARE.2010.5665788
40. Ramilli, M., Bishop, M., Sun, S.: Multiprocess malware. In: 2011 6th International Conference on Malicious and Unwanted Software, pp. 8–13 (2011). https://doi.org/10.1109/MALWARE.2011.6112320

41. Roemer, R., Buchanan, E., Shacham, H., Savage, S.: Return-oriented programming: Systems, languages, and applications. ACM Trans. Inf. Syst. Secur. **15**(1) (2012). https://doi.org/10.1145/2133375.2133377
42. Russinovich, M., Solomon, D.A.: Windows internals: including Windows server, : and Windows vista. Fifth Edition. Microsoft Press **2009**, 965–974 (2008)
43. Sun, B., Liu, J., Xu, C.: How to survive the hardware-assisted control-flow integrity enforcement. Black Hat Asia (2019). https://i.blackhat.com/asia-19/ Thu-March-28/bh-asia-Sun-How-to-Survive-the-Hardware-Assisted-Control-Flow-Integrity-Enforcement.pdf
44. Wang, T., Lu, K., Lu, L., Chung, S., Lee, W.: Jekyll on iOS: when benign apps become evil. In: 22nd USENIX Security Symposium, pp. 559–572. USENIX Security 2013, USENIX Association (2013)
45. gs Yin, H., Song, D., Egele, M., Kruegel, C., Kirda, E.: Panorama: capturing system-wide information flow for malware detection and analysis. In: Proceedin of the 14th ACM Conference on Computer and Communications Security, pp. 116–127. CCS 2007. ACM (2007). https://doi.org/10.1145/1315245.1315261

Towards Automating Code-Reuse Attacks Using Synthesized Gadget Chains

Moritz Schloegel[(✉)], Tim Blazytko, Julius Basler, Fabian Hemmer,
and Thorsten Holz

Ruhr-Universität Bochum, Bochum, Germany
{moritz.schloegel,tim.blazytko,julius.basler,
fabian.hemmer,thorsten.holz}@rub.de

Abstract. In the arms race between binary exploitation techniques and mitigation schemes, *code-reuse attacks* have been proven indispensable. Typically, one of the initial hurdles is that an attacker cannot execute their own code due to countermeasures such as *data execution prevention* (DEP, `W^X`). While this technique is powerful, the task of finding and correctly chaining gadgets remains cumbersome. Although various methods automating this task have been proposed, they either rely on hard-coded heuristics or make specific assumptions about the gadgets' semantics. This not only drastically limits the search space but also sacrifices their capability to find valid chains unless specific gadgets can be located. As a result, they often produce no chain or an incorrect chain that crashes the program. In this paper, we present `SGC`, the first generic approach to identify gadget chains in an automated manner *without* imposing restrictions on the gadgets or limiting its applicability to specific exploitation scenarios. Instead of using heuristics to find a gadget chain, we offload this task to an SMT solver. More specifically, we build a logical formula that encodes the CPU and memory state at the time when the attacker can divert execution flow to the gadget chain, as well as the attacker's desired program state that the gadget chain should construct. In combination with a logical encoding of the data flow between gadgets, we query an SMT solver whether a valid gadget chain exists. If successful, the solver provides a proof of existence in the form of a synthesized gadget chain. This way, we remain fully flexible w.r.t. to the gadgets. In empirical tests, we find that the solver often uses all types of control-flow transfer instructions and even gadgets with side effects. Our evaluation shows that `SGC` successfully finds working gadget chains for real-world exploitation scenarios within minutes, even when all state-of-the-art approaches fail.

1 Introduction

Early exploitation techniques relied on code-injection attacks, where an attacker injects shellcode into the memory space of an application and then executes it. However, quickly established mitigations forced attackers to adapt. Especially the introduction of the `W^X` policy (commonly referred to as *data execution*

© Springer Nature Switzerland AG 2021
E. Bertino et al. (Eds.): ESORICS 2021, LNCS 12972, pp. 218–239, 2021.
https://doi.org/10.1007/978-3-030-88418-5_11

prevention (DEP)) made the execution of injected code infeasible, as memory is marked as either writable or executable. This forced attackers to develop novel exploitation techniques that *reuse* already existing code (e. g., *return-to-libc*) [26,30,32]. As an additional line of defense, modern operating systems randomize a program's address space layout (ASLR). Still, a single *information leak* or small, non-randomized parts of the executable often provide an attacker the capability to mount their attack. In the past years, control-flow integrity (CFI) [1] has gained popularity. This technique enforces the property that only legitimate control-flow transitions inside a benign set required by the program are performed. While greatly limiting the attacker's freedom to chain arbitrary code snippets, so-called *code-reuse attacks* are still feasible in practice [11,24,35]. In general, code-reuse attacks have been shown to be Turing complete [22,23]. Note that in practice, attackers often only need to disable W^X before they can execute arbitrary shellcode in the context of the exploited program. This is commonly achieved by chaining so-called *gadgets*, (short) sequences of instructions ending with an indirect control-flow transfer such as ret [26]. Even medium-sized programs contain thousands of gadgets, making the process of extracting and finding a suitable combination cumbersome. Various techniques to automate the process were proposed: Initial attempts used pattern-matching-based strategies to identify a chain [20,21]; later approaches [2,8,17] make use of symbolic execution to classify gadgets and identify undesirable side effects, e. g., writing values to memory. However, even the most advanced approaches to date rely on various heuristics to confine the large search space [11,24,35]. While sometimes effective, pruning may lead to false negatives: these heuristics try to find generic chains to work across many targets, but in some cases no such chain exists.

In this paper, we propose a novel method to find gadget chains efficiently *without* pruning the search space. One category of tools that particularly excels at finding solutions for decision problems involving a large search space are SMT solvers [33]; they check if a (potentially large) set of logical formulas— so-called *constraints*—can be satisfied [15]. By building a logical formula that describes (1) the CPU and memory state before executing the first gadget, (2) the CPU and memory state desired by the attacker, and (3) the data flow between gadgets, we can model the gadget chain synthesis as a reachability problem and use an SMT solver to decide it. This approach is similar to bounded model checking [27], a software verification technique used to determine whether a system meets a given set of requirements: it combines a set of assumptions that have to hold before execution *(preconditions)* and a set of requirements that have to hold after execution *(postconditions)* with a logical encoding of the program semantics and then queries an SMT solver. If the solver returns SAT (satisfiable), it provides a *model* representing a concrete variable assignment that satisfies the given constraints. In our case, this implies that the solver successfully synthesized a gadget chain. If the result is UNSAT (unsatisfiable), the SMT solver mathematically proved that the constraints cannot be satisfied and, thus, no chain can exist for the given set of gadgets.

We introduce the design and implementation of SGC, a generic approach capable of automatically identifying gadget chains without relying on any classification or heuristics to prune the search space. At the same time, the logical formula offers a framework to specify target-specific constraints. Our evaluation demonstrates that SGC not only outperforms all state-of-the-art tools with regard to finding gadget chains, but the synthesized chains always work in real-world scenarios. For instance, we demonstrate how we can craft a gadget chain that spawns a shell for a stack-based buffer overflow in dnsmasq: After defining the concrete CPU state as preconditions, we encode the target state right before executing the system call execve(&"/bin/sh", 0, 0); running SGC provides us with a gadget chain spawning the shell without requiring any other information. We further demonstrate that even complex constraints (e.g., the sum of all values in the gadget chain must be equal to a specific value) can be satisfied by SGC.

In summary, our main contributions are:

- We introduce a generic approach to synthesize gadget chains in an automated way based on bounded model checking. Our approach does not require heuristics or pruning of the search space; instead, the SMT solver provides a proof of existence in the form of a gadget chain or proves that no gadget chain can be found for the given gadgets and constraints.
- We present the design and evaluation of our prototype SGC. We show that it not only outperforms all state-of-the-art approaches, but also works in real-world settings.
- Our approach provides unprecedented flexibility: SGC allows an attacker to specify arbitrary constraints and, thus, model even complex or unusual exploitation scenarios.

To foster further research in this area, we open-source SGC at https://github.com/RUB-SysSec/gadget_synthesis.

2   Shortcomings of State-of-the-Art Approaches

In the following, we discuss state-of-the-art approaches from academia and industry that can be used in practice to generate gadget chains automatically and analyze their shortcomings in this regard (cf. Table 1). We find that existing tools can be separated into two categories, based on their gadget chain generation:

Hardcoded Chaining Rules. Ropper [21] and ROPgadget [20] both fall into this category. Their main task is to extract gadgets, but both require hardcoded rules based on regular expressions to chain gadgets. While ROPgadget only supports a single exploitation scenario (i.e., building a system call to execve(&"/bin/sh\0", 0, 0)) , Ropper allows system calls to mprotect as well. As a result, these tools are inflexible in practice.

Symbolic Exploration. angrop [2] and ROPium [17] operate on an *intermediate representation* of gadgets, which allows them to symbolically determine side effects and perform a classification. To this end, gadgets are first lifted, then analyzed, and chained together in the last step. The latter usually involves an algorithm such as *depth-first search* (`ROPium`) or *breadth-first search* (`angrop`) to identify a sequence of gadgets that fulfills the attacker's specifications, such as specific argument values. While vastly more flexible than approaches using hardcoded rules, these tools are no panacea. They still rely on a classification of gadgets, and while they provide greater flexibility by allowing simple memory and register constraints, they lack support for more elaborate constraints. `P-SHAPE` by Follner et al. [8] also uses a symbolic exploration approach. However, it only focuses on finding gadgets useful for constructing library calls. It does neither provide a full gadget chain nor allows an attacker to specify any constraints.

Table 1. Features of different tools capable of automatically chaining gadgets.

	SGC	P-SHAPE	angrop	ROPium	ROPgadget	Ropper
Supports chains without `ret`	✓	✗	✗	✓	✓	✓
No hardcoded chaining rules	✓	✓	✓	✓	✗	✗
No classification needed	✓	✗	✗	✗	✗	✗
Supports arbitrary postconditions	✓	✗	✗	✗	✗	✗

Overall, all approaches lack flexibility; especially, they fail to support arbitrary postconditions (cf. Table 1). Instead, they rely on a classification of gadgets and pre-defined strategies to identify a gadget chain. Even when finding a chain, we empirically observe that they often crash the targeted program, e. g., through invalid memory accesses. Despite this, no tool makes any attempt at verifying the correctness of the generated gadget chains.

3 Design

In the following, we present a gadget-agnostic design that does not perform any pre-classification of gadgets while providing high flexibility by allowing to specify arbitrary, complex constraints. The nature of our approach overcomes the limitations of existing approaches. Most importantly, we can enforce an arbitrary CPU register and memory state before and after the exploitation—our design will identify a gadget chain facilitating the transition from the initial to the desired state using any gadgets available, including such using `jmp` and `call` instructions. To this end, our approach encodes the search of the gadget chain as a synthesis problem that an SMT solver decides. More specifically, our design is based on bounded model checking: preconditions and postconditions are represented by the initial and desired CPU state, while a logical formula encodes the possible gadget chain that facilitates the transition between both states.

Recall that bounded model checking is usually applied to a well-defined unit of code, such as a function with specific conditions. The goal of bounded model checking is to qualitatively assert that no diversion from the specified postconditions is possible (i. e., any diversion implies a bug that must be fixed). In other words, the goal is to find a counterexample *violating* the postconditions. For the use case of synthesizing a gadget chain, the scenario is slightly different: There is no well-defined unit of code such as a function, but a large number of individual gadgets that can be executed in an arbitrary order. As a consequence, we are not interested in knowing whether specific postconditions can be *violated* (as this most certainly is the case given the number and nature of the gadgets); instead, we are interested in whether there exists a chain of gadgets that *satisfies* the postconditions. In other words, we task the SMT solver with finding a satisfying assignment for *preconditions* ∧ *gadget_chain* ∧ *postconditions*. If the solver finds such an assignment, the produced model contains concrete values for all variables—including stack or other attacker-controlled buffers—which describe the chain of gadgets. Thus, once a model is found, converting the values into a chain becomes a trivial task. In the following, we present these steps in detail.

3.1   Gadgets

First, we must extract gadgets from the target program, which can then be further processed. This step is independent of the subsequent encoding and is covered in detail by previous works in this area [3,4,6,9,26]. As such, we omit it here for brevity. Note that we do not require the gadget extraction to be exhaustive or classify gadgets, as long as these sequences of instructions end with an indirect control-flow transfer. As assembly instructions commonly have side effects (e. g., `mul rbx` implicitly modifies the `rdx`, `rax`, and `rflags` register), we disassemble and lift the gadgets to an *intermediate representation (IR)* with explicit side effects. An example for two gadgets is visible in Fig. 1a. Noteworthy, each IR instruction has no implicit side effects. We reiterate that—other than most state-of-the-art tools—our design imposes no restrictions, ranking, or classification on the gadgets.

3.2   Logical Encoding

Given a pool of gadgets, we want to query an SMT solver to find a chain of gadgets that transitions the initial program state (formulated as preconditions) into the desired program state (formulated as postconditions). For this, we need to logically encode the semantics of gadgets and chains. Especially, we must model the semantics of gadgets, the data flow between instructions, and the data flow between gadgets. Once we have encoded all components, we must combine them into a single formula, which we then pass to an SMT solver. To construct such a formula, we connect each statement through conjunctions. In the following, we first describe how individual gadgets are encoded and then explain how gadgets are interconnected to form a chain.

Instructions and Gadgets. To use a gadget in the logical formula, we must first model all implicit state transitions on the instruction level: While a CPU executes a sequence of instructions in a row, it implicitly tracks state

```
1  gadget_a:                                  1  gadget_b:
2    mov rbx, [rsp+8] ; rbx := 064[rsp + 8]  2    pop rax ; rax := 064[rsp]
3    mov [rsp], rdx   ; 064[rsp] := rdx      3            ; rsp := rsp + 8
4    ret              ; rsp := rsp + 8       4    inc rax ; rax := rax + 1
5                     ; rip := [rsp - 8]     5    jmp rbx ; rip := rbx
```

(a) Assembly code and the corresponding intermediate representation (IR) of the instructions as comments. Note that side effects are explicitly modeled in the IR, thus a single assembly instruction may result in multiple IR instructions.

```
1  gadget_a:                                           1  gadget_b:
2    rbx_a_1 := read(M_IN, rsp_IN + 8, 64)            2    rax_b_1 := read(M_IN, rsp_IN, 64)
3                                                      3    rsp_b_1 := rsp_IN + 8
4    M_a_1 := write(M_IN, rsp_IN, rdx_IN, 64)         4
5                                                      5    rax_b_2 := rax_b_1 + 1
6    rsp_a_1 := rsp_IN + 8                             6
7    rip_a_2 := read(M_a_1, rsp_a_1 - 8)              7    rip_b_2 := rbx_IN
```

(b) SSA form of the IR representation. The variable's locality is specified by an unique identifier, here _a or _b. Suffix _IN represents the initial definition.

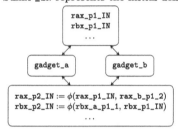

(c) Structural overview of the final SMT formula, assuming a chain of two gadgets.

Fig. 1. The high-level idea of our logical encoding: We lift assembly gadgets to an intermediate representation, make the variable and memory accesses stateful (via static single assignment form) and encode the data flow between gadgets using ϕ-functions.

changes in registers and memory. To represent this behavior in a logical formula, we must explicitly model it on the instruction and inter-instruction level. To address the instruction level, recall that we lift instruction into an IR form that explicitly handles side effects. For the latter, we have to model the data flow between instructions, e. g., when a register is assigned to another register or is defined more than once. To achieve this, we make variable assignments stateful by converting IR instructions into *static single assignment (SSA)* form [7]. This implies that each variable *definition* is assigned a new unique index, while *uses* always use the last defined index. To differentiate between gadgets, we prefix SSA variable names with an identifier that is unique to each gadget. If a gadget uses a variable that was not defined previously within this particular gadget, we postfix it by _IN to indicate that the value has been defined outside of the gadget's scope. In other words, it is an input to the gadget.

Example 1. Fig. 1b shows how rip_a_2 depends on the memory at address rsp_a_1 - 8 (line 7), which itself can be calculated as rsp_a_1 = rsp_IN + 8 (line 6). Note the identifier _a, which distinctly marks this variable as belonging to gadget a, and the postfix _IN indicating that this instruction depends on rsp's definition outside this gadget.

Memory. Similar to registers, we apply SSA to memory to make it stateful, as otherwise, the SMT solver has no context information about memory addresses and values. To transform memory into SSA form, we define memory read and write accesses as explicit operations: v_j := read(M_i, address, size) and M_i+1 := write(M_i, address, value, size). Given a stateful memory variable M, we read from and write to this variable at a given address with a given access size. Note that the write operation is stored in a new memory variable M_i+1 that encodes the previous write. Internally, these operations are expressed within a byte-wise memory model similar to the work of Sinz et al. [27], in which memory accesses with larger sizes are translated to nested byte-wise memory reads or writes. For a formal definition, we refer the interested reader to Appendix A. We initialize all memory addresses to contain the value 0.

Interconnecting Gadgets. Up until now, we described how to encode data flow within a single gadget using SSA for registers and memory. However, our goal is to combine multiple gadgets in a chain of length n without making assumptions on neither the order of gadgets nor the particular gadgets used. Especially, we allow gadgets to occur more than once in the chain. Thus, in the next step, we have to logically encode the data flow between gadgets. To achieve this, we first have to ensure that all variables are unique. So far, variables are only unique with respect to their gadget due to the SSA form's unique identifier. However, to encode the order of execution, each variable must also be unique with regard to the gadget's position within the chain. Therefore, we also include the position as index within the SSA variable names: variable_gadgetId_position_definitionIdx. This way, we can use any gadget at any position in the chain.

Example 2. If we consider the gadget for the first position in the chain, the definition rbx_a_1 (line 2 in Fig. 1b) becomes rbx_a_p1_1 (with p1 representing the first position). This way, we can use the gadget in position 2 as well, as rbx_a_p2_1 is a distinct variable.

Naturally, our encoding must consider that a gadget can be used at any position in the chain, while, at the same time, we cannot know which gadget is at a specific position within the chain. In other words, gadget_a and gadget_b can both be at positions 1 and 2, but at the time of formula generation, we do not know which of these gadgets will be at which position in the chain synthesized by the SMT solver. Therefore, we must ensure that the gadget at position $i + 1$ uses the values derived by the gadget at position i; a scenario strikingly similar to the problem of merging control flow in SSA form (for which ϕ-functions are used). We must merge the state of all gadgets at chain position i such that it can be used as input for the gadgets in the subsequent position. To achieve this, we apply the following for each register and memory variable: We first determine the variable's last definition in each gadget for position i. Then, we merge the last definitions from all gadgets via a ϕ-function and define a new variable that is used as input for the next position.

Example 3. Assume that we want to encode the gadgets for a chain of length 2 (cf. Fig. 1c). For each register, we create a ϕ-function that merges the last definitions of these variables. In the following, we consider this process exemplary for rax at position 1. The initial value of rax is rax_p1_IN—the input of rax for the first gadget position. Since we do not know if gadget_a or gadget_b is the first gadget in the chain, we must account for both possibilities and merge their last definitions of rax in a ϕ-function. gadget_a does not modify rax, thus we use rax_p1_IN; for gadget_b, we use its latest definition, rax_b_p1_2. Finally, we define a new variable—rax_p2_IN—that encodes the merged variables and is used as input for the second position in the chain: rax_p2_IN := ϕ(rax_p1_IN, rax_b_p1_2).

To model the data flow between gadgets, the logical formula has to connect each input variable of the ϕ-function with the gadget that defined the corresponding variable. On a technical level, we translate this abstract ϕ-function into nested If-Then-Else expressions that select the corresponding variable based on the program counter, which has to be equal to one of the gadget addresses. This way, we ensure that the conditions are mutually exclusive (as the program counter can only point to a single gadget) and, thus, each register's value can always be uniquely determined. This approach is based on work by Sinz et al. [27].

3.3   Preconditions and Postconditions

Following the logical encoding of the gadget chain, we now describe how to set the initial state (preconditions) and the targeted state (postconditions).

Preconditions. These conditions allow setting the initial state at the time when the attacker can divert execution flow to the gadget chain. They constraint the inputs of the first position in the gadget chain, e. g., we can encode relevant context from the target program, such as the value of specific registers or memory areas (e. g., by using a debugger). Additionally, we must specify the location where the SMT solver should place the synthesized gadget chain (and how many bytes are available), e. g., by choosing an attacker-controlled buffer on the stack. This area is then considered a free variable in the formula, such that the SMT solver can place gadget addresses and data there. We can also enforce specific characteristics for any attacker-controlled areas, such as constraining memory buffers to hold only values within a certain range.

Postconditions. While the preconditions outline the initial position, postconditions describe the desired state that the program should reach after executing the gadget chain. More specifically, we can set any register or memory address to a specific value (e. g., the system call we would like to execute and its arguments). We encode these postconditions by asserting that the outputs (i. e., register and memory variables) of the last position in the chain are equal to the given values.

Furthermore, we also support indirect constraints, so-called *pointer constraints*. These constraints support common constructs, where a reference to a specific value or string (e. g., "/bin/sh") in memory needs to reside in a specific register. To this end, we add an assertion that the memory address pointed to by this register must contain the desired value(s). This does not require us to specify the memory address itself, but we can leave the task of choosing a suitable memory address to the SMT solver. On a technical level, the values are constrained as byte-wise memory read operations relative to the address chosen by the solver.

Notably, the flexibility of our approach allows us to enforce arbitrary constraints between registers and memory locations. For instance, we could enforce that (1) certain register values must be odd, (2) the sum of registers must be equal to a specific value, or (3) the sum of two specific registers must be prime. To put it differently, our design allows to constraint exotic, target-specific conditions that may be useful in some exploitation scenarios.

3.4   Formula Generation

Our final formula consists of three main components: preconditions, gadget chain, and postconditions. The preconditions describe the initial state, which is used as input for the chain's initial gadget. The chain contains the encoding of individual instructions, the data flow between instructions within a gadget, and the data flow between gadgets—in short, the complete semantics of the gadget chain. Finally, the postconditions define the state which should be reached after executing the gadget chain. Here, the attacker encodes the desired CPU state. We combine these three components with logical conjunctions to the formula:

$$formula := preconditions \land gadget\_chain \land postconditions$$

We then pass this formula to an SMT solver that supports the combined quantifier-free theory of fixed-size bit vectors (registers) and arrays (memory), QF_ABV [28]. If the solver finds a satisfying assignment, it provides a model, i. e., concrete values for each relevant variable in the formula. For all variables of gadgets that are *not* relevant for the synthesized gadget chain, no values are assigned. As a consequence, the model describes not only the initial state (e. g., values on the stack) but register and memory values for each gadget in the chain; in other words, we receive sort of an instruction trace that includes the intermediate values for each variable in the chain. In a final step, we can extract the initial values for each controlled buffer and use them as exploitation payload. When the payload is inserted, the gadget chain is executed as described in the model. Because a satisfying assignment produced by an SMT solver is a proof of existence, the gadget chain is guaranteed to reach exactly the specified postconditions. This is in strong contrast to state-of-the-art approaches, which often use heuristics rather than proofs to construct a gadget chain.

3.5   Algorithm Configuration

A few parameters define the performance of our approach, most of which affect the SMT solver: (1) For larger numbers of gadgets, the SMT solver needs more time in its decision process. To reduce its runtime, we can sample a small subset of gadgets (e. g., 300 gadgets as determined in empirical tests). (2) Due to our logical encoding, the chain length must be defined beforehand. While this may appear inflexible, our evaluation shows that testing different chain lengths is feasible in practice; if a shorter chain is possible, the SMT solver places semantic no-operations as padding gadgets in the chain. (3) To avoid excessive runtimes, we define upper time limits for the initial gadget extraction as well as for the SMT solver. While limiting the initial gadget extraction may reduce the number of available gadgets, this has no major impact if we only sample a subset.

4   Implementation

To demonstrate the practical feasibility of our proposed approach, we implemented a prototype of SGC in roughly 5,000 lines of Python code (see https:// github.com/RUB-SysSec/gadget_synthesis). While SGC's initial gadget extraction is based on Binary Ninja [34] (version 2.3.2660), all further steps are built on top of Miasm [5] (commit 218492cd). Especially the logical encoding of gadgets is facilitated in Miasm's IR. We extended its internal memory model to be stateful. The logic formula generated in the encoding step is then passed to the SMT solver Boolector [18], which is particularly suited to solve problems within the domain theory of bit vectors and arrays [36]. As Boolector supports the const-array extension [31], we use it to model memory and initialize it with a default value of 0. As memory accesses should not happen in read/write-restricted regions, we allow the user to specify which memory addresses may be accessed. In general, the user can add any constraint they need, such as excluding specific bytes from the chain (so-called *bad bytes*).

5   Evaluation

Based on the prototype implementation of SGC, we answer the following questions:

1. Is SGC capable of automatically finding valid gadget chains in diverse exploitation scenarios? How does it compare to state-of-the-art tools?
2. How does SGC perform in real-world exploitation scenarios?
3. How flexible and target-specific are SGC's chains in comparison to other approaches?
4. In what regard do SGC's generated gadget chains differ from the ones found by state-of-the-art tools?

To answer these research questions, we conduct the following experiments.

5.1 Setup

All our experiments were performed using Intel Xeon Gold 6230R CPUs at 2.10 GHz with 52 cores and 188 GiB RAM, running Ubuntu 20.04 on x86-64. To facilitate a deterministic analysis, we disable ASLR. Even if present, we only require an attacker to leak the base address, e. g., via an information leak, which is a weaker requirement than other approaches make [11,35].

We compare SGC against the state of the art discussed in Sect. 2. While these tools work deterministically and take all gadgets into account, SGC does not: To keep the runtime of the SMT solver manageable, a subset of gadgets is randomly sampled for a provided seed. As a consequence, the sampled gadgets may be insufficient to fulfill the attacker's goals. To mitigate this problem, SGC uses by default ten different seeds, running them in parallel and reporting the first chain found. To add further variety, SGC attempts to find a chain of length 3 and 5, both for 100 and 300 gadgets, while not using more than 128 bytes of the attacker-controlled buffer. These values have been empirically chosen (cf. Sect. 5.6) In summary, 40 configurations are executed in parallel. For our evaluation, we run all configurations until completion for later analysis instead of returning the first gadget chain found. As all other tools operate deterministically, we only run them once. We emphasize that all tools are provided equal resources, i. e., CPU cores and RAM. While we restrict SGC to one hour for disassembly and the SMT solver, we define a timeout of 24 h for all other tools. To verify whether a generated chain is *valid*, we use GDB to place it in the attacker-controlled buffer within the program and then execute the chain. This way, we ensure that the gadget chain works in practice.

As targets, we use a diverse set of programs. In a first step, we replicate the experiments of Follner et al. [8] on recent versions of chromium (version 88.0.4324.182), apache2 (version 2.4.46), nginx (version 1.19.9), and OpenSSL (version 1.1.1f). All of these targets are dynamically linked and we configure SGC to ignore shared libraries, simulating a scenario where only the base address of the main executable is known but no locations of libraries. To cover scenarios where libc is present, we create an empty wrapper program that is statically linked against glibc version 2.31. To evaluate whether SGC can be used to exploit real-world vulnerabilities, we use dnsmasq (version 2.77).

5.2 Finding a Chain

Based on the experiments by Follner et al. [8], we evaluate whether SGC is capable of finding valid gadget chains. While a multitude of possible attacker goals exists, in reality, attackers mostly aim at either calling library functions such as mprotect (to change the protection flags of memory regions) and mmap (to map a RWX page in which their shellcode can be placed), or at executing system calls, such as execve with the parameter /bin/sh that spawns a shell. Therefore, we pick three exemplary attacker goals, namely (1) a library call to mprotect(addr, len, prot) with three parameters, (2) a library call to mmap(addr, length, prot, flags, fd, offset) with six parameters, and

(3) a system call to `execve(path, argv, envp)` with four parameters (one being the system call number) and the requirement to place a string in memory. On the `x86-64` architecture, these arguments are passed via registers [16]. As parameters, we use fixed exemplary values that are common in real-world exploitation scenarios, such as `execve(&"/bin/sh", 0, 0)` to spawn a shell or setting `prot` in `mprotect` to `RWX`, such that an attacker could place and execute arbitrary shellcode. To compare the tools, we run each of them in the same configuration, analyze whether it finds a chain, and check—based on our verification tooling—if the chain is *valid* in practice. Table 2 depicts the results of this experiment. As `ROPgadget` only provides fixed heuristics for `execve`, we exclude it from the other attacker goals. Similarly, `Ropper` is limited to `mprotect` and `execve`, and `P-SHAPE` focuses on library calls.

Table 2. Capability of finding a valid gadget chain to call `mprotect`, `mmap`, or `execve`. Legend: ✓ = valid chain, (✓) = chain found but crashes program, ✗ = no chain found, ^{1}) = chain found when increasing timeout to 5h, ^{2}) = `SGC` *proves* that no chain exists.

		SGC	P-SHAPE	angrop	ROPium	ROPgadget	Ropper
mprotect	chromium	✓	✗	✗	✓	–	✗
	apache2	✓	(✓)	✓	✓	–	(✓)
	nginx	✓	(✓)	✓	✓	–	✗
	OpenSSL	✓	(✓)	✗	✗	–	✗
	libc	✓	(✓)	✓	✓	–	✓
mmap	chromium	✓^{1}	✗	✗	✓	–	–
	apache2	✓	✗	✗	✓	–	–
	nginx	✓	(✓)	✗	✗	–	–
	OpenSSL	✗^{2}	✗	✗	✗	–	–
	libc	✓	(✓)	✗	✓	–	–
execve	chromium	✓	–	✗	✓	✓	✗
	apache2	✓	–	(✓)	✓	✗	(✓)
	nginx	✓	–	(✓)	✓	✗	✗
	OpenSSL	✓	–	✗	✗	✗	✗
	libc	✓	–	✓	✓	✓	✓

Most tools find a chain for `mprotect`, which is the easiest goal since only three registers have to be set. `angrop` struggled both with `chromium` and `OpenSSL` and crashed during the attempt to locate gadget chains. Likewise, `P-SHAPE` crashed for `chromium`. Although `P-SHAPE` found a chain for four targets, none of them were valid in real-world scenarios: Manual verification revealed that they cause segmentation faults (e.g., due to write attempts to inaccessible memory regions). For `mprotect`, only `SGC` identifies a valid gadget chain for all targets.

In comparison to `mprotect`, finding a chain for `mmap` is significantly more challenging since six register arguments have to be set, and thus more suitable gadgets are required. While all chains found by P-SHAPE crashed again, ROPium produced valid chains for three targets. However, this was only possible after we fixed a bug in its source code. SGC found four out of five valid chains. For chromium, we had to increase the timeout for disassembly and solving to 5h, since we initially did not find suitable gadgets to set r8 and r9, the fifth and sixth argument to mmap. We discuss the shortcomings of our disassembly and random sampling in more detail in Sect. 6. For OpenSSL, no tool was able to produce a chain. To get more insights, we performed another experiment in which SGC was given access to all 3045 available OpenSSL gadgets (instead of choosing a random subset). After 226s, the SMT solver returned UNSAT, which can be understood as proof of non-existence. In other words, SGC was able to assert that no chain for the provided gadgets exists that fulfills the postconditions. This saves the user valuable time as they are guaranteed that even manual analysis will be fruitless.

The last attacker goal, execve, models the common scenario where a shell is spawned via a system call. It differs from the previous goals in the fact that not only four register values must be prepared, but the string /bin/sh\x00 must be placed in memory. To express this behavior in ROPium, the user has to manually set a suitable memory address at which the string should be placed in memory. As such, the gadget chain construction is not completely automated. However, we include it since it is the only tool besides SGC that succeeds in finding valid chains for almost all targets.

In summary, these experiments answer research question 1.: SGC outperforms all state-of-the-art approaches and manages to find valid gadget chains for all targets, even when other tools fail. For the only case where it did not find a chain, it even provided formal proof that no chain for the available gadgets can exist.

5.3   Real-World Applicability

To answer research question 2., we are interested in whether SGC proves helpful towards finding gadget chains in real-world exploitation contexts. To this end, we conduct a case study for CVE-2017-14493 [25], which describes a stack-based buffer overflow in dnsmasq (up to version 2.77) [12]. In essence, an attacker can craft a malicious DHCPv6 packet that, when received by dnsmasq's DHCP server, triggers an overflow in the dhcp6_maybe_relay function, where the length and data of a memcpy can be controlled by the attacker. This bug allows for the injection of gadget chains of arbitrary length; if ASLR is present, an attacker can exploit an information leak in the same version, assigned CVE-2017-14494, to leak the base address [25]. For simplicity, we assume ASLR is already bypassed.

Our goal is to craft a gadget chain that calls execve(&"/bin/sh", 0, 0) to spawn a shell. Following the System V AMD64 ABI calling convention [16], register rax needs to hold the execve system call number (0x3b), while the registers rdi, rsi, and rdx pass the arguments to execve. Therefore, we set the postconditions accordingly. To define the preconditions, we have to inspect the program state at the time when the attacker can divert execution flow to the gadget chain. In detail, we dump the CPU state with GDB and constrain register values accordingly. After defining preconditions and postconditions, we logically encode the gadget chain and query the SMT solver with the formula. SGC finds a gadget chain after approximately 8m. A shell is spawned after embedding the gadget chain in a DHCPv6 packet and sending it to dnsmasq For a detailed explanation of the bug and chain found by SGC, we refer to Appendix B. To conclude research question 2., SGC assists in real-world exploitation scenarios. It only requires the initial CPU state as preconditions and the desired target state.

5.4   Target-Specific Constraints

To answer research question 3. that addresses the flexibility of our approach, we conduct two experiments that model different exploitation scenarios. In the first experiment, we aim at crafting chains that do not include so-called *bad bytes*. Such bytes cannot be used in an exploit payload since they act as terminators in the underlying program (e. g.,\x00 in C strings). We can avoid using such bytes in our payload by adding the constraint that each byte in the attacker-controlled buffer must be different from specific byte values. In this experiment, we try to craft valid gadget chains that call mprotect, mmap, and execve in the statically-linked libc wrapper, where \x0a and \x0b are considered as bad bytes. SGC produced a valid gadget chain within, on average, 512s; similarly, all other tools (excluding P-SHAPE, which does not support bad bytes) were able to produce gadget chains. This is not surprising, as avoiding bad bytes is a common requirement for many exploits and most tools consider this in their heuristics. Then, we slightly modify this experiment: We set one of the functions' parameter values to a bad byte (essentially prohibiting the tools from using this specific value directly), such that the tools must construct the value indirectly via the gadget chain. In this scenario, only ROPium and SGC manage to find valid gadget chains. This shows that even a standard feature can be problematic for heuristics-based tools.

In the second experiment, we add a more complex constraint: We require that the sum of all values (quadwords) in the attacker-controlled buffer (where the addresses and data for the gadget chain are placed) must be equal to the value 0xdeadbeef. While this constraint seems artificial, similar constraints can be found in commercial DRM systems that perform integrity checks over specific memory regions. While no other tool provides the flexibility to model this behavior, we can enforce this within a few lines of code in SGC and produce valid gadget chains for the same setup as before (within, on average, 527s).

Overall, we conclude that SGC provides great flexibility and allows to model complex constraints. Thus, it covers even unusual exploitation scenarios.

5.5   Chain Statistics

To answer research question 4., in what regard differ our gadget chains from the ones found by state-of-the-art approaches, we inspect which types of gadgets and instructions are used in the generated chains. To this end, we analyze each valid chain found during our experiment in Sect. 5.2. Since P-SHAPE found only invalid chains that crashed the program, we exclude it from this experiment.

Table 3. Statistics over all valid chains generated during experiments in Sect. 5.2.

		SGC	P-SHAPE	angrop	ROPium	ROPgadget	Ropper
avg. instructions		5.9	-	2.9	2.4	2.0	2.6
gadgets w/ mem. write		9%	-	7%	6%	3%	14%
└ excluding `execve`		9%	-	0%	0%	-	0%
gadgets w/ mem. reads		30%	-	7%	0%	0%	0%
└ excluding `execve`		32%	-	0%	0%	-	0%
CF types	`ret`	68%	-	100%	97%	100%	100%
	`call MEM`	10%	-	0%	0%	0%	0%
	`call REG`	20%	-	0%	3%	0%	0%
	`jmp REG`	2%	-	0%	0%	0%	0%

As visible in Table 3, SGC's gadgets contain on average almost six instructions, whereas the other tools use two to three instructions per gadget. Further, SGC is the only approach that makes use of explicit memory reads and writes (excluding instructions such as push and pop); all other tools only use it in the case of execve to place the string /bin/sh into the memory. Similarly, most of the tools rely exclusively on return-oriented gadgets; only ROPium uses call-oriented programming for 3% of its gadgets. Contrary, SGC only uses return-oriented programming in 68% of the cases, while it deploys call and jump-oriented gadgets in 32%. In summary, SGC has on average longer gadgets, uses more memory reads/writes, and has a significantly higher amount of non-return-oriented gadgets; in short, it includes gadgets specific to the target with side effects that are disregarded by other approaches due to their generic heuristics.

Table 4. SGC's timings for initial disassembly and chaining.

	Disassembly	Chaining	Total
`mprotect`	1845 s	363 s	2207 s
`mmap`	1617 s	2667 s	4284 s
`execve`	1845 s	494 s	2338 s

Another relevant aspect is SGC's runtime (cf. Table 4). The disassembly step is comparably slow; the time required for instruction lifting, encoding, and SMT solving is significantly lower. Our disassembly relies on a combination of Binary Ninja and Miasm: we first analyze the whole binary and disassemble then individual functions in Miasm. As it is not a focus of this work, we consider improving our disassembly component as future work. Only for mmap, finding the chain takes significantly more time since the SMT solver has to find a valid chain that prepares six function arguments. For reference, the other tools find a chain on average within 319s. However, this ignores the runtime when they found no chain (e. g., Ropper hit the timeout of 24h twice), which was often the case, especially for mmap. In summary, SGC finds a valid chain within minutes.

5.6   SGC's Configuration

After successfully answering all research questions, we would like to give a better intuition of the configuration parameters relevant for SGC. As described before, our approach is probabilistic: it randomly samples only a small subset of gadgets. As a result, the chosen subset may not be sufficient to generate a chain that fulfills the postconditions. We can select another subset of the same size or a larger number of gadgets to overcome this. The latter, however, increases the time required by the SMT solver to decide the chain synthesis problem. To get a better feeling for this trade-off, we vary the chain length and number of sampled gadgets and analyze how often the solver succeeds in deciding the synthesis problem, i. e., it finds a chain or returns UNSAT within one hour. For each configuration, we run the solver ten times with different seeds such that diverse gadgets are sampled. We do this for all target programs from Sect. 5.2 and count how often the solver finds an answer or timeouts in the process of finding chains for mprotect. In total, we perform 50 independent runs (ten different seeds for five different targets) for each configuration.

Table 5. Number of gadget chains the solver decided (i. e., considered SAT or UNSAT) vs. timeouts when building a chain to mprotect for the targets in Sect. 5.2 with ten different seeds each. Format is #Decided by SMT solver/#Timeout. We color the prevalent outcome.

		Chain Length							
		1	2	3	4	5	6	7	8
#Gadgets	100	50/ 0	50/ 0	49/ 1	31/ 19	24/ 26	16/ 34	15/ 35	12/ 38
	300	50/ 0	50/ 0	37/ 13	20/ 30	13/ 37	10/ 40	7/ 43	6/ 44
	500	50/ 0	44/ 6	31/ 19	16/ 34	10/ 40	8/ 42	5/ 45	4/ 46
	1000	50/ 0	31/ 19	25/ 25	11/ 39	9/ 41	2/ 48	0/ 50	0/ 50

As Table 5 shows, the chain length and the number of gadgets determine the SMT solver's performance: For a small number of gadgets and chain length of 1, the solver always finds an answer. However, for longer chains or more sampled gadgets, the number of timeouts increases. While the solver can decide some chains of length six or higher, it increasingly triggers the timeout of one hour. Similarly, for a larger gadget pool (e. g., 1000 gadgets), the solver already struggles for chains of length three. While the strategy of randomly sampling a small number of gadgets proved effective, an attacker can always increase the number of gadgets and set higher timeouts for the SMT solver.

6   Discussion

Limitations of SGC. While SGC has proven overall effective, various aspects can be improved: (1) Our currently used disassembly is naive since we only consider regular instruction offsets. As an improvement, we can search unaligned gadgets since any sequence of bytes can be interpreted as instructions on x86-64. (2) The SMT solver is the most significant performance bottleneck of our design as it may require a large amount of time to identify valid gadget chains. However, as our evaluation shows, randomly selecting a subset of gadgets provides an effective strategy to reduce SGC's runtime. In this scenario, an UNSAT provided by the SMT solver is *not* a formal proof that no gadget chain exists, as it only proves that no chain for the selected subset of gadgets exists.

Mitigations. To prevent exploitation, various mitigations have been proposed. (1) W^X prevents execution of injected code, however, it is ineffective against *code reuse* attacks and thus SGC. (2) Address space layout randomization (ASLR) shuffles the program's memory layout such that an attacker cannot rely on addresses. SGC requires only the base address of the code section and does not require shared libraries to find valid gadget chains, thus a single information leak suffices. (3) Lastly, control-flow integrity (CFI) prevents the redirection of control flow to arbitrary code locations. This severely hampers code-reuse attacks such as SGC because only specific gadgets can be chained together. However, related work has shown that even fine-grained CFI is insufficient to prevent code-reuse attacks in general [11,24]. We believe that an attacker could add constraints modeling the enforcement policies such that the SMT solver will only select gadget chains that pass the CFI enforcement policy. We leave this as interesting future work.

7   Related Work

After initial techniques in the domain of code-reuse focused on functions from libc [30], the concept was generalized to re-use small snippets of existing code [14,26]. These small snippets are often chained via ret instructions (ROP) [26], but other control-flow transfers work as well (JOP [3,6] and COP [4,9]). Mitigations such as ASLR have been shown to be insufficient [29]. Moving forward with new mitigations such as control-flow integrity (CFI) [1], even more advanced approaches have been proposed, e. g., counterfeit object-oriented programming (COOP) [22] or data-oriented programming (DOP) [10]. Even fine-grained CFI solutions fail to stop attackers from finding gadget chains [35].

In parallel, various techniques to automate the cumbersome task of identifying suitable gadgets have been proposed. Early approaches use pattern matching to search for desired gadgets [13,19]. Other approaches tackle the task of automating the attack itself: One of the earliest approaches, Q [23], uses software verification methods instead of pattern matching to achieve this goal. Using identification and chaining of gadgets similar to Q, Wollgast et al. [37] automate COP, which allows them to bypass coarse-grained CFI implementations. Tackling the problem imposed by fine-grained CFI solutions, Ispoglou et al. [11] propose an approach, BOPC, which automates data-only attacks. Further improving this avenue, Schwartz et al. [24] propose a generic approach, Limbo, capable of constructing chains using ROP, JOP, COP, or DOP. Their approach is similar to ours in the spirit of maintaining a generic approach to code-reuse attacks. However, their focus is on the construction of CFI-compatible gadget chains. Internally, their search relies on concolic execution and hard-coded heuristics. In contrast, our approach does not tackle the problem of identifying CFI-aware gadgets but maintains generality without relying on hard-coded heuristics. Further, Limbo only works for 32-bit Linux executables, which limits their real-world applicability. As no code is published, we cannot evaluate against Limbo.

8 Conclusion

In this paper, we presented a generic and flexible approach to automate the task of finding gadget chains. With our prototype implementation, we have shown that SGC outperforms state-of-the-art tools. It not only finds gadget chains where all other approaches fail but also allows to model complex constraints.

Acknowledgements. This work was supported by the German Research Foundation (DFG) within the framework of the Excellence Strategy of the Federal Government and the States—EXC 2092 CaSa—39078197.

A Modeling

Byte-wise memory reads and writes are modeled using single *select* and *store* operators, respectively. Larger reads are modeled by concatenating multiple *select* expressions, which we define recursively in terms of smaller read operations. Reads smaller than 64-bit into a 64-bit register are zero-extended by using *concat* with the zero bit vector bv_0. Larger writes are similarly modeled using the composition of multiple *store* expressions. Table 6 shows memory accesses of various sizes. Given an array m, address k and value v and bit size $n \in (8, 16, 32, 64)$, we use the names $mem\_read_n(m, k)$ and $mem\_write_n(m, k, v)$ to substitute the longer SMT expressions from these tables.

Table 6. Encoding of memory reads and writes (m: memory, k: address, v: value).

Name	SMT encoding
$mem\_read_8(m,k)$	$select(m,k)$
$mem\_read_{16}(m,k)$	$concat(mem\_read_8(m,k), mem\_read_8(m,k+1))$
$mem\_read_{32}(m,k)$	$concat(mem\_read_{16}(m,k), mem\_read_{16}(m,k+2))$
$mem\_read_{64}(m,k)$	$concat(mem\_read_{32}(m,k), mem\_read_{32}(m,k+4))$
$mem\_write_8(m,k,v)$	$store(m,k,v_{0:7})$
$mem\_write_{16}(m,k,v)$	$mem\_write_8(mem\_write_8(m,k,v_{0:7}), k+1, v_{8:15})$
$mem\_write_{32}(m,k,v)$	$mem\_write_{16}(mem\_write_{16}(m,k,v_{0:15}), k+2, v_{16:31})$
$mem\_write_{64}(m,k,v)$	$mem\_write_{32}(mem\_write_{32}(m,k,v_{0:31}), k+4, v_{32:63})$

B   dnsmasq CVE-2017-14493

In the following, we analyze the dnsmasq bug in more detail. The stack-based buffer overflow in dnsmasq is caused by the absence of a length check of the data copied to a static buffer on the stack. Figure 2 shows the vulnerable call to memcpy in function dhcp6_maybe_relay. Sending a malicious DHCPv6 packet allows to gain control over the instruction pointer by overflowing the mac buffer of static size DHCP_CHADDR_MAX (16) in the state structure present on the stack.

```
206    /* RFC-6939 */
207    if ((opt = opt6_find(opts, end, OPTION6_CLIENT_MAC, 3)))
208        {
209            state->mac_type = opt6_uint(opt, 0, 2);
210            state->mac_len = opt6_len(opt) - 2;
211            memcpy(&state->mac[0], opt6_ptr(opt, 2), state->mac_len);
212        }
```

Fig. 2. Vulnerable memcpy in file rfc3315.c, which overflows the mac buffer in state.

The proof-of-concept (PoC) provided alongside the bug report [25] builds up such a DHCPv6 packet containing an OPTION6_CLIENT_MAC option holding data of excessive length. While the PoC overwrites the instruction pointer with a dummy value, injecting an arbitrary amount of bytes is possible. As long as the stack is not exhausted, the packet's content is copied and remains untouched until the instruction pointer is overwritten.

In order to synthesize a gadget chain, the information needed to specify preconditions and postconditions is gathered by extracting the program state before hijacking the control flow through GDB. Table 7a shows the preconditions set for dnsmasq. The initial ret instruction, which redirects the control flow to the chain's first gadget (gadget_0), is specified by preconditioning rip. The stack pointer rsp points to the part of the controlled buffer, where the gadget chain will be copied. In the logical formula, this stack area is a free variable.

Table 7. Preconditions and postconditions used for **dnsmasq**. Registers not mentioned in the preconditions are free variables, i.e., registers an attacker controls and can set to an arbitrary value.

(a) Preconditions

Register	Value
rip	0x33dfb
rax	0x223
rcx	0x0
rdx	0x5a
rdi	0x22
r8	0x7fffffffe0e0
r9	0x0
r10	0x7fffffffbc50

(b) Postconditions

Register	Value
rip	0x461d0
rax	0x3b
rsi	0x0
rdx	0x0
rdi	&"/bin/sh"

Since we want to execute a system call to **execve** to spawn a shell, the final register values which the gadget chain needs to reach are specified accordingly. Table 7b shows the postconditions in preparation for calling **execve(&"/bin/sh", 0, 0)**. Here, **rip** holds the address of a **syscall** instruction available in the program. Using the default configuration described in Sect. 5.1, **SGC** finds a gadget chain consisting of four gadgets within approximately 8*m*. While most gadgets are straightforward, **gadget_3** (shown in Fig. 3) writes a value to the stack outside the attacker-controlled buffer, a side effect that does not harm the chain. The arithmetic operations of the first four instructions do not change register **rax**' value of 0. In line 6, the **lea** instruction is used to add 0x5 to the value present in **rbp** = 0x55555559a1cb. The resulting address, 0x55555559a1d0, is a **syscall** instruction; the address is placed on the stack at address 0x7fffffffe240 present in register **rbx**. As this address is writable memory, no harm results from this side effect.

As mentioned earlier, the PoC crafts a rogue DHCPv6 packet. In order to construct the payload with our synthesized gadget chain, the length parameter is adjusted and the dummy value is replaced with the data of the gadget chain. Sending this packet to the **dnsmasq** DHCP server successfully spawns the shell.

```
1   0x55555558a009:
2          movzx    rax, ax
3          imul     rax, ax, 0x1DCB
4          shr      eax, 0x15
5          movzx    eax, ax
6          lea      rax, qword ptr [rax + rbp + 0x5]
7          mov      qword ptr [rbx], rax
8          pop      rbx
9          pop      rbp
10         pop      r12
11         ret
```

Fig. 3. gadget_3 of the gadget chain used to spawn a shell in **dnsmasq**.

References

1. Abadi, M., Budiu, M., Erlingsson, U., Ligatti, J.: Control-flow integrity principles, implementations, and applications. ACM Trans. Inf. Syst. Secur. (TISSEC) **13**(1) (2009)
2. angr team: angrop. https://github.com/angr/angrop
3. Bletsch, T., Jiang, X., Freeh, V.W., Liang, Z.: Jump-oriented programming: a new class of code-reuse attack. In: ACM Conference on Computer and Communications Security (CCS) (2011)
4. Carlini, N., Wagner, D.: ROP is still dangerous: breaking modern defenses. In: USENIX Security Symposium (2014)
5. CEA IT Security: Miasm - reverse engineering framework. https://github.com/cea-sec/miasm
6. Checkoway, S., Davi, L., Dmitrienko, A., Sadeghi, A.R., Shacham, H., Winandy, M.: Return-oriented programming without returns. In: ACM Conference on Computer and Communications Security (CCS) (2010)
7. Cytron, R., Ferrante, J., Rosen, B.K., Wegman, M.N., Zadeck, F.K.: An Efficient method of computing static single assignment form. In: ACM Symposium on Principles of Programming Languages (POPL) (1989)
8. Follner, A., et al.: PSHAPE: automatically combining gadgets for arbitrary method execution. In: Security and Trust Management Workshop (2016)
9. Göktas, E., Athanasopoulos, E., Bos, H., Portokalidis, G.: Out of control: overcoming control-flow integrity. In: IEEE Symposium on Security and Privacy (2014)
10. Hu, H., Shinde, S., Adrian, S., Chua, Z.L., Saxena, P., Liang, Z.: Data-oriented programming: on the expressiveness of non-control data attacks. In: IEEE Symposium on Security and Privacy (2016)
11. Ispoglou, K.K., AlBassam, B., Jaeger, T., Payer, M.: Block-oriented programming: automating data-only attacks. In: ACM Conference on Computer and Communications Security (CCS) (2018)
12. Kelley, S.: dnsmasq. https://thekelleys.org.uk/dnsmasq/doc.html
13. Kornau, T.: Return-Oriented Programming for the ARM Architecture. Master's thesis, Ruhr-Universität Bochum (2010)
14. Krahmer, S.: x86–64 buffer overflow exploits and the borrowed code chunks exploitation technique (2005)
15. Kroening, D., Strichman, O.: Decision Procedures. Springer, Cham (2016). https://doi.org/10.1007/978-3-540-74105-3
16. Matz, M., Hubicka, J., Jaeger, A., Mitchell, M.: System V application binary interface. AMD64 Architecture Processor Supplement, Draft v0 99 (2013)
17. Milanov, B.: ROPium. https://github.com/Boyan-MILANOV/ropium
18. Niemetz, A., Preiner, M., Biere, A.: Boolector 2.0. J. Satisfiabil. Boolean Modeling Comput. **9**(1), 53–58 (2014)
19. Roemer, R.G.: Finding the bad in good code: automated return-oriented programming exploit discovery. Master's thesis, UC San Diego (2009)
20. Salwan, J.: ROPgadget. https://github.com/JonathanSalwan/ROPgadget
21. Schirra, S.: Ropper. https://github.com/sashs/Ropper
22. Schuster, F., Tendyck, T., Liebchen, C., Davi, L., Sadeghi, A.R., Holz, T.: Counterfeit object-oriented programming: on the difficulty of preventing code reuse attacks in C++ Applications. In: 2015 IEEE Symposium on Security and Privacy, pp. 745–762. IEEE (2015)

23. Schwartz, E.J., Avgerinos, T., Brumley, D.: Q: Exploit hardening made easy. In: USENIX Security Symposium (2011)
24. Schwartz, E.J., Cohen, C.F., Gennari, J.S., Schwartz, S.M.: A generic technique for automatically finding defense-aware code reuse attacks. In: ACM Conference on Computer and Communications Security (CCS) (2020)
25. Serna, F.J., Linton, M., Stadmeyer, K.: dnsmasq stack-based buffer overflow (CVE-2017-14493). https://security.googleblog.com/2017/10/behind-masq-yet-more-dns-and-dhcp.html
26. Shacham, H.: The geometry of innocent flesh on the bone: return-into-LIBC without function calls (on the x86). In: ACM Conference on Computer and Communications Security (CCS) (2007)
27. Sinz, C., Falke, S., Merz, F.: A precise memory model for low-level bounded model checking. In: International Conference on Systems Software Verification (2010)
28. SMT-LIB: Logics. https://smtlib.cs.uiowa.edu/logics-all.shtml#QF_ABV
29. Snow, K.Z., Monrose, F., Davi, L., Dmitrienko, A., Liebchen, C., Sadeghi, A.R.: Just-in-time code reuse: on the effectiveness of fine-grained address space layout randomization. In: IEEE Symposium on Security and Privacy (2013)
30. Solar Designer: Return-to-Libc (1997)
31. Stump, A., Barrett, C.W., Dill, D.L., Levitt, J.: A decision procedure for an extensional theory of arrays. In: IEEE Symposium on Logic in Computer Science (2001)
32. Szekeres, L., Payer, M., Wei, T., Song, D.: Sok: eternal war in memory. In: IEEE Symposium on Security and Privacy (2013)
33. Vanegue, J., Heelan, S., Rolles, R.: SMT solvers in software security. In: USENIX Workshop on Offensive Technologies (WOOT) (2012)
34. Vector 35 Inc.: Binary Ninja. https://binary.ninja/
35. van der Veen, V., Andriesse, D., Stamatogiannakis, M., Chen, X., Bos, H., Giuffrdia, C.: The dynamics of innocent flesh on the bone: code reuse ten years later. In: ACM Conference on Computer and Communications Security (CCS) (2017)
36. Weber, T., Conchon, S., Déharbe, D., Heizmann, M., Niemetz, A., Reger, G.: The SMT competition 2015–2018. J. Satisf. Boolean Model. Comput. **11**(1) (2019)
37. Wollgast, P., Gawlik, R., Garmany, B., Kollenda, B., Holz, T.: Automated multi-architectural discovery of CFI-resistant code gadgets. In: European Symposium on Research in Computer Security (ESORICS) (2016)

Peeler: Profiling Kernel-Level Events to Detect Ransomware

Muhammad Ejaz Ahmed[1](✉), Hyoungshick Kim[2], Seyit Camtepe[1], and Surya Nepal[1]

[1] Data61 CSIRO, Marsfield, NSW 2122, Australia
{ejaz.ahmed,seyit.camtepe,surya.nepal}@data61.csiro.au
[2] Sungkyunkwan University, Suwon, South Korea
hyoung@skku.edu

Abstract. Because the recent ransomware families are becoming progressively more advanced, it is challenging to detect ransomware using static features only. However, their behaviors are still more generic and universal to analyze due to their inherent goals and functions. Therefore, we can capture their behaviors by monitoring their system-level activities on files and processes. In this paper, we present a novel ransomware detection system called "Peeler" (**P**rofiling k**Ern**E**l -**L**evel **E**vents to detect **R**ansomware). Peeler first identifies ransomware's inherent behavioral characteristics such as stealth operations performed during the attack, processes execution patterns, and correlations among different kernel-level events by analysing a large-scaled OS-level provenance data collected from a diverse set of ransomware families. Peeler specifically uses a novel NLP-based deep learning model to fingerprint the contextual behavior of applications by leveraging Bidirectional Encoder Representations from Transformers (BERT) pre-trained model. We evaluate Peeler on a large ransomware dataset including 67 ransomware families and demonstrate that it achieves a 99.5% F1-score.

Keywords: Fileless malware · Ransomware detection · Deep learning · Screen-locker · Malware behavior analysis · Machine learning

1 Introduction

Ransomware is a growing threat that typically operates by either encrypting a victim's files (called *crypto* ransomware) or locking the victim's desktop screen (termed as *screen-locker* ransomware) until the victim pays a ransom. Recent statistics predict that there will be a ransomware attack every 11 s by 2021 – the global cost will be $20 billion yearly [2]. In 2019, the U.S. alone was hit by an unprecedented barrage of ransomware attacks that impacted more than 966 government agencies, educational institutions, and healthcare providers at a potential cost of around $7.5 billion [25]. As a result, a large number of proposals have recently been proposed to fight against ransomware as follows: machine learning models (e.g., [12,18,22,33,34]), use of decoy files (e.g., [12,14,27]), use

© Springer Nature Switzerland AG 2021
E. Bertino et al. (Eds.): ESORICS 2021, LNCS 12972, pp. 240–260, 2021.
https://doi.org/10.1007/978-3-030-88418-5_12

of a key escrow mechanism (e.g., [24]) and file I/O pattern profiling (e.g., [11, 12,19,21,28,30,32,33,37]). However, ransomware still remains the most popular cyber threat in the real world.

Attackers are now developing and employing various attack vectors (called *stealthy* malware) to make ransomware much stealthier than before to evade the target system [35]. For instance, Windows operating systems (OSes) are shipped with highly-trusted administrative tools, such as Windows Management Instrumentation (WMI) and Microsoft PowerShell (PS), to assist system administrators in performing their daily routine tasks. However, stealthy ransomware is trying to evade detection and prevent file recovery by impersonating benign processes. For instance, variants of Ryuk ransomware use the WMI tool to delete Windows shadow files (using the command `wmic.exe shadowcopy delete`) to prevent system restoration. Similarly, Virlock ransomware leverages the Console Registry tool for Windows (*reg.exe*) to add registry keys and values in order to disable User Account Control (UAC) check to remain stealthy. Moreover, stealthy ransomware would attempt to hide malicious code through various packing techniques and unpack only into the memory called "living off the land" attack (fileless malware) to evade disk scanning tools. Fileless malware is a type of malicious software that secretly activate pre-installed tools and applications on victims' computer to execute an attack. Recent security reports reveal that fileless malware attack rates skyrocketed by almost 900% in 2020 compared to 2019 [36]. Antivirus products may not be effective anymore in detecting such ransomware as they search for malicious payload (i.e., *signature*) on disk, whereas fileless malware is memory-based and is loaded from the remote server using pre-install utilities. Finally, the ransomware can exploit vulnerabilities in benign programs to gain control. Because attackers have many opportunities to bypass systems' security and generate new malware variants, the detection approaches based on static or behavioral signatures cannot catch up with the ever-evolving stealthy ransomware [20].

To address the shortcomings identified above, we develop a novel ransomware detection system, called "Peeler" (**P**rofiling k**Ern**El -**L**evel **E**vents to detect **R**ansomware), which relies on kernel-level provenance monitoring to capture contextual and behavioral characteristics of ransomware. Peeler intercepts kernel-level system events from the native layer of Windows OS and tracks ransomware activities from a ransomware binary execution on a victim's computer to the display of a *ransom note* on the victim's screen. To facilitate better defence against stealthy ransomware attacks on Windows OSes, Peeler profiles the contextual and behavioral characteristics of the executing processes. For instance, Hendler et al. [15,16] proposed deep learning approaches to detect malicious *PowerShell* commands. However, in practice, malicious commands could be launched not only by *PowerShell*, but also from Windows OS legitimate utilities, such as *vssadmin, wmic*, etc. We consider all malicious command sources rather than relying on malicious commands executed from a specific program. Applications perform various tasks using Windows native tools, and the context of operations depends on the commands/codes executed using these tools. Peeler determines the context of the operations by extracting the command-line argument codes/scripts from the processes and builds a natural language processing (NLP)-based deep learning model to fingerprint applications' behavior for detection. Moreover, Peeler exploits some key behavioral characteristics of ransomware relating to relationships between certain kernel-level system events. For example, file I/O's *Read* and *Write* events are strongly correlated during ransomware execution because all the *Read* events are followed by the *Write* events in order to create an encrypted version of users' files. Such characteristics are exhibited in events from other system events as well, such as *Process* provider's *Start* and *Stop* and DLL *Image* provider's *Load* and *Unload* events, respectively. Consequently, the relationships between those events could be exploited via extracting features for machine learning models that could then perform detection. We develop a highly accurate ransomware detection system for Windows operating systems (OS)[1]. Our key contributions are summarized below:

- We develop a set of methodologies based on a comprehensive analysis of ransomware from binary execution on a victim's computer to the display of a *ransom note* at the victim's computer screen and design a fast and highly accurate ransomware detection system called Peeler.
- We present a novel transformer-based language model to fingerprint the contextual behavior of applications by leveraging Bidirectional Encoder Representations from Transformers (BERT) pre-trained model. To the best of our knowledge, our work is the first to apply transformer-based deep learning model for ransomware detection.
- We evaluate the performance of Peeler. Peeler achieves 99.52% detection accuracy with a false positive rate of only 0.58% against 67 ransomware families – the largest dataset so far in terms of its diversity. To show the robustness against unseen ransomware attacks, we also use Peeler (without new training) against 70 samples from 26 new and unseen ransomware families, including crypto and screen-locker. Peeler still achieves more than 95% detection accuracy in detecting new and unseen ransomware samples.

2   Related Work

We categorize the literature regarding ransomware detection into three groups: 1) crypto ransomware detection techniques that are mainly based on specific behavioral indicators (e.g., file I/O event patterns), 2) machine learning-based approaches that build models by leveraging system behavior feature, and 3) decoy-based approaches that deploy decoy files and monitor if ransomware samples tamper with the decoy files.

Crypto Ransomware Detection. There were several proposals to monitor file I/O request patterns of applications to detect crypto ransomware.

---

[1] Windows OS is becoming the most attractive targets for ransomware writers, i.e., 87% of the existing ransomware were developed to target Windows [10].

Kharraz et al. [21] studied crypto ransomware families' file I/O request patterns and presented a dynamic analysis-based ransomware detection system called UNVEIL. UNVEIL detected 13,647 ransomware samples from a dataset of 148,223 general malware samples. Kharraz et al. [22] proposed another ransomware detection system using file I/O patterns, achieving a 100% detection rate with 0.8% false positive on 677 samples from 29 ransomware families. Scaife et al. [32] also presented a system called CryptoDrop that detects ransomware based on suspicious file activities, e.g., tampering with a large number of file accesses within a time interval. According to the experimental results, the number of lost files is ten on average. Moratto et al. [30] proposed a ransomware detection algorithm with a copy of the network traffic without impacting a user's activities. Their proposed system achieved a 100% detection rate with 19 different ransomware families after the loss of ten files.

Machine Learning Based Ransomware Detection. RWGuard [27] is a machine learning-based crypto ransomware detection system. It achieved a 0.1% false positive rate incurring a 1.9% CPU overhead with 14 crypto ransomware families. RWGuard leverages the features about processes' I/O requests and changes performed on files because RWGuard was mainly designed to detect crypto ransomware only. Sgandurra et al. [33] proposed EldeRan, another machine learning approach that builds a model using system activities such as API invocations, registry event, and file operations that are performed by applications. EldeRan achieved a 93.3% detection rate with a 1.6% false alarm rate with 582 samples from 11 ransomware families. Hirano et al. [17] and Al-rimy [11] proposed behavior-based machine learning models for ransomware detection. Hirano et al. selected five-dimensional features extracted from ransomware and benign applications' I/O log files. Nieuwenhuizen [31] proposed another behavioral-based machine learning model using a feature set that quantifies the behavioral traits for ransomware's malicious activities.

Decoy Files Based Ransomware Detection. Decoy techniques [12,14,27] have also been frequently proposed to detect ransomware attacks. For example, Gomez et al. [14] developed a tool called R-Locker using honey files to trap the ransomware. When file operations are performed on honey files by a process, the process is detected and completely blocked because benign processes do not perform any file operations on honey files. However, if decoy files are generated, which look different from genuine user files, sophisticated ransomware samples ignore decoy files [27]. Moreover, it is also unclear how those solutions would detect some ransomware families (e.g., Petya) that affect predefined system files only.

3   Key Characteristics to Detect Ransomware

Typically, a ransomware attack consists of three stages: perform stealth operations to remain undetected, launch the actual attack, and display *ransom note* after a successful attack. Peeler exploits these differences in system behavioral characteristics between ransomware and benign applications.

3.1   Application Contextual Behavior

Application Process Tree. Applications can spawn one or more processes if it is needed to perform target tasks. If a process in an application creates another process, then the creator process is called *parent* process, and the created process is called *child* process. We observe that both ransomware and benign applications spawn child processes in a specific pattern depending upon the application logic. For example, typical ransomware should create several processes to perform malicious tasks (e.g., connecting to C&C servers, modifying the Windows registry, hiding files/extensions, encrypt user files) in parallel, resulting in a specific pattern of process creation called application process tree. The sequence of process creation contains rich contextual information highlighting the context of operations performed. These actions containing malicious command-line argument command codes and embedded or referenced PS scripts play an important role in determining the application's context. Figure 1 shows a snapshot of the application process tree of VirLock ransomware during its execution. VirLock is self-reproducing ransomware that not only locks a victim's screen but also infects her files. Both behaviors – self-reproducing and infecting files – were observed in the application process tree of VirLock. We can see *locker.exe* is replicated at level 3 of the tree.

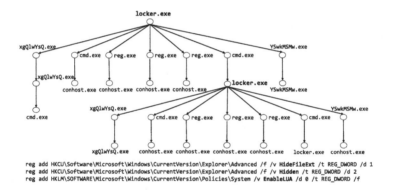

Fig. 1. Application process tree of VirLock.

To infect a victim's files, VirLock performs stealthy malicious activities to deceive victims. For instance, while creating files in the victim's computer, VirLock modifies the registry in the following ways: 1) disable Windows OS's User Account Control (UAC), which is a feature that was designed to prevent unauthorized changes in desktop computers; 2) hide all files that are created on the victim's desktop; and 3) hide all created file extensions. As shown in Fig. 1, three child processes (*reg.exe* in red color) perform the actual registry modifications. The corresponding command line execution is shown at the bottom of Fig. 1. In contrast, most benign applications create a considerably fewer number of spawned processes than stealthy ransomware. Figure 2 shows the application process trees of six benign applications (Chrome, Adobe Acrobat Reader, MS Visual Studio 2019, MS Office 365 ProPlus, Spotify, and MS Outlook).

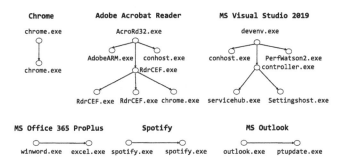

Fig. 2. Application process trees of benign applications.

Our observations on the behaviors of ransomware families show that more than 60% of samples spawn multiple processes. For instance, the VirLock ransomware sample spawns 44 processes on average. On the other hand, our observations on more than 50 most popular benign Microsoft applications show that they spawn 16 processes on average. We surmise that the processes created from both ransomware and benign apps can provide sufficient contextual information which could be leveraged to infer the intent of the underlying application.

Malicious Commands. To maximize the impact of the encryption, ransomware performs malicious activities with the following three goals: stealthiness, attack launch, payment guidance. 1) *Stealthiness:* ransomware tries to remain undetected by anti-malware services or Windows OS defenders running on the victim's computer. For example, they may disable runtime monitoring, archive scanning, automatic startup repair. Figure 1 shows the set of malicious commands executed by the Virlock ransomware to achieve stealthiness. Moreover, they may delete ransomware executable from the disk, stop all anti-malware services, or turn off User Account Control (UAC). 2) *Attack:* ransomware deletes the shadow copies and the system's backup/restore data automatically created by Windows OS. For example, vssadmin is a legitimate Windows OS utility that controls volume shadow copies of user files on a given computer. These shadow copies are regularly used as a recovery point, and additionally, they can be leveraged to re-establish or return the file to a previous state if they are destroyed or lost due to some reasons. Adversary exploits Vssadmin utility by executing the command vssadmin.exe delete shadows /all /quiet, to delete Windows OS shadow copies, making it impossible to restore the system back to its previous state. Note that an adversary can also use other legitimate tools pre-installed on Windows OS to delete shadow copies such as PowerShell, wmic, etc. The ransomware can leverage Windows OS program net.exe commands to stop or bypass detection by several popular antivirus software, in addition to defeating Windows OS Defender, e.g., `net.exe stop avpsus /y` stops Windows OS process Kaspersky Seamless Update Service, which is used by Thanos ransomware family. Moreover, ransomware sometimes tries to kill the processes related to specific programs, such as SQL server, to initiate the encryption of the user files on which these programs were operating. After encrypting user files, ransomware shows a ransom note and payment guidelines. 3) *Post-attack guidance on ransom payment* finally, a ransom note is displayed along with a read-me document to help the victim pay the ransom and restore the system files. The ransomware writer typically adds a registry key to the autorun path to show the ransom note window to achieve this. By intercepting such malicious commands at early stages, ransomware could be detected with no file losses.

3.2   Application Behavioral Characteristics

We analyzed the system events generated by ransomware samples and observed that there exist strong correlations between some events for the operations of ransomware. For example, all files read must be written (encrypted), which naturally shows a correlation between `Read` and `Write` events. Furthermore, similar correlations are exhibited among events collected from different providers such as `File`, `Process`, `Image`, and `Thread` because ransomware samples generate a large file `Read` and `Write` events to perform malicious tasks. Such relationships between certain events can be quantified by using the correlation coefficients of the events (see Table 1).

Table 1. Correlation coefficients for some events.

Events pair	Ransomware	Benign applications
(File Read, File Write)	0.9433	0.3500
(Process End, Image Unload)	0.9451	0.7174
(Process Start, Image Load)	0.9476	0.7397
(Thread Start, Thread End)	0.9560	0.6585

For example, a crypto ransomware sample generates `Read` and `Write` events regularly. As presented in Table 1, there exists a strong correlation between the number of `Read` events and the number of `Write` events. Such a correlation relationship may not appear in benign applications' `Read` and `Write` requests. Similarly, during ransomware execution, we observe the correlation between the number of `Start` processes and the number of image `Load` events, the correlation between the number of `End` processes and the number of image `Unload` events, and the correlation between the number of `Start` threads and the number of `End` thread events. These correlation coefficients are computed from the analysis performed on 206 ransomware samples and 50 most popular benign applications. Figure 3 shows correlation among three pairs of events (`Read` and `Write`, `Start` and `Load`, `End` and `Unload`). We clearly observe strong correlations for ransomware compared to benign applications. Therefore, Peeler uses those correlations to detect ransomware.

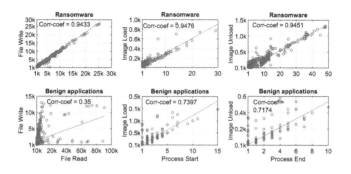

Fig. 3. Correlations among events for ransomware and benign applications.

4 System Design

4.1 Overview

Peeler has two main ransomware detection modules: 1) malicious command detector and 2) machine learning-based classifier. Figure 4 illustrates the overall design of Peeler. Peeler monitors system events continuously to detect ransomware attacks in real-time and uses them to perform ransomware detection. The malicious command detector uses predefined rules to check whether malicious commands are executed by processes in which the execution of those commands is mainly observed in ransomware activities. Machine learning-based classifier module captures contextual and behavioral features using two machine learning models. Peeler profiles the contextual information of created processes by extracting features from process command-line arguments (see Table 2). It then transforms the extracted features into contextual embedding to build an NLP-based deep learning model called BERT [13]. On the other hand, Peeler constantly monitors and extracts behavioral features the following providers: `Process`, `Image`, `File`, and `Thread` and builds another machine learning model based on support vector machine (SVM). For detection, the scores from both classification models are fused as an ensemble approach, and then detection is performed.

4.2 System Events Monitor

Peeler provides a module called *system events monitor* which relies on Event Tracing for Windows[2] (ETW) framework. ETW is a built-in, general-purpose

---

[2] ETW was first introduced in Windows 2000 and is now built-in to all Windows OS versions.

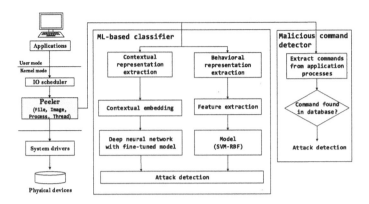

Fig. 4. Overview of Peeler.

logging and diagnostic framework in Windows OS. It is *efficient* (high speed and low overhead), *flexible* (consume events in real-time or log to a file), and provide greater *visibility* into the system such that it allows to register to more than 1,100 subsystem providers [1] to receive and consume events. ETW framework is available for usage in both APIs and command-line tools and applications. The usage of ETW-based command-line tools and applications are more common compared to ETW APIs (e.g.,TraceEvent, System.Diagnostic.Eventing, Event Tracing) to view system events [26].

We designed a module called *system events monitor* based on ETW. Our module is lightweight because it directly interacts with the native layer and performs filtering of the system events. In terms of visibility, Peeler extracts events from the following providers: Process, Image, File, Thread. The data obtained by Peeler's system events monitor are in the form of a continuous sequence of events t_i. An event is represented as: $t_i =<$ $PID, TID, Prov., EType, E_{timestamp}, E_{attrs} >$, where PID is a process identifier, TID is a thread identifier corresponding to the process PID. Prov. is provider name, EType is event name, $E_{timestamp}$ is the time of event occurrence, and E_{attrs} is a set of attributes of the event E_{name}. To implement the system events monitor in Peeler, we used an open-source project *krabsetw* [3], which is a C++ library that simplifies interactions with ETW. We modified *krabsetw* both at API and native layer to collect the events only needed for Peeler.

Table 2. Providers and events used in Peeler.

Provider	Event	Event schema	
		Common attributes	Provider-specific event attributes
Process	Start, End	PID, TID, Prov., Event, Timestamp	SessionId, ParentId ImageFileName, CommandLine

4.3 Malicious Commands Detector

Peeler uses a component called *malicious command detecter* to filter suspicious activities conducted by ransomware using the database for malicious commands which are needed to perform ransomware's activities. Peeler can collect malicious commands from the `Process`'s `Command line` argument (see Table 2). Typically, the `commandLine` attribute of the `Process` contains the actual commands. For example, Windows OS utility `net.exe` can start, stop, pause or restart any service using the command `net.exe stop ServiceName` launched via convenient script/batch file or command prompt. If an adversary leverages such commands to stop several anti-malware services, Peeler can detect the process using predefined rules. Similarly, utility *taskkill.exe* ends one or more tasks or processes. Typically, ransomware specify the image name of the process to be terminated (e.g., *taskkill.exe /IM ImageName*). The `sc.exe` utility modifies the value of a service's entries in the registry and service control manager database. Ransomware may attempt to disable several defending services on the victim's machine before starting encryption. Peeler uses rules based on utility names and actions performed in order to detect ransomware infection.

4.4 Machine Learning-Based Classifier

Peeler uses two different machine learning-based (ML-based) classifiers with contextual features and system events-based behavioral features to detect ransomware samples. The input to the algorithm is a set of events accumulated over W seconds window. In our current implementation, we empirically set $W = 5$ to optimize the speed-accuracy tradeoff. Features are extracted to build two machine learning models. The built machine learning models are then used to detect ransomware attacks.

Building the First Classifier with the Applications' Processes. As discussed in Sect. 3.1, we observed that several ransomware samples, as well as benign application samples, spawn many child processes (depending upon the application logic) to perform different tasks. However, to determine whether or not a given process's operations are malicious or not may depend on its context of operation because, like benign applications, stealthy ransomware also uses legitimate tools on Windows OS to perform various operations. To that end, Peeler profiles an application's contextual behavior by exploiting the processes creation pattern (including the commands executed during the processes runtime).

Fig. 5. Process gadget representation and normalization.

A set of semantically related processes is called *process gadget*. Process gadgets partially depict the application's contextual behavior. For instance, Fig. 5 shows the process creation pattern containing the used tools information and the command executed. To view it contextually, ransomware first scheduled a high-priority task using the *schtasks* tool to execute a malicious file. Then it deletes Windows shadow files using *Vssadmin* and *cmd* tools. Then the recovery and telemetry information is disabled using *sc.exe* and *net.exe* tools, and so on. The process gadget in Fig. 5 provides sufficient context about the intend of the executing application, which is exploited by Peeler to detect ransomware. In addition, Peeler normalizes the process gadgets by replacing numerical values with literal constants such as 'num' and absolute paths with 'PATH' constant, as shown in Fig. 5 (right). Further, we observed that in some cases, PowerShell use encoded (with Base64 encoding scheme) malicious PS commands. In such cases, Peeler first decodes (from Base64 encoding) the commands and then uses the obtained text of commands in process gadgets.

To that end, we propose to use an NLP-based deep neural network called BERT [13] that takes the process gadgets and constructs a new deep learning language model via fine-tuning. BERT [13] is pretrained by considering two main objectives: 1) Masked language modeling (MLM): the model randomly masks 15% of the words in the input, then runs the entire masked sentence through the model and has to predict the masked words. This approach is different from traditional recurrent neural networks (RNNs) that usually see the words sequentially, i.e., one after the other, or from autoregressive models like GPT, which internally mask the future tokens. BERT's main advantage is that it allows the model to learn a bidirectional representation of the sentence – providing context to the learning stage. 2) Next sentence prediction (NSP): the models concatenate two masked sentences as inputs during pretraining. The goal here is to predict if the two sentences were following each other or not.

In the fine-tuning step, the model weights are updated using our labeled dataset, which is new to the pretrained BERTbase model. BERT takes a sequence of tokens in a maximum length of 512 as input and produces a sequential representation in a 768-dimensional vector as output [13]. The network layers need to be updated to train the deep learning model on a new classification task, i.e., to identify benign/ransomware applications. The output layer is then trained to display the result intended for the fine-tuned deep learning model. We train a classifier with different layers of 768 dimensions on top of the pre-trained BERTbase transformer model to minimize task-specific parameters through the fine-tuning step.

Building the Second Classifier with the System Event Features. As discussed in Sect. 3.2, Peeler leverages four providers' (`File`, `Process`, `Image`, and `Thread`) events exhibiting casualties. In total, the following four pairs of events are used: (`Read`, `Write`), (`Start`, `Load`), (`End`, `Unload`), and (`Start`, `End`). To capture these casualties simply, Peeler extracts frequency features and trains an SVM model based on feature set FV_{SVM} for classification. We selected SVM

with RBF kernel because it is lightweight and produces the best accuracy results
with FV_{SVM}.

Features: # of process start, # of process end, # of DLL image loads, # of DLL image unloads, # of file reads, # of file writes, # of threads start, # of thread end

Attack Detection. Peeler uses two classification models (fine-tuned BERT and
SVM-RBF) and finally decides the classification outcome by fusing their scores.
Peeler extracts process command-line arguments from the stream of incoming
system events, transforms them into their normalized representations, and uses
them as input to the fine-tuned deep learning model. The constructed model
network outputs either "1" (i.e., ransomware) or "0" (i.e., benign). If a given
file event gadget is from ransomware, it will extract the process identifier and
flag the process by raising an alert to the system administrator. SVM-RBF is
trained with FV_{SVM}. The scores from the two models are fused by taking their
average for detection.

5 Dataset Collection

5.1 Ransomware

We collected 28,034 ransomware samples from VirusTotal [9], MalwareBazaar [6],
malware repository [4], malwares [5], and other online communities. However, we
excluded many malware samples from our final dataset for experiments. First,
we found that many samples were not actual ransomware samples, although
they were classified as ransomware by some vendors in VirusTotal. Therefore we
discarded such samples. This finding is consistent with the observation in the
previous work [32]. Second, ransomware often needs to interact with command-
and-control (C&C) servers to perform their malicious activities. However, several
ransomware samples did not often work appropriately because their corresponding C&C servers were inactive. Also, some sophisticated malware samples can
detect the analysis environment and remain inactive to evade detection [29].
More importantly, samples from a few ransomware families we observed were
significantly larger compared to other families. For example, we found more
than 20,000 ransomware samples from Virlock family including *Virlock Gen.1*,
VirLock Gen.4, and *VirLock Gen.8* variants. Therefore, we kept limited samples from the Virlock family and discarded other samples. Finally, we collected
292 active samples from 67 ransomware families that perform their activities
correctly. We used 206 ransomware samples from 43 ransomware families (see
Appendix A) in the first set of experiments (in Sect. 6.1). The remaining 24
ransomware families with 70 samples were collected at a later stage of data collection and used to evaluate Peeler on new and unseen ransomware samples (in
Sect. 6.3).

User Environment and Ground Truth (labeled) Dataset. We used VirtualBox 6.1 [8] to create and manage the computing environment locally for experiments. Rather than using artificially generated data, we used a real user's data running on the Windows 10 64Bit operating system (a copied version of real user data) to set up a benign user's environment realistically. Multimedia files (e.g., bmp, jpeg, png, and mp4), Microsoft office documents (e.g., docx, xlsx and pptx files), and other important files (e.g., cpp, py, pdf and wav files) were copied to various directories in different locations. We note that those files are typically most attractive targets for ransomware.

Each ransomware sample was executed and then manually labeled by each family type. We ran each ransomware sample for ten minutes or until all user files were encrypted. It took more than 90 days to run all samples and collect data. We only considered those samples that encrypted user files or locked desktop screens. If no files were modified, we excluded them from our dataset. We also obtained labeled ransomware samples from two well-known malware repositories [4,6].

Diversity in Our Dataset. Table 6 presents a list of ransomware families that are used in our evaluation. To the best of our knowledge, this is the most comprehensive dataset containing diverse ransomware families. According to previous work [31,32], the use of diverse families is more important than the number of ransomware samples from a few families for evaluating the performance of ransomware detectors. For instance, building a model on 1,000 Locky (and its variants) ransomware samples should prove no more useful than building a model on just one Locky sample [31]. Scaife et al. [32] confirmed that due to the homogeneous nature of file I/O behavior among samples within each family, a small number of representative samples in each family are sufficient to evaluate the detection performance. The core behavioral traits shown by crypto ransomware in encrypting data remain almost identical from one variant to another in a family. Since our study covered more than eight times the number of families from previous study [23], and more than two times the number of families covered in studies [21,32] and there was not much diversity within families, there was little need to collect additional samples.

5.2 Benign Applications

We also collected the dataset for popularly used applications. In addition to popularly used applications, we also considered several benign applications that could resemble ransomware in certain behavioral aspects. The reason is to investigate false-positive rates when benign applications potentially resemble ransomware. We divide the benign dataset into three main categories targeting various types of ransomware. The first category applications perform encryption or compression operations that would generate file I/O patterns similar to crypto ransomware that could result in false positives. The second category applications spawn many child processes. The third category applications are popularly used applications on Windows PCs. We collected user's system usage data under normal conditions while interacting with those applications. A user runs many different applications at the same time. For example, the user reads a document using Adobe Acrobat Reader, switched to the internet browser to view online reviews about a product, and then used Adobe Acrobat Reader again. The list of benign applications is shown in Appendix A.

6 Evaluation

We demonstrate Peeler's performance in detection accuracy, identification of legitimate tools abused by an attacker, and robustness against unseen ransomware.

For evaluation, we used the dataset described in Sect. 5. Our dataset consists of 177,236,131 system I/O events containing both ransomware samples and benign applications. Table 3 shows a detailed breakdown of our dataset. For training, 60% of both ransomware and benign applications are selected randomly. The remaining ransomware and benign samples are divided into validation (10%) and test (30%) datasets.

Table 3. Dataset statistics.

Dataset	Ransomware	Benign	Total
# system events	66,099,039	111,137,092	177,236,131
# processes	3,929	3,924	7,853
# process gadgets	1,309	1,308	2617

For training the SVM-RBF model, we used default settings to train the model. For fine-tuning the BERT model with our dataset, we used BERTbase [7] tokenizer and pretrained model. The number of commands in each process gadget is set to three because, with just three commands, BERT is able to capture the contextual information. A total 2,617 number of process gadgets are extracted from 7,853 processes from both ransomware and benign applications. The model consists of 12 layers, 12 attention heads, 768-dimensional vocabulary, and 110M parameters. The batch size and learning rate were set to 16 and 0.00002, respectively. The number of epochs was set to 10. The trained model is then used to evaluate Peeler.

6.1 Detection Accuracy

Table 4 shows the summary of Peeler's detection accuracy. Overall, Peeler achieved 99.52% accuracy with a false positive rate of only 0.58%. Similarly, Peeler achieved over 99% in both precision and F1 score.

Table 4. Peeler's detection accuracy.

Acc. (%)	TPR (%)	FPR (%)	FNR (%)	Prec. (%)	Rec. (%)	F1 (%)
99.52	99.63	0.58	0.37	99.41	99.63	99.52

False Positive Analysis. Minimizing false positives is essential to develop practically useful malware detectors because excessive false positives can annoy users and undermine the system's effectiveness. We evaluate Peeler's performance against three different types of benign application scenarios (see Table 5).

Table 5. Peeler's false positive analysis.

Scenario	TNR (%)	FPR (%)	FNR (%)
Crypto-like benign apps	98.27	1.72	0.96
Locker-like benign apps	99.5	0.31	0.5
Commonly used benign apps	99.78	0.21	0.87
All ransomware	99.42	0.58	0.37

Crypto Ransomware-Like Benign Applications. For behavior-based crypto ransomware detection solutions, a significant challenge is not to detect benign applications having compression or encryption capabilities because their system behaviors might be similar to crypto ransomware.

We deeply investigated 11 different applications using compression or encryption operations on a large number of files like crypto ransomware (see Appendix A). We observed that event sequences of some benign applications such as ZipExtractor and BreeZip are similar to those of typical crypto ransomware, but they do not restrict access to files via encryption, unlike crypto ransomware. Table 5 shows that Peeler correctly detects 98.27% with a false positive rate of 1.72% even against crypto ransomware-like benign applications.

Benign Applications Spawning Many Processes. Certain benign apps spawn many child processes. Therefore, we examine how Peeler's performance can be degraded with benign apps having such behaviors. For this analysis, we investigated 34 most popular applications from Microsoft's Windows OS Store (https://www.microsoft.com/en-us/store/apps/windows) (see Appendix A) and selected 18 applications showing such behaviors. We observe that Pycharm, Visual Studio, and Chrome spawned 140, 46, and 42 child processes, respectively. We examined the results of Peeler with those 18 applications. Table 5 shows that Peeler correctly detected 99.5% with a false positive rate of 0.31% even though these benign applications spawned many processes.

Popularly Used Benign Applications. We also evaluated Peeler's performance with commonly used benign applications such as Microsoft Office, Adobe

Acrobat Reader, email client, and instant messengers, as presented in Sect. 5.2. We show that Peeler correctly detects all benign activities performed by a user achieving a detection rate of 99.78%. The false positive and true negative rates under normal system usage are 0.21% and 0.87%, respectively. Note that the overall detection accuracy in all three scenarios is above 99%.

6.2   Effectiveness in Detecting Abused Tools/utilities

Some sophisticated ransomware samples can exploit legitimate tools/utilities, called Living-Off-The-Land techniques, to perform malicious tasks. It is therefore essential to identify such tools/utilities and the malicious tasks performed by them. To show the effectiveness of our approach, we compare Peeler with PROVDETECTOR [35] in terms of detecting the number of legitimate tools/utilities abused by ransomware. It is an anomaly-based malware detection approach that models system behavior using graphs. Total 23 legitimate tools or applications are detected by PROVDETECTOR that are abused by malware. However, Peeler detected 65 tools and applications (almost three times more than that of PROVDETECTOR) that can be abused by ransomware in performing malicious tasks. The list of abused legitimate tools and applications by ransomware is given below:

raserver.exe, SystemSettings.exe, svchost.exe, SpeechRuntime.exe, SystemSettingsBroker.exe, SearchProtocolHost.exe, SearchFilterHost.exe, cmd.exe, reg.exe, cscript.exe, backgroundTaskHost.exe, RuntimeBroker.exe, HxTsr.exe, SIHClient.exe, WmiPrvSE.exe, WindowsInternal.ComposableShell.Experiences.TextInput.InputApp.exe, provtool.exe, taskhostw.exe, rundll32.exe, DiskSnapshot.exe, cleanmgr.exe, Defrag.exe, CompatTelRunner.exe, sdiagnhost.exe, TiWorker.exe, dllhost.exe, ShellExperienceHost.exe, SearchUI.exe, mobsync.exe, MicrosoftEdgeCP.exe, ngentask.exe, ngen.exe, LogonUI.exe, makecab.exe, taskkill.exe, ruby.exe, OpenWith.exe, notepad.exe, PING.EXE, mshta.exe, consent.exe, vssadmin.exe, WMIC.exe, wscript.exe, Windows.WARP.JITService.exe, forfiles.exe, bcdedit.exe, netsh.exe, Microsoft.Photos.exe, net.exe, net1.exc, schtasks.exe, mode.com, WerFault.exe, wermgr.exe, timeout.exe, drpbx.exe, SearchIndexer.exe, MusNotificationUx.exe, icacls.exe, CsWEBftw.exe, powershell.exe, unsecapp.exe, chcp.com, attrib.exe

6.3   Robustness Against Unseen Families

To test Peeler against unseen ransomware families, we additionally collected new and *unseen* ransomware samples after three months from the first experiments and monitored online repositories for new or unseen ransomware samples. A total of 70 samples from more than 24 distinct unseen or new ransomware families are tested. We used the previously constructed Peeler without retraining. All samples tested in this experiment are manually verified from VirusTotal and other online malware repositories to confirm their family and type. Peeler correctly detected

67 samples from a total of 70 new and unseen ransomware samples achieving more than 95% detection rate. The ransomware families and the number of corresponding samples tested are given in Appendix A.

7 Conclusion

We propose a new efficient tool called Peeler to detect ransomware attacks using their system behaviors. Peeler is built on both rule-based detection and machine learning models to improve detection accuracy. To show the effectiveness of Peeler, we evaluate its performance with 43 ransomware families containing crypto ransomware and screen-locker ransomware. In the experiments, Peeler achieved a 99.52% F1 score with a false positive rate of only 0.58%. Further, we showed that Peeler is highly effective in detecting unseen or new ransomware, achieving more than 95% detection accuracy on 24 unseen ransomware families.

A Dataset

A.1 Ransomware families

We provide a comprehensive list of both ransomware families and benign applications used to evaluate Peeler. Table 6 presents two sets of ransomware families used in Sect. 6.1 and Sect. 6.3, respectively.

Table 6. Ransomware families and samples.

No.	Family	Samples	No.	Family	Samples	No.	Family	Samples	No.	Family	Samples
1	Cerber	33	12	Petya	1	23	Sodinokibi	14	34	Satana	1
2	GoldenEye	12	13	Shade	1	24	Sage	5	35	Syrk	1
3	Locky	5	14	TeslaCrypt	1	25	Dharma	3	36	ucyLocker	1
4	dotExe	3	15	Unlock92	1	26	Troldesh	1	37	Vipasana	1
5	WannaCry	3	16	Xorist	2	27	Da Vinci Code	1	38	Malevich	1
6	Shield	1	17	Jigsaw	1	28	Cryptowire	1	39	Adobe	1
7	District	1	18	Virlock.Gen.5	83	29	Gandcrab	1	40	LockScreen.AGU	12
8	GlobeImposter	1	19	Alphabet	2	30	Hexadecimal	1	41	EgyptianGhosts	1
9	InfinityCrypt	1	20	Lockey-Pay	1	31	IS (Ordinpt)	1	42	Blue-Howl	1
10	Keypass	1	21	ShellLocker	1	32	Lockcrypt	1	43	DerialLock	1
11	Pack14	1	22	Trojan.Ransom	1	33	PocrimCrypt	1		–	
Dataset for experiments in Section 6.3.											
44	Ryuk	6	50	Zeppelin	6	56	Ranzy	4	62	Netwalker	2
45	Core	3	51	Fox	3	57	Crpren	1	63	MedusaLocker	1
46	Balaclava	5	52	Crylock	7	58	Matrix	4	64	DarkSide	4
47	RagnarLocker	2	53	HiddenTear	2	59	Mespinoza	5	65	Thanos	3
48	Vaggen	3	54	Mountlocker	2	60	Nemty	2	66	Phobos	1
49	Jsworm	1	55	Winlock	1	61	Maze	1	67	Unknown	1
Total samples: 292, crypto = 188, screen-locker = 104											

A.2   Benign applications

In this section, we present benign applications that potentially show ransomware-like behaviors that are used in the evaluation of Peeler: 1) benign encryption, compression, and shredder applications (see Table 7); 2) benign application spawning multiple processes; and 3) benign applications that are most popularly used on Windows PC (see Table 8).

Table 7. Ransomware-like benign applications.

Tool	Application	Operation	Version
Compression	7-zip	Compression	19.00
	7-zip	Decompression	
	Winzip	Compression	24
	Winzip	Decompression	
	Winrar	Compression	5.80
	Winrar	Decompression	
	BreeZip	Compression	–
	BreeZip	Decompression	
	Alzip	Compression	11.04
	Alzip	Decompression	
	PeazipWinrar	Compression	7.1.1
	PeazipWinrar	Decompression	
Encryption	AESCrypt	Encryption	310.00
	AESCrypt	Decryption	
	AxCrypt	Encryption	–
	AxCrypt	Decryption	
Shredder	Eraser	Delete	6.2.0.2986
	Ccleaner	Delete	–
	Windows Delete	Delete	–

Table 8. Benign applications spawning multiple processes.

Type	Application	Version	spawn processes?
Office	MS Word	16.0.11929.20436	×
	MS Powerpoint	16.0.11929.20436	×
	MS Excel	16.0.11929.20436	×
	MS Outlook	16.0.11929.20436	✓
	Trio Office: Word, Slide, Spreadsheet	–	✓
Development	Pycharm	11.0.3+12-b304.56 amd64	✓
	Matlab	R2019a	✓
	Visual Studio C++	2019 community version	✓
	Android Studio	191.6010548	✓
Tools	Adobe Acrobat Reader	20.006.20034	✓
	Adobe Photoshop Express	3.0.316	×
	PhotoScape	3.7	×
	Cool File Viewer	–	×
	PicArt Photo Studio	–	×
	Paint 3D	–	×
Cloud and Internet	Dropbox	–	×
	Googledrive	–	×
	Internet Explorer	11.1039.17763	✓
	Google Chrome	80.0.3987.132	✓
	Remote Desktop	–	×
Messenger	Telegram	1.9.7	×
	WhatApp	0.4.930	✓
	Skype	1.9.7	×
	Facebook Messenger	–	✓
Document	Wordpad	–	×
	Notepad	–	×
	OneNote	16001.12527.20128.0	×
Media player	VLC	3.0.8	×
	Netflix	6.95.602	×
	GOM Player	2.3.49.5312	×
Miscellaneous	Spotify	–	✓
	KeePass Password manager	1.38	×
	Discord	–	×
	Facebook	–	×

References

1. About Event Tracing. https://docs.microsoft.com/en-us/windows/win32/etw/about-event-tracing
2. Global Ransomware Damage Costs Predicted To Reach $20 Billion (USD) By 2021. https://cybersecurityventures.com/global-ransomware-damage-costs-predicted-to-reach-20-billion-usd-by-2021/
3. Krabsetw. https://github.com/microsoft/krabsetw
4. A Live Malware Repository. https://github.com/ytisf/theZoo

5. Malware samples. https://github.com/fabrimagic72/malware-samples
6. MalwareBazaar. https://bazaar.abuse.ch/
7. Pretrained models. https://huggingface.co/transformers/pretrained_models.html
8. VirtualBox. https://www.virtualbox.org
9. VirusTotal. https://www.virustotal.com/
10. What systems have you seen infected by ransomware? https://www.statista.com/statistics/701020/major-operating-systems-targeted-by-ransomware/
11. Al-rimy, B.A.S., Maarof, M.A., Shaid, S.Z.M.: A 0-day aware crypto-ransomware early behavioral detection framework. In: International Conference of Reliable Information and Communication Technology, pp. 758–766 (2017)
12. Continella, A., et al.: Shieldfs: a self-healing, ransomware-aware filesystem. In: Proceedings of the 32nd Annual Conference on Computer Security Applications, pp. 336–347 (2016)
13. Devlin, J., Chang, M.W., Lee, K., Toutanova, K.: Bert: Pre-training of deep bidirectional transformers for language understanding. arXiv preprint arXiv:1810.04805 (2018)
14. Gómez-Hernández, J., Álvarez-González, L., García-Teodoro, P.: R-Locker: thwarting ransomware action through a honeyfile-based approach. Comput. Secur. **73**, 389–398 (2018)
15. Hendler, D., Kels, S., Rubin, A.: Detecting malicious powershell commands using deep neural networks. In: Proceedings of the 2018 on Asia Conference on Computer and Communications Security, pp. 187–197 (2018)
16. Hendler, D., Kels, S., Rubin, A.: Amsi-based detection of malicious powershell code using contextual embeddings. In: Proceedings of the 15th ACM Asia Conference on Computer and Communications Security, pp. 679–693 (2020)
17. Hirano, M., Kobayashi, R.: Machine learning based ransomware detection using storage access patterns obtained from live-forensic hypervisor. In: Sixth IEEE International Conference on Internet of Things: Systems, Management and Security (IOTSMS), pp. 1–6 (2019)
18. Homayoun, S., Dehghantanha, A., Ahmadzadeh, M., Hashemi, S., Khayami, R.: Know abnormal, find evil: frequent pattern mining for ransomware threat hunting and intelligence. IEEE transactions on emerging topics in computing (2017)
19. Huang, J., Xu, J., Xing, X., Liu, P., Qureshi, M.K.: Flashguard: Leveraging intrinsic flash properties to defend against encryption ransomware. In: Proceedings of the ACM SIGSAC Conference on Computer and Communications Security, pp. 2231–2244 (2017)
20. Jin, B., Choi, J., Kim, H., Hong, J.B.: Fumvar: a practical framework for generating fully-working and unseen malware variants. In: Proceedings of the 36th Annual ACM Symposium on Applied Computing (SAC) (2021)
21. Kharaz, A., Arshad, S., Mulliner, C., Robertson, W., Kirda, E.: UNVEIL: a large-scale, automated approach to detecting ransomware. In: 25th USENIX Security Symposium (USENIX Security 16), pp. 757–772 (2016)
22. Kharraz, A., Kirda, E.: Redemption: real-time protection against ransomware at end-hosts. In: International Symposium on Research in Attacks, Intrusions, and Defenses, pp. 98–119 (2017)
23. Kharraz, A., Robertson, W., Balzarotti, D., Bilge, L., Kirda, E.: Cutting the gordian knot: a look under the hood of ransomware attacks. In: International Conference on Detection of Intrusions and Malware, and Vulnerability Assessment, pp. 3–24 (2015)

24. Kolodenker, E., Koch, W., Stringhini, G., Egele, M.: Paybreak: defense against cryptographic ransomware. In: Proceedings ACM on Asia Conference on Computer and Communications Security, pp. 599–611 (2017)
25. Lab, E.M.: The State of Ransomware in the US. https://blog.emsisoft.com/en/34822/the-state-of-ransomware-in-the-us-report-and-statistics-2019/
26. Lelonek, B., Rogers, N.: Make ETW greate again. https://ruxcon.org.au/assets/2016/slides/ETW_16_RUXCON_NJR_no_notes.pdf
27. Mehnaz, S., Mudgerikar, A., Bertino, E.: RWGuard: a real-time detection system against cryptographic ransomware. In: International Symposium on Research in Attacks, Intrusions, and Defenses, pp. 114–136 (2018)
28. Milajerdi, S.M., Eshete, B., Gjomemo, R., Venkatakrishnan, V.: Poirot: aligning attack behavior with kernel audit records for cyber threat hunting. In: Proceedings of ACM SIGSAC Conference on Computer and Communications Security, pp. 1795–1812 (2019)
29. Miramirkhani, N., Appini, M.P., Nikiforakis, N., Polychronakis, M.: Spotless sandboxes: evading malware analysis systems using wear-and-tear artifacts. In: IEEE Symposium on Security and Privacy (SP), pp. 1009–1024 (2017)
30. Morato, D., Berrueta, E., Magaña, E., Izal, M.: Ransomware early detection by the analysis of file sharing traffic. J. Network Comput. Appl. **124**, 14–32 (2018)
31. Nieuwenhuizen, D.: A behavioural-based approach to ransomware detection. Whitepaper, MWR Labs Whitepaper (2017)
32. Scaife, N., Carter, H., Traynor, P., Butler, K.R.: Cryptolock (and drop it): stopping ransomware attacks on user data. In: 36th IEEE International Conference on Distributed Computing Systems (ICDCS), pp. 303–312 (2016)
33. Sgandurra, D., Muñoz-González, L., Mohsen, R., Lupu, E.C.: Automated dynamic analysis of ransomware: Benefits, limitations and use for detection. arXiv preprint arXiv:1609.03020 (2016)
34. Sivakorn, S., et al.: Countering malicious processes with process-dns association. In: Network and Distributed Systems Security (2019)
35. Wang, Q., et al.: You are what you do: Hunting stealthy malware via data provenance analysis. In: Symposium on Network and Distributed System Security (NDSS) (2020)
36. WatchGuard: Internet Security Report - Q4 2020. https://www.watchguard.com/wgrd-resource-center/security-report-q4-2020
37. Zhao, L., Mannan, M.: TEE-aided write protection against privileged data tampering. arXiv preprint arXiv:1905.10723 (2019)

User Behaviour and Underground Economy

Mingling of Clear and Muddy Water: Understanding and Detecting Semantic Confusion in Blackhat SEO

Hao Yang[1], Kun Du[1], Yubao Zhang[2], Shuai Hao[3], Haining Wang[4], Jia Zhang[1(✉)], and Haixin Duan[5,6]

[1] Tsinghua University, Beijing, China
{yang-h16,dk15}@mails.tsinghua.edu.cn,
zhangjia@cernet.edu.cn
[2] University of Delaware, Newark, DE, USA
ybzhang@udel.edu
[3] Old Dominion University, Norfolk, VA, USA
shao@odu.edu
[4] Virginia Tech, Arlington, VA, USA
hnw@vt.edu
[5] Institute for Network Science and Cyberspace, Tsinghua University, Beijing, China
duanhx@tsinghua.edu.cn
[6] Qi An Xin Group Corp., Beijing, China

Abstract. Search Engine Optimization (SEO) is a set of techniques that help website operators increase the visibility of their webpages to search engine users. However, there are also many unethical practices that abuse ranking algorithms of a search engine to promote illegal online content, called blackhat SEO. In this paper, we make the first attempt to systematically investigate a recent trend in blackhat SEO, semantic confusion, which mingles the content of a webpage to deceive existing detection of blackhat SEO. In particular, from a new perspective of content semantics, we propose an effective defense against the semantic confusion based blackhat SEO. We built a prototype of our defense called SCDS, and then we validated its effectiveness based on 4.5 million domains randomly selected from 11 zone files and passive DNS records. Our evaluation results show that SCDS can detect more than 82 thousand blackhat SEO websites with a precision of 98.35%. We further analyzed 57,477 long-tail keywords promoted by blackhat SEO and found more than 157 SEO campaigns. Finally, we deployed SCDS into the gateway of a campus network for ten months and detected 23,093 domains with malicious semantic confusion content, showing the effectiveness of SCDS in practice.

1 Introduction

Search engines are the entrance to the Internet, and search engine optimization (SEO) helps legal service/content providers improve their page ranking to be

© Springer Nature Switzerland AG 2021
E. Bertino et al. (Eds.): ESORICS 2021, LNCS 12972, pp. 263–284, 2021.
https://doi.org/10.1007/978-3-030-88418-5_13

more visible to Internet users [9,11,12]. However, underground online business such as gambling and porn may be disallowed to blatantly exhibit their content because it is banned according to the laws in some countries and regions. Thus, they adopt blackhat SEO to promote themselves. Blackhat SEO [8] is a set of unethical practices of search engine optimization, such as content spam [20], and it aims to make a page's ranking rise in a short time, no matter what kind of content is on the page. In the past decades, blackhat SEO has become the tailor-made technique for promoting underground online business.

To avoid being detected by search engines, a spate of blackhat SEO webpages recently disguise themselves by leveraging *semantic confusion*. That is to say, these webpages, on one hand, include promotion contents since their ultimate goal is to promote illegitimate products or services. On the other hand, they also mingle with some legitimate content, which is usually copied from other sources, in order to disguise themselves. Therefore, there exists a clear semantic discrepancy within these blackhat SEO webpages.

In this paper, we investigate this recent trend in blackhat SEO webpages that leverage semantic confusion to cloak illegal topics webpages. We propose an effective defense called Semantic Confusion Detection System (SCDS) to detect these blackhat SEO webpages based on semantic discrepancy. In particular, we developed two separate deep-learning classifiers to measure two coordinates with regard to legitimacy and illegitimacy, respectively. With the coordinate system built, we can identify webpages with semantic discrepancy and further check the external hyperlinks on these pages to detect blackhat SEO webpages.

Contributions. We summarize the major contributions of this work as follows:

(1) Understanding of the semantic confusion practice in blackhat SEO. We made the first attempt to systematically investigate the semantic confusion in the context of blackhat SEO. We revealed that semantic confusion has been widely adopted in practice for evading detection, posing a serious security threat to Internet users.

(2) Development of effective defense. We proposed and implemented a novel detection system, SCDS, which exploits the mingling of semantic content for accurate detection by recognizing the topics and semantic context of the text on a webpage. The evaluation results show that SCDS can effectively detect semantic confusion based blackhat SEO pages.

(3) Deployment and disclosure. We deployed our detection system on the gateway of a campus network and presented what we found to experienced security practitioners from the industry. Our findings have been confirmed and added into blacklists as seed for broader filtration.

The remainder of this paper is organized as follows. In Sect. 2, we review the background of SEO and its manipulation. In Sects. 3 and 4, we detail the architecture of SCDS and its implementation and evaluation, respectively. In Sect. 5, we present the measurement results and analysis of the ecosystem of blackhat SEO. In Sect. 6, we describe the practical issues of blackhat SEO. In Sect. 7, we discuss several related issues of this study. In Sect. 8, we survey related work, and finally, we conclude in Sect. 9.

2   Background

2.1   Search Engine Optimization (SEO)

The purpose of SEO is to increase the exposure of websites to search engine users. Websites provide content with valid semantics in tags such as `<title>` and `<meta>`, provide a valid sitemap to help crawlers retrieve content quickly and refresh the content regularly. Search engines retrieve specific content from HTML pages, and match the content with keywords from users' input. Search engines use PageRank (PR) values to evaluate a website's relevance to keywords. To avoid being abused, a search engine changes its PR algorithm from time to time [24]. Every year, search engine vendors publish guidelines for SEO [13]. Search engine vendors encourage benign SEO because this can help the spider of a search engine to crawl more effectively and help the PR algorithm to rank a page more appropriately. The SEO encouraged by search engine vendors is often called "whitehat SEO".

2.2   Blackhat SEO

While whitehat SEO advocates improving the structure of a website to make it more friendly to search engines, different unethical techniques, called *blackhat SEO*, have been exploited to manipulate ranking results on search engines. The most common practice of blackhat SEO is to directly repeat the keywords or phrases in the webpages to increase their appearance and relevance to certain terms being promoted [20]. However, such an approach can be easily recognized and penalized by search engines through detecting repeated content. Furthermore, to engage more efficient promotion, a link farm has been constructed to accumulate incoming links to a website by exploiting the vulnerabilities of other reputable websites to inject a large number of links [6]. We discuss more details about cloaking pages in blackhat SEO in Sect. 5.1.

2.3   Semantic-Based Techniques

Beyond the straightforward content manipulation, sophisticated, semantic-based content spam tied with the underground business, including illegal online gambling and pornography, has become more pervasive for evading detection. At a lower level (*i.e.*, word level), blackhat SEOers leverage automated spinning to avoid duplicate detection [30]. With the spinning, texts with similar semantic meanings but different appearances are generated and inserted into webpages.

At a higher level (*i.e.*, semantic level), blackhat SEOers fetch a large piece of normal content from legitimate websites, elaborately stuffed with a small piece of content from underground business, and assemble them into one webpage. As such, the page would be treated as a normal webpage, and the promoted content of underground business would be indexed by search engines. We call this more advanced manipulation in blackhat SEO as semantic confusion. In this study, we aim to conduct a comprehensive investigation to understand this new trend of blackhat SEO and explore the detection of semantic confusion.

Fig. 1. A typical webpage of illegal gambling site.

Fig. 2. A typical webpage of mixed content.

3 Semantic Confusion Detection

In this section, we present the architecture of SCDS and detail its components, including data source, data processor, semantic analyzer, and SEO collector.

3.1 System Overview

Our goal is to identify blackhat SEO webpages with semantic confusion, in which the illegitimate content is embedded for promotion while the legitimate content is compiled into the pages for the evasion of detection mechanisms. With regard to the legitimacy of content, we classify webpages into three different categories: normal (completely legitimate), semantic confusion (partially illegitimate), and underground (completely illegitimate).

For example, Fig. 1 shows a webpage of underground economy for illegal online gambling, which is designed for attracting visitors to play online gambling games. Figure 2 shows a webpage with semantic confusion. One part of the content is associated with education that is normal, while the other part is associated with illegal online gambling. As mentioned earlier, such a practice has been prevalent in blackhat SEO to circumvent state-of-the-art detection mechanisms such as [8].

To address this emerging threat, we propose a novel approach for classifying blackhat SEO webpages through the detection of semantic confusion. Figure 3 depicts the workflow of our proposed Semantic Confusion Detection System (SCDS), including data processing, semantics analysis, and SEO collection. In the data processing module, we build a crawler to collect the content of webpages on a large scale, and parse those pages to extract semantic-related content for further analysis. Next, such content is fed into the semantics analyzer module to determine the *semantic context (illegal and normal topics)* of webpages.

If more than one semantic contexts are recognized in a webpage at the same time, we consider the webpage possessing semantic confusion and further inspect

Table 1. Summary of datasets.

Data	Source	Purpose	Period	# Count
$Data_{news}$	THUCNEWS	Training I†	2005–2011	740,000
$Data_{nor/ugd}$	Baidu	Training II‡	2019	130,000
$Domain_{zone}$	Verisign & ICANN	Testing	2020/03	3,000,000
$Domain_{pdns}$	Farsight	Testing	2020/02 - 04	1,500,000
$Domain_{All}$	—	Testing	—	4,500,000

† Normal Semantic Coverage.
‡ Normal/Underground Classification.

whether one of semantic contexts of the webpage is associated with an underground business. As a result, we can effectively identify blackhat SEO pages that aim to promote illegitimate content with semantic confusion to deceive the search engine. Previous studies (*e.g.*, [19]) typically rely on the results from search engines to detect blackhat SEO and only focus on the pages under domain names with specific semantics (*e.g.*, .edu and .gov). However, the results from search engines may introduce inaccuracy due to outdated entries and may also cause bias when the results of search engines are incomplete or manipulated. Our method identifies blackhat SEO pages mainly based on the page content and extends the detection scope to all domains, which could significantly improve efficiency for blackhat SEO detection. In the SEO extension module, we attempt to collect more blackhat SEO pages by leveraging the elements that may present the correlation of blackhat SEO activities. Specifically, we consider two methods to extensively discover potential SEO pages: (1) we extract the external links from identified blackhat SEO pages, and (2) we use a set of blackhat SEO domains as a seed set and search the URLs under these domains that have been indexed by the search engine. We then recursively check whether these pages are also semantic-confusion-based blackhat SEO pages through the semantic analyzer.

3.2 Datasets

A summary of the datasets used in this work is listed in Table 1.

Training Datasets. The recognition of semantic contexts in webpages requires that our training dataset has complete coverage of various topics to the greatest extent possible. We collected two separate datasets for different training purposes: one for normal semantic context recognition and the other for underground economy detection.

(1) For the training dataset of semantic context classification, we use the THUCNEWS[1] dataset, which collected 740,000 pages from the RSS subscrip-

---

[1] The dataset that has been widely used in text-related studies (http://thuctc.thunlp. org/ [in Chinese]). Note that although the dataset itself was compiled based on the News pages from 2005 to 2011, the semantics of the language remains significantly stable and the accuracy of text classification holds too.

tion channel of Sina News, one of the most popular online news sites in China. The dataset, labeled as $Data_{news}$ in our study, covers 14 general news topics, including sports, entertainment, housing, home decoration, fashion, politics, gaming, society, science, finance, *etc.*

(2) For the training dataset of underground economy detection, under the help of Baidu, we collected 100,000 normal webpages and 30,000 webpages of underground economy that have been explicitly labeled by their search engine (*i.e.*, 15,000 illegal online gambling webpages and 15,000 pornographic webpages). We labeled the second dataset as $Data_{nor/ugd}$.

Testing Datasets. Liao *et al.* [19] reported that webpages with semantic inconsistency were found in all different kinds of top-level domains (TLDs). To obtain good coverage of TLDs, we collected the registered domains from 11 different TLDs from which zone files are available. Since this dataset is only for testing and there is no need to crawl the webpages from all domains, we sampled 1.64% of domains from each zone file and obtained 3,000,000 domains in total, labeled as $Domain_{zone}$. Moreover, to enrich the diversity of the testing datasets, we also retrieve DNS records through Farsight [10] DNS database APIs. Since detecting all domains is time-consuming, we select 1,500,000 domains from all A records within 2020, for producing a sufficient coverage within a reasonable time, labeled as $Domain_{pdns}$. The entire testing dataset is labeled as $Domain_{All}$.

3.3 Data Processor

With the domains listed in Table 1, we developed a crawler to obtain the webpages in each domain. We processed the content of webpages in the following steps: (1) In this research, we only consider the text content of HTML pages, so we first stripped JavaScript, CSS, and comments embedded in webpages that are irrelevant to our semantic recognition. (2) We extracted the text from HTML pages (including all text in head and body elements) and removed non-breaking spaces. Note that many pages may play "tricks" with hidden elements (*e.g.*, in <div> labels) including underground economy content to evade detection by normal users. Those hidden elements can be collected in this step. (3) Since most of the pages in our training and testing datasets are in Chinese, we performed word segmentation on the extracted text. It is worthwhile to note that our method is also applicable to webpages in English (or other languages) with no need of word segmentation. (4) We removed the stop words, as well as the words that appear only once, which dramatically decreases the scale of words and mitigates the over-fitting problem. (5) For the rest of the words on the page, we put them together to form a new piece of text for semantic analysis.

3.4 Semantic Analyzer

We are interested in two different semantic contexts: *i.e.*, legitimate topics (*e.g.*, sports and finance) and underground or illegal topics (*e.g.*, illegal online gambling and porn). Accordingly, we developed two independent classifiers to measure

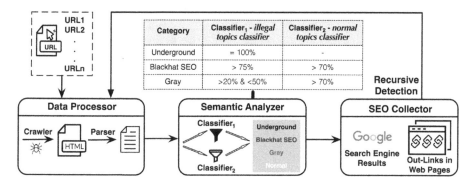

Fig. 3. Architecture of SCDS.

the semantic affinities of webpages to legitimate topics and underground topics, called a *normal topics* classifier and a *illegal topics* classifier, respectively.

The illegal topics classifier, labeled as Classifier$_1$, is trained with the dataset $Data_{nor/ugd}$, for distinguishing the normal topics from underground topics. It produces the possibility that a webpage could be associated with an underground business. The normal content classifier, Classifier$_2$, is trained with the dataset $Data_{news}$ and is used for identifying the normal topic to which the webpages belong. This classifier outputs the possibilities that a webpage belongs to each normal topic, and the sum of all the possibilities is 100%. The topics include sport, entertainment, housing, lottery, home decoration, fashion, politics, games, society, science and technology, stocks, finance, *etc.* We compare six different classification algorithms, including Naive Bayes, Logistic Regression, Random Forest, RNN, FastText and TextCNN. We use F1-measure for measuring the classification accuracy. Based on the classification results, we select TextCNN to build our classification model.

Based on the outputs of the two classifiers above, we define four categories of webpages in our study:

(1) **Underground economy page**. The content on the page is completely associated with underground economy. In this case, the output of Classifier$_1$ is positive, with a probability of 100%.

(2) **Blackhat SEO page**. The webpage contains both normal semantic context and underground economy semantic context. We found that most pages of this kind leverage semantic confusion for blackhat SEO purposes. In this case, the output of Classifier$_1$ is positive, with a probability of between 50% and 100%; and the output of Classifier$_2$ is that the web page belongs to a specific topic, with a probability greater than 70%. The selection of these threshold values is illustrated in Sect. 4. Note that this type of webpages is the primary target of our detection system.

(3) **Gray page**. This kind of webpage also has semantic confusion that is similar to blackhat SEO page. Gray page differs from blackhat SEO page in terms of the output of Classifier$_1$, which has a positive probability ranging from

Fig. 4. A blackhat SEO page with many external links.

Fig. 5. Search results with a specific keywords in Google.

20% to 50%. It indicates that gray pages have less content associated with underground economy compared to blackhat SEO pages. The threshold value we set for Classifier$_1$ is illustrated in Sect. 4. The reason why we classify blackhat SEO pages and gray pages into different categories based on the output of Classifier$_1$, lies in that these two kinds of pages have distinct goals. We will further discuss the differences in Sect. 5.

(4) **Normal page.** If (i) the probability of Classifier$_1$ output is less than 20% and (ii) the Classifier$_2$ indicates the webpage belongs to a normal topic with a probability of greater than 80%, we consider the webpage as a normal page.

Note that the primary targets of our detection are blackhat SEO pages and gray pages, because underground economy pages and normal pages are relatively easy to identify.

3.5 SEO Collector

Next, with the blackhat SEO pages detected in the semantic analyzer, the SEO collector expands the detection by recursively fetching more candidate pages from the identified SEO pages. Those extensive candidate pages are then fed back into the semantic analyzer, which will determine whether the input is a blackhat SEO page. The extension for collecting more candidate pages is achieved through the following two approaches:

(1) **Extension based on hyperlinks on webpages.** Figure 4 shows an example of a typical blackhat SEO page. We can see that the blackhat SEO pages tend to include many hyperlinks pointing to other blackhat SEO pages, which confirms the observation reported in [8]. In this study, we leveraged this feature for expanding the detection of blackhat SEO pages. Specifically, we crawled the external links in the detected blackhat SEO pages and performed the recursive detection to these newly collected pages. Moreover, if the semantic analyzer labels an expended webpage as a blackhat SEO page, it can be further expanded recursively.

(2) **Extension based on search engine results.** As mentioned above, the URLs/webpages under an SEO *domain* would also be likely to contain

SEO content. Modern search engines provide an advanced feature by which the URLs under one domain can be easily found. For example, one can search "`site:wsj.com`" in Google, which will return all URLs under `wsj.com` that have been indexed by Google. Other search engines like Baidu and Bing also provide similar services. Figure 5 shows the search results of "`site:worfwx-tx.cn`" in Google, in which the domain `wx-tx.cn` has been identified as a blackhat SEO domain. We observed that the search results exhibit a number of URLs that have similar content and page layouts. According to the discussion above, the URL under an SEO domain has a high possibility of containing SEO content. Based on the results of search engines, we can expand our detected blackhat SEO pages effectively.

With these two extension methods above, hyperlinks based extension can detect the blackhat SEO pages hosted by different domains, while search engine based extension can detect blackhat SEO pages from the same domain. All of those URLs are also classified as "blackhat SEO pages" by our analyzer, showing that we can effectively expand our detection in practice.

4   Implementation and Evaluation

In this section, we detail the implementation of SCDS, the selection of parameters, and the evaluation of its effectiveness.

4.1   Implementation

Training and Detection. We trained Classifier$_1$ and Classifier$_2$ with the datasets of $Data_{nor/ugd}$ and $Data_{news}$, respectively. First, we extracted text content from those webpages using BeautifulSoup [1], processed text segment with Jieba [2], and removed the blank words and stop words. Then, we employed the Keras library [3] and TextCNN [5] to train our classifiers with a 3:1 ratio of the training data and testing data. The training process was performed on a server with 64GB memory and 12 cores E5-CPU and took about 45 h. As a result, Classifier$_1$ achieves an accuracy of 99.993%, and Classifier$_2$ achieves an accuracy of 96.73%.

As mentioned earlier, we randomly collected 4,500,000 e2LDs (effective second-level domains) from zone files and passive DNS databases to compose the testing dataset $Domain_{All}$. We divided these domains into 10 groups, and deployed 10 crawlers built with Python Selenium Library [4] to crawl the HTML pages of these domains in 10 independent PCs equipped with 32GB memory and 1TB disk. The crawling of webpages was conducted from April 10 to April 15, 2020. We obtained 3,231,942 valid webpages. Note that we could not crawl valid content from the rest of 1.27 million domains because most of them disabled the standard web ports (*e.g.*, 80, 8080, or 443), and a few of them became expired during our experiments. Finally, we used Classifier$_1$ and Classifier$_2$ to recognize the blackhat SEO webpages and gray pages.

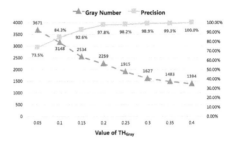

Fig. 6. Impact of different TH_{Gray}.   **Fig. 7.** Impact of different TH_{Normal}.

4.2 Evaluation

Parameter Selection. We describe our selection of key parameters in SCDS.
Gray Bound TH_{Gray}. This parameter is the lower bound for Classifier$_1$ of
the semantic analyzer. In other words, if the possibility of input text is greater
than TH_{Gray}, Classifier$_1$ will determine that the corresponding webpage includes
the content of semantics associated with an underground business. To decide a
proper threshold, we empirically set a value from 0.05 to 0.4 with a step of
0.05, and randomly selected 1,000 samples to run the classification process and
check its effectiveness. The results of precision, along with the number of total
gray pages identified by SCDS under the corresponding parameter, are plotted
in Fig. 6. We set TH_{Gray} to 0.2 since it produces a very high precision (97.8%)
while effectively capturing the most gray pages in our dataset. More specifically,
as the threshold increases greater than 0.2, the increase of precision flats, but at
the same cost of missing more pages that actually belong to the gray category.

Normal Semantic Bound TH_{Normal}. This parameter sets the lower bound
for Classifier$_2$ of the semantic analyzer to check if the input text is normal. For an
input text, if one of the topics in CNEWS is more than TH_{Normal}, we checked it
as content with a normal topic. First, we set the parameter ranging from 0.50 to
0.9 with a step of 0.05, then sampled 1,000 check results to confirm the precision.
The statistics are shown in Fig. 7. Based on the same configuration principle of
TH_{Gray}, we set TH_{Normal} to 0.75, achieving a very high precision (98.3%). The
increase of precision flats afterwards.

SEO Extension. We then deployed our detection model on 10 PCs and evaluated with the testing dataset $Domain_{All}$, which contains 3,231,942 webpages.
Our detection model identifies 75,288 blackhat SEO pages with gambling content
and 3,455 blackhat SEO pages with pornographic content, as well as 2,259 gray
pages (each blackhat SEO or gray page is with an individual domain). Because
of the time limitation, we could not query all the domains in a search engine.
We randomly selected 2,000 detected blackhat SEO domains as the input of the
SEO Collector module to expand the SEO detection. These 2,000 domains are
divided into two parts. (1) We extracted 1,000 domains and searched them in
Google. By collecting the top 10 results of each domain, we obtained 6,117 search

Table 2. Detection result of SCDS.

	#	# Domain	#Gambling URL	# Porn related	# Type of SEO pages		
					Link	iframe	Cloaking
Blackhat SEO	82,061	100,792	78,079	3,982	70,727	4,161	7,173
Gray	2,259	2,259	1,809	450	–	–	–
Total	84,320	103,051	79,888	4,432	70,727	4,161	7,173

results, 5,373 of which are valid webpages. We confirmed that 5,191 of them are blackhat SEO pages (including 4,007 gambling-related webpages and 1,184 porn-related webpages). We manually checked the other 182 pages and found that all of them are semantic confusion webpages, but the text that causes confusion is also with normal topics and no content of underground economy is included. (2) We extracted 23,317 out-links from the other 1,000 domains and confirmed that 16,857 of them are blackhat SEO pages (including 13,791 gambling-related webpages and 3,066 porn-related webpages), which belong to 3,318 e2LDs.

In total, we expanded our detection results with 100,791 blackhat SEO pages, which belong to 82,061 e2LDs. The detection results are shown in Table 2.

Evaluation Results. Due to the lack of ground truth, we manually inspected the results to validate our detection mechanism, which is also a common method used in previous studies [28]. In doing so, we randomly sampled 1,000 pages from the results of blackhat SEO and gray page detection, respectively. In order to ensure precision, two experienced researchers investigated the results independently. The guidelines of our evaluation process are as follows: (1) For gray pages, they inspected whether the page contains underground economy semantics and normal semantics simultaneously. (2) For blackhat SEO pages, they checked the mixed semantics in (1) as well as whether the pages contain hyperlinks that point to external pages, and then checked these domains in search engines to confirm if underground economy content is also indexed by search engines. In our evaluation, when both researchers agreed on a webpage being classified as an SEO page or a Gray page, we determine that the classification result is correct; otherwise, we consider the classification as a false positive case. In the end, we identified 989 blackhat SEO pages and 978 gray pages, with an precision of 98.35%. Furthermore, we deployed the detection system on our campus network for 10 months, and the detection results have been acknowledged by IT security department, justifying the effectiveness of our detection system.

5 Measurement

In this section, we present our measurement results of detecting mixed semantic pages. We first characterize blackhat SEO domains and perform an analysis on both keywords and content extracted from blackhat SEO pages. We then cluster the detected domains by external links to infer the SEO campaigns and describe our real-world deployment.

```
1  | <head>
2  |   <title>
3  |     Gambling Website_Betting
        Game_Macau Gaming
        Games_Cash Gaming
        Games_[Online
        Entertainment]_Cash games
4  |   </title>
5  | </head>
6  |
7  | <body>
8  |   <iframe scrolling ="no"
          frameborder="0"
          marginheight="0"
          marginwidth="0" width="
          100%" height="4000"
          allowtransparency="" src="
          http://www.pankou8.com/"
          ></iframe>
9  |
10 |   <ul class="nav−list" id="
        J_navlist">
11 |     <li><a href="/">Home</a
          ></li>
12 |     <li><a href="/">Education
          </a></li>
13 |     <li><a href="/">Political<
          /a></li>
14 |     ...
15 |   </ul>
16 |   ...
17 | </body>
```

Fig. 8. HTML of iframe based blackhat SEO page.

```
1  | <script type="text/javascript"  style ="display:
        none;">
2  |   var strRef=document.referrer;
3  |   var robots=['baidu ',' google ',' yahoo ',' bing
          ',' soso ',' sogou ',' so ',' youdao ',' jike
          ',' anquan ','360.cn ',' haosou '];
4  |   var ishave=false;
5  |
6  |   for(var t in robots){
7  |     if (strRef .indexOf(robots[t])!=−1){
8  |       ishave=true;
9  |       if (parent.window.opener){
10 |         parent.window.opener.location='
              https://www.tc8806.com/';
11 |   }
12 | </script>
```

Fig. 9. JS Code of cloak-based blackhat SEO page.

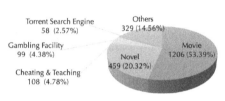

Fig. 10. Category of gray pages.

5.1   Overview

Blackhat SEO Pages. With the semantic confusion detection, we explore the features of those blackhat SEO pages and identify three major categories:

(1) *Blackhat SEO with Links.* To gain better SEO effectiveness, SEOers usually embed numerous external links that point to other blackhat SEO pages or target pages, *e.g.*, the links of gambling websites (see Fig. 4).

As discussed in Sect. 4, we discovered 100,791 blackhat SEO pages from 82,061 different e2LDs and 2,259 gray pages. The statistics of our detection results are listed in Table 2.

(2) *Blackhat SEO with iframe.* Typically in a blackhat SEO page with an iframe, an SEOer will set the width of the iframe to 100% and the height to even more than 2000px, to ensure that the iframe will be displayed in full screen and the content can be displayed to visitors in its entirety. Figure 8 shows an example of mixed semantics, where the text in the title promotes gambling webpages while the text in the body presents a normal page. When users visit this page, they will see content from another website, instead of the original page that is hidden by the full-screen iframe. To recognize this category, we first determine whether a page contains iframe tag. If it does, we check the width/height attributes of the tag. If the width is 100% and the height is higher than 2000 (covering visual areas), it is considered as a blackhat SEO page with iframe.

(3) *Blackhat SEO with cloaking.* Cloaking is a common practice exploited by blackhat SEOers to cheat the search engines [15]. When visited by human users, cloaking pages will bring them to the sites that SEOers want them to visit. However, when crawled by search engines, cloaking pages will feed them with normal content copied from other popular sites. Figure 9 shows a blackhat SEO page with cloaking, where the script embedded in the page checks if a visitor is a human user or a crawler, and then decide which strategy to adopt. From Table 2, we can see that more than 95% of blackhat SEO pages are link-based SEO, which is apparently due to its simplicity and efficiency. To recognize this category, we fetch all blackhat SEO pages twice. We first retrieve the page content normally. Then, we modify the *referrer* field of the browser to 'baidu.com' to obtain cloaked content. If the page content is different, it is considered as an blackhat SEO page with cloaking.

Gray Pages. Different from blackhat SEO pages whose potential target is the crawlers of search engines, gray pages are mainly target human users. Based on the types of their underground content, we classify gray pages into two main categories:

(1) *Gray pages with pornographic content.* These pages do not explicitly advocate unvarnished pornographic content, but offer normal content with a small portion of pornography simultaneously, *e.g.*, a movie website mainly provides normal films but also hosts pornographic videos. In addition, another group of webpages may provide seeds of Magnet URI[2] or BitTorrent[3] often suggest pornographic content to visitors.

(2) *Gray pages with gambling content.* Unlike the gambling blackhat SEO pages that usually direct visitors to gambling sites, these pages often have content about how to play gambling games, how to buy gambling facilities, or even how to cheat while gambling.

Next, we also examine the normal topics that the gray pages belong to. The statistics are shown in Fig. 10. We can see that more than 70% of gray pages are with movie or novel, indicating that not only the webpages in these two categories have the broadest visitor base, but they also have the types of content directly related to the pornographic content (*i.e.*, videos and literature).

5.2   SEO Domains

Here we group and characterize the domains hosting blackhat SEO pages with their IP geolocation, TLDs, and domain registration.

IP Geolocation. In order to analyze the IP geolocation of blackhat SEO domains, we first used the APIs provided by Farsight's passive DNS database [10] to query the current and historical IP addresses of all blackhat SEO domains.

---

[2] http://magnet-uri.sourceforge.net/, a URI-scheme in P2P file sharing for enabling resources to be referred to without an available host.

[3] https://www.bittorrent.com/, a popular file-sharing P2P tool based on distributed hash table (DHT) method.

Table 3. Top 5 countries/regions for hosting blackhat SEO domains.

No.	Country	# IP	# Domain
1	United States	43,456	52,079
2	Hong Kong	6,729	8,877
3	South Africa	2,311	2,529
4	Netherlands	1,927	2,098
5	China	722	1,136
Total	–	55,145	66,719

Then, we used the GEOLite2 database from MaxMind [21] to search the AS number and location of each IP address. We observed that most of these black-hat SEO domains are located in United States, followed by Hong Kong. This reflects the practice of blackhat SEOers for avoiding local supervision. We show the country-level IP geolocation in Table 3 and the AS information in Table 4.

Table 4. Top 5 SEO-hosting ASNs (sorted by the number of hosted domains).

NO.	ASN	Organizations	# IP	# Domain
1	AS18978	ENZUINC (US)	6,626	10,642
2	AS35916	MULTA-ASN1 (US)	6,607	7,509
3	AS15003	NOBIS-TECH (US)	6,758	7,060
4	AS40676	Psychz Networks (US)	5,096	5,648
5	AS38197	Sun Network (HongKong) Ltd. (HK)	4,846	5,217
Total	-	-	29,933	36,076

TLD distribution. We find that .com and .cn are still the most popular domains that are abused for blackhat SEO, accounting for 63.12% and 18.49%, respectively. Table 5 lists the statistics of top-level domains and predefined second-level domains.

Table 5. Top 5 TLDs/predefined-SLDs for mixed semantic domains.

No.	TLD/SLD	# Total	# SEO	# Gray	%
1	.com	53,225	51,779	1,446	63.12%
2	.cn	15,588	15,251	337	18.49%
3	.top	7,025	6,935	90	8.31%
4	.net	2,363	2,292	71	2.80%
5	.com.cn	2,349	2,319	30	2.79%
Total	–	80,550	78,576	1,974	95.51%

Domain Registration. We retrieved the domain registration information through WHOIS database. Due to the effect of GDPR [14], the registrant information like emails and telephone numbers is mostly hidden now. Finally, we obtained 56,672 valid WHOIS records showing the registrar information. Table 6 lists the top 5 registrars that operate the most domains abused for blackhat SEO. The most common registrars are Alibaba's cloud platform (aliyun.com).

Content Analysis. In order to understand the content that blackhat SEOers prefer to use, we collected the normal semantic of each blackhat SEO page. We found that the content from education websites is the most widely used by blackhat SEO pages. This is likely because the education-based content has good reputation and can easily catch the attention of human users and gain their trust to read it. The content distribution is shown in Fig. 11.

Table 6. Top 5 registrars for SEO domains.

Registrar	# Count	%
Alibaba Cloud Computing, Ltd	11,210	13.66%
Chengdu West Dimension Digital Technology Co., Ltd.	9,937	12.11%
Xin Net Technology Corporation	4,416	5.38%
GoDaddy.com, LLC	4,169	5.08%
Bizcn.COM, Inc	2,785	3.39%
Total	32,517	39.62%

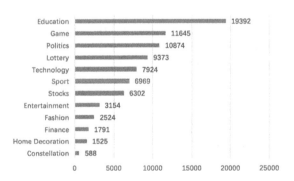

Fig. 11. Normal semantic distribution of blackhat SEO pages.

5.3   SEO Campaigns

Cluster Based on External Links. We first clustered the domains based on the external links embedded in blackhat SEO pages. *i.e.*, if a group of domains have the blackhat SEO pages that include the same link pointing to a unique target, we grouped them as a cluster. We filtered out the high-reputation domains from Alexa top 10 thousand list. Then, we crawled these target links and used Classifier$_1$ to detect whether they include underground content. If identified, we recognized it as the promotion target of a blackhat SEO campaign. Through this method, we successfully identified 157 SEO campaigns, covering 21,374 different domains that participate in these campaigns. In particular, the largest SEO campaign we detected includes 1,758 SEO domains, all of which are with iframe pages and are targeted on the domain of `7497999.com`.

Table 7. Visitor analytic service providers.

No.	Provider	# SEOer	# Domain	% Domain
1	hm.baidu.com	2,335	31,076	37.87%
2	51la.com	1,745	20,977	25.56%
3	51yes.com	279	2,497	3.04%
4	cnzz.com	432	781	0.95%
5	others	–	26,730	32.58%
Total	–	**4,791**	**82,061**	**100.00%**

Cluster Based on Statistics ID. To make a profit through the campaigns, blackhat SEOers need to embed their statistics ID in the pages and monitor the visitor count during the campaign. Typically, they insert a snippet of JavaScript into HTML source code to trigger the browser to visit a specific URL and record the visitor count. We examined the HTML source code of detected pages to extract statistics IDs based on the URL patterns presented by various service providers. For example, in an embedded JavaScript code

```
<script language="javascript" src="http://
count1.51yes.com/click.aspx?id=12345678"></script>
```

the URL points to the visitor analytic provider, and the parameter " id=12345678" presents the SEOer's ID. As shown in Table 7, the four most popular service providers for visitor analytics in China are: baidu.com, 51la.com, 51yes.com, and cnzz.com. Among those, Baidu is the most popular provider adopted by blackhat SEOers.

Comparison. We compared the clustering results between the external link-based method and the ID-based method. The former captures a group of domains that promote the same target websites while the latter identifies the domains dominated by the same blackhat SEOer. In order to improve the effectiveness of promotion, a website owner may purchase an SEO service from multiple blackhat SEOers to form a larger-scale campaign. Table 8 lists the top 5 campaigns with the most participating domains and the number of statistics ID it used. Since most of the objects we detect are blackhat SEO pages targeting Chinese users, they mainly use analytic providers in China. We also find a small portion of blackhat SEO pages using Google Analytics.

Table 8. Top 5 SEO Campaigns for promotion.

	Target	# Domain	# IP	# Country	# ID
Camp. 1	7497999.com	1,758	35	2	2
Camp. 2	hg18217.com	1,440	1,026	2	22
Camp. 3	yifageen68.cn	1,294	19	2	4
Camp. 4	jiuwuzhizun8.com	823	14	3	1
Camp. 5	187bet.com	661	335	4	3

5.4   Real-World Deployment

During our study, we deployed the SCDS at the gateway of our campus network (with more than 30K users). We collected the domains from DNS query records through the campus network, crawled the domains and checked whether their webpages contain the mingled semantic content (*i.e.*, semantic confusion). We deployed our system from April 5, 2020 to January 10, 2021, obtained 11,547,471 unique domain names, and detected 23,093 domains with semantic confusion (including 21,097 blackhat SEO and 1,996 gray pages).

6   Practical Issues

Impact on Search Engines. As illustrated in Sect. 3, for recursive detection, we extended blackhat SEO pages with semantic confusion by utilizing Google. In this step, we first selected 1,000 blackhat SEO domains (including 800 gambling and 200 pornographic domains), and searched them using Google. We then obtained 5,373 valid search results and confirmed that 5,191 blackhat SEO URLs are indexed by Google. From this, we can see that these blackhat SEO pages have an actual effect on search engine results. To compare the impact among different search engines, we randomly selected 5 SEO domains and searched them in Baidu (the most widely used search engine in China), collecting the top 20 results. We counted the number of blackhat SEO domains in the search results, as shown in Table 9. It can be seen that these sites pollute search engine results.

Table 9. Number of SEO URLs appearing in search results of SEO domains.

Domain	Category	Google	Baidu
tcppower.com	Gambling	12	20
tongyunhr.com	Gambling	20	5
skfjr.com	Gambling	0	20
flyco360.com	Gambling	20	20
jrzgxw.com.cn	Porn	20	0

Popular Website Templates. In order to enhance the cheating effect, black-hat SEO sites crawl HTML pages from authoritative sites and mix blackhat SEO content with them. To cheat search engines, blackhat SEO pages may keep part of the original title information in the new pages, *e.g.*, making a new title as a combination of Blackhat SEO keywords and original title information. We extracted all the "original title information" parts and clustered them into groups. In particular, we found that there are 771 blackhat SEO pages built based on the official webpage of "Chinese Academic of Science" and 164 pages built based on the official webpage of "Tencent," which operates the most popular Instant Messaging tools in China. Moreover, we noticed that the blackhat SEOers widely use open-source webpage templates to construct their pages. The bottom of these pages usually contain words such as "`Powered by [template provider]`", with a link to the template supply website. During the link extraction process, we found that dedecms.com, dede58.com, and adminbuy.cn are the most commonly used open-source template supply websites for constructing blackhat SEO webpages, enabling 1,703, 1,562, and 1,387 domains, respectively.

7   Discussion

Responsible Disclosure and Feedback. We reported the detection results to QiAnXin [4] and our network administration team every day. Our work can help in the following ways: (1) help search engines to identify webpages with blackhat SEO content, (2) help security practitioners to be aware of the trend of all kinds of underground economies with emerging content, (3) help security enterprises to classify webpages more accurately, especially those in "gray" host hybrid content. In the future, we will collaborate with security practitioners to deploy SCDS in real-world network environments to further investigate blackhat SEO webpages at a large scale.

Language Dependency. Our training procedure relies on the training data, and the detection result is dependent on the quality of the collected training data. Due to dataset limits, our detection mainly focused on blackhat SEO pages that promote illegal gambling/pornography content on Chinese webpages. However, we believe the identified phenomenon also exists in such SEO pages in other languages. Moreover, we demonstrated the effectiveness of our detection. If datasets belong to other languages could be obtained, our method will effectively detect the corresponding blackhat SEO pages.

Gary Page. In this study, we explicitly identified the gray pages that have not been well examined before. Limited by dataset, we only focused on gray pages related to gambling/pornography. If there are more types of training data, more gray pages related to different underground businesses could be detected.

Evasion. If blackhat SEOers had been aware of our detection mechanism, they may explore the evasion by reducing the content related to the underground

---

[4] QiAnXin is a leading Cybersecurity company in China (https://en.qianxin.com).

economy in HTML pages or adding various normal topics. However, such strategies would also significantly reduce the effectiveness of promotion, which is also a goal of our detection system.

Ethical Considerations. Since we deployed the SCDS on the gateway of our campus network, there could a concern about personal information and privacy leakage. Here we only extracted domain names and excluded any other information. Therefore, there is no risk of revealing a user's personal and private information to a third party in our study.

8 Related Work

Blackhat SEO. To understand the blackhat SEO activities, significant efforts have been spent to explore its ecosystem and practice. Wang *et al.* [27] infiltrated an SEO botnet and showed that it is quite effective in poisoning trending search terms, given its small size. Liao *et al.* [18] characterized the long-tail SEO that promotes longer and more specific keyword phrases targeting niche markets. To thwart the threat of blackhat SEO, search engines have developed many defense mechanisms. John *et al.* [16] leveraged URL signatures to identify SEO pages from a dataset of URLs provided by search engines. Lu *et al.* [20] detected search poisoning by inspecting the redirection chains unfolded when visiting a search result. The countermeasures of search engines were effective to some extent, but challenges still remain [16,17,26]. Complementary to the existing studies, our work focuses on an emerging trend of blackhat SEO, which leverages semantic confusion to disguise the content of underground economy with the text of normal topics.

Underground Economy. Prior studies have conducted in-depth analysis of different types of the underground economy, including scam [25], email spam [7], promotion infection [19], illegal commodity transaction [22] and social media spam [23]. In particular, to evade detection, the practitioners of the underground economy usually use jargon to disguise their activities. Yang *et al.* [28] and Yuan *et al.* [29] proposed different methodologies to discover such jargon or black keywords.

9 Conclusion

In this paper, we conducted the first systematic investigation of a recent trend in blackhat SEO, *semantic confusion*, by which blackhat SEOers can promote underground business by disguising their content with legitimate topics. To address this emerging threat, we developed an effective detection system that can identify such semantic-confusion-based blackhat SEO webpages with high precision. Further, we performed a comprehensive measurement study to characterize the ecosystem of blackhat SEO. Finally, we deployed our system in a gateway for real-world evaluation, showing that semantic confusion has been prevalent in blackhat SEO. Our study will help the security community to pay more serious attention to blackhat SEO detection for fighting cybercrime. In the future, we will collaborate with security practitioners to enlarge the detection scale of SCDS.

Appendix

A Practices of Semantic Confusion

We further analyzed the method of embedding mingled semantics in SEO pages and identified three main categories: (1) Modify only the `<title>` tag, and keep all other parts the same. This is because search engines often pay more attention to the `<title>` tag and the text in the title has a higher probability to be indexed. Also, blackhat SEOers do not want to be detected due to the modification of the pages or the mixed illegal content. (2) Embed the same promotion keywords into different paragraphs repeatedly. Appropriate repeats are helpful for search engines to extract keywords and give them a higher rank. These two methods mainly target search engines. (3) Replace the total paragraph with promotion content. This category mainly targets visitors and aims to attract them immediately upon arrival at the webpage. The replaced content is short-lived because it is easily noticed by search engines and webmasters.

Fig. 12. Gambling software development in GitHub.

Fig. 13. Gambling shop in JingDong (`jd.com`).

B Keyword Promotion in Other Platforms

GitHub. In our study, we found that some blackhat SEOers are promoting GitHub repositories of gambling software development services. Specifically, when we searched "`github.com+[gambling keywords]`" in Google, the results show many GitHub repositories introducing gambling software, and the descriptions of these repositories include the developer's contact information (*e.g.*, phone numbers and IM IDs). Another practice is to place a large number of gambling keywords in a repository's introduction through which search engines can index them. For example, Fig. 12 shows the search results of a gambling keyword "真人视讯" (a dark jargon that means "Live Dealer Casino Games" in

underground gambling business) with "`github.com`" in Google. The top results are mostly GitHub repositories that promote gambling development services.
E-Commerce. We also found that the keywords promoted by blackhat SEO pages were not only used in search engines, but they also appeared on E-Commerce websites. For example, when we searched the most frequent keyword, `pk10` on jd.com (a well-known E-Commerce website in China), there were shops that provide illegal gambling software development services, as shown in Fig. 13. Therefore, we recommend that E-Commerce websites should also pay attention to the identification and purification of such activities related to the underground business in search results.

References

1. Beautiful soup documentation - beautiful soup 4.9.0 documentation (2020). https://www.crummy.com/software/BeautifulSoup/bs4/doc/
2. Github - fxsjy/jieba. https://github.com/fxsjy/jieba (2020)
3. Keras: the Python deep learning API (2020). https://keras.io/
4. SeleniumHQ Browser Automation (2020). https://www.selenium.dev/
5. Textcnn - pytorch and keras — kaggle (2020). https://www.kaggle.com/mlwhiz/textcnn-pytorch-and-keras
6. Chung, Y.j., Toyoda, M., Kitsuregawa, M.: A study of link farm distribution and evolution using a time series of web snapshots. In: International Workshop on Adversarial Information Retrieval on the Web (2009)
7. Cormack, G.V.: Email spam filtering: a systematic review. Found. Trends Inf. Retr. **1**(4), 335–455 (2007)
8. Du, K., Yang, H., Li, Z., Duan, H., Zhang, K.: The ever-changing labyrinth: a large-scale analysis of wildcard DNS powered blackhat SEO. In: USENIX Security (2016)
9. Enge, E., Spencer, S., Fishkin, R., Stricchiola, J.: The Art of SEO. O'Reilly Media, Inc. (2012)
10. Farsight (2020). https://www.farsightsecurity.com/
11. Fishkin, R.: Indexation for SEO: Real Numbers in 5 Easy Steps (2010). https://moz.com/blog/indexation-for-seo-real-numbers-in-5-easy-steps
12. Google: Search Engine Optimization Starter Guide (2008). http://static.googleusercontent.com/media/www.google.com/en//webmasters/docs/search-engine-optimization-starter-guide.pdf
13. Google: Search Engine Optimization (SEO) Starter Guide (2020). https://support.google.com/webmasters/answer/7451184?hl=en
14. ICANN: Data Protection/Privacy Issues (2018). https://www.icann.org/dataprotectionprivacy
15. Invernizzi, L., Thomas, K., Kapravelos, A., Comanescu, O., Picod, J.M., Bursztein, E.: Cloak of visibility: detecting when machines browse a different web. In: IEEE S&P (2016)
16. John, J.P., Yu, F., Xie, Y., Krishnamurthy, A., Abadi, M.: deSEO: combating search-result poisoning. In: USENIX Security (2011)
17. Leontiadis, N., Moore, T., Christin, N.: A nearly four-year longitudinal study of search-engine poisoning. In: ACM CCS (2014)
18. Liao, X., Liu, C., McCoy, D., Shi, E., Hao, S., Beyah, R.A.: Characterizing Long-tail SEO Spam on Cloud Web Hosting Services. In: WWW (2016)

19. Liao, X., et al.: Seeking nonsense, looking for trouble: efficient promotional-infection detection through semantic inconsistency search. In: IEEE S&P (2016)
20. Lu, L., Perdisci, R., Lee, W.: Surf: detecting and measuring search poisoning. In: ACM CCS (2011)
21. MaxMind (2020). https://www.maxmind.com/en/home
22. Motoyama, M., McCoy, D., Levchenko, K., Savage, S., Voelker, G.M.: An analysis of underground forums. In: ACM IMC (2011)
23. Nilizadeh, S., et al.: Poised: spotting twitter spam off the beaten paths. In: ACM CCS (2017)
24. SEOmoz: Google Algorithm Change History (2016). https://moz.com/google-algorithm-change
25. Tu, H., Doupé, A., Zhao, Z., Ahn, G.J.: Users really do answer telephone scams. In: USENIX Security (2019)
26. Wang, D.Y., Der, M., Karami, M., Saul, L., McCoy, D., Savage, S., Voelker, G.M.: Search+seizure: the effectiveness of interventions on SEO campaigns. In: ACM IMC (2014)
27. Wang, D.Y., Savage, S., Voelker, G.M.: Juice: a Longitudinal Study of an SEO Botnet. In: NDSS (2013)
28. Yang, H., et al.: How to learn klingon without a dictionary: detection and measurement of black keywords used by the underground economy. In: IEEE S&P (2017)
29. Yuan, K., Lu, H., Liao, X., Wang, X.: Reading thieves' cant: automatically identifying and understanding Dark Jargons from cybercrime marketplaces. In: USENIX Security (2018)
30. Zhang, Q., Wang, D.Y., Voelker, G.M.: DSpin: detecting automatically spun content on the web. In: NDSS (2014)

An Explainable Online Password Strength Estimator

Liron David$^{(\boxtimes)}$ and Avishai Wool$^{(\boxtimes)}$

School of Electrical Engineering, Tel Aviv University, Tel Aviv, Israel
lirondavid@gmail.com, yash@eng.tau.ac.il

Abstract. Human-chosen passwords are the dominant form of authentication systems. Passwords strength estimators are used to help users avoid picking weak passwords by predicting how many attempts a password cracker would need until it finds a given password.

In this paper we propose a novel password strength estimator, called PESrank, which accurately models the behavior of a powerful password cracker. PESrank calculates the rank of a given password in an optimal descending order of likelihood. PESrank estimates a given password's rank in fractions of a second—without actually enumerating the passwords—so it is practical for online use. It also has a training time that is drastically shorter than previous methods. Moreover, PESrank is efficiently *tweakable* to allow model personalization in fractions of a second, without the need to retrain the model; and it is *explainable*: it is able to provide information on *why* the password has its calculated rank, and gives the user insight on how to pick a better password.

We implemented PESrank in Python and conducted an extensive evaluation study of it. We also integrated it into the registration page of a course at our university. Even with a model based on 905 million passwords, the response time was well under 1 s, with up to a 1-bit accuracy margin between the upper bound and the lower bound on the rank.

1 Introduction

1.1 Background

Text passwords are still the most popular authentication and are still in widespread use specially for online authentication on the Internet. Unfortunately, users often choose predictable and easy passwords, enabling password guessing attacks. Password strength estimators are used to help users avoid picking weak passwords. Usually they appear as password meters that provide visual feedback on password strength [42]. The most precise definition of password's strength is *the number of attempts that an attacker would need in order to guess it* [13].

A common way to evaluate the strength of a password is by heuristic methods, e.g., based on counts of lower- and uppercase characters, digits, and symbols (LUDS). Theses password-composition policies have grown increasingly complex [25]. Despite it being well-known that these do not accurately capture password strength [46], they are still used in practice.

© Springer Nature Switzerland AG 2021
E. Bertino et al. (Eds.): ESORICS 2021, LNCS 12972, pp. 285–304, 2021.
https://doi.org/10.1007/978-3-030-88418-5_14

Subsequently, more sophisticated, cracker-based, password strength estimators have been proposed. In a cracker-based estimator, either an actual password cracker is utilized to evaluate the password strength—or the estimator uses an accurate model of the number of attempts a particular cracker would use until reaching the given password. The main approaches have been based on, e.g., Markov models [15,31,35], probabilistic context-free grammars (PCFGs) [28,47], neural networks [34,41] and others [20,49]. Based on the well known phenomenon that people often use attributes of their personal information in their passwords (their names, email addresses, birthdays etc.), [23,29,45] have proposed to tweak the prior models, based on personal information known about a given user's password.

In this work we propose a novel addition to this line of research, called PESrank. Our goal is to provide a password strength estimator that enjoys the following properties:

- It is a cracker-based estimator, that accurately models the behavior of a powerful password cracker. The modeled cracker calculates the rank of a given password in an optimal descending order of likelihood.
- It is practical for *online* use, and is able to estimate a given password's rank in fractions of a second—i.e., without actually enumerating the passwords.
- Has reasonable training time, drastically shorter than previous methods (some of which require days of training).
- It is efficiently *tweakable* to allow model personalization, without the need to retrain the model.
- It is *explainable*, and provides feedback on *why* the password has its calculated rank, giving the user insight on how to pick a better password.

1.2   Contributions

Our idea in the design of PESrank is to cast the question of password rank estimation in a probabilistic framework used in side-channel cryptanalysis. We view each password as a point in a d-dimensional search space, and learn the probability distribution of each dimension separately. This learning process is based on empirical password frequencies extracted from leaked password corpora, that are projected onto the d dimensions. Once the d probability distributions are learned, the a-priori probability of a given password is the *product* of the d probabilities of its sub-passwords.

Using this model, optimal-order password cracking is done by searching the space in decreasing order of a-priori password probability, which is analogous to side-channel key enumeration; likewise, password strength estimation is analogous to side-channel rank estimation. There is extensive research and well known algorithms for both problems in the side-channel cryptanalysis literature. We adopt a leading side-channel rank estimation (ESrank, [10]) for use in PESrank—which accurately models an optimal key enumeration, or equivalently, password enumeration algorithm. The ESrank algorithm also has accuracy guarantees providing both upper-and lower-bounds on the true rank.

PESrank's training time is very reasonable, taking minutes-to-hours. It is also efficiently *tweakable* to allow model personalization, without the need to retrain the model. In addition, PESrank is able to *explain* the password strength value: For example, PESrank can indicate that the password newyork123 is based on a leaked word that was used by 129,023 people, and uses a very popular suffix that was used by over 17 million people. Such explainability is very important since it helps guide the user on how to pick better passwords. This is in contrast to prior methods, especially those based on neural networks, which offer little - to no explainability.

In order to demonstrate PESrank's capabilities as an online password strength estimator we implemented PESrank in Python and integrated it into the registration page of a course at our university. Even with a model based on 905 million passwords, the end-to-end response time in the browser was well under 1 s, with up to a 1-bit accuracy margin between the upper bound and the lower bound on the rank. This allowed us to run a proof-of-concept study on how students reacted to their passwords' strength estimates.

We conducted an extensive evaluation study comparing PESrank's accuracy to prior approaches. In our study we used Ur et al.'s Password Guessability Service [5] (PGS), which provides access to the Hashcat [21] and John the Ripper [36] crackers, the Markov [35] and PCFGs [47] methods, and to the neural-network method [34] (Monte-Carlo variant). We compared the ranks calculated by PESrank to the ranks obtained by these five password strength estimators. We show that PESrank (and, in fact, the optimal password cracker it models) is more powerful than previous methods: the model-based cracker can crack more passwords, with fewer attempts, than the password crackers we compared it to for crackable passwords whose rank is smaller than 10^{11}. Due to space constrains, many details have been omitted from this paper and are present in our full technical report [2].

2   Rank Estimation and Key Enumeration in Cryptographic Side-Channel Attacks

Side-channel attacks (SCA) represent a serious threat to the security of cryptographic hardware products. As such, they reveal the secret key of a cryptosystem based on leakage information gained from physical implementation of the cryptosystem on different devices. Information provided by sources such as timing [27], power consumption [26], electromagnetic emulation [39], electromagnetic radiation [1, 16] and other sources, can be exploited by SCA to break cryptosystems. A security evaluation of a cryptographic device should determine whether an implementation is secure against such an attack. To do so, the evaluator needs to determine how much time, what kind of computing power and how much storage a malicious attacker would need to recover the key given the side-channel leakages. The leakage of cryptographic implementations is highly device-specific, therefore the usual strategy for an evaluation laboratory is to launch a set of popular attacks, and to determine whether the adversary can break the implementation (i.e., recover the key) using "reasonable" efforts.

Most of the attacks that have been published in the literature are based on a "divide-and-conquer" strategy. In the first "divide" part, the cryptanalyst recovers multi-dimensional information about different parts of the key, usually called subkeys (e.g., each of the $d = 16$ AES key bytes can be a subkey). In the "conquer" part the cryptanalyst combines the information all together in an efficient way via key enumeration, for one of two purposes as follows.

The Key Enumeration Problem. The cryptanalyst obtains d independent subkey spaces $k_1, ..., k_d$, each of size n, and their corresponding probability distributions $P_{k_1}, ..., P_{k_d}$. The problem is to enumerate the full-key space in decreasing probability order, from the most likely key to the least, when the probability of a full key is defined as the product of its subkey's probabilities, and test each full key in turn until the correct secret key is found.

A naive solution for key enumeration is to take the Cartesian product of the d dimensions, and sort the n^d full keys in decreasing order of probability. However this approach is generally infeasible due to both time and space complexity. Therefore several algorithms offering better time/space tradeoffs have been devised. The currently best optimal-order key enumeration is [44], with an $O(n^{d/2})$ space complexity, and near-optimal-order key enumeration algorithms with drastically lower space complexities are those of [3,9,32,33,38].

Unlike a cryptanalyst trying to extract the secret key, a security evaluator knows the secret key and aims to estimate the number of decryption attempts the attacker needs to do before he reaches the correct key, assuming the attacker uses the SCA's multi-dimensional probability distributions. Formally:

The Rank Estimation Problem: Given d independent subkey spaces of sizes n_i for $i = 1, ..., d$ with their corresponding probability distributions $P_1, ..., P_d$ such that P_i is sorted in decreasing order of probabilities, and given a key k^* indexed by $(k_1, ..., k_d)$, let $p^* = P_1(k_1) \cdot P_2(k_2) \cdot ... \cdot P_d(k_d)$ be the probability of k^* to be the correct key. The problem is to estimate the number of full keys with probability higher than p^*, when the probability of a full key is defined as the product of its subkey's probabilities. In other words, the evaluator would like to estimate k^*'s *rank*: the position of the key k^* in the list of n^d possible keys when the list is sorted in decreasing probability order, from the most likely key to the least.

While enumerating the keys in the optimal SCA-predicted order is a correct strategy for the evaluator, it is limited by the computational power of the evaluator. Hence using algorithms to estimate the rank of a given key, without enumeration, is of great interest. Multiple rank estimation algorithms appear in the literature, the best of which are currently [10,17,33]. They all work in fractions of a second and generally offer sub 1-bit accuracy (so up to a multiplicative factor of 2).

3   Multi-dimensional Models for Passwords

3.1   Overview

The starting point in producing a password strength estimator is a leaked password corpus. The frequency of appearance of each leaked password provides an a-priori probability distribution over the leaked passwords. Given a hash of an unknown password, trying the leaked passwords in decreasing frequency order, is the optimal strategy for a password cracker—if the password at hand is in the corpus. To crack passwords that are not in the leaked corpus *as-is*, password crackers rely on the observation that people often take a word, which we shall call the *base word*, and mutate it using various transformations such as adding digits and symbols before or after the base word, capitalizing some of the base word's letters, or replacing letters by digits or symbols that are visually similar using "l33t" translations.

Our main idea is that if we can represent the list of base words as a dimension, and represent each possible class of transformations as another independent dimension, we can pose the password cracking problem as a key enumeration problem, and similarly, pose the password strength estimation as a rank estimation problem. Each dimension should have its own probability distribution. Once we pose the password strength estimation question this way, we can use existing algorithms. A multi-dimensional password cracker would enumerate combinations of base word plus a transformation in every dimension, in decreasing order of the *product* of per-dimension a-priori probabilities. For each combination it would apply the current set of transformations to the base word, and test the password. The matching multi-dimensional password strength estimator decomposes a given password into its base word and a transformation in every dimension, uses the model to calculate the a-priori probability of the password, and then estimates its rank *without enumeration*.

Thus, we arrive at the following framework: First, identify meaningful classes of transformations, and find a suitable representation for each as a dimension. Next, build a probability distribution for each dimension using the training corpus, to create a model. Finally, use a good rank estimation algorithm with the model and evaluate its performance.

3.2   The Data Corpus

To study the statistical properties of passwords, and then to train our method, we used Jason's corpus of leaked passwords [24]. This corpus contains 1.4 billion pairs of username and password, compiled from multiple leaked corpora: Yahoo, Target, Facebook, Hotmail, Twitter, MySpace, hacked PHPBB instances, and many other sources. We believe that Jason's corpus is a superset of the corpora used to train previous methods. After eliminating passwords that contain non-ASCII characters and eliminated garbage "passwords" of more than 32 characters we obtained a corpus of 905,060,363 passwords.

Table 1. Leaked password patterns in Jason's corpus

Start with digits/symbols	8.946%
End with digits/symbols	50.237%
Use capital letters	7.665%
Use l33t transformations	9.863%

From this corpus we sampled 300,000 username-password pairs, to serve as a test set. We split the test set into 10 separate samples, of 30,000 passwords each, and submitted all the sample sets to PGS for evaluation. To compare the ranks we received from PGS to those of PESrank, we trained PESrank on the same training corpora used by the PGS implementations of the various methods, as follows:

- **PGS set:** According to [5] the PCFG, Markov, hashcat and JtR algorithms were trained on 6 corpora, totalling 33 million passwords, plus 6 million natural language words, collectively called the "PGS training set". We used this set to select the dimensions of PESrank and when we compared the performance of PESrank to that of PCFG, Markov, hashcat and JtR.
- **PGS++ set:** According to [5] the Neural algorithm was trained on a passwords from a large superset of the PGS set including 26 additional corpora, called the "PGS++ training set". We used this set when comparing to the Neural algorithm.
- **Jason:** To test PESrank's training time, for the usability proof of concept and for stand-along performance evaluation we used the full Jason corpus with its 905 million leaked passwords.

3.3 Selecting Dimensions

Following [49] we chose the dimensions according to the patterns humans tend to choose in their passwords: prefixes and suffixes (e.g., iloveyou!! or 123iloveyou), mixed letter case (e.g., iLoVeyOu), and leet speak (e.g., il0v3you). We also verified the observations of [49] in Jason's corpus: Table 1 shows that significant fractions of the leaked passwords fit our choice of dimensions. After checking several options, (see technical report [2]), we chose the following five dimensions: prefix, base word, suffix, capitalization and l33t. Next we describe each dimension separately:

We define "prefix" as the string consisting of all the digits and symbols that appear to the left of the leftmost letter of the password, and define "suffix" as the string consisting of the digits and symbols that appear to the right of the rightmost letter in the password. We define "base word" as the string starting with the leftmost letter and ending with the rightmost letter of the password. For example, if password is '123Pa$$w0rd!!', the prefix is '123', the suffix is '!!' and the base word is 'Pa$$w0rd'. The base word can consist of mixed-case letters, digits and/or symbols. In case there are no letters in the password, (e.g.,

'1234567890'), the password itself is considered to be the base word, and the prefix and suffix are the empty strings. In case the password starts with a letter, (e.g., 'abc123'), the prefix is the empty string, and similarly, if the password ends with a letter, ('123abc'), the suffix is the empty string. Note that the division into these three parts is purely syntactical and is not a semantic division as in [43]. Computing a good semantic division is time and space consuming, so we elected to rely on the simpler syntax-based division.

Next we define "capitalization pattern" as the list of positions of capital letters in the base word. In order to decrease the dependency between the password length and the capitalization pattern, we elected to represent the capitalization pattern as a list of positive and negative indices at which capital letters appear: The negative indices count from the end of the base word, and the positive indices count from the base word start. To avoid ambiguity, both the negative and the positive indices do not exceed the middle index. We also added a capitalization pattern 'all-cap' for the special case in which all the letters are capitals (regardless of password length). If there is no capital letter in the base word, the capitalization pattern is empty.

Note that the capitalization-pattern dimension is not strictly independent of the base-word dimension: e.g., a capitalization pattern t may refer to indices that are outside a short base word b, or b's characters at the indexed positions may be symbols or digits (which do not have a capitalized form). In such cases the transformation t degenerates into the null transformation. For a model-based password cracker, this dependence implies some inefficiency, since the cracker will test the same password multiple times, once for each capitalization-pattern that is equivalent to the null transformation for the current base word. The rank estimation accurately accounts for such a cracker's inefficiency. This means that a more sophisticated cracker can be developed: it could skip null transformations and save itself time. Thus this dependency only increases the password strength estimation value, which is still, as we see in Sect. 5, better and lower than existing methods' estimation.

For example for '123Pa$$w0rD!!' the capitalization pattern of the base word 'Pa$$w0rD' is the first letter and the last letter, denoted by '[0, 1]', and for the base word 'PASSWORD' the capitalization pattern is 'all-cap'.

Finally, we define "l33t pattern" as a list of l33t transformation in the base word. The l33t pattern depends on the position of the letter being mutated, and on the choice of replacement (Table 2 shows that some letters have more than one l33t replacement). We elected to ignore the positionality aspect. We numbered the possible l33t replacements from 1 to 14—e.g., transforming 'a' into '4' is transformation number 3—and represent the whole l33t transformation of a base word by a tuple of l33t replacement numbers. So for '123Pa$$w0rD!!' the l33t transformation is s↔ $ and o ↔ 0. We assume that if a l33t replacement is applied then it is applied to *all* the relevant letters in the base word. So following Table 2, the l33t pattern of '123Pa$$w0rD!!' is '[1,4]' which means "replace all occurrences of o by 0 and all occurrences of s by $". If there are no l33t transformations in the base word, the base word remains as-is and the

Table 2. L33t transformations

Index	1	2,3	4,5	6	7,8	9,10	11	12,13	14
Letter	o	a	s	e	g	t	z	i	x
l33t	0	[@,4]	[\$,5]	3	[6,9]	[+,7]	2	[1,!]	%

l33t pattern is empty. Note that the l33t-pattern dimension is not independent of the base-word dimension, and as before, this dependency introduces some inefficiency to a model-based password cracker.

3.4 The Learning Phase

We learn the distributions of the prefix, base word, suffix, capitalization and l33t using the training set at hand—recall Sect. 3.2—as follows. Let these distributions be denoted by P_1, P_2, P_3, P_4, P_5 respectively. For each password in the training set, we divide the password into its five sub-passwords, as described above, and increment the dimensional-frequency of each prefix/suffix/base word/capitalization/l33t sub-password by 1. Before incrementing the base word's frequency, we "uncapitalize" and "unl33t" it, i.e., we ensure that all the base word letters are in lower case having no l33t transformation, so for the raw base word 'Pa\$\$w0rD' we increment the frequency of 'password' in the base word dimension P_2. Finally we normalize the five lists of frequencies into probability distributions, and sort them in decreasing order.

Following [14, 30, 40], we know that people have a tendency to choose passwords that contain dates and meaningful numbers. To take this observation into account, we enriched the probability distributions of the prefix, base word, and suffix dimensions (before normalizing), by adding the following strings that may not present in the training corpus: (1) All the digit sequences of up to 6 digits were added to the prefix and suffix distributions. (2) All the digit sequences of length exactly 6 were added to the base word distribution. Each extra sub-password was added with a frequency $\epsilon = 0.5$ to account for the fact that it didn't appear in the corpus.

3.5 The Estimation Phase

A model-based cracker based on, e.g., [47] goes over the password candidates using an optimal-order enumeration. We can use a matching rank estimation algorithm such as ESrank [10] to estimate the password guessability. Given a password P, we split into its sub-passwords $P = p^* || b^* || s^* || c^* || l^*$ where p^* is a prefix, b^* is a base word, s^* is a suffix, c^* is a capitalization and l^* is a l33t. With this, using the five probability distributions P_1, P_2, P_3, P_4, P_5, we can apply a rank estimation algorithm such as [10]. The algorithm estimates the number of 5-part passwords $p_i || b_j || s_k || c_w || l_t$ (split in the same way), whose probabilities obey

$$P_1(i) \cdot P_2(j) \cdot P_3(k) \cdot P_4(w) \cdot P_5(t) \geq P_1(p^*) \cdot P_2(b^*) \cdot P_3(s^*) \cdot P_4(c^*) \cdot P_5(l^*).$$

In other words, it estimates the number of guesses a model-based cracker would attempt before reaching the given password P.

For a given password which is composed only of digits, the model may include several options to reach this password by the model-based password cracker since a numeric password can be divided into prefix, base word, and suffix, in different ways. To account for this condition in the rank estimation, we added special handling of numeric passwords. For such a password, the PESrank algorithm iterates over all its possible divisions into 3 sub-passwords (of any length): for an ℓ-digit password there are exactly $(\ell+1)(\ell+2)/2$ possibilities. For each division whose 3 sub-passwords appear in the model we calculate the password's probability. Finally, we return the rank of the division with the highest probability, since this is the division that will be encountered first by the optimal enumeration algorithm.

3.6   Estimating the Ranks of Unleaked Password Parts

As described so far, if even one of a given password's five parts is not present in the relevant dimension, PESrank is unable to estimate its rank. Following Komanduri [28], we also introduce an optional "unleaked" smoothing mode to PESrank: when it's active, the model is also able to provide an estimate of the strength of passwords with unleaked parts, for which we have no empirical a-priori probability. We do this as follows: if the password part s is missing from distribution P_i, that dimension's contribution to the password's probability is taken as $\alpha P_i(n_i)$: i.e., we use the probability of the least likely value in dimension i multiplied by an arbitrary fraction $\alpha < 1$.

3.7   Performance

We tested our Python implementation of PESrank's training on a 3.40GHz core 7 PC running Windows 8.1 64-bit with 32GB RAM. The PESrank code is publicity available at GitHub [11]. We found that the PESrank training phase is quite fast—much faster than reported for previous methods. It takes only 12 min to train PESrank on the PGS set, in comparison to the days of training reported for the Markov [31] or PCFG [47] methods using the same set. To train our method on the PGS++ set, it took only 32 min, in comparison to the days it took to train the neural method [34] on the same data (see more details in Sect. 5). Because the PESrank training time is fast, we are able to train PESrank on the Jason corpus with 905 million passwords (an order of magnitude larger than the PGS++ set), and even on this corpus the training only took 4.5 h. The results are summarized in Table 3.

The table shows that on average an estimation takes 33 ms, and under 1 s in all cases, giving a good user experience. The lookup time includes: (1) dividing the password to its five dimensions' values, $v_1, \ldots, v_5$ (2) applying binary search for each dimension value v_i in its corresponding probability list P_i to obtain its probability $\Pr(v_i)$ (3) calculating the password probability $p = \prod_{i=1}^{5} \Pr(v_i)$ (4)

Table 3. PESrank performance metrics.

	PGS	Jason
Training time	12 min	4.5 h
Total space	660 MB	7.69 GB
Average estimation time per password	0.024 s	0.033 s
Maximum estimation time per password	0.690 s	0.792 s
Combined length of the two merged lists	768 integers	884 integers

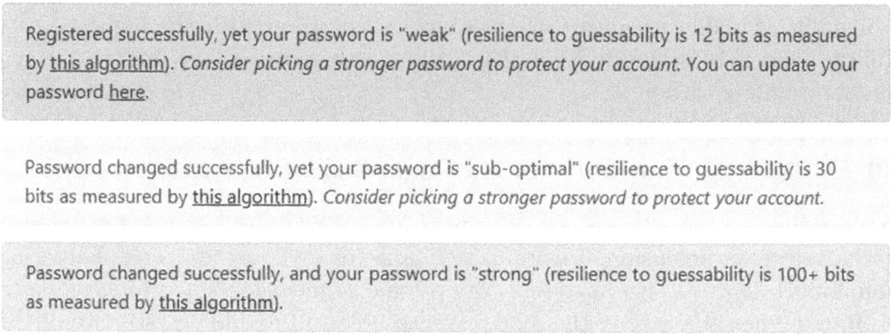

Registered successfully, yet your password is "weak" (resilience to guessability is 12 bits as measured by this algorithm). *Consider picking a stronger password to protect your account.* You can update your password here.

Password changed successfully, yet your password is "sub-optimal" (resilience to guessability is 30 bits as measured by this algorithm). *Consider picking a stronger password to protect your account.*

Password changed successfully, and your password is "strong" (resilience to guessability is 100+ bits as measured by this algorithm).

Fig. 1. The possible messages shown by the registration page.

applying the ESrank algorithm [10] to find the rank r of the given probability p. The password's strength estimation is measured in bits: $\log_2(r)$.

4   Usability of PESrank

4.1   A Proof of Concept Study

We integrated PESrank into the registration page of the Infosec course. The updated system provides users with a gentle "nudge": it accepts weak passwords, yet tells the owners they are weak, and makes it easy for them to try again. The system displays three different messages, see Fig. 1: passwords with strength below 30 bits are considered 'weak' (red), strengths between 30–50 bits are considered 'sub-optimal' (yellow) and strengths above 50 bits are considered 'strong' (green). During the registration we only saved the password strength and *not the password itself* for statistical analysis, as approved by university's ethics review board. The total time from clicking on the Register button until the browser shows the feedback message (including password registration, strength estimation, network delays, and browser rendering) is well under 1 s. The increase in registration time due to the strength estimation was negligible and qualitatively unnoticeable.

There were 98 students who registered to this course: The median password strength of the first password chosen by the students was 41.51 bits, with the

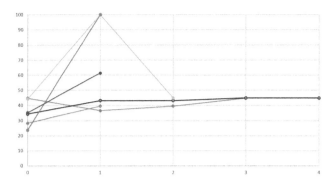

Fig. 2. The password strength versus password-change number for the 7 students who changed their password: index 0 indicates the strength of the initial password chosen by each student.

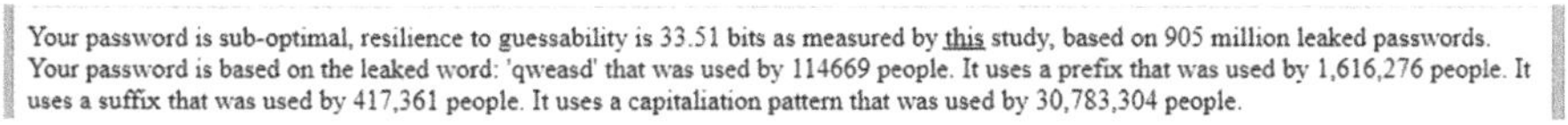

Your password is sub-optimal, resilience to guessability is 33.51 bits as measured by this study, based on 905 million leaked passwords. Your password is based on the leaked word: 'qweasd' that was used by 114669 people. It uses a prefix that was used by 1,616,276 people. It uses a suffix that was used by 417,361 people. It uses a capitaliation pattern that was used by 30,783,304 people.

Fig. 3. The PESrank implementation as a Google Cloud Function

weakest having strength of 14.14 bits. Out of the 98 students, 7 students changed their passwords to stronger passwords. The median strength of these students' first passwords was 34.32 bits, and the median strength of their final passwords was 44.88 bits: a significant improvement. In Fig. 2 we can see the evolution of passwords strengths of the seven students who changed their password (there are two students whose lines overlap due to similar strength choices). The figure shows that 5 students indeed picked a stronger password in their first change— one of whom later changed the password a second time in favor of a weaker password. Interestingly, two students changed their passwords 3 and 4 times, respectively, without significantly improving their strength.

4.2   Explainability

The anecdotal evidence from the proof of concept leads us to realize that while providing the password strength encourages some users to pick a better password, a good strength estimator should give the user guidance on *how* to pick a better password. One of the advantages of PESrank is that it is inherently very "explainable". As part of its calculation it discovers the a-priori probability (and frequency) of each sub-password - and this information can be shown to the user. E.g., in the latest version of the code, for the password NewY0rk123 we provide the following feedback: "Your password is sub-optimal, its guessability strength is 32 bits, based on 905 million leaked passwords. Your password is based on the leaked word: 'newyork' that was used by 129,023 people. It uses a suffix that was used by 17,631,940 people. It uses a capitalization pattern that was used by 592,568 people. It uses a l33t pattern that was used by 4,395,598 people".

This tells the user that (a) the transformations do not hide the leaked base word, that (b) they use a very common suffix and that (c) a simple l33t transformation is only marginally effective. And most importantly - it teaches that the split into the five dimensions is something password crackers know about and take advantage of. Furthermore, if the password has parts that are unleaked, this means the user actually selected a strong password part in that dimension—and PESrank is able to explain this. E.g. on a password "Dmmihhvk123", it would explain "Your password is strong, its guessability strength is 53 bits, based on 905 million leaked passwords. Your password is based on a good (unleaked) base word. It uses a suffix that was used by 17,631,940 people and a capitalization pattern used by 34,102,338 people". See Fig. 3 for a screenshot of the Google Cloud Function implementation. We are planning to conduct a wider scale experiment in the future using the improved code.

5   Comparison with Existing Methods

In order to test the power and accuracy of PESrank, we compared it to five cracker-based methods offered in PGS [5]: (1) the Markov model [31]; (2) the PCFGs model [47] with Komanduri's improvements [28]; (3) Hashcat [21]; (4) John the Ripper [36] mangled dictionary models. Then we compared it to the neural network-based model of Melicher et al. (with Monte-Carlo estimation) [34]. In all cases we used the algorithms' default settings and training data. To have a fair comparison, we trained PESrank on the PGS set for comparison with the PCFG, Markov, hashcat and JtR algorithms, and on the PGS++ set for comparison with the Neural algorithm. We also trained PESrank method on the full Jason corpus with its 905 million passwords in order to see how the training set size affects performance.

In order to evaluate PESrank and compare its performance to existing methods we computed for each model the percentage of passwords that would be cracked after a particular number of guesses: in other words, the Cumulative Distribution Function (CDF) of each model. More powerful guessing methods guess a higher percentage of passwords in our test set, and do so with fewer guesses: hence a better model has a CDF that rises more sharply and ultimately reaches a higher percentage.

When "unleaked" smoothing mode is active (recall Sect. 3.6), the CDF exhibits two features: first, the CDF has a sharp upward "jump" at a rank that is influenced by the choice of α, and second, the CDF by definition always reaches 100%: even a password that has unleaked parts in all 5 dimensions will receive a minimal probability of $\alpha^5 \cdot \prod_{i=1}^{5} P_i(n_i)$, which will translate to a rank equal to the models volume $\prod_{i=1}^{5} n_i$. In order to emphasize the arbitrary nature of the "unleaked" parts of the CDF, when we show figures created in "unleaked" smoothing mode, the relevant parts of the CDF are marked in a dotted line.

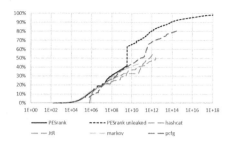

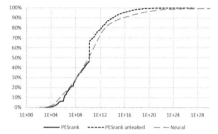

Fig. 4. The CDFs of PESrank in unleaked mode versus PCFG, Markov, Hashcat and JtR

Fig. 5. The CDFs of PESrank in unleaked mode versus Neural.

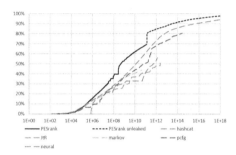

Fig. 6. The CDF of each method trained on all the passwords available to it: PESrank in unleaked mode - on Jason, Neural - on PGS++, and the rest - on PGS.

5.1   Comparison to Cracker-Based and Neural Methods

Figure 4 shows the comparing PESrank, trained on the PGS set, with PCFG, Markov, hashcat and JtR algorithms with PESrank in "unleaked" mode, with $\alpha = 10^{-3}$: note the jump around 10^9 and the dotted curve beyond it, indicating that higher ranks rely on password parts for which there is no empirical a-priori probability. We note that while PCFG does use Komanduri's smoothing [28], there is no external indication when this extrapolating calculation is applied: we speculate that it may be occurring around rank 10^{11}, where an upward "jump" can be observed in the PCFG curve.

Figure 5 shows the results comparing PESrank, in "unleaked" mode, trained on the PGS++ set, with the Neural method (with Monte Carlo estimation). We see that PESrank is on-par with the Neural method for "practically crackable" passwords (up to the "unleaked" mode jump where the dotted curve begins).

Figure 6 shows the CDFs of all the methods we compared, each trained on the maximal training set available to it (PESrank in "unleaked" mode). When PESrank is trained on a 905 million password training set, its advantage over the other methods, as provided by the PGS service [5], grows. While this figure mostly demonstrates the advantage of using a larger training set, it also shows that PESrank is actually able to digest such a large training set, due to its fast

Table 4. Storage requirements for the various methods as reported by [34] when all methods are trained on the PGS++ corpus.

PCFG	Markov	Hashcat	JtR	Neural	PESrank
4.7 GB	1.1 GB	756 MB	756 MB	60 MB	1.19 GB

Table 5. Overall performance comparison to existing methods.

	PCFG	Neural	Neural+MonteCarlo	PESrank
Training time	Hours/days	Hours/days	Hours/days	**12 min**
Lookup time	Offline	Offline	**Online**	**Online**
Tweak time	**≤ 1 s**	Hours/days	Hours/days	**≤ 1 s**
Storage requirement	Highest	Lowest	Lowest	Medium
Explainability	Maybe	No	No	**Yes**
Accuracy	**Exact**	**Exact**	Unknown	**up to 1 bit**

training time, whereas the other methods' ability to do so in reasonable time is currently unknown.

5.2 Storage Requirements

Table 4 summarizes the storage space of the different methods, as reported by [34]—where, unlike in the PGS service [5], the authors trained the earlier methods on the PGS++ training set. For comparison we provide the PESrank storage for the same set. The table shows that the Neural network requires the lowest amount of storage (60 MB) on the server-side, while PESrank requires a larger, yet very reasonable 1.19 GB storage, and significantly less than PCFG.

6 Related Work

Password strength measurement often takes one of two conceptual forms: heuristic pure-estimator approaches, and cracker-based approaches. Usually existing cracker-based methods are *generative*: they enumerate the passwords in their model either in their training phase or in their lookup phase. PESrank belongs to the cracker-based approaches, however, unlike previous methods, it is not generative. It's underlying rank estimation algorithm works directly on the multi-dimensional probability distribution *without enumerating*. This non-generative estimation is the reason why PESrank's training time and tweaking time are dramatically faster than those of [34,35,47]. In this section we describe earlier work on cracker-based approaches. Additional related work on pure-estimator methods, and about model tweaking, can be found in the Appendix.

Software tools are commonly used to generate password guesses [18]. The most popular tools transform a wordlist using mangling rules, or transformations intended to model common behaviors in how humans craft passwords.

Two popular tools of this type are Hashcat [21] and John the Ripper [36]. These tools typically run until a timeout is triggered. Since they generally take a long time to run (minutes to hours, depending on the timeout setting) their usefulness as online strength estimators is limited.

A probabilistic cracker method, based on a Markov model, was first proposed in 2005 [35], and studied more comprehensively subsequently [7,15,31]. Markov models predict the probability of the next character in a password based on the previous characters, or context characters. This method is generative: it calculates the rank of a given password by enumerating over all possible passwords in descending order of likelihood, which is computationally intensive, and makes it impractical as an online strength estimator. In addition, in order to tweak this method for each user (based the user's personal information), the model method should be retrained for each user separately [6]. Since the training takes days, it is unrealistic to tweak.

In 2009 Weir et al. [47] proposed a very influential method which uses probabilistic context-free grammars (PCFG). The intuition behind PCFG is that passwords are built with template structures (e.g., 6 letters followed by 2 digits) and terminals that fit into those structures. A password's probability is the probability of its template multiplied by those of its terminals. In 2015 the PCFG method was integrated with the techniques reported by Komanduri in his PhD thesis [28]. Conceptually, this method is similar to ours since it also assumes probability independence between model components: Our method assumes independence between the probabilities of its corresponding sub-passwords while PCFG assumes independence between the probability of the template and the terminals. Like the Markov method, the PCFG method is generative: it calculates the rank of a given password by enumerating over all possible passwords in descending order of likelihood, so it is also impractical as an online strength estimator. In contrast, PESrank calculates the rank of a given password in the descending order of likelihood *without enumerating* over the passwords themselves. Due to its 2-level model (template + terminals), which is fairly intuitive, we believe PCFG *may be* explainable—although its authors did not develop or discuss this capability.

In 2016 Melicher et al. [34] proposed to use a recurrent neural network for probabilistic password modeling. Like Markov models, neural networks are trained to generate the next character of a password given the preceding characters of a password. In its pure form this method is also generative and therefore is computationally intensive. However, the authors also describe a Monte-Carlo method to *estimate* the rank of a given password. To do so they split the algorithm into two phases: the training and sampling phase (which is generative), and a lookup phase, which uses the sampled model to provide an estimate. Therefore, like PESrank, in Monte-Carlo mode the Neural method's lookup is non-generative, making it suitable for online strength estimation. The authors do not provide bounds on the estimation error introduced by the Monte Carlo method. However, the Neural method's training phase *remains* generative: it enumerates the passwords to train the neural network. Thus, in order to personalize the neural network method for each user, it should be retrained for each user separately. Since the training takes days, this method cannot be personalized for different users in real-time. Moreover, like most neural-network-based systems, the algorithm is inherently difficult to explain, only providing a numeric rank without any hints about "why" or what to do to improve.

In Table 5 we summarize the overall differences between the leading methods according to several criteria: training time, lookup time, tweaking time, storage, explainabilty and accuracy. The information about PCFGs in this comparison is taken from [28, 47] plus [23, 29, 45] regarding its tweakability. The table shows that the PESrank method outperforms all of the leading alternatives, in different ways. Versus PCFGs, PESrank is online and its training time is significantly shorter. Versus the Neural method in its pure variant again PESrank is superior since it is online, has shorter training time, plus it is tweakable and explainable. Finally, versus the Neural method's Monte-Carlo variant (which is practical as an online estimator), PESrank retains all its other advantages in training and tweak time, explainability, and provable accuracy.

7   Conclusions

In this paper we proposed a novel password strength estimator, called PESrank, which accurately models the behavior of a powerful password cracker. PESrank calculates the rank of a given password in an optimal descending sorted order of likelihood. It is practical for *online* use, and is able to estimate a given password's rank in fractions of a second. Its training time is drastically shorter than previous methods. Moreover, PESrank is efficiently *tweakable* to allow model personalization, without the need to retrain the model; and it is *explainable*: it is able to provide information on *why* the password has its calculated rank, and gives the user insight on how to pick a better password.

PESrank casts the question of password rank estimation in a multi-dimensional probabilistic framework used in side-channel cryptanalysis, and relies on the ESrank algorithm for side-channel rank estimation. We found that an effective choice uses $d = 5$ dimensions: base word, prefix, suffix, capitalization pattern, and l33t transformation. We implemented PERrank in Python and conducted an extensive evaluation study of it. We also integrated it into the registration page of a course at our university. Even with a model based on 905 million passwords, the response time was well under 1 s, with up to a 1-bit accuracy margin between the upper bound and the lower bound on the rank.

We conclude that PESrank is a practical strength estimator that can easily be deployed in any web site's online password registration page to assist users in picking better passwords. It provides accurate strength estimates, negligible response-time overhead, good explainability, and reasonable training time.

Acknowledgments. We thank Lujo Bauer and Michael Stroucken for allowing us broad use of the PGS service and assisting us in obtaining the PGS and PGS++ sets.

A   Additional Related Work

A.1   Heuristic pure-estimator approaches

The earliest and probably the most popular methods of password strength estimation are based on LUDS: counts of lower- and uppercase letters, digits and symbols. The de-facto standard for this type of method is the NIST 800-63 standard [4,19]. It proposes to measure password strength in entropy bits, on the basis of some simple rules such as the length of the password and the type of characters used (e.g., lower-case, upper-case, or digits). These methods are known to be quite inaccurate [12].

Wheeler proposed an advanced password strength estimator [48], that extends the LUDS approach by including dictionaries, considering l33t speak transformations, keyboard walks, and more. Due to its easy-to-integrate design, it is deployed on many websites. The meter's accuracy was later backed up by scientific analysis [49].

Guo et al. [20] proposed a lightweight client-side meter. It is based on cosine-length and password-edit distance similarity. It transforms a password into a LUDS vector and compares it to a standardized strong-password vector using the aforementioned similarity measures.

Such pure-estimator approaches have the advantage of very fast estimation—typically in fractions of a second—which makes them suitable for online client-side implementation. However, they do not directly model adversarial guessing so their accuracy requires evaluation.

A.2   Tweakable extensions and variations

Several authors (cf. [23,29,45]) extended the PCFG approach to develop systems that also use personal information. The nature of the extensions was to add a new grammar variable for each type of personal information, (e.g., B for birthday, N for name and E for email) which makes the approach tweakable. However these extended methods are impractical for online use for the same reasons PCFG is impractical: they are all generative.

Personalized password strength meters (PPSMs) which rely on previous password knowledge have also been proposed [8,37]: PPSMs warns users when they pick passwords that are vulnerable based on previously compromised passwords. Similarly, PESrank can be personalized based on previous passwords, but also can be personalized based on any kind of user personal information (name, email, etc.).

Recently [22] introduced PassGAN, an approach that replaces human-generated password rules by machine learning algorithms. The PassGAN uses a Generative Adversarial Network (GAN) to learn the distribution of real passwords from actual password leaks, and to generate password guesses. The authors did not compare their results with previous rank estimators and did not report on the required training time.

References

1. Agrawal, D., Archambeault, B., Rao, J.R., Rohatgi, P.: The EM side-channel(s). In: Cryptographic Hardware and Embedded Systems-CHES 2002, 29–45 (2003)
2. David, L., Wool, A.: Online password guessability via multi-dimensional rank estimation. arXiv preprint arXiv:1912.02551 (2019)
3. Bogdanov, A., Kizhvatov, I., Manzoor, K., Tischhauser, E., Witteman, M.: Fast and memory-efficient key recovery in side-channel attacks. In: Selected Areas in Cryptography (SAC) (2015)
4. Burr, W., Dodson, D., Polk, W.: Electronic authentication guideline. Technical report, National Institute of Standards and Technology (2004)
5. Carnegie Mellon University Password Research Group. Password guessability service (pgs) (2019). https://pgs.ece.cmu.edu/
6. Castelluccia, C., Chaabane, A., Dürmuth, M., Perito, D.: When privacy meets security: Leveraging personal information for password cracking. arXiv preprint arXiv:1304.6584 (2013)
7. Castelluccia, C., Dürmuth, M., Perito, D.: Adaptive password-strength meters from markov models. In: NDSS (2012)
8. Das, A., Bonneau, J., Caesar, M., Borisov, N., Wang, X.: The tangled web of password reuse. In: NDSS 2014, pp. 23–26 (2014)
9. David, L., Wool, A.: A bounded-space near-optimal key enumeration algorithm for multi-subkey side-channel attacks. In: Handschuh, H. (ed.) CT-RSA 2017. LNCS, vol. 10159, pp. 311–327. Springer, Cham (2017). https://doi.org/10.1007/978-3-319-52153-4_18
10. David, L., Wool, A.: Poly-logarithmic side channel rank estimation via exponential sampling. In: Matsui, M. (ed.) CT-RSA 2019. LNCS, vol. 11405, pp. 330–349. Springer, Cham (2019). https://doi.org/10.1007/978-3-030-12612-4_17
11. David, L., Wool, A.: PESrank Python implementation (2020). https://github.com/lirondavid/PESrank
12. From very weak to very strong: de Carné de Carnavalet, X., Mannan, M. Analyzing password-strength meters. In: NDSS **14**, 23–26 (2014)
13. Dell'Amico, M., Filippone, M.: Monte carlo strength evaluation: Fast and reliable password checking. In: Proceedings of the 22nd ACM SIGSAC Conference on Computer and Communications Security, pp. 158–169. ACM (2015)
14. Dell'Amico, M., Michiardi, P., Roudier, Y.: Password strength: an empirical analysis. In: 2010 Proceedings IEEE INFOCOM, pp. 1–9. IEEE (2010)
15. Dürmuth, M., Angelstorf, F., Castelluccia, C., Perito, D., Chaabane, A.: OMEN: Faster Password Guessing Using an Ordered Markov Enumerator. In: Piessens, F., Caballero, J., Bielova, N. (eds.) ESSoS 2015. LNCS, vol. 8978, pp. 119–132. Springer, Cham (2015). https://doi.org/10.1007/978-3-319-15618-7_10
16. Gandolfi, K., Mourtel, C., Olivier, F.: Electromagnetic Analysis: Concrete Results. In: Koç, Ç.K., Naccache, D., Paar, C. (eds.) CHES 2001. LNCS, vol. 2162, pp. 251–261. Springer, Heidelberg (2001). https://doi.org/10.1007/3-540-44709-1_21
17. Glowacz, C., Grosso, V., Poussier, R., Schueth, J., Standaert, F.-X.: Simpler and more efficient rank estimation for side-channel security assessment. In: Fast Software Encryption, pp. 117–129 (2015)
18. Goodin, D.: Anatomy of a hack: How crackers ransack passwords like "qeadzcwrsfxv1331". Ars Technica (2013)
19. Grassi, P.A., et al.: NIST special publication 800–63b: Digital identity guidelines (2017)

20. Guo, Y., Zhang, Z.: LPSE: lightweight password-strength estimation for password meters. Comput. Secur. **73**, 507–518 (2018)
21. hashcat. Hashcat advanced password recovery (2019)
22. Hitaj, B., Gasti, P., Ateniese, G., Perez-Cruz, F.: PassGAN: a deep learning approach for password guessing. In: Deng, R.H., Gauthier-Umaña, V., Ochoa, M., Yung, M. (eds.) ACNS 2019. LNCS, vol. 11464, pp. 217–237. Springer, Cham (2019). https://doi.org/10.1007/978-3-030-21568-2_11
23. Houshmand, S., Aggarwal, S.: Using personal information for targeted attacks in grammar based probabilistic password cracking. In: IFIP Advances in Information and Communication Technology, vol. 511 (2017)
24. Jason. 1.4 billion leaked passwords in over 40GB of data (2019)
25. Kelley, P.G., et al.: Guess again (and again and again): measuring password strength by simulating password-cracking algorithms. In: 2012 IEEE Symposium on Security and Privacy, pp. 523–537. IEEE (2012)
26. Kocher, P., Jaffe, J., Jun, B.: Differential power analysis. In: Advances in Cryptology-CRYPTO 1999, pp. 388–397. Springer (1999)
27. Kocher, P.C.: Timing attacks on implementations of diffie-Hellman, RSA, DSS, and Other Systems. In: Koblitz, N. (ed.) CRYPTO 1996. LNCS, vol. 1109, pp. 104–113. Springer, Heidelberg (1996). https://doi.org/10.1007/3-540-68697-5_9
28. Komanduri, S.: Modeling the adversary to evaluate password strength with limited samples. Ph.D. thesis, Carnegie Mellon University (2016)
29. Li, Y., Wang, H., Sun, K.: Personal information in passwords and its security implications. IEEE Trans. Inf. Forensics Secur. **12**(10), 2320–2333 (2017)
30. Li, Z., Han, W., Xu, W.: A large-scale empirical analysis of Chinese web passwords. In: 23rd USENIX Security Symposium, pp. 559–574 (2014)
31. Ma, J., Yang, W., Luo, M., Li, N.: A study of probabilistic password models. In: 2014 IEEE Symposium on Security and Privacy, pp. 689–704. IEEE (2014)
32. Martin, D.P., Mather, L., Oswald, E.: Two sides of the same coin: counting and enumerating keys post side-channel attacks revisited. In: Smart, N.P. (ed.) CT-RSA 2018. LNCS, vol. 10808, pp. 394–412. Springer, Cham (2018). https://doi.org/10.1007/978-3-319-76953-0_21
33. Martin, D.P., O'Connell, J.F., Oswald, E., Stam, M.: Counting keys in parallel after a side channel attack. In: Iwata, T., Cheon, J.H. (eds.) ASIACRYPT 2015. LNCS, vol. 9453, pp. 313–337. Springer, Heidelberg (2015). https://doi.org/10.1007/978-3-662-48800-3_13
34. Melicher, W., et al.: Fast, lean, and accurate: modeling password guessability using neural networks. In: Proceedings of 25th USENIX Security Symposium, pp. 175–191 (2016)
35. Narayanan, A., Shmatikov, V.: Fast dictionary attacks on passwords using time-space tradeoff. In: Proceedings of the 12th ACM Conference on Computer and Communications Security, pages 364–372. ACM (2005)
36. OpenWall. John the ripper password cracker (2019)
37. Pal, B., Daniel, T., Chatterjee, R., Ristenpart, T.: Beyond credential stuffing: Password similarity models using neural networks. In: 2019 IEEE Symposium on Security and Privacy (SP), pp. 417–434. IEEE (2019)
38. Poussier, R., Standaert, F.-X., Grosso, V.: Simple key enumeration (and rank estimation) using histograms: an integrated approach. In: Gierlichs, B., Poschmann, A.Y. (eds.) CHES 2016. LNCS, vol. 9813, pp. 61–81. Springer, Heidelberg (2016). https://doi.org/10.1007/978-3-662-53140-2_4

39. Quisquater, J.-J., Samyde, D.: ElectroMagnetic analysis (EMA): measures and counter-measures for smart cards. In: Attali, I., Jensen, T. (eds.) E-smart 2001. LNCS, vol. 2140, pp. 200–210. Springer, Heidelberg (2001). https://doi.org/10.1007/3-540-45418-7_17

40. Shay, R., et al.: Encountering stronger password requirements: user attitudes and behaviors. In: Proceedings of the Sixth Symposium on Usable Privacy and Security (SOUPS 2010), p. 2. ACM (2010)

41. Ur, B., et al.: Design and evaluation of a data-driven password meter. In: Proceedings of the 2017 CHI Conference on Human Factors in Computing Systems, pp. 3775–3786. ACM (2017)

42. Ur, B., et al.: How does your password measure up? the effect of strength meters on password creation. In 21st USENIX Security Symposium, pp. 65–80 (2012)

43. Veras, R., Collins, C., Thorpe, J.: On semantic patterns of passwords and their security impact. In NDSS (2014)

44. Veyrat-Charvillon, N., Gérard, B., Renauld, M., Standaert, F.-X.: An Optimal Key Enumeration Algorithm and Its Application to Side-Channel Attacks. In: Knudsen, L.R., Wu, H. (eds.) SAC 2012. LNCS, vol. 7707, pp. 390–406. Springer, Heidelberg (2013). https://doi.org/10.1007/978-3-642-35999-6_25

45. Wang, D., Zhang, Z., Wang, P., Yan, J., Huang, X.: Targeted online password guessing: an underestimated threat. In: Proceedings of the 2016 ACM SIGSAC Conference on Computer and Communications Security, pp. 1242–1254 (2016)

46. Weir, M., Aggarwal, S., Collins, M., Stern, H.: Testing metrics for password creation policies by attacking large sets of revealed passwords. In: Proceedings of the 17th ACM conference on Computer and Communications Security, pp. 162–175. ACM (2010)

47. Weir, M., Aggarwal, S., De Medeiros, B., Glodek, B.: Password cracking using probabilistic context-free grammars. In: 2009 30th IEEE Symposium on Security and Privacy, pp. 391–405. IEEE (2009)

48. Wheeler, D.: zxcvbn: realistic password strength estimation. Dropbox TechBlog (2012)

49. Wheeler, D.L.: zxcvbn: low-budget password strength estimation. In: Proceedings of 25th USENIX Security Symposium, pp. 157–173 (2016)

Detecting Video-Game Injectors Exchanged in Game Cheating Communities

Panicos Karkallis[1(✉)], Jorge Blasco[1], Guillermo Suarez-Tangil[2,4], and Sergio Pastrana[3]

[1] Royal Holloway, University of London, Egham, UK
panicos.karkallis.2018@rhul.ac.uk
[2] IMDEA Networks Institute, Madrid, Spain
[3] Universidad Carlos III de Madrid, Madrid, Spain
[4] King's College London, London, UK

Abstract. Video game cheats destroy the online play experience of users and result in financial losses for game developers. Similar to hacking communities, cheat developers often organize themselves around forums where they share game cheats and know-how. In this paper, we perform a large-scale measurement of two online forums, MPGH and UnknownCheats, devoted to video game cheating that are nowadays very active and altogether have more than 7 million posts. Video game cheats often require an auxiliary tool to access the victim process, i.e., an injector. This is a type of program that manipulates the game program memory, and it is a key piece for evading cheat detection on the client side. We leverage the output of our measurement study to build a machine learning classifier that identifies injectors based on their behavioural traits. Our system will help game developers and the anti-cheat industry to identify attack vectors more quickly and will reduce the barriers to study this topic within the academic community.

Keywords: Game cheating & hacks · Underground forums · Injectors

1 Introduction

There are more than 2 billion video game players worldwide, with many of them playing online [21]. Games such as *Counter Strike: Global Offensive* (CS:GO), released in 2012, still attract more than 600K monthly average players.[1] Most modern video games also include ranking systems that prompt players to compete to get more content and features. They also offer access to exclusive in-game events, that in some cases are used as an entry point for professional e-sports.

While most players compete using their ability and experience, others use game hacks and cheats to gain advantages against their competitors. Cheating

---

[1] Data extracted from https://steamcharts.com/app/730 on 16th April 2021.

© Springer Nature Switzerland AG 2021
E. Bertino et al. (Eds.): ESORICS 2021, LNCS 12972, pp. 305–324, 2021.
https://doi.org/10.1007/978-3-030-88418-5_15

in online games undermines legitimate player's efforts, reduces their engagement in the game, and results in financial losses [9]. This affects the reputation of the games and their developers, taking players away from other games. To mitigate this, most modern games include anti-cheat software that continuously monitors the state of the game (or the system where the game runs) in the look for cheats. This has resulted in an arms race between cheaters and game developers.

Video game cheaters interact in online underground forums to share knowledge, and trade products and services, similar to other online communities focused on illicit and even illegal activities [1,14,20,24,27]. Communities dedicated to game cheats include a range of topics that go from cheating tutorials and documentation to the trading and free-sharing of cheating programs that can work with the latest game versions.

In this work, we conduct a measurement on two of the largest English-speaking online communities (forums) dedicated to game cheating: Multiplayer Game Hacking (MPGH)[2] and UnknownCheats (UC)[3]. These communities have been continuously operating since 2007. Our study provides a bi-dimensional view of the ecosystem, using both: i) social data science techniques on the forum data, and ii) binary analysis of files released for free. In a nutshell, we first shed light on how these communities are structured, the type of cheats and tools being developed, the actors involved, and the games they target. We observe that a cornerstone component of this ecosystem relies on stealthy techniques design to inject cheats into the games' program memory. Accordingly, we leverage information from our measurement to build a classifier to detect such injectors.

To the best of our knowledge, this is the first study focusing on longitudinal data on game cheats covering multiple games, years, and cheating communities (see Sect. 4). In particular, our work makes the following contributions:

- We analyze two of the most popular communities that focus on the trading and sharing of hacks and cheats using a novel methodology (see Sect. 2). Specifically, we apply text mining and to understand the topics discussed in the forums at scale, and social network analysis to describe the relationships and interests of the forum users.social network analysis to describe the relationships and interests of the forum users (as shown in Sect. 3.3).
- We propose a new taxonomy that covers modern cheats having multiple capabilities. Our taxonomy focuses on the intended effect cheats produce on a game. We use this taxonomy to perform a temporal analysis of the kind of cheats that are being developed per game and the different characteristics of each cheat.
- We build a machine learning classifier to quickly identify injectors used to execute cheats within games. Our classifier uses features extracted from the static and dynamic analysis of binaries and is able to correctly classify 91% of the 632 test samples (Sect. 3.2).
- We discuss how our work could be used to help anti-cheat analysts and discuss the limitations involved when analysing these communities (Sect. 5).

---

[2] https://www.mpgh.net/.
[3] https://www.unknowncheats.me/.

2   Methodology

We rely on data gathered from two well-known English communities dedicated to video game hacks and cheats to perform an analysis of the cheating ecosystem. In particular, we analyse how users share and distribute cheats, the type of files being shared, and the demographics and interests of such users. We then focus our analysis on files that feature code injecting capabilities. These kinds of files, normally known as *injectors*, are a key component of the cheats ecosystem, as they are needed to inject the actual cheat payload into the game's process memory. As part of our framework, we also develop a method to quickly identify cheat injectors based on their static and dynamic characteristics, using, among others, features commonly shared with malware.

Figure 1 presents an overview of the pipeline used for our analysis. Our framework starts with the data collection and pre-processing of the forum data obtained from the two online communities that are part of our analysis: *MPGH* and *UC* (Sect. 2.1). Once the data is collected and pre-processed, we analyze the content of each forum post and its corresponding attachments. These two analyses are done independently. On the one hand, the post analysis focuses on the relationships between users and video game cheats (Sect. 2.2). On the other hand, the attachment analysis looks into the kind of files that are shared by these communities for cheating purposes (Sect. 2.3), with a specific focus on attachments used to inject the cheats in the games' processes (Sect. 2.4).

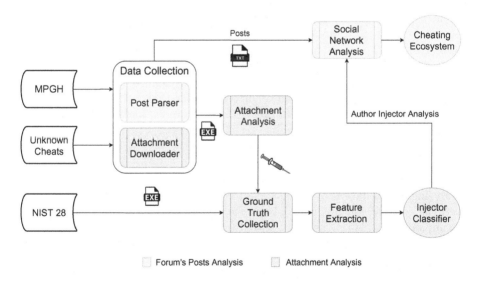

Fig. 1. Steps taken to process the posts and the attachments from the forums.

2.1 Data Collection

Acquiring data from some online communities is a daunting task. We use data from the CrimeBB dataset [25], available from the Cambridge Cybercrime Centre[4]. While this dataset contains data from various underground forums, we focus on two popular English forums for video game hacks and cheats, i.e., Multi Player Game Hacking (MPGH) and UnknownCheats (UC). Our methodology is specifically designed to cover both MPGH and UC as provided by the CrimeBB dataset. However, it can be adapted to other data sources such as non-preprocessed forums or other online communities. Our dataset includes over a decade of posts as of June 2020, totaling more than 9M posts made in 767K threads by 511K actors in MPGH, and 1.8M posts made in 120K threads by 184K actors in UC[5].

Both forums are organized around the main index page that hosts several sub-forums grouped in categories and sub-categories. For MPGH, all game forums are grouped under the "MultiPlayer Game Hacks & Cheats" category. For UC the categories group together game genres, e.g.: shooters, strategy, etc. The sub-categories match games or games from the same franchise (e.g., the Call of Duty franchise has 14 different games at the time of writing this paper). In both cases, the communities have other non-game-related forums covering a great variety of topics that go from programming to other topics outside the gaming domain. Additionally, MPGH provides specific sub-forums and marketplaces, where users can trade their hacks and cheats, and also other gaming-related goods such as virtual items, accounts, or tutorials.

Besides the text obtained from the posts, our system also analyzes the resources (cheats and auxiliary tools) shared in the forum. Both communities allow users to share files in the form of attachments (internal links to hosted resources). Links used to share attachments follow a specific format, and are thus labeled with the tag ****ATTACHMENT**** in the CrimeBB dataset. For this work, we have developed a custom crawler that automatically scrapes the text from the posts, extracts the URL of the links, and downloads all the attachments[6].

2.2 Post Analysis

Analyzing forum data is of particular interest for this research, since it provides both the context and metadata about the attachments (e.g. timestamp, game, accompanying explanations, etc.), and also the impact or popularity of the cheat providers in the community (e.g. number of downloads, reputation of the actor, number of replies, etc.) Since the dataset spans more than 15 years, processing

---

[4] https://www.cambridgecybercime.uk.

[5] In the remainder of the paper, we use the terms 'user' and 'actor' indistinguishably to refer a forum account uniquely identified by a user ID.

[6] As a result of our work, these attachments have been included in the CrimeBB catalog, and are thus available for other researchers under a legal agreement with the Cambridge Cybercrime Centre.

this data allows conducting a longitudinal analysis to analyze the evolution of the interests and discussions in the community. Accordingly, we have applied specific techniques used to analyze social media data. Concretely, we use text mining to understand the topics covered in the posts, and Social Network Analysis (SNA) to understand the roles, connections, and social interactions of the actors releasing cheats.

Game Annotation. Both communities have special sub-forums dedicated to releases and requests of hacks and cheats for each game. These typically have the structure "[GAME_TITLE] hacks and cheats". Accordingly, we annotate these sub-forums and map them to the referred game, by manually looking at forum titles and extracting the particular game where possible. For this, we used our own domain knowledge obtained from studying other gaming platforms such as Steam[7] and other gaming-specific media websites and online shops. This resulted in 238 games being identified overall from a set of 630 forums. We discard posts belonging to other forums. These may include posts that we would classify as releases but are not related to a particular game.

Social Network Analysis. To understand the relevance and impact of the cheats and also the interests of cheat providers, we conduct a Social Network Analysis on the forum data. First, for each community, we build a directed graph $G = \{U, I\}$ that represents the historical interactions (I) of the users (U). Specifically, each pair of nodes $u_i, u_j \in U$ are connected by an edge $e_{ij}(w) \in I$ where w is the number of times that the user u_i responded or interacted with a post of user u_j. Then, we extract classical network centrality measures (degree, in-degree, out-degree and eigenvector) to analyze the impact and relevance of each user in the community. Additionally, we look for posts and threads related to the actual trading of virtual items, goods and services. For this analysis, we focus on the MPGH community, since it provides dedicated boards for the market. We count the number of posts made by cheat providers on these boards, which gives us an indicator of the economic activities of actors that are releasing cheats for free.

2.3   Attachment Analysis

We annotate every attachment with the corresponding game according to the board where it is shared. For each attachment where a cheat is released, we extract information about the posts where it was released[8]. Concretely we annotate the actor, the timestamp, whether a post is starting a new thread or if it has been a response to another post (e.g. a request), the number of replies to this post, the number of downloads of the attachment, and the game associated to the post. In most cases, multiple files related to a cheat are embedded

---

[7] https://store.steampowered.com Accessed on 10th May 2021.
[8] Some attachments are duplicated or re-released in different posts.

into an archived file (e.g. zip or rar). In those cases, we annotate both, the zip file and the extracted files to the same forum. We recursively uncompressed all archive files, using a custom-made password cracking tool to inspect password-protected files. This tool scans the text from the post where the attachment is released, looks for a password reference, and saves all the successful passwords found in a passwords list. This list is used as a dictionary and all the entries are tested until the file is successfully uncompressed. All archive files that can not be uncompressed are discarded.

Apart from the context (i.e. forum-related data), for each attachment, we annotate the following information: the attachment name, its file type, a crypto-graphic hash (sha256), the author that posted the file, the number, and the list of files in the archive if the file is compressed, if the file contains an executable, if there is encryption, and the entropy [29]. Filetypes are obtained either by looking at the file extension or by interpreting their magic number using the tool *libmagic*. Initial exploratory analysis showed that various files within the attachments were not directly related to the actual cheats. These are files used either as auxiliary tools or game and system files used as backups to recover from a corrupted version. To identify these, we look for all windows binary files (exe and dll) that are digitally signed. We analysed all digital certificates and found that none of them belonged to a cheat developer (they were related to trusted developers such as Microsoft, Adobe, etc.). Because of this, we remove these files from the analysis and classify the remaining files into a global category of executable files with sub-categories depending on their kind (Java, Python, PE file, etc.)

2.4   Injector Classifier

An initial analysis of the executable files and their corresponding posts revealed that many of them were not actual cheats. As mentioned earlier, while these forums are focused on game cheating, they also include boards related to other topics such as programming, graphics, etc. Our initial exploratory analysis also showed that most of the game boards included several releases that were focused on cheat injection. These 'injectors' or 'loaders' can be used by other cheat developers to inject their cheats into the game memory, allowing them to focus on the cheating behaviour rather than on how to get the cheat into the game. Identifying these injectors quickly can allow game developers to fix or improve the detection capabilities of their anti-cheat engines sooner, reducing the window the game is susceptible to a particular cheat. Because of this, we decide to focus the rest of our analysis on these files. In particular, we develop a machine learning-based classifier capable of detecting if a particular binary has injecting capabilities. For this, we collect a series of injectors as ground truth, we extract static and dynamic properties, build a random tree-based classifier using 5-fold cross-validation.

Ground Truth Collection. We have conducted further filtering over the 45,338 executables to identify cheat-related attachments solely focusing on injecting or loading cheats in-game memory. We shortlisted a dataset of 2,543 injectors by inspecting the filename and looking for keywords like *injector*, *loader* and *injektor*. After keyword matching against the filename, a manual inspection of the files was conducted to validate the dataset.

To further validate the injector dataset, we use PEfile[9] to extract the functions and libraries imported, and also to extract strings from the binaries. Then, we match these extracted symbols against a list of methods known to be associated with code injection. The list of methods was created from the following sources: i) Feng et al. [10] described in 2008 a list of methods associated with game cheat injection; ii) A book by Nick Cano that includes and extends the methods [4] published in 2016; and iii) the tool *Capa*, an open-source security framework from FireEye that automatically identifies malware capabilities from binaries [12], and which includes some of the previously mentioned methods in their set of rules relevant to process injection. Overall our analysis includes 66 methods relevant to injection.

To train our model we include a negative class with files that are not injectors. To achieve this, we include binary files that contain as much diverse behaviours as possible. We use the files extracted from the *NIST NSRL database* [30] as our negative class files. This database collects signatures of known and traceable software applications that are meant to reduce the complexity of law enforcement and cooperate investigations, and therefore are expected to have a diverse set of behaviours without including cheat-injection characteristics.

Feature Extraction. Game cheats, and injectors in particular, are binary files obtained from *untrusted* sources (the forums we analyse). In the context of game cheating, injectors are programs designed with the purpose of loading and executing the cheat's code, either in the game memory or in a third party library used by the game. Due to the growth of anti-cheat technologies, these injectors implement techniques to remain stealthy and evade detection, such as code obfuscation or encryption of the injector's binary. The analysis of obfuscated code is hard and time consuming. Thus the classifier is trained using features derived from both static and dynamic analysis information. To get these features, we rely on existing information from VirusTotal (VT)[10]. We observe that, in order to improve the trustworthiness of their files and to probe that their cheats are *safe*, cheat providers often upload their binaries to VT, and link the corresponding report in their release post. We take advantage of this behaviour to obtain and extract static and dynamic features for our dataset. We query VT for behavioural reports from our set of injectors and non-injector files. Out of the 2,543 injectors, 1,426 produced behavioural reports containing dynamic analysis information. The behavioural reports along with the static information get parsed and converted into a feature matrix consisting of injectors (samples) as rows and information taken from the reports and static analysis as columns (features). In a similar way, we query VT for reports from non-injector files

---

[9] https://github.com/erocarrera/pefile Accessed on 10th May 2021.
[10] https://www.virustotal.com Accessed on 10th May 2021.

obtained from the NIST NSRL database. We obtain 1,731 reports that include all our required features. This means that our ground truth set consists of 1,426 injectors and 1,731 non-injectors (good-ware) files. All the files included in the dataset are unique as they have been filtered using their SHA-1 signature.

We group all our features in 7 categories: file operations, registry changes, processes & mutexes, services, functions, strings, and others (which includes a variety of features that cannot be grouped around a common theme). Table 1 shows the number of features from each category. We use one-hot encoding for all our features, except for the number of processes created which is numerical. As an example, each possible loaded module corresponds to a specific feature (e.g. *ole32.dll*) with a value of 1 if the module is actually being loaded by the binary and 0 otherwise. We provide more detailed information about the features in Appendix A.

Table 1. Summary of the features extracted from the ground truth collection using one-hot encoding.

Analysis class	Number of features
File operations	8,068
Registry changes	5,440
Strings	5,161
Processes & Mutexes	1,101
Functions	398
Services	44
Other	214

Model Creation and Validation. We use the ground-truth extracted to train a classification model. The accuracy of the model was calculated using K-fold cross-validation [26], with $K = 5$. The dataset was randomly divided to 70% training data and 30% test data. The performance of the model was measured using the f-score which takes into account the precision and recall for each class [6]. We tested different classification algorithms, i.e., SVM, random trees and neural networks, obtaining similar performances. Thus, for our experiments, we used an extremely randomized trees classifier [3]. The classifier's accuracy was tested with a different number of trees, with no significant change in performance. The performance results of our injector classifier are described in Sect. 3.2 along with a bias analysis.

3   Results

In this section, we present the results of our analysis. We start with a dataset characterization, including the type of files released in the cheats. We continue analyzing the performance of the injector classifier, and some case studies for injectors detected in our dataset. Finally, we present the results obtained from the analysis of the forums, including the demographics of the actors involved, as well as the activity related to the trading of a subset of actors that release more cheats and more injectors.

3.1   Dataset Characterization

Table 2 summarizes our dataset. In MPGH there are 86,789 posts with links to attachments, from which we have obtained 168,096 links and downloaded 160,991 attachments (some of the links were duplicated or death links). From these, 119,715 (74.3%) corresponded to images and thus were excluded from the analysis. From the remaining, 376 files were not processed; 10 files consisting of password-protected files which were not cracked by our password cracking tool (Sect. 2.3), 197 files were corrupted and 130 were multi-archives. In UC there are 16,836 posts from where we have downloaded 21,265 attachments (images excluded). A total of 146 files were not processed; 75 archives were skipped as they were multi-part and 71 were corrupted.

Table 2. Summary of the data extracted from the Multiplayer Game Hacks (MPGH) and the UnknownCheats (UC) forums.

		MPGH	UC
Structure	Forums	752	227
	Cheat Forums	555	140
	Games	191	118
	Actors	511,440	184,568
Threads in	Overall	449,832	85,454
game forums	With attachments	31,705	4,552
Posts in	Overall	5,809,108	1,203,745
game forums	With attachments	36,688	7,049

Out of all the data collected, we focus our analysis on forums that are dedicated to discussing specific games as indicated by the title of the forum, e.g. *Fortnite Hacks & Cheats*. We have mapped 630 forums to 309 game-specific forums out of a total of 238 unique games (see Table 2). We thus filter out attachments posted in forums not related to particular games (11,854 attachments). Overall, we see 5.6M game-related posts and 35K attachments in MPGH, and 1.4M posts and 7K attachments in UC.

Figure 2 shows the top 10 games in the last two years judging by the number of posts discussing each game. The total volume of posts in MPGH is much higher but is decreasing, while in UC it remains stable. This suggests that UC is becoming the principal community for cheats. Moreover, while it is more visible for UC, both communities experienced an increase in the number of posts since the beginning of March 2020 (this was more evident in MPGH). This matches the time when COVID-19 related lockdowns were imposed globally, and it is consistent with existing reports that show an increase in cheating activity by means of Denial of Service (DoS) attacks during the lockdown period [8]. When looking at individual games, we see that CS: GO is the most popular game in the two communities.

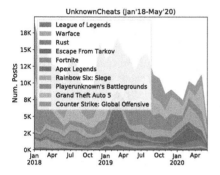 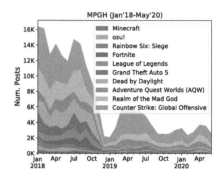

Fig. 2. Top 10 games by number of posts in UnknownCheats (left) and MPGH (right) from January 2018 until May 2020.

Table 3 provides a more detailed breakdown of the different file types found in the attachments. The *EXE* category includes all sorts of executable files, including MS-DOS, scripts, ELF and COFF (Unix), LSB, and Mach-O files. An insight that can be directly obtained from these results is the focus of each community: UC users are more interested in technical discussions around cheats, and thus they widely share the source code used to create cheats (e.g. 44% of the files from UC are C/C++ files, as opposed to MPGH where only 6% are of these types).

Table 3. Summary of attachment file types in MPGH and UC.

	MPGH Total (%)	UC Total (%)		MPGH Total (%)	UC Total (%)
Documents	363,167(37.4)	150,290(37.3)	DLL	21,760(2.2)	7,273(1.8)
Data file	164,293(16.9)	17,964(4.5)	Multimedia	20,825(2.1)	3,493(0.9)
Image	163,369(16.8)	10,513(2.6)	Game files	14,349(1.4)	4,100(1.0)
Java	59,779(6.2)	362(0.1)	Emails	13,916(1.4)	9 (0.00)
C	35,975(3.7)	51,101(12.7)	Scripts	12,357(1.3)	5,610(1.4)
C++	33,024(3.4)	127,216(31.6)	HTML	12,051(1.2)	2,892 (0.7)
EXE	26,704(2.7)	7,722(1.9)	Other	28,664(2.9)	14,099(3.5)

3.2   Injectors Classifier

Injecting code (e.g., in the form of a DLL) in a process is a widely-used method
to piggyback into the execution context of a process. While this technique can
aid programmers in the process of bypassing the restrictions of an operating
system [28], it is also used by legitimate programs (e.g., Anti Viruses).

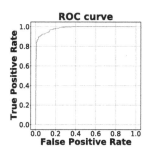

Fig. 3. Receiver Operating Characteristic (ROC) curve for the class of injectors showing 0.98 area under the curve.

We evaluate the classifier using K-fold cross-validation as described in
Sect. 2.4. We report the performance of our classifier using the average f-score
measure[6]. Overall, our system reports an f-score of 91%. The model performs
well on both classes with 0.94 *sensitivity* (TPR). When comparing the two classes
bias we can observe a 0.11 FPR on the injector class and 0.03 FPR on the good-
ware class which contributes to a *specificity* of 0.97. Figure 3 shows the ROC
curve and summarizes the trade-off between the FPR and the FPR. Having
both high *sensitivity* and *specificity* rate translates to the classifier being able
to identify injectors as well as files that are not classed as injectors. However,
obtained FPRs indicate that our classifier is better at identifying what is *not an
injector* (our goodware, negative class). If appropriately built into an automatic
analysis system, our classifier could be used by anti-cheat analysts to quickly
discard newly uploaded files that are not of interest, reducing the number of
files and posts that need to be manually reviewed.

To better understand the classifier output, we run it against the set of 12,035
binary files for which we have information from the VT sandbox. From these,
45% were classified as injectors. We applied a set of heuristics to them to further understand the output. For example, 512 (9.3%) of these files mention the
injection capabilities of the binary either in the thread title (418) and/or in
the filename of the archive where the binary is included (253). This provides
strong evidence that these files are actual injectors. Also, we confirm that some
binaries, although not released as general-purpose injectors, implement injection
capabilities. This is the case of an auxiliary tool used to change the MD5 hash
of the cheat process before it is analysed by the corresponding anti-cheat engine
to evade basic signature-based detection. Since this is done in runtime, the tool

needs to inject itself into the game process memory. Another example is one tool that is (was) used to inject code in Flash processes and replace Action-Script Bytecode (ABC) to abuse Flash-based games. This tool was first tagged as malicious by some anti-virus vendors (and then allow-listed) due to its potential to 'inject malicious code into SWF files[11]. Another example of such a file classified as an injector is a tool called LeagueDumper[12]. This tool gets injected into the League of Legends game client and stores memory components of the games' process back to disk for analysis. While this tool is not directly used to inject a game cheat, it helps cheat developers to analyse the game binaries (which are encrypted with a custom packer to avoid this kind of behaviour).

3.3   Forum Analysis

In this section, we analyze the social aspects of the two underground communities studied. We report about the demographics of the actors involved, including the social relations of these actors and their interests in the marketplace section.

Demographics. As seen in Table 2, the forum dataset is comprised of more than 511K and 184K members in MPGH and UC respectively. However, only a small proportion of these are involved in the actual provision of cheats. We consider a cheat is provided if: i) the attachment contains a binary file (e.g. DLL or EXE) and ii) the attachment is released on a game board. We found that 4,522 actors on MPGH (0.9%) and 2,476 on UC (1.3%) have shared at least one attachment in gaming forums. Figure 4 shows the distribution of actors according to the number of attachments and the number of games where these attachments are shared. A large proportion of authors have shared more than one attachment (around 51% in MPGH and 42% in UC). Also, around 8% of users in MPGH (377) have provided more than 10 attachments (and indeed, a single actor provides a total of 290 attachments). This shows that, while many users participate in the sharing of cheats, the majority of the cheats are shared by a small subset of the community. We also see differences in the specialization of users. Left-hand plots in Fig. 4 show the different games for which actors have shared attachments (we only consider those actors providing more than 2 attachments). We observe that most users (65% in MPGH and 60% in UC) are specialized in a single game (e.g. we see a single user in MPGH who has shared 218 different attachments in just one game, or one actor that has shared 286 attachments in just two games). However, there are users that are not specialized in particular games, and indeed we find that UC users tend to be less specialized, with some users sharing attachments in up to 17 different games.

Marketplace Activity. Our analysis is focused on data that is publicly released in the forums. Nevertheless, it is well known that users in underground forums

---

[11] https://community.mcafee.com/t5/Malware/quot-False-Artemis-4DD89AF63CF7-quot/m-p/521383 Accessed on 10th May 2021.

[12] https://github.com/tarekwiz/LeagueDumper Accessed on 10th May 2021.

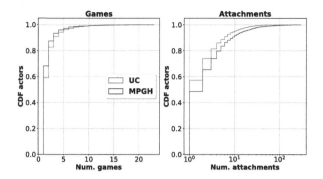

Fig. 4. Distribution of actors by number of attachments (right) and games (left) in MPGH and UnknownCheats (UC).

do share material related to cybercrime activities for free in order to increase their reputation and thus gain an advantage against competitors in the marketplace [15]. Also, underground forums have become improvised marketplaces of all sorts of virtual and online goods [20,24,27], and indeed MPGH has a set of sub-forums dedicated to trading. Estimating the actual volume of sales/benefits of a particular user is challenging—most of the actual trades occur by means of private messages and chats. However, the info gathered from these users in the market-related forums serves as a good estimation of the financial activity of these users. Accordingly, we have analyzed the number of posts made in the marketplace by the actors in MPGH that have released at least one binary attachment in gaming forums. Table 4 shows the number of actors posting and the total posts written in marketplace-related sub-forums. It can be observed that the most popular forum among cheat providers is about selling accounts/keys/items. This confirms that cheat providers are also engaged in Real Money Trading, which is a well-known practice to monetize cheats, either individually or as part of a gang or Gold Farming Group (GFG) [18]. Two other popular sub-forums are *Giveaways* and *Scammer Grave*. The former is typically used by forum users to increase their reputation and popularity by offering free goods, services, and even cryptocurrencies. The latter is a miscellaneous forum for reporting and discussing scams. The fact that cheat developers are reporting or discussing scams is another indicator of them being engaged in trading. Table 4 compares the activities of cheat providers with the top 100 actors according to the number of injectors released. Overall, we see that top cheat providers have higher interaction in the marketplace than the injector providers. Also, we observe that, rather than selling actual goods, in general, injector providers are more active in the *Giveaway* section. This might be due to the fact that we classify these actors by looking at the injectors that have been released for free (recall from Sect. 2.1 that we do not pay for these products and thus all the analysis is based on freely available attachments). Also, we see that 12 of these actors are actively engaged in the trading of eBooks, with an average of around 92 posts per author on this board.

Table 4. Activity of cheat providers in terms of number of posts and average posts per actor (P/A) in each sub-forum. *Marketplaces for specific games.

Forum	All actors			Top 100 injector providers		
	P/A	#Actors	#posts	P/A	#Actors	# posts
Selling Accounts/Keys/Items	31.14	1,278	18.10%	17.90	40	8.94%
Giveaways	49.42	886	19.91%	25.79	43	13.85%
Scammer Grave	51.70	651	15.31%	39.64	33	16.33%
Buying Accounts/Keys/Items	11.06	603	3.03%	2.35	20	0.59%
User Services	18.68	597	5.07%	12.09	23	3.47%
Trade Accounts/Keys/Items	8.21	488	1.82%	7.36	14	1.29%
eBooks For Sale	24.44	358	3.98%	92.08	12	13.80%
Marketplace Talk	14.86	335	2.26%	6.00	11	0.82%
Elite*	9.37	320	1.36%	3.15	13	0.51%
Marketplace Price Check / Questions	7.37	306	1.03%	15.38	13	2.50%
OTHERS (38)	11.86	3,828	28 %	13.90	153	37 %
TOTAL	48.62	4,522	219,854	80.10	100	8,010

Social Relations. Finally, we analyze the influence or popularity of users providing cheats and providing injectors in the entire community. For such purpose, we apply Social Network Analysis using the techniques described in Sect. 3.3. First, we build the graph of the two communities, MPGH and UC. Then, we compute the in-degree centrality metric of all the users in each forum, which indicates, for a given user, how many replies he/she has received, and from how many peers. Then, we compute three ranks: R_A, R_I and R_N. The first one ranks the actors based on the number of cheats released, the second one ranks them based on injectors, and the latter ranks actors based on their popularity in the community, derived from network centrality measures. For each actor we calculate the quartile within each rank, so we can compare whether higher positions in one rank correspond with higher positions in the other rank. Figure 5 shows the relations between the quartiles for the three ranks R_A, R_I and R_N (denoted QAi, QIi and QNi for $i \in [1, 4]$ respectively). It can be observed that most of the users that are in the first quartile of R_A are also in the first quartile of R_N, in both MPGH (55%) and UC (53%). This indicates that cheat providers are, in general, popular in their corresponding social network. A similar pattern can be observed for those providing injectors, though with a lower difference (39% and 34%n MPGH and UC respectively). However, there are also various actors which are popular and influencing users (i.e., from $QN1$), and share a few cheats and injectors, or don not share at all. Note that these forums are not used only for trading, but also for exchanging knowledge and meet peers. Thus, being socially influencing is not a sign of being a cheat provider. Instead, we observe that the free provision of cheats and injectors allows users to increase their popularity in the community.

4   Related Work

Underground Communities. Underground forums serve for the sharing and trading of illicit products and services, and also for exchange of knowledge [20]. Due to the anonymity and the sense of lack of prosecution, they are an attractive source for initiating into cybercrime activities [22,24]. Research on such forums allow to understand both old forms of cybercrimes, e.g. hacking [1,20] or game cheating [14], and also new forms of online fraud, such as e-whoring [15].

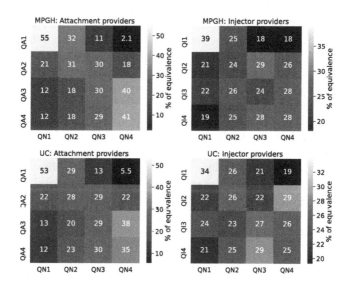

Fig. 5. Relation between number of users in each quartile according to number of attachments (QA, left-side), the number of injectors (QI, right-side) and popularity of the users in the social network (QN)

Previous works showed that cheating can be contagious within these communities, even when there is a clear social penalty associated with this practice [2,32]. The pathways into video-cheat gaming hacking were studied by Hughes et al., who analyzed the relationships of actors that are engaged both in general hacking and cheat development [14]. Fields et al. analyse cheat sites created for Whyville.net, an online gaming site to play casual science games [11]. They highlight the difference between hacks and cheats; and talk about the different types of online forums and their importance in the online gaming culture. Their work uses Grounded Theory [13] and was limited to a single community and 100 posts, which were visited weekly by the researchers to capture data for the study. In our work, we conduct quantitative analysis of two online communities with more than 7M posts overall, and also analyse the attachments shared by forum actors.

Cheat Detection. Machine learning classifiers based on static and dynamic analysis features have been widely proposed in the security domain for malware detection [5,7,16,23]. Other works have explored the use of machine learning to detect cheats based on the behavioural features exhibited by the players. Liu et al. proposed a method that uses bait targets as honeypots to detect aimbot-based cheats [19]. They performed a field measurement of two games, Counter Strike 1.6 and CS:GO. During one month and two weeks with 440 connections, they were able to identify 43 aimbots. More recently, Witschel and Wressnegger demonstrated that aimbots that introduce randomness while mimicking user improvement are capable of evading commercial anti-cheats [31]. Outside the academic world, some game developers, also provide updates on how their own games are affected by cheaters. In May 2020, Koskinas and Paloetti provided an update on the different cheats that were being reported and detected on *League of Legends* and other games from developer *Riot Games* [17]. They show how they have improved their capability to detect and remove cheaters (from 4% of games in 2015 to 1% of the players in 2020) and how cheaters are better at identifying and reporting other cheaters while playing.

To the best of our knowledge, this is the first academic work that proposes static and dynamic analysis of binary files to detect injectors used for video-game cheating.

5   Discussion and Conclusions

Limitations. Our measurement spans across two of the most popular online communities dedicated to video-game cheating and covers more than 200 games through multiple years. Our work mainly focuses on the analysis of binary files and we do not study how cheats are developed. The analysis of source code files and other scripts could provide valuable insight into the development process, but it is outside the scope of our work. Likewise, our work focuses on analyzing injectors for Windows-based games. We note however that not all game cheats affect Windows-based games. For instance, Pokemon Go, the 8th game within terms of number of cheats releases and it is only available on mobile platforms (Android and iOS). While our implementation can not currently analyze these files, our methodology is agnostic to the platform. Due to the nature of the features we use, our classifier is based on the features that these binaries exhibit today. As it happens in other domains, such as malware [16], these may change in the future as cheaters adapt to new detection techniques (e.g. Riot's Valorant[13]). While concept drift is outside of the scope of this work, the video game ecosystem provides additional data points (e.g. user-reports) that could be used to detect when the classifier becomes *outdated* and needs to be retrained.

Conclusions. In this work, we have performed a large-scale measurement of two online forums focused on video game cheating. Our study shows that these forums are widely used to distribute video game cheats, 40K since 2017 and that the majority of these cheats are developed by a small number of contributors that, in most cases, are specialized in a single game. Our results show that there is also a strong cooperation between the members of the community, which sometimes is promoted by financial incentive (i.e. selling cheats, etc. on marketplaces within the forum). Through our exploratory analysis we identify that cheat injectors are an important component gearing the cheating industry. Thus, we have developed a method to systematically detect injectors uploaded to the forum using both static and dynamic analysis features. Our classifier, which achieves a sensitivity of 0.94, could be used by anti-cheat analyst to quickly identify new injectors uploaded into these communities. Considering that between 2018 and 2020 the average number release posts per day was 7 (for each forum), using our classifier could help reduce the workload of the analyst when inspecting these new releases, preventing new cheats from becoming widespread within their games.

Acknowledgement. This work is partially supported by the Spanish grants ODIO (PID2019-111429RB-C21, PID2019-111429RB), the Region of Madrid grant CYNAMON-CM (P2018/TCS-4566), co-financed by European Structural Funds ESF and FEDER, and Excellence Program EPUC3M17, and the "Ramon y Cajal" Fellowship RYC-2020-029401.

A   Analysis Features

This appendix lists the feature categories used to train the injector classifier along with the number of features within each category. The first column describes the feature category each analysis is part of as seen on Table 1.

---

[13] https://support-valorant.riotgames.com/hc/en-us/articles/360046160933.

Table 5. Detailed categorization of features used for the injector classifier.

	Analysis name	Number of features
File Operations	files_opened	3,938
	files_deleted	1,817
	files_copied	955
	files_dropped	589
	files_written	432
	files_attribute_changed	337
Registry Changes	registry_keys_opened	2,722
	registry_keys_set	2,603
	registry_keys_deleted	115
Processes & Mutexes	processes_terminated	321
	processes_created	311
	processes_injected	12
	processes_killed	1
	processes_tree	1
	mutexes_opened	103
	mutexes_created	352
Services	services_opened	33
	services_started	6
	services_created	3
	services_stopped	1
	services_deleted	1
Functions	modules_loaded	338
	calls_highlighted	53
	signals_hooked	7
Strings	text_highlighted	4,560
	crypto_plain_text	601
Other	command_executions	155
	windows_searched	40
	permissions_requested	13
	crypto_algorithms_observed	2
	ip_traffic	1
	windows_hidden	1
	memory_pattern_domains	1
	memory_pattern_urls	1

References

1. Allodi, L.: Economic factors of vulnerability trade and exploitation. In: Proceedings of the ACM SIGSAC Conference on Computer and Communications Security, pp. 1483–1499. ACM (2017)
2. Blackburn, J., Kourtellis, N., Skvoretz, J., Ripeanu, M., Iamnitchi, A.: Cheating in online games: a social network perspective. ACM Trans. Internet Technol. (TOIT) **13**(3), 1–25 (2014)
3. Breiman, L., et al.: Arcing classifier (with discussion and a rejoinder by the author). Ann. Stat. **26**(3), 801–849 (1998)
4. Cano, N.: Game hacking: developing autonomous bots for online games. No Starch Press (2016)
5. Chen, Y., Wang, S., She, D., Jana, S.: On training robust pdf malware classifiers. In: 29th USENIX Security Symposium USENIX Security 20), pp. 2343–2360 (2020)
6. Chinchor, N., Sundheim, B.M.: Muc-5 evaluation metrics. In: Fifth Message Understanding Conference (MUC-5): Proceedings of a Conference Held in Baltimore, Maryland, 25–27 August, 1993 (1993)
7. Chumachenko, K.: Machine learning methods for malware detection and classification. The annals of statistics (2017)
8. Clayton, R.: The impact of lockdown on dos-for-hire. Tech. rep., Cambridge Cybercrime Centre COVID Briefing Papers, July 2020. https://www.cambridgecybercrime.uk/COVID/COVIDbriefing-3.pdf
9. Duh, H.B.-L., Chen, V.H.H.: Cheating behaviors in online gaming. In: Ozok, A.A., Zaphiris, P. (eds.) OCSC 2009. LNCS, vol. 5621, pp. 567–573. Springer, Heidelberg (2009). https://doi.org/10.1007/978-3-642-02774-1_61
10. Feng, W.C., Kaiser, E., Schluessler, T.: Stealth measurements for cheat detection in on-line games. In: Proceedings of the 7th ACM SIGCOMM Workshop on Network and System Support for Games, pp. 15–20. NetGames 2008. Association for Computing Machinery, New York (2008). https://doi.org/10.1145/1517494.1517497. https://doi.org/10.1145/1517494.1517497
11. Fields, D.A., Kafai, Y.B.: "stealing from grandma"or generating cultural knowledge? contestations and effects of cheating in a tween virtual world. Games Culture **5**(1), 64–87 (2010)
12. FireEye: Capa. https://github.com/fireeye/capa, https://github.com/fireeye/capa. Accessed July 2020
13. Glaser, B.G., Strauss, A.L., Strutzel, E.: The discovery of grounded theory; strategies for qualitative research. Nurs. Res. **17**(4), 364 (1968)
14. Hughes, J., Collier, B., Hutchings, A.: From playing games to committing crimes: a multi-technique approach to predicting key actors on an online gaming forum. In: 2019 APWG Symposium on Electronic Crime Research (eCrime). IEEE (2019)
15. Hutchings, A., Pastrana, S.: Understanding ewhoring. In: 2019 IEEE European Symposium on Security and Privacy (EuroS&P), pp. 201–214. IEEE (2019)
16. Jordaney, R., Sharad, K., Dash, S.K., Wang, Z., Papini, D., Nouretdinov, I., Cavallaro, L.: Transcend: detecting concept drift in malware classification models. In: 26th USENIX Security Symposium (USENIX Security 2017), pp. 625–642. USENIX Association, Vancouver, BC, August 2017. https://www.usenix.org/conference/usenixsecurity17/technical-sessions/presentation/jordaney
17. Koskinas, P., Paloetti, M.: Anti-cheat in lol (& more), May 2020 https://na.leagueoflegends.com/en-us/news/dev/dev-anti-cheat-in-lol-more/. https://na.leagueoflegends.com/en-us/news/dev/dev-anti-cheat-in-lol-more/. Accessed on May 2020

18. Lee, E., Woo, J., Kim, H., Kim, H.K.: No silk road for online gamers! using social network analysis to unveil black markets in online games. In: Proceedings of the 2018 World Wide Web Conference, pp. 1825–1834 (2018)
19. Liu, D., Gao, X., Zhang, M., Wang, H., Stavrou, A.: Detecting passive cheats in online games via performance-skillfulness inconsistency. In: 2017 47th Annual IEEE/IFIP International Conference on Dependable Systems and Networks (DSN), pp. 615–626. IEEE (2017)
20. Motoyama, M., McCoy, D., Levchenko, K., Savage, S., Voelker, G.M.: An analysis of underground forums. In: Proceedings of the 2011 ACM SIGCOMM conference on Internet Measurement Conference, pp. 71–80. ACM (2011)
21. Narula, H.: A billion new players are set to transform the gaming industry, December 2019. https://www.wired.co.uk/article/worldwide-gamers-billion-players. https://www.wired.co.uk/article/worldwide-gamers-billion-players. Accessed on May 2020
22. National Cyber Crime Unit/Prevent Team: Pathways into cyber crime, January 2017. https://www.nationalcrimeagency.gov.uk/who-we-are/publications/6-pathways-into-cyber-crime-1/file. Accessed July 2020
23. Onwuzurike, L., Mariconti, E., Andriotis, P., Cristofaro, E.D., Ross, G., Stringhini, G.: Mamadroid: detecting android malware by building Markov chains of behavioral models (extended version). ACM Trans. Privacy Secur. (TOPS) 22(2), 1–34 (2019)
24. Pastrana, S., Hutchings, A., Caines, A., Buttery, P.: Characterizing eve: analysing cybercrime actors in a large underground forum. In: Bailey, M., Holz, T., Stamatogiannakis, M., Ioannidis, S. (eds.) RAID 2018. LNCS, vol. 11050, pp. 207–227. Springer, Cham (2018). https://doi.org/10.1007/978-3-030-00470-5_10
25. Pastrana, S., Thomas, D.R., Hutchings, A., Clayton, R.: Crimebb: enabling cybercrime research on underground forums at scale. In: Proceedings of the 2018 World Wide Web Conference, pp. 1845–1854 (2018). https://doi.org/10.1145/3178876.3186178
26. Pedregosa, F., Varoquaux, G., Gramfort, A., Michel, V., Thirion, B., Grisel, O., Blondel, M., Prettenhofer, P., Weiss, R., Dubourg, V., Vanderplas, J., Passos, A., Cournapeau, D., Brucher, M., Perrot, M., Duchesnay, E.: Scikit-learn: machine learning in Python. J. Mach. Learn. Res. 12, 2825–2830 (2011)
27. Portnoff, R.S., Afroz, S., Durrett, G., Kummerfeld, J.K., Berg-Kirkpatrick, T., McCoy, D., Levchenko, K., Paxson, V.: Tools for automated analysis of cybercriminal markets. In: Proceedings of 26th International World Wide Web Conference (WWW) (2017)
28. Richter, J., Nasarre, C.: Windows via C/C++. Microsoft Press, 5th edn., November 2007
29. Shannon, C.E.: A mathematical theory of communication. Bell Syst. Tech. J. 27(3), 379–423 (1948)
30. Sherena.johnson@nist.gov: Nist special database 28, September 2020. https://www.nist.gov/srd/nist-special-database-28
31. Witschel, T., Wressnegger, C.: Aim low, shoot high: evading aimbot detectors by mimicking user behavior. In: Proceedings of the 13th European workshop on Systems Security, pp. 19–24 (2020)
32. Woo, J., Kang, S.W., Kim, H.K., Park, J.: Contagion of cheating behaviors in online social networks. IEEE Access 6, 29098–29108 (2018)

Blockchain

Revocable Policy-Based Chameleon Hash

Shengmin Xu[1,2], Jianting Ning[1,3(✉)], Jinhua Ma[1,2], Guowen Xu[4],
Jiaming Yuan[5], and Robert H. Deng[2]

[1] College of Computer and Cyber Security, Fujian Normal University,
Fuzhou 350117, China
jtning@fjnu.edu.cn
[2] School of Computing and Information Systems, Singapore Management University,
Singapore 188065, Singapore
{smxu,robertdeng}@smu.edu.sg
[3] State Key Laboratory of Information Security, Institute of Information
Engineering, Chinese Academy of Sciences, Beijing 100093, China
[4] School of Computer Science and Engineering, Nanyang Technological University,
Singapore 639798, Singapore
guowen.xu@ntu.edu.sg
[5] Computer and Information Science Department, University of Oregon, Eugene,
OR 97403, USA
jiamingy@uoregon.edu

Abstract. Policy-based chameleon hash (PCH) is a cryptographic
building block which finds increasing practical applications. Given a message and an access policy, for any chameleon hash generated by a PCH
scheme, a chameleon trapdoor holder whose rewriting privileges satisfy
the access policy can amend the underlying message without affecting the
hash value. In practice, it is necessary to revoke the rewriting privileges
of a trapdoor holder due to various reasons, such as change of positions,
compromise of credentials, or malicious behaviours. In this paper, we
introduce the notion of revocable PCH (RPCH) and formally define its
security. We instantiate a concrete RPCH construction by putting forward a practical revocable attribute-based encryption (RABE) scheme
which is adaptively secure under a standard assumption on prime-order
pairing groups. As application examples, we show how to effectively integrate RPCH into mutable blockchain and sanitizable signature for revok-
ing the rewriting privileges of any chameleon trapdoor holders. We implement our RPCH scheme and evaluate its performance to demonstrate its
efficiency.

Keywords: Policy-based chameleon hash · Revocable attribute-based
encryption · Mutable blockchain · Sanitizable signature

1 Introduction

Policy-based Chameleon Hash (PCH) generalizes the notion of chameleon hash
by giving one the ability to compute a chameleon hash and associate an access

© Springer Nature Switzerland AG 2021
E. Bertino et al. (Eds.): ESORICS 2021, LNCS 12972, pp. 327–347, 2021.
https://doi.org/10.1007/978-3-030-88418-5_16

policy to the hash. Chameleon trapdoor holders are issued rewriting privileges based on their attributes. A chameleon trapdoor holder whose rewriting privileges satisfy the access policy of a chameleon hash can find arbitrary collisions of the hash. Since PCH was proposed, it has found increasing applications in mutable blockchain and sanitizable signature to support fine-grained and controlled modifiability.

Mutable Blockchain. Most existing blockchains are designed to be immutable such that transactions in a block cannot be altered once they are confirmed. However, in many practical application scenarios, blockchain rewriting is necessary for reasons such as removing inappropriate contents [27,28] and complying legal obligations [1]. A mutable blockchain allows a certain party, called transaction modifier [4] who holds a chameleon trapdoor to process blockchain rewriting in a controlled way. By applying traditional asymmetric-key encryption and chameleon hash [24], Ateniese et al. [4] introduced the notion of mutable blockchain and proposed a construction that realizes block-level rewriting. Derler et al. [16] introduced the first construction of PCH, which supports transaction-level rewriting in a fine-grained way. Deuber et al. [17] later proposed a permissionless transaction rewriting mechanism based on consensus-based e-voting [23]. Recently, Tian et al. [36] considered the accountability in PCH-based mutable blockchain.

Sanitizable Signature. As a variant of digital signatures, sanitizable signatures allow a signer and a signer designated party, called sanitizer [3], to hold a chameleon trapdoor for rewriting signed messages in a controlled way. By replacing the traditional hash with chameleon hash [24], Ateniese et al. [3] introduced the notion of sanitizable signature and proposed a construction that realizes *unforgeability, privacy, transparency, immutability* and *accountability*. Sanitizable signature with *unlinkability* was proposed by Fleischhacker et al. [19]. Camenisch et al. [14] introduced chameleon hash with ephemeral trapdoor (CHET) to realize *invisibility*. However, the aforementioned sanitizable signatures and some following works [8,13,18] mainly concentrated on investigating additional security requirements, the sanitizer cannot be managed efficiently and flexibly. In particular, the signer needs to know the sanitizer before the signature generation phase, and sanitizing capabilities are controlled in a coarse-grained way. To address this problem, a PCH-based sanitizable signature [34] is proposed to allow the signer to define multiple sanitizers for a signed message in a fine-grained way.

Motivation. In practice, a chameleon trapdoor holder may abuse her/his rewriting privileges, maliciously rewrite the hashed objects (e.g., transaction contents in mutable blockchain and messages in sanitizable signature) to spread inappropriate/incorrect contents, or even sell the rewriting privileges to gain illegal profits. Such abused privileges must be revoked as the actions of trapdoor holders impact the security, reputation, and robustness of the entire system. However, to the best of our knowledge, current PCH proposals [16,34,36] cannot provide revocability toward rewriting privileges.

To control rewriting privileges in a versatile way, fast attribute-based message encryption (FAME) [2], as a variant of attribute-based encryption (ABE), has been used as the underlying building block of PCH [16,34,36]. However, a PCH built on standard FAME does not support user revocation. To address this issue, revocable ABE (RABE) can be used to replace the underlying FAME and realize PCH with revocability. However, one cannot naively employ the existing direct/indirect RABE to replace FAME without sacrificing the security or performance of PCH. Specifically, direct RABE incurs large overhead and is impractical in real-world scenarios while indirect RABE suffers from weak security or poor performance compared to FAME.

Direct RABE [6,7,12,26]. There are two strategies in direct revocation. The first strategy is mainly built on the key generation center (KGC) who broadcasts an updated secret key for each non-revoked user via a secure channel periodically. The secret key is bound to attributes appending a timestamp, i.e., $att\|t$, where att is an attribute and t is timestamp updated in each time epoch. This approach is impractical since a ciphertext would contain a long policy to cover all possible t values and the secure channels for a periodic secret key update to all non-revoked users are expensive. The other approach is embedding identities of all the revoked users in the ciphertexts, which is also impractical since data owners must keep the revocation list update to date and the revocation list will grow longer as time goes by.

Indirect RABE [15,31,33,37–41]. To address the problem in direct revocation, indirect revocation divides a user's decryption privilege into a secret key and a public key-updating material. A KGC issues a secret key to a user when she/he joins the system and broadcasts the key-updating material to all users periodically over a public channel. Only non-revoked users can combine their secret keys and the key-updating material to obtain decryption privileges at each time period.

Although RABE[1] offers a potential solution to realize PCH with revocation, how to realize RABE based on FAME is an open problem. FAME [2], as a basic building block for PCH [16,34,36], is an adaptively secure ABE on prime-order groups. Previous RABE solutions generally rely on the property of linear master secret sharing, named ElGamal-type ABE [40], such as adaptively secure ABE (on composite-order groups) [25] used in [33] and selectively secure ABE (on prime-order groups) [32] used in [15,31,37,39,40]. In ElGamal-type ABE, the master secret key and ciphertext are in the form of α and $m \cdot e(g,g)^{\alpha s}$, respectively. By dividing α into $\alpha - \beta$ and β, the KGC applies $\alpha - \beta$ to issue secret keys to users and uses β to generate the public key-updating material. A revoked user cannot erase β in her/his secret key to process data decryption, and a non-revoked user can easily combine the secret key and the key-updating material to erase β to reveal the sealed message. However, FAME [2] is not an ElGamal-type ABE and cannot follow this strategy. The following problem arises naturally:

---

[1] In the rest of the paper, unless otherwise specified, RABE represents indirect RABE.

"Can RABE be built from FAME and further be integrated into PCH to revoke rewriting privileges?"

Our Contributions. In this paper, we give an affirmative answer to the above problem by introducing the first formal treatment for revocability to PCH, dubbed *revocable policy-based chameleon hash* (RPCH). We present a new *revocable attribute-based encryption*, which is adaptively secure under a standard assumption on prime-order pairing groups, and then based on it we realize a practical construction of RPCH. The major contributions of the paper are three-fold.

- *Formal definition of RPCH.* RPCH extends PCH with revocability. We give a formal definition of RPCH and propose the notions of *fully indistinguishability*, *collision-resistance* and *uniqueness* in presence of attackers.
- *Adaptively secure RABE.* RABE serves as the fundamental building block to offer the properties of policy-based access control and revocability simultaneously. To instantiate an efficient RPCH construction, we present an adaptively secure RABE under a standard assumption on prime-order pairing groups.[2]
- *Practical RPCH construction.* We provide a concrete construction of RPCH with performance evaluation. Compared to PCH [16], our RPCH achieves revocability with negligible overhead. Specifically, our RPCH takes one extra exponentiation (around 3.83 ms) for hashing, and one more multiplication and pairing (around 21.19 ms) for collision finding. We also show that our RPCH is practical when integrating it into mutable blockchain and sanitizable signature.

2 Overview

In this section, we give an overview of the proposed RABE and RPCH, and the design intuitions behind them.

Overview of RABE Technique. We resort to the techniques in indistinguishability under chosen plaintext attacks (IND-CPA) secure FAME [2] and IND-CPA secure revocable identity-based encryption (RIBE) with decryption key[3] exposure resistance [35], where key exposure resistance guarantees that the exposed short-term decryption key does not affect the security of any other time periods. In our solution, the secret key follows the structure of FAME and imitates the form of a second-level secret key of the hierarchical identity-based encryption

---

[2] As explained above, previous RABE solutions are either selectively secure [15,37–41] or adaptively secure under non-standard assumptions or composite-order groups [33]. Guillevic [22] reported that bilinear pairings are 254 times slower in composite-order than in prime-order groups for the same 128-bit security. Despite dual pairing vector space [30] can transfer composite-order groups to prime-order groups, it could be paramount for enormous encoding schemes [5].

[3] In RABE, the decryption privilege is based on the decryption key, which is derived from the long-term secret key and public key-updating material.

(HIBE) [10] to achieve fine-grained access control and user revocation simultaneously. In the following, we describe the intuition behind our RABE construction from the perspectives of *secret key structure* and *key period management*.

- *Secret key structure.* We modify the structure of the FAME secret key by removing a random element g_θ, where θ is used to manage user revocation. At the beginning of each period, the key-updating material is published, and it contains g_θ with an additional time-based restriction. A non-revoked user can update her/his long-term secret key to obtain a FAME secret key with the time-based restriction, and this secret key can be used for decryption if the time-based restriction matches the timestamp associated with the ciphertext. To resist decryption key exposure attacks, we design a decryption key generation algorithm that derives a probabilistic short-term decryption key. Thus, by knowing the short-term decryption key and the public key-updating material, no one can derive the corresponding long-term secret key.
- *Key periodical management.* We rely on the key-update-nodes KUNodes algorithm [29] to reduce the size of the key-updating material from linear to the number of system users to logarithmic. Each chameleon trapdoor holder with an identifier id has $\log n$ secret keys that relate to the path of their positions in the tree-based state st to the tree root node, denoted as Path(id). The key update generation algorithm outputs a key-updating material based on KUNodes by inputting a state st, a revocation list rl, and a timestamp t. Each non-revoked user can find only one node $\theta \in$ Path(id) $\cap$ KUNodes(st, rl, t) to generate a decryption key, while revoked users cannot find it $\emptyset \in$ Path(id) $\cap$ KUNodes(st, rl, t), hence, they are revoked implicitly. Although the size of the secret key is increased from constant to logarithmic, the effect is minimal since the secret key is distributed once and the key-updating material is broadcast each period.

Overview of RPCH System Model. As shown in Fig. 1, RPCH allows a party, e.g., a data *owner*, to compute a chameleon hash associated with an access policy and a timestamp. Another party, called chameleon trapdoor holder or *modifier*, who possesses privileges and valid key-updating materials that satisfy the access policy and the timestamp in a given hash can then find arbitrary collisions. RPCH thus supports the modifiability at a fine-grained level and the revocability of the modifier rewriting privileges.

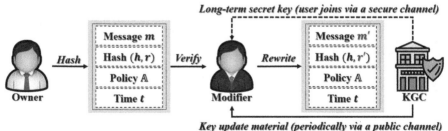

Fig. 1. System model of RPCH

Overview of RPCH Technique. We resort to the techniques in previous PCH [16], sanitizable signature [34] and our proposed RABE. Our PRCH follows the previous PCH solutions [16,34] by replacing the underlying FAME scheme with our proposed RABE, and combining with CHET [14]. In CHET, two trapdoors are used to guarantee the security of controlled rewriting: a long-term trapdoor and an ephemeral trapdoor. In RABE, we have an attribute-based long-term secret key issued when the modifier joins and a key-updating material publicly distributed each period. In the following, we describe the intuition behind our RPCH construction from the perspectives of *long-term secret key* and *ephemeral trapdoor*.

- *Long-term secret.* The long-term secret key consists of an attribute-based long-term secret key and a CHET long-term trapdoor, and both of them are issued when the modifier joins the system. The attribute-based long-term secret key is used to combine the key-updating material to enable the non-revoked modifier to derive a short-term decryption key and revoke the invalid modifier implicitly. The CHET long-term trapdoor cannot work for rewriting individually and must cooperate with the CHET ephemeral trapdoor.

- *Ephemeral trapdoor.* Each data owner picks a CHET ephemeral trapdoor during data hash and encrypts this trapdoor via hybrid encryption, where symmetric-key encryption to seal this trapdoor and RABE to seal the symmetric key. Hence, to operate the rewriting procedure, the modifier must have an attributed-based decryption key (that satisfies the access policy and the timestamp associated with the sealed ephemeral trapdoor) and the CHET long-term trapdoor. In other words, the rewriting privilege is authorized by the KGC and the data owner simultaneously. Note that, the data owner cannot process the rewriting procedure alone since the CHET long-term trapdoor is unknown to him/her.

We propose notions of *fully indistinguishability, collision-resistance* and *uniqueness* as the security requirements for RPCH. Derler et al. [16] introduced the first PCH, and its security in terms of indistinguishability and collision-resistance. Samelin and Slamanig [34] improved the security by introducing the notions of full indistinguishability, collision-resistance, and uniqueness. We refine security notations in the above works by additionally considering several different types of adversaries. In particular, in our security model, an adversary could be the combination of outsiders, insiders without valid secret keys, and insiders with valid secret keys but being revoked.

3   Preliminaries

In this section, we present the hard assumption, access structure and some building blocks, which are used in our proposed RABE and PCH schemes.

3.1 Bilinear Map

Let $\mathcal{G}$ be an asymmetric prime-order (Type-III) pairing group generator that on input 1^κ, outputs description of three groups $\mathbb{G}, \mathbb{H}, \mathbb{G}_T$ of prime order p with a bilinear map $e : \mathbb{G} \times \mathbb{H} \to \mathbb{G}_T$, and generators g and h for $\mathbb{G}$ and $\mathbb{H}$ with following properties: 1) bilinearity: for all $u \in \mathbb{G}, v \in \mathbb{H}$ and $a, b \in \mathbb{Z}_p$, $e(u^a, v^b) = e(u, v)^{ab}$; 2) non-degeneration: $e(g, h) \neq 1$; and 3) computability: it is efficient to compute $e(u, v)$ for any $u \in \mathbb{G}$ and $v \in \mathbb{H}$.

3.2 Hard Assumption

Definition 1 (DLIN). *A bilinear pairing group generator $\mathcal{G}$ satisfies the decisional linear assumption (DLIN) if for all probabilistic polynomial time adversaries $\mathcal{A}$, $\mathbf{Adv}_{\mathcal{A}}^{\mathsf{DLIN}}(\kappa) = \big| \Pr[\mathcal{A}(1^\kappa, pp, D, T_0)] - \Pr[\mathcal{A}(1^\kappa, pp, D, T_1)] \big|$ is negligible in the security parameter κ, where $pp = (p, \mathbb{G}, \mathbb{H}, \mathbb{G}_T, e, g, h) \leftarrow \mathcal{G}(1^\kappa)$; $a_1, a_2 \in \mathbb{Z}_p^*$; $s_1, s_2, s \in \mathbb{Z}_p$; $D = (g^{a_1}, g^{a_2}, h^{a_1}, h^{a_2}, g^{a_1 s_1}, g^{a_2 s_2}, h^{a_1 s_1}, h^{a_2 s_2})$; $T_0 = (g^{s_1 + s_2}, h^{s_1 + s_2})$; and $T_1 = (g^s, h^s)$.*

3.3 Access Structure

Definition 2 (Access Structure). *Let $\mathbb{U}$ denote the universe of attributes. A collection $\mathbb{A} \in 2^{\mathbb{U}} \setminus \{\emptyset\}$ of non-empty sets is an access structure on $\mathbb{U}$. The sets in $\mathbb{A}$ are called the authorized sets, and the sets not in $\mathbb{A}$ are called the unauthorized sets. A collection $\mathbb{A} \in 2^{\mathbb{U}} \setminus \{\emptyset\}$ is called monotone if $\forall B, C$: if $B \in \mathbb{A}$ and $B \subseteq C$, then $C \in \mathbb{A}$.*

3.4 Revocable Attribute-Based Encryption

Definition 3 (RABE). *Let $\mathcal{I}$ be an identifier space, $\mathcal{M}$ denote a message space and $\mathcal{T}$ be a time space. A revocable attribute-based encryption with decryption key exposure resistance $\mathcal{RABE}$ consists of the algorithms $\{\mathsf{Setup}, \mathsf{KGen}, \mathsf{KUpt}, \mathsf{DKGen}, \mathsf{Enc}, \mathsf{Dec}, \mathsf{Rev}\}$ such that:*

- $\mathsf{Setup}(1^\kappa, n) \to (mpk, msk, st, rl)$: *The probabilistic setup algorithm takes a security parameter $\kappa \in \mathbb{N}$ and the number of system users $n \in \mathbb{N}$ as input, and outputs a master public key mpk, a master secret key sk, a state st and a revocation list rl, where 1^κ and mpk are implicit input to all other algorithms.*
- $\mathsf{KGen}(msk, st, id, \mathcal{S}) \to (sk_{id}, st)$: *The probabilistic key generation algorithm takes a master secret key msk, a state st, an identifier $id \in \mathcal{I}$ and an attribute set $\mathcal{S} \subseteq \mathbb{U}$ as input, and outputs a secret key sk_{id} and an updated state st.*
- $\mathsf{KUpt}(st, rl, t) \to ku_t$: *The probabilistic key update generation algorithm takes a state st, a revocation list rl and a timestamp $t \in \mathcal{T}$ as input, and outputs a key-updating material ku_t. Note that st is kept secret by the KGC.*
- $\mathsf{DKGen}(sk_{id}, ku_t) \to dk_{id,t}$: *The probabilistic decryption key generation algorithm takes a secret key sk_{id} and a key-updating material ku_t as input, and outputs a decryption key $dk_{id,t}$.*

– $\mathsf{Enc}(m, \mathbb{A}, t) \to c$: *The probabilistic encryption algorithm takes a message* $m \in \mathcal{M}$, *an access policy* $\mathbb{A} \in 2^{\mathbb{U}}$ *and a timestamp* $t \in \mathcal{T}$ *as input, and outputs a ciphertext* c.

– $\mathsf{Dec}(dk_{id,t}, c) \to m$: *The deterministic decryption algorithm takes a decryption key* $dk_{id,t}$ *and a ciphertext* c *as input, and outputs a message* $m \in \mathcal{M}$.

– $\mathsf{Rev}(rl, id, t) \to rl$: *The deterministic revocation algorithm takes a revocation list* rl, *an identifier* $id \in \mathcal{I}$ *and a timestamp* $t \in \mathcal{T}$ *as input, and outputs an updated revocation list* rl.

Definition 4 (IND-CPA). *The security definition of* IND-CPA *for* $\mathcal{RABE}$ *between an adversary* $\mathcal{A}$ *and a challenger* $\mathcal{C}$.

Setup. $\mathcal{C}$ *runs* $\mathsf{Setup}(1^\kappa, n)$ *and gives* mpk *to* $\mathcal{A}$. $\mathcal{C}$ *keeps* msk, st *and* rl *secret.*

Phase 1. $\mathcal{A}$ *adaptively issues a sequence of following queries to* $\mathcal{C}$.

– $\mathcal{O}_{\mathsf{KGen}}(\cdot, \cdot)$: $\mathcal{A}$ *issues key generation query on an identifier* $id \in \mathcal{I}$ *and a set of attributes* $\mathcal{S} \subseteq \mathbb{U}$. $\mathcal{C}$ *returns a secret key* sk_{id} *by running* $\mathsf{KGen}(msk, st, id, \mathcal{S})$.

– $\mathcal{O}_{\mathsf{KUpt}}(\cdot)$: $\mathcal{A}$ *issues key update query on a timestamp* $t \in \mathcal{T}$. $\mathcal{C}$ *returns a key-updating material* ku_t *by running* $\mathsf{KUpt}(st, rl, t)$.

– $\mathcal{O}_{\mathsf{DKGen}}(\cdot, \cdot, \cdot)$: $\mathcal{A}$ *issues decryption key generation query on an identifier* $id \in \mathcal{I}$, *a set of attributes* $\mathcal{S} \subseteq \mathbb{U}$ *and a timestamp* $t \in \mathcal{T}$. $\mathcal{C}$ *returns a decryption key* $dk_{id,t}$ *by running* $\mathsf{DKGen}(sk_{id}, ku_t)$ *if the secret key* sk_{id} *and the key-updating material* ku_t *are available. Otherwise,* $\mathcal{C}$ *generates* sk_{id} *and* ku_t *first.*

– $\mathcal{O}_{\mathsf{Rev}}(\cdot, \cdot)$: $\mathcal{A}$ *issues revocation query on an identifier* $id \in \mathcal{I}$ *and a timestamp* $t \in \mathcal{T}$. $\mathcal{C}$ *updates the revocation list* rl *by running* $\mathsf{Rev}(rl, id, t)$.

$\mathcal{A}$ *is allowed to query above oracles with the following restrictions:*

1. $\mathcal{O}_{\mathsf{KUpt}}(\cdot)$ *and* $\mathcal{O}_{\mathsf{Rev}}(\cdot, \cdot)$ *can be queried at the time* $t \in \mathcal{T}$ *which is greater than or equal to that of all previous queries.*

2. $\mathcal{O}_{\mathsf{Rev}}(\cdot, \cdot)$ *cannot be queried at the time* $t \in \mathcal{T}$ *if* $\mathcal{O}_{\mathsf{KUpt}}(\cdot)$ *was queried at the time* $t \in \mathcal{T}$.

Challenge. $\mathcal{A}$ *outputs two messages* m_0 *and* m_1 *of the same size, an access structure* $\mathbb{A}^*$ *and a timestamp* $t^* \in \mathcal{T}$. $\mathcal{C}$ *terminates if the previous queries against the following restrictions:*

3. $\mathcal{O}_{\mathsf{DKGen}}(\cdot, \cdot, \cdot)$ *cannot be queried any identifier* $id \in \mathcal{I}$ *with any set of attributes* $\mathcal{S} \models \mathbb{A}^*$ *at the challenge time* $t^* \in \mathcal{T}$.

4. $\mathcal{O}_{\mathsf{Rev}}(\cdot, \cdot)$ *must be queried the identifier* $id \in \mathcal{I}$ *associated attributes* $\mathcal{S} \models \mathbb{A}^*$ *and the timestamp* $t \leq t^*$ *if* $\mathcal{O}_{\mathsf{KGen}}(\cdot, \cdot)$ *was queried any identifier* $id \in \mathcal{I}$ *and any set of attributes* $\mathcal{S} \models \mathbb{A}^*$.

$\mathcal{C}$ *randomly chooses* $b \in \{0, 1\}$, *and returns* c^* *to* $\mathcal{A}$ *by running* $\mathsf{Enc}(m_b, \mathbb{A}^*, t^*)$.

Phase 2. $\mathcal{A}$ *continues issuing queries to* $\mathcal{C}$ *with the previous restrictions.*

Guess. $\mathcal{A}$ *makes a guess* b' *for* b, *and it wins the game if* $b' = b$.

The advantage of $\mathcal{A}$ *in this game is defined as* $\mathbf{Adv}_{\mathcal{RABE}, \mathcal{A}}^{\mathsf{IND\text{-}CPA}}(\kappa, n) = \left| \Pr[b = b'] - 1/2 \right|$. *An* $\mathcal{RABE}$ *is* IND-CPA *secure if any probabilistic polynomial time adversary has at most a negligible advantage in* κ.

3.5   Tree-Based Structure for User Revocation

The tree-based revocation list has been widely used to reduce the computation and communication costs of key-updating materials from linear to logarithmic. The basic idea is to find a minimum of sub-tree roots to cover all non-revoked users. Specifically, as shown in Fig. 2, each data user is assigned to an individual leaf node in a binary tree and is issued secret keys from the corresponding leaf node to the root (see Step 1). To revoke users (see Step 2), we only need to find sub-tree roots that are exclusive of revoked users to generate key updates (see Step 3).

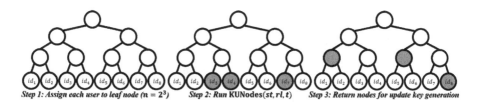

Step 1: Assign each user to leaf node $(n = 2^3)$ Step 2: Run KUNodes(st, rl, t)   Step 3: Return nodes for update key generation

Fig. 2. Tree-based revocation structure

The key-update-nodes algorithm KUNodes(st, rl, t) [29] is proposed to process the above mechanism. It takes a state st denoting the state of the binary tree, a revocation list rl, and a timestamp t, and outputs a set of nodes, where rl records a set of identifier and timestamp pairs. When a user joins the system, who will be labeled a random identifier id and assigned to an undefined leaf node. The user id will be issued a set of keys related to Path(id), where Path(id) denotes all nodes in the path from the root node to the leaf node id. The formal definition for KUNodes algorithm is referred to [9], which first introduced KUNodes algorithm in the revocable identity-based cryptosystem.

4   Revocable Policy-Based Chameleon Hash

In this section, we present the system model. Then, we present the formal definition and the security model.

4.1   System Model

PCH is a chameleon hash system with controlled rewriting privilege at a fine-grained level and involves three types of users: KGC, data owner, and data modifier. In terms of a decentralized setting, every user can play the role of a KGC and tag other users with attributes. We use data "owner" and "modifier" in presenting RPCH. In particular, we assume the number of the modifier is a small amount since the rewriting privilege should be controlled carefully and cannot be performed by the majority of users.

As shown in Fig. 1, the KGC issues the long-term secret key when the modifier joins the system via a secure channel and distributes the key-updating material periodically via a public channel. Each owner is allowed to generate chameleon hash (h, r) by setting an access policy $\mathbb{A}$ and a timestamp t for rewriting the hashed object. The modifier whose long-term secret key satisfies the policy associated with the hashed object $\mathcal{S} \models \mathbb{A}$ and the valid key-updating material in period t can operate the rewriting produce by outputting a chameleon collision.

4.2 Formal Definition

Definition 5 (RPCH). *A revocable policy-based chameleon hash $\mathcal{RPCH}$ consists of the algorithms {Setup, KGen, KUpt, DKGen, Rev, Hash, Verify, Adapt}, where the algorithms Setup, KGen, KUpt, DKGen, and Rev are described in $\mathcal{RABE}$. The definition for the rest of algorithms Hash, Verify, and Adapt is:*

- Hash$(m, \mathbb{A}, t) \rightarrow (h, r)$: *The probabilistic hash algorithm takes a message $m \in \mathcal{M}$, an access policy $\mathbb{A} \in 2^{\mathbb{U}}$ and a timestamp $t \in \mathcal{T}$ as input, and outputs a chameleon hash h and a randomness (sometimes referred to as "check value") r.*
- Verify$(m, h, r) \rightarrow b$: *The deterministic verification algorithm takes a message $m \in \mathcal{M}$, a chameleon hash h and a randomness r as input, and outputs a bit $b \in \{0, 1\}$.*
- Adapt$(dk_{id,t}, m, m', h, r) \rightarrow r'$: *The deterministic adaptation algorithm takes a decryption key $dk_{id,t}$, a message $m \in \mathcal{M}$, a message $m' \in \mathcal{M}$, a chameleon hash h and a randomness r as input, and outputs a randomness r'.*

For each $\mathcal{RPCH}$, it is required that the correctness property holds. In particular, it is required that for all $\kappa \in \mathbb{N}$, for all $(mpk, msk, st, rl) \leftarrow$ Setup$(1^\kappa, n)$, for all $\mathcal{S} \subseteq \mathbb{U}$, for all $(sk_{id}, st) \leftarrow$ KGen$(msk, st, id, \mathcal{S})$, for all $t \in \mathcal{T}$, for all $ku_t \leftarrow$ KUpt(st, rl, t), for all $dk_{id,t} \leftarrow$ DKGen(sk_{id}, ku_t), for all $m \in \mathcal{M}$, for all $(h, r) \leftarrow$ Hash$(m, \mathbb{A}, t)$, for all $m' \in \mathcal{M}$, for all $r' \leftarrow$ Adapt$(dk_{id,t}, m, m', h, r)$, we have $1 =$ Verify$(m, h, r) =$ Verify(m', h, r').

4.3 Security Model

Definition 6 (FIND). *The security definition of full indistinguishability (FIND) for $\mathcal{RPCH}$ between an adversary $\mathcal{A}$ and a challenger $\mathcal{C}$.*

Setup. *$\mathcal{C}$ runs Setup$(1^\kappa, n)$ and gives mpk and msk to $\mathcal{A}$.*

Query Phase. *$\mathcal{C}$ randomly picks $b \in \{0, 1\}$. $\mathcal{A}$ issues the following queries to $\mathcal{C}$.*

- $\mathcal{O}_{\mathsf{HashOrAdapt}}(\cdot, \cdot, \cdot, \cdot, \cdot)$: *$\mathcal{A}$ issues hash or adapt query on two messages $m, m' \in \mathcal{M}$, a decryption key $dk_{id,t}$, an access policy $\mathbb{A} \in 2^{\mathbb{U}}$ and a timestamp $t \in \mathcal{T}$. $\mathcal{C}$ generates (h_0, r_0) by running Hash$(m', \mathbb{A}, t)$, (h_1, r_1) by running Hash$(m, \mathbb{A}, t)$ and r_1 by running Adapt$(dk_{id,t}, m, m', h_1, r_1)$. $\mathcal{C}$ returns $\perp$ if $r_0 = \perp$ or $r_1 = \perp$. Otherwise, $\mathcal{C}$ returns (h_b, r_b).*

Guess. $\mathcal{A}$ *makes a guess* b' *for* b.

The advantage of $\mathcal{A}$ *in this game is defined as* $\mathbf{Adv}^{\mathsf{FIND}}_{\mathcal{RPCH},\mathcal{A}}(\kappa, n) = |\Pr[b = b'] - 1/2|$. *An* $\mathcal{RPCH}$ *is* FIND *if any probabilistic polynomial time adversary has at most a negligible advantage in* κ.

Definition 7 (ICR). *The security definition of insider collision-resistance (*ICR*) for* $\mathcal{RPCH}$ *between an adversary* $\mathcal{A}$ *and a challenger* $\mathcal{C}$.[4]

Setup. $\mathcal{C}$ *runs* Setup$(1^\kappa, n)$ *and gives* mpk *to* $\mathcal{A}$. $\mathcal{C}$ *keeps* msk, st *and* rl *secret*.

Query Phase. $\mathcal{A}$ *adaptively issues a sequence of following queries to* $\mathcal{C}$.

- $\mathcal{O}_{\mathsf{KGen}}(\cdot, \cdot)$, $\mathcal{O}_{\mathsf{KUpt}}(\cdot)$, $\mathcal{O}_{\mathsf{DKGen}}(\cdot, \cdot, \cdot)$ *and* $\mathcal{O}_{\mathsf{Rev}}(\cdot, \cdot)$ *are the same oracles defined in the* IND-CPA *security model for* $\mathcal{RABE}$ *with the same restrictions*.
- $\mathcal{O}'_{\mathsf{KGen}}(\cdot, \cdot)$: $\mathcal{A}$ *issues key generation query on an identifier* $id \in \mathcal{I}$ *and a set of attributes* $\mathcal{S} \subseteq \mathbb{U}$. $\mathcal{C}$ *runs* KGen$(msk, st, id, \mathcal{S})$ *and keeps the secret key* sk_{id}.
- $\mathcal{O}_{\mathsf{Hash}}(\cdot, \cdot, \cdot)$: $\mathcal{A}$ *issues hash query on a message* $m \in \mathcal{M}$, *an access policy* $\mathbb{A} \in 2^{\mathbb{U}}$ *and a timestamp* $t \in \mathcal{T}$. $\mathcal{C}$ *returns* (h, r) *by running* Hash$(m, \mathbb{A}, t)$.
- $\mathcal{O}_{\mathsf{Adapt}}(\cdot, \cdot, \cdot, \cdot, \cdot)$: $\mathcal{A}$ *issues adaption query on two messages* $m, m' \in \mathcal{M}$, *an access policy* $\mathbb{A} \in 2^{\mathbb{U}}$, *a timestamp* $t \in \mathcal{T}$ *and an identifier* $id \in \mathcal{I}$. $\mathcal{C}$ *returns* $\perp$ *if* id *was not queried to* $\mathcal{O}_{\mathsf{KGen}}(\cdot, \cdot)$ *before and* $\mathcal{O}'_{\mathsf{KGen}}(\cdot, \cdot)$, *or* id*'s corresponding attributes* $\mathcal{S} \not\models \mathbb{A}$. *Otherwise,* $\mathcal{C}$ *returns* r' *by running* Adapt$(dk_{id,t}, m, m', h, r)$.

Output. $\mathcal{A}$ *outputs two different messages* $m^*, m'^* \in \mathcal{M}$, *two randomnesses* r^*, r'^*, *a chameleon hash* h^* *and a timestamp* $t^* \in \mathcal{T}$, *and it wins the game if*

- $1 = $ Verify$(m^*, h^*, r^*) = $ Verify(m'^*, h^*, r'^*),
- h^* *appears in* $\mathcal{O}_{\mathsf{Hash}}(\cdot, \cdot, \cdot)$ *or* $\mathcal{O}_{\mathsf{Adapt}}(\cdot, \cdot, \cdot, \cdot, \cdot)$ *with some* $\mathbb{A}^* \in 2^{\mathbb{U}}$ *and* $t^* \in \mathcal{T}$,
- (h^*, m^*) *does not appear in* $\mathcal{O}_{\mathsf{Hash}}(\cdot, \cdot, \cdot)$ *or* $\mathcal{O}_{\mathsf{Adapt}}(\cdot, \cdot, \cdot, \cdot, \cdot)$,
- *any* $\mathcal{S} \models \mathbb{A}^*$ *and* $t^* \in \mathcal{T}$ *have not been queried to* $\mathcal{O}_{\mathsf{DKGen}}(\cdot, \cdot, \cdot)$, *and*
- *any* $id \in \mathcal{I}$ *with* $\mathcal{S} \models \mathbb{A}^*$ *was revoked in* $t \leq t^*$ *or has never been queried to* $\mathcal{O}_{\mathsf{KGen}}(\cdot, \cdot)$.

The advantage of $\mathcal{A}$ *in this game is defined as* $\mathbf{Adv}^{\mathsf{ICR}}_{\mathcal{RPCH},\mathcal{A}}(\kappa, n) = \Pr[\mathcal{A} \ wins]$. *An* $\mathcal{RPCH}$ *is* ICR *if any probabilistic polynomial time adversary has at most a negligible advantage in* κ.

Definition 8 (UNI). *The security definition of uniqueness (*UNI*) for* $\mathcal{RPCH}$ *between an adversary* $\mathcal{A}$ *and a challenger* $\mathcal{C}$.

Setup. $\mathcal{C}$ *runs* Setup$(1^\kappa, n)$ *and gives* mpk *and* msk *to* $\mathcal{A}$.

Output. $\mathcal{A}$ *outputs a message* $m^* \in \mathcal{M}$, *two randomness* r^*, r'^* *and a chameleon hash* h^*. *It wins the game if* $1 = $ Verify$(m^*, h^*, r^*) = $ Verify(m^*, h^*, r'^*) *and* $r^* \neq r'^*$.

The advantage of $\mathcal{A}$ *in this game is defined as* $\mathbf{Adv}^{\mathsf{UNI}}_{\mathcal{RPCH},\mathcal{A}}(\kappa, n) = \Pr[\mathcal{A} \ wins]$. *An* $\mathcal{RPCH}$ *is* UNI *if any probabilistic polynomial time adversary has at most a negligible advantage in* κ.

---

[4] To simplicity, the weak model, outsider collision-resistance [16] has not taken into consideration since ICR covers this weak model as in [34].

5 Revocable Policy-Based Chameleon Hash

In this section, we present the concrete constructions of RABE and RPCH, respectively. Then, we show that RPCH can be effectively integrated into mutable blockchain and sanitizable signature.

5.1 Proposed RABE

Before presenting the construction of RPCH, we introduce the construction of RABE first, which serves as an important building block to RPCH. Our RABE uses a hash function $\mathcal{H} : \{0,1\}^* \rightarrow \mathbb{G}$, and it will be modeled as a random oracle in the security proof. In particular, three types of inputs will be given to $\mathcal{H}$: inputs of the form (y, ℓ, z), (j, ℓ, z) or t, where $y \in \mathcal{S}$, $j \in \mathbb{N}$, $\ell \in \{1, 2, 3\}$, $z \in \{1, 2\}$ and $t \in \mathcal{T}$. For the seek of readability, we represent these three inputs as $y\ell z$, $0j\ell z$ and $1t$, respectively, appending 0 at the beginning of the second one and 1 at the beginning of the third one so that it is not confused each other. We assume that the inputs are appropriately encoded so that no three different tuples collide. In the following, we present the concrete construction of RABE and the sketch of the security proof.

$\underline{\mathsf{Setup}(1^\kappa, n)}$: Run $(p, \mathbb{G}, \mathbb{H}, \mathbb{G}_T, e, g, h) \leftarrow \mathcal{G}(1^\kappa)$. Pick $a_1, a_2, b_1, b_2 \in \mathbb{Z}_p^*$ and $d_1, d_2, d_3 \in \mathbb{Z}_p$. Output $mpk = (h, H_1 = h^{a_1}, H_2 = h^{a_2}, T_1 = e(g, h)^{d_1 a_1 + d_3}$, $T_2 = e(g, h)^{d_2 a_2 + d_3}, \mathcal{H}), msk = (g, h, a_1, a_2, b_1, b_2, g^{d_1}, g^{d_2}, g^{d_3}), st \leftarrow \mathsf{BT}$ and $rl \leftarrow \emptyset$, where BT denotes a binary tree with n leaf nodes.

$\underline{\mathsf{KGen}(msk, st, id, \mathcal{S})}$: Pick $r_1, r_2 \in \mathbb{Z}_p$ and compute $sk_0 = (h^{b_1 r_1}, h^{b_2 r_2}, h^{r_1 + r_2})$ using h, b_1, b_2 from msk. For all $y \in \mathcal{S}$ and $z = 1, 2$:
  1. Pick $\sigma_y, \sigma' \in \mathbb{Z}_p$.
  2. Compute $sk_{y,z} = \mathcal{H}(y1z)^{\frac{b_1 r_1}{a_z}} \cdot \mathcal{H}(y2z)^{\frac{b_2 r_2}{a_z}} \cdot \mathcal{H}(y3z)^{\frac{r_1 + r_2}{a_z}} \cdot g^{\frac{\sigma_y}{a_z}}$.
  3. Compute $sk_z' = g^{d_z} \cdot \mathcal{H}(011z)^{\frac{b_1 r_1}{a_z}} \cdot \mathcal{H}(012z)^{\frac{b_2 r_2}{a_z}} \cdot \mathcal{H}(013z)^{\frac{r_1 + r_2}{a_z}} \cdot g^{\frac{\sigma'}{a_z}}$.
  Set $sk_y = (sk_{y,1}, sk_{y,2}, g^{-\sigma_y})$ and $sk' = (sk_1', sk_2')$. Pick an unassigned left node in st and label id to it. For all $\theta \in \mathsf{Path}(id)$:
  1. Fetch g_θ if available; else pick $g_\theta \in \mathbb{G}$ and store g_θ in θ to update st.
  2. Compute $sk_\theta = g^{d_3} \cdot g^{-\sigma'}/g_\theta$.
  Output $sk_{id} = (\mathcal{S}, sk_0, \{sk_y\}_{y \in \mathcal{S}}, sk', \{\theta, sk_\theta\}_{\theta \in \mathsf{Path}(id)})$ and st.

$\underline{\mathsf{KUpt}(st, rl, t)}$: For all $\theta \in \mathsf{KUNodes}(st, rl, t)$: Fetch g_θ, pick $r_\theta \in \mathbb{Z}_p$, and compute $ku_\theta = (g_\theta \cdot \mathcal{H}(1t)^{r_\theta}, h^{r_\theta})$. Output $ku_t = (t, \{\theta, ku_\theta\}_{\theta \in \mathsf{KUNodes}(st, rl, t)})$.

$\underline{\mathsf{DKGen}(sk_{id}, ku_t)}$: Find $\theta \in \mathsf{Path}(id) \cap \mathsf{KUNodes}(st, rl, t)$. Output $\perp$ if $\theta = \emptyset$, else pick $r_\theta' \in \mathbb{Z}_p$ and compute $sk_3' = sk_\theta \cdot ku_{\theta,1} \cdot \mathcal{H}(1t)^{r_\theta'} = g^{d_3} \cdot g^{-\sigma'} \cdot \mathcal{H}(1t)^{r_\theta + r_\theta'}$ and $sk_{0,4} = ku_{\theta,2} \cdot h^{r_\theta'} = h^{r_\theta + r_\theta'}$, where $ku_{\theta,1}$ and $ku_{\theta,2}$ denote the first and the second elements of ku_θ. Set $sk'' = (sk_1', sk_2', sk_3')$ and $sk_0' = (sk_{0,1}, sk_{0,2}, sk_{0,3}, sk_{0,4})$. Here, $sk_{0,1}$, $sk_{0,2}$ and $sk_{0,3}$ denote the first, second and third elements of sk_0. Output $dk_{id,t} = (\mathcal{S}, t, sk_0', \{sk_y\}_{y \in \mathcal{S}}, sk'')$.

$\underline{\mathsf{Enc}(m, \mathbb{A} = (\mathbb{M}, \pi), t)}$: Pick $s_1, s_2 \in \mathbb{Z}_p$. Compute $c_0 = (H_1^{s_1}, H_2^{s_2}, h^{s_1 + s_2}, \mathcal{H}(1t)^{s_1 + s_2})$. Suppose $\mathbb{M}$ has n_1 rows and n_2 columns. For $i = 1, ..., n_1$ and $\ell = 1, 2, 3$, compute

$c_{i,\ell} = \mathcal{H}(\pi(i)\ell 1)^{s_1} \cdot \mathcal{H}(\pi(i)\ell 2)^{s_2} \cdot \prod_{j=1}^{n_2} [\mathcal{H}(0j\ell 1)^{s_1} \cdot \mathcal{H}(0j\ell 2)^{s_2}]^{\mathbb{M}_{i,j}}$. Set $c_i = (c_{i,1}, c_{i,2}, c_{i,3})$. Compute $c' = T_1^{s_1} \cdot T_2^{s_2} \cdot m$. Output $c = (\mathbb{A}, t, c_0, c_1, \ldots, c_{n_1}, c')$.
$\mathsf{Dec}(dk_{id,t}, c)$: If $\mathcal{S}$ in $dk_{id,t}$ satisfies $\mathbb{A} = (\mathbb{M}, \pi)$ in c, then there exist constants $\{\gamma_i\}_{i \in I}$ that satisfy $\sum_{i \in I} \gamma_i \mathbb{M}_i = (1, 0, \ldots, 0)$. Compute

$$num = c' \cdot e\left(\prod_{i \in I} c_{i,1}^{\gamma_i}, sk_{0,1}\right) \cdot e\left(\prod_{i \in I} c_{i,2}^{\gamma_i}, sk_{0,2}\right) \cdot e\left(\prod_{i \in I} c_{i,3}^{\gamma_i}, sk_{0,3}\right) \cdot e\left(c_{0,4}, sk_{0,4}\right),$$

$$den = e\left(sk_1' \cdot \prod_{i \in I} sk_{\pi(i),1}^{\gamma_i}, c_{0,1}\right) \cdot e\left(sk_2' \cdot \prod_{i \in I} sk_{\pi(i),2}^{\gamma_i}, c_{0,2}\right) \cdot e\left(sk_3' \cdot \prod_{i \in I} sk_{\pi(i),3}^{\gamma_i}, c_{0,3}\right)$$

and output num/den. Here, $c_{0,1}$, $c_{0,2}$, $c_{0,3}$ and $c_{0,4}$ denote the first, second, third and forth elements of c_0.
$\mathsf{Rev}(rl, id, t)$: Output $rl \leftarrow rl \cup \{(id, t)\}$.

Theorem 1. *The proposed RABE is* IND-CPA *secure if the* DLIN *assumption is held in the random oracle model.*

We give the sketch of our security proof and details are omitted to conserve space. Our security proof is based on the proofs in RIBE [35] and FAME [2]. We can construct a simulation $\mathcal{B}$ to simulate the security game. $\mathcal{B}$ simulates the public parameters and oracles depending on FAME with two major differences. One is that $\mathcal{B}$ needs to guess the type of $\mathcal{A}$, where $\mathcal{A}$ can play non-revoked users who can get key-updating material in the challenge time, or revoked users who must be revoked before the challenge time. The other one is that $\mathcal{B}$ needs to guess the challenge time $t^* \in \mathcal{T}$. $\mathcal{B}$ can then simulate the IND-CPA game perfectly if guess correctly. Finally, $\mathcal{B}$ can forward the guess of $\mathcal{A}$ as the result to break DLIN assumption, which is also the hard assumption of FAME.

5.2 Proposed RPCH

We present the concrete construction of RPCH directly and the sketch of the security proof. The generic construction is similar to the previous RPCH [16,34] except that the underlying ABE is replaced to RABE, and additional algorithms $\mathsf{Kupt}, \mathsf{DKGen}$ and Rev are used to manage user revocation. In our concrete construction, hybrid encryption is considered for the large-size chameleon trapdoor. In particular, an encoding method encodes a symmetric key to an RABE message, and a decoding method decodes the RABE message to a symmetric key. To simplicity, we represent the encoding and decoding method as $\mathsf{encode} : \{0,1\}^* \to \mathbb{G}_T$ and $\mathsf{encode}^{-1} : \mathbb{G}_T \to \{0,1\}^*$, respectively. Let $\mathcal{RABE} = \{\mathsf{Setup}, \mathsf{KGen}, \mathsf{KUpt}, \mathsf{DKGen}, \mathsf{Enc}, \mathsf{Dec}, \mathsf{Rev}\}$ be an IND-CPA secure RABE. The constriction of RPCH is described as follows:

$\mathsf{Setup}(1^\kappa, n)$: It includes *parameter initialization, trapdoor selection, symmetric-key encryption initialization*:
    1. Run $(mpk_{\mathcal{RABE}}, msk_{\mathcal{RABE}}, st, rl) \leftarrow \mathcal{RABE}.\mathsf{Setup}(1^\kappa, n)$. Pick $e_1 \geq N'$ with $N' = max_r\{N \in \mathbb{N} : (N, \cdot, \cdot, \cdot, \cdot) \leftarrow \mathsf{RSAKGen}(1^\kappa; r)\}$.

2. Run $(N_1, p_1, q_1, \cdot, \cdot) \leftarrow \mathsf{RSAKGen}(1^\kappa)$, choose hash functions $\mathcal{H}_1 : \{0,1\} \rightarrow \mathbb{Z}_{N_1}^*$ and $\mathcal{H}_3 : \{0,1\}^* \rightarrow \mathbb{Z}_p \times \mathbb{Z}_p$. Compute d_1 s.t. $ed_1 \equiv 1 \bmod (p_1 - 1)(q_1 - 1)$.

3. Choose a symmetric-key encryption scheme $\mathcal{SE} = \{\mathsf{KGen}, \mathsf{Enc}, \mathsf{Dec}\}$.

Output $mpk = (mpk_{\mathcal{RABE}}, N_1, e, \mathcal{H}_1, \mathcal{H}_3, \mathcal{SE}), msk = (d_1, msk_{\mathcal{RABE}}), st, rl$.

$\underline{\mathsf{KGen}(msk, st, id, S)}$: Run $(sk_{\mathcal{RABE}, id}, st) \leftarrow \mathcal{RABE}.\mathsf{KGen}(msk_{\mathcal{RABE}}, st, id, S)$.

Output $sk_{id} = (d_1, sk_{\mathcal{RABE}, id})$ and st.

$\underline{\mathsf{KUpt}(st, rl, t)}$: Output ku_t by running $ku_t \leftarrow \mathcal{RABE}.\mathsf{KUpt}(st, rl, t)$.

$\underline{\mathsf{DKGen}(sk_{id}, ku_t)}$: Run $dk_{\mathcal{RABE}, id, t} \leftarrow \mathcal{RABE}.\mathsf{DKGen}(sk_{\mathcal{RABE}, id}, ku_t)$. Output $dk_{id,t} = (d_1, dk_{\mathcal{RABE}, id, t})$

$\underline{\mathsf{Rev}(rl, id, t)}$: Output rl by running $rl \leftarrow \mathcal{RABE}.\mathsf{Rev}(rl, id, t)$.

$\underline{\mathsf{Hash}(m, \mathbb{A}, t)}$: It includes *chameleon hash parameter initialization, trapdoor selection, trapdoor encapsulation*:

1. Run $(N_2, p_2, q_2, \cdot, \cdot) \leftarrow \mathsf{RSAKGen}(1^\kappa)$, choose a hash function $\mathcal{H}_2 : \{0,1\}^* \rightarrow \mathbb{Z}_{N_2}^*$. Compute d_2, s.t. $ed_2 \equiv 1 \bmod (p_2 - 1)(q_2 - 1)$.

2. Choose $r_1 \in \mathbb{Z}_{N_1}^*$, $r_2 \in \mathbb{Z}_{N_2}^*$, compute $h_1 = \mathcal{H}_1(m, N_1, N_2)r_1^e \bmod N_1$ and $h_2 = \mathcal{H}_2(m, N_1, N_2)r_2^e \bmod N_2$. Set $h' = (h_1, h_2)$ and $r' = (r_1, r_2)$.

3. Choose $r \in \{0,1\}^\kappa$, $k \leftarrow \mathcal{SE}.\mathsf{KGen}(1^\kappa)$, $c_{\mathcal{SE}} \leftarrow \mathcal{SE}.\mathsf{Enc}(k, d_2)$, $K \leftarrow \mathsf{encode}(k, r)$. Run $c_{\mathcal{RABE}} \leftarrow \mathcal{RABE}.\mathsf{Enc}(K, \mathbb{A}, t)$ with the randomnesses $(s_1, s_2) \leftarrow \mathcal{H}_3(r, \mathbb{A}, t)$.

Output $h = (h', N_2, \mathcal{H}_2, c_{\mathcal{RABE}}, c_{\mathcal{SE}})$ and $r = r'$.

$\underline{\mathsf{Verify}(m, h, r)}$: Verify $r_1 \in \mathbb{Z}_{N_1}^*$, $r_2 \in \mathbb{Z}_{N_2}^*$ and whether $h_1 = \mathcal{H}_1(m, N_1, N_2)r_1^e \bmod N_1$ and $h_2 = \mathcal{H}_2(m, N_1, N_2)r_2^e \bmod N_2$. If all checks hold, return 1 and 0 otherwise.

$\underline{\mathsf{Adapt}(dk_{id,t}, m, m', h, r)}$: It includes *chameleon hash verification, symmetric key revelation, ciphertext verification and trapdoor revelation, message adaptation, adapted chameleon hash verification*:

1. Run $b \leftarrow \mathsf{Verify}(m, h, r)$ and return $\bot$ if $b = 0$.

2. Run $K' \leftarrow \mathcal{RABE}.\mathsf{Dec}(dk_{\mathcal{RABE}, id, t}, c_{\mathcal{RABE}})$ and set $(k', r') \leftarrow \mathsf{encode}^{-1}(K')$.

3. Run $c'_{\mathcal{RABE}} \leftarrow \mathcal{RABE}.\mathsf{Enc}(K', \mathbb{A}, t)$ with the randomnesses $(s'_1, s'_2) \leftarrow \mathcal{H}_3(r', \mathbb{A}, t)$. Output $\bot$ if $c_{\mathcal{RABE}} \neq c'_{\mathcal{RABE}}$. Otherwise, compute $d'_2 \leftarrow \mathcal{SE}.\mathsf{Dec}(k', c_{\mathcal{SE}})$ and return $\bot$ if $d_2 = \bot$.

4. Let $x_1 = \mathcal{H}_1(m, N_1, N_2)$, $x'_1 = \mathcal{H}_1(m', N_1, N_2)$, $y_1 = x_1 r_1^e \bmod N_1$ as well as $x_2 = \mathcal{H}_2(m, N_1, N_2)$, $x'_2 = \mathcal{H}_1(m', N_1, N_2)$, $y_2 = x_2 r_2^e \bmod N_2$. Compute $r'_1 \leftarrow (y_1(x_1'^{-1}))^{d_1} \bmod N_1$ and $r'_2 \leftarrow (y_2(x_2'^{-1}))^{d_2} \bmod N_2$.

5. Return $\bot$ if $h_1 \neq \mathcal{H}_1(m', N_1, N_2)r_1'^e \bmod N_1$ or $h_2 \neq \mathcal{H}_2(m', N_1, N_2)r_2'^e \bmod N_2$.

Output $r' = (r'_1, r'_2)$.

Remark. In the above constriction, we apply the well-known Fujisaki-Okamoto transform [20] to our proposed RABE. Basically, the hash algorithm takes the randomness $(s_1, s_2) \leftarrow \mathcal{H}_3(r, \mathbb{A}, t)$ based on a sufficiently large randomly sampled bitstring r to encrypt the ephemeral trapdoor and r. The adaptation algorithm applies the original decryption algorithm to receive the ephemeral trapdoor and r'. Then, it re-encrypts the ephemeral trapdoor and r' based on the randomness $(s'_1, s'_2) \leftarrow \mathcal{H}_3(r', \mathbb{A}, t)$ to validate the ciphertext. If the re-encrypted result and the original ciphertext are different, it outputs $\bot$.

Theorem 2. *The proposed RPCH is fully indistinguishable, insider collision-resistant, unique, and correct if the underlying RABE is* IND-CPA *and correct, and the underlying CHET is fully indistinguishable, strongly private collision-resistant, unique, and correct.*

All properties, but insider collision-resistance, can be proved by following the methods used in [34]. In particular, the security of fully indistinguishability and uniqueness can be reduced to the security of CHET. Only insider collision-resistance is based on strongly private collision-resistance of the underlying CHET and the security of the underlying ABE (which is RABE in our proposed RPCH). Our security proof of insider collision-resistance is a sequence of games that is similar to [34], and the security of insider collision-resistance can be reduced to the security of IND-CPA RABE and strongly private collision-resistant CHET.

5.3 Applications

We show two applications of RPCH for mutable blockchain and sanitizable signature. On a high-level, the blockchain remains intact even if a certain policy-based mutable transaction has been rewritten and a signature holds integrity when the admissible blocks of the signed message have been altered.

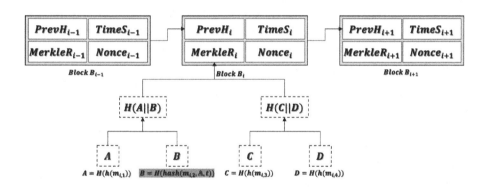

Fig. 3. RPCH for mutable blockchain

Figure 3 presents the application of RPCH for transaction-level blockchain rewriting. A block b_i has a Merkle root that accumulates four transactions: $m_{i,1}$, $m_{i,2}$, $m_{i,3}$ and $m_{i,4}$. $m_{i,1}$, $m_{i,3}$ and $m_{i,4}$ are immutable transactions hashed by the traditional collision-resistant hash function h. $m_{i,2}$ is a mutable transaction associated with an access structure $\mathbb{A}$ and a timestamp t. When $m_{i,2}$ needs to be altered to $m'_{i,2}$, a transaction modifier with PCH-based decryption key associated with the attributes $\mathcal{S}$ and timestamp t' satisfying $\mathcal{S} \models \mathbb{A}$ and $t' = t$ can compute a valid chameleon randomness r without modifying its hash value, hence, Merkle root is never modified. The transaction modifier then broadcasts

$(m'_{i,2}, r')$ to the blockchain network. All participants verify the correctness of the new randomness and update their local copy of the blockchain with the new message and randomness pair $(m'_{i,2}, r')$.

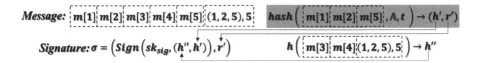

Fig. 4. RPCH for sanitizable signature

Figure 4 is an application of RPCH for sanitizable signatures. A message m has five blocks $m[1]$, $m[2]$, $m[3]$, $m[4]$ and $m[5]$, where $m[1]$, $m[2]$ and $m[5]$ are admissible blocks that can be altered. The admissible blocks are hashed via RPCH hash function $hash$ associated with an access structure $\mathbb{A}$ and a timestamp t. The non-admissible blocks and the information of admissible blocks $((1,2,5),5)$ are hashed by the traditional collision-resistant hash function h, where information of admissible blocks $((1,2,5),5)$ indicates that the 1st, 2nd and 5th blocks can be altered and the total number of blocks in m is 5. When the admissible blocks need to be altered, a sanitizer with PCH-based decryption key associated with attributes $\mathcal{S}$ and timestamp t' satisfying $\mathcal{S} \models \mathbb{A}$ and $t' = t$ can compute a valid chameleon randomness without rewriting its signature. The sanitizer then broadcasts the randomness and updates admissible blocks. The verifier then can process the verification of the updated signature.

Remark. We only consider backward secrecy in the term of revocability, where the modifier cannot alter any message after being revoked. To achieve forward secrecy, ciphertext delegation [33] can be used, where a (semi-)trusted third party updates the ciphertext periodically. However, ciphertext delegation is impractical in the application scenarios of mutable blockchain and sanitizable signature. It is hard to find a (semi-)trusted third party in the untrusted environment, and even enable them to process ciphertext update periodically.[5] The signature is hard to trace back and update once it has been released. To remedy this shortcoming, we consider processing user revocation periodically and require the mutable transaction owner and the signer of the sanitizable signature to update the timestamp in each RPCH hash in the same frequency. Hence, the compromised long-term secret key only affects several periods, and the chameleon hash under those periods may be updated before key compromization. We leave the PRCH with forward secrecy, a modifier cannot process rewriting to the hashed object generated before being revoked, without ciphertext delegation or a (semi-)trusted third party as interesting future work.

---

[5] Outsourced decryption has also not taken into consideration due to a (semi-)trusted third party is needed and processes outsourced decryption.

6   Performance Analysis

In this section, we give detailed comparisons of indirect RABE and PCH. Then, we implement PCH [16] and ours, where PCH [36] only considers accountability, and no concrete PCH construction is provided in [34].

Table 1. Comparison of RABE schemes

	Scheme	Group-order	Assumption	DKE-resistant	Security
SSW12 [33]	ABE [25]	*Composite*	SDP	✗	*adaptive*
CDLQ16 [15]	ABE [32]	*Prime*	*q-type*	✗	*selective*
QZZC17 [31]	ABE [32]	*Prime*	*q-type*	✓	*selective*
XYMD18 [38]	ABE [21]	*Prime*	DBDH	✗	*selective*
XYM19 [37]	ABE [32]	*Prime*	*q-type*	✓	*selective*
XYML19 [39]	ABE [32]	*Prime*	*q-type*	✓	*selective*
Ours	FAME [2]	*Prime*	DLIN	✓	*adaptive*

"**Scheme**" means that on which ABE the RABE is based. "**Assumption**" means that on which assumption the RABE is based. "**DKE-resistance**" means that whether the RABE is decryption key exposure resistant or not. "DBDH" means Decisional Bilinear Diffie-Hellman assumption.

Table 2. Comparison of PCH schemes

	Scheme	Revocability	Application
DSSS19 [16]	FAME [2] + RSA-Based CH [14]	✗	*Blockchain rewriting*
TLL+20 [36]	ABET [36] + DL-Based CH [14]	✗	*Blockchain rewriting*
SS20 [34]	FAME [2] + RSA-Based CH [14]	✗	*Sanitizable signature*
Ours	RABE + RSA-based CH [14]	✓	*Both*

"**Scheme**" means that on which cryptographic primitive the PCH is based. "**Revocability**" means that whether the PCH supports rewriting privilege revocation. "CH" is short for chameleon hash.

Detailed Comparisons. Table 1 compares the classical and recent indirect RABE schemes [15, 31, 33, 37–39] and ours. The previous RABE schemes, as in Table 1, are selectively secure except SSW12 [33], where SSW12 is adaptively secure under Subgroup Decision Problem (SDP) on composite-order groups. Our RABE is adaptively secure under a standard assumption on prime-order groups.

Table 2 compares the recently PCH schemes [16, 34, 36] and ours. All of them are derived from FAME [2], where TLL+20 [36] introduced attribute-based encryption scheme with traceability (ABET) based on FAME and HIBE [11], and our RABE based on FAME and RIBE. To the best of our knowledge, our RPCH is the first PCH with revocability and can be integrated into blockchain and sanitizable signatures.

Implementation and Evaluation. We implement PCH [16] and our RPCH in Java 8 using the PBC Library. We use MNT224 curve for pairings because it is the best Type-III curve in PBC and provides 96-bit security level [2]. Our experimental simulation was measured on a personal laptop with a 3.0 GHz AMD Ryzen R5 4600 processor and 16 GB RAM. To simplicity, we define the number of system users $n = 2^{10}$ in our implementation.

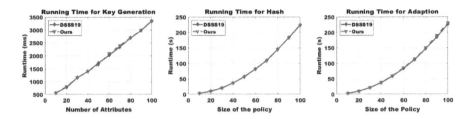

Fig. 5. Performance comparison of PCH schemes

Figure 5 compares the running time of key generation, hash and adaption for PCH schemes we consider. Our solution with a negligible performance overhead compared to DSSS19. Compared to DSSS19, our RPCH takes additional $\log_2 n - 1$ multiplications (around 0.11 ms) for key generation, additional one exponentiation (about 3.83 ms) for hash, and additional one multiplication and pairing (around 21.19 ms) for adaption.

7   Conclusion

In this work, we proposed the notion of revocable policy-based chameleon hash (RPCH) and illustrated its applications in mutable blockchain and sanitizable signature. Our RPCH allows a trusted party to effectively revoke the rewriting privileges of a chameleon trapdoor holder. We gave a practical instantiation by introducing adaptively secure revocable attribute-based encryption under a standard assumption on prime-order groups. The future work could be investigating the usability and security of RPCH, e.g., outsourced decryption and forward secrecy without any (semi-)trusted third party.

Acknowledgments. This work is supported in part by AXA Research Fund, the National Natural Science Foundation of China (Grant Nos. 62102090, 62032005, 61972094), the young talent promotion project of Fujian Science and Technology Association, and Science Foundation of Fujian Provincial Science and Technology Agency (2020J02016).

References

1. General data protection regulation. https://gdpr-info.eu/

2. Agrawal, S., Chase, M.: FAME: fast attribute-based message encryption. In: CCS, pp. 665–682 (2017)

3. Ateniese, G., Chou, D.H., de Medeiros, B., Tsudik, G.: Sanitizable signatures. In: ESORICS, vol. 3679, pp. 159–177 (2005)

4. Ateniese, G., Magri, B., Venturi, D., Andrade, E.R.: Redactable blockchain - or - rewriting history in bitcoin and friends. In: EuroS&P, pp. 111–126 (2017)

5. Attrapadung, N.: Dual system encryption framework in prime-order groups via computational pair encodings. In: ASIACRYPT, pp. 591–623 (2016)

6. Attrapadung, N., Imai, H.: Attribute-based encryption supporting direct/indirect revocation modes. In: IMA, pp. 278–300 (2009)

7. Bethencourt, J., Sahai, A., Waters, B.: Ciphertext-policy attribute-based encryption. In: IEEE S&P, pp. 321–334 (2007)

8. Bilzhause, A., Pöhls, H.C., Samelin, K.: Position paper: the past, present, and future of sanitizable and redactable signatures. In: ARES, pp. 87:1–87:9 (2017)

9. Boldyreva, A., Goyal, V., Kumar, V.: Identity-based encryption with efficient revocation. In: CCS, pp. 417–426 (2008)

10. Boneh, D., Boyen, X.: Efficient selective-id secure identity-based encryption without random oracles. In: EUROCRYPT, vol. 3027, pp. 223–238 (2004)

11. Boneh, D., Boyen, X., Goh, E.: Hierarchical identity based encryption with constant size ciphertext. In: EUROCRYPT, vol. 3494, pp. 440–456 (2005)

12. Boneh, D., Franklin, M.: Identity-based encryption from the weil pairing. In: Kilian, J. (ed.) CRYPTO 2001. LNCS, vol. 2139, pp. 213–229. Springer, Heidelberg (2001). https://doi.org/10.1007/3-540-44647-8_13

13. Bultel, X., Lafourcade, P., Lai, R.W.F., Malavolta, G., Schröder, D., Thyagarajan, S.A.K.: Efficient invisible and unlinkable sanitizable signatures. In: Lin, D., Sako, K. (eds.) PKC 2019. LNCS, vol. 11442, pp. 159–189. Springer, Cham (2019). https://doi.org/10.1007/978-3-030-17253-4_6

14. Camenisch, J., Derler, D., Krenn, S., Pöhls, H.C., Samelin, K., Slamanig, D.: Chameleon-hashes with ephemeral trapdoors. In: Fehr, S. (ed.) PKC 2017. LNCS, vol. 10175, pp. 152–182. Springer, Heidelberg (2017). https://doi.org/10.1007/978-3-662-54388-7_6

15. Cui, H., Deng, R.H., Li, Y., Qin, B.: Server-aided revocable attribute-based encryption. In: ESORICS, vol. 9879, pp. 570–587 (2016)

16. Derler, D., Samelin, K., Slamanig, D., Striecks, C.: Fine-grained and controlled rewriting in blockchains: Chameleon-hashing gone attribute-based. In: NDSS (2019)

17. Deuber, D., Magri, B., Thyagarajan, S.A.K.: Redactable blockchain in the permissionless setting. In: IEEE SP, pp. 124–138 (2019)

18. Fischlin, M., Harasser, P.: Invisible sanitizable signatures and public-key encryption are equivalent. In: Preneel, B., Vercauteren, F. (eds.) ACNS 2018. LNCS, vol. 10892, pp. 202–220. Springer, Cham (2018). https://doi.org/10.1007/978-3-319-93387-0_11

19. Fleischhacker, N., Krupp, J., Malavolta, G., Schneider, J., Schröder, D., Simkin, M.: Efficient unlinkable sanitizable signatures from signatures with re-randomizable keys. In: Cheng, C.-M., Chung, K.-M., Persiano, G., Yang, B.-Y. (eds.) PKC 2016. LNCS, vol. 9614, pp. 301–330. Springer, Heidelberg (2016). https://doi.org/10.1007/978-3-662-49384-7_12

20. Fujisaki, E., Okamoto, T.: Secure integration of asymmetric and symmetric encryption schemes. In: Wiener, M. (ed.) CRYPTO 1999. LNCS, vol. 1666, pp. 537–554. Springer, Heidelberg (1999). https://doi.org/10.1007/3-540-48405-1_34

21. Goyal, V., Pandey, O., Sahai, A., Waters, B.: Attribute-based encryption for fine-grained access control of encrypted data. In: CCS, pp. 89–98 (2006)
22. Guillevic, A.: Comparing the pairing efficiency over composite-order and prime-order elliptic curves. In: Jacobson, M., Locasto, M., Mohassel, P., Safavi-Naini, R. (eds.) ACNS 2013. LNCS, vol. 7954, pp. 357–372. Springer, Heidelberg (2013). https://doi.org/10.1007/978-3-642-38980-1_22
23. Kohno, T., Stubblefield, A., Rubin, A.D., Wallach, D.S.: Analysis of an electronic voting system. In: IEEE S&P, p. 27 (2004)
24. Krawczyk, H., Rabin, T.: Chameleon signatures. In: NDSS (2000)
25. Lewko, A.B., Okamoto, T., Sahai, A., Takashima, K., Waters, B.: Fully secure functional encryption: Attribute-based encryption and (hierarchical) inner product encryption. In: EUROCRYPT, vol. 6110, pp. 62–91 (2010)
26. Liu, J.K., Yuen, T.H., Zhang, P., Liang, K.: Time-based direct revocable ciphertext-policy attribute-based encryption with short revocation list. In: Preneel, B., Vercauteren, F. (eds.) ACNS 2018. LNCS, vol. 10892, pp. 516–534. Springer, Cham (2018). https://doi.org/10.1007/978-3-319-93387-0_27
27. Matzutt, R., et al.: A quantitative analysis of the impact of arbitrary blockchain content on bitcoin. In: Meiklejohn, S., Sako, K. (eds.) FC 2018. LNCS, vol. 10957, pp. 420–438. Springer, Heidelberg (2018). https://doi.org/10.1007/978-3-662-58387-6_23
28. Matzutt, R., Hohlfeld, O., Henze, M., Rawiel, R., Ziegeldorf, J.H., Wehrle, K.: POSTER: i don't want that content! on the risks of exploiting bitcoin's blockchain as a content store. In: CCS, pp. 1769–1771 (2016)
29. Naor, D., Naor, M., Lotspiech, J.: Revocation and tracing schemes for stateless receivers. In: Kilian, J. (ed.) CRYPTO 2001. LNCS, vol. 2139, pp. 41–62. Springer, Heidelberg (2001). https://doi.org/10.1007/3-540-44647-8_3
30. Okamoto, T., Takashima, K.: Fully secure unbounded inner-product and attribute-based encryption. In: Wang, X., Sako, K. (eds.) ASIACRYPT 2012. LNCS, vol. 7658, pp. 349–366. Springer, Heidelberg (2012). https://doi.org/10.1007/978-3-642-34961-4_22
31. Qin, B., Zhao, Q., Zheng, D., Cui, H.: Server-aided revocable attribute-based encryption resilient to decryption key exposure. In: Capkun, S., Chow, S.S.M. (eds.) CANS 2017. LNCS, vol. 11261, pp. 504–514. Springer, Cham (2018). https://doi.org/10.1007/978-3-030-02641-7_25
32. Rouselakis, Y., Waters, B.: Practical constructions and new proof methods for large universe attribute-based encryption. In: CCS, pp. 463–474 (2013)
33. Sahai, A., Seyalioglu, H., Waters, B.: Dynamic credentials and ciphertext delegation for attribute-based encryption. In: Safavi-Naini, R., Canetti, R. (eds.) CRYPTO 2012. LNCS, vol. 7417, pp. 199–217. Springer, Heidelberg (2012). https://doi.org/10.1007/978-3-642-32009-5_13
34. Samelin, K., Slamanig, D.: Policy-based sanitizable signatures. In: Jarecki, S. (ed.) CT-RSA 2020. LNCS, vol. 12006, pp. 538–563. Springer, Cham (2020). https://doi.org/10.1007/978-3-030-40186-3_23
35. Seo, J.H., Emura, K.: Revocable identity-based encryption revisited: security model and construction. In: Kurosawa, K., Hanaoka, G. (eds.) PKC 2013. LNCS, vol. 7778, pp. 216–234. Springer, Heidelberg (2013). https://doi.org/10.1007/978-3-642-36362-7_14
36. Tian, Y., Li, N., Li, Y., Szalachowski, P., Zhou, J.: Policy-based chameleon hash for blockchain rewriting with black-box accountability. In: ACSAC, pp. 813–828 (2020)

37. Xu, S., Yang, G., Mu, Y.: Revocable attribute-based encryption with decryption key exposure resistance and ciphertext delegation. Inf. Sci. **479**, 116–134 (2019)
38. Xu, S., Yang, G., Mu, Y., Deng, R.H.: Secure fine-grained access control and data sharing for dynamic groups in the cloud. IEEE Trans. Inf. Forensics Secur. **13**(8), 2101–2113 (2018)
39. Xu, S., Yang, G., Mu, Y., Liu, X.: A secure IoT cloud storage system with fine-grained access control and decryption key exposure resistance. Future Gener. Comput. Syst. **97**, 284–294 (2019)
40. Xu, S., Zhang, Y., Li, Y., Liu, X., Yang, G.: Generic construction of ElGama-type attribute-based encryption schemes with revocability and dual-policy. In: SecureComm, vol. 305, pp. 184–204 (2019)
41. Yang, Y., Liu, J.K., Liang, K., Choo, K.-K.R., Zhou, J.: Extended proxy-assisted approach: achieving revocable fine-grained encryption of cloud data. In: Pernul, G., Ryan, P.Y.A., Weippl, E. (eds.) ESORICS 2015. LNCS, vol. 9327, pp. 146–166. Springer, Cham (2015). https://doi.org/10.1007/978-3-319-24177-7_8

Fair Peer-to-Peer Content Delivery via Blockchain

Songlin He[1], Yuan Lu[2]($\boxtimes$), Qiang Tang[3], Guiling Wang[1], and Chase Qishi Wu[1]

[1] New Jersey Institute of Technology, Newark, NJ 07102, USA
{sh553,gwang,chase.wu}@njit.edu
[2] Institute of Software Chinese Academy of Sciences, Beijing, China
luyuan@iscas.ac.cn
[3] The University of Sydney, Sydney, Australia
qiang.tang@sydney.edu.au

Abstract. In comparison with conventional content delivery networks, peer-to-peer (p2p) content delivery is promising to save cost and handle high peak-demand, and can also complement the decentralized storage networks such as Filecoin. However, reliable p2p delivery requires proper enforcement of delivery fairness, i.e., the deliverers should be rewarded according to their in-time delivery. Unfortunately, most existing studies on delivery fairness are based on non-cooperative game-theoretic assumptions that are arguably unrealistic in the ad-hoc p2p setting.

We for the first time put forth an expressive yet still minimalist security notion for desired fair p2p content delivery, and give two efficient solutions FairDownload and FairStream via the blockchain for p2p downloading and p2p streaming scenarios, respectively. Our designs not only guarantee delivery fairness to ensure deliverers be paid (nearly) proportional to their in-time delivery but also ensure the content consumers and content providers are fairly treated. The fairness of each party can be guaranteed when the other two parties collude to arbitrarily misbehave. Moreover, the systems are efficient in the sense of attaining nearly asymptotically optimal on-chain costs and deliverer communication.

We implement the protocols and build the prototype systems atop the Ethereum Ropsten network. Extensive experiments done in LAN and WAN settings showcase their high practicality.

Keywords: Content delivery · Fairness · P2P · Blockchain application

1 Introduction

The peer-to-peer (p2p) content delivery systems are permissionless decentralized services to seamlessly replicate contents to the consumers. Typically these systems encompass a large ad-hoc network of deliverers to overcome the bandwidth bottleneck of the original content providers. In contrast to conventional pre-planned content delivery networks such as Akamai [1], p2p content delivery can crowdsource unused bandwidth resources of tremendous Internet peers, thus

© Springer Nature Switzerland AG 2021
E. Bertino et al. (Eds.): ESORICS 2021, LNCS 12972, pp. 348–369, 2021.
https://doi.org/10.1007/978-3-030-88418-5_17

having a wide array of benefits including robust service availability, bandwidth cost savings, and scalable peak-demand handling [2,3]. Recently, renewed attentions to p2p content delivery are gathered [2,19] due to the fast popularization of decentralized storage networks (DSNs) [5,17,34,41,42]. Indeed, most DSNs feature decentralized and robust *content storage*, but lack well-designed *content delivery* mechanisms catering for a prosperous content consumption market in the p2p setting, where the content shall not only be reliably stored but also must be always quickly *retrievable* despite potentially malicious participants [18].

The primary challenge of designing a proper delivery mechanism for complementing DSNs is to realize the strict guarantee of "fairness" against adversarial peers. In particular, it has to promise well-deserved items (e.g., retrieval of desired contents, rewards to spent bandwidth, payment for providing valid contents) to all participants [14]. Otherwise, free-riding parties can abuse the system [15,30,35] and cause rational ones to escape, eventually resulting in possible system collapse [20]. We reason as follows to distinguish two types of quintessential fairness, namely *delivery fairness* and *exchange fairness*, in the p2p content delivery setting where three parties, i.e., content *provider*, content *deliverer* and content *consumer*, are involved.

Exchange Fairness is not Delivery Fairness. Exchange fairness [4,7,10, 12,28,31], specifically for digital goods (such as signatures, videos), emphasizes that one party's input shall keep *confidential* until it does learn the other party's input. Unfortunately, in the p2p content delivery setting, merely considering it becomes insufficient, because a content deliverer would expect to receive rewards proportional to the bandwidth resources that it spends. Noticeably, exchange fairness fails to capture such new desiderata related to bandwidth cost, since it allows a deliverer to receive no reward at all after transferring a huge amount of *encrypted* data to the other party, which clearly breaks the deliverer's expectation on being well-paid but does not violate exchange fairness at all.

Consider FairSwap [12] as a concrete example: the deliverer first sends the encrypted content and semantically secure digest to the consumer, then waits for a message from the consumer (via blockchain) to confirm the receival of these ciphertexts, then the deliverer can reveal his encryption key on-chain; but, in case the consumer aborts, all bandwidth used to send ciphertexts is wasted, causing no reward for deliverer. A seemingly enticing way to mitigate the above attack could be splitting the content into n smaller chunks and run FairSwap for each chunk, but the on-chain cost would grow linearly in n, resulting in prohibitive on-chain costs for large-size content like movies. Adapting other fair exchange protocols for delivery fairness would encounter similar issues. Hence, the efficient construction satisfying delivery fairness remains unclear.

Thus, to capture the special fairness required by deliverers, we formulate delivery fairness in Sect. 4, stating that deliverers can receive rewards (nearly) proportional to the contributed bandwidth for delivering data to the consumers.

Insufficiencies of Existing "Delivery Fairness". A range of literature [29, 38–40] studied problems similar to delivery fairness in p2p delivery. However, to our knowledge, no one assures delivery fairness in the *cryptographic* sense as we seek to do. In particular, they [29,38–40] were studied in the *non-cooperative game-theoretic* settings where independent attackers free ride spontaneously without communication of their strategies, and the attackers are rational with the intentions to maximize their own benefits. Therefore, it boldly ignores an adversary that intends to break the system. Unfortunately, such rational assumptions are particularly elusive to stand in ad-hoc p2p systems accessible by all malicious evils. The occurrences of massive real-world attacks in open systems [13,32] hint us how vulnerable the earlier heavy assumptions can be and further weaken the confidence of applying the prior art to real-world p2p content delivery.

Lifting for "Exchange Fairness" Between Provider and Consumer. Besides the natural delivery fairness, it is equally vital to ensure exchange fairness for providers and consumers in a basic context of p2p content delivery, especially with the end goal to complement DSNs and enable some content providers to sell contents to consumers with delegating costly delivery/storage to a p2p network. In particular, the content provider should be guaranteed to receive payments proportional to the amount of correct data learned by the consumer; vice versa, the consumer only has to pay if indeed receiving qualified content.

Naïve attempts of tuning a fair exchange protocol [4,12,28,31] into p2p content delivery can guarantee neither delivery fairness (as analyzed earlier) nor exchange fairness: simply running fair exchange protocols twice between the providers and the deliverers and between the deliverers and the consumers, respectively, would leak valuable contents, raising the threat of massive content leakage. Even worse, this idea disincentivizes the deliverers as they have to pay for the whole content before making a life by delivering the content to consumers.

Our Contributions. Overall, it remains an open problem to realize such strong fairness guarantees in p2p content delivery to protect *all* providers, deliverers, and consumers.[1] We for the first time formalize such security intuitions into a well-defined cryptographic problem on fairness and present a couple of efficient blockchain-based protocols to solve it. In sum, our contributions are:

- We formulate the problem of p2p content delivery with desired security goals, which capture the special fairness to ensure that each party (i.e., the content provider, deliverer, and consumer) is fairly treated even if the other parties arbitrarily collude or are corrupted.
- We put forth a novel delivery fairness notion dubbed verifiable fair delivery (VFD) to quantify one party's bandwidth contribution. With the instantiation of VFD, we propose the blockchain-enabled p2p content delivery protocol FairDownload, which allows: (i) the consumers can download, i.e., *view-after-delivery*, the content with minimum involvement of the provider; (ii) one-time

---

[1] More thorough discussions about the insufficiencies of some pertinent studies (including gradual-release based fair exchange [7,10], blockchain-based fair exchange/MPC [6,9,12,25,31], fair off-chain payment channels [11,33], and some known decentralized content delivery schemes [2,19]) are provided in the online full version [21].

contract deployment and preparation while repeatable delivery of the same content to different consumers.

To further reduce the latency in FairDownload and accommodate the streaming scenario where the consumers expect *view-while-delivery*, we propose another protocol called FairStream, such that every data chunk can be retrieved by consumers in $O(1)$ communication rounds. Though FairStream requires more involvement of an on-line content provider, the provider's online workload remains much smaller than delivering the whole content by itself.

- Both FairDownload and FairStream attain only $\tilde{O}(\eta + \lambda)$ on-chain computational costs even in the worst case, which only relates to the small chunk size parameter η and the even smaller security parameter λ. Moreover, considering the fact that $\lambda \ll \eta$, both protocols essentially realize asymptotically optimal deliverer communication complexity, as the deliverer only has to send $O(\eta + \lambda)$ bits amortized for each η-bit chunk.
- We also implement FairDownload and FairStream with making various nontrivial optimizations to reduce their critical on-chain cost.[2] Extensive experiments in WAN and LAN settings showcase their real-world applicability.

2   Preliminaries

Notations. Let $[n]$ denote $\{1, \ldots, n\}$, $[a, b]$ denote $\{a, \ldots, b\}$, $x \| y$ denote concatenating x and y, $\leftarrow_{\$}$ denote uniformly random sampling, and $\preceq$ denote the prefix relationship.

Global ledger. It provides the primitive of cryptocurrency that can deal with "coin" transfers transparently. Specifically, each entry of the dictionary ledger$[\mathcal{P}_i]$ records the balance of the party $\mathcal{P}_i$, and is global (which means it is accessible by all system participants including the adversary). Moreover, the global dictionary ledger can be a subroutine of the so-called *smart contract* to transact "coins" to a designated party when some conditions are met.

Cryptographic Primitives. We consider: (i) a hash function $\mathcal{H} : \{0,1\}^* \rightarrow \{0,1\}^\lambda$ modeled as a random oracle; (ii) a *semantically secure* (fixed-length) symmetric encryption scheme consisting of (SE.KGen, SEnc, SDec); (iii) an *existential unforgeability under chosen message attack (EU-CMA)* secure digital signature scheme consisting of (SIG.KGen, Sign, Verify); (iv) a Merkle tree scheme of (BuildMT, GenMTP, VerifyMTP); (v) a specific verifiable public key encryption scheme VPKE consisting of (VPKE.KGen, VEnc, VDec, ProvePKE, VerifyPKE) allowing the decryptor to produce a proof besides the plaintext, thus attesting correct decryption in a zero-knowledge fashion, i.e., without leaking private key [8].

3   Warm-Up: Verifiable Fair Delivery

We first warm up and set forth a building block termed *verifiable fair delivery* (VFD), which enables an honest verifier to validate that a sender indeed transfers

---

[2] Code availability: https://github.com/Blockchain-World/FairThunder.git.

some amount of data to a receiver. It later acts as a key module in the fair p2p content delivery protocol (in Sect. 5). The high level idea of VFD lies in: a receiver needs to send back a signed "receipt" in order to acknowledge a sender's bandwidth contribution and continuously receives the next data chunk. Consider the data chunks of same size η are transferred *sequentially* starting from the first chunk, the sender can always use the latest receipt containing the chunk index to prove to a verifier about the contribution. Intuitively the sender *at most* wastes bandwidth of transferring one chunk.

Syntax. The VFD protocol is among an interactive poly-time Turing-machine (ITM) sender $\mathcal{S}$, an ITM receiver $\mathcal{R}$, and a non-interactive Turing-machine verifier $\mathcal{V}$, and follows the syntax:

- **Sender.** $\mathcal{S}$ can be activated by an interface $\mathcal{S}.\text{send}()$ with inputting a sequence of n data chunks and their corresponding validation strings, denoted by $((c_1, \sigma_{c_1}), \ldots, (c_n, \sigma_{c_n}))$, and there exists an efficient and global predicate $\Psi(i, c_i, \sigma_{c_i}) \rightarrow \{0, 1\}$ to check whether c_i is the i-th valid chunk due to σ_{c_i}; once activated, $\mathcal{S}$ interacts with $\mathcal{R}$ and opens an interface $\mathcal{S}.\text{prove}()$ that can be invoked to generate a proof π indicating the number of sent chunks;
- **Receiver.** $\mathcal{R}$ can be activated by an interface $\mathcal{R}.\text{recv}()$ with the input of the global predicate $\Psi(\cdot)$ to interact with $\mathcal{S}$, and outputs a sequence of $((c_1, \sigma_{c_1}), \ldots, (c_{n'}, \sigma_{c_{n'}}))$, where $n' \in [n]$ and every (c_i, σ_{c_i}) is valid due to $\Psi(\cdot)$;
- **Verifier.** $\mathcal{V}$ takes as input the proof π generated by $\mathcal{S}.\text{prove}()$, and outputs an integer $\text{ctr} \in \{0, \cdots, n\}$.

Security. The VFD protocol must satisfy the following security requirements:

- **Termination.** If at least one of $\mathcal{S}$ and $\mathcal{R}$ is honest, the VFD protocol terminates within at most $2n$ rounds, where n is the number of content chunks.
- **Completeness.** If $\mathcal{S}$ and $\mathcal{R}$ are both honest and activated, after $2n$ rounds, $\mathcal{S}$ is able to generate a proof π that can be verified by $\mathcal{V}$ to output $\text{ctr} = n$, while $\mathcal{R}$ can output $((c_1, \sigma_{c_1}), \ldots, (c_n, \sigma_{c_n}))$, which is same to $\mathcal{S}$'s input.
- **Verifiable η delivery fairness.** When one of $\mathcal{S}$ and $\mathcal{R}$ maliciously aborts, VFD shall satisfy the following delivery fairness requirements:
  - *Verifiable delivery fairness against $\mathcal{S}^*$.* The honest receiver $\mathcal{R}$ will always receive the valid sequence $(c_1, \sigma_{c_1}), \ldots, (c_{\text{ctr}}, \sigma_{c_{\text{ctr}}})$ if the corrupted $\mathcal{S}^*$ can produce the proof π that enables $\mathcal{V}$ to output ctr.
  - *Verifiable delivery fairness against $\mathcal{R}^*$.* The honest sender $\mathcal{S}$ can always generate a proof π, which enables $\mathcal{V}$ to output *at least* $(\text{ctr} - 1)$ if the corrupted $\mathcal{R}^*$ receives the valid sequence $(c_1, \sigma_{c_1}), \ldots, (c_{\text{ctr}}, \sigma_{c_{\text{ctr}}})$. At most $\mathcal{S}$ wastes bandwidth for delivering one content chunk of η-bit size.

VFD protocol Π_{VFD}. We consider the authenticated setting where the sender $\mathcal{S}$ and the receiver $\mathcal{R}$ have generated public-private key pairs $(pk_{\mathcal{S}}, sk_{\mathcal{S}})$ and $(pk_{\mathcal{R}}, sk_{\mathcal{R}})$, respectively, and they have announced the public keys to bind to themselves. Then, VFD with the global predicate $\Psi(\cdot)$ can be realized by Π_{VFD}

hereunder among $\mathcal{S}$, $\mathcal{R}$ and $\mathcal{V}$ against probabilistic poly-time (P.P.T.) and static adversary in the *stand-alone* setting[3] with the synchronous network assumption:

- **Construction of $\mathcal{S}$.** The sender, after activated via $\mathcal{S}$.send() with the input $((c_1, \sigma_{c_1}), \ldots, (c_n, \sigma_{c_n}))$, $pk_\mathcal{S}$ and $pk_\mathcal{R}$, starts a timer $\mathcal{T}_\mathcal{S}$ lasting two synchronous rounds, initializes a variable $\pi_\mathcal{S} := null$, and executes as follows:
  - For each $i \in [n]$: sends $(\mathsf{deliver}, i, c_i, \sigma_{c_i})$ to $\mathcal{R}$, and waits for $(\mathsf{receipt}, i, \sigma_\mathcal{R}^i)$ from $\mathcal{R}$. If $\mathcal{T}_\mathcal{S}$ expires before receiving the receipt, breaks the iteration; otherwise $\mathcal{S}$ verifies whether $\mathsf{Verify}(\mathsf{receipt}||i||pk_\mathcal{R}||pk_\mathcal{S}, \sigma_\mathcal{R}^i, pk_\mathcal{R}) \equiv 1$ or not, if *true*, resets $\mathcal{T}_\mathcal{S}$, outputs $\pi_\mathcal{S} := (i, \sigma_\mathcal{R}^i)$, and continues to run the next iteration (i.e., increasing i by one); if *false*, breaks the iteration;
  - Upon $\mathcal{S}$.prove() is invoked, it returns $\pi_\mathcal{S}$ as the VFD proof and halts.
- **Construction of $\mathcal{R}$.** The receiver, after activated via $\mathcal{R}$.recv() with the input $pk_\mathcal{S}$ and $(pk_\mathcal{R}, sk_\mathcal{R})$, starts a timer $\mathcal{T}_\mathcal{R}$ lasting two synchronous rounds and operates as: for each $j \in [n]$: $\mathcal{R}$ waits for $(\mathsf{deliver}, j, c_j, \sigma_{c_j})$ from $\mathcal{S}$ and halts if $\mathcal{T}_\mathcal{R}$ expires before receiving the deliver message; otherwise $\mathcal{R}$ verifies whether $\Psi(j, c_j, \sigma_{c_j}) \equiv 1$ or not; if *true*, resets $\mathcal{T}_\mathcal{R}$, outputs (c_j, σ_{c_j}), and sends $(\mathsf{receipt}, i, \sigma_\mathcal{R}^i)$ to $\mathcal{S}$ where $\sigma_\mathcal{R}^i \leftarrow \mathsf{Sign}(\mathsf{receipt}||i||pk_\mathcal{R}||pk_\mathcal{S}, sk_\mathcal{R})$, halts if *false*. Note that $\Psi(\cdot)$ is efficient as it just performs a signature verification.
- **Construction of $\mathcal{V}$.** Upon the input $\pi_\mathcal{S}$, the verifier $\mathcal{V}$ parses it into $(\mathsf{ctr}, \sigma_\mathcal{R}^{\mathsf{ctr}})$, and checks whether $\mathsf{Verify}(\mathsf{receipt}||\mathsf{ctr}||pk_\mathcal{R}||pk_\mathcal{S}, \sigma_\mathcal{R}^{\mathsf{ctr}}, pk_\mathcal{R}) \equiv 1$ or not; if *true*, it outputs ctr, or else outputs 0. Recall that Verify is to verify signatures.

The following lemma states the security of the above VFD protocol, the detailed proof of which is presented in the online full version [21].

Lemma 1. *In the synchronous authenticated network and stand-alone setting, Π_{VFD} satisfies termination, completeness and the verifiable η delivery fairness against static P.P.T. adversary corrupting one of the sender and the receiver.*

4 Formalizing P2P Content Delivery

4.1 System Model

Participating Parties. We consider the following entities (i.e., interactive Turing machines by cryptographic convention) in the context of p2p content delivery:

- *Content Provider $\mathcal{P}$* is an entity that owns the original content m composed of n chunks,[4] satisfying a public known predicate $\phi(\cdot)$,[5] and $\mathcal{P}$ is willing to

---

[3] To defend against *replay* attack in concurrent sessions, it is trivial to let the authenticated messages include a session id sid field, which, for example, can be instantiated by the hash of the transferred data identifier root_m, the involved parties' addresses and an increasing-only nonce, namely $sid := \mathcal{H}(\mathsf{root}_m||\mathcal{V}\_address||pk_\mathcal{S}||pk_\mathcal{R}||nonce)$.

[4] Remark that the content m is *dividable* in the sense that each chunk is *independent* to other chunks, e.g., the chunk is a small 10-s video fragment.

[5] Throughout this paper, we consider ϕ is in the form of $\phi(m) = [\mathsf{root}(\mathsf{BuildMT}(m)) \equiv \mathsf{root}_m]$, where root is the Merkle tree root of m. In practice, it can be acquired from a semi-trusted third party, e.g., VirusTotal [23] or BitTorrent forum sites [28].

sell to the users of interest. Also, $\mathcal{P}$ would like to delegate the delivery of m to a deliverer with promise to pay $\overset{\text{\tiny B}}{\text{B}}_{\mathcal{P}}$ for each successfully delivered chunk.

- *Content Deliverer $\mathcal{D}$* contributes its *idle* bandwidth resources to deliver the content on behalf of the provider $\mathcal{P}$ and would receive the payment proportional to the amount of delivered data.
- *Content Consumer $\mathcal{C}$* is an entity that would pay $\overset{\text{\tiny B}}{\text{B}}_{\mathcal{C}}$ for each chunk in the content m by interacting with $\mathcal{P}$ and $\mathcal{D}$.

Adversary $\mathcal{A}$. We consider the adversary with the following standard abilities [24]: (i) *Static corruptions:* $\mathcal{A}$ can corrupt some parties only before the protocol executions; (ii) *Computationally bounded:* $\mathcal{A}$ is restricted to P.P.T. algorithms; (iii) *Synchronous authenticated channel:* it describes the ability of $\mathcal{A}$ on controlling communications. W.l.o.g., we consider a global clock in the system, and $\mathcal{A}$ can delay the messages up to a clock round [25,27].

Arbiter Smart Contract $\mathcal{G}$. The system is in a hybrid model with oracle access to an arbiter smart contract $\mathcal{G}$, which is a stateful ideal functionality that leaks all its internal states to the adversary $\mathcal{A}$ and all parties, and can check some immutable conditions to transact "coins" over the cryptocurrency ledger, thus "mimicking" the contracts in real life transparently. In practice, the contract can be instantiated via real-world blockchains such as Ethereum [43]. Description of $\mathcal{G}$ in the paper follows the conventional pseudo-code notations in [27].

4.2   Design Goals

Syntax. A fair p2p content delivery protocol $\Pi = (\mathcal{P}, \mathcal{D}, \mathcal{C})$ is a tuple of three P.P.T. interactive Turing machines (ITMs) consisting of two explicit phases:

- *Preparation phase.* The provider $\mathcal{P}$ takes as input public parameters and the content $m = (m_1, \ldots, m_n) \in \{0,1\}^{\eta \times n}$ that satisfies $\phi(m) \equiv 1$, where η is chunk size in bit and n is the number of chunks, and it outputs some auxiliary data, e.g., encryption keys; the deliverer $\mathcal{D}$ takes as input public parameters and outputs some auxiliary data, e.g., encrypted content; the consumer $\mathcal{C}$ does not involve in this phase. Note $\mathcal{P}$ deposits a budget of $n \cdot \overset{\text{\tiny B}}{\text{B}}_{\mathcal{P}}$ in ledger to incentivize $\mathcal{D}$ so it can *minimize* bandwidth usage in the next phase.
- *Delivery phase.* The provider $\mathcal{P}$ and the deliverer $\mathcal{D}$ take as input their auxiliary data obtained in the preparation phase, respectively, and they would receive the deserved payment; the consumer $\mathcal{C}$ takes as input public parameters and outputs the content m with $\phi(m) \equiv 1$. Note $\mathcal{C}$ has a budget of $n \cdot \overset{\text{\tiny B}}{\text{B}}_{\mathcal{C}}$ in ledger to "buy" the content m satisfying $\phi(m) \equiv 1$, where $\overset{\text{\tiny B}}{\text{B}}_{\mathcal{C}} > \overset{\text{\tiny B}}{\text{B}}_{\mathcal{P}}$.

PROPERTIES. Besides, the protocol shall guarantee the following properties.

Completeness. For any content predicate $\phi(m) = [\text{root}(\text{BuildMT}(m)) \equiv \text{root}_m]$, conditioned on $\mathcal{P}, \mathcal{D}$ and $\mathcal{C}$ are all honest, the protocol Π attains: (i) $\mathcal{C}$ obtains the content m satisfying $\phi(m) \equiv 1$, and the balance of $\text{ledger}[\mathcal{C}]$ decreases by $n \cdot \overset{\text{\tiny B}}{\text{B}}_{\mathcal{C}}$; (ii) $\mathcal{D}$ receives the payment $n \cdot \overset{\text{\tiny B}}{\text{B}}_{\mathcal{P}}$ over the global ledger; (iii) $\mathcal{P}$ gets the payment $n \cdot (\overset{\text{\tiny B}}{\text{B}}_{\mathcal{C}} - \overset{\text{\tiny B}}{\text{B}}_{\mathcal{P}})$, as it receives $n \cdot \overset{\text{\tiny B}}{\text{B}}_{\mathcal{C}}$ from $\mathcal{C}$ and pays $n \cdot \overset{\text{\tiny B}}{\text{B}}_{\mathcal{P}}$ to $\mathcal{D}$.

Fairness. The protocol Π should satisfy the following fairness requirements:

- *Consumer Fairness.* The honest consumer $\mathcal{C}$ is ensured that: the ledger$[\mathcal{C}]$ decreases by $\ell \cdot \text{\BB}_{\mathcal{C}}$ only if $\mathcal{C}$ receives a sequence of chunks $(m_1, \ldots, m_\ell) \preceq m$ where $\phi(m) \equiv 1$, i.e., $\mathcal{C}$ pays proportional to valid chunks it *de facto* receives.
- *Deliverer η-Fairness.* The honest deliverer $\mathcal{D}$ is assured that: if $\mathcal{D}$ sent overall $O(\ell \cdot \eta + 1)$ bits during the protocol, $\mathcal{D}$ should *at least* obtain the payment of $(\ell - 1) \cdot \text{\BB}_{\mathcal{P}}$. In other words, the unpaid delivery is bounded by $O(\eta)$ bits.
- *Provider η-Fairness.* The honest provider $\mathcal{P}$ is guaranteed that: if $\mathcal{A}$ can output $\eta \cdot \ell$ bits prefixed in the content m, $\mathcal{P}$ should *at least* receive $(\ell - 1) \cdot (\text{\BB}_{\mathcal{C}} - \text{\BB}_{\mathcal{P}})$ net income. Intuitively, $\mathcal{P}$ is ensured that *at most* $O(\eta)$-bit content are revealed without being well paid.

Confidentiality Against Deliverer. A malicious $\mathcal{D}^*$ corrupted by $\mathcal{A}$ cannot output $\mathcal{P}$'s original content in a delivery session even after receiving all protocol scripts and all internal states leaked by the contract. Note that confidentiality is not captured by fairness, as it is trivial to see that a protocol satisfying fairness might not have confidentiality: upon all payments are cleared and the consumer receives the whole content, the protocol lets the consumer send the content to the deliverer.

Timeliness. When at least one of the parties $\mathcal{P}$, $\mathcal{D}$ and $\mathcal{C}$ is honest (i.e., others are corrupted by $\mathcal{A}$), the honest ones are guaranteed to halt in $O(n)$ synchronous rounds where n is the number of content chunks. At completion or abortion of the protocol, the fairness and confidentiality properties are always guaranteed.

Non-trivial Efficiency. We require the necessary efficiency to rule out possible trivial solutions: (i) the messages sent to $\mathcal{G}$ from honest parties are uniformly bounded by $\tilde{O}(1)$ bits, which excludes a trivial way of directly delivering content via smart contract; (ii) in the delivery phase, the messages sent by honest $\mathcal{P}$ are uniformly bounded by $n \cdot \lambda$ bits, where λ is a small cryptographic parameter such that $n \cdot \lambda$ is much smaller than the content size $|m|$. This makes $\mathcal{P}$ to save bandwidth after preparation phase and excludes the idea of delivering by itself.

REMARKS ABOUT DEFINITION. It is worth noticing that: (i) the predicate $\phi(\cdot)$ is a public parameter; (ii) our fairness requirements have implied the case of corrupting one party of $\mathcal{P}$, $\mathcal{D}$ and $\mathcal{C}$ instead of two since $\mathcal{A}$ can always let some corrupted one follow the original protocol; (iii) we do not consider the case that all parties are corrupted; (iv) the deliverer and the provider might lose well-deserved payment, but *at most* for one chunk, i.e., the level of unfairness is strictly bounded; (v) though we focus on the case of a *single* content deliverer, our formalism and design can be extended to capture *multiple* deliverers, e.g., by cutting the content into multiple pieces and each piece is delegated to a distinct deliverer, which forms a future extension; (vi) after the one-time preparation phase, the delivery phase becomes repeatable.

In addition, one might wonder that a probably corrupted content provider fails in the middle of a transmission, causing that the consumer does not get the entire content but has to pay a lot. Nevertheless, this is not a serious worry in the peer-to-peer content delivery setting that aims to complement decentralized content storage networks, because there essentially are a large number of deliverers, and at least some of them can be honest. As such, if a consumer encounters failures in the middle of delivery, it can iteratively ask another deliverer to start a new session to fetch the remaining undelivered chunks. Moreover, our constructions in Sect. 5 and Sect. 6 allow the consumers to fetch the content from any specific chunk instead of always starting from the first chunk, the expense of which would be nearly proportional to the actual number of retrieved chunks.

5   FairDownload: Fair P2P Downloading

5.1   FairDownload Overview

At a high level, FairDownload is constructed around the module of verifiable fair delivery (VFD) and operates in *Prepare, Deliver* and *Reveal* phases, as illustrated in Fig. 1. The core ideas are: initially the provider $\mathcal{P}$ encrypts each chunk, signs the encrypted chunks and delegates to the deliverer $\mathcal{D}$; the consumer $\mathcal{C}$ and $\mathcal{D}$ can run an instance of VFD, where the predicate $\Psi(\cdot)$ ensures each delivered chunk is correctly signed by $\mathcal{P}$; the arbiter smart contract $\mathcal{G}_d^{\text{ledger}}$ (abbr. $\mathcal{G}_d$) shown in Fig. 2 can invoke VFD verifier to check the VFD proof and realize whether $\mathcal{D}$ indeed delivers ctr chunks to $\mathcal{C}$; $\mathcal{P}$ then presents to reveal the minimum (i.e., a short $\tilde{O}(\lambda)$-bit message) number of elements (via our proposed *structured key derivation scheme* composed of Algorithms 1, 2 and 4) on-chain, so that $\mathcal{C}$ can use a small string to recover the decryption keys for all ctr chunks; the revealed on-chain elements are encrypted by the consumer's public key to ensure confidentiality against malicious $\mathcal{D}$; In case of dispute, $\mathcal{C}$ can complain to the contract $\mathcal{G}_d$ via a short $O(\eta + \lambda)$-bit message to "prove" the error of decrypted chunk and get refund, the on-chain cost of verifying which is $O(\log n)$ at worst.

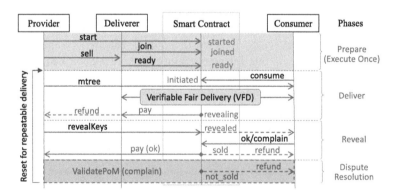

Fig. 1. The execution flow of FairDownload protocol Π_{FD}.

The Arbiter Contract Functionality $\mathcal{G}_d^{\text{ledger}}$ for P2P Downloading

The arbiter contract $\mathcal{G}_d$ has access to the ledger, and it interacts with the provider $\mathcal{P}$, the deliverer $\mathcal{D}$, the consumer $\mathcal{C}$ and the adversary $\mathcal{A}$. It locally stores the times of repeatable delivery θ, the number of content chunks n, the content digest root_m, the price $\text{\B}_\mathcal{P}$, $\text{\B}_\mathcal{C}$ and $\text{\B}_{\text{pf}}$, the number of delivered chunks ctr (initialized as 0), addresses $pk_\mathcal{P}, pk_\mathcal{D}, pk_\mathcal{C}, vpk_\mathcal{C}$, revealed keys' hash erk_{hash}, state Σ and three timers $\mathcal{T}_{\text{round}}$ (implicitly), $\mathcal{T}_{\text{deliver}}$, and $\mathcal{T}_{\text{dispute}}$.

──────── **Phase 1: Prepare** ────────

- On receive (start, $pk_\mathcal{P}$, root_m, θ, n, $\text{\B}_\mathcal{P}$, $\text{\B}_\mathcal{C}$, $\text{\B}_{\text{pf}}$) from $\mathcal{P}$:
  - assert $\text{ledger}[\mathcal{P}] \geq (\theta \cdot (n \cdot \text{\B}_\mathcal{P} + \text{\B}_{\text{pf}})) \wedge \Sigma \equiv \emptyset$
  - store $pk_\mathcal{P}$, root_m, θ, n, $\text{\B}_\mathcal{P}$, $\text{\B}_\mathcal{C}$, $\text{\B}_{\text{pf}}$
  - let $\text{ledger}[\mathcal{P}] := \text{ledger}[\mathcal{P}] - \theta \cdot (n \cdot \text{\B}_\mathcal{P} + \text{\B}_{\text{pf}})$ and $\Sigma := \text{started}$
  - send (started, $pk_\mathcal{P}$, root_m, θ, n, $\text{\B}_\mathcal{P}$, $\text{\B}_\mathcal{C}$, $\text{\B}_{\text{pf}}$) to all entities
- On receive (join, $pk_\mathcal{D}$) from $\mathcal{D}$:
  - assert $\Sigma \equiv \text{started}$
  - store $pk_\mathcal{D}$ and let $\Sigma := \text{joined}$
  - send (joined, $pk_\mathcal{D}$) to all entities
- On receive (prepared) from $\mathcal{D}$:
  - assert $\Sigma \equiv \text{joined}$, and let $\Sigma := \text{ready}$
  - send (ready) to all entities

──────── **Phase 2: Deliver** ────────

- On receive (consume, $pk_\mathcal{C}$, $vpk_\mathcal{C}$) from $\mathcal{C}$:
  - assert $\theta > 0$
  - assert $\text{ledger}[\mathcal{C}] \geq n \cdot \text{\B}_\mathcal{C} \wedge \Sigma \equiv \text{ready}$
  - store $pk_\mathcal{C}$, $vpk_\mathcal{C}$ and let $\text{ledger}[\mathcal{C}] := \text{ledger}[\mathcal{C}] - n \cdot \text{\B}_\mathcal{C}$
  - start a timer $\mathcal{T}_{\text{deliver}}$ and let $\Sigma := \text{initiated}$
  - send (initiated, $pk_\mathcal{C}$, $vpk_\mathcal{C}$) to all entities
- On receive (delivered) from $\mathcal{C}$ or $\mathcal{T}_{\text{deliver}}$ times out:
  - assert $\Sigma \equiv \text{initiated}$
  - send (getVFDProof) to $\mathcal{D}$, and wait for two rounds to receive (receipt, i, $\sigma_\mathcal{C}^i$), then execute verifyVFDProof() to let ctr $:= i$, and then assert $0 \leq \text{ctr} \leq n$
  - let $\text{ledger}[\mathcal{D}] := \text{ledger}[\mathcal{D}] + \text{ctr} \cdot \text{\B}_\mathcal{P}$
  - let $\text{ledger}[\mathcal{P}] := \text{ledger}[\mathcal{P}] + (n - \text{ctr}) \cdot \text{\B}_\mathcal{P}$
  - store ctr, let $\Sigma := \text{revealing}$, and send (revealing, ctr) to all entities

──────── **Phase 3: Reveal** ────────

- On receive (revealKeys, erk) from $\mathcal{P}$:
  - assert $\Sigma \equiv \text{revealing}$

- store erk (essentially erk's hash) and start a timer $\mathcal{T}_{\text{dispute}}$
- let $\Sigma := \text{revealed}$
- send (revealed, erk) to all entities
- Upon $\mathcal{T}_{\text{dispute}}$ times out:
  - assert $\Sigma \equiv \text{revealed}$ and current time $\mathcal{T} \geq \mathcal{T}_{\text{dispute}}$
  - $\text{ledger}[\mathcal{P}] := \text{ledger}[\mathcal{P}] + \text{ctr} \cdot \text{\B}_\mathcal{C} + \text{\B}_{\text{pf}}$
  - $\text{ledger}[\mathcal{C}] := \text{ledger}[\mathcal{C}] + (n - \text{ctr}) \cdot \text{\B}_\mathcal{C}$
  - let $\Sigma := \text{sold}$ and send (sold) to all entities

  ▷ Below is the dispute resolution
- On receive (wrongRK) from $\mathcal{C}$ before $\mathcal{T}_{\text{dispute}}$ times out:
  - assert $\Sigma \equiv \text{revealed}$ and current time $\mathcal{T} < \mathcal{T}_{\text{dispute}}$
  - if (ValidateRKeys$(n, \text{ctr}, erk) \equiv false$):
    * let $\text{ledger}[\mathcal{C}] := \text{ledger}[\mathcal{C}] + n \cdot \text{\B}_\mathcal{C} + \text{\B}_{\text{pf}}$
    * let $\Sigma := \text{not\_sold}$ and send (not_sold) to all entities
- On receive (PoM, i, j, c_i, σ_{c_i}, $\mathcal{H}(m_i)$, π_{MT}^i, rk, erk, π_{VD}) from $\mathcal{C}$ before $\mathcal{T}_{\text{dispute}}$ times out:
  - assert $\Sigma \equiv \text{revealed}$ and current time $\mathcal{T} < \mathcal{T}_{\text{dispute}}$
  - invoke the ValidatePoM$(i, j, c_i, \sigma_{c_i}, \mathcal{H}(m_i), \pi_{\text{MT}}^i, rk, erk, \pi_{\text{VD}})$ subroutine, if $true$ is returned:
    * let $\text{ledger}[\mathcal{C}] := \text{ledger}[\mathcal{C}] + n \cdot \text{\B}_\mathcal{C} + \text{\B}_{\text{pf}}$
    * let $\Sigma := \text{not\_sold}$ and send (not_sold) to all entities

  ▷ Reset to the ready state for repeatable delivery
- On receive (reset) from $\mathcal{P}$:
  - assert $\Sigma \equiv \text{sold}$ or $\Sigma \equiv \text{not\_sold}$
  - set ctr, $\mathcal{T}_{\text{deliver}}$, $\mathcal{T}_{\text{dispute}}$ as 0
  - nullify $pk_\mathcal{C}$ and $vpk_\mathcal{C}$
  - let $\theta := \theta - 1$, and $\Sigma := \text{ready}$
  - send (ready) to all entities

Fig. 2. The arbiter contract functionality $\mathcal{G}_d^{\text{ledger}}$ for downloading. "Sending to all entities" captures that the smart contract is transparent to the public.

5.2 Π_{FD}: FairDownload Protocol

Now we present the fair p2p downloading protocol Π_{FD}. The session id sid and the content digest root_m are omitted since they remain same in a delivery session.

Phase I for Prepare. The parties $\mathcal{P}$ and $\mathcal{D}$ interact with $\mathcal{G}_d$ in this phase as:

- The provider $\mathcal{P}$ with $(pk_\mathcal{P}, sk_\mathcal{P})$ deploys contracts and starts[6] Π_{FD} by sending $(\mathsf{start}, pk_\mathcal{P}, \mathsf{root}_m, \theta, n, \ddot{B}_\mathcal{P}, \ddot{B}_\mathcal{C}, \ddot{B}_{\mathsf{pf}})$ to $\mathcal{G}_d$, where root_m is the content digest in the form of Merkle tree root, θ indicates how many times of repeatable delivery are allowed for this contract, n is the number of content chunks[7], $\ddot{B}_\mathcal{P}, \ddot{B}_\mathcal{C}, \ddot{B}_{\mathsf{pf}} \in \mathbb{N}$ are price parameters, and $\ddot{B}_{\mathsf{pf}}$ is the *penalty fee*[8] in a delivery session to discrouage the misbehavior from $\mathcal{P}$.
- Upon $\Sigma \equiv \mathsf{joined}$, the provider $\mathcal{P}$ would: (i) randomly sample a master key mk, run Algorithm 1 to get the key derivation tree KT, and store mk and KT locally; (ii) use the n leaf nodes of KT to encrypt $(m_1, \ldots, m_n)$ to get $(c_1, \ldots, c_n)$; (iii) then sign the encrypted chunks to obtain a sequence of ciphertext-signature pairs $((c_1, \sigma_{c_1}), \ldots, (c_n, \sigma_{c_n}))$; compute content's Merkle tree MT and sign MT to obtain the signature $\sigma_\mathcal{P}^{\mathsf{MT}}$; locally store $(\mathsf{MT}, \sigma_\mathcal{P}^{\mathsf{MT}})$ and then send $(\mathsf{sell}, ((c_1, \sigma_{c_1}), \cdots, (c_n, \sigma_{c_n})))$ to $\mathcal{D}$ off-chain; (iv) wait for (ready) from $\mathcal{G}_d$ to enter the next phase.
- The deliverer $\mathcal{D}$ with $(pk_\mathcal{D}, sk_\mathcal{D})$ would: (i) upon receiving the $(\mathsf{started})$ message from $\mathcal{G}_d$, send $(\mathsf{join}, pk_\mathcal{D})$ to $\mathcal{G}_d$; (ii) wait for the (sell) message from $\mathcal{P}$, then verify each pair (c_i, σ_{c_i}). If valid, send $(\mathsf{prepared})$ to $\mathcal{G}_d$, and store $((c_1, \sigma_{c_1}), \cdots, (c_n, \sigma_{c_n}))$ locally, otherwise halt; (iii) wait for (ready) from $\mathcal{G}_d$ to enter the next phase.

Upon the completion of the above execution, $\mathcal{P}$ owns a master key mk, the key derivation tree KT, and the Merkle tree MT, while $\mathcal{D}$ receives the delegated encrypted content chunks and is ready to deliver the content to consumers.

Phase II for Deliver. The parties $\mathcal{C}$, $\mathcal{P}$, and $\mathcal{D}$ interact with $\mathcal{G}_d$ as follows:

- The consumer $\mathcal{C}$ with $(pk_\mathcal{C}, sk_\mathcal{C})$ and $(vpk_\mathcal{C}, vsk_\mathcal{C}) \leftarrow \mathsf{VPKE.KGen}(1^\lambda)$ would: (i) assert $\Sigma \equiv \mathsf{ready}$, and send $(\mathsf{consume}, pk_\mathcal{C}, vpk_\mathcal{C})$ to $\mathcal{G}_d$; (ii) upon receiving $(\mathsf{mtree}, \mathsf{MT}, \sigma_\mathcal{P}^{\mathsf{MT}})$ from $\mathcal{P}$, verify the signature $\sigma_\mathcal{P}^{\mathsf{MT}}$ and check whether $\mathsf{root}(\mathsf{MT}) \equiv \mathsf{root}_m$ or not, if both hold, store MT and then activate the receiver $\mathcal{R}$ in the VFD module via $\mathcal{R}.\mathsf{recv}()$ and instantiating the predicate $\Psi(\cdot)$ as $\mathsf{Verify}(i||c_i, \sigma_{c_i}, pk_\mathcal{P})$. Then $\mathcal{C}$ waits for the execution of VFD to obtain the delivered chunks $((c_1, \sigma_{c_1}), (c_2, \sigma_{c_2}), \cdots)$ and stores them; upon receiving all the n chunks, sends $(\mathsf{delivered})$ to $\mathcal{G}_d$; (iii) waits for the $(\mathsf{revealing})$ message from $\mathcal{G}_d$ to enter the next phase.
- The provider $\mathcal{P}$ would execute as follows: upon receiving $(\mathsf{initiated})$ from $\mathcal{G}_d$, asserts $\Sigma \equiv \mathsf{initiated}$, sends $(\mathsf{mtree}, \mathsf{MT}, \sigma_\mathcal{P}^{\mathsf{MT}})$ to $\mathcal{C}$, and enters the next phase.
- The deliverer $\mathcal{D}$ executes as follows: (i) upon receiving $(\mathsf{initiated})$ from $\mathcal{G}_d$, asserts $\Sigma \equiv \mathsf{initiated}$, and then activates the sender $\mathcal{S}$ in the VFD module via $\mathcal{S}.\mathsf{send}()$ and instantiating the predicate $\Psi(\cdot)$ as $\mathsf{Verify}(i||c_i, \sigma_{c_i}, pk_\mathcal{P})$, and feeds the VFD module with input $((c_1, \sigma_{c_1}), \ldots, (c_n, \sigma_{c_n}))$; (ii) upon receiving $(\mathsf{getVFDProof})$ from $\mathcal{G}_d$, sends the *latest* receipt, namely $(\mathsf{receipt}, i, \sigma_\mathcal{C}^i)$ to $\mathcal{G}_d$; (iii) waits for the $(\mathsf{revealing})$ message from $\mathcal{G}_d$ to halt.

---

[6] $\mathcal{P}$ can retrieve the deposits of $\ddot{B}_\mathcal{P}$ and $\ddot{B}_{\mathsf{pf}}$ back if no deliverers respond timely.

[7] W.l.o.g., we assume $n = 2^k$ for $k \in \mathbb{Z}$ for presentation simplicity.

[8] $\ddot{B}_{\mathsf{pf}}$ can be required proportional to $(n \times \ddot{B}_\mathcal{C})$ in case $\mathcal{P}$ deliberately lowers it.

Algorithm 1. GenSubKeys algorithm

Input: n, mk
Output: a $(2n-1)$-array KT
1: let KT be an array of length $(2n-1)$
2: $\text{KT}[0] = \mathcal{H}(mk)$
3: **if** $n \equiv 1$ **then**
4:     **return** KT

5: **if** $n > 1$ **then**
6:     **for** i in $[0, n-2]$ **do**
7:         $\text{KT}[2i+1] = \mathcal{H}(\text{KT}[i] \mathbin{\|} 0)$
8:         $\text{KT}[2i+2] = \mathcal{H}(\text{KT}[i] \mathbin{\|} 1)$
9: **return** KT

Algorithm 2. RevealKeys algorithm

Input: n, ctr, and mk
Output: rk, an array containing the minimum number of elements in KT that suffices to recover the ctr keys from $\text{KT}[n-1]$ to $\text{KT}[n + \text{ctr} - 2]$
1: let rk and ind be empty arrays
2: $\text{KT} \leftarrow \text{GenSubKeys}(n, mk)$
3: **if** $\text{ctr} \equiv 1$ **then**
4:     rk appends $(n-1, \text{KT}[n-1])$
5:     **return** rk
6: **for** i in $[0, \text{ctr}-1]$ **do**
7:     $ind[i] = n - 1 + i$
8: **while** $true$ **do**
9:     let t be an empty array
10:    **for** j in $[0, \lfloor |ind|/2 \rfloor - 1]$ **do**
11:        $p_l = (ind[2j] - 1)/2$

12:        $p_r = (ind[2j+1] - 2)/2$
           ▷ merge elements with the same parent node in KT
13:        **if** $p_l \equiv p_r$ **then**
14:            t appends p_l
15:        **else**
16:            t appends $ind[2j]$
17:            t appends $ind[2j+1]$
18:        **if** $|ind|$ is odd **then**
19:            t appends $ind[|ind| - 1]$
20:        **if** $|ind| \equiv |t|$ **then**
21:            break
22:        $ind = t$
23:    **for** x in $[0, |ind| - 1]$ **do**
24:        rk appends $(ind[x], \text{KT}[ind[x]])$
25: **return** rk

Algorithm 3. ValidateRKeys algorithm

Input: n, ctr and erk
Output: $true$ or $false$ indicating if the correct number (i.e., ctr) of keys can be recovered
1: **if** $n \equiv \text{ctr}$ and $|erk| \equiv 1$ and the position of $erk[0] \equiv 0$ **then**
2:     **return** $true$ {root of KT}
3: Initialize $chunks\_index$ as a set of numbers $\{n - 1, \cdots, n + \text{ctr} - 2\}$
4: **for** each $(i, \_)$ in erk **do**
5:     $d_i = \log(n) - |\log(i+1)|$
6:     $l_i = i, r_i = i$

7:     **if** $d_i \equiv 0$ **then**
8:         $chunks\_index$ removes i
9:     **else**
10:        **while** $(d_i\text{--}) > 0$ **do**
11:            $l_i = 2l_i + 1$
12:            $r_i = 2r_i + 2$
13:        $chunks\_index$ removes the elements from l_i to r_i
14: **if** $chunks\_index \equiv \emptyset$ **then**
15:     **return** $true$
16: **return** $false$

Algorithm 4. RecoverKeys algorithm

Input: n, ctr, and rk
Output: a ctr-sized array ks
1: let ks be an empty array
2: **for** each $(i, \text{KT}[i])$ in rk **do**

3:     $n_i = 2^{(\log n - \lfloor \log(i+1) \rfloor)}$
4:     $v_i = \text{GenSubKeys}(n_i, \text{KT}[i])$
5:     ks appends $v_i[n_i - 1 : 2n_i - 2]$
6: **return** ks

At the end of this phase, $\mathcal{C}$ receives the encrypted chunks $(c_1, c_2, \dots)$, and $\mathcal{D}$ obtains the payment for the bandwidth contribution of delivering chunks, and the contract updates and records the number of delivered chunks ctr.

Phase III for Reveal. The parties $\mathcal{P}$ and $\mathcal{C}$ interact with $\mathcal{G}_d$ as:

Algorithm 5. ValidatePoM algorithm

Input: $(i, j, c_i, \sigma_{c_i}, \mathcal{H}(m_i), \pi^i_{\mathsf{MT}}, rk, erk, \pi_{\mathsf{VD}})$;   5: assert VerifyMTP$(root_m, i, \pi^i_{\mathsf{MT}}, \mathcal{H}(m_i)) \equiv 1$
also, $(root_m, n, erk_{\mathsf{hash}}, pk_{\mathcal{P}}, vpk_{\mathcal{C}})$ are stored   6: $k_i = $ RecoverChunkKey(i, j, n, rk)
in the contract and hence accessible   7: assert $k_i \neq \perp$
Output: $true$ or $false$ 8: $m'_i = $ SDec(c_i, k_i)
  1: assert $j \in [0, |erk| - 1]$ 9: assert $\mathcal{H}(m'_i) \neq \mathcal{H}(m_i)$
  2: assert $\mathcal{H}(erk) \equiv erk_{\mathsf{hash}}$ 10: **return** $false$ in case of any assertion error
  3: assert VerifyPKE$_{vpk_{\mathcal{C}}}(erk, rk, \pi_{\mathsf{VD}}) \equiv 1$ or $true$ otherwise
  4: assert Verify$(i||c_i, \sigma_{c_i}, pk_{\mathcal{P}}) \equiv 1$

- The provider $\mathcal{P}$ executes as follows: asserts $\Sigma \equiv$ revealing, executes Algorithm 2 to obtain revealed keys rk, encrypts rk using consumer's $vpk_{\mathcal{C}}$ to obtain erk, and then sends (revealKeys, erk) to $\mathcal{G}_d$; waits for (sold) from $\mathcal{G}_d$ to halt.

- The consumer $\mathcal{C}$ in this phase would first assert $\Sigma \equiv$ revealing, and wait for (revealed, erk) from $\mathcal{G}_d$ to execute the following: (i) runs Algorithm 3 to preliminarily check erk, if $false$, sends (wrongRK) to $\mathcal{G}_d$ and halts, or if $true$ is returned, decrypts erk to obtain rk via $vsk_{\mathcal{C}}$, and then runs Algorithm 4 to recover chunk keys. Then $\mathcal{C}$ uses these keys to decrypt $(c_1, \cdots, c_{\mathsf{ctr}})$ to obtain $(m'_1, \cdots, m'_{\mathsf{ctr}})$; for each $m'_i, i \in [\mathsf{ctr}]$, checks whether $\mathcal{H}(m'_i)$ is the i-th leaf node in MT received from $\mathcal{P}$ in the *Deliver* phase. If all are consistent, $\mathcal{C}$ outputs $(m'_1, \cdots, m'_{\mathsf{ctr}})$, and then waits for (sold) from $\mathcal{G}_d$ to halt. Otherwise, $\mathcal{C}$ can raise complaint by: choosing one inconsistent position (e.g., the i-th chunk), and then sending (PoM, $i, j, c_i, \sigma_{c_i}, \mathcal{H}(m_i), \pi^i_{\mathsf{MT}}, rk, erk, \pi_{\mathsf{VD}}$) to $\mathcal{G}_d$, where i is the index of the incorrect chunk to be proved; j is the index of the element in erk that can induce k_i; c_i and σ_{c_i} are the i-th encrypted chunk and its signature received in the *Deliver* phase; $\mathcal{H}(m_i)$ is the value of the i-th leaf node in MT; π^i_{MT} is the Merkle proof for $\mathcal{H}(m_i)$; rk is decryption result from erk; erk is the encrypted revealed key; π_{VD} is the verifiable decryption proof attesting to the correctness of decrypting erk to rk.

Subroutine for Dispute Resolve. For the sake of completeness, the ValidatePoM subroutine of the arbiter contract is detailed in Algorithm 5, which is needed to handle the PoM message sent from consumer. In general, it verifies that the consumer sends the correctly decrypted elements in the key derivation tree KT, and computes the encryption key to a specific chunk (sent from the consumer) according to the KT tree elements, and then it decrypts the chunk and verifies it is essentially committed to the Merkle tree root. Its time complexity corresponds to on-chain cost and is $O(\log n)$, which minimizes the critical on-chain cost.

Analyzing FairDownload. Theorem 1 characterizes the needed security and nontrivial efficiency guarantees of Π_{FD}. The proof is provided in the full version [21].

Theorem 1. *Conditioned on that the underlying cryptographic primitives are secure, the protocol* FairDownload *satisfies the completeness, fairness,*

Algorithm 6. RecoverChunkKey algorithm

Input: (i, j, n, rk)
Output: k_i or $\perp$
1: $(x, y) \leftarrow rk[j]$
    {parse the j-th element in rk to get the key
    x and the value y}
2: let k_path be an empty stack
3: $ind = n + i - 2$ {the index in KT}
4: **if** $ind < x$ **then**
5:     **return** $\perp$
6: **if** $ind \equiv x$ **then**

7:     **return** y $\{k_i = y\}$
8: **while** $ind > x$ **do**
9:     k_path pushes 0 if ind is odd
10:     k_path pushes 1 if ind is even
11:     $ind = \lfloor (ind - 1)/2 \rfloor$
12: let $b = |k\_path|$
13: **while** $(b\text{-}\text{-}) > 0$ **do**
14:     pop k_path to get the value t
15:     $k_i = \mathcal{H}(y||t)$
16: **return** k_i

---

confidentiality against deliverer, timeliness and non-trivial efficiency properties in the synchronous authenticated network, $\mathcal{G}_d^{\mathsf{ledger}}$-hybrid and stand-alone model.

6 FairStream: Fair p2p Streaming

6.1 FairStream Overview

As shown in Fig. 3, FairStream works as *Prepare*, *Stream*, and *Payout* phases, at a high level. The core ideas are: during streaming, the consumer $\mathcal{C}$ retrieves an encrypted chunk from the deliverer $\mathcal{D}$ and a corresponding decryption key from the provider $\mathcal{P}$, yielding $O(1)$ communication rounds to obtain each chunk; any party may abort in a certain round due to, e.g., untimely response or invalid message; especially, $\mathcal{C}$ can complain during streaming to the arbiter contract $\mathcal{G}_s^{\mathsf{ledger}}$ (abbr. $\mathcal{G}_s$) illustrated in Fig. 4 and get compensated with a valid proof; the *Stream* phase finishes either any party aborts or the timer $\mathcal{T}_{\mathsf{receive}}$ in contract expires; Later, $\mathcal{D}$ and $\mathcal{P}$ can claim the deserved payment by submitting the latest receipt signed by $\mathcal{C}$ before another timer $\mathcal{T}_{\mathsf{finish}}$ (naturally $\mathcal{T}_{\mathsf{finish}} > \mathcal{T}_{\mathsf{receive}}$) in contract expires; the contract determines the ctr, namely the number of delivered chunks or revealed keys, using the *larger* index in $\mathcal{P}$ and $\mathcal{D}$'s receipts. If no receipt is received from $\mathcal{P}$ or $\mathcal{D}$ before $\mathcal{T}_{\mathsf{finish}}$ expires, the index for that party is set as 0. Such a design is critical to ensure fairness as analyzed in the full version [21].

6.2 Π_{FS}: FairStream Protocol

Phase I for Prepare. This phase executes the same as in the Π_{FD} protocol.

Phase II for Stream. The parties $\mathcal{C}$, $\mathcal{D}$ and $\mathcal{P}$ interact with $\mathcal{G}_s$ as follows:

- The consumer $\mathcal{C}$ interested in the content with root_m would initialize a variable $x := 1$ and then: (i) asserts $\Sigma \equiv \mathsf{ready}$, and sends $(\mathsf{consume}, pk_\mathcal{C})$ to $\mathcal{G}_s$; (ii) upon receiving $(\mathsf{mtree}, \mathsf{MT}, \sigma_\mathcal{P}^{\mathsf{MT}})$ from $\mathcal{P}$, verifies the signature $\sigma_\mathcal{P}^{\mathsf{MT}}$ and $\mathsf{root}(\mathsf{MT}) \equiv \mathsf{root}_m$, then stores the Merkle tree MT, or else halts; (iii) on receiving $(\mathsf{deliver}, i, c_i, \sigma_{c_i})$ from $\mathcal{D}$, checks if $i \equiv x \wedge \mathsf{Verify}(i||c_i, \sigma_{c_i}, pk_\mathcal{P}) \equiv 1$, if hold, starts (for $i \equiv 1$) a timer $\mathcal{T}_{\mathsf{keyResponse}}$ or resets (for $1 < i \leq n$) it, sends $(\mathsf{keyReq}, i, \sigma_\mathcal{C}^i)$ where $\sigma_\mathcal{C}^i \leftarrow \mathsf{Sign}(i||pk_\mathcal{C}, sk_\mathcal{C})$ to $\mathcal{P}$. If failing to check

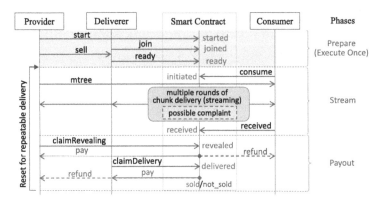

Fig. 3. The overview of FairStream protocol Π_{FS}. The dispute may arise in a certain round in the *Stream* phase, and the messages (claimDelivery) and (claimRevealing) may be sent to the contract in a different order.

or $\mathcal{T}_{\mathsf{keyResponse}}$ times out, halts; (vi) upon receiving (reveal, i, k_i, σ_{k_i}) from $\mathcal{P}$ before $\mathcal{T}_{\mathsf{keyResponse}}$ times out, checks whether $i \equiv x \wedge \mathsf{Verify}(i||k_i, \sigma_{k_i}, pk_\mathcal{P}) \equiv 1$, if failed, halts. Otherwise, starts to validate the content chunk based on received c_i and k_i: decrypts c_i to obtain m'_i ($m'_i := \mathsf{SDec}_{k_i}(c_i)$) and then checks whether $\mathcal{H}(m'_i)$ is consistent with the i-th leaf node in MT, if inconsistent, sends (PoM, $i, c_i, \sigma_{c_i}, k_i, \sigma_{k_i}, \mathcal{H}(m_i), \pi^i_{\mathsf{MT}}$) to $\mathcal{G}_s$. If it is consistent, sends the receipts (receipt, $i, \sigma^i_{\mathcal{CD}}$) to $\mathcal{D}$ and (receipt, $i, \sigma^i_{\mathcal{CP}}$) to $\mathcal{P}$, where $\sigma^i_{\mathcal{CD}} \leftarrow \mathsf{Sign}(\mathsf{receipt}||i||pk_\mathcal{C}||pk_\mathcal{D}, sk_\mathcal{C})$ and $\sigma^i_{\mathcal{CP}} \leftarrow \mathsf{Sign}(\mathsf{receipt}||i||pk_\mathcal{C}||pk_\mathcal{P}, sk_\mathcal{C})$, and sets $x := x + 1$, and then waits for the next (deliver) message from $\mathcal{D}$. Upon x is set to be $n + 1$, meaning that all chunks are received, sends (received) to $\mathcal{G}_s$; (v) waits for the messages (received) from $\mathcal{G}_s$ to halt.

- The deliverer $\mathcal{D}$ initializes a variable $y := 1$ and executes as: (i) upon receiving (initiated, $pk_\mathcal{C}$) from $\mathcal{G}_s$, sends (deliver, i, c_i, σ_{c_i}), $i = 1$ to $\mathcal{C}$ and starts a timer $\mathcal{T}_{\mathsf{chunkReceipt}}$; (ii) upon receiving (receipt, $i, \sigma^i_{\mathcal{CD}}$) from $\mathcal{C}$ before $\mathcal{T}_{\mathsf{chunkReceipt}}$ times out, checks whether $\mathsf{Verify}(\mathsf{receipt}||i||pk_\mathcal{C}||pk_\mathcal{D}, \sigma^i_{\mathcal{CD}}, pk_\mathcal{C}) \equiv 1 \wedge i \equiv y$ or not, if succeeds, continues with the next iteration: sets $y := y + 1$, sends (deliver, i, c_i, σ_{c_i}), $i = y$ to $\mathcal{C}$, and resets $\mathcal{T}_{\mathsf{chunkReceipt}}$; If fails or $\mathcal{T}_{\mathsf{chunkReceipt}}$ times out, enters the next phase.
- The provider $\mathcal{P}$ initializes a variable $z := 1$ and executes as: (i) upon receiving (initiated, $pk_\mathcal{C}$) from $\mathcal{G}_s$: sends (mtree, MT, $\sigma^{\mathsf{MT}}_\mathcal{P}$) to $\mathcal{C}$; (ii) upon receiving (keyReq, $i, \sigma^i_\mathcal{C}$) from $\mathcal{C}$, checks whether $i \equiv z \wedge \mathsf{Verify}(i||pk_\mathcal{C}, \sigma^i_\mathcal{C}, pk_\mathcal{C}) \equiv 1$, if succeeds, sends (reveal, i, k_i, σ_{k_i}), where $\sigma_{k_i} \leftarrow \mathsf{Sign}(i||k_i, sk_\mathcal{P})$, to $\mathcal{C}$ and starts (for $i \equiv 1$) a timer $\mathcal{T}_{\mathsf{keyReceipt}}$ or resets (for $1 < i \leq n$) it, otherwise enters the next phase; (iii) on receiving (receipt, $i, \sigma^i_{\mathcal{CP}}$) from $\mathcal{C}$ before $\mathcal{T}_{\mathsf{keyReceipt}}$ expires, checks whether $\mathsf{Verify}(\mathsf{receipt}||i||pk_\mathcal{C}||pk_\mathcal{P}, \sigma^i_{\mathcal{CP}}, pk_\mathcal{C}) \equiv 1 \wedge i \equiv z$, if hold, sets $z := z + 1$, otherwise enters the next phase if $\mathcal{T}_{\mathsf{keyReceipt}}$ times out.

Phase III for Payout. The parties $\mathcal{P}$ and $\mathcal{D}$ interact with $\mathcal{G}_s$ in this phase as:

The Arbiter Contract Functionality $\mathcal{G}_s^{\text{ledger}}$ for p2p Streaming

The contract $\mathcal{G}_s$ can access to ledger, and it interacts with $\mathcal{P}, \mathcal{D}, \mathcal{C}$ and the adversary $\mathcal{A}$. It locally stores $\theta, n, \text{root}_m, \mathcal{B}_{\mathcal{P}}, \mathcal{B}_{\mathcal{C}}, \mathcal{B}_{\text{pf}}, \text{ctr}_{\mathcal{D}}, \text{ctr}_{\mathcal{P}}, \text{ctr}$ (all $\text{ctr}_{\mathcal{D}}, \text{ctr}_{\mathcal{P}}, \text{ctr}$ are initialized as 0), $pk_{\mathcal{P}}, pk_{\mathcal{D}}, pk_{\mathcal{C}}$, the penalty flag plt (initialized by $false$), the state Σ and three timers $\mathcal{T}_{\text{round}}$ (implicitly), $\mathcal{T}_{\text{receive}}, \mathcal{T}_{\text{finish}}$.

——————— **Phase 1: Prepare** ———————

- This phase is the same as in $\mathcal{G}_d$.

——————— **Phase 2: Stream** ———————

- On receive (consume, $pk_{\mathcal{C}}$) from $\mathcal{C}$:
  - assert $\theta > 0$
  - assert $\text{ledger}[\mathcal{C}] \geq n \cdot \mathcal{B}_{\mathcal{C}} \wedge \Sigma \equiv \text{ready}$
  - store $pk_{\mathcal{C}}$ and let $\text{ledger}[\mathcal{C}] := \text{ledger}[\mathcal{C}] - n \cdot \mathcal{B}_{\mathcal{C}}$
  - start two timers $\mathcal{T}_{\text{receive}}$, and $\mathcal{T}_{\text{finish}}$
  - let $\Sigma :=$ initiated and send (initiated, $pk_{\mathcal{C}}$) to all entities
- On receive (received) from $\mathcal{C}$ before $\mathcal{T}_{\text{receive}}$ times out:
  - assert current time $\mathcal{T} < \mathcal{T}_{\text{receive}}$ and $\Sigma \equiv$ initiated
  - let $\Sigma :=$ received and send (received) to all entities
- Upon $\mathcal{T}_{\text{receive}}$ times out:
  - assert current time $\mathcal{T} \geq \mathcal{T}_{\text{receive}}$ and $\Sigma \equiv$ initiated
  - let $\Sigma :=$ received and send (received) to all entities

  ▷ Dispute resolution in this phase
- On receive (PoM, $i, c_i, \sigma_{c_i}, k_i, \sigma_{k_i}$, $\mathcal{H}(m_i), \pi_{\text{MT}}^i$) from $\mathcal{C}$ before $\mathcal{T}_{\text{receive}}$ expires:
  - assert current time $\mathcal{T} < \mathcal{T}_{\text{receive}}$ and $\Sigma \equiv$ initiated
  - assert $\text{Verify}(i||c_i, \sigma_{c_i}, pk_{\mathcal{P}}) \equiv 1$
  - assert $\text{Verify}(i||k_i, \sigma_{k_i}, pk_{\mathcal{P}}) \equiv 1$
  - assert $\text{VerifyMTP}(\text{root}_m, i, \pi_{\text{MT}}^i, \mathcal{H}(m_i)) \equiv 1$
  - $m_i' = \text{SDec}(c_i, k_i)$
  - assert $\mathcal{H}(m_i') \neq \mathcal{H}(m_i)$
  - let plt $:= true$
  - let $\Sigma :=$ received and send (received) to all entities

——————— **Phase 3: Payout** ———————

- On receive (claimDelivery, $i, \sigma_{\mathcal{C}\mathcal{D}}^i$) from $\mathcal{D}$:
  - assert current time $\mathcal{T} < \mathcal{T}_{\text{finish}}$
  - assert $i \equiv n$ or $\Sigma \equiv$ received or $\Sigma \equiv$ payingRevealing
  - assert $\text{ctr} \equiv 0$ and $0 < i \leq n$

- assert $\text{Verify}(\text{receipt}||i||pk_{\mathcal{C}}||pk_{\mathcal{D}}, \sigma_{\mathcal{C}\mathcal{D}}^i, pk_{\mathcal{C}}) \equiv 1$
- let $\text{ctr}_{\mathcal{D}} := i$, $\Sigma :=$ payingDelivery, and then send (payingDelivery) to all entities
- On receive (claimRevealing, $i, \sigma_{\mathcal{C}\mathcal{P}}^i$) from $\mathcal{P}$:
  - assert current time $\mathcal{T} < \mathcal{T}_{\text{finish}}$
  - assert $i \equiv n$ or $\Sigma \equiv$ received or $\Sigma \equiv$ payingDelivery
  - assert $\text{ctr} \equiv 0$ and $0 < i \leq n$
  - assert $\text{Verify}(\text{receipt}||i||pk_{\mathcal{C}}||pk_{\mathcal{P}}, \sigma_{\mathcal{C}\mathcal{P}}^i, pk_{\mathcal{C}}) \equiv 1$
  - let $\text{ctr}_{\mathcal{P}} := i$, $\Sigma :=$ payingRevealing, and then send (payingRevealing) to all entities
- Upon $\mathcal{T}_{\text{finish}}$ times out:
  - assert current time $\mathcal{T} \geq \mathcal{T}_{\text{finish}}$
  - let $\text{ctr} := \max\{\text{ctr}_{\mathcal{D}}, \text{ctr}_{\mathcal{P}}\}$
  - let $\text{ledger}[\mathcal{D}] := \text{ledger}[\mathcal{D}] + \text{ctr} \cdot \mathcal{B}_{\mathcal{P}}$
  - if plt:
    let $\text{ledger}[\mathcal{P}] := \text{ledger}[\mathcal{P}] + (n - \text{ctr}) \cdot \mathcal{B}_{\mathcal{P}} + \text{ctr} \cdot \mathcal{B}_{\mathcal{C}}$
    let $\text{ledger}[\mathcal{C}] := \text{ledger}[\mathcal{C}] + (n - \text{ctr}) \cdot \mathcal{B}_{\mathcal{C}} + \mathcal{B}_{\text{pf}}$
  - else:
    let $\text{ledger}[\mathcal{P}] := \text{ledger}[\mathcal{P}] + (n - \text{ctr}) \cdot \mathcal{B}_{\mathcal{P}} + \text{ctr} \cdot \mathcal{B}_{\mathcal{C}} + \mathcal{B}_{\text{pf}}$
    let $\text{ledger}[\mathcal{C}] := \text{ledger}[\mathcal{C}] + (n - \text{ctr}) \cdot \mathcal{B}_{\mathcal{C}}$
  - if $\text{ctr} > 0$:
    let $\Sigma :=$ sold and send (sold) to all entities
  - else let $\Sigma :=$ not_sold and send (not_sold) to all entities

  ▷ Reset to the ready state
- On receive (reset) from $\mathcal{P}$:
  - assert $\Sigma \equiv$ sold or $\Sigma \equiv$ not_sold
  - set $\text{ctr}, \text{ctr}_{\mathcal{D}}, \text{ctr}_{\mathcal{P}}, \mathcal{T}_{\text{receive}}, \mathcal{T}_{\text{finish}}$ as 0
  - nullify $pk_{\mathcal{C}}$
  - let $\theta := \theta - 1$ and $\Sigma :=$ ready
  - send (ready) to all entities

Fig. 4. The streaming-setting arbiter functionality $\mathcal{G}_s^{\text{ledger}}$. "Sending to all entities" captures that the smart contract is transparent to the public.

- The provider $\mathcal{P}$ executes as: (i) upon receiving (received) or (delivered) from $\mathcal{G}_s$, or receiving the n-th receipt from $\mathcal{C}$ (i.e., z is set to be $n + 1$), sends (claimRevealing, $i, \sigma_{\mathcal{C}\mathcal{P}}^i$) to $\mathcal{G}_s$; (ii) waits for (revealed) from $\mathcal{G}_s$ to halt.
- The deliverer $\mathcal{D}$ executes as: (i) upon receiving (received) or (revealed) from $\mathcal{G}_s$, or receiving the n-th receipt from $\mathcal{C}$ (i.e., y is set to be $n + 1$), sends (claimDelivery, $i, \sigma_{\mathcal{C}\mathcal{D}}^i$) to $\mathcal{G}_s$; (ii) waits for (delivered) from $\mathcal{G}_s$ to halt.

Analyzing FairStream. Theorem 2 characterizes the security of the protocol Π_{FS}. The proof details are given in the online version [21].

Theorem 2. *Conditioned that the underlying cryptographic primitives are secure, the protocol* FairStream *satisfies the completeness, fairness, confidentiality against deliverer, timeliness, and non-trivial efficiency properties in the synchronous authenticated network,* $\mathcal{G}_s^{\mathsf{ledger}}$*-hybrid and stand-alone model.*

Extension for Delivering from Any Specific Chunk. The protocol FairStream (as well as FairDownload) can be easily tuned to transfer the content from the middle instead of the beginning. Specifically, for the downloading setting, one can simply let the content provider reveal the elements that are able to recover a *sub-tree* of the key derivation tree KT for decrypting the transferred chunks. The complaint of incorrect decryption key follows the same procedure in Sect. 5. For the streaming setting, it is more straightforward as each chunk ciphertext and its decryption key are uniquely identified by the index and can be obtained in $O(1)$ rounds by the consumer, who can immediately complain to contract in the presence of an incorrect decryption result.

7   Implementation and Evaluations

To shed some light on the feasibility of FairDownload and FairStream, we implement, deploy and evaluate the protocols of Π_{FD} and Π_{FS} in the *Ethereum Ropsten* network. The arbiter contracts are split into *Optimistic* (no dispute) and *Pessimistic* (additionally invoked when dispute occurs) modules. Note that the contracts deployment and the *Prepare* phase can be executed only once and used multiple times to facilitate the delivery of same content to different consumers. Therefore, these one-time costs can be amortized, and we mainly report the costs after the completeness of *Prepare* phase.

In our implementations, the hash function is *keccak256* and the signature is via ECDSA over *secp256k1* curve. The encryption of each chunk m_i with key k_i is instantiated as: parse m_i into t 32-byte blocks $(m_{i,1}, \ldots, m_{i,t})$ and output $c_i = (m_{i,1} \oplus \mathcal{H}(k_i||1), \ldots, m_{i,t} \oplus \mathcal{H}(k_i||t))$. The decryption is same to the encryption. Public key encryption is based on ElGamal: Let $\mathcal{G} = \langle g \rangle$ to be G_1 group over *alt-bn128* curve [36] of prime order q, where g is group generator; the public key $h = g^k$, where $k \leftarrow_\$ \mathbb{Z}_q$ is the private key; $\mathsf{VEnc}_h(m) = (c_1, c_2) = (g^r, m \cdot g^{kr})$ represents encryption, where the message m is encoded into $\mathcal{G}$ with Koblitz's method [26] and $r \leftarrow_\$ \mathbb{Z}_q$; the decryption $\mathsf{VDec}_k((c_1, c_2)) = c_2/c_1^k$. To lift ElGamal for verifiable decryption, we adopt Schnorr protocol [37] for Diffie-Hellman tuples with Fiat-Shamir transform [16]. Specifically, $\mathsf{ProvePKE}_k((c_1, c_2))$ works as: run $\mathsf{VDec}_k((c_1, c_2))$ to obtain m; let $x \leftarrow_\$ \mathbb{Z}_q$, and compute $A = g^x$, $B = c_1^x$, $C = \mathcal{H}(g||A||B||h||c_1||c_2||m)$, $Z = x + kC$, $\pi = (A, B, Z)$, and output (m, π); $\mathsf{VerifyPKE}_h((c_1, c_2), m, \pi)$ works as: parse π to obtain (A, B, Z), compute $C' = \mathcal{H}(g||A||B||h||c_1||c_2||m)$, and verify $(g^Z \equiv A \cdot h^{C'}) \wedge (m^{C'} \cdot c_2^Z \equiv B \cdot c_2^{C'})$, and output $1/0$ to indicate whether the verification succeeds or fails.

7.1 Evaluating **FairDownload**

Table 1 presents the on-chain costs of Π_{FD}, i.e., the costs of all functions in the contract $\mathcal{G}_d$. We adopt a gas price at 10 Gwei to ensure over half of the mining power in Ethereum would mine this transaction,[9] and an exchange rate of 259.4 USD/Ether (the average market price[10] of Ether from 01/01/2020 to 11/03/2020). We stress that utilizing other cryptocurrencies such as Ethereum classic[11] can substantially decrease the actual price of the protocol execution. The price and exchange rate also apply to the streaming setting.

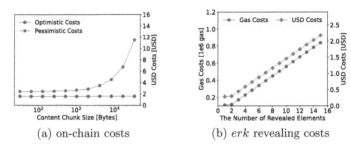

(a) on-chain costs   (b) erk revealing costs

Fig. 5. Experiment results for the Π_{FD} protocol.

Optimistic Case. Without complaint Π_{FD} executes the functions in *Deliver* and *Reveal* phases, yielding a total cost of 1.032 USD for all involving parties. The on-chain cost is *constant* regardless of the content size and the chunk size, as shown in Fig. 5a. In worse cases, up to $\log(n)$ elements in the key derivation tree KT need to be revealed (where n is the size of content), and the on-chain cost of revealing these elements in KT is depicted in Fig. 5b.

Table 1. Cost of Π_{FD}'s on chain side $\mathcal{G}_d$

Phase	$\mathcal{G}_d$'s Function	Caller	Gas	USD
Deploy	(Optimistic)	$\mathcal{P}$	2 936 458	7.617
Deploy	(Pessimistic)	$\mathcal{P}$	2 910 652	7.550
Prepare	start	$\mathcal{P}$	110 751	0.287
	join	$\mathcal{D}$	69 031	0.179
	prepared	$\mathcal{D}$	34 867	0.090
Deliver	consume	$\mathcal{C}$	117 357	0.304
	delivered	$\mathcal{C}$	57 935	0.150
	verifyVFDProof	$\mathcal{D}$	56 225	0.146
Reveal	revealKeys	$\mathcal{P}$	113 041	0.293
	payout	$\mathcal{G}_d$	53 822	0.139
Dispute	wrongRK	$\mathcal{C}$	23 441	0.061
resolve	PoM	$\mathcal{C}$	389 050	1.009

Table 2. Cost of Π_{FS}'s on-chain side $\mathcal{G}_s$

Phase	$\mathcal{G}_s$'s Function	Caller	Gas	USD
Deploy	(Optimistic)	$\mathcal{P}$	1 808 281	4.691
Deploy	(Pessimistic)	$\mathcal{P}$	1 023 414	2.655
Prepare	start	$\mathcal{P}$	131 061	0.340
	join	$\mathcal{D}$	54 131	0.140
	prepared	$\mathcal{D}$	34 935	0.091
Stream	consume	$\mathcal{C}$	95 779	0.248
	received	$\mathcal{C}$	39 857	0.103
	receiveTimeout	$\mathcal{G}_s$	39 839	0.103
	PoM	$\mathcal{C}$	90 018	0.234
Payout	claimDelivery	$\mathcal{D}$	67 910	0.176
	claimRevealing	$\mathcal{P}$	67 909	0.176
	finishTimeout	$\mathcal{G}_s$	88 599	0.230

[9] https://ethgasstation.info/.
[10] https://www.coindesk.com/price/ethereum/.
[11] https://ethereumclassic.org/.

Pessimistic Case. When some complaint arises by the consumer, the arbiter contract involves to resolve it. The cost of executing wrongRK function relates to the concrete values of n, ctr and $|erk|$, and in Table 2, the cost is evaluated on $n \equiv \text{ctr} \equiv 512$, and $|erk| \equiv 1$. The cost of PoM function validating misbehavior varies by the content chunk size η, as depicted in Fig. 5a pessimistic costs. The results demonstrate that the on-chain costs increase linearly in the chunk size.

7.2 Evaluating FairStream

Table 2 lists the costs of contract $\mathcal{G}_s$ to show the on-chain expense of the streaming protocol Π_{FS}.

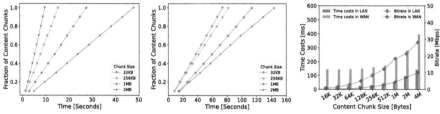

(a) Time cost of streaming 512 content chunks in LAN (b) Time cost of streaming 512 content chunks in WAN (c) Average time cost and the corresponding bitrate

Fig. 6. The performance of FairStream protocol in the LAN and WAN.

Optimistic Case. Without dispute, Π_{FS} executes the functions in *Stream* and *Payout* phases except the PoM function for verifying proof of misbehavior, yielding a total cost of 0.933 USD for all involved parties. The costs in this mode is *constant* regardless of the content size and chunk size.

Pessimistic Case. With complaint, the total on-chain cost is 1.167 USD for all involved parties. The cost of the PoM function: (i) increases slightly in number of chunks n, since it computes $O(\log n)$ hashes to verify the Merkle proof; (ii) increase linearly in the chunk size η for the chunk decryption, which follows a similar trend to Fig. 5a pessimistic costs but with lower costs as no verification of verifiable decryption proof is needed.

Streaming Efficiency. Fig. 6a and b illustrate the efficiency of streaming 512 chunks (via Π_{FS}) of various sizes in both LAN and WAN.[12] Results indicate that: (i) obviously the time costs increase due to the growth of chunk size; (ii) the delivery process remains stable with only slight fluctuation, as reflected by the slope for each chunk size in Fig. 6a and b. Furthermore, Fig. 6c depicts the average latency for delivering each chunk (over the 512 chunks) and the corresponding bitrate. It shows that the bitrate can reach 10 Mbps even in the public network, which is potentially sufficient to support high-quality content streaming. E.g., the video bitrate for HD 1080 are *at most* 8 Mbps [22].

---

[12] The experimental configuration details are described in the full version [21].

8   Conclusion

We present the first two fair p2p content delivery protocols atop blockchains to support *fair p2p downloading* and *fair p2p streaming*, respectively. They enjoy strong fairness guarantees to protect any of the content provider, the content consumer, and the content deliverer from being ripped off by other colluding parties. Essentially, our new delivery fairness notion circumvents the limit of conventional exchange fairness, thus supporting to pay the delivers according to their bandwidth usages. Detailed complexity analysis and extensive experiments are conducted to demonstrate the high efficiency of our designs. Yet still, the area is largely unexplored and has a few immediate follow-ups, for example: (i) in order to realize maximized delivery performance, it is desirable to design a mechanism of adaptively choosing deliverers during each delivery task; (ii) it is also enticing to leverage the off-chain payment channels to handle possible micropayments and further reduce the on-chain cost.

Acknowledgements. Yuan Lu is supported in part by the National Natural Science Foundation of China (No. 62102404). This work was also supported in part by NSF #1801492 and FHWA 693JJ320C000021. The authors would like to thank the anonymous reviewer for their valuable comments and suggestions.

References

1. Akamai: Akamai (2021). https://www.akamai.com/
2. Almashaqbeh, G.: CacheCash: a cryptocurrency-based decentralized content delivery network. Ph.D. thesis, Columbia University (2019)
3. Anjum, N., Karamshuk, D., Shikh-Bahaei, M., Sastry, N.: Survey on peer-assisted content delivery networks. Comput. Netw. **116**, 79–95 (2017)
4. Asokan, N., Shoup, V., Waidner, M.: Optimistic fair exchange of digital signatures. IEEE J. Sel. Areas Commun. **18**, 593–610 (2000)
5. Benet, J.: IPFS-content addressed, versioned, p2p file system. arXiv preprint arXiv:1407.3561 (2014)
6. Bentov, I., Kumaresan, R.: How to use bitcoin to design fair protocols. In: Garay, J.A., Gennaro, R. (eds.) CRYPTO 2014. LNCS, vol. 8617, pp. 421–439. Springer, Heidelberg (2014). https://doi.org/10.1007/978-3-662-44381-1_24
7. Blum, M.: How to exchange (secret) keys. In: Proceedings of the ACM STOC 1983, pp. 440–447 (1983)
8. Camenisch, J., Shoup, V.: Practical verifiable encryption and decryption of discrete logarithms. In: Boneh, D. (ed.) CRYPTO 2003. LNCS, vol. 2729, pp. 126–144. Springer, Heidelberg (2003). https://doi.org/10.1007/978-3-540-45146-4_8
9. Choudhuri, A.R., Green, M., Jain, A., Kaptchuk, G., Miers, I.: Fairness in an unfair world: fair multiparty computation from public bulletin boards. In: Proceedings of the ACM CCS, pp. 719–728 (2017)
10. Damgård, I.B.: Practical and provably secure release of a secret and exchange of signatures. J. Cryptol. **8**, 201–222 (1995). https://doi.org/10.1007/BF00191356
11. Dziembowski, S., Eckey, L., Faust, S., Malinowski, D.: Perun: virtual payment hubs over cryptocurrencies. In: Proceedings of the IEEE S&P 2019, pp. 106–123 (2019)

12. Dziembowski, S., Eckey, L., Faust, S.: FairSwap: how to fairly exchange digital goods. In: Proceedings of the ACM CCS, pp. 967–984 (2018)
13. ENISA: ENISA threat landscape 2020 -botnet (2020). https://www.enisa.europa.eu/publications/enisa-threat-landscape-2020-botnet
14. Fan, B., Lui, J.C., Chiu, D.M.: The design trade-offs of BitTorrent-like file sharing protocols. IEEE/ACM Trans. Network. **17**, 365–376 (2008)
15. Feldman, M., Lai, K., Stoica, I., Chuang, J.: Robust incentive techniques for peer-to-peer networks. In: Proceedings of the ACM EC (2004)
16. Fiat, A., Shamir, A.: How to prove yourself: practical solutions to identification and signature problems. In: Odlyzko, A.M. (ed.) CRYPTO 1986. LNCS, vol. 263, pp. 186–194. Springer, Heidelberg (1987). https://doi.org/10.1007/3-540-47721-7_12
17. Filecoin: Filecoin: a decentralized storage network. https://filecoin.io/filecoin.pdf
18. Filecoin: Filecoin spec. (2020). https://spec.filecoin.io/
19. Goyal, P., Netravali, R., Alizadeh, M., Balakrishnan, H.: Secure incentivization for decentralized content delivery. In: 2nd USENIX Workshop on Hot Topics in Edge Computing (2019)
20. Hardin, G.: The tragedy of the commons. J. Nat. Resour. Policy Res. **1**, 243–253 (2009)
21. He, S., Lu, Y., Tang, Q., Wang, G., Wu, C.Q.: Fair peer-to-peer content delivery via blockchain. arXiv preprint arXiv:2102.04685 (2021)
22. IBM: Internet connection and recommended encoding settings. https://support.video.ibm.com/hc/en-us/articles/207852117-Internet-connection-and-recommended-encoding-settings
23. Janin, S., Qin, K., Mamageishvili, A., Gervais, A.: FileBounty: fair data exchange. In: IEEE (EuroS&PW), pp. 357–366 (2020)
24. Katz, J., Lindell, Y.: Introduction to Modern Cryptography. CRC Press (2014)
25. Kiayias, A., Zhou, H.-S., Zikas, V.: Fair and robust multi-party computation using a global transaction ledger. In: Fischlin, M., Coron, J.-S. (eds.) EUROCRYPT 2016. LNCS, vol. 9666, pp. 705–734. Springer, Heidelberg (2016). https://doi.org/10.1007/978-3-662-49896-5_25
26. Koblitz, N.: Elliptic Curve Cryptosystems. Mathematics of Computation, pp. 203–209 (1987)
27. Kosba, A., Miller, A., Shi, E., Wen, Z., Papamanthou, C.: Hawk: the blockchain model of cryptography and privacy-preserving smart contracts. In: Proceedings of the IEEE (S&P), pp. 839–858 (2016)
28. Küpçü, A., Lysyanskaya, A.: Usable optimistic fair exchange. In: Pieprzyk, J. (ed.) CT-RSA 2010. LNCS, vol. 5985, pp. 252–267. Springer, Heidelberg (2010). https://doi.org/10.1007/978-3-642-11925-5_18
29. Levin, D., LaCurts, K., Spring, N., Bhattacharjee, B.: Bittorrent is an auction: analyzing and improving bittorrent's incentives. ACM SIGCOMM Comput. Commun. Rev. **38**, 243–254 (2008)
30. Locher, T., Moore, P., Schmid, S., Wattenhofer, R.: Free riding in bittorrent is cheap. In: HotNets (2006)
31. Maxwell, G.: The first successful zero-knowledge contingent payment (2016). https://bitcoincore.org/en/2016/02/26/zero-knowledge-contingent-payments-announcement/
32. Mehar, M.I., et al.: Understanding a revolutionary and flawed grand experiment in blockchain: the DAO attack. J. Cases Inf. Technol. **21**, 19–32 (2019)

33. Miller, A., Bentov, I., Bakshi, S., Kumaresan, R., McCorry, P.: Sprites and state channels: payment networks that go faster than lightning. In: Goldberg, I., Moore, T. (eds.) FC 2019. LNCS, vol. 11598, pp. 508–526. Springer, Cham (2019). https:// doi.org/10.1007/978-3-030-32101-7_30
34. Miller, A., Juels, A., Shi, E., Parno, B., Katz, J.: Permacoin: repurposing bitcoin work for data preservation. In: Proceedings of the IEEE S&P, pp. 475–490 (2014)
35. Piatek, M., Isdal, T., Anderson, T., Krishnamurthy, A., Venkataramani, A.: Do incentives build robustness in bittorrent. In: Proceedings of the NSDI (2007)
36. Reitwiessner, C.: EIP-196: precompiled contracts for addition and scalar multiplication on the elliptic curve alt_bn128. Ethereum Improvement Proposals, No. 196 (2017). https://eips.ethereum.org/EIPS/eip-196
37. Schnorr, C.P.: Efficient identification and signatures for smart cards. In: Quisquater, J.-J., Vandewalle, J. (eds.) EUROCRYPT 1989. LNCS, vol. 434, pp. 688–689. Springer, Heidelberg (1990). https://doi.org/10.1007/3-540-46885-4_68
38. Sherman, A., Nieh, J., Stein, C.: FairTorrent: a deficit-based distributed algorithm to ensure fairness in peer-to-peer systems. IEEE/ACM TON **20**, 1361–1374 (2012)
39. Shin, K., Joe-Wong, C., Ha, S., Yi, Y., Rhee, I., Reeves, D.S.: T-chain: a general incentive scheme for cooperative computing. IEEE/ACM TON **25**, 2122–2137 (2017)
40. Sirivianos, M., Park, J.H., Yang, X., Jarecki, S.: Dandelion: cooperative content distribution with robust incentives. In: Proceedings of the USENIX ATC (2007)
41. StorJ: Storj (2018). https://storj.io/storj.pdf
42. Swarm (2020). https://swarm.ethereum.org/
43. Wood, G., et al.: Ethereum: a secure decentralised generalised transaction ledger. Ethereum project yellow paper, pp. 1–32 (2014)

Conclave: A Collective Stake Pool Protocol

Dimitris Karakostas[1,3]($\boxtimes$), Aggelos Kiayias[1,3], and Mario Larangeira[2,3]

[1] University of Edinburgh, Edinburgh, UK
dimitris.karakostas@ed.ac.uk, akiayias@inf.ed.ac.uk
[2] Tokyo Institute of Technology, Tokyo, Japan
mario@c.titech.ac.jp
[3] IOHK, Hong Kong, China

Abstract. Proof-of-Stake (PoS) distributed ledgers are the most common alternative to Bitcoin's Proof-of-Work (PoW) paradigm, replacing the hardware dependency with stake, i.e., assets that a party controls. Similar to PoW's mining pools, PoS's stake pools, i.e., collaborative entities comprising of multiple stakeholders, allow a party to earn rewards more regularly, compared to participating on an individual basis. However, stake pools tend to increase centralization, since they are typically managed by a single party that acts on behalf of the pool's members. In this work we propose *Conclave*, a formal design of a *Collective Stake Pool*, i.e., a decentralized pool with no single point of authority. We formalize Conclave as an ideal functionality and implement it as a distributed protocol, based on standard cryptographic primitives. Among Conclave's building blocks is a weighted threshold signature scheme (WTSS); to that end, we define a WTSS ideal functionality and propose two constructions based on threshold ECDSA, which enable (1) fast trustless setup and (2) identifiable aborts.

1 Introduction

A major innovation of Bitcoin [31] was combining Proof-of-Work (PoW), to prevent sybil attacks, with financial rewards, to incentivize participation.

Regarding sybil resilience, Bitcoin's PoW depends on the collective network's ability to compute hashes. Thus, PoW limits each party's power and also determines how the distributed ledger is updated, i.e., which blocks can extend its blockchain. However, PoW's deficiencies, particularly its egregious environmental cost,[1] have driven research on alternative designs, most prominently Proof-of-Stake (PoS). PoS removes hardware requirements altogether and internalizes sybil resilience by relying on parties' *stake*, i.e., the assets that they own. These

---

[1] The carbon footprint of: i) a single Bitcoin transaction is equivalent to $1,202,422$ VISA transactions; ii) the total Bitcoin network is comparable to Sweden. (https://digiconomist.net/bitcoin-energy-consumption; May 2021).

This work is supported by JSPS KAKENHI No. JP21K11882.

© Springer Nature Switzerland AG 2021
E. Bertino et al. (Eds.): ESORICS 2021, LNCS 12972, pp. 370–389, 2021.
https://doi.org/10.1007/978-3-030-88418-5_18

assets are managed by the distributed ledger and serve as both the system's internal currency and consensus participation tokens. PoS systems are almost energy-free, but often rely on complex cryptographic primitives, e.g., secure Multiparty Computation [26], Byzantine Agreement [8,17,27], or Verifiable Random Functions (VRFs) [9,17].

Regarding rewards, blockchain-based financial systems, like Bitcoin, aim to incentivize participation in the consensus mechanism. The rewards comprise of newly-issued assets and of transaction fees, i.e., assets paid by parties for using the system. Interestingly, both PoW and PoS ledgers are economies of scale, who favor parties with large amounts of participating power. One reason is poorly-designed incentives, resulting in disproportionate power accumulation [13,23]. Another is temporal discounting, i.e., the tendency to disfavor rare or delayed rewards [35]. Specifically, in Bitcoin, a party is rewarded for every block it produces, so parties with insignificant amounts of power are rarely rewarded. In contrast, accumulating the power of multiple small parties in "pools" yields a steadier reward. As a result, PoW systems see the formation of mining pools,[2] while PoS systems usually favor delegation to stake pools [7,21] over "pure" PoS, where parties act independently. Finally, the ledger's performance and security are often better under fewer participants. For instance, PoS systems require participants to be constantly online, since abstaining is a security hazard; this requirement is more easily guaranteed within a small set of dedicated delegates.

A major drawback of existing stake pools is that they are typically managed by a single party, the *operator*. This party participates in consensus, claims the rewards offered by the system, and then distributes them among the pool's members (after subtracting a fee). However, the operator is a single point of failure. In this work, we explore a more desirable design, which allows players to jointly form a *collective pool*, i.e., a conclave. This design assumes no single operator, minimizing excess fees, and trust and security concerns, altogether. Collective stake pools also promote a more fair and decentralized environment. In existing incentive schemes [3], operators who can pledge large amounts of stake to the pool are preferred. Consequently, the system favors a few major pool operators and, in the long run, its wealth is concentrated around them, resulting in a "rich get richer" situation. Although this problem is inherent in all decentralized financial systems [23], a well-designed collective pool may offset the stakeholder imbalance and slightly decelerate this tendency.

Desiderata. Our design assumes a group of stakeholders who jointly create a stake pool without a single operator. Since large stakeholders typically form pools on their own, our protocol concerns smaller stakeholders, who could otherwise not participate directly. Therefore, our design could e.g., be appealing to a group of friends or colleagues, who aim for a more steady reward ratio without relying on a third party. Importantly, it should operate in a trustless environment as, unfortunately, even in these scenarios, trust is not a given. Notably, our targeted audience is parties who wish to actively participate, i.e., always be online to

---

[2] 86% of Bitcoin's hashing power and 83% of Ethereum's hashing power are controlled by 5 entities each. (https://miningpools.com; May 2021).

perform the required consensus actions; parties who wish to remain offline may instead opt for delegation schemes [7, 21].

In the absence of a central party, the responsibility of running the pool is shared among all pool's members, requiring some level of coordination which may be cumbersome. For instance, if the protocol requires unanimous actions, a single member could halt the pool's operation. To ensure good performance, the pool should allow a subset (of a carefully chosen size) to act on behalf of the whole group. The choice of such subsets depends on each party's "weight", which is in proportion to their stake. In summary, we have the following initial assumptions, which form the basis for outlining our work's desiderata:

- **small number of parties:** a collective pool is operated by a small group of players;
- **small stake disparity:** the profiles of the collective pool's members are similar, i.e., they contribute a similar amount of stake to the pool;
- **stake proportion as "weight":** each party is assigned a weight for participating in the pool's actions, relative to their part of the pool's total stake.

Next, we provide an exhaustive list of basic requirements of a collective stake pool. We note that an *admissible party set* is a set of parties with enough stake, i.e., above a threshold of the total pool's stake which is agreed upon during the pool's initialization. To the extent that some desiderata are conflicting, our design will aim to satisfy as many requirements as possible:

- **Proportional Rewards:** the claim of each member on the entire pool's protocol rewards should be proportional to their individual contribution.
- **Joint Control of Rewards:** the members of a pool should jointly control the access to its funds.
- **Unilateral Reward Withdrawal:** at any point in time, a stakeholder should be able to claim their reward, accumulated up to that point, without necessarily interacting with other members of the pool.
- **Permissioned Access:** new users can join the pool following agreement by an admissible set of pool members.
- **Robustness against Aborting:** the pool should not fail to participate in consensus, unless an admissible set of members aborts or is corrupted.
- **Public Verifiability:** stake pool formation and operation should be publicly verifiable (s.t. consensus could take into account the aggregate pool's stake).
- **Stake Reallocation:** users should freely change their personal stake allocated to the pool, without interacting with other members of the pool.
- **Parameter Updates:** an admissible set of parties should be able to update the stake pool's parameters.
- **Force Removal:** an admissible set of parties should be able to remove a member from the pool.
- **Pool Closing:** an admissible set of parties should be able to permanently close the stake pool.
- **Prevention of Double Stake Allocation:** a party should not simultaneously commit the same stake to two different stake pools.

Our Contributions and Roadmap. We propose *Conclave*, a collectively managed stake pool protocol that aims to satisfy the listed desiderata. Our first contribution is the ideal functionality $\mathcal{F}_{pool}$, a simulation-based security definition of collective stake pools, which captures the core security properties that our collective pool scheme should possess. We then describe π_{pool}, a distributed protocol executed by a set of n parties $\mathbb{P}$ which realizes $\mathcal{F}_{pool}$. π_{pool} employs certificates, which are published on the ledger, to announce its formation and closing. A major consideration and performance enhancement of our design is load balancing of transaction verification. Each transaction is verified by a (deterministically elected) committee of parties, whose size is a tradeoff between balancing workload, i.e., not requiring each party to verify every transaction, and reducing trust on the chosen validator(s). We thus construct a *distributed mempool*, i.e., a collectively managed set of unpublished transactions, s.t. if a majority of the committee's members are honest, transaction verification is secure. Our scheme uses a weighted threshold signature scheme (WTSS), to share the pool's key among its members, and a smart contract to manage the rewards. To that end, we provide a WTSS Universally Composable ideal functionality (Sect. 2), which may be of independent interest, and construct an ECDSA WTSS, based on [15,16], s.t. each party has as many shares as "units" of weight.

Related Work. In the past years a multitude of PoS protocols have been proposed. The Ouroboros family [2,9,25,26] offers, like Bitcoin, eventual guarantees of liveness and persistence. Subselection has been employed in systems like Algorand [17], which employs Byzantine Agreement to achieve transaction finality in (expected) constant time, and Snow White [8,32], which uses the notion of "robustly reconfigurable consensus" to address potential lack of participation. Our work is complementary to these protocols and can be composed with them, as it is agnostic to the underlying PoS ledger's consensus mechanism.

Real-world PoS implementations often opt for stake representation and delegation. Systems like Cardano,[3] EOS [7], and (to some extent) Tezos [19], employ different consensus protocols, but all enforce that a (relatively small) subset of representatives is elected to participate. Decred [10] takes a somewhat different approach, where stakeholders buy a ticket for participation, akin to PoS with optional participation. However, these systems typically assume single parties that act as delegates, either individually or as pool operators; our design directly aims at relaxing this restriction without requiring changes to the consensus protocol.

In cryptographic literature, pools are mostly treated from an engineering perspective. In PoW systems, SmartPool [30] is a notable design of a distributed mining pool for Ethereum, which, similar to our work, utilizes smart contracts for reward distribution. On the PoS domain, Ouroboros [26] offers a brief description of how delegation can be used within the protocol. This idea is expanded in [21], which provides a formal definition of PoS wallets and includes stake pool formation method via certificates. However, the pool's management is again centralized around the operator; our work extends this line of work by enabling the

---

[3] https://cardano.org.

formation of a collective pool. Another work, orthogonal to ours, by Brünjes
et al. [3] considers the incentives of distributing rewards among stake pools and
aims to incentivize the creation of a (pre-defined) number of pools. However, it
assumes that the pool operator commits part of their stake to make the pool
more appealing, thus favoring larger pool operators. Our work eases such wealth
concentration tendencies by enabling a collective pool to be equally competitive
to a centralized one.

2   UC Weighted Threshold Signature

In this section, we present the weighted threshold signature ideal functionality
$\mathcal{F}_{wtss}$ (Fig. 1). This functionality is used in the Collective Pool Protocol π_{pool},
which employs weighted threshold signatures for collectively signing certificates
and new blocks. The functionality $\mathcal{F}_{wtss}$ is inspired by Almansa et al. [1], which
is in turn inspired by Canetti [5]. However, unlike Almansa et al. and similar to
Canetti, during signature verification we consider the case of a corrupted signer,
i.e., a set of parties such that the majority (of weights) is corrupted.

$\mathcal{F}_{wtss}$ interacts with a set of n parties. Each party P_i is associated with an
integer w_i, i.e., its weight. $\mathcal{F}_{wtss}$ also keeps the following, initially empty, tables:
i) pubkeys: tuples $\langle sid, vk \rangle$ of sid and a public key vk; ii) sigs: tuples (m, σ, vk, f)
of message m, a signature σ, a public key vk, and a verification bit f. The
mapping $\omega[p] \to w_p$ denotes the weight of a party p, while the term ω also
denotes the set of keys the participating parties.

As highlighted in the definition, *completeness, consistency,* and *unforgeability*
are enforced upon verification, whereas *threshold completeness* is enforced upon
signature generation. Hence, it should be infeasible to issue a signature unless
using keys with enough weight, i.e., above the threshold, say, a value T.

3   The Collective Stake Pool

Our analysis is based on the UC Framework, following Canetti's formulation of
the "real world" [4]. Specifically, we define the collective pool ideal functionality
$\mathcal{F}_{pool}$, which distills the required (operational and security) properties; for readability, $\mathcal{F}_{pool}$ is divided into two parts, *management* and *consensus participation*.
The ideal functionality is realized – in the "real world" – by the distributed protocol π_{pool}, which employs various established cryptographic primitives, and,
therefore, π_{pool} can be described with auxiliary functionalities. Before proceeding with the functionality's definition, we first describe the hybrid execution of
π_{pool} and its building blocks.

3.1   Hybrid Protocol Execution

The protocol π_{pool} is performed by n parties, where each party p_i holds two
pairs of keys: (vk_{p_i}, sk_{p_i}) for issuing transactions, and (vk_{s_i}, sk_{s_i}) for staking

---

Weighted Threshold Signature Functionality $\mathcal{F}_{wtss}$

Each message is associated with $sid = \langle \mathcal{P}, \omega, T, sid' \rangle$, where $\mathcal{P}$ is the set of parties, ω is a mapping of parties to weights, T is the collective signature weight threshold, and sid' is a unique identifier.

Key Generation: Upon receiving (KEYGEN, sid) from every honest party $P \in \mathcal{P}$, send (KEYGEN, sid, P) to $\mathcal{S}$. Upon receiving a response (KEYGEN, sid, vk) from $\mathcal{S}$, record $\langle sid,$ vk$\rangle$ to pubkeys and send (KEYGEN, sid, vk) to every party in $\mathcal{P}$. Following, all messages that do not contain the established sid are ignored.

Signature Generation: Upon receiving (SIGN, sid, m) from a party p, forward it to $\mathcal{S}$. After a subset of parties $\mathcal{P}' \subseteq \mathcal{P}$ has submitted a Sign message for the same m, and upon receiving (SIGN, sid, m, σ) from $\mathcal{S}$, check that $\sum_{p \in \mathcal{P}'} \omega[p] > T$ (*Note: This condition guarantees threshold completeness.*) Next, if $(m, \sigma, vk, 0) \notin$ sigs (for the key vk that corresponds to sid in pubkeys), record $(m, \sigma, vk, 1)$ to sigs and reply with (SIGN, sid, m, σ).

Signature Verification: Upon receiving (VERIFY, sid, m, σ, vk') from P, forward it to $\mathcal{S}$. Upon receiving (VERIFIED, sid, m, σ, ϕ) from $\mathcal{S}$, set f as next:

1. If vk$' =$ vk and $(m, \sigma, vk, 1) \in$ sigs, $f = 1$. (*This guarantees completeness.*)
2. Else, if vk$' =$ vk, the aggregate weight of the corrupted parties in $\mathcal{P}$ is strictly less than T, and $(m, \sigma, vk, 1) \notin$ sigs, $f = 0$ and record $(m, \sigma, vk, 0)$ to sigs. (*This guarantees unforgeability, if the aggregate weight of the corrupted parties is below the threshold.*)
3. Else, if $(m, \sigma, vk', b) \in$ sigs, $f = b$. (*This guarantees consistency.*)
4. Else, $f = \phi$ and record (m, σ, vk', f) to sigs.

Finally, send (VERIFIED, sid, m, σ, vk', f) to P.

Fig. 1. Weighted threshold signature ideal functionality

operations, e.g., issuing delegation certificates (cf. [21]). The public key vk$_i$ is also used to generate an address α_i. Each pool member p_i pledges the funds of an address α_i (which it owns) to the pool. These funds are the player's stake in the pool and form the player's weight in the weight distribution mapping ω.

We assume the members' stake, i.e., their weight w_i in the pool, is public. Therefore, the weight distribution mapping ω is also public. Furthermore, each member of the pool has its own signature key, and can issue standard signatures through a standard signature scheme. A weighted version for a threshold signature scheme follows by having each party holding as many shares, of the original threshold scheme, as its weight. This approach has the extra advantage that security guarantees of the original scheme are carried straightforwardly into the weighted version. The full description of the WTSS Σ_{thresh} based on ECDSA is presented in Sect. 4.

Additionally, our construction relies on the consensus sub-protocol $\pi_{consensus}$ to validate a transaction by the elected committee. Specifically, the collective stake pool protocol is parameterized by: i) the validation predicate Validate, ii) the permutation algorithm π_{perm}, and iii) a consensus sub-protocol $\pi_{consensus}$.

Finally, our (modular) protocol is described in a hybrid world with auxiliary functionalities for established primitives. The functionality $\mathcal{F}_{BC}$ [20] provides a broadcast channel to all parties; $\mathcal{F}_{corewallet}$ [21] enables delegation to the pool; $\mathcal{F}_{wtss}$ (cf. Section 2) is used for weighted threshold signature operations; the Smart Contract Functionality Γ_{reward} realizes the reward distribution mechanism; $\overline{\mathcal{G}}_{simpleLedger}$ is a global Ledger Functionality [24]. Let $\mathsf{HYBRID}^{pool}_{\pi_{pool}, \mathcal{A}, \mathcal{Z}}$ denote the $\{\overline{\mathcal{G}}_{simpleLedger}, \mathcal{F}_{BC}, \mathcal{F}_{corewallet}, \mathcal{F}_{wtss}, \Gamma_{reward}\}$-hybrid execution of π_{pool} in the (global) UC Framework.

3.2   Part 1: Stake Pool Management

The functionality's first part (Fig. 3) includes all operations that are not consensus-oriented. First, establishing a stake pool consists of two parts, defined as corresponding interfaces in the ideal functionality. The pool's members *gather* and jointly decide to create a staking pool; they contact each other, e.g., via off-chain direct channels, agree on the pool's parameters, and generate its key. Importantly, the participants are aware of the total number of participants in the pool, as well as their weights. Then, the members of the pool perform a setup protocol and *register* the new pool via a *registration certificate*, which is signed by the pool's key and published on the ledger. Following, the pool receives rewards for participating in the consensus protocol. The rewards are managed by a smart contract and, at any point, each party can withdraw their part, which is proportional to the internal stake distribution. Finally, to close the pool, the members sign and publish a revocation certificate.

In more detail, the functionality $\mathcal{F}_{pool}$ interacts with n parties $p_1, \ldots, p_n$ and is parameterized by:

- the validation predicate $\mathsf{Validate}(\cdot, \cdot)$ which, given a transaction τ and a chain $\mathcal{C}$, defines whether τ can be appended to $\mathcal{C}$ (as part of a block);
- the algorithm blockify which, given a set of transactions, serializes them (deterministically) in a block;
- the probability $\Pi^{\theta, t, n}$ that the elected committee, responsible for a transaction's verification, is corrupted, dependent on the subselection parameter θ and the number of corrupted parties t out of n total parties.

It also keeps the (initially empty) variables: i) the signature threshold T; ii) the public key vk_{pool}; iii) the reward address α_{reward}; iv) the set of valid and unpublished transactions mempool; v) a mapping of parties to weights W; vi) a table of signatures sigs.

Gathering and Registration. The first step in creating a pool is the gathering of parties, in order to collectively create the pool's public key vk_{pool}. Following, the parties create and publish on the ledger the registration certificate cert_{reg}, which contains the following:

- ω: a mapping identifying each member's weight;
- α_{reward}: the address which accumulates the pool's rewards;
- vk_{pool}: the pool's threshold public key;
- σ_{pool}: the signature of $\langle \omega, \alpha_{reward} \rangle$ created by vk_{pool}.

Reward Withdrawal. During the life cycle of the pool, a member may want to withdraw the rewards received up to that point. As per the desiderata of Sect. 1, any party should be able to do so, without the explicit permission of the other pool's members. Additionally, the rewards that each party receives should be proportional to its stake, i.e., its weight within the collective pool. Reward withdrawal is implemented as the smart contract functionality Γ_{reward}. The contract is initialized with the weight distribution of the pool's members and each member's public key. We assume that the contract is associated with an address and can receive funds, similar to real-world smart contract systems like Ethereum [36]. The state transition functionality Γ_{reward} is defined in Fig. 2.

Reward Smart Contract Functionality Γ_{reward}

Γ_{reward} maintains a mapping ω, of parties to weights, and a variable b.

Initialization: Upon receiving $(\text{INIT}, sid, \omega')$, forward it to $\mathcal{S}$. Upon receiving a response $(\text{INIT-OK}, sid, \alpha_{sc})$, set $\omega \leftarrow \omega'$ and return $(\text{INIT-OK}, sid, \alpha_{sc})$.

Balance Update: On receiving $(\text{TRANSACTION}, sid, \tau)$ from $\mathcal{U}$, such that $\tau = \langle \alpha_s, \alpha_r, v, f \rangle$, if $\alpha_s = \alpha_{sc}$ set $b := b - v$, else if $\alpha_r = \alpha_{sc}$ set $b := b + v$.

Withdrawal: Upon receiving $(\text{WITHDRAW}, sid, \alpha, f)$ from the party p, set $r = \dfrac{w_p}{\sum_{p' \in \omega} w_{p'}} \cdot b$ and return $(\text{TRANSACTION}, sid, \langle \alpha_{sc}, \alpha, r, f \rangle)$.

Fig. 2. The pool's reward smart contract functionality.

Closing. Eventually, the members halt the operation of the pool. In order to do so, they revoke the pool's registration by jointly producing a revocation certificate cert_{rev}. The certificate is relatively simple, containing a timestamp x announcing the end of the pool and signed by the pool's public key vk_{pool}.

The first part of our functionality definition is given by Fig. 3, whereas the management routines, i.e., the first part of the description, of our protocol construction is given by Fig. 4.

Collective Pool Functionality $\mathcal{F}_{pool}^{T,\omega}$ (first part)

Gathering: Upon receiving (GATHER, sid) from p, forward it to $\mathcal{S}$. After every party $p_i, i \in [1, n]$ has submitted **gather**, upon receiving from $\mathcal{S}$ (GATHER-OK, sid, vk_{pool}), store T and vk_{pool}, add all party-weight pairs (p_i, ω_i) to W, and reply with (GATHER-OK, sid, vk_{pool}) to all parties.

Pool Registration: Upon receiving (REGISTER, sid, W) from p, forward it to $\mathcal{S}$. After all parties $p_i, i \in [1, n]$ have submitted **register**, upon receiving from $\mathcal{S}$ (REGISTER-OK, sid, $\alpha_{reward}, \sigma_{pool}$), set $\mathsf{cert}_{reg} = \langle (W, \alpha_{reward}, \mathsf{vk}_{pool}, \sigma_{pool}) \rangle$. Then check if $\forall (m, \sigma, b') \in$ **sigs** : $\sigma \neq \sigma_{pool}, (\mathsf{cert}_{reg}, \sigma_{pool}, 0) \notin$ **sigs**; if the checks hold, insert $(\mathsf{cert}_{reg}, \sigma_{pool}, 1)$ to **sigs**. Finally, store α_{reward} and reply with (REGISTER-OK, sid, cert_{reg}).

Reward Withdrawal: Upon receiving the message (WITHDRAW, sid, α, f) from p_i, forward it to $\mathcal{S}$. Then, compute $r = \dfrac{w_{p_i}}{\sum_{j=1}^{n} w_{p_j}} \cdot r_{pool}$, where r_{pool} is the funds of address α_{sc} as defined in $\overline{\mathcal{G}}_{simpleLedger}$. Finally, return (TRANSACTION, sid, $\langle \alpha_{sc}, \alpha, r, f \rangle$).

Closing: Upon receiving (CLOSE, sid, x) from p, forward it to $\mathcal{S}$. After a set of parties B has submitted **close** for the same x, if $\sum_{p \in B} w_p > T$, upon receiving (CLOSE-OK, sid, σ_{pool}) from $\mathcal{S}$, check if $\forall (m, \sigma, b') \in$ **sigs** : $\sigma \neq \sigma_{pool}, (x, \sigma_{pool}, 0) \notin$ **sigs**; if the checks hold, insert $(x, \sigma_{pool}, 1)$ to **sigs**. Finally, return to all parties (CLOSE-OK, sid, cert_{rev}), with $\mathsf{cert}_{rev} = \langle x, \sigma_{pool} \rangle$.

Fig. 3. The first part of the Collective Pool Functionality, parameterized with threshold T and weight mapping ω, refers to the creation and management of the pool (the second part is given by Fig. 5).

3.3 Part 2: Participation in Consensus

After a pool is set up, the functionality's second part (Fig. 5) considers participation in the system, i.e., *validating transactions* and *issuing blocks*. The pool members continuously monitor the network for new transactions, which they collect, validate, and organize in a *mempool*. As mentioned in the introduction, the pool members *remain online* for the entirety of the execution to perform the pool's operations. Specifically, when the pool is elected to participate, the mempool's transactions are serialized and published in a block. Under PoS, the pool participates proportionally to its aggregated member and delegated stake.

To improve performance, we define a distributed mechanism for transaction verification, i.e., a *distributed mempool*. Such a load balancing mechanism increases efficiency by requiring only a subset of the pool's members to verify each transaction. Notably, this is in contrast to the standard practice of Bitcoin mining pools, where the pool's operator decides the transactions to be mined by its members; instead, our approach further reduces these trust requirements.

To construct a distributed mempool, we consider a subselection mechanism to identify the parties that verify each transaction. This mechanism should be: a) *non-interactive* b) *deterministic*, c) *balanced*, i.e., every party should be chosen

---

Collective Pool Protocol $\pi_{pool}^{T,\omega}$ **(first part)**

Gathering: Upon receiving (GATHER, sid), send (KEYGEN, sid) to $\mathcal{F}_{wtss}$, with sid containing the weight mapping ω and the threshold T. Upon receiving the reply (KEYGEN, sid, vk_{pool}), return (GATHER-OK, sid, vk_{pool}).

Pool Registration: Upon receiving (REGISTER, sid, W), send (INIT, sid, W) to Γ_{reward} and wait for the reply (INIT-OK, sid, α_{reward}). Then, set $m = (W, \alpha_{reward})$ and send (SIGN, sid, m) to $\mathcal{F}_{wtss}$. Upon receiving a reply (SIGN, sid, m, σ_{pool}), return (REGISTER-OK, sid, cert_{reg}), where $\mathsf{cert}_{reg} = \langle (W, \alpha_{reward}, \mathsf{vk}_{pool}, \sigma_{pool}) \rangle$.

Reward Withdrawal: Upon receiving (WITHDRAW, sid, α, f), forward it to Γ_{reward}. Upon receiving a response (TRANSACTION, sid, $\langle \alpha_{sc}, \alpha, r, f \rangle$) return it.

Closing: Upon receiving (CLOSE, sid, x), send (SIGN, sid, x) to $\mathcal{F}_{wtss}$. Upon receiving a reply (SIGN, sid, x, σ_{pool}), return (CLOSE-OK, sid, cert_{rev}) with $\mathsf{cert}_{rev} = \langle x, \sigma_{pool} \rangle$.

Fig. 4. The first part of the Collective Pool Protocol, which describes the set of management operations (the second part is given by Fig. 6).

with the same probability. Subselection is secure if a majority of the elected committee is honest. However, since the adversary may corrupt some pool members, this may not always be the case. We model this uncertainty via the probability $\Pi^{\theta,t,n}$, which depends on the size of the committee and the power of the adversary among the pool's members.

A straightforward way to implement subselection is to assume that the pool's members are ordered in a well-defined manner, e.g., lexicographically. Given the ordered list $L = [p_1, p_2, \dots, p_n]$ of the pool's members, we use a permutation algorithm $\pi_{perm}(\cdot, \cdot, \cdot)$, which takes i) a transaction τ, ii) a chain $\mathcal{C}$, and iii) the ordered list of pool members L, and outputs a pseudorandom permuted list L_τ. For every transaction τ and a given chain $\mathcal{C}$, the committee responsible for verification consists of the θ first members in L_τ. Naturally, this proposal is rather simple, so alternative, e.g., VRF-based, mechanisms could be proposed to improve performance.

We note that using $\mathcal{C}$ during the subselection mechanism is important to avoid adaptive attacks. Specifically, the chain $\mathcal{C}$ simulates a randomness beacon, such that at least one of its last u blocks is honest, for some parameter u. If $\mathcal{C}$ was not used, the adversary could construct a malicious transaction in such a way that the subselected committee would also be malicious. By using $\mathcal{C}$ as a seed to the pseudorandom permutation, the adversary's ability to construct such malicious transactions is limited. Alternatively, cryptographic sortition [17] could be employed to fully handle adaptive adversaries.

The (honest) members need to always have the same view of the distributed mempool; this is achieved via authenticated broadcast. Assuming a Public Key Infrastructure, as is our setting, it is possible to achieve deterministic authenticated broadcast in $t+1$ rounds for t adversarial parties [12,28,33]. Each time a party adds a transaction to its mempool, it broadcasts it, such that, at any point in time, the honest members of the pool have the same view of the network w.r.t. the canonical chain and the mempool of unconfirmed transactions. We remind that, as shown by Garay *et al.* [14], $\mathcal{F}_{BC}$ can be implemented to ensure adaptive corruptions using commitments. We note that, in existing distributed ledgers, the order with which transactions are added to the mempool does not affect the choice when creating a new block; for instance, transactions of a new block are typically chosen based on a fee-per-byte score. If the order of transactions is pertinent, a stronger primitive like Atomic Broadcast [11] could be employed.

Following, the committee employs a consensus sub-protocol to agree on the transaction's validity. When a party p retrieves a new transaction τ from the network, it broadcasts it as above. Then, each party computes the permuted list L_τ. Each party, which is in the validation committee for τ, computes locally the validation predicate and submits its output to the consensus protocol. The consensus protocol should offer *strong validity*, i.e., if all honest parties should have the same input bit, they should output this bit. Finally, the output of the consensus protocol is broadcast to the rest of the pool. To verify the committee's actions, a party may request the transcript of the consensus sub-protocol.

Finally, to compute the probability of electing an honest committee, we have a hypergeometric distribution, with population size n and $n - t$ honest parties, where a sample of parties of size θ is chosen *without replacement*. Thus, the probability of honest committee majority is: $\Pi^{\theta,t,n} = 1 - \sum_{v=\lfloor \frac{\theta+1}{2} \rfloor}^{\min(\theta,t)} \frac{\binom{t}{v}\cdot\binom{n-t}{\theta-v}}{\binom{n}{\theta}}$.

Following, Fig. 5 defines the second part of our functionality, while Fig. 6 presents the second part of our protocol.

3.4   The Security of the Conclave Collective Stake Pool

Theorem 1 formalizes the security of π_{pool}; due to space constraints, the full proof is available at the paper's full version [22].

Theorem 1. *The protocol* π_{pool}, *parameterized by a validation predicate* Validate, *a permutation algorithm* π_{perm}, *and a consensus protocol* $\pi_{consensus}$ *securely realizes* $\mathcal{F}_{pool}$ *with the hybrid execution* $\mathsf{HYBRID}^{pool}_{\pi_{pool},\mathcal{A},\mathcal{Z}}$ *in the global* $\overline{\mathcal{G}}_{simpleLedger}$ *model, and* $\Pi^{\theta,t,n} = 1 - \sum_{v=\lfloor \frac{\theta+1}{2} \rfloor}^{\min(\theta,t)} \frac{\binom{t}{v}\cdot\binom{n-t}{\theta-v}}{\binom{n}{\theta}}$, *assuming* $\sum_{p \in P_\mathcal{A}} w_p < T$, *where* θ *is the subselection parameter for transaction verification,* $P_\mathcal{A}$ *is the set of* t *corrupted parties out of* n *total parties,* ω *is the weight distribution of the* n *parties, and* T *is the signature threshold.*

Proof (Sketch). There are multiple points of interest in proving the security of π_{pool}. First, when $\mathcal{A}$ advances a party in the real world, the simulator (i.e., the ideal adversary) $\mathcal{S}$ follows suit in the ideal world; importantly, $\mathcal{A}$ should advance

---

Collective Pool Functionality $\mathcal{F}_{pool}^{T,\omega}$ (second part)

Transaction Verification: Upon receiving (TRANSACTION, sid, τ, θ) from p_i, forward it to $\mathcal{S}$. Then send READ to $\overline{\mathcal{G}}_{simpleLedger}$ on behalf of p_i and wait for the reply $\mathcal{C}$. Following, set t as the number of corrupted parties; with probability $\Pi^{\theta,t,n}$ set $b := \mathsf{Validate}(\tau, \mathcal{C})$, otherwise (with probability $1 - \Pi^{\theta,t,n}$), send (TRANSACTION-VER, sid, τ) to $\mathcal{S}$, wait for a reply (TRANSACTION-OK, $sid, \mathcal{C}, \tau, f$), and set $b := f$. Finally, if $b = 1$, insert τ to mempool and send (TRANSACTION, $sid, \mathcal{C}, \tau, b$) to all parties.

Mempool Update: Upon receiving (TRANSACTION, $sid, \mathcal{C}', \tau, 1$) from p_i, forward it to $\mathcal{S}$. Then send READ to $\overline{\mathcal{G}}_{simpleLedger}$ on behalf of p_i and wait for the reply $\mathcal{C}$. If $\mathcal{C}' \prec \mathcal{C}$ and p_i is honest, insert τ to mempool and return (MEMPOOL-UPDATED, sid, τ).

Block issuing: Upon receiving (ISSUE-BLOCK, sid) from a party p, forward it to $\mathcal{S}$. When a set of parties $\mathbb{P}$ has submitted (ISSUE-BLOCK, sid), if $\sum_{j \in [1,m]} W[p_j] > T$, then for every party $p_i \in \mathbb{P}$, send READ to $\overline{\mathcal{G}}_{simpleLedger}$ on behalf of p_i and wait for the reply $\mathcal{C}_i$. If all received chains equal, i.e., are the same chain $\mathcal{C}$, remove every τ in mempool that also exists in $\mathcal{C}$. Then, set $b = \mathsf{blockify}(\mathsf{mempool})$, send (ISSUE-BLOCK, sid, b) to $\mathcal{S}$, and wait for the reply (ISSUE-BLOCK, sid, b, σ_{pool}). Following, check if $\forall (m, \sigma, b') \in T : \sigma \neq \sigma_{pool}, (b, \sigma_{pool}, 0) \notin T$; if the checks hold, insert $(b, \sigma_{pool}, 1)$ to T. Finally, reply with (BLOCK, sid, b, σ_{pool}).

Fig. 5. The second part of the proposed Pool Functionality, which defines the consensus participation operations.

Collective Pool Protocol $\pi_{pool}^{T,\omega}$ (second part)

Transaction Verification: Upon receiving (TRANSACTION, sid, τ, θ), send READ to $\overline{\mathcal{G}}_{simpleLedger}$ and wait for the reply $\mathcal{C}$. Then, set $b = \mathsf{Validate}(\mathcal{C}, \tau)$, compute $L' = \pi_{perm}(\tau, \mathcal{C}, L)$ and initiate protocol $\pi_{consensus}$ with the θ first parties in L' with input b. Upon computing the output of $\pi_{consensus}$, β, send (TRANSACTION, $sid, \mathcal{C}, \tau, \beta$) to $\mathcal{F}_{BC}$ and return it.

Mempool Update: Upon receiving (TRANSACTION, $sid, \mathcal{C}', \tau, 1$), p_i, send READ to $\overline{\mathcal{G}}_{simpleLedger}$ and wait for the reply $\mathcal{C}$. If $\mathcal{C}' \prec \mathcal{C}$, insert τ to mempool and return (MEMPOOL-UPDATED, sid, τ).

Block Issuing: Upon receiving (ISSUE-BLOCK, sid), send READ to $\overline{\mathcal{G}}_{simpleLedger}$ and wait for the reply $\mathcal{C}$. For every τ in mempool, if τ is also in $\mathcal{C}$, then remove τ from mempool. Next, set $b = \mathsf{blockify}(\mathsf{mempool})$ and send (SIGN, sid, b) to $\mathcal{F}_{wtss}$. Upon receiving a reply (SIGN, sid, b, σ_{pool}), return (BLOCK, sid, b, σ_{pool}).

Fig. 6. The second part of our protocol, which describes the set of operations for consensus participation.

parties correctly, s.t. the security of $\overline{\mathcal{G}}_{simpleLedger}$ is guaranteed and the (honest) pool members are synchronized w.r.t. the ledger state and mempool. Second, regarding the consensus sub-protocol $\pi_{consensus}$, if π_{pool} does not securely realize $\mathcal{F}_{pool}$, a transcript of an execution of $\pi_{consensus}$ exists s.t. the *validity* property of $\pi_{consensus}$ is violated. Finally, security of the *Reward Withdrawal* interface depends on the security guarantees of Kachina [24], which formalizes smart contracts and is the basis for Γ_{reward}, security of *Mempool Issuing* relies on $\mathcal{F}_{BC}$ to ensure that all members are synchronized w.r.t. the mempool and produce the same block without further coordination, while the security of the other interfaces relies on the Weighted Threshold Signature Functionality $\mathcal{F}_{wtss}$.

4 Weighted Threshold ECDSA

Our final contribution is a weighted threshold signature construction, which can be used in the implementation of π_{pool}. Our scheme is based on [15]; specifically, we introduce weights, with each party having as many shares as "units" of weight.

Our construction is a (t, n, ω)-weighted threshold ECDSA. We assume that each player p_i has a associated a weight w_i, identified by the (publicly available) weight function ω such that $\omega[p_i] = w_i$; ω is a parameter in the following two algorithms. Furthermore, we assume an index function $\mathcal{I}(i, w)$ in the secret sharing scheme, which assigns a unique index to each pair (p_i, w_i).

Following, we instantiate the algorithms Thresh-Key-Gen and Thresh-Sign. We outline the changes of our constructions to obtain identifiable abort capability based on [16], to make it suitable for an incentive-compatible pool. We note that some PoS protocols employ a Verifiable Random Function (VRF) [9,17]. Thus, this section's secret sharing techniques can also be used to distribute the VRF key in a weighted manner.

Due to space constraints, we refer to the paper's full version [22] for the computation and communication complexities of both schemes.

4.1 Key Generation Protocol Thresh-Key-Gen$_\omega$

Each party p_i is associated with a public key for the homomorphic encryption E_i and the weight w_i.

- Phase 1: Each party p_i picks its share proportionally to its weight, i.e., w_i shares. Then it commits to them and broadcast them together with its homomorphic encryption key E_i.
  - Pick uniformly random local values $u_i^{(1)}, \ldots, u_i^{(w_i)} \in \mathbb{Z}_p$
  - Compute $y_i^{(w)} =, (g^{u_i^{(w)}}) = [C_i^{(w)}, D_i^{(w)}]$, for $\forall w = \{1, \ldots, w_i\}$
  - Broadcast $C_i^{(1)}, \ldots, C_i^{(w_i)}$
  - Broadcast E_i
- Phase 2: The confirmation of the values is done through opening of commitments, and each value for each weight is secretly shared among all the players. Therefore each player executes as many secret-sharing instance as

weight "units" it has, resulting in its combined shares for the secret key $(x_i^{(1)}, \ldots, x_i^{(w_i)})$ proportionally to its weight w_i.

- Broadcast $D_i^{(1)}, \ldots, D_i^{(w_i)}$
- Receive the decommitments for $(y_j^{(1)}, \ldots, y_j^{(w_j)})$, $\forall j \in \{1, \ldots, n\}, j \neq i$
- Perform secret-sharing for each share $u_i^{(1)}, \ldots, u_i^{(w_i)}$, s.t. for each value $u_i^{(w)}$ compute the shares $u_{i, \mathcal{I}(j, w')}^{(w)}$ and secretly send to p_J, with respect to weight $1 \leq w' \leq w_j$ and index $\mathcal{I}(j, w')$, receiving back the share $u_{\mathcal{I}(j, w'), i}^{(w)}$
- Each player p_i compute its respective set of shares

$$x_i^{(1)} = \sum_{\substack{1 \leq j \leq n \\ 1 \leq w' \leq w_j}} u_{\mathcal{I}(j, w'), i}^{(1)}, \ \ldots, \ x_i^{(w_i)} = \sum_{\substack{1 \leq j \leq n \\ 1 \leq w' \leq w_j}} u_{\mathcal{I}(j, w'), i}^{(w_i)}$$

with the values received from other parties p_j.

- Phase 3: For the public key E_i, the module $N_i = p_i \cdot q_i$ for primes p_i and q_i provide zero-knowledge proof for:
  - for p_i and q_i (Proof of knowledge for factoring [34])
  - and $x_i^{(1)}, \ldots, x_i^{(w_i)}$ (Schnorr based)

Note that the joint public-key is $\mathsf{vk} = \prod_{i=1}^{i=n} \prod_{w=1}^{w=w_i} y_i^{(w)}$, whereas the joint secret-key is $\mathsf{tsk} = \sum_{i=1}^{i=n} \sum_{w=1}^{w=w_i} x_i^{(w)}$.

4.2   Signing Protocol Thresh-Sign$_\omega$

We assume a set B of parties p_i that jointly compute a signature.

- Phase 1: Each party selects two tuples of values, each with w_i values, and broadcasts w_i commitments to one of the sets.
  - Pick random values $k_i^{(1)}, \ldots, k_i^{(w_i)} \in_R \mathbb{Z}_p$
  - Pick random values $\gamma_i^{(1)}, \ldots, \gamma_i^{(w_i)} \in_R \mathbb{Z}_p$
  - Define $k = \sum_{i \in B} \sum_{w=1}^{w-w_i} k_i^{(w)}$ and $\gamma = \sum_{i \in B} \sum_{w=1}^{w=w_i} \gamma_i^{(w)}$
  - Compute w_i commitments , $(g^{\gamma_i^{(w)}}) = [C_i^{(w)}, D_i^{(w)}]$ for $\forall w = \{1, \ldots, w_i\}$
  - Broadcast $C_i^{(1)}, \ldots, C_i^{(w_I)}$
- Phase 2: Each party computes the interpolation coefficients $\lambda_i^{(w)}$ for each share it keeps, that is the shares for weights $w = \{1, \ldots, w_i\}$, taking into account its indexes $\mathcal{I}(i, w)$.
  - For $w = \{1, \ldots, w_i\}$ and $w' = \{1, \ldots, w_j\}$, compute the Lagrangian coefficients $\lambda_{i, B}^{(w)} = \prod_{j \in B, w'=1}^{w'=w_j} \frac{-\mathcal{I}(j, w')}{\mathcal{I}(i, w) - \mathcal{I}(j, w')}$
  - Compute the values

$$\mathbf{x}_i^{(1)} = (\lambda_i^{(1)}) \cdot (x_i^{(1)}), \ \ldots, \ \mathbf{x}_i^{(w_i)} = (\lambda_i^{(w_i)}) \cdot (x_i^{(w_i)}).$$

- **Phase 2A - Local Shares:** The party p_i executes locally the MtA protocol with the local shares, which are $(k_i^{(1)}, \ldots, k_i^{(w_i)})$ and $(\gamma_i^{(1)}, \ldots, \gamma_i^{(w_i)})$ to compute α and β such that $k_i^{(w)} \gamma_i^{(w')} = \alpha_{i,i}^{(w)(w')} + \beta_{i,i}^{(w)(w')}$ for p_i and $1 \leq w, w' \leq w_i$. Note that both values of the pair $k_i^{(w)}$ and $\gamma_i^{(w)}$ are used which means MtA is executed twice for a given party p_i and weight w.

- **Phase 2B - Online Shares:** Party p_i executes MtA protocol between its local shares $(k_i^{(1)}, \ldots, k_i^{(w_i)})$ and shares of the remaining parties, other than p_i:

$p_1, \ldots, p_{(i-1)}$	$p_{(i+1)}, \ldots, p_n$
$(\gamma_1^{(1)}, \ldots, \gamma_1^{(w_1)})$	$(\gamma_{i+1}^{(1)}, \ldots, \gamma_{i+1}^{(w_{i+1})})$
$\vdots$	$\vdots$
$(\gamma_{i-1}^{(1)}, \ldots, \gamma_{i-1}^{(w_{i-1})})$	$(\gamma_n^{(1)}, \ldots, \gamma_n^{(w_n)})$

Like Local Shares, there will be two MtA executions for each pair $k_i^{(w)}$ and $\gamma_i^{(w)}$, i.e., $k_i^{(w)} \gamma_j^{(w')} = \alpha_{i,j}^{(w)(w')} + \beta_{j,i}^{(w)(w')}$.

- **Phase 2C - Compute $\delta_i^{(w)}$,** for $1 \leq w \leq w_i$ and $1 \leq i \leq n$ the following values by summing the produced values from steps 2A and 2B. Second and third terms from 2A, and the remaining terms from 2B:

$$\delta_i^{(w)} = k_i^{(w)} \gamma_i^{(w)} + \sum_{\substack{w'=1 \\ w \neq w'}}^{w'=w_i} \alpha_{i,i}^{(w)(w')} + \sum_{\substack{w'=1 \\ w \neq w'}}^{w'=w_i} \beta_{i,i}^{(w)(w')}$$

$$+ \sum_{\substack{1 \leq \ell \leq i-1 \\ 1 \leq w' \leq w_\ell \\ j \in B}} \left(\alpha_{i,j}^{(w)(w')} + \beta_{j,i}^{(w)(w')} \right) + \sum_{\substack{i+1 \leq \ell \leq n \\ 1 \leq w' \leq w_\ell \\ j \in B}} \left(\alpha_{i,j}^{(w)(w')} + \beta_{j,i}^{(w)(w')} \right).$$

- **Phase 2D - Local Shares:** Party p_i executes locally the MtA protocol wi the local shares which are $(k_i^{(1)}, \ldots, k_i^{(w_i)})$ and $(\mathbf{x}_i^{(1)}, \ldots, \mathbf{x}_i^{(w_i)})$ to compute μ and ν such that $k_i^{(w)} \mathbf{x}_i^{(w')} = \mu_{i,i}^{(w)(w')} + \nu_{i,i}^{(w)(w')}$ for p_i and $1 \leq w, w' \leq w_i$.

- **Phase 2E - Online Shares:** Party p_i executes MtAwc protocol between its local shares $(k_i^{(1)}, \ldots, k_i^{(w_i)})$ and shares of the remaining parties except p_i:

$p_1, \ldots, p_{(i-1)}$	$p_{(i+1)}, \ldots, p_n$
$(\mathbf{x}_1^{(1)}, \ldots, \mathbf{x}_1^{(w_1)})$	$(\mathbf{x}_{i+1}^{(1)}, \ldots, \mathbf{x}_{i+1}^{(w_{i+1})})$
$\vdots$	$\vdots$
$(\mathbf{x}_{i-1}^{(1)}, \ldots, \mathbf{x}_{i-1}^{(w_{i-1})})$	$(\mathbf{x}_n^{(1)}, \ldots, \mathbf{x}_n^{(w_n)})$

Likewise the Local Shares, there will be two executions of the MtAwc protocol for each pair $k_i^{(w)}$ and $\mathbf{x}_i^{(w)}$, that is $k_i^{(w)} \mathbf{x}_j^{(w')} = \mu_{i,j}^{(w)(w')} + \nu_{j,i}^{(w)(w')}$.

- **Phase 2F:** Compute $\sigma_i^{(w)}$, for $1 \leq w \leq w_i$ and $1 \leq i \leq n$ the following values by summing the produced values from Steps 2D and 2E. Second and third terms from 2D, and the remaining terms from 2E:

$$\sigma_i^{(w)} = k_i^{(w)} \mathbf{x}_i^{(w)} + \sum_{\substack{w'=1 \\ w \neq w'}}^{w'=w_i} \mu_{i,i}^{(w)(w')} + \sum_{\substack{w'=1 \\ w \neq w'}}^{w'=w_i} \nu_{i,i}^{(w)(w')}$$

$$+ \sum_{\substack{1 \leq \ell \leq i-1 \\ 1 \leq w' \leq w_\ell \\ j \in B}} \left(\mu_{i,j}^{(w)(w')} + \nu_{j,i}^{(w)(w')} \right) + \sum_{\substack{i+1 \leq \ell \leq n \\ 1 \leq w' \leq w_\ell \\ j \in B}} \left(\mu_{i,j}^{(w)(w')} + \nu_{j,i}^{(w)(w')} \right).$$

- Phase 3: At this point each party p_i has two sets of values $(\delta_i^{(1)}, \ldots, \delta_i^{(w_i)})$ and $(\sigma_i^{(1)}, \ldots, \sigma_i^{(w_i)})$ from, respectively, Steps 2C and 2F. The party p_i broadcasts the former set, and all parties reconstruct the value $\delta = \sum_{\substack{w=1 \\ i \in B}}^{w=w_i} \delta_i^{(w)} = k \cdot \gamma$ (as defined in Step 1).
- Phase 4: Release w_i commitments computed in Step 1, and use them to compute the r as the first part of the signature.
  - Broadcast the values $D_i^{(w)}$ which open the commitments for $\Gamma_i^{(w)} = g^{\gamma_i^{(w)}}$
  - p_i proves in ZK the knowledge of $\gamma_i^{(w)}$ for $1 \leq w \leq w_i$
  - All compute

$$R = \left(\prod_{\substack{i \in B \\ 1 \leq w \leq w_i}} \Gamma_i^{(w)} \right)^{\delta^{-1}} = g^{\left(\sum_{\substack{i \in B \\ 1 \leq w \leq w_i}} \gamma_i^{(w)} \right) k^{-1} \gamma^{-1}} = g^{\gamma k^{-1} \gamma^{-1}} = g^{k^{-1}}$$

  - Compute the first half of the signature as $\mathrm{r} = R \mod p$
- Phase 5: Each player p_i computes $s_i^{(w)} = mk_i^{(w)} + r\sigma_i^{(w)}$, so each player p_i holds the set $(s_i^{(1)}, \ldots, s_i^{(w_i)})$ of shares of the second part of the signature.
- Phase 5A: To build the second half of the signature it is necessary to randomly sample and commit to two value sets:
  - Choose two sets of random values $(\ell_i^{(1)}, \ldots, \ell_i^{(w_i)})$ and $(\rho_i^{(1)}, \ldots, \rho_i^{(w_i)})$ such that $\ell_i^{(w)} \in \mathbb{Z}_p$ and $\rho_i^{(w)} \in \mathbb{Z}_p$.
  - Compute the set $(V_i^{(1)}, \ldots, V_i^{(w)})$ such that $V_i^{(w)} = r^{s_i^{(w)}} g^{\ell_i^{(w)}}$
  - Compute $(A_i^{(1)}, \ldots, A^{(w)_i})$ such that $A_i^{(w)} = g^{\rho_i^{(w)}}$
  - Compute the commitments $([\widehat{C}_i^{(1)}, \widehat{D}_i^{(1)}], \ldots, [\widehat{C}_i^{(w_i)}, \widehat{D}_i^{(w_i)}])$, such that $, (V_i^{(w)}, A_i^{(w)}) = [\widehat{C}_i^{(w)}, \widehat{D}_i^{(w)}]$
  - Broadcast $(\widehat{C}_i^{(1)}, \ldots, \widehat{C}_i^{(w_i)})$
- Phase 5B: Once all committed values were received, open the commits in order to joint compute V and A:
  - Broadcast $(\widehat{D}_i^{(1)}, \ldots, \widehat{D}_i^{(w_i)})$
  - Prove in ZK, for each value w, such that $1 \leq w \leq w_i$, the knowledge of $\ell_i^{(w)}$, $\rho_i^{(w)}$ and $s_i^{(w)}$ such that $V_i^{(w)} = R^{s_i^{(w)}} g^{\ell_i^{(w)}}$ and $A_i^{(w)} = g^{\rho_i^{(w)}}$
  - Compute:

$$V = g^{-m} \cdot (\mathrm{vk})^{-r} \cdot \prod_{\substack{i \in B \\ 1 \leq w \leq w_i}} V_i^{(w)}, A = \prod_{\substack{i \in B \\ 1 \leq w \leq w_i}} V_i^{(w)}$$

- Phase 5C: Like Step 5A, compute two sets of values $U_i^{(w)}$ and $T_i^{(w)}$ and prove the knowledge of them via ZK proofs. These values are used to guarantee consistency of the shares:
    - Compute the set $(U_i^{(1)}, \ldots, U_i^{(w_i)})$ such that $U_i^{(w)} = V^{\rho_i^w}$
    - Compute the set $(T_i^{(1)}, \ldots, T_i^{(w_i)})$ such that $T_i^{(w)} = A^{\ell_i^w}$
    - Compute the commitments $([\widetilde{C}_i^{(1)}, \widetilde{D}_i^{(1)}], \ldots, [\widetilde{C}_i^{(w_i)}, \widetilde{D}_i^{(w_i)}])$, such that $, (U_i^{(w)}, T_i^{(w)}) = [\widetilde{C}_i^{(w)}, \widetilde{D}_i^{(w)}]$
    - Broadcast $(\widetilde{C}_i^{(1)}, \ldots, \widetilde{C}_i^{(w_i)})$
- Phase 5D: Once the commitments are received, broadcasts their openings and verify the consistency of the shares:
    - Broadcast $(\widetilde{D}_i^{(1)}, \ldots, \widetilde{D}_i^{(w_i)})$
    - If $\prod_{\substack{i \in B \\ 1 \leq w \leq w_i}} T_i^{(w)} \neq \prod_{\substack{i \in B \\ 1 \leq w \leq w_i}} U_i^{(w)}$, then abort
- Phase 5E: Broadcast the shares of the second half of the signature, and reconstruct it:
    - Broadcast the set $(s_i^{(1)}, \ldots, s_i^{(w_i)})$
    - Compute the second signature share as $s = \sum_{\substack{i \in B \\ 1 \leq w \leq w_i}} s_i$. If (r, s) is not a valid signature, then abort.

4.3 Identifiable Abort

Here we describe the changes required to provide identifiable abort capability considering weights as it is used in our proposed construction. As mentioned earlier, weights can be also introduced in the extended version of [16]; we note that weights can be similarly applied to the scheme of [6], which extends [16]. The changes yield a similar construction as the one presented earlier, and affect only Phase 3, and the substitution of the Phases 5, 5A, 5B, 5C, 5D and 5E, to new Phases 5, 6 and 7. Identification follows similarly to [16], therefore we refer the reader to that work for a full description of the procedure.

Concretely, for the new phases with weights below, consider $w \in \{1, \ldots, w_i\}$:

- Phase 3:
    - All parties reconstruct $\delta = \sum_{\substack{w=1 \\ i \in B}}^{w=w_i} \delta_i^{(w)} = k \cdot \gamma$ and compute $\delta^{-1} \mod p$
    - Compute $(T_i^{(1)}, \ldots, T_i^{(w_i)})$ such that $T_i^{(w)} = g^{\sigma_i^{(w)}} h^{\ell_i^{(w)}}$, and provide a ZK proof of knowledge of $(\ell_i^{(1)}, \ldots, \ell_i^{(w_i)})$ and $(\sigma_i^{(1)}, \ldots, \sigma_i^{(w_i)})$
- Phase 5: All players broadcast $\widetilde{R}_i^{(w)} = R^{k_i^{(w)}}$ and a ZK proof of range (as the ones sent in the MtA on Phase 2) between $R_i^{(w)}$ and $E_i(k_i^{(w)})$. If $g \neq \prod_{\substack{i \in B \\ 1 \leq w \leq w_i}} \widetilde{R}_i^{(w)}$, the protocol aborts.
- Phase 6: All parties broadcast $S_i^{(w)} = R^{\sigma_i^{(w)}}$ and a ZK knowledge proof (as in Phase 3) between $S_i^{(w)}$ and $T_i^{(w)}$. If $y \neq \prod_{\substack{i \in B \\ 1 \leq w \leq w_i}} S_i^{(w)}$, the protocol aborts.
- Phase 7: Each player broadcasts $s_i^{(w)} = m k_i^{(w)} + r \sigma_i^{(w)}$ and sets $s = \sum_{\substack{i \in B \\ 1 \leq w \leq w_i}} s_i$. If (r, s) is not a valid signature, abort.

5 Conclusion

Our work explores a novel design for collective stake pools for Proof-of-Stake ledgers, i.e., pools without a central operator. Our first contribution is a security definition for collective stake pools, which takes the form of the ideal functionality $\mathcal{F}_{pool}$ that articulates the security properties and functions that a collective pool should offer. Following, we propose the concrete protocol *Conclave* which UC-realizes $\mathcal{F}_{pool}$. Our construction incorporates a load balancing mechanism for transaction verification, to boost performance, as well as a Weighted Threshold Signature Scheme (WTSS). Regarding the latter, we present the ideal functionality $\mathcal{F}_{wtss}$ (Sect. 2) that formalizes this new definition and might be of independent interest, and propose two constructions based on threshold ECDSA. We stress that the collective pool is modular and agnostic to the WTSS implementation, so any scheme that securely realizes $\mathcal{F}_{wtss}$ suffices.

Our design satisfies most of the desiderata outlined in Sect. 1. Some (e.g., pool proportional rewards or stake reallocation) are dependent on the underlying ledger system's details, therefore are outside of our scope; nevertheless, our design does not pose restrictions in capturing them. The reward functionality Γ_{reward} handles the reward-specific desiderata, while $\mathcal{F}_{pool}$'s first part (Fig. 3) covers the requirements for permissioned access and closing of the pool. However, $\mathcal{F}_{pool}$'s handling of stake reallocation and updating of the pool's parameters could be more dynamic, as it currently requires closing and re-creating a pool with the new parameters; a more efficient design is an interesting direction for future research. Additionally, an improvement to the WTSS scheme of Sect. 4, which would be directly applicable by π_{pool}, could assign a single weighted share to each party, instead of using multiple shares depending on each party's weight.

References

1. Almansa, J.F., Damgård, I., Nielsen, J.B.: Simplified threshold RSA with adaptive and proactive security. In: Vaudenay, S. (ed.) EUROCRYPT 2006. LNCS, vol. 4004, pp. 593–611. Springer, Heidelberg (2006). https://doi.org/10.1007/11761679_35
2. Badertscher, C., Gazi, P., Kiayias, A., Russell, A., Zikas, V.: Ouroboros genesis: composable proof-of-stake blockchains with dynamic availability. In: Lie, D., et al. (eds.) 25th Conference on Computer and Communications Security, ACM CCS 2018, pp. 913–930 (2018). https://doi.org/10.1145/3243734.3243848
3. Brünjes, L., Kiayias, A., Koutsoupias, E., Stouka, A.: Reward sharing schemes for stake pools. In: IEEE European Symposium on Security and Privacy, EuroS&P 2020, Genoa, Italy, 7–11 September 2020, pp. 256–275. IEEE (2020). https://doi.org/10.1109/EuroSP48549.2020.00024
4. Canetti, R.: Universally composable security: a new paradigm for cryptographic protocols. Cryptology ePrint Archive, Report 2000/067 (2000). https://eprint.iacr.org/2000/067
5. Canetti, R.: Universally composable signatures, certification and authentication. Cryptology ePrint Archive, Report 2003/239 (2003). https://eprint.iacr.org/2003/239

6. Canetti, R., Gennaro, R., Goldfeder, S., Makriyannis, N., Peled, U.: UC non-interactive, proactive, threshold ECDSA with identifiable aborts. In: Ligatti, J., Ou, X., Katz, J., Vigna, G. (eds.) 27th Conference on Computer and Communications Security, ACM CCS 20, Virtual Event, USA, 9–13 November 2020, pp. 1769–1787. ACM Press (2020). https://doi.org/10.1145/3372297.3423367

7. Community, E.: Eos.io technical white paper v2 (2018). https://github.com/EOSIO/Documentation/blob/master/TechnicalWhitePaper.md

8. Daian, P., Pass, R., Shi, E.: Snow white: robustly reconfigurable consensus and applications to provably secure proof of stake. In: Goldberg, I., Moore, T. (eds.) FC 2019. LNCS, vol. 11598, pp. 23–41. Springer, Cham (2019). https://doi.org/10.1007/978-3-030-32101-7_2

9. David, B., Gaži, P., Kiayias, A., Russell, A.: Ouroboros praos: an adaptively-secure, semi-synchronous proof-of-stake blockchain. In: Nielsen, J.B., Rijmen, V. (eds.) EUROCRYPT 2018. LNCS, vol. 10821, pp. 66–98. Springer, Cham (2018). https://doi.org/10.1007/978-3-319-78375-8_3

10. decred.org: Decred—an autonomous digital currency (2019). https://decred.org

11. Défago, X., Schiper, A., Urbán, P.: Total order broadcast and multicast algorithms: taxonomy and survey. ACM Comput. Surv. (CSUR) **36**(4), 372–421 (2004)

12. Dolev, D., Strong, H.R.: Authenticated algorithms for Byzantine agreement. SIAM J. Comput. **12**(4), 656–666 (1983)

13. Fanti, G., Kogan, L., Oh, S., Ruan, K., Viswanath, P., Wang, G.: Compounding of wealth in proof-of-stake cryptocurrencies. In: Goldberg, I., Moore, T. (eds.) FC 2019. LNCS, vol. 11598, pp. 42–61. Springer, Cham (2019). https://doi.org/10.1007/978-3-030-32101-7_3

14. Garay, J.A., Katz, J., Kumaresan, R., Zhou, H.S.: Adaptively secure broadcast, revisited. In: Gavoille, C., Fraigniaud, P. (eds.) 30th ACM Symposium Annual on Principles of Distributed Computing, San Jose, CA, USA, 6–8 June 2011, pp. 179–186. Association for Computing Machinery (2011). https://doi.org/10.1145/1993806.1993832

15. Gennaro, R., Goldfeder, S.: Fast multiparty threshold ECDSA with fast trustless setup. In: Lie, D., Mannan, M., Backes, M., Wang, X. (eds.) 25th Conference on Computer and Communications Security, ACM CCS 2018, Toronto, ON, Canada, 15–19 October 2018, pp. 1179–1194. ACM Press (2020). https://doi.org/10.1145/3243734.3243859

16. Gennaro, R., Goldfeder, S.: One round threshold ECDSA with identifiable abort. Cryptology ePrint Archive, Report 2020/540 (2020). https://eprint.iacr.org/2020/540

17. Gilad, Y., Hemo, R., Micali, S., Vlachos, G., Zeldovich, N.: Algorand: scaling Byzantine agreements for cryptocurrencies. In: Proceedings of the 26th Symposium on Operating Systems Principles, Shanghai, China, 28–31 October 2017, pp. 51–68. ACM (2017). https://doi.org/10.1145/3132747.3132757

18. Goldberg, I., Moore, T. (eds.): 23rd International Conference on Financial Cryptography and Data Security, FC 2019. Lecture Notes in Computer Science, Frigate Bay, St. Kitts and Nevis, 18–22 February 2019, vol. 11598. Springer, Heidelberg (2019)

19. Goodman, L.: Tezos—a self-amending crypto-ledger white paper (2014)

20. Hirt, M., Zikas, V.: Adaptively secure broadcast. In: Gilbert, H. (ed.) EUROCRYPT 2010. LNCS, vol. 6110, pp. 466–485. Springer, Heidelberg (2010). https://doi.org/10.1007/978-3-642-13190-5_24

21. Karakostas, D., Kiayias, A., Larangeira, M.: Account management in proof of stake ledgers. In: Galdi, C., Kolesnikov, V. (eds.) SCN 2020. LNCS, vol. 12238, pp. 3–23. Springer, Cham (2020). https://doi.org/10.1007/978-3-030-57990-6_1
22. Karakostas, D., Kiayias, A., Larangeira, M.: Conclave: a collective stake pool protocol. Cryptology ePrint Archive, Report 2021/742 (2021). https://ia.cr/2021/742
23. OI Karakostas, D., Kiayias, A., Nasikas, C., Zindros, D.: Cryptocurrency egalitarianism: a quantitative approach. In: Danos, V., Herlihy, M., Potop-Butucaru, M., Prat, J., Piergiovanni, S.T. (eds.) International Conference on Blockchain Economics, Security and Protocols, Tokenomics 2019, Paris, France, 6-7 May 2019, OASIcs, vol. 71, pp. 7:1–7:21. Schloss Dagstuhl - Leibniz-Zentrum für Informatik (2019). https://doi.org/10.4230/OASIcs.Tokenomics.2019.7
24. Kerber, T., Kiayias, A., Kohlweiss, M.: Kachina - foundations of private smart contracts. In: 2021 IEEE 34th Computer Security Foundations Symposium (CSF), Los Alamitos, CA, USA, pp. 47–62. IEEE Computer Society (June 2021). https://doi.org/10.1109/CSF51468.2021.00002
25. Kerber, T., Kiayias, A., Kohlweiss, M., Zikas, V.: Ouroboros Crypsinous: privacy-preserving proof-of-stake. In: 2019 IEEE Symposium on Security and Privacy, San Francisco, CA, USA, 19–23 May 2019, pp. 157–174. IEEE Computer Society Press (2019). https://doi.org/10.1109/SP.2019.00063
26. Kiayias, A., Russell, A., David, B., Oliynykov, R.: Ouroboros: a provably secure proof-of-stake blockchain protocol. In: Katz, J., Shacham, H. (eds.) CRYPTO 2017. LNCS, vol. 10401, pp. 357–388. Springer, Cham (2017). https://doi.org/10.1007/978-3-319-63688-7_12
27. Kokoris-Kogias, E., Jovanovic, P., Gailly, N., Khoffi, I., Gasser, L., Ford, B.: Enhancing bitcoin security and performance with strong consistency via collective signing. In: Holz, T., Savage, S. (eds.) 25th USENIX Security Symposium, USENIX Security 2016, Austin, TX, USA, 10–12 August 2016, pp. 279–296. USENIX Association (2016)
28. Lamport, L., Shostak, R., Pease, M.: The byzantine generals problem. ACM Trans. Program. Lang. Syst. (TOPLAS) 4(3), 382–401 (1982)
29. Lie, D., Mannan, M., Backes, M., Wang, X. (eds.): 25th Conference on Computer and Communications Security, ACM CCS 2018, Toronto, ON, Canada, 15–19 October 2018. ACM Press (2018)
30. Luu, L., Velner, Y., Teutsch, J., Saxena, P.: SmartPool: practical decentralized pooled mining. In: Kirda, E., Ristenpart, T. (eds.) 26th USENIX Security Symposium, USENIX Security 2017, Vancouver, BC, Canada, 16–18 August 2017, pp. 1409–1426. USENIX Association (2017)
31. Nakamoto, S.: Bitcoin: a peer-to-peer electronic cash system (2008)
32. Pass, R., Shi, E.: The sleepy model of consensus. In: Takagi, T., Peyrin, T. (eds.) ASIACRYPT 2017. LNCS, vol. 10625, pp. 380–409. Springer, Cham (2017). https://doi.org/10.1007/978-3-319-70697-9_14
33. Pease, M., Shostak, R., Lamport, L.: Reaching agreement in the presence of faults. J. ACM (JACM) 27(2), 228–234 (1980)
34. Poupard, G., Stern, J.: Short proofs of knowledge for factoring. In: Imai, H., Zheng, Y. (eds.) PKC 2000. LNCS, vol. 1751, pp. 147–166. Springer, Heidelberg (2000). https://doi.org/10.1007/978-3-540-46588-1_11
35. Reed, D.D., Luiselli, J.K.: Temporal discounting. In: Goldstein, S., Naglieri, J.A. (eds.) Encyclopedia of Child Behavior and Development. Springer, Boston (2011). https://doi.org/10.1007/978-0-387-79061-9_3162
36. Wood, G.: Ethereum yellow paper (2014)

Probabilistic Micropayments with Transferability

Taisei Takahashi[✉] and Akira Otsuka

Institute of Information Security, Yokohama, Japan
{dgs194102,otsuka}@iisec.ac.jp

Abstract. Micropayments are one of the challenges in cryptocurrencies. The problems in realizing micropayments in the blockchain are the low throughput and the high blockchain transaction fee. As a solution, decentralized probabilistic micropayment has been proposed. The winning amount is registered in the blockchain, and the tickets are issued to be won with probability p, which allows us to aggregate approximately $1/p$ transactions into one. Unfortunately, existing solutions do not allow for ticket transferability, and the smaller p, the more difficult it to use them in the real world. We propose a novel decentralized probabilistic micropayment *Transferable Scheme*. It allows tickets to be transferable among users. By allowing tickets to be transferable, we can make p smaller. We also propose a novel *Proportional Fee Scheme*. This is a scheme where each time a ticket is transferred, a portion of the blockchain transaction fee will be charged. With the proportional fee scheme, users will have the advantage of sending money with a smaller fee than they would generally send through the blockchain. For example, sending one dollar requires only ten cents.

Keywords: Blockchain · Micropayment · Transferability · Tamper-proof wallet

1 Introduction

Micropayments are minimal payments, e.g., less than $1, and can be used in a wide range of applications, such as per-page billing in e-book and deliver contents billed per minute. However, it is challenging to realize micropayments in the blockchain.

The problems in realizing micropayments in the blockchain are the low throughput and the high blockchain transaction fee. Since the capacity of each block is fixed, miners give priority to transactions that can generate high fees and put off micropayment transactions with low fees. In addition, the blockchain transaction fees do not depend on the amount of money to be transferred. Thus, the blockchain transaction fees can be relatively small for high-value transfers but high for micropayments.

The above problems can be solved by Layer-two [6]. Instead of registering all transactions in the blockchain, Layer-two aggregates small transactions into

© Springer Nature Switzerland AG 2021
E. Bertino et al. (Eds.): ESORICS 2021, LNCS 12972, pp. 390–406, 2021.
https://doi.org/10.1007/978-3-030-88418-5_19

a few larger ones, which can increase transaction throughput and reduce transaction fees. Decentralized probabilistic micropayments have been proposed as one of the methods for Layer-two. It is a lottery-based scheme, the amount of required payments is locked in an escrow, and micropayments are issued as lottery tickets. Let the winning amount be β, and the winning probability is p, the expected value per lottery ticket is $p \cdot \beta$, and the ticket is used as currency. Probabilistic micropayments allow us to aggregate the entire transactions by approximately p. As an example, if $10,000$ transactions are to be processed by a probabilistic micropayments scheme, only $10,000 \cdot p$ will be registered in the blockchain.

Almashaqbeh et al. have proposed MicroCash [2] which is a lightweight protocol for non-interactive and sequential payments. The disadvantage of MicroCash is that the game theory guarantees safety against double-spending attacks. Thus, the penalty escrow, which is confiscated with the double-spending attack is discovered, is expensive. As an example, when $m = 5$ and $B_{escrow} = 2000$, the penalty escrow is $B_{penalty} = 477.6$. In addition, tickets can only be sent once by the ticket issuer; in other words, the tickets can not be *transferable*.

As MicroCash, when safety is constructed using an only game-theoretic approach, considering penalty escrow, the number of beneficiary users who can receive the ticket, u, is realistically constrained to about 5. If we make u large, we need to make the penalty escrow large in proportion to u. As an alternative plan, if we assume the situation that the users can not commit malicious activity, such as tamper-resistant assumption, u can be large without penalty escrow. However, the smaller p is, the higher the gambling potential becomes and the less the payee can use it for actual economic transactions. If many tickets with a minimal winning probability are sent and not winning, the beneficiary merchants can not make any income. This is because if the ticket can not be transferable, the payee will not earn any income unless the ticket they received wins. The smaller p, the more the opportunity to get an income is lost.

If the ticket is *transferable*, p can be reduced. The payees does not lose anything since the ticket can be used to pay others even if the ticket is not won. However, it is challenging to achieve transferability with existing solutions. Since if the ticket is transferable, the double-spending attacks can be performed by the issuer and all users. Requiring game-theoretically guaranteed penalty escrow for all users is practically undesirable because of high collateral costs. Suppose the ticket transfer is limited to a tamper-proof device, malicious activities that deviate from the protocol can be prevented, and transferability can be achieved without the need for high penalty escrow.

1.1   Contribution

We propose a novel decentralized probabilistic micropayments, *Transferable Scheme*, which allows tickets to be transferable among users. Instead of a game-theoretic approach, we introduce a tamper-proof assumption, which states that all users can only issue, send, and receive tickets through tamper-proof wallets created by trusted manufactures.

Theoretically, users are not able to perform double-spending attacks through tamper-proof wallets. However, it is not possible to assume tamper-proof completely. In reality, a tamper-proof device can be broken, and a double-spending attack can be performed. For this reason, in this study, instead of assuming a tamper-proof wallet and eliminating the need for penalty escrow, we force adversaries to weigh the cost of breaking a tamper-proof wallet against the maximum expected value that can be obtained from the attack. As long as the expected value does not exceed the cost, there will be no incentives for an adversary to perform the attack. Furthermore, we propose a mechanism to detect the attack with probability $p = 1$, and that the adversary's wallet address is unavailable when the attack is detected. This creates a need for an adversary to weigh the cost of breaking the wallet against the expected utility gain of a single attack.

Furthermore, we propose a novel *Proportional Fee Scheme*. This scheme is where each user who sends and receives a ticket bears a small portion of the blockchain transaction fee required when the ticket is won. This makes it possible for payment with a smaller fee than in the blockchain.

1.2   Organization of This Paper

This paper is structured as follows: Sect. 2 surveys the works related to our proposed scheme. Section 3 outlines our payment scheme, and Sect. 4 presents the ticket winning condition. In Sect. 5 we introduce our new payment fee scheme, "Proportional Fee Scheme," and Sect. 5 presents the security design.

2   Background

Payment Channels and Networks. The payment channel establishes a private, peer-to-peer transmission protocol. Based on pre-defined rules, two parties can agree to update their state and transfer money by exchanging authenticated state transitions in a so-called 'off-chain' fashion.

In order to conduct a transaction on *Payment Channel*, two parties must first register a shared 2-of-2 multi-sig escrow fund in the blockchain and establish the channel. The payment channel enables the two parties to perform transactions through private communications. After the sending and receiving are completed in the channel, the final fixed value is registered in the blockchain. Only two transactions are registered in the blockchain per channel, escrow fund transaction, and final fixed value. A payer can send money to a user who has not established a channel with the payer through the *Payment Network* between users who have established a channel. For example, suppose Alice sends 0.1 coins to Charlie, who has not established a channel with Alice. First, Alice sends 0.1 coins to Bob, whom Alice has a channel. Next, Bob sends 0.1 coins to Charlie, whom Bob has a channel.

Unfortunately, the payment channel and the network have the disadvantage of high collateral cost [8]. Each time a channel is established, escrow is required between two parties. Also, the longer the payment network path, the more reserves are required and locked. Since the reserves can not be used during the locktime periods, the reserves represent a lost opportunity. Furthermore, in a payment network, a fee is charged for each pass through the nodes. It is impractical to adopt a payment network for micropayments since it is undesirable to incur the cost for each node.

Probabilistic Micropayment. The idea of probabilistic micropayments has been proposed by Wheeler [12] and Rivest [10]. Since small payments would be costly if settled each time, they proposed a lottery-style protocol where the ticket issuer deposit a large amount of money in the bank, and the winner could receive the money if they won. The lottery tickets can be used as currency, and the value per ticket is regarded as the expected value of the ticket. In this scheme, the existence of a bank is mandatory, and participants are limited to people who have a relationship with the bank.

MICROPAY [9] and DAM [4] have been proposed as decentralized probabilistic micropayments using blockchain. Since both have a large overhead of supporting sequential micropayments, Almashaqbeh et al. have proposed MicroCash which is a light-weight protocol for non-interactive and sequential payments.

The drawback of existing solutions is that the lottery ticket can only be sent from the ticket issuer to the recipient. Also, because of game-theoretic suppression of double-spending attacks, the penalty escrow increases proportionally with the number of recipients. Furthermore, the smaller the probability of winning p, the higher the gambling potentials becomes, and the more unstable the income-earning opportunity for the recipient.

Secure Offline Payment. The double-spending attack on fast payment is one of the fatal architectural problems in cryptocurrencies [7]. Dmitrienko et al. proposed an offline fast payment scheme that relies on tamper-proof wallets produced by trustworthy manufacturers. However, their scheme requires a trusted online time-stamp server. Takahashi et al. [11] overcome this drawback and proposed a protocol that allows secure offline payment using tamper-proof device wallet.

3 Ticket Transfer Overview

This section presents the design of our transferable scheme. We start with an outline of the lottery ticket transaction, followed by a detailed description of each part.

3.1 Outline

The outline of the system is shown in Fig. 1.

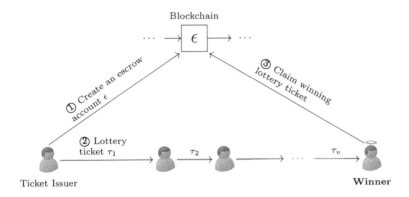

Fig. 1. Overall design

Step 1, The issuer issues a smart contract escrow account ϵ and registers and confirms that ϵ has been registered in the blockchain. **Step 2**, The issuer issues the ticket τ for probabilistic micropayments and sends it to a user. The payee verifies that the ticket came from a legitimate wallet and that the escrow account is properly registered in the blockchain. If there is no problem, the user receives the ticket and returns the service or product to the payer. Then, the payee signs the ticket with his wallet and sends it to another user. **Step 3**, If the ticket received meets the requirements for winning, the ticket is sent to the escrow account ϵ.

The sequence of procedures in this scheme, such as ticket issuance and payment with the ticket, is done using a tamper-proof wallet.

Tamper-Proof Wallet. The premise is that all users participating in the transferable scheme have tamper-proof hardware wallets.

The wallet consists of a tamper-proof device manufactured by a trusted manufacturer. It does not accept any unauthorized operation that deviates from the protocol, such as double-spent tickets.

There are two keys in the wallet. One is a key for personal use key pairs (sk^{Wx}, PK^{Wx}) for sending and receiving the ticket, we denote the hash value of PK^{Wx} be the "address" associated with the wallet owner. The other is a secret key sk^T used to prove that the ticket was created and sent from a legitimate wallet. Additionally, the wallet owner possesses a certificate $cert_T$ corresponding to the private key sk_T.

3.2 Escrow Setup

The flow diagram is shown in Fig. 2. The issuer X requests a new account w_X from the wallet (Step 1), then create the escrow transaction τ_l transferring β coins from the account x to the wallet address w_X and commit it to the networks (Step 2). As soon as τ_l is verified and integrated into the Blockchain network in

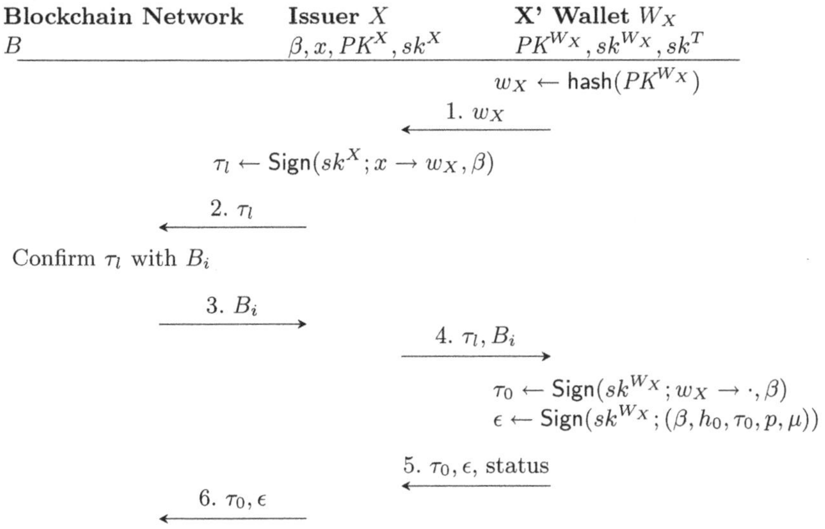

Blockchain Network   Issuer X **X' Wallet** W_X
B β, x, PK^X, sk^X PK^{W_X}, sk^{W_X}, sk^T

$$w_X \leftarrow \mathsf{hash}(PK^{W_X})$$

$$\xleftarrow{\quad 1.\ w_X \quad}$$

$$\tau_l \leftarrow \mathsf{Sign}(sk^X; x \rightarrow w_X, \beta)$$

$$\xleftarrow{\quad 2.\ \tau_l \quad}$$

Confirm τ_l with B_i

$$\xrightarrow{\quad 3.\ B_i \quad}$$

$$\xrightarrow{\quad 4.\ \tau_l, B_i \quad}$$

$$\tau_0 \leftarrow \mathsf{Sign}(sk^{W_X}; w_X \rightarrow \cdot, \beta)$$
$$\epsilon \leftarrow \mathsf{Sign}(sk^{W_X}; (\beta, h_0, \tau_0, p, \mu))$$

$$\xleftarrow{\quad 5.\ \tau_0, \epsilon,\ \text{status} \quad}$$

$$\xleftarrow{\quad 6.\ \tau_0, \epsilon \quad}$$

Fig. 2. Escrow setup

a block, say B_i, X takes B_i (Step 3), and provides τ_l and B_i to W_X (Step 4). W create the escrow account ϵ. Then, sends it to X with status (Step 5). Finally, X sends τ_0 and ϵ to the Blockchain network.[1]

3.3 Payment with Lottery Ticket

The flow diagram is shown in Fig. 3. In the payment with lottery ticket phase, the payee Y sends PK^{W_Y} (Step 1). The wallet W_X creates a ticket τ_1 and signs it with the private key sk^{W_X}, and signs the ticket τ_1 with the wallet manufacturer's private key sk^T. The wallet W_X sends ticket τ_1, $proof_1$, and $cert^T$ to the payee' wallet W_Y (Step 2). If all checks succeed, Y stores τ_1, $proof_1$, and replies to W_X with the status (Step 3). If the payee Y wants to send the received ticket to another user, the same procedure is followed from Step 1.

3.4 Ticket Winning and Revocation

The flow diagram is shown in Fig. 4. If $\tau \in$ win, Y sends τ and *proof* to the contract account ϵ (Step 1). If τ is both valid and eligible, the escrow account ϵ signs the escrow transaction τ_0 with w_Y as the destination. The payee Y observes the blockchain network and periodically updates its local chain and confirms τ_0 is valid (Step 2).

---

[1] The wallet does not check the validity of the escrow transaction τ_0 and ϵ. Payees will reject the ticket which is not transferred from ϵ.

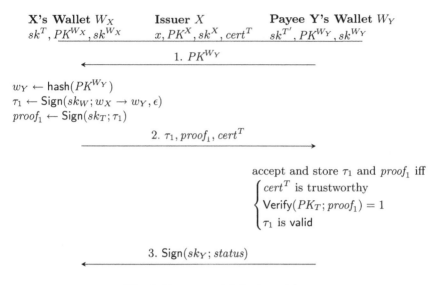

Fig. 3. Payment with lottery tickets

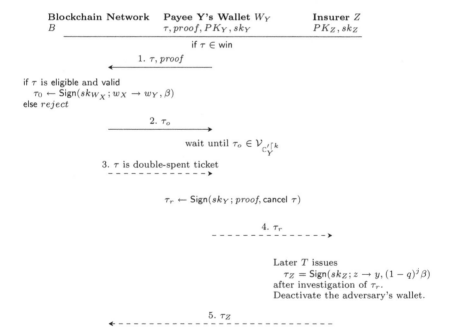

Fig. 4. Ticket redemption and double-spending wallet revocation protocol

If τ is one of the double-spent tickets created by a double-spending attack, the contract account ϵ shows that τ is double-spend one (Step 3).[2] Y initiates revocation by creating a revocation transaction $\tau_r = \mathsf{Sign}(sk_Y; proof, \mathsf{cancel}\ \tau)$ and send it to Insurer Z (Step 4). Z investigate τ_r and in order to compensate Y for the damage, issues τ_Z then committed to the Bitcoin network (Step 5).[3]

4   Ticket Winning Condition

- $\mathbb{C}$: a blockchain.
- $\mathcal{U}$: a set of users.
- $X, Y \in \mathcal{U}$: (typically, X as a payer, Y as a payee).
- l: the number of double-spent (duplicated) tickets by an adversary
- ϵ: escrow account which has several fields: $(\beta, h_0, \tau_0, p, \mu)$
  - β: the lottery winning amount
  - h_0: the block height containing the escrow account
  - τ_0: escrow creation transaction
  - p: the probability for determining of winning a ticket
  - μ: the fixed number to calculate the winning ticket$(\in \mathbb{N})$
- τ: a lottery ticket which has several fields: $(A, B, \tau_{pre}, \sigma)$
  - A: a sender
  - B: a receiver
  - τ_{pre}: a reference to a previous ticket or to an escrow account ϵ
  - σ: signature by a sender
- Φ: the cost of breaking a tamper-proof hardware wallet
- γ: the blockchain transaction fee

4.1   Structure of the Ticket

This section describes the structure of the lottery ticket and the design of the ticket winning method. If the ticket is transferable, a blockchain transaction fee is charged when the ticket is won and registered in the blockchain. We introduce a scheme where users who send and receive the ticket share the blockchain transaction fee little by little.

Definition 1. *A lottery tickets τ consists of a fivefold:*

$$\left(A, B, \tau_{pre}, \sigma^W, \sigma^T, cert^T\right) \tag{1}$$

where A and B are accounts of a sender and a receiver, respectively. τ_{pre} is a reference to a previous ticket or to an escrow account ϵ. A pair of signatures, σ^W and σ^T, is a multi-signature, where σ^W is signed with a signing key tied with a sender's account and σ^T is signed with a tamper-proof device's signing key to

---

[2] Double-spending attacks can be perfectly detected, and the adversary's address is discovered. See Sect. 6.

[3] The compensated amount is the same as the return when received the ticket. See Sect. 5 for the value of a ticket when it is in transfer.

prove that the signing device is trusted verifiable with a certificate $cert^T$ issued by a trusted manufacturer. We denote by σ_A to denote a signature signed by A. The escrow account ϵ further contains $(\beta, h_0, \tau_0, p, \mu)$ to specify the parameters of the transferable transaction, where β is the ticket winning amount, and h_0 is the block height to specify particular VDF values. τ_0 is the escrow creation transaction. p is the probability for determining of winning a ticket. μ is a fixed value used to determine the winning ticket.

For readability, we write a ticket τ as:

$$\tau = (A \rightarrow B, \tau_{pre})_X. \tag{2}$$

We define $|\tau|$ the "number of generations" of τ, which is the length of the sequence from ϵ to τ. For example, $|\tau| = n$ if there exists a sequence $\tau_1, \ldots, \tau_{n-1}$ such that $\epsilon \prec \tau_1 \prec \tau_2 \prec \cdots \prec \tau_{n-1} \prec \tau$. We define $|\tau| = \infty$ if no such sequence exists.[4] To write compactly, we denote by τ_i the i-th generation of τ.

Definition 2 (Transferred transaction). *Two tickets $\tau_i = (A \rightarrow B, \tau_{pre})_X$ and $\tau_{i+1} = (A' \rightarrow B', \tau'_{pre})_{X'}$ are said to be **transferred** if and only if following properties satisfies:*

$$\begin{cases} H(\tau_i) = \tau'_{pre} \\ A = X, \ B = A' = X' \\ cert^T_{X'} \text{ is trustworthy} \\ multi - signature \ \sigma^W_{X'} \text{ and } \sigma^T_{X'} \text{ are valid} \end{cases} \tag{3}$$

Then, we write $\tau_i \prec \tau_{i+1}$.

We write $\tau_i \lll \tau_{i+n}$ if there exists a sequence of ordered lottery tickets $\tau'_1 \prec \ldots \prec \tau'_n$ for $n \geq 1$ and they satisfy $\tau_i \prec \tau'_1$ and $\tau'_n \prec \tau_{i+n}$. In the case where τ has no previous lottery tickets, the ticket is called a 'genesis' ticket. For the genesis tickets τ_1 tied to an escrow account ϵ, we specially denote by $\epsilon \prec \tau_1$ so that a lottery tickets are simply written as:

$$\epsilon \prec \tau_1 \prec \tau_2 \prec \ldots \prec \tau_n. \tag{4}$$

Definition 3. *A lottery tickets τ is said to be valid with respect to a blockchain $\mathbb{C}$ for some security parameter k if and only if there exists an escrow account ϵ and a sequence of transactions $\tau_{i,1}, \ldots, \tau_{i,n}$ such that*

$$\epsilon \in \mathbb{C}^{\lceil k} \quad and \quad \epsilon \prec \tau_1 \prec \ldots \prec \tau_n \prec \tau. \tag{5}$$

$\mathbb{C}^{\lceil k}$ denotes the set of blocks that are k or more blocks before the beginning of the blockchain. This notion is borrowed from Garay et al. [5].

---

[4] For practical purposes, we assume that the height of τ can only be measured when all tickets in the sequence from ϵ to τ are given. Even if such sequence exists, the height of τ is considered to be ∞ unless the entire sequence is specifically presented.

4.2   Ticket Winning Condition

This section describes the design of the ticket winnings.

Definition 4. *$\tau_{i,v}$ is said to be* win *if and only if the following properties satisfies:*

$$\text{win} = \left\{ \tau_v \mid p : H\left(\text{VDF}(h_0 + v \cdot \mu)\right) < D \; for all v \in \mathbb{N} \right\} \tag{6}$$

where v is the number of generations of τ and μ is the fixed number specified in the escrow account ϵ.

h_0 is registered in ϵ, which specifies the block height at which ϵ would be registered. The probability p is calculated using a simple Verifiable Delay Function (VDF) [3]. The calculation can be done after a certain period of time has elapsed from when the ticket is transferred according to the number of generations. For example, if a ticket with $h_0 = 100$, $\mu = 5$, and $v = 3$ is received, the VDF value will be known when the block height of 115 is confirmed.

As described in the next Subsect. 5, even though the ticket meets the requirements win, the ticket may be used as payment instead of getting the winning amount β. If a ticket $\tau \in$ win has already been transferred, the user with the most recent ownership can get the winning amount β.

Definition 5. *τ_v is said to be* eligible *if and only if the following properties satisfies:*

$$\text{eligible} = \left\{ \tau_{v'} \mid \tau_{v'} = \max(\{\tau_{v''}|v'' \geq v\}) \right\} \tag{7}$$

eligible ticket will be considered as the final winning ticket. Thus, the user who has the eligible ticket can get β from the escrow account ϵ.

Fig. 5. Proportional fee scheme

5   Proportional Fee Scheme

In this section, we consider the blockchain transaction fee to transfer the winning amount to the winner's address and the value of the ticket in the transfer process.

In our transferable scheme, it is not beneficial for the issuer to bear the blockchain transaction fee. Since when the issuer bears the blockchain transaction fee, the amount available for payment is $\beta - \gamma$, which does not provide any advantage for the issuer to use the transferable scheme.

We propose a novel *Proportional Fee Scheme*. The process is depicted in Fig. 5. This scheme is where each time a payer transfers a ticket, the payer borne the fee based on the number of generations of the ticket. When a payer sends τ_j to the payee, in return, the payee gives goods or services worth $(1-q)^j\beta$.

Definition 6 (Proportional fee scheme). *Let q be the lottery ticket transaction fee rate. Suppose a payer sends a ticket τ_i, in return the payee gives goods or services worth $(1 - q)^i\beta$ to the sender. The fees borne by the payment is $(1 - q)^{i-1}q\beta$.*

Specifically, the fee for each payment is $\tau_{i-1} - \tau_i = (1-q)^{i-1}q\beta$, and the profit (income − expenditure) when τ_i = eligible is $\beta - (\tau_i + \gamma) = (1 - (1 - q)^i)\beta - \gamma$ where γ is the blockchain transaction fee.

Suppose the ticket satisfies the win condition before the accumulated fees exceed the blockchain transaction fee γ. In this case, the user may decide whether to send it to the blockchain network and get β or transfer the ticket to another user as payment. Specifically, the user can profit from the eligible ticket by getting the winning amount β under the following condition:

$$(1 - (1 - q)^i)\beta > \gamma. \tag{8}$$

If the ticket satisfies the win condition is transferred to another user, the ticket is distributed as eligible and can be sent to the blockchain in any subsequent generation. Naturally, the ticket will be sent to the blockchain network in the generation that satisfies the Eq. 8.

This scheme has the advantage that the payment fee can be smaller than the blockchain transaction fee. The average transaction fee for cryptocurrencies, especially Bitcoin, is around $11 to $15 [1].

In our transferable scheme, let $\beta = \$100$, $p = \frac{1}{100}$ and $q = \frac{1}{10}$, the ticket value per generation is depicted in Fig. 6. As we can see from Fig. 6b, the value of the ticket falls below $1 from approximately $i = 50$. Figure 7 shows the frequency of the fee, and we can see that there are more than 50 transactions whose value is less than $1. Since the fee per payment is roughly $q = \frac{1}{10}$, the fee for a $1 transfer is about 10 cents.

Both the existing Lottery scheme and our Transferable scheme can aggregate blockchain transactions by the winning probability p. The difference is that our transferable scheme does not increase the gambling potential, even makes the winning probability p smaller. In the existing scheme, the smaller p is, the lower the probability that the payee will win the ticket, which makes the income more unstable for the payees. In our transferable scheme, even if the ticket is not winning, the payee can use it for payment by paying a smaller fee than the blockchain transaction fee.

There is a concern that the sizeable winning amount β decreases the velocity of the ticket. This is because if there is a large gap between the winning amount β and the value of the ticket, the profit of winning $\beta - \gamma$ will be more significant. Therefore, it is best for recipients to decide whether to use the ticket for payment after confirming their winnings, which causes the velocity of the ticket to be slow.

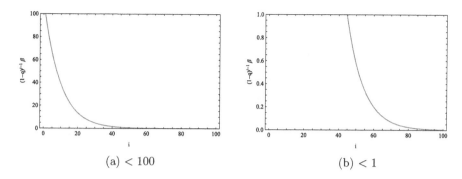

(a) < 100 (b) < 1

Fig. 6. Ticket value per generation

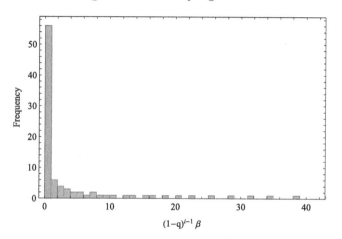

Fig. 7. Frequency of ticket value

The solution is not to make the winning amount β too high. In addition, if we set the winning amount β to a value almost equal to the blockchain transaction fee γ, the profit of winning will be very small; thus, the velocity of the ticket will not be affected.

6   Security Design

As far as the tamper-resistant assumption holds, double-spending attacks can not be performed theoretically. However, in reality, the tamper-proof hardware wallet could be broken, leading to double-spending attacks. Thus, instead of requiring a penalty escrow, we design security from the perspective of whether the utility an adversary can gain from the attack exceeds the cost of breaking the tamper-resistant hardware.

Definition 7 (κ-tamper proof). *A device is called κ-tamper proof if it satisfies the following conditions:*

1. *tamper-proof hardware is the hardware that prevents an adversary from stealing and changing stored data.*
2. *the device is either completely broken/tampered or working perfectly with probability κ and $(1 - \kappa)$, respectively.*[5]
3. *broken/tampered is a state in which all confidential information inside the device, including the private key, has been leaked to the adversary.*

We assume each device is in a state either completely broken/tampered or working perfectly. They occur with probabilities κ and $(1 - \kappa)$, respectively. As long as the behavior is observed from outside, it is not possible to distinguish between a device that is operating correctly and a device that adversary control the correct device who have an access to its internal key.

Ticket issuer

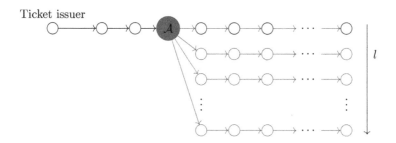

Fig. 8. Double-spending attack

Double-Spending Attack. Double-spending attacks are an attack that makes a profit by duplicating and double-spending the received ticket. In our transferable scheme, we assume that the adversary breaks the κ-tamper proof and receives or issues tickets then transfers with different addresses (wallets). We call the tickets created by the double-spending attacks "duplicated."

In our transferable scheme, we assume an adversary can gain profit up to $l \cdot \beta$ where l is the number of duplicated tickets. This is illustrated in Fig. 8.

6.1 Detection Methods

This section describes how to detect the double-spending attacks and find the adversary's address. We introduce two methods to detect the attack and find the adversary's address perfectly. When the adversary's address is found, we assume that the address is broadcasted to all users, and then the adversary's address is rejected by all users. An adversary can not profit unless the maximum expected utility he can gain from a single attack exceeds the cost of breaking the κ-tamper proof wallet.

---

[5] In reality, the adversaries are biased, but we assume it can not be distinguishable from a legitimate user from outside.

Note that the following two detection methods require that the receiver be online at the time of receipt. Conversely, the payer does not need to be online.

Definition 8 (Fork of transferred transactions)

Given two series of transactions initiated with the same escrow account $\epsilon \prec \cdots \prec \tau$ and $\epsilon \prec \cdots \prec \tau'$, the series of transactions are said to be 'fork' if and only if it satisfies both $\tau \not\prec \tau'$ and $\tau' \not\prec \tau$.

Assume the users monitor the blockchain, and after the eligible ticket is registered in the blockchain, the users check the eligible ticket against the ticket they have received.

Theorem 1 (Fork Detection). *Double-spending attacks can be perfectly detected by fork detection described in Definition 8.*

Proof. Assume there exists forked two series of transactions τ and $\tilde{\tau}$. Given τ is eligible and registered in the blockchain, the user who has $\tilde{\tau}$ reports double-spending attack. The adversary's address is confirmed from the latest common prefix of τ and $\tilde{\tau}$. $\qquad \square$

Definition 9 (Collision of transferred transactions). *Assume that each of the u users has $\alpha \, (\geq 2)$ addresses. If an adversary sends at least two duplicated tickets to any one of u users, the 'collision' occurs.*

We adopt a *round scheme* so that the adversary can not profit when the collision is detected. We divide the ticket sending procedure into three rounds. The procedure is illustrated in Fig. 9. **Round 1)** The adversary sends the tickets to the honest payees. The payee checks the received tickets for the collisions. **Round 2)** If the payee find the collision, broadcasts τ and $\tilde{\tau}$ to the honest users. **Round 3)** If the collision is not detected, the payee gives products or services to the payer in return. If the collision is detected, the adversary's address is rejected and will never be accepted by all honest users.

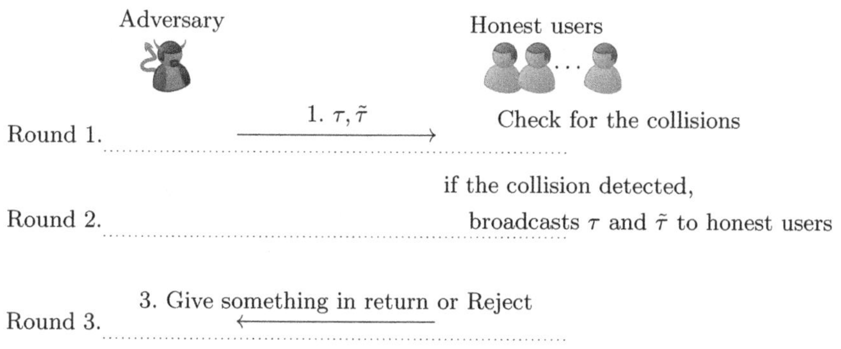

Fig. 9. Collision detection round

Theorem 2 (Collision Detection). *Let u be the number of users who participate in transfer scheme. By collision detection and round scheme, the expected utility of double-spending attack $\mathbb{E}_d$ is upper-bounded by the following inequality:*

$$\mathbb{E}_d \leq \sqrt{\frac{u}{e}}\beta. \tag{9}$$

Proof. As stated in the Definition 9, we assume a uniform distribution where each user has α addresses.[6] This must be the case where the adversary choose uniformly l different addresses from the total of αu addresses. By the round scheme, the adversary can not profit if a single user address is chosen more than once.

Let $p(l; u)$ be the probability that at least one user address is chosen more than once. This probability is described as follows:

$$p(l; u) \approx 1 - e^{-\frac{l^2}{2u}}. \tag{10}$$

Assume that the adversary double-spent l tickets with a maximum value of β per ticket. The adversary's expected utility value is

$$\mathbb{E}_d < \max_l \left\{ l\beta \cdot (1 - p(l; u)) \right\}. \tag{11}$$

Thus, $\mathbb{E}_d$ is at most $\sqrt{\frac{u}{e}}\beta$ when $l = \sqrt{u}$.   □

In our transferable scheme, double-spending attack is perfectly detected and the address used in the attack will be rejected by all users. Therefore, it is not profitable for the adversary unless the cost of breaking a single tamper-proof wallet exceeds the maximum expected value gained by the attack. Specifically, the adversary can not profit under the following conditions:

$$\sqrt{\frac{u}{e}}\beta < \Phi \tag{12}$$

where ϕ is the cost of breaking κ-tamper proof wallet.

As an example, consider the maximum expected utility value $\mathbb{E}_d$ with $u = 1,000,000$ and $\beta = \$100$. Applying the Eq. 9 produces $\mathbb{E}_d \lesssim \$60,700$.

7   Conclusions

In this paper, we introduce the first transferable decentralized probabilistic micropayment scheme and the proportional fee scheme. The feature of our scheme is that the ticket is transferable. Therefore, the ticket winning probability can be much smaller than the existing methods. Thus we can aggregate a

---

[6] In reality, the number of addresses each user has is considered more likely to follow exponential distribution. It is an unfavorable assumption that all user have the same number of addresses α.

larger number of transactions into one and can increase the blockchain throughput. Also, the proportional fee scheme can make the transaction fee smaller via the lottery ticket than on the blockchain.

Our scheme only assumes a tamper-proof device, and the ticket transfer protocol is simple, requiring only a digital signature. The tamper-proof assumptions can be achieved by SE (Secure Elements) such as SIM cards, which are widely used in Smartphones. Since the computational resources of SE are limited, the concern arises that it is not impractical to perform all operations in the SE. In our scheme, the operations to be performed in the SE can be limited to the prevention of double-spending. On the other hand, operations that are not related to double-spending prevention can be executed in the regular application area. Therefore, since the use of SE's computational resources can be minimized, it would be feasible to realize our scheme on mobile devices such as smartphones. Specifically, the operations to be performed in the SE are checking whether a ticket is valid, creating a key pair, and signing at the time of money transfer. On the regular application side, the operations are performed to avoid duplicated tickets (e.g., collision and fork detection) and check for winning tickets.

We consider that our transferable scheme is not a singular way of transferable lottery tickets but a system similar to the circulation of paper and coins issued by central banks. We will use blockchain to achieve this. We believe that our scheme can be applied not only to micropayments but also to high-value payment transactions.

References

1. Bitcoin average cost per transaction (2020). https://ycharts.com/indicators/bitcoin_average_cost_per_transaction
2. Almashaqbeh, G., Bishop, A., Cappos, J.: MicroCash: practical concurrent processing of micropayments. In: Bonneau, J., Heninger, N. (eds.) FC 2020. LNCS, vol. 12059, pp. 227–244. Springer, Cham (2020). https://doi.org/10.1007/978-3-030-51280-4_13
3. Boneh, D., Bonneau, J., Bunz, B., Fisch, B.: Verifiable delay functions. In: Shacham, H., Boldyreva, A. (eds.) CRYPTO 2018. LNCS, vol. 10991, pp. 757–788. Springer, Cham (2018). https://doi.org/10.1007/978-3-319-96884-1_25
4. Chiesa, A., Green, M., Liu, J., Miao, P., Miers, I., Mishra, P.: Decentralized anonymous micropayments. In: Coron, J.-S., Nielsen, J.B. (eds.) EUROCRYPT 2017. LNCS, vol. 10211, pp. 609–642. Springer, Cham (2017). https://doi.org/10.1007/978-3-319-56614-6_21
5. Garay, J., Kiayias, A., Leonardos, N.: The bitcoin backbone protocol: analysis and applications. In: Oswald, E., Fischlin, M. (eds.) EUROCRYPT 2015. LNCS, vol. 9057, pp. 281–310. Springer, Heidelberg (2015). https://doi.org/10.1007/978-3-662-46803-6_10
6. Gudgeon, L., Moreno-Sanchez, P., Roos, S., McCorry, P., Gervais, A.: SoK: layer-two blockchain protocols. In: Bonneau, J., Heninger, N. (eds.) FC 2020. LNCS, vol. 12059, pp. 201–226. Springer, Cham (2020). https://doi.org/10.1007/978-3-030-51280-4_12

7. Karame, G.O., Androulaki, E., Capkun, S.: Double-spending fast payments in bitcoin. In: Proceedings of the 2012 ACM conference on Computer and communications security, CCS 2012, pp. 906–917. Association for Computing Machinery (2012)
8. Miller, A., Bentov, I., Bakshi, S., Kumaresan, R., McCorry, P.: Sprites and state channels: payment networks that go faster than lightning. In: Goldberg, I., Moore, T. (eds.) FC 2019. LNCS, vol. 11598, pp. 508–526. Springer, Cham (2019). https://doi.org/10.1007/978-3-030-32101-7_30
9. Pass, R., shelat, a.: Micropayments for decentralized currencies. In: Proceedings of the 22nd ACM SIGSAC Conference on Computer and Communications Security, CCS 2015, pp. 207–218. Association for Computing Machinery (2015)
10. Rivest, R.L.: Electronic lottery tickets as micropayments. In: Hirschfeld, R. (ed.) FC 1997. LNCS, vol. 1318, pp. 307–314. Springer, Heidelberg (1997). https://doi.org/10.1007/3-540-63594-7_87
11. Takahashi, T., Otsuka, A.: Short paper: secure offline payments in bitcoin. In: Bracciali, A., Clark, J., Pintore, F., Rønne, P.B., Sala, M. (eds.) FC 2019. LNCS, vol. 11599, pp. 12–20. Springer, Cham (2020). https://doi.org/10.1007/978-3-030-43725-1_2
12. Wheeler, D.: Transactions using bets. In: Lomas, M. (ed.) Security Protocols 1996. LNCS, vol. 1189, pp. 89–92. Springer, Heidelberg (1997). https://doi.org/10.1007/3-540-62494-5_7

MINILEDGER: Compact-Sized Anonymous and Auditable Distributed Payments

Panagiotis Chatzigiannis$^{(\boxtimes)}$ and Foteini Baldimtsi

George Mason University, Fairfax, USA
{pchatzig,foteini}@gmu.edu

Abstract. In this work we present MINILEDGER, a distributed payment system which not only guarantees the privacy of transactions, but also offers built-in functionalities for various types of audits by any external authority. MINILEDGER is the *first* private and auditable payment system with storage costs independent of the number of transactions. To achieve such a storage improvement, we introduce pruning functionalities for the transaction history while maintaining integrity and auditing. We provide formal security definitions and a number of extensions for various auditing levels. Our evaluation results show that MINILEDGER is practical in terms of storage requiring as low as 70 KB per participant for 128 bits of security, and depending on the implementation choices, can prune 1 million transactions in less than a second.

1 Introduction

One of the main issues with distributed ledger-based (or else blockchain) payment schemes (e.g. Bitcoin) is the lack of privacy. All transaction information - including transacting parties' public keys and associated values - are permanently recorded on the public blockchain/ledger, and using side-channel information these keys can be clustered and eventually linked to real identities [5,30]. A number of solutions have been suggested to solve the privacy issues of distributed ledgers by hiding both the transaction graph and its associated assets and amounts [7,14,19,39], however, while privacy is a fundamental right, the need for *auditing mechanisms* is required to ensure compliance with laws and regulation [1,24] as done in traditional payment systems via auditing companies (i.e. Deloitte, KPMG). Constructing payment schemes that satisfy both privacy and auditability *at the same time*, is a rather challenging problem since these properties are often conflicting. The challenge becomes even harder when one takes *efficiency and scalability* into account. In particular, one of the most common approaches to solve the scalability issue, that of pruning old/unneeded transactions from the ledger, directly hurts auditability, as an auditor cannot possibly audit data that no longer exists in the ledger.

F. Baldimtsi—The authors have been supported by the National Science Foundation (NSF) under Grant 1717067, the National Security Agency (NSA) under Grant 204761, an IBM Faculty Award and Facebook Research Award.

© Springer Nature Switzerland AG 2021
E. Bertino et al. (Eds.): ESORICS 2021, LNCS 12972, pp. 407–429, 2021.
https://doi.org/10.1007/978-3-030-88418-5_20

While a number of solutions for accountable and private distributed payments have been proposed in the literature, they either rely on the existence of trusted authorities or do not scale for large number of participants and transactions.

Our Contributions. We present MINILEDGER: the *first space efficient*, distributed private payment system that allows an authorized set of participants to transact with each other, while also allowing for a wide set of auditing by consent operations by *any* third party auditor. We provide formal, game based definitions (in full version [15]) and a construction that relies upon a number of cryptographic primitives: a consensus protocol, semi-homomorphic encryption, compact set representation techniques (cryptographic accumulators) and non-interactive zero-knowledge proofs (NIZKs).

At a high level, MINILEDGER consists of n Banks transacting with each other through a common transaction history, or else a ledger L which is maintained by a consensus mechanism (orthogonal to our work). The ledger is modeled as a two-dimensional table with n columns, one for each participating Bank, and rows representing transactions. Whenever Bank B_j wishes to send funds of value v to another B_k, it creates a n-sized vector containing (semi)homomorphic encryptions and NIZK proofs which is appended in L. B_j encrypts the value that is sent to each participating Bank in the system using each receiving Bank's public key, i.e. the encrypted values would be v for B_k, $-v$ for B_j and 0 for any other Bank. These encryptions provide privacy in MINILEDGER since they hide values as well as the sender and recipient of each transaction, while still allowing all participating Banks to decrypt the value that corresponds to them and to compute their total assets at any point. This overcomes the need for any out-of-band communication between Banks which created security issues in previous works (ref. Sect. 4.2). Finally, the included ZK proofs guarantee that transactions are valid without revealing any information.

MINILEDGER provides auditability *by consent*. Any third party auditor with access to L can ask audit queries to a Bank and verify the responses based on the public information on L. The simplest audit is to learn the value of a cell in L, i.e. the exact amount of funds a Bank received/sent at any point. This basic audit can be used to derive more complex audit types as we discuss in Appendix A, such as transaction history, account balance, spending limit etc., without disclosing more information to the auditor than needed.

Space Efficiency. The main innovation of MINILEDGER lies in the maintenance and storage of L. In previous auditable schemes (such as zkLedger [34]) the *full L* needs to be stored at *any time* and by *all* participants. The challenge in MINILEDGER design was compacting the ledger while maintaining security and a wide set of auditing functionalities. MINILEDGER employs a smart type of transaction pruning: participating Banks can prune their own transaction history by computing a provable, *compact representation* of their previously posted history and broadcast the resulting digest to the consensus layer. Once consensus participants agree to a pruning operation (i.e. verify the digest as a valid representation of the Bank's history), that history can be erased from L and thus by all system participants (except the pruning Bank itself which always need to store its own transaction history locally). Auditing is still possible since a compact digest of transaction information is always stored in L and the Bank under audit can prove that the revealed values correctly correspond to the digest. As a result, the size of L in MiniLedger can be nearly constant (i.e. independent of the number of transactions that ever happened).

Our compact transaction history representation can lead to multiple additional benefits (besides obviously reduced storage requirements). First, a compact L makes addition of new system participants (i.e. Banks) much more efficient (typically, new parties need to download the whole L requiring large bandwidth and waiting time). Then, although the structure of L does not allow for a very large number of participating Banks n (as the computation cost of a single transaction is linear in n), the compactness of L allows augmenting MiniLedger with more fine-grained types of auditing and enabling audits in a client level (instead of a Bank level). We present MiniLedger+, an extension that serves a much larger user base in Appendix A.

Finally, we implement a prototype of the transaction layer of MiniLedger and evaluate its performance in terms of transaction costs, pruning costs and size of L which we estimate to be as low as 70KB of storage for each Bank. We show that transaction computation cost, for a system with 100 Banks, takes about 4 sec, while transaction auditing is less than 5 ms, independent of the number of Banks. Transaction computation costs increase linearly to the number of Banks (as in zkLedger) but by optimizing the underlying ZK proofs we achieve some small constant improvement. Although the linear transaction computation cost might still seem high, we note that using our MiniLedger+ extension, a small number of Banks can serve a very large user base. We perform experiments on two different types of pruning instantiations, one using Merkle trees [31] and one using batch RSA accumulators [8]. Both result in pruning measurements that are independent of the number of participating Banks. Our experiments show that we can prune 1 million transactions in less than a second using Merkle trees and in about 2 h using the RSA accumulator, and can perform audits in milliseconds in the same transaction set.

Related Work. We present an non-exhaustive overview of related works.

Anonymous Distributed Payment Systems. Zcash [7], is a permissionless protocol hiding both transacting parties and transaction amounts using zero knowledge proofs. Other notable systems are CryptoNote and the Monero cryptocurrency [39], based on decoy transaction inputs and ring signatures to provide privacy of transactions within small anonymity sets, and Quisquis [19] which provides similar anonymity level to Monero but allows for a more compact sized ledger. Zether [10] is a smart contract based payment system which only hides transaction amounts. Mimblewimble [20] uses Confidential Transactions [28] to hide transaction values in homomorphic commitments, and prunes intermediate values from the blockchain after being spent (which might be insecure in

Table 1. Confidential payment schemes comparison. By $\checkmark^S$ we denote set anonymity, $\checkmark^T$ auditing through a TP and $\checkmark^K$ through "view keys" (which reveal all private information of an account). By O: permissionless and C: permissioned we refer to the set of parties that participate in the payment scheme and not the underlying consensus.

	Record	Anon	Audit	Perm	Prune
Zcash [7,22]	UTXO	$\checkmark$	$\checkmark^T$	O	✗
Monero [26,39]	TXO	$\checkmark^S$	$\checkmark^K$	O	✗
Quisquis [19]	Hybrid	$\checkmark^S$	✗	O	$\checkmark$
MW [20]	UTXO	✗	✗	O	$\checkmark$
Solidus [14]	Accnt	$\checkmark^S$	✗	C	✗
zkLedger [34]	Accnt	$\checkmark$	$\checkmark$	C	✗
PGC [17]	Accnt	✗	$\checkmark$	O	✗
Zether [10]	Accnt	Option	✗	O	✗
MiniLedger	Accnt	$\checkmark$	$\checkmark$	C	$\checkmark$

other UTXO systems such as Bitcoin), improving its scalability. In the permissioned setting, Solidus [14] allows for confidential transactions in public ledgers, employing Oblivious RAM techniques to hide access patterns in publicly verifiable encrypted Bank memory blocks. This approach enables users to transact in the system anonymously using Banks as intermediaries.

Adding Auditability/Accountability. A number of Zcash extensions [22,25,32] proposed the addition of auxiliary information to coins to be used exclusively by a designated, trusted authority for accountability purposes. While this allows for a number of accountability functionalities, it suffers from centralization of auditing power. Additionally, all such works inherit the underlying limitations of Zcash such as the need for trusted setup and strong computational assumptions. Traceable Monero [26] attempts to add accountability features on top of Monero. In a similar idea to Zerocash, a designated "tracing" authority can link anonymous transactions with the same spending party and learn the origin or destination of a transaction. The tracing authority's role can again be distributed among several authorities to prevent single point of failure and distribute trust. PRCash [41] aims to achieve accountability for transaction volume over time. A regulation authority (can be distributed using threshold encryption) issues anonymous credentials to the system's transacting users. If transaction volume in a period exceeds a spending limit, the user can voluntarily deanonymize himself to the authority to continue transacting. PRCash however only focuses on this specific audit type. zkLedger presented a unique architecture for implementing various interactive audit types in a permissioned setting, but its linear-growing storage requirements in terms of transactions make it unpractical for real deployment. Additionally, it assumes transaction values are communicated out-of-band, creating an attack vector that could prevent participants from answering audits(further discussed in our full version [15]).

In Table 1 we summarize properties of private payment schemes and refer the reader to [16] for a systematization of knowledge on auditable and accountable distributed payment systems.

Prunable and Stateless Blockchains. Given the append-only immutability property for most ledgers, the concern for ever-growing storage requirements in blockchains was stated even in the original Bitcoin whitepaper [33], which considered *pruning* old transaction information without affecting the core system's properties. Ethereum [40], being an account-based system, supports explicit support of "old state" pruning as a default option, and defers to "archival" nodes for any history queries. Coda (Mina) [9] is a prominent example of a stateless (succinct) blockchain, which only needs to store the most recent state with recursive verifiability using SNARKs. Accumulators and vector commitments have also been proposed to maintain a stateless blockchain [8,18]. All such approaches however might negatively impact auditability and are therefore not directly applicable in our setting.

2   Preliminaries

By λ we denote the security parameter and by $z \leftarrow \mathcal{Z}$ the uniformly at random selection of an element z from space $\mathcal{Z}$. By $(\mathsf{pk}, \mathsf{sk})$ we denote a public-private key pair and by $[x_i]_{i=1}^y$ a list of elements $(x_1, x_2, ..., x_y)$. By $x \parallel y$ we denote concatenation of bit strings x and y. We denote a matrix M with m rows and n columns as M_{mn} and a i-th row and j-th column cell in the matrix as (i, j).

ElGamal Encryption Variant. MiniLedger uses a variant of ElGamal encryption (called "twisted ElGamal" (TEG) [17]). Compared to standard ElGamal, it requires an additional group generator (denoted by h below) in the public parameters pp, which makes it possible to homomorphically add ciphertexts c_2 and c_2' generated for *different* public keys pk and pk' and intentionally leak information on the relation of encrypted messages m and m' as we discuss below.

TEG is secure against chosen plaintext attacks and works as follows:

- $\mathsf{pp} \leftarrow \mathsf{SetupTEG}(1^\lambda)$: Outputs $\mathsf{pp} = (\mathbb{G}, g, h, p)$ where g, h are generators of cyclic group $\mathbb{G}$ of prime order p.
- $(\mathsf{pk}, \mathsf{sk}) \leftarrow \mathsf{GenTEG}(\mathsf{pp})$: Outputs $\mathsf{sk} \leftarrow \mathbb{Z}_p$, $\mathsf{pk} = h^{\mathsf{sk}}$.
- $(c_1, c_2) \leftarrow \mathsf{EncTEG}(\mathsf{pk}, m)$: Sample $r \leftarrow \mathbb{Z}_p$, compute $c_1 = \mathsf{pk}^r, c_2 = g^m h^r$ and output $C = (c_1, c_2)$
- $m \leftarrow \mathsf{DecTEG}(\mathsf{sk}, (c_1, c_2)$: Compute $g^m = c_2/c_1^{(1/\mathsf{sk})}$ and recover m from a look-up table (assuming that the message space is relatively small).

TEG encryption is additively homomorphic: $\mathsf{EncTEG}(\mathsf{pk}, m_1)\mathsf{EncTEG}(\mathsf{pk}, m_2) = \mathsf{EncTEG}(\mathsf{pk}, m_1 + m_2)$. Also if $(c_1, c_2) \leftarrow \mathsf{EncTEG}(\mathsf{pk}, m)$ and $(c_1', c_2') \leftarrow \mathsf{EncTEG}(\mathsf{pk}', m')$, then $c_2 c_2'$ contains an encryption of $m + m'$. This implies if $c_2 c_2' = 1$, then any external observer can deduce that $m = -m'$ (for properly chosen r, r').

Commitment Schemes. We use Pedersen commitments [36] which are additively homomorphic and allow efficient zero-knowledge proofs, are perfectly hiding and computationally binding and consist of the following algorithms:
(a) $\mathsf{ComGen}(1^\lambda)$ outputs $\mathsf{pp} = (\mathbb{G}, g, h, p)$ where g, h are generators of cyclic group $\mathbb{G}$ of prime order p, (b) $\mathsf{Com}(\mathsf{pp}, m, r)$ for a message $m \in [1...p]$ and randomness $r \in [1...p]$, outputs a commitment $\mathsf{cm} = g^m h^r$, (c) $\mathsf{Open}(\mathsf{pp}, \mathsf{cm}, m, r)$ with verifier given commitment cm and opening (m, r) returns verification bit b.

Zero-Knowledge Proofs. A zero-knowledge (ZK) proof is a two-party protocol between a prover P, holding some private data (or else *witness*) w for a public instance x, and a verifier V. The goal of P is to convince V that some property of w is true i.e. $R(x, w) = 1$, for an NP-relation R, without V learning anything more. In MINILEDGER we use non-interactive ZK proofs (NIZKs) and OR and AND compositions of them The types of ZK proofs used in MINILEDGER are:

1. ZK proof on the opening of a commitment: Using Camenisch-Stadler notation [12] (used throughout the paper): $ZKP : \{(w, r) : X = g^w h^r \bmod n\}(X, g, h, n)$ where (X, g, h, n) are the public statements given as common input to both parties, and (w, r) is the secret witness.
2. ZK proof of knowledge of discrete log: $ZKP : \{(x) : X = g^x \bmod n\}(X, g, n)$.
3. ZK proof of equality of discrete logs: $ZKP : \{(x, r, r') : X = g^x h^r \bmod n, Y = g^x h^{r'} \bmod n\}(X, Y, g, h, n)$.
4. ZK range proof that a committed value v lies within a specific interval (a, b): $ZKP : \{(v, r) : X = g^v h^r \bmod n \wedge v \in (a, b)\}(X, g, h, n)$. Such proofs can also be used to show that the value v is positive or does not overflow some modulo operation. Known range proof constructions include [11, 29, 37].

Cryptographic Accumulators. Accumulators allow the succinct and binding representation of a set of elements S and support constant-size proofs of (non) membership on S. We focus on *additive* accumulators where elements can be added over time to S and to *positive* accumulators which allow for efficient proofs of membership. We consider *trapdoorless* accumulators in order to prevent the need for a trusted party that holds a trapdoor and could potentially create fake (non)membership proofs. Finally we require the accumulator to be *deterministic*, i.e. always produce the same representation given a specific set. An accumulator typically consists of the following algorithms [6]:

- $(\mathsf{pp}, D_0) \leftarrow \mathsf{AccSetup}(\lambda_{acc})$ generates the public parameters and instantiates the accumulator initial state D_0.
- $\mathsf{Add}(D_t, x) := (D_{t+1}, \mathsf{upmsg})$ adds x to accumulator D_t, which outputs D_{t+1} and upmsg which enables witness holders to update their witnesses.
- $\mathsf{MemWitCreate}(D_t, x, S_t) := w_x^t$ Creates a membership proof w_x^t for x where S_t is the set of elements accumulated in D_t. $\mathsf{NonMemWitCreate}$ creates the equivalent non-membership proof u_x^t.
- $\mathsf{MemWitUp}(D_t, w_x^t, x, \mathsf{upmsg}) := w_x^{t+1}$ Updates membership proof w_x^t for x after an element is added to the accumulator. $\mathsf{NonMemWitUp}$ is the equivalent algorithm for non-membership.

- VerMem$(D_t, x, w_x^t) := \{0, 1\}$ Verifies membership proof w_x^t of x in D_t.

The basic security property of accumulators is *soundness* which states that for every element *not* in the accumulator it is infeasible to prove membership.

We utilize two types of accumulators: (a) the additive, universal RSA accumulator [8] and (b) additive, positive Merkle Trees [31]. We note that RSA accumulator can become trapdoorless if a trusted party (or an MPC protocol) is used to compute the primes for the modulo n, or a public RSA challenge number (i.e. from RSA Labs) is adopted. We also note that we will apply batching techniques in element additions and membership proofs [8]. In Sect. 5 we discuss the trade-offs between the two options for different implementation scenarios.

Consensus. A consensus protocol (denoted by CN) allows a set, S_{CN}, of distributed parties to reach agreement in the presence of faults. For MiniLedger we assume that the agreement is in regards to data posted on a ledger L and participation in the consensus protocol can be either *permissioned* (i.e. only authenticated parties have write access in the ledger) or *permissionless*. Consensus protocols that maintain such a fault-tolerant ledger and their details (e.g. participation credentials, incentives, sybil attack prevention etc.) are out of the scope of this paper and can be done using standard techniques [4,13]. For our construction, we assume a consensus protocol: Conscus$(x, L) := L'$ which allows all system participants given some input value x and ledger state L, to agree on a new ledger L'. We assume that consistency and liveness [21] are satisfied.

3   MiniLedger Model

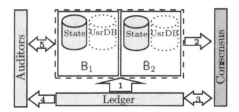

Fig. 1. MiniLedger overview. State: Bank's private database. Usr DB: optional private database for Bank's clients. Banks read Ledger to create/prune transactions (1), forward output to Consensus (2), which verifies/updates the Ledger (3). Auditor reads Ledger (4) and interacts with Banks to audit transactions (5).

We consider the following system participants: a Trusted Party TP, a set of consensus participants S_{CN}, a static set of n Banks with IDs defined by $[B_j]_{j=1}^n$ (known to everyone) and an arbitrary number of Auditors A. Each Bank has a key pair $[(pk_j, sk_j)]_{j=1}^n$ and an initial asset value $[v_j]_{j=1}^n$. Banks maintain an internal state $[st_j]_{j=1}^n$. We denote transactions by tx_i where i represents the transaction's index. We store transactions in a public ledger L maintained by a consensus layer CN and stored by all banks. We summarize the role of each participant in MiniLedger and provide the architecture overview in Fig. 1:

- TP is a trusted entity which runs an one-time setup to instantiate the system public parameters and verifies the initial assets of each Bank. TP could be replaced by an MPC protocol (i.e. [23]) executed by the Banks.
- Banks generate transactions tx that transfer some of their assets to one or more other Banks, while hiding the value and the transacting parties. Transactions are sent to the consensus layer CN (via an anonymous communications protocol, i.e. Tor) and if valid are appended on L. Banks can prune their transaction history on L and "replace" it by a digest D. The pruning Bank needs to send D to CN (incentives for the Bank to perform the pruning operation are orthogonal to our construction) and is responsible to keep a copy of the pruned transactions in its private database "State" (failing to do so can lead to audit failures). If D is valid, CN participants update L by deleting the pruned transactions and replacing them by D.
- Auditors by observing the ledger, can audit the Banks at any point for any set of transactions through interactive protocols. Auditors should be able to audit the value of a single transaction or a subset of transactions, whether these transactions are still in L or have been pruned.

Assumptions. We focus on the transaction layer and consider issues with underlying consensus and network layers and their mitigations orthogonal to this work. Specifically, we assume the fundamental consensus properties, as defined in Sect. 2, always hold. On network level, we assume a malicious Bank cannot block another Bank's view (Eclipse attacks) and transactions are sent to *all* Banks using anonymous communication channels to preserve anonymity of the sending and the receiving Bank(s). We *do not* require out-of-band communication between Banks. For simplicity, we assume the set of participating Banks is static but is easy to extend our system to dynamically add/remove Banks. We also assume the Random Oracle model to convert our ZK proofs to non-interactive.

Security Goals. MiniLedger should satisfy the following properties (formally defined in a game-based fashion in the full version [15]). *Theft prevention and balance:* When a Bank spends, we require that a) it authorized the transaction, b) its balance decreases by the appropriate amount and c) it cannot spend more than its total assets. *Secure pruning:* Ledger pruning outputs a digest that a) is only created by the respective Bank, b) contains the correct transactions in the correct order, and c) does not contain bogus transactions. *Ledger correctness:* The ledger only accepts valid transactions and pruning operations. *Correct and Sound Auditability:* An honest Bank following the protocol can always answer audits correctly and convince an Auditor, while an Auditor always rejects false claims from a malicious Bank. *Privacy:* The ledger hides both the identities of transacting parties and values of transactions from any external observer (except auditors who learn specific information during the auditing protocol).

4   MiniLedger Construction

Overview. We consider n Banks that transact with each other in an anonymous and auditable way by posting data in a common ledger L (a two-dimensional table with n columns, one for each participating Bank, and a number of rows which represent transactions). The ledger is maintained by consensus participants, who verify every submitted transaction, and is stored by all Banks. The Banks could be running consensus themselves, or outsource this operation to any external set of consensus parties.

For each tx_i, the sending Bank (i.e. the transaction creator) creates a whole row in L which includes twisted ElGamal encryptions $C_{ij} = (c_1, c_2)$ that hide the transferred value v_{ij} that corresponds to each cell (i, j). For instance, if we assume that there's only one receiving Bank in a transaction, the sending Bank would compute an encryption of $-v$ for its own cell, an encryption of v for the receiver cell, and a number of encryptions of 0 for the rest of the cells. This makes the transmitted values indistinguishable to any external observer due to ElGamal IND-CPA security. Additionally, the sending Bank accompanies each encryption with a NIZK proof π to prevent dishonest Bank behavior as discussed in details below. This specific ledger structure allows an external auditor to audit for a value sent/received by a Bank at any given point, with the Bank replying with a value v and a ZK proof π^{Aud} for its claim. This basic audit protocol can be extended to more complex queries (such as total assets held by a Bank or if a transaction exceeds a set limit) as we explain in Appendix A.

A straightforward implementation of such a transaction table, as done in zkLedger, leads to a ledger L that grows linearly to the number of posted transactions. This makes schemes like zkLedger hard to adopt in practice, since every single participant would have to store a table of size n times the total number of transactions that have ever occurred. Besides storage costs, the overall computational performance would also degrade even more over time.

Reducing Storage Costs. The main idea for MiniLedger, is that each Bank B_j periodically initiates a pruning operation, which prunes all transactions in its corresponding column on L. When a Bank performs a pruning operation, it publishes a digest D containing the pruned transactions and the consensus layer verifies that D is indeed a valid digest (i.e. contains the transactions to be pruned). Note B_j is still responsible for maintaining a private copy of *all* its pruned transactions, however, there are great storage savings for the public version of the ledger L which *everyone* in the system has to maintain. We note that the cost of a pruning operation depends on the number of transactions to be pruned but is independent of the number of participating Banks n.

When B_j is audited for a pruned transaction value v_{ij}, it would have to present the needed data to the auditor by recovering it from its private copy of its transaction history, and prove to the auditor that this data is contained in D and it had been posted on the specific row i (to maintain ordering). We implement this pruning operation using cryptographic accumulators to achieve a short, constant size representation of D.

4.1   Our Construction

For our construction we assume the following building blocks: the variant of the ElGamal encryption (SetupTEG, GenTEG, EncTEG, DecTEG), an EU-CMA signature scheme (SignGen, Sign, SVrfy), an additive, positive cryptographic accumulator (AccSetup, Add, MemWitCreate, MemWitUp, VerMem), the Pedersen commitment scheme (ComGen, Com, Open), a consensus protocol Conscus and a NIZK proof system. The phases of MINILEDGER work as follows:

Setup: Setup can be executed with the help of a trusted third party or via an MPC protocol amongst Banks.

1. SysSetup$\{\mathsf{TP}(1^\lambda) \leftrightarrow [B_j(v_j)]_{j=1}^n\}$. This interactive protocol is executed between TP and a set of n Banks. TP verifies the initial asset value v_j for each Bank and generates the public parameters for the accumulator by running AccSetup(), the key parameters of the ElGamal variant encryption scheme by executing SetupTEG() (which are also used for the Pedersen commitment scheme), the consensus protocol parameters by running TPCSetup, and the joined set of parameters denoted as pp is sent to all Banks. Each Bank generates an ElGamal key pair $(\mathsf{pk}_{B_j}, \mathsf{sk}_{B_j})$ through GenTEG() and sends pk_{B_j} to TP. Finally, TP encrypts the initial values of each Bank by running $C_{0j} = (c_1^{(0j)}, c_2^{(0j)}) \leftarrow \mathsf{EncTEG}(\mathsf{pk}_{B_j}, v_j)^1$. Then, it initializes a "running value total" which starts as $Q_{0j} = C_{0j}$ and will hold the encryption of the total assets of each Bank at any point. The vector $[Q_{0j}, C_{0j}]_{j=1}^n$ consists of the "genesis" state of the ledger L along with the system parameters pp containing the key parameters and all Bank public keys. At any point, the ledger L is agreed by the consensus participants and we assume that all Banks store it. pp and L are default inputs everywhere below.

Transaction Creation

2. $\mathsf{tx}_i \leftarrow \mathsf{CreateTx}(\mathsf{sk}_{B_k}, [v_{ij}]_{j=1}^n)$. This algorithm is run by Bank B_k wishing to transmit some (or all) of its assets to other Banks in L. For each B_j in L (including itself), B_k executes $C_{ij} \leftarrow \mathsf{EncTEG}(\mathsf{pk}_{B_j}, v_{ij})$ and computes $Q_{ij} \to Q_{(i-1)j} \cdot C_{ij}$. In order to prove *balance*, similarly to [34], B_k should pick randomness values for the ElGamal variant encryptions such that $\sum_{j=1}^n r_{ij} = 0$. Then, the sending Bank B_k generates a NIZK $\pi_{ij} \; \forall j \in (1, ..n)$ which proves the following (the exact description of π_{ij} can be found in the full version [15]):

Proof of Assets: Shows that *either* a) B_j is receiving some value ($v_{ij} \geq 0$), *or* b) B_j is spending no more than its total assets ($\sum_{k=1}^i v_{kj} \geq 0$) and within the valid range after transaction execution, while proving knowledge of its secret key sk_j showing it authorized the transfer. In both cases, an auxiliary

---

[1] To simplify notation, from now on we will drop the superscripts from the two parts of Elgamal ciphertext, i.e., we will simply write $C_{0j} = (c_1, c_2)$.

commitment cm_{ij} is used which commits to either v_{ij} or $\sum_{k=1}^{i} v_{kj}$, so the proof includes a single range proof for the commitment value to reduce computational costs, as the range proof is the most computationally expensive part of π.

Proof of Consistency: Ensures consistency for the encryption randomness r in c_1 and c_2 in both cases of the previous sub-proof, which guarantees correct decryption by Bank k.

The transaction $\mathsf{tx}_i = [C_{ik}, \mathsf{cm}_{ik}, \pi_{ik}, Q_{ik}]_{k=1}^{n}$ is sent to consensus layer CN.

3. $\mathsf{VerifyTx}(\mathsf{tx}_i) := b_i$. Verify all ZK proofs $[\pi_j]_{j=1}^{n}$, check that $\prod_{j=1}^{n} c_2^{(ij)} = 1$ (proof of balance) and that $Q_{ij} = Q_{(i-1)j} \cdot C_{ij}$. On successful verification output 1, else output $\perp$.

Transaction Pruning

4. $(D_{\beta j}, st'_j, \sigma_j) \leftarrow \mathsf{Prune}(st_j)$ This algorithm is executed by B_j when it wishes to prune its transaction history of depth $q = \beta - \alpha$ and "compact" it to an accumulator digest $D_{\beta j}$, where α is the latest digest and β is a currently posted row number (usually a Bank will prune everything between its last pruning and the latest transaction that appeared in L). It parses C_{ij} from each tx_{ij}. It fetches its previous digest $D_{\alpha j}$ (if $\alpha = 1$, sets $D \to D_{\alpha j}$ as the initial accumulator value where A is defined from pp). Then $\forall C_{ij}, i \in [\alpha, \beta]$ it consecutively runs accumulator addition $\mathsf{Add}(D_{(i-1)j}, (i \parallel C_{ij}))$ (note the inclusion of index i which preserves ordering of pruned transactions in D_j). Finally it stores all transaction encryptions $[i, C_{ij}]_{i=\alpha}^{\beta}$ to its local memory, updates st_j to st'_j, computes $\sigma_j \leftarrow \mathsf{Sign}(D_{\beta j})$ and sends $D_{\beta j}, \sigma_j$ to CN. Note that $D_{\beta j}$ does not include proofs π, and pruning breaks proofs of balance in rows for all Banks. Still "breaking" these old proofs is not an issue, as they have already been verified.

5. $\mathsf{PruneVrfy}(D_{\beta j}, \sigma_j) := b_j$ On receipt of $D_{\beta j}$, locally executes $\mathsf{Prune}()$ for the same transaction set to compute $D'_{\beta j}$. If $D'_{\beta j} = D_{\beta j}$ (given the accumulator is deterministic) outputs 1, else outputs $\perp$.

   We note that after a *successful* pruning operation (i.e. one that is agreed upon in consensus layer), all system participants that store L can delete all existing data in cells $(i, j) \forall i < \beta$ and just store $D_{\beta j}$ along with the latest $Q_{\beta j}$.

Consensus Protocol: This is handled in the consensus layer CN with its details orthogonal to our scheme. Similar to typical blockchain consensus, participants will only update L with a new tx or D if this is valid according to the corresponding verification algorithms (i.e. in Bitcoin, consensus participants validate transactions before posting them in L).

6. $\mathsf{Conscus}(\mathsf{tx} \text{ or } D) := L'$. Runs the consensus protocol among S_{CN} to update the ledger with a new tx or pruning digest D after checking their validity. If consensus participants come to an agreement, L is updated to a new state L'.

Auditing: Our auditing protocols below include a basic audit for a value v (that has either been pruned or not) and a set's sum of such values (which might be all past transactions, thus auditing Bank's total assets). These audits are interactive and require the Bank's consent. MINILEDGER can support additional audit types and/or non-interactive audits as we discuss in Appendix A.

7. Audit$\{A(C_{ij}) \leftrightarrow B_j(sk_j)\}$ is an interactive protocol between an auditor A and a Bank B_j. In this basic audit, A audits B_j for the value v_{ij} of a specific transaction tx_{ij} (that has not been pruned from L so far), encrypted as C_{ij} on the ledger L. B_j first decrypts the encrypted transaction through DecTEG() and sends v_{ij} to A, as well as a NIZK $\pi^{Aud} : \{(sk_j) : c_2/g^{v_{ij}} = (c_1)^{1/sk_j}\}(c_1, c_2, v_{ij}, pk_j, g, h)$. Then A accepts the audit for v_{ij} if π^{Aud} successfully verifies.

8. AuditSum$\{A([C_{ij}]_{i=\alpha}^{\beta}) \leftrightarrow B_j(sk_j)\}$ is an interactive protocol between an auditor A and a Bank B_j. Here A audits B_j for the sum of the values $\sum_{k=\alpha}^{\beta} v_{kj}$ for transactions $tx_{\alpha j}$ up to $tx_{\beta j}$ (that have not been pruned from L so far). This protocol is a generalization of the Audit$\{\}$ protocol outlined above, (with Audit$\{\}$ having as inputs ($\prod_{i=\alpha}^{\beta} C_{ij}$) and $\prod$ denoting direct product for ciphertexts c_1, c_2), because of ElGamal variant additive homomorphism. Note that although in this protocol the transactions are assumed to be consecutive for simplicity, its functionality is identical if the transactions are "isolated". Also if indices $\alpha = 1$ and β equals to the most recent transaction index (and no pruning has happened in the system), the audit is performed on the Bank's total assets.

9. AudPruned$\{A([(i,j)]_{i=\alpha}^{\gamma}, [C_{ij}]_{i=\gamma}^{\beta}) \leftrightarrow B_j(sk_j)\}$ is an interactive protocol between an auditor A and a Bank B_j, where transactions $[tx_{ij}]_{i=\alpha}^{\gamma}$ have been pruned from L (and thus the auditor only knows their indices and nothing else), and transactions $[tx_{ij}]_{i=\gamma}^{\beta}$ which are still public in L (i.e. not pruned) and thus the auditor still sees their encryptions. This protocol generalizes AuditSum$\{\}$. It allows the auditor to audit B_j for: (a) specific transactions (pruned or not) and, (b) sums of assets (pruned or not). For case (a), besides auditing a transaction with index in $[\gamma, \ldots, \beta]$ which is still in L, the auditor can also audit B_j for a specific transaction that has been pruned from L (i.e. ask: "Which was the value of the i-th transaction?"). The Bank would respond with the corresponding C_{ij} and depending on the underlying accumulator used, B_j would also provide a proof that C_{ij} is a member of its pruned history D_j with index i. For case (b), an auditor can audit the total (or a range of) assets of B_j no matter what transaction information of B_j remains on L. Auditing total assets works as follows: B_j fetches the stored transaction encryptions $[C_{ij}]_{i=\alpha}^{\gamma}$ from its local memory st_j, computes $[w_{ij}]_{i=\alpha}^{\gamma} \leftarrow$ MemWitCreate$(D_j, [C_{ij}]_{i=\alpha}^{\gamma}, st_j)$. Then A reads D_j from L and executes VerMem$(D_j, (i \| C_{ij}), w_{ij}) \forall i \in (\alpha, \gamma)$, outputting $[b_{ij}]_{i=\alpha}^{\gamma}$. For every i, if $b_{ij} == 1$ it executes the Audit$\{\}$ protocol with C_{ij} as input.

10. AudTotal$\{A(Q_{ij}) \leftrightarrow B_j(sk_j)\}$ is equivalent to Audit$\{\}$ for auditing B_j's total assets $\sum_{i=1}^{m} v_{ij}$ instead of a single v_{ij}.

Table 2. MiniLedger architecture and pruning.

(a) Ledger state before pruning, assuming B_1 had pruned before at tx_{10}.		
	B_1	... B_n
tx_1 ... tx_9	$D_{9,1}, Q_{9,1}$	...
tx_{10}	$C_{10,1} = (c_1 = pk_1^{r_{10,1}}, c_2 = g^{v_{10,1}} h^{r_{10,1}})$ $\pi_{10,1}, cm_{10,1}, Q_{10,1}$	...
tx_{11}	$C_{11,1} = (c_1 = pk_1^{r_{11,1}}, c_2 = g^{v_{11,1}} h^{r_{11,1}})$ $\pi_{11,1}, cm_{11,1}, Q_{11,1}$	...

(b) Ledger state after B_1 prunes at tx_{12}. Digest $D_{11,1}$ represents $C_{10,1}, C_{11,1}$ and ciphertexts that were represented in $D_{9,1}$.		
	B_1	... B_n
tx_1 ... tx_{11}	$D_{11,1}, Q_{11,1}$	...
tx_{12}	$C_{12,1} = (c_1 = pk_1^{r_{12,1}}, c_2 = g^{v_{12,1}} h^{r_{12,1}})$ $\pi_{12,1}, cm_{12,1}, Q_{12,1}$	...

MiniLedger architecture is shown in Table 2. We informally discuss its security in Appendix A and we provide a rigorous analysis in [15].

4.2 Discussion and Comparisons

Although MiniLedger architecture resembles zkLedger [34], there exist crucial differences that make MiniLedger superior both in terms of efficiency and security. We give an overview below, and a thorough analysis in the full version [15].

Storage. As already discussed, MiniLedger by leveraging consensus properties applies a pruning strategy which achieves $O(n)$ storage requirements for L, compared to $O(mn)$ for zkLedger (where m is the total number of transactions ever happened, and is a monotonically increasing value).

Security. MiniLedger does not require any out-of-band communication, as all needed information is communicated through the ledger using encryptions. On the other hand, zkLedger assumes if a Bank is actually receiving some value in a transaction, it should be notified by the sending Bank and also learn the associated value (which was hidden in the commitment) through an out-of-band channel. zkLedger however, does not require receiving Banks to be directly informed on the randomness (i.e. commitment cm_{ij} is never opened), since they can still answer the audits correctly using the audit tokens, provided that it knows its total assets precisely. This assumption is very strong and can potentially lead to attacks, such as the *"unknown value"* attack where a malicious sending Bank informs the receiving Bank on a wrong value (or does not inform it at all), which then prevents the receiving Bank from answering audits or even participate in the system. More importantly, with transaction values communicated out-of-bank, the randomness could be included with them as well. This would make the system trivial and defeat the purpose of most of its architecture, as the ledger would consist of just Pedersen commitments and proofs of assets. In this version the above attack would not work assuming all Banks are *always* online and verify the openings in real time, which is also a very strong assumption.

Computation. MINILEDGER optimizes ZK proof computation over zkLedger by combining disjunctive proof of assets and proof of consistency into a single proof, giving an efficiency gain of roughly 10% in space and computation. Additionally, while zkLedger's computation performance degrades over time (as the monotonically-increasing ledger requires more operations to construct transactions), MINILEDGER achieves steady optimal performance.

On Setup Parameters. We argue that even with the use of a TP, the trust level is rather low. The parameters of ElGamal are just random generators (similar to Pedersen commitments in zkLedger) and for certain accumulator instantiations (such as Merkle trees) there is no trapdoor behind the parameter generation. Finally, the consensus setup essentially consists of choosing trapdoorless parameters (i.e. block specifics etc.) and the set of participating parties. Thus, the only trust placed in TP is to pick a valid set of participants – something that all participants can check, exactly as in zkLedger. In comparison to zkLedger (given that ElGamal parameters are the same as Pedersen commitment parameters), the only additional setup is that of the accumulator which as discussed, for certain instantiations can be completely trapdoorless.

5   Evaluation

We implement a prototype of the transaction layer of MINILEDGER in Python over the secp256k1 elliptic curve. We use the *zksk* library [27] for the ZK and implement range proofs using the Schoenmakers' Multi-Base Decomposition method [38][2]. The measurements were performed on Ubuntu 18.04 - i5-8500 3.0 GHz CPU - 16 GB RAM using a single thread[3].

Accumulator Instantiation
A critical implementation choice is how to instantiate the accumulator needed for the pruning operations. For efficiency reasons, we require schemes with constant size public parameters and no upper bound on the number of accumulated (i.e. pruned) elements. We only consider schemes that have at most sublinear computation and communication complexity (in the number of pruned elements) for opening/proving a single transaction to the auditor and where the auditor's verification cost is also at most sublinear.

We first consider Merkle trees [31]. Assuming a Bank prunes q transactions, the Merkle root provides $O(1)$ representation in terms of storage with $O(1)$ public parameters. Opening and verification complexity of Merkle proofs for a single transaction audit involves $O(\log q)$ hashing operations. However although hashes are relatively cheap operations, the over-linear verification complexity might be

---

[2] By using twisted ElGamal [17], MINILEDGER is fully-compatible with Bulletproofs [11] which can further reduce its concrete storage requirements.

[3] A basic implementation of MINILEDGER is available at https://github.com/ PanosChtz/Miniledger.

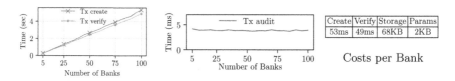

Fig. 2. Transaction creation, verification and auditing costs.

a concern when auditing a series of transactions. Finally, it should be noted that Merkle trees only support membership proofs.

We then consider the batch-RSA accumulator [8]. Given that all RSA accumulators can only accumulate primes p, we use a deterministic prime mapping hash function (as in [8]) to accumulate arbitrary inputs. The batch-RSA accumulator has $O(1)$ storage for its digest with $O(1)$ public parameters as well. Proving membership for a single element p in the standard RSA accumulator, requires the prover computing a witness w equal to the primes' product in the accumulator without p (an $O(q)$ operation as shown in Fig. 4), and the verifier checking that $(g^w)^p = A$ where A is the current state of the accumulator. Therefore, batch-RSA achieves same complexity $O(q)$ for a set of elements $(p_1, ..., p_\ell)$ as when proving membership of a single element (while Merkle Trees have $O(\ell \log q)$ complexity). Consequently, the basic pruning operations Prune() and PruneVrfy() are about two orders of magnitude more expensive compared to Merkle trees as we show in Fig. 3. However they are efficient when auditing large amounts of transactions especially if auditing the total sum. Then, batching allows for negligible computation costs for the proving Bank, and negligible audit verification cost for a single transaction. Thus, choice between Merkle trees and batch-RSA accumulators ultimately relies on the use-case requirements.

For our batch-RSA implementation, we use the SHA-256 hash function and the Miller - Rabin primality test for hashing to prime numbers, and we use an RSA-3072 modulo to maintain the same level of security [35]. We decouple the witness computation cost from the proof of membership cost for the Bank, as the Bank might elect to pre-compute the witnesses before its audit (assuming however that it does not prune again until the audit, since that would require the witnesses to be recomputed again). Note the auditor needs to run the hashing to prime mapping function again for all audited values (i.e. the auditor cannot rely on the "honesty" of a Bank presenting pre-computed prime numbers for its pruned transactions). For Merkle trees, we use SHA-256 as well.

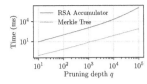

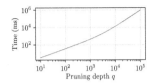

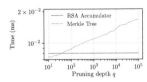

Fig. 3. Pruning computation cost

Fig. 4. RSA witness Generation cost

Fig. 5. Audit open cost for one tx

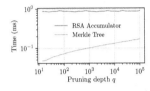

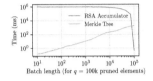

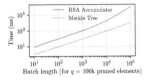

Fig. 6. Audit verify cost

Fig. 7. Batch audit open costs

Fig. 8. Batch audit verify costs

Transaction Creation, Verification and Auditing. Every MINILEDGER transaction includes an ElGamal ciphertext C, a commitment cm, a NIZK π and a running total Q for *each* Bank. Naturally, this results in linearly-increasing computation costs in terms of number of Banks as shown in Fig. 2 for both transaction creation and verification. Storing the running total Q leads to constant transaction creation and verification computational costs (for fixed number of Banks), making total assets auditing much more efficient. In contrast, zkLedger's growing ledger size also implies linearly-increasing NIZK verification costs, as the verifier would need to compute the product of all transaction elements for each Bank. The transaction creation and verification costs are 53 ms and 49 ms respectively (for a single cell in L), roughly comparable with [34].

Auditing any single value on the ledger takes about 4 ms as shown in Fig. 2. This is the cost for the complete auditing protocol, namely the decryption and proving cost for the Bank and the verification cost for the Auditor. In contrast to [34], the auditing cost is constant without being impacted either by the number of Banks or the number of past transactions.

Transaction Pruning. We evaluate the computation requirements of the pruning operation which involves executing Prune() and PruneVrfy() to create the digest D_j. Our results in Fig. 3 show it is possible to prune and verify about 1 million transactions in less than a second using Merkle trees and in about 2 h using RSA accumulator. Note prime number multiplication costs dominate the total costs (which also include hashing to primes and an exponentiation) when the pruning depth becomes large. We also stress that these computation requirements are *independent* of the number of Banks n in the system.

For transaction auditing in AudPruned{} interactive protocol, auditing opening and verification costs are shown in Figs. 5 and 6 respectively. As previously discussed, we do not include the RSA accumulator's witness creation costs (which can be pre-computed) and are shown in Fig. 4.

For auditing sums of values (i.e. "batch" auditing), the associated costs for opening and verifying a 100K transaction digest are shown in Figs. 7 and 8 respectively, with x-axis representing the number of audited transactions. Note that for auditing 10^5 transactions (i.e. the whole sum), RSA accumulator opening is significantly cheaper compared to Merkle trees, as the audited Bank would only need to retrieve the respective transactions from its local memory (which implies nearly $O(1)$ cost) and send them to the auditor (who would in turn need to recompute all primes and perform the exponentiation of their product).

Based on our evaluation results and the discussion above, the choice between Merkle tree and batch RSA accumulator depends on use-case. Merkle trees fit a system expected to incorporate sparse audits on individual transactions, while RSA accumulator is preferred on deployments with frequent auditing on many transactions at a time (e.g. sums of assets or value thresholds over a time period).

Storage Costs. The storage cost for L has a $64n$-byte lower bound for the ElGamal variant encryptions (which represent the running total Q), plus the needed storage for each digest D and the system's pp, assuming all n Banks have pruned their transaction history and the ledger is made of a single row. Concretely, in our implementation each transaction's communication and storage cost is 68 KB per Bank (actual memory footprint), which includes the ElGamal variant encryption, the auxiliary commitment, the NIZK and the running total. A MiniLedger instantiation including the necessary public parameters, one transaction and a digest requires only 70 KB of storage per Bank.

Network and Consensus Costs. MiniLedger design focuses in the transaction layer. The consensus layer, which can be instantiated by *any* consensus protocol that satisfies the basic properties of consistency and liveness, is orthogonal to our work and providing a full implementation including a consensus layer is out of scope (note previous works [17,19,34,41] take a similar evaluation approach and do not include consensus measurements). Still for showcasing an implementation scenario, we discuss below how MiniLedger could be implemented using Hyperledger Fabric and also provide some rough cost estimations.

For simplicity and efficiency, we consider Banks only acting as "clients", outsourcing ledger storage and consensus operations to an arbitrary number of "peer" and "orderer" nodes respectively. These numbers are entirely dependent on the use-case and does not affect MiniLedger performance or scalability. This separation between Banks and consensus participants

Table 3. Consensus costs

Banks	Peers	Tx/s	Network
10	80	21	LAN
100	4	2	WAN

is quite natural (e.g. Diem [2], uses similar approach i.e. decoupled permissioned consensus and provider-intermediated transactions [3]). Given Hyperledger requires at least 0.5 s to complete a full consensus operation with 4 peers and 256-bit ECDSA [4], we derive conservative estimations of the expected transaction throughput, shown in Table 3. These estimations are more than sufficient for intra-Bank transactions in a deployed system (in MiniLedger+, any number of client-to-client transactions can be aggregated in a single MiniLedger transaction). Note although permissioned consensus generally seems more fitting to MiniLedger, permissionless consensus could also be utilized when implemented on top of an smart contract.

6   Conclusion

We present MiniLedger, the first *private and auditable payment system with storage independent to the number of transactions*. MiniLedger utilizes existing cryptographic tools and innovates on the meticulous design of optimized ZK proofs to tackle important scalability issues in auditable, private payments. We achieve huge storage savings compared to previous works that store information for each transaction ever happened. Using our pruning techniques, the overall MiniLedger size can be impressively compacted to 70KB per Bank, no matter how many transactions have ever occurred. Note that our storage and computation costs could be further improved, e.g. by using Bulletproofs [11] (instead of Schoenmakers multi-base decomposition [38]), more efficient programming languages (e.g. Rust) and libraries, or by utilizing CPU parallelization. However, as in related systems [2,34] our goal is not to support "thousands" of Banks, but an arbitrary number of clients as discussed in Appendix A which does not affect the computation/storage costs in the public ledger. MiniLedger can currently serve a small consortium of Banks (e.g. the world's Central Banks) with an *arbitrary* number of clients, or build a hierarchy of a large number of Banks and clients in accordance with MiniLedger+. Evaluating MiniLedger in such a large scale or achieving its properties in a permissionless setting are interesting directions for future work.

A   MiniLedger Security and Extensions

A.1   MiniLedger security

We achieve the security of MiniLedger construction as follows: *Theft prevention and balance:* relies on NIZK soundness of π (e.g. prevent a cheating prover to make false claims such as knowledge of sk or v in range) and consensus consistency. *Secure pruning:* relies on accumulator soundness (e.g. prevent accepting a digest not representing the exact set of pruned transactions) and consensus consistency. *Ledger correctness:* relies on consensus consistency. *Correct and Sound auditability:* relies on NIZK soundness (e.g. preventing convincing an auditor for a false claim), accumulator soundness and consensus consistency. *Privacy:*

relies on IND-CPA security of ElGamal variant, Pedersen commitment hiding and NIZK zero-knowledgeness (e.g. prevent distinguishing information on the ledger or leaking private information during transaction creation).

A.2   Adding Clients for Fine-grained Auditing (MiniLedger+)

At a high level, each Bank B_j maintains a *private* ledger of clients L_{B_j} (denoted as "UsrDB" in Fig. 1), independent of the public ledger L. For each client m, B_j stores its transactions in encrypted format. For a B_s client to transfer value v to a B_r client, she creates a transaction that includes encryptions of the recipient client's pk, the receiver's Bank B_r and v, as well as appropriate NIZKs to prove consistency with the protocol, which is recorded on the private ledger L_{B_s}. Then B_s constructs a transaction on L that transfers v to B_r, which in turn decrypts the information and allocates v to its recipient client. MiniLedger+ preserves anonymity while enabling fine-grained auditing at a client level, including checks that Banks allocated the funds correctly. It also has minimal overhead compared to MiniLedger while still maintaining a ledger of constant size. We provide a detailed description and analysis in the full version [15].

A.3   Additional Types of Audits

As shown in Sect. 4.1, MiniLedger basic audit functionality Audit{} is on the value v_{ij} of specific transaction tx_{ij}. Several more audit types can be constructed which reduce to that basic audit. We discuss some of those below, and provide more details for audit extensions in the full version [15]. Note these audits can still be executed for pruned data.

Full Transaction Audit: For an auditor to learn the full details of a transaction (sender, receiver and values), they would have to audit the entire row (i.e. perform n audits on v_{ij} $\forall j$).

Statistical Audits: Audits such as average or standard deviation are supported by utilizing "bit flags" to disregard zero-value transactions, proved for correctness in zero knowledge.

Value or Transactions Exceeding Limit: Utilizing appropriate range proofs, an auditor can learn if a sent or received value exceeds some limit t. Multiple range proofs can show a Bank has not exceeded the limit over a time period.

Transaction Recipient: The goal of this audit type is for a sending Bank to prove the recipients for one of its transactions. While a Bank doesn't know (and therefore cannot prove) where a *received* value came from (unless learning it out-of-band as in zkLedger), for *outbound* transactions the Bank can keep an additional record of its transaction recipients in its local memory. As an example, for proving in tx_i that the Bank really sent v_{ij} to B_j, it could send this claim to the auditor who in turn would simply then audit B_j to verify this claim.

Client Audits: Audits in a client level (e.g. statistical audits or transaction limits) can be performed similar to the respective audits in a Bank level, however the auditor needs first to learn and verify the Bank's private ledger L_B as discussed above. From that point, the auditor can perform all audits in a client level in a similar fashion to the respective audits in a Bank level. For instance, to learn if some MINILEDGER+ client exceeded a value transaction threshold within a time period or over a number of transactions, this audit can be executed by selecting the client's transactions from the Bank's private table that happened within this period by their id's. The audit would then be on the sum of the values represented by the product of the respective ciphertexts, and the client would produce a range proof for that ciphertext product as above. and select those with the appropriate timestamp. A special useful audit would be to learn if a MINILEDGER+ client has sent assets to some specific client pk or not. The transactions would need to be augmented with an additive universal accumulator, with each sender adding the end client recipient's pk to the accumulator, while also providing its Bank a ZK proof of adding the correct public key. During an audit, the client would have to prove membership (or non membership) to the auditor. An important note is that the receiving client *does not* directly learn the original sender of a specific transaction in-band, which implies the above approach cannot work for a client to prove if he has *received* (or not) assets from another client.

Non-interactive Audits: The audit proof π^{Aud} described in Sect. 4 is interactive and require the Bank's consent. While can treat a Bank's refusal to cooperate as a failed audit, we could still enable non-interactive audits by including an encryption of π^{Aud} and its statement for each transaction cell under a pre-determined trusted auditor's public key (which preserves privacy). Our full version [15] provides more details.

References

1. Privacy coins face existential threat amid regulatory pinch. https://www.bloomberg.com/news/articles/2019-09-19/privacy-coins-face-existential-threat-amid-regulatory-crackdown
2. The libra blockchain (2020). https://developers.libra.org/docs/assets/papers/the-libra-blockchain/2020-05-26.pdf
3. Libra roles and permissions (2020). https://lip.libra.org/lip-2/
4. Androulaki, E., et al.: Hyperledger fabric: a distributed operating system for permissioned blockchains. In: Oliveira, R., Felber, P., Hu, Y.C. (eds.) Proceedings of the Thirteenth EuroSys Conference, Porto, Portugal, 23–26 April 2018, pp. 30:1–30:15. ACM (2018)
5. Androulaki, E., Karame, G.O., Roeschlin, M., Scherer, T., Capkun, S.: Evaluating user privacy in bitcoin. In: Sadeghi, A.-R. (ed.) FC 2013. LNCS, vol. 7859, pp. 34–51. Springer, Heidelberg (2013). https://doi.org/10.1007/978-3-642-39884-1_4

6. Baldimtsi, F., et al.: Accumulators with applications to anonymity-preserving revocation. In: 2017 IEEE European Symposium on Security and Privacy, Paris, France, 26–28 April 2017, pp. 301–315. IEEE (2017)
7. Ben-Sasson, E., et al.: Zerocash: decentralized anonymous payments from bitcoin. In: 2014 IEEE Symposium on Security and Privacy, pp. 459–474. IEEE Computer Society Press (2014). https://doi.org/10.1109/SP.2014.36
8. Boneh, D., Bünz, B., Fisch, B.: Batching techniques for accumulators with applications to IOPs and stateless blockchains. In: Boldyreva, A., Micciancio, D. (eds.) CRYPTO 2019. LNCS, vol. 11692, pp. 561–586. Springer, Cham (2019). https://doi.org/10.1007/978-3-030-26948-7_20
9. Bonneau, J., Meckler, I., Rao, V., Shapiro, E.: Coda: decentralized cryptocurrency at scale. Cryptology ePrint Archive, Report 2020/352 (2020)
10. Bünz, B., Agrawal, S., Zamani, M., Boneh, D.: Zether: towards privacy in a smart contract world. In: Bonneau, J., Heninger, N. (eds.) FC 2020. LNCS, vol. 12059, pp. 423–443. Springer, Cham (2020). https://doi.org/10.1007/978-3-030-51280-4_23
11. Bünz, B., Bootle, J., Boneh, D., Poelstra, A., Wuille, P., Maxwell, G.: Bulletproofs: Short proofs for confidential transactions and more. In: 2018 IEEE Symposium on Security and Privacy, pp. 315–334. IEEE Computer Society Press (2018)
12. Camenisch, J., Stadler, M.: Efficient group signature schemes for large groups. In: Kaliski, B.S. (ed.) CRYPTO 1997. LNCS, vol. 1294, pp. 410–424. Springer, Heidelberg (1997). https://doi.org/10.1007/BFb0052252
13. Castro, M., Liskov, B.: Practical byzantine fault tolerance. In: Proceedings of the Third USENIX Symposium on Operating Systems Design and Implementation (OSDI), New Orleans, Louisiana, USA, 22–25 February 1999, pp. 173–186 (1999)
14. Cecchetti, E., Zhang, F., Ji, Y., Kosba, A.E., Juels, A., Shi, E.: Solidus: confidential distributed ledger transactions via PVORM. In: Thuraisingham, B.M., Evans, D., Malkin, T., Xu, D. (eds.) ACM CCS 2017, pp. 701–717. ACM Press (2017). https://doi.org/10.1145/3133956.3134010
15. Chatzigiannis, P., Baldimtsi, F.: Miniledger: compact-sized anonymous and auditable distributed payments. Cryptology ePrint Archive, Report 2021/869 (2021). https://ia.cr/2021/869
16. Chatzigiannis, P., Baldimtsi, F., Chalkias, K.: SoK: auditability and accountability in distributed payment systems. In: Sako, K., Tippenhauer, N.O. (eds.) ACNS 2021. LNCS, vol. 12727, pp. 311–337. Springer, Cham (2021). https://doi.org/10.1007/978-3-030-78375-4_13
17. Chen, Yu., Ma, X., Tang, C., Au, M.H.: PGC: decentralized confidential payment system with auditability. In: Chen, L., Li, N., Liang, K., Schneider, S. (eds.) ESORICS 2020. LNCS, vol. 12308, pp. 591–610. Springer, Cham (2020). https://doi.org/10.1007/978-3-030-58951-6_29
18. Chepurnoy, A., Papamanthou, C., Zhang, Y.: Edrax: a cryptocurrency with stateless transaction validation. Cryptology ePrint Archive, Report 2018/968 (2018). https://eprint.iacr.org/2018/968
19. Fauzi, P., Meiklejohn, S., Mercer, R., Orlandi, C.: Quisquis: a new design for anonymous cryptocurrencies. In: Galbraith, S.D., Moriai, S. (eds.) ASIACRYPT 2019. LNCS, vol. 11921, pp. 649–678. Springer, Cham (2019). https://doi.org/10.1007/978-3-030-34578-5_23
20. Fuchsbauer, G., Orrù, M., Seurin, Y.: Aggregate cash systems: a cryptographic investigation of mimblewimble. In: Ishai, Y., Rijmen, V. (eds.) EUROCRYPT 2019. LNCS, vol. 11476, pp. 657–689. Springer, Cham (2019). https://doi.org/10.1007/978-3-030-17653-2_22

21. Garay, J., Kiayias, A.: SoK: a consensus taxonomy in the blockchain era. In: Jarecki, S. (ed.) CT-RSA 2020. LNCS, vol. 12006, pp. 284–318. Springer, Cham (2020). https://doi.org/10.1007/978-3-030-40186-3_13

22. Garman, C., Green, M., Miers, I.: Accountable privacy for decentralized anonymous payments. In: Grossklags, J., Preneel, B. (eds.) FC 2016. LNCS, vol. 9603, pp. 81–98. Springer, Heidelberg (2017). https://doi.org/10.1007/978-3-662-54970-4_5

23. Gennaro, R., Jarecki, S., Krawczyk, H., Rabin, T.: Secure distributed key generation for discrete-log based cryptosystems. In: Stern, J. (ed.) EUROCRYPT 1999. LNCS, vol. 1592, pp. 295–310. Springer, Heidelberg (1999). https://doi.org/10.1007/3-540-48910-X_21

24. Heasman, W.: Privacy coins in 2019: True financial freedom or a criminal's delight? (2020). https://cointelegraph.com/news/privacy-coins-in-2019-true-financial-freedom-or-a-criminals-delight

25. Jiang, Y., Li, Y., Zhu, Y.: Auditable zerocoin scheme with user awareness. In: Proceedings of the 3rd International Conference on Cryptography, Security and Privacy, Kuala Lumpur, Malaysia, 19–21 January 2019, pp. 28–32 (2019)

26. Li, Y., Yang, G., Susilo, W., Yu, Y., Au, M.H., Liu, D.: Traceable monero: anonymous cryptocurrency with enhanced accountability. IEEE Trans. Depend. Secure Comput. (2019). https://doi.org/10.1109/TDSC.2019.2910058

27. Lueks, W., Kulynych, B., Fasquelle, J., Bail-Collet, S.L., Troncoso, C.: zksk: a library for composable zero-knowledge proofs. In: Proceedings of the 18th ACM Workshop on Privacy in the Electronic Society, pp. 50–54 (2019)

28. Maxwell, G.: Confidential transactions (2015). https://people.xiph.org/~greg/confidential_values.txt

29. Maxwell, G., Poelstra, A.: Borromean ring signatures (2015). https://github.com/Blockstream/borromean_paper/blob/master/borromean_draft_0.01_34241bb.pdf

30. Meiklejohn, S., et al.: A fistful of bitcoins: characterizing payments among men with no names. Commun. ACM **59**(4), 86–93 (2016)

31. Merkle, R.C.: A digital signature based on a conventional encryption function. In: Pomerance, C. (ed.) CRYPTO 1987. LNCS, vol. 293, pp. 369–378. Springer, Heidelberg (1988). https://doi.org/10.1007/3-540-48184-2_32

32. Naganuma, K., Yoshino, M., Sato, H., Suzuki, T.: Auditable zerocoin. In: 2017 IEEE European Symposium on Security and Privacy Workshops, pp. 59–63 (2017)

33. Nakamoto, S.: Bitcoin: A peer-to-peer electronic cash system (2008)

34. Narula, N., Vasquez, W., Virza, M.: zkledger: privacy-preserving auditing for distributed ledgers. In: 15th USENIX Symposium on Networked Systems Design and Implementation, pp. 65–80. USENIX Association, Renton (2018)

35. National Institute of Standards and Technology: Recommendation for Key Management: NIST SP 800-57 Part 1 Rev 4. USA (2016)

36. Pedersen, T.P.: Non-interactive and information-theoretic secure verifiable secret sharing. In: Feigenbaum, J. (ed.) CRYPTO 1991. LNCS, vol. 576, pp. 129–140. Springer, Heidelberg (1992). https://doi.org/10.1007/3-540-46766-1_9

37. Poelstra, A., Back, A., Friedenbach, M., Maxwell, G., Wuille, P.: Confidential assets. In: Zohar, A., et al. (eds.) FC 2018. LNCS, vol. 10958, pp. 43–63. Springer, Heidelberg (2019). https://doi.org/10.1007/978-3-662-58820-8_4

38. Schoenmakers, B.: Interval proofs revisited. In: Workshop on Frontiers in Electronic Elections (2005)

39. Van Saberhagen, N.: Cryptonote v 2.0 (2013). https://cryptonote.org/whitepaper.pdf

40. Wood, G.: Ethereum: a secure decentralized generalised transaction ledger (2021). https://ethereum.github.io/yellowpaper/paper.pdf, Accessed 14 Feb 2021
41. Wüst, K., Kostiainen, K., Čapkun, V., Čapkun, S.: PRCash: fast, private and regulated transactions for digital currencies. In: Goldberg, I., Moore, T. (eds.) FC 2019. LNCS, vol. 11598, pp. 158–178. Springer, Cham (2019). https://doi.org/10.1007/978-3-030-32101-7_11

Succinct Scriptable NIZK via Trusted Hardware

Bingsheng Zhang[1]([✉]), Yuan Chen[1], Jiaqi Li[1], Yajin Zhou[1], Phuc Thai[2], Hong-Sheng Zhou[2], and Kui Ren[1,3]

[1] Zhejiang University, Hangzhou, China
{bingsheng,yajin_zhou,kuiren}@zju.edu.cn
[2] Virginia Commonwealth University, Richmond, USA
{thaipd,hszhou}@vcu.edu
[3] Key Laboratory of Blockchain and Cyberspace Governance of Zhejiang Province, Hangzhou, China

Abstract. Non-interactive zero-knowledge proof or argument (NIZK) systems are widely used in many security sensitive applications to enhance computation integrity, privacy and scalability. In such systems, a prover wants to convince one or more verifiers that the result of a public function is correctly computed without revealing the (potential) private input, such as the witness. In this work, we introduce a new notion, called succinct scriptable NIZK, where the prover and verifier(s) can specify the function (or language instance) to be proven via a script. We formalize this notion is UC framework and provide a generic trusted hardware based solution. We then instantiate our solution in both SGX and Trustzone with Lua script engine. The system can be easily used by typical programmers without any cryptographic background. The benchmark result shows that our solution is better than all the known NIZK proof systems w.r.t. prover's running time (1000 times faster), verifier's running time, and the proof size. Finally, we show how the proposed scriptable succinct NIZK can be readily deployed to solve many well-known problems in the blockchain context, e.g. verifier's dilemma, fast joining for new players, etc..

1 Introduction

Collaboration is one of the main driving forces for the sustainable advancement of our civilization, growing from small-size tributes, to cities, and then to large-scale states. Being a part of the modern society, we are interacting with hundreds of known/unknown entities either physically or remotely. The main motivation of this work is to introduce new concepts and frameworks to enable more effective collaborations. One potential candidate tool is a well-known cryptographic primitive—zero knowledge (ZK) proof/argument system. In a ZK system, two players, the prover and the verifier, are involved; one hand, the prover who holds a valid witness of an NP statement, is able to convince the verifier that the statement is true without revealing the corresponding witness; on the other hand, if

© Springer Nature Switzerland AG 2021
E. Bertino et al. (Eds.): ESORICS 2021, LNCS 12972, pp. 430–451, 2021.
https://doi.org/10.1007/978-3-030-88418-5_21

the prover does not know any valid witness of the statement, then he cannot convince the verifier. ZK systems can be used to enable trustworthy collaborations: all players in a protocol are required to prove the correctness of their behaviors in the protocol execution. However, to enable effective collaborations, desired properties are expected, and we will elaborate them below.

Our Design Choices. In a large-scale collaboration network, it is infeasible for a party to prove the correctness of its computation to all other parties one by one. The first property we need from ZK systems, is *(1) non-interactiveness* in the sense that the prover only needs to prove the correctness of the computation once, and the prover then can send the same proof to all other parties i.e., the verifiers. From now on, we use NIZK to denote non-interactive ZK systems. The second desirable property we need is *(2) succinctness*, given the fact that the bottleneck for large-scale collaboration is the capacity of the underlying peer-to-peer network communication. Furthermore, as already mentioned, we note that in a typical application scenario a single prover will prove the same statement to many verifiers. In this *unbalanced* setting, a desirable NIZK proof system should have the property of *(3) lightning fast verifier*.

Up to now, those properties have already been achieved by a number of existing NIZK proof systems, such as zk-SNARK [15,33], zk-STARK [3], etc. However, these NIZK systems have not been widely used in practice yet. A significant barrier is the that the computation of prover is very heavy. The state-of-the-art NIZK systems need hours to prove large statement even on a powerful PC (32 cores and 512 GB RAM [3]), let alone portable devices such as smartphones, tablets, and IoT devices. We aim to develop a NIZK system with the property of *(4) truly lightweight prover*.

To enable wide adoption of NIZK in the real world, the design must be *(5) deployment friendly*. The underlying cryptographic machinery should be transparent to the developers, and the protocol can be operated without cryptographic background. Unfortunately, all existing NIZK proof systems for universal language require re-compilation of both prover and verifier's executable binary files for every new language instance.

Our Approach. We propose a new primitive, called *succinct scriptable NIZK*, with the goal of achieving all desirable properties above. This new primitive allows the developers to specify the language instance or computation to be verified *via a script without any re-compilation*. Similar to NIZK proof systems for universal language, a scriptable NIZK system can support multiple language instances, depending on the script language design and the script engine execution environment. Different from existing succinct NIZK systems for universal language, our scriptable NIZK is very easy to use; for a new language instance, the players can easily define the scripts and no further compilation is required.

Defining Scriptable NIZK. We assume both the prover and the verifiers have agreed on the *function/script*, denoted as $\mathcal{C}$, the *public input*, denoted as $\mathsf{Input}_{\mathrm{pub}}$, and the *(public) output*, denoted as Output; in addition, the prover keeps a *private input*, denoted as $\mathsf{Input}_{\mathrm{priv}}$, such that $\mathcal{C}(\mathsf{Input}_{\mathrm{pub}}, \mathsf{Input}_{\mathrm{priv}}) = \mathsf{Output}$. The prover is able to prove to the verifiers that he knows a private input $\mathsf{Input}_{\mathrm{priv}}$ that would make the script execution $\mathcal{C}(\mathsf{Input}_{\mathrm{pub}}, \mathsf{Input}_{\mathrm{priv}})$ to generate output Output.

We note that not all scripts can be supported; each scriptable NIZK system is parameterized by a predicate Q, and $\mathsf{Q}(\mathcal{C}, \mathsf{Input}_{\mathrm{pub}}, \mathsf{Input}_{\mathrm{priv}}, \mathsf{Output}) = 1$ for any valid script $\mathcal{C}$. The predicate Q is defined by the script language design and the script engine execution environment.

An NP language $\mathcal{L}$ is defined by its polynomial-time decidable relation $\mathcal{R}$; namely, $\mathcal{L} := \{x : \exists w \text{ s.t. } (x, w) \in \mathcal{R}\}$. In practice, for each relation $\mathcal{R}$, we assume there exists a corresponding script $\mathcal{C}_{\mathcal{R}}$ such that $\mathcal{C}_{\mathcal{R}}(x, w) = 1$ iff $(x, w) \in \mathcal{R}$; otherwise, $\mathcal{C}_{\mathcal{R}}(x, w) = 0$. To use the scriptable NIZK system for an NP language, the prover and the verifiers set $\mathsf{Input}_{\mathrm{pub}} := x$, $\mathsf{Input}_{\mathrm{priv}} := w$, $\mathsf{Output} := 1$, and the script as $\mathcal{C}_{\mathcal{R}}$. The notion is formally modeled in the UC framework.

Constructing Succinct Scriptable NIZK. We then present a generic succinct scriptable NIZK construction in the trusted hardware model. Trusted hardware can enable an isolated and trusted computation environment where security sensitive data can be stored and processed with confidentiality and integrity guarantees. Most existing trusted hardware based applications, e.g., [14] emphasize on the confidentiality aspect, while the security of our construction mainly relies on the computational integrity guaranteed by trusted hardware. The main idea is as follows. Recall that in a NIZK proof, the prover and the verifier have common input $(\mathcal{C}_{\mathcal{R}}, \mathsf{Input}_{\mathrm{pub}} := x)$. The potentially malicious prover wants to convince the verifiers that he knows a witness $\mathsf{Input}_{\mathrm{priv}} := w$ such that $\mathcal{C}_{\mathcal{R}}(\mathsf{Input}_{\mathrm{pub}}, \mathsf{Input}_{\mathrm{priv}}) = 1$. Since the trusted hardware can guarantee computation integrity even when the host is malicious, we can let $\mathcal{O}_{\mathrm{HW}}^{\mathsf{Q}}$ to execute the relationship decision algorithm $b \leftarrow \mathcal{C}_{\mathcal{R}}(x, w)$ and sign the output b. To bind the decision algorithm and statement, we let $\mathcal{O}_{\mathrm{HW}}^{\mathsf{Q}}$ sign $(\mathcal{C}_{\mathcal{R}}, x, b)$ without revealing the witness w. Therefore, by checking the signature, the verifier is convinced that the prover must know a witness w such that $\mathcal{C}_{\mathcal{R}}(x, w) = 1$ if $(\mathcal{C}_{\mathcal{R}}, x, 1)$ is signed by $\mathcal{O}_{\mathrm{HW}}^{\mathsf{Q}}$. Similarly, for general computation, the private input $\mathsf{Input}_{\mathrm{priv}}$ is not signed; therefore, zero-knowledge property is preserved even if the signature leaks the signed message.

Although there are a number of works in the literature studying how to speed up secure computing via trusted hardware, such as Intel SGX, we emphasize that this problem has not been solved by previous works. The closest related work is sealed-glass proof introduced by Tramer *et al.* [38], where the authors try to explore some use cases even if the isolated execution environment has unbounded leakage, i.e., arbitrary side-channels. We note that, their primitive is interactive, thus not scalable; in their protocol, for each verification, the trusted hardware must be interacted with. Our primitive is non-interactive, and in our construction, the verifier can verify the proof without interacting with the trusted hardware. There are also many theoretical differences between interactive ZK and non-interactive ZK, such as the minimum assumptions needed to realize the primitive; therefore, this work is not covered by [38]. Most importantly, ours is the first work to investigate *scriptable* NIZK, which is developer-friendly.

Instantiation. We instantiate our succinct scriptable NIZK proof system on two most popular trusted hardware platforms: Intel SGX and Arm TrustZone. The main component is the Q-compliant hardware functionality $\mathcal{O}_{HW}^Q$. In terms of Intel SGX, the $\mathcal{O}_{HW}^Q$ functionality is instantiated by three entities: the (trusted) Intel server, the prover, and the SGX hardware device. In terms of Arm Trust-Zone, currently only manufacture has the privilege to access TrustZone root keys; nevertheless, our system uses Hikey 960 TrustZone development board. The $\mathcal{O}_{HW}^Q$ functionality is instantiated by two entities: the (trusted) authority server, and the TrustZone development board.

With regard to scriptability, in practice, it is a challenge for a third party to verify the consistency between an executable binary and its software specification. That is, the binary contains no bug, no trapdoor, and it is not subverted. Even if it is possible, it dramatically increases the verifier's complexity. On the other hand, it is implausible to assume a trusted third party that is available to generate a certified binary for each language instance. To address this issue, we decide to adopt a scripting language, called Lua. Lua is a lightweight script language. We implemented modified Lua script engine for both Intel SGX enclave computation environment and the TrustZone environment. At a high level, we let the Intel server and/or the setup authority server to prepare and sign a Lua engine enclave/binary. The signed Lua engine is published as a common reference string (CRS). In addition, the hardware is initialized with a signing key, and it corresponding public key is also published as a part of the CRS. The modified Lua engine takes input as a script $\mathcal{C}$, a public input Input_{pub}, a private input Input_{priv}, and a tag tag that can be used to store auxiliary information, such as session id. The Lua engine runs $\mathsf{Output} \leftarrow \mathcal{C}(\mathsf{Input}_{pub}, \mathsf{Input}_{priv})$ and signs $\langle \mathcal{C}, \mathsf{Input}_{pub}, \mathsf{Output} \rangle$. Therefore, any verifier who has the public key can verify the signature. The predicate Q is restricted by the Lua engine constrain. For instance, there is a fixed heap size, e.g., 32MB when the Lua engine enclave is built. It limits the maximum script size. Moreover, as security requirement, one may want to introduce a maximum running time to prevent the script from running forever. Such a running time cap would also reflected by Q.

Recall that scriptable NIZK proofs are typically deployed in a one-to-many scenario, where the prover only needs to invoke the trusted hardware once and many verifiers can check the validity of the proof; however, currently, the remote attestation of Intel's SGX requires the verifier to interact with the Intel Attestation Service (IAS) server. If each verifier needs to query the Intel IAS server to check the proof, the overall performance is limited by the throughput of Intel's IAS. Moreover, the validity of a NIZK proof should be consistent over time, i.e., if a NIZK proof is verifiable at this moment, the same proof should remain verifiable in the future. Unfortunately, this would not be the case if we invoke the Intel IAS in the verification process; certifying an old quote (say, generated 1 year ago) is never the design goal of Intel's remote attestation. This is because the quote needs to contain a non-revoked proof for each item on the signature revocation list, and the proof is no longer verifiable once the revocation list is updated at the Intel side. That means a quote is only valid until the next revocation list update. To resolve this issue, in our design, after generating the quote, the prover immediately queries the Intel IAS server for the attestation verification report on behave of a verifier. Since the attestation verification report is signed by Intel, given Intel's public key, anyone can verify the validity of the attached signature. This tweak also makes the verification process non-interactive.

Performance. The performance of our succinct scriptable NIZK system is theoretically and experimentally evaluated and compared with the other NIZK proof systems. Table 1 illustrates the asymptotic efficiency comparison measured by the circuit size. $|C|$ is the circuit size; $|w|$ is the witness size; $|c|$ is the problem instance size; s is the number of copies of the subcircuits; d is the width of the subcircuits. As we can see, our construction can achieve constant CRS size, constant verifier's complexity, and constant proof size. The prover's complexity is also minimum, which is $|C|$. Note that in theory, the verifier's complexity cannot be sublinear to the statement size $|x|$, but as a convention, it is ignored in the table.

Table 1. Asymptotic efficiency comparison of different NIZK proof/argument systems. $|C|$ is the circuit size; $|w|$ is the witness size; $|c|$ is the problem instance size; s is the number of copies of the subcircuits; d is the width of the subcircuits. DL stands for discrete logarithm assumption, CRHF stands for collision-resistant hash functions, SIS stands for shortest integer solution assumption, KE stands for knowledge-of-exponent assumption, HW stands for trusted hardware model, and AGM stands for algebraic group model.

Scheme	Setup size	Proof size	Prover's time	Verifier's time	Setup Asm	Comp. Asm
Ligero	1	$\sqrt{|C|}$	$|C|\log|C|$	$s\log s + d\log d$	RO	CRHF
Bootle et al.	1	$\sqrt{|C|}$	$|C|$	$|C|$	RO	CRHF
Baum et al.	$\sqrt{|C|}$	$\sqrt{|C|}\log|C|$	$|C|\log|C|$	$|C|$	CRS	SIS
zk-STARKs	1	$\log^2|C|$	$|C|\operatorname{polylog}(|C|)$	$\operatorname{polylog}(|C|)$	RO	CRHF
Aurora	1	$\log^2|C|$	$|C|\log|C|$	$|C|$	RO	CRHF
Bulletproof	$|C|$	$\log|C|$	$|C|\log|C|$	$|C|\log|C|$	CRS + RO	DL
SNARKs	$|C|$	1	$|C|\log|C|$	$|c|$	CRS/AGM	KE
This work	1	1	$|C|$	1	HW	Signature

In terms of the actual experimental performance. The prover's running time for evaluating a Boolean circuit consisting of 2^{39} NAND gates only takes less than 10 mins, which is 900 times faster than the state of the art, zk-STARK, for circuits larger than 2^{35} gates. Note that this performance result is tested through Lua script, and native code for circuit evaluation is 10 times faster in our experiment. The verifier's running time is merely a signature verification, which takes approximately 1.5 ms – better than all the other existing succinct NIZK systems. The proof size is 297 Bytes with current Intel SGX signature, where 256 Bytes are the signature. Hence, we envision it is possible to further reduce the proof size by replacing the signature scheme. The TrustZone based system uses ECDSA on the `secp256k1` curve, so the proof size is only 32 Bytes.

Applications. Finally, we discuss applications of our succinct scriptable NIZK. We note that, many applications have been previously investigated. However, it is very challenging to deploy them in practice due to the performance barrier.

Sound and Scalable Blockchain. As discussed at the very beginning of the Introduction, lots of heated discussions are taking place in blockchain community, with the goal of improving the performance in a sound manner. This consists of two parts. First, we should address the existing issues, since many blockchain scalability proposals have been implemented even the community is aware of the security concerns. Again, we note that, these issues were not addressed probably due to the missing of fast and succinct NIZK.

Second, we will enable new design paradigm for the interesting "one-to-many" unbalanced computation scenarios. Using our NIZK, typically, a single node as prover, can generate in very short time a proof that will convince all other nodes to accept the validity of the current state of the ledger, without requiring those nodes to naively re-execute the computation, nor to store the entire blockchain's state, which would be required for such a naive verification.

Privacy Preserving Smart Contracts. The zero-knowledge properties of ZK proofs has already been intensively used in blockchain projects, with the goal of ensuring the anonymity and protecting financial privacy. Notably, Succinct Non-interactive ARguments of Knowledge (zk-SNARK) has been used in Zcash and Ethereum; Bulletproofs has been used in Monaro. Recently, Ethereum has the plan to explore the feasibility zk-STARK in its future version of their platform. We note that, it is still not clear if zk-STARK can be widely adopted in blockchain platforms given the fact that, the current proof size is $1000\times$ longer than zk-SNARKs. Fortunately, our NIZK is super succinct, and super fast.

2   Preliminaries

Trusted Execution Environment. Trusted execution environment (TEE) refers to a range of technologies that can establish an isolated and trusted environment where security sensitive data can be stored and processed with confidentiality and integrity guarantees. TEE needs to be instantiated on top of a trusted computing base (TCB), which consists of hardware, firmware and/or software. Minimizing the size (attack surface) of TCB with reasonable assumptions is the common goal of this line of research. In practice, TEE can be realized on top of several promising trusted hardware technologies, such as ARM TrustZone and Intel SGX. Although recently a few side-channel attacks, e.g. [9,28], have been explored against those TEE candidates, new designs and fixes are proposed on a monthly basis. Hence, we envision that TEE will be a cheap and acceptable assumption in the near future. In this work, our benchmarks are mainly based on the Intel SGX platform for its readily deployed remote attestation infrastructure; however, our technique can also be implemented on any other TEE solutions.

Intel SGX. Intel Software Guard Extensions (SGX) is a widely used trusted hardware solution to enable TEE. It provides a hardware enforced isolated execution environment against malicious OS kernels and supervisor software. The SGX processor sets aside an exclusive physical memory space, called processor reserved memory (PRM) to ensure the confidentiality and integrity of enclave's memory. Each SGX hardware holds two root keys: root provisioning key and root seal key. The actual attestation keys are deviated from those root keys via PRF. Intel's (anonymous) attestation is based on an anonymous group signature scheme called Intel Enhanced Privacy ID (EPID) [8]. In this work, we are particularly interested in SGX's ability to enable attested computation, i.e. any third party can audit an outcome is computed by a pre-agreed program in a genuine SGX. More specifically, the application enclave first uses EREPORT to generate a report for *local attestation* (identifying two enclaves are running on the same platform). The report is then sent to a special enclave called Quoting Enclave (QE) to produce a *quote* by signing the report with the group signature. In theory, given the group public key (and the up-to-date revocation list), any verifier can check the validity of the signed quote non-interactively; however, currently, one must contact the Intel Attestation Service (IAS) for verification. IAS will first verify the group signature and then create the corresponding attestation verification report with its own signature.

NIZK Proof/Argument Systems. Let $\mathcal{R}$ be a polynomial time decidable binary relation. We call x the statement and w the witness, if $(x, w) \in \mathcal{R}$. $\mathcal{L} := \{x \mid \exists w : (x, w) \in \mathcal{R}\}$ is the NP language defined by $\mathcal{R}$. In a zero-knowledge (ZK) proof/argument system, the prover wants to convince one or more verifier(s) $x \in \mathcal{L}$, where $\mathcal{L}$ is an arbitrary NP language. The ZK system is called non-interactive (NIZK) [6] if the prover can generate the proof without interacting with a verifier, and any verifier(s) can check the validity of the proof. However, it is not possible to realize a NIZK proof/argument system unless the language is in BPP in the plain model (a.k.a. standard model) [18]. To circumvent this impossibility result, all NIZK proof/argument systems must rely on some trusted setup assumptions, such as the common reference string model, random oracle model, and generic group model, etc. A NIZK system is called *succinct* if the proof size is asymptotically less than $|w| + |x|$ (cf. Sect. 3). Unfortunately, it is also shown in [16] that succinct NIZK proof/argument systems cannot be based on any falsifiable assumptions, i.e. an assumption that can be written as a game. That means one must embrace "strong assumptions" to enjoy the benefit of succinctness. In addition, many NIZK proof/argument systems have a so-called *unbalanced* property, where the verifier's complexity is minimized (sometimes maybe at the cost of increasing the prover's complexity). This property is desirable when the number of verifiers is large, such as the blockchain scenarios.

3   Security Definition

In this section, we formally define the scriptable NIZK. Our definition is through an ideal functionality $\mathcal{F}_{\mathrm{sNIZK}}^{\mathsf{Q}}$. In addition, we present a setup functionality $\mathcal{O}_{\mathrm{HW}}^{\mathsf{Q}}$.

We note that the two functionalities will be realized in Sect. 4 and instantiated in Sect. 5, respectively.

Functionality $\mathcal{F}_{\text{sNIZK}}^{\text{Q}}$

The functionality interacts with a set of parties $\mathcal{P} := \{P_1, \ldots, P_n\}$ and adversary $\mathcal{S}$. It is parameterized with a predicate Q.

Proof: Upon receiving $(\text{PROVE}, \text{sid}, \text{ssid}, \langle \mathcal{C}, \text{Input}_{\text{pub}}, \text{Input}_{\text{priv}}, \text{Output}\rangle)$ from a party $P_i \in \mathcal{P}$:

- Assert $Q(\mathcal{C}, \text{Input}_{\text{pub}}, \text{Input}_{\text{priv}}, \text{Output}) = 1$ and $\mathcal{C}(\text{Input}_{\text{pub}}, \text{Input}_{\text{priv}}) = \text{Output}$;
- Send $(\text{PROVE}, \text{sid}, \text{ssid}, \langle P_i, \mathcal{C}, \text{Input}_{\text{pub}}, \text{Output}\rangle)$ to $\mathcal{S}$;
- Upon receiving $(\text{PROVE}, \text{sid}, \text{ssid}, \pi)$ from $\mathcal{S}$, record tuple $(\mathcal{C}, \text{Input}_{\text{pub}}, \text{Output}, \pi)$ and return $(\text{PROVE}, \text{sid}, \text{ssid}, \langle \mathcal{C}, \text{Input}_{\text{pub}}, \text{Output}, \pi\rangle)$ to P_i.

Verification: Upon receiving $(\text{VERIFY}, \text{sid}, \text{ssid}, \langle \mathcal{C}, \text{Input}_{\text{pub}}, \text{Output}, \pi\rangle)$ from a party $P_j \in \mathcal{P}$:

- If tuple $(\mathcal{C}, \text{Input}_{\text{pub}}, \text{Output}, \pi)$ is not recorded, send $(\text{VERIFY}, \text{sid}, \text{ssid}, \langle P_j, \mathcal{C}, \text{Input}_{\text{pub}}, \text{Output}, \pi\rangle)$ to $\mathcal{S}$;
- Upon receiving $(\text{VERIFY}, \text{sid}, \text{ssid}, \text{Input}_{\text{priv}})$ from $\mathcal{S}$:
  - Assert $Q(\mathcal{C}, \text{Input}_{\text{pub}}, \text{Input}_{\text{priv}}, \text{Output}) = 1$ and $\mathcal{C}(\text{Input}_{\text{pub}}, \text{Input}_{\text{priv}}) = \text{Output}$;
  - Record the tuple $(\mathcal{C}, \text{Input}_{\text{pub}}, \text{Output}, \pi)$;
- If a tuple $(\mathcal{C}, \text{Input}_{\text{pub}}, \text{Output}, \pi)$ has been recorded, return $(\text{VERIFY}, \text{sid}, \text{ssid}, 1)$; else, return $(\text{VERIFY}, \text{sid}, \text{ssid}, 0)$.

Fig. 1. The scriptable functionality $\mathcal{F}_{\text{sNIZK}}^{\text{Q}}$.

Scriptable NIZK Ideal Functionality. The scriptable NIZK ideal functionality $\mathcal{F}_{\text{sNIZK}}^{\text{Q}}$ is depicted in Fig. 1. The functionality is parameterized by a predicate Q. Given a script $\mathcal{C}$, a public input $\text{Input}_{\text{pub}}$, a private input $\text{Input}_{\text{priv}}$, and an output Output, the functionality $\mathcal{F}_{\text{sNIZK}}^{\text{Q}}$ allows the prover to obtain a proof π if $Q(\mathcal{C}, \text{Input}_{\text{pub}}, \text{Input}_{\text{priv}}, \text{Output}) = 1$ and $\mathcal{C}(\text{Input}_{\text{pub}}, \text{Input}_{\text{priv}}) = \text{Output}$. Once a proof π is generated, it will always is verified. Notice that the proof π is generated without the knowledge of the private input $\text{Input}_{\text{priv}}$; therefore, the proof generated by $\mathcal{F}_{\text{sNIZK}}^{\text{Q}}$ has the conventional zero-knowledge. Since $\mathcal{F}_{\text{sNIZK}}^{\text{Q}}$ must obtain a private input $\text{Input}_{\text{priv}}$ such that $\mathcal{C}(\text{Input}_{\text{pub}}, \text{Input}_{\text{priv}}) = \text{Output}$ before recording a proof π. Hence, $\mathcal{F}_{\text{sNIZK}}^{\text{Q}}$ also capture the (knowledge) soundness property. In addition, the scriptable property is reflected by the predicate Q, which restricts the class of functions that $\mathcal{F}_{\text{sNIZK}}^{\text{Q}}$ supports. For instance, Q could be the total execution steps is less than a certain bound.

The functionality $\mathcal{F}_{\text{sNIZK}}^{\text{Q}}$ interacts with a set of players $\mathcal{P} := \{P_1, \ldots, P_n\}$ as well as ideal adversary $\mathcal{S}$. To generate a proof π, the prover needs to submit the command $\langle \mathcal{C}, \text{Input}_{\text{pub}}, \text{Input}_{\text{priv}}, \text{Output}\rangle$ to $\mathcal{F}_{\text{sNIZK}}^{\text{Q}}$. After checking the validity, $\mathcal{F}_{\text{sNIZK}}^{\text{Q}}$ will inform the adversary $\mathcal{S}$ using command $(\text{PROVE}, \text{sid}, \text{ssid}, P_i, \mathcal{C}, \text{Input}_{\text{pub}}, \text{Output})$. If the adversary $\mathcal{S}$ allows, she will then send the proof π to $\mathcal{F}_{\text{sNIZK}}^{\text{Q}}$. $\mathcal{F}_{\text{sNIZK}}^{\text{Q}}$ records the message $(\mathcal{C}, \text{Input}_{\text{pub}}, \text{Output}, \pi)$ and returns it to the requestor. To verify a proof π, the functionality $\mathcal{F}_{\text{sNIZK}}^{\text{Q}}$ first checks if the tuple $(\mathcal{C}, \mathsf{Input}_{\mathrm{pub}}, \mathsf{Output}, \pi)$ is recorded. If not, which means the proof is not generated by the functionality itself, then $\mathcal{F}_{\mathrm{sNIZK}}^{\mathsf{Q}}$ asks the adversary $\mathcal{S}$ for the private input. Once a private input $\mathsf{Input}_{\mathrm{priv}}$ is submitted, $\mathcal{F}_{\mathrm{sNIZK}}^{\mathsf{Q}}$ checks $\mathsf{Q}(\mathcal{C}, \mathsf{Input}_{\mathrm{pub}}, \mathsf{Input}_{\mathrm{priv}}, \mathsf{Output}) = 1$ and $\mathcal{C}(\mathsf{Input}_{\mathrm{pub}}, \mathsf{Input}_{\mathrm{priv}}) = \mathsf{Output}$. If it is the case, $\mathcal{F}_{\mathrm{sNIZK}}^{\mathsf{Q}}$ records the tuple $(\mathcal{C}, \mathsf{Input}_{\mathrm{pub}}, \mathsf{Output}, \pi)$, and the proof is accepted.

Remark on Succinctness. We say a NIZK proof system is succinct if the size of the proof $|\pi| = \mathrm{poly}(\lambda)(|x| + |w|)^{o(1)}$.

Functionality $\mathcal{O}_{\mathrm{HW}}^{\mathsf{Q}}$

The functionality interacts with a set of parties $\mathcal{P} := \{P_1, \ldots, P_n\}$ and adversary $\mathcal{S}$. It is parameterized with a predicate Q and a digital signature scheme $\mathsf{DS} := (\mathsf{KeyGen}, \mathsf{Sign}, \mathsf{Verify})$.

- Upon receiving $(\mathrm{INIT}, \mathsf{sid})$ for the first time from any party $P_i \in \mathcal{P}$:
  - Generate $(\mathsf{PK}, \mathsf{SK}) \leftarrow \mathsf{DS.KeyGen}(1^\lambda)$;
  - Record $(\mathsf{sid}, \mathsf{PK}, \mathsf{SK})$;
- Upon receiving $(\mathrm{GETPK}, \mathsf{sid})$ from a party $P_i \in \mathcal{P}$:
  - If $(\mathsf{sid}, \mathsf{PK}, \cdot)$ is recorded, return $(\mathrm{GETPK}, \mathsf{sid}, \mathsf{PK})$ to the requestor P_i.
- Upon receiving $(\mathrm{COMPUTE}, \mathsf{sid}, \mathsf{ssid}, \langle \mathcal{C}, \mathsf{Input}_{\mathrm{pub}}, \mathsf{Input}_{\mathrm{priv}} \rangle)$ from a party $P_i \in \mathcal{P}$ for some ssid, if $(\mathsf{sid}, \cdot, \mathsf{SK})$ is recorded, send $(\mathrm{COMPUTE}, \mathsf{sid}, \mathsf{ssid}, \langle P_i, \mathcal{C}, \mathsf{Input}_{\mathrm{pub}} \rangle)$ to the adversary $\mathcal{S}$; Once receiving $(\mathrm{PROCEED}, \mathsf{sid}, \mathsf{ssid})$ from $\mathcal{S}$, do:
  - Execute $y \leftarrow \mathcal{C}(\mathsf{Input}_{\mathrm{pub}}, \mathsf{Input}_{\mathrm{priv}})$;
  - Assert $\mathsf{Q}(\mathcal{C}, \mathsf{Input}_{\mathrm{pub}}, \mathsf{Input}_{\mathrm{priv}}, y) = 1$;
  - Sign $\sigma \leftarrow \mathsf{DS.Sign}(\mathsf{SK}, \langle \mathsf{ssid}, \mathcal{C}, \mathsf{Input}_{\mathrm{pub}}, y \rangle)$;
  - Return $(\mathrm{COMPUTE}, \mathsf{sid}, \mathsf{ssid}, \langle y, \sigma \rangle)$ to the requestor P_i.

Fig. 2. The Q-compliant trusted hardware functionality $\mathcal{O}_{\mathrm{HW}}^{\mathsf{Q}}$.

Q-Compliant Trusted Hardware Model. Our scheme is built in the Q-*compliant trusted hardware model* (Q-HW model), where Q is a predicate that specifies the class of functions that the hardware is allowed to compute. In the Q-HW model, all parties have access to an ideal functionality $\mathcal{O}_{\mathrm{HW}}^{\mathsf{Q}}$, which on input queries, executes a given Q-compliant function and returns the execution results. The predicate Q depends on the setup, which may vary from protocol to protocol. In this work, we abstract our requirement as the functionality $\mathcal{O}_{\mathrm{HW}}^{\mathsf{Q}}$ (cf. Fig. 2, below). The $\mathcal{O}_{\mathrm{HW}}^{\mathsf{Q}}$ functionality is parameterized with a predicate Q and a digital signature scheme, denoted $\mathsf{DS} := (\mathsf{KeyGen}, \mathsf{Sign}, \mathsf{Verify})$. $\mathcal{O}_{\mathrm{HW}}^{\mathsf{Q}}$ can be initialized once by sending the $(\mathrm{INIT}, \mathsf{sid})$ command to it. It then generates $(\mathsf{PK}, \mathsf{SK}) \leftarrow \mathsf{DS.KeyGen}(1^\lambda)$ and record $(\mathsf{sid}, \mathsf{PK}, \mathsf{SK})$. After initialization, anyone can query the public key PK using the GETPK command. Anyone can then send $(\mathrm{COMPUTE}, \mathsf{sid}, \mathsf{ssid}, \mathcal{C}, \mathsf{Input}_{\mathrm{pub}}, \mathsf{Input}_{\mathrm{priv}})$ request to the functionality $\mathcal{O}_{\mathrm{HW}}^{\mathsf{Q}}$, where $\mathcal{C}$ is the polynomial-time algorithm, $\mathsf{Input}_{\mathrm{pub}}$ is the public input, and $\mathsf{Input}_{\mathrm{priv}}$ is the private input. The functionality first computes $\mathcal{C}(\mathsf{Input}_{\mathrm{pub}}, \mathsf{Input}_{\mathrm{priv}}) = y$ and then asserts $\mathsf{Q}(\mathcal{C}, \mathsf{Input}_{\mathrm{pub}}, \mathsf{Input}_{\mathrm{priv}}, y) = 1$; it then returns (y, σ), where the signature $\sigma \leftarrow \mathsf{DS.Sign}(\mathsf{SK}, \langle \mathsf{ssid}, \mathcal{C}, \mathsf{Input}_{\mathrm{pub}}, y \rangle)$. Note that the private input is not signed.

4   Our Succinct Scriptable NIZK Construction

In this section, we present our succinct scriptable NIZK construction in the $\mathcal{O}_{\mathrm{HW}}$-hybrid world. Before presenting our intuition and construction, we first set up the context for succinct scriptable NIZK.

Common Information. Unlike most existing NIZK proof systems, the script $\mathcal{C}$ (or language $\mathcal{L}$ to be proven) is not hardcoded in the prover and verifier executable files. Our script NIZK proof system allows the users to configure the language instance. This implicitly assumes that the prover and the verifier(s) have some common information in addition to the statement x before the protocol execution. For instance, they all know the description of the NP language $\mathcal{L}$, which is usually represented by its polynomially decidable binary relation $\mathcal{R}$. Without loss of generality, for a relation $\mathcal{R}$, we assume there exists an efficiently computable algorithm $\mathcal{C}_{\mathcal{R}}$ such that $\mathcal{C}_{\mathcal{R}}(x, w) = 1$ if $(x, w) \in \mathcal{R}$ and otherwise $\mathcal{C}_{\mathcal{R}}(x, w) = 0$. $\mathcal{C}_{\mathcal{R}}$ is the common public input to both the prover and the verifier. Depending on the concrete implementation, different NIZK proof systems use different $\mathcal{C}_{\mathcal{R}}$ representation; most popular NIZK proof systems use arithmetic circuit representation, while some, e.g. [4], allows more developer-friendly representations, e.g., in C programming language. Although, in principle, one can convert any RAM model program into a circuit representation, this transform imposes $O(\log n)$ overhead.

Intuition. Trusted hardware offers two important features: (i) data confidentiality and (ii) computation integrity. Most existing trusted hardware (TEE) based applications, e.g., [14] mainly explore the data confidentiality aspect; whereas, in this project, we emphasize the computation integrity aspect. Recall that in a NIZK proof, the prover and the verifier have common input $(\mathcal{C}_{\mathcal{R}}, \mathsf{Input}_{\mathrm{pub}} := x)$. The potentially malicious prover wants to convince the verifiers that he/she knows a witness $\mathsf{Input}_{\mathrm{priv}} := w$ such that $\mathcal{C}_{\mathcal{R}}(\mathsf{Input}_{\mathrm{pub}}, \mathsf{Input}_{\mathrm{priv}}) = 1$. Since the trusted hardware can guarantee computation integrity even when the host is malicious, we can let $\mathcal{O}_{\mathrm{HW}}^{\mathsf{Q}}$ to execute the relationship decision algorithm $b \leftarrow \mathcal{C}_{\mathcal{R}}(x, w)$ and sign the output b. To bind the decision algorithm and statement, we let $\mathcal{O}_{\mathrm{HW}}^{\mathsf{Q}}$ signs $(\mathcal{C}_{\mathcal{R}}, x, b)$ without revealing the witness w. Therefore, by checking the signature, the verifier is convinced that the prover must know a witness w such that $\mathcal{C}_{\mathcal{R}}(x, w) = 1$ if $(\mathcal{C}_{\mathcal{R}}, x, 1)$ is signed by $\mathcal{O}_{\mathrm{HW}}^{\mathsf{Q}}$. Similarly, for general computation, the private input $\mathsf{Input}_{\mathrm{priv}}$ is not signed; therefore, zero-knowledge property is preserved even if the signature leaks the signed message.

What is the difference between the above NIZK construction and trusted computation in the $\mathcal{O}_{\mathrm{HW}}^{\mathsf{Q}}$ functionality setting? Recall that NIZK proofs are typically deployed in a one-to-many scenario, so the prover only needs to invoke the $\mathcal{O}_{\mathrm{HW}}^{\mathsf{Q}}$ once and many verifiers can check the validity of the proof; on the contrary, the other existing TEE based trusted computation applications mostly focus on one-to-one setting. Our crs is just the public key of $\mathcal{O}_{\mathrm{HW}}^{\mathsf{Q}}$.

Construction. Our Succinct Scriptable NIZK construction utilizes the Q-compliant hardware functionality $\mathcal{O}_{\mathrm{HW}}^{\mathsf{Q}}$ as defined in Fig. 2.

Succinct scriptable NIZK protocol Π_{NIZK}^{Q}

Proof: Upon receiving (PROVE, sid, ssid, $\langle \mathcal{C}, \text{Input}_{\text{pub}}, \text{Input}_{\text{priv}}, \text{Output} \rangle$) from the environment $\mathcal{Z}$, $P_i \in \mathcal{P}$ does:

- If the functionality $\mathcal{O}_{HW}^{Q}$ is not initialized yet, send (INIT, sid) to $\mathcal{O}_{HW}^{Q}$;
- Assert $Q(\mathcal{C}, \text{Input}_{\text{pub}}, \text{Input}_{\text{priv}}, \text{Output}) = 1$ and $\mathcal{C}(\text{Input}_{\text{pub}}, \text{Input}_{\text{priv}}) = \text{Output}$;
- Send query (COMPUTE, sid, ssid, $\mathcal{C}, \text{Input}_{\text{pub}}, \text{Input}_{\text{priv}}$) to $\mathcal{O}_{HW}^{Q}$ and obtain (COMPUTE, sid, ssid, $\langle \text{Output}, \sigma \rangle$) from $\mathcal{O}_{HW}^{Q}$;
- Output (PROVERETURN, sid, ssid, σ) to the environment $\mathcal{Z}$.

Verification: Upon receiving (VERIFY, sid, ssid, $\langle \mathcal{C}, \text{Input}_{\text{pub}}, \text{Output}, \pi \rangle$) from the environment $\mathcal{Z}$, $P_j \in \mathcal{P}$ docs:

- Query (GETPK, sid) to $\mathcal{O}_{HW}^{Q}$, obtaining (GETPK, sid, PK);
- Parse π as σ;
- Compute $b \leftarrow \text{DS.Verify}(\text{PK}, \langle \text{ssid}, \mathcal{C}, \text{Input}_{\text{pub}}, \text{Output} \rangle, \sigma)$;
- Output (VERIFYRETURN, sid, ssid, b) to the environment $\mathcal{Z}$.

Fig. 3. The succinct scriptable NIZK protocol Π_{NIZK}^{Q} in the $\mathcal{O}_{HW}^{Q}$-hybrid model.

We aim to achieve constant verification time; light-weight device can perform the verification. In addition, the verifier is only required to query the $\mathcal{O}_{HW}^{Q}$ functionality once to obtain the public key PK; when PK has already been fetched, the verification can be executed offline. As depicted in Fig. 3, our succinct scriptable NIZK proof protocol Π_{NIZK}^{Q} uses a digital signature scheme DS := (KeyGen, Sign, Verify) as its building block. At the beginning of the protocol, the hardware functionality needs to be initialized. In Fig. 3, this step is performed by the prover (marked in grey) if it is not done yet. The prover then asserts $Q(\mathcal{C}, \text{Input}_{\text{pub}}, \text{Input}_{\text{priv}}, \text{Output}) = 1$ and $\mathcal{C}(\text{Input}_{\text{pub}}, \text{Input}_{\text{priv}}) = \text{Output}$; it sends (COMPUTE, sid, ssid, $\mathcal{C}, \text{Input}_{\text{pub}}, \text{Input}_{\text{priv}}$) to $\mathcal{O}_{HW}^{Q}$ and obtains (COMPUTE, sid, ssid, $\langle \text{Output}, \sigma \rangle$) from $\mathcal{O}_{HW}^{Q}$. σ is the proof.

To verify a proof π, the verifier needs to know the public key PK. This step can be performed by a trusted setup, and PK is published as the common reference string. Otherwise, the verifier can query $\mathcal{O}_{HW}^{Q}$ to fetch it (marked in grey). In the verification phase, the verifier V accepts the proof if $\text{DS.Verify}(\text{PK}, \langle \text{ssid}, \mathcal{C}, \text{Input}_{\text{pub}}, \text{Output} \rangle, \sigma) = 1$.

Security. We show the security of our succinct scriptable NIZK construction via Theorem 1, below. Its proof can be found in the full version.

Theorem 1. *Assume signature scheme* DS := (KeyGen, Sign, Verify) *is EUF-CMA secure. The scriptable NIZK protocol Π_{NIZK}^{Q} described in Fig. 3, UC-realizes the $\mathcal{F}_{\text{sNIZK}}^{Q}$ functionality depicted in Fig. 1 in the $\mathcal{O}_{HW}^{Q}$-hybrid world.*

5 $\mathcal{O}_{HW}^{Q}$ Instantiations

In this section, we realize the Q-compliant trusted hardware functionality $\mathcal{O}_{HW}^{Q}$ via Intel SGX and Arm TrustZone.

Challenges. In both platforms, there are a number of challenges need to be resolved. In terms of SGX, the remote attestation of Intel SGX currently requires the verifier to contact the Intel IAS server. On the other hand, in a typical NIZK proof system usage case, the prover aims to prove the truth of the statement to a great number of verifiers. If each verifier needs to query the Intel IAS server to check the proof, the overall performance is limited by Intel's throughput. Moreover, the validity of a NIZK proof should be consistent over time, i.e., if a NIZK proof is verifiable at this moment, the same proof should remain verifiable in the future. Unfortunately, this would not be the case if we invoke the Intel IAS in the verification process; certifying an old quote (say, generated 1 year ago) is never the design goal of Intel's remote attestation. This is because the quote needs to contain an *non-revoked proof* for each item on the signature revocation list, and the proof is no longer verifiable once the revocation list is updated at the Intel side. That means a quote is only valid until the next revocation list update. To resolve this issue, in our design, after generating the quote, the prover immediately queries the Intel IAS server for the attestation verification report on behave of a verifier. Since the attestation verification report is signed by Intel, given Intel's public key, anyone can verify the validity of the attached signature. This tweak also makes the verification process non-interactive.

Secondly, the existing SGX-based proof system, e.g., [38], requires the prover and the verifiers agree on the executable binary (enclave) for the language to be proven. It would make it impossible to build a universal NIZK system in practice. Note that SGX only signs the measure of the enclave, which cannot be directly compared with the corresponding algorithm. Imaging a verifier who is checking a NIZK proof generated some time ago, how would the verifier know the executable binary (enclave) is faithfully compiled? Therefore, NIZK systems, like [38], would need a trusted party to generate an executable binary (enclave) for a given problem instance, and the binary is served as the concrete CRS for the given instance.

In terms of TrustZone, unlike the ecosystem of SGX that is controlled by Intel, the fragmentation of the ARM TrustZone ecosystem may make it hard to have a unique setup standard. To resolve this issue, we need to introduce a trusted setup authority to serve as an attestation server.

SGX-Based System Overview. In our system, the protocol Π_{SGX} involves three entities: the (trusted) Intel server, denoted as IS, the prover P, and the SGX hardware, denoted as $\mathsf{HW}_{\mathrm{SGX}}$. In practice, it is still a challenge for a third party to verify the consistency between an executable binary and its software specification.

That is, the binary contains no bug, no trapdoor, and it is not subverted. Even it is possible, it dramatically increases the verifier's complexity. On the other hand, it is implausible to assume a trusted third party that is available to generate a certified binary for each

---

Enclave $\mathcal{SE}$

$\mathsf{VerifySign}(\mathcal{C}, \mathsf{Input}_{\mathrm{pub}}, \mathsf{tag})$:

- (OCALL) Load $\mathsf{Input}_{\mathrm{priv}}$;
- Execute script $y \leftarrow \mathcal{C}(\mathsf{Input}_{\mathrm{pub}}, \mathsf{Input}_{\mathrm{priv}})$;
- Set $\mathsf{ReportData} = (\mathsf{tag}, \mathsf{hash}(\mathcal{C}, \mathsf{Input}_{\mathrm{pub}}, y))$;
- (EREPORT) Create report r for QE to sign;
- Return (y, r);

Fig. 4. The script engine enclave $\mathcal{SE}$.

problem instance. To address this issue, we decide to adopt a scripting language, called Lua. Lua is a lightweight script language, which is ideal for the SGX enclave computation environment. We let a trusted party, i.e., the (trusted) Intel server IS, to produce a Lua script engine enclave $\mathcal{SE}$. IS then signs $\mathcal{SE}$ so that no one can tamper with its functionality. As depicted in Fig. 4, $\mathcal{SE}$ has one main function called VerifySign[1]. It takes three arguments: (i) a script $\mathcal{C}$, (ii) a public input $\mathsf{Input}_{\mathrm{pub}}$ (iii) a tag, tag, that can be used to specify the proof context, such as $ssid$, etc. The VerifySign function first loads the private input $\mathsf{Input}_{\mathrm{priv}}$ from the prover; it then executes the script $y \leftarrow \mathcal{C}(\mathsf{Input}_{\mathrm{pub}}, \mathsf{Input}_{\mathrm{priv}})$ using the script interpreter. Abort if $y = \bot$, which means the execution error happened; that is considered as $\mathsf{Q}(\mathcal{C}, \mathsf{Input}_{\mathrm{pub}}, \mathsf{Input}_{\mathrm{priv}}, y) = 0$. Otherwise, it sets $h := \mathsf{hash}(\mathcal{C}, \mathsf{Input}_{\mathrm{pub}}, y)$ and $\mathsf{ReportData} := (\mathsf{tag}, h)$; it then invokes EREPORT to create a report r for QE to sign. Finally, it returns (y, r).

Remark. Technically, the private input $\mathsf{Input}_{\mathrm{priv}}$ can be input to the VerifySign function together with the script $\mathcal{C}$ and the public input $\mathsf{Input}_{\mathrm{pub}}$ as another argument. We choose to load $\mathsf{Input}_{\mathrm{priv}}$ separately during the enclave execution for the sake of uniformity: (i) for some applications, we could choose to hard code $\mathcal{C}$ and $\mathsf{Input}_{\mathrm{pub}}$ for efficiency; and (ii) in case that the prover needs to use an SGX enabled server from a third party, it is possible to load $\mathsf{Input}_{\mathrm{priv}}$ in to the enclave via secure channels to ensure privacy.

The hardware functionality $\mathcal{O}_{\mathrm{HW}}^{\mathsf{Q}}$ is instantiated by the protocol $\Pi_{\mathrm{SGX}}^{\mathsf{Q}}$ shown in Fig. 5. The INIT functionality is realized by the Intel server IS and the hardware $\mathsf{HW}_{\mathrm{SGX}}$. Upon receiving (INIT, sid), IS invokes the EPID provisioning key procedure [25] with $\mathsf{HW}_{\mathrm{SGX}}$. The root seal key of $\mathsf{HW}_{\mathrm{SGX}}$ was generated during the processor manufacturing, and Intel claims that they are oblivious to it; the root provisioning key is set up by a special purpose offline key generation facility. The actual procedure is complicated; $\mathsf{HW}_{\mathrm{SGX}}$ is registered to the Intel server IS via a blind joining protocol. We refer interested reader to [25] for details. Hereby, we simplify the description – at the end, $\mathsf{HW}_{\mathrm{SGX}}$ stores a group signature secret key GSK, and the Intel server IS stores the corresponding group signature public key GPK that allows it to verify the signatures generated by $\mathsf{HW}_{\mathrm{SGX}}$. Note that the group signature is only used to authenticate $\mathsf{HW}_{\mathrm{SGX}}$ to the Intel, rather than to the public. Therefore, it is possible to replace the group signature scheme with some symmetric key cryptographic primitive, e.g., MAC. In addition, IS also generates $(\widetilde{\mathsf{PK}}, \widetilde{\mathsf{SK}}) \leftarrow \mathsf{DS}.\mathsf{KeyGen}(1^{\lambda})$. It then creates the script engine enclave $\mathcal{SE}$ as depicted in Fig. 4 and signs it $\tilde{\sigma} \leftarrow \mathsf{DS}.\mathsf{Sign}(\widetilde{\mathsf{SK}}, \mathcal{SE})$. The public key is defined as $\mathsf{PK}^* := (\widetilde{\mathsf{PK}}, \mathcal{SE}, \tilde{\sigma})$. Anyone can query (GETPK, sid) to the Intel server IS to fetch the public key PK^*. The COMPUTE command is realized by all three parties. Upon receiving $(\mathrm{COMPUTE}, sid, ssid, \langle \mathcal{C}, \mathsf{Input}_{\mathrm{pub}}, \mathsf{Input}_{\mathrm{priv}} \rangle)$, the prover P_i creates an enclave instance of $\mathcal{SE}$ to $\mathsf{HW}_{\mathrm{SGX}}$; it then invokes $\mathsf{VerifySign}(\mathcal{C}, \mathsf{Input}_{\mathrm{pub}}, \mathsf{tag})$ (supplying $\mathsf{Input}_{\mathrm{priv}}$ during the execution). $\mathsf{HW}_{\mathrm{SGX}}$ executes the script $y \leftarrow \mathcal{C}(\mathsf{Input}_{\mathrm{pub}}, \mathsf{Input}_{\mathrm{priv}})$; Abort, if $y = \bot$,

---

[1] The enclave also has a GetQEInfo function to receive the target information of QE. It is omitted for simplicity.

Protocol $\Pi_{\mathrm{SGX}}^{\mathrm{Q}}$

Init: Upon receiving (INIT, sid), the Intel server IS interacts with HW_{SGX} invoking the EPID provisioning key procedure (Cf. [26]); At the end of the protocol:

- The Intel server IS stores GPK;
- HW_{SGX} stores GSK;

The Intel server IS also does:

- Generate $(\widetilde{PK}, \widetilde{SK}) \leftarrow \mathsf{DS.KeyGen}(1^\lambda)$;
- Create the script engine enclave $\mathcal{SE}$ as depicted in Fig. 4;
- Sign $\tilde{\sigma} \leftarrow \mathsf{DS.Sign}(\widetilde{SK}, \mathcal{SE})$;

GetPK: Upon receiving (GETPK, sid), the Intel server IS sets $PK^* := (\widetilde{PK}, \mathcal{SE}, \tilde{\sigma})$ and return (GETPK, sid, PK^*);

Prove: Upon receiving (COMPUTE, sid, $ssid$, $\langle \mathcal{C}, \mathsf{Input}_{\mathrm{pub}}, \mathsf{Input}_{\mathrm{priv}} \rangle$):

- The prover P_i creates an enclave instance of $\mathcal{SE}$ to HW_{SGX};
- The prover P_i invokes VerifySign($\mathcal{C}, \mathsf{Input}_{\mathrm{pub}}, \mathsf{tag} := (sid, ssid)$); (Supply $\mathsf{Input}_{\mathrm{priv}}$ during the execution);
- HW_{SGX} runs $y \leftarrow \mathcal{C}(\mathsf{Input}_{\mathrm{pub}}, \mathsf{Input}_{\mathrm{priv}})$ and aborts if $y = \perp$ (i.e. $Q(\mathcal{C}, \mathsf{Input}_{\mathrm{pub}}, \mathsf{Input}_{\mathrm{priv}}, y) = 0$); Otherwise, it outputs a quote $q(\mathcal{C}, \mathsf{Input}_{\mathrm{pub}}, y, \mathsf{tag})$;
- The prover P_i sends the quote $q(\mathcal{C}, \mathsf{Input}_{\mathrm{pub}}, y, \mathsf{tag})$ to the Intel server IS to verify.
- The Intel server IS checks the validity of the quote; it then signs and returns $\sigma \leftarrow \mathsf{DS.Sign}(SK, \langle \mathcal{C}, \mathsf{Input}_{\mathrm{pub}}, y, \mathsf{tag} \rangle)$;
- The prover P_i outputs (y, σ);

Fig. 5. Protocol $\Pi_{\mathrm{SGX}}^{\mathrm{Q}}$ realizing $\mathcal{O}_{\mathrm{HW}}^{\mathrm{Q}}$ via Intel SGX.

which is considered as $Q(\mathcal{C}, \mathsf{Input}_{\mathrm{pub}}, \mathsf{Input}_{\mathrm{priv}}, y) = 0$. Otherwise, it outputs a report $r(\mathcal{C}, \mathsf{Input}_{\mathrm{pub}}, y, \mathsf{tag})$ for local attestation. The prover P_i sends the report $r(\mathcal{C}, \mathsf{Input}_{\mathrm{pub}}, y, \mathsf{tag})$ to the QE of HW_{SGX} to produce a quote $q(\mathcal{C}(\mathsf{Input}_{\mathrm{pub}}, \mathsf{Input}_{\mathrm{priv}}))$; the prover P_i sends the quote $q(\mathcal{C}, \mathsf{Input}_{\mathrm{pub}}, y, \mathsf{tag})$ to the Intel server IS to verify. The above steps are simplified in Fig. 5. The Intel server IS checks the validity of the quote, i.e., checking the group signature and that the SGX platform generating the quote is not revoked; it then signs and returns $\sigma \leftarrow \mathsf{DS.Sign}(SK, \langle \mathcal{C}, \mathsf{Input}_{\mathrm{pub}}, y, \mathsf{tag} \rangle)$; The prover P_i outputs (b, v), Fig. 6 summaries the basic flow for the INIT, GETPK, and COMPUTE protocols.

TrustZone-Based System Overview. ARM TrustZone is another popular trusted hardware platform that can also be leveraged (as long as a device-unique, asymmetric key pair signed by the device's vendor exists). ARM TrustZone provides isolated execution by separating the CPU into two different worlds, i.e., normal world and secure world. The code running inside the normal world cannot directly access the resource inside the secure world. Also only the application inside the secure world can access the protected resource.

Specifically, the device-unique key pair can be used to sign the attention blob that indicates the attestation data originates from the secure world. The attestation data in this case contains $\langle \mathcal{C}, \mathsf{Input}_{\mathrm{pub}}, y, \mathsf{tag} \rangle$. The signed data will be passed to the attestation server of device vendor (like Intel IAS). If the signature verification passes on the device vendor's attestation server, the prover generates proof.

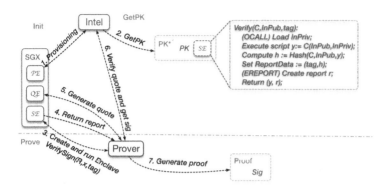

Fig. 6. SGX based trusted hardware instantiation

The Lua script engine design and system architecture is similar to the SGX-based solution. However, it is more efficient, as the attestation data can be verified without interacting with the the attestation server if the verifier already fetched the public key PK from it.

6   Implementation and Evaluations

Our SGX-based prototype is implemented in C++ using the Intel(R) SGX SDK v2.5 for Linux. Our implementation is built on top of [34], and we added OpenSSL lib functions for common cryptographic primitives, such as SHA256, ECDSA, etc. Since system call is not allowed in enclave, we also simulated a simple file system to support the Lua interpreter. The size of the compiled enclave binary is approximately 3.2 MB. In Appendix A, we will present more detail on our SGX-based prototype.

Our TrustZone-based prototype is developed on the Hikey 960 development board, which is powered by Huawei Kirin 960 SoC with 4 ARM Cortex-A73 cores and 4 1.8 GHz ARM Cortex-A53 cores. There are 4 GB DDR4 memory and 32 GB UFS flash on our board. In our experiment, we choose OPTEE (v3.6) as the OS in the secure world, which is open source and well maintained. For the normal world OS, we use a Linux distribution, which is developed by Linaro Security Working Group based on Linux kernel v5.1 and able to corporate with OPTEE. Then, we implement a Trusted App (TA) for the secure world, which will be managed by OPTEE. The Client Application (CA) in the normal world can invoke the TA through specific interface. Lua Intrepreter (v5.3.2) is adopted and modified. The default secure memory size supported by OPTEE is 16 MB, which restricts the script size. A signing key is stored in the TrustZone for the experiment. The enclave structure and system design is similar to the SGX-based solution, except we adopt ECDSA signature over the secp256k1 curve. Therefore, the signature/proof size is only 32 Bytes.

Figure 7a, 7b, 7c shows the performance comparison of different succinct NIZK proof systems w.r.t. prover's running time, verifier's running time, and proof size, respectively. The complexity is measured by the number of multiplication gates. Our work and BCCGP are 128bit security; libSNARK and SCI are 80-bit security; Ligero and zk-STARK are 60-bit security. Our system is tested on a SGX-equipped processor (i7-8700 @ 3.2 GHz and 16 GB RAM, single thread) and Hikey 960 TrustZone development board. All the other systems were tested on a server with 32 AMD cores @ 3.2 GHz and 512 GB RAM, and the data was reported by [3]. For libSNARK, the hollow marks (libSNARK*) in verifier time and proof size measure only count the post processing phase; while solid marks also count CRS generation time. For our SGX based scheme, the prover's running time includes network time for Intel IAS verification; SGX-A (TZ-A) stands for arithmetic circuit over ring $\mathbb{Z}_{2^{64}}$, and SGX-B (TZ-B) stands for Boolean circuit (NAND gates) w.r.t. SGX and TrustZone platforms.

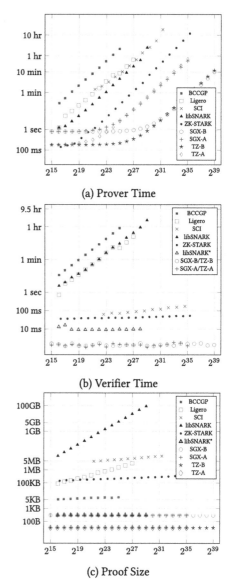

(a) Prover Time

(b) Verifier Time

(c) Proof Size

Fig. 7. Performance comparison of different succinct NIZKs.

Although our NIZK proof system support RAM model computer program, we implemented circuit evaluation as Lua script to facilitate comparison. We emphasize that the reported time is tested using Lua scripts. If the circuit is written in native C, the performance is approximate 10 times better on both SGX and TrustZone platforms. The complexity is measured by the number of multiplication gates. We provide 'SGX-A' and 'TZ-A' as the benchmark for arithmetic circuit over ring $\mathbb{Z}_{2^{64}}$ for SGX and TrustZone, respectively; 'SGX-B' and 'TZ-B' as the benchmark for Boolean circuit, using SIMD to implement NAND gates. The measure of the enclave is assumed to be precomputed and announce by Intel, so it is not counted into the verifier's running time; moreover, the problem instance consists of the Lua script and its hash; otherwise, the verifier can also compute the hash at a small cost. As shown in [13], SHA256 can be performed at 2.1–3.5GB/s on most platforms.

7   Related Work

Universal NIZK. Now we briefly describe several different practical approaches for universal NIZK (i.e., can be applied to general computations and languages in NP). We note that our description here are based on a large body of existing results, and unfortunately we cannot cover the entire body research in this line. We mainly compare the performance related properties, including prover scalability, verifier scalability, setup/initialization scalability, and communication scalability. Additionally, we also compare the underlying setup assumptions and computational assumptions. We note that, in the existing approaches, each setup only support one language instance. Meanwhile, our scriptable NIZK can support multiple language instances in a single setup.

There are multiple approaches to scalable NIZK. The *first approach* is based on homomorphic public-key cryptography, by Ishai et al. [23] and Groth [20]. Then Gennaro et al. [15] introduced an extremely efficient instantiation, based on Quadratic Span Programs, which later been implemented in Pinocchio [33]; see also [4,5,11,26]. Note that, this technique has been used in Zcash. We note that, the homomorphic public-key cryptography based approach can be combined with other techniques to improve the performance. For example, Valiant, [40] suggested to reduce prover space consumption via knowledge extraction assumptions; This combined method can inherit most of the properties from the underlying proof system. We note that our scriptable NIZK system is more efficient.

The *second approach* is based on the hardness of the DLP, originally proposed by Groth [21] and then implemented in [7,10]. [10] Note that, the communication complexity in the DLP approach is logarithmic. However, the verifier complexity in this approach is not scalable. The *third approach* is based on efficient Interactive Proofs (IP) [19,35]. The line of realizations can be found in [42] and [41]. Note that, the verifier in this approach is not scalable. The *fourth approach* is via the so-called "MPC in the head", originally suggested by Ishai et al. [24] and then implemented in ZKBoo [17], and in Ligero [1]. "MPC in the head" based systems have a non-scalable verifier; in addition, communication complexity is non-scalable. A recent proposal called STARK [3], attempts to simultaneously minimize proof size and verifier computation. However, their proof sizes are not small.

In [22,29], an updatable and universal reference string is used. The main goals of this approach is to address risks surrounding setups and many other security challenges in practice. It does not improve the efficiency. Another method to achieve universal setup is using universal circuit [27,39]. In [4,5], a TinyRAM architecture is used to describe universal computations as simple programs. A universal circuit is built based on a specific universal language (i.e., a set of tuples, where each tuple consists of a TinyRAM program, an input string, and a time-bound to run the program). Unfortunately, this approach incur a large overhead on the prover computation.

Trusted Hardware. Many previous works have proposed using trusted hardware to build cryptographic algorithms and systems, including protection of cryptographic keys [30], functional encryption [14], digital rights management [37], map-reduce jobs [12,31], machine learning [32], data analytics [36], and protecting unmodified Windows applications [2].

8   Conclusion

In this work, we introduce a new notion called succinct script NIZK proof system. We formally model this notion in the UC framework. We then propose a generic scriptable NIZK solution based on trusted hardware. We also instantiated our scheme in both Intel SGX and Arm TrustZone. To the best of our knowledge, the proposed succinct scriptable NIZK is better than all the existing succinct NIZK proof systems w.r.t. the prover running time (1000 times faster for Lua script, 10000 times faster for Native C), the verifier's running time (10 times faster), and the proof size (10 times smaller). Most importantly, our NIZK proof system can be readily deployed and used by any developers without the need of cryptographic background.

Acknowledgement. Bingsheng Zhang is supported by the Key (Keygrant) Project of Chinese Ministry of Education. (No. 2020KJ010201) and the National Natural Science Foundation of China (Grant No. 62072401). Hong-Sheng Zhou and Phuc Thai are supported by NSF grant CNS-1801470, a Google Faculty Research Award and a research gift from Ergo Platform. Yajin Zhou and Kui Ren are also supported by the Open Project Program of Key Laboratory of Blockchain and Cyberspace Governance of Zhejiang Province. Yajin Zhou is the corresponding author.

A   SGX implementation

As we mentioned in Sect. 6, our SGX-based prototype is implemented in C++ using the Intel(R) SGX SDK v2.5 for Linux. Our implementation is built on top of [34], and we added OpenSSL lib functions for common cryptographic primitives, such as SHA256, ECDSA, etc. Since system call is not allowed in enclave, we also simulated a simple file system to support the Lua interpreter. The size of the compiled enclave binary is approximately 3.2 MB.

Up on execution, the prover first creates an instance of the Lua script engine enclave in the SGX and transfers the target information of QE into the Lua script engine enclave, which will be used later to generate the report for QE. The prover then produces his proof by calling specific function interface of the enclave, VerifySign, taking the script C and the public input Input_{pub} as the arguments of the function. In our prototype, the script C and statement Input_{pub} are preloaded into the simulated filesystem. After loading Input_{priv} from the prover and putting it into the simulated filesystem, the enclave invokes the Lua interpreter

Table 2. QuoteBody structure

uint16_t	version;
uint16_t	sign_type;
sgx_epid_id_t	epid_group_id;
sgx_isv_svn_t	qe_svn;
sgx_isv_svn_t	pce_svn;
uint32_t	xeid;
sgx_basename_t	basename;
sgx_cpu_svn_t	cpu_svn;
sgx_mise_select_t	misc_select;
uint8_t	reserved1[28];
sgx_attributes_t	attributes;
sgx_measurement_t	mr_enclave;
uint8_t	reserved2[32];
sgx_measurement_t	mr_signer;
uint8_t	reserved3[96];
sgx_prod_id_t	isv_prod_id;
sgx_isv_svn_t	isv_svn;
uint8_t	reserved4[60];
sgx_report_data_t	report_data;

to process the script $y \leftarrow \mathcal{C}(\mathsf{Input}_{\mathrm{pub}}, \mathsf{Input}_{\mathrm{priv}})$, where the script can access the statement and witness through Lua file operations. Note that Lua heap size need to be predefined while compiling the Lua script engine enclave, such as 32 MB, which restrict the class of script it can support.

After the script execution, the enclave hashes $h := \mathsf{hash}(\mathcal{C}, \mathsf{Input}_{\mathrm{pub}}, \mathsf{Input}_{\mathrm{priv}})$ and then put (tag, h) in to the REPORTDATA field of the report structure, and generate the report $r(\mathsf{tag}, h)$ for QE to sign. The prover will then fetch the report $r(\mathsf{tag}, h)$ and send it together with signature revocation list (which can be obtained from the Intel IAS and SPID (which is assigned by the Intel IAS when user registers to the Intel IAS) to the QE. The QE will verify the report using its report key and compute an non-revoked proof for the signature revocation list, generating a quote consisting of the ReportBody field of the report, the non-revoke proof and some other necessary information. The prover then will send the quote to the Intel IAS server for attestation verification report.

Reducing Proof Size. Naively, the prover can send the entire signed attestation verification report as the NIZK proof. The proof size is 731 Bytes (IAS report size) + 256 Bytes (the signature size). To reduce proof size, we observe that Intel's signature is signed on top of the hash of the attestation verification report, so the prover does not need to give the entire report as a part of the proof as far as the verifier can reproduce the hash of the report. However, the verifier is interested in some field of in the isvEnclaveQuoteBody, such as REPORTDATA. Notice that SHA256 uses Merkle-Damgård structure, i.e., the final hash digest is calculated by iteratively calling a compression function over trunks of the signing document. Therefore, the prover can give the partial hash digest of the first part of the signing report, including ID, timestamp, version, isvEnclaveQuoteStatus. The isvEnclaveQuoteBody structure is shown in Table 2. The verifier is only interested in the five fields marked in grey background, and they can be reconstructed from the public input of the verifier. Moreover, currently, all the reserved fields must be 0. Moreover, the verifier also wants to check isvEnclaveQuoteStatus = OK; nevertheless, we observe that the attestation verification report whose isvEnclaveQuoteStatus = OK has a fixed length n. Otherwise, the length of the attestation verification report is different from n. Based on that observation, we can regard the length n as another public input of the verifier. Then when the verifier receives a proof, he/she can check whether the isvEnclaveQuoteStatus field of the associated attestation verification report is OK by putting the length n into the end of the report as the total hashed length. then if the isvEnclaveQuoteStatus field is not OK, the report hash is not aligned probably, resulting a wrong hash digest.

We let the prover give the partial hash digest until misc_select field. Denote the partial hash digest of the report as ph. The prover needs to provide the attributes field, denoted as attr, which is 16 Bytes[2]. The proof is $(ph, \text{attr}, \sigma)$. The verifier can use reconstruct the hash of the report and then check the validity of the signature. The proof size is now reduced to 41 Bytes + 256 Bytes (the signature size), which is 297 Bytes.

References

1. Ames, S., Hazay, C., Ishai, Y., Venkitasubramaniam, M.: Ligero: Lightweight sublinear arguments without a trusted setup. In: ACM CCS 2017, pp. 2087–2104 (2017)
2. Baumann, A., Peinado, M., Hunt, G.: Shielding applications from an untrusted cloud with haven. ACM Trans. Comput. Syst. (TOCS) **33**(3), 8 (2015)
3. Ben-Sasson, E., Bentov, I., Horesh, Y., Riabzev, M.: Scalable, transparent, and post-quantum secure computational integrity. Cryptology ePrint Archive, Report 2018/046 (2018). https://eprint.iacr.org/2018/046
4. Ben-Sasson, E., Chiesa, A., Genkin, D., Tromer, E., Virza, M.: SNARKs for C: verifying program executions succinctly and in zero knowledge. In: Canetti, R., Garay, J.A. (eds.) CRYPTO 2013. LNCS, vol. 8043, pp. 90–108. Springer, Heidelberg (2013). https://doi.org/10.1007/978-3-642-40084-1_6
5. Ben-Sasson, E., Chiesa, A., Tromer, E., Virza, M.: Succinct non-interactive zero knowledge for a von neumann architecture. In: USENIX Security 2014, pp. 781–796 (2014)
6. Blum, M., Feldman, P., Micali, S.: Non-interactive zero-knowledge and its applications (extended abstract). In: 20th ACM STOC, pp. 103–112 (2019)

---

[2] In fact, there are 56 bits reserved area, whose default value is 0 in the attributes field. Hence, the size can be further reduced by 56 bits.

7. Bootle, J., Cerulli, A., Chaidos, P., Groth, J., Petit, C.: Efficient zero-knowledge arguments for arithmetic circuits in the discrete log setting. In: Fischlin, M., Coron, J.-S. (eds.) EUROCRYPT 2016. LNCS, vol. 9666, pp. 327–357. Springer, Heidelberg (2016). https://doi.org/10.1007/978-3-662-49896-5_12

8. Brickell, E., Li, J.:Enhanced privacy id from bilinear pairing for hardware authentication and attestation. In: 2010 IEEE Second International Conference on Social Computing, pp. 768–775 (2010)

9. Van Bulck, jJ., et al.: Foreshadow: extracting the keys to the intel sgx kingdom with transient out-of-order execution. In: USENIX Security Symposium (2018)

10. Bünz, B., Bootle, J., Boneh, D., Poelstra, A., Wuille, P., Maxwell, G.: Bulletproofs: short proofs for confidential transactions and more. In: 2018 IEEE Symposium on Security and Privacy, pp. 315–334 (2018)

11. Danezis, G., Fournet, C., Groth, J., Kohlweiss, M.: Square span programs with applications to succinct NIZK arguments. In: Sarkar, P., Iwata, T. (eds.) ASIACRYPT 2014. LNCS, vol. 8873, pp. 532–550. Springer, Heidelberg (2014). https://doi.org/10.1007/978-3-662-45611-8_28

12. Dinh, T.T.A., Saxena, P., Chang, E.C., Ooi, B.C., Zhang, C.: M2R: enabling stronger privacy in MapReduce computation. In: USENIX Security 2015, pp. 447–462 (2015)

13. ECRYPT. ebacs: Ecrypt benchmarking of cryptographic systems (2018). https://bench.cr.yp.to/results-hash.html, Accessed 11 May 2019

14. Fisch, B., Vinayagamurthy, D., Boneh, D., Gorbunov, S.: IRON: functional encryption using intel SGX. In: ACM CCS 2017, pp. 765–782 (2017)

15. Gennaro, R., Gentry, C., Parno, B., Raykova, M.: Quadratic span programs and succinct NIZKs without PCPs. In: Johansson, T., Nguyen, P.Q. (eds.) EUROCRYPT 2013. LNCS, vol. 7881, pp. 626–645. Springer, Heidelberg (2013). https://doi.org/10.1007/978-3-642-38348-9_37

16. Gentry, C., Wichs, D.: Separating succinct non-interactive arguments from all falsifiable assumptions. In: 43rd ACM STOC, pp. 99–108 (2011)

17. Giacomelli, I., Madsen, J., Orlandi, C.: ZKBoo: Faster zero-knowledge for boolean circuits. Cryptology ePrint Archive, Report 2016/163 (2016). http://eprint.iacr.org/2016/163

18. Goldreich, O., Oren, Y.: Definitions and properties of zero-knowledge proof systems. J. Cryptol. **7**(1), 1–32 (1994). https://doi.org/10.1007/BF00195207

19. Goldwasser, S., Kalai, Y.T., Rothblum, G.N.: Delegating computation: interactive proofs for muggles. In: 40th ACM STOC, pp. 113–122 (2015)

20. Groth, J.: Fully anonymous group signatures without random oracles. In: Kurosawa, K. (ed.) ASIACRYPT 2007. LNCS, vol. 4833, pp. 164–180. Springer, Heidelberg (2007). https://doi.org/10.1007/978-3-540-76900-2_10

21. Groth, J.: Efficient zero-knowledge arguments from two-tiered homomorphic commitments. In: Lee, D.H., Wang, X. (eds.) ASIACRYPT 2011. LNCS, vol. 7073, pp. 431–448. Springer, Heidelberg (2011). https://doi.org/10.1007/978-3-642-25385-0_23

22. Groth, J., Kohlweiss, M., Maller, M., Meiklejohn, S., Miers, I.: Updatable and universal common reference strings with applications to zk-SNARKs. In: Shacham, H., Boldyreva, A. (eds.) CRYPTO 2018. LNCS, vol. 10993, pp. 698–728. Springer, Cham (2018). https://doi.org/10.1007/978-3-319-96878-0_24

23. Ishai, Y., Kushilevitz, E., Ostrovsky, R.: Efficient arguments without short pcps. In: Twenty-Second Annual IEEE Conference on Computational Complexity (CCC'07), pp. 278–291 (2007)

24. Ishai, Y., Kushilevitz, E., Ostrovsky, R., Sahai, A.: Zero-knowledge from secure multiparty computation. In: 39th ACM STOC, pp. 21–30 (2007)
25. Johnson, S.P., Scarlata, V.R., Rozas, C.V., Brickell, E., McKeen, F.; Intel sgx: epid provisioning and attestation services. Intel (2016)
26. SCIPR Lab. libsnark: a c++ library for zksnark proofs (2019)
27. Lipmaa, H., Mohassel, P., Sadeghian, S.: Valiant's universal circuit: Improvements, implementation, and applications. Cryptology ePrint Archive, Report 2016/017 (2016). https://eprint.iacr.org/2016/017
28. Lipp, M., Gruss, D., Spreitzer, R., Maurice, C., Mangard, S.: ARMageddon: cache attacks on mobile devices. In: USENIX Security 2016, pp. 549–564 (2016)
29. Maller, M., Bowe, S., Kohlweiss, M., Meiklejohn, S.: Sonic: zero-knowledge snarks from linear-size universal and updateable structured reference strings. IACR Cryptology ePrint Arch. **2019**, 99 (2019)
30. McCune, J.M., Parno, B.J., Perrig, A., Reiter, M.K., Isozaki, H.: Flicker: an execution infrastructure for tcb minimization. In: ACM SIGOPS Operating Systems Review, vol. 42, pp. 315–328. ACM (2008)
31. Ohrimenko, O., Costa, M., Fournet, C., Gkantsidis, C., Kohlweiss, M., Sharma, D.: Observing and preventing leakage in MapReduce. In: ACM CCS 2015, pp. 1570–1581 (2015)
32. Ohrimenko, O., et al.: Oblivious multi-party machine learning on trusted processors. In: USENIX Security 2016, pp. 619–636 (2016)
33. Parno, B., Howell, J., Gentry, C., Raykova, M.: Pinocchio: nearly practical verifiable computation. In: 2013 IEEE Symposium on Security and Privacy, pp. 238–252 (2013)
34. Pires, R., Gavril, D., Felber, P., Onica, E., Pasin, M.: A lightweight mapreduce framework for secure processing with sgx. In: Proceedings of the 17th IEEE/ACM International Symposium on Cluster, Cloud and Grid Computing, CCGrid 2017, pp. 1100–1107 (2017)
35. Reingold, O., Rothblum, G.N., Rothblum, R.D.: Constant-round interactive proofs for delegating computation. In: 48th ACM STOC, pp. 49–62 (2019)
36. Schuster, F., et al.: VC3: trustworthy data analytics in the cloud using SGX. In: 2015 IEEE Symposium on Security and Privacy, pp. 38–54 (2015)
37. Suh, G.E., Clarke, D., Gassend, B., Van Dijk, M., Devadas, S.: Aegis: architecture for tamper-evident and tamper-resistant processing. In: ACM International Conference on Supercomputing 25th Anniversary Volume, pp. 357–368. ACM (2014)
38. Tramer, F., Zhang, F., Lin, H., Hubaux, J., Juels, A., Shi, E.: Sealed-glass proofs: using transparent enclaves to prove and sell knowledge. In: Euro S&P 2017, pp. 19–34 (2017)
39. Valiant, L.G.: Universal circuits (preliminary report). In: Proceedings of the Eighth Annual ACM Symposium on Theory of Computing, STOC 1976, pp. 196–203 (1976)
40. Valiant, P.: Incrementally verifiable computation or proofs of knowledge imply time/space efficiency. In: Canetti, R. (ed.) TCC 2008. LNCS, vol. 4948, pp. 1–18. Springer, Heidelberg (2008). https://doi.org/10.1007/978-3-540-78524-8_1
41. Wahby, R.S., Tzialla, I., Shelat, A., Thaler, J., Walfish, M.: Doubly-efficient zkSNARKs without trusted setup. In: 2018 IEEE Symposium on Security and Privacy, pp. 926–943 (2018)
42. Zhang, Y., Genkin, D., Katz, J., Papadopoulos, D., Papamanthou, C.: vSQL: verifying arbitrary SQL queries over dynamic outsourced databases. In: 2017 IEEE Symposium on Security and Privacy, pp. 863–880 (2017)

Machine Learning

CONTRA: Defending Against Poisoning Attacks in Federated Learning

Sana Awan, Bo Luo, and Fengjun Li$^{(\boxtimes)}$

The University of Kansas, Lawrence, KS, USA
{sanaawan,bluo,fli}@ku.edu

Abstract. Federated learning (FL) is an emerging machine learning paradigm. With FL, distributed data owners aggregate their model updates to train a shared deep neural network collaboratively, while keeping the training data locally. However, FL has little control over the local data and the training process. Therefore, it is susceptible to poisoning attacks, in which malicious or compromised clients use malicious training data or local updates as the attack vector to poison the trained global model. Moreover, the performance of existing detection and defense mechanisms drops significantly in a scaled-up FL system with non-iid data distributions. In this paper, we propose a defense scheme named CONTRA to defend against poisoning attacks, e.g., label-flipping and backdoor attacks, in FL systems. CONTRA implements a cosine-similarity-based measure to determine the credibility of local model parameters in each round and a reputation scheme to dynamically promote or penalize individual clients based on their per-round and historical contributions to the global model. With extensive experiments, we show that CONTRA significantly reduces the attack success rate while achieving high accuracy with the global model. Compared with a state-of-the-art (SOTA) defense, CONTRA reduces the attack success rate by 70% and reduces the global model performance degradation by 50%.

Keywords: Federated learning · Data poisoning · Label-flipping attacks · Backdoor attacks · Adversarial machine learning

1 Introduction

As an emerging machine learning paradigm, federated learning (FL) is considered a promising solution for privacy-preserving distributed learning. In FL, individual clients first train local models with local training data and a shared global model, and then send the updates to an aggregation server to update the global model for the next training iteration [6,21,24]. In this way, a shared model is learned over data from multiple clients without sharing the raw data by any means. Besides ensuring data privacy, FL also improves the efficiency and scalability of machine learning tasks by parallelizing the training among multiple clients and reducing communication costs. This new collaborative machine

© Springer Nature Switzerland AG 2021
E. Bertino et al. (Eds.): ESORICS 2021, LNCS 12972, pp. 455–475, 2021.
https://doi.org/10.1007/978-3-030-88418-5_22

learning trend is adopted in many applications such as mobile keyboards [6,25] and medical imaging [20]. As a result, federated learning becomes a new target of various adversarial machine learning attacks, such as poisoning attacks [9,29] and exploratory attacks [3,15,32].

In fact, FL is particularly susceptible to poisoning attacks since the clients can fully control the local data and the local training process. In poisoning attacks, malicious clients can poison local model updates by injecting poisoned instances into the training data (i.e., *data poisoning attacks* [14,34]) or directly manipulating model updates (i.e., *model poisoning attacks* [2,7,8,13,36]). As a result, the attacker can tamper with the weights of the global model or inject a backdoor into it. While data poisoning is considered a special case of model poisoning [14], the latter is more effective [7] since it can cause the trained model to produce wrong predictions with only a few malicious clients. In general, the impact of poisoning attacks is related to two factors, the ratio of malicious clients among all clients in FL tasks and the amount of poisoned local training data. For example, 3% poisoned data could cause an 11% reduction in test accuracy [33]. Therefore, it is critical to design solutions to defend against poisoning attacks in federated learning.

The goal of the poisoning attacks is to cause the global model to produce attacker-chosen outputs on specific attacker-chosen inputs (i.e., *targeted attacks*) or wrong outputs on all the inputs (i.e., *untargeted attacks*). Since untargeted attacks attempt to reduce the test accuracy of the main task, they deteriorate the benign performance of the aggregated model across all classes and thus could be detected or mitigated by robust aggregation schemes [10,12,37] operated on the server. However, the robust aggregation techniques may perform poorly or even fail to work when the number of Byzantine adversaries exceeds certain explicit bound [14]. On the contrary, the adversary in targeted attacks expects the poisoned model to output attacker-chosen predictions for specific attacker-chosen inputs while behaving normally on other inputs. Most of the existing defenses leverage the difference between benign and malicious model updates to distinguish between the benign and potentially malicious client groups using clustering-based [31,34] or behavior-based [14] model checking schemes. While these approaches demonstrate their effectiveness in detecting or mitigating targeted poisoning attacks, their performance is often evaluated under simplified, less practical settings (discussed in Sect. 3.2). Moreover, all these schemes adopt very specific assumptions about the training data distributions on honest and malicious clients. For example, [10,31] assumed independent and identically distributed training data while [14,27] assumed non-i.i.d. distributions, which indicate that the reported effectiveness were achieved only in specific situations [28].

In this paper, we aim to answer two research questions: *(i)* what is the impact of training data distributions and adversary populations on existing defenses against targeted poisoning attacks in FL? And *(ii)* how to design a generic and reliable solution against targeted poisoning attacks in FL? To answer the first question, we adopt the Dirichlet distribution [38] to synthesize i.i.d. and non-i.i.d. data distributions in federated learning and investigate the effectiveness of three defense schemes, i.e., Krum [10], PCA-based clustering [34], and FoolsGold [14]

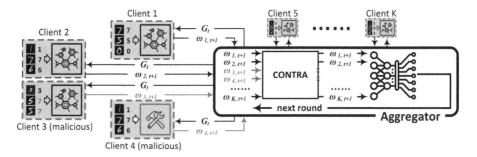

Fig. 1. An overview of FL architecture and the proposed CONTRA approach.

under different assumptions about the data distribution and adversarial population. Our results show that they either fail to prevent the attacks when specific assumptions do not hold, become less effective, or cause a reduction in overall model accuracy. Next, we propose a generic defense scheme, called CONTRA, to thwart poisoning attacks in federated learning. Compared with a state-of-the-art defense, CONTRA reduces the attack success rate by 70% and reduces the global model performance degradation by 50%.

2   Background and Related Work

2.1   Federated Learning

Federated learning (FL) aims to build a global model G over data distributed across multiple clients without sending the raw data to any centralized server. Similar to other modern learning algorithms, FL algorithms rely on stochastic gradient descent (SGD), which minimizes the cost function based on the stochastic estimates of its gradient. Given a dataset $\mathcal{D}$ with n data samples (x_i, y_i), where $y_i \in \mathcal{C}$ is the class label, training a DNN model is to find an optimal set of the parameters $\mathbf{w} = (w^1, ..., w^p)$ that minimizes a chosen loss function $\mathcal{L} = \frac{1}{n} \sum_{i=1}^{n} \mathcal{L}(\mathbf{w}; x_i, y_i)$. In SGD, $\mathcal{D}$ is divided into multiple batches where each data sample only appears in one batch. In a training round, SGD computes the gradient $g_j = \frac{1}{b} \sum_{(x_i, y_i) \in \mathbf{B_j}} \nabla \mathcal{L}(\mathbf{w}; x_i, y_i)$ for each batch $\mathbf{B_j}$, where $\nabla \mathcal{L}$ is the gradient of the loss function and b is the batch size, and updates $\mathbf{w} = \mathbf{w} - g_j$ iteratively until the DNN model converges.

[24] proposes to combine local SGD on each client with a server that performs model averaging using the *federated averaging* (FedAvg) algorithm. As shown in Fig. 1, a FL system consists of K clients and an aggregation server S (called aggregator). In a training round $t \in [1, T]$, a fraction of clients (denoted by the reporting fraction C) are randomly selected to train the global model G_t (with parameters $\mathbf{w}_t$). In particular, a client k trains a local model based on G_t and her local data $\mathcal{D}_k$ as: $\mathbf{w}_{k,t+1} = \mathbf{w}_t - \eta \cdot g_k = \mathbf{w}_t - \eta \cdot b \sum_{j=1}^{n_k/b} g_j$, where η is a fixed local learning rate, and n_k and b denote the size of $\mathcal{D}_k$ and the local mini-batches, respectively. Then, the server S (called aggregator) computes the

weighted average of the local model updates from all K clients to update the parameters of the global model G_{t+1} as: $\mathbf{w}_{t+1} = \sum_{k=1}^{K} \frac{n_k}{n} \mathbf{w}_{k,t+1}$. The FedAvg algorithm also allows a client to iterate the local training process multiple times (i.e., E training passes in each local epoch) before sending the local update to the aggregator. Finally, when $C = 1$, the algorithm degrades to the baseline *federated SGD* algorithm.

2.2 Poisoning Attacks on Federated Learning

The FL paradigm enlarges the attack surface of the model training process since the clients with full control over local data and local training processes can submit arbitrary updates to change the model. If an attack is to reduce the test accuracy of the model across all classes, it is an untargeted poisoning attack, whereas a targeted attack aims to change the model and cause it to misclassify specific inputs into the target class(es) of the attacker's choice, while not affecting the accuracy of the classes unrelated to the attack. In this paper, we mainly focus on the targeted poisoning attacks, since untargeted attacks can be easily detected or mitigated by state-of-the-art robust aggregation techniques [10,12,37].

Data Poisoning Attacks. FL is vulnerable to data poisoning attacks. An attacker (e.g., client 3 in Fig. 1) can modify its local data by directly flipping the labels of honest training instances of one class (i.e., the source class) to another class (i.e., the target class) while keeping the features of the training data unchanged. It is known as the *label-flipping* attack [9,14,34], which can cause substantial drops in global model accuracy and recall even with a small percentage of malicious clients [34]. A *backdoor poisoning attack* was proposed in [17] to break distributed learning schemes based on synchronized SGD, in which the attacker injects backdoored inputs into local data to modify individual features of the training data and embed backdoors into the global model. Recently, Xie et al. proposed a distributed backdoor attack that split a global trigger pattern into separated local patterns and embedded them into local training data of multiple attackers [36]. Other data poisoning attacks leverage the back-gradient descent to generate adversarial training examples [26].

Model Poisoning Attacks. In FL, a malicious client (e.g., client 4 in Fig. 1) can directly manipulate the local model update to influence the global model, or manipulate the local training algorithm or its parameters to inject poisoning neurons into the global model. For example, the attacker can scale up its poisoning model by a factor of $\frac{n}{\eta}$ to cancel out the model updates from benign clients and replace the global model with its backdoored model [2]. In a subsequent study, Bhagoji et al. proposed an alternating minimization approach to make the attack stealthy [8], which first trained the local model using a benign dataset for the main task and then refined it using a poisoned dataset for the adversarial task. Formulating model poisoning as an optimization problem, [13] proposed to craft local models that force the global model to deviate the most towards the inverse of the direction along which the global model parameter would change without attacks. This attack was effective with synthetic non-i.i.d.

datasets, however, it performed poorly on i.i.d. and highly imbalanced non-i.i.d. datasets, as reported in [30]. Meanwhile, an aggregation-agnostic attack, which consistently applies small changes (i.e. noise) to many parameters to introduce backdoors or perturb the model's convergence, was developed in [5]. It was shown to be robust against statistics-based defenses in the i.i.d. setting.

2.3   Existing Defenses Against Poisoning Attacks

Conventional defenses against poisoning attacks in centralized learning involve discovering rare features in the training data that influence the model [19] or small input perturbations that consistently change the outputs [4]. However, these techniques require access to local training data and thus are not applicable in FL. Recently, several detection or defense approaches have been proposed to prevent poisoning attacks in FL, which can be mainly categorised into three directions, *Byzantine robust aggregation*, *clustering-based detection*, and *behavior-based defense*. All of them adopt a common assumption that the attacker population is less than 50%. We will discuss their effectiveness and limitations in Sect. 3.2.

Byzantine Robust Aggregation. In SGD-based federated learning algorithms, the aggregator computes the average of the local models to update the weights of the global model. To eliminate incorrect local updates due to Byzantine errors, robust aggregation schemes proposed different aggregation rules to replace the average of the model updates with a robust estimate of the mean, such as median aggregation [12,37], trimmed mean aggregation [37], or the Krum aggregation that minimizes the Euclidean distances between selected local models [10].

Byzantine robust aggregation schemes demonstrate promising results against untargeted poisoning attacks and targeted model poisoning attacks using boosted learning rates [2], but they are less effective in preventing adaptive poisoning attacks [13], causing a reduction in test accuracy of the global model. Moreover, they work poorly or even fail when a large number of Byzantine adversaries exist in the system [14]. Finally, robust aggregation implicitly assumes the training data is independent and identically distributed. *Our study on Krum shows extremely high attack success rates (e.g. 70% to 90%) with non-i.i.d. training data.*

Clustering-Based Detection. In targeted poisoning attacks, a common observation is that the model updates from malicious clients have unique characteristics compared to the ones from honest clients [31,34]. Therefore, we can re-write the averaging step of FedAvg as:

$$\mathbf{w}_{t+1} = \sum_{k=1}^{K} \frac{n_k}{n} \mathbf{w}_{k,t+1} = \sum_{\mathcal{D}_i \subset \mathcal{D}_M} \frac{|\mathcal{D}_i|}{n} \mathbf{w}_{i,t+1} + \sum_{\mathcal{D}_j \subset \mathcal{D}-\mathcal{D}_M} \frac{|\mathcal{D}_j|}{n} \mathbf{w}_{j,t+1} \quad (1)$$

where $\mathcal{D}_M$ denotes the union of the training data held by all malicious clients. $\mathbf{w}_{i,t+1}$ and $\mathbf{w}_{j,t+1}$ represent local model updates submitted by malicious and honest client populations, respectively.

The clustering-based approaches propose to check model updates at the aggregator and then cluster them into two groups, for example, using dimensionality reduction techniques such as principal component analysis (PCA) [34], k-means [31] or DBSCAN [28] clustering algorithms. Thus, the clusters with less than $n/2$ clients are identified as suspicious clusters of malicious clients.

However, these approaches also assume that the training data is independent and identically distributed. *Our study on the PCA-based defense shows that when the data are non-i.i.d., the clustering-based defense schemes fail to distinguish between model updates submitted by malicious clients and honest clients.* Intuitively, this is because the model updates from the honest clients may diverge in most iterations if they have highly imbalanced non-i.i.d. training data.

Behavior-Based Defense. As honest and malicious clients act differently in targeted poisoning attacks, behavior-based approaches measure the behavioral difference (in terms of local model updates) between the malicious clients and the majority using the Euclidean distance or cosine similarity. For example, adaptive federated averaging (AFA) was proposed in [27], which computed the cosine similarity between the gradients of each local model and the weighted average of all the local models in each round. Based on a range determined by the mean, median, and standard deviation of the calculated cosine similarities, local updates with out-of-range similarities were discarded from the aggregation. However, AFA suffers from the same problem as previous approaches to penalize honest clients with imbalanced non-i.i.d. training data. Recently, Cao et al. proposed to measure the cosine similarity between a local model and the server model trained with a small clean root dataset [11] and assign a trust score to each client. Then, the average of local model updates weighted by the clients' trust scores is used to update the global model. This scheme relies on the root dataset, which has a non-negligible impact on the final global model. Moreover, honest clients whose data distributions are different from the root dataset distribution may be incorrectly penalized.

Another observation about the targeted poisoning attacks is that the groups of honest and malicious clients have distinct contributions to the global model, which would drive the global model towards two different objectives. Moreover, compared with honest clients, malicious clients with the same adversarial objective will produce model updates that are more similar to each other. As pointed out in [14], the distance between the local models submitted by any two malicious clients is smaller than the ones between a malicious client and an honest client. So, FoolsGold [14] proposes to limit contributions of potentially malicious clients with similar model updates to the global model by reducing their learning rates. The FoolsGold scheme shows promising results when the training data is non-i.i.d., since the local models from honest clients may be far from the global model and far from each other too. *However, our study shows that when the training data is i.i.d., it may incorrectly penalize honest clients with similar data distributions and therefore result in substantial drops in test accuracy.*

Besides, recent "structure-based" defenses such as [35] demonstrated promising results in detecting "backdoor neurons" that can be triggered only by backdoored inputs but not clean inputs. However, our work is different from this line of research, which attempt to mitigate backdoor attacks in FL after the training phase. Moreover, as they target the backdoor attacks, they are less effective in detecting non-backdoor poisoning attacks.

3 The Threat Model and the Problem

3.1 Threat Model and Assumptions

Attacker's Goal. In poisoning attacks, the attackers aim to indirectly manipulate the parameters of the learned model by injecting malicious updates to the aggregator. In this paper, we focus on the *label-flipping* and *backdoor data poisoning* attacks [2,17] in federated classification tasks. In a label-flipping attack, the attacker flips the labels of the training samples from one selected class (i.e., source) to another class (i.e., target), while keeping the features unchanged. Therefore, the attack is independent of the model characteristics, the loss function, or the SGD algorithm. A backdoor attack, on the other hand, embeds special patterns such as patches of pixels or shadows into the original training samples and relabels them with the attacker-chosen label. The patterns act as triggers for the target class, which is exploited by the attacker at test time.

Attacker's Capability. We assume that the aggregator is honest while a subset of FL clients is malicious. The proportion of these Sybil-controlled clients among all the participants is denoted by $m\%$. We also assume that each malicious client can manipulate her own training data, but she cannot access or manipulate other clients' data or their learning processes, e.g., the loss function computation, the optimization algorithm, or server's aggregation process. We further assume that the honest clients possess training data that represents every class in the dataset. For an attack to succeed, an attacker must exert more influence on the target class than the total influence from the honest clients. The attacker may target any class by recruiting more malicious clients to outweigh the influence of honest clients. Therefore, we expect a defense to be robust against a significant proportion of malicious clients.

Training Data Distribution. FL allows us to train deep models with real-world data from distributed, heterogeneous sources, where the statistical characteristics of individual data may differ significantly from each other. Therefore, we assume the training data can be independent and identically distributed or non-identically distributed.

3.2 Factors Impacting Defense Designs Against Poisoning Attacks

Existing defense approaches demonstrated promising results in mitigating the poisoning attacks in FL. However, they often made specific assumptions about training data distributions or adopted simplified settings (e.g., small number of clients and extreme synthesis of non-i.i.d. data distributions) when evaluating

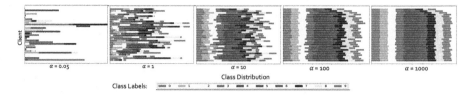

Fig. 2. Synthetic data distributions of 30 clients derived from the Dirichlet distribution with different α, using the MNIST dataset with 10 classes.

the performance of the proposed schemes. It remains an open question if these defenses could achieve the same level of effectiveness when some assumptions do not hold. Therefore, in this section, we investigate the factors and limitations that may impact the effectiveness of the defenses. In particular, we implement the label-flipping attack and three representative defenses of robust aggregation (e.g., Krum [10]), clustering-based (e.g., PCA [34]) and behavior-based detection (e.g., FoolsGold [14]) and then compare their effectiveness under different settings with varying malicious client populations and data distributions.

Settings and Impacting Factors. To obtain a fair understanding of the defenses' performance under a more realistic setting, we adopt a federated learning system with 100 clients and the MNIST dataset with 10 classes, 60K training, and 10K test data samples [23]. We consider four attacker populations to simulate the scenarios with very few Sybils (i.e. $m = 5\%$ and 10%) to theoretic upper bound of robust aggregation schemes (i.e. $m = 33\%$) and all defenses (i.e. $m = 50\%$). In the label-flipping attack, we randomly select a pair of source and target labels and flip the label of the training samples of the malicious clients who are randomly chosen from the 100 clients.

To evaluate the effectiveness of the defenses, we use two metrics, *model accuracy* (MA) and *attack success rate* (ASR), which assess the final global model performance on the testing data. Detailed definitions are presented in Sect. 5.1. As a baseline, the accuracy of the global model trained with FEDAVG without and under the label-flipping attack on MNIST is 90% and 76.81%, respectively.

Training and Test Data Distributions. Previous works on FL often assume the training data is independent and identically distributed across the clients [2, 10,28,31,36]. To synthesize a population with i.i.d. data, they usually subsample a population of homogeneous clients with an equal number of samples per class and randomly assign a uniform distribution over all the classes to each client. However, in practice, FL is exposed to statistical heterogeneity such that the training data are unbalanced and usually follow non-representative distribution of the total population. To synthesize a population with non-i.i.d. data, a widely-used approach is "sort-and-partition" [24], which represents a pathologically extreme case of non-identicalness [1]. However, partitions cannot represent complex non-i.i.d. distributions in practical FL scenarios.

In this work, we adopt the *Dirichlet distribution* to synthesize data distributions [2,18,36]. We assume that every client's training samples are drawn

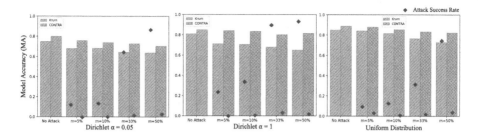

Fig. 3. Model accuracy and attack success rate of Krum and CONTRA under the label-flipping attack with different data distributions and attacker populations.

independently with class labels following a categorical distribution over N classes parameterized by a vector q: ($q_i \geq 0, i \in [1, N]$ and $\|q_1\| = 1$). Specifically, to synthesize a population of non-identical clients, we draw $q \sim Dir(\alpha p)$ from a Dirichlet distribution, where p characterizes a prior class distribution over N classes and $\alpha > 0$ is a concentration parameter controlling the identicality among clients. With $\alpha \rightarrow \infty$, all clients have identical distributions to the prior; with $\alpha \rightarrow 0$, each client holds samples from only one class chosen at random.

For example, we generate unbalanced populations from the training images of the MNIST dataset and distribute them to 100 clients. We set the prior distribution to be uniform across 10 classes. For each client, with a given α, we sample q and assign the corresponding number of images from 10 classes to her. To understand the generated distributions, we visualize the sample distributions drawn from the Dirichlet distribution with different values of the concentration parameter α in Fig. 2. Here, we use 30 clients for neat presentation. We can see that the distribution is extremely non-i.i.d. with $\alpha = 0.05$ and i.i.d. with $\alpha = 1000$. With an α between 1 and 10, the distributions are typically non-i.i.d., but when α is larger than 100, they lean towards i.i.d. Therefore, we believe the Dirichlet distribution with an α between 1 and 100 can better represent the real-world data distributions than previous approaches.

The Learning Process. In each training round, the federated learning schemes randomly select a group of C clients to train the model. C is known as the reporting fraction, which is typically set as 0.1 or 0.2 for scalability purpose. In the local training process, FL applies SGD with a mini-batch size b (e.g., 50–100) and iterates the local training process through E (e.g., 1–5) training passes in a local epoch to accelerate the convergence of the global model. Therefore, we should also consider the impact of these parameters.

Effectiveness and Limitations of Three Defense Approaches. Next, we evaluate the effectiveness of Krum [10], PCA-based detection [34], and Fools-Gold [14] under the label-flipping attack. We consider settings with different malicious client populations and synthesized data distributions and compare their performance without and under the attack.

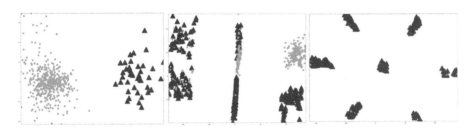

Fig. 4. Two-dimensional PCA plots demonstrate the clusters of honest and malicious gradients (*Left*: $m = 10\%$, uniform distribution; *Middle*: $m = 33\%$, Dirichlet distribution with $\alpha = 1$; *Right*: $m = 50\%$, Dirichlet distribution with $\alpha = 1$).

Krum. We implement Multi-Krum [24], a variant of Krum. For each local model update, it computes the total Euclidean distance from the $n - f - 2$ nearest neighbors and uses the average of the best k updates to compute the global model, where n and f denote the number of total and malicious clients, respectively. When $k = 1$, multi-Krum is the same as Krum, and it reduces to the basic FedAvg aggregation rule when $k = n$.

As shown in Fig. 3, Krum is not effective in defending against the targeted poisoning attacks. Moreover, its performance is strongly influenced by the parameter f and is significantly worse in the non-i.i.d. settings with high malicious clients ratio. Even with a small number of malicious clients (e.g., $m = 10\%$), the attack success rate is 38% and 14% in the non-i.i.d. and i.i.d. settings, respectively. The model accuracy is 81% (the average of 10 runs) in the i.i.d. setting, but it drops to 68% under the the Dirichlet distribution with $\alpha = 0.05$. With more malicious clients (e.g., $m = 33\%$ and 50%), Krum works very poorly in both i.i.d. and non-i.i.d. settings.

PCA-Based Detection. We implement the scheme in [34]. In each training round, the aggregator computes the difference between a client's model update and the global model (i.e. $\theta_{\Delta,i} \leftarrow \theta_{r,i} - \theta_r$) and extracts the relevant subset of the parameter space using PCA dimensionality reduction. Figure 4 visualizes the gradients of the local models with two components (i.e. dimensions), where the orange and blue colors denote the gradients of the honest and malicious updates, respectively. As we can see, the honest and malicious models highly overlap in the non-i.i.d. settings. As a result, the two groups cannot be distinguished by any clustering-based detection approach.

FoolsGold. FoolsGold demonstrates a promising result with non-i.i.d. and i.i.d. training data. However, its evaluation adopts over-simplified settings, such as a small set of clients (10 honest clients and 5 malicious clients), non-stochastic SGD (using $C = 1$), and pathological extreme cases to synthesize the i.i.d. and non-i.i.d. distributions. So, we set $C = 0.1$ and evaluate its performance under the more realistic settings used in this work. The results in Tables 2 and 3 show a reduction in model accuracy and an increased attack success rate in all settings.

4   The **CONTRA** Approach

In this section, we present a new defense mechanism against poisoning attacks in federated learning, called CONTRA. We will first explain the design rationale of CONTRA and then elaborate its building blocks and the algorithm. Finally, we will discuss the strengths and limitations of CONTRA.

4.1   Overview of the **CONTRA** Design

In federated learning, the local gradients, which are computed to minimize the local objectives, are expected to align with the direction that approaches the optimal of the global objective. However, in each training round, the directions of client i's local objective and the global objective may not align well due to the dynamics in local data distributions, where the angle between the two can be denoted as θ_i. In a targeted attack, malicious clients have a poisoning objective to classify data with a specific feature-space pattern into a target class. Therefore, their local gradients should approach the direction of the poisoning objective but not the one of the global objective. We denote the angle between the directions of a malicious client's gradient and the global objective as δ_j. Intuitively, many clustering-based detection schemes distinguish the clusters of honest and malicious clients, assuming θ_is are similar to each other but different from δ_js.

However, this assumption may not hold, especially when the data are non-i.i.d, as shown in our study on the PCA-based detection scheme (in Sect. 3.2). Motivated by [14], we consider the alignment among the clients' updates in this work. In particular, we consider the angle between the directions of the gradients of two malicious clients (denoted by γ) in each round. Since malicious clients have the same poisoning objective throughout the training process, γ of any two malicious clients should always be smaller than the angle between the gradients of a malicious and an honest clients and the angle between any two honest clients.

Therefore, we propose to measure the alignment level among clients using pairwise cosine similarity. In each round, a higher alignment level means that the client's local objective is closer to the one of another client and thus the client is more suspicious to be malicious. To eliminate the impact of malicious clients to the global model, we introduce a reputation system with two penalty mechanisms based on the alignment level, by reducing the learning rate of a suspicious client and her chance of being selected into the FL process in the future training round. CONTRA enables a high model accuracy and a low attack success rate against targeted poisoning attacks even in cases with a large attacker population (to be discussed in Sect. 5). Meanwhile, as a server-side defense, it is running on the aggregator and does not introduce any changes or overhead at the client.

4.2   The **CONTRA** Algorithm

Next, we explain the detailed design of CONTRA which consists of three components, alignment level measurement, adaptive learning rates, and reputation-based aggregation. The algorithm of CONTRA is illustrated in Algorithm 1.

Alignment Level Measurement. CONTRA calculates the cosine similarity between the normalized gradient vectors of two local updates to measure their angular distance, which reflects the similarity of the indicative features in the output layer of the local models [31]. These features are relevant to the correctness of the model and the success of a targeted attack, because they map directly to the output probabilities. In federated learning, as many clients update the global model collaboratively and iteratively, the gradient of a single client may change drastically over the training rounds. So, CONTRA maintains local updates from each client over several consecutive training rounds and computes the *pairwise similarity between the aggregated historical updates* (Lines 3–8 in Algorithm 1). For malicious clients approaching the poisoning objective, the directions of their aggregated historical updates are more likely to align with each other. Finally, we set the *alignment level* of a client j as the average of its top-k pairwise cosine similarity, denoted as τ_j, where k can be determined based on the estimated attacker population.

Adaptive Learning Rate. CONTRA employs dynamic learning rate at each local model and adaptively adjusts a client's local learning rate as $lr_j = 1 - \tau_j$ based on her alignment level (Line 20). Local learning rates are typically used to adjust the speed towards global model convergence. So, we reduce the learning rates of suspicious clients to limit their contributions to the global model in each round. The learning rates are further normalized by the maximum learning rate in each round (Lines 23). This is to ensure that if no malicious client exists in the system, the honest clients will not be penalized by our scheme. To avoid incorrectly penalizing honest clients, we also implement the pardon function (Lines 18) proposed in [14] that applies a ratio $min(1, \frac{\tau_j}{\tau_i})$ to each cosine similarity.

Reputation-Based Aggregation. CONTRA uses a reputation-based aggregation scheme to reduce the chance that a suspicious client is selected to participate in the FL process. In FEDAVG [24], given a reporting fraction $C \in (0, 1]$, $K \times C$ clients are randomly selected to participate in every training round. Therefore, each client has an equal probability $p_i = C$ to be selected. CONTRA employs a reputation-based aggregation scheme that dynamically adjusts a client's probability as $p_i = C + \lambda \cdot r_i$, where r_i is the reputation score of client i. In each round, we rank the clients by p_i and select the top $K \times C$ clients to join the next round. When $\lambda = 0$, the scheme reduces to FEDAVG; otherwise, the client with a higher trust score is more likely to be selected to participate in the next training round. The initial trust scores of all clients are set to 1, so that each client has an equal probability of being selected. In a later round, the trust score of a client j is adjusted by a small Δ if its alignment level τ_j is higher than a preset threshold t (Lines 10–14 in Algorithm 1). The normalized trust scores are then used to adjust the selection probability of the clients. Empirically, we set $\lambda = C(1 - C)$ and use $\Delta = 0.1$ for the image classification tasks and $\Delta = 0.05$ for the Loan dataset (discussed in Sect. 5).

4.3   Discussions

We evaluate the performance of CONTRA in Sect. 5. It can effectively mitigate targeted poisoning attacks in both i.i.d. and non-i.i.d. settings, with a
performance better than existing approaches such as Krum and FoolsGold. However, CONTRA may be less effective or even fail in a special case where there
is only one malicious client in the system. For example, under the label-flipping

---

Algorithm 1. The CONTRA algorithm

Input: Initial model w_0 and local updates $\delta = \{\delta_{i,j}\}$: $\delta_{i,j}$ from client j at iteration i
Set reporting fraction $C = 0.1$; for client j: initial reputation score $r_j = 1$, $G_j = \delta_{1,j}$.
At Server:
1: **for** iteration i **do**
2:    $S_i \leftarrow$ select top-J clients with probability $p_j = C + \lambda \cdot r_j$; $J = K \times C$
3:    **for** every client $j \in S_i$ **do**
4:       $\delta_{i,j} = ClientUpdate(j, w_i)$
5:       compute historical aggregate: $G_j = G_j + \delta_{i,j}$
6:       **for** every client $p \neq j$ **do**
7:          cosine similarity $cs_{j,p} = dot(G_j/||G_j||, G_p/||G_p||)$
8:       **end for**
9:       set τ_j as the average of the top-k cosine similarity $cs_{j,p}$ between client j and
          all other clients
10:      **if** $\tau_j > t$ **then**
11:         $r_j = r_j - \Delta$
12:      **else**
13:         $r_j = r_j + \Delta$
14:      **end if**
15:    **end for**
16:    **for all** client m **do**
17:       **for all** client n **do**
18:          $cs_{m,n}* = min(1, \frac{\tau_m}{\tau_n})$ // re-weighing the cosine similarity
19:       **end for**
20:       $lr_m = (1 - \tau_m)$
21:       $r_m = r_m/max(r)$ //normalize the reputation score to $[0, 1]$
22:    **end for**
23:    $lr_m = lr_m/max_m(lr)$ //normalize the learning rate to $[0, 1]$
24:    $lr_m = (log[\frac{lr_m}{1-lr_m}] + 0.5)$ //logit function to enlarge the divergence
25:    $w_{i+1} \leftarrow w_i + \sum_{l=1}^{L} lr_l \times \delta_{i,l}$
26: **end for**
At Client: Run $ClientUpdate(j, w)$
27: $\mathbf{B} \leftarrow$ split local dataset into batches of size $|\mathbf{B}|$
28: **for** local epoch i from 1 to E **do**
29:    **for all** $b \in \mathbf{B}$ **do**
30:       $w \leftarrow w - \eta \Delta l(w; b)$
31:       $\delta_j \leftarrow (w_i - w_{init})$
32:    **end for**
33: **end for**
34: **return** δ_j

---

attack, its accuracy drops from 85.22% (with 20 malicious clients) to 81.23% (with 1 malicious client), while the attack success rate increases from 1.9% to 8.43%. This is because CONTRA relies on similarity (i.e. alignment) among malicious clients with the same poisoning objective to identify suspicious clients in FL. To address this single-attack case, we can integrate CONTRA with an existing robust aggregation scheme such as median aggregation [37] and Krum [10], which is powerful in detecting outliers. For example, an integrated scheme with Multi-Krum can improve CONTRA's test accuracy to 84.88% and reduce the ASR to 2.7% in the single-attacker case.

Recently, intelligent perturbation-based model poisoning attacks [13] are proposed, which could be extended to defeat CONTRA. For example, malicious clients can submit carefully-crafted updates in pairs with perturbations that cancel out in aggregation, i.e., $\delta_1' = \delta_1 + \varphi$ and $\delta_2' = \delta_2 - \varphi$, where φ is drawn from orthogonal perturbation vectors. Therefore, δ_1' and δ_2' are not similar to each other, but they achieve the same impact on the aggregated global model as δ_1 and δ_2. As pointed out by [14,31], this type of attack is more effective if φ is applied to features that are not important to the model or the attack. Therefore, Fung et al. suggested filtering for indicative features in the model and use a weighted scheme based on the feature importance to mitigate the intelligent attacks [14]. We will explore the solution in this direction in our future work.

5   Experiments

5.1   Datasets, Settings, and Baseline

CONTRA is evaluated on three popular ML datasets: MNIST [23], CIFAR-10 [22], and Loan [16], as summarized in Table 1. Referring to the convergence rate reported in the literature [34,36], we set the training process to 100, 300, and 200 rounds for the MNIST, CIFAR, and Loan models, respectively.

Data Distribution and Training. For MNIST and CIFAR-10, a Dirichlet distribution is used to divide training images among 100 clients. The distribution hyperparameter α varies from 0.05 to 1000. Meanwhile, the 2,223,300 samples in the Loan dataset are divided into 50 US states, each of whom represents an FL client. FL prototype is implemented in Python using PyTorch. Each experiment is repeated five times on different populations under the same configuration (e.g., α) and the average results are reported. In the experiments, every party uses SGD as optimizer and trains for E local epochs with local learning rate l_r, and a batch size of 50. 10% of the participants are randomly selected in each round to submit locally computed SGD updates for aggregation.

Attack Settings. In the label-flipping attack, a proportion $m = 5\%$, 10%, 20%, 33% and 50% of the clients are malicious. We simulate two types of poisoning attacks: (1) Label-flipping attacks: the adversaries attempt to flip a randomly selected source label (S) of the training samples to a target (adversarial) label (T), while keeping the features unchanged (Sect. 5.2). And (2) Pixel-pattern backdoor attacks: the adversaries embed trigger patterns to the selected training samples before flipping their labels (Sect. 5.3).

Metrics. We evaluate the *model accuracy* (MA) and the *attack success rate* (ASR) on the testing data. ASR is defined as: $ASR = N_T/N_S$, where N_S denotes the number of testing samples with source label S and N_T denotes the number of testing samples mislabeled as T. The attack succeeds if the poisoned model outputs the desired target label T for a source label S, otherwise the attack fails.

Table 1. Datasets and performance of unattacked models. Model Accuracy: MA.

	#clients	#classes	Train/Test	Feature	Model used	MA	$l_{r/E}$
MNIST	100	10	60K/10K	784	1-layer softmax [14]	90%	0.01/1
CIFAR-10	100	10	50K/10K	1024	Lightweight Resnet-18	84%	0.1/2
LOAN	50	3	1,778K/444K	127	3 fc	85%	0.001/1

Table 2. FoolsGold [14] performance with varying client data distributions and Dirichlet-distributed non-iid data. A-5 attack; 10 honest and 5 malicious clients.

	Shared data [14]			Dirichlet-distributed non-iid data				
	$s = 0\%$	$s = 50\%$	$s = 100\%$	$\alpha = 0.05$	$\alpha = 1$	$\alpha = 10$	$\alpha = 100$	$\alpha = 1000$
MA (%)	81.9	89.1	87.8	75.4	74.2	79.9	79.0	79.5
ASR (%)	0.0	1.7	6.7	1.7	1.8	2.1	2.8	3.1

Baseline. We employ FoolsGold [14] as the baseline. We first implement the A-5 label-flipping attack on MNIST with the same settings as [14]. Table 2 demonstrates FoolsGold's performance with various sharing ratios (s), where s=0% implies that each client owns a single label of samples, while s=100% implies that each client's dataset is uniformly sampled from all classes (iid data). Meanwhile, we also evaluate FoolsGold with more realistic, Dirichlet-distributed non-iid data (when $\alpha \to \infty$, data distributions are close to iid). As shown in Table 2, the model accuracy drops significantly with Dirichlet-distributed data.

5.2 Defense Against Label-Flipping Attacks

Label-Flipping Attack on Dirichlet-Distributed Client Data. We evaluate CONTRA and FoolsGold [14] with Dirichlet-distributed non-iid data. We simulate 100 clients for MNIST and CIFAR, and 50 clients for Loan, which is more practical than 15 clients in [14]. The results are shown in Table 3. First, FoolsGold's model accuracy drops significantly with increased clients, as benign inputs are mistakenly penalized. CONTRA outperforms FoolsGold in all settings. FoolsGold achieves an overall average accuracy of 76.3% and ASR of 3.2%, while

CONTRA increases model accuracy to 80.8% and reduces ASR to 0.9%. In particular, the average model accuracy degradation (compared with unattacked models) is 9.9% with FoolsGold and 5.5% with CONTRA. We also compare the performance of CONTRA and Krum under the label-flipping attack and show the results in Fig. 3. The results indicate that CONTRA is robust and effective, and it outperforms state-of-the-art solutions.

Coordinated Attack. We simulate the scenario that malicious clients coordinate and manipulate their data. Similar to [14], we denote the data sharing rate among the malicious clients as x_s, i.e., $x_s\%$ of the samples at each malicious client are uniformly distributed from all classes, while the rest $(1-x_s)\%$ are attack samples that are exclusive to this client. Data at the honest clients follow Dirichlet distribution with various α. Results on MNIST data (Table 4) indicate that both FoolsGold and CONTRA effectively reduce ASR, while CONTRA out-

Table 3. Performance comparison of CONTRA and FoolsGold [14] under a label-flipping attack: MA and ASR at model convergence.

| | | MNIST | | | | CIFAR-10 | | | | LOAN | | | |
| | | MA (%) | | ASR (%) | | MA (%) | | ASR (%) | | MA (%) | | ASR (%) | |
m	α	FG	Ours	FG	Ours	FG	Ours	FG	Ours	FG	Ours	FG	Ours
5%	0.05	73.35	75.98	**0.0**	**0.0**	68.23	72.41	1.3	**0.0**	80.76	83.11	2.1	0.00
	1	81.86	84.21	1.2	**0.0**	73.63	76.88	1.8	**0.0**				
	10	**84.60**	**89.52**	1.8	**0.0**	78.81	83.27	1.4	**0.0**				
	100	83.72	88.16	1.9	1.1	**81.34**	**84.41**	1.4	**0.0**				
	1000	83.69	88.02	2.1	1.0	80.55	83.22	2.8	0.1				
10%	0.05	70.18	73.92	**1.1**	**0.0**	68.45	71.48	1.4	**0.0**	79.34	82.44	3.1	0.0
	1	81.77	83.59	1.3	**0.0**	74.84	77.95	2.2	1.0				
	10	**81.79**	**85.93**	2.3	0.8	78.04	82.19	1.5	1.3				
	100	80.67	85.47	2.6	1.3	78.54	82.14	1.7	0.7				
	1000	80.75	85.44	2.8	**0.0**	**78.80**	**83.47**	3.8	1.2				
20%	0.05	67.98	73.22	4.2	**0.0**	66.29	71.28	2.9	**0.0**	77.35	83.25	3.5	0.9
	1	74.58	82.18	**1.6**	**0.0**	72.21	74.66	1.9	**0.0**				
	10	79.54	**85.65**	2.7	1.1	**78.04**	**83.19**	1.7	1.3				
	100	**80.40**	85.32	3.0	1.1	77.69	82.34	2.9	0.5				
	1000	79.64	85.22	4.3	1.9	77.76	82.63	3.8	1.5				
33%	0.05	69.32	72.82	5.6	1.4	67.82	70.42	3.1	**0.0**	76.42	81.47	5.4	1.8
	1	77.24	80.16	**2.2**	0.9	70.08	72.97	**2.0**	0.4				
	10	**79.20**	83.63	3.1	1.7	73.63	79.87	2.6	1.7				
	100	78.34	**83.86**	3.5	**0.8**	73.86	80.43	5.9	1.3				
	1000	78.55	83.20	3.4	1.7	**74.59**	**81.04**	4.8	1.3				
50%	0.05	66.57	70.42	3.2	1.5	67.75	70.41	3.3	1.8	74.88	81.23	6.1	2.3
	1	75.66	81.64	**1.4**	**0.3**	69.11	73.70	**2.4**	**0.8**				
	10	75.32	81.44	2.9	1.4	71.47	74.62	2.5	1.8				
	100	**76.13**	81.56	4.1	1.5	72.12	**78.41**	6.6	1.9				
	1000	74.55	**82.34**	4.2	2.2	**72.53**	77.38	7.8	2.0				
Mean		77.41	82.15	2.66	0.87	73.85	78.03	2.94	0.82	77.75	82.30	4.04	1

Table 4. CONTRA performance against coordinated attacks on MNIST.

	FoolsGold				Ours			
	$\alpha = 0.05$		$\alpha = 1000$		$\alpha = 0.05$		$\alpha = 1000$	
x_s	MA	ASR	MA	ASR	MA	ASR	MA	ASR
0%	0.6835	0.034	0.8322	0.042	0.7313	0.00	0.8704	0.00
50%	0.6981	0.033	0.81	0.038	0.7287	0.012	0.852	0.011
100%	0.7012	0.00	0.7919	0.056	0.7502	0.00	0.8414	0.021

performs FoolsGold in all settings, as CONTRA's reputation system increases the likelihood of honest clients to be recruited for FL training.

Hyperparameters. We evaluate CONTRA on MNIST with local epoch count $E \in \{1, 5\}$ and reporting fraction $C \in \{0.1, 0.2, 0.4\}$, which corresponds to 10, 20, and 40 clients participating in each round, respectively. Note that $C=0.1$ is the most common setting in the literature, which is used in all previous experiments. Table 5 shows the classification performance. With the increase of C, for similarly distributed client data (larger α), more honest clients are likely to be penalized by the detection scheme resulting in drops in model accuracy. Meanwhile, with smaller α (non-iid data), honest client updates are diverse and differentiated from the sybil updates, therefore, increasing C improves model accuracy by involving more honest clients. Moreover, synchronizing the weights after 5 local epochs significantly improves the model accuracy, especially for larger α.

Table 5. Model accuracy (%) for different parameter settings. Total client population: 100; malicious clients: 33%; C: reporting fraction.

	Local epoch count $E = 1$					Local epoch count $E = 5$				
C	$\alpha=1000$	$\alpha=100$	$\alpha = 10$	$\alpha = 1$	$\alpha=0.05$	$\alpha=1000$	$\alpha=100$	$\alpha = 10$	$\alpha = 1$	$\alpha=0.05$
0.40	78.48	76.72	84.19	81.32	76.33	87.92	86.59	84.21	84.06	78.73
0.20	76.85	75.43	85.04	82.20	78.40	88.96	87.43	87.65	83.21	79.14
0.10	83.20	83.86	83.63	80.16	75.38	86.70	85.86	85.41	83.90	75.67

Table 6. Performance comparison of CONTRA (ours) and FoolsGold [14] under backdoor attacks. Malicious clients: 33%; $\alpha = 100$.

MNIST				CIFAR-10				LOAN			
MA (%)		ASR (%)		MA (%)		ASR (%)		MA (%)		ASR (%)	
FG	Ours	FG	Ours	FG	Ours	FG	Ours	FG	Ours	FG	Ours
81.4	87.4	18	2.86	79.6	82	3.85	0.9	81.29	83.2	6.14	1.95

Computing and Communication Overhead. Last, we evaluate the runtime overhead introduced by CONTRA. All experiments are performed on a machine with a 2.6 GHz Intel core i5 processor and 128 GB RAM. The baseline FL system with 100 honest clients takes 18.43 s, on average, to run 100 training rounds. With 33% of malicious clients and CONTRA deployed, the average runtime increases to 29.36 s. This corresponds to a relative slowdown of approximately 1.60x compared to the baseline, which is very acceptable. The size of the messages exchanged is less than 7 MB in both cases.

5.3   Defense Against Backdoor Attacks

For MNIST and CIFAR, adversarial images are selected from a random class. We embed a 4×4 pattern with gray-scale 255 (or 255 in all RGB channels) to the top left corner of each adversarial image, and assign it with an adversarial label. For the Loan dataset, six low-importance features from a random label are chosen. They are replaced with new values that are slightly larger than the maximum value of the feature. To remain stealthy, each attacker's batch has 20 backdoored samples mixed with correctly labeled data.

Experimental results are reported in Table 6. For the lightweight Resnet-18 model on CIFAR-10, the ASR is 3.85% for FoolsGold and under 1% for CONTRA. Meanwhile, with the 1-layer softmax model on MNIST, the ASR is 18% with FoolsGold, while CONTRA reduces it to 2.86%. The accuracy on Loan does not drop much because of the simple fully-connected model architecture. The ASR is 6.14% and 1.95% with FoolsGold and CONTRA, respectively.

6   Conclusion

Federated learning systems are vulnerable to poisoning attacks, in which adversaries manipulate their local data/label/model and contribute maliciously generated updates to the aggregator, with the intention to degrade the accuracy of the global model or to inject a backdoor into it. We have observed that existing defense mechanisms fall short when the experiment configurations are akin to real world settings, e.g., with larger number of FL clients and non-iid data distributions. In this paper, we present CONTRA, a reputation-based defense against poisoning attacks in federated learning systems. In particular, we identify the different optimization objectives of the honest and adversarial FL participants. In response, we develop a cosine-based similarity measurement for client contributions. We further design a reputation-based approach to dynamically and adaptively limit the contribution of the potentially malicious clients. Through extensive experiments with three popular ML datasets, we demonstrate that CONTRA provides outstanding performance: it reduces the attack success rate to 1%, and maintains significantly higher model accuracy than state-of-the-art defense mechanisms.

Acknowledgements. The authors were sponsored in part by NSF IIS-2014552, DGE-1565570, DGE-1922649, and the Ripple University Blockchain Research Initiative. The authors would like to thank the anonymous reviewers for their valuable comments and suggestions.

References

1. Arnold, S., Yesilbas, D.: Demystifying the effects of non-independence in federated learning. arXiv preprint arXiv:2103.11226 (2021)
2. Bagdasaryan, E., Veit, A., Hua, Y., Estrin, D., Shmatikov, V.: How to backdoor federated learning. In: International Conference on Artificial Intelligence and Statistics, pp. 2938–2948. PMLR (2020)
3. Barreno, M., Nelson, B., Sears, R., Joseph, A.D., Tygar, J.D.: Can machine learning be secure? In: ACM Symposium on Information Computer and Communication security (2006)
4. Barreno, M., Nelson, B., Joseph, A.D., Tygar, J.D.: The security of machine learning. Mach. Learn. **81**(2), 121–148 (2010). https://doi.org/10.1007/s10994-010-5188-5
5. Baruch, G., Baruch, M., Goldberg, Y.: A little is enough: circumventing defenses for distributed learning. Adv. Neural Inf. Process. Syst. **32**, 8635–8645 (2019)
6. Beaufays, F., Rao, K., Mathews, R., Ramaswamy, S.: Federated learning for emoji prediction in a mobile keyboard (2019). https://arxiv.org/abs/1906.04329
7. Bhagoji, A.N., Chakraborty, S., Mittal, P., Calo, S.: Model poisoning attacks in federated learning. In: Workshop on Security in Machine Learning (SecML) (2018)
8. Bhagoji, A.N., Chakraborty, S., Mittal, P., Calo, S.: Analyzing federated learning through an adversarial lens. In: the 36th International Conference on Machine Learning (2019)
9. Biggio, B., Nelson, B., Laskov, P.: Poisoning attacks against support vector machines. In: Proceedings of the 29th International Conference on International Conference on Machine Learning, pp. 1467–1474 (2012)
10. Blanchard, P., El Mhamdi, E.M., Guerraoui, R., Stainer, J.: Machine learning with adversaries: Byzantine tolerant gradient descent. In: the 31st International Conference on Neural Information Processing Systems, pp. 118–128 (2017)
11. Cao, X., Fang, M., Liu, J., Gong, N.Z.: FLTrust: byzantine-robust federated learning via trust bootstrapping (2020)
12. Chen, Y., Su, L., Xu, J.: Distributed statistical machine learning in adversarial settings: byzantine gradient descent. POMACS **1**, 44:1-44:25 (2017)
13. Fang, M., Cao, X., Jia, J., Gong, N.: Local model poisoning attacks to byzantine-robust federated learning. In: 29th USENIX Security Symposium (2020)
14. Fung, C., Yoon, C.J.M., Beschastnikh, I.: The limitations of federated learning in sybil settings. In: 23rd International Symposium on Research in Attacks, Intrusions and Defenses (RAID), pp. 301–316 (2020)
15. Ganju, K., Wang, Q., Yang, W., Gunter, C.A., Borisov, N.: Property inference attacks on fully connected neural networks using permutation invariant representations. In: ACM Conference on Computer and Communication Security, pp. 619–633 (2018)
16. George, N.: Lending club loan data (version 3) (2019). https://www.kaggle.com/wordsforthewise/lending-club
17. Gu, T., Dolan-Gavitt, B., Garg, S.: Badnets: identifying vulnerabilities in the machine learning model supply chain (2019)

18. Hsu, T.M.H., Qi, H., Brown, M.: Measuring the effects of non-identical data distribution for federated visual classification. arXiv preprint arXiv:1909.06335 (2019)
19. Jagielski, M., Oprea, A., Biggio, B., Liu, C., Nita-Rotaru, C., Li, B.: Manipulating machine learning: poisoning attacks and countermeasures for regression learning. In: the 39th IEEE Symposium on Security and Privacy (2018)
20. Kaissis, G.A., Makowski, M.R., Rückert, D., Braren, R.F.: Secure, privacy-preserving and federated machine learning in medical imaging. Nat. Mach. Intell. **2**(6), 305–311 (2020)
21. Konečný, J., McMahan, H.B., Yu, F.X., Richtárik, P., Suresh, A.T., Bacon, D.: Federated learning: strategies for improving communication efficiency. arXiv preprint arXiv:1610.05492 (2016)
22. Krizhevsky, A., Hinton, G., et al.: Learning multiple layers of features from tiny images (2009)
23. Lecun, Y., Bottou, L., Bengio, Y., Haffner, P.: Gradient-based learning applied to document recognition. Proc. IEEE **86**(11), 2278–2324 (1998)
24. McMahan, B., Moore, E., Ramage, D., Hampson, S., Arcas, B.A.: Communication-efficient learning of deep networks from decentralized data. In: Artificial Intelligence and Statistics, pp. 1273–1282. PMLR (2017)
25. McMahan, B., Ramage, D.: Federated learning: collaborative machine learning without centralized training data (2017). https://ai.googleblog.com/2017/04/federated-learning-collaborative.html
26. Muñoz-González, L., et al.: Towards poisoning of deep learning algorithms with back-gradient optimization. In: the 10th ACM Workshop on Artificial Intelligence and Security, pp. 27–38 (2017)
27. Muñoz-González, L. Co, K.T., Lupu, E.C.: Byzantine-robust federated machine learning through adaptive model averaging. arXiv preprint arXiv:1909.05125 (2019)
28. Nguyen, T.D., et al.: FLGUARD: secure and private federated learning. arXiv preprint arXiv:2101.02281 (2021)
29. Shafahi, A., et al.: Poison frogs! targeted clean-label poisoning attacks on neural networks. In: 32nd International Conference on Neural Information Processing Systems, pp. 6106–6116 (2018)
30. Shejwalkar, V., Houmansadr, A.: Manipulating the byzantine: optimizing model poisoning attacks and defenses for federated learning. In: Network and Distributed Systems Security (NDSS) Symposium 2021 (2021)
31. Shen, S., Tople, S., Saxena, P.: Auror: defending against poisoning attacks in collaborative deep learning systems. In: In Proceedings of the 32nd Annual Conference on Computer Security Applications, ACSAC 2016, Los Angeles, CA, USA, 5–9 December 2016, pp. 508–519 (2016)
32. Shokri, R., Stronati, M., Song, C., Shmatikov, V.: Membership inference attacks against machine learning models. In: 2017 IEEE Symposium on Security and Privacy (SP), pp. 3–18 (2017)
33. Steinhardt, J., Koh, P.W., Liang, P.: Certified defenses for data poisoning attacks. In: Proceedings of the 31st International Conference on Neural Information Processing Systems, NIPS'17, pp. 3520–3532 (2017)
34. Tolpegin, V., Truex, S., Gursoy, M.E., Liu, L.: Data poisoning attacks against federated learning systems. In: Chen, L., Li, N., Liang, K., Schneider, S. (eds.) ESORICS 2020. LNCS, vol. 12308, pp. 480–501. Springer, Cham (2020). https://doi.org/10.1007/978-3-030-58951-6_24
35. Wu, C., Yang, X., Zhu, S., Mitra, P.: Mitigating backdoor attacks in federated learning. arXiv preprint arXiv:2011.01767 (2020)

36. Xie, C., Huang, K., Chen, P.Y., Li, B.: Dba: distributed backdoor attacks against federated learning. In: International Conference on Learning Representations (2020)
37. Yin, D., Chen, Y., Kannan, R., Bartlett, P.: Byzantine-robust distributed learning: towards optimal statistical rates. In: 35th International Conference on Machine Learning (2018)
38. Yurochkin, M., Agarwal, M., Ghosh, S., Greenewald, K., Hoang, N., Khazaeni, Y.: Bayesian nonparametric federated learning of neural networks. In: International Conference on Machine Learning, pp. 7252–7261. PMLR (2019)

Romoa: <u>Ro</u>bust <u>M</u>odel <u>A</u>ggregation for the Resistance of Federated Learning to Model Poisoning Attacks

Yunlong Mao[✉], Xinyu Yuan, Xinyang Zhao, and Sheng Zhong

State Key Laboratory for Novel Software Technology, Nanjing University,
Nanjing 210023, China
maoyl@nju.edu.cn

Abstract. Training a deep neural network requires substantial data and intensive computing resources. Unaffordable price holds back many potential applications of deep learning. Besides, it is risky to gather user's private data for training centrally. Then federated learning appears as a promising solution to having users learned jointly while keeping training data local. However, security issues keep coming up in federated learning applications. One of the most threatening attacks is the model poisoning attack which can manipulate the inference result of a jointly learned model. Some recent studies show that elaborate model poisoning approaches can even breach the existing Byzantine-robust federated learning solutions. Hence, it is critical to discuss alternative solutions to secure federated learning. In this paper, we propose to protect federated learning against model poisoning attacks by introducing a robust model aggregation solution named Romoa. Unlike previous studies, Romoa can deal with targeted and untargeted poisoning attacks with a unified approach. Moreover, Romoa achieves more precise attack detection and better fairness for federated learning participants by constructing a new similarity measurement. We conclude that through a comprehensive evaluation of standard datasets, Romoa can provide a satisfying defense effect against model poisoning attacks, including those attacks breaching Byzantine-robust federated learning solutions.

Keywords: Model poisoning attack · Robust model aggregation · Federated learning

1 Introduction

The breakthrough of deep neural networks (DNNs) largely depends on substantial training data. As the data volume grows rapidly, it becomes inefficient to gather the Internet end users' data to a central server. Meanwhile, explicitly collecting users' private data may lead to various privacy threats [30]. At this point, the federated learning (FL) concept [21,28] emerges to meet the demands

© Springer Nature Switzerland AG 2021
E. Bertino et al. (Eds.): ESORICS 2021, LNCS 12972, pp. 476–496, 2021.
https://doi.org/10.1007/978-3-030-88418-5_23

of learning models collaboratively. FL is a promising concept to achieve collaborative learning with participants' private data kept locally. However, training DNNs collaboratively creates a new attack surface in the FL setting [23].

Among various attacks recently identified in FL, the poisoning attack is one of the most threatening attacks. The adversary of poisoning attacks is capable of manipulating the collaboratively learned model to classify input incorrectly. The input can be a specifically targeted sample or an arbitrary sample depending on the poisoning attack is targeted [8] or untargeted [9]. According to the poisoning approach, poisoning attacks can be categorized into data poisoning [8,12,26,31] and model poisoning [1,3,9]. Many efforts have been made to eliminate the adversarial effect of data poisoning attacks. But solutions to defeating model poisoning attacks are still under discussion. Several robust model aggregation methods [15,36] have been proved effective when dealing with model poisoning attacks. However, recent studies [3,9] have shown that Byzantine-robust aggregation solutions are still vulnerable to model poisoning attacks if these solutions are not integrated into FL properly.

Meanwhile, the existing robust model aggregation solutions [9,15,36] largely depend on the member selection for model aggregation, which only allows a small fraction of the participants (sometimes just one participant) has the right to contribute to the global model each time. This strategy causes other participants' training efforts to be wasted. In this way, the individual fairness [16,35] of all participants will be at risk. Meanwhile, new maneuvers of model poisoning attacks keep coming up. The existing defense studies cannot catch up with the rapid evolution of these attacks. Hence, it is essential to integrate an effective defense scheme into FL, preventing potential model poisoning attacks.

But designing a proper defense solution for FL is quite challenging. The first question is how to identify model poisoning attacks precisely. Since deep learning uses some techniques with randomness in the training process, like stochastic gradient descent (SGD) optimizer and dropout operation, it is difficult to distinguish the attack from normal training fluctuations, especially when participants' data are not independent and identically distributed (non-i.i.d.). Additionally, the adversary could conceal the attack by lowering the degree of model manipulation or performing the attack opportunistically [3]. If we use some rigorous detecting rules, then false alarms are unavoidable. However, if we use some loose detecting rules, the adversarial participant will be missed. Furthermore, handling suspicious participants is another tricky problem. Using a subset of participants for aggregation can avoid the adversarial effect. But a sizable portion of learned knowledge will be discarded. In the end, some participants cannot make fair contributions to the jointly learned model.

To defend FL against model poisoning attacks and solve these problems at the same time, we propose an alternative solution for robust model aggregation, named Romoa. The basic idea of Romoa comes from two observations of model poisoning attacks: ① the global learning convergence will be slowed down by model poisoning attacks. In most cases, when the adversary tries to poison the global model, significant fluctuations will occur on the learning curve. The global model needs more training iterations to overcome these fluctuations introduced by the poison. ② model poisoning attacks cannot be accomplished at once.

To maintain the adversarial effect on the global model, the adversary needs to interfere with the learning procedure frequently. Romoa uses a hybrid method based on several similarity measurements and a lookahead strategy. Although related work [1,11] has used distance or similarity metrics to detect poisoning attacks, letting a similarity measurement work well with FL together is still under discussion. Romoa gives the first attempt to use hybrid similarity measurements in a lookahead way for identifying adversarial behaviors precisely and timely. Then we design a sanitizing factor in Romoa to eliminate the poisoning effect in FL model aggregation. For the concerns of FL fairness, Romoa calculates the sanitizing factors with momentum, which will lead to heavy punishment to significantly adversarial participants while honest participants can retain voting rights even if there are false alarms. In summary, we make following contributions in this paper:

- To protect FL against model poisoning attacks, we propose Romoa, a robust model aggregation solution. In Romoa, we design a hybrid similarity measurement method to identify the attacks precisely. Meanwhile, Romoa can ensure defensive effectiveness and individual fairness of FL simultaneously.
- We propose an alternative approach for the security analysis of FL by formalizing model poisoning attacks into a repeated game. Then we give a detailed analysis of Romoa in a game manner. The analysis result shows that the robustness of Romoa can be ensured based on Nash equilibrium.
- We evaluate Romoa with two standard datasets in image classification tasks. Meanwhile, we compare our solution with a well-known Byzantine-robust solution in the same attack settings. The experimental results verify the effectiveness of Romoa even in both solo and collusive attacks.

2   Problem Statement

2.1   Federated Learning

In federated learning (FL) [21,28], a central parameter server (PS) will coordinate n participants who join the same FL task such as image classification. For simplicity, we assume that each participant $P_i, i \in [1, n]$ has private training data x^i held by P_i only and all participants share the same DNN architecture and learning hyper-parameters. Generally, a mini-batch SGD optimizer is used by P_i to minimize a loss function $\mathcal{L}(\theta^i)$ for model parameters θ^i. To update the local model, the gradient ∇_{θ^i} of θ^i should be estimated as

$$g^i(\theta^i) = \frac{1}{m} \sum_{j=1}^{m} \nabla_{\theta^i} \mathcal{L}(\theta^i, x_j), \ x_j \in x^i. \tag{1}$$

A globally shared iteration counter $t \in [1, T]$ should be maintained by the PS. Given P_i's local gradient g_{t-1}^i, P_i's model parameter θ^i for the next iteration should be updated by $\theta_t^i = \theta_{t-1}^i - \eta g^i$, where t indicates training iteration and η is a predefined learning rate. After the local training of all participants has been done, the PS will perform model aggregation by following a predefined strategy such as averaging. In this way, the PS gives the model aggregation result as $\bar{\theta}_t = \frac{1}{n} \sum_{i=1}^{n} \theta_t^i$. At the beginning of the $(t+1)$-th training iteration, all participants download the latest global model $\bar{\theta}_t$ from the PS and update local models. After synchronizing with the PS, the above procedure should be repeated until the global model has achieved an expected usability or the maximum training iteration limit.

2.2 Model Poisoning Attack

Generally, all participants in a FL task can only exchange knowledge through a trusted PS[1]. Any legal participant can be an adversary who wants to poison the jointly learned model. It has been proved that collusive attacks can promote poisoning attacks significantly [9,11,31]. For collusive poisoning, we assume that the total amount of adversarial participants should be less than $\lceil n/2 \rceil$. Moreover, the adversary has stealth capability to avoid detection schemes. We note there are several ways for the adversary to attack stealthily. Here we will consider a general approach where the adversary mitigates the adversarial effect by reducing poison dosage. This approach can be characterized by a stealth factor for model poisoning attacks.

Adversarial Goal. The adversarial goal is not to destroy the FL framework. Instead, the adversarial goal is to corrupt the jointly learned model to behave abnormally. According to recent studies, there are two main categories of the adversarial goal, *targeted poisoning attack* [3] and *untargeted poisoning attack* [9]. The adversary of an untargeted poisoning attack aims to cause the misclassification of all input samples indiscriminately while the targeted poisoning adversary aims to cause the misclassification of specific (targeted) input samples. The existing defense studies commonly discuss two adversarial goals separately [1,9]. But we will take into account them at the same time and give a unified solution.

Untargeted Poisoning Attack (UPA). The most powerful UPA yet is established by Fang et al. in [9]. By replacing the local model with a compromised one, UPA can breach several Byzantine-robust solutions. Specifically, the adversary in UPA is to solve an optimizing problem for finding the opposite direction of model updating. This optimizing problem can be customized regarding a specific Byzantine-robust solution. Taking one adversary P_a as an example, the objective function of UPA[2] is

$$
\begin{aligned}
\mathcal{O}^{\mathrm{UPA}} &= \arg\max_{\theta_a} s^T (\bar{\theta} - \bar{\theta}_{\mathrm{adv}}), \\
\text{subject to } \bar{\theta} &= \sum_{i=1}^{n} \theta_i, \bar{\theta}_{\mathrm{adv}} = \theta_a + \sum_{i=1, i \neq a}^{n} \theta_i,
\end{aligned}
\tag{2}
$$

---

[1] This assumption is reasonable since there are many effective solutions [2,5,17] that can protect participants from an untrusted central server. Discussion of an untrusted PS needs an exclusive study.

[2] For more details of this approach, please refer to [9]. We will use UPA as a general notation in this paper.

where s^T is a vector of the changing directions of the global model from the before-attack state $\bar{\theta}$ to the after-attack state $\bar{\theta}_{adv}$.

Targeted Poisoning Attack (TPA). Targeted poisoning attacks have been widely studied recently [1,3,29]. Different from UPA, TPA has specific interests in some data samples. Assume these samples all in one set $x_{TPA} = \{x_1, x_2, \ldots, x_r\}$. Given the corresponding labels $y_{TPA} = \{y_1, y_2, \ldots, y_r\}$, the adversary aims to have each sample $x_i \in x_{TPA}$ misclassified as label y_i' after poisoning the global model, $y_i' \neq y_i$. Then the TPA objective function for the adversary P_a is

$$\mathcal{O}^{TPA} = \arg\min_{\theta_a} \mathcal{L}(\{x_i, y_i'\}_{i=1}^r, \bar{\theta}_{adv}),$$
$$\text{subject to } \bar{\theta}_{adv} = \theta_a + \sum_{i=1, i \neq a}^n \theta_i, \tag{3}$$

where $\mathcal{L}(\cdot)$ is the loss function used in P_a's local training. We remark that a boost factor in original TPA [1,3] is omitted here, which will be combined with our stealth factor.

Stealth Factor. In the existing studies, the concealment of poisoning attacks is barely discussed because this will mitigate adversarial effect significantly. Previous work [3] uses a boost factor to enlarge the adversarial effect, but we find it also helpful for adversary's stealth. Generally, we define the adversary's goal in the t-th iteration as $\mathcal{A}_t = \theta_{t-1}^a - \alpha_t(\theta_{t-1}^a - \mathcal{O}_t^b)$, $t \in [1, T]$, $\alpha_t \in [0.0, 1.0]$, subjecting to the corresponding constraint. Specifically, when $\alpha_t = 1$, the adversary's goal $\mathcal{A}_t$ is to replace the local model with a poisoning model completely. When $\alpha_t = 0$, the adversary chooses not to attack this time. In other cases, $\mathcal{A}_t$ can be seen as a mixture of the global model and local poison model since $\mathcal{A}_t$ can be written as $(1 - \alpha_t)\theta_{t-1}^a + \alpha_t\mathcal{O}_t^b$ equivalently.

Attack Evaluation. To demonstrate the effect of model poisoning attacks, we use the following experimental setting by default. A *baseline* FL task consists of a central PS and 10 participants. Two standard datasets and corresponding DNNs[3] are used, i.e., MNIST [19] and CIFAR-10 [18]. By default, we assume training datasets for participants are independent and identically distributed (i.i.d.) while a non-i.i.d. case will be discussed further. In each baseline task, a cross-entropy loss function and a SGD optimizer are used while the learning rate and the batch size are 0.001 and 64. These is one adversary (9 benign participants) using the same training setting as others by default, mounting UPA or TPA in the task. Two key metrics are commonly used to evaluate the effect of model poisoning attacks, model *accuracy* (for UPA and TPA) and target label *confidence* (for TPA only). Evaluation results for baseline tasks are shown in Fig. 1 and 2, which clearly demonstrate the effect of UPA and TPA in baseline tasks.

We will use *error rate* as a unified metric later for both TPA and UPA to measure the defense performance. The lower the error rate, the greater probability the adversary fails and the better the defense performance is. As for TPA, the error rate equals the attack confidence of the target class. The confidence score

---

[3] Detailed information of DNN architectures we used is given in the appendix.

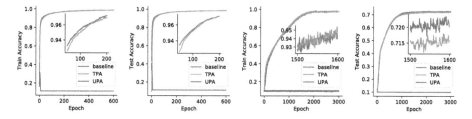

Fig. 1. Model accuracy compromised by model poisoning attacks with MNIST (left two) and CIFAR-10 (right two) datasets (one adversary).

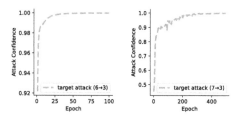

Fig. 2. Confidence of TPA with MNIST (left) and CIFAR-10 (right) datasets (one adversary). The TPA adversary intends to flip label 6 (number 6) to label 3 (number 3) in MNIST and label 7 (frog) to label 3 (bird) in CIFAR-10.

can be calculated by the probability of a sample being classified to a poisoned label. The error rate of UPA is calculated by one minus average accuracy across all input samples.

3   Robust Model Aggregation

The design of Romoa is inspired by some experimental observations of model poisoning attacks. In a compromised FL task, the learning procedure will be interfered by the adversary as long as the poison takes effect, whether in a stealthy manner or not. The interference can be observed from two aspects: notably extra training iterations for the global convergence and more unexpected fluctuations on the global learning curve. Given these abnormal appearances, it is still challenging to identify the adversary from normal FL participants especially when randomness and non-i.i.d. datasets are used. Recent studies [4,8,11,31] have investigated the feasibility of similarity measurement based solutions. These solutions are effective but the defensive effect is thwarted when dealing with attacks which are designed against Byzantine-robust solutions [3,9,15,31,32].

To tackle this problem, we propose a novel similarity measurement by combining hybrid similarity measurements with a lookahead strategy. On the basis of this lookahead similarity measurement, Romoa can identify the adversary precisely with negligible interference to training. After quantifying the divergence between participants, Romoa will assign a sanitizing factor to each participant.

The sanitizing factor is constructed based on temporal similarity measurement result and historical behaviors of each participant. Then local model parameters will be sanitized by corresponding factors during the model aggregation. Different from the existing solutions, Romoa uses a lookahead strategy to capture potential threats and no labors of any participant will be dropped simply. This feature provides FL with both robustness and individual fairness. Now, we will introduce Romoa in a constructing order.

3.1 Asynchronous Model Updating

Asynchronous parameter updating schemes (asynchronous updating for short) are effective in specific learning cases [34,40]. In asynchronous updating, the PS performs model aggregation every τ iterations to sync model states of all FL participants. For the period between two adjacent syncing points, participants are allowed to explore model states locally [33,34,40]. Apart from this, the syncing operation is the same as the original FL. Briefly, we give a general asynchronous updating in Algorithm 1, which will be the basis of Romoa.

Algorithm 1: Asynchronous updating algorithm.

Input : learning rate η, amount of participants n, moving rate γ, syncing period τ, maximal iteration T.
Output: globally learnt model $\bar{\theta}$.

```
1  for i ← 1 to n do
2  |   θ₀ⁱ ← rand(0, 1)                                        /* initialization */
3  end

   Participant Pᵢ:
4  for i ← 1 to n do
5  |   for t ← 1 to T do
6  |   |   θₜⁱ ← θₜ₋₁ⁱ − ηgₜⁱ(θₜ₋₁ⁱ)                          /* local training */
7  |   |   if τ divides t then
8  |   |   |   upload θₜⁱ
9  |   |   |   download θ̄ₜ                                    /* syncing */
10 |   |   |   θₜⁱ ← θₜⁱ − γ(θₜⁱ − θ̄ₜ)
11 |   |   end
12 |   end
13 end

   Parameter Server:
14 for t ← 1 to T do
15 |   if τ divides t then
16 |   |   θ̄ₜ ← (1/n) Σⁿᵢ₌₁ θₜⁱ                               /* averaging aggregation */
17 |   end
18 end
```

3.2   Lookahead Similarity Measurement

Previous studies have discussed the possibility of using Euclidean distance or cosine similarity to measure the differences of DNN models between FL participants [1,4,11]. However, we find that simply calculating distance or similarity is not sufficient. Different from previous work, we design a novel similarity measurement method by using a lookahead strategy. The original lookahead strategy proposed in [39] is an alternative optimizer for improving the learning stability. We will use the lookahead strategy in a different way. In asynchronous updating, all participants are allowed to explore locally between two adjacent syncing points. We will take advantage of this feature and let the PS monitor the exploration stage. Then the PS can be aware of poisons generated in local exploration ahead of aggregation.

Assuming the whole asynchronous updating process can be divided into numerous periods, $T = K\tau, K \in \mathbb{N}$. All participants are required to upload local models during exploration. If t' counts continuously from the last syncing point t, P_i will perform τ local training iterations and upload $\boldsymbol{\theta}_{t'}^i$ to the PS for lookahead similarity measurement before the next syncing point, i.e., $t' \in [k\tau + 1, (k + 1)\tau]$. But only local model parameters in the $((k + 1)\tau)$-th iteration will be used for synchronization. After collecting all local models, the PS should perform parameter selection first. Specifically, parameters with high absolute values will be selected at the ratio of γ (generally assuming $\gamma = \frac{1}{n}$ if no further explanation is given). The selection result of $\boldsymbol{\theta}_{t'}^i$ is denoted by $\tilde{\boldsymbol{\theta}}_{t'}^i$, $|\tilde{\boldsymbol{\theta}}_{t'}^i| = \gamma|\boldsymbol{\theta}_{t'}^i|$. Let $[\boldsymbol{\theta}_{t'}^{j,w}]$ denote the index of w-th parameter of $\boldsymbol{\theta}_{t'}^j$ and $\left\{[\boldsymbol{\theta}_{t'}^{j,w}]\right\}$ as the corresponding index set. Finally, merge all participants' parameter selection results:

$$\hat{\boldsymbol{\theta}}_{t'}^i = \tilde{\boldsymbol{\theta}}_{t'}^i \cup \left\{\boldsymbol{\theta}_{t'}^j \big| [\boldsymbol{\theta}_{t'}^{j,w}] \in \left\{[\tilde{\boldsymbol{\theta}}_{t'}^{j,w}]\right\}, j \in [1, n], i \neq j\right\}. \tag{4}$$

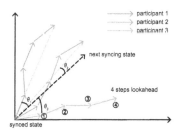

Fig. 3. Cosine similarity using a lookahead strategy ($\tau = 4$).

In the t'-th iteration, the PS calculates a lookahead aggregation of the selected parameters, $\bar{\boldsymbol{\theta}}_{t'} = \frac{1}{n}\sum_{i=1}^n \hat{\boldsymbol{\theta}}_{t'}^i$. If we treat the state of an expanded selection of parameters as a planar point, then we can illustrate the calculation of lookahead similarity in Fig. 3. The angle to be calculated is formed by two edges. One is from the last syncing state (e.g., syncing point t) to the last lookahead state of a participant. The other one is from the last syncing state to the lookahead aggregation of all participants. Given these two updating paths both started with last synced state $\bar{\theta}_t$, one ended with next syncing state $\bar{\theta}_{t'}$, the other ended with participant P_i's selected parameters $\hat{\theta}_{t'}^i$, we can define two non-zero vectors $[\bar{\theta}_t^w, \bar{\theta}_{t'}^w]$ and $[\bar{\theta}_t^w, \hat{\theta}_{t'}^{i,w}]$ (w denotes the index of parameters). Then element-wise cosine similarity measurement for any participant P_i is

$$S_{cosine}^{i,w} = \frac{(\hat{\theta}_{t'}^{i,w} - \bar{\theta}_t^w)(\bar{\theta}_{t'}^w - \bar{\theta}_t^w)^T}{(\sum_{\theta \in \{\hat{\theta}_{t'}^{i,w} - \bar{\theta}_t^w\}} \theta^2)^{(\frac{1}{2}} \times \sum_{\theta \in \{\bar{\theta}_{t'}^w - \bar{\theta}_t^w\}} \theta^2)^{\frac{1}{2}}}. \tag{5}$$

The above definition gives similarity measurement for parameters $\hat{\theta}_{t'}^i$ which are selected according to absolute values. But the remaining unselected parameters also need to be measured properly. We use cosine similarity and Pearson correlation in a layer-wise way to capture divergences of the unselected parameters. If all parameters in the l-th layer of a DNN model is denoted by $\theta_{t'}^{i[l]} \in \mathbb{R}^{M_l}$ (M_l is the total number of parameters in the l-th layer) and function $std(\cdot)$ yields standard deviation, then these two measurements are defined as

$$L_{cosine}^{i[l]} = \frac{(\theta_{t'}^{i[l]} - \bar{\theta}_t^{[l]})(\bar{\theta}_{t'}^{[l]} - \bar{\theta}_t^{[l]})^T}{(\sum_{\theta \in \{\theta_{t'}^{i[l]} - \bar{\theta}_t^{[l]}\}} \theta^2)^{\frac{1}{2}} \times \sum_{\theta \in \{\bar{\theta}_{t'}^{[l]} - \bar{\theta}_t^{[l]}\}} \theta^2)^{\frac{1}{2}}}, \tag{6}$$

$$L_{pearson}^{i[l]} = \frac{L_{cosine}^{i[l]}}{std(\{\theta_{t'}^{i[l]} - \bar{\theta}_t^{[l]}\}) \times std(\{\bar{\theta}_{t'}^{[l]} - \bar{\theta}_t^{[l]}\})}. \tag{7}$$

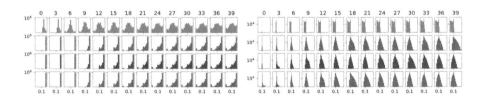

Fig. 4. Distributions of similarity measurement (left) and sanitizing factors (right) for 4 participants training with MNIST dataset (UPA adversary in the first row). X-axis is value of the results and Y-axis is the corresponding density. Indicator $0, 3, 6...$ is the number of epoch.

An example of the lookahead similarity measurement is given in Fig. 4. Obviously, the adversary (in the first row) has a totally different measurement distribution when compared with other honest participants.

3.3   Model Aggregation with Sanitizing Factor

To eliminate the adversarial effect of poisoning attacks while maintaining a unanimous model updating tendency, we introduce a sanitizing factor F. The sanitizing factor is a weight vector for each parameter, which is constructed on the basis of lookahead similarity measurement results. Each parameter should be sanitized by a sanitizing factor when the PS performs model aggregation. In this manner, sharp fluctuations in the global learning process are supposed to be moderated. For converting similarity measurement results into sanitizing factors, we use a mean shift algorithm [10], which can estimate the density of model parameters and measurement results. Specifically, the mean shift algorithm takes the similarity measurement result as its input and yields clusters and corresponding centroids. For any $\theta_w \in \boldsymbol{\theta}$, if θ_w belongs to some cluster, then the centroid is denoted by c_w (the same centroid may be referred to as different identifiers). The generating function for element-wise sanitizing factors is

$$f^i_{S_{cosine}}(\theta_w) = \begin{cases} S^i_{cosine}(\theta_w) - c_w, & \text{if } \theta_w \text{ in } \hat{\boldsymbol{\theta}}^i, \\ 0, & \text{otherwise.} \end{cases} \tag{8}$$

Similarly, we can define two generating functions for layer-wise sanitizing factors. For θ_w in the l-th layer,

$$f^i_{L_{cosine}}(\theta_w) = L^{i[l]}_{cosine}(\theta_w) - c_w, \tag{9}$$

$$f^i_{L_{pearson}}(\theta_w) = L^{i[l]}_{pearson}(\theta_w) - c_w. \tag{10}$$

When three measurements results are combined, the minimum result is selected as a representative. Then sanitizing factor F^i_t for θ^i can be defined as

$$F^i_t = \{\min\{f^i_{S_{cosine}}(\theta_w), f^i_{L_{cosine}}(\theta_w), f^i_{L_{pearson}}(\theta_w)\}\}_{\theta_w \in \theta^i_t},$$

$$F^i_t = \beta e^{F^i_t} / \sum_{j=1}^n e^{F^j_t} + (1 - \beta) F^i_{t-1}, \tag{11}$$

where β is a residual rate, accumulating F^i_t with its historical observations accumulatively ($\beta = 1/2$ if no further explanation is given). For the initialization, we set $F^i_0 \leftarrow \frac{1}{n}$ since each participant is assumed to be honest from the very beginning. By integrating the sanitizing factors into parameter aggregation, we have Romoa as shown in Algorithm 2. Meanwhile, Fig. 4 shows distributions of sanitizing factors for the adversary and honest participants. It is shown that the adversary's sanitizing factors are totally different from others. And sanitizing factors will not affect honest participants since the historical records can prevent false positives.

4   Security Analysis

In this section, we will formalize model poisoning attacks and Romoa's defense into a game. Informally, FL can be seen as a finitely repeated game. We will first construct a strategic game for one training iteration with potential adversaries in FL, named federated learning game (FLG). Then we show that all participants in FLG will choose to be honest or adversarial at the same time if no defense exists. Next, we extend FLG to a finitely repeated game, named repeated federated learning game (rFLG). Finally, we will show that Romoa is secure in rFLG if a Nash equilibrium can be achieved with all participants being honest (i.e., no attacks). We give the conclusion first and then show how to prove it.

Theorem 1. *FL with robust model aggregation (Romoa) is secure against model poisoning attack if the number of adversarial participants is less than $\lceil n/2 \rceil$, where n is the total number of FL participants.*

4.1   FLG: Federated Learning Game

The FLG is a strategic game, denoted by G, containing the interactions of all participants in each iteration. We assume that all participants are rational and should take actions simultaneously. The adversary can make the attack subtle or effective by controlling the poison dosage. All participants want to get a finally well-trained DNN model when the game ends. If the model functionality achieves higher than a threshold, then honest participants win. If an adversary gets a higher attack score, then the adversary wins. Furthermore, the adversary prefers to attack than learning honestly because the adversary is supposed to get extra revenues from a compromised model aggregation. Besides, the adversary can still win the game even if honest participants lose.

Each participant in a FL task is a natural player in FLG. Participant P_i has an action set A_i, which contains all available actions, $i \in [1, n]$. A utility function mapping an action set to a real-value utility score is $u_i : \boldsymbol{A} \leftarrow \mathbb{R}$. Please note that $u_i(\boldsymbol{a}) \geq u_i(\boldsymbol{a'})$ if and only if P_i has preference for action set $\boldsymbol{a}$ over action set $\boldsymbol{a'}$, where $\boldsymbol{a}$ and $\boldsymbol{a'} \in \boldsymbol{A}$. Now we can define FLG as a strategic game $G =< \mathcal{P}, \{A_i\}_{i=1}^n, \{u_i\}_{i=1}^n >$. The player set is denoted by $\mathcal{P} = \{P_1, P_2, \ldots, P_n\}$. For a general purpose of model poisoning attacks, we define available action set A_i as $\{q_0, q_1, q_2, \ldots, q_d\}$, where d is the maximal degree of the poison dosage. Specifically, the action q_0 indicates no poison while the rest actions $\{q_1, q_2, \ldots, q_d\}$ indicate the poison dosage increasing linearly (the player can choose any action by adjusting the stealth factor α). We use $|a_i|/d \in [0.0, 1.0]$ to represent the poison percentage of action a_i.

The utility function in FLG consists of two parts. The first part is information gain from model aggregation, denoted by $\frac{1}{n} \sum_{i=1}^n g(a_i)$, where $g(a_i) = 1 - |a_i|/d$ is a set-valued mapping. The second part is attack score, which is another set-valued mapping, denoted by $h(a_i) = |a_i|/d$. Then the corresponding utility function of P_i can be defined as

$$u_i(\boldsymbol{a}) = \frac{1}{n} \sum_{j=1}^n g(a_j) + h(a_i), \tag{12}$$

where $a_i \in A_i$. We now give some intuitive interpretations about the utility function. Normally, P_i can get knowledge from other players through the model aggregation. But this knowledge will be hidden in a mixture of all participants'

Algorithm 2: FL with robust model aggregation (Romoa).

Input : learning rate η, amount of participants n, residual rate β, moving rate γ, syncing period τ, maximal iteration T.

Output: globally learnt model $\bar{\theta}$.

```
 1  for i ← 1 to n do
 2  │   θ₀ⁱ ← rand(0, 1)                                    /* initialization */
 3  │   F₀ⁱ ← 1/n
 4  end
```

Participant P_i:

```
 5  for i ← 1 to n do
 6  │   for t ← 1 to T do
 7  │   │   θₜⁱ ← θₜ₋₁ⁱ − ηgₜⁱ(θₜ₋₁ⁱ)
 8  │   │   upload θₜⁱ                                    /* lookahead updating */
 9  │   │   if τ divides t then
10  │   │   │   download θ̄ₜ                                      /* syncing */
11  │   │   │   θₜⁱ ← θₜⁱ − γ(θₜⁱ − θ̄ₜ)
12  │   │   end
13  │   end
14  end
```

Parameter Server:

```
15  for t ← 1 to T do
16  │   calculating Fₜⁱ for Pᵢ                             /* sanitizing factor */
17  │   for i ← 1 to n do                                     /* normalization */
18  │   │   Fₜⁱ ← βe^{Fₜⁱ} / ∑ⱼ₌₁ⁿ e^{Fₜʲ} + (1 − β)Fₜ₋₁ⁱ
19  │   end
20  │   if τ divides t then
21  │   │   θ̄ₜ ← ∑ᵢ₌₁ⁿ θₜⁱFₜⁱ                            /* sanitized aggregation */
22  │   end
23  end
```

---

information. Hence, the information gain from the aggregation should be scaled by $\frac{1}{n}$. Obviously, if all participants take normal action, then the total social welfare will equal to n while each player yields 1 utility.

We design the attack score carefully so that the adversary can get extra revenues for attack action while players' cooperation is still possible. Considering all possible outcomes, the adversary prefers to take the most effective action q_d if all the other participants act normally. In this case, the adversary can get $2 - \frac{1}{n}$ utility while other players get $1 - \frac{1}{n}$ utility. Since all players are rational, they will choose to take take the most effective poisoning action and end in 1 utility from the attack eventually, which also yield a total social welfare n.

4.2 rFLG: Repeated Federated Learning Game

Now we extend the FLG into a finitely repeated game rFLG to characterize players' interactions repeatedly for the recursive learning. Aiming at secure aggregation, it is crucial to have undesirable behaviors punished. The sanitizing factors introduced in Romoa are designed exactly for this purpose. Given $G =< \mathcal{P}, \{A_i\}_{i=1}^n, \{u_i\}_{i=1}^n >$, rFLG can be defined as a finitely repeated game of G as $G_0 =< \mathcal{P}, H, S, \{u_i\}_{i=1}^n >$, where $\mathcal{P}$ and $\{u_i\}_{i=1}^n$ are the same player set and utility function set as G, $H = \{\varPhi\} \cup \{\cup_{t=1}^T A^t\}$ is the set of historical action profiles, $\varPhi$ is the initial profile, T is a given positive integer, and $A = \{A_i\}_{i=1}^n$. Additionally, S is the set of strategies for each player, which assigns an action in A_i to every finite sequence of action history. It should be noted that if $\boldsymbol{a}^t = (a^1, a^2, \ldots, a, \ldots, a^t)$, $a \in A_i$, $a' \in A_i$ and $u_i(a) \geq u_i(a')$, we will say that P_i has a preference for action sequence $(a^1, a^2, \ldots, a, \ldots, a^t)$ over action sequence $(a^1, a^2, \ldots, a', \ldots, a^t)$. To put Romoa into the rFLG, we make an abstraction of the sanitizing factors and use it to reconstruct original utility functions as

$$u_i^*(\boldsymbol{a}) = \sum_{j=1}^n \frac{e_j}{n} g(a_j) + h(a_i), \tag{13}$$

where e_j can be seen as a predefined price of each player P_j charging for P_i's unsuitable behaviors. To have e_j worked in the same way as the sanitizing factors, we assume that e_j can be determined by the similarity between action profiles of P_i and P_j. Specifically,

$$e_j = \begin{cases} 1, & \text{if } g(a_i) \geq g(a_j), \\ g(a_i), & \text{otherwise.} \end{cases} \tag{14}$$

In this way, the adversary who takes attack action will be punished by other participants. Given e_j, we can derive another strategic game G^* from G. $G^* =< \mathcal{P}, \{A_i\}_{i=1}^n, \{u_i^*\}_{i=1}^n >$. Different from the original G, we can easily conclude that G^* has a unique Nash equilibrium where all players choose to take action q_0, which means no attacks. Then a FL task with Romoa can be defined as another rFLG $G_0^* =< \mathcal{P}, H, S, \{u_i^*\}_{i=1}^n >$. Furthermore, by following the theorem about Nash equilibrium of finitely repeated game, we can directly conclude that the outcome of the G_0^* consists of the Nash equilibrium of G^* repeated T times.

5   Evaluation

We evaluate Romoa in two aspects, defense capability and model usability. For the purpose of comparison, we use a FL task without any defense as a baseline where 9 participants use the default setting as previously introduced while one model poisoning adversary. We also compare Romoa with two well-known Byzantine-robust solutions Krum [4] and RFA [9] in the same settings[4] with participants scale from 10 to 200. All experimental results are averaged across multiple runs with MNIST [19] and CIFAR-10 [18] datasets respectively.

Recall that UPA aims to increase the error rate for all labels indiscriminately while TPA aims to increase the error rate only for the target samples.

---

[4] Since our FL setting is different from Krum and RFA, the results may vary slightly. But this does not hurt major conclusions.

Figure 5 shows error rates of UPA regarding different solutions. Note that both Romoa and RFA achieve nearly perfect defense on MNIST dataset but Romoa can outperform RFA on CIFAR-10 dataset. Meanwhile, UPA error rate reaches significantly high in the baseline in early stage and the performance of Krum shows that Byzantine-robust solution could be broken quickly. Defense results against TPA are shown in Fig. 6. All solutions are evaluated by confidences of true label and the poisoning label. True label confidence of the baseline is compromised quickly. But Romoa and Krum can provide strong protect in the same case. Note that Romoa has explicit advantage over RFA and outperforms Krum in poisoning label confidence.

As for the model usability evaluation, UPA and TPA may have different focuses. UPA influences global model accuracy seriously while TPA barely has influences on global model accuracy. Figure 7 and Fig. 8 are evaluation results of model accuracy in training and test regarding UPA and TPA respectively. As

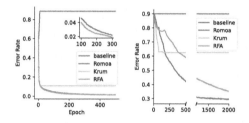

Fig. 5. Error rates of UPA with MNIST (left) and CIFAR-10 (right) datasets.

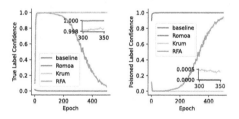

Fig. 6. Confidence of true label (left) and poisoned label (right) for the samples targeted by TPA with MNIST dataset.

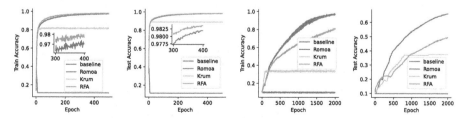

Fig. 7. Global model accuracy of the model attacked by UPA with MNIST (left two) and CIFAR-10 (right two).

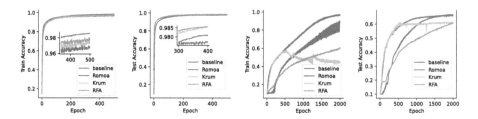

Fig. 8. Global model accuracy compromised by TPA with MNIST (left two) and CIFAR-10 (right two) datasets.

Table 1. Average error rate for FL tasks on different scales. Romoa can outperform Krum and RFA in most cases and achieve competitive in other cases.

Participants (n)			10			20		
Adversarial participants			1	3	4	1	6	9
MNIST	TPA	baseline	0.969517	0.944382	0.985758	0.973807	0.963074	0.990942
		Romoa	0.008289	**0.000183**	**0.000571**	0.021465	**0.013944**	**0.001301**
		RFA	**0.004690**	0.564633	0.687104	**0.009044**	0.61265	0.61265
		Krum	0.046238	0.062209	0.360937	0.058969	0.094315	0.461042
	UPA	baseline	0.884297	0.886125	0.886371	0.881747	0.886246	0.886527
		Romoa	**0.014700**	**0.043952**	**0.042849**	0.087651	**0.068632**	**0.108119**
		RFA	0.033200	0.105942	0.884133	**0.048608**	0.143554	0.886077
		Krum	0.111384	0.171478	0.898100	0.137760	0.160500	0.899100
CIFAR10	TPA	baseline	0.976524	0.993349	0.969406	0.942245	0.993748	0.988471
		Romoa	0.106586	0.116066	0.128794	0.105491	0.110650	0.19591
		RFA	0.101637	0.36399	0.713695	**0.009044**	0.171790	0.738469
		Krum	**0.100348**	**0.103137**	**0.100276**	0.099465	**0.099167**	**0.100321**
	UPA	baseline	0.899990	0.900000	0.900000	0.900000	0.900000	0.900000
		Romoa	**0.390807**	**0.473752**	**0.483586**	**0.497820**	**0.589919**	**0.675593**
		RFA	0.411122	0.899662	0.899919	0.527069	0.899814	0.900000
		Krum	0.631414	0.915900	0.899800	0.706112	0.881600	0.899300
Participants (n)			100			200		
Adversarial participants			1	33	49	1	66	99
MNIST	TPA	baseline	0.995910	0.995476	0.995090	0.995910	0.995476	0.995090
		Romoa	0.051435	0.136652	**0.152566**	0.108603	**0.189824**	**0.211517**
		RFA	**0.034294**	0.532786	0.988208	**0.091589**	0.682731	0.995961
		Krum	0.106764	**0.102102**	0.999547	0.131459	0.767544	0.987186
	UPA	baseline	0.867507	0.886444	0.886500	0.873398	0.886481	0.886500
		Romoa	**0.122615**	**0.189103**	**0.225616**	**0.188722**	**0.291795**	**0.292397**
		RFA	0.138354	0.885578	0.887790	0.195785	0.682731	0.995961
		Krum	0.296960	0.884200	0.931200	0.853001	0.875300	0.870700
CIFAR10	TPA	baseline	0.995910	0.995476	0.995090	0.995910	0.995476	0.995090
		Romoa	0.107185	0.117845	**0.126996**	0.117252	**0.112823**	**0.211517**
		RFA	0.102496	0.194651	0.914630	0.100821	0.234961	0.941820
		Krum	**0.101537**	**0.102102**	0.999547	**0.100606**	0.908100	0.902900
	UPA	baseline	0.899408	0.900000	0.900000	0.898762	0.900000	0.900000
		Romoa	**0.740108**	**0.834114**	**0.834114**	0.875135	**0.884951**	**0.888772**
		RFA	0.743340	0.899804	0.900000	**0.860587**	0.899931	0.900000
		Krum	0.900200	0.898500	0.908600	0.905888	0.911900	0.913200

Table 2. Error rate of UPA and TPA with non-i.i.d. datasets.

		No attack	TPA	UPA
MNIST	baseline	0.149003	0.880771	0.895005
	Romoa	0.133656	0.432999	0.16347
CIFAR10	baseline	0.460900	0.972004	0.900100
	Romoa	0.424200	0.738158	0.570603

we can see, Romoa can protect global model accuracy against UPA and TPA effectively. RFA can achieve the best performance on MNIST dataset but both RFA and Krum fail on CIFAR-10 dataset. We remark this failure may be caused by the neglect of training data diversity. We give more experimental results in Table 1, which takes into account more adversarial participants. Basically, we can conclude that Romoa can outperform Krum and RFA in most cases and Romoa has better performance when dealing with more adversarial participants.

To be more practical, we also evaluate Romoa with non-i.i.d. datasets. Intuitively, defense solutions based on similarity measurement methods cannot deal with participants' non-i.i.d. datasets. But Romoa can use hybrid similarity measurements in a lookahead manner to overcome this problem. The result in Table 2 is obtained by replacing the identical training data in default setting for 10 participants with assigning to each participant a distinct label and the corresponding data. Then the rest setting is the same as default with one adversary. In this case, we find Romoa can still frustrate UPA and TPA significantly.

6   Related Work

In recent years, the emergence of Federated learning [21,28] has attracted much attention and gives a new solution to better use the Internet end-users' big data. However, security issues keep coming up. Among all these threats, the poisoning attack [7,9,11,14,31,32,38] is highly threatening. According to different approaches used for poisoning, there exist two main categories, data poisoning attacks [8,12,26,31] and model poisoning attacks [1,3,9]. Despite different adversarial goals, the most significant feature shared by all poisoning attacks is that the model usability will be sabotaged, regarding some specific samples or all data samples.

On the other side, there are also many insightful studies of defensive solutions to poisoning attacks. To eliminate the adversarial effect, many efforts have been made to implement Byzantine-robust federated learning [22,24,25,27,36,37]. FLTrust [6] adopts the idea that the parameter server assign trust scores computed by cosine similarity to each participants, the global model is based on bootstrapping trust local models. However, in [6] it assumes that the parameter server must keep a small clean training dataset for robust aggregation. Apart from above-mentioned methods, another approach tends to apply knowledge distillation. Han et al. [13] introduced another robust federated learning method called CoMT(Collaborative Machine Teaching), where the learner (parameter server) is taught by distributed teachers (participants) with collaboratively fine-tuning. Lin et al. [20] investigated the ensemble distillation algorithm, a more flexible model fusion aggregation rule under heterogeneous federated learning scenario. Although lots of new solutions have been proposed, the game of attack and defense continues. Recent studies have reported two model poisoning attacks [3,9], which can breach Byzantine-robust solutions easily. Now it is urgent to think about alternative solutions to the defense of federated learning. That is also a major motivation of our work.

7   Conclusion

Model poisoning attacks are critical threats to FL. The best solution to defeating poisoning attacks is still under discussion. We give a practical solution based on similarity measurement in this paper. Through the analysis in a game-theory manner, we show the correctness of Romoa. Based on comparative experiments, we find that Romoa can defend against poisoning attacks effectively and outperforms Byzantine-robust solutions Krum and RFA in most cases. But we also note that collusive poisoning attacks become unbeatable when the proportion of adversarial participants is relatively large, like about 50%. How to protect FL in this case is quite challenging, and we will take this into account in our future work.

Acknowledgement. The authors would like to thank the reviewers for their helpful comments. This work was supported in part by National Key R&D Program of China under Grant 2020YFB1005900, NSFC-61902176, BK20190294, NSFC-61872176, and Leading-edge Technology Program of Jiangsu Natural Science Foundation (No. BK20202001).

Appendix

1 DNN Architectures

The DNN architectures for baseline FL tasks with MNIST and CIFAR-10 datasets are shown in Fig. 9 and Fig. 10, respectively.

Layer	Output Shape	Param #
Conv2D(64,5)+ReLU	(None, 24, 24, 64)	1664
Conv2D(64,5)+ReLU	(None, 20, 20, 64)	102464
Dropout(0.25)	(None, 20, 20, 64)	0
Flatten	(None, 25600)	0
Dense(128)+ReLU	(None, 128)	3276928
Dropout(0.5)	(None, 128)	0
Dense(10)+Softmax	(None, 10)	1290

Fig. 9. DNN architecture for MNIST tasks.

Layer	Output Shape	Param #
Conv2D(64,3)+ReLU	(None, 32, 32, 64)	1792
Conv2D(64,3)+ReLU	(None, 32, 32, 64)	36928
MaxPooling2D(2,2)	(None, 16, 16, 64)	0
Conv2D(128,3)+ReLU	(None, 16, 16, 128)	73856
Conv2D(128,3)+ReLU	(None, 16, 16, 128)	147584
Conv2D(128,3)+ReLU	(None, 16, 16, 128)	147584
MaxPooling2D(2,2)	(None, 8, 8, 128)	0
Conv2D(256,3)+ReLU	(None, 8, 8, 256)	295168
Conv2D(256,3)+ReLU	(None, 8, 8, 256)	590080
Conv2D(256,3)+ReLU	(None, 8, 8, 256)	590080
MaxPooling2D(2,2)	(None, 4, 4, 256)	0
Flatten	(None, 4096)	0
Dense(1024)+ReLU	(None, 1024)	4195328
Dropout(0.5)	(None, 1024)	0
Dense(10)+Softmax	(None, 10)	10250

Fig. 10. DNN architecture for CIFAR-10 tasks.

References

1. Bagdasaryan, E., Veit, A., Hua, Y., Estrin, D., Shmatikov, V.: How to backdoor federated learning. In: International Conference on Artificial Intelligence and Statistics, pp. 2938–2948 (2020)
2. S S Bell, J.H., Bonawitz, K.A., Gascón, A., Lepoint, T., Raykova, M.: Secure single-server aggregation with (poly) logarithmic overhead. In: Proceedings of the 2020 ACM SIGSAC Conference on Computer and Communications Security, pp. 1253–1269 (2020)

3. Bhagoji, A.N., Chakraborty, S., Mittal, P., Calo, S.: Analyzing federated learning through an adversarial lens. In: International Conference on Machine Learning, pp. 634–643 (2019)
4. Blanchard, P., El Mhamdi, E.M., Guerraoui, R., Stainer, J.: Machine learning with adversaries: byzantine tolerant gradient descent. In: Proceedings of the 31st International Conference on Neural Information Processing Systems, pp. 118–128 (2017)
5. Bonawitz, K., et al.: Practical secure aggregation for privacy-preserving machine learning. In: Proceedings of the 2017 ACM SIGSAC Conference on Computer and Communications Security, pp. 1175–1191 (2017)
6. Cao, X., Fang, M., Liu, J., Gong, N.Z.: Fltrust: byzantine-robust federated learning via trust bootstrapping. In: 28th Annual Network and Distributed System Security Symposium, NDSS (2021)
7. Cao, X., Jia, J., Gong, N.Z.: Data poisoning attacks to local differential privacy protocols. In: 30th {USENIX} Security Symposium ({USENIX} Security 21) (2021)
8. Chen, X., Liu, C., Li, B., Lu, K., Song, D.: Targeted backdoor attacks on deep learning systems using data poisoning. arXiv preprint arXiv:1712.05526 (2017)
9. Fang, M., Cao, X., Jia, J., Gong, N.: Local model poisoning attacks to byzantine-robust federated learning. In: 29th {USENIX} Security Symposium ({USENIX} Security 20), pp. 1605–1622 (2020)
10. Fukunaga, K., Hostetler, L.: The estimation of the gradient of a density function, with applications in pattern recognition. IEEE Trans. Inf. theory $21(1)$, 32–40 (1975)
11. Fung, C., Yoon, C.J., Beschastnikh, I.: The limitations of federated learning in sybil settings. In: 23rd International Symposium on Research in Attacks, Intrusions and Defenses ({RAID} 2020), pp. 301–316 (2020)
12. Gu, T., Dolan-Gavitt, B., Garg, S.: Badnets: identifying vulnerabilities in the machine learning model supply chain. arXiv preprint arXiv:1708.06733 (2017)
13. Han, Y., Zhang, X.: Robust federated learning via collaborative machine teaching. In: Proceedings of the AAAI Conference on Artificial Intelligence, vol. 34, pp. 4075–4082 (2020)
14. Huang, H., Mu, J., Gong, N.Z., Li, Q., Liu, B., Xu, M.: Data poisoning attacks to deep learning based recommender systems. In: 28th Annual Network and Distributed System Security Symposium, NDSS (2021)
15. Jagielski, M., Oprea, A., Biggio, B., Liu, C., Nita-Rotaru, C., Li, B.: Manipulating machine learning: poisoning attacks and countermeasures for regression learning. In: 2018 IEEE Symposium on Security and Privacy (SP), pp. 19–35 (2018)
16. John, P.G., Vijaykeerthy, D., Saha, D.: Verifying individual fairness in machine learning models. In: Conference on Uncertainty in Artificial Intelligence, pp. 749–758 (2020)
17. Kadhe, S., Rajaraman, N., Koyluoglu, O.O., Ramchandran, K.: Fastsecagg: scalable secure aggregation for privacy-preserving federated learning. arXiv preprint arXiv:2009.11248 (2020)
18. Krizhevsky, A., Hinton, G.: Learning multiple layers of features from tiny images (2009)
19. LeCun, Y., Bottou, L., Bengio, Y., Haffner, P.: Gradient-based learning applied to document recognition. Proc. IEEE $86(11)$, 2278–2324 (1998)
20. Lin, T., Kong, L., Stich, S.U., Jaggi, M.: Ensemble distillation for robust model fusion in federated learning. In: Advances in Neural Information Processing Systems 33: Annual Conference on Neural Information Processing Systems (2020)

21. McMahan, B., Moore, E., Ramage, D., Hampson, S., Arcas, B.A.: Communication-efficient learning of deep networks from decentralized data. In: Artificial Intelligence and Statistics, pp. 1273–1282 (2017)
22. Muñoz-González, L. Co, K.T., Lupu, E.C.: Byzantine-robust federated machine learning through adaptive model averaging. arXiv preprint arXiv:1909.05125 (2019)
23. Nasr, M., Shokri, R., Houmansadr, A.: Comprehensive privacy analysis of deep learning: Passive and active white-box inference attacks against centralized and federated learning. In: 2019 IEEE symposium on security and privacy (SP), pp. 739–753 (2019)
24. Portnoy, A., Hendler, D.: Towards realistic byzantine-robust federated learning. arXiv preprint arXiv:2004.04986 (2020)
25. Reisizadeh, A., Farnia, F., Pedarsani, R., Jadbabaie, A.: Robust federated learning: the case of affine distribution shifts. In: Advances in Neural Information Processing Systems 33: Annual Conference on Neural Information Processing Systems (2020)
26. Shafahi, A., et al.: Poison frogs! targeted clean-label poisoning attacks on neural networks. In: Advances in Neural Information Processing Systems, pp. 6103–6113 (2018)
27. Shen, S., Tople, S., Saxena, P.: Auror: defending against poisoning attacks in collaborative deep learning systems. In: Proceedings of the 32nd Annual Conference on Computer Security Applications, pp. 508–519 (2016)
28. Shokri, R., Shmatikov, V.: Privacy-preserving deep learning. In: Proceedings of the 22nd ACM SIGSAC Conference on Computer and Communications Security, pp. 1310–1321 (2015)
29. Suciu, O., Marginean, R., Kaya, Y., Daume III, H., Dumitras, T.: When does machine learning {FAIL}? generalized transferability for evasion and poisoning attacks. In: 27th {USENIX} Security Symposium ({USENIX} Security 18), pp. 1299–1316 (2018)
30. Toch, E., et al.: The privacy implications of cyber security systems: a technological survey. ACM Comput. Surv. (CSUR) 51(2), 1–27 (2018)
31. Tolpegin, V., Truex, S., Gursoy, M.E., Liu, L.: Data poisoning attacks against federated learning systems. In: European Symposium on Research in Computer Security, pp. 480–501 (2020)
32. Wang, H., et al.: Attack of the tails: yes, you really can backdoor federated learning. In: Advances in Neural Information Processing Systems (2020)
33. Wu, W., He, L., Lin, W., Mao, R., Maple, C., Jarvis, S.A.: Safa: a semi-asynchronous protocol for fast federated learning with low overhead. IEEE Trans. Comput. (2020)
34. Xie, C., Koyejo, S., Gupta, I.: Asynchronous federated optimization. arXiv preprint arXiv:1903.03934 (2019)
35. Yeom, S., Fredrikson, M.: Individual fairness revisited: transferring techniques from adversarial robustness. In: Proceedings of the Twenty-Ninth International Joint Conference on Artificial Intelligence, IJCAI, pp. 437–443 (2020)
36. Yin, D., Chen, Y., Kannan, R., Bartlett, P.: Byzantine-robust distributed learning: towards optimal statistical rates. In: International Conference on Machine Learning, pp. 5650–5659 (2018)
37. Yin, D., Chen, Y., Kannan, R., Bartlett, P.: Defending against saddle point attack in byzantine-robust distributed learning. In: International Conference on Machine Learning, pp. 7074–7084 (2019)

38. Zhang, J., Chen, J., Wu, D., Chen, B., Yu, S.: Poisoning attack in federated learning using generative adversarial nets. In: 18th IEEE International Conference on Trust, Security and Privacy in Computing and Communications/13th IEEE International Conference on Big Data Science and Engineering (TrustCom/BigDataSE), pp. 374–380 (2019)
39. Zhang, M.R., Lucas, J., Hinton, G., Ba, J.: Lookahead optimizer: k steps forward, 1 step back. In: Advances in Neural Information Processing Systems, pp. 9597–9608 (2019)
40. Zheng, S., et al.: Asynchronous stochastic gradient descent with delay compensation. In: International Conference on Machine Learning, pp. 4120–4129 (2017)

FLOD: Oblivious Defender for Private Byzantine-Robust Federated Learning with Dishonest-Majority

Ye Dong[1,2], Xiaojun Chen[1,2(✉)], Kaiyun Li[1,2], Dakui Wang[1], and Shuai Zeng[1]

[1] Institute of Information Engineering, Chinese Academy of Sciences, Beijing, China
{dongye,chenxiaojun,likaiyun,wangdakui,zengshuai}@iie.ac.cn
[2] School of Cyber Security, University of Chinese Academy of Sciences, Beijing, China

Abstract. *Privacy* and *Byzantine-robustness* are two major concerns of federated learning (FL), but mitigating both threats simultaneously is highly challenging: privacy-preserving strategies prohibit access to individual model updates to avoid leakage, while Byzantine-robust methods require access for comprehensive mathematical analysis. Besides, most Byzantine-robust methods only work in the *honest-majority* setting.

We present FLOD, a novel oblivious defender for private Byzantine-robust FL in dishonest-majority setting. Basically, we propose a novel Hamming distance-based aggregation method to resist $> 1/2$ Byzantine attacks using a small *root-dataset* and *server-model* for bootstrapping trust. Furthermore, we employ two non-colluding servers and use additive homomorphic encryption (AHE) and secure two-party computation (2PC) primitives to construct efficient privacy-preserving building blocks for secure aggregation, in which we propose two novel in-depth variants of Beaver Multiplication triples (MT) to reduce the overhead of Bit to Arithmetic (Bit2A) conversion and vector weighted sum aggregation (VSWA) significantly. Experiments on real-world and synthetic datasets demonstrate our effectiveness and efficiency: (i) FLOD defeats known Byzantine attacks with a negligible effect on accuracy and convergence, (ii) achieves a reduction of $\approx 2\times$ for offline (resp. online) overhead of Bit2A and VSWA compared to ABY-AHE (resp. ABY-MT) based methods (NDSS'15), (iii) and reduces total online communication and run-time by 167–1416$\times$ and 3.1–7.4$\times$ compared to FLGUARD (Crypto Eprint 2021/025).

Keywords: Privacy-preserving · Byzantine-robust · Federated Learning · Dishonest-majority

1 Introduction

Federated Learning (FL) is an emerging collaborative machine learning trend, in which the training is distributed and executed in parallel, and used in real-world applications, e.g., next word prediction [17], medical imaging [15]. More

© Springer Nature Switzerland AG 2021
E. Bertino et al. (Eds.): ESORICS 2021, LNCS 12972, pp. 497–518, 2021.
https://doi.org/10.1007/978-3-030-88418-5_24

importantly, FL offers an appealing solution to privacy preservation by enabling clients to train a global model via an aggregator (a.k.a server) while keeping private data at local to avoid violating related regulations and laws [28,35].

Despite its benefits, FL has been shown to be vulnerable to Byzantine and inference attacks [16,26]. In the former, the adversary $\mathcal{A}^c$, who controls some clients, aims to manipulate the global model, e.g., compromise the model performance. In the latter, adversary $\mathcal{A}^s$, who corrupts the aggregator, follows the execution transcript honestly but tries to learn additional information about the clients' private local data by analyzing their model updates. Mitigating both kinds of attacks simultaneously is highly challenging: Defending Byzantine attacks require access to the clients' model updates [1,6,25,38], while privacy-preserving strategies, such as the methods based on secure computation which is provable security, prohibit this to avoid information leakage [8,12,31,33]. Additionally, existing Byzantine-robust methods mainly rely on clients *honest-majority* assumption, which means $\mathcal{A}^c$ controls $< 1/2$ clients.

Recently, Cao *et al.* proposed FLTrust [11] to overcome the honest-majority limitation by using a small clean *root-dataset* to compute server-model update for bootstrapping trust. But it requires complex calculation operations such as cosine distance, rescaling, and comparison, which are very expensive when evaluated in secure computation.

Nguyen *et al.* employed two servers P_0 and P_1 as aggregators and proposed FLGUARD [27] to preserve privacy while thwarting Byzantine attacks by combining a novel robust aggregation approach with 2PC, but it only works under honest-majority assumption. Worsely, FLGUARD results in a severe P-P overhead and increases the client-aggregator (C-P) communication by $3\times$, which is also a serious burden since the C-P connection is usually in WAN and bandwidth limited. In terms of reducing C-P communication, quantization is one promising approach that approximates float model updates with low-bit precision. Among these researches, SIGNSGD [5] transmits only the sgn model update (-1 for negative and 1 otherwise), and a majority vote decides the global update. However, SIGNSGD is also suffering from inference and Byzantine attacks (in dishonest-majority). What is worse, it introduces significant convergence degradation compared to traditional FL (cf. Sect. 5.1). Therefore, it is urgent and challenging to propose a solution to adequately tackle these obstacles simultaneously.

To address the challenge, we propose FLOD, a novel oblivious defender for private Byzantine-robust FL in a dishonest-majority setting based on bootstrapping trust and sgn quantization techniques. Though bootstrapping trust and quantization are inspired by prior works, our technical innovation lies in the novel in-depth aggregation method. Unlike existing works, our key insight is that Hamming distance [9] is highly more suitable and efficient than others to measure the similarity of binary vectors. Therefore, we aim to compute the Hamming distance between each local model update and the aggregator's to measure the similarity and remove local model updates with relatively a large hamming distance (small similarity). To this end, we introduce a sgn/Boolean conversion method to support XOR and propose to use ReLU with a pre-defined threshold τ for clipping the distance. The aggregated model update is the weighted average of all sgn model updates based on corresponding clipped results.

In terms of privacy preservation, we employ two non-colluding servers as aggregators and design efficient privacy-preserving blocks based on 2PC primitives to protect the immediate results. Concretely, we construct CXOR and PCBit2A to evaluate correlated XOR for free and realize Bit2A conversion efficiently. Hence, we can compute the Hamming distance privately. Then, we use garbled circuits (GC) with *single instruction multiple data* (SIMD) optimization to implement private τ-Clipping. Finally, we compute the weighted average of all secret-shared sgn model updates as CSWA securely. Specially, we propose two variants of MT [13] based on the correlations of secret-shared values to reduce the offline and online overheads of Bit2A and VSWA by $\approx 2\times$, respectively. Notably, these secure blocks are of independent interest and can be useful in other works.

Contributions. In brief, we summarize our main contributions as follows.

- **Byzantine-robustness:** We propose FLOD, a novel Hamming distance-based aggregation method in the dishonest-majority setting. In contrast to existing works, FLOD is much more efficient, especially evaluated in 2PC, since our solution is mainly composed of lightweight operations, e.g., XOR, ADD, and MUL. Moreover, we achieve the same level of Byzantine-robustness as FLTrust for sgn model updates in theory.
- **Privacy Preservation:** To impede inference attacks by a semi-honest aggregator, we construct privacy-preserving building blocks based on 2PC and AHE for each component of FLOD. Furthermore, we propose two novel variants of MTs based on the correlations of secret-shared values to reduce the overhead (including communication and run-time) of Bit2A and VSWA by $\approx 2\times$. We also give a detailed analysis of the correctness and privacy of FLOD.
- **Evaluations:** We implement a proof-of-concept prototype and give the experimental results on neural networks: (i) FLOD defeats known Byzantine attacks with a negligible effect on accuracy and convergence, (ii) achieves a reduction of $\approx 2\times$ for offline (resp. online) overhead compared to ABY-AHE (resp. ABY-MT) based method [13], (iii) and reduces total online communication and run-time by $167-1416\times$ and $3.1-7.4\times$ compared to FLGUARD [27].

Roadmap. We present the preliminaries and definitions in Sect. 2. Then, we formulate our scope and threat model in Sect. 3. In Sect. 4, we give the concrete design of FLOD, including the proposed aggregation rule (cf. Sect. 4.1) and privacy-preserving building blocks (cf. Sect. 4.2). The prototype and experimental results are presented in Sect. 5. We discuss existing works in Sect. 6 and conclude this work in Sect. 7.

2   Background and Preliminaries

2.1   Federated Learning

Workflow. Federated learning (FL) [19,20,22] enables K distributed clients to collaboratively build a global model $\mathbf{W}$. In each training round, client C_i locally computes model updates $\mathbf{w}_i$ based on previous global model $\mathbf{W}$ and local dataset D_i, and sends $\mathbf{w}_i$ to the aggregator. Then, the aggregator aggregates all $\mathbf{w}_i$ as $\mathbf{w}$ according to the particular aggregation method, such as average $\mathbf{w} = \frac{1}{n} \cdot \sum_{i=1}^{K} \mathbf{w}_i$. Finally, the aggregator dispatches $\mathbf{w}$ to all clients for model update.

Inference Attack. FL provides *data locality* such that D_i can be confined within its owner C_i. Despite this, clients still entail sharing locally trained $\mathbf{w}_i$, in order to synthesize the final global model $\mathbf{W}$. However, these local $\mathbf{w}_i$ are subject to information leakage. Specially, one semi-honest aggregator $\mathcal{A}^s$ can attempt to infer sensitive information and even restore private D_i from received $\mathbf{w}_i$ [39]. Therefore, it is an essential requirement to keep $\mathbf{w}_i$ confidential.

Byzantine Attacks. In Byzantine attacks, adversary $\mathcal{A}^c$ controls some clients and manipulates $\mathbf{w}_i'$ to affect the final $\mathbf{W}$'s behavior. As the main accuracy (MA) is one of the dominant metrics in machine learning, we focus on the Byzantine attacks aiming at compromising MA in this work. To attack FL, existing work mainly uses *data poisoning* [38] and *model poisoning* [6] attacks. In the former, $\mathcal{A}^c$ poisons the instances of training data, e.g., *label flipping*. While in the latter, $\mathcal{A}^c$ can add well manipulated noises, e.g., *Gaussian noises*, to $\mathbf{w}_i$.

Hamming Distance. For two bit vectors $\mathbf{x}, \mathbf{y} \in \{0,1\}^d$ of equal length, their Hamming distance hd is the number of positions where $x_i \neq y_i$ for $x_i \in \mathbf{x}$ and $y_i \in \mathbf{y}$. Formally, $hd = \sum_{i=1}^{d} x_i \oplus y_i$.

2.2 Cryptographic Preliminaries

Secure 2-Party Computation (2PC). allows two parties to jointly compute a function without leaking private inputs. Basically, there are three techniques: **A**rithmetic sharing, **B**oolean sharing, and **Y**ao's garbled circuits.

Arithmetic/Boolean Sharing. For one ℓ-bit value x in finite ring $\mathcal{R}$, party P_t for $t \in \{0,1\}$ holds an additive share $\langle a \rangle_t^{\mathsf{A}}$ such that $a = \langle a \rangle_0^{\mathsf{A}} + \langle a \rangle_1^{\mathsf{A}}$. For two arithmetic shared value $\langle a \rangle^{\mathsf{A}}$ and $\langle b \rangle^{\mathsf{A}}$, addition (ADD) can be evaluated locally. And multiplication (MUL) gate relies on Beaver's Multiplication Triples (MTs): P_0 and P_1 prepare triple $(\langle x \rangle^{\mathsf{A}}, \langle y \rangle^{\mathsf{A}}, \langle z \rangle^{\mathsf{A}})$ where $z = xy$ and P_t holds the t-th share. Then P_t computes $\langle e \rangle_t^{\mathsf{A}} = \langle a \rangle_t^{\mathsf{A}} - \langle x \rangle_t^{\mathsf{A}}$ and $\langle f \rangle_t^{\mathsf{A}} = \langle b \rangle_t^{\mathsf{A}} - \langle y \rangle_t^{\mathsf{A}}$. Both parties reconstruct e and f, and compute $\langle ab \rangle_t^{\mathsf{A}} = -tef + f\langle a \rangle_t^{\mathsf{A}} + e\langle b \rangle_t^{\mathsf{A}} + \langle z \rangle_t^{\mathsf{A}}$ [3]. Note we omit the modular operation for brevity. The triples can be generated offline using Additive Homomorphic Encryption (AHE) or Oblivious Transfer (OT) as [13]. *Boolean Sharing* can be seen as arithmetic sharing in $\mathbb{Z}_2$, and hence all operations carry over: addition is replaced by XOR ($\oplus$), and multiplication is replaced by AND ($\wedge$).

Yao's Garbled Circuits (GC) is run between two parties called *garbler* and *evaluator*. The garbler generates the garbled circuits corresponding to the Boolean circuit by associating two random keys K_0^w, K_1^w for each wire w to represent bit value $\{0,1\}$, and then sends GC together with the keys for its inputs to the evaluator. While the evaluator obliviously obtains keys for its inputs via Oblivious Transfer (OT) [30], it evaluates the circuit to obtain the output key, which is used to decode the real output. For more details, please refer to [4,37].

Additive Homomorphic Encryption (AHE). A public key encryption scheme is additively homomorphic if given two ciphertexts $\widehat{x} = \mathsf{AHE.Enc_{pk}}(x)$ and $\widehat{y} = \mathsf{AHE.Enc_{pk}}(y)$, there is a public-key operation $\boxplus$ such that $\mathsf{AHE.Enc_{pk}}(x + y) = \widehat{x} \boxplus \widehat{y}$, e.g., Paillier's encryption [29], exponential ElGamal encryption [14]. Besides, adding or multiplying a ciphertext by a constant c is also efficiently supported: $\mathsf{AHE.Enc_{pk}}(c+x) = c \boxplus \widehat{x}$ and $\mathsf{AHE.Enc_{pk}}(c \cdot x) = c \boxtimes \widehat{x}$. Furthermore, we use *single instruction multiple data* (SIMD) technique [34] to pack multiple messages into one ciphertext for better efficiency.

Semi-honest Model. A semi-honest adversary runs the protocol honestly but try to learn additional information from received messages. Let π be a two-party protocol running in real-world and $\mathcal{F}$ be the ideal functionality completed by a trusted party. The ideal-world adversary is referred to as a simulator Sim. We define the two interactions as follows:

- $\mathsf{Real}_\pi(\kappa, C; x_1, x_2)$ run protocol π with security κ, where P_t inputs x_t and C is the corrupted party.
  Output $\{View_t, t \in C\}, (y_1, y_2)$. The P_t's view and output are $View_t$ and y_t.
- $\mathsf{Ideal}_{\mathcal{F},\mathsf{Sim}}(\kappa, C; x_1, x_2)$ compute $(y_1, y_2) \leftarrow \mathcal{F}(x_1, x_2)$.
  Output $\mathsf{Sim}(C, \{x_i, y_i\}_{i \in C})$ and (y_1, y_2)

In the semi-honest model, a protocol π is secure as long as the ideal-world adversary's view is indistinguishable from the view in the ideal-world.

3 Scope and Threat Model

We focus on the widely deployed horizontal scenario where the data is independent and identically distributed (*i.i.d.*) among clients, e.g., financial institutions or medical centers. Our goal is to preserve Byzantine-robustness and privacy at the same time in FL.

Additionally, we follow previous works [27] and consider two kinds of adversaries: $\mathcal{A}^c$ and $\mathcal{A}^s$, as follows:

- Adversary $\mathcal{A}^c$ controls K' ($\leq K - 2$) (if $K' = K - 1$, the aggregated result is likely to be the honest model update) clients and tries to compromise the global model performance. However, $\mathcal{A}^c$ has no control over the aggregators and honest clients. Note that $\mathcal{A}^c$ is not involved in the computation between the servers and only receives the aggregated results in each update. Thus, it learns nothing beyond what can be inferred from the aggregated results and its own inputs.
- The second adversary $\mathcal{A}^s$, which runs our protocols honestly, has access to no more than one server (two non-colluding servers) and does not perform Byzantine attacks (semi-honest). The non-colluding assumption can be guaranteed between two competing companies as it is in their interest to not

give their customer's data to the competitor for protecting business secrets. Additionally, it is reasonable to assume that the two servers are semi-honest because cloud providers/companies are strictly regulated and threatened with severe financial and reputation damages once malicious behavior is detected.

4   Design of **FLOD**

FLOD follows the workflow of typical FL except maintaining a root-dataset and server-model as FLTrust [11], we hence elaborate our aggregation method, privacy-preserving building blocks, and the analysis of correctness and privacy.

4.1   Aggregation Method

In each round of model update, client C_i (resp. aggregator) computes the sgn model update $\widetilde{\mathbf{w}}_i$ (resp. $\widetilde{\mathbf{w}}_s$) in $\{-1,1\}$ as SIGNSGD [5]. The sgn value can limit scaling attacks [2], but naively adding them up will ignore their direction property. Specially, an attacker can manipulate the direction of $\widetilde{\mathbf{w}}_i$ such that the global model might be updated towards the opposite of correct direction. FLTrust resolved a similar issue using *cosine similarity* and ReLU clipping [11], but it requires many expensive non-linear operations. When combining them with secure computation, the overhead will be much more serious.

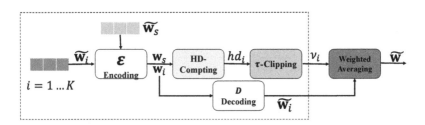

Fig. 1. Overview of FLOD aggregation method.

To this end, we propose an efficient aggregation method as Fig. 1. First, we introduce sgn/Boolean conversion so that C_i (resp. aggregator) can convert the $\widetilde{\mathbf{w}}_i$ (resp. $\widetilde{\mathbf{w}}_s$) in $\{-1,1\}$ to Boolean representation $\mathbf{w}_i$ (resp. $\mathbf{w}_s$) and back. Then, aggregator computes their Hamming distance with mostly XOR/ADD and τ-clip the distance with little comparison, where τ is the threshold. Finally, aggregator converts $\mathbf{w}_i$ back to $\widetilde{\mathbf{w}}_i$ and aggregates them based on clipping results.

sgn/**Boolean Conversion.** Recall $\widetilde{\mathbf{w}}_i$ is in $\{-1,1\}^d$, it is not suitable for XOR operation. Therefore, for $\widetilde{w}_{ij} \in \widetilde{\mathbf{w}}_i$ we propose encoding method $\mathcal{E}$ as:

$$\mathcal{E}(\widetilde{w}_{ij}) = \begin{cases} 0, \ if \ \widetilde{w}_{ij} = 1; \\ 1, \ otherwise. \end{cases} \tag{1}$$

And to aggregate $\widetilde{\mathbf{w}}_i$ in the last step of aggregation, we need to decode $\mathcal{E}(\widetilde{w_{ij}})$. To this end, we propose the decoding method $\mathcal{D}$ as:

$$\mathcal{D}(\mathcal{E}(\widetilde{w_{ij}})) = 1 - 2\mathcal{E}(\widetilde{w_{ij}}) \tag{2}$$

It is straightforward to see that we can guarantee $\mathcal{D}(\mathcal{E}(\widetilde{w_{ij}})) = \widetilde{w_{ij}}$.

Algorithm 1. FLOD Aggregation Method

Input: C_i inputs $\widetilde{\mathbf{w}}_i$ for $i \in [1, K]$ and aggregator inputs $\widetilde{\mathbf{w}}_s$.
Output: $\widetilde{\mathbf{w}} = \frac{1}{\sum_{i=1}^{K} \nu_i} \cdot (\sum_{i=1}^{K} \nu_i \cdot \widetilde{\mathbf{w}}_i)$.
1: Encode $\widetilde{\mathbf{w}}_s \in \{-1, 1\}^d$ using $\mathcal{E}$ into $\{0, 1\}^d$ as $\mathbf{w}_s = \mathcal{E}(\widetilde{\mathbf{w}}_s)$.
2: **for** $i \in [1, K]$ **do**
3:    Encode $\widetilde{\mathbf{w}}_i \in \{-1, 1\}^d$ using $\mathcal{E}$ into $\{0, 1\}^d$ as $\mathbf{w}_i = \mathcal{E}(\widetilde{\mathbf{w}}_i)$.
4:    Compute $hd_i = \sum_{j=1}^{d} w_{ij} \oplus w_{sj}$ for $w_{ij} \in \mathbf{w}_i$ and $w_{sj} \in \mathbf{w}_s$.
5:    Clip hd_i as $\nu_i = \mathrm{ReLU}(\tau - hd_i)$.
6: **end for**
7: **return** $\widetilde{\mathbf{w}} = \frac{1}{\sum_{i=1}^{K} \nu_i} \cdot (\sum_{i=1}^{K} \nu_i \widetilde{\mathbf{w}}_i)$, where $\widetilde{\mathbf{w}}_i = \mathcal{D}(\mathbf{w}_i)$.

HD-Computing. After computing and $\mathcal{E}$-encoding sgn model update, we have the Boolean representation in $\mathbb{Z}_2^d$. Now, for each C_i, we let the aggregator compute the Hamming distance between $\mathbf{w}_i$ and $\mathbf{w}_s$ as:

$$hd_i = \sum_{j=1}^{d} w_{ij} \oplus w_{sj}. \tag{3}$$

τ-**Clipping.** We let the aggregator use threshold τ to clip hd_i and assign weight ν_i to $\mathbf{w}_i$ as:

$$\nu_i = \mathrm{ReLU}(\tau - hd_i), \tag{4}$$

where $\mathrm{ReLU}(x)$ returns x if $x > 0$, and 0 otherwise. Therefore, if $hd_i > \tau$, which indicates the difference between $\mathbf{w}_i$ and $\mathbf{w}_s$ is huge, ReLU will return 0 and we will exclude $\mathbf{w}_i$ from the aggregation. Otherwise, we assign positive weight $\tau - hd_i$ to $\mathbf{w}_i$. Hence, when hd_i is smaller, which means $\mathbf{w}_i$ is more similar to $\mathbf{w}_s$, the corresponding weight ν_i is bigger.

Weighted Averaging. Finally, we compute $\widetilde{\mathbf{w}} = \frac{1}{\sum_{i=1}^{K} \nu_i} (\sum_{i=1}^{K} \nu_i \cdot \widetilde{\mathbf{w}}_i)$ as the aggregated result to update the global model. The formulation is in Algorithm 1, and the analysis of our Byzantine-robustness is illustrated in Appendix A.

4.2   Privacy-Preserving Building Blocks

We construct the privacy-preserving blocks of FLOD as Fig. 2: We employ two non-colluding servers, P_0 and P_1, as aggregators. In each round of aggregation,

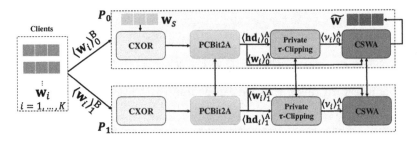

Fig. 2. Workflow of privacy-preserving FLOD. Without losing generality, we let P_0 maintain root-dataset and server-model. As $\mathcal{E}$ can be evaluated locally by each party and secure $\mathcal{D}$ is implemented in CSWA, we omit them for brevity.

P_0 computes and $\mathcal{E}$ encodes $\mathbf{w}_s$, and C_i sends the Boolean share of $\mathcal{E}$-encoded $\mathbf{w}_i$ to P_t. P_0 and P_1 firstly compute the coordinate-wise XOR of $\mathbf{w}_i$ and $\mathbf{w}_s$ privately using CXOR. Then, they jointly convert the Boolean shares to arithmetic shares using PCBit2A for efficient weighted averaging aggregation. Next, P_t sum up all coordinates of $\langle \mathbf{hd}_i \rangle^{\mathsf{A}}$ as $\langle hd_i \rangle^{\mathsf{A}}$, and jointly clip it with τ to obtain ν_i as private τ-Clipping. Finally, two servers aggregate $\widetilde{\mathbf{w}}_i$s based on ν_i as $\widetilde{\mathbf{w}}$ in CSWA, where we compute the arithmetic shares of $\widetilde{\mathbf{w}}_i$ through the shares of $\mathbf{w}_i$. And $\widetilde{\mathbf{w}}$ is revealed to P_0 and all clients for model update.

Algorithm 2. PCBit2A

Input: For $t \in \{0,1\}$, P_t inputs $\langle \mathbf{w}_i \rangle^{\mathsf{B}}_t$ and $\langle \mathbf{hd}_i \rangle^{\mathsf{B}}_t$ for $i \in \{1, ..., K\}$.
Output: For $t \in \{0,1\}$, P_t outputs $\langle \mathbf{w}_i \rangle^{\mathsf{A}}_t$ and $\langle \mathbf{hd}_i \rangle^{\mathsf{A}}_t$ for $i \in \{1, ..., K\}$.
1: **for** $i = 1$ to K **do**
2:    **Offline:**
3:    P_0 samples length-d vectors $\mathbf{x}_i$, $\mathbf{x}'_i$, $\mathbf{r}_i$, and $\mathbf{r}'_i$ at random.
4:    P_1 samples length-d vectors $\mathbf{y}_i$ at random.
5:    P_1 encrypts and sends $\widehat{\mathbf{y}}_i = \mathsf{AHE.Enc}_{\mathsf{pk}_1}(\mathbf{y}_i)$ to P_0.
6:    P_0 computes and sends $\boldsymbol{\xi}_i = (\mathbf{x}_i \boxtimes \widehat{\mathbf{y}}_i) \boxplus \mathbf{r}_i$, $\boldsymbol{\xi}'_i = (\mathbf{x}'_i \boxtimes \widehat{\mathbf{y}}_i) \boxplus \mathbf{r}'_i$ to P_1.
7:    P_1 sets $\langle \mathbf{z}_i \rangle^{\mathsf{A}}_1 = \mathsf{AHE.Dec}_{\mathsf{sk}_1}(\boldsymbol{\xi}_i)$, $\langle \mathbf{z}'_i \rangle^{\mathsf{A}}_1 = \mathsf{AHE.Dec}_{\mathsf{sk}_1}(\boldsymbol{\xi}'_i)$. P_0 sets $\langle \mathbf{z}_i \rangle^{\mathsf{A}}_0 = -\mathbf{r}_i$, $\langle \mathbf{z}'_i \rangle^{\mathsf{A}}_0 = -\mathbf{r}'_i$.
8:    **Online:**
9:    P_0 computes and sends $\langle \mathbf{w}_i \rangle^{\mathsf{B}}_0 + \mathbf{x}_i$ and $\langle \mathbf{hd}_i \rangle^{\mathsf{B}}_0 + \mathbf{x}'_i$ to P_1.
10:    P_1 computes and sends $\langle \mathbf{w}_i \rangle^{\mathsf{B}}_1 + \mathbf{y}_i$ to P_0.
11:    P_0 locally computes $\langle \mathbf{u}_i \rangle^{\mathsf{A}}_0 = -\mathbf{x}_i(\langle \mathbf{w}_i \rangle^{\mathsf{B}}_1 + \mathbf{y}_i) + \langle \mathbf{z}_i \rangle^{\mathsf{A}}_0$ and $\langle \mathbf{u}'_i \rangle^{\mathsf{A}}_0 = -\mathbf{x}'_i(\langle \mathbf{hd}_i \rangle^{\mathsf{B}}_1 + \mathbf{y}_i) + \langle \mathbf{z}'_i \rangle^{\mathsf{A}}_0$, and P_1 sets $\langle \mathbf{u}_i \rangle^{\mathsf{A}}_1 = \langle \mathbf{w}_i \rangle^{\mathsf{B}}_1(\langle \mathbf{w}_i \rangle^{\mathsf{B}}_0 + \mathbf{x}_i) + \langle \mathbf{z}_i \rangle^{\mathsf{A}}_1$ and $\langle \mathbf{u}'_i \rangle^{\mathsf{A}}_1 = \langle \mathbf{hd}_i \rangle^{\mathsf{B}}_1(\langle \mathbf{hd}_i \rangle^{\mathsf{B}}_0 + \mathbf{x}'_i) + \langle \mathbf{z}'_i \rangle^{\mathsf{A}}_1$.
12:    P_t computes $\langle \mathbf{w}_i \rangle^{\mathsf{A}}_t = \langle \mathbf{w}_i \rangle^{\mathsf{B}}_t - 2\langle \mathbf{u}_i \rangle^{\mathsf{A}}_t$ and $\langle \mathbf{hd}_i \rangle^{\mathsf{A}}_t = \langle \mathbf{hd}_i \rangle^{\mathsf{B}}_t - 2\langle \mathbf{u}'_i \rangle^{\mathsf{A}}_t$.
13: **end for**
14: **return** For $t \in \{0,1\}$, P_t outputs $\langle \mathbf{w}_i \rangle^{\mathsf{A}}_t$ and $\langle \mathbf{hd}_i \rangle^{\mathsf{A}}_t$ for $i \in \{1, ..., K\}$.

Correlated XOR (CXOR). After model evaluation and $\mathcal{E}$, P_0 has $\mathbf{w}_s \in \{0,1\}^d$, P_t has $\langle \mathbf{w}_i \rangle_t^{\mathsf{B}}$ for $t \in \{0,1\}$. To compute the Hamming distance between $\mathbf{w}_i$ and $\mathbf{w}_s$, we need to compute their coordinate-wise XOR firstly. As $\mathbf{w}_i = \langle \mathbf{w}_i \rangle_0^{\mathsf{B}} \oplus \langle \mathbf{w}_i \rangle_1^{\mathsf{B}}$, we have $\mathbf{hd}_i = \mathbf{w}_s \oplus \mathbf{w}_i = \mathbf{w}_s \oplus \langle \mathbf{w}_i \rangle_0^{\mathsf{B}} \oplus \langle \mathbf{w}_i \rangle_1^{\mathsf{B}}$. Therefore, we let P_0 computes $\langle \mathbf{hd}_i \rangle_0^{\mathsf{B}} = \mathbf{w}_s \oplus \langle \mathbf{w}_i \rangle_0^{\mathsf{B}}$ and $\langle \mathbf{hd}_i \rangle_1^{\mathsf{B}} = \langle \mathbf{w}_i \rangle_1^{\mathsf{B}}$ with no communication.

Partial Correlated Bit to Arithmetic Conversion (PCBit2A). To achieve practical aggregation, we need to convert $\langle \mathbf{w}_i \rangle^{\mathsf{B}}$ and $\langle \mathbf{hd}_i \rangle^{\mathsf{B}}$ to arithmetic shares since the latter is more efficient for ADD and MUL. Considering $w_{ij} \in \mathbf{w}_i$ is 0 or 1, we have $w_{ij} = \langle w_{ij} \rangle_0^{\mathsf{B}} + \langle w_{ij} \rangle_1^{\mathsf{B}} - 2\langle w_{ij} \rangle_0^{\mathsf{B}} \langle w_{ij} \rangle_1^{\mathsf{B}}$. As P_t has $\langle w_{ij} \rangle_t^{\mathsf{B}}$, the main challenge is computing the arithmetic shares of $\langle w_{ij} \rangle_0^{\mathsf{B}} \langle w_{ij} \rangle_1^{\mathsf{B}}$ securely.

To this end, a naive approach is generating MT using AHE as ABY library [13] and computing the product in element-wise as Sect. 2.2, where we view $\{\langle \mathbf{a}_i \rangle_0^{\mathsf{A}} = \langle \mathbf{w}_i \rangle_0^{\mathsf{B}}, \langle \mathbf{a}_i \rangle_1^{\mathsf{A}} = 0\}$, $\{\langle \mathbf{b}_i \rangle_0^{\mathsf{A}} = 0, \langle \mathbf{b}_i \rangle_1^{\mathsf{A}} = \langle \mathbf{w}_i \rangle_1^{\mathsf{B}}\}$, and compute $\langle \mathbf{a}_i \mathbf{b}_i \rangle^{\mathsf{A}} = \langle \mathbf{w}_i \rangle_0^{\mathsf{B}} \langle \mathbf{w}_i \rangle_1^{\mathsf{B}}$. But this method requires P_1 encrypts $4K$ length-d vectors and sends $4K\lceil d/s \rceil$ ciphertexts to P_0 in offline phase, and P_t sends $4Kd\ell$ bits to P_{1-t} in online phase for all $\langle \mathbf{w}_i \rangle^{\mathsf{B}}$ and $\langle \mathbf{hd}_i \rangle^{\mathsf{B}}$ conversions totally. To improve efficiency, we propose a novel partial correlated Bit2A (PCBit2A) method requires $4\times$ less encryption and $\approx 2\times$ less communication in offline, and reduces $P_0 \rightarrow P_1$ (resp. $P_1 \rightarrow P_0$) communication by $2\times$ (resp. $4\times$) in online.

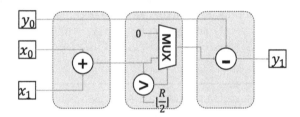

Fig. 3. Boolean circuit for private τ-Clipping. "+" refers to integer addition and "−" refers to integer subtraction. The "MUX" is multiplexer and ">" outputs 1 i.f.f. the input is larger than $\lfloor \mathcal{R}/2 \rfloor$.

Firstly, as P_t holds $\langle \mathbf{w}_i \rangle_t^{\mathsf{B}}$ for $\langle \mathbf{w}_i \rangle_0^{\mathsf{B}} \langle \mathbf{w}_i \rangle_1^{\mathsf{B}}$, we propose a variant of MT (partial MT) $(\mathbf{x}_i, \mathbf{y}_i, \mathbf{z}_i)$ inspired by [7] such that P_0 holds $\{\mathbf{x}_i, \langle \mathbf{z}_i \rangle_0^{\mathsf{A}}\}$, P_1 holds $\{\mathbf{y}_i, \langle \mathbf{z}_i \rangle_1^{\mathsf{A}}\}$, and $\mathbf{z}_i = \mathbf{x}_i \mathbf{y}_i$. In online, P_0 computes and sends $\langle \mathbf{w}_i \rangle_0^{\mathsf{B}} + \mathbf{x}_i$ to P_1, while P_1 sends $\langle \mathbf{w}_i \rangle_1^{\mathsf{B}} + \mathbf{y}_i$ to P_0. P_0 computes $\langle \mathbf{u}_i \rangle_0^{\mathsf{A}} = -\mathbf{x}_i(\langle \mathbf{w}_i \rangle_1^{\mathsf{B}} + \mathbf{y}_i) + \langle \mathbf{z}_i \rangle_0^{\mathsf{A}}$ and P_1 computes $\langle \mathbf{u}_i \rangle_1^{\mathsf{A}} = \langle \mathbf{w}_i \rangle_1^{\mathsf{B}}(\langle \mathbf{w}_i \rangle_0^{\mathsf{B}} + \mathbf{x}_i) + \langle \mathbf{z}_i \rangle_1^{\mathsf{A}}$ to obtain $\langle \mathbf{u}_i \rangle_0^{\mathsf{A}} + \langle \mathbf{u}_i \rangle_1^{\mathsf{A}} = \langle \mathbf{w}_i \rangle_0^{\mathsf{B}} \langle \mathbf{w}_i \rangle_1^{\mathsf{B}}$ in secret. And $\langle \mathbf{hd}_i \rangle_0^{\mathsf{B}} \langle \mathbf{hd}_i \rangle_1^{\mathsf{B}}$ computation is likewise.

The above method complete $\langle \mathbf{w}_i \rangle^{\mathsf{B}}$ and $\langle \mathbf{hd}_i \rangle^{\mathsf{B}}$ conversions independently. As $\langle \mathbf{w}_i \rangle_1^{\mathsf{B}} = \langle \mathbf{hd}_i \rangle_1^{\mathsf{B}}$, we further let P_1 prepare $\mathbf{y}_i = \mathbf{y}_i'$, while P_0 generate $\mathbf{x}_i$, $\mathbf{x}_i'$, $\mathbf{r}_i$, and $\mathbf{r}_i'$ independently at random. In offline, P_1 only encrypts and sends $\widehat{\mathbf{y}}_i$ to P_0. While P_0 uses $(\mathbf{x}_i, \widehat{\mathbf{y}}_i, \mathbf{r}_i)$ (resp. $\mathbf{x}_i', \widehat{\mathbf{y}}_i, \mathbf{r}_i'$) to compute $\boldsymbol{\xi}_i$ (resp. $\boldsymbol{\xi}_i'$). And P_t computes $\langle \mathbf{z}_i \rangle_t^{\mathsf{A}}$ and $\langle \mathbf{z}_i' \rangle_t^{\mathsf{A}}$ locally as the offline in Algorithm 2. Note that we can also generate the MTs using OT with much more communication and less run-time. As the network costs are charged much more than computation [18], we adopt AHE based method to minimize the monetary cost. In online, P_0 sends $\langle \mathbf{w}_i \rangle_0^B + \mathbf{x}_i$ and $\langle \mathbf{hd}_i \rangle_0^B + \mathbf{x}_i'$ to P_1, while P_1 only sends $\langle \mathbf{w}_i \rangle_1^B + \mathbf{y}_i$ to P_0. Thus P_t can complete $\langle \mathbf{w}_i \rangle^B$ and $\langle \mathbf{hd}_i \rangle^B$ conversions simultaneously as illustrated in online of Algorithm 2. Therefore, we need $2Kd\ell$ (resp. $Kd\ell$) bits for $P_0 \rightarrow P_1$ (resp. $P_1 \rightarrow P_0$) online communication.

Private τ-Clipping. To evaluate τ-Clipping privately, we use GC to clip $\langle hd_i \rangle^A = \sum_{j=1}^d \langle hd_{ij} \rangle^A$. The Boolean circuit is illustrated in Fig. 3: P_0 inputs $x_0 = \tau - \langle hd_i \rangle_0^A$ and $y_0 = r$ (chosen at random), P_1 inputs $x_1 = -\langle hd_i \rangle_1^A$. The first block computes the arithmetic sum of $\tau - hd_i = x_0 + x_1$ over integers. The second block computes the ReLU function. And the third block subtract y_0 from the result to obtain the P_1's share y_1. Finally, P_t sets $\langle \nu_i \rangle_t^A = y_t$.

Correlated Secure Weighted Aggregation (CSWA). To weighted average all $\widetilde{\mathbf{w}}_i$ privately, we first let P_t computes $\langle \widetilde{\mathbf{w}}_i \rangle_t^A = t - 2\langle \mathbf{w}_i \rangle_t^A$ to implement $\mathcal{D}$ securely in batch. With $\langle \nu_i \rangle^A$ and $\langle \widetilde{\mathbf{w}}_i \rangle^A$, P_0 and P_1 are capable to compute $\langle \widetilde{\mathbf{w}} \rangle^A$ where the main challenge is computing $\langle \nu_i \widetilde{\mathbf{w}}_i \rangle^A$ for $i \in \{1, ..., K\}$. A trivial method is using MT for each scalar-product as ABY [13], but this needs Kd triples in total, which requires P_t to encrypt (and send) $2K\lceil d/s \rceil$ ciphertexts to P_{1-t} in offline, and $2Kd\ell$ bits online communication for each P_t in online. Hence, we propose an efficient method which achieves $\approx 2\times$ reduction in communication.

Our key insight is that ν_i is fixed for all coordinates of $\widetilde{\mathbf{w}}_i$. Therefore, we construct MT $(x_i, \mathbf{y}_i, \mathbf{z}_i)$ subject to $\mathbf{z}_i = x_i \mathbf{y}_i$ using AHE, where P_t has $(\langle x_i \rangle_t^A, \langle \mathbf{y}_i \rangle_t^A, \langle \mathbf{z}_i \rangle_t^A)$. P_t thus only sends $1 + K\lceil d/s \rceil$ ciphertexts to P_{1-t} in

---

Algorithm 3. CSWA

Input: For $t \in \{0, 1\}$, P_t inputs $\langle \mathbf{w}_i \rangle_t^A$ and $\langle \nu_i \rangle_t^A$ for $i \in \{1, ..., K\}$.
Output: P_0 outputs $\widetilde{\mathbf{w}} = \frac{1}{\sum_{i=1}^K \nu_i} \cdot (\sum_{i=1}^K \nu_i \cdot \widetilde{\mathbf{w}}_i)$.
1: **for** $i = 1$ to K **do**
2:     **Offline**
3:     P_t locally samples scalar $\langle x_i \rangle_t^A$, length-d vector $\langle \mathbf{y}_i \rangle_t^A$ and $\mathbf{r}_{i,t}$.
4:     P_t encrypts and sends $\widehat{\langle x_i \rangle_t^A} = \mathsf{AHE.Enc}_{\mathrm{pk}_t}(\langle x_i \rangle_t^A)$ to P_{1-t}.
5:     P_t computes and sends $\boldsymbol{\xi}_{i,t} = \langle \mathbf{y}_i \rangle_t^A \boxtimes \widehat{\langle x_i \rangle_t^A} \boxplus \mathbf{r}_{i,t}$ to P_{1-t}.
6:     P_t decrypts and sets $\langle \mathbf{z}_i \rangle_t^A = \langle x_i \rangle_t^A \langle \mathbf{y}_i \rangle_t^A + \mathsf{AHE.Dec}_{\mathrm{sk}_t}(\boldsymbol{\xi}_{i,1-t}) - \mathbf{r}_{i,t}$.
7:     **Online**
8:     P_t computes $\langle \widetilde{\mathbf{w}}_i \rangle_t^A = t - 2\langle \mathbf{w}_i \rangle_t^A$ to implement $\mathcal{D}(\langle \mathbf{w}_i \rangle^A)$ securely.
9:     P_t sends $(\langle e_i \rangle_t^A = \langle \nu_i \rangle_t^A - \langle x_i \rangle_t^A, \langle \mathbf{f}_i \rangle_0^A = \langle \widetilde{\mathbf{w}}_i \rangle_t^A - \langle \mathbf{y}_i \rangle_t^A)$ to P_{1-t}.
10:    P_0 & P_1 reconstruct $(e_i, \mathbf{f}_i)$ locally.
11:    P_t locally computes $\langle \nu_i \widetilde{\mathbf{w}}_i \rangle_t^A = -te_i \mathbf{f}_i + e_i \langle \widetilde{\mathbf{w}}_i \rangle_t^A + \langle \nu_i \rangle_t^A \mathbf{f}_i + \langle \mathbf{z}_i \rangle_t^A$.
12: **end for**
13: P_t computes $\sum_{i=1}^K \langle \nu_i \widetilde{\mathbf{w}}_i \rangle_t^A$, $\sum_{i=1}^K \langle \nu_i \rangle_t^A$, and P_1 sends its shares to P_0.
14: **return** P_0 reconstructs and computes $\widetilde{\mathbf{w}} = \frac{1}{\sum_{i=1}^K \nu_i} \cdot (\sum_{i=1}^K \nu_i \widetilde{\mathbf{w}}_i)$.

offline. Note that we let P_t duplicate $\langle x_i \rangle_t^{\mathsf{A}}$ into s copies and pack these copies into one ciphertext to support SIMD technique, and we use denotation $\widehat{\langle x_i \rangle_t^{\mathsf{A}}} = \mathsf{AHE.Enc}_{pk_t}(\langle x_i \rangle_t^{\mathsf{A}})$ for brevity. In online, P_t sends $\langle e_i \rangle_t^{\mathsf{A}} = \langle \nu_i \rangle_t^{\mathsf{A}} - \langle x_i \rangle_t^{\mathsf{A}}$, $\langle \mathbf{f}_i \rangle_t^{\mathsf{A}} = \langle \widetilde{\mathbf{w}}_i \rangle_t^{\mathsf{A}} - \langle \mathbf{y}_i \rangle_t^{\mathsf{A}}$ to P_{1-t}, reconstruct both, and computes $\langle \nu_i \widetilde{\mathbf{w}}_i \rangle_t^{\mathsf{A}} = -te_i\mathbf{f}_i + e_i\langle \widetilde{\mathbf{w}}_i \rangle_t^{\mathsf{A}} + \langle \nu_i \rangle_t^{\mathsf{A}}\mathbf{f}_i + \langle \mathbf{z}_i \rangle_t^{\mathsf{A}}$. Finally, P_t adds up $\sum_{i=1}^{K} \langle \nu_i \widetilde{\mathbf{w}}_i \rangle_t^{\mathsf{A}}$ and $\sum_{i=1}^{K} \langle \nu_i \rangle_t^{\mathsf{A}}$, and P_1 reveals its shares to P_0, who computes $\widetilde{\mathbf{w}} = \frac{1}{\sum_{i=1}^{K} \nu_i} \cdot (\sum_{i=1}^{K} \nu_i \widetilde{\mathbf{w}}_i)$. This requires $K(d+1)\ell$ bits for P_0 and $(K+1)(d+1)\ell$ bits for P_1 in online. The details are in Algorithm 3.

4.3   Correctness and Privacy

Correctness. FLOD is correct as long as the core building blocks are correct. First, it is straightforward that CXOR is correct. Then, PCBit2A conversion is correct since AHE and partial MT based secure multiplication are correct. Afterwards, GC guarantees that P_t can obtain the shares of $\nu_i = \mathsf{ReLU}(\tau - hd_i)$ for $\mathbf{w}_i$. Finally, AHE and MT also guarantee the correctness of CSWA.

Privacy. We analyze the privacy of FLOD against semi-honest adversary $\mathcal{A}^s$, who corrupts one server, in Theorem 1. The proof is illustrated in Appendix B.

Theorem 1 (Privacy of FLOD). FLOD *guarantees that adversary $\mathcal{A}^s$ learns nothing beyond what can be inferred from the aggregated results $(\sum_{i=1}^{K} \nu_i \widetilde{\mathbf{w}}_i, \sum_{i=1}^{K} \nu_i)$ with $1 - \epsilon$ probability where ϵ is negligible, as long as there are no more than one corrupted server in semi-honest model.*

Additionally, we can guarantee privacy even in the $\mathcal{A}^c$-$\mathcal{A}^s$ collusion threat model. The reason is that $\mathcal{A}^s$ learns nothing no more than the aggregated results with an overwhelming probability, and $\mathcal{A}^c$ only receives the aggregated results (cf. Sect. 3). Therefore, they learn nothing more than what can be inferred from the aggregated results and their own inputs with an overwhelming probability.

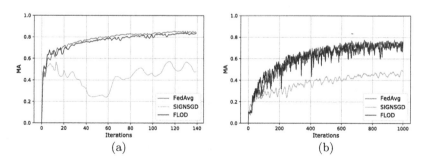

Fig. 4. MA along with the training iterations with $\delta = 0$. 4(a) is for FNet on Fashion-MNIST, 4(b) is for ResNet-18 on CIFAR10.

Table 1. MA of FedAvg, Krum, Median, T-Mean, FLGUARD, FLTrust, and FLOD with $\delta = 30\%$. Note that we evaluate FedAvg with no Byzantine attack.

MA, $\delta = 30\%$		FedAvg	Krum	Median	T-Mean	FLGUARD	FLTrust	FLOD
GA	FNet	0.86	0.85	0.85	0.85	0.77	0.85	0.84
	ResNet-18	0.79	0.76	0.75	0.76	0.74	0.76	0.76
LF	FNet	0.86	0.85	0.83	0.83	0.78	0.85	0.84
	ResNet-18	0.79	0.76	0.64	0.66	0.75	0.75	0.75

5   Evaluation

Evaluation Setup: We implement FLOD in C++ and Python3. We use ABY library [13] for 2PC and SIMD circuits, and rely on SEAL library [32] for AHE. Parameters for both schemes are set with 128-bit security level. And we employ widely used Convolutional Neural Networks: FNet with $\approx$507K parameters on Fashion-MNIST [36] and ResNet-18 light with $\approx$2.07M parameters on CIFAR-10 [21]. Experiments are executed on Intel(R) Xeon(R) CPU E5-2650 v3@ 2.30 GHz servers with 64 GB RAM, and we use PyTorch v1.4.0 equipped with CUDA v10.2 and two 12G memory TITAN Xp GPUs for model training. The *P-P* connection is equipped with 10 Gbps LAN with 0.2 ms RTT. And the *C-P* connection is over 50 Mbps WAN with 50 ms RTT.

5.1   Effectiveness Analysis

We evaluate FLOD against state-of-the-art Byzantine attacks: Gaussian Attack (GA) and Label Flipping attack (LF). In GA, the poisoned model updates are drawn from a Gaussian distribution (model poisoning). While in LF, we replace training label y on the Byzantine machines with $9 - y$ (data poisoning). We measure the main task Top-1 accuracy (MA) as the effectiveness metric.

First, we measure MA with training iterations of FLOD, FedAvg [24], and SIGNSGD with $\delta = \frac{K'}{K} = 0\%$ to show our model performance under no Byzantine attacks. Then, we fix $\delta = 30\%$ and compare the MA of FLOD to Krum [6], Median [38], T-Mean [38], FLGUARD [27], and FLTrust [11] to show our robustness in honest-majority. Finally, we measure the MA with dynamic δ to present our robustness is comparable to FLTrust, which is better than other works when $\delta > 50\%$. We train FNet for 150 iterations and ResNet-18 Light for 1,000 iterations, and set $\tau = \frac{d}{3}$ and $\frac{d}{2}$ for FNet and ResNet-18 for best MA, respectively. Determining the optimal τ is a interesting task, and we leave it for future work.

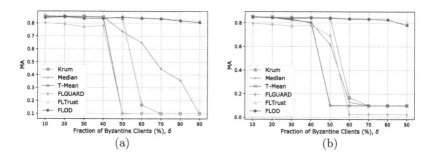

Fig. 5. MA of FNet with $\delta = 10\%$–90% for all Byzantine-robust aggregation methods, where 5(a) is for GA and 5(b) is for LF.

Performance Analysis with $\delta = 0$. One Byzantine-robust aggregation method should also apply to no attack cases in real applications: it should introduce little degradation to model performance when $\delta = 0$. As FedAvg achieves the optimal performance, we compare FLOD to it. Also, we measure the MA of SIGNSGD since we encode model updates similar to it.

As shown in Fig. 4, FLOD converges to a similar MA level as FedAvg achieved within the same training iterations for both FNet and ResNet-18 Light. The reason is that FLOD utilizes the root dataset to bootstrap trust; thus, it can almost aggregate all sgn model updates when $\delta = 0$. Although the sgn encoded values lose some information, it has merely impacts on the overall model training. However, SIGNSGD converges much slower than FedAvg and ours because SIGNSGD only returns the sgn of the sum of all individual model updates to resist Byzantine attacks, which is equivalent to Median method for sign encoded model updates. As Median excludes $\approx K - 1$ values for each coordinate, SIGNSGD introduces significant degradation to model convergence.

Performance Analysis with $\delta = 30\%$. Table 1 shows the MA of FLOD and existing methods: Krum, Median, T-Mean, FLGUARD, and FLTrust, in honest-majority ($\delta = 30\%$), under both attacks. As SIGNSGD converges much slower and is equivalent to Median for sign encoded model updates, we omit it here. And we present the MA of FedAvg without attack for a comprehensive comparison.

FLOD introduces little MA loss compared to FedAvg and other Byzantine-robust FL methods. Compared to FedAvg, the MA loss is no more than 0.02 for FNet and 0.04 for ResNet-18. Moreover, the MA degradation is within 0.01 for all cases compared to FLTrust. The degradation has two main sources: (i) With Byzantine attacks, the correct model updates (or clean data) is less than that of FedAvg. Therefore, FLOD and FLTrust with $\delta = 30\%$ both introduce MA degradation compared to FedAvg with $\delta = 0$. (ii) For FLOD, sgn encoding introduces information loss compared to original model updates. Hence, FLOD achieves a slightly lower MA than FLTrust. However, this degradation is so little that it can be acceptable in practical with enhancements on privacy preservation.

Table 2. *P-P* communication of PCBit2A (resp. CSWA) and ABY based methods for Bit2A (resp. VSWA) in one round of aggregation, where $K = 10, 50, 100$, models are FNet and ResNet-18, offline (resp. online) communication is in GB (resp. MB), and X denotes AHE for offline and MT for online.

Comm.		Bit2A				VSWA			
Model		FNet		ResNet-18		FNet		ResNet-18	
Method		PCBit2A	ABY-X	PCBit2A	ABY-X	CSWA	ABY-X	CSWA	ABY-X
Off., K	10	1.43	2.90	7.44	15.28	0.74	1.45	4.03	7.64
	50	7.44	14.77	33.86	91.74	3.94	7.39	22.81	44.99
	100	14.07	30.60	67.93	153.13	7.64	15.30	38.63	76.56
On., K	10	58.16	151.22	237.17	616.64	41.07	81.14	165.83	329.58
	50	290.06	754.16	1185.06	3081.16	194.41	387.62	797.55	1594.78
	100	580.16	1508.42	2370.45	6163.17	387.69	772.38	1587.20	3173.68

Besides, compared to Krum, Median, T-Mean, and FLGUARD, we achieve a similar or better MA in honest-majority. Therefore, FLOD has much broader application prospects for resisting Byzantine attacks in FL.

Performance Analysis with Dynamic δ. Fig. 5(a)–5(b) show the MA with the fraction of Byzantine clients for all methods. To completely test the Byzantine-robustness, we alter $\delta = 10\%$–90%. Firstly, we see FLOD can reach a similar or even higher level of MA as other FL methods in honest-majority, which is consistent with our analysis. Secondly, when $\delta > 50\%$ the MA of Krum, Median, and FLGUARD drops sharply, e.g. MA ≈ 0.1 when $\delta = 90\%$. The reason is that these methods all rely on the honest-majority assumption, and thus with $\delta > 50\%$, the poisoned model updates will be aggregated into the final result. However, FLOD and FLTrust can still maintain a high MA since both methods utilize a root-dataset to bootstrap trust, and thus can exclude the poisoned model updates even in dishonest-majority. Similar results for ResNet-18 are illustrated as Fig. 8 in Appendix C.

5.2 Efficiency Analysis

We test the costs and scalability of FLOD by varying the number of clients ($K = 10, 50, 100$) and size of model updates. Concretely, we measure the communication overhead and run-time in respective offline and online phases.

Communication. We test the *P-P* communication costs of Bit2A and VSWA for offline, and compare our costs to ABY-AHE based method. For online, we measure each block communication and compare it to ABY-MT based method, and further compare our total online communication overhead, including the *C-P* overhead, of one aggregation to FLGUARD to demonstrate our improvements. *P-P Offline Communication.* We measure the *P-P* communication costs for the offline of PCBit2A and CSWA, and compare our costs to ABY-AHE based method as the offline part of Table 2. Firstly, our PCBit2A reduces the communication

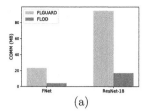 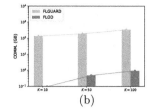 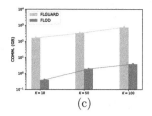

(a)   (b)   (c)

Fig. 6. Total online C-P and P-P communication of FLOD and FLGUARD for FNet and ResNet-18 in one aggregation. 6(a) shows each C-P communication, 6(b) shows the P-P costs for FNet, and 6(c) shows the P-P costs for ResNet-18. Note the y-axis of 6(b) and 6(c) is in log-scale.

costs by $\approx 2\times$ for Bit2A. This is because we propose partial MTs and reuse $\mathbf{y}_i$ to generate correlated partial MTs for $\langle \mathbf{w}_i \rangle^{\mathsf{B}}$ and $\langle \mathbf{hd}_i \rangle^{\mathsf{B}}$ conversions simultaneously. Secondly, we also reduce the VSWA offline communication costs by $\approx 2\times$ since we reuse the same $\langle x_i \rangle^{\mathsf{A}}$ for all coordinates of $\mathbf{w}_i$ in CSWA. Hence, we improve the total offline communication efficiency in one aggregation by $\approx 2\times$ compared to ABY-AHE method.

Online Communication. Table 2 online part shows the online communication between P_0 and P_1 caused by PCBit2A and CSWA in one aggregation, and we compare our costs to ABY-MT based method. For PCBit2A, we reduce the communication by around 2.5× due to our partial correlated triples optimization. And for CSWA we reduce the communication by $\approx 2\times$ as ν_i is same for all coordinates of $\mathbf{w}_i$. Additionally, the costs of PCBit2A and CSWA are determined by K and model size since P_0 and P_1 need to conduct multiplication for each coordinate of $\mathbf{w}_i$. Besides, private τ-Clipping introduces little online communication, and thus we present it as Table 4 in Appendix D due to page limitation.

Besides, we present the total online C-P and P-P communication costs of FLOD (including private τ-Clipping) in one aggregation, and compare our overhead to FLGUARD as Fig. 6. Firstly, Fig. 6(a) shows that we reduce the C-P communication by $\approx 6\times$ compared to FLGUARD. This reason is that FLGUARD encodes the model updates and aggregated results as 64-bit integers, while we use 1 bit to represent each share of the $\mathcal{E}$-encoded binary sgn model update and 32 bits to encode the aggregated results (which is enough to achieve a comparable accuracy as FedAvg). Secondly, in Fig. 6(b)–6(c), we compare the P-P communication in one aggregation of FLOD to FLGUARD to show our improvements: FLOD requires 361–1416× less communication for FNet and 167–417× less communication for ResNet-18. The reason is that our methods are mainly composed of arithmetic operations and require a little GC for private τ-Clipping. While FLGUARD requires much tremendous expensive garbled circuits for cosine distance calculation, clustering, and Euclidean distance calculation/clipping/aggregation. Thirdly, with K being increased, the communication of FLGUARD increases more sharply than FLOD. Therefore, our FLOD is much more communication efficient than FLGUARD.

Run-Time. We test the run-time, including the computation, data transferring, and network latency, for offline and online phases. Also, we compare our offline run-time to ABY-AHE based method, and online run-time to ABY-MT based method and FLGUARD in one aggregation.

Table 3. Run-time in seconds of PCBit2A (resp. CSWA) and ABY based methods for Bit2A (resp. VSWA) in one aggregation for FNet and ResNet-18, where $K = 10, 50, 100$ and X denotes AHE for offline and MT for online.

Run-time		Bit2A				VSWA			
Model		FNet		ResNet-18		FNet		ResNet-18	
Method		PCBit2A	ABY-X	PCBit2A	ABY-X	CSWA	ABY-X	CSWA	ABY-X
Off., K	10	22.82	50.83	113.47	241.28	16.56	25.42	78.57	120.64
	50	114.36	241.28	582.13	1194.15	80.39	121.76	386.87	558.65
	100	222.54	479.47	1151.29	2381.73	157.71	289.78	766.14	1696.35
On., K	10	9.34	23.35	22.42	56.05	5.16	5.22	20.75	21.84
	50	45.52	113.76	106.43	266.08	23.43	25.66	96.33	98.15
	100	94.19	235.98	213.50	533.75	48.36	49.78	192.66	193.75

Offline Run-Time. Table 3 offline part shows the offline run-time of PCBit2A, CSWA and ABY-AHE based method for Bit2A and VSWA. Compared to ABY-AHE based method, our approaches reduce the run-time by around 2× and 1.5×. The reason is that we propose partial MTs and utilize the correlations for $(\langle \mathbf{w}_i \rangle^{\mathsf{B}}, \langle \mathbf{hd}_i \rangle^{\mathsf{B}})$ in PCBit2A, and use $\langle x_i \rangle^{\mathsf{A}}$ for all $w_{ij} \in \mathbf{w}_i$ in CSWA, and hence we reduce the total instances of AHE operations by ≈2× for Bit2A and by 1.5× for VSWA. Moreover, it reduces the run-time of data transfer, which is consistent with offline communication analysis.

Online Run-Time. Table 3 online part presents the online run-time per aggregation of PCBit2A and CSWA, and we compare our costs to ABY-MT based method. As can be seen, we reduce the run-time of Bit2A by around 2.5× due to our reduction on the numbers of multiplication and communication. However, the online run-time improvements of CSWA is limited. The reasons are as follows: (i) We do not reduce the multiplication invocations, and the efficiency of scalar-vector and vector-vector element-wise multiplication is almost the same in batch processing; (ii) The reduction of communication saves little time in our LAN P_0-P_1 network setting. CXOR and private τ-Clipping introduce little overhead due to the efficient XOR operation and model update size independent GC invocations, respectively. We thus present their costs in Appendix D.

Figure 7 presents the total online run-time of FLOD (including CXOR and private τ-Clipping) and FLGUARD in one aggregation. As the ML training is executed in plaintext and can be significantly accelerated using GPU, we omit its overhead as **FLGUARD**. As illustrated in the experimental results, we reduce the online run-time significantly compared to **FLGUARD**: (i) **FLOD** reduces the run-time by 3.9–7.4× for FNet and 3.1–6.2× for ResNet-18. (ii) Besides, we also observe that with K being increased, the run-time of **FLGUARD** increases much more significantly than **FLOD**. Therefore, our methods are more practical in real applications.

6   Related Works

Here, we review the work in the area of privacy preservation and Byzantine-robustness of FL. In terms of privacy preservation, the main used technologies are differential privacy (DP), (additively) homomorphic encryption ((A)HE), secret sharing, and etc. Shokri *et al.* used DP to protect model update to achieve the balance between privacy and accuracy [33]. Liu *et al.* further combined the local DP with Top-k gradients selection to improve the performance [23]. Phong *et al.* proposed to protect the clients' gradients utilizing **AHE** [31]. Bonawitz *et al.* designed a secure aggregation scheme for sum function by exploiting secret sharing and key agreement protocol [8]. Besides, Gibbs *et al.* combined secret sharing with Zero-Knowledge Proof to verify the validity of clients' gradients [12]. But these schemes all focus on simple linear aggregation, e.g., average.

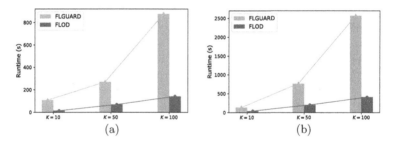

Fig. 7. Total online run-time of **FLOD** and **FLGUARD** for FNet and ResNet-18 in one aggregation. 7(a) is for FNet and 7(b) is for ResNet-18.

Meanwhile, Byzantine-robust aggregation rules have been extensively studied using clear gradients. Among these methods, the main mechanism is to compare gradients received and remove the outliers. Blanchard *et al.* proposed **Krum** combining the intuitions of *majority*-based and *squared-distance*-based methods to guarantee convergence tolerating $K' \leq \lfloor K/2 \rfloor - 1$ adversaries [6]. Mhamdi *et al.* showed that convergence is not enough and introduced **Bulyan** to reduce the attacker's leeway to narrow $\mathcal{O}(1/\sqrt{d})$ bound [25]. Alistarh *et al.* proposed a variant of SGD which finds ε-approximate minimizers of convex functions in $\tilde{O}(\frac{1}{\varepsilon^2 m + \alpha^2/\varepsilon^2})$ iterations [1]. Yin *et al.* developed trimmed mean and median based robust distributed learning algorithms with a focus on optimal statistical performance [38]. Bernstein *et al.* proposed SIGNSGD where clients transmit only the sign of their gradient vector to a server, and the overall update is decided by a majority vote [5]. But these method all depends on the clients honest-majority assumption. Cao *et al.* proposed FLTrust to break this limitation by collecting a small clean dataset on the aggregation server to bootstrap trust, but this method also provides no privacy guarantee for clients [11].

To our best knowledge, only Nguyen *et al.* proposed a similar work, FLGUARD [11], as ours. But they requires much more significant overhead, including computation and communication, which limits their real application seriously.

7   Conclusion

We propose FLOD, an efficient oblivious defender for private Byzantine-robust FL in dishonest-majority. We introduce a Hamming distance-based aggregation method and then use 2PC and AHE based protocols, with several novel in-depth optimizations, to protect privacy. Evaluations show our effectiveness and efficiency. We aim to verify the correctness of the aggregated results in future.

Acknowledgements. We are grateful to the anonymous reviewers for their comprehensive comments. This work was supported by the Strategic Priority Research Program of Chinese Academy of Sciences, Grant No. XDC02040400.

A   Byzantine-Robustness Analysis

Cosine similarity is one of the best metrics to measure the similarity of two vectors. Recall the cosine similarity of two sgn $\widetilde{\mathbf{w}}_i$ and $\widetilde{\mathbf{w}}_s$ is $c_i = \frac{\langle \widetilde{\mathbf{w}}_i, \widetilde{\mathbf{w}}_s \rangle}{\|\widetilde{\mathbf{w}}_i\| \cdot \|\widetilde{\mathbf{w}}_s\|}$, and FLTrust clips c_i using ReLU function to remove the poisoned model updates with negative c_i [11]. Based on $\widetilde{\mathbf{w}}_i$, $\widetilde{\mathbf{w}}_s$ in $\{-1, 1\}^d$ and Eq. (2, 3), we have

$$
c_i = \frac{\sum_{j=1}^d \widetilde{w}_{ij} \cdot \widetilde{w}_{sj}}{\sqrt{d} \cdot \sqrt{d}} = \frac{1}{d} \cdot \left(\sum_{j=1}^d (1 - 2\mathcal{E}(\widetilde{w}_{ij})) \cdot (1 - 2\mathcal{E}(\widetilde{w}_{sj})) \right)
$$

$$
= 1 - \frac{2}{d} \cdot \left(\sum_{j=1}^d (\mathcal{E}(\widetilde{w}_{ij}) + \mathcal{E}(\widetilde{w}_{sj}) - 2\mathcal{E}(\widetilde{w}_{ij})\mathcal{E}(\widetilde{w}_{sj})) \right)
$$

$$
= 1 - \frac{2}{d} \cdot \left(\sum_{j=1}^d \mathcal{E}(\widetilde{w}_{ij}) \oplus \mathcal{E}(\widetilde{w}_{sj}) \right) = 1 - 2\frac{hd_i}{d}.
$$

Thus, we have $c_i > 0 \Leftrightarrow 1 - 2 \cdot \frac{hd_i}{d} > 0 \Leftrightarrow hd_i < \frac{d}{2}$. Therefore, with $\tau = \frac{d}{2}$ we have $\nu_i > 0 \Leftrightarrow c_i > 0$, which means τ-clipping Hamming distance-based method is capable to exclude the poisoned sgn model updates equivalent to that the cosine similarity-based method achieved. What is more, our τ-clipping Hamming distance-based method is more flexible than the cosine similarity-based one since we can alter τ for different tasks to achieve the best Byzantine-robustness.

B   Proof of Theorem 1

Proof (of Theorem 1). The universal composability framework [10] guarantees the security of arbitrary composition of different protocols. Therefore, we only need to prove the security of individual protocols. We give the proof of the security under the semi-honest model in the real-ideal paradigm [10].

Privacy of CXOR. There is nothing to simulate as the protocol is non-interactive.

Privacy of PCBit2A. In offline phase, P_0's view in real-world is composed of $\{\mathbf{x}_i, \mathbf{r}_i, \mathbf{x}'_i, \mathbf{r}'_i, \text{AHE.Enc}_{\text{pk}_0}(\mathbf{y}_i)\}$. To simulate it in ideal-world, the Sim can simply return $\{\boldsymbol{\Delta}^x_i, \boldsymbol{\Delta}^r_i, \boldsymbol{\Delta}^{x'}_i, \boldsymbol{\Delta}^{r'}_i, \text{AHE.Enc}_{\text{pk}'_0}([0, 0, ..., 0])\}$ where $\boldsymbol{\Delta}^x_i, \boldsymbol{\Delta}^r_i, \boldsymbol{\Delta}^{x'}_i, \boldsymbol{\Delta}^{r'}_i$ are chosen from $\mathcal{R}^d$ at random and pk'_0 is generated by Sim. Due to the semantic security of AHE, these two views are computationally indistinguishable from each other. And P_1's view in real execution can also be simulated by Sim which outputs two random vectors in $\mathcal{R}^d$ since the real-world view $\{\boldsymbol{\xi}_i, \boldsymbol{\xi}'_i\}$ are masked by random vectors $\mathbf{r}_i$ and $\mathbf{r}'_i$. In online, the output of Sim for corrupted P_t is one share which is uniformly chosen from $\mathcal{R}^d$, and thus P_t's view in the real-world is also indistinguishable from that in ideal-world.

Privacy of Private τ-Clipping. As the underlying garbled circuits are secure, P_t's view composed of *labels* in real-world is indistinguishable from the ideal-world view, which comprises of simulated labels.

Privacy of CSWA. In the offline, the view of P_t in the real-world is computationally indistinguishable from the ideal-world view because of the semantic security of AHE. Moreover, in the online, the real-world view of P_t is also masked random values. Sim can simulate it with random values of the same size.

Therefore, we guarantee that the adversary $\mathcal{A}^s$ (when corrupts P_0) learns nothing beyond what can be inferred from the aggregated results $(\sum_{i=1}^{K}\langle \nu_i \widetilde{\mathbf{w}}_i \rangle^A_t, \sum_{i=1}^{K}\langle \nu_i \rangle^A_t)$ with an overwhelming probability. Completing the proof.

C   MA of ResNet-18 on CIFAR10 with Altering δ

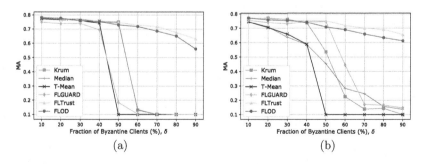

(a)   (b)

Fig. 8. MA of ResNet-18 on CIFAR10 with $\delta = 10\%$–90% for all Byzantine-robust aggregation methods, where 8(a) is for GA and 8(b) is for LF.

D   Online Overhead of Free-HD and Private τ-Clipping

Table 4. Comm. and Run-time of Free $-$ HD and Private τ-Clipping.

K	Comm (MB)			Run-time (s)					
	10	50	100	10		50		100	
Model				FNet	ResNet-18	FNet	ResNet-18	FNet	ResNet-18
CXOR	0	0	0	0.02	0.07	0.08	0.34	0.15	0.64
Private τ-Clipping	0.06	0.28	0.56	0.006		0.012		0.020	

References

1. Alistarh, D., Allen-Zhu, Z., Li, J.: Byzantine stochastic gradient descent. arXiv preprint arXiv:1803.08917 (2018)
2. Bagdasaryan, E., Veit, A., Hua, Y., Estrin, D., Shmatikov, V.: How to backdoor federated learning. In: International Conference on Artificial Intelligence and Statistics, pp. 2938–2948. PMLR (2020)
3. Beaver, D.: Efficient multiparty protocols using circuit randomization. In: Feigenbaum, J. (ed.) CRYPTO 1991. LNCS, vol. 576, pp. 420–432. Springer, Heidelberg (1992). https://doi.org/10.1007/3-540-46766-1_34
4. Bellare, M., Hoang, V.T., Rogaway, P.: Foundations of garbled circuits. In: Proceedings of the 2012 ACM Conference on Computer and Communications Security, pp. 784–796 (2012)
5. Bernstein, J., Wang, Y.X., Azizzadenesheli, K., Anandkumar, A.: signSGD: compressed optimisation for non-convex problems. In: International Conference on Machine Learning, pp. 560–569. PMLR (2018)
6. Blanchard, P., El Mhamdi, E.M., Guerraoui, R., Stainer, J.: Machine learning with adversaries: byzantine tolerant gradient descent. In: Proceedings of the 31st International Conference on Neural Information Processing Systems, pp. 118–128 (2017)
7. Bogdanov, D., Laur, S., Willemson, J.: Sharemind: a framework for fast privacy-preserving computations. In: Jajodia, S., Lopez, J. (eds.) ESORICS 2008. LNCS, vol. 5283, pp. 192–206. Springer, Heidelberg (2008). https://doi.org/10.1007/978-3-540-88313-5_13
8. Bonawitz, K., et al.: Practical secure aggregation for privacy-preserving machine learning. In: Proceedings of the 2017 ACM SIGSAC Conference on Computer and Communications Security, pp. 1175–1191. ACM (2017). https://doi.org/10.1145/3133956.3133982
9. Bookstein, A., Kulyukin, V.A., Raita, T.: Generalized hamming distance. Inf. Retrieval 5(4), 353–375 (2002)
10. Canetti, R.: Universally composable security: a new paradigm for cryptographic protocols. In: Proceedings 42nd IEEE Symposium on Foundations of Computer Science, pp. 136–145. IEEE (2001)
11. Cao, X., Fang, M., Liu, J., Gong, N.Z.: FLTrust: byzantine-robust federated learning via trust bootstrapping. arXiv preprint arXiv:2012.13995 (2020)
12. Corrigan-Gibbs, H., Boneh, D.: Prio: private, robust, and scalable computation of aggregate statistics. In: 14th {USENIX} Symposium on Networked Systems Design and Implementation ({NSDI} 2017), pp. 259–282 (2017)

13. Demmler, D., Schneider, T., Zohner, M.: Aby-a framework for efficient mixed-protocol secure two-party computation. In: NDSS (2015)
14. ElGamal, T.: A public key cryptosystem and a signature scheme based on discrete logarithms. IEEE Trans. Inf. Theory **31**(4), 469–472 (1985)
15. Erickson, B.J., Korfiatis, P., Akkus, Z., Kline, T.L.: Machine learning for medical imaging. Radiographics **37**(2), 505–515 (2017)
16. Fang, M., Cao, X., Jia, J., Gong, N.: Local model poisoning attacks to byzantine-robust federated learning. In: 29th {$USENIX$} Security Symposium ({$USENIX$} Security 2020), pp. 1605–1622 (2020)
17. Hard, A., et al.: Federated learning for mobile keyboard prediction. arXiv preprint arXiv:1811.03604 (2018)
18. Ion, M., et al.: On deploying secure computing: private intersection-sum-with-cardinality. In: 2020 IEEE European Symposium on Security and Privacy (EuroS&P), pp. 370–389. IEEE (2020)
19. Kairouz, P., et al.: Advances and open problems in federated learning. arXiv preprint arXiv:1912.04977 (2019)
20. Konečný, J., McMahan, H.B., Yu, F.X., Richtárik, P., Suresh, A.T., Bacon, D.: Federated learning: strategies for improving communication efficiency. arXiv preprint arXiv:1610.05492 (2016)
21. Krizhevsky, A., Hinton, G., et al.: Learning multiple layers of features from tiny images (2009)
22. Li, M., et al.: Scaling distributed machine learning with the parameter server. In: 11th {$USENIX$} Symposium on Operating Systems Design and Implementation ({$OSDI$} 2014), pp. 583–598 (2014)
23. Liu, R., Cao, Y., Yoshikawa, M., Chen, H.: FedSel: federated SGD under local differential privacy with top-k dimension selection. In: Nah, Y., Cui, B., Lee, S.-W., Yu, J.X., Moon, Y.-S., Whang, S.E. (eds.) DASFAA 2020. LNCS, vol. 12112, pp. 485–501. Springer, Cham (2020). https://doi.org/10.1007/978-3-030-59410-7_33
24. McMahan, B., Moore, E., Ramage, D., Hampson, S., y Arcas, B.A.: Communication-efficient learning of deep networks from decentralized data. In: Artificial Intelligence and Statistics, pp. 1273–1282. PMLR (2017)
25. Mhamdi, E.M.E., Guerraoui, R., Rouault, S.: The hidden vulnerability of distributed learning in byzantium. arXiv preprint arXiv:1802.07927 (2018)
26. Nasr, M., Shokri, R., Houmansadr, A.: Comprehensive privacy analysis of deep learning: passive and active white-box inference attacks against centralized and federated learning. In: 2019 IEEE Symposium on Security and Privacy (SP), pp. 739–753. IEEE (2019)
27. Nguyen, T.D., et al.: FLGUARD: secure and private federated learning. arXiv preprint arXiv:2101.02281 (2021)
28. Nosowsky, R., Giordano, T.J.: The health insurance portability and accountability act of 1996 (HIPAA) privacy rule: implications for clinical research. Annu. Rev. Med. **57**, 575–590 (2006). https://doi.org/10.1146/annurev.med.57.121304.131257
29. Paillier, P.: Public-key cryptosystems based on composite degree residuosity classes. In: Stern, J. (ed.) EUROCRYPT 1999. LNCS, vol. 1592, pp. 223–238. Springer, Heidelberg (1999). https://doi.org/10.1007/3-540-48910-X_16
30. Peikert, C., Vaikuntanathan, V., Waters, B.: A framework for efficient and composable oblivious transfer. In: Wagner, D. (ed.) CRYPTO 2008. LNCS, vol. 5157, pp. 554–571. Springer, Heidelberg (2008). https://doi.org/10.1007/978-3-540-85174-5_31

31. Phong, L.T., Aono, Y., Hayashi, T., Wang, L., Moriai, S.: Privacy-preserving deep learning via additively homomorphic encryption. IEEE Trans. Inf. Forensics Secur. **13**(5), 1333–1345 (2018). https://doi.org/10.1109/TIFS.2017.2787987
32. Microsoft SEAL (release 3.6), November 2020. https://github.com/Microsoft/ SEAL Microsoft Research, Redmond, WA
33. Shokri, R., Shmatikov, V.: Privacy-preserving deep learning. In: Proceedings of the 22nd ACM SIGSAC Conference on Computer and Communications Security, pp. 1310–1321. ACM (2015). https://doi.org/10.1145/2810103.2813687
34. Smart, N.P., Vercauteren, F.: Fully homomorphic SIMD operations. Des. Codes Cryptogr. **71**(1), 57–81 (2012). https://doi.org/10.1007/s10623-012-9720-4
35. Team, I.P.: EU general data protection regulation (GDPR): an implementation and compliance guide. IT Governance Ltd (2017). https://doi.org/10.2307/j.ctt1trkk7x
36. Xiao, H., Rasul, K., Vollgraf, R.: Fashion-MNIST: a novel image dataset for benchmarking machine learning algorithms. arXiv preprint arXiv:1708.07747 (2017)
37. Yao, A.C.C.: How to generate and exchange secrets. In: 27th Annual Symposium on Foundations of Computer Science (SFCS 1986), pp. 162–167. IEEE (1986)
38. Yin, D., Chen, Y., Kannan, R., Bartlett, P.: Byzantine-robust distributed learning: towards optimal statistical rates. In: International Conference on Machine Learning, pp. 5650–5659. PMLR (2018)
39. Zhu, L., Han, S.: Deep leakage from gradients. In: Yang, Q., Fan, L., Yu, H. (eds.) Federated Learning. LNCS (LNAI), vol. 12500, pp. 17–31. Springer, Cham (2020). https://doi.org/10.1007/978-3-030-63076-8_2

MediSC: Towards Secure and Lightweight Deep Learning as a Medical Diagnostic Service

Xiaoning Liu[1], Yifeng Zheng[2(✉)], Xingliang Yuan[3], and Xun Yi[1]

[1] RMIT University, Melbourne, Australia
{maggie.liu,xun.yi}@rmit.edu.au
[2] Harbin Institute of Technology, Shenzhen, China
yifeng.zheng@hit.edu.cn
[3] Monash University, Clayton, Australia
xingliang.yuan@monash.edu

Abstract. The striking progress of deep learning paves the way towards intelligent and quality medical diagnostic services. Enterprises deploy such services via the neural network (NN) inference, yet confronted with rising privacy concerns of the medical data being diagnosed and the pre-trained NN models. We propose MediSC, a system framework that enables enterprises to offer secure medical diagnostic service to their customers via an execution of NN inference in the ciphertext domain. MediSC ensures the privacy of both parties with cryptographic guarantees. At the heart, we present an efficient and communication-optimized secure inference protocol that purely relies on the lightweight secret sharing techniques and can well cope with the commonly-used linear and non-linear NN layers. Compared to the garbled circuits based solutions, the latency and communication of MediSC are $24\times$ lower and $868\times$ less for the secure ReLU, and $20\times$ lower and $314\times$ less for the secure Maxpool. We evaluate MediSC on two benchmark and four real-world medical datasets, and comprehensively compare it with prior arts. The results demonstrate the promising performance of MediSC, which is much more bandwidth-efficient compared to prior works.

Keywords: Secure computation · Privacy-preserving medical service · Neural network inference · Secret sharing

1 Introduction

Recent thriving deep learning techniques have been fueling a wide spectrum of medical endeavors, ranging from the radiotherapy [5], clinical trial and research [7], to medical imaging diagnostics [6]. Enterprises capitalize on neural networks (NNs) to offer medical diagnostic services, facilitating hospitals and researchers to produce faster and more accurate decisions over their medical data. With the growth in such offerings comes rapidly growing awareness of

© Springer Nature Switzerland AG 2021
E. Bertino et al. (Eds.): ESORICS 2021, LNCS 12972, pp. 519–541, 2021.
https://doi.org/10.1007/978-3-030-88418-5_25

daunting privacy concerns. The medical data is of sensitive nature and must be always kept confidential [8,13,24,25]. Meanwhile, NN models used in these services are seen as lucrative intellectual properties and encode knowledge of private training data [14].

The general setup of the above NN-powered service scenario fits within the field of secure multi-party computation (MPC). By designing specialized MPC protocols, recent works [15,19,21,22,28] enable the joint execution of secure NN inference systems over encrypted customer's data and/or the service provider's model. Nevertheless, these systems still come at a steep performance overhead that may not be amiable for the real-world medical scenario. During inference, they all require customers to conduct heavy cryptographic computations like homomorphic encryption (HE) and garbled circuits (GC), imposing intensive computational and communication overheads. These performance hurdles are further exacerbated when, e.g., the service is deployed to a hospital with resource-constrained devices (like portable medical imaging scanners [18]). Furthermore, some of their protocols [15,19] are not directly compatible with the widely-adopted non-linear functions (like ReLU), causing limitations of applicability for modern NN architectures.

We design, implement, and evaluate MediSC, a lightweight and secure NN inference system tailored for medical diagnostic services. MediSC proceeds by having the hospital and the medical service engage in a tailored secure inference protocol over their encrypted inputs. Only the hospital learns the diagnostic result; and the privacy of the medical data and model is ensured against each other. In particular, we combine insights from cryptography and digital circuit design, making an efficient and low-interaction service suitable for realistic medical scenarios. Our contributions are summarized as follows.

- We propose a secure NN inference system framework MediSC relying only on the lightweight secret sharing techniques, which requires neither heavy cryptographic computation nor large-size ciphertext transmissions.
- We present a hybrid protocol design that consists of a preprocessing phase and an online phase where the preprocessing phase conducts as much computation as possible to ease the online phase. Moreover, the preprocessing only involves lightweight computation in the secret sharing domain.
- We devise an efficient and communication-optimized secure comparison function to support the most challenging and widely adopted non-linear functions (ReLU and Max-pool), harnessing the insights from cryptography and the field of digital circuit design. Compared to the commonly-used GC solutions, MediSC's secure ReLU is 24× faster and requires 868× less communication, and the secure Max-pool is 20× faster and uses 314× less communication.
- We conduct formal security analysis. We implement a prototype of MediSC and conduct comprehensive evaluations over two benchmarking datasets and four realistic medical datasets. Our experiment results show that MediSC requires the least network resources compared to prior works with up to 413×, 19× and 10× bandwidth savings for MNIST, CIFAR-10,

and the medical applications, respectively. MediSC outperforms the state-of-the-art (SOTA) [28] by 10× in bandwidth cost, with comparable latency[1].

2   Related Works

The past few years have seen an increased interest in secure neural network inference. A plethora of prior works [12,15,19,21,22,28,34,36] focus on a scenario where an *interactive* protocol is run between the service provider and the customer. Some other works [23,29,31] rely on a security assumption where two *non-colluding cloud servers* are employed to jointly conduct secure inference over outsourced model and data. Despite their different system models, these works require to use heavy cryptographic tools (like HE and GC) during the latency-sensitive online inference procedure. Moreover, some of these works do not fully support the modern NN models [15,19]. Instead, these works approximate the non-linear functions into the crypto-friendly polynomials, trading the accuracy and applicability for efficiency [20,26], which could cause critical consequences in the medical scenario.

The SOTA work [28] presents a hybrid and interactive inference protocol, preprocessing some cryptographic operations to accelerate the online inference execution. However, this work still demands intensive workloads on the customer to conduct heavy cryptographic computations during preprocessing, and relies on expensive GC based approach to evaluate the ReLU. MediSC adopts a similar hybrid setting yet only involves the lightweight secret sharing techniques during the entire secure inference procedure, which has an prominent advantage of *rather simplified* implementation for easy real-world deployment, compared to the SOTA which requires heavy optimization in GC and homomorphic encryption implementation.

3   Preliminaries on Additive Secret Sharing

Additive secret sharing [9] protects an ℓ-bit value $x \in \mathbb{R}_{2^\ell}$ as two secret shares $\langle x \rangle_0 = r \pmod{2^\ell}$ and $\langle x \rangle_1 = x - r \pmod{2^\ell}$ such that $\langle x \rangle_0 + \langle x \rangle_1 \equiv x \pmod{2^\ell}$, where $\mathbb{Z}_{2^\ell}$ is a ring and r is a random value from the ring ($r \in_R \mathbb{Z}_{2^\ell}$). It perfectly hides x as each share is a random value and reveals no information of x. Given two parties P_0 and P_1, each party holds the corresponding shares of two secret values x and y. Additive secret sharing supports efficient local addition/subtraction over shares $\langle z \rangle_i = \langle x \rangle_i \pm \langle y \rangle_i$ and scalar multiplication $\langle z \rangle_i = \eta \cdot \langle x \rangle_i$ (η is a public value). They are calculated by each party P_i ($i \in \{0,1\}$) without interactions. Multiplication over two shares $\langle z \rangle = \langle x \rangle \cdot \langle y \rangle$ is enabled with the secret-shared Beaver's triple [11], i.e., P_i holds ($\langle t_1 \rangle_i, \langle t_2 \rangle_i, \langle t_3 \rangle_i$) in a way that $t_3 = t_1 \cdot t_2$. Such a multiplication with Beaver's triple is a standard secure protocol, whereby P_i

---

[1] From a direct comparison with results reported in SOTA which demands highly optimized implementations with GPU acceleration. Our performance result is not based on such optimization.

obtains the shares $\langle z \rangle_i$ of xy at the end. Note that Beaver's triples are data independent and can be efficiently generated via one-off computation by a third party [31, 37]. Additive secret shares can support boolean operations over binary values. Given the bit length $\ell = 1$ and the ring $\mathbb{Z}_2$, a secret binary value x is shared as $[\![x]\!]_0 = r \in \mathbb{Z}_2$ and $[\![x]\!]_1 = r \oplus [\![x]\!]_0$. The bitwise XOR ($\oplus$) and AND ($\wedge$) over shares are calculated in the same way as the above addition and multiplication, respectively.

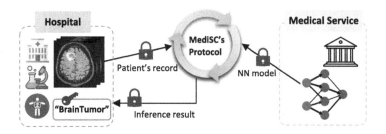

Fig. 1. System architecture.

4 System Overview

4.1 Architecture

MediSC targets a typical scenario of secure NN inference based medical diagnostic service. As shown in Fig. 1, MediSC operates between two parties: the *hospital* (customer) and the *medical service* provider. The *medical service* holds a proprietary NN model that is pre-trained on medical datasets. The *hospital* holds confidential medical records (e.g., brain MRI images) and intends to leverage the deep learning service to facilitate a medical conclusion. In practice, the role of hospital in MediSC can actually be any healthcare institutes, medical research laboratories, or life-science organizations. To initiate a secure medical diagnostic service, the two parties execute MediSC's secure NN inference protocol over their encrypted model and encrypted medical record. At the end, an encrypted inference result is returned to the hospital which can then decrypt to get the plaintext inference result. MediSC ensures that the hospital learns the inference result and nothing else, while the medical service learns no information about the hospital's medical records.

4.2 Threat Model

MediSC is designed for the *semi-honest* two-party model: the hospital and the medical service will faithfully follow the protocol, yet attempting to deduce information about the counterparty's private input from the messages seen from protocol execution. It is noted that the behavior of hospital is enforced by the ethics, law and privacy regulations [8,13]. The medical service is usually offered by well-established companies (e.g., Microsoft Project InnerEye [6], Google DeepMind Health [5]) and would not take their business model and reputation at risk to act maliciously [10]. Such an adversarial model is also adopted in prior secure NN inference works [22,28]. MediSC strives to ensure the privacy of the hospital's medical records and the NN model (values of trained weights). Like prior work [22,23,28], MediSC does not hide the data-independent model architecture, such as kernel size and number of layers. Lastly, MediSC deems thwarting adversarial machine learning attacks orthogonal, which attempt to exploit the inference procedure as a blackbox oracle to extract private information. Mitigation strategies can be differentially private learning [35].

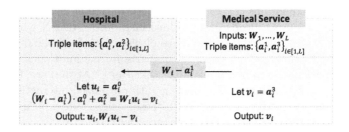

Fig. 2. MediSC's preprocessing phase.

5   Our Proposed Design

In this section, we introduce MediSC's secure NN inference protocol for medical diagnostic applications. At a high level, our design consists of two types of secure layer evaluations: secure *linear* and *non-linear* layers, which can well support the typical NN layers, i.e., the convolutional/fully-connected/batch normalization/average pooling layers (linear), and the ReLU activation/max pooling layers (non-linear). Each secure layer evaluation conducts a certain function on the encrypted inputs (features) and yields encrypted outputs passed to the next secure layer. Our overarching goal is to devise a lightweight protocol for secure neural network inference, while minimizing interactions in between the hospital and the medical service for a low-latency diagnosis. Atop such goal, we have two prominent design insights.

Eliminating Heavy Cryptography for Linear Layers. We first split MediSC's protocol into a preprocessing phase and an online phase, and shift as much computation as possible to preprocessing phase. Inspired by [28], we preprocess the model as secret shares and deliver corresponding shares to the hospital before medical record becomes available. So, the online phase can directly work over secret shares without any heavy cryptographic techniques (like HE) or multi-round ciphertext transmissions. Yet we are aware that the protocol in

[28] involves heavy HE during preprocessing to produce and send the model shares as ciphertexts, which may not be amiable for the resource-limited hospital, like COVID-19 pandemic screening centers with handheld medical imaging scanners [18]). Instead, our protocol delicately leverages the insight from Chameleon [31] and enables the preprocessing to be purely based on lightweight computation in the secret sharing domain. As a result, our entire protocol works only with small shares, which immediately gains 20× improvement on preprocessing and 10× on overall communication costs over [28].

Eliminating the Usage of GC for Non-linear Layers. For secure evaluation of non-linear layers, prior works either resort to the heavy cryptographic techniques (i.e., garbled circuits) [22,28], or circumvent the non-linearities with their polynomial approximations [15,19]. Unfortunately, such methods may introduce high communication overheads or introduce instabilities of NN when handling complex tasks [20,26]. In MediSC, we make observations from the field of digital circuit design [17] and present a secure comparison function that can efficiently evaluate comparison-based non-linear layers like ReLU. At the core, this function is fully based on lightweight secret sharing with optimized interactions between the hospital and the medical service. With these designs, our experiment demonstrates a 413× bandwidth reduction compared with prior works.

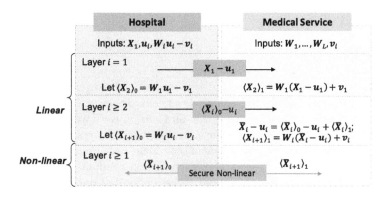

Fig. 3. MediSC's online phase.

5.1 Secure Linear Layers

This subsequent section presents MediSC's secure inference protocol, which comprises two phases: the *preprocessing* phase and the *online inference* phase. Before diving in to the details, we first note that MediSC works over the secret sharing domain. That is, any float-point number v (i.e., model weights and medical record values) is projected to a signed fixed-point integer $\bar{v} = \lfloor v \cdot 2^s \rfloor \bmod 2^\ell$ in ring $\mathbb{Z}_{2^\ell}$, where 2^s is the scaling factor. The most significant bit (MSB) indicates the sign ($1 \rightarrow$negative; $0 \rightarrow$non-negative)[2]. Through such a conversion, both the value and sign information are perfectly hidden.

Preprocessing Phase. The preprocessing phase is illustrated in Fig. 2. The hospital and the medical service pre-generate secret shares of the NN model in an appropriate form which are to be used during online inference. This is a one-off computation and conducted independent of the hospital's medical record. Let L be number of layers. The hospital takes as input the L sets of randomnesses (in tensor form) $\{\mathbf{a}_i^0, \mathbf{a}_i^2\}$, where $i \in [1, L]$. Similarly, the medical service takes as input the tensors of model weights for each layer $\mathbf{W}_1, ..., \mathbf{W}_L$ and randomnesses tensors $\{\mathbf{a}_i^1, \mathbf{a}_i^3\}$. Such randomness tensors $\{\mathbf{a}_i^0, \mathbf{a}_i^1, \mathbf{a}_i^2, \mathbf{a}_i^3\}$ are independent to any party's input and can be pre-distributed to the parties, and satisfy the relationship: $\mathbf{a}_i^3 = \mathbf{a}_i^0 \cdot \mathbf{a}_i^1 - \mathbf{a}_i^2$. Note that the dimension of each randomness tensor is in line with the dimension of each layer's filter. Given these inputs, the two parties perform the following steps.

1. For each $i \in [1, L]$, the medical service computes $\mathbf{W}_i - \mathbf{a}_i^1$ over the weight tensors and sends to the hospital.
2. The hospital computes $(\mathbf{W}_i - \mathbf{a}_i^1) \cdot \mathbf{a}_i^0 = \mathbf{W}_i \mathbf{a}_i^0 - \mathbf{a}_i^0 \mathbf{a}_i^1 + \mathbf{a}_i^2$ for each layer.
3. Let $\mathbf{u}_i$ denote $\mathbf{a}_i^0$, and $\mathbf{v}_i$ denote $\mathbf{a}_i^3$. The medical service thus holds $\mathbf{v}_i$, and the hospital holds $\mathbf{W}_i \mathbf{u}_i - \mathbf{v}_i$, i.e., an additively secret-shared weight tensors $\mathbf{W}_i \mathbf{u}_i$.

Online Inference Phase. During online inference, the hospital takes as input the tensor of a medical record $\mathbf{X}_1$, the randomnesses $\mathbf{u}_i$, and weight shares $\mathbf{W}_i \mathbf{u}_i - \mathbf{v}_i$, as shown in Fig. 3. The medical service takes as input the weight tensors $\mathbf{W}_1, ..., \mathbf{W}_L$ and the randomnesses $\mathbf{v}_i$. They then perform the secure layer function in pipeline as follows.

The first linear layer $i = 1$:

1. The hospital computes and sends $\mathbf{X}_1 - \mathbf{u}_1$ to the medical service, and uses $\langle \mathbf{X}_2 \rangle_0$ to denote $\mathbf{W}_1 \mathbf{u}_1 - \mathbf{v}_1$.
2. The medical service computes $\langle \mathbf{X}_2 \rangle_1 = \mathbf{W}_1(\mathbf{X}_1 - \mathbf{u}_1) + \mathbf{v}_1 = \mathbf{W}_1 \mathbf{X}_1 - \mathbf{W}_1 \mathbf{u}_1 + \mathbf{v}_1$.
3. At this point, the hospital and the medical service hold the additive secret shares (i.e., $\langle \mathbf{X}_2 \rangle_0$, $\langle \mathbf{X}_2 \rangle_1$) of features[3] outputted from the first linear layer $\mathbf{W}_1 \mathbf{X}_1$.

Remaining linear layers $i \geq 2$:

1. Similar to the first layer, the hospital computes $\langle \bar{\mathbf{X}}_i \rangle_0 - \mathbf{u}_i$ over its share $\langle \bar{\mathbf{X}}_i \rangle_0$ of activation produced from the secure ReLU evaluation (which we will detail later), and sends it to the medical service. Such a treatment can perfectly hide the hospital's share, and protect the activation $\bar{\mathbf{X}}_i$ against the medical service. It then sets $\langle \mathbf{X}_{i+1} \rangle_0 = \mathbf{W}_i \mathbf{u}_i - \mathbf{v}_i$.

---

[2] We refer the readers to more details in Appendix Sect. A.
[3] Biases can be added to the medical service's shares locally.

2. The medical service computes $\mathbf{X}_i - \mathbf{u}_i = \langle\bar{\mathbf{X}}_i\rangle_0 - \mathbf{u}_i + \langle\bar{\mathbf{X}}_i\rangle_1$. Then it gets $\langle\mathbf{X}_{i+1}\rangle_1 = \mathbf{W}_i(\mathbf{X}_i - \mathbf{u}_i) + \mathbf{v}_i$, ensuring both parties hold additive secret shares (i.e., $\langle\mathbf{X}_{i+1}\rangle_0$, $\langle\mathbf{X}_{i+1}\rangle_1$) of layer result $\mathbf{W}_i\mathbf{X}_i$.

Non-linear layers: The shares form secure linear layer evaluation can be fed into the secure non-linear layer (e.g., ReLU), which outputs shares $\langle\bar{\mathbf{X}}_{i+1}\rangle_0$, $\langle\bar{\mathbf{X}}_{i+1}\rangle_1$ of activations to each party.

Output layer: The medical service sends $\langle\mathbf{X}_L\rangle_1$ to the hospital, who can then integrate $\langle\mathbf{X}_L\rangle_0$ for reconstruction of the final inference result $\mathbf{X}_L$.

5.2 Secure Non-linear Layers

MediSC supports highly efficient evaluation of the secure non-linear layers in the secret sharing domain. As mentioned above, MediSC denotes all values as the signed fixed-point integers with MSB indicating the sign, i.e., the MSB would be '0' for a non-negative value and '1' for a negative value. With such a representation, we observe that all non-linear layers mainly relying on the comparison operation can be simplified to an MSB extraction problem along with some linear operations (addition and multiplication). For the ease of presentation, we focus on the most-widely adopted ReLU function. The ReLU function can be converted to a simplified MSB extraction problem via

$$max(x, 0) \rightarrow \neg\mathsf{MSB}(x) \cdot x = \begin{cases} 1 \cdot x & \text{if } x \geq 0 \\ 0 \cdot x & \text{if } x < 0 \end{cases}, \tag{1}$$

where x is the feature on each neuron outputted from previous linear layer. Through such a conversion, we observe that it consists of four atomic steps: the *secure* $\mathsf{MSB}(\cdot)$ *extraction*, the *secure NOT*, the *secure* B2A (i.e., Boolean-to-Additive shares conversion), and the *secure multiplication*. The most challenging computation is the secure $\mathsf{MSB}(\cdot)$ extraction, of which we propose an efficient and

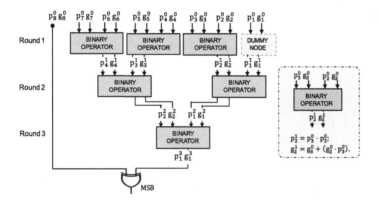

Fig. 4. An illustration of 8-bit parallel prefix adder (PPA).

communication-optimized construction and present the details in the subsequent section. For the rest steps, the secure B2A converts boolean shares $[\![x]\!]$ in ring $\mathbb{Z}_2$ to additive shares in $\mathbb{Z}_{2^\ell}$, i.e., $\langle x \rangle \leftarrow \mathsf{B2A}([\![x]\!])$. Meanwhile, the *secure NOT* and the *secure multiplication* are linear operations and well handled by additive secret sharing.

Communication-Optimized Secure MSB Extraction. The secure $\mathsf{MSB}(\cdot)$ extraction function is used to securely extract the MSB of an additive-shared data $\langle x \rangle$ and generate a boolean-shared MSB $[\![x_\ell]\!]$, where ℓ is the bit length. The idea is that extracting the MSB in the secret sharing domain can be performed via binary addition over two secret shares' bit strings by an ℓ-bit full adder, as expatiated below. Suppose an ℓ-bit value x with its decomposed bit string $x = \{x_\ell, ..., x_1\}$ and the secret shares $\langle x \rangle_0, \langle x \rangle_1$. Let $e = \{e_\ell, ..., e_1\}$ and $f = \{f_\ell, ..., f_1\}$ denote the bit strings of $\langle x \rangle_0$ and $\langle x \rangle_1$, respectively. In this way, $x = e + f \pmod{2^\ell}$. Then, an ℓ-bit full adder is used to perform the binary addition $(\{e_k\} + \{f_k\})$ in the secret sharing domain to produce the carry bits $c_\ell, ..., c_1$, and finally the MSB is calculated via $x_\ell = c_\ell \oplus e_\ell \oplus f_\ell$, where $k \in [1, \ell]$. The key takeaway to extract the MSB is producing the most significant carry bit c_ℓ via the full adder logic. In the following section, without specifically mentioned, the operator '$+$' over two binary values (including boolean shares) denotes the bitwise-XOR operation for the ease of demonstration.

We make an observation from the field of digital circuit design that the parallel prefix adder [17] (PPA) offers an efficient realization of the full adder logic in logarithm round complexity $O(\log \ell)$. To construct PPA, we introduce a *signal tuple* (g_i, p_i): the carry generate signal g_i and the carry propagate signal p_i, which can be derived in parallel via

$$g_i = e_i \cdot f_i; \; p_i = e_i + f_i. \tag{2}$$

Then the full adder logic $c_{i+1} = (e_i \cdot f_i) + c_i \cdot (e_i + f_i)$ is reformulated as $c_{i+1} = g_i + c_i \cdot p_i$, and the ℓ-th carry bit can be generated via $c_\ell = g_{\ell-1} + (p_{\ell-1} \cdot g_{\ell-2}) + ... + (p_{\ell-1}...p_2 \cdot g_1)$. Through this reformulation, PPA can extract the MSB in $O(\log \ell)$ communication round latency.

A concrete illustration of 8-bit PPA is given in Fig. 4. As shown, it constructs a $\log \ell$-depth (3-depth) binary tree with a binary operator $\odot$ adhering to each node. Each layer of the tree indicates one round of communication. The binary operator $\odot$ takes as input the two adjacent signal tuples $(g_{in_1}, p_{in_1}), (g_{in_2}, p_{in_2})$, performs the following computations:

$$(g_{out}, p_{out}) = (g_{in_1}, p_{in_1}) \odot (g_{in_2}, p_{in_2});$$
$$g_{out} = g_{in_2} + g_{in_1} \cdot p_{in_2}; \; p_{out} = p_{in_2} \cdot p_{in_1}, \tag{3}$$

and outputs a signal tuple (g_{out}, p_{out}). PPA iteratively performs the above binary operation over the input tuples associated with each leaf node, and propagates the outputted signal tuples to the next layer's nodes as inputs. Such computations are terminated until the root node is reached, i.e., the node with (p_1^3, g_1^3)

Algorithm 1. Secure MSB($\cdot$) Extraction Function.

Input: Arithmetic shared integer feature $\langle x \rangle \in \mathbb{Z}_{2^\ell}$.
Output: Boolean shared MSB $[\![x_\ell]\!] \in \mathbb{Z}_2$.

Decompose $\langle x \rangle$ into bit strings:

1: Let e denote $\langle x \rangle_0$ and f denote $\langle x \rangle_1$.
2: Decompose to bit strings $e \to e_\ell, ..., e_1$ and $f \to f_\ell, ..., f_1$.
3: **for** $k \in [1, \ell]$ **do**
4:    Set $[\![e_k]\!]_0 = e_k$, $[\![e_k]\!]_1 = 0$ and $[\![f_k]\!]_0 = 0$, $[\![f_k]\!]_1 = f_k$.

Compute signal tuples (g, p) in Eq. 2:

5:    $[\![g_k^0]\!] - [\![e_k]\!] \cdot [\![f_k]\!]$, $[\![p_k^0]\!] - [\![e_k]\!] + [\![f_k]\!]$.
6: **end for**

Compute PPA tree based on Eq. 3:

Round $\mathcal{R} = 1$:

7: **for** $k \in [2, \ell/2]$ **do**
8:    Set $([\![g_1^1]\!], [\![p_1^1]\!]) = ([\![g_1^0]\!], [\![p_1^0]\!])$ as a dummy node.
9:    Let $in_1 = 2k - 2$, $in_2 = 2k - 1$.
10:    $([\![g_k^1]\!], [\![p_k^1]\!]) = ([\![g_{in_1}^0]\!], [\![p_{in_1}^0]\!]) \odot ([\![g_{in_2}^0]\!], [\![p_{in_2}^0]\!])$.
11: **end for**

Round $\mathcal{R} = 2, ..., \log \ell$:

12: **for** $k \in [1, \ell/2^{\mathcal{R}}]$ **do**
13:    Let $in_1 = 2k - 1$, $in_2 = 2k$.
14:    $([\![g_k^{\mathcal{R}}]\!], [\![p_k^{\mathcal{R}}]\!]) = ([\![g_{in_1}^{\mathcal{R}-1}]\!], [\![p_{in_1}^{\mathcal{R}-1}]\!]) \odot ([\![g_{in_2}^{\mathcal{R}-1}]\!], [\![p_{in_2}^{\mathcal{R}-1}]\!])$.
15: **end for**

Compute MSB:

16: Set $[\![c_\ell]\!] = [\![g_1^{\log \ell}]\!]$, $[\![x_\ell]\!] = [\![p_\ell^0]\!] + [\![c_\ell]\!]$.

---

in Fig. 4. To this end, the carry bit c_ℓ is obtained and the MSB is calculated via $x_\ell = c_\ell + p_\ell = c_\ell + (e_\ell + f_\ell)$. In light of above philosophy, we present details of the secure MSB extraction function in Algorithm 1.

Secure B2A Function. Given a secret value x, the secure B2A function is used to convert its boolean shares $[\![x]\!]$ in ring $\mathbb{Z}_2$ to the corresponding additive secret shares $\langle x \rangle$ in ring $\mathbb{Z}_{2^\ell}$. Recall that our proposed secure ReLU function over each feature x is formulated as follows: $max(x, 0) \to \neg \mathsf{MSB}(x) \cdot x$. The secure B2A function is invoked after securely extracting the boolean shares of NOT MSB $[\![\neg x_\ell]\!]$. However, the produced boolean shares cannot be directly multiplied with the additively-shared feature $\langle x \rangle$ as they are shared with different moduli, i.e., $[\![\neg x_\ell]\!] = [\![\neg x_\ell]\!]_0 + [\![\neg x_\ell]\!]_1 \pmod 2$ and $\langle x \rangle = \langle x \rangle_0 + \langle x \rangle_1 \pmod{2^\ell}$. So we need to convert $[\![\neg x_\ell]\!]$ to its additive form $\langle \neg x_\ell \rangle$.

Our secure B2A function follows the standard realization [37]. Given two parties the hospital (denoted as P_0) and the medical service (denoted as P_1), the secure B2A($[\![x]\!]$) function is performed as follow:

1. P_0 sets $\langle e \rangle_0 = [\![x]\!]_0$, $\langle f \rangle_0 = 0$, and P_1 sets $\langle e \rangle_1 = 0$, $\langle f \rangle_1 = [\![x]\!]_1$;
2. P_0 and P_1 compute $\langle x \rangle_i = \langle e \rangle_i + \langle f \rangle_i - 2 \cdot \langle e \rangle \cdot \langle f \rangle$.

Secure ReLU Function. For the ease of presentation, we show the secure ReLU function attached on each neuron over single feature element x. Given the above secure MSB extraction function and the shares of a single input feature $\langle x \rangle$, the hospital (denoted as P_0) and the medical service (denoted as P_1) perform the secure ReLU function as follows:

1. Secure MSB extraction: P_0 and P_1 invoke Algorithm 1 to get $[\![x_\ell]\!] \leftarrow$ MSB($\langle x \rangle$).
2. Secure NOT: P_i computes NOT MSB $[\![\neg x_\ell]\!] = [\![x_\ell]\!] + i$.
3. Secure B2A: P_0 and P_1 run $\langle \neg x_\ell \rangle \leftarrow$ B2A($[\![\neg x_\ell]\!]$) to convert the boolean-shared NOT MSB into additive shares.
4. Secure multiplication: P_0 and P_1 compute to produce the activation on each neuron $\langle \bar{x} \rangle = \langle \neg x_\ell \rangle \cdot \langle x \rangle$.

Secure Pooling Layer. Within an n-width pooling window, the max pooling layer $\max(x_1, \cdots, x_n)$ can be transformed to the pairwise maximum operation and realized based on the secure MSB($\cdot$) extraction via $\mathfrak{b} \leftarrow$ MSB($x_1 - x_2$) and $\max(x_1, x_2) = (1-\mathfrak{b}) \cdot x_1 + \mathfrak{b} \cdot x_2$. Given the above secure MSB extraction function, the secure B2A function, and the shares of a set of activations $\langle x_1 \rangle, ..., \langle x_n \rangle$ within the n-width pooling window, the hospital (denoted as P_0) and the medical service (denoted as P_1) perform the secure MaxPool function as follows:

1. For $k \in [1, n-1]$:
2. Secure MSB extraction: P_0 and P_1 invoke Algorithm 1 to get the boolean shares of MSB $[\![\mathfrak{b}]\!] \leftarrow$ MSB($\langle x_k \rangle - \langle x_{k+1} \rangle$).
3. Secure B2A: P_0 and P_1 run $\langle \mathfrak{b} \rangle \leftarrow$ B2A($[\![\mathfrak{b}]\!]$) to convert the boolean-shared MSB into additive shares.
4. Secure branching: P_0 and P_1 use the MSB to choose the maximum value as follows: $\langle \mathfrak{b}' \rangle_i = i - \langle \mathfrak{b} \rangle_i$, where $i \in \{0, 1\}$ is the identifier of party P_i, and then compute $\langle z_k \rangle = \langle \mathfrak{b}' \rangle \cdot \langle x_k \rangle + \langle \mathfrak{b} \rangle \cdot \langle x_{k+1} \rangle$. P_i sets $\langle x_{k+1} \rangle := \langle z_k \rangle$.
5. Finally, P_i outputs $\langle z_n \rangle_i$ as the shares of MaxPool result.

The average pooling layer $\lfloor (x_1+, ..., +x_n)/n \rfloor$ can be directly computed over additive secret shares via secure addition, where n is a cleartext hyper-parameter.

5.3 Security Analysis

MediSC properly encrypts the medical data, NN model (i.e., the weights), and any intermediate values as secret shares uniformly distributed in ring $\mathbb{Z}_{2^\ell}$ via standard secret sharing techniques [9,16]. It ensures that throughout the service procedure, the hospital only learns the inference result and nothing else, while the medical service learns nothing. Formally, we present the ideal functionality and the formal security definition, and then prove the security of MediSC's secure NN inference protocol under the ideal/real world paradigm. We first define the ideal functionality $\mathcal{F}^{\mathsf{SNNI}}$ capturing our targeted security properties.

Definition 1. *The ideal functionality $\mathcal{F}^{\mathsf{SNNI}}$ of secure neural network inference comprises the following parts:*

- **Input.** *The medical service submits the neural network model $\mathcal{W}$ to $\mathcal{F}^{\text{SNNI}}$. The hospital submits the medical record $\mathbf{X}$ to $\mathcal{F}^{\text{SNNI}}$.*
- **Computation.** *Upon receiving the neural network model $\mathcal{W}$ from the medical service and the medical record $\mathbf{X}$ from the hospital, $\mathcal{F}^{\text{SNNI}}$ performs neural network inference and generates the prediction $\mathcal{W}(\mathbf{X})$.*
- **Output.** *The $\mathcal{F}^{\text{SNNI}}$ returns the prediction $\mathcal{W}(\mathbf{X})$, and outputs nothing to the medical service.*

Given above ideal functionality, we formally provide the security definition.

Definition 2. *A protocol Π securely realizes the $\mathcal{F}^{\text{SNNI}}$ if it provides the following guarantees in the presence of a probabilistic polynomial time (PPT) semi-honest adversary with static corruption:*

- **Corrupted hospital.** *A corrupted and semi-honest hospital should learn nothing about the service's model weights and coefficients beyond the generic architecture hyper-parameter. Formally, there should exit a PPT simulator $\mathsf{Sim_H}$ that $\mathsf{View}_{\mathsf{H}}^{\Pi} \overset{c}{\approx} \mathsf{Sim_H}(\mathbf{X}, \mathcal{W}(\mathbf{X}))$, where H is the hospital and $\mathsf{View}_{\mathsf{H}}^{\Pi}$ indicates the view of the semi-honest hospital in real-world protocol execution.*
- **Corrupted medical service.** *A corrupted and semi-honest medical service should learn nothing about the values of the medical record $\mathbf{X}$ inputted by the hospital. Formally, there should exist a PPT simulator $\mathsf{Sim_S}$ that $\mathsf{View}_{\mathsf{S}}^{\Pi} \overset{c}{\approx} \mathsf{Sim_S}(\mathcal{W})$, where S is the medical service and $\mathsf{View}_{\mathsf{S}}^{\Pi}$ indicates the view of the semi-honest medical service in the real-world protocol execution.*

Theorem 1. *MediSC's secure neural network inference protocol securely realizes the ideal functionality $\mathcal{F}^{\text{SNNI}}$ under Definition 2.*

Proof. We show a simulator for the corrupted medical service or hospital, such that the distribution of real protocol execution is computationally indistinguishable to the simulated distribution according to our security definition.

- **Simulator for the corrupted hospital:** Let $\mathsf{Sim_{BM}}$ denote the simulator of Beaver's multiplication procedure. Its emulated view is indistinguishable from the real view of hospital H in the multiplication procedure. $\mathsf{Sim_H}$ chooses an uniform random tape for the hospital.
  i) During preprocessing of Π, $\mathsf{Sim_H}$ produces and outputs the randomness $\mathbf{r} \overset{\$}{\leftarrow} \mathbb{Z}_{2^\ell}$ to emulate the message in real protocol, i.e., $\mathcal{W} - \mathbf{a}^1$. As both messages are uniformly distributed in ring $\mathbb{Z}_{2^\ell}$ and given the security of additive secret sharing, the hospital cannot distinguish the simulated message with the one received from real protocol. The hospital calculates $\langle \tilde{\mathbf{X}}_2 \rangle_0 = \mathbf{a}^0 \cdot \mathbf{r} + \mathbf{a}^2$ and sets $\mathbf{u} = \mathbf{a}^0$.
  ii) During online inference of Π, the corrupted hospital inputs the shares of medical record $\mathbf{X} - \mathbf{u}$ or protected activation shares $\langle \bar{\mathbf{X}}_i \rangle_0 - \mathbf{u}$ and the shares $\langle \mathbf{X}_{i+1} \rangle_0$ and receives no messages for the linear layers. $\mathsf{Sim_H}$ works in a dummy way by directly outputting inputs of the hospital, and thus the output of $\mathsf{Sim_H}$ is identically distributed to the view of the semi-honest hospital. For the non-linear layers, $\mathsf{Sim_H}$ produces $\langle \tilde{\mathbf{X}}_{i+1} \rangle_1 \overset{\$}{\leftarrow} \mathbb{Z}_{2^\ell}$

and invokes $\mathsf{Sim}_{\mathsf{BM}}$ to conduct secure multiplication over $\langle \tilde{\mathbf{X}}_{i+1} \rangle_1$ and $\langle \mathbf{X}_{i+1} \rangle_0$ whenever interactions are involved in the secure ReLU function. $\mathsf{Sim}_{\mathsf{H}}$ outputs the simulated shares of activation returned from the secure ReLU function. $\mathsf{Sim}_{\mathsf{H}}$ performs the above operations for each layer. At the end, $\mathsf{Sim}_{\mathsf{H}}$ outputs the simulated last layer's result shares $\langle \tilde{\mathbf{X}}_L \rangle_0, \langle \tilde{\mathbf{X}}_L \rangle_1$. The combination of these two shares is uniformly distributed in ring $\mathbb{Z}_{2^\ell}$, same as the result from the real protocol execution. Thus, the output of $\mathsf{Sim}_{\mathsf{H}}(\mathbf{X}, \mathcal{W}(\mathbf{X}))$ is indistinguishable to the view $\mathsf{View}_{\mathsf{H}}^{\Pi}$ of the semi-honest hospital.

– **Simulator for the corrupted medical service:** $\mathsf{Sim}_{\mathsf{S}}$ chooses an uniform random tape for the medical service.

  i) During preprocessing of Π, the medical service inputs only the shares of model $\mathcal{W} - \mathbf{a}^1$ and does not receive any messages. $\mathsf{Sim}_{\mathsf{S}}$ works in a dummy way by directly outputting inputs of the medical service $\mathbf{v} = \mathbf{a}^1$. Thus, the output of $\mathsf{Sim}_{\mathsf{S}}$ is identically distributed to the view $\mathsf{View}_{\mathsf{S}}^{\Pi}$ of the semi-honest medical service.

  ii) During online inference of Π, $\mathsf{Sim}_{\mathsf{S}}$ produces and outputs the randomness $\mathbf{r} \xleftarrow{\$} \mathbb{Z}_{2^\ell}$ to simulate the real world message $\mathbf{X} - \mathbf{u}$ (or $\bar{\mathbf{X}} - \mathbf{u}$). Given the security of additive secret sharing, the medical service cannot distinguish the simulated message with the one received from real protocol. For the non-linear layers, $\mathsf{Sim}_{\mathsf{S}}$ produces $\langle \tilde{\mathbf{X}}_{i+1} \rangle_0 \xleftarrow{\$} \mathbb{Z}_{2^\ell}$. Whenever interactions are involved in the secure ReLU function, $\mathsf{Sim}_{\mathsf{S}}$ invokes $\mathsf{Sim}_{\mathsf{BM}}$ to conduct secure multiplication over $\langle \tilde{\mathbf{X}}_{i+1} \rangle_0$ and $\langle \mathbf{X}_{i+1} \rangle_1$ received from the medical service. $\mathsf{Sim}_{\mathsf{S}}$ outputs the simulated shares of activation returned from the secure ReLU function. $\mathsf{Sim}_{\mathsf{S}}$ performs the above operations for each layer. Since all simulated intermediary messages are uniformly distributed in ring $\mathbb{Z}_{2^\ell}$, and given the security of additive secret sharing and Beaver's secure multiplication procedure, the output of $\mathsf{Sim}_{\mathsf{S}}(\mathcal{W})$ is indistinguishable to the view $\mathsf{View}_{\mathsf{S}}^{\Pi}$ of the corrupted medical service.

6 Performance Evaluation

We implement a prototype of MediSC in Java and evaluate the prototype to two computational nodes emulating the hospital and the medical service. Each computational node runs CentOS Linux 7 with Intel Xeon Gold 6150 CPU at

Table 1. Performance of secure layer functions.

Secure layer	Conv.		BN	ReLU	MaxPool	AvgPool
	3×3	5×5			2×2	2×2
Time (ms)	1.25	2.16	1.74	22.7	31.2	0.05
Comm. (Bytes)	36	100	4	32	144	0

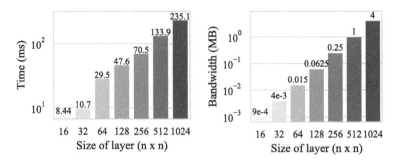

Fig. 5. Performance of the secure FC layer. Left: time (ms). Right: bandwidth (MB).

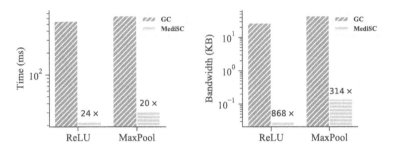

Fig. 6. Performance comparison of the secure non-linear layers. Left: time. Right: bandwidth. Baseline: GC realizations.

2.7 GHz, 384 GB RAM, Mellanox Spectrum network. In our experiment, we set the data filed size to be 32-bit integers, i.e., the additively secret shared data in ring $\mathbb{Z}_{2^{32}}$. We follow most of the prior secure inference works [15,22,30] to evaluate MediSC in fast networks, as the hospital and the medical service can communicate via dedicated connections. We evaluate MediSC with two benchmarking datasets (MNIST and CIFAR-10) with three NN models, and four real-world medical datasets (Breast Cancer, Diabetes, Liver Disease, and Thyroid). For training, we use PyTorch backend on a NVIDIA Tesla V100 GPU. More implementation details and model architectures are available in Appendix Sect. A.

6.1   Microbenchmarks

Secure Layer Functions. We evaluate MediSC's secure layer functions: the secure convolutional (Conv.), fully connected (FC), batch normalization (BN), ReLU, max pooling (MaxPool), and average pooling (AvgPool) layers. They are the main building blocks in MediSC's secure inference. For demonstration, we choose to evaluate the Conv. with the commonly-used 3×3 and 5×5 filter sizes, and the MaxPool and AvgPool with 2×2 pooling window. As Table 1 benchmarks, all functions are demonstrated lightweight, where the linear and non-linear layers can be finished within 2.5 ms and 35 ms respectively, consuming less than 150 Bytes bandwidth. Figure 5 plots the performance of the $n \times n$ fully

Table 2. Performance summary of the benchmarking networks.

Dataset	Model	Time (s)		Comm. (MB)		Accu.	Layers
		Preprocess[a]	Online	Preprocess[a]	Online		
MNIST	M1	0.07	0.57	0.45	0.45	98%	3FC-2ReLU
	M2	1.21	4.42	2.54	2.62	99%	4CONV/FC-8ReLU-2AP
CIFAR-10	C1	17.01	130.02	243.0	246.4	81%	8CONV/FC-8ReLU-2AP

[a] One-time cost during preprocessing.

Table 3. Performance summary of the medical applications.

Dataset/model	Time (s)		Comm. (KB)		Accu.	Layers
	Preprocess	Online	Preprocess	Online		
Breast cancer	0.10	0.20	3.13	4.13	93%	3FC-2ReLU-3BN
Diabetes	0.03	0.16	2.34	3.59	74%	3FC-2ReLU
Liver disease	0.06	0.32	19	23	72%	3FC-2ReLU
Thyroid	0.28	0.64	49.2	55.5	98%	3FC-2ReLU-3BN

Table 4. Bandwidth (MB) comparison of MediSC with prior art.

Model M1		Model M2		Model C1	
MiniONN	15.8	MiniONN	657.5	MiniONN	9272
CryptoNets	372.2	FALCON	62.1	FALCON	1278
XONN	4.29	XONN	32.13	XONN	2599
Chameleon	10.5	Gazelle (ReLU)	70	Chameleon	2650
				Gazelle (ReLU)	∼5000
				Delphi (ReLU)	∼5100
MediSC	**0.9**	**MediSC**	**5.16**	**MediSC**	**489**
Breast cancer		Diabetes		Liver disease	
XONN	0.35	XONN	0.16	XONN	0.3
MediSC	**0.007**	**MediSC**	**0.005**	**MediSC**	**0.04**

connected layer. The time (left figure) and bandwidth (right figure) ascend in linear with the growth of the input and output feature size n.

Non-linear Layers Comparison with GC. Figure 6 demonstrates that MediSC's design achieves $24\times$, $20\times$ speedup and consumes $868\times$, $314\times$ less communication for the ReLU and MaxPool over the GC-based approaches. This GC baseline realizes equivalent functionalities to ours. For a fair comparison, we use the Java based GC framework [33] which integrates modern free-XOR and half-AND optimizations. Such achievements validate that MediSC's purely secret sharing based design is lightweight and much more practical, compared with the prior works involving GC [22,28,30,31].

Table 5. Performance breakdown of M1.

Layers	Preprocess	FC1	ReLU1	FC2	ReLU2	FC3
Time (s)	0.072	0.123	0.198	0.055	0.198	0.001
Comm. (MB)	0.45	0.383	0.0039	0.0625	0.0039	0.0048

Table 6. Performance breakdown of M2.

Layers	Preprocess	CONV1	ReLU1	AP1	CONV2	ReLU2	AP2	FC3	ReLU3	FC4
Time (s)	1.21	0.80	3.04	0.002	0.15	0.28	1.4E−4	0.029	0.087	0.024
Comm. (MB)	2.54	0.87	0.07	0	1.56	0.008	0	0.097	0.003	0.0038

Table 7. Performance breakdown of C1.

Layers	Preprocess	CONV1	ReLU1	CONV2	ReLU2	AP1	CONV3	ReLU3	CONV4
Time (s)	17.0	6.99	68.32	6.45	14.2	0.008	1.104	17.29	1.07
Comm. (MB)	243.0	6.75	2.0	144.0	0.5	0.0	36.0	0.5	36.0
Layers	ReLU4	AP2	CONV5	ReLU5	CONV6	ReLU6	CONV7	ReLU7	FC1
Time (s)	4.3	0.002	0.21	4.35	0.17	4.35	0.056	1.08	0.003
Comm. (MB)	0.125	0.0	9.0	0.125	9.0	0.125	2.25	0.03	0.04

6.2 MediSC's Protocol Performance

Evaluations on MNIST and CIFAR-10. We evaluate MediSC's secure inference protocol on MNIST and CIFAR-10 datasets with three models, and summarize the performance in Table 2. For MNIST, MediSC produces high-quality predictions with 0.47 s (98%) and 4.42 s (99%) online processing time for M1 (3FC-ReLU) and M2 (4CONV/FC-ReLU-2AP). For CIFAR-10, MediSC consumes 2.1 min to produce a 81% accurate prediction for the model C1 (8CONV/FC-ReLU-2AP). Note that the costs of preprocessing are one-time overhead and are determined by the model size.

Evaluations on Medical Datasets. To showcase MediSC's applicability for the real-world medical diagnostic applications, we deploy and evaluate our secure NN inference protocol over the publicly available healthcare datasets. As shown in Table 3, MediSC produces the robust diagnoses within 1s for all medical applications and consumes <60KB. Besides, the workload during preprocessing conducted mainly at the hospital side is light (within 0.3 s and 50 KB), which confirms that MediSC is amiable for resource constrained devices.

Comparison with Prior Art. We compare MediSC's performance with notable prior secure NN inference works in Table 4 to demonstrate MediSC's performance efficiency. MediSC requires the least network resources among all other prior works with up to 413× bandwidth saving for MNIST and up to 19× bandwidth saving for CIFAR-10. For the medical datasets, MediSC achieves at

Table 8. Performance breakdown of breast cancer.

Layers	Preprocess	FC1	BN1	ReLU1	FC2	BN2	ReLU2	FC3	BN3
Time (ms)	100	7	27	110	75	1.8	5.4	0.2	0.2
Comm. (KB)	3.13	1.84	0.062	0.49	1	0.0625	0.5	0.12	0.007

Table 9. Performance breakdown of diabetes.

Layers	Preprocess	FC1	ReLU1	FC2	ReLU2	FC3
Time (ms)	62.2	38.5	146.3	47.8	92.9	0.3
Comm. (KB)	18.94	2.50	2.00	16.00	16.00	0.50

Table 10. Performance breakdown of liver disease.

Layers	Preprocess	FC1	ReLU1	FC2	ReLU2	FC3
Time (ms)	34.8	6.1	102.4	4.1	47.3	0.2
Comm. (KB)	2.05	0.63	0.62	1.54	0.63	0.16

least 10× improvement over XONN, the notable prior work considering medical scenario.

For the SOTA - Delphi [28] (all ReLU version for keeping accuracy), it consumes overall 5100MB while MediSC only needs 489MB, with a 10× improvement[4]. Such significant improvement stems from the fact that MediSC only involves lightweight secret sharing based secure computation through out the whole service procedure, while Delphi involves the use of heavy homomorphic encryption and garbled circuits. Regarding the overall runtime, we note that it is not fair to make a direct comparison with results reported in [28] as Delphi is implemented in a different programming language (Rust) with significant optimizations and acceleration from GPU computing. Our performance results are not based on such optimizations.

It is worth noting that secure evaluation of non-linear layers is the *performance bottleneck* in secure neural network inference [28]. For evaluation of the original ReLU function, Delphi adopts a GC-based approach. Note that we have provided above in Fig. 6 a (fair) comparison between our design and the GC-based approach, which has demonstrated a significant performance boost of our design over the GC-based approach (24× in runtime and 868× in communication). On another hand, even when a direct (unfair) comparison is made with their reported runtime driven by aforementioned significantly *optimized* and *sophisticated* implementations, the overall runtime of MediSC with much simplified implementations is still comparable (147 s in MediSC against 140 s in Delphi).

---

[4] Preprocessing: 243MB in MediSC and 4915MB in Delphi.

Table 11. Performance breakdown of thyroid.

Layers	Preprocess	FC1	BN1	ReLU1	FC2	BN2	ReLU2	FC3	BN3
Time (ms)	287.2	46.1	21.7	248.8	28.0	21.1	262.8	27.3	0.3
Comm. (KB)	49.23	8.20	0.39	3.13	39.06	0.39	3.13	1.17	0.01

Performance Breakdown. The breakdown of time and bandwidth costs of the preprocessing and each layer during online inference are given in this section. Table 5 and Table 6 report the performance breakdown of M1, M2 for MNIST. Table 7 reports the performance breakdown of C1 for CIFAR-10. Table 8, Table 9, Table 10 and Table 11 report the performance breakdown of Breast Cancer, Diabetes, Liver Disease, and Thyroid.

7   Conclusion

In this paper, we present MediSC, a secure and lightweight NN inference system towards secure intelligent medical diagnostic services. Our protocol fully resorts to the lightweight additive secret sharing techniques, free of heavy cryptographic operations as seen in prior art. The commonly-used non-linear ReLU and max pooling layer functions are well supported in a secure and efficient manner. With MediSC, the privacy of the medical record of the hospital and the NN model of the medical service is provably ensured with practical performance.

Acknowledgment. This work was supported in part by Australian Research Council (ARC) Discovery Projects (No. DP200103308, No. DP180103251, and No. DP190102835), ARC Linkage Project (No. LP160101766), and HITSZ Start-up Research Grant (No. BA45001023).

A   Further Implementation Details

A.1   More Details of Implementation Setting

MediSC is implemented in Java. Recall that MediSC's secure NN inference protocol is computed in the secret sharing domain over ring $\mathbb{Z}_{2^\ell}$, i.e., all real-valued model weights are converted into ℓ-bit signed fixed-point integers and secretly shared in $\mathbb{Z}_{2^\ell}$. In MediSC, we follow the state-of-the-art work [28] to choose the ring size as $\mathbb{Z}_{2^{32}}$, a 32-bit ring by the modulus 4294967296. To represent the signed integers, we split the ring into two halves, where the lower-half ring $[0, 2^{31} - 1]$ represents the non-negative values and the upper-half ring $[2^{31}, 2^{32} - 1]$ represents the negative values. In this way, both the sign and the secret value is well protected. Besides, to convert the real-valued model weights to 32-bit fixed-point integers, we scale and quantize the weight with a scaling factor s to represent the bit length of the fractional part. For M1, M2, and C1, the factor is set as 1024, 128, and 64, respectively. For all medical datasets, the factor is set as 1024.

Multiplication over two fixed-point integers can overflow the capacity of the ring $\mathbb{Z}_{2^{\ell}}$, since the fractional part is increased to $2s$ bits in the resulting product. To assure the correctness, all intermediate results after multiplying over two shares should be rescaled down by 2^s before subsequent operation. We follow prior works [28, 32] to adopt a secure local truncation scheme proposed in the work [29], which simply discard the last s fractional bits to adjust the product to ℓ bits.

A.2   Training Details

We provide in Table 12 the detailed setting of training over plaintext datasets. Recall that we train the models M1 and M2 on MNIST, the model C1 on CIFAR-10, and the models over four publicly available medical datasets: Breast Cancer [1], Diabetes [2], Liver Disease [3] and Thyroid Disease [4]. Our training procedure is executed on NVIDIA Tesla V100 GPU with PyTorch backend. We adopt the SGD for M1, M2, C1, and Breast Cancer, and Adam optimizer for Diabetes, Liver Disease, and Thyriod. They are with adaptive learning rate with cosine learning rate decay every 50 epoches. For all datasets, all image pixels and the medical features are normalized to integers in $[0, 255]$. In this way, the hospital's inputs do not need to be preprocessed in our secure NN inference protocol.

Table 12. Summary of training settings.

Learning rate	Weight decay	Momentum	Optimizer	Epoch	Batch size
MNIST (M1, M2)					
1×10^{-3}	5×10^{-4}	0.9	SGD	600	128
CIFAR-10 (C1)					
1×10^{-3}	5×10^{-4}	0.9	SGD	000	128
Breast cancer					
1×10^{-3}	5×10^{-4}	0.9	SGD	9000	453
Diabetes					
1×10^{-5}	–	–	Adam	50000	615
Liver disease					
1×10^{-4}	–	–	Adam	50000	467
Thyroid					
1×10^{-5}	–	–	Adam	30000	3772

A.3   More Details of Model Architecture

In this section, we present the detailed model architectures used in our paper. The models M1 and M2 are trained on MNIST. In general, M1 is a Multi-Layer Perception consisting of 3 fully connected (FC) layers with ReLU activation, which has been used in prior works [15,19,22,30,31]. The architecture of M1 is summarized in Table 13. As shown in Table 14, M2 comprises 3 convolutional (CONV) layers with ReLU, 2 average pooling (AP) layers and an FC layer, which has been adopted in prior works [19,22,27,30]. For CIFAR-10, the model C1 (minionn network) consists of 7 CONV layers with ReLU, 2 AP layers and an FC layer as shown in Table 15. Is has been adopted in prior works [19,22,27, 30,31] for a benchmarking evaluation. Table 16, Table 17, and Table 18 report the architectures of the models on Breast Cancer, Diabetes, and Liver Disease, respectively. They have been adopted in prior work [30]. Table 19 reports the model architecture evaluating on Thyroid disease.

Table 13. Model architecture of M1.

Layers	Padding	Stride
FC (input: 784, output: 128)+ ReLU	–	–
FC (input: 128, output: 128)+ ReLU	–	–
FC (input: 128, output: 10)	–	–

Table 14. Model architecture of M2.

Layers	Padding	Stride
CONV (input: 1 × 28 × 28, kernel: 1 × 16 × 5 × 5 feature: 16 × 24 × 24) + ReLU	–	1
AP (input: 16 × 24 × 24, window: 16 × 2 × 2 output: 16 × 12 × 12)	–	2
CONV (input: 16 × 12 × 12, kernel: 16 × 16 × 5 × 5 feature: 16 × 8 × 8) + ReLU	–	1
AP (input: 16 × 8 × 8, window: 16 × 2 × 2 output: 16 × 4 × 4)	–	2
FC (input: 256, output: 100) + ReLU	–	–
FC (input: 100, output: 10)	–	–

Table 15. Model architecture of C1.

Layers	Padding	Stride
CONV (input: 3 × 32 × 32, kernel: 3 × 64 × 3 × 3 feature: 64 × 30 × 30) + ReLU	0	1
CONV (input: 64 × 32 × 32, kernel: 64 × 64 × 3 × 3 feature: 64 × 32 × 23) + ReLU	0	1
AP (input: 64 × 32 × 32, window: 64 × 2 × 2 output: 64 × 16 × 16)	–	2
CONV (input: 64 × 16 × 16, kernel: 64 × 64 × 3 × 3 feature: 64 × 16 × 16) + ReLU	0	1
CONV (input: 64 × 16 × 16, kernel: 64 × 64 × 3 × 3 feature: 64 × 16 × 16) + ReLU	0	1
AP (input: 64 × 16 × 16, window: 64 × 2 × 2 output: 64 × 8 × 8)	–	2
CONV (input: 64 × 8 × 8, kernel: 64 × 64 × 3 × 3 feature: 64 × 8 × 8) + ReLU	0	1
CONV (input: 64 × 8 × 8, kernel: 64 × 64 × 3 × 3 feature: 64 × 8 × 8) + ReLU	0	1
CONV (input: 64 × 8 × 8, kernel: 16 × 64 × 3 × 3 feature: 16 × 8 × 8) + ReLU	0	1
FC (input: 1024, output: 10)	–	–

Table 16. Model architecture of breast cancer.

Layers	Padding	Stride
FC (input: 30, output: 16) + BN + ReLU	–	–
FC (input: 16, output: 16) + BN + ReLU	–	–
FC (input: 16, output: 2) + BN	–	–

Table 17. Model architecture of diabetes.

Layers	Padding	Stride
FC (input: 8, output: 20) + ReLU	–	–
FC (input: 20, output: 20) + ReLU	–	–
FC (input: 20, output: 2)	–	–

Table 18. Model architecture of liver disease.

Layers	Padding	Stride
FC (input: 10, output: 32) + ReLU	–	–
FC (input: 32, output: 32) + ReLU	–	–
FC (input: 32, output: 2)	–	–

Table 19. Model architecture of thyroid.

Layers	Padding	Stride
FC (input: 21, output: 100) + BN + ReLU	–	–
FC (input: 100, output: 100) + BN + ReLU	–	–
FC (input: 100, output: 3) + BN	–	–

References

1. Breast cancer. https://www.kaggle.com/uciml/breast-cancer-wisconsin-data/
2. Diabetes. https://www.kaggle.com/uciml/pima-indians-diabetes-database
3. Liver disease. https://www.kaggle.com/uciml/indian-liver-patient-records
4. Thyroid. https://archive.ics.uci.edu/ml/datasets/Thyroid+Disease
5. Google DeepMind Health (2020). https://deepmind.com/blog/announcements/deepmind-health-joins-google-health
6. Microsoft Project InnerEye (2020). https://www.microsoft.com/en-us/research/project/medical-image-analysis/
7. PathAI (2020). https://www.pathai.com/
8. 104th United States Congress: Health Insurance Portability and Accountability Act of 1996 (HIPPA) (1996). https://www.hhs.gov/hipaa/index.html
9. Atallah, M., Bykova, M., Li, J., Frikken, K., Topkara, M.: Private collaborative forecasting and benchmarking. In: Proceedings of WPES (2004)

10. Barni, M., Failla, P., Lazzeretti, R., Sadeghi, A.R., Schneider, T.: Privacy-preserving ECG classification with branching programs and neural networks. IEEE Trans. Inf. Forensics Secur. **6**, 452–468 (2011)
11. Beaver, D.: Efficient multiparty protocols using circuit randomization. In: Feigenbaum, J. (ed.) CRYPTO 1991. LNCS, vol. 576, pp. 420–432. Springer, Heidelberg (1992). https://doi.org/10.1007/3-540-46766-1_34
12. Brutzkus, A., Gilad-Bachrach, R., Elisha, O.: Low latency privacy preserving inference. In: Proceedings of ICML, pp. 812–821. PMLR (2019)
13. European Parliament and the Council: The General Data Protection Regulation (GDPR) (2016). http://data.europa.eu/eli/reg/2016/679/2016-05-04
14. Fredrikson, M., Jha, S., Ristenpart, T.: Model inversion attacks that exploit confidence information and basic countermeasures. In: Proceedings of ACM CCS (2015)
15. Gilad-Bachrach, R., Dowlin, N., Laine, K., Lauter, K., Naehrig, M., Wernsing, J.: CryptoNets: applying neural networks to encrypted data with high throughput and accuracy. In: Proceedings of ICML (2016)
16. Goldreich, O., Micali, S., Wigderson, A.: How to play ANY mental game or a completeness theorem for protocols with honest majority. In: Proceedings of STOC (1987)
17. Harris, D.: A taxonomy of parallel prefix networks. In: The Thrity-Seventh Asilomar Conference on Signals, Systems & Computers 2003, vol. 2, pp. 2213–2217. IEEE (2003)
18. Jacobi, A., Chung, M., Bernheim, A., Eber, C.: Portable chest X-ray in coronavirus disease-19 (COVID-19): a pictorial review. Clin. Imaging **64**, 35–42 (2020)
19. Juvekar, C., Vaikuntanathan, V., Chandrakasan, A.: GAZELLE: a low latency framework for secure neural network inference. In: Proceedings of 27th USENIX Security (2018)
20. Leshno, M., Lin, V.Y., Pinkus, A., Schocken, S.: Multilayer feedforward networks with a nonpolynomial activation function can approximate any function. Neural Netw. **6**(6), 861–867 (1993)
21. Li, S., et al.: FALCON: a Fourier transform based approach for fast and secure convolutional neural network predictions. In: Proceedings of IEEE/CVF CVPR (2020)
22. Liu, J., Juuti, M., Lu, Y., Asokan, N.: Oblivious neural network predictions via MiniONN transformations. In: Proceedings of ACM CCS (2017)
23. Liu, X., Wu, B., Yuan, X., Yi, X.: Leia: A lightweight cryptographic neural network inference system at the edge. IACR Cryptology ePrint Archive 2020, 463 (2020)
24. Liu, X., Yi, X.: Privacy-preserving collaborative medical time series analysis based on dynamic time warping. In: Sako, K., Schneider, S., Ryan, P.Y.A. (eds.) ESORICS 2019. LNCS, vol. 11736, pp. 439–460. Springer, Cham (2019). https://doi.org/10.1007/978-3-030-29962-0_21
25. Liu, X., Zheng, Y., Yi, X., Nepal, S.: Privacy-preserving collaborative analytics on medical time series data. IEEE Trans. Dependable Secur. Comput., 1 (2020). https://doi.org/10.1109/TDSC.2020.3035592
26. Lou, Q., Jiang, L.: SHE: a fast and accurate deep neural network for encrypted data. In: Proceedings of NeurIPS, pp. 10035–10043 (2019)
27. Lou, Q., Lu, W.j., Hong, C., Jiang, L.: FALCON: fast spectral inference on encrypted data. In: Proceedings of NeurIPS, pp. 2364–2374 (2020)
28. Mishra, P., Lehmkuhl, R., Srinivasan, A., Zheng, W., Popa, R.A.: Delphi: a cryptographic inference service for neural networks. In: USENIX Security Symposium (2020)

29. Mohassel, P., Zhang, Y.: SecureML: a system for scalable privacy-preserving machine learning. In: Proceedings of IEEE S&P (2017)
30. Riazi, M.S., Samragh, M., Chen, H., Laine, K., Lauter, K., Koushanfar, F.: XONN: XNOR-based oblivious deep neural network inference. In: Proceedings of 28th USENIX Security (2019)
31. Riazi, M.S., Weinert, C., Tkachenko, O., Songhori, E.M., Schneider, T., Koushanfar, F.: Chameleon: a hybrid secure computation framework for machine learning applications. In: Proceedings of AsiaCCS (2018)
32. Wagh, S., Gupta, D., Chandran, N.: SecureNN: 3-party secure computation for neural network training. In: Proceedings of PETS (2019)
33. Wang, X.: Flexsc (2018). https://github.com/wangxiao1254/FlexSC
34. Xie, P., Wu, B., Sun, G.: BAYHENN: combining Bayesian deep learning and homomorphic encryption for secure DNN inference. In: Proceedings of IJCAI, pp. 4831–4837 (2019)
35. Yu, L., Liu, L., Pu, C., Gursoy, M.E., Truex, S.: Differentially private model publishing for deep learning. In: Proceedings of S&P. IEEE (2019)
36. Zhang, Q., Wang, C., Wu, H., Xin, C., Phuong, T.V.: GELU-Net: a globally encrypted, locally unencrypted deep neural network for privacy-preserved learning. In: Proceedings of IJCAI, pp. 3933–3939 (2018)
37. Zheng, Y., Duan, H., Wang, C.: Towards secure and efficient outsourcing of machine learning classification. In: Sako, K., Schneider, S., Ryan, P.Y.A. (eds.) ESORICS 2019. LNCS, vol. 11735, pp. 22–40. Springer, Cham (2019). https://doi.org/10.1007/978-3-030-29959-0_2

TAFA: A Task-Agnostic Fingerprinting Algorithm for Neural Networks

Xudong Pan, Mi Zhang$^{(\boxtimes)}$, Yifan Lu, and Min Yang$^{(\boxtimes)}$

Fudan University, Shanghai, China
{xdpan18,mi_zhang,luyf17,m_yang}@fudan.edu.cn

Abstract. Well-trained deep neural networks (DNN) are an indispensable part of the intellectual property of the model owner. However, the confidentiality of models are threatened by *model piracy*, which steals a DNN and obfuscates the pirated model with post-processing techniques. To counter model piracy, recent works propose several model fingerprinting methods, which are commonly based on a special set of adversarial examples of the owner's classifier as the fingerprints, and verify whether a suspect model is pirated based on whether the predictions on the fingerprints from the suspect model and from the owner's model match with one another. However, existing fingerprinting schemes are limited to models for classification and usually require access to the training data. In this paper, we propose the first **T**ask-**A**gnostic **F**ingerprinting **A**lgorithm (TAFA) for the broad family of neural networks with rectified linear units. Compared with existing adversarial example-based fingerprinting algorithms, TAFA enables model fingerprinting for DNNs on a variety of downstream tasks including but not limited to classification, regression and generative modeling, with no assumption on training data access. Extensive experimental results on three typical scenarios strongly validate the effectiveness and the robustness of TAFA.

Keywords: Fingerprinting · Intellectual property · Deep learning

1 Introduction

The past decade witnesses the boom of deep learning in a number of typical intelligent tasks related to computer vision [1] and natural language processing [2], which lays the ground for the wide use of deep learning models in various safety-/security-critical application domains including traffic [3], finance [4], healthcare [5] and many more. In recent years, to obtain more performant and generalizable deep learning models, IT corporations are devoting increasingly more computing power and private data resources to the training process of deep neural networks (DNN), which usually contain billions of trainable parameters, with the training process lasting for weeks even on a cluster of high-demanding computing devices [2]. Widely recognized as an important intellectual property (IP) of the model owner, a well-trained neural network needs to be safeguarded against potential model piracy or improper model redistribution [3,6,7].

© Springer Nature Switzerland AG 2021
E. Bertino et al. (Eds.): ESORICS 2021, LNCS 12972, pp. 542–562, 2021.
https://doi.org/10.1007/978-3-030-88418-5_26

In face of the urgent call on protecting the IP of DNN, *model watermarking* [8] and *model fingerprinting* [9] are two major developing techniques against model piracy. Following the general scheme of digital watermarking [10], the model owner who adopts model watermarking techniques would in prior embed secrets into a released version of his/her owned original model (i.e., the *target* model). If one claims the ownership of a DNN model (i.e., the *suspect model*), the ownership of the suspect model can be verified by a trusted third party based on the consistency between the secrets provided by the claimer and the secrets encoded in the suspect model. A number of recent works on model watermarking explore various types of secrets to be embedded into different parts of a DNN (e.g., [7,8,11]). However, as existing watermarking techniques require to modify the original parameters of a well-trained DNN to embed the watermark, the accuracy of the DNN model would be slightly impacted, which is usually unacceptable for safety-/security-critical tasks in, e.g., finance and healthcare [9].

As a complement to model watermarking, model fingerprinting aims at determining whether the suspect model is pirated from the target model, which intuitively works by testing whether fingerprints of the target model are also present in the suspect one. Different from the embedded secrets used in watermarking, fingerprints are designed as innate properties of the target model, instead of being manually embedded into the model. As a result, no modifications are conducted on the original model, which provably preserves the functionality of the original model, a highly desiring characteristic for critical scenarios. Still in its infancy, existing model fingerprinting schemes focus on fingerprinting DNN classifiers and mostly consider the usage of a special set of *adversarial examples* [12], i.e., samples with human-imperceptible perturbations which cause misclassification of the target classifier, as its fingerprints [9,13,14]. However, their heavy dependence on adversarial examples may cause the following limitations in practical usages:

- *Limited to Classification Settings.* Existing methods frequently leverage notions like adversarial example and decision boundary, which are almost exclusively defined for classification settings. As a result, most existing fingerprinting algorithms could hardly be applied to DNNs for other downstream tasks except for classification, which excludes many important application scenarios.
- *Dependence on Training Data.* Besides, existing fingerprinting algorithms usually require access to the training data to produce suitable adversarial examples as fingerprints. However, such an assumption can hardly be realistic especially when the model owner is not allowed or is unwilling to share the training data as it may contain highly sensitive personal information or be curated with huge manual costs.

As the distribution and redistribution of various types of DNNs become a rather common practice in nowadays deep learning ecosystem (e.g., Torch Hub [15] and Amazon AWS [16]), how to audit and verify the improper reuse of DNNs in more general scenarios is an urging open challenge to address.

Our Work. In this paper, we propose the first **T**ask-**A**gnostic **F**ingerprinting **A**lgorithm (TAFA) which leverages innate properties of a DNN with rectified linear units (ReLU) to construct and verify fingerprints. Compared with existing adversarial example-based fingerprinting methods, TAFA substantially extends the capability of model fingerprinting to a much wider range of DNNs for different downstream tasks. As widely recognized, ReLU is probably the most popular activation function used in modern deep learning due to its good numeric properties [17], and arouses increasing interests in our community to demonstrate novel attack and defense insights on this model family (e.g., [18–20]).

By design, TAFA is expected to be both *independent from the downstream tasks and from the training data*. To be task-agnostic, we propose to construct and verify fingerprints by exploiting the *piecewise linear* property of a DNN with ReLU [21], an innate property to a DNN wherever ReLU is applied. Intuitively, the piecewise linear property states, the input space of a DNN with ReLU can be divided into pieces of *linear regions* (Fig. 1(a)), where the DNN behaves as a linear function when the input is constrained to one of the regions. As observed by [22], the arrangement of linear regions of a DNN can be rather divergent even when the DNN is trained on the same dataset but with different weight initialization. Inspired from this observed uniqueness of linear region arrangements, we suggest to determine whether a suspect model is stolen from the target model by verifying the similarity in the linear region arrangements formed by the *first* ReLU layer, which is expected to exhibit by-design robustness even when the stolen model has been fine-tuned or retrained as long as the parameters in the first layer are not intensively modified.

However, the direct comparison of linear region arrangement is challenging. As one major technical contribution of our work, we alternatively propose a novel linear programming-based fingerprint extraction algorithm to construct special pairs of samples (i.e., *fingerprinting pairs*) for the target model such that, any two of samples in a pair lie in the same linear region formed by the first ReLU layer. Intuitively, when a suspect model is unrelated with the target model, the samples in the same fingerprinting pair have almost no chance to coincide in the same linear region, while, for a pirated model post-processed from the target one, the samples are very likely to be preserved in the same region unless the post-processing hugely modifies the linear region arrangement. Moreover, as the generation process of fingerprinting samples starts from random points in the input space, TAFA is by design independent from the training data.

Under both *white-box* and *black-box* access to the suspect model, we propose the accompanying fingerprint verification algorithms which report the confidence score of a suspect model's being pirated from the target model. In general, the verification algorithms work by estimating whether samples in one constructed fingerprinting pair indeed lie in the same linear region of the suspect model. Specifically, in the white-box setting, we verify the similarity of the *activation pattern* of samples in the same fingerprinting pair at the first ReLU layer, which is one-to-one correspondent to the linear region and has the form of a binary vector where each bit denotes the activation/deactivation of the corresponding neuron.

In the black-box setting, we are inspired by a recent technique in [20] which exactly calculates the number of intersection points of a linear segment with the boundary hyperplanes when the suspect model is queried as a prediction API only. We simplify this previous technique to implement our black-box verification algorithm, which determines whether the line segment between samples in a fingerprinting pair has no intersection point with the boundary by comparing the local gradients to the samples in a fingerprinting pair.

In summary, we mainly make the following contributions:

- We propose TAFA, the first task-agnostic fingerprinting algorithm with no assumptions on training data access. Compared with existing fingerprinting algorithms, TAFA substantially extends the capability of model fingerprinting to a much wider range of DNN models for different downstream tasks including classification, regression and generative modeling.
- As a major technical contribution, we propose a linear programming-based algorithm to efficiently generate pairs of samples lying in the same linear regions to form the fingerprinting pairs (Sect. 3.3). Correspondingly, we propose verification schemes to determine the presence of the fingerprint under both white-box and black-box accesses to the suspect model (Sect. 3.4).
- We validate the effectiveness and the hyperparameter sensitivity of TAFA on three practical scenarios, namely, skin cancer diagnosis, warfarin dose prediction and fashion generation (Sect. 4), which correspond to classification, regression and generative modeling tasks respectively. For example, in fingerprinting a ResNet-18 trained for skin cancer diagnosis [5], TAFA outperforms the state-of-the-art model fingerprinting algorithm IPGuard [9] by about 20% in terms of ARUC (Sect. 5).

2   Deep Neural Networks with Rectified Linear Units

Notations. Formally, a $(H+1)$-layer deep neural network (DNN) $F(\cdot; \Theta) : \mathcal{X} \to \mathcal{Y}$ can be written as a chain of mappings (i.e., layers) applied to the data input x: $F(x; \Theta) := f_H \circ \sigma_H \circ f_{H-1} \circ \ldots f_1 \circ \sigma_1 \circ f_0(x)$, where $f_i : \mathbb{R}^{d_i} \to \mathbb{R}^{d_{i+1}}$ is called the i-th layer of the DNN model, with d_0 (d_{H+1}) the input (output) dimension. Here, $\sigma_i : \mathbb{R}^{d_i} \to \mathbb{R}^{d_{i+1}}$ is the activation function at the i-th layer. For convenience, we denote the first i layers as F_i, i.e., $F_i := f_i \circ \ldots f_1 \circ \sigma_1 \circ f_0$. The above formulation covers a wide range of neural networks applied in real-world scenarios, including a variety of learning tasks such as classification, regression and generative modeling [23]. Appendix A presents more background information.

Activation Function. In modern deep learning practices, rectified linear unit (ReLU [23,24]) is probably the most common choice of an activation function, which is defined as $\sigma_{\mathrm{ReLU}}(x) = \begin{cases} x & \text{if } x \geq 0 \\ 0 & \text{if } x < 0 \end{cases}$. Intuitively, a ReLU can be viewed as a gate structure which allows nonnegative inputs to pass forward to the next layer without modifications while it blocks the negative inputs by setting it as 0. When we apply σ_{ReLU} to a vector, the ReLU function is applied in an elementwise manner. From fully-connected neural networks and shallow convolutional neural networks (CNN) to deep CNN like GoogLeNet [25] and ResNet [1], a very broad class of popular neural network architectures is now implemented with ReLU. Due to the wide application of DNNs with ReLU in practice, our current work mainly targets at fingerprinting DNN models with ReLUs, i.e., $\sigma_i \equiv \sigma_{\text{ReLU}}$ for $i = 1, 2, \ldots, H$. In the rest of this paper, we abbreviate σ_{ReLU} as σ for simplicity.

Layer Architecture. In a wide range of learning tasks, a fully-connected layer and a *convolutional layer* are commonly implemented as the first layer of a fully-connected neural network (FCN) and a convolutional neural network (CNN). For a self-contained introduction to the formulation of a fully-connected layer and a convolutional layer, please refer to Appendix A.

– *Fully-Connected Layer (Def. A1):* A fully-connected layer is a key module of fully-connected neural networks (FCN), which is a common choice for learning tasks where the input are flat feature vectors from the dataset itself (e.g., the demographic feature of a patient can be viewed as a flat feature vector where each element represents attributes like gender, age and blood type) or from an upstream feature extraction module as in transfer learning [26].
– *Convolutional Layer (Def. A2):* A convolutional layer is ubiquitous in most commercial deep convolutional neural networks (CNN) including the well-known VGGNet [27], ResNet [1] and GoogLeNet [19]. These CNNs are especially suitable for handling visual data inputs, applicable to popular learning tasks like image classification and image generation. Mathematically, a convolutional layer can also be viewed as a special form of a fully-connected layer (i.e., as a matrix-vector multiplication), if one vectorizes the input and converts correspondingly the filters into a matrix form [28]. In Sect. 3.3, without loss of generality, we mainly describe our methodology with respect to a DNN model which implements a fully-connected layer as its first layer.

Activation Pattern and Linear Region Arrangement. Activation pattern and linear region arrangement are two sides of the gate-like behavior of ReLU. Microscopically, when a data input is forwarded through a ReLU layer, each ReLU in the layer is activated or deactivated based on the sign of the input, which as a whole presents a binary pattern, i.e., the *activation pattern*, formally written as $A_i(x; \Theta) = \mathcal{I}[F_i(x; \Theta) \succeq 0] \in \{0, 1\}^{d_i}$. Macroscopically, if we group data inputs with the same activation pattern into subsets, the total input space is divided into a number of regions which are disjoint yet adjacent to one another (Fig. 1). For an arbitrary region, the complicated DNN degrades to a local linear function, which is called the *piecewise linear* property of ReLU. The piece linear property of ReLU has aroused wide theoretical researches [21,22,29]. For example, [22] interestingly observed that the configuration of linear regions (i.e., *linear region arrangement*) are mostly unique to a neural network.

3   Task-Agnostic Fingerprinting Algorithm

3.1   Security Settings of Model Fingerprinting

Threat Model. A model fingerprinting task is a security game between two parties, namely a *defender* and an *attacker*. Prior to the game, a model owner trains its own DNN model F for a certain downstream task, costing a considerable amount of computing power or utilizing a private training dataset. In these cases, the trained model F is reasonably viewed as the IP of the model owner. Following the nomenclature in [9], we refer to the model F as the *target model*. In the ecosystem of machine-learning-as-a-service (MLaaS), the model owner can deploy the target model at a third-party platform (e.g., Amazon AWS [16]) to gain monetary profits by answering queries. However, such potential profits may also tempt an attacker to pirate the target model via, e.g., software/hardware vulnerabilities and social engineering, and deploy the pirated model as its own MLaaS for profiting, which essentially infringes the IP of the model owner.

In general, model fingerprinting is a scheme adopted by the defender to verify whether a suspect model $\tilde{F}$ is pirated from the target model F or not. When a suspect model is indeed pirated from the target model, an attacker may apply a number of model post-processing techniques to obfuscate the ownership of the pirated model, producing a so-called *positive suspect model*. In our current work, following [3], we assume an attacker may apply pruning, fine-tuning or retraining for ownership obfuscation, with the details introduced later. Otherwise, if a suspect model is not a post-processed version of the target model but is independently trained from scratch by another honest model owner, it is called a *negative suspect model*. Following the threat model in [9], we assume the defender has a white-box access to the target model, which is reasonable when the defender is the model owner itself or a trusted third party, and has either white-box or black-box (i.e., via a prediction oracle) access to the suspect model.

Typically, a model fingerprinting scheme consists of a *fingerprint extraction* phase and a *verification* phase: 1) In a fingerprint extraction phase, a *fingerprint* which is expected be to be unique to the target model and robust against adversarial post-processing techniques, is extracted from the target model F. 2) In a verification phase, the model owner attests the suspect model with either a white-box or a black-box access to determine whether and with what confidence the fingerprint is also present in the suspect model $\tilde{F}$.

Existing Fingerprinting Schemes and Their Limitations. As an emerging research topic, the development of model fingerprinting is still in its infancy. To the best of our knowledge, existing schemes are all designed for fingerprinting DNN classifiers [9,13,14,30,31]. These schemes are commonly based on constructing *adversarial examples* [12] for the target classifier as its fingerprint. Intuitively, one constructs an adversarial example by adding humanly imperceptible perturbations which cause the target model to misclassify the adversarial example into an incorrect class, while the major difference of existing fingerprinting schemes lie in their diverse requirements on the constructed adversarial examples. Section 6 presents a more detailed survey on existing model finger-printing algorithms.

Despite the novelty of previous works in designing different types of adversarial examples as fingerprints, the dependence on adversarial examples also brings the following limitations which may inhibit their practical usages: 1) The notion adversarial example is only defined for classification tasks. This inherently limits the applicability of existing fingerprinting schemes to DNNs for other typical learning tasks like regression and generation, which however represent a non-trivial proportion of practical usages of DNNs in the wild. 2) Adversarial examples are by definition generated from clean data samples, which to some degree eliminates the existence of a third-party to provide model fingerprinting service, especially for data-sensitive scenarios. Although [9] also tried to generate samples near the decision boundary from randomly initialized samples, they however find the decision boundary close to random points is less unique than that close to training data points. From our perspective, to design a task-agnostic data-free model fingerprinting would be ideal to enable an authorized third-party to protect the IP of learning models in future deep learning ecosystem.

Post-Processing Techniques for Model Piracy. In the security game of model fingerprinting, instead of using the pirated target model as it is, the adversary may apply a variety of model post-processing techniques to prevent the pirated model from being detected. In this paper, we mainly consider the following set of post-processing techniques.

- *Pruning*: Pruning is a conventional model compression technique which removes a certain proportion of less significant weights [32] or filters [33] in a DNN. For example, Han et al. proposed to mask out a specified proportion of weights of the smallest absolute value from the DNN and retrain the masked model to preserve the utility on the learning task [32].
- *Fine-Tuning*: To fine-tune the last K layers of an H-layer DNN which is already trained, the parameters of the first $H - K$ layers are fixed, while the parameters of the last K layers are further updated by optimizing the learning objective on the training data.
- *Retraining*: Different from fine-tuning, to retrain the last K layers of an H-layer DNN, the learned parameters of the last layer are first reset and randomly initialized. Then the last K layers are updated by fitting the training data, with the first $H - K$ layers frozen.

As the first step towards a task-agnostic fingerprinting scheme, TAFA in our current work is designed to fight against model piracy techniques which do not modify the architecture of the target model. We admit it may leave the cases where the adversary conducts model extraction [18] with a surrogate model of a different architecture uncovered. Considering a number of recent research efforts in defending against model extraction (e.g., [34]), we focus on model fingerprinting under the same threat model as in [9] where the adversary has successfully stolen the target model as a whole via, e.g., system attacks or social engineering, and leverages the above model post-processing techniques for obfuscation.

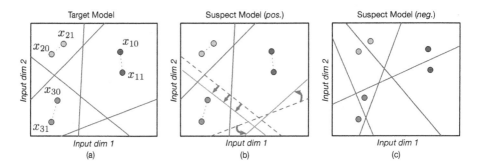

Fig. 1. The arrangement of linear regions formed by the first ReLU layer of (a) the target model, (b) the positive suspect model and (c) the negative suspect model, where the solid lines represent the boundary hyperplanes and the pairs of filled circles of the same color represent the fingerprinting pairs generated by TAFA.

3.2   Overview of TAFA

Compared with existing fingerprinting schemes via adversarial examples, we devise our fingerprinting scheme TAFA based on the linear region arrangement formed by ReLU layers of the target DNN. Ideally, when a fingerprint scheme is based on the linear regions, it is by design independent from the specific task where a DNN is applied, and is naturally robust against fine-tuning-based or retraining-based post-processing techniques especially when the fine-tuning and retraining do not intensively modify the parameters in the layers for deriving the fingerprint. Instantiating the generic fingerprinting scheme in Sect. 3.1, we provide below an overview on the key procedures of TAFA.

1. **Fingerprint Extraction of TAFA:** The model fingerprint used in TAFA consists of N pairs of samples $\{(x_{i0}, x_{i1})\}_{i=1}^{N}$ (i.e., *fingerprinting pairs*) which share the same activation pattern at the first ReLU layer. As Fig. 1 illustrates, behind our design of this fingerprint is the rationale that the target model should share a similar arrangement of linear regions with the target model, while the arrangement of linear regions of negative suspect models, usually initialized with random weights and trained independently from scratch, should be almost unrelated with that of the target model [22], which ensures the uniqueness of the constructed fingerprint. However, to exactly parametrize the linear regions is almost intractable due to a variety of permutation/scaling isomorphisms present in the activation region arrangement [20]. As an alternative, we use a pair of samples sharing the activation pattern to represent the linear region where they belong. In the extraction phase, a key technique is a primitive to generate samples which hold the same activation pattern at the first ReLU layer (Fig. 1(a)).

2. **Fingerprint Verification of TAFA:** To verify whether the arrangement of linear regions are preserved or highly similar between the target model and a suspect model, our verification algorithms generally check whether the samples (x_{i0}, x_{i1}) constructed in the same linear region of the target model still stays in the same region of the suspect model. By design, the verification is: 1) unique

for the target model and its pirated version, as for each of the N fingerprinting pairs, a negative suspect model has almost no chance to have the two samples to be preserved in the same linear region (Fig. 1(c)) and 2) robust against slight perturbations on parameters, as the arrangement of linear regions is relatively stable to small changes in the boundary hyperplanes. As Fig. 1(b) shows, a small translation or rotation transformation on the boundary hyperplane is not likely nullify the validity of the verification condition, especially when the constructed samples lie in the center of the linear region. Intuitively, when a third-party authority is allowed to interfere the fingerprinting procedure and ask the owner of the suspect model to provide an additional oracle to reveal the activation pattern at the first ReLU layer for the fingerprints (i.e., *a white-box setting*), the verification can be straightforward by comparing the revealed activation patterns, which we briefly introduce in the first part of Sect. 3.4 as an appetizer. Interestingly, we suggest an even more robust verification scheme could be devised when the model owner only has access to the suspect model via its prediction oracle (i.e., *a black-box setting*). Our black-box verification is mainly based on strategically querying the prediction oracle multiple times for numerically determining the identity of the linear region where the samples belong, as we introduce in the second part of Sect. 3.4.

3.3   Fingerprint Extraction

We detail how to construct a fingerprinting pair where the samples share the same activation pattern at the first ReLU layer of a DNN $F(\cdot; \Theta)$. Given a random seed x_0 (i.e., by sampling a random point from $\mathcal{X}$) with its first activation pattern $\hat{A} := A_1(x_0; \Theta)$, we consider the following optimization problem,

$$\max_{\Delta} \|\Delta\|_1, \text{ s.t., } A_1(x_0 + \Delta; \Theta) = \hat{A}; x_0 + \Delta \in \mathcal{X}, \tag{1}$$

where the first constraint in Eq. (1) means we need to find a perturbation Δ which preserves the activation pattern of x_0 and the second constraint requires the perturbed sample still lies in the problem space $\mathcal{X}$. In the optimization objective above, we expect the perturbation Δ is maximized so that the generated fingerprint sample $x_1 := x_0 + \Delta$ can be sufficiently diverse to represent the linear region indexed by $\hat{A}$. However, the constraint $A_1(x_0 + \Delta; \Theta) = \hat{A}$ is combinatorial, which in general has no efficient solvers. Alternatively, we exploit the definition of A_1 in Sect. 2 to convert the constraint into the equivalent form:

$$(2\hat{A} - 1) \odot f_1(x_0 + \Delta; \theta) \succeq \epsilon I, \tag{2}$$

where the *margin* ϵ is a positive constant which controls the distance from the region boundary. Usually, a larger ϵ produces a fingerprint sample more distant from the boundary and therefore more robust (Sect. 5.2).

Finally, we show the optimization problem above can be reformulated as a standard linear programming (LP) problem, which is based on the following observations: (a) When the first layer of the target model is a fully-connected layer or a convolutional layer, the constraint in Inequality (2) is a set of linear inequality w.r.t. the elements in the perturbation Δ. (b) The problem space $\mathcal{X}$ can be usually written as a box constraint. For example, for image-related tasks, the normalized RGB values of each pixel of an image are constrained in $[-1, 1]$. (c) The current optimization objective $\|\Delta\|_1 = \sum_j |\Delta_j|$ can be converted into a linear form by introducing an additional variable Z_j for each Δ_j and adding a pair of constraints $Z_j \geq \Delta_j$ and $Z_j \geq -\Delta_j$ to replace the absolute value term $|\Delta_j|$. As a demonstration, we write the final form of the LP problem for the fully-connected layer on image-related tasks below.

$$\max_{\Delta} \sum_{j=1}^{d_1} Z_j, \text{ s.t., } \forall j = 1, ..., d_1, -Z_j \leq \Delta_j \leq Z_j, \tag{3}$$

$$(2\hat{A}_j - 1)(\langle W_0^j, X + \Delta \rangle + b_0^j) \geq \epsilon, \quad -1 \leq (x_0)_j + \Delta_j \leq 1. \tag{4}$$

Moreover, as a convolutional layer can be written as a sparse fully-connected layer, the corresponding LP problem can be analogously derived as above. In practice, LP problems in the standard form can be efficiently solved with mature black-box solvers such as Gurobi [35], which ensures the efficiency of the fingerprint extraction phase. Repeating the procedure above with N different seed samples $\{x_{i0}\}_{i=1}^N$ produces the full fingerprint for the target model.

3.4 Fingerprint Verification

In general, the verification stage determines whether a fingerprinting pair (x_{i0}, x_{i1}) of the target model is still in the same linear region of the suspect model. Given the generated samples and a white-box/black-box access to the suspect model, the verification routine should output a confidence score in $[0, 1]$ (or called the *matching rate* of the two models) to tell whether the suspect model is pirated from the target model or not. If the matching rate is over a certain threshold, the fingerprint algorithm will consider the suspect model is pirated. *(1) White-Box Verification:* In the white-box setting, the verification is straightforward because the verifier is allowed to obtain the ground-truth first activation pattern by querying the exposed interface A_1 of the suspect model to obtain the first activation patterns of the fingerprint samples. Provided with the set of the first activation patterns $(A_1(x_{i0}), A_1(x_{i1}))$, we leverage the *normalized Hamming distance* to derive the confidence score, which writes

$$\text{MR}_{\text{wb}} = 1 - \frac{1}{Nd_1} \sum_{i=1}^N \text{tr}(|A_1(x_{i0}) - A_1(x_{i1})|). \tag{5}$$

(2) Black-Box Verification: In the black-box setting, we are inspired by a primitive recently proposed in [20], which allows the calculation of the number of intersection points of a line segment $u(t) = x_0 + t(x_1 - x_0)$ with the boundary hyperplanes corresponding to the first ReLU layer, via only a black-box access to the prediction oracle of a model M. We denote the primitive as

$PointsOnLine(x_0, x_1, M) \in \mathbb{N}$. Specifically, once the line segment between an arbitrary pair of samples x_0 and x_1 has no intersection points with any region boundary, i.e., $PointsOnLine(x_0, x_1, M) = 0$, then x_0 and x_1 are in the same linear region. In our context, as the verifier is only curious about whether the samples are in the same linear region, we simplify the full implementation of the primitive $PointsOnLine(x_0, x_1, M)$ in [20] to checking whether the directional gradients local to the pair samples in a fingerprinting pair, i.e., x_0 and x_1, are identical to one another within a given numerical tolerance η, which formally writes $PointsOnLine(x_0, x_1, M) := \mathbf{1}\{|\|F(u(\delta)) - F(u(0))\| - \|F(u(1)) - F(u(1-\delta))\|| \geq \eta\delta\}$. Based on this simplified primitive, the matching rate is defined as

$$\mathrm{MR_{bb}} = \frac{1}{N} \sum_{i=1}^{N} \mathbf{1}\{PointsOnLine(x_{i0}, x_{i1}, M) = 0\}. \tag{6}$$

4   Evaluation Settings

• **Scenarios.** Table 1 provides an overview of the three scenarios covered in our evaluation. More details on the scenarios are provided in Appendix B.1.

Table 1. Datasets and tasks used in our experiments. (*The word in *italic* is used as the identifier for each scenario)

Task	Type	Dataset	Model
Skin Cancer Diagnosis	Classification	DermaMNIST [36]	ResNet-18 [1]
Warfarin Dose Prediction	Regression	IWPC Dataset [37]	FCN (31-100-1)
Fashion Generation	Generative Modeling	FashionMNIST [38]	FCN (64-128-256-512-768)

• **Construction of Suspect Models.** Following Cao et al. [9], we construct the positive suspect models with the following configurations of the three common model post-processing techniques which we introduce in Sect. 3.1.

(1) Fine-Tuning. We consider two types of fine-tuning configurations, i.e., fine-tuning the last layer (FTLL) and fine-tuning all layers (FTAL). An FTLL version of the target model only has its last layer to be fine-tuned for additional epochs on the training data, with the parameters in other layers fixed. As a contrast, all the layers of the target model are fine-tuned during an FTAL process.

(2) Retraining. Similarly, we consider two types of retraining configurations, i.e., retraining the last layer (RTLL) and retraining all layers (RTAL). The essential difference between RTLL/RTAL and FTLL/FTAL is whether the last one layer is first reset as a randomly initialized layer. We set the number of epochs for fine-tuning and retraining both as 10.

(3) Pruning. We consider two types of parameter pruning schemes, i.e., weight pruning (WP) [32] and filter pruning (FP) [33]. For weight pruning, we choose the ratio of pruned weights from 0.1 to 0.9 with a stride of 0.1. For filter pruning, we choose the ratio of pruned filters from $1/16$ to $15/16$ with a stride of $1/16$.

To construct the set of negative suspect models, we use different random seeds to initialize models of the same architecture as the target model. We then train the models from scratch on the same training set as the set of negative suspect models. In all the three scenarios, the number of negative suspect models is 20. Besides, as our current work focuses on detecting pirated models without modifications on the architecture, we do not construct and evaluate our fingerprint algorithm on positive/negative suspect models of different architectures. By default, our fingerprint algorithm considers suspect models of different architectures as negative. Figure 6 summarizes the performance of the target model, the positive and the negative suspect models on the primary learning tasks.

• **Metrics and Other Details.** Denoting the decision threshold as $\rho \in (0,1)$, we view a suspect model with its predicted matching rate higher than ρ as *positive* and otherwise as negative. In the evaluation, we follow the evaluation protocol in [9], which, namely, measures the following performance metrics:

(1) Robustness ($R(\rho)$). It measures the proportion of positive suspect models which are also verified as positive by the fingerprinting algorithm.
(2) Uniqueness ($U(\rho)$). It measures the proportion of negative suspect models which are also verified as negative by the fingerprinting algorithm.
(3) Area under the Robustness-Uniqueness Curves (ARUC). It measures the area of the intersecion region under the robustness and uniqueness when the threshold varies in $(0,1)$, i.e., ARUC $= \int_0^1 \min\{R(\rho), U(\rho)\}d\rho$, and is empirically calculated as the average $\min\{R(\rho), U(\rho)\}$ on $\{0, \frac{1}{L}, \ldots, \frac{L-1}{L}, 1\}$ with $L = 100$ as in [9]. For other detailed settings, we by default set the number of fingerprinting pairs, i.e., N, as 100 and the margin hyperparameter, i.e., ϵ in Inequality (2), as 0.1 for all the experiments below. Section 5.2 evaluates the sensitivity of TAFA with respect to the hyperparameters.

5   Evaluation Results

5.1   Effectiveness of TAFA

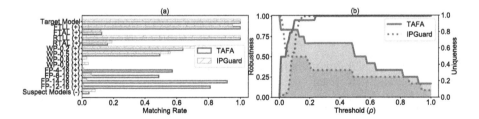

Fig. 2. Comparisons of (a) matching rates, (b) curves of robustness and uniqueness and the ARUC of TAFA and IPGuard on Skin.

Comparison with Baseline. In the first part, we compare the effectiveness of TAFA with the state-of-the-art model fingerprinting scheme IPGuard [9], which for the first time presents the idea of using a set of adversarial examples at the decision boundary of a classifier as fingerprints, with its general methodology adopted by a series of follow-up works [13,14,30]. As IPGuard does not release an official implementation, we implemented IPGuard according to the description in the original paper and validated the correctness of the implementation by reproducing the reported results on CIFAR-10 and CIFAR-100. As the highlight of TAFA is in enabling fingerprinting on DNNs for more general downstream tasks other than classification, we mainly view IPGuard as one representative baseline to measure the effectiveness of TAFA in fingerprinting DNN classifiers. We set the number of fingerprinting samples for IPGuard as 100. Figure 2 reports the matching rates for the positive and negative suspect models on Skin.

As we can see from Fig. 2(a), compared with IPGuard, TAFA on the one hand predicts much higher matching rates on positive suspect models post-processed by FTLL, RTLL and filter pruning. Especially on FTLL and RTLL, the pre-dicted matching rate from TAFA is 100%, which is because TAFA relies on the linear region arrangement of the first ReLU layer for fingerprinting and hence is inherently robust to FTLL and RTLL as long as the first layer is not modified. In the meanwhile, the usage of a fingerprinting pair in the same linear region ensures a stronger robustness of TAFA against filter pruning. It is mainly because when a redundant filter is pruned, the original linear arrangement is only modi-fied by the elimination of the boundary hyperplane corresponding to the pruned filter. Consequently, the samples mostly remain in the same linear region, which results in a high matching rate (uniformly over 50%). On the other hand, the utilization of the first ReLU layer for fingerprinting in TAFA does not sacrifice the uniqueness of the constructed fingerprints, which conforms to the finding in [22] that the arrangement of linear regions in two independently trained DNNs is highly unrelated. Compared with IPGuard, the average predicted matching rates of TAFA (i.e., the bottom bar of Fig. 2(a)) is lower than IPGuard by a non-trivial margin ($\sim$4%). To present a more intuitive comparison on the over-all performance of TAFA and IPGuard, Fig. 2(b) plots the robustness curve $R(\rho)$ and the uniqueness curve $U(\rho)$ when the threshold ranges from 0 to 1, where the shaded parts represent the ARUC. As we can see, both the robustness and the uniqueness curves are uniformly higher than those of IPGuard, resulting in a larger ARUC (i.e., $0.492 > 0.216$). Figure 4 further provides a more compre-hensive comparison of IPGuard and TAFA in terms of the ARUC metric.

Task-Agnostic Fingerprinting. As one of our major contributions, TAFA works independently from the downstream tasks where the target model is applied. Figure 3 reports the performance of TAFA on regression (i.e., Warfarin) and generative modeling (i.e., Fashion), when the suspect model is accessed as white-box (i.e., $w.b.$) and black-box (i.e., $b.b.$) for verification.

As we can see from Fig. 3, under both the white-box and the black-box set-tings, the predicted matching rates from TAFA remain high for positive suspect models post-processed with FTLL, RTLL or after pruning redundant weights by a ratio smaller than 0.5. For these post-processed models, the parameters at the first layer of the target model are only slightly modified, which ensures

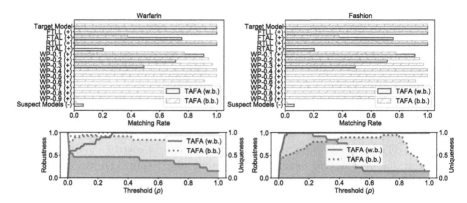

Fig. 3. Matching rates, curves of robustness and uniqueness and the ARUC of TAFA and IPGuard on Warfarin and Fashion when the suspect model is accessed as a white-box (i.e., $w.b.$) and a black-box (i.e., $b.b.$).

each fingerprinting pair is largely preserved in one linear region. Comparing the performance between white-box and black-box verification, we observe the white-box verification is advantageous in fingerprinting models post-processed with FTAL and RTAL (i.e., the parameters of all the layers are slightly updated), while the black-box verification is observed to be more robust against intensive model pruning (i.e., over 50% of weights are pruned). We infer the main reason as, the white-box verification verifies a suspect model to be positive if the activation pattern of samples in the same fingerprinting pair is identical, which is a more effective indicator compared with the approximated local gradient when the perturbation on parameters remains slight (Fig. 1(b)). However, when a large proportion of weights are pruned, the activation pattern for different samples in a pair may also change radically, which may weaken the white-box verification from verifying an intensively pruned target model. In contrast, the black-box verification is based on checking whether the local gradient at each sample in a pair is identical, a more intrinsic characterization on the linear region arrangement without referring to relatively transient features of the linear regions such as the activation pattern. In the meantime, compared with the white-box verification, the improvement in the robustness of the black-box verification has no clear trade-off with the uniqueness of verification.

5.2 Hyperparameter Sensitivity

We further evaluate the effectiveness of TAFA when the number of the generated fingerprinting pairs N and the margin ϵ in Inequality (2) are varied during the fingerprint extraction stage.

(1) Influence of Number of Fingerprinting Pairs N. On the three scenarios, we vary the number of generated fingerprint samples/pairs N from 10 to 100 with a stride of 10. Figure 4 reports the corresponding ARUC curves. From the

results on Skin, we observe TAFA with both white-box and black-box verification outperforms IPGuard in terms of ARUC by 20% for each tested N. When the number of fingerprinting pairs is as small as 10, the verification of TAFA still achieves over 50% ARUC. Furthermore, from the ARUC curves we observe the white-box verification algorithm is relatively stable with N, while the performance of the black-box verification on Warfarin and Fashion increases by a noticeable margin when N is enlarged from 10 to 100. For example, the improvement in ARUC is about 15% on Fashion. Such a feature is especially desirable for users of TAFA, because, with more computing power devoted to generating the fingerprint, the user would usually expect more effective fingerprinting. Finally, despite the fluctuation of ARUC when N varies, we observe the ARUC of TAFA mostly stays over 40% on Skin and over 60% on the other two scenarios when N is over 50, which implies that one could expect TAFA to provide an accurate and relatively robust model fingerprinting primitive for other practical scenarios when the number of fingerprinting pairs is no smaller than 50 as we recommend.

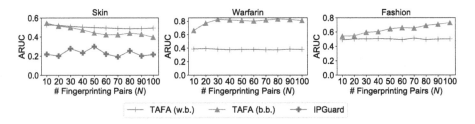

Fig. 4. The curves of ARUC with a varied number of fingerprinting pairs.

(2) Influence of Margin ϵ. Besides, we vary the margin hyperparameter ϵ in the linear programming problem in Inequality (2) from 1×10^{-1} to 1×10^{-6} by decreasing 10 times per step, which produces 6 different groups of fingerprinting pairs, with $N = 100$. Figure 5 reports the corresponding ARUC curves on Warfarin and Fashion. As we can see, for both the white-box and the black-box settings, the ARUC of TAFA has a downward trend when ϵ decreases. In other words, the generated fingerprint is more effective when the samples in the pair have a larger margin to the boundary hyperplane. As is stated in Sect. 3.3, a fingerprinting pair which is distant to the boundary hyperplane is less likely to be scattered to different linear regions if slight perturbations are conducted on the boundary hyperplanes, and therefore provides a more robust characterization of the linear region arrangement.

Additionally, we also study the influence of the pairwise distance between samples in fingerprinting pairs on the performance of TAFA. Due to the space limit, we present the corresponding results in Fig. 7 of Appendix B, where TAFA exhibits a more desirable performance when the pairwise distance is sufficiently large. Otherwise, samples in a fingerprinting pair would be identical or rather close to one another, which deteriorates its distinguishing power in representing the uniqueness of the linear region arrangement. Practically, according to

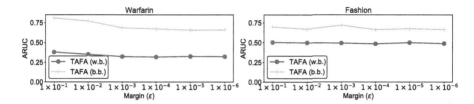

Fig. 5. The curves of ARUC with a varied margin ϵ during the fingerprint generation.

the validated effectiveness of TAFA in Fig. 2 and 3, we actually do not require a manual control on the pairwise distance between samples, as the maximization objective in our fingerprint generation algorithm ensures the samples in a constructed fingerprinting pair are well-conditioned in terms of the distance.

6   Related Work

Model Fingerprinting. Previous fingerprinting schemes focus on fingerprinting DNN models designed for classification tasks, mainly based on constructing different types of adversarial examples as model fingerprints. For example, one of the earliest fingerprinting schemes IPGuard [9] proposes an optimization objective to find adversarial examples near the decision boundary of the target classifier. Underlying IPGuard is the assumption that the target classifier should share a more similar decision boundary with a positive suspect model than a negative one. As a result, IPGuard chooses adversarial examples near the decision boundary to represent the decision boundary. Differently, Lucas et al. [13] and Zhao et al. [14] indendpently propose to use an ensemble of the target classifiers and a set of locally post-processed positive suspect classifiers to construct so-called *conferrable* adversarial examples, a special class of adversarial examples that *exclusively* transfer from the target model to the positive suspect model. In other words, conferrable adversarial examples can be viewed as a unique link between the target model and the positive suspect model. During the preparation of this paper, we also notice some more parallel works present different fingerprinting schemes for DNN classifiers [30,31]. For example, Wang et al. leverages DeepFool [39] to generate adversarial examples as fingerprints [30], while Li et al. utilizes the similarity between models in terms of the probability vectors on test inputs for piracy detection [31]. More detailed surveys can be found in [40,41]. As a strong complement to the aforementioned fingerprinting techniques, our proposed TAFA is based on the notion of activation patterns, which is more common to a broad family of DNNs with ReLU and can be applied to DNNs in a task-agnostic way.

Model Watermarking. Different from model fingerprinting, model watermarking is a more active protection for the confidentiality of DNN models, which works by directly embedding secrets of the model owner into a trained model before it is released. A number of recent works on model watermarking explore various types of secrets (e.g., random bit strings [7,42], generated serial number [43] or random sample sets [8]) as possible watermarks to be encoded into, e.g., the least significant bit of the weight [7], the distribution of outputs at the intermediate layer [42], or the full parameters [8,43].

7 Conclusion and Future Directions

In this paper, we present TAFA, the first task-agnostic model fingerprinting algorithm which achieves a noticeable improvement over the state-of-the-art model fingerprinting scheme and enables the fingerprinting of DNN models in a broader set of application scenarios, including but not limited to important learning tasks such as regression and generative modeling. As a future work, it would be meaningful to consider extend TAFA to fingerprint other neural network family, such as Transformer-based pretrained language models (e.g., BERT [2]), which consist of Gaussian error linear units that share a similar mathematical property as ReLU. Besides, future works may also consider to enhance the design of TAFA by incorporating more in-depth properties of the linear regions (e.g., the volume of a region, the occurrence frequency of normal samples in a region) for fingerprint construction. Moreover, it is promising to further evaluate and apply TAFA for fingerprinting DNNs on other typical learning tasks such as ranking, information retrieval and feature extraction.

Acknowledgement. We sincerely appreciate the shepherding from Kyu Hyung Lee. We would also like to thank the anonymous reviewers for their constructive comments and input to improve our paper. This work was supported in part by National Natural Science Foundation of China (61972099, U1836213,U1836210, U1736208), and Natural Science Foundation of Shanghai (19ZR1404800). Min Yang is a faculty of Shanghai Institute of Intelligent Electronics & Systems, Shanghai Institute for Advanced Communication and Data Science, and Engineering Research Center of CyberSecurity Auditing and Monitoring, Ministry of Education, China.

A   More Backgrounds on Deep Learning

• **Learning Tasks.** In a general deep learning scenario, we denote a deep neural network (DNN) as $F(\cdot; \Theta)$, a parametric model which maps a *data input* x in $\mathcal{X} \subset \mathbb{R}^{d_{in}}$ to prediction $y = F(x; \Theta)$ in $\mathcal{Y} \subset \mathbb{R}^{d_{out}}$. The concrete choice of the prediction space $\mathcal{Y}$ depends on the nature of the downstream task to which the DNN is applied. In this paper, we mainly evaluate our proposed fingerprinting algorithm on the following three popular learning tasks.

(1) **Classification:** In a K-class classification task, a DNN learns to classify a data input x (e.g., an image) into one of the N classes (e.g., based on the contained object). Usually, a DNN for classification has its prediction space as a N-dimensional simplex $\Delta_N := \{(p_1, p_2, \ldots, p_N) : 0 \leq p_i \leq 1, \sum_{i=1}^{N} p_i = 1\}$, where each prediction $(p_1, \ldots, p_N)$ is called a *probability vector* with p_i giving the predicted probability of x belonging to the i-th class.

(2) Regression: In a regression task, a DNN learns to predict the corresponding d_{out}-dimensional value y (e.g., drug dosing) based on the d_{in}-dimensional input x (e.g., demographic information).

(3) Generative Modeling: In a generative modeling task, a DNN learns to model the distribution of a given dataset (e.g., hand-written digits) for the purpose of data generation (e.g., generative adversarial nets [44]). Once trained, the DNN is able to output a prediction (e.g., a realistic hand-written digit) which has the same shape as the real samples in the dataset, when a random noise is input to the model. Although there are a few more typical learning tasks (e.g., ranking and information retrieval) in nowadays deep learning practices, the above three tasks already cover a majority of use cases of DNNs [23].

• **Formulation of Layer Structures.** To be self-contained, we formalize the two typical neural network layers below.

Definition A1 (Fully-Connected Layer). *A fully-connected layer f_{FC} is composed of a weight matrix $W_0 \in \mathbb{R}^{d_1 \times d_{in}}$ and a bias vector $b_0 \in \mathbb{R}^{d_1}$. Applying the fully-connected layer to an input $x \in \mathbb{R}^{d_{in}}$ computes $f_{FC}(x) := W_0 x + b_0$.*

Definition A2 (Convolutional Layer). *For the simplest case [1], a convolutional layer f_{Conv} is composed of C_{out} filters, i.e., $W^c \in \mathbb{R}^{C_{in} \times K \times K}$, and a bias vector $b \in \mathbb{R}^{C_{out}}$. For each output channel $c = 1, 2, \ldots, C_{out}$, applying the convolutional layer to an input $x \in \mathbb{R}^{C_{in} \times H_{in} \times W_{in}}$ computes $f_{Conv,c}(x) = \sum_{k=1}^{C_{in}} W^c * x^k + b_c$, where $[W^c * x^k]_{ij} := \sum_{m=1}^{K} \sum_{n=1}^{K} [W^c]_{m,n} [x^k]_{i-m,j-n}$, the cross-correlation between the c-th filter W^c and the k-th input channel x^k.*

B   More Evaluation Details and Results

B.1   Details of Scenarios

We introduce the details of the tasks, the datasets and the model architectures studied in our work.

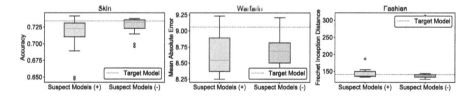

Fig. 6. Performance of the target model, the positive and the negative suspect models on the three scenarios.

(1) Skin Cancer Classification (*abbrev.* **Skin**). The first scenario covers the usage of deep CNN for skin cancer diagnosis. According to [36], we train a

---

[1] Without loss of generality, we only formalize a convolutional layer with its stride equal to 1, its padding equal to 0 and its kernel of a square shape.

ResNet-18 [1] as the target model on DermaMNIST [36], which consists of 10005 multi-source dermatoscopic images of common pigmented skin lesions imaging dataset. The input size is originally $3 \times 28 \times 28$, which is upsampled to $3 \times 224 \times 224$ to fit the input shape of a standard ResNet-18 architecture implemented in torchvision. The task is a 7-class classification task.

(2) Warfarin Dose Prediction (*abbrev.* **Warfarin**). The second scenario covers the usage of FCN for warfarin dose prediction, which is a safety-critical regression task that helps predict the proper individualised warfarin dosing according to the demographic and physiological record of the patients (e.g., weight, age and genetics). We use the International Warfarin Pharmacogenetics Consortium (IWPC) dataset [37], which is a public dataset composed of 31-dimensional features of 6256 patients and is widely used for researches in automated warfarin dosing. According to [45], we use a three-layer fully-connected neural network with ReLU as the target model, with its hidden layer composed of 100 neurons. The target model learns to predict the value of proper warfarin dosing, a non-negative real-valued scalar in $(0, 300.0]$.

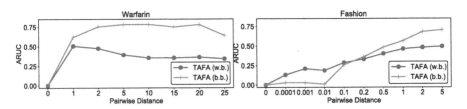

Fig. 7. The curves of ARUC when we control the distance between samples in each fingerprinting pair during the fingerprint generation.

(3) Fashion Generation (*abbrev.* **Fashion**). The final scenario covers the usage of FCN for generative modeling. We choose [38], which consists of 28×28 images for 60000 articles of clothing. Following the paradigm of Wasserstein generative adversarial networks (WGAN [46]), we train a 5-layer FCN of architecture $(64 - 128 - 256 - 512 - 768)$ as the generator and a 4-layer FCN of architecture $(768 - 512 - 256 - 1)$. We view the FCN-based generator as the target model, because a well-trained generator represents more the IP of the model owner as it can be directly used to generate realistic images without the aid of the discriminator.

References

1. He, K., Zhang, X., et al.: Deep residual learning for image recognition. In: CVPR, pp. 770–778 (2016)
2. Devlin, J., Chang, M.W., et al.: Bert: pre-training of deep bidirectional transformers for language understanding. In: NAACL-HLT (2019)
3. Cao, Y., Xiao, C., et al.: Adversarial sensor attack on lidar-based perception in autonomous driving. In: CCS (2019)

4. Heaton, J.B., Polson, N.G., et al.: Deep learning for finance: Deep portfolios. iN: Econometric Modeling: Capital Markets - Portfolio Theory eJournal (2016)
5. Esteva, A., Kuprel, B., et al.: Dermatologist-level classification of skin cancer with deep neural networks. In: Nature (2017)
6. Wenskay, D.L.: Intellectual property protection for neural networks. In: Neural Networks (1990)
7. Uchida, Y., Nagai, Y., et al.: Embedding watermarks into deep neural networks. In: ICMR (2017)
8. Adi, Y., Baum, C., et al.: Turning your weakness into a strength: watermarking deep neural networks by backdooring. In: USENIX Security Symposium (2018)
9. Cao, X., Jia, J., et al.: Ipguard: protecting the intellectual property of deep neural networks via fingerprinting the classification boundary. In: AsiaCCS (2021)
10. Cox, I., Miller, M., et al.: Digital watermarking. In: Lecture Notes in Computer Science (2003)
11. Wang, J., Wu, H., et al.: Watermarking in deep neural networks via error back-propagation. In: Electronic Imaging (2020)
12. Szegedy, C., Zaremba, W., Sutskever, I., Bruna, J., et al.: Intriguing properties of neural networks. ArXiv (2014)
13. Lukas, N., Zhang, Y., et al.: Deep neural network fingerprinting by conferrable adversarial examples. ArXiv (2019)
14. Zhao, J., Qingyue, H., et al.: Afa: adversarial fingerprinting authentication for deep neural networks. Comput. Commun. **150**, 488–497 (2020)
15. Pytorch hub. https://pytorch.org/hub/, Accessed 01 Feb 2021
16. Amazon aws. https://aws.amazon.com/, Accessed 01 Feb 2021
17. Nair, V., Hinton, G.E.: Rectified linear units improve restricted boltzmann machines. In: ICML (2010)
18. Tramèr, F., Zhang, F., et al.: Stealing machine learning models via prediction apis. In: USENIX Security (2016)
19. Jagielski, M., Carlini, N., et al.: High accuracy and high fidelity extraction of neural networks. In: USENIX Security Symposium (2020)
20. Rolnick, D., Kording, K.P.: Reverse-engineering deep relu networks. In: ICML (2020)
21. Montúfar, G., Pascanu, R., et al.: On the number of linear regions of deep neural networks. In: NIPS (2014)
22. Hanin, B., Rolnick, D.: Complexity of linear regions in deep networks. In: ICML (2019)
23. Goodfellow, I., Bengio, Y., et al.: Deep Learning. MIT Press, Cambridge (2016)
24. Jarrett, K., Kavukcuoglu, K., et al.: What is the best multi-stage architecture for object recognition? In: ICCV (2009)
25. Szegedy, C., Liu, W., et al.: Going deeper with convolutions. In: CVPR (2015)
26. Pan, S.J., Yang, Q.: A survey on transfer learning. In: TKDE (2010)
27. Simonyan, K., Zisserman, A.: Very deep convolutional networks for large-scale image recognition. ArXiv (2015)
28. Ren, J., Xu, L.: On vectorization of deep convolutional neural networks for vision tasks. In: AAAI (2015)
29. Serra, T., Tjandraatmadja, C., et al.: Bounding and counting linear regions of deep neural networks. In: ICML (2018)
30. Wang, S., Chang, C.H.: Fingerprinting deep neural networks - a deepfool approach. In: ISCAS (2021)
31. Li, Y., Zhang, Z., et al.: Modeldiff: testing-based DNN similarity comparison for model reuse detection. In: ISSTA (2021)

32. Han, S., Pool, J., et al.: Learning both weights and connections for efficient neural network. ArXiv (2015)
33. Li, H., Kadav, A., et al.: Pruning filters for efficient convnets. ArXiv (2017)
34. Juuti, M., Szyller, S., et al.: Prada: protecting against dnn model stealing attacks. In: EuroS&P (2019)
35. Gurobi linear programming optimizer. https://www.gurobi.com/, Accessed 01 Feb 2021
36. Yang, J., Shi, R., et al.: Medmnist classification decathlon: a lightweight automl benchmark for medical image analysis. ArXiv (2020)
37. Whirl-Carrillo, M., McDonagh, E., et al.: Pharmacogenomics knowledge for personalized medicine. In: Clinical Pharmacology & Therapeutics (2012)
38. Xiao, H., Rasul, K., et al.: Fashion-mnist: a novel image dataset for benchmarking machine learning algorithms. ArXiv (2017)
39. Moosavi-Dezfooli, S.M., Fawzi, A., et al.: Deepfool: a simple and accurate method to fool deep neural networks. In: CVPR (2016)
40. Boenisch, F.: A survey on model watermarking neural networks. ArXiv (2020)
41. Regazzoni, F., Palmieri, P., et al.: Protecting artificial intelligence ips: a survey of watermarking and fingerprinting for machine learning. In: CAAI Transactions on Intelligence Technology (2021)
42. Rouhani, B., Chen, H., et al.: Deepsigns: a generic watermarking framework for ip protection of deep learning models. ArXiv (2018)
43. Xu, X., Li, Y., et al.: "identity bracelets" for deep neural networks. IEEE Access (2020)
44. Goodfellow, I., Pouget-Abadie, J., et al.: Generative adversarial nets. In: NeurIPS (2014)
45. Truda, G., Marais, P.: Warfarin dose estimation on multiple datasets with automated hyperparameter optimisation and a novel software framework. ArXiv (2019)
46. Arjovsky, M., Chintala, S., et al.: Wasserstein generative adversarial networks. In: ICML (2017)

DA3G: Detecting Adversarial Attacks by Analysing Gradients

Jan-Philipp Schulze[1,2](✉) ⓘ, Philip Sperl[1,2](✉) ⓘ, and Konstantin Böttinger[2] ⓘ

[1] Technical University of Munich, Munich, Germany
{jan-philipp.schulze,philip.sperl}@aisec.fraunhofer.de
[2] Fraunhofer Institute for Applied and Integrated Security, Garching, Germany
konstantin.boettinger@aisec.fraunhofer.de

Abstract. Deep learning models are vulnerable to specifically crafted inputs, called adversarial examples. In this paper, we present DA3G, a novel method to reliably detect evasion attacks on neural networks. We analyse the behaviour of the network under test on the given input sample. Compared to the benign training data, adversarial examples cause a discrepancy between visual and causal perception. Although visually close to a benign input class, the output is shifted at the attacker's will. DA3G detects these changes in the pattern of the gradient using an auxiliary neural network. Our end-to-end approach readily integrates with a variety of existing architectures. DA3G reliably detects known as well as unknown attacks and increases the difficulty of adaptive attacks.

Keywords: Adversarial machine learning · Attack detection · Defence methods · Evasion attacks · Deep learning · Neural network security

1 Introduction

In the past years, deep learning (DL) models have led to significant performance increases in common machine learning (ML) tasks like computer vision, natural language processing, and behavioural analysis. Progressively, these systems are applied in real-world scenarios interacting with their users, e.g. as voice assistants or autonomous systems. Although critical decision processes may depend on DL-based models, they are known to be prone to attacks. These so-called adversarial examples [3,28,37] are specifically crafted inputs that steer the decision to the target of an attacker. In this paper, we present DA3G: a method to reliably detect adversarial attacks on neural networks (NNs).

Adversarial ML is a crucial intersection of IT security and AI research. With each improvement on the attack side, new defence methods are necessary to protect AI-based applications. DA3G is based on the following intuition: Adversarial attacks explore the decision boundaries of a target NN. A successful attack is visually close to the original input, but causes a misclassification. During the

---

J.-P. Schulze and P. Sperl—Co-first authors.

© Springer Nature Switzerland AG 2021
E. Bertino et al. (Eds.): ESORICS 2021, LNCS 12972, pp. 563–583, 2021.
https://doi.org/10.1007/978-3-030-88418-5_27

training of NNs, backpropagation is used to minimise this discrepancy for the benign training data. Thus, we believe it is a natural choice to analyse the gradient to detect and prevent attacks. The gradient contains information about the direction, magnitude and origin of prediction losses. Previous work using manually selected features based on this information [10,25] suggests the relation between the networks' gradients and their distinct behaviour during attacks. In DA3G, we introduce an end-to-end method, automatically learning which parts of the gradient are most important to distinguish between benign inputs and adversarial examples.

Throughout our research, we were inspired by another end-to-end attack detection method called DLA [34]. Here, the hidden activations of a target NN's dense-layers were inspected by an auxiliary NN, which the authors called alarm network. Whereas we use a similar architecture, our analysis is based on the gradient caused by the input samples. Based on this principle, we call our novel adversarial example detection method DA3G: detecting adversarial attacks by analysing gradients. In summary we make the following contributions:

- We introduce DA3G, a general end-to-end method to detect adversarial examples based on the analysis of neural networks' gradients.
- We implement and evaluate our approach to successfully detect previously unseen adversarial examples of various attack methods.
- We thoroughly investigate adaptive white-box attacks on DA3G and find a significant increase of robustness compared to unprotected models.

2   Background and Related Work

2.1   Adversarial Examples

In this paper, we present a novel defence method reliably detecting evasion attacks on NNs. Adversarial examples are specifically perturbed inputs, which fool the network under attack, but look unsuspicious to human observers. More formally, adversarial examples can be defined as follows: Let $f(\mathbf{x}; \boldsymbol{\theta})$ be a trained NN used for classification tasks and let $H(\mathbf{x})$ be a human oracle with comparable classification capabilities. For a benign input $\mathbf{x}$:

$$f(\mathbf{x}; \boldsymbol{\theta}) = H(\mathbf{x}).$$

Let $\tilde{\mathbf{x}}$ be a slightly perturbed version of $\mathbf{x}$ such that $\|\tilde{\mathbf{x}} - \mathbf{x}\|_p \leqslant \epsilon$ for some small $\epsilon \in \mathbb{R}^+$. Here, $\|\cdot\|_p$ denotes the l_p-norm. Then, $\tilde{\mathbf{x}}$ is an adversarial example if the following holds:

$$H(\mathbf{x}) = H(\tilde{\mathbf{x}}) \quad \wedge \quad f(\mathbf{x}; \boldsymbol{\theta}) \neq H(\tilde{\mathbf{x}}).$$

2.2   Attack Methods

Research on adversarial attack methods is rapidly evolving, providing a wide range of concepts. In the following, we summarise important findings of recent years. We adopt the categorisation presented by Zhang et al. [43] dividing the attacks in gradient-based, decision-based, and optimisation-based approaches.

In 2014, Goodfellow et al. presented their FGSM attack method together with first principles on why adversarial examples exist [15]. This one-step method pushes the input in the direction of the gradient. Further refined and extended, Kurakin et al. presented the iterative version of FGSM, called BIM [22]. Here, the gradient is reevaluated after each iteration step, thus resulting in more robust adversarial examples. Similarly to BIM, in 2018 Madry et al. introduced PGD [26]. The authors argue that their method poses the strongest first order attack.

In 2015, Moosavi-Dezfooli et al. introduced DeepFool [27]. Instead of relying on the gradient, this decision-based method iteratively pushes the inputs towards the decision boundary of the attacked network. During the attack, the NN's decision boundary is linearised resulting in polyhedrons.

Finally, the optimisation-based C&W attack introduced by Carlini and Wagner [7] is currently considered to be the most powerful white-box attack. Opposed to other gradient-based approaches, the authors introduced a substitute cost function steering the input to the desired target class.

Other important methods are the One-Pixel-Attack [36] and the Boundary Attack [4]. In the former attack, only one pixel of the original images is changed to craft adversarial examples. The latter attack does not require the gradients of the attacked NN, nor its probability distribution.

2.3   Defence Methods

The stronger attacks became, the more attention adversarial defence methods received in research. In the following, we introduce important adversarial defences with a focus on adversarial example detection methods, i.e. the category DA3G belongs to.

Currently, adversarial training is considered to be the most effective countermeasure to protect against adversarial examples. Here, adversarial examples are added to the training data, using the original labels of the samples. Shown by Madry et al., the PGD attack method provides the most robust NNs when used as the generator in adversarial training [26]. During this iterative process of adversarial generation and retraining, the following min-max problem is solved:

$$\min_{\theta} \rho(\theta), \text{where } \rho(\boldsymbol{\theta}) = \mathbb{E}_{(\mathbf{x},y)\sim P_{\mathcal{D}}}[\max_{\boldsymbol{\delta}\in\mathcal{S}} \mathcal{L}(f(\mathbf{x}+\boldsymbol{\delta};\boldsymbol{\theta}),y)].$$

$P_{\mathcal{D}}$ denotes the data distribution, $\mathcal{S}$ the perturbation budget, $\mathcal{L}$ the loss function and $\boldsymbol{\theta}$ the trained model parameters. Shortcomings of adversarial training include the high computational cost and the limited generalisation, increasing the security only under one particular threat model [5]. For example, NNs retrained on PGD_{∞} might still be vulnerable to l_2 attacks.

Alternatively, a series of defence methods is based on data preprocessing steps and random processes. Such defences break the adversarial features added to the benign inputs reducing the efficacy of attacks. Sharad et al. provide an extensive overview of this area of research and introduce their defence method called Randomised Squeezing [33]. The authors conclude that randomised methods increase the robustness in black-box and grey-box settings, but can be bypassed using adaptive white-box attacks. For example, Expectation Over Transformation [2] or Backward Pass Differentiable Approximation [1] generate robust adversarial examples circumventing randomised defences.

Robustness certification techniques [11,17,29,30,39] pose a promising alternative to the heuristic methods introduced above. The approaches guarantee that no adversarial example can be found for a given perturbation budget. Downsides of certified robustness techniques are their computational cost and their limitation to certain NN architectures. Furthermore, the resulting certificates are only valid for known samples $\mathbf{x} \in \mathcal{X}$ [5]. Finally, Ghiasi et al. [14] presented an attack method bypassing certified defences.

Adversarial Example Detection. With DA3G, we present a novel adversarial example detection method. In the following, we introduce recent findings in this area in more detail. For the interested reader, we refer to the survey of Zhang et al. [43]. The authors provide a comparative study analysing state-of-the-art detection methods.

ML-LOO is currently considered the most reliable detection method presented by Yang et al. [42]. The authors leverage methods from explainable AI, namely leave-one-out (LOO). Here, the importance of each input pixel is quantified by erasing it and measuring the change in the output prediction. ML-LOO uses the interquartile range of the LOO distribution as decision variable. The authors discovered that benign inputs have a significantly narrower LOO distribution, i.e. a few input pixels are important for the output. Other notable adversarial detection methods with its origin in explainable AI are based on SHAP signatures [12] and robust features [13].

DA3G is based on the analysis of a NN's gradients. Closely related to this approach are the methods Gradient Similarity [10] and GraN [25]. Both adversarial detection methods use predefined metrics calculated on the gradient as input to a logistic regression classifier. In GraN, the authors calculate the layer-wise l_1-norm, whereas Gradient Similarity use the l_2-norm enriched by the cosine similarity to certain training samples. Both feature sets seem useful to detect known and unknown adversarial attacks. In our method, DA3G, we extend the research by showing that the *raw gradient* is useful to detect adversarial attacks. Without predefined metrics, our method uses the entire information content present in the NN's gradient. We believe compressing the gradient to a l_p-norm diminishes its information content. DA3G is more flexible and scalable as it readily integrates with complex NN architectures. In contrast to the aforementioned research, we consider advanced threat models like adaptive attacks, where DA3G delivers considerably performance increase. With DA3G, we hope to further contribute to the research on gradient-based adversarial detection.

DA3G automatically analyses the gradients of the NNs to detect adversarial examples. For this, we adapt the target-alarm architecture introduced by

Sperl et al. [34]. The authors presented an adversarial example detection method called DLA. This method is based on the analysis of a target network's dense-layer activations by an auxiliary NN called the alarm network. Follow-up work ported the idea to other use-cases, e.g. anomaly detection [35]. We build upon this method and use a separate network similar to the alarm network to process the gradients of our target networks. In DA3G, we introduce an end-to-end approach that works for a wide range of data sets and target models. Furthermore, our evaluation of adaptive white-box attacks shows that DA3G increases the level of security so that potential attackers need significantly more resources to fool the protected models.

3   Threat Models

As the research on attack methods progresses, defence methods like ours are required to provide robustness under ever more challenging threat models. Following the current best-practices provided by Carlini et al. [5]., we introduce the two threat models based on which we built and evaluated DA3G. Our threat models cover the following three aspects defining the type of attackers DA3G protects against:

1. *Goals of the adversary.* Either the classification is forced to a certain output, i.e. a targeted attack, or to any class different to the original one, i.e. an untargeted attack.
2. *Capabilities of the adversary.* DA3G protects against evasion attacks. Here, the attacker may change any part of the input fed to the NN during inference. The changes are measured using an l_p-norm.
3. *Knowledge of the adversary.* We distinguish between grey-box setting, where the attacker has access to the NN's parameters, and white-box settings, with an omniscient adversary also knowing the applied countermeasures.

3.1   Grey-Box Threat Model

During grey-box attacks, adversaries have access to the parameters of the NNs and hence are capable of using the model's gradients. In our threat model, the attackers alter the classification output of the attacked NNs in an untargeted manner bound by the l_2 and l_∞ norm. Here, the attackers are not aware of the defence method, however, they have unrestricted access to the NN under attack. We use untargeted attacks as these are the easiest for the attacker: any other class than the original one results in an successful attack. This setting evaluates DA3G's detection performance prior to adaptive attacks.

3.2   White-Box Threat Model

In white-box settings, the adversaries are aware of all parameters of the NN under attack including the countermeasures used. Thus, attackers can bypass the defence and steer the decision to their target. These adaptive attacks are known to circumvent many past defence methods [5,6,38], thus are a main evaluation point for DA3G. We use l_2 and l_∞ bounded attacks and consider targeted attacks using the least-likely target class [41] similar to Carlini et al. [6].

4   Detecting Adversarial Attacks by Analysing Gradients

Adversarial attacks explore the boundaries of the victim NN's decision surface. Although visually close to benign samples, adversarial inputs cause different outputs of the NN. We expect this discrepancy between the adversarial input, which is close to a benign class, and its output, which the attacker shifted to a wrong class, to be measurable in the gradient. Intuitively, these differences may be the magnitude, direction, variance, or other shifts in the distribution. Instead of manually defining what these differences may be, we analyse the raw gradient by a second NN, which automatically combines suitable features to distinguish benign from adversarial inputs. In the following, let $\hat{f}$ denote the one-hot encoded maximum transform of f, i.e.

$$\hat{f}_i(\mathbf{x}; \boldsymbol{\theta}) = \begin{cases} 1 & \text{if } f_i(\mathbf{x}; \boldsymbol{\theta}) = \max_{j=1,\dots,N} f_j(\mathbf{x}; \boldsymbol{\theta}), \\ 0 & \text{otherwise}, \end{cases}$$

where N is the dimension of the output and f_i denotes the probability of f's ith output class. Then, DA3G's core assumption can be formulated as:

Let $f(\mathbf{x}; \boldsymbol{\theta})$ be a neural network, which was trained using the loss function $\mathcal{L}(y, y')$. Analysing the gradient $\nabla_{\boldsymbol{\theta}} \mathcal{L}(f(\mathbf{x}; \boldsymbol{\theta}), \hat{f}(\mathbf{x}; \boldsymbol{\theta}))$ caused by an input sample $\mathbf{x}$, we can distinguish between benign inputs and adversarial attacks.

4.1   Architecture

DA3G comprises two NNs: 1) the pretrained target network f_t and 2) the alarm network f_a. The alarm network analyses the target network's gradient caused by the current input. As output, it returns a score, where adversarial examples are closer to 1. During training, the alarm network learns to generalise the gradient of the known benign and adversarial samples to yet unseen inputs. We give an overview about our architecture in Fig. 1.

According to our intuition, there are measurable differences in the gradient for benign and adversarial inputs. An NN's gradient is based on its loss function $\mathcal{L}(y, y')$, which compares the current output y to the expected output y'. However, during inference, y' is not known. Instead, we use the estimated output $\hat{y} = \hat{f}(\mathbf{x}; \boldsymbol{\theta})$, which is always available for the pretrained target model. In other words, we compare the predicted output to the most likely output class. The overall mapping function becomes:

$$f_a(\mathbf{x}; \boldsymbol{\theta}_a) : \nabla_{\boldsymbol{\theta}_t} \mathcal{L}_t \left(f_t(\mathbf{x}; \boldsymbol{\theta}_t), \hat{f}_t(\mathbf{x}; \boldsymbol{\theta}_t) \right) \mapsto [0, 1]$$

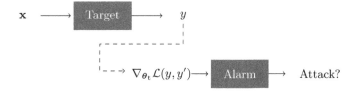

Fig. 1. Overview about DA3G: The alarm network analyses the gradients caused by the current input sample in the target network. We evaluate the loss between the predicted labels y and the target labels y'. As y' is not known during inference, we approximate it with the maximum $\hat{y} = \hat{f}(\mathbf{x}; \boldsymbol{\theta})$ of the prediction.

4.2 Training Objectives

The two components of DA3G, i.e. the target and alarm network, are trained separately. Whereas the target network fulfills its original task, e.g. a classification, the alarm network is trained to detect attacks on the target network. In the following, we assume an existing target model with fixed parameters $\boldsymbol{\theta}_t$.

Let $\tilde{\mathbf{x}} \in \tilde{\mathcal{X}}$ denote an adversarial example successfully fooling the target network by modifying the benign input $\mathbf{x} \in \mathcal{X}$. This attack may be precomputed or be part of the optimisation process during training of DA3G. The alarm network's task is to distinguish between benign inputs and adversarial examples. Using the binary cross-entropy loss, this objective becomes:

$$\underset{\boldsymbol{\theta}_a}{\operatorname{argmax}} \, \mathbb{E}_{\mathbf{x} \sim P_{\mathcal{X}}, \tilde{\mathbf{x}} \sim P_{\tilde{\mathcal{X}}}} [\log(1 - f_a(\mathbf{x}; \boldsymbol{\theta}_a)) + \log(f_a(\tilde{\mathbf{x}}; \boldsymbol{\theta}_a))]$$

5   Experimental Setup

In the following, we carefully describe the settings, which we evaluated DA3G in. It will serve as basis for our evaluation in Sect. 6.

5.1   Architectural Choices

DA3G comprises the target and alarm network. We evaluated a range of popular NN architectures for the target network, each serving as classifier on the respective data set. An in-depth overview can be found in Appendix A, Table 4. For MNIST and Fashion-MNIST, we chose the well established and tested LeNet5 architecture together with an example model provided by Keras. Similarly, we trained a ResNet model and again a Keras example architecture for CIFAR10.

To show the general applicability of DA3G, we use a common architecture for the alarm network. Across all experiments, we chose a simple, fully connected, and SELU-activated [20] NN with the following dimensions: 100, 50, 10. We trained for 500 epochs using Adam with a learning rate of 5×10^{-5}. In order to lower the resource demands, we limited our analysis to the gradient of the last two target network's layers. We did not perform an evaluation, which layers result in the best detection performance, but expect last two layers to influence the output the most.

5.2 Data Sets

For easier comparison to prior work, we chose the publicly available and commonly applied [43] data sets MNIST [24], Fashion-MNIST [40], and CIFAR10 [21]. All three data sets contain images, differing in complexity and size. MNIST pictures handwritten digits for which each sample is composed of 28×28 grey-scale pixels. Fashion-MNIST depicts more complex shapes like clothes and shoes. CIFAR10 further increases the complexity with coloured samples of shape $32 \times 32 \times 3$. The data sets comprise a predefined train and test split, which we used throughout our evaluation. During the training of DA3G, we introduced a validation set for which we drew 20% from the training data. As preprocessing step, we scaled input data to the range $[0, 1]$.

5.3 Attack Methods

In accordance with common guidelines [5], we evaluated DA3G on three attack methods of different types: PGD [26], DeepFool (DF) [27], and the C&W [7] attack. Because of similarities among attacks of the same type, our evaluation contains a sufficiently diverse set of methods. We profited from the attack categorisation introduced in [43]. Here, the authors divided the attacks into gradient-based, decision-based, and optimisation-based examples. PGD represents gradient-based multi-step attacks, DF decision-based and C&W optimisation-based methods. For PGD and DF, we considered both the l_2 and l_∞ versions of the attacks, while concentrating on the l_2 version of the C&W attack. Please note that DF and C&W generate adversarial examples in an unbounded manner. Hence, the attacks try to find minimally altered samples fooling the attacked NN within the given perturbation budget ϵ. PGD, on the other hand, is a bounded method and therefore generates adversarial examples $\tilde{x}$ with the property $\|\tilde{x} - x\| \approx \epsilon$. For MNIST and Fashion-MNIST, we set ϵ to 0.3 and 4.0 for the l_2 and l_∞ attacks, respectively. Similarly, for CIFAR10 we set ϵ to 0.03 and 0.9. For all attacks, we selected the parameters such that a 100% success rate is reached when attacking the unprotected targets.

5.4 Baseline Methods

In our first experiment, we compared the performance of DA3G to the two adversarial example detection methods ML-LOO [42] and DLA [34]. We selected ML-LOO based on the thorough evaluation presented in the survey on adversarial example detection by Zhang et al. [43]. In this survey, the authors compared five different methods using three data sets. The authors concluded that ML-LOO provided the best detection capabilities, outperforming the remaining four methods in the majority of the evaluated test cases. A drawback of ML-LOO are its computation times. To mitigate this problem, we concentrated on the last two layers of each target model as source of information as also done in DA3G. We trained ML-LOO's logistic regression models for 1000 iterations each.

As DA3G uses the target-alarm architecture first introduced by Sperl et al. [34], we also added DLA to our experiment pipeline. By comparing DA3G to DLA, we can directly assess the impact of using the gradients instead of the dense-layer activations as source of information. In our experiments, we used the same alarm models for DLA and DA3G. We trained DLA's alarm models for 50 epochs each, again using Adam with a learning rate of 5×10^{-5}.

5.5   Experimental Setup

We carefully designed a set of experiments to evaluate the performance of DA3G. Each one considers a different attack surface, where the attacker's abilities and knowledge increase. If not stated otherwise, we used 40 000 adversarial examples to train DA3G and the two baseline methods. In our evaluation, we consider the following four experiments. For the first three settings, we assumed the grey-box threat model (Sect. 3.1), while we used the white-box threat model (Sect. 3.2) for the final experiment.

1. *Basic Grey-Box Detection.* Detection of the same attack type that DA3G was trained on. We compared DA3G's performance against ML-LOO and DLA as examples of state-of-the-art adversarial detection methods.
2. *Combined Grey-Box Detection.* Detection of multiple attack types that DA3G was trained on. Additionally, we evaluated the influence of the number of known adversarial examples to simulate environments, where it is infeasible to generate a large amount of training samples.
3. *Leave-One-Out Grey-Box Detection.* Detection of other kinds of attacks methods than the ones known during training. This measures the protection against yet unknown attacks.
4. *Adaptive White-Box Attacks.* Protection against adversaries that are aware of DA3G and adapt their attack accordingly. Simulates a setting with an omniscient attacker, who knows the countermeasures used.

Adaptive Attacks. We based our adaptive attacks on the findings of Carlini et al. [6] and Sperl et al. [34]. Let $Z_t(\cdot)$ and $Z_a(\cdot)$ be the output logits of the target and alarm network, respectively. And let N be the number of output classes, then an adversary attacks the combined function $G(\cdot)$:

$$G(\mathbf{x})_i = \begin{cases} Z_t(\mathbf{x})_i, & \text{if } i \leq N \\ (Z_a(\mathbf{x}) + 1) \cdot \max_j Z_t(\mathbf{x})_j, & \text{if } i = N + 1 \end{cases}$$

We distinguish between inputs considered benign by the alarm network, i.e. $Z_a(\mathbf{x}) < 0$, and malicious inputs, i.e. $Z_a(\mathbf{x}) > 0$. In the respective cases, DA3G's decision becomes:

$$\operatorname*{argmax}_{i}(G(\mathbf{x})_i) = \begin{cases} \operatorname*{argmax}_{i}(Z_{\mathrm{t}}(\mathbf{x})_i), & Z_{\mathrm{a}}(\mathbf{x}) < 0 \\ N + 1, & Z_{\mathrm{a}}(\mathbf{x}) > 0 \end{cases}$$

Naturally, the global detection threshold of 0 may not be the optimal decision boundary for DA3G, yet increases simplicity and readability. As we performed targeted white-box attacks, we omitted DF and evaluated the robustness of DA3G against PGD and the C&W attacks. The alarm models were trained on 40 000 adversarial examples generated with C&W and both versions of PGD.

6   Evaluation

In the following, we analyse the performance of DA3G. For the first three experiments, we show the mean area under the ROC-curve (AUC) for three runs of each experiments. The AUC measures the performance independent of an output threshold, thus allows to judge the general detection capabilities. For the adaptive attacks using PGD, we visualise the attack success as a function of the attack steps. In the case of adaptive adversaries using C&W, we visualise the required perturbations.

6.1   Basic Grey-Box Detection

We started our evaluation with the simplest scenario: the detection of known attack types. Here, we motivate that the raw gradient indeed contains information to distinguish between benign and malignant inputs. The results are summarised in Table 1. We are happy to report near perfect results on all experiments except for PGD on MNIST. Indeed, for DF and C&W, DA3G was the best performing method across all three data sets beating both baseline methods. The performance of DA3G was especially striking on F-MNIST, where our method was the only one scoring 100% detection for all three attack types.

Motivated by these results, we further analysed why DA3G's performance was lower for PGD on MNIST. Looking at the gradients, we saw nearly vanishing values when the PGD-generated adversarial examples were at the input. This was in stark contrast to the adversarial examples of DF and C&W, where the gradient values showed more variance. We believe this phenomenon is similar to the findings of Tramer et al. [38], who showed that PGD creates adversarial examples of high confidence. DA3G uses the loss between the output probabilities and the maximum output – hence, the loss and thus the gradients vanish for outputs of high confidence, i.e. close to the arguments of the maxima. MNIST promotes high confidence outputs as the classes are well separated and well preprocessed unlike real-world inputs. As we can see in the results, more realistic and thus complex data sets like F-MNIST and CIFAR10 do not show the same performance drop for PGD. We conclude that the low detection rate for PGD is likely inherent to MNIST and not a general problem of DA3G.

The results of our first experiment motivated the validity of our core assumption: indeed, the raw gradients can be used to distinguish between benign inputs

Table 1. Test results for experiment 1: mean AUC with the according standard deviation after three runs for the basic grey-box detection. We highlighted the best result for each experiment.

Data	Target	Method	PGD_∞	PGD_2	DF_∞	DF_2	$C\&W_2$
MNIST	LeNet5	DA3G	$.94 \pm .00$	$.93 \pm .00$	$1.0 \pm .00$	$1.0 \pm .00$	$1.0 \pm .00$
		ML-LOO	$1.0 \pm .00$	$1.0 \pm .00$	$.98 \pm .00$	$.91 \pm .00$	$.91 \pm .00$
		DLA	$1.0 \pm .00$	$1.0 \pm .00$	$1.0 \pm .00$	$1.0 \pm .00$	$1.0 \pm .00$
	KerasExM	DA3G	$.94 \pm .00$	$.93 \pm .00$	$1.0 \pm .00$	$1.0 \pm .00$	$1.0 \pm .00$
		ML-LOO	$1.0 \pm .00$	$1.0 \pm .00$	$1.0 \pm .00$	$.99 \pm .00$	$.99 \pm .00$
		DLA	$.99 \pm .00$	$.98 \pm .00$	$1.0 \pm .00$	$1.0 \pm .00$	$1.0 \pm .00$
F-MNIST	LeNet5	DA3G	$1.0 \pm .00$	$1.0 \pm .00$	$1.0 \pm .00$	$1.0 \pm .00$	$1.0 \pm .00$
		ML-LOO	$1.0 \pm .00$	$.99 \pm .00$	$.86 \pm .00$	$.82 \pm .00$	$.82 \pm .00$
		DLA	$1.0 \pm .00$	$1.0 \pm .00$	$.99 \pm .00$	$.99 \pm .00$	$.99 \pm .00$
	KerasExM	DA3G	$1.0 \pm .00$	$1.0 \pm .00$	$1.0 \pm .00$	$1.0 \pm .00$	$1.0 \pm .00$
		ML-LOO	$1.0 \pm .00$	$1.0 \pm .00$	$.95 \pm .00$	$.93 \pm .00$	$.94 \pm .00$
		DLA	$1.0 \pm .00$	$1.0 \pm .00$	$.99 \pm .00$	$.99 \pm .00$	$.99 \pm .00$
CIFAR10	KerasExC	DA3G	$.98 \pm .00$	$.97 \pm .00$	$.98 \pm .00$	$.98 \pm .00$	$.98 \pm .00$
		ML-LOO	$1.0 \pm .00$	$1.0 \pm .00$	$.81 \pm .00$	$.81 \pm .00$	$.82 \pm .00$
		DLA	$1.0 \pm .00$	$1.0 \pm .00$	$.97 \pm .00$	$.97 \pm .00$	$.97 \pm .00$
	ResNet	DA3G	$.99 \pm .00$	$.99 \pm .00$	$.99 \pm .00$	$1.0 \pm .00$	$1.0 \pm .00$
		ML-LOO	$1.0 \pm .00$	$1.0 \pm .00$	$.74 \pm .00$	$.73 \pm .00$	$.78 \pm .00$
		DLA	$1.0 \pm .00$	$1.0 \pm .00$	$.98 \pm .00$	$.98 \pm .00$	$.98 \pm .00$

and adversarial examples. We observed high detection performance across all three attack types especially for more complex data sets.

6.2 Combined Grey-Box Detection

Motivated by our first experiment, we increased the difficulty by detecting all three attack types at once. We randomly sampled adversarial examples generated by the different attack methods to train DA3G. To further investigate the real-world application, we show the detection performance as function of the number of adversarial training samples. For large data sets, it may be infeasible to generate large amounts of adversarial examples under limited hardware resources. We summarise the results in Table 2.

DA3G followed the intuitive behaviour: the more adversarial examples were available during training, the better the detection performance. Even for 1000 adversarial examples, we saw promising results. We report that DA3G's detection performance remained strong when trained on multiple attacks at once. Indeed, we saw near perfect results of more than 98% for the more complex

Table 2. Test results for experiment 2: mean AUC with the according standard deviation after three runs for the combined grey-box detection using different amounts of adversarial examples during training.

Data	Target	100	1000	10000	40000
MNIST	LeNet5	.65 ± .01	.84 ± .01	.94 ± .00	.96 ± .00
	KerasExM	.56 ± .04	.89 ± .01	.98 ± .00	.99 ± .00
F-MNIST	F-LeNet5	.62 ± .01	.87 ± .01	.98 ± .00	.99 ± .00
	F-KerasExM	.72 ± .02	.87 ± .00	.98 ± .00	.99 ± .00
CIFAR10	KerasExC	.64 ± .01	.79 ± .01	.89 ± .00	.93 ± .00
	ResNet	.67 ± .01	.87 ± .00	.97 ± .00	.98 ± .00

target networks across all data sets. This experiment shows that DA3G reliably detects known adversarial attacks of multiple types.

6.3   Leave-One-Out Grey-Box Detection

In this experiment, we expanded our evaluation to the detection of yet unknown attacks. We evaluated DA3G in multiple leave-one-out settings. Here, DA3G was trained on two attack types, yet evaluated on adversarial examples of the unknown type. In Table 3 we summarise the leave-one-out experiments for all possible combinations.

Again, we report near perfect results for a wide range of combinations. As seen in experiment 1, DA3G performs especially well when detecting the decision- and optimisation-based attacks DF and C&W. Indeed, the only combination resulting in inferior performance was the detection of PGD without known examples in the training data. We believe this is due to the aforementioned observation that PGD-generated adversarial examples have nearly vanishing gradients. Nonetheless, our evaluation showed that DA3G's detection performance significantly increased when PGD was among the training set – without any degradation for the left-out attack type. We may conclude that a gradient-based method should combined with either a decision- or optimisation-based attack during training. Then, DA3G allows reliable detection of yet unknown attacks.

6.4   Adaptive White-Box Attacks

In our final experiment, we evaluated the robustness increase by DA3G against an omniscient adversary. This scenario is especially challenging as both the target model and our defence method were attacked. We closely followed the available guidelines in research [5,6,38]. Our optimisation function was introduced in Sect. 5.5, on which we performed PGD_∞, PGD_2, and $C\&W_2$ attacks. For a strong adversary, we took special care to optimise the attack hyperparameters as summarised in Table 5. Previous work has shown that especially the attack step size may further increase the attack success of PGD [9].

Table 3. Test results for experiment 3: mean AUC with the according standard deviation after three runs for the leave-one-out grey-box detection.

Data	Target	Trained With	Tested With		
			$\mathbf{PGD}_{\infty,2}$	$\mathbf{DF}_{\infty,2}$	$\mathbf{C\&W}_2$
MNIST	LeNet5	$DF_{\infty,2}$, $C\&W_2$	$.66 \pm .00$	$1.0 \pm .00$	$1.0 \pm .00$
		$PGD_{\infty,2}$, $C\&W_2$	$.93 \pm .00$	$.99 \pm .00$	$1.0 \pm .00$
		$PGD_{\infty,2}$, $DF_{\infty,2}$	$.92 \pm .00$	$.99 \pm .00$	$.99 \pm .00$
	KerasExM	$DF_{\infty,2}$, $C\&W_2$	$.45 \pm .02$	$1.0 \pm .00$	$1.0 \pm .00$
		$PGD_{\infty,2}$, $C\&W_2$	$.98 \pm .00$	$1.0 \pm .00$	$1.0 \pm .00$
		$PGD_{\infty,2}$, $DF_{\infty,2}$	$.98 \pm .00$	$1.0 \pm .00$	$1.0 \pm .00$
F-MNIST	LeNet5	$DF_{\infty,2}$, $C\&W_2$	$.56 \pm .01$	$1.0 \pm .00$	$1.0 \pm .00$
		$PGD_{\infty,2}$, $C\&W_2$	$.99 \pm .00$	$.99 \pm .00$	$.99 \pm .00$
		$PGD_{\infty,2}$, $DF_{\infty,2}$	$.99 \pm .00$	$.99 \pm .00$	$.99 \pm .00$
	KerasExM	$DF_{\infty,2}$, $C\&W_2$	$.48 \pm .02$	$1.0 \pm .00$	$1.0 \pm .00$
		$PGD_{\infty,2}$, $C\&W_2$	$.99 \pm .00$	$.98 \pm .00$	$.98 \pm .00$
		$PGD_{\infty,2}$, $DF_{\infty,2}$	$.99 \pm .00$	$.99 \pm .00$	$.99 \pm .00$
CIFAR10	KerasExC	$DF_{\infty,2}$, $C\&W_2$	$.59 \pm .07$	$.98 \pm .00$	$.98 \pm .00$
		$PGD_{\infty,2}$, $C\&W_2$	$.93 \pm .00$	$.91 \pm .01$	$.92 \pm .00$
		$PGD_{\infty,2}$, $DF_{\infty,2}$	$.93 \pm .00$	$.94 \pm .00$	$.93 \pm .00$
	ResNet	$DF_{\infty,2}$, $C\&W_2$	$.63 \pm .02$	$.99 \pm .00$	$1.0 \pm .00$
		$PGD_{\infty,2}$, $C\&W_2$	$.98 \pm .00$	$.97 \pm .00$	$.99 \pm .00$
		$PGD_{\infty,2}$, $DF_{\infty,2}$	$.96 \pm .01$	$.99 \pm .00$	$.99 \pm .00$

We show our results on MNIST and CIFAR10 in Fig. 2. The interested reader finds the plots for Fashion-MNIST in Appendix B. The robustness of bounded attacks, e.g. PGD, is measured as attack success for a fixed attack budget. For unbounded attacks, e.g. C&W, we show the l_2 perturbation required for successful attacks. As general – and natural – observation, we see all adaptive attacks bypassing DA3G after certain attack effort. Hence, our evaluation does not seem to overestimate the robustness due to obfuscated gradients [1].

Robustness Against PGD Adaptive Attacks. As expected, all unprotected target models could be attacked within the minimum number of steps. The DA3G-protected models showed more resilience, either by increasing the attack effort or by lowering the attack success rate. Especially on MNIST and Fashion-MNIST, the differences were striking. For PGD_∞, DA3G could lower the attack success to less than 90% under increased attack effort. Our evaluation suggested that the target network architecture has an impact on the vulnerability. For KerasExM, the attack success rate increased slowly, then converged to 66.8% after 1000 steps. In contrast, the attacker achieved an attack success rate of around 80%

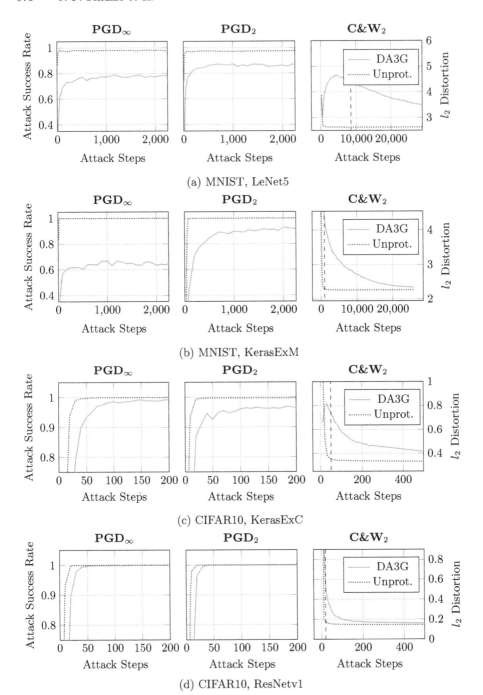

Fig. 2. Adaptive attacks on the MNIST and CIFAR10 models. The dashed lines show the number of C&W steps required such that at least 80% of all attacks on the protected model were successful.

on LeNet5. After the attacks have converged, even doubling the number of steps did not further increase the success rate. For ResNet on CIFAR10, both PGD_2 and PGD_∞ reached 100% attack success. In the more resilient case, attacks on KerasExC did not reach perfect success rates. Here, PGD_2 converged to 96.1% after 100 iterations. Although improving on the unprotected MNIST models, DA3G seemed more vulnerable to PGD_2 attacks. For the CIFAR10 target models, the adaptive attacks approached 100% success. The difference between PGD_2 than on PGD_∞ was less severe on MNIST and Fashion-MNIST. Here, the attack could not attack all inputs. Throughout the experiments, strictly more attack steps were needed to achieve successful attacks. We conclude that DA3G successfully increased the level of security of the NNs and often prevents a notable fraction of the performed attacks. Furthermore, the adversaries' attack effort, i.e. attack steps, considerably increased compared to the unprotected cases.

Robustness Against C&W Adaptive Attacks. For the unbounded C&W attack, we expressed the level of protection by measuring the required perturbation budget. As seen in Fig. 2, severe perturbation was needed for a successful attack even after thousands of attack steps. During our evaluation, we saw that the attack did not reach a perfect success rate immediately – even though the C&W method is unbounded and thus could alter the input by any extend. In such cases, we calculated the l_2 perturbations using the successful adversarial attacks only. We saw similar results across all data sets: whereas the unprotected model was easily attacked, the distortion needed for the DA3G-protected model nearly doubled. Depending on the properties of the data and underlying use-case, the increased amount of required perturbations may prevent the attacker from successfully crafting human-imperceptible adversarial examples. We conclude that DA3G improves the robustness against optimisation-based attacks and forces adversaries to induce more changes to the inputs.

7   Discussion and Future Work

With DA3G, we present a new end-to-end method reliably detecting adversarial examples under challenging threat models. Summarising our evaluation, we report that DA3G forces potential adversaries to invest more computational power to fool our protected NNs. For some attacks, even considerable attack effort did not result in overall attack success. Interestingly, we report a notable difference in the level of security against adversaries using either PGD_∞ or PGD_2. For bounded attacks, the reported success rates depend on the fixed values of ϵ, quantifying the allowed perturbation budgets. In real-world applications, ϵ highly depends on the underlying use-case and definition of the imperceptibly of adversarial examples. Hence, we argue that even though DA3G may seem to provide a limited robustness towards PGD in our experiments, it may find its application in real-world scenarios in which adversaries face a more limited perturbation space. We encourage future work to further investigate the robustness of DA3G in other potential use-cases. In our evaluation, we applied DA3G to a wide range of target networks indicating the applicability independent of the NN architecture. We envision the detection of e.g. audio adversarial examples using sequential target models.

In DA3G, we analysed the gradients based on the loss between the predicted probability distribution and the maximum distribution. Our empirical evaluation showed that the gradient is indeed suitable to reliably detect adversarial examples. As theoretical foundation, we believe that the gradient contains information about the location of robust and non-robust features similar to the work of Ilyas et al. [18]. When adversarial examples exploit non-robust features to shift the output, corresponding neurons may be subject to abnormal change, quantified by the gradient. We hope that future work will further evaluate the theoretical foundation and shed more light on the differences between benign inputs and adversarial examples.

8   Conclusion

In this paper, we presented a new end-to-end adversarial example detection method called DA3G. Our detection method automatically analyses the gradients of the network under test for potential attacks. With our evaluation under challenging threat models, we showed that DA3G reliably detects known and yet unknown attacks. Even adaptive adversaries are forced to invest significantly more computational effort to successfully bypass DA3G when attacking protected NNs. Thanks to the general target-alarm architecture, it is readily applicable to a wide range of NNs. With DA3G, we provide a reliable way to protect NNs from adversarial attacks.

A   Network Architectures

For our evaluation, we applied DA3G on a variety of common NN architectures. We give an in-depth overview of the respective parameters in Table 4.

Table 4. Architectures, training settings, and clean accuracy of the target NNs.

	Model	Architecture	Settings
(Fashion-) MNIST	LeNet5 [23]	– 2 conv. layers with filter sizes 6 and 16 – each conv. layer is followed by a average-pooling layer – finally, 1 flatten layer and 3 dense layers with 120, 84, and 10 neurons each	– learning rate: 0.001 – epochs = 20 – batch size: 128 – accuracy mnist: 98.9% – accuracy fmnist: 90.8%
	KerasExM [8]	– 2 conv. layers with filter sizes 32 and 64 – each conv. layer is followed by 1 max-pooling layer – finally, a flatten layer, a 0.5 dropout layer and a dense layers 10 neurons	– learning rate: 0.001 – epochs: 12 – batch size: 128 – accuracy mnist: 99.3% – accuracy fmnist: 90.8%
CIFAR10	KerasExC [19]	– 4 conv. layers, the first pair with filter size 32, the second pair with filter size 64 – max-pooling after each pair – 0.25 and 0.5 dropout, flatten layer, and 2 dense layers with 512 and 10 neurons	– learning rate: 0.0005 – epochs: 100 – batch size: 32 – accuracy: 85.0%
	ResNet [16]	– ResNet20, version 1 – for further details: [16]	– epochs: 200 – batch size: 32 – accuracy: 91.8%

B   Adaptive Attacks

We show our results for F-MNIST in Fig. 3.

C   PGD Attack Step Size

We evaluated multiple hyperparameters to increase the strength of the adaptive attacks. In Table 5, we list the PGD step sizes chosen for the final models. For the grey-box experiments, we used Foolbox's [31,32] default values relative to ϵ.

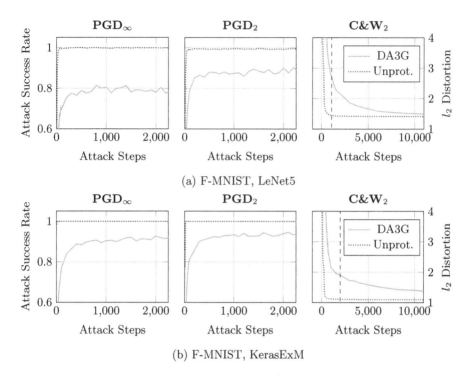

(a) F-MNIST, LeNet5

(b) F-MNIST, KerasExM

Fig. 3. Adaptive attacks on the Fashion-MNIST models. The dashed lines show the number of C&W steps required such that at least 80% of all attacks on the protected model were successful.

Table 5. PGD step sizes during the adaptive attacks.

Data	Target	PGD$_2$	PGD$_\infty$
MNIST	LeNet5	.50/ϵ	.04/ϵ
	KerasExM	.075/ϵ	.025/ϵ
F-MNIST	F-LeNet5	.30/ϵ	.015/ϵ
	F-KerasExM	.20/ϵ	.015/ϵ
CIFAR10	KerasExC	.15/ϵ	.0015/ϵ
	ResNet	.05/ϵ	.001/ϵ

References

1. Athalye, A., Carlini, N., Wagner, D.: Obfuscated gradients give a false sense of security: circumventing defenses to adversarial examples. In: 35th International Conference on Machine Learning, ICML 2018, vol. 80, pp. 274–283 (2018). http://proceedings.mlr.press/v80/athalye18a.html
2. Athalye, A., Engstrom, L., Ilyas, A., Kevin, K.: Synthesizing robust adversarial examples. In: 35th International Conference on Machine Learning, ICML 2018, vol. 80, pp. 284–293 (2018). http://proceedings.mlr.press/v80/athalye18b.html

3. Biggio, B., et al.: Evasion attacks against machine learning at test time. In: Machine Learning and Knowledge Discovery in Databases, pp. 387–402 (2013). https://doi.org/10.1007/978-3-642-40994-3_25

4. Brendel, W., Rauber, J., Bethge, M.: Decision-based adversarial attacks: reliable attacks against black-box machine learning models. In: International Conference on Learning Representations (2018). https://openreview.net/forum?id=SyZI0GWCZ

5. Carlini, N., et al.: On evaluating adversarial robustness. arXiv (2019). http://arxiv.org/abs/1902.06705

6. Carlini, N., Wagner, D.: Adversarial examples are not easily detected: bypassing ten detection methods. In: AISec 2017 - Proceedings of the 10th ACM Workshop on Artificial Intelligence and Security, pp. 3–14 (2017). http://doi.acm.org/10.1145/3128572.3140444

7. Carlini, N., Wagner, D.: Towards evaluating the robustness of neural networks. In: Proceedings - IEEE Symposium on Security and Privacy, pp. 39–57. IEEE (2017). https://doi.org/10.1109/SP.2017.49

8. Chollet, F.: Simple MNIST convnet (2015). https://keras.io/examples/vision/mnist_convnet/

9. Croce, F., Hein, M.: Reliable evaluation of adversarial robustness with an ensemble of diverse parameter-free attacks. In: Proceedings of Machine Learning Research, pp. 2206–2216. PMLR (2020). http://proceedings.mlr.press/v119/croce20b/croce20b.pdf

10. Dhaliwal, J., Shintre, S.: Gradient similarity : an explainable approach to detect adversarial attacks against deep learning (2018). https://arxiv.org/pdf/1806.10707.pdf

11. Dvijotham, K.D., et al.: Training verified learners with learned verifiers (2018). https://arxiv.org/pdf/1805.10265.pdf

12. Fidel, G., Bitton, R., Shabtai, A.: When explainability meets adversarial learning: detecting adversarial examples using SHAP signatures. In: 2020 International Joint Conference on Neural Networks (IJCNN) (2020). https://doi.org/10.1109/IJCNN48605.2020.9207637

13. Freitas, S., Chen, S.T., Wang, Z.J., Horng Chau, D.: UnMask: adversarial detection and defense through robust feature alignment. In: Proceedings - 2020 IEEE International Conference on Big Data, pp. 1081–1088 (2020). https://doi.org/10.1109/BigData50022.2020.9378303

14. Ghiasi, A., Shafahi, A., Goldstein, T.: Breaking certified defenses: semantic adversarial examples with spoofed robustness certificates. In: International Conference on Learning Representations (2020). https://openreview.net/forum?id=HJxdTxHYvB

15. Goodfellow, I.J., Shlens, J., Szegedy, C.: Explaining and harnessing adversarial examples (2015). http://arxiv.org/abs/1412.6572

16. He, K., Zhang, X., Ren, S., Sun, J.: Deep residual learning for image recognition. In: Proceedings of the IEEE Computer Society Conference on Computer Vision and Pattern Recognition, pp. 770–778 (2016). https://doi.org/10.1109/CVPR.2016.90

17. Hein, M., Andriushchenko, M.: Formal guarantees on the robustness of a classifier against adversarial manipulation. In: Advances in Neural Information Processing Systems (2017). https://proceedings.neurips.cc/paper/2017/file/e077e1a544eec4f0307cf5c3c721d944-Paper.pdf

18. Ilyas, A., Santurkar, S., Tsipras, D., Engstrom, L., Tran, B., Madry, A.: Adversarial examples are not bugs, they are features. In: Advances in Neural Information Processing Systems, vol. 32 (2019). https://proceedings.neurips.cc/paper/2019/file/e2c420d928d4bf8ce0ff2ec19b371514-Paper.pdf

19. Keras: CIFAR-10 CNN (2020). https://keras.io/examples/cifar10_cnn/
20. Klambauer, G., Unterthiner, T., Mayr, A.: Self-normalizing neural networks. In: NIPS 2017: Proceedings of the 31st International Conference on Neural Information Processing Systems, pp. 972–981 (2017). https://papers.neurips.cc/paper/2017/file/5d44ee6f2c3f71b73125876103c8f6c4-Paper.pdf
21. Krizhevsky, A.: Learning multiple layers of features from tiny images. Technical report (2009). https://www.cs.toronto.edu/~kriz/learning-features-2009-TR.pdf
22. Kurakin, A., Goodfellow, I.J., Bengio, S.: Adversarial examples in the physical world. In: International Conference on Learning Representations, ICLR, pp. 99–112 (2016). https://doi.org/10.1201/9781351251389-8
23. LeCun, Y., Bottou, L., Bengio, Y., Haffner, P.: Gradient-based learning applied to document recognition. Proc. IEEE **86**(11), 2278–2323 (1998). https://doi.org/10.1109/5.726791
24. LeCun, Y., Cortes, C., Burges, C.: MNIST handwritten digit database. ATT Labs, February 2010. http://yann.lecun.com/exdb/mnist
25. Lust, J., Condurache, A.P.: GraN: an efficient gradient-norm based detector for adversarial and misclassified examples. In: 28th European Symposium on Artificial Neural Networks, Computational Intelligence and Machine Learning (2020)
26. Madry, A., Makelov, A., Schmidt, L., Tsipras, D., Vladu, A., Science, C.: Towards deep learning models resistant to adversarial attacks. In: International Conference on Learning Representations (2018). https://openreview.net/forum?id=rJzIBfZAb
27. Moosavi-Dezfooli, S., Fawzi, A., Frossard, P.: DeepFool: a simple and accurate method to fool deep neural networks. In: 2016 IEEE Conference on Computer Vision and Pattern Recognition (CVPR), pp. 2574–2582 (2016). https://doi.org/10.1109/CVPR.2016.282
28. Nguyen, A., Yosinski, J., Clune, J.: Deep neural networks are easily fooled: high confidence predictions for unrecognizable images. In: Proceedings of the IEEE Computer Society Conference on Computer Vision and Pattern Recognition, pp. 427–436 (2015). https://doi.org/10.1109/CVPR.2015.7298640
29. Raghunathan, A., Steinhardt, J., Liang, P.: Certified defenses against adversarial examples. In: International Conference on Learning Representations (2018). https://openreview.net/forum?id=Bys4ob-Rb
30. Raghunathan, A., Steinhardt, J., Liang, P.: Semidefinite relaxations for certifying robustness to adversarial examples. In: Advances in Neural Information Processing Systems (2018). https://proceedings.neurips.cc/paper/2018/file/29c0605a3bab4229e46723f89cf59d83-Paper.pdf
31. Rauber, J., Brendel, W., Bethge, M.: Foolbox: a Python toolbox to benchmark the robustness of machine learning models. In: Reliable Machine Learning in the Wild Workshop, 34th International Conference on Machine Learning (2017). http://arxiv.org/abs/1707.04131
32. Rauber, J., Zimmermann, R., Bethge, M., Brendel, W.: Foolbox native: fast adversarial attacks to benchmark the robustness of machine learning models in PyTorch, Tensorflow, and JAX. J. Open Source Softw. **5**(53), 2607 (2020). https://doi.org/10.21105/joss.02607
33. Sharad, K., Marson, G.A., Truong, H.T.T., Karame, G.: On the security of randomized defenses against adversarial samples. In: Proceedings of the 15th ACM Asia Conference on Computer and Communications Security, pp. 381–393 (2020). https://doi.org/10.1145/3320269.3384751

34. Sperl, P., Kao, C.Y., Chen, P., Lei, X., Bottinger, K.: DLA: dense-layer-analysis for adversarial example detection. In: Proceedings 5th IEEE European Symposium on Security and Privacy, pp. 198–215 (2020). https://doi.org/10.1109/EuroSP48549.2020.00021

35. Sperl, P., Schulze, J.P., Böttinger, K.: Activation anomaly analysis. In: Machine Learning and Knowledge Discovery in Databases, pp. 69–84 (2021). https://doi.org/10.1007/978-3-030-67661-2_5

36. Su, J., Vargas, D.V., Sakurai, K.: One pixel attack for fooling deep neural networks. IEEE Trans. Evol. Comput. **23**(5), 828–841 (2019). https://doi.org/10.1109/TEVC.2019.2890858

37. Szegedy, C., et al.: Intriguing properties of neural networks. In: International Conference on Learning Representations (2014). https://openreview.net/forum?id=kklr_MTHMRQjG

38. Tramèr, F., Carlini, N., Brendel, W., Madry, A.: On adaptive attacks to adversarial example defenses. In: Advances in Neural Information Processing Systems, pp. 1633–1645 (2020). https://proceedings.neurips.cc/paper/2020/file/11f38f8ecd71867b42433548d1078e38-Paper.pdf

39. Wong, E., Zico Kolter, J.: Provable defenses against adversarial examples via the convex outer adversarial polytope. In: Proceedings of the 35th International Conference on Machine Learning, pp. 5286–5295 (2018). http://proceedings.mlr.press/v80/wong18a/wong18a.pdf

40. Xiao, H., Rasul, K., Vollgraf, R.: Fashion-MNIST: a novel image dataset for benchmarking machine learning algorithms. arXiv pp. 1–6 (2017). https://arxiv.org/pdf/1708.07747.pdf

41. Xu, W., Evans, D., Qi, Y.: Feature squeezing: detecting adversarial examples in deep neural networks. In: Network and Distributed System Security Symposium, NDSS (2018). https://doi.org/10.14722/ndss.2018.23198

42. Yang, P., Chen, J., Hsieh, C.J., Wang, J.L., Jordan, M.I.: ML-LOO: detecting adversarial examples with feature attribution. In: AAAI Conference on Artificial Intelligence (2020). https://doi.org/10.1609/aaai.v34i04.6140

43. Zhang, S., et al.: Detecting adversarial samples for deep learning models: a comparative study. IEEE Trans. Netw. Sci. Eng. **4697** (2021). https://doi.org/10.1109/tnse.2021.3057071

Common Component in Black-Boxes Is Prone to Attacks

Jiyi Zhang[1]([✉]), Wesley Joon-Wie Tann[1], Ee-Chien Chang[1], and Hwee Kuan Lee[1,2,3,4,5,6]

[1] School of Computing, National University of Singapore, Singapore, Singapore
{jzhang93,wesleyjtann,changec}@comp.nus.edu.sg
[2] Bioinformatics Institute, A*STAR Singapore, Singapore, Singapore
leehk@bii.a-star.edu.sg
[3] Singapore Eye Research Institute (SERI), Singapore, Singapore
[4] Image and Pervasive Access Lab (IPAL), Singapore, Singapore
[5] Rehabilitation Research Institute of Singapore, Singapore, Singapore
[6] Singapore Institute for Clinical Sciences, Singapore, Singapore

Abstract. Neural network models are getting increasingly complex. Large models are often modular, consisting of multiple separate sharable components. The development of such components may require specific domain knowledge, intensive computation power, and large datasets. Therefore, there is a high incentive for companies to keep these components proprietary. However, when a common component is included in multiple black-box models, it could potentially provide another attack vector and weaken security. In this paper, we present a method that "extracts" the common component from black-box models, using only limited resources. With a small number of data samples, an attacker can (1) obtain accurate information about the shared component, stealing propriety information of the intellectual property, and (2) utilize this component to train new tasks or execute subsequent attacks such as model cloning, class inversion, and adversarial attacks more effectively. Comprehensive experiments demonstrate that our proposed method successfully extracts the common component through hard-label and black-box access only. Moreover, the consequent attacks are also effective against straightforward defenses that introduce noise and dummy classifiers.

1 Introduction

Machine learning models, in particular, deep neural network models, have achieved significant progress in the past few years. As the learning tasks are getting increasingly complex, instead of training an end-to-end network for every single task, there is a recent trend of modular designs whereby composite models are built using smaller common components. For example, FaceNet [32] generates human face embeddings which can be used for verification, classification, and searching tasks.

Nonetheless, the adoption of modular design comes with new threats. Firstly, the development of some common components requires specific domain

© Springer Nature Switzerland AG 2021
E. Bertino et al. (Eds.): ESORICS 2021, LNCS 12972, pp. 584–604, 2021.
https://doi.org/10.1007/978-3-030-88418-5_28

knowledge, intensive computing resources, and high-value datasets. Hence, there is a huge incentive for companies to keep those components proprietary. When multiple models based on the same component are exposed to the public as black-boxes, it leads to a concern of whether an adversary could "extract" the component by querying the black-boxes. Secondly, the existence of a common component could be exploited by an adversary to enhance the effectiveness of known attacks such as model cloning [18, 22, 27, 28, 30, 34, 35], adversarial attacks [1, 3–5, 8, 12, 16, 20, 23, 33], and inversion attacks [9–11, 17, 19, 21, 25, 36].

In this paper, we investigate component extraction from a set of composite models that share some commonality, then employing it for other subsequent adversarial attacks. We assume the adversary has no knowledge about the models' architecture, no access to the training data of any of the models, and can only view the hard labels (i.e., index of the largest soft label) released by the black-box models. The adversary, via black-box access to multiple composite models, first extracts the common component of black-box composite models. Then, we consider a few scenarios whereby the adversary attempt to leverage the extracted component by either (1) training a composite model for new task, (2) cloning each individual composite victim, (3) conducting a class inversion attack on each composite victim, or (4) organizing adversarial attacks on each composite victim. While there are many ways to build a composite model, we focus on the common embed-then-classify workflow which consists of an embedder in the first few layers and an embedding classifier in the last remaining layers. This workflow can be found in many applications.

Similar to Papernot *et al.* [30], our method creates substitute models from black-box accesses. For the embed-then-classify workflow, we employ a tree-like structure that consists of a "trunk" and some "branches" where the trunk resembles the embedder, and the branches resemble the embedding classifiers.

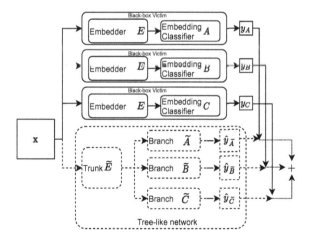

Fig. 1. Using a tree-like substitute to attack victims containing a common embedder. The three victims share the same embedder E, but each of the victims uses a different embedding classifier (A, B, C). Using input $\mathbf{x}$ and outputs (y_A, y_B, y_C), we train a substitute model and extracts its embedding trunk $\widetilde{E}$.

Figure 1 illustrates the attack where a common embedder E is used in three targeted black-box classifiers A, B, and C. Let $(\mathbf{x}, (y_A, y_B, y_C))$ be the input-output pair obtained by an adversary, where $\mathbf{x}$ is the input sample and (y_A, y_B, y_C) are the respective hard-labels from A, B and C. These input-output pairs can then be used to train the substitute model. During training, the losses are computed separately for each pair of substitute and target model, then added together for backpropagation. Using such a training method, the common functionalities of the victims are squeezed into the trunk, which is the extracted embedder. We observe through empirical evidence (See Tables 1, 2, 3) that it supports this squeezing of commonalities into the embedder trunk, and we provide an explanation for it in Sect. 4.6. The branches of the extracted embedder can be further used by an adversary for other subsequent attacks.

The proposed method is generic and applicable to different types of data and neural network architecture. Our evaluation results show it is possible to extract embedders that are sufficiently accurate to meet the attack goals. For example, let us consider the attack scenario where an embedder E was trained using 3.3 million images, and black-box access to three composite classifiers is made available to the public. In our experiments, if we train a new embedder from scratch using $7,280$ images[1], the classification accuracy is only 15.8% when used in a new classification task. However, if we utilize an embedder $\widetilde{E}$ extracted from the three classifiers, accuracy increases to 82.6% (See Table 1). Note that there is room for further improvement of the extraction since a composite with the fully trained E could achieve an accuracy of 99.2%.

This paper has the following contributions:

1. We highlight that common components in black-box classifiers make it possible for potential attacks in the black-box settings, and we provide various attack scenarios to demonstrate this vulnerability (Sect. 2).
2. We propose an attack that employs a tree-like substitute architecture with a trunk and multiple branches. Common functionality are squeezed into the trunk by adaptively lowering the size of the branches while attaining the required accuracy (Sect. 3).
3. We evaluate the effectiveness of our approach in stealing the common component (Sect. 4). We suggest two methods of evaluation: clustering capability and degree of distance preservation (Sect. 4.4). We observe that, as expected, the effectiveness improves as the number of victims increases. We also provide an explanation for this observation (Sect. 4.6).
4. We evaluate the effectiveness of subsequent attacks using the extracted common component (Sect. 4.5).

2   Threat Model

We consider four attack scenarios. In all scenarios, the victims form a set of composite models, $M_1, M_2, \ldots, M_n$, containing a common embedder E. The adversary's goal differs in each scenario.

---

[1] We assume the adversary does not have the resources to get a large number of training data.

2.1 Embedder, Composite and Victim Models

The embedder E is a neural network model which could be used in multiple tasks, for example, a face embedding algorithm FaceNet [32] that can be used for different tasks such as face recognition or emotion detection. The output of E can be consumed by other neural network models. For example, additional layers C takes the output of E as input and produces the final soft label, a.k.a, the prediction scores. Therefore, the whole workflow can be represented as a composite $M = C \circ E$. Given an input sample $\mathbf{x}$, its corresponding soft label is $M(\mathbf{x}) = (C \circ E)(\mathbf{x}) = C(E(\mathbf{x}))$. For clarity in exposition, we call E, C, M, the *embedder*, *embedding classifier*, and *composite classifier*, respectively. In the context of the threat model, when M is exposed to the adversary, M is also called the *victim*.

The embedder is trained using a large and high-value dataset $\mathcal{D}_e$, where there could be multiple embedding classifiers $C_1, C_2, ..., C_n$ used for different tasks. These embedding classifiers are trained independently. During the training of an embedding classifier C_i, a data sample $\mathbf{x}$ with ground truth label y is picked from a dataset $\mathcal{D}_i$. This sample $\mathbf{x}$ is then fed into the embedder E to generate the embedding $E(\mathbf{x})$. $(E(\mathbf{x}), y)$ is the input-output pair used to train C_i. Each trained embedding classifier C_i connects to the embedder E to form the composite model $M_i = C_i \circ E$.

2.2 Adversary's Knowledge and Capability

We consider adversaries with very limited knowledge and access to the victims. An adversary has black-box access to a set of victims: M_1, M_2, ..., M_n, where each M_i is the composite $C_i \circ E$. The adversary can adaptively feed samples to each black box and obtain the hard label. That is, for any input $\mathbf{x}$, the adversary can obtain $\arg\max M_i(\mathbf{x})$ for any i. We highlight that the adversary is not given the soft label $M_i(\mathbf{x})$.

Moreover, the adversary has no knowledge about the internal architecture of the victims. We also assume the adversary has no access to the training dataset $\mathcal{D}_e$ of the embedder or the training dataset $\mathcal{D}_1, \mathcal{D}_2, ..., \mathcal{D}_n$ of the embedding classifiers. The adversary has a very limited amount of data from a distribution the same or similar to that of $\mathcal{D}_e$. We discuss the details of the exact settings used in our evaluation in Sect. 4.

2.3 Attack Scenarios

Our main goal is to investigate the component extraction of a common embedder from a set of composite models that share some commonality; we demonstrate the threat of subsequent attacks that leverage this extracted common embedder. The following four attack scenarios give concrete illustrating examples of the threat. The settings of victims and adversary capability are the same across all scenarios.

S1. Training a Composite Model for New Task. An adversary has black-box and hard-label-only access to composite models $M_1, M_2, ..., M_n$, consisting of a common embedder E. The adversary's goal is to extract the embedder E and learn a new classification task on a different, small, labelled dataset D' using this extracted embedder, without obtaining a legal copy of embedder from the owner.

S2. Model Cloning. An adversary has black-box and hard-label-only access to composite models M_1, M_2, ..., M_n with a common embedder E. The adversary wants to "clone", that is, find a substitute $\widetilde{M}_i$ for each of the M_i such that they produce the same hard label on samples from $\mathcal{D}_i$. That is, on sample $\mathbf{x}$ from some sample distribution of adversary's choice, $\arg\max M_i(\mathbf{x}) = \arg\max \widetilde{M}_i(\mathbf{x})$.

S3. Class Inversion Attack. An adversary has black-box and hard-label access to composite models M_1, M_2, ..., M_n with a common embedder E. For each victim M_i, the adversary attempt to find a representative sample for each class of M_i. Note that class inversion differs from traditional model inversion, whose goal is to reconstruct the input image from the soft labels.

S4. Adversarial Attacks. An adversary has black-box and hard-label-only access to composite models M_1, M_2, ..., M_n with a common embedder E. The adversary attempt to find adversarial samples for each composite M_i.

3   Proposed Attack

3.1   Substitute Architecture

Tree-Like Network. To extract the commonality from a set of victims, we propose a tree-like architecture that consists of a "trunk" and some "branches", one branch representing each victim (Fig. 1). The intuition is to squeeze the functionalities shared by the victims into the trunk and leave functionalities specific to each victim in the branches. Let us denote $\widetilde{E}$ as the trunk and $\widetilde{C}_i$ as the i-th branch, where the composite $\widetilde{C}_i \circ \widetilde{E}$ is to be trained as the victim $M_i = C_i \circ E$.

Trunk. The trunk $\widetilde{E}$ has the same input dimension as the victim embedder E, therefore also the same input dimension as each victim model $M_i = C_i \circ E$. The selection of the trunk model depends on the type of input data and the nature of the task. For example, CNN could be used for image tasks. There is no specific requirement for the model architecture, but a general principle is that the trunk should at least have enough parameters to achieve the function of the common component, which adversary aims to extract. Previous research in model stealing [30] shows that the choice of model architecture has only limited impact on whether the attack would be successful. A few different candidates can be tested and the best will be chosen.

Branches. Each branch $\widetilde{C_i}$ is a shallow neural network with the same output dimension as the respective victim $M_i = C_i \circ E$, and input dimension same as the output dimension of the trunk $\widetilde{E}$. As mentioned earlier, common functionality are to be squeezed to the trunk $\widetilde{E}$ and hence the branches should be smallest viable model, that is, the number of parameters within the branches should be sufficiently small while attaining an accepted classification accuracy. In the proposed attack, this is done by searching over different choices of layers and choosing the best performing architecture.

3.2 Training

Data. Our attack only requires a small amount of unlabeled data from a similar distribution as the victims' training data. The data can either be natural samples or synthesized. In our evaluation, to ensure fairness, we carefully divide the dataset such that the adversary uses unlabeled data that are not in victims' training data. The details of data we used in the attacks can be found in Sect. 4.

Querying. The adversary queries victim models as black-boxes to label its data. For each input $\mathbf{x}$ and each composite model M_i, the hard label $\arg\max M_i(\mathbf{x})$ can be obtained. The input and output pair $(\mathbf{x}, [\arg\max M_1(\mathbf{x}), ..., \arg\max M_n(\mathbf{x})])$ can then be used to train the tree-like substitute model.

Loss Function. To train the substitute model, CrossEntropy loss is computed at each branch end and then aggregated together. The overall loss function to train the composite cloned model, therefore, is:

$$loss = \sum_{k=1}^{n} L_{CrossEntropy}(\widetilde{C_k}(\widetilde{E}(\mathbf{x})), \arg\max M_k(\mathbf{x}))$$

In such a way, both the trunk and branches can be updated in one back-propagation. The parameters of trunk and each branch can also be frozen individually in order to fine-tune and squeeze the commonality into the trunk.

Pretraining and Fine-Tuning. We found that it is beneficial to use a general pre-trained model as the trunk to kick-start the training. For example, when attacking victim models on face tasks, we use MobileNet V2 [31], pretrained on the ImageNet dataset [7]. Though the ImageNet dataset is quite different from human faces, it still helped the training to converge much faster. We also found common transfer learning techniques can help. We freeze the trunk to train the branches first quickly, then unfreeze and train the whole tree after a certain number of epochs.

3.3 Adoption in Each Attack Scenario

The proposed method extracts the common component through hard-label and black-box access, and it can be directly adopted for the following attacks in the scenarios discussed in Sect. 2.

S1. Training a Composite Model for New Task. After the tree-like substitute network is trained, trunk $\widetilde{E}$ can be used as an embedder in another new task. Given a new dataset D', we can compute embeddings for all samples. While keeping the weights of the $\widetilde{E}$ unchanged, a new embedding classifier can then be trained to classify these embeddings. This new embedding classifier, when combined with $\widetilde{E}$, gives a new composite classifier.

S2. Model Cloning. After finish training the tree-like substitute network, the trunk $\widetilde{E}$ can be connected to any of the branch $\widetilde{C_i}$ to form a composite classifier $\widetilde{C_i} \circ \widetilde{E}$. This composite classifier is a clone for the respective victim $M_i = C_i \circ E$.

S3. Class Inversion Attack. There are two ways to apply our approach and conduct a class inversion attack.

– *Attack on Cloned Models.* In attack scenario S2, an adversary is able to get a clone for each of the victims. Existing white-box inversion attacks can then be applied to these cloned models. Note the outputs of victims are hard labels, so the inversion model is only able to generate a representative for each class in the victim model.
– *Inverted Tree-Like Network.* An inverted tree-like network can be trained directly. The method is almost exactly the same as what we proposed in Sect. 3, except that direction of the tree is now swapped. The branches are individual decoders that take in victims' outputs. The outputs are then fed into the trunk, which is a shared common decoder that generates the image as the inversion result. For each branch, the mean square error loss between the generated output $\mathbf{x}'$ and the original input $\mathbf{x}$ is computed. The losses for all branches are computed and added together for backpropagation. This training process squeezes the commonality of inversion into the trunk and stores information unique to each classifier's inversion inside the branches.

S4. Adversarial Attacks. In attack scenario S2, an adversary is able to get a clone for each of the victims. Adversarial attacks, including both gradient-based or non-gradient based, can then be directly applied to the clones. The adversarial samples generated by the clones can be transferred and applied to the original victim models.

4   Evaluation on Face Classification Task

In this section, we analyze the effectiveness of the proposed attack on various face classification tasks using face image data.

4.1   Dataset

We test our approach using the FaceScrub [26] dataset. FaceScrub contains human faces of 530 identities: 265 male celebrities and 265 female celebrities. There are 106,863 images in total. We crop out the faces in the images and resize them to dimension $160 \times 160 \times 3$.

4.2   Model Setup

We choose a FaceNet Inception ResNet V1 model [32] pre-trained on VGGFace2 [2], which contains 3.3 million images of 8,631 identities, as the embedder model in victim composite models. The weights are directly obtained from the FaceNet GitHub repository[2]. Note that the model of FaceNet is public, and hence it is meaningless to "extract" it. For the purpose of evaluation, the ground truth of the embedder is required, and thus we choose FaceNet for our experimentation.

For victim embedding classifier models, we use simple neural networks with only two fully connected layers. These models take in the embeddings generated by the pre-trained FaceNet model and run classification on the identities. We train these embedding classifiers independently. We use a few different combinations of settings, which consist of different classes and different classifiers. For example, in one setting, there are 3 victim classifiers where each victim is trained to classify 10 identities. There is no overlap of training data for any two victims. When training each victim, we use 80% data for training and reserve 20% data for testing.

During the attack, we use MobileNet V2 [31] as the architecture of the trunk. We load pre-trained weights on ImageNet [7]. For the branches, we use shallow, fully connected networks.

4.3   Attack Process

We query the victim composite models as black-boxes. There are 7,280 unlabeled images from 100 identities that have no overlap with the training dataset of victim models used for the attack. The number of images we use is around 0.221% of the original dataset used to train the victim embedder, and the number of identities we use is around 1.16% of the original dataset. For all combinations of settings, we train 100 epochs and save the best models.

4.4   Benchmark of Embedder Extraction

We benchmark the extracted embedder $\widetilde{E}$ using two indicators: (Q1) clustering capability and (Q2) degree of distance preservation.

Clustering Capability of Embedder (Q1). We visualize the clustering capability of an embedder by feeding in 648 images of 10 identities from a separate testing dataset. The embeddings generated by the embedder are then projected to 2D space using t-Distributed Stochastic Neighbor Embedding (t-SNE) [14].

Here, we are using settings where each victim is trained to classify 10 classes. In Fig. 2, we show the clustering capability of seven embedders we extracted when 1, 2, 3, 6, 10, 20, 40 victims are made available for an adversary to query.

We also include the performance of training a face embedder from scratch using the same amount of data (7,280 images of 100 identities) we used to query

---

[2] https://github.com/timesler/facenet-pytorch.

the victim model. We use the same training procedure and loss function as the FaceNet paper [32]. Its clustering capability is shown in Fig. 2(i).

The results show that, with only a limited amount of data, the proposed attack is able to extract an embedder that can achieve decent clustering capability by querying some black-box victim models. Without querying the victim models, such few data points are insufficient to train a working embedder from scratch.

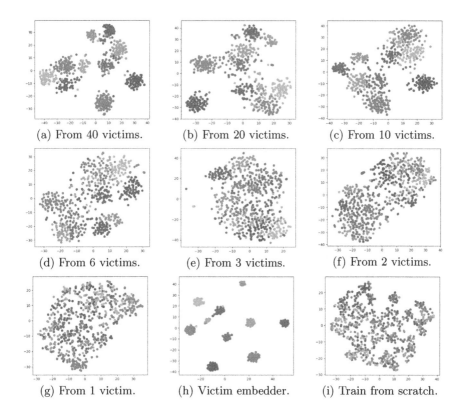

(a) From 40 victims.   (b) From 20 victims.   (c) From 10 victims.

(d) From 6 victims.   (e) From 3 victims.   (f) From 2 victims.

(g) From 1 victim.   (h) Victim embedder.   (i) Train from scratch.

Fig. 2. Comparison of the clustering capabilities of various embedders in clustering faces from testing identities. In (a)–(g), it shows the extracted embedders when 40, 20, 10, 6, 3, 2, 1 victims are made available to an adversary. The victim embedder and embedder trained from scratch are shown in (h) and (i), respectively. Each color represents one of the ten identities.

Degree of Distance Preservation (Q2). We measure the degree of distance preservation using a ratio of pairwise distances $DR(\cdot, \cdot)$. For any two samples $\mathbf{x}_1$ and $\mathbf{x}_2$, this distance ratio is computed using the embeddings generated by the extracted embedder $\widetilde{E}$ and original victim embedder E, $DR(\mathbf{x}_1, \mathbf{x}_2) = \frac{\|E(\mathbf{x}_1) - E(\mathbf{x}_2)\|}{\|\widetilde{E}(\mathbf{x}_1) - \widetilde{E}(\mathbf{x}_2)\|}$. Note that we normalize the output of each embedder first before we compute the distance ratio.

For this evaluation, we use 648 images from 10 testing identities. We compute the distance ratio for all pairs of images. In Fig. 3, we plot the distribution of distance ratio for eight extracted embedders, each from 1, 2, 3, 6, 10, 20, 30, 40 victim classifiers of 10 classes, respectively.

From Fig. 3, we can see that when there is a sufficient amount of victim models available to attack, the distance ratio distributions have small dispersion, indicating that the extracted embedders are able to generate similar embeddings as the original victim embedder.

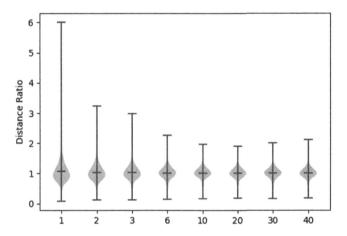

Fig. 3. Ratio of pairwise distances among embeddings generated by victim embedder and by extracted embedders. As the number of victims increases, the distance ratio distributions are closer, indicating the similarity in embeddings.

4.5 Performance in Attack Scenarios

In this section, we evaluate the performance of each attack scenario proposed in Sect. 2.3.

Training a Composite Model for New Task (S1). Here we use the embedders extracted from victims containing embedding classifiers of 10 classes. We train new embedding classifiers in three settings, each with a different number of classes. For each setting, we train 10 classifiers and take the average testing accuracy. Each embeddings classifier is trained for 30 epochs, and the best testing accuracy is recorded.

Table 1. Accuracy of classification of the extracted embedders across a various number of classes and victims. Classification accuracies increase as the number of victims increase.

Average accuracy		Original model	From scratch	No. of victims available							
				1	2	3	6	10	20	30	40
No. of classes	10	99.2%	15.8%	57.8%	75.7%	82.6%	89.0%	93.4%	94.8%	94.7%	95.5%
	20	99.2%	8.70%	43.0%	64.9%	73.0%	81.2%	88.5%	91.7%	93.3%	93.5%
	30	99.2%	6.03%	38.5%	58.4%	68.2%	78.1%	86.0%	89.2%	91.4%	92.1%

In Table 1, we can see that when there are enough victim classifiers to attack, the extracted embedder is able to achieve competitive performance as the original victim embedder, especially in tasks with a small number of classes.

Model Cloning (S2). We can observe that the accuracy of the cloned model generally increases with the number of available victims and decreases with the increase in the number of classes in each victim in Table 2. In addition, in the first row, we can see that once a certain number of victims are exposed to the attacks, we can achieve a high testing accuracy. However, after that, having access to more victims may not necessarily increase the accuracy much more.

Table 2. Accuracy of cloned models across a various number of classes and victims.

Average accuracy		Original model	No. of victims available							
			1	2	3	6	10	20	30	40
No. of classes	10	99.2 ± 0.8%	62.7%	66.6 ± 4.2%	69.9 ± 6.5%	75.1 ± 5.6%	79.3 ± 5.6%	84.4 ± 5.7%	85.8 ± 4.6%	87.0 ± 4.3%
	20	99.2 ± 0.5%	56.4%	62.5 ± 3.5%	63.5 ± 0.7%	68.9 ± 2.8%	71.6 ± 4.7%	76.8 ± 3.5%	–	–
	30	99.2 ± 0.4%	50.2%	55.4 ± 2.3%	58.1 ± 2.2%	60.1 ± 2.0%	66.1 ± 4.3%	–	–	–

Class Inversion Attack (S3). We use the same 7,280 images to query the victim model and train the inverted tree-like substitute. After we obtain this inversion model, we then convert class IDs into one-hot embeddings. For example, the embedding of the first class of a victim model is $[1,0,0,...,0]$. We feed these embeddings into the inversion model to visualize each data class. In Fig. 4, we show the inverted representatives for all classes in one of the victim classifiers. The first row shows training samples for each of the 10 classes, while the second row shows the inverted representatives for each class. We can see that even with only class IDs, the inverted images leak quite some information. For example, the genders and hairstyles match well.

Fig. 4. Inversion results for each class in a victim. First row shows sample training images for each of the 10 classes. Second row shows inverted representatives for each class.

Adversarial Attacks (S4). There are many settings of adversarial attacks; here, we only demonstrate a particular setting. An adversary first conducts model cloning. In this case, a white-box adversarial attack, an un-targeted version of Fast Gradient Sign Attack (FGSM), is then applied to the clones to generate a set of adversarial samples. We compute the transfer rate, which is the attack success rate of these adversarial samples when applied to the corresponding original victim classifiers.

We first run the attack for all testing images on the cloned classifier for each victim in each setting. The magnitude of perturbation is set to 0.1. Samples that can cause the wrong classification on the cloned classifier are then transferred and applied to the original victim. The attack success rate of these samples on the original victims (transfer rate) is shown in Table 3.

Table 3. Transfer rate of generated adversarial samples. It demonstrates the attack success rate of adversarial samples when applied to the cloned classifiers and their corresponding victim classifiers.

Transfer rate		No. of victims available							
		1	2	3	6	10	20	30	40
No. of classes	10	5.71%	7.02%	7.82%	8.80%	12.7%	10.6%	17.1%	19.0%
	20	5.05%	7.21%	8.30%	11.9%	12.1%	16.0%	–	–
	30	5.61%	7.43%	7.59%	13.8%	21.9%	–	–	–

In Table 3, we can see the transfer rates are significantly higher when the cloned models are obtained from multiple victim models. For example, for victim classifiers with 10 classes, the transfer rate is only 5.71% in a conventional single model stealing setting, while our approach is able to achieve a 19.0% transfer rate if there are 40 victims available for attack. Note the transfer rate is also higher when there are more classes in the classifier as it becomes easier for the un-targeted attack to change the result to any other class.

4.6   Observation from Empirical Evidence

From the results in the previous sections on Clustering Capability (Fig. 2), Degree of Distance Preservation (Fig. 3), Training a Composite Model for New Task (Table 1), and Model Cloning (Table 2), we observe that there is a general trend of increased performance of extracted embedder $\widetilde{E}$, as the number of victims increases. This trend holds across a various number of classes. While this observation, where the similarity of extracted $\widetilde{E}$ gets closer to the original victim embedder E as more victim classifiers are used, is intuitively true, we provide an explanation for this intuition.

In our proposed attack setting, the adversary queries victim classifier models with a small set of data. For each query input sample $\mathbf{x}$ in the data, the embedder first maps it into a particular point in the embedding space. Next, each victim classifier, with its specific task, classifies this same point by setting a plane in the embedding space to designate the boundaries. With multiple victim classifiers, each classifier delineates a plane that cuts this same embedding space, resulting in many different planes acting as constraints on the position of this point in the embedding space. Hence, as the adversary uses more victim classifiers, the performance of the extracted embedder $\widetilde{E}$ improves as each victim adds a constraint on $\widetilde{E}$ to reinforce similarity to the original embedder.

5   Analysis and Potential Defense

In Sect. 4, we evaluated the effectiveness of the proposed attack on image data. In this section, we are interested in analyzing the performance of the proposed attack under a set of special conditions. We would like to find out whether there is a weakness that we can exploit to defend against such attacks.

5.1   Similar vs Same Component

So far, we have evaluated the performance of the proposed attack against victim models containing the same component. Nonetheless, there could be different versions of a component with the same functionality. For example, in the case of face classification, the model owners may choose different face embedders. In addition, the model owner may deliberately deploy different variants of the embedders as an attempt of defense. Here we evaluate the performance of the proposed attack when victim classifiers use components with the same functionality but different models and parameters instead of using the exact same component.

We use two different face embedders to simulate these scenarios. One is trained using the VGGFace2 dataset, and the other is trained using the CASIA WebFace dataset. We create 6 victim models by training 3 embedding classifiers for each of these two face embedders. We then apply the proposed attack on these victims and compare its performance with the reference setting, where 6 victim classifiers all use the same face embedder trained on VGGFace2.

Table 4. Comparison of performance between embedders extracted from victims using the exact same embedder and victims using two different embedders with the same functionality.

	6 classifiers with embedder trained on VGGFace2	3 classifiers with embedder trained on VGGFace2 + 3 classifiers with embedder trained on CASIA WebFace	
Model cloning accuracy	75.1± 5.6%	VGGFace2	CASIA WebFace
		81.5± 4.7%	81.7± 1.1%
Performance in new tasks (No. of classes) 10	89.0%	91.8%	
20	81.2%	84.5%	
30	78.1%	81.6%	

In Table 4, we can see the outcomes for the proposed attack are consistent no matter whether the same embedder is used or different embedders with the same functionality are used. By extracting from victim classifiers with different embedders, it actually results in better model cloning accuracy. The embedder extracted from victims using different embedders with the same functionality also performs better in new classification tasks.

As the proposed attack only looks for the hard labels produced by the black-box victims, using different variants of the embedder is unlikely to cause any drawback in performance.

5.2   Noisy Victims

When the adversary tries to collect a set of victims sharing the same component, irrelevant models may be accidentally included and make the set of victim models noisy. In addition, model owners may deliberately set up additional models as an attempt to mislead the attacking process and protect the victims. Here we conduct an experiment where some other models which do not share the same common component are also treated as victims and test how this may affect the performance of the proposed attack.

In this experiment, we create 6 victim face classifiers where each of them uses FaceNet's embedder to generate embeddings for a different set of face images and then uses an embedding classifier to classify these embeddings into 10 classes. We consider two different ways to add additional models into this clean set of victims and make it noisy: (1) Deploy dummy composite models with the same architecture but share an embedder that is randomly initialized. The embedding classifier inside each dummy model is also randomly initialized. (2) Include random pickers, which pick random numbers sampled from a uniform distribution and return as results.

We test four different settings where 0, 6, 60, 120 fake victims are included in the set, making the ratio of real and fake victims 1:0, 1:1, 1:10, 1:20. For each setting, we test both additional dummy models and random pickers and compare the performance of the proposed attack on these two versions of a noisy set of victims against the performance on a clean set of victims.

Table 5. Performance of proposed attack on noisy sets of victims containing different number of additional victims.

No. of additional victims			0	6	60	120
Model cloning accuracy		Dummy classifier	75.1 ± 5.6%	77.2 ± 7.2%	75.2 ± 7.1%	73.2 ± 9.0%
		Random picker		76.1 ± 7.9%	75.9 ± 6.6%	76.5 ± 6.7%
Performance in new tasks (No. of classes)	10	Dummy classifier	89.0%	91.1%	89.9%	90.5%
		Random picker		89.8%	87.7%	86.1%
	20	Dummy classifier	81.2%	84.0%	83.9%	83.8%
		Random picker		83.4%	79.2%	77.5%
	30	Dummy Classifier	78.1%	81.7%	80.6%	81.0%
		Random Picker		80.9%	75.6%	74.7%

In Table 5, we repeat the experiment in Sect. 4.5 on the noisy sets of victims. We show the (a) model cloning accuracy and (b) performance of each embedder when used to train new embedding classifiers. On the one hand, while we observe some slight drop in model cloning accuracy, it seems that the decrease is rather limited. On the other hand, the extracted embedders obtained the same or even better performance when the victim sets are noisier. Intuitively, when there is an overwhelming amount of fake victims, the attack will eventually be ineffective. Therefore, it is interesting to find out the number of fake victims required to break the proposed attack. It seems even when the ratio of real and fake victims reaches 1:20, there is still no significant decrease in attack performance.

5.3   Complexity of Victim Models

We are interested in knowing whether the success of the attack depends on the simplicity of victim models. In other words, we would like to know whether making the victims more complicated can mitigate the proposed attack.

One method of making the model more complicated is to add more layers. Since we have already used quite complicated embedders in our previous evaluations, we replace the simple embedding classifiers and add more layers. We repeat the experiments in Sect. 4 and create 6 victim models using the same ResNet face embedder trained on VGGFace2 but replace the 2-layer embedding classifier with 5 layers. We then apply the proposed attack on these victims and compare the performance.

Table 6. Comparison of performance between embedders extracted from clean and noisy sets of victims.

		ResNet embedder + 2 Layer	ResNet embedder + 5 Layer
Model cloning accuracy		75.1 ± 5.6%	74.5 ± 4.1%
Performance in new tasks (No. of classes)	10	89.0%	88.4%
	20	81.2%	81.1%
	30	78.1%	76.5%

In Table 6, we can see that for the same task, the depth of the model does not seem to affect the performance of the proposed attack a lot. The model cloning accuracy and performance of the embedder in new classification tasks remains unchanged. In fact, as the proposed attack only utilizes the hard labels, the internals of the victims do not matter much, especially when the victim composite classifiers have reached high accuracy.

Another way of making the victim classifier more complicated is to add dummy output classes and make the output dimension larger. In Sect. 4, we observe that for victims with more output classes, it requires more victim classifiers to be available such that the proposed attack can be effective. This property could be explored as a potential direction of defense. Nonetheless, certain techniques must be applied to make it difficult for an adversary to distinguish real output units and dummy ones.

5.4   Data Distribution

We found that attacking the victim models using data from a wrong distribution makes the attack less successful. We conducted an experiment on composite classifiers on face classification tasks.

We created 6 victim face classifiers where each of them uses FaceNet's embedder to generate embeddings for a different set of face images and then uses an embedding classifier to classify these face embeddings into 10 classes. We attack these victims using the CIFAR-10 [15] data and compare its performance with attacks conducted using face images.

Table 7. Performance of proposed attack when using data from same (Face Images) and different (CIFAR-10) distributions.

	Attack using face images	Attack using CIFAR-10
Model cloning accuracy	$75.1 \pm 5.6\%$	$36.3 \pm 7.6\%$

In Table 7, we can see that querying the victims using data from a wrong distribution significantly decreases the model cloning accuracy, indicating decreased similarity between the extracted embedder and the original victim embedder.

In Fig. 5, we can also observe that the embedder extracted using samples from a wrong distribution is not able to cluster the face images well.

The above results show that it is important to know the data distribution of victims for the proposed attack to work. It is arguably easy to guess the distribution of a model when the victim is exposed as a white-box model or when soft labels are given. However, for the setting in this paper, the adversary only has access to hard labels. This means that for any given input, the victim classifier always returns a class index without any confidence score, which makes guessing the correct input distribution much more difficult.

While this could be a possible direction for defense, building a defense based on this property may cause many limitations. For example, the classifier models could not be deployed as public APIs since the data distribution has to be made public in such cases.

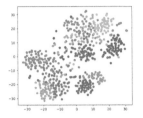 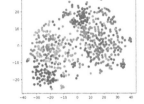

(a) Extracted using face images.   (b) Extracted using CIFAR-10 images.

Fig. 5. Comparison of clustering capabilities between embedders extracted using face and CIFAR-10 images.

6   Conclusion

We present a new angle of black-box attack on neural network models. Instead of attacking just one victim, we exploit the fact that a common component, possibly proprietary, is often used in multiple different victim models. We propose an attack that allows us to extract a common component that has more capability than the end-to-end victims. We conducted extensive experiments and the results have demonstrated that our approach is highly effective, requires minimum access to the victims, and is quite robust even under a noisy setting.

As neural network models are getting increasingly complex, modular design is becoming an increasingly popular trend. It is interesting to determine whether such kinds of design would lead to a new security threat or even opportunities to harden the security. Our attack shows that reusing a common proprietary component while exposing the overall classifier as black-boxes could allow an adversary to steal this component. In addition, the common functionality could be exploited to enhance the effectiveness of some known attacks. While modularity is essential in complex design, we hope that this work would bring attention to the security of the modular design.

Acknowledgement. This research is supported by the National Research Foundation, Singapore under its Strategic Capability Research Centres Funding Initiative. Any opinions, findings and conclusions or recommendations expressed in this material are those of the author(s) and do not reflect the views of National Research Foundation, Singapore. This work is partly supported by the Biomedical Research Council of the Agency for Science, Technology, and Research, Singapore.

A   Evaluation on Time Series Audio Data and Speaker Classification

The proposed strategy is generic and can be applied on different types of data and neural network architecture. We repeat a similar set of experiments as Sect. 4 on audio data and voice classification tasks.

A.1   Dataset

This evaluation was done using LibriSpeech [29] dataset. The version we use contains 100 h of English speech from 251 unique speakers. We use 100 speakers to train the victim embedding classifiers and use 100 speakers to attack the victims. The remaining speakers are reserved for analysis.

A.2   Model Setup

We choose a SpeakerNet model [6] trained on development set of VoxCeleb2 [24] which contains 145,569 voice recordings of 5,994 speakers with data augmentation, as the victim embedder. The weights are directly obtained from GitHub repository[3]. For embedding classifiers, we also use simple models with only two fully connected layers and same train and test splitting as Sect. 4. Similar to our evaluation on image dataset, we also test a set of different combinations of settings for victims. During the attack, to construct the tree-like substitute, we use the ResNet34Half [13] as the trunk and shallow fully connected networks as branches.

A.3   Attack Process

We query the victim classifiers as black-boxes. We use 9,061 unlabeled voice recordings from 100 speakers which have no overlap with the training data of victims for the attack. The number of recordings we use is around 6.22% of the original dataset used to training the victim embedder and the number of speakers we use is around 1.67% of the original dataset. For all combination of settings, we train 100 epochs and save the best models.

A.4   Benchmark of Embedder Extraction

Clustering Capability of Embedder (Q1). We visualize the clustering capability of the extracted embedders using 964 voice recordings of 10 speakers from a separate testing dataset. Here we are using the embedders extracted from victims with 10 classes. The embeddings generated by the original embedder and extracted embedder are projected to 2D space using t-Distributed Stochastic Neighbor Embedding (t-SNE) [14]. We also try training from scratch using the

---

[3] https://github.com/clovaai/voxceleb_trainer.

same amount of data we used to query the victim model. However, the amount of data is too little to generate any meaningful result.

In Fig. 6, we can see that embedders extracted from multiple victim classifiers indeed have significantly better clustering capabilities. The embedder extracted from a single victim performs poorly.

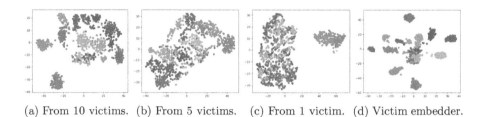

(a) From 10 victims.   (b) From 5 victims.   (c) From 1 victim.   (d) Victim embedder.

Fig. 6. Comparison of capabilities in clustering voice of 10 testing speakers. Each color represents a speaker.

Degree of Distance Preservation (Q2). Here we did a similar experiment as in Sect. 4.4 to compute ratio of pairwise distances among embeddings generated by both the extracted embedders and victim embedder. We use 964 voice recordings of 10 speakers for this experiment.

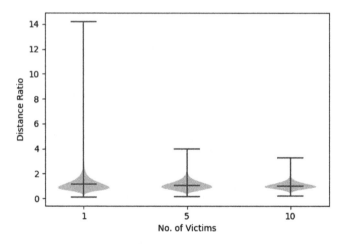

Fig. 7. Ratio of pairwise distances among embeddings generated by victim embedder and by extracted embedders.

In Fig. 7, we plot the distribution of distance ratio for 3 embedders, each extracted from 1, 5, 10 victim classifiers of 10 classes respectively. Extracting from more victim models yields much smaller dispersion, indicating the distances are better preserved.

A.5   Performance in Attack Scenarios

Training a Composite Model for New Task (S1). We evaluate the performance of the extracted embedders when used in new voice classification tasks. Here we use the embedders we extracted from victims with 10 classes. They are the models visualized in Fig. 6(a)(b)(c). In Table 8, we can see performance of the embedder increases with the amount of victims available for extraction, and decreases with the number of classes.

Table 8. Accuracy of classification when using extracted embedders to create embedding.

Average accuracy		Original model	No. of victim classifiers available		
			1	5	10
No. of classes	5	99.1%	77.0%	93.2%	96.7%
	10	98.4%	60.6%	83.8%	91.8%
	20	98.0%	44.9%	76.4%	85.7%

References

1. Brendel, W., Rauber, J., Bethge, M.: Decision-based adversarial attacks: reliable attacks against black-box machine learning models. In: ICLR (2018)
2. Cao, Q., Shen, L., Xie, W., Parkhi, O.M., Zisserman, A.: Vggface2: a dataset for recognising faces across pose and age. In: FG, pp. 67–74 (2018)
3. Carlini, N., Wagner, D.A.: Towards evaluating the robustness of neural networks. In: IEEE S&P, pp. 39–57 (2017)
4. Chen, P., Sharma, Y., Zhang, H., Yi, J., Hsieh, C.: EAD: elastic-net attacks to deep neural networks via adversarial examples. In: AAAI, pp. 10–17 (2018)
5. Chen, S., He, Z., Sun, C., Huang, X.: Universal adversarial attack on attention and the resulting dataset damagenet. arXiv preprint 2001.06325 (2020)
6. Chung, J.S., et al.: In defence of metric learning for speaker recognition. In: Interspeech (2020)
7. Deng, J., Dong, W., Socher, R., Li, L., Li, K., Li, F.: Imagenet: a large-scale hierarchical image database. In: CVPR, pp. 248–255 (2009)
8. Dong, Y., Liao, F., Pang, T., Hu, X., Zhu, J.: Discovering adversarial examples with momentum. arXiv preprint 1710.06081 (2017)
9. Dosovitskiy, A., Brox, T.: Generating images with perceptual similarity metrics based on deep networks. In: NIPS, pp. 658–666 (2016)
10. Dosovitskiy, A., Brox, T.: Inverting visual representations with convolutional networks. In: CVPR, pp. 4829–4837 (2016)
11. Fredrikson, M., Jha, S., Ristenpart, T.: Model inversion attacks that exploit confidence information and basic countermeasures. In: ACM CCS, pp. 1322–1333 (2015)
12. Goodfellow, I.J., Shlens, J., Szegedy, C.: Explaining and harnessing adversarial examples. In: ICLR (2015)
13. He, K., Zhang, X., Ren, S., Sun, J.: Deep residual learning for image recognition. CoRR abs/1512.03385 (2015)

14. Hinton, G.E., Roweis, S.T.: Stochastic neighbor embedding. In: NIPS, pp. 833–840 (2002)
15. Krizhevsky, A.: Learning multiple layers of features from tiny images. Technical report (2009)
16. Kurakin, A., Goodfellow, I.J., Bengio, S.: Adversarial examples in the physical world. In: ICLR (2017)
17. Lee, S., Kil, R.M.: Inverse mapping of continuous functions using local and global information. IEEE Trans. Neural Netw. 5(3), 409–423 (1994)
18. Lowd, D., Meek, C.: Adversarial learning. In: ACM SIGKDD, pp. 641–647 (2005)
19. Lu, B., Kita, H., Nishikawa, Y.: Inverting feedforward neural networks using linear and nonlinear programming. IEEE Trans. Neural Netw. 10(6), 1271–1290 (1999)
20. Madry, A., Makelov, A., Schmidt, L., Tsipras, D., Vladu, A.: Towards deep learning models resistant to adversarial attacks. In: ICLR (2018)
21. Mahendran, A., Vedaldi, A.: Understanding deep image representations by inverting them. In: CVPR, pp. 5188–5196 (2015)
22. Milli, S., Schmidt, L., Dragan, A.D., Hardt, M.: Model reconstruction from model explanations. In: FAT*, pp. 1–9 (2019)
23. Moosavi-Dezfooli, S., Fawzi, A., Frossard, P.: Deepfool: a simple and accurate method to fool deep neural networks. In: CVPR, pp. 2574–2582 (2016)
24. Nagrani, A., Chung, J.S., Xie, W., Zisserman, A.: Voxceleb: large-scale speaker verification in the wild. Comput. Speech Lang. 60, 101027 (2020)
25. Nash, C., Kushman, N., Williams, C.K.I.: Inverting supervised representations with autoregressive neural density models. In: AISTATS, vol. 89, pp. 1620–1629 (2019)
26. Ng, H., Winkler, S.: A data-driven approach to cleaning large face datasets. In: ICIP, pp. 343–347 (2014)
27. Oh, S.J., Schiele, B., Fritz, M.: Towards reverse-engineering black-box neural networks. In: Samek, W., Montavon, G., Vedaldi, A., Hansen, L.K., Müller, K.-R. (eds.) Explainable AI: Interpreting, Explaining and Visualizing Deep Learning. LNCS (LNAI), vol. 11700, pp. 121–144. Springer, Cham (2019). https://doi.org/10.1007/978-3-030-28954-6_7
28. Orekondy, T., Schiele, B., Fritz, M.: Knockoff nets: stealing functionality of black-box models. In: CVPR, pp. 4954–4963 (2019)
29. Panayotov, V., Chen, G., Povey, D., Khudanpur, S.: Librispeech: an ASR corpus based on public domain audio books. In: ICASSP, pp. 5206–5210 (2015)
30. Papernot, N., McDaniel, P.D., Goodfellow, I.J., Jha, S., Celik, Z.B., Swami, A.: Practical black-box attacks against machine learning. In: AsiaCCS, pp. 506–519 (2017)
31. Sandler, M., Howard, A.G., Zhu, M., Zhmoginov, A., Chen, L.: Mobilenetv 2: inverted residuals and linear bottlenecks. In: CVPR, pp. 4510–4520 (2018)
32. Schroff, F., Kalenichenko, D., Philbin, J.: Facenet: a unified embedding for face recognition and clustering. In: CVPR, pp. 815–823 (2015)
33. Szegedy, C., et al.: Intriguing properties of neural networks. In: ICLR (2014)
34. Tramèr, F., Zhang, F., Juels, A., Reiter, M.K., Ristenpart, T.: Stealing machine learning models via prediction apis. In: USENIX (2016)
35. Wang, B., Gong, N.Z.: Stealing hyperparameters in machine learning. In: IEEE S&P, pp. 36–52 (2018)
36. Yang, Z., Zhang, J., Chang, E., Liang, Z.: Neural network inversion in adversarial setting via background knowledge alignment. In: ACM CCS, pp. 225–240 (2019)

LiMNet: Early-Stage Detection of IoT Botnets with Lightweight Memory Networks

Lodovico Giaretta[1]([⊠]) , Ahmed Lekssays[2] , Barbara Carminati[2] ,
Elena Ferrari[2] , and Šarūnas Girdzijauskas[1]

[1] KTH Royal Institute of Technology, Stockholm, Sweden
{lodovico,sarunasg}@kth.se
[2] University of Insubria, Varese, Italy
{alekssays,barbara.carminati,elena.ferrari}@uninsubria.it

Abstract. IoT devices have been growing exponentially in the last few years. This growth makes them an attractive target for attackers due to their low computational power and limited security features. Attackers use IoT botnets as an instrument to perform DDoS attacks which caused major disruptions of Internet services in the last decade. While many works have tackled the task of detecting botnet attacks, only a few have considered early-stage detection of these botnets during their propagation phase.

While previous approaches analyze each network packet individually to predict its maliciousness, we propose a novel deep learning model called LiMNet (**Li**ghtweight **M**emory **Net**work), which uses an internal memory component to capture the behaviour of each IoT device over time. This memory incorporates both packet features and behaviour of the peer devices. With this information, LiMNet achieves almost maximum AUROC classification scores, between 98.8% and 99.7%, with a 14% improvement over state of the art. LiMNet is also lightweight, performing inference almost 8 times faster than previous approaches.

Keywords: IoT · Botnet detection · Memory networks · Recurrent networks

1 Introduction

IoT devices are gaining popularity thanks to their usefulness in gathering and processing data. They have become an important pillar in Industry 4.0, which

This project has received funding from the European Union's Horizon 2020 research and innovation programme under the Marie Skłodowska-Curie grant agreement No 813162. The content of this paper reflects the views only of their author(s). The European Commission/ Research Executive Agency are not responsible for any use that may be made of the information it contains.

© Springer Nature Switzerland AG 2021
E. Bertino et al. (Eds.): ESORICS 2021, LNCS 12972, pp. 605–625, 2021.
https://doi.org/10.1007/978-3-030-88418-5_29

led to an exponential growth in terms of IoT deployments worldwide. As a result, the number of IoT connections is expected to reach 83 billions by 2024.[1]

Their growing number is one reason IoT devices have become an attractive target for attackers. Another reason is that cybersecurity practices for IoT deployments are still not well understood and often not applied. For instance, IoT devices often use weak passwords and unencrypted network traffic[2]. Moreover, their low computational power limits their ability to run sophisticated security solutions. Thus, vulnerable IoT devices are exploited by attackers by injecting malicious software (malware) to perform various attacks (e.g., Distributed Denial of Service (DDoS)) on different targets. For example, the DNS provider Dyn faced one of the largest known DDoS attacks that reached 1.2 Tbps [2]. The attack was performed by Mirai, a type of malware that spreads across IoT devices to form a network of compromised devices referred to as a botnet.

There are several contributions in the literature focusing on detecting IoT botnet attacks based on network traffic patterns [3,9,12,19], using different machine learning (ML) techniques (e.g., Recurrent Neural Networks (RNN), Convolutional Neural Networks (CNN), etc.). Yet, few works focus on detecting IoT botnets during their spreading phase, before any attacks. These approaches typically use shallow ML techniques [7] or recurrent neural networks [1] to analyze network packet headers. Unfortunately, while these models provide good accuracy, their architectures exhibit several limitations, such as low inference speed and the inability to account for temporal and topological information.

In this paper, we expose the issues and limitations of these state-of-the-art models for early-stage botnet detection, propose changes to mitigate these issues, and propose an alternative model called LiMNet (**Li**ghtweight **M**emory **Net**work). LiMNet is a novel device-centric model for early-stage botnet detection. It uses an internal memory to understand the behaviour of each IoT device and employs mutually-recurrent units to capture the causal interactions among the devices over time. This allows it to classify infected and under-attack devices, in addition to malicious packets. LiMNet is designed to be a lightweight model suitable for large-scale IoT deployments. It achieves better results than state-of-the-art recurrent models, while being smaller in memory footprint and faster during inference.

Contributions. The main contributions of this work can therefore be summarized as follows, in order of importance:

1. A a novel lightweight model for early-stage IoT botnet detection based on memory networks and mutually-recurrent units, which achieves near maximum scores ($\sim$99% AUROC), 14% better than state of the art, while being almost 8 times faster in inference;
2. novel device classification tasks to aid the deployment of targeted countermeasures in infected Iot networks;

---

[1] https://www.juniperresearch.com/press/iot-connections-to-reach-83-bn-by-2024.
[2] https://www.enisa.europa.eu/publications/baseline-security-recommendations-for-iot.

3. a critical analysis of the issues and limitations of state-of-the art recurrent models for early-stage IoT botnet detection;
4. a modification to the input representations of existing recurrent models, mitigating some generalization issues while providing 4 times faster inference.

The rest of the paper is organized as follows. Section 2 provides background on IoT botnets and ML techniques. Section 3 introduces the state of the art for early-stage botnet detection. Section 4 presents LiMNet, while Sect. 5 analyzes the limitations of recurrent models for botnet detection. Sections 6 and 7 present the evaluation methodology and experimental results, respectively. Sections 8 and 9 provide insights and conclusions. Finally, Appendix A further analyses the datasets used, while Appendices B and C present additional results.

2 Background

To understand the limitations of existing recurrent models for botnet detection and the architecture of LiMNet, we first introduce some background information on IoT botnets (Sect. 2.1) and several concepts from the ML field, namely Recurrent Neural Networks (Sect. 2.2), Memory Networks (Sect. 2.3) and Graph Representation Learning (Sect. 2.4).

2.1 IoT Botnets

Botnets present four main components: the bot, the C&C server, the loader, and the report server [12]. The bot is a malicious executable that infects IoT devices and is responsible for executing commands issued by the botmaster (i.e., the owner of the botnet). The C&C server is a dashboard that communicates with all compromised devices. It is managed by the botmaster and allow him/her to issue commands to the bot to, for example, orchestrate an attack. The loader is the component that helps in disseminating the malware in different computer architectures (e.g., ARM, x86, etc.) by communicating with potential new victims. Finally, the report server stores information about the bots.

Botnets are designed with different architectures. While some botnets like Torii, Mirai and its variants are based on a centralized architecture where there is only one central C&C server, other botnets, such as Hajime, employ decentralized communication patterns [12].

While IoT botnets present similar ways of attacking and infecting devices, they often differ in how they identify potential victims. Certain botnets can random Internet devices (e.g. Bashlite/gafgyt), while others prioritize scanning the local network. There are also botnets with unknown or non-trivial behaviour, such as Torii, for which the source code is not available, and Hajime, for which no attacks have been observed yet.

Mirai is one of the largest botnets currently active in IoT environments, with over 600k bots and attacks surpassing 1 Tbps in traffic volume, making it an important target for analysis. Infected devices scan random IPv4 addresses by sending TCP SYN probes on Telnet using TCP/23 or TCP/2323, ignoring a list of hard-coded IP addresses. If a device responds, its credentials are brute-forced using a hard-coded list of 62 username and password combinations, which are extracted from default configurations of IoT devices. Upon a successful login attempt, the credentials and IP address of the device are sent to the report server. Then, the loader can log into the new victim, determine its architecture and download the appropriate build of the bot. After that, the malware hides itself by changing its process name and kills all processes using TCP/23 or TCP/2323, or processes of other competing bots. In parallel, it listens for commands from the C&C server while scanning for new victims [2].

The spreading phase and the attack phase of a botnet are independent. The spreading phase starts when a device is infected and tries to recruit new victims. On the other hand, the attack phase begins when the botmaster issues commands via the C&C to the bots to perform an orchestrated attack on a target, usually in the form of a distributed denial of service (DDoS).

2.2   Recurrent Neural Networks

Recurrent neural networks (RNNs) [20] are a type of deep learning model that takes sequential data as input. RNNs can be used to process a variety of sequential inputs, such as sentences in language translation, sounds in speech recognition, or time-series in financial analysis. RNN models typically have small sizes, as the same operations and internal weights (referred to as a *cell*) are reused to process each entry in the sequence. The entries are processed one at a time, as each cell takes as an additional input a *memory* produced by the previous cell and outputs an updated memory for the next cell. This allows RNNs to model the evolution of the sequence and interpret later entries based on earlier ones, but it also makes RNNs slower than non-sequential models.

Several RNN cell types have been introduced over the years. For instance, LSTMs (Long Short Term Memory) use two memory vectors to remember important facts over longer sequences, compared to the original RNN cells [4]. GRUs (Gated Recurrent Units) achieve similar results but use a single memory vector and less internal weights [4]. Finally, FastGRNN cells [14] are even smaller and faster, while maintaining good output quality.

RNNs are often used in conjunction with *embedding layers*. These are responsible for converting arbitrary tokens into numerical vectors that can then be input to the RNN, or to other deep learning models, using a lookup table. For example, in a language translation application, a word embedding layer maps each word to a low-dimensional space, where its position with respect to other words encodes the meaning and usage of the word itself. This position is trained jointly with the rest of the ML model. Embedding layers are often very large, as a separate vector is needed for each possible input token.

2.3   Memory Networks

Memory networks [25] were introduced to address the limited capability of deep learning models to store and organize long-term memories. They introduce a novel long-term memory component that can be dynamically updated based on new input facts, which are stored and then retrieved to respond to queries.

In addition to the internal memory, memory networks have four components. First, an *input feature map* converts the input to an internal representation, which is then used by a *generalization layer* to update the internal memory of the model. The updated memory and the input representation are then combined by an *output feature map* into an output representation, which is finally used by a *response layer* to produce the actual output.

Memory networks have been effectively applied in several fields, including question answering [25] and recommender systems [6].

2.4   Graph Representation Learning on Temporal Interaction Networks

Graph Representation Learning (GRL) is the field of extracting low-dimensional representations from graph-structured data, in order to apply ML techniques on them [8]. Temporal Interaction Networks are graphs where an edge between two nodes indicates that they interacted at a specific time. These networks naturally evolve over time to incorporate new interactions. Several techniques have been proposed to capture both short-term and long-term behaviour of these graphs, with a focus on recommender systems. In particular, JODIE [13] and DGNN [16] employ mutually-recurrent neural networks to update the short-term representations of the nodes involved after each interaction. DeepRed[11] is conceptually similar, but forgoes recurrent networks in favor of dynamically generating short-term representations from long-term embeddings.

While the literature on GRL for temporal interaction networks and that of memory models are mostly separate, we note that the described GRL techniques can be seen as particular instances of the broader memory model concept, as they dynamically update their internal knowledge in response to incoming information, and subsequently use this updated knowledge to perform predictions.

3   Related Work

Many works have tackled the issue of IoT botnet detection using ML models. One popular direction, which also applies to other types of malware, consists in performing static or dynamic analysis of the executable file on the infected device itself. For instance, in [22], a Convolutional Neural Network is used to detect printable string information stored in the executable code of IoT botnets.

A different direction explored in the broader domain of malware detection consists of analyzing traffic at the network level to identify which nodes in a network are infected. In particular, a number of features are extracted from each network packet and fed to an ML model which classifies the packet as benign or malicious. In the context of IoT botnets specifically, several works used network-level analysis to detect botnets in the attack phase, with the goal of mitigating these attacks by filtering malicious traffic. Different ML techniques have been employed, including deep autoencoders fed with statistical packet features [18] and recurrent models fed with packet headers [9,17].

Another research direction focuses on exploiting graph theory to detect botnets, not only in IoT but also in more traditional settings. As P2P bots frequently communicate with each other, community detection techniques have proven effective in detecting them [5,23,27]. Statistical approaches have also been used to identify correlations between nodes and thus infer botnet affiliations [15,26].

Yet, few work have focused on detecting botnets during their propagation phase, before any large-scale attacks. MedBIoT[7] is a dataset explicitly designed for this task. Its authors evaluate the performance of simple techniques including k-Nearest Neighbours classifiers, decision trees and random forests. Recurrent models have also been shown to be very effective for early-stage detection on MedBIoT [1]. These models, like the ones for detection of botnet attacks by which they are inspired [9], treat packet headers as sequences of fields, such as IP address, source port, packet length, etc. The low-dimensional representations of these fields, obtained from an embedding layer, are passed to layers of recurrent cells, with the last output being fed to a classifier for botnet detection.

Our approach, LiMNet, focuses on IoT botnet spreading, but differs from the discussed works [1,7] in several aspects. First, LiMNet is a memory network which learns device representations, rather than a recurrent network focused on packet representations. This allows it to more easily identify not only malicious packets, but also devices that have been, or will soon be, infected. Furthermore, it uses few key packet features, rather than all header fields.

4   LiMNet: A Lightweight Memory Network for Early-Stage Botnet Detection

LiMNet is a novel Lightweight Memory Network that can extract causal relationships from a stream of interactions between nodes in a graph, store relevant node-level information in an internal memory and use this information to solve node- and interaction-level tasks.

While LiMNet should be able to generalize to temporal interaction networks from various domains, here we focus solely on early-stage detection of IoT botnets, where the interactions are network packets and the nodes are IoT devices.

In this context, LiMNet substantially differs from previous works in that it is device-centric, rather than packet-centric. It builds and tunes over time an internal representation of the behaviour of each device and then uses this, combined with packet features, to identify bots. This provides it with important additional information compared to state-of-the-art models that analyze each packet in isolation.

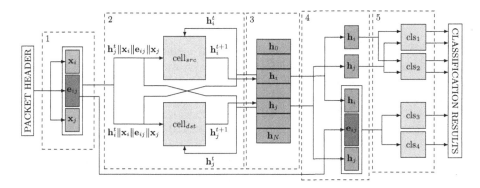

Fig. 1. Structure of LiMNet with two device classifiers and two packet classifiers. Colored boxes are: blue) memory representations green) packet features orange) device features grey) trainable networks. Dashed numbered boxes are: 1) input feature map 2) generalization layer 3) memory 4) output feature map 5) response layer.

4.1 LiMNet Architecture

Figure 1 provides an overview of LiMNet. We subdivide its description following the four main components of any memory model (cfr. Section 2.3): input feature map, generalization layer, output feature map and response.

Input Feature Map. Given an incoming packet, tshark[3] is used to extract the packet length and the IP addresses of source and destination devices, and also to infer the application-level communication protocol, or the transport-level protocol if the former cannot be detected. A feature vector for the packet is then built by concatenating its normalized length with the one-hot encoding of the detected protocol. For each of the source and destination addresses, a feature vector is built containing two binary features: whether they are unicast or multicast and whether they are public or private addresses.

Generalization Layer. The generalization layer consists of two mutually-recurrent cells, inspired by JODIE [13] and DGNN [16]. These can be LSTM, GRU or FastGRNN cells, as introduced in Sect. 2.2. The memory of the model is a dictionary mapping IP addresses to the memory of the recurrent cells. The source cell (resp. destination cell) updates the memory representation of the source node (resp. destination node), using as input the concatenation of the edge features, address features of both devices and previous memory of the destination node (resp. source node). More precisely, when a new packet is sent from IP address i to IP address j, the following update is performed:

$$\mathbf{h}_i^{t+1} = \text{cell}_{\text{src}}\left(\mathbf{h}_j^t \| \mathbf{x}_i \| \mathbf{e}_{ij} \| \mathbf{x}_j \,,\, \mathbf{h}_i^t\right) \tag{1}$$

$$\mathbf{h}_j^{t+1} = \text{cell}_{\text{dst}}\left(\mathbf{h}_i^t \| \mathbf{x}_i \| \mathbf{e}_{ij} \| \mathbf{x}_j \,,\, \mathbf{h}_j^t\right) \tag{2}$$

where $\mathbf{e}_{ij}$, $\mathbf{x}_i$ and $\mathbf{x}_j$ are the feature vectors for, respectively, the packet, the device i and device j, and $\mathbf{h}_i^t$ (resp. $\mathbf{h}_j^t$) is the memory representation of device i

---

[3] https://www.wireshark.org/docs/man-pages/tshark.html.

(resp. j) after t packets have been processed. This representation is the memory of the recurrent cell, and thus consists of a single vector for FastGRNN and GRU cells, or two vectors (short and long term memories) for LSTM cells. For IP addresses not seen before, the memory representation is initialized with zeros.

To prevent excessive memory usage in large deployments, if an IP address is not seen for a long period of time, its representation can be removed from the memory dictionary. This is a sensible decision, as external public servers may change IP address or stop being accessed by the local IoT devices. Furthermore, if an internal IP address remains silent for a long time, it is likely that the IoT device was removed from the network and the address reassigned to a new IoT device, therefore rendering the previous memory useless and even detrimental.

Output Feature Map. The output feature map is responsible for extracting the new packet and device representations to be used to generate the model responses. For the device representation, the updated contents of the memory are used directly. For cell types that produce multiple memory vectors, such as the LSTM, only the short-term representation is passed forward to the response layer. The packet representation is obtained by concatenating the new representations of the source and destination devices with the original features of the packet from the input feature map.

Response Layer. The response layer is responsible for computing the desired model outputs, in this case, device and packet classifications. To achieve device classifications, the device representations from the output feature map are passed to a single-layer feed-forward classifier. A separate classifier is trained for each classification task. The same process is used for packet-level classification, using the packet representation from the output feature map.

4.2   Training LiMNet

The trivial approach to train LiMNet would be to order all packets in the network trace and then feed the entire sequence to the model, packet by packet. However, this leads to two issues: 1) scalability, as the training hardware parallelism cannot be exploited, and 2) vanishing gradients, as the contribution of early packets is lost in the backpropagation process.

We overcome these issues using truncated backpropagation through time (p-BPTT) [10], a well-known RNN training technique in which the input trace is split into shorter, partially-overlapping subtraces, which are treated as independent inputs. Batches of subtraces can be trained in parallel, while each of them is processed sequentially to ensure causal consistency. In general, p-BPTT can hinder the ability of a model to capture long-term relations [24]. However our analysis, reported in Appendix B, does not show generalization issues and training can be performed efficiently on very long subtraces, up to $\sim 10^5$ packets.

5 Limitations of Existing Recurrent Models for Early-Stage Botnet Detection

While existing recurrent models from [1] and [9] have been shown to perform well, they present several issues that make their deployment in real-world IoT scenarios challenging. This motivates the contributions of this work: a review of these recurrent models to analyze their limitations and the proposal of the novel LiMNet architecture. Here we provide an overview of these issues.

Issue 1: packet headers contain specific device IDs, such as MAC and IP addresses, that should not be used to classify traffic in local networks. A model trained with these features might, for example, learn that the packets sent from a certain local IP are malicious based on the training dataset, while in the real IoT network that local IP might not be malicious. Therefore, existing recurrent models might fail to generalize to different or evolving networks. LiMNetdoes not use any device IDs in its training and so is not affected by this issue.

Issue 2: by employing an input embedding layer, recurrent models assume that the same token appearing in different input positions represents the same, or similar, concept. However, the number 22 appearing as source port, destination port or packet length carries very different meanings. Therefore, these models might fail to capture complex scenarios where these distinctions become fundamental. Furthermore, the embedding layer treats the packet headers as a categorical variable, with each value mapped to an independent embedding. This prevents it from capturing patterns in numerical fields, such as the similarity between packet length 22 and 23. By not using an embedding layer to parse the headers, LiMNet avoids these pitfalls.

Issue 3: recurrent models are well-known to incur high inference latency. This is because the recurrent cell must be applied sequentially to each element of the input sequence, which in this case is a sequence of packet header fields. High throughput can be achieved by increasing the batch size used for inference, but only at the cost of additional latency introduced by the batching process. By contrast, the source and destination cells in LiMNet are independent and can be processed in parallel, speeding up inference.

Issue 4: by ignoring the temporal and topological relations among packets, focusing on a single header at a time, these models miss the overall evolution of the network. This may hinder their ability to accurately classify traffic flows, especially when malicious traffic looks similar to benign traffic at the level of individual packets. LiMNet is designed specifically to exploit these relations.

6 Evaluation Methodology

6.1 Deployment Environment

The use case targeted in this work is that of early detection of botnet propagation at the network level. Therefore, a suitable solution should fulfill a number of requirements. First, inference should be performed on a stream of packets with

Table 1. Datasets summary

Dataset	# Of Devices	# Of Packets	Botnets
MedBIoT	83	17,845,567	Mirai, Bashlite, Torii
Kitsune	12	764,137	Mirai

both low-latency and high throughput, in order to scale to large IoT deployments while still being able to react quickly to incoming threats.

Second, inference should not require any specialized hardware to achieve the desired performance level. This is because the inference should be able to run on simple, low-power hardware such as smart routers and smart switches, as close as possible to the actual IoT devices, to have real-time access to all packets being exchanged in the network. These network devices typically provide simple x86 or ARM CPUs with low core counts and small amounts of RAM. On the other hand, training can be done offline, by replaying captured network traffic on GPU-accelerated training servers.

Therefore, unlike previous work [1], we focus our performance testing on single-core CPU inference, and use a batch size of 1. In these conditions, light-weight models that can fit in the small private cache of the core and only require small matrix multiplications gain a substantial performance advantage.

6.2 Datasets

In order to evaluate the effectiveness of the recurrent models and of LiMNet, we use two different datasets: MedBIoT and Kitsune. Both datasets, summarized in Table 1, focus on the spreading phase of IoT botnets, rather than on the attacks driven by these botnets, and are therefore the most suitable to evaluate early-stage detection models.

The MedBIoT dataset [7] is gathered from a medium-size network with 83 devices. These devices are a combination of real and emulated devices, spanning categories such as smart locks, switches, fans, and light bulbs. Real, working botnets, namely Mirai, Bashlite/Gafgyt, and Torii, are injected in the controlled environment at different times. The network traffic of the spreading phases is captured, including communication between bots and controlled C&C servers.

The Kitsune dataset [21] is gathered in a small network of 3 PCs and 9 IoT devices, including a thermostat, a baby monitor, a webcam, low-cost security cameras and doorbells. One of these is infected with the Mirai malware and the network traffic is subsequently captured.

6.3   Tasks

Previous works [1, 7] consider the classification of malicious packets as the only task for botnet detection. However, device-level tasks may play an important role as well. Classifying a device as infected or under attack allows administrators to identify vulnerable devices and deploy more targeted countermeasures.

Therefore, in addition to the binary classification of malicious packets based on ground-truth labels, we consider the classification of infected and under attack devices, with device labels generated from the packet labels and headers using simple heuristics. While the datasets do not present any overlap of multiple malware types, this is a possibility in real networks, and a device may therefore be infected and under attack at the same time. Thus, we consider these as two independent binary classification tasks. The metric used is the area under the ROC curve (AUROC), as it provides a good indication of the possible tradeoffs between sensitivity and fallout achievable by the models.

6.4   State-of-the-Art Recurrent Models for Early-Stage Botnet Detection

We test state-of-the-art recurrent models from [9] and [1] with two goals: to evaluate the impact of the issues discussed in Sect. 5 and to establish baseline accuracy and inference speed when evaluating LiMNet.

However, these recurrent models are only designed to perform packet-level classification, while LiMNet also performs the device-level tasks described above. In the original models, the output representation of the last recurrent cell is fed to a shallow feed-forward decoder which classifies the input packet. We extend this by adding a pair of decoders which take the same representation as input and are trained to classify the source and destination node of the packet, respectively. As for the memory model, we allow multiple packet classification tasks by training multiple packet classifiers and we allow multiple device classification tasks by training multiple pairs of source and destination classifiers.

The implementation of LiMNet, the modified baselines and the complete evaluation code used in this paper are freely available online[4].

7   Experimental Results

7.1   Experiment 1: Parameter Selection for Recurrent Models

In their original formulation, the recurrent models from [9] and [1] take all packet header fields as inputs. As discussed in Sect. 5, this may lead to overfitting due to the presence of device identifiers (Issue 1). Furthermore, due to the sheer length of the header (33 fields in [9]), inference latency is high (Issue 3).

---

[4] https://github.com/lodo1995/LiMNet.

Table 2. Combinations of datasets and hyperparameters employed in the evaluation

Datasets	MedBIoT (Torii subset), MedBIoT (Mirai subset), MedBIoT (BashLite subset), MedBIoT (complete), Kitsune
Cell types	LSTM, GRU, FastGRNN
Layers	3, 1
Layer sizes	64, 32
Input features	Full header, Full header except MACs and IPs, Only ports and length

To alleviate these issues, we test the recurrent models with smaller subsets of the packet headers. In particular, we test them with all headers expect for MAC and IP addresses, to prevent overfitting, and with only the UDP/TCP ports and packet length, providing a level of input information similar to LiMNet.

Motivated by the results in [1], we test both deep models with 3 recurrent layers and shallow models with a single layer, as well as three different recurrent cells, namely LSTM, GRU and FastGRNN. According to [1], both using shallower models and using smaller recurrent cells, such as GRU and FastGRNN, can achieve similar performance to the deep LSTM-based model in [9], while being much faster. Finally, in the same spirit of minimizing size without loss of quality, we test smaller layers of size 32, in addition to the size 64 used in previous works. Considering the different datasets, the total number of parameter combinations to test is 180, summarized in Table 2.

Unfortunately, the results on the MedBIoT dataset do not allow for meaningful comparisons, as all combinations lead to over 99.9% AUROC scores on all three tasks. In contrast, on the Kitsune dataset, the results are much lower and present a meaningful spread. Particularly interesting is the fact that feeding the recurrent model with only port and length information provides consistently better results than using all features as done in previous work, with up to 2% better AUROC scores, as seen in Table 3. On the contrary, providing all features except the IDs leads to the worst results.

Table 3. AUROC scores of recurrent models with different hyperparameter combinations, fed with ports and length features on the Kitsune dataset. "best of ..." indicates the best results obtained by models fed with more features (not necessary the same model in all columns). All results are averages over 5 runs. Bold results are the best, underlined results are within 0.5%.

Layers	Layers size	Cell	Device malicious	Device attacked	Packet malicious
Best with all headers except IDs			84.27	95.77	75.88
Best with all headers			84.99	96.6	78.02
1	32	FastGRNN	<u>85.66</u>	96.91	80.63
1	32	GRU	<u>85.72</u>	<u>97.11</u>	80.76
1	32	LSTM	<u>85.75</u>	<u>97.2</u>	80.66
1	64	FastGRNN	<u>85.71</u>	<u>97.09</u>	80.86
1	64	GRU	<u>85.74</u>	<u>97.44</u>	80.86
1	64	LSTM	**85.83**	<u>97.38</u>	<u>81.04</u>
3	32	FastGRNN	<u>85.48</u>	96.83	80.79
3	32	GRU	<u>85.56</u>	<u>97.26</u>	80.83
3	32	LSTM	<u>85.62</u>	<u>97.28</u>	80.9
3	64	FastGRNN	<u>85.8</u>	<u>97.22</u>	**81.37**
3	64	GRU	<u>85.82</u>	**97.52**	<u>81.23</u>
3	64	LSTM	<u>85.7</u>	<u>97.45</u>	<u>81.12</u>

We therefore focus on the comparison of these low-features models, summarized in Table 3. A larger layer size of 64 provides consistently better results than 32. Using a 3 layers network as in [9] provides a slight advantage compared to the single-layer network from [1], although the margin is slim. On the other hand, the choice of recurrent cell seems to have almost no impact, with the best per-task results achieved by three different cell types.

In summary, the key takeaway of this experiment is that reducing the amount of input features provides measurably better results and should be considered even if inference speed is not an issue. However, further time and space savings by reducing number of layers and layer sizes may have a slight negative effect on model quality.

7.2 Experiment 2: Recurrent Vs Memory Models

The next experiment aims at comparing the best recurrent models identified above with LiMNet. Our model is always fed with minimal features extracted from port and length headers and always has a single layer, as explained in Sect. 4. Thus, the only parameters that need to be evaluated are layer size and cell type, for which the same values presented in Table 2 are used.

As was the case for the recurrent models, LiMNet also easily achieves over 99.9% AUROC score on all tasks in MedBIoT, and we therefore focus our attention on the harder and more indicative Kitsune dataset.

As can be seen in Table 4, LiMNet with layer size of 64 and GRU recurrent units achieves an almost maximum score of ∼99%, outperforming the best low-features recurrent models by a large margin of over 12% on average on the three tasks. When compared to the original recurrent models that use all packet headers, the advantage of LiMNet grows to over 14%. Similarly to recurrent models, LiMNet also provides better results with larger layers. However, while the former were not significantly affected by the choice of recurrent cell, LiMNet appears to strongly favor GRU units. In general, the results present a wider spread, indicating a higher sensitivity of LiMNet to its hyperparameters.

Table 4. AUROC scores of different configurations of recurrent models and of LiMNet. All results are averaged over 5 runs. Bold results are the best, underlined results are within 0.5% of the best.

Type	Layers	Layers size	Cell	Device malicious	Device attacked	Packet malicious
Best recurrent with all headers				84.99	96.6	78.02
Recurrent	1	64	LSTM	85.83	97.38	81.04
Recurrent	3	64	FastGRNN	85.8	97.22	81.37
Recurrent	3	64	GRU	85.82	97.52	81.23
LiMNet	1	32	FastGRNN	85.52	95.97	92.8
LiMNet	1	32	GRU	<u>98.73</u>	<u>98.72</u>	<u>99.72</u>
LiMNet	1	32	LSTM	85.91	96.7	88.82
LiMNet	1	64	FastGRNN	98.21	97.87	<u>99.48</u>
LiMNet	1	64	GRU	**99.13**	**98.84**	**99.75**
LiMNet	1	64	LSTM	84.54	97.09	86.36

7.3   Experiment 3: Inference Speed

The third and final experiment aims at comparing the inference speed of the best configuration of both recurrent models and LiMNet.

Given the characteristics of the deployment environment described in Sect. 6.1, the inference is performed on a single x86 CPU core[5], as low-power smart network equipment typically lacks more powerful resources. Furthermore, the batch size is set to 1, effectively disabling batching, as it is undesirable for two reasons. First, it substantially increases latency by queuing messages, while

---

[5] More precisely, a single core of an Intel Cascade Lake-SP CPU with 2.2 GHz base clock, 3.2 GHz max. turbo clock, 32 KB L1d cache and 1 MB L2 private cache.

providing little throughput improvements due to the low level of data parallelism available on a single x86 core. Second, batching puts additional pressure on the RAM, which might be limited in these low-power devices.

Table 5 summarizes the results obtained by the recurrent and LiMNet configurations that ranked best in previous experiments. We report the numbers from the MedBIoT dataset, as it includes a more diverse (and more realistic) range of devices, ports and protocols, therefore slightly increasing the size and reducing the speed of both recurrent and LiMNet models. However, the same conclusions could be drawn on the Kitsune dataset, albeit at a lower scale.

Table 5. Inference speed and model size of different model configurations on the MedBIoT dataset. Models marked with * are trained on all packet headers, while the others are trained with the minimal amounts of features as described in the text.

Type	Layers	Layer size	Cell	Model size [kiB]				Infer. speed [packets/s]
				Embed.	Cells	Classif.	Total	
Recurrent*	1	64	LSTM	16384	130	1.3	16515	429
Recurrent	1	64	LSTM	9178	130	1.3	9309	1814
Recurrent	3	64	FastGRNN	9178	98	1.3	9277	948
Recurrent	3	64	GRU	9178	293	1.3	9472	972
LiMNet	1	32	GRU	–	64	0.6	**65**	**3381**
LiMNet	1	64	FastGRNN	–	75	1.0	76	3067
LiMNet	1	64	GRU	–	225	1.0	226	3037

The fastest LiMNet model (GRU cell, layer size 32) achieves over 3300 packets per second. However, it is not the best performing model in terms of quality. Based on Table 4. A layer size of 64 would achieve marginally better average scores. However, this comes at a 10% speed reduction. Depending on the specific deployment setting, this may be an important tradeoff to consider.

The fastest recurrent model is around 46% slower. This difference has three causes. First, the LSTM recurrent unit is slightly larger and slower than the GRU unit. Second, LiMNet requires 2 recurrent units (for source and target devices), while the recurrent models require one unit for each feature, and thus 3 units when considering ports and packet length. Finally, the large size of the embedding layer (over 95% of the total) means that the recurrent model cannot fit in the private L2 cache of a CPU core and must instead reside in the slower and shared L3 cache, or in main memory. This introduces a memory bottleneck compared to LiMNet, as large embedding representations need to be fetched from distant memory locations and, due to the random access patterns, speculative pre-fetching is not effective.

Furthermore, moving from the fastest to the highest-quality recurrent model brings an additional 46% speed reduction, from 1814 to 972 packets per second. This is due to the switch from 1 layer to 3 layers, which triples the number of recurrent cells that need to be evaluated during inference.

For completeness, we also take the fastest hyperparameter combination for the recurrent model and train it with all features instead of just ports and packet length. The results is a model that is 76% slower, as due to the much larger number of input headers the recurrent units grow in number from 3 to 33.

To summarize, LiMNet not only achieves much better scores than the original recurrent models from [9] and [1], but can do so at an almost 8 times higher speed. On the other hand, the speedup that these models can achieve with less input features stops at 4 times their original speed.

8   Discussion and Limitations

8.1   Dataset Limitations

Unfortunately, the number of open-access datasets that focus on the spreading phase (rather than the attack phase) of IoT botnets and that provide enough devices to extract network-level interactions is very limited. Each of the two datasets used in this paper presents its limitations.

MedBIoT is a large dataset with multiple devices and malware types. However, as discussed in Sect. 7 and as already hinted by previous results [1,7], the distinction between benign and malicious traffic is too obvious, with any deep learning-based approach achieving near-perfect scores, making comparisons difficult. Kitsune, on the other hand, appears to present a harder challenge, making it a useful benchmark for comparisons. However, it is several orders of magnitude smaller and lacks diverse malware and IoT devices. It may thus not provide a complete picture of a real IoT deployment.

We further analyze these two datasets in Appendix A and find that Kitsune provides a more balanced, and thus more challenging, mix of network protocols. However, more work is necessary to fully understand these dataset dynamics and to develop more open-access datasets suitable for advanced IoT botnet detection.

8.2   Issues of Recurrent Models for Early-Stage Botnet Detection

Section 5 discussed a number of potential issues in the architecture of state-of-the-art recurrent models for IoT botnet detection. While the limitations of the datasets do not allow for a complete, in-depth analysis of each issue, the results presented in Sect. 7 provide some hints to the extent of these issues.

Issue 1, that is, the incorrect use of device IDs that may prevent model generalization, seems to be confirmed by the results in Table 3. Models trained without those IDs perform worse than those trained with them, indicating that the model is exploiting these dataset-specific information in its embeddings.

However, that issue is rendered moot by the fact that removing almost all features achieves even better performance. This may be related to **Issue 2**. As most packet headers reuse the same numerical values with different meaning (e.g. port 22 vs packet length 22 vs packet checksum 22), reducing the number of input headers reduces the number of different meanings that a single numerical value can have. This allows the embedding layer to better capture the semantics of these numerical values. Intuitively, the model is able to better focus on the few relevant fields selected, without being confused by insignificant headers such as checksums and reserved fields.

Issue 3 is also partially mitigated by the reduced number of features. However, the inference speed of recurrent models is still inferior to that of LiMNet, as shown in Sect. 7.3.

Finally, the substantially better results obtained by LiMNet confirm the relevance of **Issue 4**, indicating the presence of useful information in the temporal and topological relationships between different packet flows.

9 Conclusion

Securing IoT networks from malicious botnets is an important step towards the widespread deployment of IoT devices in the Industry 4.0 and in smart homes.

In this work, we analyzed the issues and limitations of state-of-the art recurrent models for early-stage detection of devices infected and under attack. Our proposed modifications to mitigate these issues slightly improved classification performance, while increasing inference speed by 4 times.

However, we have shown that an increase of 14% in classification scores, up to a nearly maximum value of ~99%, and an almost 8 times speedup can be achieved by switching to a completely different model. Based on memory networks and mutually-recurrent units, our LiMNet architecture can understand and exploit the crucial temporal and topological relationships in the network, while being incredibly lightweight in both size and computational requirements.

Furthermore, the LiMNet architecture proposed in this work is not specific to malware detection and could be applied in any temporal interaction network that presents strong causal relationships. Therefore, the potential use of LiMNet in other areas of security should be explored in future works. One such area could be the detection of fraudulent behaviour in financial transactions on cryptocurrency networks such as Bitcoin and Ethereum.

Acknowledgements. The authors would like to thank Stefanos Antaris (affiliated with KTH and Hive Streaming AB) for the insightful discussions and literature recommendations that helped shape the direction of this work.

A Kitsune vs MedBIoT: Challenges for ML Models

To effectively and fairly compare early-stage botnet detection models, large, realistic and challenging datasets are required. We therefore analyze Kitsune and MedBIoT, to understand why the former is more challenging than the latter.

In [1], the authors hypothesize that their balancing of the different malware classes in MedBIoT may cause their very high scores. However, in our work, we do not perform any balancing and still achieve near-perfect scores for both our approach and the baseline from [1], thus disproving this hypothesis.

Table 6. Distribution of protocols in the datasets, as identified by `tshark`. When the application-level protocol is not identified, the transport-level protocol is reported.

MedBIoT				Kitsune			
Protocol	Legitimate	Malicious	% Of total packets	Protocol	Legitimate	Malicious	% Of total packets
TCP	14971443	4747941	89.1	UDP	39650	23904	41.2
MQTT	1732790	2210	7.8	TCP	20669	30048	32.9
TELNET	0	350431	1.6	DNS	23608	14305	24.6
HTTP	266377	4769	1.2	SSDP	636	416	0.7
DNS	17994	34016	0.2	TELNET	0	435	0.3
10 others	2848	3616	<0.1	7 others	282	144	<0.3

The breakdown of the protocol distributions of the datasets, reported in Table 6, shows that MedBIoT is dominated by a single protocol and that within most protocols legitimate packets are one order of magnitude more (or less) than malicious ones, with the overall dataset being skewed towards legitimate traffic. A model can easily achieve high scores by focusing on the dominating protocol, and by providing simple majority answers for the others. Kitsune, on the other hand, is fairly well-split across three dominant protocols and fairly balanced between legitimate and malicious traffic, both overall and within each protocol. Any model therefore needs to capture multiple legitimate behaviours and learn to discern malicious traffic within each protocol based on additional signals. It is thus unsurprising that Kitsune proved more challenging in our experiments, as it better tests the modelling capabilities of botnet detection approaches.

B   Effect of Truncated Backpropagation Through Time

Truncated Backpropagation Through Time (p-BPTT) [10] has gained traction in the RNN field as a simple technique to quickly and efficiently train model on very long sequences. However, this technique is known to reduce the ability of a model to capture long-range relations, as inputs that are very far in the original sequence never co-appear in the same subsequence after splitting [24].

To ensure that this issue is not affecting LiMNet, we train it with different combinations of length and stride for the subsequences. For a fair comparison, it is important to consider the length/stride ratio. A higher ratio indicates more overlaps between the subsequences and thus leads to more training data points per epoch. The results are reported in Table 7.

Keeping the ratio fixed at 5, Table 7 shows that longer subsequences lead to worse results, not better. If there are any gains from modelling long-term relations, they are offset by the larger strides, which cause most packets to never appear close to the end of any subsequence, where the backpropagation gradients are stronger. This issue can be mitigated by reducing the stride and thus

Table 7. AUROC scores of LiMNet with GRU units and layer size 32 on the Kitsune dataset, with varying subsequence length and stride for p-BPTT.

Sequence length	Sequence stride	Length/stride ratio	Device malicious	Device attacked	Packet malicious
1000	200	5	98.68	<u>98.93</u>	98.97
5000	1000	5	98.38	98.07	<u>99.59</u>
10000	2000	5	96.37	97.37	98.64
20000	4000	5	64.77	90.89	86.26
10000	1000	10	**99.42**	**99.26**	**99.93**
20000	1000	20	<u>99.2</u>	<u>98.99</u>	<u>99.84</u>

increasing the ratio. This bring performance up, but at much higher computational costs. Furthermore, even with high ratios, increasing sequence length over 10k packets does not seem to provide any benefit, indicating that, at this length p-BPTT does not negatively impact LiMNet performance.

C   Cross-dataset Model Generalization

As an additional experiment, in Table 8 we consider the performance of LiMNet when trained on one dataset and tested on another. The results show once more how different the scenarios presented by Kitsune and MedBIoT are.

As the datasets present different protocol mixes (as shown in Appendix A), the one-hot protocol encoding of the testing dataset needs to be modified to match that of the training dataset, which is the one the model expects. For protocols present in both datasets, this "alignment" amounts to a simple reshuffle of the features. For application-level protocols that are present in the testing dataset but not in the training one, we consider two options: 1) replacing them with their transport-level protocol, as TCP and UDP are present in both datasets, or 2) setting all protocol features to zero, effectively marking the packet as having no protocol. Our results show no substantial differences between these two options.

A model trained on Kitsune has no knowledge of the Torii and Bashlite malware present in MedBIoT, while one trained on the latter is aware of the Mirai malware in Kitsune. This explains why training on MedBIoT and testing on Kitsune provide better results than the opposite in the malicious packet detection task. However, the results on this task are still extremely low, probably because the model also faces different patterns of legitimate traffic, which it cannot recognize. The device-level tasks, present much better (although still low) results. This may be due to the memory component of LiMNet: while a single packet may be hard to judge in these conditions, the model still memorizes enough knowledge over time to correctly flag at least part of the devices.

Table 8. AUROC scores of LiMNet with GRU units and layer size 32, trained and tested on different combinations of datasets

Training dataset	Testing dataset	Protocol alignment	Device malicious	Device attacked	Packet malicious
Kitsune	Kitsune	–	98.73	98.72	99.72
Kitsune	MedBIoT	Transport	58.92	60.39	28.64
Kitsune	MedBIoT	No proto	58.83	59.98	28.52
MedBIoT	MedBIoT	–	99.79	99.79	99.84
MedBIoT	Kitsune	Transport	42.87	60.99	35.62
MedBIoT	Kitsune	No proto	42.87	60.99	35.63

References

1. Alzahrani, H., Abulkhair, M., Alkayal, E.: A multi-class neural network model for rapid detection of IoT botnet attacks. Int. J. Adv. Comp. Sci. Appl. **11**(7), 688–696 (2020)
2. Antonakakis, M., et al.: Understanding the mirai botnet. In: 26th {USENIX} security symposium ({USENIX} Security 17), pp. 1093–1110 (2017)
3. Bahşi, H., Nõmm, S., La Torre, F.B.: Dimensionality reduction for machine learning based iot botnet detection. In: 2018 15th International Conference on Control, Automation, Robotics and Vision (ICARCV), pp. 1857–1862. IEEE (2018)
4. Chung, J., Gulcehre, C., Cho, K., Bengio, Y.: Empirical evaluation of gated recurrent neural networks on sequence modeling. arXiv preprint arXiv:1412.3555 (2014)
5. Coskun, B., et al.: Friends of an enemy: Identifying local members of peer-to-peer botnets using mutual contacts. In: Proceedings of the 26th Annual Computer Security Applications Conference, ACSAC 2010, pp. 131–140. Association for Computing Machinery, New York (2010)
6. Ebesu, T., Shen, B., Fang, Y.: Collaborative memory network for recommendation systems. In: The 41st international ACM SIGIR Conference on Research & Development in Information Retrieval, pp. 515–524 (2018)
7. Guerra-Manzanares, A., Medina-Galindo, J., Bahsi, H., Nomm, S.: Medbiot: generation of an IoT botnet dataset in a medium-sized IoT network. In: ICISSP (2020)
8. Hamilton, W.L., Ying, R., Leskovec, J.: Representation learning on graphs: Methods and applications. arXiv preprint arXiv:1709.05584 (2017)
9. Hwang, R.H., Peng, M.C., Nguyen, V.L., Chang, Y.L.: An lstm-based deep learning approach for classifying malicious traffic at the packet level. Appl. Sci. **9**(16) (2019). https://doi.org/10.3390/app9163414
10. Jaeger, H.: Tutorial on training recurrent neural networks, covering BPPT, RTRL, EKF and the echo state network approach, vol. 5. GMD-Forschungszentrum Informationstechnik Bonn (2002)
11. Kefato, Z.T., Girdzijauskas, S., Sheikh, N., Montresor, A.: Dynamic embeddings for interaction prediction. In: Proceedings of The Web Conference 2021 (2021)
12. Kolias, C., Kambourakis, G., Stavrou, A., Voas, J.: Ddos in the IoT: mirai and other botnets. Computer **50**(7), 80–84 (2017)
13. Kumar, S., Zhang, X., Leskovec, J.: Predicting dynamic embedding trajectory in temporal interaction networks. In: Proceedings of the 25th ACM SIGKDD International Conference on Knowledge Discovery and Data Mining. ACM (2019)

14. Kusupati, A., Singh, M., Bhatia, K., Kumar, A., Jain, P., Varma, M.: Fastgrnn: a fast, accurate, stable and tiny kilobyte sized gated recurrent neural network, NIPS 2018, pp. 9031–9042. Curran Associates Inc., Red Hook, NY, USA (2018)

15. Li, J., et al.: Distributed threat intelligence sharing system: a new sight of p2p botnet detection. In: 2019 2nd International Conference on Computer Applications & Information Security (ICCAIS), pp. 1–6. Riyadh, Saudi Arabia (2019)

16. Ma, Y., Guo, Z., Ren, Z., Tang, J., Yin, D.: Streaming graph neural networks. In: Proceedings of the 43rd International ACM SIGIR Conference on Research and Development in Information Retrieval, pp. 719–728 (2020)

17. McDermott, C.D., Majdani, F., Petrovski, A.V.: Botnet detection in the internet of things using deep learning approaches. In: 2018 International Joint Conference on Neural Networks (IJCNN), pp. 1–8 (2018). https://doi.org/10.1109/IJCNN.2018.8489489

18. Meidan, Y., et al.: N-baiot-network-based detection of IoT botnet attacks using deep autoencoders. IEEE Pervasive Comput. **17**(3), 12–22 (2018). https://doi.org/10.1109/MPRV.2018.03367731

19. Meidan, Y., et al.: N-baiot-network-based detection of IoT botnet attacks using deep autoencoders. IEEE Pervasive Comput. **17**(3), 12–22 (2018)

20. Mikolov, T., Karafiát, M., Burget, L., Černockỳ, J., Khudanpur, S.: Recurrent neural network based language model. In: Eleventh Annual Conference of the International Speech Communication Association (2010)

21. Mirsky, Y., Doitshman, T., Elovici, Y., Shabtai, A.: Kitsune: an ensemble of autoencoders for online network intrusion detection. Network and Distributed System Security Symposium (NDSS) (2018)

22. Nguyen, H., Ngo, Q., Le, V.: IoT botnet detection approach based on psi graph and dgcnn classifier. In: 2018 IEEE International Conference on Information Communication and Signal Processing (ICICSP), pp. 118–122 (2018). https://doi.org/10.1109/ICICSP.2018.8549713

23. Sagirlar, G., Carminati, B., Ferrari, E.: Autobotcatcher: blockchain-based p2p botnet detection for the internet of things. In: 2018 IEEE 4th International Conference on Collaboration and Internet Computing (CIC), pp. 1–8. IEEE (2018)

24. Tallec, C., Ollivier, Y.: Unbiasing truncated backpropagation through time. CoRR abs/1705.08209 (2017). http://arxiv.org/abs/1705.08209

25. Weston, J., Chopra, S., Bordes, A.: Memory networks. arXiv preprint arXiv:1410.3916 (2014)

26. Yang, Z., et al.: P2p botnet detection based on nodes correlation by the mahalanobis distance. Information **10**(5), 160 (2019)

27. Zhuang, D., et al.: Peerhunter: detecting peer-to-peer botnets through community behavior analysis. In: 2017 IEEE Conference on Dependable and Secure Computing, pp. 493–500. Taipei (2017)

Adversarial Activity Detection Using Keystroke Acoustics

Amin Fallahi[(⊠)] and Vir V. Phoha

Syracuse University, Syracuse, NY 13244, USA
{afallahi,vvphoha}@syr.edu

Abstract. Using keystroke acoustics to predict typed text has significant advantages, such as being recorded covertly from a distance and requiring no physical access to the computer system. Recently, some studies have been done on keystroke acoustics, however, to the best of our knowledge none have used them to predict adversarial activities, such as password dictionary attacks, data exfiltration, etc. We show that keystrokes in an adversarial environment have unique characteristics that distinguish it from benign environments and these differences can be used to predict adversarial activities and threat levels against a computer system. On a dataset of two million keystrokes consisting of seven adversarial and one benign activity, we use a signal processing approach to extract keystrokes from the audio and a clustering method to recover the typed letters followed by a text recovery module to regenerate the typed words. Furthermore, we use a neural network model to classify the benign and adversarial activities and achieve significant results: (1) we extract individual keystroke sounds from the raw audio with 91% accuracy and recover words from audio recordings in a noisy environment with 71% average top-10 accuracy. (2) We classify adversarial activities with 93.11% to 98.07% average accuracy under different operating scenarios.

Keywords: Attack detection · Adversarial activity classification · Keystroke acoustics

1 Introduction

Keystroke acoustics can be used to detect adversarial activities and threats against a system by monitoring users' behavior without interrupting their interaction with the computer. There is no need to install specific software or hardware, such as a keylogger on the users' machines to monitor their activity. Therefore, the typing activity of a malicious attacker may be monitored covertly without the attacker's awareness. So, it is less likely that the attacker takes preventive measures to evade being detected. In Sect. 4.2, we discuss how our method compares with installing a simple keylogger on the users' machines which is one of the traditional monitoring methods.

© Springer Nature Switzerland AG 2021
E. Bertino et al. (Eds.): ESORICS 2021, LNCS 12972, pp. 626–648, 2021.
https://doi.org/10.1007/978-3-030-88418-5_30

In this research, we propose a model consisting of multiple components that gets the audio data of the users' typing sessions as input and detects the type of their activity and the threat level against the system as output. As depicted in Fig. 1, we use audio signals collected using multiple recording devices to recover the keystrokes and typed words of the users. Then, we develop an LSTM-based neural network model to identify the user's activity type based on the typed words. Finally, we use the user's activity and its preassigned threat level to generate a threat score for the session.

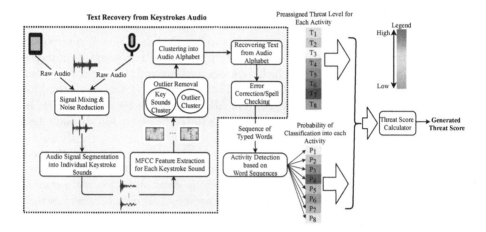

Fig. 1. Overview of our proposed components from recording the typing session audio to quantifying the threat level.

Table 1. Comparison of the prior work on text recovery using keystrokes audio with our work.

Research	Data quality	Data type	Data collection method	Recovery method	No. of Mics
Asonov & Agrawal [1]	Clean & Noisy	Random	Fixed	Keys	2
Zhuang et al. [23]	Moderate Noise	Benign	Fixed	Words	1
Berger et al. [8]	Clean	Benign	Fixed	Words	1
Liu et al. [14]	Moderate Noise	Random	Random	Keys	2
Roth et al. [18,19]	Clean & Noisy	Benign	Free & Fixed	N/A	1
Campagno et al. [9]	Clean & Noisy	Random	Fixed	Keys	1
This Work	**Very Noisy**	**Adversarial & Benign**	**Free**	**Words**	**2**

1.1   Related Work

Prior studies have proposed multiple approaches for recovering letters and words using audio recordings of typing sessions. In a classic approach to this problem,

Asonov and Agrawal [1] propose a method to extract individual keystroke sounds from raw audio using amplitude threshold and signal peaks. Then, they extract FFT (Fast Fourier Transform) coefficients from each keystroke as a feature vector and train a neural network to detect the keystrokes. Zhuang et al. [23] improve Asonov and Agrawal's work using an unsupervised approach instead of a labeled training set. They use Mel-frequency Cepstral Coefficients (MFCC) instead of FFT coefficients. Berger et al. [8] further improve the previous work by proposing a dictionary attack to extract words based on the keystroke audio recordings and achieve 73% overall accuracy for recovering the words. However, their approach is not applicable for recovering random text like passwords. In another effort, Liu et al. [14] combine time of arrival and acoustic features of keystrokes to extract individual keystrokes from audio recordings with a mobile phone. They recover 97% of the text without training or depending on linguistic context. Campagno et al. [9] propose Skype & Type which focuses on recovering the keystrokes using audio transmitted over VoIP applications. They use a peak detection method for individual keystroke sound extraction and MFCC features for classification. In another noteworthy work, Wang et al. [22] study the detection of combined keystrokes using acoustic signals.

Another application that has been studied by the prior work is attack detection and classification using keystrokes. Belman et al. [6] extract several features from keystroke dynamics of benign and malicious users and train conventional classifiers for adversarial activity detection. However, their method assumes that they have access to keystroke dynamics, including the exact pressed keys and the timing of keystrokes. In our method, we use audio recordings instead of keystroke dynamics and pay attention to the context of the typed text.

Furthermore, in another series of studies, Roth et al. [18,19] use keystroke audio emanations for user identification. They use a threshold-based method and MFCC features for building an authentication model based on keystroke acoustics.

2   The Significance of Our Work

Although prior studies have addressed the use of keystroke acoustics for various applications, none have used them for malicious activity and threat level detection to the extent of our knowledge. As summarized in Table 1, this study stands out from prior work and contributes to the research in multiple aspects:

- We present a model for text recovery from raw audio data of users' typing sessions, especially suited to noisy environments, such as where multiple people are present in a room (similar to a real-world office environment). Our results on a particularly challenging dataset with multiple inaudible keystrokes and a noisy environment show that our text recovery model is able to recover the typed words with an average 71% top-10 accuracy.
- We show that it is possible to classify a sequence of typed words which are recovered from audio into 8 different activities with up to 98.07% accuracy by proposing an LSTM-based model which is unique for our application. While

the number of activities is limited to our dataset, our work is easily extendable to other activities.

- Our large dataset of near two million keystrokes is collected during both adversarial and benign sessions from 103 and 117 users respectively. The users have interacted with the keyboard freely, without having to type certain fixed words several times in contrast to most of the prior studies.
- Although other studies have collected and used data from noisy environments, as discussed in Sect. 5.1, the amount of noise in our data is significantly high, making the text recovery task very challenging.

Table 2. A comparison between the characteristics of the attack and the benign dataset. The numbers show the averages for the entire dataset.

	Attack	Benign
Duration	4884.62 s	2915.32 s
Enters	160.21	68.57
Enters/hour	119.5	85.44
Letters/Sentence	11.18	65.28
Words/Sentence	2.65	13.1
Words in Dict	21.46%	31.59%

Table 3. The number of audible, inaudible, and noisy keystroke sounds out of 100 randomly selected ones for 5 users of the dataset as discussed in Sect. 5.1.

User	Audible	Inaudible	Noisy
1	39	57	4
2	50	43	7
3	56	42	2
4	71	25	4
5	65	32	3

3   Typing Differences in Adversarial and Benign Environments

User interaction with the input devices varies during different activities. In benign activities like web browsing, email writing, etc., the usage of specific keys and the overall usage of the keyboard are different. For example, the use of the enter key is more frequent in adversarial activities because the commands are separated by the enter key and are shorter than sentences typed in a benign session. Also, the use of special characters is more frequent in adversarial activities and dictionary words appear more in benign activities. Table 2 shows a few statistical differences between the two datasets. The average number of enters per hour is higher for the attack sessions which can show higher terminal usage with shorter commands. The average numbers of letters and words are higher for the benign activity showing longer words and sentences. Also, a higher percentage of the words typed during the benign session appear in an English dictionary. Therefore, several features can distinguish between the benign and adversarial activities as studied in [6]. However, these features may misclassify benign terminal sessions with a lot of safe commands, resulting in a high false positive rate. Also, they cannot distinguish between different types of adversarial activities.

Benign and adversarial environments are also different in terms of the typed words and commands. Some of the commands typed in a terminal are more dangerous in nature. For example, "sudo" is used to gain administrative privileges and is more common in malicious activities than daily tasks. Similarly, the commands for creating filesystems, installing applications, etc. can be more dangerous than a simple execution of "ls" to list the files in a directory.

3.1   How These Differences Are Useful in Our Application?

The presence of specific words which are unique to one environment and are absent from another, helps us train a neural network model to distinguish between the adversarial and benign activities as discussed in Sect. 7. Since a single malicious command may not be sufficient for evaluating the threat level of the entire typing session, we assign a threat level to each activity instead of each command. Our model learns to classify a sequence of words (which may form multiple commands) into an activity. Then, we use the threat level of the activity to detect the maliciousness level of the entire typing session (Sect. 7.1).

4   Threat Model and Adversarial Capabilities

We assume the adversary has limited access to a system, network, or sensitive data for a legitimate purpose and can use a Linux terminal to exploit the system and a web browser to search for attack instructions and downloading malware. However, we do not make any assumptions about the presence of any vulnerabilities in the system. The adversary works with a mouse and a keyboard and can recognize if any eavesdropping or surveillance software or hardware have been directly installed on the machine. The only information captured is the environment sound.

4.1   Real World Attack Scenario

This work addresses any attack that can be done in public spaces with a keyboard on a computer. A routine scenario can be an employee working with a computer in an office or a college student using a public computer available on campus. After authentication, the user will have limited access to the computer and the network. The type of the keyboard is fixed for the specific public computer and the user is identified through authentication. A voice recorder has been set up in the room which records the environment audio and broadcasts it to a server that runs our model for threat level evaluation.

4.2 Using Keystroke Acoustics Versus Keylogger

A common eavesdropping method to detect potentially harmful behavior is to install software or hardware keyloggers on the users' machines. The keylogger reads all the keystrokes and broadcasts them to a server for processing. However, audio recording can be done covertly and from distance without physical access to the computer and the user's awareness. So, it is more practical in the real-world scenario.

5 Description of Benign and Adversarial Datasets

Following Institutional Review Board (IRB) approval, two separate datasets have been collected in our lab. In both, several modalities have been collected from a variety of participants. The SU-AIS BBMAS [7] dataset is collected from the participants during their everyday routines which we consider as benign activity. The second dataset is collected from participants while performing predefined malicious tasks on a computer to gain access to a remote machine and extract sensitive information. This dataset is expected to be published and made publicly available by December 2021 in IEEE Dataport by our lab. In both datasets, the user has used a standard computer QWERTY keyboard (Dell KB212-B). Two devices have been used for recording the audio: a Blue Yeti Professional Wired Microphone which was placed 1 in. away from the top of the keyboard and a Samsung Galaxy S6 smartphone which was placed 1 foot to the left of the keyboard.

The benign data is collected from 117 participants during regular daily tasks like text transcription, online shopping, note-taking, and typing the answers to a set of questions. Most of the participants were students with computer science or related majors with ages of 19 to 35 years. Among the participants 72 were male and 45 were female. The adversarial dataset has been collected from 103 students in the age range of 19–46 years among which 22 were female and 81 were male, mostly with computer science background during a sequence of activities that result in discovering a vulnerability in a remote machine, getting access to it, and extracting information from it. The tasks are defined in a way to reproduce a regular procedure for a common form of attack in a network. The users were asked to do 7 different activities to eventually succeed in the attack. They were given a Linux machine with a web browser to search for information and tutorials to aid them to fulfill the requirements of the tasks. The users were free to use their method for completing the tasks and were not asked to follow a fixed set of instructions or commands. Among the available data, we use keystrokes data and audio data which is recorded using a standalone microphone and a mobile phone in this work. The activities and their threat level against the system which are manually set by us are described in detail in Table 4.

Table 4. Description of activities performed by the users in the adversarial and benign datasets, example command that may be entered by the user, and their threat level. Example commands only show one method of doing a specific task and the participants were asked to use their own method for fulfilling the task.

Welcome Activity	Description	Opening a terminal on a Linux machine
	Example	Use GUI, CTRL+T, gnome-terminal, xterm
	Threat Level	Low
Network Discovery	Description	Identifying IP addresses and open ports
	Example	nmap -sV 192.0.1.1/24
	Threat Level	Medium
Target Identification	Description	Identifying an attack to access a vulnerable machine
	Example	ssh 192.0.1.3
	Threat Level	Medium
Password Dictionary Attack	Description	Cracking a user/pass of the remote machine
	Example	hydra –L user.txt –P pass.txt 192.0.1.3 ssh
	Threat Level	High
Privilege Escalation	Description	Obtaining root access to the remote machine
	Example	sudo, chown, chmod, scp
	Threat Level	High
Data Exfiltration	Description	Downloading sensitive files from the remote machine
	Example	chown, chmod, scp
	Threat Level	High
Credential Stealing	Description	Accessing the remote machine by stealing credentials
	Example	ssh -i id_rsa jesse@192.0.1.12
	Threat Level	High
Benign	Description	Daily tasks like online shopping, note-taking, etc.
	Example	Arbitrary benign command/text
	Threat Level	Low/Benign

5.1   Noisiness of the Data

Our data is collected in a lab room with the presence of other researchers and an instructor directing the participant to do the tasks and their voice is also recorded in the background. Based on the typing behavior of the user, some keys may be pressed gently without making any audible sound to be recorded. Furthermore, our data is collected using simple and cheap equipment like mobile phones, making it more noisy and challenging. Therefore, several keystroke sounds are inaudible or overlap with human voice and background noise. To evaluate the quality of the data, we use the exact keystrokes times to extract their sound from the session audio. Then, we listen to 100 random keystroke sounds from

5 users manually to see if they are audible by the human ear. We refer to a keystroke sound as inaudible if nothing can be heard from the audio and refer to it as noisy if some noise from the environment such as human voice talking in the background overlaps with the keystroke sound in a way it cannot be heard and recognized by the human ear. We show the statistics for this experiment in Table 3.

6   Text Extraction from Audio

As shown in Fig. 1, to recover the typed text from audio, first we preprocess the raw audio signal to improve the quality and reduce the noise. Then, we extract individual keystroke sounds from it. Next, we generate features for each keystroke audio signal, remove the outliers, and cluster them into a set of audio letters. Finally, we present a mathematical model to recover the words using the audio alphabet and use a spell-checking method to fix the errors in the recovered words. In this section, we go over each component in detail. Since the audio recordings from the benign dataset are not available, we only use the attack dataset for extracting text from audio.

6.1   Audio Signal Preprocessing by Signal Mixing and Noise Reduction

We process and clean the audio file by mixing audio data from two separate recording devices to improve the signal quality. In summary, these are the steps taken to preprocess the raw audio:

- Matching and time synchronizing the recordings from the microphone and the smartphone. Because the exact start times of the recordings are available in the dataset and both tracks have been recorded with equal sample rates, there is no need for up-sampling or down-sampling and the effect of distance from the keyboard is diminished.
- Mixing both signals into one stereo audio track using Sound eXchange (SoX) mixing tool [5].
- Obtaining a noise profile to reduce the background noise such as human voice, fan, door sound, etc.
- Using a generic spectral noise gating algorithm with the noise profile to reduce the background noise in the audio.
- Applying voice reduction and isolation filter using Audacity [3] tool to remove the human voices.
- Normalizing the amplitude using two passes of ffmpeg loudnorm filter with EBU R 128 [21] algorithm.

6.2   Audio Signal Segmentation into Individual Keystroke Sounds

Each keystroke event is composed of three stages: touch, press, and release [23]. Since the most distinguishable and significant peak of the signal is the press event, we use it for detecting the keystroke signal. We use a similar approach to prior research [14,18,19,23] with different parameters and modifications to fit our data and application. First, we calculate FFT coefficients for small sliding windows of 10 ms. With a 44100 Hz signal sample rate, we slide the window in steps of 1 Hz (0.02 ms). Then, we get the sum of FFT coefficients for each window as the signal energy and calculate the 99% percentile of the resulting sum values from all the windows. Finally, we accept the windows greater than the 99% percentile as peaks. As a result, each keystroke sound will be detected multiple times. To avoid this, we use a threshold of 5000 Hz (113 ms) which is obtained through experiments as the minimum delay between two press events. We take the past 10ms and the future 90 ms of the peak from the signal to include the touch event, assuming each keystroke event takes 100 ms. The 100 ms keystroke delay has shown to be sufficient for our purpose in prior research [1,14,23].

To further improve the accuracy of our method, we use an amplitude and a frequency filter to accept the detected keystroke sounds. Based on experiments, a minimum cutoff of 12000 for amplitude and a maximum cutoff of 150 Hz for frequency achieve the best results.

This process is only used with the testing data because the ground truth for all the keystroke timings is available in the dataset. Thus, instead of using this process to extract the individual keystroke sounds, we directly use the timings to extract them from the preprocessed audio and extend them to 100 ms.

6.3   Using MFCCs as Audio Features

MFCCs have been frequently used as features in speech recognition applications [11]. Research has shown that they can also be effective for recovering keystrokes using their sound [14,18,19,22,23]. Thus, we generate MFCCs as features for each individual keystroke sound. We use a window length of 10 ms and 2.5 ms step between windows, 32 filters in the filter bank, and 16 coefficients with a frequency range of 400–14000 Hz. The shape of the MFCC feature set will be 30 × 13 for each keystroke sound which we flatten to get a linear feature vector of length 390.

6.4   Removing Inaudible and Noisy Keystrokes

After generating the feature vectors, we use the K-Means clustering algorithm to split keystroke sounds into two clusters. As a result, one cluster includes all the correctly recorded keystroke sounds and the other cluster includes noisy or inaudible ones. For each cluster, we calculate the mean of the absolute amplitude values. The cluster with the lower mean contains the outliers which we remove from the data.

6.5   Clustering Keystroke Sounds into Audio Alphabet

The sound a keystroke makes is not always unique. So, similar to [18,19], we define an audio alphabet containing a set of audio letters. Our audio alphabet size is larger than the number of keys, allowing each key to be assigned to different audio letters. We use the Gaussian Mixture clustering algorithm (implemented in Python sklearn.mixture.GaussianMixture package) to assign keystroke sounds into 104 different clusters (the number of clusters is chosen through experiments reported in Appendix A). We only use alphanumeric, special character, space, and enter keys (total 52 keys) for generating the clusters using training data. For each user, the training data consists of individual keystroke sounds extracted from the audio recordings using the ground truth timings and values available in the dataset.

Table 5. (a) Example of 22 keystroke sounds clustered into 8 audio letters. (b) The value of h'_{kc_j} probability for each letter. (c) Assigned keys to each cluster during the training session, sorted by h'_{kc_j} probability. The values for the clusters which are not among the example query discussed in Sect. 6.6 are not shown in (b) and (c).

(a)

Cluster	Keys
c_1	d b d d
c_2	e b b e
c_3	e a a e c
c_4	b a a
c_5	a c
c_6	c c
c_7	a
c_8	d

(b)

Key (k)	Probability		
	h'_{kc_1}	h'_{kc_2}	h'_{kc_3}
a	0	0	2/5
b	1/4	1/2	0
c	0	0	1/5
d	3/4	0	0
e	0	1/2	2/5

(c)

Cluster	Keys
c_1	d b
c_2	b e
c_3	a e c

6.6   Text Recovery Using Audio Alphabet

Let $T - \{t_1, t_2, ..., t_n\}$ be the set of all the training samples, the probability that keystroke sound t_i being assigned to cluster c_j calculated by the Gaussian Mixture clustering method be $g_{c_j t_i}$, the total number of training samples assigned to cluster c_j be N_j, and $A = \{a_1, a_2, ..., a_n\}$ be the set of all keystroke sounds (t_i's) that represent key k. We calculate h_{kc_j} which is the probability of key k in cluster c_j:

$$h_{kc_j} = p(k|c_j) = \frac{\sum_{i=1}^{n} g_{c_j a_i}}{N_j} \tag{1}$$

For each a_i representing k, Gaussian Mixture clustering method generates a vector $v_{a_i} = \{g_{c_1 a_i}, g_{c_2 a_i}, ..., g_{c_j a_i}\}$. We take the maximum $g_{c_j a_i}$ for each a_i, set it to 1, and set the rest to zero. So, we assign each keystroke sound to only one cluster:

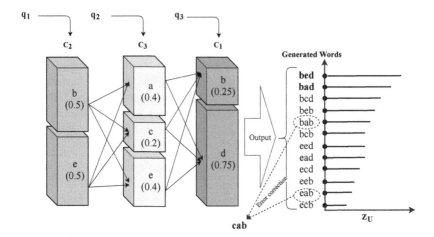

Fig. 2. Generating words for the query $Q = \{q_1, q_2, q_3\}$ clustered into $Y = \{c_2, c_3, c_1\}$ where each c_i is a letter from the audio alphabet (clusters). All the possible permutations from the clusters are generated and then sorted by Z_U which shows the correctness probability of the word. "bad" and "bed" are already correct English words. "bab" and "eab" will be corrected to "cab" by the error correction module.

$$J = \{j | g_{c_j a_i} = max(v_{a_i})\} \qquad\qquad G_{c_j a_i} = \begin{cases} 0 & j \neq J \\ 1 & j = J \end{cases}$$

Then, we define h'_{kc_j} and H_{kc_j} probabilities:

$$N'_j = \sum_{i=1}^{n} G_{c_j t_i} \qquad h'_{kc_j} = \frac{\sum_{i=1}^{n} G_{c_j a_i}}{N_j} \qquad H_{kc_j} = max(h_{kc_j}, h'_{kc_j})$$

We sort the keys in each cluster by H_{kc_j}. So, the keys in cluster c_j will be $K_{c_j} = \{k_1, k_2, ..., k_{52}\}$ where $H_{k_1 c_j} \geq H_{k_2 c_j} \geq ... \geq H_{k_{52} c_j}$. Note that samples representing some keys will never be assigned to some of the clusters and the majority of h probabilities will be zero resulting in $h = h'$ for most of the samples and clusters.

Now, if we have a query of keystroke sounds $Q = \{q_1, q_2, ..., q_m\}$ where each q_i is a keystroke sound sample from a testing set, we use the Gaussian Mixture clustering method with the already trained model to classify each q_i to the clusters. Then, we only take the cluster c_j with the highest $H_{c_j q_i}$ for each q_i. As a result, we assign each q_i to only one cluster. So we have a set of clusters $Y = \{y_1, y_2, ..., y_m\}$ where $q_1 \in y_1, q_2 \in y_2, ..., q_m \in y_m$. Now, we generate all the permutations of keys from the clusters, taking one key from each cluster, starting with the key with the highest H_{kc_j} in each cluster c_j.

We use a dictionary of English words [2] combined with a list of Linux commands and common words typed in terminals [15]. If we have k_i representing letter l_i, we define $d_{k_i} = p(l_i | l_{i-1})$. If the number of times l_i and l_{i-1} appear sequentially in all the words in the dictionary is j and the number of all occurrences of l_i in the dictionary is L, we calculate $d_{k_i} = j/L$.

Let $U = k_1, k_2, ..., k_m$ be a permutation of keys (word) where k_i is selected from c_i. We define:

$$Z_U = \prod_{i=1}^{m} \frac{\alpha d_{k_i} + \beta H_{k_i c_i}}{\alpha + \beta} \qquad (2)$$

Z_U represents the correctness probability of a permutation retrieved from a query of clusters based on the probability of the letters in the dictionary (d) and the probability of each key in each cluster (H). α and β are factors for changing the weight of d and H and are manually set through experiments (Appendix C). We calculate Z_U for each permutation and sort them based on Z_U. As a result, our model generates words that are recovered from the query of keystroke sounds sorted by their correctness probability.

A Simplified Example: We show an example of the training and testing procedure with a limited number of samples. To minimize the number of possible permutations generated from a query of clusters, we assume that each training sample is only assigned to one cluster, so $H_{kc_j} = h'_{kc_j}$. Let $T = \{t_1, ..., t_{22}\}$ and $T' = \{l_1, ..., l_{22}\}$ where T contains all the keystroke sounds in the training set and T' is the set of letters represented by the keystroke sounds in T and l_n is the key represented by t_n. In our example, we set $T' = \{b, d, d, d, e, b, a, e, c, b, c, a, b, a, e, a, a, c, e, c, a, d\}$ and assume there are 8 clusters and each sample has been assigned to one of the clusters as shown in Table 5a. Also, we have query $Q = \{q_1, q_2, q_3\}$ clustered into $Y = \{c_2, c_3, c_1\}$. Then, we calculate h'_{kc_j} for all keys in all clusters which shows the probability of key k, if cluster c_j is selected. We show the calculated h' values in Table 5b for c_1, c_2, c_3 because these are the only clusters that have appeared in our sample query. By sorting the keys in each cluster based on h', we get the clusters in Table 5c. Then, we generate all the permutations of keys as shown in Fig. 2. Next, we calculate Z_U based on d_k and h'. For simplicity, we just illustrate the Z_U values for each permutation in Fig. 2 as the calculations are redundant and straightforward.

6.7   Error Correction Using Dictionary

Having a set of words sorted by Z_U, we still recover words that are not completely correct or not in the dictionary. So, after generating the possible words, we use a spell-checking algorithm [16] with the same dictionaries used in the text recovery module [2, 15]. We filter out the words with numbers and special characters using regular expressions and do not pass them to this module.

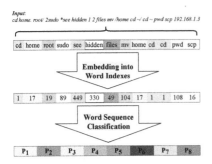

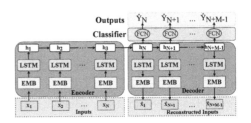

Fig. 3. An example of a sequence of words typed by one of the users during activity 6. Red shows higher probability while green indicates lower probability. (See Appendix D) (Color figure online)

Fig. 4. Data flow over N time-steps with inputs x_1, x_2, x_N (words) for the encoder/decoder LSTM architecture as discussed in Sect. 7.

7   Adversarial Activity Detection and Classification

Among the different prominent architectures of Artificial Neural Networks (ANNs) that have been implemented as software and hardware components [20], recurrent neural networks are the preferred methods of learning from temporally correlated datasets. Long Short-Term Memory (LSTM) is a variant of RNN that has shown notable performance in the classification of sequential data. Hence, we propose an LSTM-based model to classify each sequence of words into one of the 8 classes. To build the training dataset, first, we get all the keystrokes from all the users and take each sequential set of letter keys (separated by space or enter) as a typed word. Then, we use every n sequential words for each activity of each user as one data sample. To feed the sequence into the network, we fix its length to n words. When n words are not available, we pad the sequence with zeros and when a sequence is longer than n words, we break it into segments of n words. As a result, we have fixed-length sequences of words and their corresponding activity to be used for training the model. Also, we get all the words from the dataset and sort them based on their frequency. Then, we assign an index to each word, with the most frequent word indexed with 1. The procedure for classifying a sample sequence of words has been demonstrated in Fig. 3.

Figure 4 shows the flow of the data across three time steps. Similar to the previous work on time series data classification [4,13], each input word x is fed to an embedding layer (EMB) to be represented in a lower-dimensional space. Then, the word embedding is passed to an LSTM layer that performs the main task of classification using Adam optimizer [12]. Pavllo et al. [17], show that regularizing the model by adding another network to form an encoder-decoder architecture that learns to reconstruct the input data increases the robustness and generalization capability of the LSTM layer and helps the model to learn and represent the features of the data in a more effective way. So, we add such a component to our network. The latent state of the LSTM, which is represented by h_t in Fig. 4, is shared among the encoder and the decoder. For the classification task, h is passed through a fully connected network (FCN) with one hidden layer. During the training process, h is also used for reconstruction of the input data $\hat{x}_t$.

Equation 3 shows the loss function that is used for training the model. L_R denotes the loss value obtained for the reconstruction of input in the output of the decoder and L_C represents the classification loss, which is calculated by comparing the expected output with the predicted class from the model. α and β are coefficients for controlling the effect of L_C and L_R on the total loss.

$$L_{total} = \alpha L_C(y, \hat{y}) + \beta L_R(x, \hat{x}) \tag{3}$$

7.1 Quantifying the Threat Level

The output of the activity classification network is a probability vector $v = \{p_1, p_2, ..., p_8\}$ indicating the probability that word sequence B belongs to each activity a_1 to a_8 respectively. We also define $D = \{d_1, d_2, ..., d_8\}$ where d_i indicates the threat level for each activity and is manually set. Since d_8 represents the benign activity, we set it to a small value ϵ. Finally, we define $X = d_1 p_1 + d_2 p_2 + ... + d_8 p_8$ as a measure for threat level of B. After calculating the threat level score in each time step, it is possible to utilize a separate scoring model such as BehavioSec trust model [10] to continuously monitor and update the threat level against the system in real-time.

8   Performance Evaluation of the Proposed Components

In this section, we evaluate and analyze the performance of each module in our proposed method through several experiments.

8.1   Audio Signal Segmentation into Individual Keystroke Sounds

After preprocessing and outlier removal, we use the audio segmentation module to extract the keystroke times. For each keystroke time in the ground truth, we find the closest value from the audio segmentation module predictions. Then, we use an error threshold to consider the predicted time as correct or incorrect. With a threshold of 100 ms, our audio segmentation module can detect 91% of the keystroke sounds on average. The mean squared error averaged for all the users is 0.09.

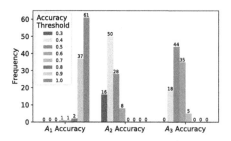

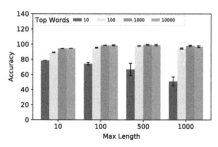

Fig. 5. Distribution of the number of users based on A_1, A_2, A_3 accuracy metrics as discussed in Sect. 8.2.

Fig. 6. Accuracy of the activity classifier with different word sequence lengths and number of most frequent words.

8.2   Clustering into Audio Alphabet

To evaluate the clustering method, we assume each training sample is assigned to only one cluster and define three metrics to calculate the accuracy. For all test samples $t_1, t_2, ..., t_n$ representing keys $k_1, k_2, ..., k_n$ clustered into $c_1, c_2, ..., c_n$ respectively, we calculate A_1 as an accuracy metric by considering a classification correct if at least one training sample that represents k_i has been assigned to c_i during the training procedure ($h'_{c_i k_i} > 0$). We also define A_2 as another accuracy metric:

$$A_1 = \frac{\sum_{i=0}^{n} \begin{cases} 0 & h'_{k_i c_i} = 0 \\ 1 & h'_{k_i c_i} \neq 0 \end{cases}}{n} \qquad A_2 = \frac{\sum h'_{k_i c_i}}{n}$$

We consider sample t_i representing key k_i clustered into c_i as correct if k_i has the highest probability $h'_{k_i c_i}$ among all the keys that have been clustered into c_i during the training procedure. If N is the total number of the keys we calculate A_3:

$$A_3 = \frac{\sum_{i=0}^{n} \begin{cases} 0 & h'_{k_i c_i} \neq max_{j=0}^{N}(h'_{k_j c_i}) \\ 1 & h'_{k_i c_i} = max_{j=0}^{N}(h'_{k_j c_i}) \end{cases}}{n} \qquad (4)$$

As an example, take the clusters of Table 5a. Assume we have a set of testing samples t_1, t_2, t_3 representing keys a, b, c clustered into c_1, c_2, c_3. Then, we have:

$$h'_{ac_1}, h'_{bc_2}, h'_{cc_3} = 0, 1/2, 1/5 \implies \begin{cases} A_1 = \frac{0+1+1}{3} = 0.66 \\ A_2 = \frac{0+1/2+1/5}{3} = 0.23 \\ A_3 = \frac{0+1+0}{3} = 0.33 \end{cases}$$

We take 70% of keystroke sounds for each user and group them into 104 clusters. Then, we predict the cluster for each sample keystroke sound from the test set. It is possible that the keystroke sounds representing a specific letter be assigned to different clusters. Also, multiple keystroke sounds representing the same character can be assigned to the same cluster. The average A_1, A_2, and A_3 values for all the users are 90%, 38%, 48% respectively. We show the distribution of the number of users based on the accuracy values in Fig. 5. Note that an A_2 value of 100% is only possible when all the samples that have been assigned to each cluster only represent a specific letter. In this case, each cluster represents only one letter. Similarly, an A_3 value of 100% means all the samples from the test set that represent a specific key are assigned to only one cluster. This also leads to each cluster representing only one letter. As a result, A_2 and A_3 can reach 100% in theory while it is not possible in practice and values of 38% and 48% do not necessarily show a low accuracy for the model.

We evaluate the effect of the number of the clusters on the performance of the model which is reported in Appendix A. Furthermore, we compare our method for detecting individual keystrokes based on audio with a similar work *Skype & Type* [9] in Appendix B.

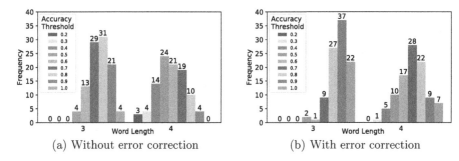

(a) Without error correction   (b) With error correction

Fig. 7. Distribution of the number of users based on the top-1000 accuracy of the word recovery module for 3-letter and 4-letter words before and after using the error correction module.

8.3   Recovering Text from Clusters

For each user, we get the keystroke sounds from 70% of the typed words to train the clusters and use the remaining 30% for testing. While we use the ground truth for identifying words using spaces and enters as separators for our evaluation, in a real-world scenario, we identify the separators by assigning them to a specific cluster that represents them. The cluster with the highest number of enters (or spaces) assigned to it in the training session, represents enter (or space). Later, when a keystroke sound is assigned to such cluster, we consider it as a possible separator. We take the words with a fixed length. Most of the typed words are between 2 to 4 letters, so we use those in most of our experiments. The distribution of words length in the datasets is shown in Fig. 12 in Appendix E.

In Fig. 7, we show the distribution of the top-1000 accuracy for all of the users for 3 and 4-letter words with and without using the error correction module. With

3-letter words, the accuracy for most of the users is 80–90% while for 4-letter words it is 50–60%. The average accuracy for all the users is 72% for 3-letter words and 53% for 4-letter words. The average top-10 accuracy for words of length 2–4 and all the users is 54% which will later be improved by the error correction module.

Error Correction. We apply the error correction method (Sect. 6.7) to the guessed words in the previous experiment. Figure 7 shows how the error correction module improves the performance of the word recovery module. With error correction, the average top-10 accuracy for words of 2 to 4 letters will be improved to 71% which is an acceptable accuracy considering our noisy dataset. Also, since text recovery is not the final goal of our model and the recovered words will be passed to the activity detection module, the effect of accuracy for the text recovery module will be lowered. In Sect. 8.4, we show that if we use our activity detection model with the words directly fetched from the dataset (without extracting them from audio), the accuracy gain in comparison with using the words produced by the text recovery module is insignificant.

8.4   Adversarial Activity Detection and Classification

We directly take the ground truth for all the typed word sequences from the attack and benign datasets instead of the words generated by the text recovery module and fix their length. We only take the n most frequent words (top words) typed by all the users and discard (zero out) the rest. We train and test our model with different sequence lengths and top words and show the results in Fig. 6. The best accuracy gained is 98.07% when we take only the 1000 top words and fix the sequence length to 50 words. The training and validation loss and accuracy of the model for sequences of 50 words and considering the 1000 most frequent words are shown in Fig. 13 in Appendix E.

Furthermore, we use the words generated by the text recovery module to evaluate our activity detection model. We use sequences of 2 to 4 letter words from the dataset to train the activity detection model. Then, we use the text recovery module to generate words of length 2–4 using keystroke audio samples and feed them as test data to the activity detection module. We use sequences of 50 subsequent words for this experiment. Since we do not have the audio for the benign dataset, we directly get the words from it without recovering them from the audio. As a result of this evaluation, our model achieves 93.11% accuracy in detecting and classifying the activities.

In another experiment, we fine-tune the hyper-parameters of our model and compare the best-performing configuration with other classifiers. We use the fixed-length zero-padded sequences of words as features, and activities as labels for the training and testing data. For each classifier, we fine-tune the hyper-parameters separately to get the best possible accuracy. Among the several algorithms and configurations we used, decision tree results in the best performance with 75% accuracy which is significantly less than our model's performance. Detailed results of this experiment are reported in Table 6 in Appendix E.

9   Conclusion and Future Work

We showed that it is possible to detect different adversarial activities and evaluate the threat level against a computer system using the audio recordings of typing sessions with significant accuracy. To show that, we proposed a model with multiple components to extract text from typing audio, detect activity based on extracted words, and quantify the threat level based on the activity. While we used a limited set of activities for classification, our model is easily extendable to other classes of adversarial and benign activities. There are possible extensions to this work that we have left for future research. In our model, we only use a limited number of keys (alphanumerical, special characters, space, and enter) for classification. While we showed that it is possible to classify the activity and measure the threat level using those keys with notable performance, the use of other keys on the keyboard (like tab which is used to auto-complete commands in the terminal) and their effects on the model performance is left for the future research. Also, studying the detection of keystroke combinations which is partially addressed in [22] and its effects on our model performance remains for the future research. Another possible extension to this work is building a continuous threat level monitoring model and using real-time audio. However, as we discussed in Sect. 7.1, our work can be easily expanded to support real-time data. Prior work [23] have shown that it is possible to use unsupervised learning methods for recovering text from the audio which can be studied for our application. Since our model prioritizes dictionary words, whether random sequences of keystrokes can contribute to activity detection is also subject to further research.

A   Choosing the Number of the Clusters

To find the optimal number of clusters, we take 30% of all the keystroke sounds from all the users as test data and classify them into the pre-trained clusters. Figure 8 shows the evaluation results using our three metrics. When the number of clusters grows, the probability that a keystroke sound representing a key k be assigned to a cluster with at least one sample representing k from the training set decreases. At the same time, if a keystroke sound is clustered correctly because the number of samples is lower in each cluster, the probability of the key in the cluster (h') would be higher, resulting in higher A_2 and A_3 values. Overall, the results show that using 104 and 208 clusters achieves the best performance. In another experiment, we run the word extraction algorithm for each user with different word lengths and number of clusters. First, we get 70% of the words for each user and generate the clusters using the keystroke sounds from each word. Then, we take 30% of the words as the test data and classify them into clusters. Next, we use the predicted cluster to regenerate the words and consider a prediction correct if it is among the 1000 most probable words predicted by the algorithm. As shown in Fig. 9, 104 and 208 clusters achieve the best overall performance and the sum of performance metrics for 104 clusters is the highest.

Therefore, based on the findings in Fig. 8 and Fig. 9, we choose to use 104 clusters for the rest of our experiments.

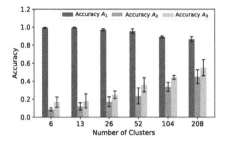
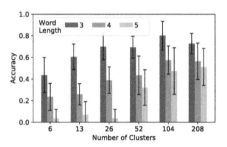

Fig. 8. Accuracy of the clustering method evaluated using three metrics, changing number of the clusters.

Fig. 9. Top-1000 accuracy of the word recovery module for different word lengths and number of clusters.

B   Comparison with Other Work

There are a limited number of prior studies with publicly available source code to be evaluated with our data. Among those, we evaluate a similar work *Skype & Type!* (S&T) [9] with our dataset. S&T has different components similar to our work. The audio segmentation module uses a peak detection method to extract individual key sounds from the raw audio file. However, this component as implemented does not work on our dataset because of the presence of noise and inaudible keys. So, we remove this component and use already extracted individual key sounds and their labels with their classification model. S&T generates MFCC features with similar hyper-parameters to ours and uses a feature selection algorithm to reduce the number of features. We run their model using different classifiers with the audio data from 5 of the users in our dataset separately and once with the audio data of all the users combined. Note that their model directly classifies the feature vector and assigns it to a key while our classification method generates a probability for multiple possible audio letters (clusters) representing each MFCC feature vector and does not give an explicit key for each sample. We use A_3 as the metric for calculating the accuracy of our work. Using this metric is fair for comparison because for each sample key audio, we output one cluster and for each cluster, we only take the most probable letter as correct. So, in this evaluation method, our classifier gets a keystroke sound as input and outputs a key (letter) like what S&T does. The results for all users and 5 users are presented in Fig. 10 showing significantly better accuracy for our model in comparison to S&T for single users and similar accuracy for all users combined. In Fig. 11, we show the frequency of the users based on the classification accuracy of their key sound samples for both S&T and our method. We need to mention that our method can achieve even better accuracy because we build a probability model to consider all the possible letters in the cluster and do not only take the most probable letter as the result of the classification. So, our model does not assign a specific key to a keystroke sound sample and the subsequent modules (text extraction, error correction) will decide about the final chosen key.

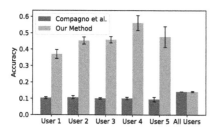

Fig. 10. Comparison of the performance of our method with S&T [9] for retrieving single letters from keystroke sounds.

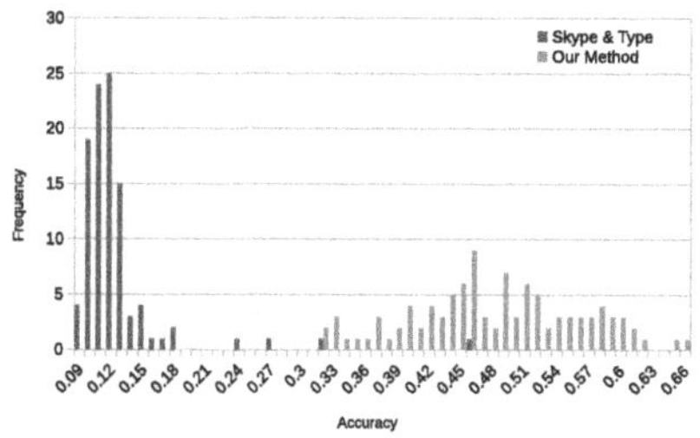

Fig. 11. Distribution of users based on accuracy for classifying each user's key sounds using S&T [9] method and our method.

C   Choosing the Values of α and β

To choose the best values for α and β in Eq. 2 which control the effect of probability in the dictionary and the probability in the clusters for each recovered word, we run the same experiment that we used for evaluating the text recovery module, varying the values of α and β between 1 to 1000. Based on the experiment on the 3-letter and 4-letter words, the best results are achieved when $\alpha = 1$ and $\beta = 10$. So, we use these values for the rest of the experiments.

D   Examples of Adversarial Activity Detection Using Typed Sentences

We obtain a set of sequentially typed words from the attack dataset: {how, to, scan, open, ports, in, kali}

The set of words will be embedded into word indexes. In this example, we only consider the top 1000 words, so, the word"ports" is embedded to zero because it is not among the top 1000 words in the dataset: {121, 12, 720, 150, 0 ,10, 990}

Finally, the adversarial activity probability vector will be generated by the attack detection module: {0.1, 0.7, 0.4, 0.3, 0.2, 0.2, 0.2, 0.5}

As can be seen, the typed sentence will be classified to the network discovery activity (Table 4) with the highest probability. Also, the benign activity probability is relatively high which is expected as the typed sentence is not necessarily threatening.

Similarly, we show an example of a sentence taken from the benign dataset. Here, we also show the sentence before error correction, so, the effect of error correction module can be seen: {slice, it, and, then, place, a, layer, of, tomato, on, top, of, the, laye, rof, onion} → {slice, it, and, then, place, a, layer, of, tomato, on, top, of, the, layer, of, onion} → {818, 17, 5, 21, 220, 4, 561, 14, 0, 16, 41, 14, 6, 561, 14, 0} → {0.1, 0.0, 0.0, 0.0, 0.1, 0.1, 0.0, 0.9}

E   Supplementary Figures and Tables

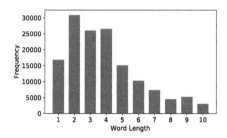

Fig. 12. Word length distribution in benign and attack datasets combined.

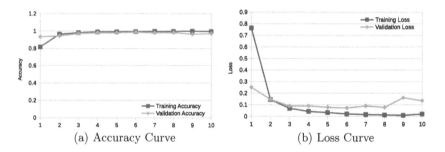

(a) Accuracy Curve   (b) Loss Curve

Fig. 13. Training and validation loss and accuracy for activity detection algorithm with word sequences of length 50 and considering only the 1000 top words.

Table 6. Comparison of the performance of different algorithms for classifying word sequences to activities. The input data is fixed-length zero-padded sequences of 50 words considering only the 2000 most frequent words in the dataset.

Model	Hyper-parameters		Accuracy	
			Mean	STD
Nearest Neighbor	Number of Neighbors	3	0.65	0.01
RBF SVM	Regularization	2	0.67	0.10
	gamma	1		
Decision Tree	Max depth	5	0.75	0.04
Random Forest	Max depth	5	0.69	0.09
	Number of estimators	10		
	Max features	1		
AdaBoost	Number of estimator	50	0.38	0.8
	Base estimatior	1		
Naive Bayes	Variance smoothing	1e−9	0.28	0.04
QDA	Threshold	1e−4	0.46	0.03
Our Model	Embedding vector length	512	0.98	0.01
	LSTM layer size	100		
	Number of epochs	10		
	Batch size	32		

References

1. Asonov, D., Agrawal, R.: Keyboard acoustic emanations. In: IEEE Symposium on Security and Privacy, 2004. Proceedings. 2004, pp. 3–11 (2004). https://doi.org/10.1109/SECPRI.2004.1301311
2. Atkinson, K.: Scowl (spell checker oriented word lists) and friends (2020). http://wordlist.aspell.net/
3. Audacity Team: Audacity. https://www.audacityteam.org/
4. Baghaei, K.T., Rahimi, S.: Sepsis prediction: an attention-based interpretable approach. In: 2019 IEEE International Conference on Fuzzy Systems (FUZZ-IEEE), pp. 1–6 (2019). https://doi.org/10.1109/FUZZ-IEEE.2019.8858808
5. Barras, B.: Sox : Sound exchange (01 2012)
6. Belman, A.K., Sridhara, S., Phoha, V.V.: Classification of threat level in typing activity through keystroke dynamics. In: 2020 International Conference on Artificial Intelligence and Signal Processing (AISP), pp. 1–6 (2020). https://doi.org/10.1109/AISP48273.2020.9073079
7. Belman, A.K., et al.: Insights from bb-mas - a large dataset for typing, gait and swipes of the same person on desktop, tablet and phone (2019)
8. Berger, Y., Wool, A., Yeredor, A.: Dictionary attacks using keyboard acoustic emanations. In: Proceedings of the 13th ACM Conference on Computer and Communications Security, CCS 2006, pp. 245–254. Association for Computing Machinery, New York (2006). https://doi.org/10.1145/1180405.1180436, https://doi.org/10.1145/1180405.1180436

9. Compagno, A., Conti, M., Lain, D., Tsudik, G.: Don't skype & type! acoustic eavesdropping in voice-over-ip (2017)
10. Deutschmann, I., Nordström, P., Nilsson, L.: Continuous authentication using behavioral biometrics. IT Professional **15**(4), 12–15 (2013). https://doi.org/10.1109/MITP.2013.50
11. Ganchev, T., Fakotakis, N., Kokkinakis, G.: Comparative evaluation of various mfcc implementations on the speaker verification task. In: Proceedings of the SPECOM-2005, pp. 191–194 (2005)
12. Kingma, D.P., Ba, J.: Adam: A method for stochastic optimization (2017)
13. Kopuru, M., Rahimi, S., Teimouri Baghaei, K.: Recent approaches in prognostics: State of the art (08 2019)
14. Liu, J., Wang, Y., Kar, G., Chen, Y., Yang, J., Gruteser, M.: Snooping keystrokes with mm-level audio ranging on a single phone. In: Proceedings of the 21st Annual International Conference on Mobile Computing and Networking, MobiCom 2015, pp. 142–154. Association for Computing Machinery, New York (2015). https://doi.org/10.1145/2789168.2790122, https://doi.org/10.1145/2789168.2790122
15. Nguyen, B.: Linux Dictionary. The Linux Documentation Project. https://tldp.org/LDP/Linux-Dictionary/html/index.html
16. Norvig, P.: How to write a spelling corrector (August 2016), http://norvig.com/spell-correct.html
17. Pavllo, D., Feichtenhofer, C., Grangier, D., Auli, M.: 3d human pose estimation in video with temporal convolutions and semi-supervised training (2019)
18. Roth, J., Liu, X., Ross, A., Metaxas, D.: Biometric authentication via keystroke sound. In: 2013 International Conference on Biometrics (ICB), pp. 1–8 (2013). https://doi.org/10.1109/ICB.2013.6613015
19. Roth, J., Liu, X., Ross, A., Metaxas, D.: Investigating the discriminative power of keystroke sound. IEEE Trans. Inf. Forensics Secur. **10**(2), 333–345 (2015). https://doi.org/10.1109/TIFS.2014.2374424
20. Shakiba, F.M., Zhou, M.: Novel analog implementation of a hyperbolic tangent neuron in artificial neural networks. IEEE Trans. Ind. Electron. 1 (2020). https://doi.org/10.1109/TIE.2020.3034856
21. Union, E.B.: R 128 - loudness normalisation and permitted maximum level of audio signals (August 2020). https://tech.ebu.ch/docs/r/r128.pdf
22. Wang, J., Ruby, R., Wang, L., Wu, K.: Accurate combined keystrokes detection using acoustic signals. In: 2016 12th International Conference on Mobile Ad-Hoc and Sensor Networks (MSN), pp. 9–14 (2016). https://doi.org/10.1109/MSN.2016.010
23. Zhuang, L., Zhou, F., Tygar, J.D.: Keyboard acoustic emanations revisited. ACM Trans. Inf. Syst. Secur. **13**(1) (2009). https://doi.org/10.1145/1609956.1609959

Automotive

Tell Me How You Re-Charge, I Will Tell You Where You Drove To: Electric Vehicles Profiling Based on Charging-Current Demand

Alessandro Brighente[(✉)], Mauro Conti, and Izza Sadaf

University of Padova, Human Inspired Technologies Research Center, Padova, Italy
alessandro.brighente@unipd.it, conti@math.unipd.it,
izza.sadaf@studenti.unipd.it

Abstract. Charging an EV (Electric Vehicle) comprises two phases: a) resource negotiation, and b) actual charging. While the former phase runs over secure communication protocols, the latter is usually assumed not to be a threat to security and privacy. However, we believe that the physical signals exchanged between the EV and the EVSE (Electric Vehicle Supply Equipment) represent information that a malicious user could exploit for profiling. Furthermore, as a large number of EVSEs has been deployed in public places to ease out-of-home EV charging, an attacker might easily have physical access to unsecured data.

In this paper, we propose EVScout, a novel attack to profile EVs during the charging process. By exploiting the physical signals exchanged by the EV and the EVSE as a side-channel to extract information, EVScout builds a set of features peculiar for each EV. As an EVScout component, we also propose a novel feature extraction framework, based on the intrinsic characteristics of EV batteries, to identify features from the exchanged electric current. We implemented and tested EVScout over a set of real-world measurements (considering 100 charging sessions of 22 EVs). Numerical results show that EVScout could profile EVs, attaining a maximum of 0.9 recall and 0.85 precision. To the best of authors' knowledge, these results set a benchmark for upcoming privacy research for EVs.

Keywords: User privacy · Electric vehicles · Profiling · Cyber-physical systems · Machine learning

1 Introduction

EVs (Electric Vehicles) sales are predicted to represent 30% of the global market share by 2030 [6]. In fact, as EVs represent an ecological substitute to gas-fueled transportation, some countries have set their goal in terms of number of adopted EVs. For instance, Canada targets to reach 1 million EVs by 2030 [1]. Together with the increasing demand for EVs, also demand for their charging equipment,

© Springer Nature Switzerland AG 2021
E. Bertino et al. (Eds.): ESORICS 2021, LNCS 12972, pp. 651–667, 2021.
https://doi.org/10.1007/978-3-030-88418-5_31

i.e., EVSEs (Electric Vehicle Supply Equipments) is rising. In fact, to cope with the increasing adoption of EVs, countries are asked to invest in EVSEs to be placed in public facilities. Furthermore, some countries also started their initiatives to increase the number of public available EVSEs. For instance, with the "workplace charging challenge", USA is encouraging the installation of EVSEs at the workplace [20]. EVSEs should provide a safe and secure means for users to charge their EV, the same way as gas stations do. In order to both automate and secure the charging process, EVSEs are organized in a network. Communication protocols are here exploited to ease the interaction between users and end-level service provider, i.e., the power distributor. Users can therefore charge their EV to publicly available EVSEs by previously booking a charging session. The booking process includes multiple steps, such as the login of the user into the system, the negotiation of power between the EVSE and power distributor, the eventual acknowledgment to the user and eventually the actual charging process. All these steps can be grouped in two major phases: the negotiation phase, and the charging phase. Most of the security and privacy effort has been put on the negotiation phase, as it involves communications and sharing of private information between the actors involved. The overall system has been analyzed in literature from a CPS (Cyber-Physical System) security point of view, and several threats have been identified [1,9]. However, security and privacy analysis should also focus on the charging phase. Even though no personal data is exchanged during the actual charging phase, an attacker may be able to exploit these signals to infer users' private information. Furthermore, the attacker may easily exploit these signals as they are transmitted inherently in clear. In fact, as their purpose is indeed not to transfer bits, but energy, they are neither coded nor authenticated.

Profiling is the process of extracting features that are representative of a certain group or individual, such that a single user or a group can be later identified based on their generated data. Profiling can be employed in different scenarios. For instance, services targeted for the particular needs of a user may be provided after profiling. On the other hand, profiling has the drawback of undermining users' privacy. In fact, monitoring users' activities is essential in both preliminary feature extraction and later use. To prevent malicious users to gather and exploit data for profiling purposes, data is usually exchanged using secure communication protocols. However, exchanged signals not including bits can be exploited for feature extraction. While researchers exploited energy consumption in other domains, we are the first to explore this in the EVs domain. An example of power consumption as side channel is given by [5], where the attacker implements laptop user recognition by exploiting the current drawn by a smart wall socket during users' activity. In [13] user presence in a smart home is detected based on raw data measured by smart meters deployed in different sectors of the house. In [16] user's activity is inferred based on the power delivered via USB cable during smartphone charging, while a similar concept has been exploited in [23] to infer users' browsing activities. However, to the best of the author's knowledge, this is the first time that the exchanged electric current during the charging process of an EV is exploited to jeopardize users' privacy.

In this paper we show how the signals exchanged during the charging phase can be exploited by a malicious actor to profile an EV. In a scenario in which an increasing number of EVSEs are placed in public premises [3] and are therefore not supervised, an attacker may easily have physical access to the premises and hence to the transferred signals. We propose *EVScout*, an attack to profile EVs based on the electric current values exchanged during the charging phase. To the best of our knowledge, this is the first implementation of such attack for EVs. The main idea behind EVScout is that each EV presents unique physical features when exchanging signals with the EVSE. In particular, when the battery's SoC (State of Charge) goes from 70–80% to full charge, the current exchanged highly depends on the battery implementation, and therefore differs from an EV to another. As part of EVScout, we hence propose a novel feature extraction framework based on the intrinsic behavior of EVs' battery.

To summarize, the contributions of this paper are:

- We propose EVScout, an attack to profile EVs based on the current exchanged during the charging session. We hence highlight the threat given by non protected exchange of signals between EV and EVSE.
- As part of EVScout, we propose a novel feature extraction framework, suitably designed based on EVs' battery behavior.
- We provide a prototype implementation of EVScout, comprising different learning algorithms.
- We test EVScout on real-world measurement of 100 charging sessions for each of the 22 considered EVs, further assessing the validity of our proposed attack.
- Through thorough testing, we show that EVScout could profile EVs based on their charging behaviors, obtaining a maximum precision value of 0.85 and 0.9 recall. These results set a benchmark for future investigation on EV users' privacy.

The rest of the paper is organized as follows. In Sect. 2 we introduce the preliminary knowledge needed for the comprehension of the EV charging infrastructure, and describe the threat model. In Sect. 3 we describe the EVScout attack, showing how it leverages current values from charging sessions to profile EVs. In Sect. 4 we introduce the dataset used to assess the validity of EVScout. We then present and discuss numerical results, showing the feasibility of profiling based on charging sessions data. In Sect. 5 we discuss possible countermeasures to EVScout. Lastly, in Sect. 6 we derive the conclusions.

2   System and Threat Model

In order to be efficient, the feature extraction process should target the specific behavior of the analyzed system. In this section we present the preliminary knowledge needed for the implementation of EVScout. First, in Sect. 2.1 we introduce the system model, where we define the main blocks of an EV charging infrastructure. Along with the system model, we also show the signaling needed during the charging phase, as well as the physical behavior of an EV's battery. Then, in Sect. 2.2, we present the threat model, defining the basic assumptions on the the attacker's knowledge and behavior.

2.1 System Model

The charging infrastructure for EVs can be seen as a network, where a central controller (power distributor) distributes power based on nodes demand, while accounting for the maximum supported load by the electric grid. Nodes in the network are characterized by their deployment site, being it a customer premise, public stations, or office buildings. Each EV is both physically and logically connected to the grid via the EVSE, which manages communications between the user (i.e., the owner of the EV) and the power distributor. For public charging infrastructures and office stations, multiple EVSEs are connected to the power distributor through a central control, that copes with the demand of a large number of connected users [1]. EVSEs are typically equipped with communication interfaces (wireless or wired) to allow communication with the user. By means of modules in the EV or smartphone, the user can communicate with the EVSE and, in turn, with the power supplier.

Current implementations of EVSEs are organized in three levels [9,21] . Level 1 and 2 use a 5 lead connector based on SAE J1772 standard [19], where 3 leads are connected to the grid via relays in the EVSE. The remaining 2 pins, i.e., pilot and proximity lines, are used for signaling. While the proximity line gives an indication of whether a good physical connection has been established, the pilot line provides a basic communication means between the EV and the EVSE. The combination of signals collected from all the pins is used to provide the main computer of the EVSE information about the charging process, allowing for metering used to assess the charging session state. If a problem arises at one of the two sides of the charging process, the EVSE computer hardware will remove power from the adapter to prevent injuries on both sides. Level 3 EVSEs are instead more complex, comprising bigger pins for power delivery and allowing power line communications via the pilot line.

Typical batteries employed for EVs belong to the class of Li-ion (lithium-ion) [2,22]. Current and voltage values exchanged during the charging process depend on the SoC of the EV battery, and can be divided into two classes: constant current/ constant voltage and constant power/constant voltage [12]. We here consider the first class, where the charging process can be further divided into two phases: a) the constant current phase; where the current level is constant while the voltage value increases and b) the constant voltage phase, where voltage is constant whereas current decreases. The switch point between the two phases is given by the SoC of the battery. Typical SoC switching values lie between 60% and 80% of the full charge. An example of a charging profile for an EV's Li-ion battery is shown in Fig. 1. We here remark that constant current and constant voltage phases are mutually exclusive in time, as this will be exploited by EVScout.

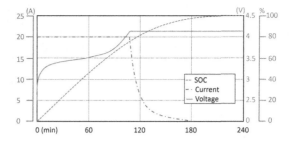

Fig. 1. Charging profile of a Li-ion battery [18]: we see that, as the SoC increases, the charging mode switches from constant current to constant voltage.

2.2   Threat Model

We assume that the attacker is equipped with a small measuring device which can be connected on one side to the EVSE plug, and the other side to the EV plug, to measure the exchanged current at the connection point between the EV and EVSE. Similar to attacks based on ATM skimming, we assume that this device is hard to be noticed by users. The device is assumed to be equipped with a wireless communication module or having storage capabilities, such that it can deliver the collected information to the attacker. The attacker has hence access to the TS (time series) of the current values that the EVSE exchanges with the EV during the charging phase. Such values are recorded for each pin of the EV charger. In this paper, we assume that the attacker trains a different classifier for each target EV. Therefore, in order to properly train the classifier, a sufficient number of TSs shall be collected for each single EV. In order to speed up this process, a single device shall be plugged to each EVSE, such that the attacker gets access to data from multiple points. This is motivated by the fact that the target EV may be plugged to different EVSEs in successive charging sessions, e.g., in the parking spaces at work places or shopping malls the target user often visits. The attacker has hence access to multiple charging sessions of the same EV, and exploits them to build a training set for feature characterization and extraction. Furthermore, the attacker collects data generated from the charging sessions of multiple EVs.

We assume that the attacker targets public premises, accessible to anyone. In this case, since there is no regulation on access to EVSEs, the attacker is able to attach the measuring devices. Furthermore, the attack is facilitated by the fact that typical users are not going to modify in any way the charging system. Therefore, the attacker is not limited in being the company running the EVSEs network, but can be anyone interested in obtaining such information. However, we notice that the EVSE devices can be routinely checked by the staff of the running company. Therefore, the most successful attacks are expected to involve collusion in two different scenarios, i.e., a) with the running company, or b) with the EVSE builders such that measuring devices are natively built in. To build a set with sufficient features we assume that the attacker collects: the TS of the exchanged current values, the TS of the pilot signals, the total kW exchanged, and the time duration of the charging phase. Notice that, in order to retrieve this data, the attacker does not need to perform elaborate network intrusion schemes, as signals are exchanged outside the network. Furthermore, notice that the attacker is not modifying in any way the charging process. Hence, the system is not able to automatically detect the presence of the attacker.

Figure 2 shows the assumed system and threat model. Multiple EVSEs are connected to the central control, which provides coordination and power distribution. A single EV is connected to each EVSE. The attacker gets access to the physical quantities exchanged by multiple EVs during the charging phase, and exploits them for profiling. Notice that, if the attacker can remotely access to the current exchanged in different nodes of the network, it can also locate users. Therefore, profiling may also lead to user tracking. The knowledge of the physical signal features associated with each EV (and hence user) can also be exploited for impersonation attacks. Considering EVSEs which are automated based on the specific user needs, an attacker could steal assets from a target user by generating a signal with the same physical features of the target user. Scenarios in which this may harm the target user include billing and misbehaving users exclusion from the system. Therefore, the motivation behind the attack can be multiple. As an illustrative example, consider advertising: the attacker has both information on a certain user's typical movements and the amount of energy she consumes on a regular basis. This information can be sold to EVSE owners, which will target their advertisement to the profiled user according to its demand. Notice that, although a single classifier is trained for each EV, the attacker collects information regarding multiple EVs, such that more than a single classifier can be implemented with the gathered data. Therefore, the attacker can also sell information about collective use of the EVSE charging stations by EVs to EVSE companies. Although profiling can be implemented by means of cameras, this would not allow for collection of energy traces, therefore losing some of the information available with the proposed attack. Such information can be obtained by means of EVScout. A further threat is given by the possibility of tracking a user. In fact, thanks to EVScout, a malicious user is able to detect the presence of a target user in a certain place and time based on the fact that her EV is connected to a particular EVSE. Although this attack can be implemented by meas of cameras, the envisioned device used to gather the data needed for EVScout is less noticeable, and hence less detectable by the running company's staff.

3   The EVScout Attack

In this section we describe the EVScout attack. We give a high level description of the attack in Sect. 3.1. In Sect. 3.2 we present the concept of tails as features, and propose a novel feature extraction algorithm. In Sect. 3.3, we show how tails are exploited for feature extraction. Lastly, in Sect. 3.4, we show how machine learning classifiers can be exploited to provide EVs' identity based on the previously extracted features.

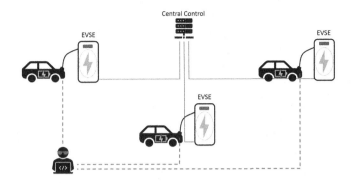

Fig. 2. System and threat model. Multiple EVSEs are connected to the central control which provides coordination and power distribution among them. A single EV is connected to each EVSE. The attacker gets access to the physical quantities exchanged by multiple EVs during the charging phase.

3.1   Attack Overview

As previously stated, in the context of EVs charging infrastructures, users' data is authenticated and secured. However, signals not representing bits are not deemed to be a security issue, and are hence in clear. Since the exchanged current during the charging phase includes the user's generated data, it also comprises features and recurrent behaviors that can be exploited for profiling. EVScout identifies and extracts those physical features which are representative of every single EV, such that we can state with sufficient confidence if and when a certain user is connected to the charging grid.

Figure 3 shows the block diagram of EVScout's steps. EVScout starts with data collection. In fact, in order for the attacker to profile EVs, multiple charging sessions for each EV must be collected. Once built the dataset, EVScout identifies those features that are peculiar to each EV. To this goal, we here propose to exploit the behavior of the batteries during the charging process. In particular, assuming that the attacker has access only to the ampere-based electrical quantities, we exploit the current behavior during the constant voltage phase. Leveraging the nomenclature in [17], we name the current TS during the constant voltage phase as tail. The first feature to be extracted is therefore the tail. Notice that, the choice of exploiting tails is due to the assumption that the attacker has only access to the ampere-based TS. If the attacker has access to voltage values, the corresponding features can not be extracted during the tail. In fact, as tail correspond to the constant voltage phase, features extracted may be under-representative of the battery's behavior. Therefore, if the attacker has access to both current and voltage TS, current features are extracted from tails, whereas voltage features are extracted during the constant current phase.

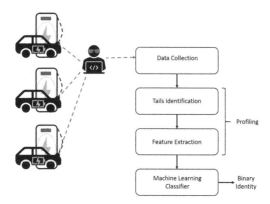

Fig. 3. Block diagram of EVScout's steps.

3.2 Tail Identification

Charging sessions are not necessarily comprehensive of the constant voltage phase, as a user may need to leave before full charge is reached. Since EVScout exploits the tails, we propose an algorithm to identify whether the session includes a constant voltage phase. The presence of a tail implies that the session terminates with full SoC, and eventually zero-current exchanged between EV and EVSE. Tails however can not be identified by the presence of zeros in the current TS, as this may be due to idle phases during the scheduling process. Furthermore, scheduling may cause shot noise in the TS also after full SoC, leading to spikes as shown in Fig. 4. Therefore, we designed a suitable tail reconnaissance algorithm. In order to mitigate the effects of scheduling and to highlight the trends in the considered TS, we propose to apply a suitable filter. In particular, we filter both the current TS and the pilot TS with a length N_{avg} moving average filter. Given time instant t and denoting the electric current value at time t as $c(t)$, the output value $y(t)$ of the moving average filter at time t is given by

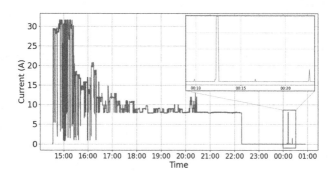

Fig. 4. Example of a realization of a CTS. We notice that, after the CTS reaches a steady zero-values state, noise spikes are present.

$$y(t) = \frac{1}{N_{\text{avg}}} \sum_{m=0}^{N_{\text{avg}}-1} c(t-m). \tag{1}$$

Notice that different filter implementations can be considered, e.g., low pass filter. However, a low pass filter requires a more accurate design, and it also leads to ringing effects, which may be misleading for trend, and hence tail identification.

If the filter has a sufficient length, its effect includes also spikes removal. This eases the identification of tails in the TS, as we can rely on the presence of steady zero values. In detail, if the current TS assumes zero values from t_{start} on to its end, then we say that full SoC has been reached. Tails are characterized by a descending trend in the TS, as shown from the current behavior during the constant voltage phase in Fig. 1. By forward analysis of the current TS, it is difficult to identify the time instant corresponding to the beginning of the tail. Therefore, we propose to proceed backward from the point where full SoC is obtained. Proceeding from t_{start} backwards, we identify the tail by accounting for the number of samples in the current TS reporting an ascending trend. Notice that, even though scheduling and noise could affect the trend of the TS, its effects are mitigated by the moving average filter. A perfectly backward-ascending trend is given by a negative difference between the values at time t and $t - 1$, i.e., $y(t)-y(t-1) < 0$. However, we notice that tails do not always exhibit a perfectly backward-ascending trend, as they may still be heavily affected by noise after filtering. Therefore, we relax the concept of perfect backward-ascending trend including samples for which $y(t) - y(t - 1) \leq \varepsilon$, with ε being a small positive value. Furthermore, we also allow for short descending trends by accounting for T_{max} consecutive segments for which $y(t) - y(t - 1) > \varepsilon$. If this is the case for T_{max} consecutive samples, the trend is considered fully descending and hence discarded.

The steps of the tail extraction algorithm are shown in Algorithm 1. We denote as $\mathcal{I}$ the set of EV indexes and as $\mathcal{C}(i)$, $\mathcal{P}(i)$ the set of current and pilot TS associated with ID i, respectively. For each TS $c \in \mathcal{C}(i)$, we compute the filtered current and pilot TS, respectively denoted as $\tilde{c}$ and $\tilde{p}$, and we search for the steady zero values instant t_{start}. If t_{start} is found, we proceed by identifying the number of samples of the tail. Given our definition of backward ascending trend, we compute the number of samples for which $\tilde{c}(t) - \tilde{c}(t - 1) \leq \varepsilon$. As short descending trends are also allowed, we account for the number n of consecutive descending samples, and if it exceeds T_{max} we stop the counter. However, if an ascending segment is found after a descending samples series, the counter is reset. Given the number S of tail's samples, the tail $\tilde{c}(t_{\text{start}}, s)$ is obtained from the filtered current TS, starting from $t_{\text{start}} - s$ up to t_{start}. The tail $\tilde{p}(t_{\text{start}}, s)$ associated to the pilot TS is analogously obtained, starting from $t_{\text{start}} - s$ up to t_{start}. Both current and pilot TS are eventually added respectively to the set $\mathcal{T}_c(i)$ and $\mathcal{T}_p(i)$ of current and pilot TS tails associated with EV ID i.

Algorithm 1: Tail extraction algorithm.

Data: $\mathcal{C}, \mathcal{P}, \mathcal{I}, C_{max}, T_{max}, N_{avg}$

Result: $\mathcal{T}_c, \mathcal{T}_p$

```
1  for i ∈ I do
2  |   for c ∈ C(i) do
3  |   |   compute c̃ and p̃ via (1);
4  |   |   compute t_start;
5  |   |   if t_start found then
6  |   |   |   n = 0, s = 0 ;
7  |   |   |   for t = t_start, t_start − 1, . . . , 1 do
8  |   |   |   |   if c̃(t) − c̃(t − 1) > ε then
9  |   |   |   |   |   n = n + 1;
10 |   |   |   |   else
11 |   |   |   |   |   n = 0;
12 |   |   |   |   |   s = s + 1;
13 |   |   |   |   end
14 |   |   |   |   if n = T_max then
15 |   |   |   |   |   exit loop;
16 |   |   |   |   end
17 |   |   |   end
18 |   |   |   T_c(i) = T_c(i) ∪ c̃(t_start, s);
19 |   |   |   T_p(i) = T_p(i) ∪ p̃(t_start, s);
20 |   |   else
21 |   |   |   go to next c;
22 |   |   end
23 |   end
24 end
```

3.3 Tail's Features Extraction

Once identified the tails, EVScout extracts from them features used for profiling. A classical approach for TSs feature extraction is given by segmentation [4,5,7]. The main idea is to divide each TSs into non-overlapping segments, such that each contains meaningful statistical features for classification purposes. However, tails are rather short TS, with no stationary component. By segmentation, we may obtain short segments whose features are highly variable across different segments. Therefore, we do not further process tails before extracting features. In particular, for each tail, we compute mean, mode, median, max value, standard deviation, the slope of the linear approximation, auto-correlation, and length of the tail. Furthermore, for each session, we use as an additional feature the total kW delivered, and the overall session time duration. Since we consider both current and pilot time-series features as input, the total number of considered features is 18. Notice that, although deep learning-based feature extractors are available in the literature, we here consider manual feature extraction due to the limited size of the available dataset, which is not sufficient to properly train deep learning algorithms.

3.4   Classification Algorithms

Once features have been identified, EVScout feeds them to a machine learning classifier. Profiling can be formulated as a supervised classification problem, where a two-class classifier is trained with both tails from the target EV and tails from all other EVs. In particular, we assume that a classifier whose input is the features vector of a tail from the target EV shall return output value 1, otherwise shall return output value 0.

In this paper, we compare four different classifiers, namely SVM (support vector machine), kNN (k-Nearest Neighbors), DT (Decision Tree), and RF (Random Forest). Hyper-parameters optimization is obtained via cross-validation, where the training set is suitably divided into parameters training and validation sets. Each hyper-parameter values is obtained by averaging over the optimal values obtained for each cross-validation iteration. Notice that all four classifiers are standard learning algorithms, without deep architectures. Although deep learning automates the feature extraction process, a large number of samples shall be used to effectively train deep architectures. The use of non-deep structures allows us to show the feasibility of EVScout over our currently available dataset. The same motivation resides behind the choice of binary classifiers. In fact, a single multi-class classifier can be designed to have a single class for each EV. However, multi-class classifiers require a larger dataset for training purposes compared to binary classifiers.

4   Evaluation

In this Section we show the feasibility of EVScout. In particular, in Sect. 4.1 we present the ACN (Adaptive Charging Network), whose charging session are exploited for numerical evaluation. Then, in Sect. 4.2, we specify EVScout's parameter and its implementation over the ACN dataset. Lastly, in Sect. 4.3, we assess the validity of EVScout via numerical evaluation. We show that, by analyzing the charging sessions, EVScout builds a set of features that can be classified according to the EV they belong to.

4.1   The ACN Infrastructure and Dataset

In order to test EVScout, we exploit the ACN proposed in [11]. It consists of level 2 EVSEs connected with a central controller that regulates power exchanges in the grid. Employing an online optimization framework, the ACN allows to adapt the power exchanged in the grid, satisfying users power demand while coping with the grid's capacity limits. The dataset comprises charging sessions from actually deployed ACNs, each reporting user-specific measurements such as the arrival and departure time, the kw/h delivered, current and pilot TSs collected between the EV connection and disconnection time. Notice that, although the user may have planned for a full recharge during the selected period, this may not be reflected in the TS. In fact, due to the variable number of connected EVs, the upper power limit of the grid, and premature departure of the user, the battery may not be fully-charged at disconnection time. Notice that, in the ACN dataset, not all TS are sampled with the same period. However, we avoid upsampling, as the risk is to introduce statistical features that are not representative of the considered battery. Each user in the dataset is identified by a unique ID, which is associated with the owned EV.

4.2 Algorithm

The first step of EVScout is to build a suitable dataset to be exploited for profiling. The ACN dataset comprises charging sessions for a large number of EVs, and we select a subset of them for EVScout testing. In particular, we extract the current and pilot TS, kW/h delivered and session duration associated to 100 sessions for each EV in the set $\mathcal{I} = \{$000000022, 000000061, 000000066, 000000067, 000000068,   000000069,   000000162,   000000216,   000000222,   000000234, 000000242,   000000248,   000000290,   000000291,   000000292,   000000300, 000000324, 000000342, 000000364, 000000515, 000000560, 000000562$\}$, for a total number of 22 EVs. Notice that the dataset does not provide any information regarding the make and model of the analyzed EVs. However, since the energy behavior highly depends on the chemical reactions of the single battery, we think EVScout could be able to distinguish EVs of the same model. Furthermore, the batteries employed by the analyzed EVs all belong to the same class, i.e., constant current / constant voltage. However, since both classes show particular behaviors in time, we believe that our attack could be easily extended to the non-analyzed class. The effectiveness of EVScout in these cases will be investigated in future work.

For each session, EVScout first identifies whether a tail is present, and discards all the other sessions. Then it builds a feature vector for each tail, associating it with the ID of its corresponding EV. EVScout is tested across all EVs in the dataset, by averaging the performance attained with each single classifier. In particular, we implement a binary classifier for each EV, and we associate each feature vector of the target EV to label 1, otherwise with label 0. The overall performance of the obtained classifiers are averaged considering 100 randomly created training and testing sets. The overall performance of EVScout is obtained by averaging the results obtained for each ID's classifier. Let us denote as Q the ratio between the number of feature vectors associated with the target EV and the number of feature vectors associated with other EVs. Hence, Q measures the amount of unbalancing in the considered dataset. In order to further assess the performance of EVScour, each classifier is tested for multiple Q values. Regardless of the value Q, 80% of the dataset has been used for training and the remaining 20% for testing. As the number of feature vectors of a single EV is smaller than the overall number of feature vectors, when considering small Q values, the set of feature vectors associated with other EVs is randomly created from the overall set. Results are averaged over 150 random set creations.

4.3   Numerical Results

We exploit the implementation of the classification algorithms in [14]. Results are assessed in terms of precision P, recall R, and $F1$. Numerical results assessing the validity of EVScout are presented as a function of Q, the amount of unbalancing in the dataset. Since traditional performance measures such as $F1$ may be misleading when considering highly unbalanced datasets, the geometric mean (G-Mean) between recall and specificity has been proposed as a suitable performance metric [8]. Therefore, we consider G-Mean as a proper indicator of the validity of EVScout for large Q values. By denoting as TP, TN, FP and FN respectively the number of true positive, true negative, false-positive and false-negative outcomes, we can express the recall as $R = \frac{TP}{TP+FN}$, and specificity as $\alpha = \frac{TN}{FP+TN}$. G-Mean is hence obtained as G-Mean $= \sqrt{\alpha R}$.

Since not every session is associated to a tail, the number of useful sessions associated with each EV is reduced. Furthermore, since the tail extraction process is automated, the number of extracted tails also depends on the parameter values. Figure 5 shows the effect of the length N_{avg} of the moving average filter on the average number of extracted tails per EV. We see that, as the filter length increases, the effects of scheduling noise are mitigated, and a larger number of tails is identified. However, we notice that after $N_{\text{avg}} = 25$, the average number of extracted tails is constant. This hence represents the maximum average number of tails that can be drawn from the current dataset. We notice that, even though 100 sessions have been extracted for each EV, the average number of tails is significantly lower. This confirms the fact that sessions are not necessarily associated with a tail, and a suitable tail extraction algorithm is needed. The filter length not only mitigates the effect of spikes after the tail, but it also leads to different extracted tails and, hence, features used for classification. We recall that all samples in the TS may be affected by noise. Since a tail may be compromised by such fluctuations, noise may mislead the tail extraction algorithm for sub-optimal filter lengths. Figure 6 shows the performance of the kNN classifier in terms of precision and recall for different filter length values N_{avg} and different amounts of unbalancing Q. We notice that, for both precision, recall and all Q values, the best performance is obtained for $N_{\text{avg}} = 25$, showing that averaging over too many samples leads to feature deterioration. Thus, we henceforth consider results obtained with $N_{\text{avg}} = 25$.

Figure 7 shows the results obtained by EVScout for different Q values. We notice that, as Q increases, the performance of EVScout decrease for all classifiers implementation. As the number of considered EVs increases with Q, the chance of two users having the same EV model or having EVs with similar charging profiles increases. This is reflected in a worsening of classifiers' performance. However, we notice that for the maximum $Q = 5$, precision and recall are respectively 0.75 (with RF) and 0.7 (with kNN), meaning that EVs can still be profiled with sufficient confidence. We further notice that, whereas in terms of P the RF classifier attains the best performance, when considering R we notice that some classifiers are more robust than others to increasing unbalancing. In fact, as Q increases, kNN attains better performance than RF. Hence, EVScout

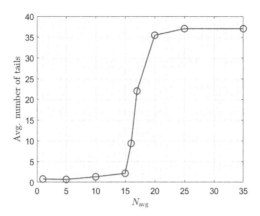

Fig. 5. Average number of tails extracted per EV considering different filter lengths N_{avg}.

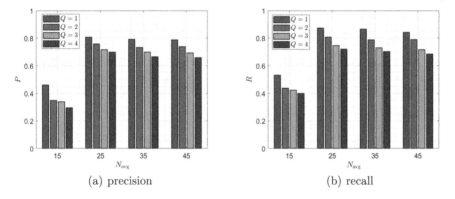

(a) precision   (b) recall

Fig. 6. Performance of EVScout for different filter lengths N_{avg} and different amount of unbalancing Q. Performance obtained with kNN classifier.

shall be design with a proper classifier based on the unbalancing in the available dataset. Regarding $F1$, we notice that the performance of EVScout degrades for increasing values of Q for all classifiers. However, this is not the case in terms of G-Mean, confirming its validity for unbalanced datasets. This is particularly true when considering the performance of kNN and DT, which does not present high variability as Q increases. This shows that profiling can be achieved irrespective of the amount of unbalancing in the dataset, i.e., a single user can still be profiled based on its charging profile also in largely populated networks.

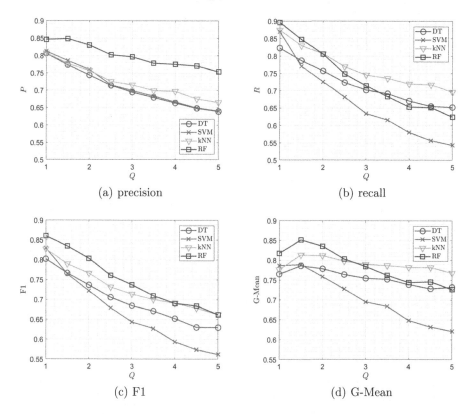

Fig. 7. Performance of EVSCout for different amount of unbalancing in the dataset. Results are shown for the different classifier algorithms, and $N_{avg} = 25$. We see that good classification performance are obtained for all classifier. As Q increases, results show different some classifiers are more robust that others to increasing unbalancing. Results on G-Mean show that profiling can be achieved also in largely populated networks.

5   Possible Countermeasures

In order to deal with information leakage from smart meters, [10] proposes to obfuscate the communication between user and supplier through rechargeable batteries. This solution is effective to modify the demand-response correlation in the measured data. This approach can be leveraged to mitigate the effects of EVScout, where the EV's battery drains current from a secondary battery which communicates with the EVSE, masquerading the original battery's tail behavior. However this approach incurs in a higher implementational cost at both EV and EVSE sides, as the number of involved batteries doubles. Furthermore, the attacker may be able to extract features from the secondary battery, and hence still be able to perform profiling. A similar concept is exploited in [15], where noise is added to smart meters data via an adversarial learning framework. This idea can be exploited to mitigate the effects of EVScout, by adding a suitable amount of noise to the current required by the EV's battery during the tail phase. However, this would imply redesigning how EVSEs manage the current required by EVs, as the added noise may mislead both the attacker and the EVSE. The risk is therefore that the recharging process's efficiency drops. Other non-technical countermeasures are also possible. For instance, EV owners can be educated to check the presence of suspicious devices attached to the EVSE. Furthermore, running companies should often inspect their equipment to check the presence of illegitimate devices, as well as install closed-circuit TV to detect the presence of such devices. Different solutions can hence be adopted to prevent users profiling. However, research should design proper countermeasures to ease the spreading of privacy-preserving EVs and EVSEs.

6   Conclusions

In this paper, we analyzed the EV charging infrastructure and its main components. After identifying the two phases of a charging session, we discussed how security and privacy research should focus also on the actual charging phase. In particular, we discussed the privacy concerns arising when a user gets access to the physical signals exchanged from EV and EVSE in public premises. We proposed EVScout, a profiling attack that exploits the electric current exchanged during the charging process to profile EVs. Together with EVScout, we also proposed a feature extraction algorithm based on the intrinsic characteristics of the EVs' battery. We then tested EVScout on real world-data. By thoroughly numerical evaluation, we showed that EVs can be profiled based on their charging session, with sufficient confidence despite the increasing number of costumers in the network.

References

1. Antoun, J., Kabir, M.E., Moussa, B., Atallah, R., Assi, C.: A detailed security assessment of the EV charging ecosystem. IEEE Network **34**(3), 200–207 (2020)
2. Bai, Y.s., Zhang, C.N.: Experiments study on fast charge technology for lithium-ion electric vehicle batteries. In: 2014 IEEE Conference and Expo Transportation Electrification Asia-Pacific (ITEC Asia-Pacific), pp. 1–6. IEEE (2014)
3. Brown, A., Lommele, S., Schayowitz, A., Klotz, E.: Electric vehicle charging infrastructure trends from the alternative fueling station locator: First quarter 2020. Technical report, National Renewable Energy Lab. (NREL), Golden, CO (United States) (2020)
4. Christ, M., Kempa-Liehr, A.W., Feindt, M.: Distributed and parallel time series feature extraction for industrial big data applications. arXiv preprint arXiv:1610.07717 (May 2016)
5. Conti, M., Nati, M., Rotundo, E., Spolaor, R.: Mind the plug! laptop-user recognition through power consumption. In: Proceedings of the 2nd ACM International Workshop on IoT Privacy, Trust, and Security, pp. 37–44 (2016)
6. Deloitte: Electric vehicles: setting a course for 2030. In: https://www2.deloitte. com/us/en/insights/focus/future-of-mobility/electric-vehicle-trends-2030.html (July 2020)

7. Deng, H., Runger, G., Tuv, E., Vladimir, M.: A time series forest for classification and feature extraction. Inf. Sci. **239**, 142–153 (2013)
8. Ferri, C., Hernández-Orallo, J., Modroiu, R.: An experimental comparison of performance measures for classification. Pattern Recogn. Lett. **30**(1), 27–38 (2009)
9. Gottumukkala, R., Merchant, R., Tauzin, A., Leon, K., Roche, A., Darby, P.: Cyber-physical system security of vehicle charging stations. In: Proceedings of IEEE Green Technologies Conference (GreenTech), pp. 1–5 (April 2019)
10. Kalogridis, G., Efthymiou, C., Denic, S.Z., Lewis, T.A., Cepeda, R.: Privacy for smart meters: Towards undetectable appliance load signatures. In: 2010 First IEEE International Conference on Smart Grid Communications, pp. 232–237. IEEE (2010)
11. Lee, Z.J., Li, T., Low, S.H.: ACN-data: analysis and applications of an open EV charging dataset. In: Proceedings of the Tenth ACM International Conference on Future Energy Systems, pp. 139–149 (June 2019)
12. Marra, F., Yang, G.Y., Træholt, C., Larsen, E., Rasmussen, C.N., You, S.: Demand profile study of battery electric vehicle under different charging options. In: 2012 IEEE Power and Energy Society General Meeting, pp. 1–7. IEEE (November 2012)
13. Molina-Markham, A., Shenoy, P., Fu, K., Cecchet, E., Irwin, D.: Private memoirs of a smart meter. In: Proceedings of the 2nd ACM Workshop on Embedded Sensing Systems for Energy-Efficiency in Building, pp. 61–66 (November 2010)
14. Pedregosa, F., Varoquaux, G., Gramfort, A., Michel, V., Thirion, B., Grisel, O., Blondel, M., Prettenhofer, P., Weiss, R., Dubourg, V., Vanderplas, J., Passos, A., Cournapeau, D., Brucher, M., Perrot, M., Duchesnay, E.: Scikit-learn: machine learning in python. J. Mach. Learn. Res **12**, 2825–2830 (2011)
15. Shateri, M., Messina, F., Piantanida, P., Labeau, F.: Real-time privacy-preserving data release for smart meters. IEEE Trans. Smart Grid **11**(6), 5174–5183 (2020)
16. Spolaor, R., Abudahi, L., Moonsamy, V., Conti, M., Poovendran, R.: No free charge theorem: a covert channel via usb charging cable on mobile devices. In: Gollmann, D., Miyaji, A., Kikuchi, H. (eds.) ACNS 2017. LNCS, vol. 10355, pp. 83–102. Springer, Cham (2017). https://doi.org/10.1007/978-3-319-61204-1_5
17. Sun, C., Li, T., Low, S.H., Li, V.O.: Classification of electric vehicle charging time series with selective clustering. Electric Power Syst. Res. **189**, 106695 (2020)
18. ThunderSky: Instruction manual for LFP/LCP/LMP lithium power battery. Technical report, Thunder Sky (2007)
19. Troepfer, C.: SAE electric vehicle conductive charge coupler, SAE J1772. Technical report, Society of Automotive Engineers (2009)
20. U.S.D.O.E.: EV everywhere grand challenge: Road to success. Technical report, U. S. Department of Energy (January 2014)
21. Wang, L., Qin, Z., Slangen, T., Bauer, P., Van Wijk, T.: Grid impact of electric vehicle fast charging stations: Trends, standards, issues and mitigation measures-an overview. IEEE Open J. Power Electron. **2**, 56–74 (2021)
22. Wu, H., Pang, G.K.H., Choy, K.L., Lam, H.Y.: An optimization model for electric vehicle battery charging at a battery swapping station. IEEE Trans. Veh. Technol. **67**(2), 881–895 (2017)
23. Yang, Q., Gasti, P., Zhou, G., Farajidavar, A., Balagani, K.S.: On inferring browsing activity on smartphones via usb power analysis side-channel. IEEE Trans. Inf. Forensics Secur. **12**(5), 1056–1066 (2016)

CAN-SQUARE - Decimeter Level Localization of Electronic Control Units on CAN Buses

Bogdan Groza$^{(\boxtimes)}$, Pal-Stefan Murvay, Lucian Popa, and Camil Jichici

Faculty of Automatics and Computers, Politehnica University Timisoara,
Timisoara, Romania
{bogdan.groza,pal-stefan.murvay,lucian.popa,camil.jichici}@aut.upt.ro

Abstract. The CAN bus survived inside cars for more than three decades due to its simplicity and effectiveness while protecting it calls for solutions that are equally simple and effective. In this work we propose an efficient mechanism that achieves decimeter-level precision in localizing Electronic Control Units (ECUs) on the CAN bus. The proposed methodology requires two connections at the ends of the bus and a single rising edge, i.e., the start of a dominant bit. Since several such rising edges are present in every frame, malicious devices may be easily localized with high accuracy from single frame injections. Our methodology requires only elementary computations, e.g., additions and multiplications, which are trivial to perform and implement. We prove the feasibility of the proposed methodology inside a real car and perform more demanding experiments in a laboratory setup where we record modest overlaps only between nodes that are 10 cm apart. We prove resilience against replacement and insertion attacks as well as against temperature variations in the range of 0–60 °C.

1 Introduction and Motivation

There is really not much more that needs to be said to convince readers on the insecurity of modern vehicles and their communication buses, e.g., [2,17,18], etc. It is apparent that a bus designed by BOSCH in the 80s, the Controller Area Network (CAN), cannot cope with modern security needs. With new vulnerabilities reported each year, the challenge in designing security for this widely spread bus that proved its efficiency for more than three decades remains open. The difficulty of embedding cryptographic elements inside the 64-bit CAN frames was so tremendous that researchers looked at various alternatives such as authentication data embedded in the ID field [11,24], covert timing channels [25], etc. The industry did not hesitate to proceed in this direction as proved by recently released AUTOSAR standards for secure in-vehicle communication [1] which introduces truncated authentication tags of 24–28 bits in each frame and a 0–8 bits freshness parameter (see SecOC profiles 1–3 in [1]). Hopefully, the time for such compromises may come to an end with the release of CAN-FD that carries

© Springer Nature Switzerland AG 2021
E. Bertino et al. (Eds.): ESORICS 2021, LNCS 12972, pp. 668–690, 2021.
https://doi.org/10.1007/978-3-030-88418-5_32

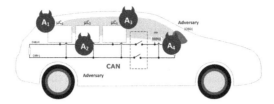

Fig. 1. Addressed setting: an in-vehicle CAN bus with adversaries at several possible locations

512 bit payloads and sets room for regular sized cryptographic elements. Clearly, the high-bandwidth CAN-FD will make the use of CAN inside cars even more attractive and the deployment of cryptographic security easier.

But adding cryptography is far from solving the problem as ECUs may be compromised and engaged in malicious activities, i.e., impersonating other nodes, cryptographic keys may be extracted by memory dumps or side-channel attacks, etc. In this context, using physical layer techniques to identify [3], localize [20] and eventually isolate nodes [9] is of prime importance.

Motivation and Contributions. In-vehicle networks are controlled environments where it is somewhat unlikely that an adversary will tap the bus at any random location due to obvious physical access difficulties. All of the attacks reported so far come from open ports, e.g., the OBD port, corrupted control units, e.g., the infotainment or telematic unit, etc. Therefore the most likely scenario is that an attack will originate at a predictable location. Figure 1 suggests such a setting in which an in-vehicle CAN bus is tapped by an adversary on the OBD port or possibly by corrupting an existing electronic control unit (insertion of malicious nodes or tapping the bus in accessible locations is not excluded from our experiments). In-vehicle networks are not necessarily flat, i.e., multiple buses can be linked via gateways, a case in which the solution presented in this work can be easily extended by placing probes at the ends of each bus. Freshly emerged works [9] have proved the feasibility of disconnecting parts of the bus in real time without damaging real-time communication. In this context, localizing intruders on the bus becomes an immediate problem. In this work, we propose a technique based on frame timing and signal characteristics. This technique was previously explored in [20] but the results were not so successful in detecting node replacement and insertions on the bus. We use the same setting as the one in [20] and achieve high precision in localizing the devices regardless to the type of attack: node corruption, replacement or insertion. If intruder nodes can be localized then other countermeasures such as bus segment disconnection can be applied. Moreover, given the small localization error, a visual inspection will immediately point to the maliciously planted device. We briefly summarize the contributions of our work as follows:

1. we prove localization to be feasible with high precision, i.e., most of the times in the order of a decimeter or less according to the inter-distance matrix, even

when sampling from the CAN-H line alone without needing the additional CAN-L voltage (this halves the wiring costs),

2. while other proposals require statistical tests or more demanding machine learning algorithms, we reduce computational costs to virtually nothing, i.e., our localization scheme requires only buffering some samples and one subtraction/division for each sample (these are trivial to implement),

3. we prove the resilience of the technique in front of node replacement and insertions, a possible attack scenario or an innocuous circumstance called by a faulty device, to which previous works did not offer much resilience,

4. we provide experiments on a setup built with a new professional CAN bus cable and prove the resilience of the proposed method in front of multiple adversaries and environmental changes, i.e., temperature variations, in addition to validating against our previous dataset from [20] where such an analysis was not performed,

5. we further endorse the use of double bus taps which originates from the work in [9] although in a very distinct context, i.e., that of isolating segments of the bus, which opens numerous roads for future security solutions.

The rest of the paper is organized as follows. We briefly present the related work in the next subsection. Section 2 provides some background on CAN and a comprehensive description of our experimental setup. In Sect. 3 we begin by presenting the methodology in our work and then proceed to the experimental results in Sect. 4. Finally, Sect. 5 holds the conclusions of our work.

1.1 Related Works

Since it was not designed to include security mechanisms, the CAN standard provides no means of uniquely identifying the transmitter of a frame which opens door for attacks. An analysis of CAN bus attacker capabilities can be found in [8]. To overcome this design limitation, various solutions have been proposed starting from regular cryptographic security which has been also recently adopted by the industry [1], placing additional ECUs to act as gateways [10], destroying malicious frames by legitimate senders that recognize their IDs [6] and, as a distinctive line of work, physical fingerprinting CAN nodes and determining their location on the bus which we discuss next.

One research direction considered by multiple related works is fingerprinting CAN nodes based on their unique physical layer behavior. CAN physical signaling is influenced by unique characteristics of CAN transceiver chips and even by power supply circuitry. The idea of fingerprinting CAN nodes based on voltage measurements of the CAN differential signal was introduced in [19]. The paper illustrates the concept by applying simple signal processing on a dataset obtained by sampling signals from a CAN bus working at a bit rate of 125 kbps with an oscilloscope at a sample rate of 2 GS/s. The results obtained in this initial work are improved by Choi et al. in [4]. They extract a set of 17 features from the signals sampled at 2.5 GS/s on a 500 kbps CAN bus and use classification algorithms to fingerprint and identify nodes. Using a similar setup, the same authors propose using only voltage data from rising and falling edges of the recorded frames [5]. In a more pragmatic approach, the Viden mechanism proposed in [3] is based on a very low sampling rate (50 kS/s) and its efficiency is demonstrated by a proof of concept implementation. Viden uses multiple measurements of dominant levels sampled at different points during the frame transmission to build voltage profiles for uniquely identifying transmitter nodes.

The automotive industry also showed interest in this type of approaches. A series of papers authored by Kneib et al. comes as a proof of research efforts at Bosch on this subject. In Scission [14], further improvements are made on using voltage signatures for fingerprinting by focusing on characteristics exhibited by signals around rising and falling edges sampled from CAN frame sections following the arbitration field. Further improvements are presented in EASI [16] which is tailored to the capabilities of automotive-grade microcontrollers. The required sampling rate in this case is as low as 2 MS/s when using randomly interleaved sampling. Their more recent proposal, VALID [23], aims to reduce the required sampling rate even more for the purpose of achieving a solution that can be implemented on currently available automotive-grade microcontrollers. In [15], the authors also evaluate the effect of temperature on the accuracy of their proposed mechanisms. The effect of environmental factors, e.g. temperature, voltage, was also considered by authors of [7] in the design of SIMPLE, a voltage-based IDS that accounts for temperature and voltage variations by updating node fingerprints.

The work in [20] uses features extracted from voltage data to estimate the location of the transmitter for several attack scenarios with adversaries at various locations on the bus. A different approach proposed for adversary localization and isolation by having a bus guardian control relays placed near each node is detailed in [9]. Rumez et al. [21] take another approach and propose the use of time domain reflectometry to evaluate the network structure and estimate node locations. Their approach is based on measuring the network response to a pulse which is sent when the network is offline, i.e., before starting communication. While their results prove the ability to identify disconnected nodes or newly added network nodes, the mechanism is unable to correlate message transmissions to node locations on the bus.

2 CAN Background and Experimental Setup

This section gives a brief background on CAN then proceeds to a detailed presentation of our experimental testbed.

2.1 CAN Background

The CAN protocol is still the most widely used for communication between ECUs found inside contemporary vehicles. Its simple two-wire (CAN-High, CAN-Low) physical layer, support for bit rates up to 1 Mbit/s (a maximum bit rate of 500 kbit/s is employed for in-vehicle application) and maximum payload of 8 bytes make it suitable for a wide range of applications [12,13]. The standard CAN data frame, depicted in Fig. 2 (i) is divided into several main fields: arbitration, control, data, CRC and acknowledgment. The name of the arbitration field comes from its use in the arbitration mechanism which is employed for deciding which node should win the bus in case two or more nodes start transmission at the same time. A dominant bit, i.e. SOF (Start-of-Frame) marks the beginning of the frame followed by the 11 bit frame identifier (ID) which is used to identify CAN messages and, as part of the arbitration field, also contributes to frame arbitration, i.e. lower IDs indicate higher priority. The payload length (DLC) is encoded in the control field. The data field is followed by a 15 bit CRC and the ACK bit which is used to ensure that a transmitted frame was properly received by network nodes. An extended data frame also exists which allows the use of 29 bit IDs with no changes in the payload size. A newer extension of the protocol, i.e. CAN-FD (CAN with Flexible Data-rate), allows the use of bit rates higher than 1 Mbps after the arbitration field along with payloads of up to 64 bytes. Currently available CAN-FD compatible transceivers are capable of bit rates of up to 8 Mbps.

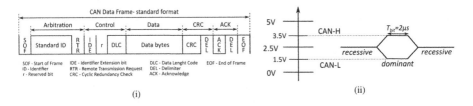

Fig. 2. Standard CAN frame format (i) and physical bit representation (ii)

At the physical layer, CAN is implemented as a 2-wire differential line. Data representation at the physical layer is based on two symbols: recessive and dominant. Figure 2 (ii) depicts bit representation at the physical level for high-speed CAN. The dominant state (logical '0'), is reached when the CAN-High and the CAN-Low lines are actively driven by the transceiver. During the dominant state the CAN-H line reaches a voltage of about 3.5 V while the CAN-L line goes down to 1.5 V. These values may differ (e.g., when working with 3.3 V levels) and will still properly represent a dominant bit as long as the differential voltage is above 0.9 V. In contrast, the recessive (1) state occurs when the bus is not driven, both lines exhibiting a similar voltage level which is usually around 2.5 V.

2.2 Experimental Setup

An abstract representation of our experimental setup is shown in Fig. 3. The CAN bus is constructed from a professional CAN cable with a total length of 5 ms. The bus is divided into 9 segments with lengths of 10-10-50-50-100-100-130-30-20 cm providing 10 connection points in the form of DB9 connectors. Due to space constraints, we defer the pictures with our setup for Appendix A. In Scenario A we used 10 devices, each connected to one of the entry points, while in Scenario B we use 5 legitimate devices connected to the following 5 connection points, A, C, E, G, I and the rest of the points are dedicated for adversaries. This along with some of the distances depicted in the figure are detailed in the next section which addresses the methodology in our work.

The employed network nodes consist of two types of USB-to-CAN devices: 5 x USB-CAN modules from SYSTEC electronic and 2xVN5610A from Vector Informatik. The USB-CAN modules are equipped with a high-speed CAN transceiver capable of transmitting data at up to 1 Mbps, while the VN5610A devices support both high-speed CAN and CAN-FD. In our experiments the bit rate was configured to 500 kbps for all devices considering that this is the recommended data rate for use in high-speed CAN buses in automotive [22]. Periodic data frames were transmitted from the USB-CAN modules using the PcanView, application from SYSTEC electronic and from the VN5610A devices using Vector CANoe environment. For bus monitoring and sample acquisition we used a PicoScope 5444D with four probes connected to the two bus lines, i.e., CAN-Low and CAN-High, on both ends of the bus, close to the termination on each side as shown on the left side of Fig. 3. We configured the PicoScope to sample voltage data at 250 MS/s which is the maximum rate when using all 4 channels.

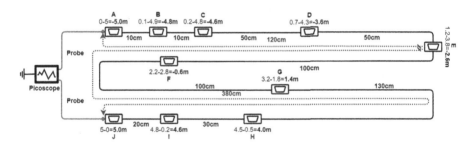

Fig. 3. Abstract view of the experimental setup with nodes connected to the CAN bus in 10 distinct locations (white boxes) and a PicoScope

3 Methodology and Results

We now present the proposed methodology for fingerprint extraction and discuss some limitations in existing approaches.

3.1 Concept and Limitations in Previous Approaches

To localize the nodes on the bus we use the difference in propagation time to the left and right probes. The difference in propagation time, referred by us as *differential delay* and denoted as Δ can be used to compute the exact position of each node on the network. The *differential delay* multiplied with the propagation speed, i.e., 5 ns/m, leads to the *differential position* denoted as π which can be also obtained by subtracting the distance to the right probe from the distance to the left probe. Figure 3 depicts the *differential position* of each node. For example, node A is located 0 cm from the left probe and 5 m from the right probe which results in $0-5 = -5$ m. Node E is located 120 cm from the left and 380 cm from the right probe which results in $120-380 = -260$ cm, etc. The *differential position* can be immediately converted to the physical position toward the left probe by adding the cable length and dividing by 2, i.e., the physical position to the left probe is $\frac{\pi+\ell}{2}$ where ℓ is the cable length.

The more complicated task is the correct estimation of the propagation delay for which in our previous work [20] we used a threshold based separation that did not cope well with adversarial attacks on the bus. Figure 4 presents some details regarding voltage levels which lead to issues in computing differential delays based on a simple threshold. While the voltage appears to rise sharply on both the left and right sides of the bus (i) the detailed view in (ii) proves that the rising slopes are not perfectly parallel and by very small changes in the threshold used to calculate the differential delay (in the order of 0.1 V or less) significant changes in the reported distance may occur. As a concrete numerical example, in (iii) we show that localization errors may vary from 80 cm up to 1.2 m which is very high for a threshold between 2.7 V and 3.4 V. So ideally, one would choose the lowest possible threshold value. Based on the data that we recorded, setting a threshold as low as 0.2 V above the expected CAN-H voltage for a recessive state (2.5 V) which gave the small error was most of the times unusable due to electrical noise on the bus. For example, in (iv) we show anomalies during the start of the bit that may greatly affect the computed differential delay (note that the voltage actually dips before the bit starts which would result in a delayed identification of the start when using a threshold), then in (v) we show the recessive voltage (before the starting bit of the same node) for a clean bus (blue) and the same bus with 2 adversaries (green) and 3 adversaries (dark green) while (vi) shows the voltage when the temperature variates between 0 °C (light blue), 24 °C (blue), 50 °C (green) and 60 °C (dark green). On a CAN bus, nodes may disconnect when entering in a bus-off state and thus the recessive voltage may change due to innocuous circumstances. Clearly, temperature variations are even more common as components may heat-up while running and a car may operate in various climatic conditions. Fluctuations in the order of 0.2 V or even more are to be expected so using a simple voltage threshold as we previously used in [20] is not sufficient to cope with adversaries and environmental variations. To achieve resilience to such variations, we need to use the recessive voltage of the bus and subtract it from the threshold. Essentially, this is what we do in CAN-SQUARE and in addition we also use a sliding window w to jump over short-lived fluctuations of the voltage.

As a more practical example regarding delays, Fig. 5 contrasts between the delays computed with a threshold based separation shown in (i), similar to the

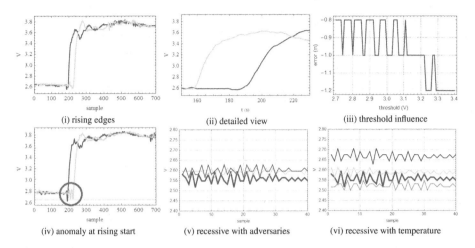

Fig. 4. Voltage values on the left and right rising edges (i), detail view of the rising portion (ii), threshold influence on delay (iii), anomaly before rising time (iv), recessive level variation with adversaries tapping the bus (v) and temperature variations (vi)

attempt in [20], and the slope-based separation from CAN-SQUARE (this work) shown in (ii). Note that the purple points significantly overlap with the blue points on the left side of the figure. On the right side of the plot, by using the methodology in this work, the separation becomes clearer with no overlap between the magenta and blue points. Small overlaps remain between the cyan and green points but these correspond to nodes separated by only 20 cm of wire. As it will be shown later in our experiments, by averaging over multiple values, separation will be possible even for nodes that are 10 cm apart.

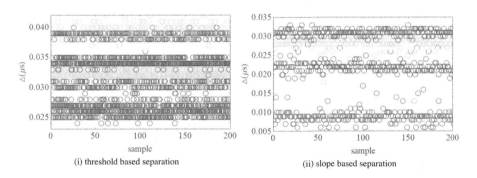

Fig. 5. Separation based on thresholds (i) and based on slopes (ii) as proposed in this work (Color figure online)

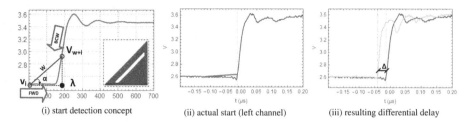

(i) start detection concept   (ii) actual start (left channel)   (iii) resulting differential delay

Fig. 6. CAN-SQUARE bit start-time extraction: concept (i), actual start on the left channel (ii) and the resulting differential delay of 0.028 μs (iii)

3.2   Intrusion Detection and Localization Algorithm

Let the voltage samples recorded from the left side of the bus be $\widetilde{v}_l = \{\widetilde{v}_l[0], \widetilde{v}_l[1], \widetilde{v}_l[2], ..., \widetilde{v}_l[b-1]\}$ and the voltage from the right side of the bus be $\widetilde{v}_r = \{\widetilde{v}_r[0], \widetilde{v}_r[1], \widetilde{v}_r[2], ..., \widetilde{v}_r[b-1]\}$ at time $\widetilde{t} = \{\widetilde{t}[0], \widetilde{t}[1], \widetilde{t}[2], ..., \widetilde{t}[b-1]\}$ (the time runs identically for both sides of the bus). As a general notation, we use a tilde to separate between vectors and scalars. We assume a buffer of size b which in our experiments was set at 2–4 thousand samples to cover the duration of 1 bit, e.g., for a 500 kbps CAN the duration of a bit is $2\,\mu s$ which would require a buffer of 4000 values at a 500 MS/s sampling rate (note that we are interested only in the start of the bit so the buffer does not need to cover the entire bit duration). Since the recording is done at some fixed sample rate δ, then the time for sample i is actually $i \times \delta$. Then for a fixed window $w < b$ we define the left and right slopes of the signal as: $\widetilde{s}_l[i] = \frac{\widetilde{v}_l[i]-\widetilde{v}_l[i+w]}{\widetilde{t}[i]-\widetilde{t}[i+w]} = \frac{\widetilde{v}_l[i+w]-\widetilde{v}_l[i]}{w\delta}$, $\widetilde{s}_r[i] = \frac{\widetilde{v}_r[i]-\widetilde{v}_r[i+w]}{\widetilde{t}[i]-\widetilde{t}[i+w]} = \frac{\widetilde{v}_r[i+w]-\widetilde{v}_r[i]}{w\delta}$, $\forall i \in [0..b-w-1]$. That is, computing the slope requires only one subtraction and one division (considering that the sampling rate is fixed and thus $w\delta$ is constant). Having the left and right slopes defined, for a target slope α we define the *fingerprint indexes* λ_l, λ_r as the minimum indexes for which it holds that $s_l[\lambda_l] > \alpha$ and $s_r[\lambda_r] > \alpha$. The *differential delay* of a rising edge is the time difference between the two fingerprint indexes, i.e., $\Delta = \widetilde{t}[\lambda_l] - \widetilde{t}[\lambda_r] = (\lambda_l - \lambda_r)\delta$ and the position of the sender node is $\pi = \frac{\Delta}{5 \times 10^{-9}}$ (we consider the usual propagation speed of 5 ns/m).

Figure 6 (i) provides a suggestive graphical overview on how the timing fingerprint is constructed. This figure suggests a window w and a slope $\alpha = 1$, i.e., $\tan(45°)$, formed between voltage levels at indexes i and $i + w$. This figure also explains the title of our work which is a reminiscence of a *speed square*, i.e., a triangular marking tool, as shown in the right side of the figure. This simple procedure came out as the best to get a clean cut of the node distances on the bus. In our experiments we use two types of moving squares, i.e., the forward square FWD-SQUARE and the backward BCW-SQUARE which are moving from left to right and right to left respectively (the conducted experiments showed that the BCW-SQUARE method is more precise). Due to space constraints, we defer the pseudocode description of the FWD and BCW-SQUARE to Appendix B. Figures 6 (ii) and (iii) show the actual indexes at which the signal is cut on the left and right channels for a window set to $w = 100$ in our experiments. The actual fingerprint, i.e., the timing difference between the two indexes on the left and right channels, is $\Delta = 0.028\,\mu s$. This difference was recorded for a node that is located 20 cm from one end of the bus and 480 cm from the other. Given a signal propagation speed of 5 ns per meter this results in theory in a theoretical differential delay of about 23 ns (the measured 28 ns in the experiments are very close to the expected value and is in fact a worst case from our experiments).

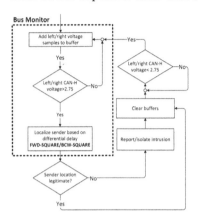

Fig. 7. Flowchart of the intrusion localization procedure

Having the description of the localization procedure, the conceptual description of the proposed intrusion detection and localization algorithm easily follows. Figure 7 provides an overview for this. The algorithm continuously adds voltage samples from the bus to a buffer and checks that the CAN-H voltage on the left and right sides did not exceed 2.75 V (this threshold is selected based on CAN physical layer specification in ISO 14229-2 which set this as the minimum CAN-H voltage during a dominant bit). Once such change occurs, the algorithm proceeds to the forward or backward square algorithms which will localize the nodes. If the recorded location is not a legitimate one, then an intrusion will be signaled (possibly isolated with techniques such as those presented in [9]). Regardless, the buffer is subsequently cleaned and the monitor waits for the voltage to drop below the 2.75 V which will happen when returning to a recessive state. The monitoring continues in the same fashion. As stated, the pseudocode description of the FWD and BCW-SQUARE can be found in Appendix B.

4   Experimental Evaluation

In this section we present the scenarios that we consider and then provide concrete experimental data for each of them.

4.1   Evaluation Scenarios

As an additional step to prove the correctness of our approach, we also verify the methodology inside a real car. Note that the correctness of our approach is supported by the laws of physics which cannot be refuted by practical deployments of CAN buses inside cars. Propagation delays are also used in numerous security applications, e.g., distance-bounding protocols. Still, experimenting inside the car gives convincing arguments in support of our approach. For this purpose we placed two bus taps inside a Renault Megane as depicted in Figs. 8 (i) and (ii): one in the vicinity of the engine ECU which called for additional wirings done

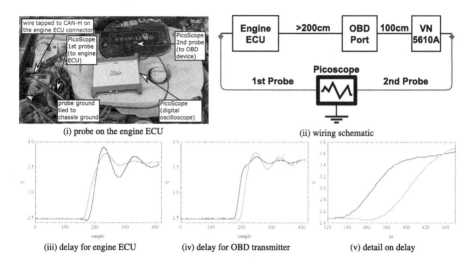

Fig. 8. Experiments inside a Renault Megane: (i) probe on the engine ECU, (ii) wiring schematic, (iii) differential delays for the engine ECU, (iv) differential delays for the OBD transmitter and (v) detailed view of delays (Color figure online)

by us and the other on the OBD port which was already accessible and linked to the engine ECU. To verify that the differential delays are similar, besides the incoming frames from the engine ECU we also inject frames from the OBD port with a VN5610A. Figures 8 (iii) and (iv) show the differential delays from the engine ECU as well as from the VN5610A plugged on the OBD port. Note that the differential delays are identical while the blue and green edges are flipped between (iii) and (iv) since the engine ECU and the VN5610A are placed at opposite sides of the bus. The measured differential delays, detailed in Fig. 8 (v), are of around 34 ns which corresponds to an interdistance of 6.8 m that further translates to a physical distance of 3.4 m (as later explained in subsection 4.2). This roughly corresponds to the wire length of slightly more than 2 m from the engine ECU, that we could measure with a tape line inside the car, plus the 1 m extension of the OBD wire where we placed the second probe.

Since it is much harder to perform insertion and replacement attacks at various distances inside the car due to access difficulties and it is also harder to control temperature variations in the range of 0–60 °C, we perform the rest of the data collection on an experimental bus. The attacks and environmental changes that we account for are realistic and the laboratory setup facilitates the collection of a much larger experimental basis. Concretely, we test the proposed mechanism on two distinct network configurations based on [20]: a 10 ECU network in Scenario A and a 5 ECU network in scenario B. Figure 9 shows a schematic representation of ECU locations in each scenario. The first network configuration allows data collection from a larger number of ECUs while the second network configuration allows more insertion points for adversary nodes. We apply our mechanism both on our previous datasets from [20] and on fresh datasets from the newly implemented network (pictured in Appendix A) that follows the same configuration with a professional CAN bus cable. On this new setup we also test the response to multiple adversaries and environmental variations, i.e., temperature changes which are known to influence voltage fingerprints.

Scenario A: Replacement Attacks on a Large Network with 10 ECUs. It is the first legitimate network containing 10 ECUs for which we use our datasets from [20]. This is a somewhat high number of ECUs for a single bus. Note that while more than 100 ECUs are claimed to be present inside some cars, and this is indeed correct, they are always grouped on several CAN buses that may further communicate via a gateway.

Attack Scenario A.1: Multiple ECU Replacements in the 10 ECUs (identical devices). This represents the first alteration of our clean network in which we consider the malicious (or innocuous action in case that ECU replacement is done by an authorized garage) to be the *replacement* of some existing ECUs which is emulated simply by mixing the devices from the first setup.

Attack Scenario A.2: Multiple ECU Replacements in the 10 ECUs (distinct devices). This scenario pushes the limit of the previous by replacing 6 out of the 10 legitimate ECUs from Scenario 1 with distinct devices.

Scenario B: Single or Multiple Insertions and Temperature Variations on a Smaller Network with 5 ECUs. Since this scenario requires multiple measurements as well as open locations in the network, i.e., for the insertion attacks, we will use a smaller network. Note that this is still a realistic number of ECUs since existing reference works such as [7,14] have physically fingerprinted real cars that had 4–6 ECUs. Also, the results that we obtain hold even for larger number of ECUs as they are comparable to the 10 ECU network in Scenario A.

Attack Scenario B.1: Temperature Variations. In this scenario we keep our experimental setup inside a box, at 50 °C and 60 °C in order to observe the influence of environmental temperature. This scenario is very realistic given the various conditions in which cars, and CAN buses in particular, may operate.

Attack Scenario B.2: Single Insertions in the Clean Network with 5 ECUs (Distinct devices). This scenario tries to determine how fingerprinting will be altered by the addition of new ECUs to the bus and thus we consider inserting two distinct devices (one at a time) on the clean network from Scenario B.

Attack Scenario B.3: Multiple Insertions in the Clean Network with 5 ECUs (Distinct devices). Each node that is added to the bus will change the impedance which immediately affects propagation timings. Previously, we were only concerned with single adversaries on the bus, now we extend the experiments with data for 2 and 3 adversaries. Such a scenario is less likely, but we need to determine its influence on timings.

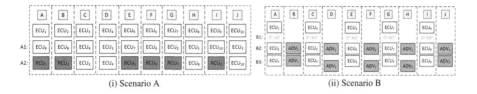

(i) Scenario A   (ii) Scenario B

Fig. 9. ECU placement in Scenario A (i) and Scenario B (ii)

4.2 Results

We first prove the robustness of our localization algorithms in front of network modifications, i.e., ECU replacement and position changes, for the large 10 ECU network. Then we proceed to a finer grained analysis against replacement, multiple ECU insertions and temperature variations on the 5 ECU network.

As a general procedure, we quantify the distances between locations π', π'' on the bus as the Euclidean distance between the evaluated locations of the reporting ECUs to the bus ends, i.e., $\mathbb{D}^{\blacklozenge}(\pi', \pi'') = \left\{ \sqrt{(\delta(\pi') - \delta(\pi''))^2} : \forall \pi', \pi'' \in \{A, B, ..., J\} \right\}, \blacklozenge \in \{\text{intra}, \text{inter}\}$. The intra-distances refer to distances between experiments performed on the same (clean) network while inter-distance refer to distances between measurements taken on the clean network when compared to the network affected by adversarial/environmental actions. Whenever $\pi' = \pi''$, i.e., the evaluated positions are the same, the distance represents an intra-distance and whenever $\pi' \neq \pi''$, i.e., the evaluated positions are distinct, the distance represents an inter-distance. The distances $\mathbb{D}^{\blacklozenge}(\pi', \pi'')$ is further computed as the mean of 1000 random experiments and in the following tables we are going to present either the mean interdistance over single rising edges denoted as $\overline{\mathbb{D}}_1$ or the mean value of the medians for 15 consecutive rising edges denoted as $\widehat{\mathbb{D}}_{15}$. The reason for choosing the median of 15 consecutive values is that an 8 byte CAN frame will have an average of 15 transitions from 0 to 1 (due to the stuffing rule, each 5 consecutive identical bits will be followed by a 6-th that differs). Thus, 15 rising edges will be generally available in each frame to establish the node location.

Important Note. Since we work with the differential delays at the two bus ends, the position of each node $\delta(\pi), \forall \pi \in \{A, B, ..., J\}$ is reported in the range of $[-5\,\text{m}, 5\,\text{m}]$ to which some error is added due to cable imperfections, measurement imprecisions and noise that affects our algorithms. The inter-distance $\mathbb{D}^{\blacklozenge}(\pi', \pi'')$ may report values of up to $10\,\text{m}$ plus some measurement error for a $5\,\text{m}$ cable which may seem puzzling but it is nevertheless correct. For example in case of node A placed at $-5\,\text{m}$ and node J at $+5\,\text{m}$ we have $\mathbb{D}^{\text{inter}}(A, J) = \sqrt{(-5 - 5)^2} = 10\,\text{m}$. The *physical distance* $\mathbb{D}^{\text{phy}}(\pi', \pi'')$ between two nodes is actually half the inter-distance, i.e., $\mathbb{D}^{\text{phy}}(\pi', \pi'') = \frac{\mathbb{D}^{\text{inter}}(\pi', \pi'')}{2}$. This can be easily proved as follows. Consider positions π', π'' and position π'

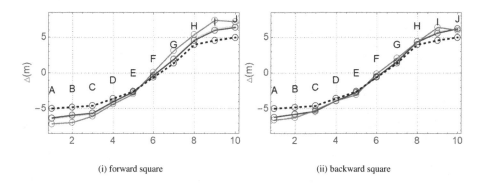

(i) forward square   (ii) backward square

Fig. 10. Reported distances over 3 distinct experiments in Scenario A: clean network (blue), replacements with identical nodes (green) and replacements with distinct nodes (magenta) with the forward (i) and backward (ii) square method (Color figure online)

located at distance d'_l from the left side of the bus and d'_r from the right side, while π'' is at d''_l from the left and d''_r from the right. The physical distance between them is $\mathbb{D}^{phy}(\pi', \pi'') = \sqrt{(d'_l - d''_l)^2}$ and since for our cable of length ℓ we have $d'_l = \ell - d'_r, d''_l = \ell - d''_r$ it also holds that $\mathbb{D}^{phy}(\pi', \pi'') = \sqrt{(d'_l - d''_l)^2} = \sqrt{(\ell - d'_r - \ell + d''_r)^2} = \sqrt{(d''_r - d'_r)^2} = \sqrt{(d'_r - d''_r)^2}$. The inter-distance however is $\mathbb{D}^{inter}(\pi', \pi'') = \sqrt{[(d'_l - d'_r) - (d''_l - d''_r)]^2}$ and by substituting d'_r, d''_r

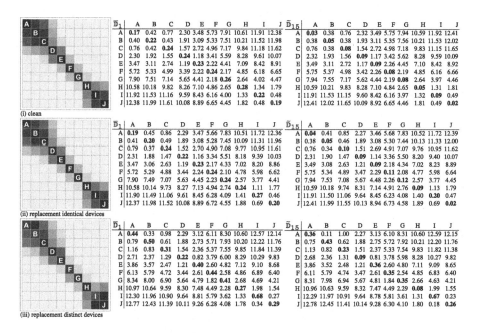

(i) clean

$\bar{\mathbb{D}}_1$

	A	B	C	D	E	F	G	H	I	J
A	**0.17**	0.42	0.77	2.30	3.48	5.73	7.91	10.61	11.91	12.38
B	0.40	**0.22**	0.43	1.91	3.09	5.33	7.51	10.21	11.52	11.98
C	0.76	0.42	**0.24**	1.57	2.72	4.96	7.17	9.84	11.18	11.62
D	2.30	1.92	1.55	**0.24**	1.18	3.41	5.59	8.28	9.61	10.07
E	3.47	3.11	2.74	1.19	**0.23**	2.22	4.41	7.09	8.42	8.91
F	5.72	5.33	4.99	3.39	2.22	**0.24**	2.17	4.85	6.18	6.65
G	7.90	7.51	7.14	5.65	4.41	2.18	**0.26**	2.64	4.02	4.47
H	10.58	10.18	9.82	8.26	7.10	4.86	2.65	**0.28**	1.34	1.79
I	11.92	11.53	11.16	9.59	8.43	6.16	4.00	1.33	**0.22**	0.48
J	12.38	11.99	11.61	10.08	8.89	6.65	4.45	1.82	0.48	**0.19**

$\bar{\mathbb{D}}_{15}$

	A	B	C	D	E	F	G	H	I	J
A	**0.03**	0.38	0.76	2.32	3.49	5.75	7.94	10.59	11.92	12.41
B	0.38	**0.05**	0.38	1.93	3.11	5.35	7.56	10.21	11.53	12.02
C	0.76	0.38	**0.08**	1.54	2.72	4.98	7.18	9.83	11.15	11.65
D	2.32	1.93	1.56	**0.09**	1.17	3.42	5.62	8.28	9.59	10.09
E	3.49	3.11	2.72	1.17	**0.09**	2.26	4.45	7.10	8.42	8.92
F	5.75	5.37	4.98	3.42	2.26	**0.08**	2.19	4.85	6.16	6.66
G	7.94	7.55	7.17	5.62	4.44	2.19	**0.08**	2.64	3.97	4.46
H	10.59	10.21	9.83	8.28	7.10	4.84	2.65	**0.05**	1.31	1.81
I	11.91	11.53	11.15	9.60	8.42	6.16	3.97	1.32	**0.09**	0.49
J	12.41	12.02	11.65	10.09	8.92	6.65	4.46	1.81	0.49	**0.02**

(ii) replacement identical devices

$\bar{\mathbb{D}}_1$

	A	B	C	D	E	F	G	H	I	J
A	**0.19**	0.45	0.86	2.29	3.47	5.66	7.83	10.51	11.72	12.36
B	0.41	**0.20**	0.49	1.89	3.08	5.28	7.45	10.09	11.31	11.96
C	0.79	0.37	**0.24**	1.52	2.70	4.90	7.08	9.77	10.95	11.61
D	2.31	1.88	1.47	**0.22**	1.16	3.34	5.51	8.18	9.39	10.03
E	3.47	3.06	2.63	1.19	**0.23**	2.17	4.33	7.02	8.20	8.86
F	5.72	5.29	4.88	3.44	2.24	**0.24**	2.10	4.78	5.98	6.62
G	7.90	7.49	7.07	5.63	4.45	2.23	**0.24**	2.57	3.77	4.41
H	10.58	10.14	9.73	8.27	7.13	4.94	2.74	**0.24**	1.11	1.77
I	11.90	11.49	11.06	9.61	8.45	6.28	4.09	1.41	**0.27**	0.46
J	12.37	11.98	11.52	10.08	8.89	6.72	4.55	1.88	0.69	**0.20**

$\bar{\mathbb{D}}_{15}$

	A	B	C	D	E	F	G	H	I	J
A	**0.04**	0.41	0.85	2.27	3.46	5.68	7.83	10.52	11.72	12.39
B	0.38	**0.05**	0.46	1.89	3.08	5.30	7.44	10.13	11.33	12.00
C	0.76	0.34	**0.10**	1.51	2.69	4.91	7.07	9.76	10.95	11.62
D	2.31	1.90	1.47	**0.09**	1.14	3.36	5.50	8.20	9.40	10.07
E	3.49	3.08	2.63	1.21	**0.09**	2.18	4.34	7.02	8.23	8.89
F	5.75	5.34	4.89	3.47	2.29	**0.11**	2.08	4.77	5.98	6.64
G	7.94	7.53	7.08	5.67	4.48	2.26	**0.12**	2.57	3.77	4.45
H	10.59	10.21	9.74	8.31	7.14	4.91	2.76	**0.09**	1.13	1.79
I	11.91	11.50	11.06	9.64	8.45	6.23	4.08	1.40	**0.20**	0.47
J	12.41	11.99	11.55	10.13	8.94	6.73	4.58	1.89	0.69	**0.02**

(iii) replacement distinct devices

$\bar{\mathbb{D}}_1$

	A	B	C	D	E	F	G	H	I	J
A	**0.44**	0.33	0.98	2.29	3.12	6.11	8.30	10.60	12.57	12.14
B	0.79	**0.50**	0.61	1.88	2.73	5.71	7.93	10.20	12.22	11.76
C	1.16	0.83	**0.31**	1.54	2.36	5.37	7.55	9.85	11.84	11.39
D	2.71	2.37	1.29	**0.22**	0.82	3.79	6.00	8.29	10.29	9.83
E	3.86	3.57	2.47	1.21	**0.40**	2.60	4.82	7.12	9.10	8.68
F	6.13	5.79	4.72	3.44	2.61	**0.44**	2.58	4.86	6.89	6.40
G	8.34	8.00	6.90	5.64	4.79	1.82	**0.41**	2.68	4.69	4.21
H	10.97	10.64	9.59	8.30	7.48	4.49	2.28	**0.27**	1.98	1.54
I	12.30	11.96	10.90	9.64	8.81	5.79	3.62	1.33	**0.68**	0.27
J	12.77	12.43	11.39	10.11	9.26	6.28	4.08	1.78	0.34	**0.29**

$\bar{\mathbb{D}}_{15}$

	A	B	C	D	E	F	G	H	I	J
A	**0.36**	0.11	1.00	2.27	3.13	6.10	8.31	10.60	12.59	12.15
B	0.75	**0.43**	0.62	1.88	2.75	5.72	7.92	10.21	12.20	11.76
C	1.13	0.82	**0.23**	1.51	2.37	5.33	7.54	9.83	11.82	11.38
D	2.68	2.36	1.31	**0.09**	0.81	3.78	5.98	8.28	10.27	9.82
E	3.86	3.52	2.48	1.21	**0.36**	2.60	4.80	7.11	9.09	8.65
F	6.11	5.79	4.74	3.47	2.61	**0.35**	2.54	4.85	6.83	6.40
G	8.31	7.98	6.94	5.67	4.81	1.84	**0.35**	2.66	4.63	4.21
H	10.96	10.63	9.59	8.32	7.47	4.49	2.29	**0.08**	1.99	1.79
I	12.29	11.97	10.91	9.64	8.78	5.81	3.61	1.31	**0.67**	0.23
J	12.78	12.45	11.41	10.14	9.28	6.30	4.10	1.80	0.18	**0.26**

Fig. 11. Reported distances over 3 experiments in Scenarios A.1 and A.2: clean network, replacements with the identical devices and replacement with distinct devices

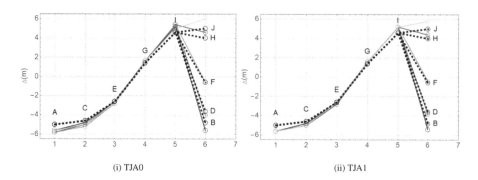

(i) TJA0   (ii) TJA1

Fig. 12. Insertion attacks: TJA0 (i) vs. TJA1 (ii) with the BCW-SQUARE method

for cable of length ℓ we get $\mathbb{D}^{\text{inter}}(\pi', \pi'') = \sqrt{[(d'_l - \ell + d'_l) - (d''_l - \ell + d''_l)]^2} = \sqrt{(2d'_l - 2d''_l)^2} = 2\sqrt{(d'_l - d''_l)^2} = 2\mathbb{D}^{\text{phy}}(\pi', \pi'') \Rightarrow \mathbb{D}^{\text{phy}}(\pi', \pi'') = \frac{\mathbb{D}^{\text{inter}}(\pi', \pi'')}{2}\square.$

Scenario A. In Fig. 10 we present the intra and inter-distances results for the clean 10 ECU network (blue) in as well as for replacements with identical devices (green) and replacement with distinct devices (magenta). The black dotted line denotes the real position of the nodes. The backward square has a slightly improved accuracy. For replacements with the same devices there is almost no change in the reported distances. When replacing with distinct devices the change becomes visible and the locations may shift with at most 30cm. ECU replacement is a rare procedure inside a vehicle and if such change occurs, it will likely be done with identical devices. In Fig. 11 we present the intra and inter-distance between the three configurations as numerical values and also as heatmap for the values on the left. Additional plots for replacements in Scenario A can be found in Appendix C.

To establish a more concrete view on the accuracy of the localization methods, in Tables 1 and 2 we present numerical data on the estimated distances as medians **M**, means μ over all the reported distances and errors with respect to the true location on the network. Note that as the impedance of the cable does affect the propagation speed which we consider to be fixed at a reference of 5 ns/m, and thus the reported distance may vary based on the cable impedance, we expect for such variations to be present. The fact that the errors at the bus ends, i.e., locations A vs. J are symmetric prove that our method has very good precision. Finally, the accuracy can be corrected by interpolating with the expected error but this would be out of scope.

Scenario B. In Scenario B we investigate both single and multiple node insertions attacks as well as the influence of temperature variations. First, in Fig. 12 we present the influence of single node insertions based on applying the new methodology on our past dataset from [20]. Insertions are performed with two distinct transceivers TJA0 and TJA1. For brevity, we defer part of the numerical data for Scenario B to Appendix D.

Figure 13 presents these in terms of inter-distances when using the backward square method. The first device, i.e., TJA0, has a slightly larger effect on the distances but the results are close. This shows that off-line calibration during production with innocuous adversarial devices may be useful in calibrating the detection algorithm for future attacks by unknown devices. It can be easily seen from the heatmaps that the adversary device easily positions close to the target node while it is still possible to distinguish it from the legitimate node.

Table 1. Scenarios A.1 and A.2 - node replacements FWD-SQUARE $\alpha = 2.5, w = 100$

Scenario	A	err.	B	err.	C	err.	D	err.	E	err.	F	err.	G	err.	H	err.	I	err.	J	err.
clean ntw. (M)	-6.40	1.40	-6.00	1.20	-5.80	1.20	-4.20	0.60	-2.60	0.00	-0.40	0.20	2.00	0.60	4.80	0.80	6.20	1.60	6.60	1.60
clean ntw. (μ)	-6.42	1.42	-6.09	1.29	-5.79	1.19	-4.10	0.50	-2.68	0.08	-0.31	0.29	2.04	0.64	4.80	0.80	6.20	1.60	6.60	1.60
replacement-same (M)	-6.40	1.40	-6.00	1.20	-5.60	1.00	-4.00	0.40	-2.60	0.00	-0.40	0.20	2.00	0.60	4.60	0.60	6.00	1.40	6.40	1.40
replacement-same (μ)	-6.32	1.32	-5.94	1.14	-5.64	1.04	-4.03	0.43	-2.67	0.07	-0.33	0.27	1.94	0.54	4.60	0.60	6.00	1.40	6.40	1.40
replacement-distinct (M)	-7.20	2.20	-7.00	2.20	-6.00	1.40	-4.40	0.80	-3.00	0.40	0.20	0.80	3.20	1.80	5.40	1.40	7.40	2.80	7.20	2.20
replacement-distinct (μ)	-7.14	2.14	-6.95	2.15	-6.07	1.47	-4.37	0.77	-2.96	0.36	0.13	0.73	3.15	1.75	5.40	1.40	7.40	2.80	7.20	2.20

Table 2. Scenarios A.1 and A.2 - node replacements BCW-SQUARE $\alpha = 1, w = 25$

Scenario	A	err.	B	err.	C	err.	D	err.	E	err.	F	err.	G	err.	H	err.	I	err.	J	err.
clean ntw. (M)	-6.20	1.20	-5.80	1.00	-5.40	0.80	-3.80	0.20	-2.80	0.20	-0.40	0.20	1.80	0.40	4.40	0.40	5.80	1.20	6.20	1.20
clean ntw. (μ)	-6.21	1.21	-5.81	1.01	-5.45	0.85	-3.89	0.29	-2.71	0.11	-0.47	0.13	1.72	0.32	4.40	0.40	5.80	1.20	6.20	1.20
replacement-same (M)	-6.20	1.20	-5.80	1.00	-5.40	0.80	-4.00	0.40	-2.80	0.20	-0.60	0.00	1.60	0.20	4.40	0.40	5.60	1.00	6.20	1.20
replacement-same (μ)	-6.20	1.20	-5.77	0.97	-5.35	0.75	-3.91	0.31	-2.73	0.13	-0.54	0.06	1.64	0.24	4.40	0.40	5.60	1.00	6.20	1.20
replacement-distinct (M)	-6.60	1.60	-6.20	1.40	-5.20	0.60	-4.00	0.40	-3.00	0.40	0.00	0.60	2.00	0.60	4.40	0.40	6.40	1.80	6.00	1.00
replacement-distinct (μ)	-6.60	1.60	-6.25	1.45	-5.20	0.60	-3.92	0.32	-3.08	0.48	-0.09	0.51	2.11	0.71	4.40	0.40	6.40	1.80	6.00	1.00

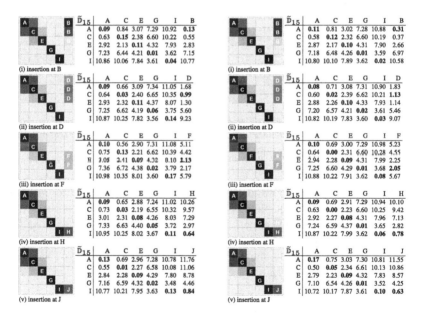

Fig. 13. Reported inter-distances in case of the node insertion attack from Scenario B.2 with TJA0 (left) and TJA1 (right)

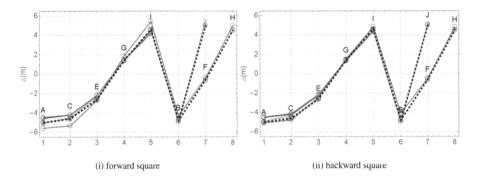

(i) forward square   (ii) backward square

Fig. 14. Reported distances over 5 distinct experiments in Scenario B: clean network (blue), heated 50 C (blue), heated 60 C (magenta), 2 adversaries (orange) and 3 adversaries (red) with the forward (i) and backward (ii) square method (Color figure online)

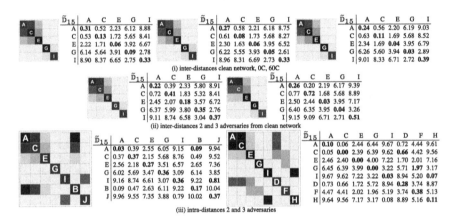

$\tilde{D}_{15}$	A	C	E	G	I
A	**0.31**	0.52	2.23	6.12	8.88
C	0.53	**0.13**	1.72	5.65	8.41
E	2.22	1.71	**0.06**	3.92	6.67
G	6.14	5.64	3.91	**0.09**	2.78
I	8.90	8.37	6.65	2.75	**0.33**

$\tilde{D}_{15}$	A	C	E	G	I
A	**0.27**	0.58	2.21	6.18	8.75
C	0.61	**0.08**	1.73	5.68	8.27
E	2.30	1.63	**0.06**	3.95	6.52
G	6.22	5.55	3.93	**0.05**	2.61
I	8.96	8.31	6.69	2.73	**0.33**

$\tilde{D}_{15}$	A	C	E	G	I
A	**0.24**	0.56	2.20	6.19	9.03
C	0.63	**0.11**	1.69	5.68	8.52
E	2.34	1.69	**0.04**	3.95	6.79
G	6.26	5.60	3.94	**0.03**	2.89
I	9.01	8.33	6.71	2.72	**0.39**

(i) inter-distances clean network, 0C, 60C

$\tilde{D}_{15}$	A	C	E	G	I
A	**0.22**	0.39	2.33	5.80	8.91
C	0.72	**0.41**	1.83	5.32	8.41
E	2.45	2.07	**0.18**	3.57	6.72
G	6.37	5.99	3.80	**0.35**	2.76
I	9.11	8.74	6.58	3.04	**0.37**

$\tilde{D}_{15}$	A	C	E	G	I
A	**0.26**	0.20	2.19	6.17	9.39
C	0.77	**0.72**	1.68	5.68	8.89
E	2.50	2.44	**0.03**	3.95	7.17
G	6.40	6.35	3.95	**0.04**	3.26
I	9.15	9.09	6.71	2.71	**0.51**

(ii) inter-distances 2 and 3 adversaries from clean network

$\tilde{D}_{15}$	A	C	E	G	I	B	J
A	**0.03**	0.39	2.55	6.05	9.15	**0.09**	9.94
C	0.37	**0.37**	2.15	5.68	8.76	0.49	9.52
E	2.56	2.18	**0.27**	3.51	6.57	2.65	7.36
G	6.02	5.69	3.47	**0.36**	3.09	6.14	3.85
I	9.16	8.74	6.61	3.07	**0.36**	9.22	0.81
B	0.09	0.47	2.63	6.11	9.22	**0.17**	10.04
J	9.96	9.55	7.35	3.88	0.79	10.02	**0.37**

$\tilde{D}_{15}$	A	C	E	G	I	D	F	H
A	**0.10**	0.06	2.44	6.44	9.67	0.72	4.44	9.61
C	0.05	**0.00**	2.39	6.39	9.62	**0.66**	4.42	9.56
E	2.46	2.40	**0.00**	4.00	7.22	1.70	2.01	7.16
G	6.45	6.39	3.99	**0.00**	3.22	5.71	**1.97**	3.17
I	9.67	9.62	7.22	3.22	**0.03**	8.94	5.20	0.07
D	0.73	0.66	1.72	5.72	8.94	**0.28**	3.74	8.87
F	4.47	4.41	2.02	1.96	5.19	3.74	**0.38**	5.13
H	9.64	9.56	7.17	3.17	0.08	8.89	5.16	**0.11**

(iii) intra-distances 2 and 3 adversaries

Fig. 15. Reported distances over 3 experiments in Scenario B.1 and B.3: (i) clean network and temperature variations, (ii) inter-distances to the clean network with 2, 3 adversaries and (iii) intra-distances for 2, 3 adversaries

We now extend these experiments with new ones in which we account for temperature variations and multiple adversaries. In Fig. 14 we present the reported distances over the 5 distinct experiments: clean network (blue), heated 50 °C (blue), heated 60 °C (magenta), 2 adversaries (orange) and 3 adversaries (red). The black dotted line denotes the real position of the nodes. Figure 15 shows the inter and intra-distances both as numerical values and heatmaps with the more effective backward square method.

5 Conclusions

The methodology proposed in this work is very simple and extremely effective in localizing nodes on the CAN bus. Since a single rising edge is sufficient and one frame carries more than a dozen such edges, localization can be done after a single frame with extremely high accuracy. The correctness of our approach is confirmed by data collection in a real car where we used two probes: one connected near the OBD port and the other near the engine ECU where we did a minor modification by slightly extending the wire from the existing connector. Further experiments performed on a realistic laboratory setup suggest decimeter level precision with slight overlaps only between nodes that are 10 cm apart. This short localization range clearly sets room for physical inspection of the exact device that is responsible for injecting frames on the bus. The proposed method seems to be highly resilient to temperature variations despite voltage changes on the bus. The computational overhead is also insignificant, the only possible limitation is the required high sampling rate but this is clearly achievable with modern signal processing devices.

Appendix A - Experimental Setup

Figure 16 (i) provides a depiction of our newly built experimental setup which uses an industry grade CAN bus cable. The bus is terminated at each end by a split termination as commonly employed in industry applications with two $60\,\Omega$ resistors in series (totaling $120\,\Omega$) and a capacitor of 10 nF to remove noise.

To avoid overloading the picture, only 5 devices are connected to the bus which corresponds to the clean network in Scenario B. Figure 16 (ii) shows the network placed inside the refrigerator where it was kept for 1 h. We intentionally placed the cable and devices in the refrigerator with no attempt to preserve the bus geometry as in the original setup. Somewhat surprising for us, even if the geometry of the bus was changed drastically and the temperature dropped from room temperature 24 °C to 0 °C, the impact on the reported lengths was insignificant (variations in the order of several centimeters at most). To record data at higher temperature, the clean setup was placed inside a sealed box to avoid heat dissipation and 4 hair-driers were used to heat it for 30 min at 50 °C and 60 °C.

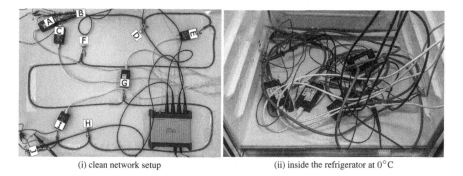

(i) clean network setup   (ii) inside the refrigerator at 0°C

Fig. 16. The clean network (i) and the network dropped inside a refrigerator at 0 °C (ii)

Appendix B - BCW and FWD-SQUARE Algorithms

Algorithm 1 presents the bus monitor which reads voltage samples on CAN-H to the left and right sides of the bus v_l, v_r and appends them to the buffers $\widetilde{v}_l, \widetilde{v}_r$ (lines 2–3) until a threshold τ is exceeded on both side (line 5). The threshold τ was set to 2.75 V which is the minimum acceptable dominant voltage on CAN-H according to ISO specifications. When this threshold is met, the FWD or BCW functions extract the time of the rising edge to the left and right of the bus, i.e., t_l, t_r, and the position π is computed (lines 6–8).

Algorithms 2, 3 present the FWD and BCW functions. The FWD-SQUARE function proceeds from the left to the end of the array (indexes 0 to $b-1$) until the slope exceeds the value of α (lines 3–4). The BCW-SQUARE function first proceeds from the left to right until the voltage reaches the threshold τ to avoid a start on a bit plateau (line 3). Then the index is decremented until the slope drops below the value of α (line 5).

Algorithm 1. Bus Monitor

```
1: procedure          MONITORLOCA-
   TION(v_l, v_r, t)
2:      ṽ_l ← add(ṽ_l, v_l)
3:      ṽ_r ← add(ṽ_r, v_r)
4:      t̃ ← add(t̃, t)
5:      if v_l ≥ τ ∧ v_r ≥ τ then
6:          t_l ← SQUARE(ṽ_l, t̃, w, α)
7:          t_r ← SQUARE(ṽ_r, t̃, w, α)
8:          π  ←  (t_l  −  t_r) × (5 ×
        10^{-9}s/m)^{-1}
9:      else
10:         π ← ⊥
11:     end if
12:     return π
13: end procedure
```

Algorithm 2. FWD SQUARE

```
1: function FWDSQUARE(ṽ, t̃, w, α)
2:      i ← 0
3:      while (ṽ[i] − ṽ[i − w])/wδ < α do
4:          i ← i + 1
5:      end while
6:      return t̃[i]
7: end function
```

Algorithm 3. BCW SQUARE

```
1: function BCWSQUARE(ṽ, t̃, w, α)
2:      i ← 0
3:      while ṽ[i] < τ do i ← i + 1
4:      end while
5:      while (ṽ[i] − ṽ[i − w])/wδ > α do
6:          i ← i − 1
7:      end while
8:      return t̃[i]
9: end function
```

Appendix C - Complementary Data Regarding Distances

In Fig. 17 we also present the raw distances and their histogram distributions as computed for Scenario A for the 10 ECUs. Note that there are overlaps between the first three and the last two devices, but these are separated by only 10 cm and respectively 20 cm of wire. This is an extremely small distance and even so, the devices can be distinguished over multiple samples.

Figure 18 shows the convergence of the mean values in contrast to the median values with the number of samples. It can be easily seen that the median value converges faster, generally a dozen samples being sufficient to establish the location and these can be extracted from a single frame. The plots are for the BCW-SQUARE method applied on the nodes in Scenario B. The FWD-SQUARE method has lesser accuracy as previously discussed.

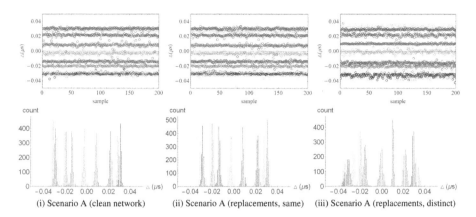

(i) Scenario A (clean network)   (ii) Scenario A (replacements, same)   (iii) Scenario A (replacements, distinct)

Fig. 17. Reported distances for the 10 devices in Scenario A and their histogram distributions

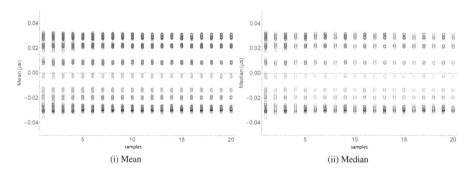

(i) Mean   (ii) Median

Fig. 18. Convergence of mean (i) and median (ii) values toward the real distance

Appendix D - Additional Numerical Data for Scenario B

Tables 3 and 4 give the numerical values as medians **M** and means μ over all the collected samples for each node with the forward and backward square methods. The backward square method is more accurate.

Tables 5 and 6 provide the true distances along with the resulting errors. Again, note that since no cable has exactly the 5 ns/m propagation speed, small variations are expected. The results clearly indicate that the professional CAN bus cable has lower propagation delays and the distances appear smaller than in the previous experiments. The FWD-SQUARE provided less accuracy and we have attempted a software interpolation to increase the sampling rate by 2x–8x but the benefits were little, the BCW-SQUARE remaining still more accurate.

Interestingly, the distances are almost unaffected by temperature variations. The effects of 2 adversaries are similarly low, only when 3 adversaries are connected to the bus the distances are more visibly affected. Such a scenario with 3 adversaries would be less likely on an in-vehicle bus.

Table 3. Scenario B.2 - single insertions FWD-SQUARE $\alpha = 2, w = 100$

Scenario	A	err.	C	err.	E	err.	G	err.	I	err.
clean (M)	-6.00	1.00	-5.40	0.80	-2.80	0.20	1.80	0.40	5.60	1.00
clean (μ)	-5.95	0.95	-5.35	0.75	-2.75	0.15	1.80	0.40	5.67	1.07
TJA0-B (M)	-6.00	1.00	-5.20	0.60	-2.60	0.00	2.00	0.60	5.80	1.20
TJA0-B (μ)	-5.94	0.94	-5.21	0.61	-2.54	0.06	1.95	0.55	5.74	1.14
TJA0-D (M)	-6.20	1.20	-5.60	1.00	-2.40	0.20	2.00	0.60	6.00	1.40
TJA0-D (μ)	-6.19	1.19	-5.61	1.01	-2.42	0.18	2.09	0.69	5.94	1.34
TJA0-F (M)	-6.20	1.20	-5.60	1.00	-3.00	0.40	2.20	0.80	6.00	1.40
TJA0-F (μ)	-6.23	1.23	-5.67	1.07	-3.01	0.41	2.10	0.70	6.03	1.43
TJA0-H (M)	-6.20	1.20	-5.60	1.00	-3.00	0.40	1.60	0.20	6.00	1.40
TJA0-H (μ)	-6.13	1.13	-5.58	0.98	-3.00	0.40	1.51	0.11	5.94	1.34
TJA0-J (M)	-6.00	1.00	-5.40	0.80	-3.00	0.40	1.60	0.20	5.40	0.80
TJA0-J (μ)	-5.99	0.99	-5.39	0.79	-2.90	0.30	1.59	0.19	5.41	0.81
TJA1-B (M)	-5.80	0.80	-5.20	0.60	-2.60	0.00	1.80	0.40	5.60	1.00
TJA1-B (μ)	-5.82	0.82	-5.20	0.60	-2.63	0.03	1.86	0.46	5.51	0.91
TJA1-D (M)	-6.00	1.00	-5.40	0.80	-2.60	0.00	2.00	0.60	5.60	1.00
TJA1-D (μ)	-5.97	0.97	-5.41	0.81	-2.52	0.08	1.96	0.56	5.63	1.03
TJA1-F (M)	-6.00	1.00	-5.40	0.80	-2.80	0.20	2.00	0.60	5.60	1.00
TJA1-F (μ)	-5.95	0.95	-5.41	0.81	-2.89	0.29	1.96	0.56	5.69	1.09
TJA1-H (M)	-6.00	1.00	-5.40	0.80	-2.80	0.20	1.60	0.20	5.80	1.20
TJA1-H (μ)	-5.92	0.92	-5.38	0.78	-2.89	0.29	1.63	0.23	5.70	1.10
TJA1-J (M)	-5.80	0.80	-5.20	0.60	-2.80	0.20	1.80	0.40	5.40	0.80
TJA1-J (μ)	-5.79	0.79	-5.24	0.64	-2.80	0.20	1.70	0.30	5.47	0.87

Table 4. Scenario B.2 - single insertions BCW-SQUARE $\alpha = 1, w = 25$

Scenario	A	err.	C	err.	E	err.	G	err.	I	err.
clean (M)	-5.60	0.60	-5.00	0.40	-2.80	0.20	1.60	0.20	5.20	0.60
clean (μ)	-5.69	0.69	-5.01	0.41	-2.70	0.10	1.60	0.20	5.25	0.65
TJA0-B (M)	-5.60	0.60	-4.80	0.20	-2.60	0.00	1.60	0.20	5.20	0.60
TJA0-B (μ)	-5.65	0.65	-4.84	0.24	-2.63	0.03	1.63	0.23	5.24	0.64
TJA0-D (M)	-5.60	0.60	-5.00	0.40	-2.60	0.00	1.60	0.20	5.40	0.80
TJA0-D (μ)	-5.66	0.66	-5.03	0.43	-2.61	0.01	1.65	0.25	5.35	0.75
TJA0-F (M)	-5.80	0.80	-5.20	0.60	-2.80	0.20	1.60	0.20	5.40	0.80
TJA0-F (μ)	-5.76	0.76	-5.13	0.53	-2.77	0.17	1.64	0.24	5.39	0.79
TJA0-H (M)	-5.80	0.80	-5.00	0.40	-2.80	0.20	1.60	0.20	5.40	0.80
TJA0-H (μ)	-5.71	0.71	-5.04	0.44	-2.80	0.20	1.60	0.20	5.32	0.72
TJA0-J (M)	-5.60	0.60	-5.00	0.40	-2.80	0.20	1.60	0.20	5.00	0.40
TJA0-J (μ)	-5.53	0.53	-4.99	0.39	-2.74	0.14	1.57	0.17	5.07	0.47
TJA1-B (M)	-5.60	0.60	-4.80	0.20	-2.60	0.00	1.60	0.20	5.20	0.60
TJA1-B (μ)	-5.56	0.56	-4.88	0.28	-2.68	0.08	1.60	0.20	5.19	0.59
TJA1-D (M)	-5.60	0.60	-5.00	0.40	-2.60	0.00	1.60	0.20	5.20	0.60
TJA1-D (μ)	-5.60	0.60	-4.95	0.35	-2.66	0.06	1.64	0.24	5.25	0.65
TJA1-F (M)	-5.60	0.60	-5.00	0.40	-2.60	0.00	1.60	0.20	5.20	0.60
TJA1-F (μ)	-5.67	0.67	-5.01	0.41	-2.69	0.09	1.61	0.21	5.28	0.68
TJA1-H (M)	-5.60	0.60	-5.00	0.40	-2.80	0.20	1.60	0.20	5.20	0.60
TJA1-H (μ)	-5.65	0.65	-4.99	0.39	-2.73	0.13	1.58	0.18	5.25	0.65
TJA1-J (M)	-5.60	0.60	-5.00	0.40	-2.60	0.00	1.60	0.20	5.20	0.60
TJA1-J (μ)	-5.50	0.50	-4.93	0.33	-2.67	0.07	1.63	0.23	5.10	0.50

Table 5. Scenarios B.1 and B.3 temperature variations and multiple insertions FWD SQUARE $\alpha = 2, w = 200$ (8x)

Scenario	A	err.	C	err.	E	err.	G	err.	I	err.
cln. ntw. (M)	-4.60	0.40	-4.20	0.40	-2.20	0.40	1.50	0.10	4.50	0.10
cln. ntw. (μ)	-4.56	0.44	-4.19	0.41	-2.15	0.45	1.46	0.06	4.42	0.18
cln. ntw. 0 °C (M)	-4.50	0.50	-4.20	0.40	-2.20	0.40	1.50	0.10	4.50	0.10
cln. ntw. 0 °C (μ)	-4.50	0.50	-4.17	0.43	-2.19	0.41	1.49	0.09	4.48	0.12
cln. ntw. 50 °C (M)	-4.60	0.40	-4.20	0.40	-2.20	0.40	1.50	0.10	4.40	0.20
cln. ntw. 50 °C (μ)	-4.54	0.46	-4.22	0.38	-2.21	0.39	1.46	0.06	4.21	0.39
cln. ntw. 60 °C (M)	-4.60	0.40	-4.20	0.40	-2.20	0.40	1.50	0.10	4.40	0.20
cln. ntw. 60 °C (μ)	-4.45	0.55	-4.21	0.39	-2.21	0.39	1.46	0.06	4.24	0.36
2 adv. B, J (M)	-5.00	0.00	-4.50	0.10	-2.20	0.40	1.40	0.00	4.50	0.10
2 adv. B, J (μ)	-5.05	0.05	-4.52	0.08	-2.25	0.35	1.43	0.03	4.54	0.06
3 adv. D,F,H (M)	-5.50	0.60	-5.30	0.70	-2.70	0.10	1.90	0.50	5.50	0.90
3 adv. D,F,H (μ)	-5.57	0.57	-5.33	0.73	-2.70	0.10	1.86	0.46	5.44	0.84

Table 6. Scenario B.1 and B.3 temperature variations and multiple insertions BCW SQUARE $\alpha = 0.25, w = 25$

Scenario	A	err.	C	err.	E	err.	G	err.	I	err.
cln. ntw. (M)	-4.80	0.20	-4.00	0.60	-2.40	0.20	1.60	0.20	4.00	0.60
cln. ntw. (μ)	-4.50	0.50	-4.23	0.37	-2.27	0.33	1.41	0.01	4.36	0.24
cln. ntw. 0 °C (M)	-4.80	0.20	-4.00	0.60	-2.40	0.20	1.60	0.20	4.00	0.60
cln. ntw. 0 °C (μ)	-4.51	0.49	-4.11	0.49	-2.19	0.41	1.41	0.01	4.33	0.27
cln. ntw. 50 °C (M)	-4.80	0.20	-4.00	0.60	-2.40	0.20	1.60	0.20	4.00	0.60
cln. ntw. 50 °C (μ)	-4.48	0.52	-4.13	0.47	-2.17	0.43	1.43	0.03	4.39	0.21
cln. ntw. 60 °C (M)	-4.80	0.20	-4.00	0.60	-2.40	0.20	1.60	0.20	4.80	0.20
cln. ntw. 60 °C (μ)	-4.53	0.47	-4.18	0.42	-2.22	0.38	1.45	0.05	4.40	0.20
2 adv. B, J (M)	-4.80	0.20	-4.80	0.20	-2.40	0.20	1.60	0.20	4.00	0.60
2 adv. B, J (μ)	-4.88	0.12	-4.31	0.29	-2.24	0.36	1.32	0.08	4.33	0.27
3 adv. D,F,H (M)	-4.80	0.20	-4.80	0.20	-2.40	0.20	1.60	0.20	4.80	0.20
3 adv. D,F,H (μ)	-5.05	0.05	-4.79	0.19	-2.44	0.16	1.51	0.11	4.84	0.24

References

1. AUTOSAR: Specification of Secure Onboard Communication, 4.3.1 edn. (2017)
2. Checkoway, S., et al.: Comprehensive experimental analyses of automotive attack surfaces. In: USENIX Security Symposium. San Francisco (2011)
3. Cho, K.T., Shin, K.G.: Viden: attacker identification on in-vehicle networks. In: ACM SIGSAC Conference on Computer and Communications Security, pp. 1109–1123. ACM (2017)
4. Choi, W., Jo, H.J., Woo, S., Chun, J.Y., Park, J., Lee, D.H.: Identifying ECUs using inimitable characteristics of signals in controller area networks. IEEE Trans. Veh. Technol. **67**(6), 4757–4770 (2018)

5. Choi, W., Joo, K., Jo, H.J., Park, M.C., Lee, D.H.: VoltageIDS: low-level communication characteristics for automotive intrusion detection system. IEEE Trans. Inf. Forensics Secur. **16**(8), 2114–2129 (2018)
6. Dagan, T., Wool, A.: Parrot, a software-only anti-spoofing defense system for the CAN bus. ESCAR EUROPE **34** (2016)
7. Foruhandeh, M., Man, Y., Gerdes, R., Li, M., Chantem, T.: SIMPLE: single-frame based physical layer identification for intrusion detection and prevention on in-vehicle networks. In: Proceedings of 35th Annual Computer Security Applications Conference, pp. 229–244 (2019)
8. Fröschle, S., Stühring, A.: Analyzing the capabilities of the CAN attacker. In: Foley, S.N., Gollmann, D., Snekkenes, E. (eds.) ESORICS 2017. LNCS, vol. 10492, pp. 464–482. Springer, Cham (2017). https://doi.org/10.1007/978-3-319-66402-6_27
9. Groza, B., Popa, L., Murvay, P.S., Yuval, E., Shabtai, A.: CANARY - a reactive defense mechanism for controller area networks based on active RelaYs. In: 30th USENIX Security Symposium (2021)
10. Humayed, A., Li, F., Lin, J., Luo, B.: CANSentry: securing CAN-based cyber-physical systems against denial and spoofing attacks. In: Chen, L., Li, N., Liang, K., Schneider, S. (eds.) ESORICS 2020. LNCS, vol. 12308, pp. 153–173. Springer, Cham (2020). https://doi.org/10.1007/978-3-030-58951-6_8
11. Humayed, A., Luo, B.: Using ID-hopping to defend against targeted DoS on CAN. In: International Workshop on Safe Control of Connected and Autonomous Vehicles, pp. 19–26. ACM (2017)
12. ISO: 11898-1-Road vehicles-Controller area network (CAN)-Part 1: Data link layer and physical signalling. Technical report, International Organization for Standardization (2015)
13. ISO: 11898-2, Road vehicles Controller area network (CAN) Part 2: High-speed medium access unit. Technical report, International Organization for Standardization (2016)
14. Kneib, M., Huth, C.: Scission: signal characteristic-based sender identification and intrusion detection in automotive networks. In: Proceedings of the 2018 ACM SIGSAC Conference on Computer and Communications Security, pp. 787–800. ACM (2018)
15. Kneib, M., Schell, O., Huth, C.: On the Robustness of Signal Characteristic-Based Sender Identification. arXiv preprint arXiv:1911.09881 (2019)
16. Kneib, M., Schell, O., Huth, C.: EASI: edge-based sender identification on resource-constrained platforms for automotive networks. In: Network and Distributed System Security Symposium (NDSS), pp. 1–16 (2020)
17. Koscher, K., et al.: Experimental security analysis of a modern automobile. In: Security and Privacy (SP), 2010 IEEE Symposium on, pp. 447–462. IEEE (2010)
18. Miller, C., Valasek, C.: Adventures in automotive networks and control units. DEF CON **21**, 260–264 (2013)
19. Murvay, P.S., Groza, B.: Source identification using signal characteristics in controller area networks. IEEE Signal Process. Lett. **21**(4), 395–399 (2014)
20. Murvay, P.S., Groza, B.: TIDAL-CAN: differential timing based intrusion detection and localization for controller area network. IEEE Access **8**, 68895–68912 (2020)
21. Rumez, M., et al.: CAN Radar: Sensing Physical Devices in CAN Networks based on Time Domain Reflectometry (2019)
22. SAE: J2284-3 High-Speed CAN (HSC) for Vehicle Applications at 500 KBPS. Standard, SAE International (November 2016)

23. Schell, O., Kneib, M.: VALID: voltage-based lightweight intrusion detection for the controller area network. In: 2020 IEEE 19th International Conference on Trust, Security and Privacy in Computing and Communications (TrustCom), pp. 225–232 (2020)

24. Wu, W., et al.: IDH-CAN: a hardware-based ID hopping CAN mechanism with enhanced security for automotive real-time applications. IEEE Access **6**, 54607–54623 (2018)

25. Ying, X., Bernieri, G., Conti, M., Poovendran, R.: TACAN: transmitter authentication through covert channels in controller area networks. In: Proceedings of the 10th ACM/IEEE International Conference on Cyber-Physical Systems, pp. 23–34. ACM (2019)

Shadow-Catcher: Looking into Shadows to Detect Ghost Objects in Autonomous Vehicle 3D Sensing

Zhongyuan Hau$^{(\boxtimes)}$, Soteris Demetriou, Luis Muñoz-González, and Emil C. Lupu

Imperial College London, London, UK
{zy.hau17,s.demetriou,l.munoz,e.c.lupu}@imperial.ac.uk

Abstract. LiDAR-driven 3D sensing allows new generations of vehicles to achieve advanced levels of situation awareness. However, recent works have demonstrated that physical adversaries can spoof LiDAR return signals and deceive 3D object detectors to erroneously detect "ghost" objects. Existing defenses are either impractical or focus only on vehicles. Unfortunately, it is easier to spoof smaller objects such as pedestrians and cyclists, but harder to defend against and can have worse safety implications. To address this gap, we introduce Shadow-Catcher, a set of new techniques embodied in an end-to-end prototype to detect both large and small ghost object attacks on 3D detectors. We characterize a new semantically meaningful physical invariant (3D shadows) which Shadow-Catcher leverages for validating objects. Our evaluation on the KITTI dataset shows that Shadow-Catcher consistently achieves more than 94% accuracy in identifying anomalous shadows for vehicles, pedestrians, and cyclists, while it remains robust to a novel class of strong "invalidation" attacks targeting the defense system. Shadow-Catcher can achieve real-time detection, requiring only between 0.003 s–0.021 s on average to process an object in a 3D point cloud on commodity hardware and achieves a 2.17x speedup compared to prior work.

Keywords: Autonomous vehicle · LiDAR Spoofing · Attack detection

1 Introduction

High-precision depth sensors are increasingly being used for mapping the environment in various application domains, such as robotics [23], security surveillance [11] and augmented reality applications [16]. LiDARs (derived from light detection and ranging) are popular such depth sensors. They are pervasively deployed [3,5] in autonomous vehicles (referred to as AVs henceforth) where a new class of Deep Neural Network (DNN) 3D classifiers leverage their measurements (processed in batches called 3D point clouds) to detect objects – a necessary task for downstream safety-critical driving decision-making [17,20,21,29].

© Springer Nature Switzerland AG 2021
E. Bertino et al. (Eds.): ESORICS 2021, LNCS 12972, pp. 691–711, 2021.
https://doi.org/10.1007/978-3-030-88418-5_33

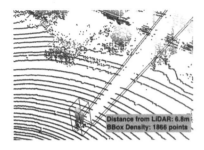
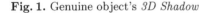
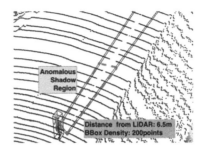

Fig. 1. Genuine object's *3D Shadow*   **Fig. 2.** Ghost object's *3D Shadow*

Recent studies have shown that it is possible to attack LiDAR-based perception systems by spoofing LiDAR return signals [4,15,22]. To defend against model-level LiDAR spoofing attacks, prior works suggested using sensor fusion [4], view fusion (SVF) [24], or leveraging 3D-point statistical anomaly detection based on physical invariants such as object occlusions and free space (CARLO) [24]. Unfortunately, sensor fusion approaches [13,31] rely on the assumption that a majority of the sensors are not under attack. SVF makes fewer assumptions but requires expensive retraining of the classifiers and has reduced classification accuracy, which is more dangerous than failing to detect ghost objects. CARLO is a backward compatible method, agnostic to the adversary and achieves good accuracy in detecting spoofed vehicles with an acceptable performance overhead. However, CARLO depends on the size of the object's bounding box and on the fact that genuine vehicles exhibit a high points' density. This approach does not work for smaller objects such as pedestrians and cyclists. Lastly, there is no approach to date which uses semantically meaningful information which can be crucial in reasoning and explaining system decisions.

In this work, we introduce a new approach to detect model-level LiDAR spoofing attacks on both large and small objects that assumes neither the presence nor the cooperation of other sensors. Our mechanism is agnostic to the classification model targeted: any detected object, either genuine or fake (*ghost*), will be subjected to verification. We observe that real 3D objects are closely followed by 3D shadows, which exhibit different characteristics than the shadows of spoofed objects (see Figs. 1 and 2). We use this observation to design an efficient and effective detection mechanism that verifies the presence of objects only when they exhibit the expected 3D shadow effect.

We design, develop and evaluate a system, Shadow-Catcher, which firstly employs ray optics to map the expected *shadow region* of a detected 3D object. Then, it uses a scoring algorithm leveraging exponential decay weight estimation to reduce the importance of measurement artifacts and determine whether the proposed shadow region corresponds to (a) a real shadow or (b) an anomalous shadow. In the latter case, it uses a binary classifier trained on density features extracted from the proposed shadow region, to further classify a shadow region as a *ghost object shadow* or as a *poisoned shadow* (thus verifying the presence of a true object). Our evaluation shows that more than 98% of the 3D objects in our dataset have meaningful shadows, and that Shadow-Catcher's shadow region estimation closely captures their true shape. We also show that Shadow-Catcher consistently achieves more than 94% accuracy in identifying anomalous shadows. Shadow-Catcher can further classify with 96% accuracy whether the anomalous shadow corresponds to a ghost attack. In addition, we also design a novel, strong, *object invalidation adversary* which follows an optimal strategy to launch an evasion attack that poisons a genuine shadow such that it is misclassified as a ghost shadow, thus invalidating genuine objects. We demonstrate that Shadow-Catcher remains robust. Lastly, Shadow-Catcher achieves real-time detection (2.17x improvement compared to related work [24] for processing ghost vehicles) rendering it suitable for deployment both online to provide hints to vehicle passengers, operators or end-to-end AI systems and offline for forensic analysis. Visual examples of Shadow-Catcher are shown online [2].

2   Background and Related Work

LiDAR Sensors. To scan the environment, LiDARs emit a pulse in the invisible near-infrared wavelength (900–1100 nm), which is reflected on incident objects before returning to the receiver. Based on the time of flight, LiDARs calculate the distance between the sensor and the incident object. LiDARs used in AVs (e.g. Velodyne LiDARs) emit a number of light pulses from an array of vertically arranged lasers (16, 32, 64, etc.) that rotate around a center axis to obtain a 360-view of the surroundings of the sensor unit. The sensor translates a return signal to a measurement 3D point consisting of coordinates (x,y,z) and a reflection value (R) corresponding to the return signal's reflectivity or signal strength. 3D point clouds are commonly projected to 2D in a more compact representation called *birds-eye view* or BEV for short.

3D Object Detector Attacks. Prior work showed that 3D object detectors based on point-clouds are vulnerable to LiDAR spoofing attacks [4,15,22,24] and point cloud perturbation attacks [14,26,28,30,32]. Wicker and Kwiatkowska [27] further found that 3D object detectors are trained to learn object representations from a "critical point set", and subtle changes in the input greatly impact the model's performance. More closely related to our work are LiDAR spoofing attacks. Petit *et al.* [15] first introduced physical attacks to generate noise, fake echos and fake 3D objects by relaying and replaying LiDAR signals. However, they were unable to spoof objects closer than 20 m from the LiDAR receiver. Subsequently, Shin *et al.* [22] managed to inject 10 3 D points that are up to 12 m in front of the LiDAR receiver. Cao *et al.* [4] then demonstrated the capability to spoof up to 100 points and proposed a model-level spoofing methodology that can fool a target AV simulator. Recently Sun *et al.* [24] successfully used up to 200 points to launch model-level attacks which leverage 3D points of occluded or distant vehicles to spoof front-near vehicles. Such attacks can have severe repercussions as they can force a vehicle to brake abruptly [4]. This might physically injure passengers, halt traffic or induce a crash with the vehicle behind it.

3D Object Detector Defenses. Existing defenses for 3D point cloud object detection focus on defending against point cloud perturbations [14, 30, 33]. More related to our work are point injection (or LiDAR spoofing) attacks in AV settings, where suggestions were made to use multi-modal sensor fusion [13, 31], view fusion [24] and to leverage occlusion patterns [24]. Multi-modal sensor fusion makes strong assumptions about the integrity of sensors, Sun *et al.*'s [24] SVF approach is promising but not backward compatible, and requires expensive retraining to deal with a noticeable penalty in its classification performance which may prove more dangerous than the attack it tries to address. Sun *et al.* [24] also proposed (CARLO) which is similar to our approach as it can be applied orthogonally to the object classifier. However it is significantly slower than Shadow-Catcher for vehicles. More importantly, CARLO is not robust against smaller objects, such as pedestrians and cyclists. Lastly, our work introduces a new semantically meaningful physical invariant, 3D shadows.

3 Threat Model

We adopt the threat model from [4, 24] and assume a physical adversary who can spoof LiDAR return signals to fool an AV's 3D object detector model. The adversary can spoof the signals either by placing an attacker device on the roadside or by mounting it on an attack vehicle driving in front of the target vehicle in an adjacent lane [4]. The attacker's device can capture the LiDAR signal, and emit a return signal with a delay which controls where in the resulting point cloud the spoofed point will appear. This has been proven as a realistic attack surface [4, 15, 22, 24]. Below we define the adversary's ($\mathcal{A}$) capabilities and goals.

$\mathcal{A}$'s Capabilities. $\mathcal{A}$ enjoys state of the art sensor spoofing capabilities and can inject ≤ 200 points within a horizontal angle of $10°$ [24] in a 3D scene. $\mathcal{A}$ can launch model-level spoofing attacks able to emulate distant and occluded vehicles [4, 24]. In addition, we consider attacks spoofing smaller objects with ≤ 200 injected points. $\mathcal{A}$ is a white-box adversary with full knowledge of the internals of both the victim model and the detection mechanism.

Extending the Threat Model: Considering Smaller Objects. Prior work introduced a defense (CARLO) against attacks aiming to spoof vehicles [24]. However CARLO is limited when considering smaller objects, such as pedestrians, cyclists or motorcycles. Our experiments evaluating CARLO's limitations to detect spoofed pedestrian objects are given in Appendix A. Our approach considers vehicle spoofing but also spoofing of smaller objects such as pedestrians and cyclists. The latter is an even easier target for $\mathcal{A}$ but harder to defend; genuine pedestrian and cyclist objects consist of ∼200 points on average—by analyzing the full KITTI dataset we found an average number of points of 478, 206 and 174 in the bounding boxes of cars, pedestrians and cyclists respectively. Considering such objects is paramount, as they are commonly encountered, and the safety repercussions can be more severe in the case of an accident. In the KITTI dataset, which contains LiDAR measurements from real-world driving scenarios, more than 30% of the objects detected on the road are pedestrians and cyclists, with pedestrians being the second most predominant object after cars [10]. Failing to reliably detect (or verify) such objects (e.g. in an invalidation attack), has a higher probability of leading to human injuries and even fatalities [25] than accidents involving only vehicles.

Extending the Threat Model: Object Invalidation Attacks. Using shadows to verify true objects, might incentivize attacks where the adversary's goal changes from injecting ghost objects to invalidating genuine objects by poisoning their shadow. This could lead to an erroneous safety-critical decision with potentially dire consequences. Our defense mechanism recognizes this. In contrast with related work, it considers for the first time an even stronger adversary which is capable of launching both ghost object injection and object invalidation attacks. To test the robustness of our system against object invalidation attacks, we formulate a novel, strong attack with full knowledge of the detection mechanism, and evaluate the success of this attack against our system.

4   3D Shadows as a Physical Invariant

We observe that any 3D object representation in a point cloud is closely followed by a respective region void of measurements. We call this the *3D shadow effect*. Object detectors do not take into account shadow effects and only learn point representations of objects for the detection task. 3D shadow effects occur because LiDAR sensors record measurements (3D points) from return light pulses reflected off an object in a direct line of sight that return within a constrained time period to the receiver of the sensor unit. Thus, anything behind the incident object cannot be reached by the light rays and cannot be measured, resulting in void (shadow) regions. This observation leads us to hypothesize that *the presence and characteristics of shadows can be used to verify genuine 3D objects*. In this section we systematically analyze real 3D driving scenes to verify the presence of shadows in genuine 3D objects, obtain ground truth for such shadow regions and to verify that ghost objects cannot have realistic shadows.

Presence of 3D Shadows. To verify the presence of 3D shadows we randomly sampled 120 scenes from the KITTI dataset [10]. The dataset includes LiDAR measurements (point cloud scenes) from real driving scenarios in Karlsruhe, Germany. The dataset is accompanied by a set of object labels for training 3D object detectors. We used these labels to locate true objects in each scene. We then converted each scene to its birds-eye-view (BEV) representation by projecting each 3D point to a 2D plane. Then, we went through all 120 scenes and (1) manually annotated shadow regions, if present, using the VIA annotation tool [6], and (2) assigned shadow regions to objects.

In the 120 sampled scenes, we found a total of 607 objects (see Table 1). All objects are located in the frontal view of the vehicle and include objects both on the road and on sidewalks. Out of the 607 objects, we have identified shadows for 597 or 98.3% of the objects, the details by object type can be found in Table 1.

We could not identify shadows for the remaining 10/607 (1.6%) objects, due to the objects' location in the environment. For example, if one object is directly in front of another but not fully occluding it (e.g., a person is standing in front of a vehicle), the first object cannot be unequivocally assigned a shadow region because of the second object.

Table 1. Objects and their shadows in 120 KITTI scenes.

	Count in dataset	% of total objects	Labeled shadows	% of object type
Car	444	73.1	439	98.9
Pedestrian	45	7.4	41	91.1
Cyclist	17	2.8	17	100
Van	56	9.2	55	98.2
Truck	17	2.8	17	100
Tram	6	1.0	6	100
Sitting person	1	0.2	1	100
Miscellaneous	21	3.5	21	100
Total	607	N.A.	597	N.A.

Conclusion. By manually labeling shadow regions for objects, we found strong evidence of co-occurrence of objects and shadow regions. This supports our hypothesis that the presence of shadows is a physical invariant that can be potentially used to verify genuine objects in 3D scenes.

3D Shadows of Genuine vs. Ghost Objects. LiDARs default operating mode records the *Strongest Return Signal*. Thus, successfully spoofing a signal, is equivalent to transforming a measurement point in the original point cloud to the desired spoofed position [4]. In other words, following the physics of the LiDAR, spoofing a point should result in a corresponding point behind the injected point (in the laser ray direction) to be removed from the point cloud. This would result in a void region that might resemble a 3D shadow behind a concentrated attack trace. However, the resolution of LiDAR varies with distance. Ground reflections and objects nearer to the LiDAR have higher density of points. This density decreases as the distance from the sensor increases. Due to the limitations of the attacker's $\mathcal{A}$ capabilities, and the LiDAR's resolution (point density per distance), there exists an effective distance where the attacker would be unable to successfully spoof an object while mimicking a genuine shadow. This presents an opportunity to leverage 3D shadows to develop a robust detection mechanism.

To characterise the LiDAR resolution, we used a scene where the ego-vehicle is in an object-free environment and analysed the ground reflection measurements recorded. A 2 m × 2 m region of analysis was used to calculate the density of points as a measure of the LiDAR's resolution. We used the objects manually labeled in the KITTI dataset of 7481 scenes, categorised the objects by type, counted the number of points in the object's bounding box and binned them by distance from the ego-vehicle. Table 2 shows the results of the analysis of average point-cloud density with respect to distance for both ground reflection measurements in clean environment and point measurements in the respective object's bounding box for the whole KITTI dataset. The LiDAR's ground reflection resolution (Row 1 of Table 2) decreases sharply as the distance increases. At a distance of 15 m–20 m, the density is about 200 points in a 2 m × 2 m region (which corresponds to a horizontal angle of $\leq 10°$ at that distance). To have 200 points in their bounding box, Cars would need to be at a distance of 20–25, whilst Pedestrians and Cyclists would need to be at a distance of 10–15. Thus, the analysis shows that at a distance of 10 m and higher, the resolution of the LiDAR (KITTI data were captured using a Velodyne HDL-64E LiDAR) is insufficient compared to the attacker's capability and the attacker is able to spoof objects with a corresponding shadow region that would be indistinguishable from a real shadow. Therefore, the effective distance of Shadow-Catcher is determined to be 10 m which is sufficient to detect the strongest adversary known to date, who tries to spoof a front-near obstacle to cause an unsafe reaction by the AV. Undoubtedly, both LiDAR and adversarial capabilities will evolve. The use of higher-end LiDARs with more laser channels might introduce more attack opportunities, however, the attacker's current capabilities to inject points reliably is limited by hardware. Moreover, higher-end lasers also mean a higher resolution (i.e. a denser point-cloud), which would require the adversary to reliably inject significantly more points to spoof an object that exhibits a realistic shadow. If the adversary's capability matches the LiDAR point density, no defense would be viable.

Table 2. Distance vs Avg. point density in object's bounding box and clean environment

	Distance from LiDAR (m)/Avg. points								
	0–5	5–10	10–15	15–20	20–25	25–30	35–40	40–45	45–50
Env (2 m × 2 m)	1295	859	288	196	103	73	42	28	10
Car (BBox)	4858	2040	865	405	208	117	73	51	36
Ped (BBox)	1187	455	207	99	62	42	27	29	16
Cycl (BBox)	1718	651	263	125	78	53	37	17	12

Conclusion. We characterised the LiDAR (Velodyne HDL-64E) scan resolution of ground reflection and objects for the KITTI dataset. The result was used to determine the effective distance which was found to be 10 m (conservative), where $\mathcal{A}$ would not be able to reconstruct a legitimate looking object that subverts a shadow detection mechanism. This distance can be further increased with higher resolution LiDARs such as the Velodyne VLS-128.

5   Shadow-Catcher Design

High Level Architecture. Shadow-Catcher's overall architecture and decision workflow is summarized in Fig. 3. Shadow-Catcher is agnostic to the sensor spoofing methodology and the victim model. It takes as input, the output of a 3D object detector (bounding boxes of detected objects in 3D scene's point cloud) and the original point cloud of the scene, and performs a three-phase analysis to determine whether the detected objects are genuine or ghosts. Shadow-Catcher can further distinguish between ghost objects and genuine objects whose shadow regions are being poisoned. In Phase 1, it employs a *shadow region proposal* algorithm which uses geometrical optics (or ray optics) to generate proposed shadow regions for each of the 3D objects detected by the 3D object detector. By tracing rays from the reference point of the LiDAR unit, Shadow-Catcher can determine the boundaries of shadow regions for 3D objects. However, the shadow region can be imprecise and can include 3D point artifacts which in principle should not be present. To deal with these imprecisions, in Phase-2, Shadow-Catcher's *genuine shadow verification* component, performs a point-wise analysis in each shadow region to determine whether the region is indicative of a genuine shadow. For this, it uses a novel 3D-point scoring mechanism. If the genuine shadow verification fails, which would mean the system is under attack, Shadow-Catcher uses an *adversarial shadow classification* model to determine whether the shadow region is indicative of a ghost object's shadow (thereby detecting a ghost attack) or a genuine object's shadow (thereby detecting an invalidation attack). Below we elaborate on Shadow-Catcher's three main components: (a) shadow region proposal; (b) genuine shadow verification; and (c) adversarial shadow classification.

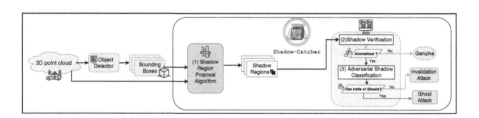

Fig. 3. 3D scene perception pipeline with Shadow-Catcher integrated.

2D Shadow Region Proposal. Intuitively, if a scene is converted into its 2D representation, then, using ray optics, we can obtain an area (2D shadow region) behind an object that rays cannot reach since they would have already reflected off the incident surface of the object. To compute the shadow region, we first convert a 3D scene into its 2D birds-eye view (BEV) compact representation. Next, we compute the boundary lines of the shadow region. We first take the coordinates of the bounding box for the detected object from the 3D object detector. Using the coordinates of the corners of the bounding box, we compute the gradients of the lines from the reference point (position of the LiDAR unit) to each of the corners. Let (x_i, y_i), $\forall i = 1, \ldots, 4$, be the 4 anchoring corners of a 3D bounding box on the ground. The gradients (m_i) of lines connecting the reference point (0,0) to corner coordinates are computed with $m_i = \frac{y_i - 0}{x_i - 0}$. The minimum and maximum gradient lines define the *shadow boundary lines* for the shadow region. To simulate the fact that LiDAR has a finite range we define a maximum *shadow length* (l). The shadow length (l) can be derived from the height of the object (h), with respect to the height of the LiDAR unit (H) and the furthest distance of the object from LiDAR unit (d_{obj}). Using similar triangles, the shadow length (l) can be derived as $l = d_{obj} \times \frac{h}{H-h}$. The shadow boundary lines and the shadow length determine the full shadow region of the object.

In principle, shadow regions should be completely void of points. Hence, it would suffice to project all the points onto the 2D ground plane before examining the 2D shadow regions. However, 2D shadow regions can only define a 2D area behind the object, which corresponds to the projection of the shadow on the ground. This can result in noisy points contaminating the shadow regions in lieu of taller objects behind the target 3D object.

3D Shadow Region Proposal. To address the aforementioned limitation of 2D shadow regions we introduce the 3D shadow region estimation. With 3D shadow regions, we examine a volume of space for the presence of points. The base area of the 3D shadow region is the 2D region obtained using the 2D shadow region proposal algorithm. To account for the height of the shadow region, we explore two approaches: (a) simulate LiDAR light rays as in 2D shadow region estimation, but this time analyze the points in the region of space bounded from the ground to the non-occluded incident rays; and (b) use of a uniform height above the ground level to obtain a short volume of space for analysis of points (Illustrations on our website [2]). The choice of 3D shadow region estimation method and their effects on detection performance are evaluated in Sect. 6.

Genuine Shadow Verification. After the shadow regions are identified, Shadow-Catcher performs an analysis inside each region to determine whether the shadow is genuine or not. As mentioned previously, in principle there should be no measurements inside shadow regions, as light rays cannot reach there. However, inaccuracies of the shadow estimation, and noisy artifacts due to physical effects, the placement and shape of objects can result in points being recorded inside genuine shadow regions. Thus, a trivial approach which expects those regions to be completely empty would be frequently flagging real objects as ghosts, resulting in high error rates.

To mitigate this, we propose a method which reduces the significance of noisy measurements inside shadow regions and assigns the shadow region an anomaly score. Our genuine shadow verification method classifies a shadow as genuine if its anomaly score is below a threshold. It first assigns a weight to each point inside the shadow region. Intuitively, points due to noise are assigned a lower weight, but points found in non expected regions (i.e. along the center-line or close to the start-line) are assigned higher weights. Specifically, we use two exponential decay equations (Eq. (1) and (2)) on two axis of analysis to assign weights to the points, where x_{start}, x_{end}, x_{mid} and x_{bound} are the distances of the point from the start-line, end-line, center-line and closest boundary line of the shadow region and α is a parameter that tunes the rate of exponential decay. The aggregate anomaly score of the shadow region is computed using Eq. (4), where w_{min} is the minimum weight a point can obtain in any axis of analysis (i.e. point at boundary line) and T is the total number of points in shadow.

$$w_{start} = \exp\left(\frac{\ln(0.5)}{\alpha} \times \frac{x_{start}}{(x_{start} + x_{end})}\right) \tag{1}$$

$$w_{mid} = \exp\left(\frac{\ln(0.5)}{\alpha} \times \frac{x_{mid}}{(x_{mid} + x_{bound})}\right) \tag{2}$$

$$w_{min} = \exp\left(\frac{\ln(0.5)}{\alpha}\right) \tag{3}$$

$$score = \frac{\sum_{i=1}^{T}(w_{start,i} \times w_{mid,i}) - (T \times w_{min}^2)}{T \times (1 - w_{min}^2)} \tag{4}$$

The anomaly score threshold is set empirically. An extensive analysis was performed and the Receiver Operating Characteristic (ROC) curve was used to determine the threshold that produces an acceptable True Positive and False Positive Rate (see Sect. 6). An object is verified as genuine by Shadow-Catcher if its shadow region gets a lower score than the anomaly threshold, otherwise the shadow is flagged as anomalous. At this point Shadow-Catcher can already detect that the system is under a LiDAR poisoning attack. However, we take this a step further and also try to determine the type of attack against the system.

Adversarial Shadow Classification. A high shadow anomaly score indicates either a ghost attack or an object invalidation attack. Shadow-Catcher distinguishes between the two. We observe that during ghost attacks, the shadow regions of ghost objects exhibit a high density of points while points are sparse in the shadow regions of true objects during invalidation attacks. Therefore, we expect the distribution of points within the shadow regions of ghost vs invalidated objects to be distinguishable. Leveraging these observations we use clustering to extract density features from shadow regions, which we then use to train a binary adversarial shadow classifier. Shadow-Catcher uses this classifier to determine whether an anomalous shadow is the result of a ghost attack or an invalidation attack.

Feature Extraction. To characterize the density of the measurements in a shadow region, we cluster points that are in spatial proximity. We use "Density-Based Spatial Clustering of Applications with Noise" (DBSCAN) [7] for this purpose as it is able to identify points that are clustered in arbitrary shapes and does not require to pre-specify the number of clusters. This suits our use-case well, as point clusters in 3D point clouds are irregular and the number of clusters in a region is not known a priori.

Clustering points in shadow regions with DBSCAN, allows us to extract the number of clusters found by controlling the density of clusters. Intuitively we would expect the shadow regions of ghost objects to exhibit multiple clusters with regular and similar shapes. On the other hand, during an object invalidation attack, we would expect the shadow region to be mainly void with points injected by the attacker eliciting a high aggregated score near the region of high weighting as modeled by the exponential decay equations in the axis of analysis. Thus, a distinguishable characteristic of shadows for an invalidation attack would be a small number of or no clusters detected (Example in [2]). From DBSCAN, we then derive the following features to characterize the shadows of objects: (a) *number of clusters* in the shadow region obtained from DBSCAN; (b) *average density of points in clusters* obtained by taking the total number of points in clusters and averaging out by the number of clusters.

Attack Classification Model. The shadow characteristic features are then used as input to a binary classification model to distinguish between shadows of ghost objects and shadows of genuine objects under an invalidation attack. Note that the attacker can elicit a high anomaly score by opportunistically injecting a single point at the shadow location of highest weighting. Whilst this triggers the anomaly detection, it fails to elicit a ghost attack classification. To defeat the mechanism, an attacker would have to effectively emulate shadows representative of ghost attack shadows, which requires both injecting points at regions of high weighting and creating multiple clusters with sufficient density of points (i.e. to emulate the shadow features of ghost shadows). We define the *object invalidation attack* in the following sub-section.

Object Invalidation Attack. Shadow-Catcher's use of shadows, can incentivize a new class of object invalidation attacks targeting genuine objects' shadows. We formulate this as an evasion attack (test-time) on the adversarial shadow classification model. We consider a strong adversary who has state-of-the-art LiDAR spoofing capabilities and knowledge of the classifier's decision boundary and feature representation (i.e. shadow characteristics features). Their goal is to introduce points in the shadow region of a genuine object to change the shadow's characteristics and cause the classification model to misclassify a genuine shadow as a ghost object shadow, effectively invalidating the real object.

We can evaluate the robustness of the classification according to the capability of the adversary. In our case, we define the attacker's capability as the total number of points that can be injected in a target shadow region in a single point cloud scene. We refer to this as the adversary's "point budget". We then define the invalidation adversary's budget $B_{\mathcal{A}}$ as:

$$n_0 + n_p = N_c \times \rho_c, \quad \text{s.t.} \ n_p \leq B_{\mathcal{A}} \tag{5}$$

where n_0 is the original number of points in the shadow region, n_p is the number of injected malicious points, N_c is the number of clusters after injection, and ρ_c is the average cluster density after injection.

Intuitively, the invalidation adversary's optimal strategy against Shadow-Catcher can be defined as follows: Given a set of features for a genuine shadow, inject the minimum number of points, n_p, to deceive the classifier by modifying the combination of cluster density and number of clusters, subjected to a point budget B_A and the configuration parameters of DBSCAN used by Shadow-Catcher. This optimal attack strategy can be formalized as:

$$\min n_p, \quad \text{s.t. } \exists\, N_c \in \mathcal{Z}^+ \mid F((n_0 + n_p)/N_c, N_c) = 1 \tag{6}$$

where $F(\cdot, \cdot)$ is the output of the classifier, which is one if an attack is identified as a ghost and zero otherwise. As the complexity of the optimization problem in Eq. (6) is reduced, $n_p \in \mathcal{Z}^+$ is a scalar and the classifier has only 2 features, the problem can be solved using simple techniques such as the bisection method. We evaluate the robustness of Shadow-Catcher to such an adversary in Sect. 6.

6   Evaluation

We evaluate Shadow-Catcher's effectiveness and efficiency in detecting ghost and invalidation attacks. We also evaluate its accuracy in estimating shadow regions, but due to space limitations we present that analysis in Appendix B.

Ghost Object Injection for Shadow-Catcher Evaluation. Shadow-Catcher is agnostic to the adversarial strategy and is applied on the output of 3D object detectors. Therefore, it suffices to evaluate its response on the products of object spoofing attacks: bounding boxes of detected spoofed objects and resulting point cloud. Our attacks follow $\mathcal{A}$'s capabilities and generate large (cars) and small (pedestrians, cyclists) spoofed objects in front-near locations of 5–8 in-front of the victim vehicle. To create a ghost object of a particular type (e.g. pedestrian), we first extract the point clouds of genuine objects from real-world point clouds (from KITTI [10]) and prune them to $\mathcal{A}$'s capabilities, the maximum physical capabilities demonstrated in the related work (200 points within a spoofing angle of 10°). The resulting attack trace is then added into the target scene's point cloud. We then remove any points behind the attack trace (to obey the LiDAR single return signal measurement mode) effectively recreating the result of a real-world spoofing attack. For each object type, its attack trace is injected in 200 random scenes from the KITTI dataset, resulting in an *Adversarial Dataset* containing a total of 600 scenes (200 scenes × 3 objects injected).

Anomalous Shadow Detection. We used the Adversarial Dataset to evaluate Shadow-Catcher's ability to correctly detect ghost objects' shadows as anomalous and real objects' shadows as non-anomalous. Ground truth labels of scenes together with ghost object label were used for the bounding box generation. We evaluated Shadow-Catcher's scoring method using 2D shadow Regions (BEV) and 3D Shadow Regions (Ray Height and Uniform Height with different height values ranging from 0.1 m to 0.6 m above ground level). Our main results are summarized in Fig. 4. A more detailed report on our evaluation is presented in [2] due to space limitations.

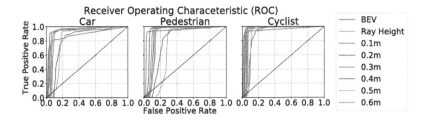

Fig. 4. ROC curves for detection of injected objects.

2D vs 3D Shadow Regions. We found that 3D shadow regions with uniform height above the ground level outperform the other shadow regions of interest. Noisy points (stray reflections or overhanging objects such as tree branches and sign posts) are reduced when we only consider a small volume above ground which only captures the LiDAR scan reflections off the ground when there are no objects. This results in a more accurate scoring of the shadow region to detect anomalous shadows that have points in sub-regions of high weighting.

Height Sensitivity Analysis and Anomaly Detection Threshold. For shadow regions with uniform height above ground, we performed a sensitivity analysis to find the optimal height for detecting ghost objects. The height that yields the best AUC-ROC is 0.2 m above the ground with a score of 0.94, 0.95 and 0.96 for detection of injected Car, Pedestrian and Cyclist respectively. Shadow regions with uniform height of 0.2 m also result in the maximum F1 Score and Accuracy for the detection of injected objects. Finally, we parametarized the detection threshold and found that an anomaly score threshold of 0.2 provide the best trade-off of TPR vs FPR for all injected objects.

Utility. Overall, we found that 3D shadows, with a uniform height of 0.2m above the ground and an anomaly score threshold of 0.2 provide the best overall trade-off of TPR vs FPR for all injected objects. In particular, with the above configuration, we obtain an overall accuracy of 0.94, TPR of 0.94 and FPR of 0.069 for anomalous shadow regions due to Ghost Attacks. This is comparable to CARLO's performance [24], which reports a reduced attack success rate of 5.5% for Car objects. CARLO was not evaluated on smaller objects [24], however our experiments suggest that it will severely underperform(see Appendix A).

We also took a closer look into the sources of errors (illustration of examples in [2]). False negatives (ghost objects not detected by Shadow-Catcher) in the dataset can typically be attributed to injected objects being implanted in regions that are already void of points due to incomplete LiDAR measurements. Note that this is due to the LiDAR's failure to take measurements of the ground level. As LiDAR technology gets better, our approach's accuracy will also improve. False positives (real objects flagged as potential ghosts by Shadow-Catcher) are due to their shadows having points from other larger objects behind them. Although, this may (very rarely) happen, the safety repercussions are less important as the second object (right behind the first) will be correctly validated.

Attack Classification. Next, we evaluate Shadow-Catcher's ability to distinguish between ghost attacks and object invalidation attacks. We first show how the features extracted from shadow regions by Shadow-Catcher's differ between shadows of ghost and genuine objects, and that they can be used to train an effective binary classifier. Then we evaluate Shadow-Catcher's classification robustness against a novel, strong invalidation adversary with LiDAR spoofing capabilities and full knowledge of the classification method aiming to misclassify a genuine shadow as a ghost shadow.

Feature Characteristics of Shadows. We used genuine object shadows for comparison with ghost object shadows for two reasons. (a) Shadow-Catcher's anomaly detection might (but very rarely) incorrectly mark a genuine object's shadow as anomalous. Being able to distinguish between the two, acts as a second line of validation which can correct Shadow-Catcher's mistake in the previous phase. This can lead to better utility. (b) An invalidation attack adversary targets genuine object shadows. Thus the distinction between genuine and ghost shadows can serve as a baseline for detecting against invalidation attacks (in the next subsection we use this baseline to design a strong invalidation adversary).

We use the Adversarial Dataset for evaluation. Shadow-Catcher was used to generate object shadows of uniform height (0.2 m) and then we compute the *number of 3D point clusters* in each shadow region and *density of the clusters* using DBSCAN ($\epsilon = 0.2$, min_pts $= 6$). The shadows are labeled (ghost vs genuine) and split into a training set and a test set (80:20) to train six different binary classifiers and evaluate their performance on the test set. As we are most concerned with the TPR and FPR of classifiers for best utility, we use AUC-ROC as the decision criteria to choose the model.

We found that the prevalence rate of feature combination of 0 clusters and 0 cluster density for genuine shadows is 86.2% (1899/2202) and for ghost shadows is 4.4% (24/543). We further observe that 91.7% (2020/2202) of the genuine object shadows have <5 clusters and 95.4% (2101/2202) have <10 clusters. Of those genuine shadows with clusters, 91.6% (2019/2202) have average clusters density of <10 points and 98.6% (2172/2202) have average cluster densities of <20 points. These genuine shadow regions are opportunities for an adversary to perform an invalidation attack. A least effort adversary will target shadows which will likely be incorrectly marked as anomalous or force triggering anomaly detection with a single 3D point injected in sub-regions of high importance.

We trained six classifiers and compare their performance (Table 3). We chose these classifiers as they tend to do well for low dimensionality data. We found that a SVM Model with polynomial degree $= 2$ provided the best AUC-ROC performance in distinguishing between ghost and genuine shadows.

Table 3. Performance metrics for shadow classifiers

	Accuracy	F1-Score	AUC-ROC
Logistic regression	0.962	0.909	0.953
Random forest	0.969	0.921	0.938
SVM- linear	0.960	0.906	0.978
SVM-poly (deg = 2)	0.965	0.918	**0.981**
SVM-poly (deg = 3)	0.967	0.923	0.971
SVM-RBF	0.974	0.938	0.967

Robustness Against Evasion Attacks on Shadow Classification Model. We further evaluate the robustness of the adversarial shadow classifier against the invalidation adversary defined in Sect. 5, setting the DBSCAN parameters as before ($\epsilon = 0.2$, min_pts = 6). To visualize the maximum cluster-density combination the attacker can introduce given a budget $B_{\mathcal{A}}$ (Eq. 5), we use the *Maximum Operating Curve* (MOC), which shows the set of valid (ρ_c, N_c) combinations on the feature space that can be reached for a given $B_{\mathcal{A}}$ (we use 20, 40, 60, 100 and 200 points). In our previous experiments we found that 86.2% of the genuine shadows have cluster-density combination on the feature space of value 0 for both N_c and $\rho_c = (n_0 + n_p)/N_c$. Thus, for solving the problem in Eq. (6), we start exploring this cluster-density combination on the feature space.

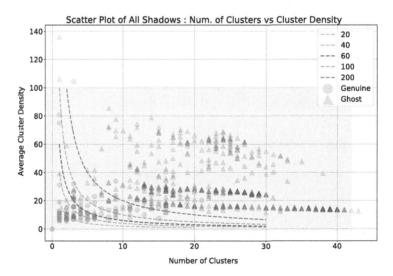

Fig. 5. Scatter plot of shadow features and decision regions from SVM Classifier with a polynomial kernel with degree = 2. Dashed lines are operating curve of adversary according to their budget from (0,0).

This is a very strong adversary because we assume that: (a) the adversary can predict the optimal cluster-density combinations; (b) the adversary can identify where the 3D points should be introduced in the environment to achieve that combination; (c) it is feasible to introduce those measurements.

Figure 5 shows all shadow features and the decision regions from the boundary of the non-linear SVM classifier (poly deg = 2). A point in the red region is the feature combination where the classifier model will label the shadow as a ghost attack and blue region an invalidation attack. The dashed curves represent MOCs[1] for different budgets from the origin (0,0), which is the predominant feature combination (86.2%) for all genuine shadows in our dataset. We observe that for MOCs of up to 200 points, the curves lie within the decision region for non-ghost shadows. Thus, an attacker needs to inject 200 or more points to evade the non-linear SVM model which shows that our model is robust against an adversary that can reliably spoof up to 200 points. With technological improvements, adversarial capabilities can potentially improve beyond 200 points, but there are also ample opportunities to improve Shadow-Catcher accordingly. When higher resolution LiDARs are used, Shadow-Catcher robustness improves, as long as adversarial spoofing capabilities do not match the LiDARs' resolution.

Runtime Efficiency. To evaluate Shadow-Catcher's runtime efficiency, we use the same Adversarial Dataset. We measure Shadow-Catcher's end-to-end analysis time for each identified object (genuine and ghost), starting from the time Shadow-Catcher receives the 3D objects bounding box coordinates until Shadow-Catcher labels the object. We also measure the execution time for each component of Shadow-Catcher. Shadow-Catcher is configured to use 3D shadow generation with a uniform height of 0.2 m above ground, an anomaly score threshold of 0.2, DBSCAN for feature extraction with $\epsilon = 0.2$, min_pts = 6, and our pre-trained SVM binary classifier with a polynomial kernel of degree = 2. Shadow-Catcher's prototype implementation is written in Python with 1200 lines of code. We measure the execution time on a machine equipped with an Intel Core i7 Six Core Processor i7-7800X (3.5 GHz) and 32 GB RAM.

Table 4. Shadow-Catcher's object processing times (in ms)

	Shadow generation	Shadow scoring	Shadow verification	Total time
Car	0.4 ± 0.3	4 ± 10	N.A.	4.4 ± 10.3
Pedestrian	0.3 ± 0.1	6 ± 8	N.A.	6.4 ± 8.1
Cyclist	0.3 ± 0.1	3 ± 4	N.A.	3.3 ± 4.1
Car (ghost)	0.4 0.1	10 ± 6	10.06 ± 20.05	20.46 ± 26.15
Ped. (ghost)	0.3 0.1	7 ± 5	10.06 ± 17.05	17.36 ± 22.15
Cyc. (ghost)	0.3 ± 0.1	7 ± 6	12.06 ± 24.05	19.36 ± 24.15

---

[1] The MOC contains discrete values, given the set of valid combinations (ρ_c, N_c). For illustration purposes, we plot the MOC as a continuous contour.

Table 4 summarizes our results. On average, Shadow-Catcher processes objects in a scene in 0.003 s–0.021 s. This is only a small fraction of the time a 3D object detector takes to analyze a scene—Point-GNN has an average inference time of 0.6 s [9]. Genuine objects are processed much faster than adversarial objects, which is important as this corresponds to most frequently encountered cases. The longer duration taken to process adversarial object shadows is mainly due to the feature extraction step, which is triggered when a shadow is deemed anomalous by the shadow scoring mechanism, requiring 10.7 ms on average. The variation observed in the total execution time, comes from the different object sizes and the different point densities in their shadows. Notably, Shadow-Catcher can process a spoofed car in 46.6 ms (worst case), which compared to prior work (100 ms on average) [24] constitutes at least a 2.17x speedup. Moreover, Shadow-Catcher's is implemented in Python and thus, can be readily improved even further if more efficient languages are used (e.g. C).

7 Conclusion

In this work we introduced 3D shadows, a new semantically meaningful physical invariant for verifying the presence of objects in a 3D scene. Then we introduced a set of new techniques embodied in an end-to-end system (Shadow-Catcher) which leverage shadows to tackle spoofing attacks against 3D object detectors. Our evaluation shows that Shadow-Catcher achieves 94% and 96% average accuracy in identifying anomalous shadows and classifying them as either ghost or invalidation attacks. We further design a strong, novel invalidation adversary aiming to evade classification and found that Shadow-Catcher remains robust up to 200 points. Shadow-Catcher can analyze objects in real time (0.003 s–0.021 s on average, a 2.17x speedup compared to the state of the art).

Appendices

A   Limitation of Prior Art

Recently, Sun et al. proposed CARLO [24], a system for detecting model-level LiDAR spoofing attacks. CARLO consists of two components. The first, Laser Penetration Detection (LPD), serves as a quick anomaly detector to filter fake and valid objects. Objects for which LPD is not confident in its decision are sent for further analysis to a second component, the Free Space Detection (FSD), which is computationally more expensive. LPD's design intuition is that points in the frustum correlate with occlusion patterns, and hence, uses the ratio of the number of points behind the object's bounding box over the total the number of points in the frustum of an object; objects with high ratio are classified as suspicious or definitely fake. This approach uses points in the bounding box (as part of the frustum), and for smaller objects, the ratio is small and heavily influenced by noisy LiDAR measurements. Moreover, the approach does not take into account the location and characteristics of points in the region behind the bounding box, and could be susceptible to false positives from noise artifacts. FSD's detection is based on the intuition that genuine vehicles have high density of points and hence, low free space in the bounding boxes as most of the space in the bounding box should be occluded by points in front. However, for smaller objects, this approach might be ineffective as the original space in the bounding box is small and mostly occupied by the points. Hence there are limited regions for analysis of free space. We implemented CARLO and evaluated its effectiveness to distinguish genuine from spoofed pedestrian objects.

LPD Evaluated on Pedestrians. To evaluate the LPD ratios of genuine and spoofed pedestrians, we collected the LPD ratios of genuine pedestrian objects in the KITTI dataset as well 200 spoofed front-near pedestrians (6 m in front of ego-vehicle). Figure 6 shows the distribution of LPD ratios of genuine and spoofed pedestrians. We observe that there is an overlap of the two distributions from 0.5 to 0.8, which presents opportunities for attackers to invoke FSD. Additionally, as the LPD ratio's denominator accounts for all the points in the frustum, and for small objects the number of points in frustum is small, there is a possibility of an attacker to inject points (within the total adversary $\mathcal{A}$ budget) in the frustum to lower the ratio to trigger FSD.

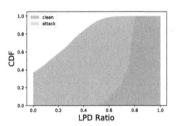

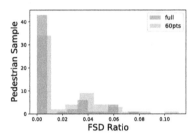

Fig. 6. LPD ratio distribution of genuine and spoofed pedestrian objects. Genuine object's *3D Shadow*

Fig. 7. FSD ratio distribution of pedestrian objects with full and down-sampled point cloud.

FSD Evaluated on Pedestrians. We randomly sampled 60 genuine pedestrian objects from KITTI and injected their point cloud 6 m in front of the ego-vehicle to spoof a front-near obstacle. Using the same 60 pedestrian objects, these objects' point clouds were also down-sampled to the size of 60 points (below adversary $\mathcal{A}$'s budegt of 200 points) and were similarly injected (Point-GNN detected all down-sampled traces as pedestrians). We then used the implementation of Free Space Detection (FSD) in CARLO to evaluate the FSD ratio of spoofed objects with the full-sized and down-sampled point clouds. Figure 7 shows that the distribution of FSD ratio overlaps for pedestrians objects of full and down-sampled point clouds, with the majority of them having an FSD ratio of 0. This shows that the approach of FSD will not result in a separable distribution to effectively distinguish small spoofed pedestrians from genuine pedestrians. FSD expects ghost objects to result in very high FSD ratios which as we showed does not happen for small objects.

B   2D Shadow Region Estimation

We analyze Shadow-Catcher's accuracy of 2D shadow region generation by comparing it with the 597 manually labeled shadows (see Sect. 4). We evaluate the 2D region generation separately since 3D regions build on top of it. The significance of 2D vs 3D region estimations in the detection performance is evaluated separately in Subsect. 6. To quantify how closely Shadow-Catcher can match the objects' observed shadows, we measure their Intersection over the Union (IoU) and perform a Procrustes shape analysis. An IoU value of 1 means that the two regions are perfectly matched and 0 means the two regions are disjoint. Procrustes provides us with two metrics: (a) similarity of the shapes; and (b) scale differences of the shapes [1,12,19]. For similarity, values close to 1 mean that the shapes are identical. For scale, a value of 1 means that the size of the shapes are identical and anything less than 1 means the ground-truth shadow shape is smaller, and larger than 1 is the opposite.

Table 5. Aggregated correspondence metrics of all objects

	IoU	Similarity	Scale
Mean	0.728	0.713	1.286
Median	0.760	0.969	0.970
Standard deviation	0.152	0.376	2.08

Table 5 summarizes our results across all object types. Detailed results are deferred to the project website [2]. From the median values of the corresponding metrics, it can be observed that, for more than half the objects, the computed shadow matches closely with the ground-truth shadow—IoU, Similarity and Scale values are well above 0.5 which indicates a good prediction (object detection bounding box accuracy is commonly evaluated at IoU $\geq$ 0.5 [8,18]). We do observe some variation in the results which can be attributed to measurement inaccuracies and human-errors in the labeling process, and to overestimation of shadow areas (Illustration provided on the project's website [2]). Shadow-Catcher uses bounding boxes which are larger than the actual objects and this results in larger shadow regions. However, Shadow-Catcher's exponential decay approach to weighting the significance of 3D points in shadows (see Sect. 5) compensates for this. This is verified with Shadow-Catcher's overall accuracy in detecting genuine shadows, ghost and invalidation attacks (see Sect. 6).

References

1. Procrustes analysis. https://www.mathworks.com/help/stats/procrustes.html
2. Shadow-catcher project website. https://sites.google.com/view/shadow-catcher
3. Google spin-off waymo to sell lidar it fought uber on. https://www.bbc.co.uk/news/47482028, March 2019
4. Cao, Y., et al.: Adversarial sensor attack on lidar-based perception in autonomous driving. In: Proceedings of the 2019 ACM SIGSAC Conference on Computer and Communications Security, pp. 2267–2281 (2019)
5. Coldewey, D.: Here's how Uber's self-driving cars are supposed to detect pedestrians. https://techcrunch.com/2018/03/19/heres-how-ubers-self-driving-cars-are-supposed-to-detect-pedestrians/, March 2018
6. Dutta, A., Zisserman, A.: The VIA annotation software for images, audio and video. In: Proceedings of the 27th ACM International Conference on Multimedia, MM 2019, New York, NY, USA. ACM (2019)
7. Ester, M., Kriegel, H.-P., Sander, J., Xiaowei, X., et al.: A density-based algorithm for discovering clusters in large spatial databases with noise. In KDD **96**, 226–231 (1996)
8. Everingham, M., Van Gool, L., KI Williams, C., Winn, J., Zisserman, A.: The pascal visual object classes (VOC) challenge. Int. J. Comput. Vis. **88**(2), 303–338 (2010)
9. Geiger, A.: Object detection evaluation. http://www.cvlibs.net/datasets/kitti/eval_object.php
10. Geiger, A., Lenz, P., Stiller, C., Urtasun, R.: Vision meets robotics: The KITTI dataset. Int. J. Robot. Res. (IJRR) **32**, 1231–1237 (2013)
11. Gips, M.: The future of lidar and security. https://www.securitymagazine.com/articles/91907-the-future-of-lidar-and-security, March 2020
12. Gower, J.C.: Generalized procrustes analysis. Psychometrika **40**(1), 33–51 (1975)
13. Ivanov, R., Pajic, M., Lee, I.: Attack-resilient sensor fusion. In: 2014 Design, Automation & Test in Europe Conference & Exhibition (DATE), pp. 1–6. IEEE (2014)
14. Liu, D., Yu, R., Su, H.: Extending adversarial attacks and defenses to deep 3D point cloud classifiers. In: 2019 IEEE International Conference on Image Processing (ICIP), pp. 2279–2283 (2019)
15. Petit, J., Stottelaar, B., Feiri, M., Kargl, F.: Remote attacks on automated vehicles sensors: experiments on camera and lidar. Black Hat Europe **11**, 2015 (2015)
16. Porter, J.: Go read this analysis of what the iPad Pro's LiDAR sensor is capable of. https://www.theverge.com/2020/4/16/21223626/ipad-pro-halide-camera-lidar-sensor-augmented-reality-scanning, April 2020
17. Qi, C.R., Yi, L., Su, H., Guibas, L.J.: PointNet++: deep hierarchical feature learning on point sets in a metric space. In: Advances in Neural Information Processing Systems, pp. 5099–5108 (2017)
18. Redmon, J., Divvala, S., Girshick, R., Farhadi, A.: You only look once: unified, real-time object detection. In: Proceedings of the IEEE Conference on Computer Vision and Pattern Recognition, pp. 779–788 (2016)
19. Ross, A.: Procrustes analysis. Course report, Department of Computer Science and Engineering, University of South Carolina, 26 (2004)
20. Shi, S., et al.: PV-RCNN: point-voxel feature set abstraction for 3D object detection. In: CVPR (2020)

21. Shi, W., Rajkumar, R.: Point-GNN: graph neural network for 3D object detection in a point cloud. ArXiv, abs/2003.01251 (2020)
22. Shin, H., Kim, D., Kwon, Y., Kim, Y.: Illusion and dazzle: adversarial optical channel exploits against lidars for automotive applications. In: Fischer, W., Homma, N. (eds.) CHES 2017. LNCS, vol. 10529, pp. 445–467. Springer, Cham (2017). https://doi.org/10.1007/978-3-319-66787-4_22
23. RT Staff: What is lidar and how does it help robots see? https://www.roboticsbusinessreview.com/rbr/what_is_lidar_and_how_does_it_help_robots_see/, October 2019
24. Sun, J., Cao, Y., Chen, Q.A., Mao, Z.M.: Towards robust lidar-based perception in autonomous driving: general black-box adversarial sensor attack and countermeasures. In: 29th USENIX Security Symposium (USENIX Security 20), pp. 877–894. USENIX Association, August 2020
25. Wakabayashi, D.: Self-driving Uber car kills pedestrian in Arizona, where robots roam. https://www.nytimes.com/2018/03/19/technology/uber-driverless-fatality.html, March 2018
26. Wen, Y., Lin, J., Chen, K., Jia, K.: Geometry-aware generation of adversarial and cooperative point clouds. arXiv preprint arXiv:1912.11171 (2019)
27. Wicker, M., Kwiatkowska, M.: Robustness of 3D deep learning in an adversarial setting. In: Proceedings of the IEEE Conference on Computer Vision and Pattern Recognition, pp. 11767–11775 (2019)
28. Xiang, C., Qi, C.R., Li, B.: Generating 3D adversarial point clouds. In: Proceedings of the IEEE Conference on Computer Vision and Pattern Recognition, pp. 9136–9144 (2019)
29. Yang, B., Luo, W., Urtasun, R.: PIXOR: real-time 3D object detection from point clouds. CoRR, abs/1902.06326 (2019)
30. Yang, J., Zhang, Q., Fang, R., Ni, B., Liu, J., Tian, Q.: Adversarial attack and defense on point sets. arXiv preprint arXiv:1902.10899 (2019)
31. Yang, K., Rui Wang, Yu., Jiang, H.S., Luo, C., Guan, Y., Li, X., Shi, Z.: Sensor attack detection using history based pairwise inconsistency. Futur. Gener. Comput. Syst. **86**, 392–402 (2018)
32. Zeng, X., et al.: Adversarial attacks beyond the image space. In: Proceedings of the IEEE Conference on Computer Vision and Pattern Recognition, pp. 4302–4311 (2019)
33. Zhou, H., Chen, K., Zhang, W., Fang, H., Zhou, W., Yu, N.: DUP-Net: denoiser and upsampler network for 3D adversarial point clouds defense. In: 2019 IEEE/CVF International Conference on Computer Vision (ICCV), pp. 1961–1970. IEEE (2019)

Anomaly Detection

AutoGuard: A Dual Intelligence Proactive Anomaly Detection at Application-Layer in 5G Networks

Taous Madi[1(✉)], Hyame Assem Alameddine[1(✉)], Makan Pourzandi[1],
Amine Boukhtouta[1], Moataz Shoukry[2], and Chadi Assi[2]

[1] Ericsson Security Research, Ericsson Canada, Montreal, QC, Canada
`{taous.madi,hyame.a.alameddine,makan.pourzandi,`
`amine.boukhtouta}@ericsson.com`
[2] Concordia University, CIISE, Montreal, QC, Canada
`moataz.shoukry@mail.concordia.ca, chadi.assi@concordia.ca`

Abstract. Application-layer protocols are widely adopted for signaling in telecommunication networks such as the 5G networks. However, they can be subject to application-layer attacks that are hardly detected by existing traditional network-based security tools that often do not support telecommunication-specific applications. To address this issue, we propose in this work AutoGuard, a proactive anomaly detection solution that employs application-layer Performance Measurement (PM) counters to train two different Deep Learning (DL) techniques, namely, Long Short Term Memory (LSTM) networks and AutoEncoders (AEs). We leverage recent advancements in Machine Learning (ML) that show the advantages brought by combining multiple ML models to build a dual-intelligence approach allowing the proactive detection of application layer anomalies. Our proposed dual-intelligence solution promotes signaling workload forecasting and anomaly prediction as a proactive security control in 5G networks. As a proof of concept, we implement our approach for the proactive detection of Diameter-related signaling attacks on the Home Subscriber Server (HSS) core network function. To evaluate our solution, we conduct a set of experiments using data collected from a real 5G testbed. Our results show the effectiveness of our dual intelligence approach on proactively detecting signaling anomalies with a precision reaching 0.86.

Keywords: Proactive anomaly detection · Forecasting · 5G networks · Diameter protocol · Deep Learning

1 Introduction

The Fifth Generation (5G) technology services that are massively pervading every area of our lives are possible due to a significant structural change in the mobile network. Nonetheless, to enable a short time to market of 5G networks, the third Generation Partnership Project (3GPP) proposed a Non-Standalone (NSA) deployment in which the 5G New Radio (NR) will be supported by the

© Springer Nature Switzerland AG 2021
E. Bertino et al. (Eds.): ESORICS 2021, LNCS 12972, pp. 715–735, 2021.
https://doi.org/10.1007/978-3-030-88418-5_34

Evolved Packet Core (EPC) of the 4G network as a first step towards a full StandAlone (SA) deployment of 5G. This phased adoption of 5G brings attention towards its security that is dependent on the security of its protocols [1]. In fact, the NSA 5G deployment adopts application-layer signaling protocols that are used in the 4G EPC such as the Diameter protocol, which is vulnerable to application-layer Denial of Service (DoS) attacks if the attacker gets access to the interconnect network [2]. Thus, securing 5G networks against signaling attacks is imperative.

Multiple works in the literature proposed reactive anomaly detection solutions using Machine Learning (ML) models that leverage network-layer information (e.g., flows, packets) in order to detect DoS attacks on their networks [3,4]. However, application-layer DoS attacks such as those signaling attacks exploiting vulnerabilities in the Diameter protocol are more difficult to be detected using only network-layer information. This is due to the fact that those attacks are based on legitimate application-layer requests which are indistinguishable from other legitimate ones at the network-layer [5,6]. Furthermore, due to the widespread use of encryption in the Internet in general, network appliance detection solutions (e.g., web application firewall, etc.) are not able to detect all application-layer attacks [7]. In addition, Diameter-based filtering techniques, which were suggested to minimize the risk of Diameter signaling attacks, can be easily bypassed by spoofing Diameter application-layer information such as the origin-host of the Mobile Network Operator (MNO) [2] as illustrated in the following example.

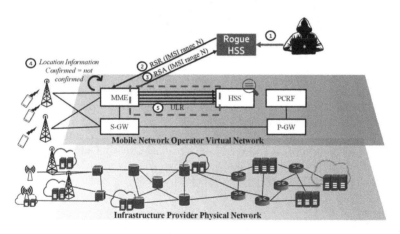

Fig. 1. Reset request diameter attack [2].

Motivating Example. *Figure 1 presents an example of application-layer DoS attacks [2,8]. More precisely, it depicts a Diameter-based signaling attack that causes a DoS on the Home Subscriber Server (HSS) by sending a spoofed ReSet Request (RSR) towards the Mobility Management Entity (MME). To perform this attack, we assume that an adversary managed to compromise a network function running on top of a virtualized environment [9,10] by exploiting a virtualization layer vulnerability (e.g., CVE-2019-5736 [11], see more vulnerabilities* *in [10]) to impersonate the victim HSS through spoofing (step ①). After retrieving the identity of the target MME, the attacker sends an RSR with a range of International Mobile Subscriber Identities (IMSIs) (step ②). Upon receipt, the MME responds with a ReSet Answer (RSA) (step ③) and sets the location information confirmed indicator of the subscribers with these identities as not confirmed (step ④). Due to the hop-by-hop routing vulnerability in Diameter protocol [2], the RSA message will be routed back to the Virtual Network Function (VNF) under control of the attacker instead of being routed to the legitimate HSS, which makes it impossible for the victim to detect the spoofing. At the next authentication radio of the subscribers whose IMSIs were specified in the hostile RSR message, the MME will send Update Location Requests (ULRs) to the legitimate HSS to update their locations (step ⑤). Given the high number of ULR messages, the HSS will potentially suffer from a DoS or an Economical Denial of Sustainability (EDoS) [8] affecting the operator's network availability and/or operational costs. The dashed red box in Fig. 1 highlights this attack.*

In the above example, the ULRs look like legitimate messages which will make them hardly detectable at the network-layer. However, an application-layer detection method can monitor the nature of exchanged messages and therefore dramatically increase the chances of detecting this type of attacks. In this work, we address the problem of application-layer DoS anomaly detection in NSA 5G network by leveraging application-layer information, mainly Performance Measurements (PM) counters that can be collected at the EPC network functions (e.g., HSS, MME, etc.). We believe our approach of using application-layer counters to detect application-layer attacks is deemed useful in today's and future networks where encryption is adopted (Fig. 1).

Furthermore, we depart from existing reactive anomaly detection solutions [3,4] that detect anomalies after their occurrence and propose AutoGuard, a proactive anomaly detection approach[1] to protect applications from attacks. AutoGuard predicts the upcoming system anomalies in the future before they happen based on the current application-layer information trend. It does this by 1) forecasting future signaling workload, then, 2) using the forecast signaling trend to predict future anomalies (i.e., possible attacks). To achieve this, we leverage recent advancements in ML and neural networks that show the advantages brought by combining multiple ML models (e.g., [12,13]). Thus, we build a novel dual-intelligence solution composed of a Long Short Term Memory (LSTM) responsible for forecasting future signaling trend by capturing patterns in both benign and anomalous data; along with an Autoencoder (AEs) aiming at profiling the normal signaling workload. Once trained using application-layer PM counters, both models interact together to predict future possible anomalies. More precisely, the AE tries to detect anomalies in the forecast signaling trends provided by the LSTM. This is particularly useful to predict the attacks, such as signaling storms, which show specific trends before they actually occur. Such a proactive anomaly detection solution enables appropriate prevention and mitigation measures before the actual occurrence of these anomalies.

---

[1] Throughout the paper, we use the expressions *anomaly prediction* and *proactive anomaly detection* interchangeably.

While there exist many research works investigating the 5G control plane-related threats [14–16], we believe that this is the first attempt of a dual-intelligence solution that promotes signaling workload forecasting and anomaly prediction as a proactive security control in 5G networks. The following summarizes the main contributions of this work:

- We propose AutoGuard, a data-driven application-layer proactive anomaly detection solution that predicts signaling anomalies before they happen or in their early stages in NSA 5G networks.
- We exploit the advantages of application-layer information, mainly PM counters in detecting application-layer DoS attacks exploiting vulnerabilities in signaling protocols.
- We propose a dual-intelligence engine combining both the LSTM networks forecasting capabilities and the AEs profiling capabilities to achieve the proactive anomaly detection.
- As a proof of concept, we leverage real network data collected from our NSA 5G testbed to train our models and evaluate the performance of AutoGuard.
- Through multiple experimental results, we validate the efficiency of AutoGuard in proactively detecting Diameter-based DoS signaling attack.

The rest of the paper is organized as follows: Sect. 2 summarizes the related works. Section 3 provides a background on NSA 5G, the Diameter protocol and the threat model. Section 4 presents the architecture of AutoGuard. Section 5 discusses our feature engineering. Our AutoGuard dual intelligence solution is detailed in Sect. 6. Section 7 describes our dataset and experimental settings, and discusses the results. Finally, Sect. 8 concludes the paper.

2   Related Works

Many works in the literature studied the next generation telecommunication networks threat landscape and security implications (e.g., [14,15,17]) but only few proposed security controls in this regard [18].

Core Network Control Plane Security Controls. In [19], the authors propose a generic Diameter security framework discussing security controls accounting for Diameter signaling and subscriber malicious activities. In [20], a Network Intrusion Prevention System (NIPS) for EPC has been proposed leveraging Software Defined Networks (SDN) and Network Function Virtualization (NFV) to enforce flow-level security controls. A DL-based Distributed Denial of Service (DDoS) signature-based attack detection approach has been proposed in [18] to detect silent calls, signaling attacks and Short Message Service (SMS) spamming attacks. While the described solutions can be categorized as signature-based, our solution is anomaly-based, which allows detecting unknown signaling threats.

Time Series Forecasting. Parametric (e.g., ARIMA) and non-parametric models [21] have been widely applied for time series forecasting. In [22], support vector regression has been used for travel time forecasting while authors of

[23] used ARIMA for predicting electricity demand changes due to the increased use of electrical vehicles. Recently, DL techniques have gained momentum due to their capability to deal with multivariate and noisy datasets [21,24], thus, resulting in various neural network architectures claiming highly improved forecasting accuracy. An experimental comparison between linear models, namely, ARIMA, SARIMA, ARMAX, and a network-based LSTM models has shown that LSTM outperforms the aforementioned methods [25]. In [24,26], variants of convolutional LSTM (ConvLSTM) models have been successfully applied for univariate time series forecasting. In [21], authors propose an LSTM model for traffic speed forecasting. Likewise, in this work, we leverage LSTM networks for forecasting the Diameter signaling trends.

Time Series Anomaly Detection. Time series anomaly detection has been addressed in [3] using a variant of stacked LSTM networks in which prediction error distributions have been used to detect anomalies. Authors of [27] applied federated learning to detect anomalies in Industrial Internet of Things (IIOT) context using attention mechanism-based convolutional LSTM networks. In [28], a hybrid model combining variational AE and LSTM has been proposed to improve the anomaly detection accuracy. In [29], unsupervised learning using sparsely connected RNN-based ensemble approaches has been applied for outlier detection. An ensemble approach along with a weighted anomaly window have been adopted in [30] for earliest detection results. In [31], authors propose an LSTM-based anomaly detection using prediction errors. Each time an outlier is detected, the model is retrained to differentiate novelties from anomalies. The authors of [32] convert time series data into image frames and use Residual UNet model to detect anomalies. In all those works the prediction errors are used to detect anomalies. As calculating the prediction errors requires comparing the predicted values with the actual values, all those works identify anomalies after the fact once the actual values are available, contrarily to our work where we add an additional intelligence layer on top of the forecasting model to anticipate potential anomalies before they happen or in their early stages.

Application-Layer Attack Detection. Many works in the literature addressed DDoS attacks exploiting vulnerabilities in application-layer protocols such as HTTP, FTP, DNS, VoIP and SMTP [6]. These attacks were addressed using statistical methods [33], ML techniques such as stacked autoencoder to detect HTTP attacks using HTTP-based features (e.g., URL, responseCode, etc.) [34], and autoregressive models and support vector machine to detect HTTP DDoS attacks using the entropy of HTTP GET requests per source IP address [5]. Nonetheless, these solutions do not consider attacks exploiting vulnerabilities in signaling protocols nor explore protocol-specific statistics as features.

Combining ML Models. Many works have recently proposed ensemble approaches where the results of multiple ML models for anomaly detection are combined (e.g., [12,13]). Those solutions aim at building a consensus of judgments between multiple models to increase the overall anomaly detection performance. However, in this work, we combine two models with the purpose of anticipating potential anomalies, which is a first attempt of its kind.

3   Background and Threat Model

In this section, we provide a background on our context, namely, the NSA 5G core and the Diameter protocol. We also present the threat model we consider. Further, we briefly discuss the DL techniques (LSTM and AEs) used for time series prediction and anomaly detection.

3.1   NSA 5G Core Signaling - Diameter Protocol

In order to accelerate the adoption of 5G networks, operators can leverage their existing EPC core network through adopting a NSA deployment of 5G [35]. The EPC employs the Diameter protocol, defined by the 3GPP, for signaling between its network functions at multiple interfaces [36]. For example, the HSS communicates with other control plane entities at the core network through multiple 3GPP Diameter interfaces, such as S6a [37], S6m and S6t [38].

The Diameter base protocol is an Authentication, Authorization and Accounting (AAA) protocol for applications such as network access or IP mobility in both local and roaming situations [1,39]. It acts at the application layer of the Open Systems Interconnection (OSI) model and runs on top of the Transport Control Protocol (TCP) or Stream Control Transmission Protocol (SCTP) [39]. The Diameter protocol adopts a peer-to-peer architecture in which Diameter nodes, a client and a server, communicate in order to grant or deny access to a user. A Diameter client (i.e., a network access server) sends an access request with the user's credentials to a Diameter server, which performs the user authentication procedure [40]. The Diameter base protocol is implemented in all Diameter nodes and provides basic functionalities such as error notification, user sessions handling and accounting. It can be extended to support other applications through Attribute Value Pairs (AVPs) that can be added to the Diameter message. AVPs bear different kinds of information such as user authentication information, transportation of service specific authorization information, resource usage information, etc. [39].

3.2   Threat Model

The threat landscape of the NSA core network is bounded to the use of virtualization technologies hosting its VNFs along with the vulnerabilities attributed to the Diameter protocol used for signaling between these VNFs. For this work, we pose the following assumptions:

- VNFs (e.g., the HSS) can be compromised by an attacker exploiting the virtualization software vulnerabilities (e.g., CVE-2019-5736 [11]) or from the misconfiguration issues in the cloud virtualized infrastructure. More details on virtualization-based NFV attacks can be found in [10].
- An attacker can spoof a network function by getting access to some information such as the IP address, the host and realm information (i.e., origin-realm and destination-realm of the Diameter protocol depicting the origin and destination MNOs domains) of the target network function. For example, the identity of the HSS can be found via press releases on roaming agreements or roaming documents shared on the internet.

– It is possible for an attacker to recover the IMSIs of a set of subscribers by using an IMSI catcher for example [41]. Man-in-the-middle attacks within the core network are also in-scope since no end-to-end security is ensured [2].
– Diameter protocol has several vulnerabilities (e.g., the hop-by-hop routing mechanisms) [2], which can be exploited to perform different types of attacks causing disturbances at core-level network functions leading them to deviate from their normal behavior. An example of such attacks is the RSR attack that is illustrated in Fig. 1.
– There is no application-layer checks allowing to detect spoofing attacks.

Finally, the in-scope anomalies for AutoGuard are the ones exhibiting specific temporal patterns over time such as the signaling storm (e.g., RSR attack). This scope can be extended to all attacks showing specific event sequences which can be captured with application layer logs. We leave the investigation in this direction for future work. Furthermore, we believe that AutoGuard can be adopted to detect signaling attacks with temporal patterns targeting the 5G SA network such as HTTP/2 DoS [16]. Beside predicting anomalies in the 5G NSA and SA control plane, AutoGuard can also be applied at different parts of the 5G network such as 5G applications, 5G edge network and 5G networks slices with a tuning of the considered application-layer features.

4 AutoGuard - Architecture

In this section, we present AutoGuard architecture (Fig. 2). AutoGuard is mainly composed of two modules:

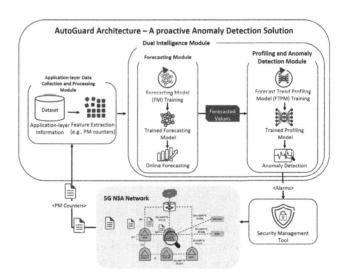

Fig. 2. AutoGuard architecture.

Application-Layer Data Collection and Processing Module. The data collection and processing module collects application-layer information that we leverage for training the DL models of our solution. The use of application-layer information in our approach better reflects the Diameter signaling characteristics as the Diameter protocol acts at the application-layer. Further, it comes inline with the current trend of network openness and infrastructure sharing in which cloud tenants (e.g., MNOs) lease resources from an infrastructure provider. In such a setting, our solution comes in hand to cloud tenants as it allows them detecting anomalies at the application-layer which they have direct access to, complementing hence the network-layer security solutions enforced by the infrastructure providers. The data collection and processing module identifies the relevant data sources such as log files available at the target network functions (e.g., HSS, MME, etc.) to collect the application-layer information. The latter is then processed for feature extraction. We account for PM counters along with other statistical information (Sect. 5) as features extracted by this module.

Dual Intelligence Module. The features extracted by the data collection and processing module are provided to the dual intelligence module which performs the proactive anomaly detection. The dual intelligence module accounts for a forecasting module that forecasts future signaling trends over a number of time steps using a trained Forecasting Model (FM). The forecast trends are sent to the anomaly detection module (part of the dual intelligence module), which evaluates whether the forecast trend is potentially anomalous or not using a trained normal Forecast Trend Profiling Model (FTPM). Upon the detection of anomalous data points, alarms can be raised to the security management tool, which will enforce the appropriate prevention and mitigation measures. While the security management tool is out of the scope of this paper, we envision that upon the receipt of AutoGuard alarms, such tool can opt for scaling the resources to contain a DoS attack for example (e.g. scale up HSS resources in case of RSR attack). Further, it can opt for routing the suspicious incoming workload within the predicted time window towards deep inspection tools, which would enable to filter out and drop attack flows.

Novel Dual Intelligence Interaction. The main novelty of our solution lies in feeding the forecasting output into an additional intelligence layer, namely, the AE, for proactively detecting the anomalies based on the forecast sequences. Existing solutions for time series anomaly detection using DL techniques (e.g., [3,28]) apply the approach illustrated in Fig. 3a. First, the future sequence (the signaling trend in our case) is predicted at time t by the forecasting model for a number of future time steps, then once the complete actual sequence is recorded (at $t+3$ in the example of Fig. 3a), the prediction error is calculated using the predicted and the actual sequences and used as a measure to detect anomalies. As the prediction error can only be calculated after the actual sequence is collected, anomalies are detected only after the fact. Note that existing works train their forecasting model on benign data only and thus, their forecast trend will be similar to benign ones which results in high prediction errors in case of anomalies. In our solution, however, the dual intelligence module introduces proactiveness in the detection by first training the FM on benign and anomalous data, then training the second model, namely, FTPM, to recognize the anomalous forecast sequences before they are manifested or in their early stages using the FTPM reconstruction error as illustrated in Fig. 3b (note that the prediction is done at time t in Fig. 3b, while it is done at time $t+3$ in Fig. 3a). We should emphasize that training the forecasting model in our solution on both benign and anomalous data enables capturing both normal and abnormal patterns, and hence forecasting potentially anomalous data points. Thus, instead of having to wait for the actual data to calculate the prediction error, we detect anomalies in the forecast sequence by feeding it to FTPM.

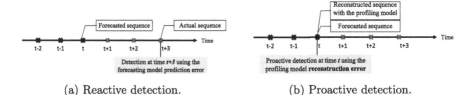

(a) Reactive detection. (b) Proactive detection.

Fig. 3. Reactive versus proactive anomaly detection.

5 PM Counters and Statistical Features

In this section, we discuss the application-layer PM counters and statistical attributes we account for in our feature engineering.

Performance Measurement Counters. Our feature engineering is based on Diameter-related PM counters, which report on statistics regarding the Diameter messages exchanged between peer applications. There exist two categories of PM counters: generic counters and interface-specific counters maintained per peer application. For example, when the HSS has Diameter sessions established with multiple MMEs over the S6a interface, a set of S6a-specific counters is maintained for each MME separately at the HSS. Examples of PM counters are the number of sent requests, the number of received answers and the number of sent/received successful/unsuccessful answers. PM counters are collected through time-stamped log files recorded at the application layer over a time window. The latter is specific to the MNO logging configuration and can be defined manually depending on the density of the network traffic.

For each collected PM counter, p, a univariate time series $uTS_p = \{O_p^{(1)}, O_p^{(2)}, \ldots, O_p^{(n)}\}$ is recorded, where $O_p^{(i)}$ is the value of the PM counter p at the time step i. Since anomalies are rare events, forecasting them might be very challenging. To improve the predictive performance of rare events, we further aggregate the univariate time series observations over a time window and extract a set of statistical features as discussed next.

Statistical Multivariate Time Series. To better characterize the time dependencies over different observations of a univariate time series, we derive a statistical multivariate time series. More precisely, using uTS_p, we generate a multivariate time series $mTS = \{x^{(1)}, x^{(2)}, \ldots, x^{(n-s+1)}\}$ composed of a set of F statistical features calculated over a sliding time window of size s, where each point $x^{(t)} \in \mathbb{R}^F$ in the time series is an F-dimensional vector $\{x_1^{(t)}, x_2^{(t)}, \ldots, x_F^{(t)}\}$ providing a statistical summary of the original observations covered by the current sliding time window. The latter is shifted by one for each statistical observation. Finally, note that the multivariate time series may contain statistical features extracted from multiple univariate time series, each corresponding to a different PM counter. The multivariate time series are used as a ground truth for models training. The statistical features we consider are the variance, the mean, the standard deviation, the 75th percentile, the 95th percentile, the maximum, the minimum and the entropy.

6 Dual Intelligence Solution

We present AutoGuard, a dual intelligence solution based on the combination of FM and FTPM models illustrated in Fig. 2 to enable a proactive anomaly detection. In the following, we discuss our dual intelligence approach, detail the choices of our models and explain their interaction.

6.1 Forecasting with LSTM Networks

LSTM networks have been widely applied for forecasting. They are known to be highly skillful for learning dependencies over temporal sequences containing long term patterns of unknown length [42, 43].

Given a statistical multivariate time series mTS, our objective is to train an LSTM network, which forecasts a set of statistical features for the target PM counters for a given number of future time steps (*predict forward pf* parameter) based on a number of lag/historical time steps (*look back lb* parameter). To this end, we first transform the multivariate time series (mTS) into a dataset composed of input sequences X and output sequences Y, which can be used for supervised learning (Fig. 4). The input sequence refers to the lag observation and its length is defined by lb. The output sequence refers to the future time steps to forecast and its length is defined by pf. For example, in Fig. 4, we use the statistical features described in Sect. 5 as input and we want to forecast the total number (sum) of the PM counter p (x_1) for the three next steps. In this example, lb and pf are fixed to three.

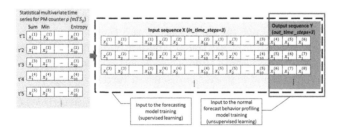

Fig. 4. Training datasets for the FM and the FTPM.

Since our objective is to predict for multiple time steps ahead given a number of lag observations, our forecasting problem can be considered as a sequence-to-sequence prediction problem. Therefore, we adopt the LSTM encoder-decoder architecture which has proven effective for this purpose [44]. As suggested by its name, an LSTM encoder-decoder model is composed of two sub-models: 1) the encoder which reads the input sequence and generates a fixed-dimensional vector internal representation; 2) the decoder that interprets this internal representation to predict the output sequence.

6.2   Profiling and Anomaly Detection with Autoencoders

AEs have been recently applied for anomaly detection [45] and have provided superior performance compared to traditional approaches [46]. An AE is a multi-layer neural network belonging to the class of unsupervised learning algorithms. Thanks to its symmetric architecture composed of an encoder and a decoder, an AE learns an approximation of the identity function $h_{w,b}(x) \approx x$ in a way to output $\tilde{x}$ which is the closest possible to the original input x; w and b being respectively the weight and the noise vectors. In other words, the AE learns to minimize the *reconstruction error*.

In this work, we employ an AE to implement the FTPM (Fig. 2). The basic idea behind applying AEs for anomaly detection is that outliers are harder to be accurately represented in the latent space than the normal data points since they deviate from the discovered latent characteristics. Therefore, it is expected that the error on outliers' reconstruction will be much larger than the error on the reconstruction of inliers [47]. To build the FTPM, we train our AE using the output sequences (Y) from the training dataset after transformation (Fig. 4). For illustration, in Fig. 4, the LSTM model is trained to forecast the output sequences Y given the input sequences X. Thus, we use the same output sequence Y to train the AE in an unsupervised way.

6.3   Online Proactive Anomaly Detection

Once trained, FM and FTPM can be deployed in the network to proactively detect anomalies before their occurrence using the observed signaling trends. In fact, the online proactive anomaly detection phase is composed of two steps. In the first step, the forecasting engine receives the input data and feeds it into the forecasting model. The latter generates the predicted output sequence for the number of future time steps defined by the predict forward parameter. In the next step, the forecast sequence is fed into the profiling model, which outputs the reconstructed vector of the forecast sequence. Then, the reconstruction error is calculated based on the forecast sequence and the reconstructed one. If the reconstruction error exceeds a given threshold, σ, the forecast sequence is flagged as a potential upcoming anomaly.

Anomaly Identification. As previously discussed, anomalies are captured based on the reconstruction error. The Root Mean Squared Error (RMSE) can be used to define anomaly scores. The latter provides errors in the unit of the input which could be particularly useful for univariate time series analysis. A detection threshold σ needs to be defined to discriminate anomalous and normal observations. More details on threshold selection are provided in Sect. 7.3. Algorithm 1 presents the steps of AE-based anomaly detection. The algorithm assigns an anomaly score to each data point. If the anomaly score is greater than the threshold then the data point is flagged as anomalous, otherwise it is considered as normal.

Algorithm 1. Anomaly detection with AE

Input- training_data: X, test_data: x , threshold: σ
Output- outliers
Model=TrainAutoEncoder(X)
outliers $\leftarrow$ []
for $x_i \in x$ **do**
    $\tilde{x}_i$ =Model.predict(x_i)
    $Score_i = RMSE(x_i, \tilde{x}_i)$
    if $Score_i > \sigma$ **then**
        outliers.add($[x_i, \tilde{x}_i]$)
    end if
end for
Return outliers

---

7   Experiments

In this section, we first provide a description of our dataset and experimental settings, then we discuss different experimental results for evaluating the performance of AutoGuard.

7.1   Dataset Description

In this work, we leverage a 5G control plane dataset collected from ENCQOR NSA 5G testbed[2]. To showcase the efficiency of our approach, we simulate multiple RSR attacks on our testbed. For that, we vary the number of subscribers that try to reconnect to the network in order to trigger the authentication radio causing multiple ULR messages to be sent to the HSS. Our application-layer data collection and processing module (Sect. 4) parses a set of time-stamped XML log files extracted from the HSS, and generates a time series dataset composed of 2000 entries. Each data point contains PM counters of five minutes aggregate. Then, the statistical multivariate time series are generated (Sect. 5). To improve our models' performance, we augment our original time series dataset using several techniques (e.g., time wrapping, scaling, jittering) [48–50] and finally choose

---

[2] ENCQOR 5G is a Canada-Québec-Ontario partnership which focuses on research and innovation in the field of 5G technologies. https://quebec.encqor.ca.

the jittering technique as it best fits our dataset. We keep the discussion of data augmentation details as part of the future work.

We transform the statistical multivariate time series into a format which fits the sequence-to-sequence supervised learning (Sect. 6.1) based on the predict forward (pf) and the look back (lb) parameters. We finally split the augmented dataset into 70% for training, 10% for validation and 20% for testing. We further split the test dataset into an optimization test dataset (50%) for threshold tuning, and evaluation test dataset (50%) for detection performance evaluation. Note that the FM is trained with both benign and anomalous data to be able to capture anomalous trends, while the FTPM is trained with benign data only. In addition, for all the experiments, we fix the number of batches to 10 as the latter does not have a significant impact on the performance, and we fix the number of epochs to 300 and use the early stopping option with the *validation loss* as the metric to monitor. The latter will enable to control the models' over-fitting and reduce the training time. We also set the aggregation time window that is used for generating the statistical multivariate time series to 12 as this value has been proven empirically to be the best for our dataset (Appendix 9.1).

7.2   Experimental Settings

In our solution, we define both the encoder and the decoder of the LSTM forecasting model to be one LSTM layer with 200 neurons. Furthermore, for the FTPM, we employ an AE composed of one input layer with cardinality equal to pf, one hidden layer and one output layer with cardinality equal to pf. As detailed next, our experimental results show that the chosen neural networks' configurations provide good performance. Therefore, and given the space limitation, we keep the evaluation of other neural network architectures for future work. All the experiments are conducted on a single large Ubuntu virtual machine running in a community data center with 4 virtual CPUs, 28 GB of memory and NVIDIA GPU to accelerate the models' training. The development was performed using Python 3.6.7 and TensorFlow 2.2.0.

7.3   Experimental Results

In this section, we first evaluate the predictive performance of the LSTM FM (Fig. 2), then we assess the detection capability of the FTPM (Fig. 2) without and within the dual intelligence engine.

AutoGuard Forecasting Capability Evaluation. In this set of experiments, we evaluate the training time and performance of the FM based on the values of the look back (lb) and predict forward (pf) parameters. More specifically, we consider different pairs *(lb, pf)*, where both lb and pf vary within the set {1, 2, 3, 4, 5}. Based on our experimental findings (Appendix 9.2), we fix the learning rate to 0.001 and avoid using the dropout for model training.

Figure 5 reports the predictive performance and the training time of the FM for different values of the prediction parameters. We can see in Fig. 5a that when

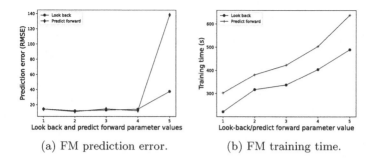

(a) FM prediction error.   (b) FM training time.

Fig. 5. FM evaluation based on the look back and predict forward parameters.

the *pf* and *lb* are less or equal to four, the predictive performance is plateau and
the RMSE slightly varies between 12 and 14. This means that the FM has good
prediction performance capabilities when considering short historical lags and
future time steps to predict. However, for larger prediction parameter's values, we
start observing a significant degradation especially with respect to the increase
in *pf* parameter (RMSE reaches 138 when *pf* is equal to five). This is mainly
due to the fact that farther time steps forecasts are predicted with significantly
larger errors. Furthermore, as illustrated in Fig. 5b, the training time of the FM
increases when increasing *lb* or *pf* prediction parameters. This is expected since
the prediction parameters along with the number of features define the size of
input and output layers of the LSTM network, and larger layers lead to longer
training time.

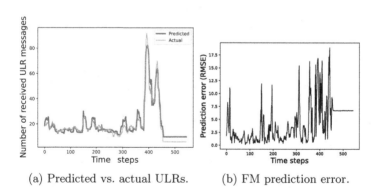

(a) Predicted vs. actual ULRs.   (b) FM prediction error.

Fig. 6. FM prediction performance with prediction parameters *(lb, pf) = (3,3)*.

For better illustration, Fig. 6 shows the predictive performance of the FM
for *(lb, pf) = (3, 3)*. Figure 6a illustrates the actual values of the number of
received ULR messages in blue and the forecast values in orange for the first
future time step, and Fig. 6b illustrates the corresponding prediction error in
terms of RMSE. We observe that the FM is able to predict the fluctuation of the

number of received ULR messages at the HSS thanks to its ability at capturing long-term dependencies. Note that the mean and the standard deviation for the RMSE on the predicted trends are respectively 14.82, and 17.64, which indicates the good prediction capability.

Based on the above discussed results, we conclude that for *lb* and *pf* less than five, the FM is able to forecast the signaling storm patterns that might occur within the next a*(s+pf−1) minutes, *a* being the aggregation window at log recording (fixed to five in our testbed), and *s* is the aggregation time window for the statistical time series generation. For example, in our setting, the RSR attack can be detected up to 70 min ahead.

AutoGuard Proactive Detection Capability Evaluation. In this section, we evaluate the detection performance of FTPM. To evaluate the loss due to the prediction error introduced by FM, we compare the reactive detection scenario with the AutoGuard proactive detection scenario. In the reactive scenario, the FTPM is fed with the ground truth (actual) sequences from the test dataset, whereas in the proactive detection scenario, the FTPM is fed with the sequences predicted by the FM for the same test dataset. Note that for this set of experiments, the AE learning rate is fixed to 0.001 and the number of epochs to 300. To prevent over-fitting, we implement the early stopping option to monitor the validation loss. With this configuration, the AE converges on average after 23 epochs with an average training time equal to 8.82 s. In both scenarios, we use the optimization test dataset to find the optimal detection threshold, then we use the identified threshold to evaluate the F1-score of the FTPM.

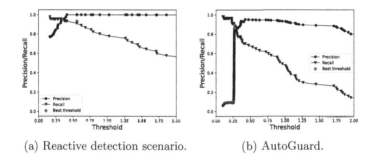

(a) Reactive detection scenario.   (b) AutoGuard.

Fig. 7. Threshold selection for the best precision/recall of the profiling model.

According to the precision-recall curve in Fig. 7a, the threshold providing the best precision-recall trade-off for the reactive detection scenario is 0.55 resulting in an F1-score equal to 0.97, a precision equal to 0.98 and a recall equal to 0.91. For the proactive detection scenario (Fig. 7b), the best threshold is 0.27 and the corresponding F1-score when tested on the evaluation dataset is 0.84, the precision reaches 0.86 and the recall is equal to 0.85. We observe that in spite of the fact that AutoGuard may predict an incoming attack 70 min ahead of the time, the precision loss is less than 12.1%, which shows the effectiveness of AutoGuard in predicting the possible future attacks even with the errors introduced at the forecasting step.

To further evaluate the detection performance of AutoGuard, we consider the authentication synchronization failure attack described in [51]. This attack aims at causing a DoS against a target User Equipment (UE) by sending many attach requests to the MME. For each one of those requests, the MME issues an Authentication Information Request (AIR) Diameter message containing the IMSI of the victim UE towards the HSS. The latter responds with an authentication vector which is generated using a per UE maintained counter called the sequence number. Further, the HSS increments this number. Then, when the legitimate UE sends an attach request, its authentication fails because of the out-of-sync sequence numbers, hence causing a DoS on the legitimate UE.

We simulate the authentication synchronization failure attack as described in [51] by reconnecting a UE many times to cause multiple AIR messages to be sent by the MME to the HSS to generate a new test dataset. The experimental result recorded on the corresponding test dataset presents comparable F1-score (0.84), precision (0.89) and recall (0.83) to those reported for the RSR attack. This is mainly due to the fact that the authentication synchronization failure exhibits similar temporal patterns that can be captured by the forecasting model through the Diameter PM counter features.

Note that, we recorded an average response time equal to 0.51 s for Auto-Guard. We therefore show that AutoGuard may predict future attacks in a reasonable time and with low losses in precision compared to the reactive detection scenario. Given the complexity and the ever changing 5G environment, model refreshment is deemed an efficient solution to maintain the robustness of Auto-Guard against varying network activities. Due to space limitation, we report such discussion to future works.

8   Conclusion

In this work, we proposed AutoGuard, a data-driven proactive anomaly detection approach against application-layer signaling attacks targeting the NSA 5G core network. To this end, we leveraged Diameter-related PM counters and DL techniques to devise a dual intelligence engine combining forecasting and anomaly detection capabilities. As a proof of concept, we implemented our approach for the prediction of signaling attacks on the HSS core network function and evaluated it using data collected from a real NSA 5G testbed. Our results showed the effectiveness of our dual intelligence engine at proactively detecting anomalies with high performance, which would help triggering early mitigation actions to avoid potential damage. We hope that this work will act as a first step towards exploring proactive anomaly detection solution for other types of application-layer attacks in mobile networks. As future work, we plan to analyze the effect of the prediction errors at different future time steps on the detection accuracy of the dual intelligence engine. We also plan to evaluate other forecasting models such as the deep transformer models [52].

9   Appendix

9.1   Effect of the Aggregation Time Window on the Forecasting

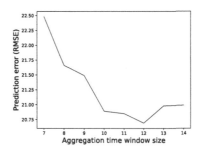

Fig. 8. Effect of the time window on the predictive performance of the FM.

The objective of this set of experiments is to evaluate the effect of the aggregation time window that is used for the generation of the statistical multivariate time series. To this end, we fix the look back and predict forward parameters to the pair (3, 3). From our empirical analysis, we found that when the time window is small (between two and six), the FM performs well in the prediction of the recurrent observations but fails in predicting the rare events compared with the same model trained using time series generated with larger time window values. This is mainly due to the fact that the statistical features generated over large time windows provides a better characterization of the time dependencies over sequences of observations. Since in our solution we are interested in forecasting anomalies, which are considered as rare event, we focus on evaluating the predictive performance related to larger time windows (beyond six). As illustrated in Fig. 8, the value 12 provides the best predictive performance among the large time window values. As such, we set the time window size to 12 for the remaining sets of experiments.

9.2   Hyper-parameters Tuning for the Forecasting Model

The objective of this set of experiments is to study the impact of the learning rate and the dropout regularization technique on the FM's performance. While the learning rate controls how rigorous the model's learning should be, the dropout allows preventing neural network models from over-fitting [53]. Following common practices, we vary the learning rate $1.00E-04$ to $1.00E-01$ and the dropout within the set $\{0.0, 0.2, 0.4, 0.6\}$. As reported in Table 1a, the best predictive performance is reached when the learning rate is equal to 0.001 with a negligible increase in the training time compared to larger learning rate values (i.e., 0.1 and 0.01).

We remark a notable increase in the training time between 1.00E−4 and 1.00E−3 for a marginal decrease in the prediction error. Though, the performance gain (in terms of RMSE) is significant from 1.00E−1 to 1.00E−2 and 1.00E−3 while the increase in time for 1.00E−2 and 1.00E−3 is marginal, therefore, the learning rate 1.00E−3 seems to achieve the best trade-off training time/predictive performance.

As for the dropout regularization, we consider the input dropout, which is applied to the input layer and the recurrent dropout that is applied to the recurrent input signal on the LSTM nodes. As depicted in Table 1b, both the input and the recurrent dropout do not have a significant impact on the model performance, however a slight improvement (smaller error) is achieved when no dropout is considered. Based on those findings, we fix the learning rate to 0.001 and avoid using the dropout for the remaining sets of experiments.

Table 1. Evaluating the effect of learning rate and dropout on the FM.

Learning rate	Training time	RMSE
1.00E−04	131.23	14.58
1.00E−03	53.74	14.64
1.00E−02	51.42	14.83
1.00E−01	50.28	26.02

(a) Effect of the learning rate on the training time (s) and the prediction error.

Dropout	RMSE	
	Input dropout	Recurrent dropout
0.0	14.73	14.64
0.2	14.80	14.76
0.4	14.89	14.75
0.6	15.01	14.84

(b) Effect of the input and recurrent dropout on the prediction error.

References

1. The European Union Agency for Network and Information Security (ENISA). Signalling security in telecom ss7/diameter/5g (2018)
2. Global System for Mobile Communications Association (GSMA). FS.19 Diameter Interconnect Security (2019)
3. Malhotra, P., Vig, L., Shroff, G., Agarwal, P.: Long short term memory networks for anomaly detection in time series. In: ESANN (2015)
4. Salahuddin, M.A., Faizul, B.M., Alameddine, H.A., Pourahmadi, V., Boutaba, R.: Time-based anomaly detection using autoencoder. In: 16th International Conference on Network and Service Management (CNSM), pp. 1–9 (2020)
5. Ni, T., Gu, X., Wang, H., Li, Y.: Real-time detection of application-layer DDoS attack using time series analysis. J. Control Sci. Eng. **2013**, 6 p. (2013). https://doi.org/10.1155/2013/821315. Article ID 821315
6. Mantas, G., Stakhanova, N., Gonzalez, H., Jazi, H.H., Ghorbani, A.A.: Application-layer denial of service attacks: taxonomy and survey. Int. J. Inf. Comput. Secur. **7**(2/3/4), 216–239 (2015)
7. Canard, S., Diop, A., Kheir, N., Paindavoine, M., Sabt, M.: BlindIDS: market-compliant and privacy-friendly intrusion detection system over encrypted traffic. In: Proceedings of the 2017 ACM on Asia Conference on Computer and Communications Security, ASIA CCS 2017, pp. 561–574, New York, NY, USA, 2017. Association for Computing Machinery

8. Chowdhury, F.Z., Kiah, L.B.M., Ahsan, M.A.M., Idris, M.Y.I.B.: Economic denial of sustainability (EDoS) mitigation approaches in cloud: analysis and open challenges. In: 2017 International Conference on Electrical Engineering and Computer Science (ICECOS), pp. 206–211 (2017)
9. Raza, M.T., Lu, S., Gerla, M.: vEPC-sec: securing LTE network functions virtualization on public cloud. IEEE Trans. Inf. Forensics Secur. **14**(12), 3287–3297 (2019)
10. Madi, T., Alameddine, H.A., Pourzandi, M., Boukhtouta, A.: NFV security survey in 5G networks: a three-dimensional threat taxonomy. Comput. Netw/. **197**, 108288 (2021)
11. National Vulnerability Database. Cve-2019-5736. https://nvd.nist.gov/vuln/detail/CVE-2019-5736. Accessed 21 Dec 2019
12. Affeldt, S., Labiod, L., Nadif, M.: Spectral clustering via ensemble deep autoencoder learning (SC-EDAE). Pattern Recogn. **108**, 107522 (2020)
13. Chaurasia, S., Goyal, S., Rajput, M.: Outlier detection using autoencoder ensembles: a robust unsupervised approach. In: 2020 International Conference on Contemporary Computing and Applications (IC3A), pp. 76–80 (2020)
14. Mavoungou, S., Kaddoum, G., Taha, M., Matar, G.: Survey on threats and attacks on mobile networks. IEEE Access **4**, 4543–4572 (2016)
15. Jover, R.P., Marojevic, V.: Security and protocol exploit analysis of the 5g specifications. IEEE Access **7**, 24956–24963 (2019)
16. Hu, X., Liu, C., Liu, S., You, W., Zhao, Y.: Signalling security analysis: is http/2 secure in 5g core network? In: 2018 10th International Conference on Wireless Communications and Signal Processing (WCSP), pp. 1–6(2018)
17. Ahmad, I., Shahabuddin, S., Kumar, T., Okwuibe, J., Gurtov, A., Ylianttila, M.: Security for 5g and beyond. IEEE Commun. Surveys Tutorials **21**(4), 3682–3722 (2019)
18. Hussain, B., Du, Q., Sun, B., Han, Z.: Deep learning-based DDoS-attack detection for cyber-physical system over 5G network. IEEE Trans. Industr. Inf. **17**(2), 860–870 (2021)
19. Thanh, T.Q., Rebahi, Y., Magedanz, T.: A diameter based security framework for mobile networks. In: 2014 International Conference on Telecommunications and Multimedia (TEMU), pp. 7–12 (2014)
20. Jarvis, K.: Network Intrusion Prevention in the Evolved Packet Core utilising Software Defined Networks and Network Function Virtualisation (2019)
21. Essien, A., Petrounias, I., Sampaio, P., Sampaio, S.: Improving urban traffic speed prediction using data source fusion and deep learning. In: 2019 IEEE International Conference on Big Data and Smart Computing (BigComp), pp. 1–8 (2019)
22. Wu, C., Ho, J., Lee, D.T.: Travel-time prediction with support vector regression. IEEE Trans. Intell. Transp. Syst. **5**(4), 276–281 (2004)
23. Amini, M.H., Kargarian, A., Karabasoglu, O.: ARIMA-based decoupled time series forecasting of electric vehicle charging demand for stochastic power system operation. Electr. Power Syst. Res. **140**, 378–390 (2016)
24. Essien, A., Giannetti, C.: A Deep learning framework for univariate time series prediction using convolutional LSTM stacked autoencoders. In: 2019 IEEE International Symposium on INnovations in Intelligent SysTems and Applications (INISTA), pp. 1–6 (2019)
25. Muzaffar, S., Afshari, A.: Short-term load forecasts using LSTM networks. Energy Procedia **158**, 2922–2927 (2019)

26. Essien, A., Giannetti, C.: A deep learning model for smart manufacturing using convolutional LSTM neural network autoencoders. IEEE Trans. Industr. Inf. **16**(9), 6069–6078 (2020)
27. Liu, Y., et al.: Deep anomaly detection for time-series data in industrial IoT: a communication-efficient on-device federated learning approach. IEEE Internet Things J. **8**, 6348–6358 (2021). https://doi.org/10.1109/JIOT.2020.3011726
28. Lin, S., Clark, R., Birke, R., Schönborn, S., Trigoni, N., Roberts, S.: Anomaly detection for time series using VAE-LSTM hybrid model. In: ICASSP 2020–2020 IEEE International Conference on Acoustics, Speech and Signal Processing (ICASSP), pp. 4322–4326 (2020)
29. Kieu, T., Yang, B., Guo, C., Jensen, C.S.: Outlier detection for time series with recurrent autoencoder ensembles. In: Proceedings of the Twenty-Eighth International Joint Conference on Artificial Intelligence, IJCAI-19, pp. 2725–2732. International Joint Conferences on Artificial Intelligence Organization (2019)
30. Buda, T.S., Assem, H., Xu, L.: ADE: an ensemble approach for early anomaly detection. In: 2017 IFIP/IEEE Symposium on Integrated Network and Service Management (IM), pp. 442–448 (2017)
31. Lee, M.-C., Lin, J.-C., Gran, E.G.: RePAD: real-time proactive anomaly detection for time series. In: Barolli, L., Amato, F., Moscato, F., Enokido, T., Takizawa, M. (eds.) AINA 2020. AISC, vol. 1151, pp. 1291–1302. Springer, Cham (2020). https://doi.org/10.1007/978-3-030-44041-1_110
32. Doan, M., Zhang, Z.: Deep learning in 5G wireless networks-anomaly detections. In: 2020 29th Wireless and Optical Communications Conference (WOCC), pp. 1–6. IEEE (2020)
33. Ranjan, S., Swaminathan, R., Uysal, M., Knightly, E.W.: DDoS-resilient scheduling to counter application layer attacks under imperfect detection. In: INFOCOM, pp. 1–14. Citeseer (2006)
34. Yadav, S., Subramanian, S.: Detection of application layer DDoS attack by feature learning using stacked autoencoder. In: 2016 International Conference on Computational Techniques in Information and Communication Technologies (ICCTICT), pp. 361–366. IEEE (2016)
35. Ericsson: Core network evolution from EPC to 5G core made easy. https://www.ericsson.com/en/digital-services/5g-core. Accessed 23 Dec 2020
36. 3GPP. 3gpp TS 29.230 v16.3.0 diameter applications; 3gpp specific codes and identifiers (release 16)
37. 3GPP. 3gpp TS 29.272 version 16.3.0. evolved packet system (eps); mobility management entity (MME) and serving GPRS support node (SGSN) related interfaces based on diameter protocol (release 16)
38. 3GPP. 3gpp TS 29.336 v16.2.0 home subscriber server (HSS) diameter interfaces for interworking with packet data networks and applications (release 16)
39. Internet Engineering Task Force (IETF). Diameter Base Protocol. Available at: https://tools.ietf.org/html/rfc6733 (2012)
40. Jeffrey, L., Steven, J., Hicks, L.: Introduction to diameter. https://www.ibm.com/developerworks/library/wi-diameter/wi-diameter-pdf.pdf
41. Dabrowski, A., Pianta, N., Klepp, T., Mulazzani, M., Weippl, E.: IMSI-catch me if you can: IMSI-catcher-catchers. In: Proceedings of the 30th Annual Computer Security Applications Conference, ACSAC 2014, pp. 246–255, New York, NY, USA, 2014. Association for Computing Machinery
42. Yu, R., Li, Y., Shahabi, C., Demiryurek, U., Liu, Y.: Deep Learning: A Generic Approach for Extreme Condition Traffic Forecasting, pp. 777–785 (2017)

43. Zhao, Z., Chen, W., Wu, X., Chen, P.C.Y., Liu, J.: LSTM network: a deep learning approach for short-term traffic forecast. IET Intell. Transp. Syst. **11**, 68–75 (2017)
44. Sutskever, I., Vinyals, O., Le, Q.V.: Sequence to sequence learning with neural networks. CoRR, abs/1409.3215 (2014)
45. Zhao, Y., Nasrullah, Z., Li, Z.: PyOD: a python toolbox for scalable outlier detection (2019)
46. Munir, M., Chattha, M.A., Dengel, A., Ahmed, S.: A comparative analysis of traditional and deep learning-based anomaly detection methods for streaming data. In: 2019 18th IEEE International Conference On Machine Learning And Applications (ICMLA), pp. 561–566 (2019)
47. Chen, J., Sathe, S., Aggarwal, C., Turaga, D.: Outlier detection with autoencoder ensembles. In: SDM (2017)
48. Iwana, B.K., Seiichi, U.: An empirical survey of data augmentation for time series classification with neural networks. arXiv preprint arXiv:2007.15951 (2020)
49. Wen, Q., Sun, L., Song, X., Gao, J., Wang, X., Xu, H.: Time series data augmentation for deep learning: a survey. ArXiv, abs/2002.12478 (2020)
50. Rashid, K.M., Louis, J.: Time-warping: a time series data augmentation of IMU data for construction equipment activity identification. In: Al-Hussein, M. (ed.) Proceedings of the 36th International Symposium on Automation and Robotics in Construction (ISARC), pp. 651–657. International Association for Automation and Robotics in Construction (IAARC), May 2019
51. Hussain, S.R., Chowdhury, O., Mehnaz, S., Bertino, E.: LTEInspector: a systematic approach for adversarial testing of 4G LTE. In: Proceedings 2018 Network and Distributed System Security Symposium (2018)
52. Wu, N., Green, B., Ben, X., O'Banion, S.: Deep transformer models for time series forecasting: the influenza prevalence case (2020)
53. Srivastava, N., Hinton, G., Krizhevsky, A., Sutskever, I., Salakhutdinov, R.: Dropout: a simple way to prevent neural networks from overfitting. J. Mach. Learn. Res. **15**(1), 1929–1958 (2014)

MORTON: Detection of Malicious Routines in Large-Scale DNS Traffic

Yael Daihes[1,2], Hen Tzaban[2], Asaf Nadler[1,2(✉)], and Asaf Shabtai[1]

[1] Software and Information Systems Eng., Ben-Gurion University of the Negev, Be'er Sheba, Israel
asafnadl@post.bgu.ac.il
[2] Akamai Technologies Inc., Tel Aviv, Israel

Abstract. We present MORTON, a method that identifies compromised devices in enterprise networks based on the existence of routine DNS communication between devices and disreputable host names. With its compact representation of the input data and use of efficient signal processing and a neural network for classification, MORTON is designed to be accurate, robust, and scalable. We evaluate MORTON using a large dataset of corporate DNS logs and compare it with two recently proposed beaconing detection methods aimed at detecting malware communication. The results demonstrate that while MORTON's accuracy in a synthetic experiment is comparable to that of the other methods, it outperforms those methods in terms of its ability to detect sophisticated bot communication techniques, such as multistage channels. Additionally, MORTON was the most efficient method, running at least 13 times faster than the other methods on large-scale datasets, thus reducing the time to detection. In a real-world evaluation, which includes previously unreported threats, MORTON and the two compared methods were deployed to monitor the (unlabeled) DNS traffic of two global enterprises for a week-long period; this evaluation demonstrates the effectiveness of MORTON in real-world scenarios where it achieved the highest F1-score.

Keywords: DNS · PSD · Neural networks · Botnet

1 Introduction

Enterprise networks are prominent targets of malware bots [22]. After a malware bot has been downloaded and executed on an enterprise device, the device effectively becomes part of a botnet controlled by a remote attacker. The attacker exchanges control messages with its bots through a command and control (C&C) channel, by which the attacker instructs the bots to perform attacks, such as data theft [28] and DDoS attacks [40]. To protect against these attacks, numerous studies have focused on the detection of bots' C&C communication [42].

Bots often rely on the DNS protocol to acquire the IP address of their C&C server. Modern botnets frequently change their C&C servers' IP addresses and domain names using techniques, such as fast flux [12,32] and domain generation algorithms (DGA) [29], in order to avoid being detected. The fact that in

© Springer Nature Switzerland AG 2021
E. Bertino et al. (Eds.): ESORICS 2021, LNCS 12972, pp. 736–756, 2021.
https://doi.org/10.1007/978-3-030-88418-5_35

many cases the botnet utilizes the DNS protocol has led to extensive research on the detection of malicious domain names in DNS logs, by tracking the patterns of fast flux and DGA techniques and identifying devices that query these domain names [42]. Despite the fact that the practice of classifying bots based on the DNS protocol through malicious domain name detection has been widely adopted, it fails to detect all botnet communication, and less than 20% of all malicious domain names are reported and eventually added to DNS blacklists [23]. Given this, in this study we are interested in developing a method to detect bots (infected devices) if they engage in routine communication to disreputable host names, by analyzing large-scale enterprise DNS traffic. Prior studies [13,33] that attempted to identify bots without relying on malicious domain name detection focused on the detection of "beaconing"—a bot communication technique in which a recurring message is sent from the bots to predetermined host names so that the attacker can know the latest time at which a bot was available. *Connection pairs (CPs)*, i.e., the outgoing DNS queries from a *specific device* about a *specific host name*, that exhibit periodicity are suspected as beaconing communication which should be further investigated.

Existing beaconing detection methods suffer from a couple of limitations. First, the number of CPs in large-scale enterprises is extremely large. Therefore, these methods must either filter the CPs with less suspicious host names prior to classification to provide acceptable performance, and/or, must be executed less frequently, which will lead to longer detection times and delayed detection. Second, attackers may try and evade the above-mentioned periodicity detection methods by communicating through multiple host names, which, despite being periodic, are not captured within any single CP. One notable example of a bot communication technique that involves multiple host names is multistage channels [26] (MSC), in which a bot communicates with a set of host names throughout its lifecycle; for instance, the TrickBot and Emotet banking Trojans [30] make use of MSCs, thus demonstrating the importance of identifying bot communication that involves multiple host names. Further details on bot communication that involve multiple host names is provided in Appendix 35.A.

In this paper, we present **MORTON**: a method for malicious routine detection on large-scale DNS traffic. MORTON analyzes the DNS communication logs of large enterprise networks and identifies devices that periodically communicate with a set of disreputable domains. Compared to prior studies, MORTON classifies devices at least 13 times faster and thus is able to scan a large-scale, growing stream of DNS logs with less resources and/or faster than other proposed methods. Specifically, MORTON classifies the outgoing DNS requests made by a device directly, rather than indirectly classifying CPs. Direct classification of devices as bots has two main advantages: (1) it is faster, because it involves fewer classification tasks (i.e., the number of enterprise devices is significantly smaller than the number of CPs), and (2) it can be used to detect malicious routines that include multiple host names, such as MSC and multihop attacks.

The evaluation presented in this study compares MORTON with two recently proposed methods designed to identify malware bot beaconing: Baywatch [13] and the adaption of WARP [8] to DNS logs, as proposed by Shalaginov *et al.* [33]. Two experiments were performed to compare the performance of the three methods: a labeled evaluation (using synthetic data) and an unlabeled real-world evaluation. The results demonstrate that while MORTON's accuracy in a synthetic experiment is comparable to that of the other methods, it outperforms those methods in terms of its ability to detect sophisticated bot communication techniques, such as MSCs. In a real-world evaluation, MORTON obtained the highest precision, recall and accordingly F1-score.

We summarize our paper's contributions as follows:

1. We introduce an effective, robust, and efficient method for detecting routine bot communication in large-scale DNS traffic. MORTON is capable of detecting an MSC bot communication technique similar to the one that was involved in the recent SolarWinds attack, which have thus far been overlooked by other detection methods. Furthermore, MORTON was optimized to identify a variety of bot controller framework configurations and therefore can be deployed without further fitting as described in this study.

2. We provide a comparison of MORTON and two recently proposed methods on two large-scale DNS datasets: (a) a dataset with simulated bots to evaluate accuracy, robustness, and efficiency, and (b) a real-world dataset labeled using VirusTotal to evaluate performance and value in real-world scenarios. To the best of our knowledge, such a comparison is lacking in the literature, making it difficult to compare and select an appropriate method.

2   Related Work

The topic of botnet detection in DNS traffic has been thoroughly studied over the last decade [36]. To identify botnet, relevant studies focused on either host-based detection (malicious domain name detection), device-based detection, or their combination (CPs). Table 1 summarizes the studies based on these categories.

Host-Based Detection: The majority of studies targeted just external host names by identifying hosts involved in fast flux networks [12], data exfiltration [28], or DGAs [29,35]. These studies are effective in identifying malicious hosts [42], but they are limited to specific use cases that do not adequately cover the threat landscape. For example, studies on DGA or flux-based detection were not designed for identifying beaconing and MSC communication used by bots.

Device-Based and CP Detection: Another category of studies focuses on bot-infected devices that engage in periodic communication with disreputable hosts. Device detection studies are often concerned with the potential inaccuracy of malicious activity detection based only on periodic communication. Prior work [13,15,24,33] addressed these concerns by making some assumptions. First, it was assumed that a number of devices within the analyzed network would be infected with the same threat, and therefore analyzing and detecting devices as groups would be feasible. Another assumption is that the bots are all communicating with a single external host. These strong assumptions result in methods that focus on detecting groups of devices periodically communicating to one external host. While these assumptions result in greater confidence in the detection being related to security threats and specifically botnets, they also result in far less data to analyze and consequently far less coverage of malware bots. The drawbacks of the abovementioned techniques, as shown in this study, are decreased effectiveness against bot communication that involves multiple external host names (e.g., MSC) and reduced efficiency on large-scale DNS traffic. MORTON addresses these drawbacks by directly classifying the outgoing DNS queries made by a device rather than performing indirect classification of connection pairs; this is accomplished by combining signal processing with a neural network, to efficiently and accurately classify compromised devices.

Using Data Sources Other than DNS: Other studies attempt to improve detection performance by using other data sources in addition to DNS logs [3, 6, 20, 37]. The use of other data sources (e.g., HTTP or NetFlow logs), however, is considered out of the scope of this study.

Table 1. Summary of related research on botnet detection using DNS traffic.

Studies	Targets	Conditions
MORTON	Devices	Periodic communication to disreputable hosts
[11, 14, 18, 33, 38, 41]	CPs	Periodic communication to disreputable hosts
[3, 6, 20, 37]	Devices or Hosts	+ Non-DNS logs (e.g., NetFlow)
[10, 12, 28, 29, 35, 42]	Hosts	DGA, Fast flux or Data exfiltration

3 MORTON

3.1 Overview

MORTON consists of two phases: data processing and classification (see Fig. 1). The data processing phase transforms the input, a time series of outgoing DNS queries, to a power spectral density (PSD) vector that characterizes the intensity of periodic communication at various frequencies. In this phase, we first filter the time series of DNS queries from reputable host names that are not likely to be involved in malicious activity. Then, the filtered time series of DNS queries are aggregated by time. The data processing ends by applying discrete Fourier transform (DFT) on the aggregated DNS queries to produce the PSD vector. In the classification phase, a neural network model classifies the PSD vector based on whether the device that made the DNS queries is a bot or not.

3.2 Definitions

An outgoing DNS query (Q) made by internal device (D) to a host name H at time (T) is represented as a tuple $Q =< D, H, T >$.

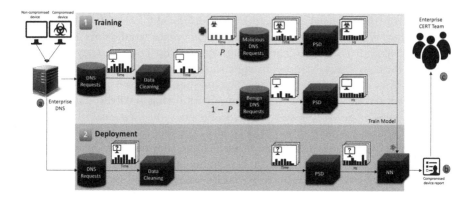

Fig. 1. MORTON training and deployment. Training (1) includes legitimate DNS traffic which is divided into the traffic of benign devices and the traffic of devices into which malicious bot communication was injected. The synthetic labeled data is used to train a neural network that classifies a newly observed time series of DNS requests, based on whether the requests were made by a bot or not. In deployment (2) a neural network processes and classifies new DNS requests series. In turn, (a) MORTON identifies new bots, and (b) reports them for further investigation by an enterprise's CERT team (c).

3.3 Data Processing

Filtering: MORTON's input might contain queries to host names that are assumed to be trusted. Accordingly, the goal of data filtering is to remove queries to reputable host names from the input to improve the accuracy and decrease the processing time. These benefits make data filtering processes very common in methods that attempt to detect malicious routines [13,33]. The data filtering process applied in MORTON is based on the ideas of global and local reputation ranking as described in [13]. Global reputation dictates that a host name is reputable and therefore should be trusted if it is listed in publicly available lists that are often associated with benign host names (e.g., the Alexa Top 1M list). Local reputation complements global reputation by dictating that the host names are also regarded as trusted if they are queried by a sufficiently large portion of devices in the network.

We define a *filtering function* C that outputs a true value indicating if a Q should remain. The filtering function respects both the global reputation and the local reputation, using special parameters, ϕ_G and ϕ_L. ϕ_G defines the number of highest-ranking Alexa top 1M domains that are regarded as trusted. ϕ_L defines the minimal rate of querying devices to consider a host name as trusted. For instance, if ϕ_G is set at 100,000 and ϕ_L is set at 0.3, then host names that are ranked below 100,000 in the Alexa top 1M list or are accessed by at least 30% of the devices within the examined timeframe are regarded as trusted and are filtered from the input. Formally, the filtering is applied to the input using the filtering function: $I^c_{(D_i,T_s,T_e)} = \{Q|(D = D_i) \wedge (T_s \leq T < T_e) \wedge (C(Q) \text{ is True})\}$.

DNS Query Aggregation: The DNS query aggregation stage transforms a filtered input, which is a series of outgoing DNS queries, into an aggregate series of DNS queries, counting the number of DNS queries made by a device within each timeframe. Aggregating the original signal inherently consists of a loss of information, but it has several important advantages. First, the resulting aggregation is dramatically smaller than the filtered input, thereby reducing the required processing time of such data. Second, aggregating the data generates new input of a *constant* size which is the number of timeframes examined, *regardless* of the filtering function configuration, thus allowing MORTON to observe the signal without information-less padding (usually used for varied sized inputs). Lastly, *aware* attackers can design their bots so they jitter (i.e., wait for a random period of time before every communication) to appear less periodic and evade detection. Our use of aggregating results to discrete timeframes (e.g., hourly query counts) limits an aware attacker's ability to evade our detection. For instance, an aware attacker that knows MORTON was configured to use hourly timeframes would have to choose between communicating within an hour of the communication time and becoming detected or delaying communication by over an hour thus reducing the botnet's effectiveness.

Formally, $T_{(D_i, T_s, T_e)} = (t_1, t_2, t_3, .., t_i, .., t_N)$ defines the aggregation of the filtered input, where t_i represents the number of overall DNS queries that were made in the i-th timeframe, and N is the overall number of λ seconds timeframes. MORTON can be configured to use different values of N and λ. Lower λ values will result in shorter timeframes that provide better data granularity for accuracy, while higher values will result in longer timeframes that provide greater efficiency through a smaller representation. Higher N values will result in the method inspecting more timeframes, thus making it more sensitive to detections that occur over a period of time, but less efficient, because the input becomes larger. For brevity, for the remainder of the paper we refer to the DNS query aggregation $T_{(D_i, T_s, T_e)}$ simply as T.

PSD Computation: A power spectral density (PSD) vector is a common data representation form for periodicity detection tasks. The PSD vector is defined as the squared magnitude of the discrete Fourier transform (DFT) coefficients for a given input. PSD vectors are used to estimate the spectral density within a time series signal, which later allows classifiers to more easily identify periods in which a repetitive behavior takes place. Intuitively, a PSD vector can be thought of as the "intensity" of the rate of events at particular time frequencies. Accordingly, a frequency entry within the PSD vector that has a high value indicates a routine event occurring within that frequency.

First, DFT is applied to the DNS query aggregation T as shown in Eq. 1:

$$DFT(T, k) = \sum_{n=0}^{N-1} t_n e^{-i2\pi \frac{kn}{N}}$$

(1)

where $k = 0, 1, ..., N - 1$.

By definition, every PSD vector entry (frequency) is defined as described in Eq. 2:

$$F_k = \left\| DFT\left(T, k\right) \right\|^2$$

(2)

resulting in a PSD vector of the form 3:

$$PSD(T) = \left(F_0, F_1, ..., F_{\frac{N-1}{2}-1} \right) \tag{3}$$

For example, if the number of timeframes is $N = 168$, then the output PSD will have $\frac{N-1}{2} = 83$ entries, as shown below:

$$(F_0 = 0.145, F_1 = 0.03, .., F_{82} = 0.01)$$

Normalization: The values of the PSD vectors are unbounded and of different magnitudes, and therefore they must be normalized prior to classification. The normalization of PSD vectors scales the amplitude of every frequency to a value between zero and one, which is proportional to the original values that appear in the training set. The resulting normalized PSD vector is guaranteed to maintain the same "distribution of energy" for every frequency and a consistent scale for classification. The normalized PSD vector is henceforth referred to as $\overline{PSD(T)}$.

Classification: MORTON trains a vanilla feedforward neural network (NN); this type of NN is commonly used for classification tasks with well structured input due to its performance. The NN parameters (θ) are learned in training, and the network is applied as a function (F) on the normalized PSD vector which captures the behavior of a single device. The output is a classification result (Y); formally, $Y = F(\theta, \overline{PSD(T)})$. The result ($Y$) is a continuous value ranging from zero to one, where higher values indicate greater certainty that the input DNS queries were made by a bot.

4   Labeled Evaluation

4.1   Dataset

DNS Logs: To generate labeled data we used a dataset consisting of *real* DNS logs collected over a seven day period at the end of May 2020 from Akamai's DNS traffic (that cover eight enterprise networks in a variety of time zones). The DNS logs describe queries made by 16,000 devices to 1,262,527 host names. The number of unique connection pairs (i.e., device to host name) is 1,893,221. Every DNS log line contains the DNS query timestamp, the device identifier, and the queried host names, as described in Sect. 3.2.

Labeling: Managed enterprise devices are rarely part of a botnet [22]. Therefore, we label all of the devices in the dataset as benign, except for a random subset of devices (5%) into which we inject synthetic malicious bot communication traffic. The injected traffic mimics the periodic queries made by known botnet control frameworks, such as Cobalt Strike [7] and Empire [17], as further explained below. Specifically, for each of the randomly selected devices, we generate synthetic DNS queries and combine these within the device's real DNS queries by aligning the start time of the generated DNS queries with the timestamp of the original (real) DNS queries. The 16,000 devices are split into a training set of 10,000 devices and a test set of 6,000, while maintaining the proportion of labels.

Synthetic Data: The injected bot communication is synthetically generated to cover possible configurations of known bot control frameworks such as Cobalt Strike [7] and Empire [17]. Each bot has a configuration that dictates the rate of DNS queries, the inter-arrival time between consecutive queries, the random waiting time before issuing a query (referred to as "jitter"), and the list of malicious host names to which the DNS queries are sent. The configuration for each bot is sampled as described below. The inter-arrival time is sampled uniformly, with possible values ranging from one minute (i.e., communicating every minute) to 1,440 min (i.e., communicating once every 24 h), as allowed by the abovementioned frameworks. The number of queries made for each interval is also sampled uniformly, with values ranging from one to four. The maximal jitter in seconds was uniformly sampled with values ranging from zero to 900 (i.e., between zero and 15 min of waiting time). The list of queried host names was either one new domain name for mimicking beaconing or three to six different new domain names randomly chosen each time for mimicking multistage channel communication.

Data Cleaning: The filtering of the dataset is performed using the following configuration: $\phi_G = 500,000$ and $\phi_L = 0.03$, i.e., only the top 500,000 host names on the Alexa Top 1M list and host names that are queried by at least 3% of the devices throughout the past week are omitted from the dataset. The value of ϕ_L represents an upper bound on the estimated rate of devices compromised with the same bot within the organization at any given point in time. In managed enterprise networks, the most prevalent malware (including bots) family appear on at most 0.57% of enterprise devices within a time span of three consecutive years [22]. Accordingly, we set $\phi_L = 3\%$, which is a large enough value to eliminate bots that are up to five times more prevalent in enterprise devices than that described in [22]. Note that if more than 3% of the devices are infected, MORTON should have been able to identify and alert the infection at an earlier stage.

4.2 Methods Compared

The experiment compares the following three methods on the task of detecting infected devices that exhibit beaconing and MSC.

Baywatch: Baywatch [13] has a confidence parameter ($m \in \mathbb{N}$) that sets a tradeoff between accuracy and efficiency (higher m result in a slower but more accurate detection). We evaluate Baywatch using two different settings, fast and accurate, which we refer to Baywatch-10 ($m = 10$) and Baywatch-100 ($m = 100$) respectively, to account for the range of achievable results by this method.

WARP: Shalaginov et al. [33] presented a general method for periodicity detection. Within the general method, CPs of internal devices and external host names are extracted and processed to return the length of the minimal periodic cycle. Processing specific CPs consists of computing the time difference between consecutive DNS queries, smoothing the time difference, and replacing the smoothed time difference values with unique symbols that form a string. The string formed is provided to an underlying periodicity detection algorithm that processes strings.

Shalaginov *et al.* proposed four potential underlying periodicity detection algorithms, and our implementation relies on one of them, namely, WARP [8].

MORTON: Within the scope of this evaluation, we defined the time window size (λ) to be exactly one hour due to system constraints. As a result, a dataset of one week translates into $N = 168$ hourly time windows. MORTON classifies whether a device is a bot or not based on its PSD vector which captures the behavior of the device within N ($N = 168$) consecutive one hour time windows (i.e., the PSD vector is computed based on one week of data from the device). As mentioned in Eq. 3, the size of the PSD vector is $\frac{N-1}{2} = 83$, which is the exact number of input neurons in the NN architecture.

The neural network architecture consists of three hidden layers with 25, 55, and 25 neurons respectively, the ReLU activation function, and an output layer with the sigmoid activation function. The training of the neural network is conducted with a dropout setting on the hidden layers with a rate of 0.01; this is done to regulate the training, so it will use all of the neurons and achieve its optimal performance. Early stopping is defined so that if the validation loss remains roughly unchanged for five consecutive epochs, the training stops. The Adam optimizer is used to minimize the binary cross-entropy loss.

The architecture and the learning rate were selected, because they performed best with regard to the area-under-curve metric when compared against more than 25 alternative architectures originating from an ablation study and the use of AutoML for structured data [19], as can be seen in Appendix 35.B.

The entire evaluation is conducted on a cloud computing instance (AWS EC2 C5.x18 xlarge[1]), with extensive computational and memory resources, to correctly simulate the hardware of a large-scale enterprise network. The specification of the instance includes 72 virtual CPUs (vCPU), 144 GB of memory, and a 550 GB EBS disk.

4.3   Evaluation Results

Performance: We compare the performance of the evaluated methods using the area under the curve (AUC) measure (as presented in Fig. 2). We also report on the TPR for a fixed and low FPR (1%). While typically the sensitivity of security systems is set according to the resources available for analyzing alerts and the organization's security policy (in terms of the trade-off between the FPR and FNR), we examined the performance at FPR = 1%, since it is considered a practical configuration for intrusion detection systems [5], in order to reduce the number of false alarms requiring investigation by an enterprise CERT.

For beaconing detection, WARP is the most accurate method (AUC = 0.97), followed by MORTON (AUC = 0.85), Baywatch-100 (AUC = 0.85), and finally by the fast Baywatch-10 (AUC = 0.64). The AUC scores show that all methods are capable of detecting beaconing with high accuracy, with WARP performing best. Despite that, for a low FPR value of 1%, only MORTON was able to

---

[1] https://aws.amazon.com/ec2/instance-types/c5/.

produce adequate results, with a TPR value of 77%, compared to the other methods that were unable to produce any detection with the low FPR of 1%. For Baywatch, setting the confidence parameter C to 1.0 resulted in a minimal FPR of 14.4% thus reflecting Baywatch's lack of sensitivity, which is addressed by the authors who mentioned the need to apply additional methods to reduce the FPR further. For WARP, the lowest s value of zero (i.e., highest confidence) results in a minimal FPR of 3%, which is more sensitive than Baywatch but less sensitive than MORTON. Effectively, the automated use of these methods to detect beaconing with an acceptable FPR of less than 3% can only be achieved by either using MORTON, or by applying one of the other two methods with new additional filtering to reduce the FPR after detection.

For MSC detection, MORTON (AUC = 0.85) is the most accurate method; it is followed by the accurate Baywatch-100 (AUC = 0.72), Shalginov-WARP (AUC = 0.58), and the fast Baywatch-10 (AUC = 0.56). Similarly to the beaconing experiment, methods other than MORTON were unable to produce any detection when configured to a low FPR value of 1%. The lowest possible FPR value for which the two methods produced a detection is as follows: FPR = 14.4% for Baywatch and FPR = 3% for WARP. In contrast to the beaconing accuracy test, MORTON dominates the accuracy evaluation for MSC, with higher TPR values for every FPR value, thus making MORTON more suitable for the detection of MSC in general and for automatic detection in particular.

Robustness: Bots that are configured to periodically communicate with their C&C server are not always able to do so (e.g., when a compromised device is turned off). In addition, an attacker may attempt to evade detection methods by preventing an installed bot from sending some communication. Accordingly, an important aspect to consider when evaluating bot communication detection methods is their ability to detect bots even when some of their routine communication logs are incomplete. To evaluate the robustness of the detection methods, we designed an experiment that simulates dropped communication and defined a new metric that we refer to as the *robustness score*, which is explained below.

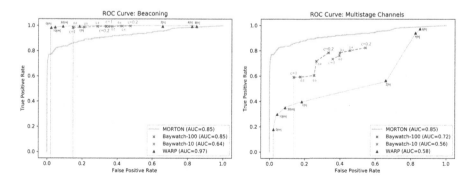

Fig. 2. Receiver operating characteristic curve of MORTON, Baywatch, and WARP, with different m values, on the test set.

The experiment for evaluating robustness is similar to the experiment for evaluating accuracy, with two modifications. First, we define the notion of a *drop rate* – the rate at which malicious DNS queries are dropped from the dataset. This experiment was conducted with 10 different drop rate values ranging from 0% (i.e., no drop) and increasing by 10% until a 90% drop is reached. Second, we define a acceptable false positive rate that applies for all of the methods, which is crucial for a comparison of the detection rate. The acceptable false positive rate is determined to be 0.144, because it is the lowest FPR value for which all of the methods are capable of detecting at least one bot in the test set (see Fig. 2). Eventually, the rate of bots successfully detected while maintaining the specified FPR are reported as the *detection rate*.

The experiment results in a function that maps drop rate values to detection rates, which is henceforth referred to as the *robustness function*. The area that is captured between the robustness function and the x-axis is referred to as the *robustness score*. The robustness score is a scalar that describes the level of robustness provided by a system that detects periodic signals. The score ranges between zero and one, and a perfect score of one signifies a system with a perfect detection rate when dealing with varying rates of dropped traffic. Accordingly, the evaluation of robustness deals with the robustness score of the different methods for both beaconing and MSC.

The robustness scores of all of the methods evaluated are presented in Fig. 3. For beaconing detection, the highest robustness score (0.697) was achieved by both MORTON and Baywatch, whereas WARP received a score of 0.402. For MSC, MORTON (0.697) performed best and was followed by Baywatch (0.393) and WARP (0.211).

Efficiency: To better understand the relationship between the number of devices in the dataset and the run-time performance of the compared methods, we select subsets of the original dataset where the number of devices varies. This sampling results in 11 subsets of the original datasets with $2^1, 2^2, 2^4, ...2^{10}$, and 2^{11} device IDs that were randomly selected from the original dataset. The methods are then applied on each of the datasets sampled to estimate the total number of seconds required for bot communication detection. The results are portrayed in Fig. 3. The largest sample consists of 2,048 devices and slightly more than 700,000 CPs. The fastest method based on the time it took to classify the largest sample (with the same resources) was MORTON (70 s), followed by Baywatch-10 (16 min), Baywatch-100 (three hours), and WARP (24 h). Based on the results, we conclude that MORTON is at least 13 times faster than other methods, on large-scale datasets.

Hyperparameters N and λ: To further investigate the impact of N and λ on MORTON's performance, we evaluate MORTON's effectiveness for different values of N (when $\lambda = 1$ h). The analysis (i.e., tested values of N) is limited by the data retention policy of the enterprises monitored by Akamai that delete data older than one week. From the results we conclude that if only two days of data are available, MORTON's detection rate will be limited to 74%, and when using four days of data ($N = 96$) MORTON's detection rate reaches almost 90%.

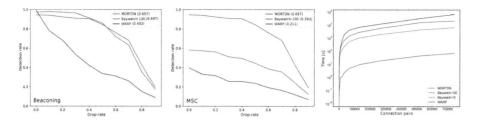

Fig. 3. The robustness scores of MORTON, Baywatch, and WARP for beaconing (left) and MSC (middle), and their run-time (in seconds) with different m values on the test set (right).

Because of the large scale DNS traffic collected and monitored by Akamai, the data is aggregated into one hour time intervals; i.e., the granularity of the data available is one hour. For this reason, we couldn't evaluate the impact of λ smaller than one hour on MORTON's performance. In addition, since our goal is to detect the attack as fast as possible we would like to set λ to be as small as possible (in our case one hour) and therefore, we didn't test larger values of λ (as it will results in a longer time to detect). Alternatively, we conducted an addition evaluation of MORTON, when $\lambda = 1\,h$ and $N = 168$, on a threat landscape where H (the bot parameter that refers to the malicious communication inter-arrival-time) changes. Specifically, we tested with $H=1,2,..,3600\,min$ between consecutive communication attempts.

The results of the evaluation demonstrate that MORTON maintains a fair detection rate (above 75%) for communication attempts that occur at most once every 36 h. Our interpretation of this is that an attacker seeking to evade detection by MORTON in its current setting would be forced to communicate infrequently, i.e., more than 36 h between consecutive communication attempts (+1,200% increase in operation time), thus dramatically reducing the effectiveness of the attack. This demonstrates that the selected $\lambda = 1\,h$ and $N=168$ are robust and effective. A summary of the labeled experiment evaluation results is presented in Table 2.

Table 2. Summary of the results. The best performing method in every category is marked in bold.

Category		MORTON	Baywatch-10	Baywatch-100	WARP
AUC	Beaconing	0.85	0.64	0.85	**0.97**
TPR (FPR = 1%)	Beaconing	**0.77**	0	0	0
Robustness score	Beaconing	**0.697**	<0.697	**0.697**	0.402
AUC	MSC	**0.85**	0.56	0.72	0.58
TPR (FPR = 1%)	MSC	**0.77**	0	0	0
Robustness score	MSC	**0.697**	<0.393	0.393	0.211
CP classifications/sec	General	**10,000**	729.1	64.8	8.1

5   Real-World Evaluation

5.1   Methodology

We provide a complementary analysis, by comparing the methods on an unlabeled DNS dataset, to evaluate its performance in a real-world setting. The methodology of the real-world analysis involves applying the compared methods, namely, MORTON, Baywatch-100, and WARP on a real-world, unlabeled dataset, and comparing their achieved precision, recall and F1-scores scores. For consistency, the setting matches the description in Sect. 4. Specifically, the Baywatch setting that optimizes accuracy, namely, Baywatch-100, is compared to analyze performance rather than efficiency.

The dataset for evaluating the real-world efficacy of the methods consists of DNS logs that were produced by two worldwide enterprises consisting of 20,000 devices over the course of a week at the end of December 2020. There are no labels within the dataset to indicate whether a device is a bot or not. After applying each method on the above-mentioned dataset, a list of identified devices by each method is generated.

Labeling: In order to label the identified devices as either bot or benign devices we opted to use VirusTotal (VT), since this is a common practice in most academic research and industry in this domain. According to the labeling approach we used, a device is considered infected by a bot only if: (1) an automatic (periodic) communication to a host name is detected, (2) the detected host name is considered a non-reputable one (as explained in Sect. 3.3, in a preliminary preprocessing phase, reputable domains are eliminated), and (3) the host name was either identified as malicious by VT or accessed by at least two malicious files. Similar to previous studies [16,21,34], we consider a file to be malicious if it was detected by at least two security vendors in VT, a standard which results in reliable classification of the files [43]. A malicious file accessing a host name is not necessarily a bot. In addition, VT does not provide sufficient evidence to classify the malware type. Therefore, since as a best practice, beaconing and multi-stage channels used by bots employ more than a single malicious file [27], we require that at least two malicious files have accessed the host name. Note that in order to further validate our results, we repeated the labeling process using VT four months after the dataset was collected. The results did not change significantly (the label of 10 devices was changed from benign to bot, which is less than 2.5%), which shows that the proposed labeling is robust.

5.2   Evaluation Results

The three methods were evaluated using the same dataset which includes data of 20,000 devices. When all models' thresholds were tuned based on the labeled evaluation to an acceptable false alarm rate of 1%, MORTON detected 77 devices (precision = 66%), Baywatch-100 detected 293 (precision=26%), and WARP detected 42 devices (precision = 23%). Additionally, to conduct a fair comparison of the precision, recall, and F1-score, we aim to compare all of the methods with a similar support i.e., the number of detected devices. To that end, we select the 42 highest scored devices detected by each method, which is the maximal amount possible due to WARP's detection rate. In this comparison, all of the methods combined detected 85 out of 20,000 devices as malicious, out of which 43 were verified as malicious. Table 3 summarizes the results. From the results, we can see that MORTON detected almost 70% of the infected devices (i.e., false negative rate of 30%), while Baywatch-100 detected almost 49% of the infected devices (i.e., false negative rate of 51%), and WARP detected 23.2% of the infected devices (i.e., false negative rate of 77%).

Table 3. Real-world evaluation summary

Method	Precision	Recall	F1-score
Baywatch-100	21 out of 42 (50%)	21 out of 43 (48.8%)	0.489
MORTON	30 out of 42 (71.4%)	30 out of 43 (69.7%)	**0.699**
WARP	10 out of 42 (23.2%)	10 out of 43 (23.2%)	0.230

5.3 Case Studies

We analyze three use cases detected during the real-world experiment to understand the nature of the precision and recall associated with the compared methods, and further show that there is no significant difference between the verified use cases and the synthetic cases described in Sect. 4.

"Gandalf": gammawizard.com is a website that provides legitimate online analytics tools for trading. Baywatch-100 incorrectly detected one of these tools, called "Gandalf". This legitimate activity is in fact periodic (i.e., queried every two minutes). However, despite being periodic, the queries made to "Gandalf" do not constitute malware bot beaconing; Specifically, it is described by the following features: time interval of two minutes and 15 queries per beacon (on average). This situation in which there is a high volume of queries made within a very short timeframe, as illustrated in Fig. 4, does not conform with malicious activity generated by frameworks such as Cobalt Strike or Empire. This demonstrates that MORTON overcomes incorrect detection of this form because it is trained only on periodic queries that match beaconing behavior.

uBlock: *uBlock* [4] is a malicious add-on for the Chrome browser. It uses cloned legitimate code to disguise as a legitimate ad blocker while in fact facilitating a malicious backdoor for cookie stuffing, a technique used to commit ad fraud. uBlock performs 2 DNS queries (on average) every 15 min to learn the hosting IP address of its servers, to which it sends a "heartbeat" messsage (see Fig. 4). The message is sent as HTTPS GET requests to various URLs that start with "https://ublockerext.com/heartbeat." MORTON is the only method to identify uBlock, thus demonstrating successful detection of bot communication to a single host name, as shown in Sect. 4.

IsErik: IsErik [1] is a sophisticated and modular adware [39], that uses MSC to communicate with its servers. IsErik's infection process involves the automated and periodic execution of code through WScript on a victim's device. The code execution includes communication to a *variety* of host names, as is also documented in public security reports [1,31]. A time series plot of the DNS queries made by IsErik to its C&C servers is presented in Fig. 4 which depicts its communication consisting of two DNS queries (on average) every five minutes. The IsErik case study demonstrates the importance of detecting routine communication made to multiple host names—a feature that distinguishes MORTON from the compared methods.

In order to show that there is no significant difference between real-world bot traffic and the generated bot traffic, we conducted a two sample Kolmogorov–Smirnov (K-S) test [25]. We compared the distributions of interarrival time between queries of the two real-world bots we were able to manually verify, uBlock and IsErik, with that of synthetically generated bot samples as described in Sect. 4. We hypothesized that there is no significant difference between the real-world samples and the synthetic data. The K-S test resulted in a p-value greater than 72% and 87% for the two cases of IsErik and uBlock respectively, thus we can conclude that the hypothesis cannot be rejected, and therefore, there is no significant difference between real-world bot traffic and the generated bot traffic (i.e., the samples are likely to have come from the same distribution).

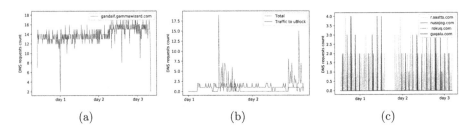

(a)   (b)   (c)

Fig. 4. Outgoing DNS requests for analyzed threats: (a) "Gandalf" mistakenly detected by Baywatch-100 (b) uBlock uses a single host name technique (c) IsErik adware communicates with its servers using multiple host names.

6   Deployment Considerations and Limitations

Data collection: To train the model, an enterprise customer would have to obtain a dataset of its own enterprise DNS logs, for instance, by using a DNS tap or a DNS logging service. The dataset must then be processed, cleaned, and labeled for training as explained in detail in Sect. 3. The resulting dataset will contain DNS logs made by enterprise devices, similarly to that of the dataset described in this study. The only expected difference between a dataset obtained by an enterprise customer and the dataset described in this study could be the number of samples, due to a smaller number of monitored devices. In such cases, the organizations can use a transfer learning approach and retrain a pretrained model with the enterprise DNS logs or obtain data over a longer period of time.

Model Training and Deployment: MORTON was optimized for the detection of infected devices involved in beaconing and multistage channel communication using various configurations of the Empire and Cobalt Strike bot controller frameworks. These configurations cover a wide variety of bot communication patterns, including the specific Cobalt Strike configuration that was used in the recent SolarWinds breach [9]. Also, note that the model was not trained and fitted to a specific enterprise network. Therefore, we conclude that a new enterprise can use the same model architecture trained in this research and used by Akamai Technologies, with the data collected by that enterprise.

Resilience and Limitations Against an Aware Attacker: Our evaluation shows that an attacker must wait at least 36 h between consecutive communication attempts to reduce the detection rate of MORTON to 75% (see Subsect. 4.3); this makes the attack significantly less effective, even for an aware attacker. In cases in which an enterprise wants to consider a threat model where the communication is performed at a very low frequency (i.e., a message sent every 36 h or more), the enterprise can simply collect new data using the known bot controller frameworks (when the controller framework parameters are configured according to the new threat model) and retrain the model.

Another key challenge is that an aware attacker can attempt to evade detection by programming its malware bots to make DNS requests over HTTPS or through an unknown resolver. For such scenarios, MORTON, WARP, Baywatch, and other similar security solutions for DNS requests will be ineffective. Enterprises can overcome this by blocking encrypted traffic that cannot be inspected by a proxy or on the endpoint, or by disabling the use of all resolvers other than the enterprise DNS resolver, as proposed by the National Security Agency [2].

7 Discussion

Labeled evaluation: The labeled (supervised) evaluation indicates that MORTON is comparable to the two methods in terms of accuracy for the detection of malware bot beaconing but outperforms those methods when detecting bots that communicate using advanced techniques, such as multistage channels. Additionally, MORTON was found to be more robust and efficient than the other methods evaluated.

Real-World Evaluation: The unlabeled (unsupervised) evaluation on two large enterprises with 20,000 devices demonstrated MORTON's effectiveness for malicious bot detection in a real-world, unlabeled environment and showed that MORTON's precision, recall, and F1-score values exceed that of the other two methods. Our interpretation of both the empirical results (see Subsect. 5.2) and the investigated case studies (see Subsect. 5.3) is that MORTON is better suited for detecting verified malicious periodic communication. Furthermore, we witnessed that despite the higher recall rate ofBaywatch-100 compared to

MORTON that was observed in the labeled beaconing evaluation, MORTON has a higher recall rate in the real-world because of the multi-stage channel data involved and the periodic non-bot communication that are inaccurately detected byBaywatch-100 (as seen in Subsect. 5.3). As mentioned in the analyzed cases, this stems from MORTON's training process and the use of a supervised classifier, which distinguish MORTON from the other methods examined.

To summarize, the experiment results obtained on real-world DNS traffic demonstrate MORTON's effectiveness for malicious bot detection in a real-world, unlabeled environment and show that MORTON's precision score exceeds that of the two other proposed methods for bot periodicity detection by as much as three times. Furthermore, MORTON also has a proven unique ability to detect bot communication of both a single host name, as demonstrated by the uBlock example, and multiple host names, as demonstrated in the IsErik use case.

8   Conclusions and Future Work

We present MORTON, a system that detects bots by analyzing DNS communication logs and identifying routine DNS queries to disreputable host names that are queried by a bot on behalf of an enterprise device. MORTON is designed for large-scale enterprise networks, and accordingly, it was evaluated on two large-scale DNS datasets and compared to two recently proposed methods, Baywatch, proposed by Hu *et al.* [13], and WARP, as proposed by Shalaginov *et al.* [33], which were also designed for large-scale networks. Based on the comparison results, we conclude that MORTON is comparable to the other methods in terms of accuracy for the detection of beaconing, but while outperforming them in detecting multistage channels, and performing at least thirteen times faster.

In future work, we plan to consider the ability to incorporate cybersecurity experts' feedback into the model. In addition, we plan to extend our research and to apply MORTON to network logs other than DNS logs (e.g., HTTP or network access logs).

Appendix 35.A   Detecting Multiple Host Names

The primary drawback of bot communication techniques that use a single host name (e.g., malware beaconing technique with single host name C&C communication) is their lack of robustness. The single host name is effectively a single point of failure, and if the host name is unavailable for any reason, the attackers cannot control their bots. An additional drawback is that communication with a single host name may be less covert. For instance, in DNS data exfiltration, every exfiltration message is sent to an attacker's host name. A single host name that receives a large volume of exfiltration messages is more detectable by security systems [28]. Therefore, the activities of bots that split their DNS exfiltration messages and send them to multiple host names are less suspicious.

The most well-known use of multiple host names for botnet communication is through domain generation algorithms [26] (DGAs), which are used by over 40 known botnets [29]. Most bots that use DGAs generate new domain names on a daily basis [29], thus pointing to the importance of detecting bot communication that uses multiple domain names.

Multistage channels (MSC) are another bot communication technique in which multiple host names are used. The initial installation of the bot on a compromised device is referred to as the first stage of the infection. Throughout the first stage, the bot communicates with its C&C through either a single host name or multiple host names. However, the host names will change when the first stage bot requires an upgrade. A bot upgrade typically involves communicating with a new host name to download a module that enhances the bot's capabilities. The process of upgrading the bot is referred to as the second stage of the infection. The MSC bot communication technique often involves several stages, where multiple host names are gradually upgrading the bot. The use of MSC improves the robustness of a botnet's infrastructure, because security researchers cannot easily identify the different host names that will be used by a botnet in order to shut down its operation (i.e., prevent bots from upgrading).

Other cases of bot communication techniques in which multiple host names are used include fallback channels and multihop proxies [26]. In fallback channels, a bot that fails to communicate with its C&C host name attempts to communicate to the host name next in line, based on a prioritized list of host names. Multihop proxies is a bot communication technique in which the C&C channel is established through a series of proxy servers that are associated with different host names. The series of proxy servers between bots and their C&C servers prevents security researchers from easily matching a bot communicating with its C&C server based on network logs. MORTON is designed to detect every multiple host communication technique mentioned, as long as it is used in a periodic manner.

Appendix 35.B   Neural Network Parameters

The architecture and the learning rate were selected, because they performed best with regard to the area-under-curve metric when compared against more than 25 alternative architectures originating from an ablation study and the use of AutoML for structured data [19], as can be seen in Table 4. (note that all of the settings were trained and evaluated on a smaller subset of the data to reduce training time).

Table 4. Neural network parameters

	# Layers	# Neurons	Learning rate	AUC
Ablation study	3	25–55–25	0.01	**0.581**
	2	25–55	0.01	0.566
	1	25	0.01	0.561
	3	25–55–25	0.001	0.532
AutoML for structured data [19]	2	25–352	0.01	0.554
	1	352	0.01	0.554

References

1. Stefana Gal -Software Engineer, Bitdefender ATD Team: Who iserik: A resurface of an advanced persistent adware? https://www.bitdefender.com/files/News/CaseStudies/study/284/Bitdefender-WhitePaper-Erik-CREA3910-en-EN-GenericUse.pdf
2. Agency, N.S.: Adopting Encrypted DNS in Enterprise Environments. https://media.defense.gov/2021/Jan/14/2002564889/-1/-1/0/CSI_ADOPTING_ENCRYPTED_DNS_U_OO_102904_21.PDF (2021)
3. Alina, O., Li, Z., Norris, R., Bowers, K.: MADE: security analytics for enterprise threat detection. In: Proceedings of the 34th Annual Computer Security Applications Conference, pp. 124–136. ACM (2018)
4. Meshkov, A.: AdGuard Research: Fake ad blockers 2: Now with cookies and ad fraud. https://adguard.com/en/blog/fake-ad-blockers-part-2.html
5. Axelsson, S.: The base-rate fallacy and the difficulty of intrusion detection. ACM Trans. Inf. Syst. Secur. (TISSEC) 3(3), 186–205 (2000)
6. Bilge, L., Balzarotti, D., Robertson, W., Kirda, E., Kruegel, C.: Disclosure: detecting botnet command and control servers through large-scale netflow analysis. In: Proceedings of the 28th Annual Computer Security Applications Conference, pp. 129–138 (2012)
7. Cobalt Strike.com: Cobalt strike release notes. https://www.cobaltstrike.com/releasenotes.txt
8. Elfeky, M.G., Aref, W.G., Elmagarmid, A.K.: WARP: time warping for periodicity detection. In: Fifth IEEE International Conference on Data Mining (ICDM 2005), p. 8. IEEE (2005)
9. FireEye: Highly Evasive Attacker Leverages SolarWinds Supply Chain to Compromise Multiple Global Victims With SUNBURST Backdoor (2020). https://www.fireeye.com/blog/threat-research/2020/12/evasive-attacker-leverages-solarwinds-supply-chain-compromises-with-sunburst-backdoor.html
10. Gao, H., et al.: An empirical reexamination of global DNs behavior. In: Proceedings of the ACM SIGCOMM 2013 Conference on SIGCOMM, pp. 267–278 (2013)
11. Haffey, M., Arlitt, M., Williamson, C.: Modeling, analysis, and characterization of periodic traffic on a campus edge network. In: 2018 IEEE 26th International Symposium on Modeling, Analysis, and Simulation of Computer and Telecommunication Systems (MASCOTS), pp. 170–182. IEEE (2018)
12. Holz, T., Gorecki, C., Rieck, K., Freiling, F.C.: Measuring and detecting fast-flux service networks. In: NDSS (2008)

13. Hu, X., et al.: BAYWATCH: robust beaconing detection to identify infected hosts in large-scale enterprise networks. In: 2016 46th Annual IEEE/IFIP International Conference on Dependable Systems and Networks (DSN), pp. 479–490. IEEE (2016)
14. Hubballi, N., Goyal, D.: FlowSummary: summarizing network flows for communication periodicity detection. In: Maji, P., Ghosh, A., Murty, M.N., Ghosh, K., Pal, S.K. (eds.) PReMI 2013. LNCS, vol. 8251, pp. 695–700. Springer, Heidelberg (2013). https://doi.org/10.1007/978-3-642-45062-4_98
15. Huynh, N.A.: Frequency analysis and online learning in malware detection. Ph.D. thesis, Nanyang Technological University (2019)
16. Invernizzi, L., et al.: Nazca: detecting malware distribution in large-scale networks. In: NDSS, vol. 14, pp. 23–26. Citeseer (2014)
17. Johnson, J.: Purple team: About beacons, https://ci.security/resources/news/article/purple-team-about-beacons
18. Jiang, J., Yin, Q., Shi, Z., Li, M., Lv, B.: A new c&c channel detection framework using heuristic rule and transfer learning. In: 2019 IEEE 38th International Performance Computing and Communications Conference (IPCCC), pp. 1–9. IEEE (2019)
19. Jin, H., Song, Q., Hu, X.: Auto-Keras: an efficient neural architecture search system. In: Proceedings of the 25th ACM SIGKDD International Conference on Knowledge Discovery & Data Mining, pp. 1946–1956 (2019)
20. Khan, R.U., Zhang, X., Kumar, R., Sharif, A., Golilarz, N.A., Alazab, M.: An adaptive multi-layer botnet detection technique using machine learning classifiers. Appl. Sci. 9(11), 2375 (2019)
21. Kolodenker, E., Koch, W., Stringhini, G., Egele, M.: PayBreak: defense against cryptographic ransomware. In: Proceedings of the 2017 ACM on Asia Conference on Computer and Communications Security, pp. 599–611 (2017)
22. Kotzias, P., Bilge, L., Vervier, P.A., Caballero, J.: Mind your own business: a longitudinal study of threats and vulnerabilities in enterprises. In: NDSS (2019)
23. Kührer, M., Rossow, C., Holz, T.: Paint it black: evaluating the effectiveness of malware blacklists. In: Stavrou, A., Bos, H., Portokalidis, G. (eds.) RAID 2014. LNCS, vol. 8688, pp. 1–21. Springer, Cham (2014). https://doi.org/10.1007/978-3-319-11379-1_1
24. Manasrah, A.M., Domi, W.B., Suppiah, N.N.: Botnet detection based on DNs traffic similarity. Int. J. Adv. Intell. Paradigms 15(4), 357–387 (2020)
25. Massey, F.J., Jr.: The Kolmogorov-Smirnov test for goodness of fit. J. Am. Stat. Assoc. 46(253), 68–78 (1951)
26. MITRE ATT&CK: MITRE ATT&CK tactics and techniques for enterprise. https://attack.mitre.org/matrices/enterprise/
27. MITRE ATT&CK: Multi-stage channels technique. https://attack.mitre.org/techniques/T1104/
28. Nadler, A., Aminov, A., Shabtai, A.: Detection of malicious and low throughput data exfiltration over the DNs protocol. Comput. Secur. 80, 36–53 (2019)
29. Plohmann, D., Yakdan, K., Klatt, M., Bader, J., Gerhards-Padilla, E.: A comprehensive measurement study of domain generating malware. In: 25th {USENIX} Security Symposium ({USENIX} Security 16), pp. 263–278 (2016)
30. Rendell, D.: Understanding the evolution of malware. Comput. Fraud Secur. 2019(1), 17–19 (2019)

31. Caragay, R., Cureg, F., Lagrazon, I., Mendoza, E., Yaneza, J.: (Threats Analysts): Exposing modular adware: How dealply, iserik, and managex persist in systems. https://blog.trendmicro.com/trendlabs-security-intelligence/exposing-modular-adware-how-dealply-iserik-and-managex-persist-in-systems

32. Schales, D.L., Hu, X., Jang, J., Sailer, R., Stoecklin, M.P., Wang, T.: FCCE: highly scalable distributed feature collection and correlation engine for low latency big data analytics. In: 2015 IEEE 31st International Conference on Data Engineering, pp. 1316–1327. IEEE (2015)

33. Shalaginov, A., Franke, K., Huang, X.: Malware beaconing detection by mining large-scale DNs logs for targeted attack identification. In: 18th International Conference on Computational Intelligence in Security Information Systems. WASET (2016)

34. Sharif, M., Urakawa, J., Christin, N., Kubota, A., Yamada, A.: Predicting impending exposure to malicious content from user behavior. In: Proceedings of the 2018 ACM SIGSAC Conference on Computer and Communications Security, pp. 1487–1501 (2018)

35. Sidi, L., Mirsky, Y., Nadler, A., Elovici, Y., Shabtai, A.: Helix: DGA domain embeddings for tracking and exploring botnets. In: Proceedings of the 29th ACM International Conference on Information & Knowledge Management, pp. 2741–2748 (2020)

36. Singh, M., Singh, M., Kaur, S.: Issues and challenges in DNs based botnet detection: a survey. Comput. Secur. **86**, 28–52 (2019)

37. Sivakorn, S., et al.: Countering malicious processes with process-DNs association. In: NDSS (2019)

38. Tran, M.C., Nakamura, Y.: In-host communication pattern observed for suspicious http-based auto-ware detection. Int. J. Comput. Commun. Eng. **4**(6), 379 (2015)

39. Urban, T., Tatang, D., Holz, T., Pohlmann, N.: Towards understanding privacy implications of adware and potentially unwanted programs. In: Lopez, J., Zhou, J., Soriano, M. (eds.) ESORICS 2018. LNCS, vol. 11098, pp. 449–469. Springer, Cham (2018). https://doi.org/10.1007/978-3-319-99073-6_22

40. Welzel, A., Rossow, C., Bos, H.: On measuring the impact of DDoS botnets. In: Proceedings of the Seventh European Workshop on System Security, pp. 1–6 (2014)

41. Yeh, Y.R., Tu, T.C., Sun, M.K., Pi, S.M., Huang, C.Y.: A malware beacon of botnet by local periodic communication behavior. In: 2018 IEEE 42nd Annual Computer Software and Applications Conference (COMPSAC), vol. 2, pp. 653–657. IEEE (2018)

42. Zhauniarovich, Y., Khalil, I., Yu, T., Dacier, M.: A survey on malicious domains detection through DNs data analysis. ACM Comput. Surveys (CSUR) **51**(4), 1–36 (2018)

43. Zhu, S., et al.: Measuring and modeling the label dynamics of online anti-malware engines. In: 29th {USENIX} Security Symposium ({USENIX} Security 20), pp. 2361–2378 (2020)

Iterative Selection of Categorical Variables for Log Data Anomaly Detection

Max Landauer[1]([✉]), Georg Höld[1], Markus Wurzenberger[1], Florian Skopik[1], and Andreas Rauber[2]

[1] Austrian Institute of Technology, Giefinggasse 4, Vienna, Austria
{max.landauer,georg.hoeld,markus.wurzenberger,florian.skopik}@ait.ac.at
[2] Vienna University of Technology, Favoritenstraße 9-11, Vienna, Austria
rauber@ifs.tuwien.ac.at

Abstract. Log data is a well-known source for anomaly detection in cyber security. Accordingly, a large number of approaches based on self-learning algorithms have been proposed in the past. Most of these approaches focus on numeric features extracted from logs, since these variables are convenient to use with commonly known machine learning techniques. However, system log data frequently involves multiple categorical features that provide further insights into the state of a computer system and thus have the potential to improve detection accuracy. Unfortunately, it is non-trivial to derive useful correlation rules from the vast number of possible values of all available categorical variables. Therefore, we propose the Variable Correlation Detector (VCD) that employs a sequence of selection constraints to efficiently disclose pairs of variables with correlating values. The approach also comprises of an online mode that continuously updates the identified variable correlations to account for system evolution and applies statistical tests on conditional occurrence probabilities for anomaly detection. Our evaluations show that the VCD is well adjustable to fit properties of the data at hand and discloses associated variables with high accuracy. Our experiments with real log data indicate that the VCD is capable of detecting attacks such as scans and brute force intrusions with higher accuracy than existing detectors.

1 Introduction

Modern computer systems are permanently exposed to cyber threats, such as intrusions or denial-of-service attacks. Consequently, cyber security experts develop intrusion detection systems that monitor system behavior through analysis of continuously generated log events and autonomously disclose any malicious activity. Thereby, anomaly detection is particularly interesting, because it employs self-learning techniques that are capable of recognizing unknown attacks without the need for pre-existing or manually coded knowledge [4].

Log data is a suitable source for such techniques as it keeps track of almost all events and thus provides detailed insights into the state of a computer system. Most existing analysis techniques thereby focus on network traffic, because it

© Springer Nature Switzerland AG 2021
E. Bertino et al. (Eds.): ESORICS 2021, LNCS 12972, pp. 757–777, 2021.
https://doi.org/10.1007/978-3-030-88418-5_36

contains numeric features such as packet count or duration that fit well-known machine learning methods, e.g., support vector machines or neural networks. Few approaches use categorical variables, because they lack intuitive distance metrics and comprise of immense amounts of possible combinations [5,19].

However, categorical variables are common in system logs and complement the detection of anomalous events. In particular, variables such as user identifiers, IP addresses, service names, system operations, or program states, occur in regular patterns that are expected to persist over time as long as the system behavior remains steady. For example, services utilize specific subsets of all available system operations and execute them with particular relative frequencies. Unexpected deviations from such conditional occurrence distributions indicate a change of system behavior and should therefore be reported to the system operators as anomalies. Unfortunately, the selection of variables suitable for such a detection mechanism is non-trivial, because it usually relies on expert knowledge about the system at hand and is difficult to automatize.

We propose the Variable Correlation Detector (VCD) as a solution to aforementioned issues. The approach comprises of a sequence of selection constraints to reduce the search space and identify interesting correlations between categorical variables. In addition, the VCD reuses conditional distributions of value occurrences computed in the selection phase for the disclosure of deviations in a subsequent detection phase. Our approach has several advantages over state-of-the-art methods. First, it identifies interesting correlations independent from the total occurrences of the involved values, which is different to approaches based on frequent itemset mining [19]. This is especially important for the detection of stealthy attacks that only produce infrequent values. Second, our approach does not generate strict rules for value co-occurrences, but instead involves fuzzy rules that do not always have to be fulfilled by employing statistical tests on chunks of events. Third, our approach is designed for online detection in streams of log data, which is essential for application in real-world scenarios.

This paper presents the correlation selection and anomaly detection mechanisms of the VCD. An implementation is available online as part of our log-based anomaly detection system [21]. We summarize our contributions as follows:

- An iterative method for selecting useful correlations of categorical variables.
- An online anomaly detection technique based on identified correlations.
- An evaluation of our open-source implementation of the proposed concepts.

The remainder of this paper is structured as follows. Section 2 reviews the state-of-the-art of correlation analysis in categorical log data. In Sect. 3, we outline the concept of the VCD. We then provide details of our proposed correlation selection constraints in Sect. 4. We present the evaluation of our algorithm in Sect. 5 and discuss the results in Sect. 6. Finally, Sect. 7 concludes the paper.

2   Related Work

Research on association mining between categorical variables in database transactions has been ongoing for many years. One of the main issues prevalent in this field is the immense search space arising from the many possible combinations of variables and values [19]. Accordingly, approaches such as the well-known Apriori algorithm [1] are usually designed for efficient searching and pruning.

To enable outlier or anomaly detection in categorical data, it is usually necessary to adjust or extend association mining algorithms. For example, Narita and Kitagawa [15] propose techniques to detect records that fail to occur in expected associations and to compute outlier scores that are also suitable for speeding up the search. Khalili and Sami [12] show that the Apriori algorithm is suitable to be used for intrusion detection, in particular, by identifying critical states of industrial systems with sensor outputs as variables. One of the downsides of algorithms based on frequent itemset mining is that they require multiple passes over the data, which prevents online processing. Djenouri et al. [7] therefore propose a single-pass technique with improved parameter selection and use pruning to limit the search space to itemsets that cover the largest amount of events.

The problem with such approaches based on frequent itemset mining is that they omit infrequent values, because they are not interesting for the associations. Anomalies are then considered as infrequent combinations of otherwise frequent values [19]. However, infrequent values are important for anomaly detection, as long as they occur consistently with their associated values. Accordingly, Das and Schneider [6] replace rare values with placeholders and use conditional probabilities to disclose associations. While our approach also employs conditional probability distributions, we propose a sequence of selection steps rather than value replacement to reduce complexity without loosing precision.

Distance-based techniques are commonly used for anomaly detection in numeric data, however, it is non-trivial to compute distances between categorical values. Eiras-Franco et al. [8] solve this problem by encoding categories as binary vectors to apply maximum likelihood analysis. Similarly, one-hot encoding is also used by Moustafa and Slay [14], who measure the association strength between variables using the Pearson correlation coefficient as well as Information Gain. Ren et al. [18] support anomaly detection on data streams by computing cluster references on chunks of data, where a distance function based on value equality is used. Our approach also analyzes chunks of data rather than individual lines, but employs statistical tests on conditional probability distributions.

A different strategy to tackle the lack of a distance metric and large event space is pursued by Chen et al. [5], who embed the data in a latent space and mine associations between pairs of variables, which include user IDs, IP addresses, and URLs. Similarly, Pande and Ahuja [16] use an embedding method based on word2vec for anomaly classification in HTTP logs. Alternatively, Ienco et al. [11] measure the similarity between value co-occurrences by applying distance metrics on their conditional occurrence probabilities. The advantage of this method is that it enables anomaly score computation for ranking. Conditional probabilities are also used by Tuor et al. [20], who show that neural networks are suitable for anomaly detection in categorical user data. We argue that the downside of these approaches is that they suffer from lower explainability than frequent itemset methods, where variable associations are more intuitive.

Table 1. Value co-occurrences of syscall types and items in Audit logs.

Items	Syscall type									
	0	1	2	20	42	49	59	90	105	Σ
0	6097	860	0	189	34	14	0	0	1	7195
1	0	0	2592	0	104	0	0	5	0	2701
2	0	0	90	0	0	0	14	0	0	104

Most aforementioned approaches rely on the assumption that their data involves only categorical variables or that these variables have been manually pre-selected. However, log files involve various data types, including discrete, continuous, static, and unique variables. Gupta and Kulariya [9] therefore use a Chi-squared test to select variables with sufficiently distinct value co-occurrences before comparing regression, support vector machines, naive bayes, and decision trees for anomaly detection. Our approach employs a sequence of constraints to limit the search space and then makes use of statistical tests to disclose anomalies. In the following section, we outline an overview of this procedure.

3 Concept

This section outlines the concept of the Variable Correlation Detector (VCD). First, we explain important aspects of correlations of variables. Then, we state definitions relevant for this paper and outline the overall procedure of the VCD.

3.1 Correlations of Variables

Log data are chronological sequences of events. Most log data sets comprise of a certain number of different event types, where each type defines the syntax of the corresponding log lines. Accordingly, simple log data such as comma-separated-values only consist of a single event. In any way, each event type specifies a sequence of variables or features. For example, the syscall event in Audit logs consists of a sequence of key-value pairs, such as "syscall=2" that specifies the syscall type or "items=1" that specifies the number of associated path records.

Some variables are strongly correlated, meaning that the occurrence of a value in one variable indicates the occurrence of a specific value in another variable. Given a sufficiently large time frame, these conditional probabilities should be more or less constant on a system with stable behavior. Any changes to these occurrence patterns indicate potentially malicious activities, i.e., anomalies.

Table 1 shows the number of occurrences of syscall types and items extracted from 10000 Audit logs that are also used in the evaluation in Sect. 5.1. With 7195 total occurrences, the majority of these events involve "items = 0" (sum of first row). However, it is visible that syscall type 2 ("open") mostly occurs with "items=1" (2592 occurrences) and sometimes "items = 2" (90 occurrences), but never with "items = 0". Since other value pairs exhibit similar dependencies, it

Table 2. Definitions of symbols used in this paper.

Symbol	Definition
E	Log event type from the set of all event types $\mathcal{E}$, i.e., $E \in \mathcal{E}$.
V_i	Variable of log event type E, with $V_1, ..., V_n \in E$.
$\mathcal{V}_i$	Set of distinct values attained by V_i.
$v_{i,j}$	Value j of variable V_i, i.e., $\mathcal{V}_i = \left\{ v_{i,1}, ..., v_{i,m_i} \right\}$.
$P(v_{i,j})$	Probability that value j occurs in V_i.
$P(v_{i,j} \mid v_{k,l})$	Probability that value j occurs in V_i given that value l occurs in V_k.
$V_i \rightsquigarrow V_k$	Correlation between variables V_i and V_k.
$v_{i,j} \rightsquigarrow v_{k,l}$	Correlation between values of variables, i.e., occurrence of value j in V_i correlates with value l of V_k.
θ_i	Threshold parameter for correlation selection.
N	Size of the sample for computing correlations during initialization.
M	Size of the sample for updating and testing in online mode

is reasonable to monitor the conditional probability distributions of the variable "items" with respect to "syscall" for improved detection over monitoring the occurrences of "items" alone. The same reasoning applies for the other direction, i.e., monitoring the occurrences of syscall types given the number of items.

Different to existing approaches, we do not only focus on the selection of variables that are suitable for such correlations, but monitor the co-occurrences of their values. Thereby, we are not solely interested in frequent values or value combinations, but instead calculate the conditional probability distributions of all values that are useful for anomaly detection. Consider syscall type 59 ("exec") as an example: Even though the value only occurs in 14 events, it always co-occurs with "items = 2" and thus indicates a strong correlation. Due to the large number of possible combinations of variables and distinct values, a brute-force solution is computationally not feasible in practice, especially for high-volume log data with diverse values. This paper therefore presents an iterative selection strategy for interesting correlations that is presented in the following sections.

3.2 Definitions

As mentioned in the previous section, most log files comprise of several events $\mathcal{E}$, each containing a unique set of variables. For simplicity, we only consider a single event $E \in \mathcal{E}$ in the following and assume that the procedure is applicable to all other events analogously. Moreover, we assume that event E involves n variables $V_1, .., V_n$, each comprising of an arbitrary number of values $v_{i,1}, ..., v_{i,m_i}$ from the unique value set $\mathcal{V}_i$. We compute the estimated value occurrence probability as $P(v_{i,j}) = |\{V_i = v_{i,j}\}| / N$ in a sample of size N and the conditional probabilities as $P(v_{i,j} \mid v_{k,l}) = |\{V_i = v_{i,j} \wedge V_k = v_{k,l}\}| / |\{V_k = v_{k,l}\}|$. Correlations are denoted using the $\rightsquigarrow$ operator. Table 2 summarizes all symbol definitions.

3.3 Procedure

Our approach selects variable fields of log events and performs statistical tests on value occurrences in these fields for the purpose of anomaly detection. To limit

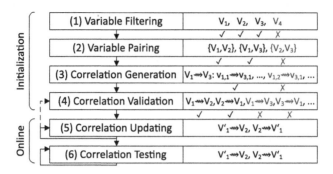

Fig. 1. Procedure of the Variable Type Detector. Correlations between variables and values are filtered iteratively.

the search space, we propose several sequential analysis steps that act as filters for all possible variable and value combinations. Figure 1 shows these steps as a state chart, with an in-depth description of each step following in Sects. 4.2-4.6.

For the initialization phase in steps (1)–(4), the VCD first collects a sample of N log lines. We assume that all available variables of a log event are possible choices for correlations and that there is no manual pre-selection. Step (1) *Variable Filtering* sorts out variables that are unlikely to yield useful correlations, such as variables with many unique or static values. This step is exemplarily visualized in the figure by removing variable V_4 for subsequent analyses steps.

Step (2) *Variable Pairing* then generates pairs of the remaining variables V_1, V_2, V_3. This step removes pairs with dissimilar value probability distributions or disjoint value sets. In the figure, the variable pair $\{V_2, V_3\}$ is not considered for correlation. Remaining pairs are transformed to correlation hypotheses in step (3) *Correlation Generation*, where conditional occurrence probabilities of all involved values are computed. Correlations between values denoted by $\rightsquigarrow$ that exhibit weak associations are omitted, e.g., values that occur in many combinations or have similar conditional probabilities to other correlated values. In the figure, value correlation $v_{1,2} \rightsquigarrow v_{3,1}$ of variable correlation $V_1 \rightsquigarrow V_3$ is removed. Note that correlations are directed, i.e., $V_1 \rightsquigarrow V_3$ is different from $V_3 \rightsquigarrow V_1$.

Step (4) *Correlation Validation* then evaluates whether all resulting value correlations indicate a sufficiently strong dependency between the correlated variables, in particular, whether the valid value correlations have independent probability distributions and involve sufficiently many occurring values. For example, assuming that several value correlations such as $v_{1,2} \rightsquigarrow v_{3,1}$ were removed in step (3), the variable correlation $V_1 \rightsquigarrow V_3$ is removed. This marks the end of the initialization phase, which is only executed once for every log event type.

For online anomaly detection, all correlation hypotheses that remain after step (4) are transformed into rules, which are repeatedly evaluated using samples of size M. For this, we perform statistical tests in step (5) *Correlation Updating* and go back to step (3) to re-initialize the correlation rules if value distributions change or new values appear, e.g., V_1 is replaced by V_1' in Fig. 1. Once correlation rules are stable for a sufficiently long time period and should not be updated anymore, they are tested in step (6) for the purpose of anomaly detection.

Table 3. Sample data.

ID	V_1	V_2	V_3	V_4	ID	V_1	V_2	V_3	V_4	ID	V_1	V_2	V_3	V_4
1	1	1	1	1	5	1	1	3	1	9	3	3	3	1
2	1	1	2	1	6	2	2	2	2	10	2	2	1	1
3	1	1	3	3	7	1	2	1	1	11	2	2	1	3
4	1	2	1	1	8	2	3	2	1	12	1	1	2	1

4 Approach

This section presents detailed explanations of all aforementioned steps of the VCD procedure. We also provide examples for the various selection criteria.

4.1 Sample Data

We provide a small sample to make the equations in the following sections easier to understand and to obtain a rough estimate for reasonable choices for threshold parameters θ_i. The data shown in Table 3 comprises of one event with four variables, i.e., $E = \{V_1, V_2, V_3, V_4\}$, and a sample size of $N = 12$. We point out that this data is only for illustrative purposes and that the application of the VCD in practice requires sufficiently large sample sizes for appropriate probability estimation. Each variable involves three possible values, in particular, $\mathcal{V}_1 = \mathcal{V}_2 = \mathcal{V}_3 = \{1, 2, 3\}$. The occurrence probabilities of the values of V_1 are computed as $P(v_{1,1}) = \frac{7}{12}, P(v_{1,2}) = \frac{4}{12}, P(v_{1,3}) = \frac{1}{12}$. The data is set up so that V_1 and V_2 correlate, i.e., the occurrence of any value in V_1 usually co-occurs with the same value in V_2. This is also reflected in the conditional probabilities, e.g., $P(v_{2,1} \mid v_{1,1}) = \frac{5}{7}, P(v_{2,2} \mid v_{1,2}) = \frac{3}{4}$. On the other hand, V_3 and V_4 do not show a strong correlation with any other variable. Accordingly, the following examples usually set the thresholds θ_i so that correlations involving V_3 and V_4 are removed, but $V_1 \rightsquigarrow V_2$ and $V_2 \rightsquigarrow V_1$ are selected as relevant for detection.

4.2 Variable Filtering

This section covers heuristics for variables. The first criterion targets variables with many unique values and the second criterion addresses dominating values.

Diversity of Values. Correlation analysis as it is done by the VCD requires categorical variables to reasonably calculate occurrence probabilities from the sample. Accordingly, we assume that there is a finite number of different values attained by each variable and that the sample size is large enough to obtain an estimate on their occurrence probabilities, i.e., $|\mathcal{V}_i| \ll N$. Variables with a large number of unique values are likely discrete rather than categorical, e.g., event IDs or timestamps, and do not yield stable correlations as described in Sect. 3.1. The reason for this is that they result in a high number of infrequent value co-occurrences that do not represent any actual correlation between the variables, e.g., an event ID is usually a random value. Equation 1 thus defines an upper limit for the number of unique values in V_i, where $\theta_1 \in [0, 1]$. From all available variables, we select all V_i that fulfill Eq. 1, and omit all others.

$$|\mathcal{V}_i| \leq \theta_1 \cdot N \tag{1}$$

The small sample size of the data in Table 3 requires $\theta_1 \geq 0.25$ to retain the variables, e.g., $\theta_1 = 0.25$ yields a critical value of 3 and $|\mathcal{V}_1| \leq 3$ is fulfilled.

Distribution Probabilities. In some variables, one or few values are occurring more often than others and are thus dominating the value probability distribution. These variables usually have weaker correlation with other variables, since most correlated values co-occur with the same dominating value. An extreme case of this situation are static variables, where the same value occurs in every log line and is thus trivially useless for correlation. We therefore use Eq. 2 to select only variables V_i where no occurrence probability of $v_{i,j}$ exceeds a certain limit. To allow more unique values $\theta_2 \in [0, 1]$ should be selected closer to 1.

$$P(v_{i,j}) < \theta_2 + \frac{1 - \theta_2}{|\mathcal{V}_i|} \tag{2}$$

We point out that this heuristic causes that variables with similarly dominated value probability distributions that may have a strong association between the values are omitted. Since this heuristic is mainly used to efficiently limit the search space, it is possible to set θ_2 to a sufficiently large value to include these variables and use subsequent analysis steps to omit incorrect variable pairings.

The data from Table 3 involves value $v_{4,1}$ which dominates V_4. Setting $\theta_2 = 0.6$ excludes only this variable, since $P(v_{4,1}) = 0.75$ exceeds $0.6 + \frac{1-0.6}{3} = 0.73$.

4.3   Variable Pairing

This section describes criteria for selecting pairs of variables suitable for correlation. The first criterion matches variables with similar probability distributions and the second criterion addresses common value spaces.

Similarity of Distributions. As pointed out in the previous section, variables with similar value probability distributions are more likely to exhibit associations between their values than other variable pairs. The reason for this is that similar distributions imply that for each value in V_i there exists another value in V_k that occurs roughly the same amount of times and may thus have a direct relationship with the former value. On the other hand, comparing the value occurrences of one dominated distribution and another evenly distributed distribution, there is necessarily at least one value in one variable that co-occurs with more than one value in another variable, which indicates a weaker association.

We therefore generate variable pair $\{V_i, V_k\}$ if the occurrence probabilities $P(v_{i,j})$ of all values in V_i do not differ from $P(v_{k,l})$ in V_k, where each value is only used once. Equation 3 describes this rule formally, where $\theta_3 \in [0, \infty)$ and $p = 1, ..., min(|\mathcal{V}_i|, |\mathcal{V}_k|)$ is the index of the order statistic so that $v_{i,(1)}$ is the most occurring value of V_i, $v_{i,(2)}$ is the second most occurring value of V_i, etc.

$$|P(v_{i,(p)}) - P(v_{k,(p)})| \leq \frac{\theta_3}{max(|\mathcal{V}_i|, |\mathcal{V}_k|)} \tag{3}$$

Setting $\theta_3 = 0.6$ yields a critical value of $\frac{0.6}{3} = 0.2$. In this case, variables V_1 and V_2 from Table 3 are correctly paired, since all probability differences $|P(v_{1,1}) - P(v_{2,1})| = 0.16$, $|P(v_{1,2}) - P(v_{2,2})| = 0.08$, and $|P(v_{1,3}) - P(v_{2,3})| = 0.08$ are lower than 0.2, where values are compared in decreasing order of their occurrences. Assuming that V_4 is not removed in the variable filtering phase, the pair $\{V_2, V_4\}$ is omitted since $|P(v_{2,1}) - P(v_{4,1})| = 0.33$ which exceeds 0.2.

Common Values. Another heuristic is that variables sharing common values are likely related in some way. For example, log lines that involve separate variables for source and destination IP addresses often have the same value space, since data is sent and received from the same IP addresses. This also applies to state transitions in logs, such as network logs that contain messages like "inactive $->$ scanning", "scanning $->$ authenticating", etc. As an alternative in case that Eq. 3 is not fulfilled, we select pairs $\{V_i, V_k\}$ where both variables share a certain fraction of common values. This corresponds to selecting variable pairs that fulfill Eq. 4, where $\theta_4 \in [0, 1]$. For the sample data displayed in Table 3, this constraint is trivially fulfilled since all variables have the same value space.

$$|\mathcal{V}_i \cap \mathcal{V}_k| \geq \theta_4 \cdot min(|\mathcal{V}_i|, |\mathcal{V}_k|) \tag{4}$$

4.4   Correlation Generation

This section outlines the generation of correlation hypotheses for values of variable pairs. Note that each pair $\{V_i, V_k\}$ is considered as the two hypotheses $V_i \rightsquigarrow V_k$ and $V_k \rightsquigarrow V_i$ that are analyzed separately.

Diversity of Correlations. For optimal variable correlation, each value of one variable only occurs with a particular value of another variable and vice versa. Conversely, values that co-occur with many different values from the correlated variable indicate weak or random associations as pointed out in Sect. 4.2 and should not be considered for correlation hypotheses. We therefore select only value correlations $v_{i,j} \rightsquigarrow v_{k,l}$ for hypothesis $V_i \rightsquigarrow V_k$ if the relative amount of co-occurring values of $v_{i,j}$ does not exceed $\theta_5 \in [0, 1]$, i.e., if Eq. 5 is fulfilled.

$$\frac{|\{v_{k,l} : P(v_{k,l} \mid v_{i,j}) > 0\}|}{|\mathcal{V}_k|} \leq \theta_5 \tag{5}$$

Selecting $\theta_5 = 0.7$ for the data from Table 3 yields that $v_{1,1} \rightsquigarrow v_{2,l}$ of $V_1 \rightsquigarrow V_2$ are fulfilled for all l, since $v_{1,1}$ only occurs with $v_{2,1}, v_{2,2}$ and $\frac{2}{3} \leq \theta_5$. Similarly, $v_{1,2} \rightsquigarrow v_{2,l}$ yield $\frac{2}{3}$ and $v_{1,3} \rightsquigarrow v_{2,l}$ yield $\frac{1}{3}$, thus all possible value correlations from $V_1 \rightsquigarrow V_2$ are selected. On the other hand, all $v_{1,1} \rightsquigarrow v_{3,l}$ of $V_1 \rightsquigarrow V_3$ are omitted since $v_{1,1}$ co-occurs with three values in V_3 and $\frac{3}{3}$ exceeds θ_5.

Skewness of Distributions. If Eq. 5 from the previous section is not fulfilled, we use an alternative selection constraint to avoid that useful correlations are omitted too easily. In particular, we check the shape of the conditional distributions to identify dependencies between values, i.e., if one of the values in V_k occurs with relatively high frequency given that $v_{i,j}$ occurs, we add $v_{i,j} \rightsquigarrow v_{k,l}, \forall l$ to the hypothesis $V_i \rightsquigarrow V_k$. Equation 7 shows that this constraint is realized by subtracting the highest from the lowest of all conditional probabilities given $v_{i,j}$ (cf. Eq. 6), where $\theta_6 \in [0, \infty)$. The idea behind this is that the difference is large for skewed distributions where some values co-occur frequently and others only rarely, and small for evenly distributed values. Note that this does not take into consideration that dominating values in V_k could incorrectly cause that the constraint is fulfilled, which is addressed in the following section.

$$\mathcal{P}_{i,j,k} = \{P(v_{k,l} \mid v_{i,j}) : P(v_{k,l} \mid v_{i,j}) > 0, \forall l\} \tag{6}$$

$$\max(\mathcal{P}_{i,j,k}) - \min(\mathcal{P}_{i,j,k}) > \frac{\theta_6}{|\{v_{k,l} : P(v_{k,l} \mid v_{i,j}) > 0\}|} \tag{7}$$

We use $\theta_6 = 0.8$ as a sample for the data in Table 3 and assume that $v_{1,2} \rightsquigarrow v_{2,l}, \forall l$ was omitted by the constraint from Eq. 5. Then $P(v_{2,1} \mid v_{1,1}) - P(v_{2,2} \mid v_{1,1}) = 0.42$ and $P(v_{2,2} \mid v_{1,2}) - P(v_{2,3} \mid v_{1,2}) = 0.5$ both exceed the critical value of $\frac{0.8}{2} = 0.4$. However, $v_{1,1} \rightsquigarrow v_{3,l}, \forall l$ is not fulfilled, because $P(v_{3,1} \mid v_{1,1}) - P(v_{3,3} \mid v_{1,1}) = 0.14$ does not exceed the critical value of $\frac{0.8}{3} = 0.27$ and is therefore correctly omitted from hypothesis $V_1 \rightsquigarrow V_3$.

4.5 Validation of Correlations

This section presents hypothesis validation constraints that omit correlations without sufficiently strong dependencies between values or few correlating values.

Dependencies of Distributions. As pointed out in Sect. 4.4, a valid correlation $V_i \rightsquigarrow V_k$ should imply that the conditional value probabilities $P(v_{k,l} \mid v_{i,j})$ differ from each other depending on the value $v_{i,j}$ attained by V_i. Otherwise, the values in V_k are independent from the attained values in V_i, which means that the correlation hypothesis should be discarded. We address this by measuring the variances of all conditional distributions in V_k with respect to the overall distribution of V_k. Equation 8 shows that the variances are added for all value correlations selected by one of the constraints from Sect. 4.4. Since variances of more frequently occurring value correlations are more representative for the variable and should therefore have a higher influence on the result, Eq. 9 with $\theta_7 \in [0, \infty)$ weights all variances by the occurrence probabilities of $v_{i,j}$ and checks whether their sum exceeds a threshold. In this case, the conditional distributions involved in the correlation hypothesis are sufficiently dependent and thus selected, otherwise the correlation is omitted from further analysis.

$$\mathbb{V}_k(v_{i,j}) = \sum_l \left\{ (P(v_{k,l} \mid v_{i,j}) - P(v_{k,l}))^2 : v_{i,j} \rightsquigarrow v_{k,l} \right\} \tag{8}$$

$$\sum_j \{\mathbb{V}_k (v_{i,j}) \cdot P (v_{i,j}) : v_{i,j} \rightsquigarrow v_{k,l}\} \geq \theta_7 \tag{9}$$

We first consider correlation $V_1 \rightsquigarrow V_2$ from Table 3 as an example and use $\theta_7 = 0.2$ as a threshold. The variances $\mathbb{V}_2 (v_{1,1}) = 0.13$, $\mathbb{V}_2 (v_{1,2}) = 0.29$, and $\mathbb{V}_2 (v_{1,3}) = 1.04$ are weighted by probabilities $P (v_{1,1}) = 0.58$, $P (v_{1,2}) = 0.33$, and $P (v_{1,3}) = 0.08$ respectively to yield a total of 0.26 that exceeds $\theta_7 = 0.2$. Accordingly, the conditional value distributions in V_2 sufficiently depend on the attained values in V_1, thus $V_1 \rightsquigarrow V_2$ is selected as a valid correlation. On the other hand, the weighted sum of variances for $V_3 \rightsquigarrow V_1$ yields 0.06, which does not exceed the threshold and thus indicates that the correlation should be omitted.

Value Coverage. The second selection criterion for value correlations from one of the constraints from Sect. 4.4 ensures that only variable correlations supported by sufficiently many correlating values are selected. In other words, a correlation $V_i \rightsquigarrow V_k$ is omitted if only a small fraction of the values in V_i have corresponding correlations. Thereby, we use the occurrence probabilities of $v_{i,j}$ to weight frequent values higher. According to Eq. 10, we only select $V_i \rightsquigarrow V_k$ if the relative amount of correlating values exceeds a threshold $\theta_8 \in [0, 1]$.

$$\sum_j \{P (v_{i,j}) : v_{i,j} \rightsquigarrow v_{k,l}\} \geq \theta_8 \tag{10}$$

We use data from Table 3 and consider the variable correlation $V_1 \rightsquigarrow V_3$ with $\theta_8 = 0.5$. We assume that all correlations from $v_{1,1}$ to values from V_3 were removed as outlined in the example in Sect. 4.4, but correlations from $v_{1,2}$ and $v_{1,3}$ to V_3 exist. The sum of probabilities for these values is then $P (v_{1,2}) + P (v_{1,3}) = 0.416$. Since this sum does not exceed the threshold of 0.5, correlation $V_1 \rightsquigarrow V_3$ is omitted from further analysis. Assuming that all value correlations were selected for $V_1 \rightsquigarrow V_2$ the constraint is trivially fulfilled since the sum of all occurrence probabilities always equals 1 and thus exceeds the threshold.

4.6 Correlation Updating and Testing

The previous sections outlined the initialization phase of the VCD, where correlations are selected by a sample of N log lines. Afterwards, the VCD switches to online mode, where samples of M log lines are repeatedly collected and tested with respect to the previously generated correlation rules. In the following, we use $\widetilde{P}$ to denote occurrence probabilities of values from these test samples. We use a two-sample Chi-squared test for homogeneity [3] to determine whether a test sample corresponds to the rules. For this, we first compute a test statistic t by comparing the conditional probabilities of the training and test samples with the expected probability P_e based on the mean as shown in Eq. 11 and Eq. 12.

$$P_e = \frac{N \cdot P (v_{k,l} \mid v_{i,j}) + M \cdot \widetilde{P} (v_{k,l} \mid v_{i,j})}{N + M} \tag{11}$$

$$t = \sum_l \left(N \cdot \frac{(P(v_{k,l} \mid v_{i,j}) - P_e)^2}{P_e} + M \cdot \frac{(\widetilde{P}(v_{k,l} \mid v_{i,j}) - P_e)^2}{P_e} \right) \qquad (12)$$

For a given $v_{i,j}$, we then define an indicator function $I_k(v_{i,j})$ in Eq. 13 that is 1 if the test statistic does not exceed a critical value given by the Chi-squared distribution with confidence $\alpha_1 \in [0,1]$, i.e., there is no significant difference between the conditional distributions of the training and test samples, and is 0 otherwise. We then store these indicators for all $v_{i,j} \in \mathcal{V}_i$ in a list $r_{i,j}$, so that $r_{i,j}^{(t-d)}, ..., r_{i,j}^{(t)}$ are the d most recent indicators after t tests of $v_{i,j}$, and compute another test statistic $s_{i,j}^t = \sum_{x=t-d}^t r_{i,j}^{(x)}$ on these values. The purpose of this is to reduce the number of false positives, i.e., anomalies are only reported when a certain number of Chi-squared tests fail. Since r is a binomial process, we use Eq. 14 to compute a critical value λ, where $\alpha_2 \in [0,1]$ is the confidence of the binomial test and α_1 is reused as the success probability of the Chi-squared test. If $s_{i,j}^t \geq \lambda$ holds, there is no significant change of the conditional probabilities of $v_{i,j} \rightsquigarrow v_{k,l}, \forall l$ at test t, and vice versa. Note that the runtime can be reduced by computing λ a single time in advance when d, α_1, and α_2 remain constant.

$$I_k(v_{i,j}) = \begin{cases} 1 & \text{if } t < \chi^2_{\alpha_1, |\mathcal{V}_k|-1} \\ 0 & \text{otherwise} \end{cases} \qquad (13)$$

$$\lambda = min \left\{ k_{max} : \sum_{k=0}^{k_{max}} \frac{d!}{k! \cdot (d-k)!} \cdot \alpha_1^k (1-\alpha_1)^{d-k} > 1 - \alpha_2 \right\} \qquad (14)$$

The aforementioned computations are carried out for updating as well as testing correlations. The main difference between both phases is that step (6) *Correlation Testing* only reports anomalies when tests fail, i.e., $s < \lambda$, meaning that all changes of correlations are reported every time after processing the test samples as long as they persist. On the other hand, step (5) *Correlation Updating* adjusts the base line for comparison by updating distributions with newly observed values, removing correlations if the binomial test fails, and periodically repeating steps (3)–(4) to identify new correlations. Accordingly, this phase is seen as an extended training phase that is essential for online learning.

5   Evaluation

This section outlines the evaluation of our approach. We first compare variable correlations selected from a real data set with two well-known correlation metrics. We then showcase the detection capabilities of the VCD.

5.1   Comparison with Association Metrics

This section compares the selected correlations of the VCD with well-known association metrics. We first describe the data and then show the results.

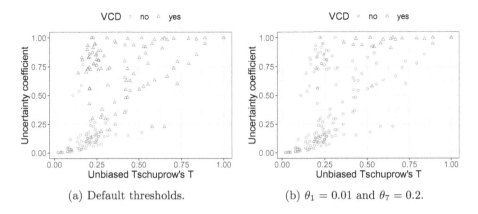

(a) Default thresholds.   (b) $\theta_1 = 0.01$ and $\theta_7 = 0.2$.

Fig. 2. Comparison of VCD selection with association metrics.

Data. We use 10000 Audit logs of type syscall from the publicly available AIT-LDSv1.1 [13] for this evaluation. We select Audit logs, because they are a common source for log analysis and are sufficiently complex to be representative for all kinds of log data. In addition, they contain many categorical variables that correlate with varying strength and have diverse value occurrence distributions. Out of all 27 variables, we remove the timestamp as well as 6 static variables that only attain one value, because it is not possible to generate useful correlations with them. The VCD always omits these variables due to Eq. 1 and Eq. 2.

We use the remaining 20 variables to generate all 380 possible variable pairs and measure their association strength. For this, we employ two association metrics for nominal values with arbitrary many categories, (i) the Uncertainty Coefficient U [17] based on conditional entropy, and (ii) the Unbiased Tschuprow's T [2] based on the Pearson Chi-squared statistic. Both metrics are in the range $[0,1]$, where 0 indicates no association between the variables, and 1 indicates the highest possible dependency. However, while T is symmetrical, U is non-symmetrical and measures how well the dependent variable is predictable by the given variable. For example, the data in Table 1 yields $T(\{\text{syscall}, \text{items}\}) = 0.53$ as well as $U(\text{syscall} \mid \text{items}) = 0.58$ and $U(\text{items} \mid \text{syscall}) = 0.93$.

Results. We run the sequential selection steps of the VCD on the raw event logs and analyze the variable correlations that remain after the initialization phase. In Figs. 2a and 2b, these remaining correlations are marked "yes" (blue triangles), while all variable pairs that are omitted by one of the selection constraints are marked "no" (red circles). Each point in the scatter plots represents one of the 380 variable pairs displayed by their respective U and T, i.e., points closer to the top right corner of the plot indicate stronger association between the two involved variables, while points closer to the bottom left indicate weaker association.

The VCD was used with default settings (cf. Appendix A.1) to classify the variable pairs in Fig. 2a. From all variable pairs, 222 were selected as interesting after the initialization phase and 158 were omitted. Since all of the omitted pairs received a relatively low association score by at least one of the metrics, we conclude that the VCD achieved to correctly omit irrelevant correlations. For example, among the omitted correlations is "syscall" $\rightsquigarrow$ "pid", which is reasonable as the process id "pid" is mostly random and independent from syscall types.

It is possible to further narrow down the set of tracked variable correlations by adjusting the thresholds. In particular, some of the variables involve large numbers of distinct values, which means that the number of monitored value correlations for pairs of these variables is immense. The default value $\theta_1 = 0.3$ allows 3.000 unique values in each variable, which is limited to 100 by setting $\theta_1 = 0.01$. This causes that the number of remaining correlations drops from 222 to 126, where most of the rejected pairs are located close to the top left corner of the plot. Closer examination of these rejected pairs shows that they involve variables with many distinct values on the left side of the correlation and thus achieve a high U score, e.g., syscall arguments such as "a1" $\rightsquigarrow$ "items" with around 1000 unique "a1" values. Since their prediction strengths merely emerge from the large value space, adjusting θ_1 successfully omits these correlations.

In addition to adjusting θ_1, we increase θ_7 from 0.05 to 0.2 in Fig. 2b so that only variable pairs with strong dependency remain. This further reduces the amount of monitored correlations to 97 and omits correlations involving IDs such as "ppid" $\rightsquigarrow$ "exe", while more interesting correlations such as the sample correlation between "syscall" and "items" from Table 1 remains in both directions. We conclude that these experiments show the VCD is capable of selecting useful and strong correlations based on user-defined thresholds.

5.2   Anomaly Detection

This part of the evaluation validates the anomaly detection capabilities of the VCD. We first provide information on the log data and then present the results.

Data. We use Apache access logs from the AIT-LDSv1.1 [13] for this part of the evaluation. These logs are relevant, because they involve several categorical variables, including IP addresses, request methods (e.g., "GET", "POST"), resource names, status codes, etc. In addition, web-based attacks frequently manifest themselves as changes of multiple sequential values in these variables. In particular, we select (i) a brute-force login attack using Hydra[1] that repeatedly requests the login web page with arbitrary user data, and (ii) a Nikto vulnerability scan[2] that requests non-available resources and thereby causes multiple redirects that correspond to status code 302. To evaluate detection accuracy with respect to different attack executions, we simulate varying intensities by injecting only a certain amount of events at particular times. Precisely, we inject batches of 5, 10, 20, 50, and 200 events for each attack in intervals of 10000 lines (around 12 h). We label log line samples containing these batches as anomalous to measure the detection accuracy of the VCD in the following.

[1] https://tools.kali.org/password-attacks/hydra, accessed: 2021-04-21.
[2] https://cirt.net/Nikto2, accessed: 2021-04-21.

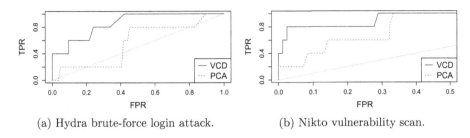

(a) Hydra brute-force login attack.   (b) Nikto vulnerability scan.

Fig. 3. Anomaly detection ROC plots for two attack scenarios.

Results. For both attack cases, we configure the VCD to use the first $N = 10000$ lines of the Apache Access log files for initialization of the correlations. Thereby, we set $\theta_3 = 0.7$ and $\theta_7 = 0.005$ since the involved variables usually have different distributions and are relatively independent. All other parameters are used with default values (cf. Appendix A.1). After initialization, we use a test sample size of $M = 1000$ to update the correlations on the remaining lines of the first day (20000 lines) using empirically determined confidences $\alpha_1 = 0.001$ and $\alpha_2 = 0.05$, and an indicator list size $d = 30$. This phase omits correlations that appear interesting during initialization, but are too unstable for anomaly detection. With the beginning of the second day, we switch the VCD from updating to testing mode, i.e., correlations that fail tests are no longer changed or omitted. We experiment with different values for α_1 in the test phase and count true positives (TP) as detected samples containing injected lines, false positives (FP) as detected normal samples, false negatives (FN) as undetected samples containing injected lines, and true negatives (TN) as undetected normal samples.

For comparison, we select Principal Component Analysis (PCA) as a baseline, because it allows to handle categorical data through one-hot encoding of values. Similar to the VCD, we use samples of 1000 lines to generate value count vectors and use the first 30000 lines for model building. In the subsequent detection phase, we measure the squared prediction error of test samples and mark them as anomalies if the error exceeds threshold Q_α, where confidence α is varied [10].

Figure 3a shows the trade-off between true positive rate $(TPR = \frac{TP}{TP+FN})$ and false positive rate $(FPR = \frac{FP}{FP+TN})$ of VCD and PCA in the first attack scenario. The results indicate that the VCD successfully detects the attack and yields $TPR = 60\%$ (corresponding to the detection of the samples containing 20, 50, and 200 injected lines) at only $FPR = 10\%$. Closer inspection of the anomalies shows that involved variables are mainly "request" and "referer". In the training phase, the request to the login page "/login.php" occurs in 1.2% of all lines, half of these times with referer "http://mail.insect.com/login.php" and with "–" otherwise. However, requests to the login page made by the Hydra attack always have referer "–" and thus distort this distribution within the test sample, which is detected by the VCD. On the other hand, the PCA ROC curve indicates that it is only slightly better than random guessing. The reason for this is that the one-hot encoded data becomes very high-dimensional and PCA is thus unable to detect slight changes of single values in such complex models.

For the second attack scenario, relevant variables include the request method, where values "GET", "POST", and "OPTIONS" occur with 74%, 21%, and 5% in the training data respectively, as well as the status code, where 200 occurs in 96% and 302 in 4% of these lines. The Nikto scan generates lines with request method "GET" and status code "302", a combination that only occurs in 0.5% of all lines. Since the VCD is better suited to detect changes of occurrences conditioned by infrequent values such as "302"$\rightsquigarrow$"GET" of correlation "status"$\rightsquigarrow$"method", it performs better than PCA as visible in Fig. 3b.

6   Discussion

The evaluation in the previous section ascertains that the VCD selects appropriate variables for correlation analysis and detects anomalies by monitoring co-occurrences of correlated values over time. Thereby, the VCD makes use of a sequence of filtering steps that are separately configured by thresholds. We recognize that such a large number of parameters usually complicates practical application [19], however, we argue that this is not the case for the VCD since the thresholds are set relatively independent and specific to certain properties of the data (cf. Appendix A.1). In addition, it is possible to omit single selection steps and iteratively refine the limits of the search space as we show in Sect. 5.1.

This paper focuses on the correlation between pairs of variables rather than correlations where more than two variables are involved, e.g., $V_1 \rightsquigarrow \{V_2, V_3\}$ or $\{V_1, V_2\} \rightsquigarrow V_3$. However, we argue that this is trivial to achieve, since our selection criteria work analogously with combined occurrences of values. In fact, our implementation [21] supports correlation analysis of specific subsets of variables.

Finally, we suggest to develop selection strategies similar to the one presented in this paper, but with a focus on mixes of categorical and continuous variables, i.e., categorical values indicate that values of another variable origin from a particular continuous distribution. For example, logged measurement data such as memory usage could follow a normal distribution with mean and variance depending on an active user. We leave this task for future research.

7   Conclusion

This paper presents the Variable Correlation Detector (VCD), a novel approach for anomaly detection based on value co-occurrences in categorical variables of log events. The VCD comprises two modes. First, an initialization mode where variable and value correlations are iteratively selected by multiple factors, such as skewness, similarity, and dependency of value occurrence probabilities as well as diversity and coverage of values. Second, an online learning and detection mode that continuously updates the identified correlations and reports anomalies based on deviations of the conditional occurrences. Other than state-of-the-art approaches, the VCD also analyzes infrequent values and recognizes system behavior changes that occur over long time spans. We foresee several extensions for future work, including an anomaly score and automatic threshold selection.

Acknowledgements. This work was partly funded by the FFG projects INDICAET-ING (868306) and DECEPT (873980), and the EU H2020 project GUARD (833456).

A   Appendix

A.1   Threshold Parameter Selection

The filtering steps for correlations between variables and values presented in Sect. 4 make use of threshold parameters θ_1-θ_8 to narrow down the search space and select only those correlations that are likely to positively contribute to the detection of anomalies. This section investigates the influence of these threshold parameters on the resulting correlations and thereby supports the manual parameter selection process, in particular, by relating each parameter to specific properties of the data at hand. In the following, we first explain the generation of synthetic data for this evaluation and then describe our experiments.

Data. To measure the influence of thresholds on the correlation selection, it is necessary to control properties of the input data. Therefore, we generate synthetic data for our experiments. We use three variables V_1, V_2, and V_3, of which only V_1 and V_2 correlate with varying strength, and monitor the correlations found by the VCD for different threshold settings. We use values $V_i = \{0, 1, ..., x\}$, $x \in \mathbb{N}$ for each variable and compute their occurrence probabilities as normalized geometric series. Equation 15 shows how the probabilities for values in V_1 and V_3 are computed, where $p_i = 1$ means that all values are equally likely to occur, and lower values mean that one or more values are dominating the probability distribution. Equation 16 shows how the conditional probabilities of values in V_2 given values from V_1 are computed. Thereby, ρ specifies the correlation strength, i.e., larger values for ρ indicate that the same values co-occur more frequently with each other, and ζ is a damping factor that reduces the correlation strength for larger $v_{i,j}$, i.e., higher values for ζ cause more co-occurrences between different values.

$$P\left(v_{i,j}\right) = \frac{p_i^j}{\sum_{j'=0}^{|\mathcal{V}_i|} p_i^{j'}} \tag{15}$$

$$P\left(v_{k,l} \mid v_{i,j}\right) = \frac{(1-\rho)^{|j-l|} + \zeta^{||\mathcal{V}_i|-j|}}{\sum_{l'=0}^{|\mathcal{V}_k|} (1-\rho)^{|j-l'|} + \zeta^{||\mathcal{V}_i|-j|}} \tag{16}$$

Figure 4 shows the co-occurrences of values from V_1 and V_2 for a sample configuration of $x = 9$, $p_1 = 0.7$, $\rho = 0.9$, and $\zeta = 0.4$. Due to the relatively strong correlation factor, most values in V_1 occur with the same value of V_2. The figure also shows that higher values of V_1 co-occur with more values of V_2 due to the damping factor, e.g., while $v_{1,1}$ only occurs with four different values of V_2, $v_{1,9}$ occurs with each value of V_2 at least once.

To evaluate the accuracy of the correlation selection procedure, we generate a ground truth of expected value correlations that contains all $v_{1,j} \rightsquigarrow v_{2,l}$ and

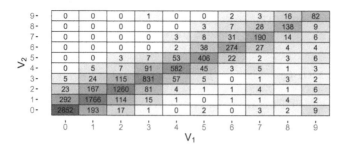

Fig. 4. Value co-occurrences of damped correlation.

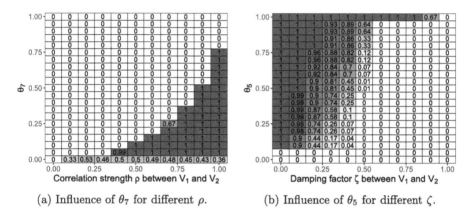

(a) Influence of θ_7 for different ρ. (b) Influence of θ_5 for different ζ.

Fig. 5. Influence of thresholds on accuracy of correlation selection.

$v_{2,l} \rightsquigarrow v_{1,j}$ that occur at least once in the data. We count correlations selected by the VCD and present in the ground truth as true positives (TP), correlations not present in the ground truth as false positives (FP), correlations missed by the VCD as false negatives (FN), and all other correlations as true negatives (TN). We use the F-score $F_1 = TP/(TP + 0.5 \cdot (FP + FN))$ to measure the accuracy in the next section.

Results. We first experiment with θ_7, which is essential for selecting correlations that represent actual dependencies between the values and do not spuriously emerge from skewed value probability distributions. To analyze the relationship between θ_7 and the correlation strength, we increase θ_7 in steps of 0.05 and ρ in steps of 0.1 in the range $[0, 1]$ while leaving $p_1 = 0.7, p_3 = 0.7, \zeta = 0.4$ constant, generate 10 data samples with 10000 events respectively as outlined in the previous section, and then compute the average F-score of these simulation runs. The results visualized in Fig. 5a show that weaker correlation strengths require θ_7 to be sufficiently low to select all correct correlations and achieve the highest possible F-score of 1. However, setting θ_7 to 0 causes a decrease of the F-score independent of the correlation strength. The reason for this is that

Table 4. Dependencies and default values of thresholds.

Thresh.	Infl. by	Default	Thresh.	Infl. by	Default
θ_1	$|\mathcal{V}|, N$	0.3	θ_5	ρ, ζ	0.5
θ_2	p	0.4	θ_6	ρ, ζ	1
θ_3	p, ρ	0.5	θ_7	ρ	0.05
θ_4	$\mathcal{V}$	0	θ_8	θ_5, θ_6	0.7

correlations involving V_3 are not checked for dependency and are thus incorrectly selected, which increases the number of FP. We therefore conclude that θ_7 should be set to a low, but non-zero value, e.g., 0.05. Note that the selection of θ_7 is not affected by ζ, since additional value co-occurrences only have little influence on the sum of variances as long as they are not dominating the distribution.

Threshold θ_5 on the other hand relies on the total number of co-occurrences for a given value and is thus influenced by ζ in addition to ρ. Figure 5b shows the F-score for various combinations of θ_5 and ζ, while $\rho = 1$ is fixed. As expected, increasing values for ζ yield lower F-scores for a given θ_5, because the number of distinct co-occurring values for any given value increases quickly (cf. Fig. 4). Accordingly, it is necessary to set $\theta_5 \geq 1$ for $\zeta > 0.5$ to select any correlations. For $\zeta \leq 0.5$, θ_5 effectively steers the allowed number of distinct co-occurrences, e.g., for $\theta_5 = 0.5$ at most 5 co-occurring values are allowed since $|\mathcal{V}_i| = 10, \forall i$.

We argue that the influence of other thresholds is trivial and therefore omit the plots for brevity. Table 4 shows a summary of all thresholds and the data properties with the highest influence on their selection. Note that θ_8 is most influenced by θ_5 and θ_6 rather than a property of the input data, because these thresholds regulate the generation of value correlations that affect the selection criterion involving θ_8. The table also provides default values that we identified as useful during our experiments and are used in the evaluations in Sect. 5.

These results indicate that the large number of parameters does not impede practical application of the VCD, since the thresholds are mostly independent from each other and allow to configure the correlation selection constraints specifically to counteract otherwise problematic properties of the data. For example, a high number of correlations involving many distinct values (i.e., $|\mathcal{V}|$ is large) or weakly correlated variables (i.e., ρ is low) should be addressed by adjusting θ_1 and θ_7 accordingly to reduce the total number of correlations that are considered for anomaly detection as shown in Sect. 5.1.

References

1. Agrawal, R., Srikant, R., et al.: Fast algorithms for mining association rules. In: Proceedings of the 20th International Conference on Very Large Data Bases, vol. 1215, pp. 487–499. Citeseer (1994)
2. Bergsma, W.: A bias-correction for cramér's v and tschuprow's t. J. Kor. Stat. Soc. **42**(3), 323–328 (2013)

3. Bolboacă, S.D., Jäntschi, L., Sestraş, A.F., Sestraş, R.E., Pamfil, D.C.: Pearson-fisher chi-square statistic revisited. Information **2**(3), 528–545 (2011)
4. Chandola, V., Banerjee, A., Kumar, V.: Anomaly detection: a survey. ACM Comput. Surv. **41**(3), 1–58 (2009)
5. Chen, T., Tang, L.A., Sun, Y., Chen, Z., Zhang, K.: Entity embedding-based anomaly detection for heterogeneous categorical events. arXiv preprint arXiv:1608.07502 (2016)
6. Das, K., Schneider, J.: Detecting anomalous records in categorical datasets. In: Proceedings of the 13th ACM SIGKDD International Conference on Knowledge Discovery and Data Mining, pp. 220–229 (2007)
7. Djenouri, Y., Belhadi, A., Fournier-Viger, P.: Extracting useful knowledge from event logs: a frequent itemset mining approach. Knowl.-Based Syst. **139**, 132–148 (2018)
8. Eiras-Franco, C., Martinez-Rego, D., Guijarro-Berdinas, B., Alonso-Betanzos, A., Bahamonde, A.: Large scale anomaly detection in mixed numerical and categorical input spaces. Inf. Sci. **487**, 115–127 (2019)
9. Gupta, G.P., Kulariya, M.: A framework for fast and efficient cyber security network intrusion detection using apache spark. Procedia Comput. Sci. **93**, 824–831 (2016)
10. He, S., Zhu, J., He, P., Lyu, M.R.: Experience report: system log analysis for anomaly detection. In: Proceedings of the 27th International Symposium on Software Reliability Engineering, pp. 207–218. IEEE (2016)
11. Ienco, D., Pensa, R.G., Meo, R.: A semisupervised approach to the detection and characterization of outliers in categorical data. IEEE Trans. Neural Netw. Learn. Syst. **28**(5), 1017–1029 (2016)
12. Khalili, A., Sami, A.: Sysdetect: a systematic approach to critical state determination for industrial intrusion detection systems using apriori algorithm. J. Process Control **32**, 154–160 (2015)
13. Landauer, M., Skopik, F., Wurzenberger, M., Hotwagner, W., Rauber, A.: Have it your way: generating customized log datasets with a model-driven simulation testbed. IEEE Trans. Reliab **70**(1), 402–415 (2021)
14. Moustafa, N., Slay, J.: The evaluation of network anomaly detection systems: statistical analysis of the unsw-nb15 data set and the comparison with the kdd99 data set. Inf. Secur. J. Glob. Perspect. **25**(1–3), 18–31 (2016)
15. Narita, K., Kitagawa, H.: Detecting outliers in categorical record databases based on attribute associations. In: Zhang, Y., Yu, G., Bertino, E., Xu, G. (eds.) APWeb 2008. LNCS, vol. 4976, pp. 111–123. Springer, Heidelberg (2008). https://doi.org/10.1007/978-3-540-78849-2_13
16. Pande, A., Ahuja, V.: Weac: word embeddings for anomaly classification from event logs. In: Proceedings of the International Conference on Big Data, pp. 1095–1100. IEEE (2017)
17. Press, W.H., Teukolsky, S.A., Vetterling, W.T., Flannery, B.P.: Numerical Recipes. The Art of Scientific Computing, 3rd edn. Cambridge University Press, Cambridge (2007)
18. Ren, J., Wu, Q., Zhang, J., Hu, C.: Efficient outlier detection algorithm for heterogeneous data streams. In: Proceedings of the 6th International Conference on Fuzzy Systems and Knowledge Discovery, vol. 5, pp. 259–264. IEEE (2009)

19. Taha, A., Hadi, A.S.: Anomaly detection methods for categorical data: a review. ACM Comput. Surv. **52**(2), 1–35 (2019)
20. Tuor, A., Kaplan, S., Hutchinson, B., Nichols, N., Robinson, S.: Deep learning for unsupervised insider threat detection in structured cybersecurity data streams. arXiv preprint arXiv:1710.00811 (2017)
21. Wurzenberger, M., et al.: Logdata-anomaly-miner. https://github.com/ait-aecid/logdata-anomaly-miner, Accessed 21 Apr 2021

Author Index

Printed in the United States
by Baker & Taylor Publisher Services